THE FAIRCHILD DICTIONARY OF FASHION

THE FAIRCHILD

Dictionary *of* Fashion

THIRD EDITION

CHARLOTTE MANKEY CALASIBETTA

PHYLLIS TORTORA

Illustrated by BINA ABLING

FAIRCHILD PUBLICATIONS, INC.
NEW YORK

Executive Editor: Olga T. Kontzias

Development Editor: Sylvia L. Weber

Art Director: Adam B. Bohannon

Production Manager: Priscilla Taguer

Production: Chernow Editorial Services, Inc.

Copy Editor: Suzanne Lander

Interior Design: Adam B. Bohannon

Cover Design: Adam B. Bohannon

Cover Illustration: Bina Abling

Seventh Printing, 2009
Sixth Printing, 2008
Fifth Printing, 2008
Fourth Printing, 2007
Third Printing, 2007
Copyright © 2003

Fairchild Publications, Inc.

Second Edition, Revised © 1998, Fairchild Publications

Second Edition, © 1988, Fairchild Publications

First Edition, © 1975, Fairchild Publications

Library of Congress Catalog Card Number: 2002103884

ISBN: 1-56367- 235-9

GST R 133004424

Printed in the United States of America

CONTENTS

PREFACE TO THE THIRD EDITION

Origins of the Fairchild Dictionary of Fashion

This third edition of *The Fairchild Dictionary of Fashion* stands on the foundation of two previous editions that were originated and developed by Charlotte Mankey Calasibetta. Since 1975, the work has served as an invaluable reference for students, scholars, authors, designers, those in the fashion business, and anyone with an interest in fashion past and present. Professor Calasibetta's description of how she created the first edition will provide insight into the formidable task that she undertook:

> This dictionary evolved from a college course in fashion. In an attempt to teach students a vocabulary of fashion terms that would not become outdated, lists were assembled of collars, necklines, sleeves, skirts, and so on, and each was considered in the light of the existing fashion trends—which were "in," and which were "out." The basic categories for this dictionary grew from these lists. The addition of historical terms and some of the vocabulary of clothing manufacturers rounded out the entries.

The second edition added approximately 1,700 entries and 11 more categories. In 1998 a revised second edition was published that included an appendix containing not only fashion terms new since the previous edition, but also terms used in the manufacture, merchandising, and distribution of apparel; entries describing types of retail organizations; and business terms relating to the fashion industry.

The Third Edition

Categories

The third edition preserves what is best of the earlier editions, but a number of changes make the book even more comprehensive and useful. One of the strengths of the dictionary has been the organization of entries into categories. A reader who is interested in a definition of a "peg-top skirt," for example, will find that entry in the Skirts category and can compare that definition with those for other types of skirts. Illustrations of a variety of skirt types also appear with the category, allowing for visual comparisons.

Should readers not know the category into which an item fits, they can consult the alphabetical listing, where a cross-reference will direct them to the appropriate location.

In past editions, however, some categories tended to overlap other categories and/or entries in the alphabetical listing. After careful analysis of the categories, the author and editors of this edition have merged some, discarded others, and added a few new categories. For example, prior editions had separate categories for SHOES, BOOTS, SANDALS, and SLIPPERS. In this edition, the more general category of FOOTWEAR now contains all of the aforementioned types of foot coverings. The categories of COATS and of JACKETS had a considerable amount of duplication, and so the two categories have been merged into one called COATS AND JACKETS. The table of contents provides a complete list of the categories utilized in this edition.

Another change is in the transfer of historical terms from the alphabetical listing to the appropriate category. If a historical term, for example, "hennin" (a type of hat), clearly fits into a category, it is placed there. Readers will now find "hennin" in the category of HEADWEAR.

Exceptions to this practice include garments that may be similar to modern garments in their function, but different in construction, that were worn before the categorical heading term was used. For example, the category heading PANTS is a relatively recent term that came into use only in the 19th c. Trunk hose, a 16th c. garment for men, differed in form and shape from 19th and 20th c. pants, although they both served as lower body coverings. Such terms are listed separately in the alphabetical listing. Likewise, the category BLOUSES AND TOPS does not include those items designated as "bodices" or other upper-body coverings that were worn before the term "blouse" became widely used in the second half of the 19th c.

DRESSES, LOOKS, and SUITS are examples of categories that contained a number of duplications of alphabetical entries. As a means of eliminating this repetition, the entries contained in these aforementioned categories have been placed in the alphabetical listing.

Kinds of Words Defined in the Dictionary

Contemporary Fashion Terms
As in the earlier editions, a major focus is fashion terms currently in use and those that tend to be revived periodically. Fashion designers often derive inspiration from the past, and words from earlier decades and even previous centuries may still be in use. For many of the entries, the derivation of the term is noted.

Fashion Terms from Non-Western Cultures and Folk Costume
The focus of this dictionary is fashion in the Western world. To be comprehensive and cover non-Western apparel would require a book far larger than this one. For these reasons, non-Western apparel terms are defined only if they have become part of Western fashion or have some current importance. Folk costume terms are included only if they are used in mainstream fashion.

Historic Fashion Terms
Another important aspect of earlier editions has been the inclusion of historic fashion terms. Historic terms that are no longer in current usage are

designated by a special archival symbol, an infinity symbol (∞), as in the following example:

Andalusian casaque ∞ (an-da-loó-zee-an cask) Woman's evening tunic, fastened down center with series of ribbons, with the front of the skirt cut away, and sloping to knee-length in the back. Worn over another skirt c. 1809.

Several unique aspects of historic terms should be noted. One of these is spelling. Before the publication of standardized dictionaries in English in the 18th and 19th c., spelling could be quite erratic. For example, a popular hair and wig style of the 18th c. can be spelled *cadogan, catogan,* or *catagan.* Medieval terms, some of which derive from English and others from French, tend to have many spelling variations. Those with Latin roots tend to be more stable.

Dictionary users will find many fashion elements from the 19th century that are named after royalty or famous persons of the past. As fashion changes accelerated and periodicals provided more coverage of fashions, there was a tendency to assign names to styles. Also, costume historians and other writers of the 19th c. originated many names for styles of earlier centuries. Where possible, definitions of such terms will incorporate a brief explanation of who the historical personage was or note that a particular term was coined at a time long after the costume was worn.

Merchandising and Retailing Terms

Fashion design, production, and marketing terms were introduced in the revised 2nd edition in an appendix. These and additional entries have been incorporated into the alphabetical listing. The terms included are those with specific application to some segment of the fashion industry. General business terms are not included.

Textile Terms

The number of textile terms has decreased significantly in this edition. Entries have been limited to some basic textile terms, to standard textiles that continue to be widely used, and to new textile materials that have had a recent impact on fashion.

Those textile terms that have been retained are identified by a dagger (†).

angora † Soft fuzzy yarn made from the underhair of the angora rabbit that is used for knitwear and for trimmings.

Since the publication of the 2nd edition of *Fairchild's Dictionary of Fashion,* a new edition of the *Fairchild Dictionary of Textiles* has been issued. That work provides comprehensive listings of textile terms, both contemporary and historic, and users who require a more complete definition of textile terms are advised to consult that work.

Fashion Designers

Previous editions of the *Dictionary of Fashion* have included an appendix of fashion designers and discussion of their work. In the present edition, that appendix has been reduced, so as to provide more space for new fashion entries, and now provides only a brief biographical note about each designer. A very thorough examination of the life and work of important fashion designers past and present is to be found in the Fairchild publication, *Who's Who in Fashion,* 3rd edition. Names of fashion designers listed in the appendix are included in the alphabetical listing and are designated by an asterisk (*).

Dior, Christian * See APPENDIX/DESIGNERS.

Limitations on Entries Included in the Dictionary

In any book, space imposes some limits on content. The following are some of the kinds of terms not included in this work. Definitions of colors have been eliminated because the author and editors felt that it is virtually impossible to define a color; it must be shown.

As previously noted, non-Western apparel terms and folk costume terms are included only if they have become part of Western fashion. Foreign terms do not appear unless they are used in English in fashion or scholarship about fashion. Foreign words used in English in a fashion context *are* included.

Weapons (e.g., swords, daggers, guns) are not included, even when carried ceremonially. Registered trademark names have been eliminated, insofar as that is possible. The constant addition and deregistration of trademarks makes it very difficult to include such entries and be both up-to-date and accurate. Some trademarks, however, are so significant to fashion that they must be included.

Illustrations

The Fairchild Dictionary of Fashion includes 800 drawings, all new, illustrating fashion terms. When an entry is illustrated at some other place in the book, a notation is made of where that illustration can be found.

Format and Organization of Definitions

The following entries will serve to illustrate the organization and format features of the third edition of *The Fairchild Dictionary of Fashion*.

abilements/abillements   See BILLIMENTS.

Entries are printed in boldface. Where more than one spelling is current, alternate spellings are placed behind a slash in the main entry. Cross-references are in small caps. This cross-reference is to an entry in the alphabetical listing.

baseball cap   See HEADWEAR.

When an entry in the alphabetical listing is to be found in a category under the same name as the entry, the category alone is cross-referenced and the term can be found in that category. If the term is a synonym or is defined within another entry, it is listed as follows:

cadogan net   See HEADWEAR: SNOOD.

ACADEMIC COSTUME
Outfits consisting of caps, called mortarboards (see ACADEMIC COSTUME: MORTARBOARD); gowns; . . . Also called *academic regalia*.

Category headings are printed in capital letters. They are set off from the alphabetical text by borders. Cross-references to items in categories are printed in small caps, with the category given first, followed by a colon, and the individual entry listed after the colon. Synonyms are printed in italics. Any cross-reference that does not include a category designation will be found in the alphabetical listing.

bikini **1.** Two-piece swimsuit introduced in 1946 by designer Jacques Heim, who called it the atom because of its small size. Soon after, a version was advertised as "smaller than the atom." Eventually the name was changed to bikini after Bikini Atoll, a small coral island in the Pacific where atomic tests were made from 1946 to 1956. Bikinis were worn on Riviera beaches, but not accepted on U.S. public beaches until the early 1960s. By the 1980s these suits became still smaller and a number of variations had developed. These were: **string bikini,** consisting of a minimal halter bra with bikini panties, worn low on hips, and made of two triangular-shaped pieces attached to an elastic band or string ties; **teardrop bikini,** made up of bikini pants worn with a bra composed of two tiny triangles with straps at neck and around the body; **tankini** (tan′-kee-nee), a woman's bathing suit with a tank top and a bikini bottom; **corset bikini,** a top that looks like an underwire bra and a bikini bottom; **camikini,** with a camisole top and a bikini bottom. **2.** Man's very brief swim trunks.

In some entries, closely related terms are defined within the definition of the primary entry. Such terms also serve as primary entries and are printed in boldface type. When an entry has more than one definition, each definition for the entry is preceded by a number in boldface.

babushka (bah-boosh′-ka) Triangular-shaped scarf or square folded diagonally, worn draped over the head and tied under the chin in the manner of Russian peasant woman. *Der.* Russian, "grandmother." So-called because it was worn by older Russian immigrants to the United States. Also called a *kerchief.*

When derivations for entries are given, they are placed at the end of the entry and preceded by *Der.*

bandeau (ban-doe′)

Pronunciation of the entry, rendered phonetically, follows the main entry. It is printed in nonbold typeface and is placed inside parentheses. Pronunciations are not provided for all terms, but are given when pronunciations may not be obvious to the user. These phonetic renderings are, at best, approximations of the actual pronunciation. Many are foreign language words that are nearly impossible to interpret phonetically. So all terms are rendered in the closest phonetic equivalent in the way that an English-speaker would pronounce the syllables. The accent mark shown in any pronunciation is given after the syllable that should be emphasized.

Acknowledgments

Many individuals assisted in the preparation of this new edition of *The Fairchild Dictionary of Fashion.* I would like to thank them for the expertise they brought to the project.

My gratitude goes first to my husband, Vincent Tortora, for lending his linguistic skills to his development of the pronunciations included in the work.

A number of individuals contributed both general reviews of the dictionary and specialized reviews of individual categories. The general reviewers ae Lynda Campbell, Fairfax County Public Schools; Mary Morris, G Street Fabrics; and Robert Woods, Berkeley College. Reviewers of individual categories include Kate Achelpohl, Vision Council of America, Eyewear; Jerry Anderson, The Neckwear Association of America, Ties; Edith Anderson Feisner, The Embroiderers' Guild of America, Embroidery; Adam Graham, American Gem Society, Gems, Gem Cuts, and Settings and Jewelry; Keith Kaplan, Fur Information Council of America, Furs; Sally Kay, The Hosiery Association, Hosiery; Jeryl Spear, *Salon News* Contributing Editor, Hairstyles and Hair Accessories; and Bella Veksler, Drexel University, Belts, Handbags, Headwear, and Scarves.

Working with Bina Abling, the illustrator of this edition, was a pleasure. The results of her excellent and illuminating contributions are to be found in the pages of this book. And, as always, Merle Thomason, archivist for Fairchild Publications, was ready and able to locate a basis for elusive illustrations.

I offer my special thanks to the staff of Fairchild Books. Olga Kontzias, Executive Editor, worked through the steps necessary to get the new edition started and provided input to and evaluation of reorganization ideas. Mary McGarry, Acquisitions Editor, also took part in the planning stages. Sylvia L. Weber, Development Editor, became a guide in questions of style, and was a most valuable source of advice and encouragement throughout the writing and editing. Adam Bohannon, Art Director, originated an effective and appealing design for the interior of the book and Priscilla Taguer was the Production Manager.

In the production phase, Chernow Editorial Services, Inc., coordinated a smooth transition from manuscript to printed text. Barbara Chernow, President, was always ready with answers to questions about organization and Steve Bedney, Managing Editor, handled the flow of work with what seemed like effortless attention to the many essential details.

Working with these professionals was always rewarding. And I appreciate all of their help.

Numerous libraries also provided assistance. These were the Briarcliff Manor, NY, Public Library and the Westchester, NY, Library System and its numerous branches, the library of the Fashion Institute of Technology, the Queens College Benjamin Rosenthal Library, the New York Public Library and Picture Collection, and the Port Washington, NY, Public Library.

Internet sources of information and confirmation are too numerous to cite, but without use of the World Wide Web, this project would have required far more time and energy.

THE FAIRCHILD DICTIONARY OF FASHION

A **1.** Shoe size: Letter indicating a width; widths run from AAAA to EEEEE with AAAAs being the narrowest and EEEEEs the widest. **2.** Pajama size: Men's regular height (5′8″–5′11″) size corresponding to 32″–36″ chest measurement. For other sizes, see BIG, REGULAR, EXTRA-TALL, and TALL. **3.** Shirt size: For men's extra-tall with 15–15½ collar measurement. **4.** Bra cup size. Standard sizes run AAA, AA, A, B, C, D, the A sizes being the smallest and D the largest. There is no industry agreement on cup sizes larger than D. Different manufacturers use different designations.

abalone See CLOSURES: ABALONE BUTTON.

abilements/abillements See HEADWEAR: BILLIMENT.

abstract See PRINTS, STRIPES, AND CHECKS: ABSTRACT PRINT.

ACADEMIC COSTUME

Outfits consisting of caps, called mortarboards (see ACADEMIC COSTUME: MORTARBOARD); gowns; and hoods traditionally worn at Commencement exercises or other ceremonial occasions by students and faculty. Although simple gowns and mortarboards may be worn by secondary-school students, those in higher education wear more

mortarboard
gown
hood

Academic costume

elaborate regalia consisting of caps, gowns, and hoods that are most often black with color trim on hoods. American academic costume was designed by Gardner Cotrell Leonard of Albany, NY, in 1887 and adopted by the American Intercollegiate Code of 1894, revised in 1932. The code states the style of cap, gown, and hood to be worn by persons with bachelor's, master's, and doctor's degrees along with the colors to be used on the hood. Academic costume originated at the Universities of Oxford and Cambridge more than 600 years ago. Also called *academic regalia* (ak-ah-dem′-ik ree-gale′-ee-yah).

academic hood Decorative drape that comes close to the neck in front and hangs down the back of academic gowns. Made in various lengths and shapes according to the degree held, hoods are usually black with a colored facing indicating the degree granted, while lining colors represent the school colors of the institution conferring the degree, and the outer band of velvet shows the field of study. *Der.* From the cowl cape attached to gowns of undergraduates since end of 15th c. Also see under ACADEMIC COSTUME: BACHELOR'S, MASTER'S, and DOCTOR'S HOODS, and ACADEMIC HOOD COLORS.

academic hood colors The lining colors at the back of the academic hood represent the school colors of the college or institution conferring the degree. The outer band of velvet that extends around the front of the neck indicates the different faculties, or fields of study, as follows: Agriculture, maize; Arts and Letters, white; Chiropody, nile green; Commerce and Accounting, drab; Dentistry, lilac; Economics, copper; Engineering, orange; Fine Arts, brown; Forestry, russet; Humanities, crimson; Law, purple; Library Science, lemon; Medicine, green; Music, pink; Nursing, apricot; Optometry, seafoam; Oratory, silver gray; Pedagogy, light blue; Pharmacy, olive green; Philanthropy, rose; Philosophy, blue; Physical Education, sage green; Public Administration, drab; Public Health, salmon pink; Science, golden yellow; Social Science, citron; Theology, scarlet; and Veterinary science, gray.

bachelor's gown Academic gown, formerly of black worsted or similar fabric, opening in front with two wide box pleats extending to the hem; large flowing sleeves ending in points; back and sleeves set into square yoke with cartridge pleats. Worn with the bachelor's hood and mortarboard at graduation by candidates, or former recipients, of a bachelor's degree. Since the 1970s colored gowns are sometimes worn instead of black. Also see under ACADEMIC COSTUME: BACHELOR'S HOOD, ACADEMIC HOOD COLORS, and MORTARBOARD.

bachelor's hood Black decorative drape, 3' long in back with a 2″ colored velveteen band around the neck in front and a pendant tail in the back that is turned over to reveal colors of the institution granting the degree. Worn with the bachelor's gown and mortar board at graduation by candidates, or former recipients, of bachelor's degree. Also see ACADEMIC COSTUME: ACADEMIC HOOD COLORS.

doctor's gown Black unclosed academic gown with wide bands of velvet down the front. The full sleeves are set in with cartridge pleats and have three bands of velvet at the upper arm. Worn as part of academic costume by candidates for, and holders of, doctoral degrees.

doctor's hood Black academic hood with colored velvet band at neck to indicate type of degree. This velvet band extends down the back and is rolled over to show the school colors of the wearer. Square cut at hem and larger than bachelor's and master's hoods. See ACADEMIC COSTUME: ACADEMIC HOOD COLORS.

master's gown Black open-front gown with a square yoke and long closed hanging sleeves. The arms emerge through slits above elbows of the sleeves, which have crescents cut out near the sleeve hems. In the back cartridge pleats join a full back and sleeves to the yoke. Worn with master's hood and mortarboard by candidates for, and holders of, master's degrees.

master's hood Black cowl-drape 3½-feet long in back with band of colored velveteen around the edge that is turned over in back to show a lining denoting the institution granting the degree. Worn with master's gown. Also see ACADEMIC COSTUME: ACADEMIC HOOD and ACADEMIC HOOD COLORS.

mortarboard Academic headgear consisting of large, square black brim attached horizontally to a cap. A large tassel in center of the flat top hangs to right side before graduation, to the left after. Worn all over United States today and since 14th c. at such universities as Oxford and Cambridge in England. Formerly called by various names including *cater cap, cornercap, cornet, Oxford cap,* and *trencher cap.*

accordion pleats See CLOTHING CONSTRUCTION DETAILS: ACCORDION, PANTS: PARTY PANTS, and SKIRTS: ACCORDION-PLEATED SKIRTS.

acetate † (as′-uh tayt) Generic fiber category established by the FTC for manufactured fibers that are chemical variants of cellulose called cellulose acetate and that are manufactured from cellulose materials, such as wood chips. The term also refers to fabrics or yarns made from acetate fibers. Used in a wide variety of apparel, acetate fabrics have a crisp hand and a high luster. Current trademarks for acetate fiber include Chromespun®, Estron®, and Celanese® acetate.

achilles tendon protector See FOOTWEAR: A.T.P.
acrobatic slipper See FOOTWEAR.

A

acrylic † (uh krihl′ ihk)   Generic fiber category established by the FTC for a manufactured fiber primarily composed of a polymer material called acrylonitrile. Also refers to fabrics or yarns made from acrylic fibers. Acrylic fabrics have a soft, wool-like hand, good wrinkle resistance, wash and dry quickly, and therefore are often used in easy-care apparel products such as sweaters and socks. Current trademarks for acrylic fiber include Acrilan®, Duraspun®, and Creslan®.

action back   Term used to describe the extra fullness incorporated into the back of a jacket, coat, or dress that extends from the shoulder blades to the waist usually in form of pleats, to permit freedom of movement. See COATS AND JACKETS: BI-SWING.

action gloves   See GLOVES AND GLOVE CONSTRUCTIONS.

ACTIVEWEAR

Any of a wide variety of apparel items designed to be worn for active sports. Not to be confused with official athletic uniforms worn by professional athletes, although such uniforms may serve as the inspiration for the design of some activewear. Many consumers wear activewear apparel not only for sports but also as casual dress.

aerobic ensemble (uh-roh′-bik)   Headband, leotards, tights, and leg warmers worn for aerobic dancing. In this costume the headband is usually a brow band of terry cloth; leotards are a tight-fitting, torso-length garment with high or low neck and long or short sleeves; tights are made with or without feet and/or stirrups and are usually made of stretch nylon; leg warmers are knitted leg coverings without feet. Also called *workout suit* or *exercise suit.*

athletic clothes   At one time designated apparel worn solely for active sports, however now that clothes for active sports are also worn for other activities, the term ACTIVEWEAR is more often used.

bathing dress   See SWIMWEAR: category heading.

bathing suit   See SWIMWEAR: category heading.

bike suit   Tight-fitting leggings and colorful tops worn for bike riding. Also see ACTIVEWEAR: TRI-SUIT and SHORTS.

bike-tards   Tightly fitted, one-piece garment, often worn for bicycling, that extends from the top of the torso to the hem, which is located above the knee. Worn for bicycling, the garment fit is achieved by using SPANDEX yarns.

bike suit

camouflage suit   Two-piece suit consisting of a hip-length jacket, tapered pants, and sometimes a matching cap with ear flaps. Made of soft waterproofed duck fabric printed in abstract pattern of greens and browns to blend with surrounding terrain. Used by combat soldiers in World War II.

camouflage suit

Accepted for sportswear, particularly for duck hunting, in mid-1960s. After the early 1980s accepted for general wear.

cat suit   One-piece, skintight, long-sleeved suit with feet; variation of the UNITARD (see under ACTIVEWEAR.

cross-country skiing   See PANTS: KNICKERS #1.

cycling suit/cycling costume   ∞ Any costume worn for bicycling in the late 19th c. Boys: jacket, similar to PATROL JACKET, worn with tight knee pants. Women: RATIONALS (see ACTIVEWEAR) or a divided skirt with tailored or NORFOLK JACKET, leggings, and a straw sailor hat. Men: KNICKERBOCKERS and NORFOLK JACKET. See COATS AND JACKETS: NORFOLK JACKET and PATROL JACKET.

exercise suit   See under ACTIVEWEAR: AEROBIC ENSEMBLE and SAUNA SUIT.

fencing suit   Two-piece white suit with close-fitting pants and waist-length jacket made with a standing collar, diagonal closing, and small red heart on left breast. Top is quilted

A

or padded to prevent injury from the fencing foil.

gaiter See FOOTWEAR.

gym suit Suits worn by students for physical education classes; the acceptable style being determined by individual schools. When gym was first introduced, women wore blue serge or sateen pleated BLOOMERS (see under PANTS), white MIDDY BLOUSES (see under BLOUSES AND TOPS), and long black stockings. During the 1930s, ROMPER suits were worn. Since mid-1970s any type pull-on shorts and T-shirts are acceptable.

gymnastic suit Suit worn for gymnastic competitions. Women wear leotards. Men wear athletic shirts and long slim tapered pants with a stirrup strap under the instep.

hunt breeches Riding breeches with drop front, legs cut wide from thighs to hips and tight at knees. Usually made in canary or tan cavalry twill with buckskin patches at inside of knees.

informal habit Suit worn by adults and children for horse shows consisting of a *riding coat* and *jodhpurs,* sometimes matched as to fabric, sometimes contrasting. Colors worn are usually black, tan, blue, and gray. DERBY hat (see HEADWEAR) may be worn to complete costume. Also see ACTIVEWEAR: RIDING HABIT.

jockey pants Below the knee breeches with drop front and jodhpur-type legs worn tucked into boots by jockeys in horse races.

jodhpurs (jod′ poors) Riding pants, with drop front or zipper closing, that flare at thighs and have narrow straight-cut legs below knee with cuffs at ankles. Similar to men's breeches worn in India and popular for men and women horseback riders since 1920s. *Der.* Jodhpur, city in India. Also see RIDING BREECHES.

jodhpurs 1930s

jogging suit Suit worn for a slow, steady type of running called "jogging," popular since the 1960s. Various types of suits are worn: (a) sweatsuits (b) suit consisting of a zippered jacket, crew-necked sweater, and pants, and (b) warmup suits. Often made of fleece, terrycloth, or velour. See ACTIVEWEAR: SWEATSUITS and WARMUP SUITS.

jogging suit

judo suit Suit, similar in style to karate suit, which is worn for judo, a form of Japanese martial arts. See ACTIVEWEAR: KARATE SUIT.

jumpsuit 1. Shirt and ankle-length pants in a one-piece suit with zip-front and long or short sleeves. Originally worn by flyers in World War I, also by parachute jumpers and flyers in World War II. In the late 1960s adopted for sports- and leisurewear by men and women. **2.** Sleeveless one-piece swimsuit with tank or V-top combined with shorts. Introduced in 1985.

jumpsuit 1981

karate suit Two-piece suit made of white cotton or cotton and polyester, called a *gi* or *ghi* (ghee), that is worn for practicing the martial art of karate. The garment consists of a pair of drawstring pants and a wrap top that ties shut with a belt. As practiced in Asia, the uniform closed with either a white belt, for beginners, or a black belt, for advanced practitioners. For teaching non-Asians, a belt ranking system was invented. Each different karate system has different colors with one fairly common system being white for beginners, then progressing through yellow, green, and brown, to black.

karate suit

leotard (lee′-ah-tard′) Originally a two-piece, knit, body-hugging garment worn by the French acrobat Jules Leotard in the 19th c. Now a formfitting one-piece knitted garment with high or low neck, long or short sleeves, and ending in brief panties that is worn alone or over ankle-length *tights* as practice garment. Adopted by dancers, acrobats, and for exercising. Claire McCardell first introduced it in fashionable dress in 1943, although it did not catch on until the 1960s.

leotard

playsuit Shorts and shirt combined to make a suit with a waistline seam, worn with a coordinating skirt. Introduced in 1930s and fashionable at intervals since.

rationals ∞ Popular name for full pleated serge bloomers or knickerbockers worn by women for bicycling in 1890s.

playsuit and skirt
1930s

riding breeches Pants full-cut at hips and thigh and tightly fitted at knee, sometimes made of stretch fabric, some with zipper closure, and others with buttoned drop front. Worn by men and women with high boots for horseback riding. When made in a yellow fabric called *canary breeches*. Also called HUNT BREECHES (see under ACTIVE-WEAR) and *show breeches*. Also see ACTIVEWEAR: JODHPURS and ACTIVEWEAR: RIDING SMALLS.

rationals

riding habit **1.** Any combination of jacket and breeches or jodhpurs worn for horseback riding. The occasion determines the type of costume worn. Also see ACTIVEWEAR: INFORMAL HABIT. **2.** Women's riding costume showed these changes over time. In the early 17th c. composed of long hose, or CALENÇONS, worn with doublet and petticoat, and later in the century, the man's JUSTAUCORPS. In the 18th and 19th c., a number of named riding-dress styles were worn. See AMAZONE, BRUNSWICK, and EQUES-TERIENNE COSTUME in the alphabetical listing

and COATS AND JACKETS: JOSEPH #1. Riding trousers were introduced in the early 1880s for women and worn under the riding dress or skirt. RIDING BREECHES without the skirt were worn with a longer jacket about 1914. By the early 1920s, JODH-PURS (see under ACTIVE-WEAR) were popular.

riding habit

riding skirt ∞ Calf-length wraparound skirt worn by women who rode sidesaddle in late 19th and early 20th c.

riding smalls ∞ Man's riding BREECHES worn from 1814 to 1835 made of light-colored doeskin, with wide hips but tight from knees down.

rodeo suit. Suit worn at a western-type rodeo. Combination of western shirt, western pants, neckerchief, cowboy hat, and boots. Some suits are very elaborately trimmed with embroidery, fringe, or beads.

sauna suit Exercise suit made of soft flexible vinyl in jumpsuit or two-piece style with zip-front and knitted cuffs at wrists and ankles. Worn around the house, it seals in body heat, acting like a steambath and encouraging loss of weight. An innovation of the late 1960s. Also called an *exercise suit.*

sea legs Man's below-the-calf–length tightly fitted beach pants with elasticized cuffs. Made in brilliant horizontal stripes in varying widths and many colors.

shorts suit **1.** Shorts and tops made of matching or contrasting material for sportswear. **2.** See SHORTS.

ski pants Pants or leggings worn for skiing and other winter sports. The styles vary, generally following the trend in trouser leg styles and varying from wide to tight-fitting, and often having straps under the feet. First introduced with jodhpur-type legs in the late 1920s; narrow styles in stretch fabrics appeared in 1950s. For downhill racing and jumping competitions, see ACTIVEWEAR: UNITARD and SKI SUIT.

A

ski suit Any type jumpsuit or two-piece pants suit worn for winter sports. The first ski pants made their appearance for women in late 1920s and were styled similar to JODHPURS (see under ACTIVEWEAR). In the 1930s ski suits were made of wool with medium-width trousers and knitted bands at the ankles. Jackets were close-fitting

ski suit

and usually zippered. In the 1968 Winter Olympics®, fitted jumpsuits with a contrasting stripe extending down the side were introduced. In the 1984 Winter Olympics®, UNITARDS (see under activewear) were worn. Insulated jackets may be added for extra warmth. While competitive skiers seek to reduce wind resistance as much as possible with close-fitting garments, recreational skiers wear bulkier jumpsuits with high collars and belted waistlines or two-piece pants suits.

snowboarding suit Two-piece pants suit or JUMPSUIT (see under ACTIVEWEAR) worn for the sport of snowboarding. Similar to SKI SUIT (see SKI SUIT), but more loosely fitted.

snowmobile suit Jumpsuit with attached hood made of wind-resistant nylon and polyester fiberfill insulation. Made with two-way zippers to hips or one-way zipper to knees. Has snap closed pockets on chest, self-fabric belt, and knitted cuffs at wrists. Sometimes has stripes around sleeves which reflect lights of cars. Worn with snowmobile boots and gloves.

snowsuit Two-piece suit, or one-piece jumpsuit, worn by infants up to two years of age. Jumpsuit has a zipper that extends part way up the leg, making access easier. Suits have attached hoods and ribbing at ankles and wrists, some are insulated and waterproofed.

snowsuit 1933

stormsuit Two-piece sport suit made of rubberized nylon consisting of pants and jacket

with hood worn for hunting and fishing in inclement weather.

sunsuit Child's or infant's summer playsuit made with romper pants and a bib top.

surfing suit See ACTIVE-WEAR: WETSUIT.

sweatclothes Apparel worn primarily for exercising and jogging. Also worn as leisure wear.

stormsuit

sweatsuit Two-piece suit with fleece lining. Consists of a sweatshirt that pulls over the head or a sweatjacket that zips, plus sweatpants with legs gathered into ribbing or elastic at the ankles. Used by athletes for practicing running and also worn after boxing, or other exercise, to prevent sore muscles. Also worn for jogging.

swimsuit See SWIMWEAR: category heading.

tankini See SWIMWEAR: BIKINI.

teardrop bikini See SWIMWEAR: BIKINI.

tennis clothes/tennis dress First played in France in the Middle Ages, tennis was introduced in the United States as lawn tennis in 1874 with the basic rules, height of net, and dimensions of court not changing since that time. For lawn tennis, women wore fitted jackets and full skirts coming to boot tops. When bustles were in fashion (1870s and 1880s) and when leg-of-mutton sleeves were stylish (1890s), tennis dress reflected the current styles. Men wore long, white flannel trousers and white shirts. For many years it was traditional for players to wear only white. Tailored shorts were worn in 1930s. Player Gussie Moran introduced short dresses with ruffled panties for tennis in 1940s. By the 1960s mini- or micro-skirted dresses, initially white but also made in colors by the 1970s, were worn when playing tennis. Contemporary tennis fashions consist of tennis dresses or shorts and tops for women and shorts and tops for men. These change from season to season with various colors and cuts being popular, often based on what professional players have been wearing in tournaments.

tri-suit Tight-fitting suit made with stretch yarns in color-blocked style similar to a TANK SUIT (see under SWIMWEAR) but with midthigh-length legs. Worn particularly by athletes participating in Triathlon competitions, which include swimming, bike riding, and running. *Der.* Shortened form of "Triathlon."

trunks **1.** Man's shorts made loose-legged with drawstring at waist. Worn from late 19th c. on for boxing and other sports, sometimes over full-length tights. **2.** See SWIMWEAR.

tutu See alphabetical listing.

unitard One-piece BODYSUIT made of patterned, knitted fabric. Combines leotards and tights into one suit. Worn for exercising and aerobics, sometimes with small bikini pants on top. (See ACTIVEWEAR: LEOTARD and HOSIERY: TIGHTS. *Der.* From *uni*, meaning "one," and *leotard.*

unitard

warm-up **1.** *Adj.* Describes apparel, most often jackets, pants, or jumpsuits, modeled after those worn by athletes when warming up for sports events. Generally made of knitted fabrics, jackets have raglan sleeves and zipper-front closings; pants have drawstring or elastic waists and elastic or knitted cuffs at ankles. In the 1980s, fabrics used expanded to include terrycloth and velour, and the styles were adopted for outdoor sports, beachwear, indoor exercises, and casual wear. **2.** Interlined overpants worn for skiing with zippers down the sides for easy removal.

wetsuit Garment made of neoprene, a synthetic rubber, that is used for protection against cold water in sports such as scuba diving, windsurfing, white-water rafting. They are generally available in one- or two-piece styles. One-piece styles may be full wetsuits with arms and legs and sometimes with a hood and boots, or suits may be full-length without sleeves. This latter style is called a **farmer John.** A jacket can be worn over farmer Johns or with a high-waisted trouser. One-piece suits with short legs and short sleeves are also available. Some suits close with a **beaver-tail** construction, which is a large flap of material that comes from the back, through the crotch to fasten at the front. Most close with long zippers. Wetsuits are rated according to thickness in millimeters, or "mils," with thicker suits being appropriate for colder water.

workout suit See ACTIVEWEAR: AEROBIC ENSEMBLE.

---

acton See ARMOR.

adaptation **1.** Dress designing term for an interpretation of an expensive designer dress reproduced in a less expensive model. Not a direct copy but made with modification of design and fabric. Compare with KNOCKOFF and LINE-FOR-LINE COPY. **2.** Costume for a play or film made in an historic period style, e.g., 18th c., but which differs from the original styles in elements such as design and fabric.

Adelaide boot See FOOTWEAR.

adjustable Adjective indicating that some aspect of apparel can be modified to change aspects such as fit, appearance, size. See JEWELRY: ADJUSTABLE RING and VESTS: ADJUSTABLE VEST.

adjustments Reductions in the retailer's cost for goods either because of returns of merchandise to the manufacturer or as a result of problems with the merchandise.

admiral coat See COATS AND JACKETS.

Adolfo * See APPENDIX/DESIGNERS.

Adri * See APPENDIX/DESIGNERS.

Adrian, Gilbert * See APPENDIX/DESIGNERS.

Adrienne gown See SACK #1.

aegis (ee´-jis) ∞ In ancient Greek mythology a garment serving as a piece of armor that was made of the skin of a goat worn with the head to the front of the body. In depictions of Zeus, king of the gods, and Athena, goddess of wisdom, the aegis became a shield. In some depictions of Athena, it was a breastplate covered with goatskin that had the image of the head of Medusa in the center bordered with snakes.

aerobic (uh-roh´-bik) Adjective describing exercises sufficiently intense to contribute to the strengthening of the vascular system. This adjective is sometimes used with the names of items of apparel intended to be worn for aerobic exercise. See ACTIVEWEAR: AEROBIC ENSEMBLE and FOOTWEAR: AEROBIC SHOES.

aesthetic dress (s-thet′-ik) Styles of dress for men and women adopted by a small group in England who were seeking reform in the arts in late 19th c. Loosely based on historic costume of the Middle Ages, features of women's dress included elimination of corseting, large sleeves, and softer, more fluid lines than the then-fashionable bustle dresses. The writer Oscar Wilde, a proponent of this movement, wore a velvet suit with knee breeches, a loosely fitted jacket, a soft, wide collar, and flowing tie. His costume was said to serve as the inspiration for LITTLE LORD FAUNTLEROY STYLES. The Gilbert and Sullivan operetta *Patience* satirized aesthetic styles, calling these "**greenery yallery, Grosvenor gallery**" (gro′vener) costumes.

aesthetic dress 1880s

Afghanistan-inspired apparel Clothing derived from or inspired by apparel worn in the country of Afghanistan. See COATS AND JACKETS, VESTS, and SHIRTS.

afghan stitch See EMBROIDERIES AND SEWING STITCHES.

African dress Straight cut or A-line dress made of African printed fabric (sometimes of raffia) elaborately trimmed with wooden or glass beads or sequins. Made in mini- and full-length styles, some with midriffs, others with see-through midriffs with strands of beads connecting top and skirt. Introduced by Paris couturier Yves Saint Laurent in 1967.

Afro styles/Afro look Hairstyles, clothes, and accessories derived from African or African-American cultures. Usually adopted first by African-Americans, many Afro styles make their way into mainstream fashion. Beginning in late 1960s, influential examples include garments such as the BUBA, DASHIKI, and SELOSO. Also see HAIRSTYLES: AFRO and AFRO PUFFS, PRINTS, STRIPES, AND CHECKS: AFRICAN PRINTS, WIGS AND HAIRPIECES: AFRO WIG, and JEWELRY: AFRO CHOKER.

afternoon dress ∞ **1.** Term used during the 19th c. to indicate a type of dress suitable for visiting in the afternoons. **2.** In the early 20th c. indicated a dressy dress, frequently full-length in the 1920s and 1930s, suitable for a garden party or formal tea. Usually worn with a large picture hat.

after-ski See APRÈS-SKI.

agal See KAFFIYEH-AGAL.

agate See GEMS, GEM CUTS, AND SETTINGS.

age See EDGE #2.

agile manufacturing Technological innovations in apparel manufacturing that use MODULAR PRODUCTION techniques rather than the more common BUNDLE SYSTEM. With agile manufacturing, special orders can be accommodated more readily. Also called *modular manufacturing* and *flexible manufacturing.*

aggravators See HAIRSTYLES.

aglet (egg′-let) /aiglet/aiguillette Ornamental metal tag, frequently of gold or silver, similar to modern shoelace tip at end of lacing. Called POINTS in the 15th c. and used for joining men's doublet and hose; later used in bunches for a decorative effect.

Agnès * See APPENDIX/DESIGNERS.

Agnès Sorel (1422–1450) The name of the mistress of King Charles VII of France who was renown for her lavish wardrobe. Her name was used as an adjective when describing certain 19th-c. fashion terms. See AGNÈS SOREL BODICE, HAIRSTYLES: AGNÈS SOREL COIFFURE, AGNÈS SOREL CORSAGE, AGNÈS SOREL DRESS STYLE.

Agnès Sorel bodice ∞ Woman's dress bodice of 1861 with square neckline front and back, and full bishop sleeves.

Agnès Sorel corsage ∞ Woman's loose-fitting bodice or a PELISSE ROBE similar to a jacket, fastened high at neck or worn open, revealing waistcoat. Worn in 1851 and named after Agnès Sorel.

Agnès Sorel dress style PRINCESS-STYLE dress worn in early 1860s.

A

agraffe (ah′-graf) **/agraf/agrafe** ∞ **1.** Circular, square, or diamond-shaped clasp, used in pairs to fasten the mantle at the neck in the Middle Ages; and made of bronze, gold, or silver embossed in elaborate patterns, set with jewels. **2.** Pin used to fasten slashes in garments in 16th c. Compare with FERMAIL. *Der.* Norman, *aggrape*, "clasp on medieval armor."

aide memoire fan See FANS.

aiglet See AGLET.

aigrette See FEATHERS.

aiguillette (ah-gwel-let) **/aiguille 1.** Shoulder decoration made of gilt cord, frequently braided, used on military dress uniforms. The cord (aiguillette) has AGLETS at the end. **2.** See AGLET.

aigulet See AGLET.

aile de pigeon See WIGS AND HAIRPIECES: PIGEON-WING.

ajour See LACES: JOURS.

aketon See ARMOR: ACTON.

alarm watch See WATCHES.

Alaska See FOOTWEAR.

Alaskan seal See FURS: FUR SEAL.

alb See CLERICAL DRESS.

albernous/albernoz See CAPES, CLOAKS, AND SHAWLS: BURNOOSE.

Albert (1819–1861) First name of the husband of Queen Victoria, which was used as an adjective in certain 19th-c. men's fashion terms. He was Prince of Saxe-Coburg-Gotha and, after his marriage, Prince Consort of Great Britain. See these entries: FOOTWEAR: ALBERT BOOT; COATS AND JACKETS: ALBERT DRIVING CAPE, ALBERT JACKET, ALBERT OVERCOAT, ALBERT RIDING COAT, ALBERT SAC, ALBERT DRIVING CAPE, and ALBERT TOP FROCK; and FOOTWEAR: ALBERT SLIPPER.

Alençon lace See LACES.

alexandrite See GEMS, GEM CUTS, AND SETTINGS.

Alice in Wonderland dress See PINAFORE DRESS.

A-line Apparel styled close and narrow at the shoulders or waist and flaring gently away from the body to the hem in a line resembling the letter A. Introduced in 1955 by Paris couturier Christian Dior, the term is used as an adjective in describing a wide variety of apparel with this shape, including coats, dresses, jumpers, and skirts. See A-LINE DRESS, JUMPERS: A-LINE JUMPER, and SKIRTS: A-LINE SKIRT.

A-line dress Dress style that flares gently from under the arms to hem of skirt, resembling the letter A. Usually made with narrow shoulders, a high round neckline, and is similar to a SKIMMER. Introduced in 1955 by Paris couturier Christian Dior.

A-line dress 1955

Allard, Linda * See APPENDIX/DESIGNERS.

alligator See LEATHERS.

alligator-grained See LEATHERS.

alligator lizard See LEATHERS.

all-in-one 1. Child's full-length, knitted garment with legs that may or may not have feet. **2.** See UNDERGARMENTS: FOUNDATIONS. **3.** See SHOULDERS AND SLEEVES.

all-in-one

all-in-one pantyhose See HOSIERY: PANTYHOSE.

allover See LACES and PRINTS, STRIPES AND CHECKS.

all-purpose poncho See CAPES, CLOAKS, AND SHAWLS: RAIN PONCHO.

all rounder See NECKLINES AND COLLARS: DOG COLLAR.

all-sheer pantyhose See HOSIERY.

all-weather Adjective used for clothing and accessories suitable for dry or wet weather and for varying temperatures. See COATS AND JACKETS: ALL-WEATHER COAT and ALL-WEATHER RAINCOAT, and FOOTWEAR: ALL-WEATHER BOOT.

almain coat jacket See COATS AND JACKETS.

almain hose See TRUNK HOSE.

almandine garnet/spinel See GEMS, GEM CUTS, AND SETTINGS.

almoner See HANDBAGS AND RELATED ACCESSORIES: AULMONIÈRE.

almuce 1. See HEADWEAR. **2.** See CAPES, CLOAKS, AND SHAWLS. Also spelled *amuce, almusse, aunice, aumusse.*

aloe (ahl′-loh) **1.** A fiber obtained from the leaves of several tropical plants. **2.** See EMBROIDERY AND SEWING STITCHES. **3.** See LACES.

aloha shirt See SHIRTS: HAWAIIAN SHIRT.

alpaca † A sheeplike animal of the camel family, related to the llama, native to the Andes in South America. Yarn spun from fleece is lustrous and shiny.

alpargata See FOOTWEAR.

Alpine Adjective used to describe apparel inspired by or derived from the clothing of the European mountains called the Alps. See FOOTWEAR: ALPINE BOOT, HEADWEAR: ALPINE HAT, and COATS AND JACKETS: ALPINE JACKET.

alum tanning See LEATHERS.

amadis sleeve See SHOULDERS AND SLEEVES.

amazon Adjective attached to the names of certain items of women's fashionable apparel. The Amazons were a legendary race of warlike women. The use of the term in the 19th c. was part of a tendency of the period to name fashions for historical or legendary figures. See NECKLINES AND COLLARS: AMAZON COLLAR, AMAZON CORSAGE, UNDERGARMENTS: AMAZON CORSET, and FEATHERS: AMAZON PLUME.

amazon corsage ∞ Plain bodice buttoned up front to high neckline and trimmed with small white cambric collar and cuffs; tailored style for women in 1842.

amazone ∞ Woman's scarlet riding habit with high waistline and full-length skirt worn in early part of 19th c. in U.S., France, and England. *Der.* From legendary Greek women warriors called *Amazons.*

amber See GEMS, GEM CUTS, AND SETTINGS.

American buskins See FOOTWEAR.

American coat See COATS AND JACKETS.

American Fashion Critics' Award Original name for the COTY AWARD.

American Indian One of the terms used to refer to the indigenous people of the Americas. Used as an adjective to describe fashion items inspired by or derived from Native American dress. See BELTS: AMERICAN INDIAN, HAIRSTYLES: AMERICAN INDIAN HAIRSTYLE, HANDBAGS AND RELATED ACCESSORIES: SQUAW BAG, HEADWEAR: AMERICAN INDIAN HEADBAND, JEWELRY: INDIAN BEADS and AMERICAN INDIAN NECKLACE, and PRINTS, CHECKS, AND STRIPES: AMERICAN INDIAN PRINT.

American Indian beadwork Tiny glass beads in various colors woven to make headbands, necklaces, and used for trimmings—sometimes in shape of medallions—by various Native American tribes.

American Indian dress 1. Dress made of suede or buckskin with simple lines and trimming of beads and fringe, originally worn by North American Indian women. 2. Modern interpretation of Native American dress in leather, suede, or fabric. Also called *Pocahontas dress.*

American marten See FURS.

amethyst See GEMS, GEM CUTS, AND SETTINGS.

amice See CLERICAL DRESS.

Amies, Hardy * See APPENDIX/DESIGNERS.

amorphous See GEMS, GEM CUTS, AND SETTINGS.

amuce See ALMUCE.

amulet Small object believed to possess magical powers—a good-luck charm worn as protection against evil by primitive people and surviving to present time in various forms of jewelry.

anadem See HAIR ACCESSORIES.

anchor store A large, popular retail store usually located at the end of the mall (hence the name "anchor").

Andalouse cape See CAPES, CLOAKS, AND SHAWLS.

Andalusian casaque ∞ (an-dah-loo′-zee-an cask) Woman's evening tunic fastened down center with series of ribbons with front of skirt cut away, sloping to knee-length in the back. Worn over another skirt in 1809.

Andean shift Native dress from Peru made in straight-cut style of native fabrics and trimmed with embroidery. Sold in U.S. in late 1960s. Also called an *ocepa. Der.* Dress from Andes Mountains in South America.

andradite garnet See GEMS, GEM CUTS, AND SETTINGS.

androgynous/androgynous look (an-droj′-eh-nus) Possessing both male and female characteristics. Styles of various periods may include androgynous elements. Examples for women include short boyish bob hairstyles; man-tailored suits of men's wear fabrics; tailored trousers; trenchcoats; slouch hats, neckties, and button-down collars. For men,

androgynous look
1990s

the adoption of more traditionally feminine styles has included long hair, makeup, jewelry, and clothes with more color.

angel overskirt ∞ Woman's short overskirt having two long points on either side used as part of daytime dress in 1894.

angel sleeve   See SHOULDERS AND SLEEVES.

angled pocket   See POCKETS: HACKING POCKET.

angled shawl collar   See COLLARS AND NECKLINES.

angle-fronted coat   See COATS AND JACKETS.

anglesea hat   See HEADWEAR.

Angleterre, point d' lace   See LACES: POINT D'ANGLETERRE.

Anglo-Greek bodice ∞ Woman's bodice with wide lapels placed far apart and edged with lace. Worn in 1820s with FICHU-ROBINGS.

Anglo-Saxon embroidery   See EMBROIDERIES AND SEWING STITCHES.

angora † Soft fuzzy yarn made from the under-hair of the angora rabbit used for knitwear and for trimmings.

Angoulême bonnet   See HEADWEAR.

animal print   See PRINTS, CHECKS, AND STRIPES.

ankh   Egyptian symbol for eternal life, some what like a cross with vertical bar forming a loop at top. Popular as jewelry motif, especially as necklaces and rings, in late 1960s and 1970s. Also called *ansate cross*. See JEWELRY: ANKH RING.

ankle boots   See FOOTWEAR.

ankle bracelet   See JEWELRY.

ankle-jack   See FOOTWEAR.

ankle length   See LENGTHS.

ankle-length hose   See HOSIERY.

ankle sock   See HOSIERY.

ankle-strap   See FOOTWEAR.

anklet   **1.** See JEWELRY: ANKLE BRACELET. **2.** See HOSIERY: ANKLE SOCK.

ankle watch   See WATCHES.

Annette Kellerman   See SWIMWEAR.

Annie Hall look   Style of dressing for women inspired by clothing worn by Diane Keaton in the film *Annie Hall*, written and directed by Woody Allen. Typical styles included such elements as baggy pants, men's

Annie Hall look 1978

shirts and vests, and the idea of wearing clothes in an uncoordinated manner.

annular brooch   See PENANNULAR BROOCH.

anorak   See COATS AND JACKETS.

ansate cross   See ANKH.

anslet   See DOUBLET.

antelope   See FURS and LEATHERS.

antelope-finished lambskin   See LEATHERS.

Anthony, John   * See APPENDIX/DESIGNERS.

anti-embolism stocking   See HOSIERY.

antigropolis   See FOOTWEAR.

antique bodice ∞ Long-waisted, tight bodice with low décolletage and deep point at front waistline; worn for evening by women in 1830s and 1840s.

antique couching   See EMBROIDERIES AND SEWING STITCHES: ORIENTAL COUCHING.

antique finish   See LEATHERS.

antique lace   See LACES.

antique satin   See SATIN.

antique taffeta † Crisp taffeta that may have irregular slubs throughout in imitation of 18th-c. fabrics. Also made in iridescent effects with lengthwise and crosswise yarns of different colors.

antireflective coating   See EYEWEAR.

Antoinette fichu   See SCARVES: FICHU #1.

Antwerp lace   See LACES.

ao dai   Pantsuit consisting of a long-sleeved mid-calf tunic, slashed on side seams (or one side), and full-length pants; worn by men and women in Vietnam.

apache (ah-patch'-ee) **1.** Styles similar to clothes worn by American Southwest tribe of Native Americans from Arizona and New Mexico. **2.** In France, *apache* (ah'-pash) is slang for gangster or thug, especially as depicted by French nightclub dancers. *Der.* The French word was taken from the Native American tribe of the same name, which was thought to be very fierce. Also see HANDBAGS AND RELATED ACCESSORIES: SQUAW BAG, SCARVES, and SHIRTS.

ape drape   See HAIRSTYLES: SHAG.

apex   See HEADWEAR.

apollo corset   See UNDERGARMENTS.

apollo knot   See HAIRSTYLES.

apparel   **1.** Any type of clothing worn by men, women, and children. Synonyms: *attire, clothes, costume, dress, garb, garment, habit, uniform,* *robe, raiment,* and *vestments,* the latter used particularly for clerical dress. **2.** Used since early 14th c. to denote clothing, particularly a suit of clothes. **3.** Late 14th c.: embroidered borders of ecclesiastical garments. **4.** Late 14th c.: embellishment of armor.

apparel industry The manufacturers, jobbers, and contractors engaged in the manufacture of ready-to-wear clothing for men, women, and children. Also called *cutting-up trade, garment trade, needle trade,* and *rag business.*

apparel price ranges Prices in the apparel industry may be designated as falling into one of the following categories that form a sort of continuum of prices from low to high: **low end, budget, moderate, better, bridge,** and **designer.**

Appenzell See EMBROIDERIES AND SEWING STITCHES.

applejack cap See HEADWEAR: NEWSBOY CAP.

appliqué (ap-plee-kay) **1.** Surface pattern made by cutting out fabric or lace designs and attaching them to another fabric or lace by means of embroidery or stitching. **2.** See LACES. **3.** Applied leather designs on shoes and handbags.

appurn See APRONS: NAPRON.

après ski/après ski look (ah-pray') French term meaning "after-ski." Used as a fashion adjective with clothing and accessories typically worn when relaxing after skiing. This look first became popular in the 1950s at famous resorts such as Sun Valley, Lake Placid, and San Moritz. As more people began to ski, the look increased in popularity. Elements included colorful, glamorous sportswear items such as vests of fur or embroidery; pants of velvet, printed fabrics, and suede; sweaters in jacquard knits; and unusual boots. *Der.* French, "after skiing." See FOOTWEAR: APRÈS-SKI BOOT.

apron checks See PRINTS, STRIPES, AND CHECKS.

apron dress Any dress worn with a decorative apron. Also see PINAFORE DRESS.

apron jumper See JUMPERS: WRAP JUMPER.

APRONS

apron **1.** Item of apparel designed to protect clothing or used as a decorative accessory. Historically, aprons were worn from the 13th c. on by men and women. They originated in Middle Ages from an extra piece of cloth tied over skirt by women before sitting down at the table. See APRONS: BARMECLOTH. This style was later adopted by servants and worn with a bib top. In the 16th to 18th c., color of the apron denoted the trade of workman or artisan. See CHECKERED APRON MAN, BLUE-APRONED MAN, and GREEN-APRONED MAN. Decorative aprons of lace and embroidery were worn over dresses in the first half of the 17th c., throughout the 18th c., and in the 1870s. *Der.* Old French, *napperon,* the diminutive *nappe* meaning "cloth." During the Middle Ages, a *napperon,* or napkin, became apron. (Older spelling *appurn.*) **2.** Dress with a free-hanging panel attached to the front of a skirt, which resembles an apron. **3.** See TIES.

barber's apron Long circular cape, fastening at the neckline in back, originally made of cotton fabric and now sometimes of plastic, worn to protect clothes while hair is being cut.

barmecloth ∞ Early medieval term for an apron. Gradually replaced by the word apron after the end of the 14th c. Also called *barmhatre.*

barmfell ∞ Term for a leather apron from 14th to 17th c. Also called *barmskin.*

belly-chete ∞ 16th-c. slang term for apron.

bib apron Apron that extends high on chest, held by straps over the shoulders crossing in center back and attached at the waistline. First worn in the 17th c.

bib apron

butcher's apron Apron made of heavy fabric—usually white. Styled all-in-one piece coming to the chest in front, having a strap going around the back of the neck, curved under the arms, and tied at center back. *Der.* From apron worn by butchers when cutting meat. Also see APRONS: CHEF'S APRON.

carpenter's apron Characterized by having a large pocket made of fabric or leather divided into sections and mounted on a belt. Worn to carry nails, small tools, etc.

A

cartoon apron Usually a butcher's type apron printed with humorous pictures or slogans.

chef's apron Apron of canvas, terrycloth, or other type of fabric styled like a butcher's apron and worn by cooks for outdoor barbeques as well as in the kitchen. May have a KANGAROO POCKET (see under POCKETS) across the center front and be screen printed with a name or message.

cobbler's apron Hip-length, large-pocketed apron originally worn by shoemakers, carpenters and other workmen to hold nails. Popular as woman's fashion in late 1960s, and usually made of fabric. Also see APRONS: CARPENTER'S APRON.

cobbler's apron

cocktail apron Tiny half-apron made of net, lace, or fabric.

fig leaf ∞ Small black silk apron worn by women in 1860s and 1870s.

half-apron Bibless apron coming only to waist.

Hoover apron Utility wrap-around dress with two half-fronts and attached sash that goes through slot at each side seam to tie in back. *Der.* Originated during World War I when Herbert Hoover was food administrator in the United States.

Hoover apron 1935

laissez-tout-faire ∞ (le′-zay-too-fare) Long apron worn over the dress for home wear in 17th c.

lawn-tennis apron ∞ Drab-colored bib apron worn for tennis by women in 1880s with skirt pulled up on left side and draped at back where there was a large patch pocket for holding tennis balls. Another pocket was placed low on the right side of the skirt. Both pockets were decorated with embroidery.

napron ∞ Used in 14th c. and first half of 15th c. for *apron. Der.* Old French, *naperon,* diminutive of *nape* or *nappe,* "tablecloth" or "apron." From about 1460, words *apron* or *appurn* were used.

pinafore apron Apron worn by young girls made with a gathered skirt, bib top, and suspender straps. Sometimes made with ruffles over the shoulders extending to waistline.

Priscilla apron ∞ Young girl's apron of 1890s styled with full skirt shirred into waistband. Bib top extended around neck in broad, lace-trimmed, sailor-collar effect. Had straps from shoulder blades to waistband in back. Frequently made of lightweight cotton fabrics.

safeguard ∞ Man's colored apron worn by bakers and tradesmen from 16th to 18th c.

tea apron ∞ White lawn apron with small pocket, which ties around waist and is trimmed with ruffles, VALENCIENNES LACES (see under LACES), and HEM-STITCHING (see under EMBROIDERIES AND SEWING STITCHES). Used when sewing, or to protect the dress, in early 20th c.

trucker's apron Shaped similar to a butcher's apron with large pockets in front. Has a slit in center front and ties around each leg.

tyes ∞ American term for girl's apron in late 19th c.

work apron Any apron designed to cover the clothes amply while the wearer is working at a job that might soil or harm garments.

---

apron swimsuit See SWIMWEAR: PINAFORE SWIMSUIT.

apron tongue See FOOTWEAR: TONGUE.

apron wrap jumper See JUMPERS: WRAP JUMPER.

aquamarine See GEMS, GEM CUTS, AND SETTINGS.

Arabian Nights look See HAREM LOOK.

araneum lace See LACES.

Aran Isle sweater See SWEATERS.

arba kanfoth (ar′ba kan-foth) Undergarment worn by Orthodox Jewish men, consisting of a rectangle of cloth with hole or slit in center for head and tassels or fringe at the corners.

arch cushion See FOOTWEAR.

arctics See FOOTWEAR.

argentan lace See LACES.

Argentina borregos lamb See FURS: LAMB.

argyle See **1.** PLAIDS AND TARTANS. **2.** HOSIERY. **3.** SWEATERS.

Arizona ruby See GEMS, GEM CUTS, AND SETTINGS: RUBY.

A

Armani, Giorgio * See APPENDIX/DESIGNERS.
armband bracelet See JEWELRY.
Armenian lace See LACES.
Armenian mantle See COATS AND JACKETS.
armhole Section of garment through which arm passes or into which sleeve is fitted. Usually round but may be squared underneath the arm. Older synonyms include *armscye* (arm′-sye), *armseye, arm's eye.*

ARMOR

Protective garments worn by soldiers and knights from early times, especially those made of CHAIN MAIL and cast metal from Middle Ages through 17th c.

acton (ak′-tun) **1.** A padded, sleeveless jacket worn under CHAIN MAIL in the 12th and 13th c. Term is used interchangeably with GAMBESON by experts on Medieval costume and armor. **2.** Later applied to a steel-plated jacket worn as armor. Also spelled *ackton, acketon, aketon, auqueton, hacketon, haqueton.*

Armor with parts labeled

(labels: burgonet, visor, shoulder cop, gorget, breastplate, vambrace, skirt, gauntlet, tasset, cuisse, poleyn or knee cop, greave, sabaton)

basinet Pointed steel helmet worn as armor from 1350 to 1450. Also spelled *bascinet, bacinet, basnet.*
bouchette (boo-shet) Large buckle used in medieval times to fasten breastplate of armor.
brassart (brass′-are) Piece of armor worn on upper arm for protection from mid-14th to 15th c.
brayette Metal CODPIECE worn as armor in 16th c. Also spelled *braguette.*
burgonet (bur′gon-ay) Metal helmet worn as armor in the 16th c. Has a brim that projects over the eyes, called an *umbril,* and a metal projection to protect the back of the neck. It may have hinged earflaps and one or more standing pieces or *combs* on the crown. Some are decorated with elaborate ham- mered designs. Of Burgundian origin and adopted by England, Germany, Italy, and France. Compare with armor: morion.

camail (ka-mal′) Shoulder cape of CHAIN MAIL laced to helmet worn as part of armor during first half of 14th c.
cannon Piece of protective plate armor for the upper arm or forearm, cylindrical or semi-cylindrical.
capeline (cap-leen) Iron or steel skullcap worn by foot soldiers in Middle Ages.
cervellière (ser′-vel-yair) Close-fitting steel cap usually worn under helmet during Middle Ages. *Der.* French, *cervelle,* "brains."
chain mail See ARMOR: MAIL.
chapel de fer (sha-pel de fehr) Armor for head, a skullcap of iron or steel, sometimes with brim; worn by medieval knights. *Der.* French, "cap of iron."
chausse (sho′sez) Stockings of CHAIN MAIL (see under ARMOR), worn by knights and soldiers in last quarter of the 13th c.
coat of mail See ARMOR: HAUBERK.
coiffe de mailles (qwaff de mile) Hood of MAIL worn by Norman war lords from late 11th to mid-12th c. Later worn under helmet and, in 15th c., by ordinary soldiers. Also called *coif of mail.*
coiffette (kwah-fet′) Iron or steel skullcap worn by soldiers during 14th c.
cointise (kwan-teez′) Lappet or scarf under the crest of helmet worn in late 12th c. Also spelled *quaintise, quintise.*
collaret Armor worn in the Middle Ages to protect the neck.
corselet Originally leather armor; later in 16th c. metal-plate armor worn by pikemen, made of cast metal—lighter than the cuirass. See ARMOR: CUIRASS.
coutes (koot) Armor for the elbows worn over CHAIN MAIL in early 13th c. Also plate armor for elbows in latter 14th c. *Der.* French, *coude,* "elbow."
cuirass (kew-rass′) **1.** Sleeveless leather thigh-length tunic worn as armor by ancient Greeks and Romans. **2.** Armor consisting of breastplate and backplates of steel worn either under or over other garments from mid-

14th to mid-17th c. At first over a mail shirt and *jupel* (see GIPON) and under a TABARD, later worn outside with metal TASSETS (see under ARMOR) forming a skirt. Similar to CORSELET (see under ARMOR) or breastplate.

cuisse (qwees) Piece of armor or padding shaped to protect the thigh that was worn during the Middle Ages.

culet (ku′-lit) Piece of armor consisting of a skirt of articulated plate fastened to a backplate to protect the loins worn from mid-16th to mid-17th c.

demi brassard Armor worn in early 14th c. consisting of a metal plate worn to protect the upper arm.

demi-jamb Armor consisting of a metal plate over front of leg from ankle to knee connected to the SOLLERET (see under ARMOR), or shoe. Worn by knights and soldiers in the early 14th c. Also see ARMOR: GREAVE.

demi-vambrace Armor worn on front of forearm from elbow to the wrist.

épaulière (ep′-ool-yehr) Armor consisting of single piece of unarticulated shoulder plate, first worn about 1300, smaller in size than the pauldron. See ARMOR: PAULDRON. Also called *epaulet* and *shoulder cop.*

gauntlet Armor of MAIL, or PLATE (see under ARMOR), worn on the hand from 15th to 17th c.

gorget (gorge′-et) Armor worn on throat in Middle Ages.

greave Metal-plate leg covering reaching from ankle to knee. Worn from 11th to 17th c. as armor. Also called *jamb (jambe)* (zham). When made of leather in the 14th c., called a *jambeau* (zham-bow′). When worn just on the front of the leg, called a *demijamb (jambe)* (dem-ee zham).

hauberk (ho′-berk) Knee-length shirt made of mail worn as armor in 11th, 12th, and 13th c. Sometimes covering hands ending in mail mittens. Sides were split from waist down in front and back for convenience in riding horseback and worn over quilted gambeson (see DOUBLET). Sometimes called *coat of mail.* Also see ARMOR: VAMBRACE.

jamb/jambe See ARMOR: GREAVE.

jambeau (zham′-bow) Leather armor worn to protect leg in 14th c. See ARMOR: GREAVE.

jazerant (jazz′-er-ant) Armor worn in 14th c. consisting of a leather or cloth tunic covered with overlapping plates of leather, metal, or horn. Also spelled *jazeran, jazerine, jesseraunt.*

knee-piece Armor worn to protect the knee. Called *poleyn* (pol′-ain) or *knee cop.*

lame (lah-may) Armor composed of thin overlapping plates used for covering the hands. Also see ARMOR: GAUNTLET.

mail The earliest form of mail in armor consisted of metal rings sewn to foundation of leather in parallel rows. By the Middle Ages, metal rings were interlinked and called *chain mail. Der.* Middle English, *maille,* one of the "rings" from which it was made.

mentonnière (mohn-ton′-yehr) Protective armor for lower part of face or chin worn in tournaments in Middle Ages.

morion Lightweight helmet, with brim forming peaks front and back. Turned down on sides with high comb in center extending from front to back over crown of head. Popular in 16th c. throughout Europe, and associated with Spanish conquistadors in Mexican conquest. Also called *comb morion.* Compare with ARMOR: BURGONET.

pauldron (pol′drum) Armor worn in late 15th c. consisting of single large rigid shoulder plate lapping over armor at chest and back. Also called *épaulière* (eh-pol yair′) and *shoulder cop.*

plastron Iron breastplate worn as armor between HAUBERK and GAMBESON. See under ARMOR.

plate Armor made from solid sections of metal.

poleyn Piece of armor consisting of a metal plate (originally leather) worn over knee cap, introduced in 13th c. Also called *knee cop* and *genouillière* (zhe-no-yair′).

rerebrace (rer′bras) Plate armor worn on the upper arm. See ARMOR: CANNON or VAMBRACE.

sabaton Broad-toed armor of mid-16th c. strapped over top of foot. Also called *bear paw* or *duckbill solleret.* Also spelled *sabatayne.* Also see ARMOR: SOLLERET.

A

sallet (sal′-ay) Helmet worn in 15th c. by Germans, French, and British, usually cast in one piece in potlike shape flaring somewhat at neck in front and sometimes in back. Covered entire face with small slit to see through, sometimes had a moveable visor. Also spelled *celata, salade, salet.*

shoulder cop Small plates covering front of shoulder. Later they were small pieces of articulated metal. Still later consisted of a single large plate called a PAULDRON (see under ARMOR). Also called *épaulière.*

solleret (sol′-er-ay) Piece of armor worn during the Middle Ages to protect foot. Consisted of jointed flexible pieces of iron. In the 15th c. had a long pointed toe—then called *solleret à la poulaine* (sol′-er-ay ah lah poo-layn′). Also spelled *soleret, solaret.* Also see ARMOR: SABATON.

tasset Armor for the upper thigh made either of a single plate or of several narrow flexible plates joined together by rivets. Also spelled *tace, tasse.*

tonlet Flaring skirt of metal plates or of solid metal, sometimes fluted with deep vertical folds, worn as armor in 16th c. Also called *lamboy, jamboy,* or *base.*

vambrace **1.** Armor consisting of metal plate worn on forearm, under the HAUBERK or over it, in early 13th c. **2.** Later, plate armor for entire arm made up of upper and lower CANNONS and COUTES for the elbow. (See cross-references under ARMOR.)

ventail Armor for lower part of face on 16th-c. helmet. If face guard is made in three pieces, ventail is middle piece.

visor Movable part of helmet that could be lowered to cover the face.

---

armseye/arm's eye See ARMHOLE.

armur raccoon See FUR: USSURIAN RACCOON.

army cap See HEADWEAR: FATIGUE CAP, OVERSEAS CAP, or SERVICE CAP.

Army/Navy clothes Surplus items of new clothing of the types worn by men and women of the U.S. Army and Navy that are sold in special stores called "Army/Navy stores."

Arrasene See EMBROIDERIES AND SEWING STITCHES.

Arrow® Collar man See NECKLINES AND COLLARS: DETACHABLE COLLAR.

arrowhead See EMBROIDERIES AND SEWING STITCHES.

Art Deco/Art Deco look A nonrepresentational style in the arts of the 1920s and 1930s that relies on geometric and stylized forms drawn from diverse sources ranging from Aztec motifs to animal and floral patterns. The term came into use only in 1968 when an author, Bevis Hillier, writing about the style, derived the term from the name of a Paris exposition of 1925 that featured designs of this period: Exposition International des Arts Décoratifs et Industriels Modernes. In fashion the style was most evident in textiles and jewelry. Art Deco design experienced a revival in the late 1960s and has continued to appear since then. Also called *Art Moderne, Modernistic, Jazz Modern, Skyscraper Style.* See HOSIERY: ART DECO HOSE, JEWELRY: ART DECO EARRING, and PRINTS, STRIPES, AND CHECKS: ART DECO.

Art Deco designs 1920s

artichoke See HAIRSTYLES.

artificial crinoline See UNDERGARMENTS: HOOPS.

artificial silk † Used before 1925 to describe rayon and acetate. Also called *art silk.*

artillery twill † Synonym for WHIPCORD.

artist's smock **1.** Traditionally a SMOCK used by artists. Usually three-quarter length with full sleeves gathered into band at wrist and a large round collar and, sometimes, with black tie around the neck. **2.** Any smock worn when painting.

Art Moderne See ART DECO.

Art Nouveau/Art Nouveau look (noo′vo) Design style of the period 1890 to 1910 that represented an attempt by artists and artisans to develop a style with no roots in the past. Designs emphasized curved, waving lines; stylized natural forms of plants, animals, and women; and a strong sense of motion. Revived in later periods, especially in jewelry and textiles. The style was known as *stile liberty* (stee´-lay lee-bare-tay´) in Italy, as *Jugendstil* (Yu´-gend-stil) in Germany, and as *modernismo* (moh-der-nees´-moh) in Spain. See HOSIERY:

Art Nouveau designs 1898

ART NOUVEAU HOSE and PRINTS, STRIPES, AND CHECKS: ART NOUVEAU PRINTS.

artois See CAPES, CLOAKS, AND SHAWLS.

artois buckle See CLOSURES: BUCKLES D'ARTOIS.

art silk See ARTIFICIAL SILK.

art to wear See WEARABLE ART.

Ascot Fashionable horse-racing spot, Ascot Heath, in England, for which a number of fashions have been named. See COATS AND JACKETS: ASCOT JACKET, NECKLINES AND COLLARS: ASCOT NECKLINE/COLLAR, SCARVES: ASCOT SCARF, and TIES: ASCOT.

A-shirt See SHIRTS: ATHLETIC SHIRT.

Ashley, Laura * See APPENDIX/DESIGNERS.

asooch 17th-c. term meaning "sash-wise" or "scarf-wise"; draped diagonally from shoulder to hip. Also spelled *aswash.*

assasins See PATCHES #3.

Assisi embroidery See EMBROIDERIES AND SEWING STITCHES.

associated buying office An office that offers consultation services and buys merchandise for a group of independently owned stores. Participating stores are shareholders in the buying office. Also called a *cooperative buying office.*

assortment The merchandise available in a store at any given time. Assortments are often described in terms of **breadth** (i.e., numbers of styles) and **depth** (i.e., numbers of sizes and colors available for each style).

asterism See GEMS, GEM CUTS, AND SETTINGS.

astrakhan/astrakan † **1.** Fabric with a heavy, curly pile made to imitate karakul lamb fleece. May be woven or knitted. Used as trimming or

for men's hats. **2.** Wool from the karakul lamb. **4.** See FURS: KARAKUL.

astrolegs hose See HOSIERY.

astronaut's cap See HEADWEAR.

aswash See ASOOCH.

asymmetric/asymmetric dress The principle of informal balance, rather than formal balance, with each side of the garment offering a different silhouette. In women's dresses, examples would include drapery arranged more to one side, a side closing, one shoulder uncovered, or trimming arranged differently on each side of the dress. Other examples include SWIMWEAR: ASYMMETRIC SWIMSUIT; CLOSURES: ASYMMETRIC, CLOTHING CONSTRUCTION DETAILS: ASYMMETRIC HEM, COLLARS AND NECKLINES: ASYMMETRIC COLLAR/NECKLINE, SKIRTS: ASYMMETRIC SKIRT.

asymmetric dress 1994

Ata See TALLITH.

atef See HEADWEAR.

atelier de couture Workrooms in which Parisian haute couture designers and their staff design and produce their COLLECTIONS.

athletic clothes See ACTIVEWEAR.

athletic pants See PANTS: SWEATPANTS.

athletic shirt See UNDERWEAR: ATHLETIC SHIRT and SHIRTS: ATHLETIC SHIRT.

athletic shoes See FOOTWEAR.

athletic shorts See SHORTS.

athletic socks See HOSIERY: SWEATSOCKS.

at-home wear Informal clothing worn at home, particularly when entertaining. See SLEEPWEAR AND LOUNGEWEAR: CAFTAN and HOSTESS ROBE.

atours See HEADWEAR.

A.T.P. See FOOTWEAR.

attaché case See HANDBAGS AND RELATED ACCESSORIES: BRIEFCASE.

attached collar See NECKLINES AND COLLARS.

attic look Early 1970's term for apparel that looked like clothes and accessories found in the attics of old houses. Also see VINTAGE LOOK.

attifet See HEADWEAR.

attire 1. Synonym for APPAREL. **2.** See HEAD-WEAR.

Aubusson stitch See EMBROIDERIES AND SEWING STITCHES: REP STITCH.

Audubon Plumage Law Law passed in early 20th c. prohibiting use and importation of feathers from rare birds, such as the egret, that were used as fashionable trim on women's hats from late 19th to early 20th c. *Der.* Named for John James Audubon, American ornithologist who died in 1851.

Augustabernard * See APPENDIX/DESIGNERS.

aulmoniere See HANDBAGS AND RELATED ACCESSORIES.

aumusse/aunice See HEADWEAR: ALMUCE.

auqueton See ARMOR: ACTON.

aurora borealis crystal See JEWELRY.

Australian opossum See FURS.

Austrian crystal See JEWELRY.

Austrian seal See FURS.

automobile Adjective used to describe apparel used by drivers in the early days of automobile use. See HEADWEAR: AUTOMOBILE CAP and AUTOMOBILE VEIL.

automobile coat See COATS AND JACKETS: DUSTER.

avant-garde (ah-vant′ gard) French term commonly used in English meaning new, unconventional, ahead of its time. Used as an adjective to describe apparel that may be provocative or startling.

aviator Adjective applied to apparel or accessories that are copied from or inspired by clothing worn by airplane pilots. See EYEWEAR: AVIATOR'S GLASSES and HEADWEAR: AVIATOR'S HELMET.

award sweater See SWEATERS: LETTER SWEATER.

awning stripe See PRINTS, STRIPES, AND CHECKS.

Ayrshire embroidery See EMBROIDERIES AND SEWING STITCHES: MADEIRA EMBROIDERY.

Aztec Adjective describing apparel ornamented with designs and motifs associated with the Aztec civilization of ancient Mexico. See PRINTS, STRIPES, AND CHECKS: AZTEC PRINTS and SWEATERS: AZTEC SWEATER.

B **1.** Shoe size: Letter indicating a width; widths run from AAAA to EEEEE with AAAAs being the narrowest and EEEEEs the widest. **2.** Pajama size: Men's regular height (5′8″–5′11″) size corresponding to 37″–40″ chest measurement. For other sizes, see BIG, EXTRA-TALL, REGULAR, and TALL. **3.** Shirt size: For men's extra-tall size with 16–16½ collar measurement. **4.** Bra cup size. Standard sizes run AAA, AA, A, B, C, D, the A sizes being the smallest and D the largest. There is no industry agreement on cup sizes larger than D. Different manufacturers use different designations.

babet bonnet See HEADWEAR.

babet cap See HEADWEAR.

babushka See SCARVES.

baby Adjective describing apparel or textiles that implies something of smaller size.

baby beads See JEWELRY: BABY BRACELET.

baby bodice ∞ Daytime bodice introduced in 1878 with lingerie features similar to baby's dress such as vertical pleats down front, a wide sash, basques (see BASQUE #2) below waistline, and a square neck. Later in 1897, worn with a high drawstring neckline fastened with ribbon and a wide sash.

baby bonnet See HEADWEAR.

baby boomers Those 76 million Americans born after World War II and between the years 1946 and 1964.

baby boot See FOOTWEAR.

baby bunting Infant's outdoor combination blanket-sack with zipper-up front and separate or attached hood, frequently made of blanket cloth and bound with satin. Also called *bunting* and *grow bag*. Contemporary baby buntings may be made with legs instead of a sack bottom.

baby bunting c. 2000

baby-doll dress/baby-doll look **1.** Woman's dress cut like a smock, with a high neckline and gathers or pleats hanging from a tiny yoke, similar to children's, infant's, and dolls' dresses of the 1930s. Introduced in early 1960s by English designers and used again in late 1970s by French ready-to-wear designers. Shown at MOD DRESS. Elements that made up the entire look included baby-doll shoes, with straps over the instep, and mini purses on long chains. Also carried over to very short pajamas and nightgowns. Popularity enhanced by movie *Baby Doll* (1956), in which Carroll Baker played the lead. *Der.* Term used to refer to clothing and accessories used for children's dolls and infants' clothes in the early 20th c. **2.** Revived in fall 1985 when British designer *Vivienne Westwood* introduced a collection of dresses called by this name. Dresses were similar to children's and dolls' dresses of 1930s and 1940s—some with collars, cuffs and wide belts, others

baby doll dress #2

with full skirts over crinoline petticoats. Patou, in Paris in the fall of 1986, introduced a style with long sleeves, wrapped draped bodice, and sometimes worn over petticoats made with ruffles.

baby-doll pajamas See SLEEPWEAR AND LOUNGE-WEAR.

baby-doll sleeve See SHOULDERS AND SLEEVES: PUFFED SLEEVE.

baby dress Dresses popular until mid-20th c. for infants, regardless of sex, usually made of fine white cotton in loose-fitting style and trimmed with tucks, embroidery, and lace. At present such dresses are usually reserved for female infants.

baby Irish lace See LACES.

baby lace See LACES.

baby Louis heel See FOOTWEAR: LOUIS HEELS.

baby ribbon Narrow ribbon ⅛″ to ¼″ in width, sometimes made of reversible satin. Originally used for baby clothes and also to thread through insertion, lace, and beading in late 19th and early 20th c.

baby sash ∞ Woman's sash of ribbon tied in bow at back; popular at end of 19th c.

baby skirt See SKIRTS.

Baby Stuart cap See HEADWEAR.

Bachelor's gown See ACADEMIC COSTUME.

Bachelor's hood See ACADEMIC COSTUME.

bachlick See SCARVES.

bacinet See ARMOR: BASINET.

back 1. The rear or underside of a fabric or garment, as opposed to the front or upper side. 2. ∞ 14th-c. term sometimes used to describe any outer garment.

back-combing See HAIRSTYLES.

backing See CLOTHING CONSTRUCTION DETAILS.

backless bra See UNDERGARMENTS.

backless dress Dress with extremely low back, sometimes dipping to below the waist, used mainly for evening gowns. Made in many different styles with high front that sometimes has a cutout.

backpack See HANDBAGS AND RELATED ACCESSORIES.

backs ∞ Term used in the 14th c. to refer to clothing in general.

backless dress 1998

backstay See FOOTWEAR.

back stitch/backstitch See EMBROIDERIES AND SEWING STITCHES.

back strings 18th-c. synonym for LEADING STRINGS.

back-wrap dress See WRAP DRESS.

badger See FURS.

bäffchen See CLERICAL DRESS: GENEVA BANDS.

bag 1. Any one of various kinds of luggage. 2. Shortened form of word HANDBAG. See HANDBAGS AND ACCESSORIES. 3. Shortened form of bagwig. See WIGS AND HAIRPIECES: BAGWIG.

bag bodice ∞ Woman's bodice with PLASTRON (see PLASTRON # 2) cut to blouse over belt or waistband, worn in daytime in 1883.

bag bonnet See HEADWEAR.

bag cap See HEADWEAR.

baggies See PANTS: BAGGY PANTS.

bagging shoe See FOOTWEAR: STARTUP.

baggy pants See PANTS.

bag-irons ∞ Iron, bronze, or silver frames with suspension units made of a crossbar and swivel. Lower section of concentric semi-circular rings act as stiffeners for opening and closing. Used for medieval pouches worn hanging from belt in 15th and 16th c. Also called bag-rings.

bag-rings See BAG-IRONS.

bag-waistcoat See VESTS.

bagnolette See HEADWEAR.

bagpipe sleeve See SHOULDERS AND SLEEVES.

bags Slang term for men's trousers in 19th and early 20th c. See PANTS: OXFORD BAGS.

baguette See GEMS, GEM CUTS, AND SETTINGS: BAGUETTE CUT.

bagwig See WIGS AND HAIRPIECES.

bakelite Plastic that may be clear and uncolored or colored and opaque. Used for jewelry and for handbags and/or their fittings.

Bakst, Leon Nikolaevich (1868–1924) Russian artist who, after leaving Russia for Paris in 1909, won international fame designing sets and costumes for the Ballets Russes produced by Diaghilev. Helped to start a wave of Orientalism in women's dresses in the pre–World War I era.

bal/Balmoral See FOOTWEAR.

balaclava See HEADWEAR.

balas ruby See GEMS, GEM CUTS, AND SETTINGS: SPINEL.

balayeuse   See DUST RUFFLE.

balbriggan   † Soft, lightweight tubular knit fabric made of cotton, manufactured, or blended yarns in a plain stitch. It may be slightly napped on the reverse side. Used for pajamas and SNUGGIES (see UNDERGARMENTS). *Der.* Named for Balbriggan, Ireland, where name was first used for type of unbleached hosiery.

baldric/baldrick   See BELTS.

Balenciaga, Cristobal   * See APPENDIX/DESIGNERS.

ballantine   See HANDBAGS AND RELATED ACCESSORIES: RETICULE.

ball earring   See JEWELRY.

ballerina length   See LENGTHS.

ballerina shoe   See FOOTWEAR.

ballet laces   See FOOTWEAR.

ballet neckline/ballerina neckline   See NECKLINES AND COLLARS.

ballet skirt   See SKIRTS.

ballet slipper   See FOOTWEAR.

ball fringe   See BRAIDS.

ball gown   See FORMAL ATTIRE.

ball heel   See FOOTWEAR.

balloon   Adjective used to describe apparel that has the rounded shape of a balloon. See HEADWEAR: BALLOON HAT, SHORTS: BALLOON SHORTS, SKIRTS: BUBBLE SKIRT, and SHOULDERS AND SLEEVES: BALLOON SLEEVE.

ballpoint embroidery   See EMBROIDERIES AND SEWING STITCHES: LIQUID EMBROIDERY.

ballroom neckcloth   See TIES.

balmacaan coat   (bal-má-can)   See COATS AND JACKETS.

Balmain, Pierre   * See APPENDIX/DESIGNERS.

Balmoral   (bahl-mor'-al)   Castle near Braemar, Aberdeenshire, Scotland, purchased by Queen Victoria in 1852. She built another granite castle on this site, using it as a fashionable retreat. The name of the castle was used as an adjective when describing certain fashionable items of Victorian apparel.

Balmoral bodice   ∞ (bahl-mor'-al)   Tight-fitting jacket-type bodice with long sleeves worn by women in early 1860s and early 1880s. Made with high neck and a series of double box pleats in back, one over the other to form fullness over hips; or made with long tabs over the bustle in back. Usually worn with contrasting skirt in

1880s, at which time it was also called *postillion corsage.*

Balmoral boot   See FOOTWEAR.

Balmoral cap/bonnet   See HEADWEAR.

Balmoral jacket   See COATS AND JACKETS.

Balmoral mantle   See CAPES, CLOAKS, AND SHAWLS.

Balmoral petticoat   See UNDERGARMENTS.

Balmoral tartan   See PLAIDS AND TARTANS.

Baltic seal   See FURS.

Baltic tiger   See FURS.

bamberges   See FOOTWEAR.

bambin/bambino hat   See HEADWEAR.

band   1. See NECKLINES AND COLLARS. 2. See CLERICAL DRESS: GENEVA BANDS.

bandanna   (ban-dan'-nah)   † 1. Cotton calico fabric usually made by RESIST PRINTING on red or navy-blue with black-and-white designs. 2. See SCARVES. 3. Silk printed square from India used as neckcloth or snuff handkerchief in 18th and 19th c. 4. See PRINTS, STRIPES, AND CHECKS. *Der.* From Hindu *bandhnu,* a "method of tie-dyeing cloth."

band bow   See TIES.

bandbox   ∞ 1. In the 16th and 17th c., a box in which collars, called bands (see NECKLINES AND COLLARS: FALLING BAND), were kept. Bandboxes developed for use in Europe from mid-18th c. on. Used in the United States for storage and transportation of clothing, hats, etc., during the 19th c. After the Civil War they declined in popularity, and by late 19th c. were replaced by more utilitarian trunks, portmanteaux, and hatboxes. 2. Hatbox, usually round, of cardboard or thin wood covered with stiff paper that in the United States by the 1820s was printed with pictorial panoramas. European boxes were plainer. Both were used to carry small items as well as hats.

band briefs   See UNDERGARMENTS.

band cuff   See CUFFS.

bandeau   1. See HEADWEAR. 2. See UNDERGARMENTS: BRA. 3. See SWIMWEAR.

bandeau d'amour   See HAIRSTYLES.

bandeau slip   See UNDERGARMENTS: BRA SLIP.

banded agate   See GEMS, GEM CUTS, AND SETTINGS: AGATE.

banded bottom sleeve   See SHOULDERS AND SLEEVES: BANDED BOTTOM SLEEVE.

banded collar   See NECKLINES AND COLLARS.

B

banded neckline   See NECKLINES AND COLLARS.
banded sleeve   See SHOULDERS AND SLEEVES.
bandelet   **1.** See GLOVES AND GLOVE CONSTRUCTIONS. **2.** See SCARVES.
band-leg panties   See UNDERGARMENTS: BAND BRIEFS.
bandoleer   See BELTS.
bandolier   **1.** Shoulder bag carried by women of Great Plains Native American tribes. Made in pouch style and used to carry small items, e.g., combs, needle and thread. **2.** See BELTS: BANDOLEER.
bandore and peak   See HEADWEAR.
banging chignon   See HAIRSTYLES.
bangle bracelet   See JEWELRY.
bangle watch   See WATCHES: BRACELET WATCH.
bangs   See HAIRSTYLES.
banian/banjan   See BANYAN.
Banton, Travis   *   See APPENDIX/DESIGNERS.
b a n y a n   ∞ Comfortable, loose-fitted dressing gown worn by men in the late 17th through the early 19th c. Often very decorative, these garments were made from a wide variety of fabrics, including cotton calicos, elaborate silks, and glazed wool. Although this garment was made for indoor wear, it was not unheard of for a man to go outside in his banyan. *Der.* From *banian*, a caste of Hindu merchants from the subcontinent of India. Also spelled *banian, banjan*.

banyan

bar drop pin   See JEWELRY.
barbe   See HEADWEAR.
barber's apron   See APRONS.
barbette/barbet   See HEADWEAR.
barbs   See introduction to FEATHERS.
barbula   See BEARD.
Barcelona handkerchief   ∞ Colored or black silk handkerchief made in checks or fancy designs in twill weave. Worn around neck or head, or carried in hand, in 18th and 19th c. *Der.* From Barcelona, Spain, where first made.
Bardot, Brigitte (bar′-doe)   French movie actress who became a sex symbol of the 1950s and 1960s after the movie *And God Created Woman* (1956). Responsible for a wave of interest in tousled hairstyles, tight jeans, body sweaters, and blue-and-pink–checked gingham little-girl dresses.
Bardot hair   See HAIRSTYLES.
bare bra   See UNDERGARMENTS.
bare look   Styles in which large areas of the body that are customarily covered are revealed. Examples include tiny halters, tiny bikinis, halter necklines on dresses and evening gowns, bare midriff styles, and low, plunging décolletage. Often used as a descriptive term in the 1970s and after.
bare midriff   Adjective describing clothing that exposes the body from under the bust, baring the rib cage, to the waist or hips. Introduced in the U.S. in the late 1920s and early 1930s, made popular by film star Carmen Miranda in the 1940s, and revived in the 1960s and 1980s after interest developed in the fashions of India such as the SARI and the short-waisted blouse worn with it. See

bare midriff 1936

SLEEPWEAR AND LOUNGEWEAR: BARE-MIDRIFF PAJAMAS and BLOUSES AND TOPS: BARE-MIDRIFF TOP.
bare top   See BLOUSES AND TOPS.
barège shawl   See CAPES, CLOAKS, AND SHAWLS.
barette   See HAIR ACCESSORIES: BARRETTE.
bargello stitch   See EMBROIDERIES AND SEWING STITCHES.
bark cloth   See TAPA CLOTH.
bark tanning   See LEATHERS: VEGETABLE TANNING.
barmecloth   See APRONS.
barmfell   See APRONS.
barmhatre   See APRON: BARMECLOTH.
barmskin   See APRONS: BARMFELL.
barn coat   See COATS AND JACKETS: FIELD COAT.
barong tagalog   See SHIRTS.
baroque (bahr′-oke)   Art and decorative style in the 17th and first half of 18th c. that was characterized by heavy ornate curves and excessive ornamentation. Term is applied to certain jewelry and
baroque design

embroidery designs that derive from the baroque style.

baroque pearl See GEMS, GEM CUTS, AND SETTINGS: PEARLS.

barouche coat See COATS AND JACKETS.

bar pin See JEWELRY.

barré † (ba-ray´) 1. Defect in woven fabric consisting of differences in warps or filling as to color or texture. Also spelled *barry*. **2.** French adjective for fabrics or knits with horizontal stripes in two or more colors. Used for neckwear.

barred buttonhole See CLOTHING CONSTRUCTION DETAILS: WORKED BUTTONHOLES.

barrel Adjective used to describe cylindrically shaped objects. See CLOSURES: BARREL SNAPS, CUFFS: BARREL, HAIRSTYLES: BARREL CURLS, HANDBAGS AND RELATED ACCESSORIES: BARREL BAG, TIES: OSBALDISTAN TIE, SHOULDERS AND SLEEVES: BARREL SLEEVE, and TRUNK HOSE.

barrel-shaped muff ∞ Large muff made of or trimmed in fur, sometimes concealing arms to elbows. Illustrated in paintings such as *Madame Molé-Raymond* by Vigée-Lebrun and *Mrs. Siddons* by Gainsborough.

barrette (ba-ret) 1. See HAIR ACCESSORIES. **2.** See HEADWEAR.

barrister's wig See WIGS AND HAIRPIECES.

barrow ∞ 19th-c. covering for infant consisting of a piece of flannel wrapped around the body and covering the feet. By the early 20th c. this had become a LAYETTE item: a long wraparound strapless petticoat set onto a wide underarm band that pinned shut. Generally it was worn with the hem pinned up with large safety pins.

barry See BARRÉ.

Barrymore collar See NECKLINES AND COLLARS.

bar-shaped tie See TIES.

bar tack See EMBROIDERIES AND SEWING STITCHES.

bas de chausses See CHAUSSE and NETHER STOCKS.

bascinet See ARMOR: BASINET.

base **1.** See GEMS, GEM CUTS, AND SETTINGS: BASE. **2.** See ARMOR: TONLET.

baseball Adjective used to describe any item of clothing that is derived from or influenced by clothing worn for the American sport of baseball. See HEADWEAR: BASEBALL CAP, COATS AND JACKETS: BASEBALL JACKET, and SHIRTS: BASEBALL SHIRT.

base coat See COATS AND JACKETS.

bases ∞ **1.** Man's separate skirt, hung in unpressed tubular pleats, that was worn with a padded doublet or under armor from about 1490 to 1540. Sometimes simulated in steel in armor. **2.** Skirt of a jacket or jerkin, hanging in unpressed pleats. **3.** See COATS AND JACKETS: BASE COAT.

bases

basic dress Dress of simple cut with no ornamentation, usually colored black. Jewelry, collars, and other accessories can be added to change the appearance. Introduced in the 1930s, worn through 1940s, and revived in early 1970s. Also called "L.B.D." (little black dress).

basic dress

little black dress 2001

basics In retailing refers to those products for which there is a constant and continuing demand. Examples: hosiery, jeans, T-shirts. Also called *staples*.

basinet See ARMOR.

basket See HEADWEAR.

basket bag See HANDBAGS AND RELATED ACCESSORIES.

basketball shoe See FOOTWEAR.

basket button See CLOSURES.

basket stitch See EMBROIDERIES AND SEWING STITCHES.

basket weave † Variation of plain weave, made by weaving two or more crosswise yarns over and under same number of lengthwise yarns to produce a checkerboard effect.

basket weave diagram

basket-weave stitch See EMBROIDERIES AND SEWING STITCHES.

basque (bask) ∞ **1.** In the 17th c. originally referred to a part of a man's doublet extending below the waist that was made with a series of vertical slashes forming tabs. **2.** By mid-19th c., used for that part of a woman's bodice that extended below the waistline. **3.** In the early 20th c., referred to a woman's waist-length jacket or dress that fits tightly through waist and rib cage.

basque #2

basque beret See HEADWEAR: BERET #1.

basque-habit ∞ Bodice worn from 1860s on with square-cut tabs below the waistline.

basque shirt See SHIRTS.

basque waistband See BELTS.

basquina See BASQUINE #2.

basquin body ∞ Woman's daytime bodice of 1850s without a waistline seam that extended below the waistline.

basquine ∞ (bas′-keen) **1.** See COATS AND JACKETS. **2.** Wide underskirt of rich fabric held out by hoops worn in 16th c. Also called *basquina* in Spain.

Bass Weejuns® See FOOTWEAR.

baste/basting stitch See EMBROIDERIES AND SEWING STITCHES.

bateau neckline (ba-toe′) See NECKLINES AND COLLARS.

bathing cap See HEADWEAR.

bathing dress See SWIMWEAR: BATHING SUIT.

bathing slipper See FOOTWEAR.

bathing suit See SWIMWEAR.

bathrobe See SLEEPWEAR AND LOUNGEWEAR.

bathrobe dress Wraparound dress with shawl collar, no buttons, front lapped over and held in place with a sash. Worn since the mid-1960s.

batik † **1.** A method of dyeing in which the pattern area is covered with wax and the fabric placed in a dyebath where the uncovered areas take up the color. Additional colors can be added by selectively covering and uncovering areas of the cloth. Because the wax sometimes cracks during handling and dye leaks through these cracks, fabrics often show fine lines or streaks in the patterns. **2.** See PRINTS.

bating See LEATHERS.

batiste † A plain weave, lightweight sheer fabric usually made of cotton or a cotton and polyester blend. Made in a variety of colors and printed designs and used for men's and women's shirts, handkerchiefs, infants' clothing, women's blouses, dresses, nightgowns, and lingerie.

batswing tie See TIES.

batt See FOOTWEAR.

battant l'oeil See HEADWEAR.

Battenberg jacket See COATS AND JACKETS.

Battenberg lace See LACES.

batter's cap See HEADWEAR.

batting † Matted sheets of fibers used in quilting or stuffing. Fibers used include cotton, wool, kapok, spun rayon, or FIBERFILL.

battle jacket See COATS AND JACKETS.

battlements ∞ Trimming consisting of square-cut tabs used in same manner as scallops on dresses, skirts, jackets, and basques in the 19th c.

batwing sleeve See SHOULDERS AND SLEEVES.

baum marten See FURS.

bautte/bautta See CAPES, CLOAKS, AND SHAWLS.

Bavarian dress ∞ Woman's carriage dress, trimmed with bands of fabric down the front, that was worn in 1820s.

Bavarian lace See LACES.

bavolet See HEADWEAR.

bayadère See SCARVES.

bayadère stripe (bah-yah-deer′) ∞ **1.** In 1850s, flat velvet trimming used either woven in or applied to dresses. **2.** Name of fabric with brilliant contrasting horizontal stripes. **3.** See CHECKS, PRINTS, AND STRIPES. *Der.* Costume of Indian *bayadère*, or "dancing girl."

B-boys See HIP-HOP.

beach Adjective used to describe clothing for wearing at the beach. See ACTIVEWEAR: BEACH ROBE, CAPES, CLOAKS, AND SHAWLS: BEACH PONCHO, HEADWEAR: BEACH HAT, WIGS AND HAIRPIECES: BEACH WIG, ACTIVEWEAR: BEACH WRAP-UP.

beach coat See ACTIVEWEAR: BEACH ROBE.

beach pajamas Full-length culottes often made of printed fabric worn sometimes with matching bolero as sportswear in 1920s and 1930s, revived in 1970s.

beach pajamas
1929

beach shift Simple cover-up designed to be worn over a

bathing suit, often in matching fabric. Also called *beach dress.*

beach toga   See ACTIVEWEAR: BEACH COAT.

beachwear   Items of apparel or accessories specifically for use at the beach.

beaded   Adjective used to describe items decorated with beads. See HANDBAGS AND RELATED ACCESSORIES: BEADED BAG, SWEATERS: BEADED SWEATER.

beaded necklace   See JEWELRY: AMERICAN INDIAN NECKLACE.

beaded velvet   See CUT VELVET.

beading   **1.** See EMBROIDERIES AND SEWING STITCHES. **2.** See LACE.

beads   See JEWELRY.

beanie   See HEADWEAR.

bear paw   See ARMOR: SABATON.

beard   The hair that grows on the lower part of a man's face that, when not shaved off, may be trimmed and shaped around the jaw and chin in various ways that may be given fashion names. The following are some specific types of beards: **bodkin beard** Beard with long point in center of chin; worn by men from early 1520 to early 17th c. **favourite** Small tuft of hair worn on man's chin from 1820 to 1840. **goatee** Small pointed beard similar to tuft of hair on a goat's chin. **imperial** Man's small pointed tuft of hair under lower lip. Fashion set by Emperor Napoleon III of France from 1852 to 1871. **newgate fringe** Colloquial term in 19th c. for men's short whiskers that formed a fringe around the jaw. **pique devant** (peeay´k deh´-vahn) Short pointed beard worn with a moustache by men from 1570s to 1600. Also called *pickdevant* and *barbula.* **vandyke beard** Small pointed beard. *Der.* Named for the type of beards depicted by Flemish painter Sir Anthony Van Dyke (1599–1641) in his portraits of men.

goatee

vandyke beard

beard box   ∞ Early American device made of pasteboard, worn at night over beard to preserve its shape.

beard brush   ∞ Term used for small brush used in public to comb the beard; popular during the first half of 17th c.

bearer   See UNDERGARMENTS.

bearskin   **1.** See HEADWEAR. **2.** See FURS.

Beatles/Beatle   Rock-music group from Liverpool, England, that became very popular in early 1960s. Members were George Harrison, John Lennon, Paul McCartney, and Ringo Starr. They appeared in Mod clothing and long hairstyles that started a trend for young people in England, the United States, and throughout the world. Clothing derived from styles associated with the group often were described with the adjective "Beatle." See HAIRSTYLES: BEATLE CUT and FOOTWEAR: BEATLE BOOT.

beatnik   Young, radical bohemians of the 1950s who were influenced by the so-called beat poets and French existentialist writers. Men wore working men's clothes and women wore their hair very long and dressed in black leotards and black skirts with ballet shoes.

Beaton, Sir Cecil (1904–1980)   An English-born photographer and illustrator for *Vogue* magazine. In 1928 Beaton creating drawings of clothes worn at society parties as well as caricatures of well-known English actresses. As a photographer he did both fashion and portrait photos, becoming a favorite of the British royal family. During World War II he photographed in North Africa, Burma, and China for Ministry of Information. He designed scenery and costumes for ballet, opera, and theater productions in both London and New York. Beaton designed the costumes for stage productions of *My Fair Lady* and the film *Gigi.* Queen Elizabeth II knighted him in 1972.

beau (boh) (*pl.* beaux)   Term used from 1680s to mid-19th c. for a gentleman who was fastidious about his clothes and accessories, similar to but not as effeminate as *fop.* Also see DANDY.

Beau Brummel (Boh Brum´-ul)   Somewhat derogatory term used to refer to a man who takes an unusually strong interest in his appearance and his clothes (*e.g.,* "He's a Beau Brummel.").

beau of the time of George "Beau" Brummel

B

Term derives from the nickname of George "Beau" Brummel (1778–1840), an English dandy who was a court favorite and men's fashion leader during the Regency Period (1811–1820). Brummel insisted on impeccable grooming, absence of showy fabrics or excessive decoration, and superb tailoring.

beau monde (bow mond)   French term meaning the "world of fashion"; literally, "the beautiful world."

Beaufort coat   See COATS AND JACKETS.

Beaulard   *   See APPENDIX/DESIGNERS.

Beautiful People   Expression coined by writer Rebecca Warfield in *Vogue* magazine in 1962 to describe rich and fashionable people.

beauty spot   Mark on the face either natural (such as small mole) or artificial, drawing attention to a good feature. Also see PATCH #3.

Beauvais embroidery   See EMBROIDERIES AND SEWING STITCHES.

beaux   Plural of BEAU.

beaver   See FURS.

beaverette   See FURS.

beaver hat   See HEADWEAR.

beaver tail   See SWIMWEAR: WETSUIT.

bebe bonnet   See HEADWEAR.

bebop cap   See HEADWEAR: NEWSBOY CAP.

becca   See HEADWEAR: ROUNDLET.

Bedale jacket   See COATS AND JACKETS: BEDALE COAT.

Bedford cord   † Heavyweight cotton or manufactured fiber fabric characterized by heavy lengthwise cords or stripes. The ribs are formed by heavy yarns used as backing or stuffer yarns. Carded single or two-ply yarns are used in face of fabric. Popular for women's and men's summer suits where word is shortened to *cord*. Also made by knitting and called *cord knit*. Lighter weights are called *warp piqué* (pee-kay′).

bedgown   See SLEEPWEAR AND LOUNGEWEAR.

bed jacket   See SLEEPWEAR AND LOUNGEWEAR.

bedroom slipper   See FOOTWEAR.

bed socks   See HOSIERY.

beefeater's uniform   Tudor-period uniform consisting of knee-length red DOUBLET with white ruffle at neck. The doublet is elaborately trimmed with gold and black and is worn with red TRUNK HOSE, red stockings with garters below

the knees, a black hat with a soft, high crown flared slightly at top that is pleated into headband with a narrow brim, and black shoes trimmed with rosettes. Worn since 1485 by Yeoman of the Guard of the royal household in England, appointed by Henry VII. Same costume worn today by Yeoman Extraordinary of the Guard, appointed Wardens of the Tower of London by Edward VI. *Der.* Term in use from about the middle of the 17th c. alluding to British fondness for roast beef.

beehive   See HAIRSTYLES.

beehive hat   See HEADWEAR.

Beene, Geoffrey   *   See APPENDIX/DESIGNERS.

beer jacket   See COATS AND JACKETS.

beggarbeads   See JEWELERY.

beggar's lace   See LACES: TORCHON LACE.

beguin   See HEADWEAR.

Belcher handkerchief   See TIES AND NECKCLOTHS.

belette   ∞ An ornament or jewel; a term from the 13th to 16th c. Also spelled *bilett*.

Belgian lace   See LACES.

Belgrave shoe   See FOOTWEAR.

bell   Adjective used to describe a wide variety of apparel details or items that have the approximate shape of a bell. See CAPES, CLOAKS, AND SHAWLS: BELL, FOOTWEAR: BELL-BOTTOM HEEL, PANTS: BELL-BOTTOM TROUSERS, SHOULDERS AND SLEEVES: BELL SLEEVE, SKIRTS: BELL SKIRT, UMBRELLAS: BELL UMBRELLA, and UNDERGARMENTS: BELL HOOP.

bellboy/bellhop   Adjective used to describe garments inspired by or modeled after the clothing worn by hotel employees, called bellboys. Although uniforms worn by these employees now differ from hotel to hotel, at one time most wore a distinctive uniform consisting of waist-length red jacket with high Chinese collar closing diagonally, trimmed with gold braid and button, and small red pillbox hat.

bellboy hat   See HEADWEAR.

bellied doublet   See PEASCOD-BELLIED DOUBLET.

bellows   Adjective used to describe apparel details or items that expand and contract like a bellows, an instrument used to produce a stream of air. See FOOTWEAR: BELLOWS TONGUE, POCKETS: BELLOWS POCKET, and SHOULDERS AND SLEEVES: BELLOWS SLEEVE.

belly-chete   See APRON.

belly piece   ∞ At the front of man's DOUBLET, a stiffened triangular ridge lined with buckram, pasteboard, or whalebone. Worn from 1620 to 1660s.

belt bag   See HANDBAGS AND RELATED ACCESSORIES.

BELTS

belt   Decorative or functional item worn circling above, below, or at the natural waistline. Also worn over the shoulder in military fashion. May be made of fabric, leather, plastic, chain, etc. In the past and in poetic writings also called a *girdle*. Belts in classical antiquity were mostly of the sash type. In the Middle Ages, as fitted garments were made, belts became important and a man's or woman's wealth could be determined by the richness of his or her linked, elaborately jeweled belt.

American Indian belt   Leather belt decorated with woven American Indian beadwork in bright colors and motifs.

baldric/baldrick   ∞ Wide decorative belt used to hold dagger worn at hip level. Worn diagonally from right shoulder to left hip, where sword was placed from 13th to 17th c.

bandoleer   Wide belt having loops to hold cartridges with one or two straps extending over shoulders. Also spelled *bandolier.*

basque waistband   ∞ Belt or waistband decorated with five pointed tabs worn on afternoon dresses by women in latter half of 19th c.

bikini chain belt   Fine gold chain worn with bikini or hip-hugger pants. Introduced in late 1960s.

black belt   See ACTIVEWEAR: KARATE CLOTHING.

braided belt   Belt made by plaiting narrow strips of leather, vinyl, elastic, thong, or fabric that may buckle or tie.

brown belt   See ACTIVEWEAR: KARATE CLOTHING.

cartridge belt   Webbed or leather belt, worn by armed forces and law enforcement officers, with individual spaces

cartridge belt

for ammunition. The belt may have an attached holster for a gun. This style without a holster but with a row of fake bullet cartridges was adopted as a fashion fad.

chain belt   Belt made of various sizes of chain. May be a single chain or a series of chains looped to medallions or imitation jewels at intervals.

chain belt

cinch belt   Wide belt worn pulled tight, usually of elastic or fabric, either laced or clasped in front, popular in 1940s and 1950s.

cinch belt

cincture (sink´-cher)   1. See CLERICAL DRESS. 2. Synonym for *belt. Der.* Latin, *cinctur,* "a girdle."

cingulum (sing´-oo-luhm)   ∞ 1. Belt or girdle worn under the breasts by women in ancient Rome. 2. Belt worn by men in Rome on tunic to adjust the length of garment. 3. Roman sword belt. 4. See CLERICAL DRESS.

contour belt   Any belt that is curved so that it conforms to the body shape. It may be wider in the front or the back and various versions have been fashionable periodically. One type called a **dip belt** was usually of stiffened fabric, cut wider in the front with a pointed lower edge. It fastened by strings attached to each end that came from back around to the front and tied under the belt and was fashionable in late 19th and early 20th c.

contour belt

corselet belt   Wide belt, sometimes enclosing the rib cage, frequently laced up front in manner similar to peasant's bodice. Called *swiss belt* in the 19th c.

cowboy belt   Wide leather belt, sometimes with tooled designs, worn at top of hipbone by frontier cowboy to hold gun holster. Adapted for women's and men's sportswear.

cross-girdling   See GREEK BELT.

cummerbund   Wide fabric belt, sometimes pleated lengthwise and fastened in back. Worn with men's semiformal dinner suit, also worn by women. Copied from wrapped cloth belts worn

cummerbund

B

in Eastern countries. *Der. kamarband,* "loin-band."

dip belt See BELTS: CONTOUR BELT.

D-ring belt A narrow belt closed by pulling the end through two D-shaped rings.

gaucho belt (gow'-cho) Belt made of medallions of leather and metal joined with chain; introduced in late 1960s. *Der.* Spanish, "cowboy" of South America.

gobelin corselet Woman's belt in form of a corselet (see BELTS: CORSELET BELT) worn in mid-1860s, coming up high under the bust to a point in front at waistline, narrowing in back and trimmed with a ruffle of lace.

Greek belt Long narrow sash that crosses over chest and winds around waist, a fashion innovation of the 1960s copied from sash worn in ancient Greece. Also called *cross-girdling.*

half belt ∞ Belt that does not extend around the entire waistline. It may be used in the back only. One such belt is the **martingale belt,** a half belt worn on back of garment above or below normal waistline. *Der.* Part of horse's harness designed to hold head down.

judo belt See ACTIVEWEAR: KARATE CLOTHING.

karate belt See ACTIVEWEAR: KARATE CLOTHING.

kidney belt Extremely wide belt, similar to a POLO BELT (see under BELTS), worn when motorcycling to prevent injury.

Marguerite girdle Stiff belt laced in back and wider in front, forming two points above and below waistline. Sometimes made with butterfly arrangement in front and with a ruffle, PEPLUM, or bow in back to give a BUSTLE effect (see BUSTLE #2). Popular in 1860s and worn at intervals since.

martingale belt See BELTS: HALF BELT.

mesh belt Belt made of extremely small metal links fastened together to form a flexible fabriclike band.

money belt Belt worn under or over clothing when traveling, with hidden zippered compartment for money.

money belt

monk's belt **1.** See CLERICAL DRESS: CINCTURE. **2.** Fashion term for a belt of cincture-

type made of rope, braided rayon, or nylon with tassels on the ends.

obi See OBI-STYLED SASH.

obi-styled sash Sash that is approximately 4″ to 5″ wide at the center and tapers to 1″ to 1½″ at the ends. It is worn wrapped around the waist twice and tied, with the ends hanging down the front. The tapered ends may be of contrasting colors or fabrics. Although it is a single piece of fabric, it gives the appearance of a double sash. Adapted in 1980s from the **obi,** which is a sash approximately 15″ wide and 4 to 6 yards long, worn by Japanese men, women, and children on top of KIMONO. It is folded lengthwise with the fold toward hem, is wrapped twice around waist, and tied in a flat butterfly bow in back. Style of tying and design of fabric vary according to age and sex. Sometimes spelled *obe.*

polo belt Wide leather belt covering the rib cage; it fastens in front with three small buckles on narrow leather straps. Originally worn by polo players for protection. Also see BELTS: KIDNEY BELT.

Pompeian silk sash ∞ Wide black silk belt woven with allegorical figures, usually worn by women with a bodice, colored skirt, and white summer jacket in 1860s.

safari belt Wide belt with attached flap pockets in front.

Sam Browne belt Belt around waist with extension strap over right shoulder, worn by U.S. Army officers, guards, and some policemen. Also called *shoulder belt. Der.* From British general, Sir Samuel Browne, who, having lost his left arm, couldn't support his sword without this special belt.

sash Any belt of soft material that loops over and ties in a knot or bow rather than buckling.

self-covered belt Any belt cut out of the same fabric as garment, usually stiffened with a liner. Available in kits for the home sewer. If tied, it is called a *self sash.*

sash

self sash See BELTS: SELF-COVERED BELT.

serpentine belt Belt made in wavy design, zigzagging around the body.

shoulder belt   See BELTS: SAM BROWNE BELT.

skirt-belt   Belt with attached PEPLUM forming a short skirt. Introduced in late 1960s to wear over jumpsuits, body stockings, and pants.

spaghetti sash   A sash made of a long narrow piece of fabric, with cording inserted as filler to give a rounded effect, sometimes knotted at the ends.

surcingle belt   A webbed belt woven in plain or striped fabric fastened with a metal buckle through which a harness leather tab is pulled. Sometimes has a zippered pocket for money. *Der.* From the girth that fastens a horse's saddle or blanket.

swiss belt   See BELTS: CORSELET BELT.

thong belt   **1.** Wide leather belt with eyelets at each end through which a piece of rawhide is laced. **2.** Belt made of braided rawhide.

tooled leather belt   **1.** Handmade leather belt of various widths embossed with various motifs. May be purchased in kits. **2.** Belts imitating the above, stamped out by machine, sometimes imported from Mexico and Central America. **3.** Belts from India in intricate designs that are inked in various colors.

webbed belt   Belt of heavy canvas webbing, usually wide and fastened with a clip buckle, worn by military. Used in a narrower width on bathing suits in the 1920s. Adapted for casual wear by men and women in various widths and colors from 1960 on.

weight belt   **1.** Belt of nylon webbing fitted with approximately twelve pound weights. Used for scuba diving and underwater swimming. Extra weights may be added. **2.** Wide leather-textured vinyl or fabric belt with eight to ten pound weights worn under or over clothing as a reducing aid or figure improver.

white belt   See ACTIVEWEAR: KARATE CLOTHING.

zone (zo-knee) ∞ Belt worn by ancient Greek women around the hips, usually the lower one of two.

---

belt buckle   See CLOSURES.

beluque   See CAPES, CLOAKS, AND SHAWLS.

Ben Casey   Television series of the 1950s with physician Ben Casey as the central character. Because of its popularity, certain of the clothes worn by the doctor served as the inspiration for fashionable clothes, most notably the *Ben Casey collar* and the *Ben Casey shirt.* See NECKLINES AND COLLARS: MEDIC and SHIRTS: MEDIC.

bench coat   See COATS AND JACKETS: BENCHWARMER.

benchwarmer   See COATS AND JACKETS.

bench wig   See WIGS AND HAIRPIECES.

bend   **1.** See LEATHERS. ∞ **2.** Term used from 11th to end of 15th c. for band of fabric on a dress, fillet for hair, or a hat band. **3.** See PRINTS, STRIPES, AND CHECKS.

Ben Franklin glasses   See EYEWEAR.

bengaline   † Heavy weight fabric characterized by large corded effect in the crosswise direction. Often made of lustrous fibers and used for more formal women's apparel such as suits or coats, for millinery, and ribbons.

benjamin   See COATS AND JACKETS.

benjy   **1.** See VESTS. **2.** See HEADWEAR.

benny   See COATS AND JACKETS: BENJAMIN.

Benoiton coiffure   See HAIRSTYLES.

berber   † Fabric of moderate weight similar to CHINCHILLA CLOTH that is used for skirts and jackets.

berdash   See BURDASH.

beret   See HEADWEAR

beret sleeve   See SHOULDERS AND SLEEVES.

bergère hat   See HEADWEAR.

Berlin gloves   See GLOVES AND GLOVE CONSTRUCTIONS.

Berlin wool work   See EMBROIDERIES AND SEWING STITCHES.

Bermuda collar   See NECKLINES AND COLLARS.

bermuda shorts   See SHORTS.

Bernhardt mantle   See CAPES, CLOAKS, AND SHAWLS.

Bernhardt, Sarah   (búrn-hart) (1845–1923) Famous French actress known as the "Divine Sarah," whose elaborate costumes, hairstyles, and jewels influenced fashion in Europe and the United States in late 19th c. Her name is sometimes used as an adjective describing styles that were associated with or inspired by her.

Bernhardt sleeve   See SHOULDERS AND SLEEVES.

bernos   See CAPES, CLOAKS, AND SHAWLS: BURNOOSE.

berretino   See HEADWEAR: ROUNDLET #1.

berretta/berrette See CLERICAL DRESS: BIRETTA.

bertha See NECKLINES AND COLLARS.

bertha pelerine See NECKLINES AND COLLARS.

Bertin, Rose * See APPENDIX/DESIGNERS.

beryl See GEMS, GEM CUTS, AND SETTINGS.

besom pocket See POCKETS: WELT POCKET.

bespoke British tailoring term that refers to men's custom-made garments such as suits and coats.

Bessarabian lamb See FURS: LAMB.

betrothal ring See JEWELRY.

Betsie ruff See NECKLINES AND COLLARS.

better goods See APPAREL PRICE RANGES.

bevel See GEMS, GEM CUTS, AND SETTINGS.

Bewdley cap See HEADWEAR: Monmouth cap.

bezel See GEMS, GEM CUTS, AND SETTINGS: CROWN.

biarritz gloves See GLOVES AND GLOVE CONSTRUCTIONS.

bias † The direction in fabrics diagonal to the lengthwise or crosswise directions. When woven fabrics are pulled in the bias direction, they exhibit greater stretch than in the other directions.

bias

bias binding Narrow strips of fabric cut on the bias, thus pliable for use in covering raw edges of curved necklines and armholes, or used at trimming. May be either hand-cut or sold in packages.

bias-cut A technique used by designers for cutting clothing to utilize the greater stretch in the bias or diagonal direction of the fabric, thereby causing it to accentuate body lines and curves and drape softly. For example, a full-skirted dress cut on the bias will hang more gracefully or a narrow dress will cling to the figure. Bias-cut garments were an important feature of the designs of Madeleine Vionnet in 1920s and 1930s and bias-cut styles are revived periodically. In the Middle Ages, before the development of knitting, hose were cut on the bias in order to make them fit better. Old spelling was *byesse.*

bias pleat See CLOTHING CONSTRUCTION DETAILS.

bias skirt See SKIRTS.

bias slip See UNDERGARMENTS.

bib 1. Square, rounded, or otherwise shaped piece of fabric or flexible plastic that is tied around the neck to protect clothing when the wearer is eating. Usually for children, bibs have been worn since the 16th century. When a similar-shaped element is introduced into apparel, the term "bib" may be used in the name. See NECKLINES AND COLLARS, JEWELRY, BLOUSES AND TOPS. 2. Extra piece of cloth attached to waist of apron, pants, or skirt extending upward over chest. See APRONS: BIB APRON, JUMPERS: BIB JUMPER, SHORTS: BIB SHORTS. 3. See JEWELRY.

bib cravat See TIES.

bibi bonnet See HEADWEAR.

bicorne/bicorn See HEADWEAR.

bicycle Adjective used to describe any item of clothing derived from or influenced by clothing worn for bicycling. See GLOVES AND GLOVE CONSTRUCTION: BICYCLE GLOVE and HEADWEAR: BICYCLE HELMET.

bicycle bal See FOOTWEAR.

bicycle clip hat See HEADWEAR.

bifocals See EYEWEAR.

bifurcated garments Garments constructed with legs.

big coat See COATS AND JACKETS.

big easy sweater See SWEATERS.

biggin/biggonet See HEADWEAR.

big look See V-SHAPE LOOK.

big regular Men's size for pajamas, corresponding to a chest measurement of 48″ or more, and a height of 5′7″ to 5′11″.

big shirt See under SHIRTS: OVERSIZED SHIRT and BIG TEE SHIRT

bike jacket See COATS AND JACKETS.

bike shorts See SHORTS.

bike suit See ACTIVEWEAR.

bike-tards See ACTIVEWEAR.

bikini 1. See SWIMWEAR. 2. Adjective describing garments, other than swimwear, influenced by the cut of bikini swimwear. See BLOUSES AND TOPS: BIKINI TOP, BELTS: BIKINI CHAIN, HOSIERY: BIKINI PANTYHOSE, and UNDERGARMENTS: BIKINI PANTIES and BIKINI BRIEF.

bilett See BELETTE.

bill See HEADWEAR: VISOR.

billfold See HANDBAGS AND RELATED ACCESSORIES: WALLET.

billiment/billment See HEADWEAR: BILLIMENT.

billycock/billicock See HEADWEAR.

binche (bansh) See LACES.

B

binding **1.** See CLOTHING CONSTRUCTION DETAILS. **2.** See GLOVES AND GLOVE CONSTRUCTION.

binding off Knitting term for removing stitches from the needles on a hand-knitted article in such a way that the piece of knitting will not ravel.

binette See WIGS AND HAIRPIECES.

bingle See HAIRSTYLES.

biot See FEATHERS.

bird cage See HEADWEAR.

bird-of-paradise feathers See FEATHERS.

bird's-eye † **1.** Fabric woven in linen or cotton on a loom with a DOBBY ATTACHMENT (see DOBBY WEAVE) in small diamond design with dot in center. Crosswise yarns are heavier and loosely twisted to make fabric more absorbent to use for diapers. Also called *diaper cloth.* **2.** Clear-finished worsted suiting woven with a geometrical design in diamond effect with small dot in center. Used for men's and women's suits.

biretta **1.** See CLERICAL DRESS. **2.** See HEADWEAR.

birlet See HEADWEAR: BOURRELET.

birrus See CAPES, CLOAKS, AND SHAWLS.

birthday suit **1.** ∞ Man's court suit worn in 18th c. for a royal birthday. **2.** (slang) Naked, as when born.

birthstone See GEMS, GEM CUTS, AND SETTINGS.

birthstone necklace See JEWELRY.

birthstone ring See JEWELRY.

bisette † (bee-set') **1.** ∞ Term used in Lyons, France, in the mid-16th c. to describe the silver thread trim on apparel. **2.** See LACES.

bishop collar See NECKLINES AND COLLARS.

bishop sleeve See SHOULDERS AND SLEEVES.

bi-swing See COATS AND JACKETS.

bivouac mantle See CAPES, CLOAKS, AND SHAWLS.

black belt See ACTIVEWEAR: KARATE CLOTHING.

black fox See FURS.

Blackglama® See FURS: MUTATION MINK.

black opal See GEMS, GEM CUTS, AND SETTINGS: OPAL.

black tie Abbreviated term designating a man's semiformal evening attire. Compare with WHITE TIE.

Black Watch tartan See PLAIDS AND TARTANS.

black work See EMBROIDERIES AND SEWING STITCHES.

blade jacket See COATS AND JACKETS.

Blahnik, Manolo * See APPENDIX/DESIGNERS.

Blake See FOOTWEAR: MCKAY METHOD.

blanchet ∞ Long white cotton camisole with sleeves, collar, and fur lining; worn over the shirt in the 15th c.

blanket See FURS.

blanket sleepers See SLEEPWEAR AND LOUNGE-WEAR.

blanket stitch See EMBROIDERIES AND SEWING STITCHES.

Blass, Bill * See APPENDIX/DESIGNERS.

blazer See COATS AND JACKETS: BLAZER.

blazer button See CLOSURES.

blazer costume ∞ Tailored suit with matching jacket and skirt; worn with a shirtwaist by girls and women in mid-1890s. Jacket usually had wide lapels and did not fasten in front.

blazer sock See HOSIERY.

blazer stripe See PRINTS, STRIPES, AND CHECKS.

blazer sweater See SWEATERS.

bleached jeans See PANTS: BLUE JEANS.

bleaching The process of removing color from some substance. Among the materials that are sometimes bleached are textiles and furs.

bleeding † Tendency of dyed fabric to lose color or run when wet.

bleeding madras See MADRAS.

blehand/blehant See BLIAUT.

blended yarn † Yarns that are composed of two or more fibers mixed together then spun to form one yarn, e.g., cotton fibers and polyester staple. When such a yarn is used to make a fabric, the fabric possesses some of the qualities of both fibers.

blending **1.** See BLENDED YARN. **2.** See FURS.

bliaut (blee-o') ∞ **1.** Overgown worn long or knee-length by men and long by women, from 12th to early 14th c. Made with a tight-fitting bodice that laced up sides or back; it had a full skirt attached at a low waistline; long sleeves that sometimes had PENDANT CUFFS (see under CUFFS); and was worn with a belt at the hip. **2.** For men another variation was narrow-sleeved, slit from hem to knee, and often worn under a coat of chain mail. Also spelled *bliaud, bliaunt, blehant, blehand.*

bliaut
12th century

blind eyelet See CLOSURES.

blind stitch See EMBROIDERIES AND SEWING STITCHES: SLIP STITCH.

bling See HIP-HOP.

blistered See SLASHING.

block/block pattern See SLOPER.

block heel See FOOTWEAR.

blocking **1.** Process of shaping knitted clothing after completion or washing by drawing its outline on paper and shaping article to conform. **2.** Millinery term for placing a felt or straw hood over a block of wood, then using heat or steam for desired shape.

block printing See PRINTS, STRIPES, AND CHECKS.

blonde See LACES.

blonde de fil See LACES: MIGNONETTE LACE.

bloodstone See GEMS, GEM CUTS, AND SETTINGS.

Bloomer, Amelia Jenks See BLOOMER COSTUME.

bloomer costume Knee-length dress worn over pants gathered at the ankle. Costume adopted by women's rights advocates of the 1850s that was modeled after clothing worn in health sanitariums. Although she did not originate the style, Amelia Jenks Bloomer (1818–1894), writer and lecturer on women's rights, wrote favorably about and wore this costume for her lectures and so it was named after her. Although the costume did not continue in general use after the 1850s, full pants gathered at the hem are still called BLOOMERS.

bloomer costume

bloomer dress Dress popular for children after World War I worn with matching bloomers underneath.

bloomers **1.** See PANTS. **2.** Slang for underpants. See UNDERGARMENTS: PANTIES.

bloomer swimsuit See SWIMWEAR.

BLOUSES AND TOPS

blouse Clothing for the upper part of the body, usually softer and less tailored than a *shirt*, worn with matching or contrasting skirt, pants, suit, or jumper. The practice of wearing the same blouse with different skirts was new in the mid-19th c. Prior to this even if dresses were made in two parts, a bodice and a skirt, both parts were generally of the same fabric and intended to be worn together. Originally the term blouse was applied to a type of shirt worn by a member of the armed forces of the United States, e.g., an Army blouse or Navy middy blouse. When the middy blouse was adopted for boys in 1860s, *blouse* first came into Civilian use. Its usage in reference to women's fashion expanded when women's *shirtwaists* were introduced in the 1890s; however, that garment was more likely to be called a *waist* until the 1920s, when more sportswear and suits were worn and blouses became an essential part of a woman's wardrobe. *Der.* French, *blouson*, "to blouse."

top Clothing worn as a blouse or shirt substitute with pants or a skirt mainly for sportswear, and sometimes for evening. The term comes into use in the 1930s when HALTER TOPS (see under BLOUSES AND TOPS) were popular for both sportswear and evening. A synonym for *blouse.*

bare-midriff top Top that ends below bust and bares the rib cage. Often made with strapless, halter, or tank neckline. Similar to CROPPED TOP. See under BLOUSES AND TOPS.

bare top Strapless evening bodice tightly fitted and boned.

bib blouse Blouse with high collar and an inset of contrasting color or fabric in front that has the appearance of a bib.

bib blouse

bib top Bare-back top, just covering front of body, as in, for example, the top of overalls.

bib top

bikini top Brief top, using a minimum of fabric, covering the bust and tying in back and around the neck in halter fashion.

blouse-slip See UNDERGARMENTS.

B

blousette (blooz-et′) Sleeveless blouse for wear under cardigans or suits. Popular from 1930s to 1940s. Also see DICKEY 1.

blouson blouse (blue zohn′) Type of OVERBLOUSE (see under BLOUSES AND TOPS) with fullness at the waist usually gathered into a band.

blouson blouse

bodyshirt See SHIRTS: BODY-SHIRT #3.

bolero blouse ∞ Long-waisted blouse with attached pieces of fabric forming a false bolero, popular for women during 1920s and 1930s.

bow blouse Blouse with band around neck having two long ends in front that tie in a bow.

bow blouse

bustier Tight-fitting top sometimes laced similar to a corset or camisole. Used separately or for the top of a dress.

bustier

butcher boy blouse Woman's blouse, hip-length or longer, shaped like a smock, usually yoked and buttoned either front or back. Popular in 1940s, and used later for maternity blouse. *Der.* Garment worn by French butchers' delivery boys.

camisole top 1. Top made with straps over the shoulder, or strapless, cut straight across with elastic drawn through a heading. May hang free or have elastic at waistline. Sometimes made with built-in bra. 2. Top with spaghetti straps and low scoop neckline in front and back. *Der.* From word *camisole*, formerly a lingerie item.

camisole top

capelet blouse Blouse with a double-tiered collar in the shape of a cape and is sometimes made in bow-tie style with BISHOP SLEEVES (see under SHOULDERS AND SLEEVES).

chemisette Sleeveless blouse worn under a suit in early 20th c.

choli Blouse worn with Indian SARI, reaching just to the ribs, made with short tight sleeves and scooped neckline. Frequently made of fine silk and sometimes trimmed with gold braid or embroidery. Worn by Hindu women and popular in the United States since 1968, when bare-midriff styles became popular. Also spelled *cholee, coli. Der.* Hindu, *coli.*

cossack blouse Long over-blouse made with a high standing collar, full sleeves, fastened asymmetrically in front, and secured with a belt or sash. Embroidery is frequently used for trim on collar, down front, and on cuffs. Same as *Zhivago blouse* and *Russian blouse.*

cossack blouse

cropped top Any top cut short to bare the midriff section. Similar to BARE-MIDRIFF TOP (see under BLOUSES AND TOPS), although not as likely to be fitted. This top may be a cut-off shirt, t-shirt, or sweatshirt and is a style adopted by men, as well as women and children from the early 1980s and after.

cropped top

dandy blouse Ruffle-trimmed blouse reminiscent of DANDY styles of early 19th c.

dashiki See DASHIKI in alphabetical list.

diamanté top (dya-mahn-tay′) Top made entirely (or partly) of sparkling sequins, beads, or paillettes. Very popular in mid-1980s. *Der.* French, "made of diamonds."

drawstring blouse Blouse that fastens at neckline with drawstring, e.g., gypsy or peasant blouse.

dueling/fencing blouse Blouse borrowed from European man's shirt of the 17th c. worn by men and women generally in white cotton, crepe, or jersey. Tailored with notched collar, dropped shoulder, and long full sleeves gathered into tight cuffs.

flashdance top Knit shirt similar to conventional sweatshirt with sleeves cut short and neckline cut low in various styles. Both are left in unfinished state with seams overcast on right side of shirt. *Der.* From designs by Michael Kaplan for the movie *Flashdance*, 1983.

flip-tie blouse See BLOUSES AND TOPS: STOCK-TIE BLOUSE.

Gabrielle waist ∞ (ga-bree-el′) Woman's fitted waist of 1870s buttoned down center front. Sometimes made with a small fluted ruff and sleeves in a series of puffs.

Garibaldi shirt/blouse ∞ (gar-ih-bawl′-dee) Red merino wool high-necked shirt of 1860s. While some examples had EPAULETS on the shoulders and were trimmed with black braid, bloused, belted, and worn with a black CRAVAT (see TIES AND NECK-CLOTHS), the name was also applied to any red blouse made with full sleeves gathered into wristband and having a small collar. *Der.* Inspired by clothes worn by Italian patriot Giuseppe Garibaldi (1807–1882) and his troops during their campaign to unite Italy in the 1840s and 1850s.

Giribaldi blouse 1862

Gibson waist ∞ **1.** Blouse styled like a man's shirt with a small turned-over collar, small black bow tie, and leg-of-mutton sleeves. Popular in the 1890s and worn with separate skirt and belt. **2.** Blouse with high neckline that buttoned down the back, had leg-of-mutton sleeves, and Gibson pleats. Made in LAWN, SATIN, BOBBINETTE, and other fabrics, it was elaborately decorated with lace, insertion, and tucks. *Der.* Named after Charles Dana Gibson who portrayed "The Gibson girl."

Gibson girl blouse, 1899

granny blouse See BLOUSES AND TOPS: VICTORIAN BLOUSE.

granny waist Fitted bodice of 1890s with lace insert in front, large lace ruffles around a low neckline, and optional large lace ruffles falling over the arms from puffed sleeves. *Der.* Named for the styles worn by one's grandmother.

guimpe (gamp) ∞ Separate blouse worn under a low-necked dress in the 1890s, similar to a CHEMISETTE (see under BLOUSES AND TOPS).

gypsy blouse Full blouse with drawstring neckline and either short puffed or long full sleeves. Popular in late 1960s. *Der.* Originally worn by gypsies, a nomadic people of Europe, Asia, and North America. Similar to *peasant blouse.*

halter top Top with front supported by narrow ties or straps around the back and neck, leaving the back bare.

halter top

Hubbard blouse ∞ Loose-fitting tunic blouse with ruffles at hem, sleeves, and neck with a cord used to pull in fullness at waist. Worn by young girls in 1880s over kilt-pleated skirt.

Indian wedding blouse Blouse with a neckline like that on a CAFTAN, long set-in sleeves flaring at wrist, and rounded shirttails. Elaborately embroidered (currently by machine chain stitch) around neckline, down front, around hems of sleeves, and hem. Usually imported from India in a cotton fabric.

jabot blouse (zha-bo′) **1.** Back-buttoned blouse having standing band collar with attached ruffle or jabot in center front. **2.** Front-buttoned blouse with jabot-like ruffles on either side of opening.

jumper Sailor's OVERBLOUSE or MIDDY BLOUSE (see under BLOUSES AND TOPS).

Martha Washington waist ∞ V-necked blouse of late 1890s with dickey that has a choker collar. It was made with surplice front gathered at shoulder seams, draped to one side, and tied in back with a bow. Sleeves varied from full double puff to single puff coming to elbow and fitted to wrist. *Der.* For Martha Washington, wife of first U.S. president, George Washington.

maternity blouse/maternity top Overblouse that is worn by pregnant women. The earlier versions, c. 1940s, were designed to hang loosely from a yoke, but by the 1980s maternity tops were styled similarly to any type of blouse, shirt, t-shirt, or top.

matinee See BLOUSES AND TOPS: TEA JACKET.

middy blouse **1.** Slip-on blouse made with a braid-trimmed SAILOR COLLAR (see under necklines and collars) and cuffs worn with a SAILOR TIE (see under TIES) slipped through a loop on blouse. Sometimes has an insignia on left sleeve. Worn in blue serge and white duck by members of the U.S. Navy and by boys since the 1860s. By the 1890s it was adopted for women for lawn tennis, canoeing, boating, and yachting. In 1906 worn with black sateen or serge-pleated BLOOMERS (see under PANTS) as a GYMNA-SIUM SUIT (see ACTIVEWEAR: GYM SUIT). From World War I period on worn with KNICKERS for biking and sportswear. In 1920s worn for gym classes and camping. Also see PETER THOMPSON DRESS. **2.** Any slip-on blouse made with a sailor collar. Also called a *nautical blouse.*

middy blouse #1 1910

nautical blouse See BLOUSES AND TOPS: MIDDY BLOUSE.

overblouse Any blouse or top worn over the skirt or pants rather than tucked inside.

oversized top Extra large slip-on top made in many styles, sometimes hip-length with full sleeves.

peasant blouse Folkloric woman's blouse called by national names (e.g., Rumanian, Polish, or Swedish). Usually white with puffed or long rag-lan sleeves made with embroidered borders. Neckline is some-times square and trimmed with embroidery or round and made with elastic or draw-string. Also see BLOUSES AND TOPS: GYPSY BLOUSE.

peasant blouse

peek-a-boo waist ∞ Woman's waist made of eyelet embroidery popular in early 20th c.

peplum blouse OVERBLOUSE (see under BLOUSES AND TOPS) made in two ways: (a) with separate seam at waist to which ruffle or bias-cut circular piece is added for fullness, or (b) long and full with elasticized waistline thus making a ruffle waistline.

pullover/pull-on blouse Any blouse that has no fasteners and pulls on over the head. Also called a *slip-on blouse.*

Russian blouse See BLOUSES AND TOPS: COS-SACK BLOUSE.

screen-print top Knit top screen-printed with animals, hearts, and other designs—often popular cartoon characters, idols, or slogans are used.

see-through blouse Blouse of transparent fabric worn by women with or without a bra or body stocking underneath.

shell Sleeveless or cap-sleeved slip-on collarless blouse that may have one or several buttons in back. Made in woven or knitted fabric, this classic style may be colored so as to match or contrast in an ensemble with a skirt and jacket.

shell

shirtwaist **1.** Any blouse cut similarly to a contemporary man's shirt. **2.** Term originating in 1890s for women's blouses styled like men's shirts with buttons down front, tailored collar, and sometimes worn with a black tie. **3.** A woman's blouse with a high choker neckline buttoned in back—one of the first items produced by the ready-to-wear industry.

shirtwaist #1 1943

sleeveless blouse Any style of blouse that has no sleeves.

slip-blouse See UNDERGARMENTS: BLOUSE-SLIP.

slip-on blouse See BLOUSES AND TOPS: PULLOVER BLOUSE.

smock top Full OVERBLOUSE (see under BLOUSES AND TOPS) with full sleeves, similar to a smock.

squaw blouse Heavily embroidered blouse resembling PEASANT BLOUSE (see under BLOUSES AND TOPS) inspired by Native American styles. *Der.* White settlers' name for a Native American woman.

stocking bodice Knitted or shirred elastic tube pulled over woman's torso as a *strapless top* to wear with pants, shorts, or an evening skirt.

stocking bodice or tube top

Popular in the 1940s, revived in late 1960s and 1980s. By the 1990s more likely to be called a **tube top.**

stock-tie blouse Plain blouse with an ascot neckline (see NECKLINES AND COLLARS: ASCOT). Also called *flip-tie blouse* and *stock-tie shirt.*

strapless top An elastic or stretch top made without straps. Also See BLOUSES AND TOPS: STOCKING BODICE.

stretch top Close-fitting blouse made of stretchy knit fabric. Also see BODY SUIT in alphabetical listing.

sweater blouse Sweater made of fine yarn and worn as blouse, sometimes having ruffled details or dressmaker styling and worn tucked inside skirt. Worn intermittently since 1930 and particularly popular in 1980s.

tailored blouse Any style of blouse with little or no ornamentation or trimming. Similar in style to a man's shirt.

tank top Similar to men's undershirt with U neckline and deep armholes shaped toward shoulder to form narrow straps. Similar to athletic shirt (see UNDERGARMENTS: ATHLETIC SHIRT). *Der.* From top of tank suit, a bathing suit worn in early indoor swimming pools called "tanks."

tank top

tea jacket ∞ Loose informal jacket or bodice with close-fitting back. Sometimes made with tight sleeves and loose-hanging front profusely trimmed with lace. Worn by women from late 1880s to end of 19th c. replacing the tailor-made bodice of the dress for afternoon tea. Also called *matinee.*

top See definition under category heading BLOUSES AND TOPS.

torso blouse OVERBLOUSE (see under BLOUSES AND TOPS) that fits snugly and extends to hips.

trapeze top TANK TOP (see BLOUSES AND TOPS) with a flared bottom.

tube top See BLOUSES AND TOPS: STOCKING BODICE.

tunic blouse Thigh-length, sleeved or sleeveless overblouse, worn over a skirt,

tunic blouse

slacks, or alone as a short dress. Popular in 1940s and revived in 1960s.

tuxedo blouse Woman's blouse styled like a man's formal shirt. There are many variations of this blouse: (a) a bib style with contrasting collar; (b) a blouse with tucked front; and (c) a blouse trimmed with vertical ruffles. A black bow tie and black coat styled like a tuxedo jacket are sometimes worn to complete the costume.

twinset A matched set of blouses designed to be worn together; these may be made of the same fabric or contrasting fabric. The outermost blouse is usually long-sleeved with a buttoned front, while the other blouse is styled like a shell or with a camisole top.

Vassar blouse ∞ Woman's blouse worn in 1890s similar to a peasant blouse. Had a drawstring neckline with upstanding ruffle and bouffant sleeves—either three-quarter or full-length—ending in a ruffle. Sometimes decorated with embroidery, ribbon suspender straps, or with clusters of bows on the shoulders.

Victorian blouse 1. Blouse inspired by late Victorian era blouses that had high necklines, long sleeves, and yokes. Sometimes trimmed with tucks, lace, insertion and/or ruffles; they were usually white. Introduced in late 1960s as a version of the SHIRTWAIST (See under BLOUSES AND TOPS) of late Victorian era and also called *granny blouses.* **2.** Front-buttoned blouse with lace-edged high standing collar, lace-edged yoke, and leg-of-mutton sleeves. Usually made of plaid or printed fabric.

waist ∞ BLOUSE or SHIRTWAIST (See under BLOUSES AND TOPS); term in use from about 1890 to the 1920s.

wifebeater Slang originating in the early 1990s for a plain white ATHLETIC SHIRT (see under UNDERGARMENTS) that became a fashionable women's top. *Der.* Comes from the stereotype of working-class violent men in plays, films, or TV who are often costumed in athletic shirts.

wrap blouse Blouse with two bias-cut front sections extended into long sash ends that are crossed and wrapped around waist. Worn in mid-1960s and revived in 1980s.

wrapped top Diagonal piece of fabric, about 1½ to 2 yards long and 1 yard wide, worn folded in half and wrapped around the body with ends tied in front to make a strapless top. Two long ends hang down at waist. May be stitched to front of shorts to make rompers or attached to pants to make a jumpsuit.

yoke blouse ∞ Woman's waist or blouse worn from mid-1860s to 1890s with square yoke in front and back outlined with a ruffle. Also has fullness below yoke, elastic at waist, and a ruffle below waist or a waistband. Also called a *yoke waist* or *yoke shirtwaist*.

Zhivago blouse (zhi-vah′go) Blouse for men and women inspired by the film *Dr. Zhivago* in 1965. Same as COSSACK or *Russian blouse*. See under BLOUSES AND TOPS.

---

blouse coat See COATS AND JACKETS.

blouse dress ∞ Boy's or girl's dress of 1870s and 1880s made with BLOUSON top (see BLOUSON #1) and low waistline. Usually the short skirt was pleated. Also called a *blouse costume*. For later versions, see FRENCH DRESS.

blouse-slip/blouse-top See UNDERGARMENTS.

blousette See BLOUSES AND TOPS.

blouson (blue-zohn′) **1.** Bloused-top dress with low waistline seam. A style introduced in 1920s and reintroduced in 1950s. *Der.* French "to blouse." **2.** Dress, suit jacket, or blouse with full back. Popular style of about 1960. See BLOUSES AND TOPS: BLOUSON BLOUSE, COATS AND JACKETS: BLOUSON JACKET, SWIMWEAR: BLOUSON SWIMSUIT.

blouson #2

blucher/blucher bal See FOOTWEAR.

blue-aproned men English tradesmen of 16th to 18th c. who were recognized by their aprons of blue fabric—a color not worn by the upper classes. Also see BLUE COAT.

blue billy See SCARVES.

bluebonnet See HEADWEAR.

blue coat ∞ **1.** Coat worn by apprentices and servants from end of 16th c. to end of 17th c., a color avoided by gentlemen as an indication of

lower class. Also see BLUE-APRONED MEN and GREEN-APRONED MEN. **2.** Slang for a policeman.

blue fox See FURS.

blue jeans See PANTS.

blue pelt See FURS.

boa See SCARVES.

boarded finish See LEATHERS.

boater See HEADWEAR.

boater tie See TIES.

boating shoe See FOOTWEAR.

boat neckline See NECKLINES AND COLLARS: BATEAU.

bob See HAIRSTYLES.

bobbinet **1.** † A machine-made net fabric with hexagonal meshes. **2.** See LACES.

bobbin lace See category heading for LACES.

bobby pin See HAIR ACCESSORIES.

bobby's hat See HEADWEAR.

bobby socks See HOSIERY.

bobby soxer ∞ Slang for teenager of the 1940s who followed current fashion fads such as bobby socks and saddle shoes. (See HOSIERY: BOBBY SOX and FOOTWEAR: SADDLE SHOES.)

bobtailed coat See COATS AND JACKETS.

bob-wig See WIGS AND HAIRPIECES.

bodice **1.** The upper part of a woman's dress, often close-fitting. Synonyms: *body, corsage.* **2.** See UNDERGARMENTS: PAIR OF BODIES.

bodice en coeur ∞ (bod′ees on cur) Upper part of a woman's evening dress of the mid 19th c. that has a low, heart-shaped neckline. Also called *Marquise bodice* (mar-kees′ bod-iss).

bodkin **1.** Long flat needle with blunt end used to string elastic and ribbon through eyelet INSERTION, HEADINGS, or WAISTBANDS. **2.** ∞ 16th to 19th c.: long hairpin used by women. **3.** Instrument for punching holes in leather or fabric.

bodkin beard See BEARD.

body **1.** *adj.* Used to describe apparel that fits the body closely. Examples: body stocking, body shirt. **2.** See BODICE # 1. **3.** † *n.* Quality of a fabric implying firmness, both stiffness and flexibility.

body boot See FOOTWEAR.

body briefer See UNDERGARMENTS.

body clothes Tightly fitted clothes with built-in comfort, e.g., stretch jeans, leotards, body stockings, bodysuits made of basic yarns combined with elastomeric fibers (see ELASTOMERS) to give stretch.

body coat See COATS AND JACKETS.

body hose See BODY STOCKING.

body jewelry Highly decorative accessories designed to be worn on all parts of the body, face, and head, over body stockings or clothing. Includes items which may be pasted on as well as elaborate pieces of metal jewelry and decorative chains; or a cape, dress, cap, pants, coat, or scarf made of loose strands of pearls. Popular in late 1960s. Designed by Bill Smith, Kenneth J. Lane, Quasar Khanh, and Paco Rabanne. Also see UNDERGARMENTS: CADORO BRA and JEWELRY: BODY PIERCING.

body painting Fad of late 1960s for painting face and body with fantasy flowers, geometric, and other designs. See TATTOO and CASTE MARK.

body-piercing See JEWELRY.

body shaper See UNDERGARMENTS.

bodyshaper pantyhose See HOSIERY: PANTYHOSE.

body shirt See BODYSUIT and SHIRTS: BODY SHIRT #3.

body shorts See SHORTS.

body stocking Introduced in early 1960s as a one-piece knitted body garment with legs and feet, with or without sleeves. In 1964, Warners won a Coty Fashion Award for a filmy nude-colored Lycra tricot-knit stretch garment designed with shoulder straps and no legs. Legless variety is also known as *bodysuit, body shirt,* or *body sweater.* When designed as a control undergarment, called BODY BRIEFER (see under UNDERGARMENTS).

body stocking

bodysuit 1. One-piece fitted garment without legs having a snap crotch. Made in a variety of plain, patterned, or ribbed knits. Made sleeveless or with long or short sleeves, and with many styles of collars and necklines. Sometimes substitutes as a blouse or sweater. Also called a *body shirt* or *body sweater.* **2.** See UNDERGARMENTS. **3.** In 1986, Donna Karan changed the concept of the bodysuit silhouette somewhat to include "blouse" or "shirt" styles in a variety of fabrics, suede, or leather.

bodysuit #1

body sweater See BODY STOCKING.

body wave See HAIRSTYLES: PERMANENT WAVE.

Bohan, Marc * See APPENDIX/DESIGNERS.

Bohemian lace See LACES.

boiled shirt See SHIRTS.

boiled wool Contemporary name for FULLED WOOL.

Bokhara shawl See CAPES, CLOAKS, AND SHAWLS.

bold look Menswear look of the late 1940s and 1950s. Not a radical change in style but rather a continuation of the ENGLISH DRAPE SUIT with greater emphasis on coordination among the shirt, accessories, and the suit.

Boldini See HAIRSTYLES: POMPADOUR.

bolero (bo-lehr′-o) **1.** See COATS AND JACKETS. **2.** Adjective used to describe garments derived from or inspired by an above-the-waist jacket that was named for a dance called the "bolero." See BLOUSES AND TOPS: BOLERO BLOUSE, CAPES, CLOAKS, AND SHAWLS: BOLERO CAPE or MANTLE, HEADWEAR: BOLERO TOQUE, and SWEATERS: BOLERO SWEATER.

bolero costume ∞ Dress with matching bolero, reaching nearly to the waist, or separate jacket and skirt worn with a shirtwaist. Worn from early 1900s to 1920. Some boleros were fitted, some had elaborate full caped sleeves. Also see COATS AND JACKETS: BOLERO.

bollinger See HEADWEAR.

bolo tie See TIES.

bolster collar See NECKLINES AND COLLARS.

Bolton thumb See GLOVES AND GLOVE CONSTRUCTIONS.

bombast ∞ Stuffing material used in apparel, especially TRUNK HOSE, in the 16th and 17th c. It could consist of such diverse materials as horsehair, wool, rags, flax, cotton, or bran.

bomber jacket See COATS AND JACKETS: FLIGHT JACKET.

bonaid See HEADWEAR: BLUEBONNET.

Bonaparte, Napoleon (1769–1821) Napoleon I, Emperor of France, 1804–1815. He encouraged use of French textiles and established military fashions for men, e.g., tight cream-colored breeches, BICORNE hat (see HEADWEAR), high rolled collared jackets. His first wife, the Empress Josephine, influenced Empire Period dress and accessory styles, most notably cashmere shawls.

Also see NECKLINES AND COLLARS: NAPOLEONIC COLLAR.

bone lace   See LACES.

boned foundation   See UNDERGARMENTS.

bones   See CLOTHING CONSTRUCTION DETAILS: STAY #1.

bongrace   See HEADWEAR.

bonnaz embroidery   See EMBROIDERIES AND SEWING STITCHES.

bonnet   See HEADWEAR.

bonnet à bec   See HEADWEAR.

bonnet en papillon   See HEADWEAR: BONNET À BEC.

bonnet rouge   See HEADWEAR.

Bonnie and Clyde look   Styles inspired by the film *Bonnie and Clyde* in 1967. Essentially a revival of the 1930s silhouette with late-1960s, above-the-knee skirt length. Characteristic styles included three-piece suit with V-neck, long waistline, and unbuttoned jacket; pinstriped gangster suits; and the beret worn on the side of the head. *Der.* Named after movie by the same name with costumes designed by Theadora Van Runkel.

Bonnie and Clyde look

book bag   See HANDBAGS AND RELATED ACCESSORIES.

bookbinder print   See PRINTS, STRIPES, AND CHECKS.

boot   1. See FOOTWEAR. 2. See HOSIERY.

boot blow-up   Plastic or rubber boot form inserted to retain shape when boots are not being worn.

boot bracelet   See JEWELRY.

boot cuff   See CUFFS.

boot-cut pants   See PANTS.

bootee/bootie   See FOOTWEAR.

boot garters   See FOOTWEAR.

boot hook   See FOOTWEAR.

boot hose   See HOSIERY.

boot hose tops   See HOSIERY: BOOT HOSE.

boot jack   Implement used to aid the wearer in removing his boots, introduced in the 18th c.

bootlace tie   See TIES: STRING TIE.

boot leg   See PANTS: BOOT CUT.

boots   See FOOTWEAR.

boot sleeve   See SHOULDERS AND SLEEVES.

boot stocking   See HOSIERY: BOOT HOSE.

boot strap   See FOOTWEAR: BOOT HOOK #1.

Borazon®   See GLOVES AND GLOVE CONSTRUCTIONS.

bord   See GLOVES AND GLOVE CONSTRUCTION: BANDELET.

border   1. Trimming at edge, or just above edge, on an item of apparel or an accessory. 2. Decorative woven cords or stripes in handkerchiefs. 3. Decorative edge on fabric or edge used for identification purposes.

border prints   See PRINTS, STRIPES, AND CHECKS.

borders   See HEADWEAR: BILLIMENT.

borel   ∞ 14th-c. term for clothing.

bosom   1. Synonym for the human breast. 2. That part of a garment that covers the breast.

bosom bottles   ∞ Tiny bottles holding water, worn by ladies in the latter half of 18th c. to keep bouquets of flowers fresh. Bottle was formed like a small vial that could be fastened to shoulder or tucked into the neckline of dress.

bosom flowers   ∞ Artificial flowers worn by men and women in the 18th c., usually with full evening dress. Also worn by the dandies in daytime. Also see BOUTONNIERE and CORSAGE.

bosom friends   See FALSIES.

bosom knot   See BREASTKNOT.

bosom shirt   See SHIRTS.

bosses   See HEADWEAR.

Boss, Hugo   *   See APPENDIX/DESIGNERS.

boteh   See CAPES, CLOAKS, AND SHAWLS: CASHMERE SHAWL.

botews   See FOOTWEAR: BUSKINS #2.

bottine   See FOOTWEAR.

bottom-up theory of fashion change   The idea that some fashion changes result from the adoption by older or more affluent individuals of styles that originated with groups or individuals who are young, less affluent, or from the counterculture. Compare with TRICKLE-DOWN THEORY OF FASHION CHANGE.

bottomweight   †   Fabric suitable for such garments as pants, skirts, winter dresses.

bouchette   See ARMOR.

bouclé (boo-klay′) † **1.** A rough, curly, knotted yarn made by twisting together two fine foundations threads with a thicker yarn that is delivered in such a way as to cause the thick yarn to twist up on the surface. **2.** Any fabric made with these yarns. *Der.* French for buckle or curl.

boudoir cap See HEADWEAR.

boudoir slippers See FOOTWEAR.

bouffant Adjective meaning full or puffed in French (boo-fahn′) that is also used in English (boo-fahnt′) to describe apparel or hairstyles that are full or puffed out. See BOUFFANT DRESS, HAIRSTYLES: BOUFFANT, SCARVES: BUFFON, SHOULDERS AND SLEEVES: BOUFFANT MÉCHANIQUE, SKIRTS: BOUFFANT, and UNDERGARMENTS: BOUFFANT PETTICOAT.

bouffant dress (boo-fahnt′) Dress with tight-fitting bodice and full, gathered, pleated, or ruffled skirt. Sometimes skirt is shaped like a bubble, a bell, or a cone and may be worn with hoops or petticoats. *Der.* French "full" or "puffed." Also see BUBBLE and PAPER DOLL DRESSES.

bouffant dress 1949

boulevard heel See FOOTWEAR.

Boulogne hose See TRUNK HOSE.

bound See CLOTHING CONSTRUCTION DETAILS.

bound buttonhole See CLOSURES.

bound pocket See POCKETS.

bound seam See CLOTHING CONSTRUCTION DETAILS.

Bourbon hat See HEADWEAR.

Bourbon lock See HAIRSTYLES: LOVE LOCK.

bourdon lace See LACES.

bournouse See CAPES, CLOAKS, AND SHAWLS: BURNOOSE.

bourrelet (boor-lay′) **1.** See HEADWEAR. **2.** Stuffed, rolled trimming. **3.** See UNDERGARMENTS: BUM ROLL.

bourse (boorce) **1.** See HANDBAGS AND RELATED ACCESSORIES. **2.** See WIGS AND HAIRPIECES.

boutique (boo-teek′) Small shop selling a variety of merchandise including dresses, jewelry, accessories, antique bibelots, or object d'art. Ever since Parisian designer Lucien Lelong opened his *Boutique de la Maison Couture* in 1929, haute couture designers have taken up the practice of selling a variety of designer label merchandise in boutiques. The term has been applied to small shops everywhere since the 1950s; and now such shops are often contained within large department stores.

boutonnière (boo-ton-yair′) **1.** Flower worn in lapel buttonhole. The practice was initiated by wealthy men about town and has been popular for formal functions since the 19th c. **2.** Small bouquet, or flower, worn by women on left shoulder or lapel. *Der.* French, "buttonhole."

bow 1. Knot usually having two loops and two ends—often a narrow fabric, ribbon, or string; used for sashes, neckties, or decorative trim. Also called *bow knot.* **2.** An adjective applied to garments in which a bow is an important element. See BLOUSES AND TOPS: BOW BLOUSE, NECKLINES AND COLLARS: BOW COLLAR, and TIES: BOW TIE. **3.** See EYEWEAR: TEMPLE.

Bow, Clara American film star of 1920s, called "the It Girl" in 1926. A round-eyed beauty with small cupid's-bow lips, she typified sex appeal and inspired several hats of the late 1920s. See HEADWEAR: Clara Bow hat.

bow knot See BOW #1.

bowl crop See HAIRSTYLES.

bowl cut See HAIRSTYLES.

bowler See HEADWEAR: DERBY.

bowling Adjective used to describe apparel designed for the sport of bowling or influenced by apparel used for bowling, which is played at a bowling alley—a long hardboard runway with ten pins set up at the end. For special clothing worn, see SHIRTS and FOOTWEAR.

box bag See HANDBAGS AND RELATED ACCESSORIES.

box bottoms ∞ Men's close-fitting below-the-knee breeches made with stiffened lining; worn in 19th c.

box calf See LEATHERS.

box cape See CAPES, CLOAKS, AND SHAWLS.

box coat See COATS AND JACKETS.

boxer Adjective used for undergarments or shorts styled similarly to those worn for sport of boxing. See BOXER under the categories of ACTIVEWEAR, SHORTS, and UNDERGARMENTS.

boxes See FOOTWEAR: GALOSHES.

box jacket See COATS AND JACKETS.

box pleat See CLOTHING CONSTRUCTION DETAILS and SKIRTS.

Boy George See ANDROGYNOUS LOOK.

boyish bob See HAIRSTYLES.

boy coat See COATS AND JACKETS.

boy-leg See LENGTHS.

boy shorts See ACTIVEWEAR.

boys' sizes Sizes 8 to 20, each size available in slim, regular, and husky. Sizes are determined by height, weight, and circumference of chest and waist.

bra See UNDERGARMENTS.

bracae ∞ (brak′ay) Latin word for loose-fitting pants or hose worn by northern European tribes. Adopted for use by Roman soldiers when fighting in cold, northern regions. Called *broc* by Anglo-Saxons. See BRAIES.

bracelet **1.** Ornament usually worn on the arm or wrist. See JEWELRY. **2.** Adjective applied to elements of apparel that bear some relationship in length, appearance, or function to a bracelet. See HANDBAGS AND RELATED ACCESSORIES: BRACELET BAG, FOOTWEAR: BRACELET-TIE SHOE, GLOVES AND GLOVE CONSTRUCTIONS: BRACELET LENGTH, SHOULDERS AND SLEEVES: BRACELET SLEEVE, and WATCHES: BRACELET WATCH.

bracelet ring See JEWELRY: SLAVE BRACELET.

braces British term for SUSPENDERS, first worn about 1787. Also called *gallowses*.

bractiate ∞ Pin used to fasten garments from 6th to mid-8th c.

braguette See ARMOR: BRAYETTE.

BRAIDS

braid **1.** *n.* Narrow woven band for use as trimming, binding, or for outlining lace and embroidery. **2.** *v.* To plait or interweave strands of hair, fabric, or straw. **3.** See HAIRSTYLES.

ball fringe Type of braid with little fuzzy balls suspended at regular intervals. Used on beach ponchos and robes, and fashionable in late 1870s and 1880s for dress trimming.

coronation braid Firmly woven mercerized cord braid, alternately wide and narrow, used to outline a pattern in embroidery or lace.

Also used for COUCHING (see under EMBROIDERIES AND SEWING STITCHES).

diamanté braid (dya-mahn-tay′) Fake sparkling jewels, e.g., rhinestones, sewn on strips of fabric. Used as trimming on dresses, blouses, evening wear, etc. *Der.* French, "set with diamonds."

embroidered braid Tape with decorative motifs embroidered at regular intervals used for trimming.

galloon **1.** Narrow tape or braid made of cotton, silk, rayon, wool, or man-made fibers (sometimes with metallic threads added) used for trimming. **2.** Double-edged lace made in various widths. **3.** Double-edged wide braid frequently made of gold or metallic yarn with jewels sometimes spaced at regular intervals. A highly decorative rich braid used profusely in 1969. *Der.* French, *galon*, "braid."

gimp Braid made from heavy core yarn arranged in a pattern and stitched to create a raised effect.

Hercules braid Worsted braid heavily corded from ½″ to 4″ in width; several widths often used together.

horsehair braid Permanently stiff coarse braid made originally from horsehair, now of nylon. Used for stiffening bouffant skirts at the hemline and in millinery.

lacet Braid of silk or cotton woven in various widths, frequently with looped edges. Used for trimming and edging, and sometimes combined with crochet work or tatting.

ladder braid Braid with open stitches crossed by bars creating a ladderlike effect, made with a bobbin.

middy braid Narrow, flat white braid originally used to trim collars and cuffs on middy blouses and sailor collars.

military braid Flat ribbed worsted or gold braid sometimes in twill weave in various widths. Used to designate rank on military uniforms.

rapolin (rap′-o-lin) Swiss millinery braid made in triple rows and having an uneven surface.

rat-tail braid Silk braid of tubular shape used for trimming.

rice braid Firmly woven highly mercerized braid with wide parts alternating with narrow, to give the appearance of grains of rice. Used for trimming. Similar to BRAIDS: CORONATION BRAID.

rickrack Braid usually made of cotton or blends and having a zigzag form. Widths may vary.

Russian braid See BRAIDS: SOUTACHE BRAID.

soutache braid (soo-tash′) Narrow flat decorative braid. Used for borders and for all-over ornamental patterns. Also called *Russian braid.* *Der.* Hungarian, *sujtas,* "flat trimming braid."

---

braided belt See BELTS.

braie girdle See BREECH GIRDLE.

braies ∞ Medieval term, from which the term BREECHES derives, for loose-fitting pants that were either full-, knee-length, or short and were worn by men as an undergarment. Earlier forms were called *bracae* by the Romans and *broc* by the Anglo-Saxons.

braies

brand **1.** *n.* A manufacturer or distributor-assigned name, mark, or label assigned to a product in order to encourage consumer-recognition of the product. Brands may be TRADEMARKS. **2.** *adj.* Having an assigned name, mark, or label, as in "brand merchandise."

Brandenburg See COATS AND JACKETS.

Brandenburgs See CLOSURES: FROGS.

brand loyalty Consumer preference for a particular brand of merchandise.

brand-name fiber † Fiber sold under a specific trademark name, e.g., Lycra®.

bra-shift Sleeveless, loose-fitting dress with top of dress fitted to the figure like a bra. An innovation of the mid-1960s.

bra-slip See UNDERGARMENTS.

brassart (brass′are) **1.** See ARMOR. **2.** See SHOULDERS AND SLEEVES. **3.** Wide white silk ribbon bow with streamers worn by first communicants. **4.** ∞ 19th-c: mourning band of black cloth worn on upper left arm. **5.** ∞ Ribbon bow worn in the 19th c. on the elbow of an evening dress.

brass button See CLOSURES.

brassiere See UNDERGARMENTS: BRA.

bratt See CAPES, CLOAKS, AND SHAWLS.

brayette See ARMOR.

bray girdle See BREECH GIRDLE.

Brazilian emerald See GEMS. GEM CUTS, AND SETTINGS.

Brazilian peridot See GEMS. GEM CUTS, AND SETTINGS.

Brazilian sapphire See GEMS. GEM CUTS, AND SETTINGS.

breadth See ASSORTMENT.

breaker pants See PANTS.

breakfast cap See MORNING CAP.

breakfast coat See SLEEPWEAR AND LOUNGEWEAR: BRUNCH COAT.

breakfast wrapper See SLEEPWEAR AND LOUNGEWEAR: ROBE DE CHAMBRE.

breasted heel See FOOTWEAR.

breast hook See STAY HOOK.

breast kerchief See SCARVES.

breast knot ∞ Bunch of ribbons or ribbon bow worn at bosom of woman's dress in 18th and early 19th c. Also called *bosom knot.*

breastplate See JEWELRY.

breast pocket See POCKETS.

breasts See CLOSURES: BREASTS.

breech/breeches **1.** Garment that extends from the waist to just below the knee where it fastens with a buckle or buttons. Traditionally worn by men, breeches were replaced by full-length PANTS in the early 19th c. By the latter part of the 19th c., garments cut like breeches were more likely to be referred to as KNICKERS. **2.** Colloquial term that can refer to any two-legged garment covering the lower half of the body. Sometimes called *britches.* **3.** ∞ Derived from the word BRAIES, and used in the 14th to 16th c. to refer to the upper part of hose that fit the trunk of the body, and in the 16th c. as synonymous with TRUNK HOSE or HOSE.

breeches #1

breech belt Waistband of the BREECH or BREECHES. Also see BREECH GIRDLE.

breechcloth/breechclout See LOIN CLOTH.

breech girdle ∞ Belt or string pulled through wide hem at top of breech in drawstring fashion—at waist or a little below. Worn from 13th to 15th c.

by men. Also called *braie girdle, bray girdle, bregirdle.*

breeching A ritual carried out in Renaissance in England when a boy of age 5 or 6 was given his first pair of breeches.

bregirdle See BREECH GIRDLE.

bretelles **1.** An ornamental trimming on womens' dresses that consists of REVERS (see under NECKLINES AND COLLARS) or ruffles that extend in a diagonal line from the outer edge of the shoulder to the waist at close to the center of the front and back. Especially popular from 1814 to 1835. Synonym: *suspender trimming.* **2.** Decorative bands with the appearance of functional straps or suspenders that extend from the waist in back over the shoulders to the waist in front. *Der.* French, "suspenders."

bretelles #1

Breton See HEADWEAR.

Breton costume See COATS AND JACKETS: BRETON JACKET.

Breton jacket See COATS AND JACKETS.

Breton lace See LACES.

Breton work See EMBROIDERIES AND SEWING STITCHES.

brick stitch/brick work See EMBROIDERIES AND STITCHES.

bridal Adjective used to describe clothing and accessories worn by a bride at a wedding. See HEADWEAR: BRIDAL VEIL, LACES: BRIDAL LACE, JEWELRY: BRIDAL SET.

bridal dress See WEDDING DRESS.

bride lace ∞ Blue ribbon used in 16th and 17th c. to tie sprigs of rosemary given as wedding favors, to the arm; later used on hat.

brides **1.** ∞ 1830s and 1840s: ribbons attached to inside brim of bonnet, or broad-brimmed hat, that were loosely tied or hung free. Sometimes by extension refers to the bonnet itself. **2.** See LACES.

bride's garter See WEDDING GARTER.

bridesmaid's dress Any type of dress worn by a bride's attendant at a wedding, usually selected by the bride. May match in style and color with other attendants, and is usually selected to complement the bride's dress.

bridge jewelry See JEWELRY.

bridge line A line at the upper end of the apparel price range that is made with fewer details and less expensive fabrics than designer clothing. See APPAREL PRICE RANGES.

bridles Strings attached to mobcap for tying under the chin in the 18th c. Also called *kissing strings.*

briefcase See HANDBAGS AND RELATED ACCESSORIES.

briefers See ACTIVEWEAR.

briefs See UNDERGARMENTS.

brigadier wig See WIGS AND HAIRPIECES: MAJOR WIG.

Brigance, Tom * See Appendix/Designers.

brilliant cut See GEMS, GEM CUTS, AND SETTINGS.

brim See HEADWEAR.

britches See BREECHES #2.

British look **1.** Conservative elegant look for men reflecting the influence of London tailors of Savile Row that included narrow shoulders, three-button suit coats with narrow lapels, and narrow trousers without cuffs popular in 1960s. **2.** Contemporary men's wear influenced by London tailors. Many of the finest men's custom tailoring shops are located on Savile Row, a street in London's West End. They have catered to a wealthy international clientele with quality and conservative men's apparel ever since Henry Poole & Co. opened in 1843. Also called *London look* and *Savile Row look.*

British warm See COATS AND JACKETS.

Brittany work See EMBROIDERIES AND SEWING STITCHES: BRETON WORK.

broadbrim See HEADWEAR.

broadcloth † **1.** Closely woven plain weave fabric with a fine rib in the crosswise direction. Usually made from cotton or cotton blends but can also be made of other fibers. **2.** Wool or wool blend fabric made in plain or twill weave with a napped (brushed) surface that is brushed in one direction.

broad-stitched seam See CLOTHING CONSTRUCTION DETAILS.

broadtail lamb See FURS.

broc See BRAIES.

brocade † A heavy fabric with a complex, raised pattern that is woven on a JACQUARD loom.

Electronic or mechanical controls in this loom can manipulate yarns to combine into many different types of weaves in a single fabric. Often made with decorative and lustrous yarns, the resulting fabric is especially suitable for evening and formal wear.

brocade embroidery See EMBROIDERIES AND SEWING STITCHES.

brocatelle † Medium-weight dress fabric woven on a JACQUARD loom with a pattern that stands out in high relief giving a blistered effect. Some fabrics give the appearance of being quilted. Made of filament yarns on its face, with cotton yarns in the backing.

broché See CAPES, CLOAKS, AND SHAWLS.

brodekin/brodkin/brotiken See FOOTWEAR: BRODEKIN.

broderie anglaise See EMBROIDERIES AND SEWING STITCHES: MADEIRA WORK.

broderie russe See EMBROIDERIES AND SEWING STITCHES: RUSSIAN EMBROIDERY.

brogan See FOOTWEAR.

brogue See FOOTWEAR.

broken hat See HEADWEAR: CHAPEAU BRAS.

broken twill weave See HERRINGBONE WEAVE.

broker A person (often called a *middleman*) who acts as an intermediary in business deals between the retailer and the manufacturer.

bronzed leather See LEATHERS.

Bronx jacket See COATS AND JACKETS: PERFECTO JACKET.

brooch See JEWELRY: PIN.

Brooks Brothers® look 1. Traditional well-tailored look of a successful businessman featuring classic men's styles as sold by Brooks Brothers®, a New York specialty store, originally for men, founded in 1818. **2.** Women's classics, including tailored suits, shirts with button-down collars, and tailored skirts, were added to the Brooks Brothers® products in 1949 when they added a small women's department. Currently the store and its branches sell classic clothes in stores and on the Internet for both men and women. *Der.* Trade name and name of famous store in New York City originally catering only to men.

Brooks, Donald * See APPENDIX/DESIGNERS.

broomstick skirt See SKIRTS.

brow band See HEADWEAR.

brown belt See ACTIVEWEAR: KARATE CLOTHING.

brown George See WIGS AND HAIRPIECES.

Bruce tartan See PLAIDS AND TARTANS.

Bruges lace See LACES.

Brummel, Beau See BEAU BRUMMEL.

Brummel bodice See UNDERGARMENTS.

brunch coat See SLEEPWEAR AND LOUNGEWEAR.

Brunswick ∞ Close-fitting riding coat-dress with mannish collar worn by women in 18th c. *Der.* Said to have originated in Brunswick, Germany.

Brunswick gown See SACK #1.

brush See FURS.

brush cut See HAIRSTYLES: CREW CUT.

brush-dyeing See FURS and LEATHERS.

brushed † Adjective applied to woven or knitted fabrics that have had fibers pulled or brushed up to the surface to create a soft texture or nap.

Brussels lace See LACES.

Brussels net See LACES.

Brutus head/wig See HAIRSTYLES.

buba An Afro-inspired dress of 1969 worn by women. Styled in a large panel print and wide decorative borders and with the same design on front and back. Sleeves are usually fitted at armholes, widely flared at wrists, and frequently ending in a long point.

bubble 1. *Adj.* Used to describe any item of apparel or hair-styling with a balloonlike shape. See CAPES, CLOAKS, AND SHAWLS: BUBBLE CAPE, HAIRSTYLES: BUBBLE CURLS, JEWELRY: BUBBLE BRACELET, SLEEPWEAR AND LOUNGEWEAR: BUBBLE COVER-UP, and SKIRTS: BUBBLE SKIRT. **2.** *n.* Child's garment with short or long lengths that are slightly balloon-shaped.

bubble #2

bubble beret See HEADWEAR: BERET # 3.

bubble bob See HAIRSTYLES: BEE-HIVE.

bubble dress Dress style of 1959 with fitted bodice, sometimes strapless, with skirt bubbling out at hips and tapering in closely at hem. *Der.* Literally the skirt was shaped like a "bubble." Reintroduced in 1984.

bubble dress

B

bubble-up theory of fashion change   See BOT-TOM-UP THEORY OF FASHION CHANGE.

Buchanan tartan   See PLAIDS AND TARTANS.

bucket bag   See HANDBAGS AND RELATED ACCESSORIES.

bucket hat   See HEADWEAR.

bucket-top boot   See FOOTWEAR: FRENCH-FALL BOOT.

Buckingham/Buckinghamshire lace   See LACES.

buckle   See CLOSURES.

buckled jumper   See JUMPERS.

buckled wig   See WIGS AND HAIRPIECES.

buckles d'Artois   See CLOSURES.

Bucko calf   See LEATHERS.

buck oxfords   See FOOTWEAR.

buckram   † Loosely woven, heavily sized fabric in a plain weave used for stiffening. Similar to crinoline but heavier and much stiffer. Sizing will wash out, making fabric unsuitable for washable garments. *Der.* From costly material made in Bokhara, a city in Uzbekistan.

bucksain   See COATS AND JACKETS.

buckskin/buckskins   1. See LEATHERS. 2. 15th to 19th c.: used to refer to buckskin gloves, breeches, or riding gaiters.

buckskin jacket   See COATS AND JACKETS.

buckskin jumper   See JUMPERS.

buckskin vest   See VESTS.

bucky pelts   See FURS.

budget   See HANDBAGS AND RELATED ACCESSORIES.

budget goods   See APPAREL PRICE RANGES.

buffalo checks   See PLAIDS, STRIPES, AND CHECKS.

buff coat   See COATS AND JACKETS.

buffing   See LEATHERS.

buffins, pair of   See TRUNK HOSE.

buff jerkin   See COATS AND JACKETS: BUFF COAT.

buffon   See SCARVES.

bug-eyed glasses   See EYEWEAR.

bugle beads   See JEWELRY.

bugle bracelet   See JEWELRY.

bugle chain   See CHAIN.

built-in bra   See UNDERGARMENTS.

built-up heel   See FOOTWEAR: STACKED HEEL.

built-up slip   See UNDERGARMENTS.

built-up straps   Shoulder straps constructed in continuous curve as part of garment, usually used for a slip or swimsuit.

bulgare pleat   ∞ (bool′gar pleet)   Term used in mid-1870s for double box pleats kept in place with elastic on inside of skirt.

bulky   1. † Adjective used to describe yarns or fabrics made with yarns that have been crimped, curled, or otherwise treated to make them larger and softer. 2. Adjective used to describe anything that is exceptionally large.

bulldog toe   See FOOTWEAR.

bulletproof jacket   See COATS AND JACKETS.

bull head   See HAIRSTYLE.

bullion   See EMBROIDERIES AND SEWING STITCHES and LACES.

bullion-hose   See TRUNK HOSE.

bully-cocked   See HEADWEAR: COCKED HAT.

bumper   See FOOTWEAR.

bumper/bumper brim   See HEADWEAR.

bumper collar   See NECKLINES AND COLLARS.

bum roll   See UNDERGARMENTS.

bun   See HAIRSTYLES.

bundle   See BUNDLE SYSTEM.

bundle stitch   See EMBROIDERIES AND SEWING STITCHES.

bundle system   In the garment trade, a method of garment production using an unorganized flow of work from one employee to another. Garment pieces are tied together into a **bundle.** The operator takes the bundle, performs one or more operations, bundles the finished work, then passes the work to the next employee. In the **development bundle system**, items move in units or bundles in a more highly organized manner from one operator to another.

Bunka embroidery   See EMBROIDERIES AND SEWING STITCHES.

bunny suit   See SLEEPWEAR AND LOUNGEWEAR.

bun snood/bun-warmer   See HEADWEAR: CHIGNON CAP.

bunting   See BABY BUNTING.

Burberry®   1. Originally a trademark for a heavy or lightweight British fabric treated to resist rain, snow, and wind. Used in officers' coats during World War I, the fabric was also made into raincoats and people often referred to raincoats manufactured from this fabric as Burberrys. The trademark is still registered and as currently described covers a wide variety of apparel produced by this company. 2. See COATS AND

JACKETS. **3.** See PLAIDS AND TARTANS: BURBERRY PLAID.

burdash/berdash ∞ Fringed sash worn by fashionable young men over the coat in late 17th and early 18th c.

burgonet See ARMOR.

burka See CHADOR # 1.

burlap † Loosely constructed, plain woven fabric made of jute or other minor bast fibers. Originally considered a utility fabric for bags and sacks. Now sometimes embroidered and used for handbags and items of apparel.

burlet See HEADWEAR: BOURRELET #1.

burnet/burnette See HEADWEAR.

burn grace See HEADWEAR: BONGRACE.

burnoose/burnouse See CAPES, CLOAKS, AND SHAWLS.

burn-out/burnt-out † Adjective describing fabric or lace that has a patterned effect produced by using yarns of two different fibers and destroying all or part of one of the yarns. Chemicals that dissolve one of the fibers are printed onto the fabric in the design areas. A burn-out pattern effect may be produced on velvet by dissolving parts of the pile but leaving other pile areas and the ground intact.

Burnsides Side whiskers and full moustache with clean-shaven chin worn from 1860s to end of 19th c. *Der.* Named for Major General Ambrose Everett Burnside, commander of Army of the Potomac in 1862 under General Grant.

Burnsides

burn-out lace See LACES: PLAUEN LACE.

burnt-out See BURN-OUT.

buros See CAPES, CLOAKS, AND SHAWLS: BIRRUS.

burr cut See HAIRSTYLES: INDUCTEE'S CUT.

Burrows, Stephen * See APPENDIX/DESIGNERS.

burse See HANDBAGS AND RELATED ACCESSORIES.

burunduki See FURS.

busby See HEADWEAR.

bush coat/jacket See COATS AND JACKETS.

bush cut See HAIRSTYLES: CREW CUT.

busheling ∞ Formerly used to refer to the alteration or repair of men's clothing.

bush hat See HEADWEAR.

bush shirt See SHIRTS: SAFARI SHIRT.

business man's cut See HAIRSTYLES.

business sheer hose See HOSIERY: SHEER HOSE.

business suit Man's suit, conservative in style and color, suitable for daytime wear at the office and also worn for other occasions—with exception of formal and semi-formal occasions. So called and cut to distinguish it from a sport suit, which may be made of plaids and brighter colors. May be single- or double-breasted and made in one-, two-, or three-button style. Traditionally worn with a dress shirt and tie; however, in the late 1990s, as casual dress became more common in the business world, some men wore business suits with t-shirts.

business suit 2000

busk ∞ Long, flat piece of wood, whalebone, steel, and sometimes horn that was inserted into a casing in the front of a woman's bodice or corset to maintain a flat line. Some busks were highly ornamented with low relief carvings or engravings. Used from the second half of the 16th c. to the 19th c.

buskins See FOOTWEAR.

bust A woman's breasts.

Buster Brown© **1.** See FOOTWEAR. **2.** See HAIRSTYLES: BUSTER BROWN. **3.** See NECKLINES AND COLLARS: BUSTER BROWN.

bustier **1.** See BLOUSES AND TOPS. **2.** See UNDERGARMENTS.

bustle **1.** See UNDERGARMENTS. **2.** General term describing exceptional fullness at the back of the skirt of a woman's dress.

bustle back **1.** See HEADWEAR. **2.** See SKIRTS.

bustle curls See HAIRSTYLES.

bustle dress Any dress with fullness protruding in back from waist to hips or waist to hem. A style characteristic of 1870 to 1890, which is often called "The Bustle Period" by costume historians. Bustles also appeared in some clothes of the 1940s and was reintroduced in early 1980s. A 1980s version, designed by Christian Lacroix for Jean Patou, consisted of a knee-length dress

bustle dress 1885

with large pouf in back and long floor-length hanging panel.

bust measurement See CHEST MEASUREMENT.

bust pads See FALSIES.

butcher boy blouse See BLOUSES AND TOPS.

butcher linen † **1.** Heavyweight durable fabric made in plain weave. Originally of linen for butcher's aprons, later made in cotton. Under current labeling legislation, the fiber from which the fabric is made must be identified. Used for summer suits and sportswear. **2.** Spun rayon fabrics which imitate linen by using yarn of uneven thickness. Term is a misnomer and term *butcher rayon* should be used.

butcher rayon See BUTCHER LINEN #2.

butcher's apron See APRONS.

butch haircut See under HAIRSTYLES: CREW CUT.

butterfly An adjective used to describe an item or element of apparel that is shaped like a butterfly. See EYEWEAR: BUTTERFLY GLASSES, FOOTWEAR: BUTTERFLY BOW, HEADWEAR: BUTTERFLY CAP and BUTTERFLY HEADDRESS, NECKLINES AND COLLARS: BUTTERFLY COLLAR, SHOULDERS AND SLEEVES: BUTTERFLY SLEEVE, and TIES: BUTTERFLY BOW TIE.

Butterick, Ebenezer Merchant tailor who is said to have invented the sized, tissue paper pattern. In 1863, he cut out a pattern for his son's trousers using heavy paper similar to cardboard. His wife suggested women would like ready cut-out patterns for all clothes. As the cardboard was bulky, he next tried a lighter weight paper and finally tissue paper. By 1890s patterns were available for anything made of cloth from a wedding gown to a pin cushion. There were Butterick designers in New York, Paris, London, Berlin, and Vienna to develop the newest ideas of great modistes. Also see DELINEATOR.

button **1.** See CLOSURES. **2.** See GLOVES AND GLOVE CONSTRUCTIONS.

button-down See NECKLINES AND COLLARS and SHIRTS: IVY LEAGUE SHIRT.

button earrings See JEWELRY.

buttoned shoe See FOOTWEAR.

buttonhole/buttonholes See CLOSURES.

buttonhole stitch See EMBROIDERIES AND SEWING STITCHES.

button hook **1.** Small metal hook attached to long handle formerly used to pull buttons through buttonholes of shoes or gloves. **2.** Small metal hooks first used in the 1860s instead of eyelets on shoes, the laces winding around hooks, crisscrossing to fasten shoes. Used now on skating and other types of boots and called *speed lacing* or *lacing studs*. See CLOSURES: SPEED LACING.

button shoes See FOOTWEAR.

button-tab sleeve See SHOULDERS AND SLEEVES.

B.V.D.'s® See UNDERGARMENTS: ENVELOPE COMBINATION.

buyer An individual authorized to make purchases for a retailer.

buying Making purchases of goods from a manufacturer for a retailer who will sell them to the ultimate consumer. Often done through a RESIDENT BUYING OFFICE.

buying office See RESIDENT BUYING OFFICE.

buzz cut See HAIRSTYLES: CREW CUT.

bycocket See HEADWEAR.

byesse See BIAS.

Byron Adjective derived from the name of Lord George Gordon Byron (1788–1814) who was an important English poet of the Romantic Period. He became famous not only for his poetry, but also for behavior that was considered outrageous at the time. His name was used as a fashion adjective not during his lifetime, but well after his death, to describe apparel that was thought to be "romantic." See TIES: BYRON TIE, COLLARS AND NECKLINES: BYRON COLLAR.

byrrus See CAPES, CLOAKS, AND SHAWLS: BIRRUS.

byzance See JEWELRY.

Byzantine embroidery See EMBROIDERIES AND SEWING STITCHES.

Byzantine stitch See EMBROIDERIES AND SEWING STITCHES.

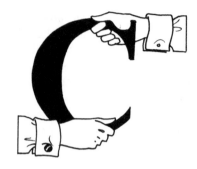

C **1.** Shoe size: Letter indicating a width; widths run from AAAA to EEEEE with AAAAs being the narrowest and EEEEEs the widest. **2.** Pajama size: Men's regular height (5′8″–5′11″) size corresponding to 41″–44″ chest measurement. For other sizes, see BIG, REGULAR, EXTRA-TALL, and TALL. **3.** Shirt size: For men's extra-tall size with 17–17½ collar measurement. **4.** Bra cup size. Standard sizes run AAA, AA, A, B, C, D, the A sizes being the smallest and D the largest. There is no industry agreement on cup sizes larger than D. Different manufacturers use different designations.

caban **1.** See COATS AND JACKETS. **2.** See COATS AND JACKETS: GABERDINE.

cabana set See ACTIVEWEAR.

cabas See HEADWEAR.

cabbage ruff See RUFF.

cabin-boy breeches See PANTS.

cable hatband ∞ Band of gold yarn twisted to resemble a rope or cable; worn in the late 16th c.

cable stitch See EMBROIDERIES AND SEWING STITCHES.

cable sweater See SWEATERS.

cable yarn See CORD YARN.

cabochon See GEMS, GEM CUTS, AND SETTINGS.

cabretta See LEATHERS.

cabriole headdress See HAIR ACCESSORIES.

cabriolet bonnet See HEADWEAR.

cache-folies See WIGS AND HAIRPIECES.

cache-laid See MASKS.

cache-peigne See HEADWEAR.

cack See FOOTWEAR.

CAD See COMPUTER-AIDED DESIGN.

CAD/CAM See COMPUTER-AIDED DESIGN/COMPUTER-AIDED MANUFACTURING.

caddie/caddy See HEADWEAR: BUSH HAT.

cadenette (cad-net′) French term for a "lock of hair." See HAIRSTYLES: COIFFURE EN CADENETTES.

Cadogan See HAIRSTYLES: GEORGE and WIGS AND HAIRPIECES: CLUBWIG.

cadogan net See HEADWEAR: SNOOD.

Cadoro® bra See UNDERGARMENTS.

Caesar haircut See HAIRSTYLES.

caftan Long, full robe with a slit neckline that is often decorated with embroidery and has long or three-quarter-length sleeves that widen to the end. Based on a North African or Middle Eastern garment, the caftan was adopted by American women in the 1960s and after and worn as at-home or evening dress.

caftan

caftan neckline See NECKLINES AND COLLARS.

cage **1.** Overblouse or dress made out of lattice-like or transparent fabric. **2.** See UNDERGARMENTS: HOOPS.

cage-americaine See UNDERGARMENTS.

cage dress Woman's garment made in two layers with inner layer opaque and cut close to body, and outer layer of sheer or latticed fabric hanging loosely. Such dresses, introduced in late

1960s by Paris couturier Yves Saint Laurent, were similar to dresses designed by Spanish couturier Cristobal Balenciaga in Paris in the 1940s. Popular again in the 1990s.

cage empire   See UNDERGARMENTS.

cage petticoat   See UNDERGARMENTS.

caging   See FURS.

cagoule   See CAPES, CLOAKS, AND SHAWLS.

cainsil (kane-sil)   See CHAINSE.

cairngorm   See GEMS, GEM CUTS, AND SETTINGS.

cake hat   See HEADWEAR.

calamanco   See FOOTWEAR: CALAMANCO SHOES.

calamanco shoes   See FOOTWEAR.

calash   See HEADWEAR

calasiris   See KALASIRIS.

calcarapedes   See FOOTWEAR.

calceus   See FOOTWEAR.

calculator watch   See WATCHES.

calèche   See HEADWEAR: CALASH.

calençons ∞ (kal'sen)   Worn by women in early 17th c., a type of long drawers or hose worn with doublet and petticoat that later developed into the breeches and trousers of women's contemporary riding habit.

calender   † Passing fabric between two heated rollers in order to produce a smooth, even appearance.

calendar watch   See WATCHES.

calf-length   See LENGTHS.

calfskin   See FURS and LEATHERS.

calgoule   See CAPES, CLOAKS, AND SHAWLS.

calico   † Plain weave, light- to medium-weight cotton or cotton-blend fabric usually printed with very small designs such flowers or geometric forms. Also see PRINTS, STRIPES, AND CHECKS: CALICO PRINT.

calico button   See CLOSURES.

California embroidery   See EMBROIDERIES AND SEWING STITCHES.

calisthenic costume   ∞ Knee-length dress worn with Turkish trousers similar to BLOOMER COSTUME. Worn in late 1850s by women and girls for such sports as archery, iceskating, and exercising with dumbbells. Later, a version of this dress was called *gymnasium costume*.

calk   See FOOTWEAR.

calligraphic scarf   See SCARVES.

Callot Soeurs   *   See APPENDIX/DESIGNERS.

calotte   ∞ **1.** See HEADWEAR. **2.** See CLERICAL DRESS.

calypso chemise ∞ (ca-lip-so)   Woman's dress of the 1790s made in two parts: a dress of colored muslin worn under a loose robe.

calypso shirt   See SHIRTS.

CAM   See COMPUTER-AIDED MANUFACTURING.

camail   **1.** See ARMOR. **2.** See CAPES, CLOAKS, AND SHAWLS.

Camargo   See COATS AND JACKETS.

Camargo hat   See HEADWEAR.

camauro   See CLERICAL DRESS.

cambric   † Fine, closely woven cotton fabric made with mercerized yarns given a calendered finish. May also be made of linen and used for handkerchiefs. *Der.* From Cambrai, France.

Cambridge coat   See COATS AND JACKETS.

Cambridge paletot   See COATS AND JACKETS.

camelaurion   See HEADWEAR.

cameleons   See FOOTWEAR.

camel hair   † **1.** Fibers from the crossbred Bactrian camel of Asia, which produces soft luxurious yarn that is resistant to heat and cold. **2.** Cloth made of these fibers.

cameo   **1.** A small low relief carving usually made from a banded two-layered gemstone such as onyx or sardonyx that gives a raised design, usually in white with another color left as the background. Most common subject is a woman's head and shoulders. The opposite of INTAGLIO. See GEMS, GEM CUTS, AND SETTINGS: CAMEO and INTAGLIO. **2.** Carving a two-tone shell in the same manner as above to produce a **shell cameo**. **3.** Using colored pottery material similar to that used by Josiah Wedgwood and molded to produce a WEDGEWOOD® CAMEO (see under JEWELRY).

Cameron tartan   See PLAIDS AND TARTANS.

cames   See UNDERGARMENTS: CHEMISE.

camikini   See SWIMWEAR: BIKINI.

camise   See UNDERGARMENTS: CHEMISE.

camisette   See UNDERGARMENTS.

camisia   ∞ Medieval British term for chemise. See UNDERGARMENTS: CHEMISE.

camisole   **1.** See UNDERGARMENTS. **2.** See BLOUSES AND TOPS: CAMISOLE TOP. **3.** See NECKLINES AND COLLARS: CAMISOLE NECKLINE. **4.** ∞ Sleeved jacket or jersey formerly worn by men.

cami-tap set   See UNDERGARMENTS: TAP PANTIES.

camouflage pants   See PANTS.

camouflage suit   See ACTIVEWEAR.

camp   **1.** Deliberate adoption of styles or behavior that are generally considered to be vulgar, artificial, or humorous. *adj.* Also used as an adjective to describe such styles. **2.** See SHIRTS and SHORTS.

campagus   See FOOTWEAR.

campaign coat   See COATS AND JACKETS.

campaign hat   See HEADWEAR.

campaign wig   See WIGS AND HAIRPIECES.

camp shirt   See SHIRTS.

camp shorts   See SHORTS.

canadienne   See COATS AND JACKETS.

canary breeches   See ACTIVEWEAR: RIDING BREECHES.

canary diamond   See GEMS, GEM CUTS, AND SETTINGS.

cancan dress   Contemporary version of the traditional costume of Parisian cancan dancers of the 1890s. The bodice has a bustier effect and laces up the back. The skirt has an overskirt in apronlike effect tapering to center back with a large bow, and is worn over underskirt made with rows of ruffles.

cancan dress

Designed by Victorine for Karl Lagerfeld of Chanel for fall 1986. *Der.* Similar to dresses worn by Music Hall dancers in film and stage show *Can-Can* and those shown in paintings by Henri Toulouse-Lautrec.

candlewick embroidery   See EMBROIDERIES AND SEWING STITCHES.

candy stripes   See PRINTS, STRIPES, AND CHECKS.

cane   Staff or walking stick to assist walking or to carry as a fashionable accessory. Canes vary from rough rustic wood for country use, e.g., **shillelagh** (sha-lay′-lee), to polished woods with elaborately decorated heads. Carried from 16th c. to present by men and occasionally by women, specific types included: **malacca cane** (mah-lah′-kah), also called a *clouded cane*, carried in 18th c. and made from the mottled stem of the malacca palm; **rattan canes,** carried in 17th and 18th c. and made from an East Indian palm; **constable,** a small cane with a gold-plated top carried by men in 1830s and 1840s; **penang lawyer,** a walking stick used by men in 19th c. made from a palm stem with a bulbous top.

canezou   ∞ (can-zoo′)   Refers to any of several types of 19th-c. accessory garments that were sometimes worn as a means of extending the life of an older garment. **1.** A woman's waist-length spencer jacket of 1820s without sleeves, this sleeveless overblouse style continued in use until the 1860s. **2.** In 1830s a cape, cut short and pointed, extending down center front and back but not covering the arms. Also called *canezou pelerine.* **3.** By mid-19th c. an elaborate fichu or scarf of muslin, ribbons, and lace covering bodice of dress.

canezou pelerine   See CANEZOU #2.

canions   ∞ Tubular garments worn on the thighs as extensions of men's TRUNK HOSE from 1570 to 1620. Frequently of different fabric or color than the trunk hose. Shown at ELIZABETHAN STYLES.

cannetille (can-tee)   **1.** Military braid of gold or silver thread that looks like lace. Also spelled *cantile.* **2.** Fine spiral-twisted gold or silver thread, used for embroidery.

cannon   **1.** See CANNONS. **2.** See ARMOR.

cannons   ∞ Frills of lace or bunches of ribbons that fell down over tops of wide boots worn by men during 1660s and 1670s. Also called *port canons, canons.* Also worn with low shoes and PETTICOAT BREECHES. Shown at PETTICOAT BREECHES.

cannon sleeve   See SLEEVES AND SHOULDERS.

canotier   See HEADWEAR.

canteen bag   See HANDBAGS AND RELATED ACCESSORIES.

cantile   See CANNETILLE #1.

canvas embroidery   See EMBROIDERIES AND SEWING STITCHES: BERLIN WORK.

cap   See HEADWEAR.

capa   See CAPES, CLOAKS, AND SHAWLS.

CAPES, CLOAKS, AND SHAWLS

cape   Sleeveless outerwear of various lengths usually opening in center front; cut in a full circle, in a segment of a circle, or on the straight—usually with slits for arms. A classic type of outerwear worn in one form or another throughout history. During the Middle Ages, a cape was more generally called a *mantle.* Important from then on in various eras in various lengths as a separate item or attached to coats. Shown at CAPES, CLOAKS, AND SHAWLS: BURNOOSE.

cloak   Loose outer garment not clearly distinguishable from outer garments that might also be classed as *capes, mantles,* or *loose coats* with vestigial sleeves. This term appears often during last half of 19th c.

shawl   Decorative or utilitarian wrap, larger than a scarf, worn draped over the shoulders and sometimes the head. May be oblong, square, or a square folded diagonally. Believed to have originated in Bukhara, it was worn in Kashmir as early as late 16th c. Also worn in Persia and India, and worn by country people for utilitarian purposes. Did not become fashionable in Europe until second half of 18th c. Very popular throughout the 19th c. and worn intermittently since. *Der.* Persian and Hindu, "shal." Shown at CAPES, CLOAKS, AND SHAWLS: SPANISH SHAWL.

all-purpose poncho   See CAPES, CLOAKS, AND SHAWLS: RAIN PONCHO.

almuce   ∞ Small fur-lined Medieval cape with attached hood that tied under the chin. Also spelled *amuce, almusse, aunice, aumusse.*

Andalouse cape   ∞ (an'-da-looz') Cape worn outdoors by women in 1846, made of silk and trimmed with fringe.

artois   ∞ (ahr-twah') Long loose cloak with lapels and several capes, the longest ending near the waistline; worn by men and women in late 18th c.

Balmoral mantle   ∞ Cloak of velvet, cashmere, or wool styled like an INVERNESS CAPE (see under CAPES, CLOAKS, AND SHAWLS) and popular for outdoor wear in the 1860s.

barège shawl   ∞ (ba-rezh') A printed shawl made in France in the 1850s from fabric with worsted crosswise yarns and silk lengthwise yarns.

bautte/bautta   ∞ (bah-oot'ta) Black cloth wrap of 18th c. with hood that could be drawn down over face to form a half mask.

beach poncho   Oblong terrycloth poncho that can be laid flat for use as a towel at the beach.

bell   ∞ Circular cape used as traveling cloak, sometimes hooded, sometimes with side and back vents; worn by men and women from late 13th to early 15th c.

beluque   ∞ Woman's cape or mantle worn in the 15th c.

Bernhardt mantle   ∞ Woman's short outdoor cape with loose front and dolman or sling sleeves that was popular in 1886. Named after Sarah Bernhardt, a famous French actress of the period.

birrus   ∞ Hooded cape of rough cloth, worn in bad weather by Romans of all classes under the last emperors. Also spelled *byrrus, buros.*

bivouac mantle   ∞ (biv-oo-wak') Full-length loose cape of scarlet cloth, styled with high collar, padded and lined with ermine. Worn by women in 1814.

Bokhara shawl   (bo-kar'-a) Shawls made in Bokhara, Uzbekistan, of camel's hair spun into yarn. Dyed with vegetable dyes and woven into 8-inch strips of patterned fabric joined invisibly to form shawls.

bolero cape   ∞ Elbow-length cape, worn by women at end of 19th c., cut like a bolero in front and tapered to waistline in back. Also called *bolero mantle.*

box cape   Straight cut, elbow- or hip-length cape with broad padded shoulders and square silhouette. Made of fur or wool and fashionable in late 1930s.

bratt   ∞ **1.** Mantle or cape made of coarse material worn by peasants in Ireland in 9th and 10th c. Also called *Irish mantle.* **2.** Term used in latter part of 14th c. for wrap or blanket for an infant.

broché   ∞ (bro-shay') Paisley-type shawl made in Scotland, woven in alternating stripes of pattern and plain color. See CASHMERE SHAWL #2. Very popular in 1830s.

bubble cape   Elbow-length fur cape often made with skins worked in the round. Popular in 1950s and early 1960s.

burnoose/burnouse Circular three-quarter length cape of wool that had a pointed hood or fabric cut and sewn to simulate a hood. The hood often had a tassel attached at the point. The garment was derived from capes worn by indigenous people of North Africa. Especially popular in the 1840s to the 1860s, the style is occasionally revived.

burnoose

cagoule ∞ (ka-gool′) Cloth or fur semicircular cape with attached hood worn by peasants from 11th to 13th c.

capa 1. ∞ Wide, circular, full-length hooded cape worn by Spanish men from Middle Ages to early 17th c. In the Romantic era in France (c. 1830s and 1840s), it was called *cape a l'espagnole* (les-pan-yol′) and worn by women. **2.** Full cape worn by bullfighters in Spain, used to attract bull's attention. *Der.* Latin, *capa*, "hooded cloak."

capelet Any small cape, e.g., a cape collar, attached or detachable, on a coat, dress, or suit. Also see CAPES, CLOAKS, AND SHAWLS: TIPPET.

capote (kah-pote′) **1.** Full circular cape with wide cape collar and red lining. Used as a working cape by matadors at Spanish and Mexican bullfights. Also spelled *capot*. **2.** ∞ Generic term for hooded coat or cloak worn from Middle Ages on.

capuchon ∞ (kap′-oo shon) Woman's waist-length outdoor evening mantle with wired hood and long tight sleeves worn in 1837. Also called *carmeillette* (kar-may′-yet).

cardinal ∞ **1.** In 18th c. three-quarter-length scarlet cloak with hood that resembled the MOZETTA worn by cardinals in Roman Catholic church. See CLERICAL DRESS: MOZETTA. **2.** Woman's waist-length red cloak without hood or collar worn in 1840s.

carmeillette See CAPES, CLOAKS, AND SHAWLS: CAPUCHON.

casaweck See COATS AND JACKETS.

cashmere shawl 1. Extremely fine, soft shawl handmade from hair of the Tibetan cashmere goat. In the Kashmir Valley of northwestern India weaving was under the direction of the Maharaja from c. 1586 and for over 200 years shawls were woven for the court and never left India. Two main types were made: (a) Those with woven designs that were made in sections and sewn together in square and oblong shapes. Often they were woven in pairs so that they were reversible. These were called *twin* or *double shawls*. (b) Others woven in a color scheme of white, red, or green and afterward embroidered in gold, silver, and silk threads. The characteristic design is a cone or leaf pattern called a **boteh**. Such shawls were extremely popular during French consulate (1799–1804) and Empire period (1804–1814). **2.** Machine-made sheep's wool imitations of cashmere shawls produced in France and Scotland and popular during the 19th c. Known also as **paisley shawls** (pay′-slee) after the town of Paisley in Scotland, where large numbers of these shawls were manufactured. The characteristic boteh design became known as a *paisley design*.

paisley shawl

cassock mantle ∞ Woman's knee-length short-sleeved cloak, with shirring at shoulders and down the center back, of 1880s.

cawdor cape See CAPES, CLOAKS, AND SHAWLS: GLENGARRY CAPE.

chambord mantle/chambard mantle ∞ Three-quarter-length hooded woman's cloak of 1850s that resembled a shawl with fullness in back, made of satin or velvet.

chaussee hood See CAPES, CLOAKS, AND SHAWLS: EPITOGA #2.

chlaine ∞ (klain) Woolen cape worn in Greece during Homeric period by shepherds and warriors.

chlamys ∞ (klay′-mis or klahm′-is) Oblong mantle approximately 5′ or 6′ × 3′, fastened in front or on one shoulder with a pin. Worn in ancient Greece by travelers, youths, soldiers, hunters, and in Greek mythology by the god Hermes. Chlamys continued to be worn in more semicircular shape in Byzantium and in later centuries for sports and traveling.

circular ∞ Long cape or mantle of silk, satin, or other fine fabric in extra wide widths, and frequently lined with rabbit or gray squirrel combined with bright fabric. Fashionable in late 19th c.

clerical cape See CLERICAL DRESS.

chlamys

cloak See under category heading for CAPES, CLOAKS, AND SHAWLS: CLOAK.

Colleen Bawn cloak ∞ Woman's cloak of 1860s to 1890s made of white grenadine with large cape pulled up in center back and caught with rosettes or bowknots. *Der.* After the title of a melodrama by Dion Boucicault.

cope **1.** See CLERICAL DRESS. **2.** Style worn as a coronation robe by English sovereigns. **3.** Originally a hooded cloak designed as a rain cape sometimes made with sleeves and fastened in center front. After adoption by clergy, it was always sleeveless and richly decorated.

compass cloak See CAPES, CLOAKS, AND SHAWLS: FRENCH CLOAK.

cottage cloak ∞ Woman's hooded cloak of 19th c. tied under chin, similar to those seen in pictures of the fairy-tale character Little Red Riding Hood.

crispin ∞ **1.** Cloak without a collar worn by actresses waiting in the theater wings in early 19th c., later adopted for men, women, and children. First worn in mid 1820s. **2.** Man's evening cloak, with full sleeves and quilted lining, worn in late 1830s. **3.** Woman's short mantle of early 1840s with close-fitting back and small PELERINE cape (see under CAPES, CLOAKS, AND SHAWLS)—sometimes with sleeves—made of bias-cut satin, velvet, or cashmere and often padded.

crocheted shawl Fringed shawl made by hand crocheting usually in a lacy pattern. Popular in late 1960s and early 1970s in oblong, semicircular, or triangular shapes.

domino **1.** Originally, a large hood worn by monks. Later, a cloak with attached hood for men and women. **2.** A large cloak, usually black, worn with a small mask for traditional carnival and masquerade costume. Popular in 18th and 19th c.

domino #2

Dorothy cloak Wool cape manufactured and sold to the public after 1890 by the Shakers, a religious community. Full length, with a short shoulder cape, and without arm slits, it opened down the front and closed with silk ribbon ties. It had a very full, attached hood and was made in a variety of colors. *Der.* Named after the designer Shaker Eldress Dorothy Durgin.

epitoga ∞ **1.** Originally an ancient Roman cloak worn over the toga sometimes having bell-shaped sleeves. **2.** Cloak of the 13th c. similar to above but cut more like a robe and worn as academic dress. Also called *chausse* or *chaussee hood.* **3.** The medieval hood reduced to symbolic form as a part of academic and ceremonial robes.

Esmeralda cloak ∞ Waterproof wrap of the late 1860s worn in U.S. Introduced from Paris in both plain and tartan designs. In England, worn only in the rain. In Paris it had two capes, no sleeves, and was ornamented with bows, frills, fringe, satin braid, and rosettes.

Eugénia, The ∞ Voluminous woman's cape of early 1860s, of seven-eighths length. Usually black with second cape reaching to waist in back and shorter in front. Both capes were edged with fancy box-pleated ribbon.

faldetta ∞ Waist-length colored taffeta women's mantle trimmed with wide lace ruffle worn in 1850.

fichu-pelerine ∞ Large cape or shawl-like covering for woman's shoulders worn from mid-1820s to 1860s. Usually white and frequently made with a double cape and turned-down collar and tied in front with the

fichu-pelerine 1834

ends reaching below the waist and sometimes as far as the knee.

fishnet poncho Square medium-sized poncho made of fishnet or see-through fabric with a high large turtleneck collar. The edge of the collar and the hem is trimmed with ball fringe.

French cloak ∞ Long circular or semi-circular cape, sometimes with a square flat collar or shoulder cape worn in 16th and 17th c. One type of French cloak was the **compass cloak**, a full circular cape worn by men. When made in semi-circular shape, it was called a **half-compass cloak**. In the 16th c., any of these cloaks was also called a *manteau*.

French policeman's cape Circular-cut knee-length cape worn by French policemen, made of heavy black wool and rubber. Heavy enough to be swung like a club. Authentic cape was sold as sportswear in boutiques and Army surplus stores in U.S. in late 1960s. Also called *gendarme cape*.

frileuse ∞ Women's cape or pelerine wrap, with a fitted back and loose sleeves, made of quilted satin or velvet. Used indoors or at the theater in 1847.

froufrou mantle ∞ Woman's shoulder cape of late 1890s made in three tiers trimmed with RUCHING. Had a high, standing collar and rosettes and long ribbon streamers in front. Also called *froufrou cape. Der.* From the name of the comedy *Froufrou*, written by Henri Meilhac and Ludovic Halévy in 1869.

fur stole Term used in 20th c. for waist-length fur cape with elongated ends in front, sometimes trimmed with tails of animals. Formerly called *pelerine* or *tippet*. Very popular in late 1940s, 1950s, and 1960s, especially in mink.

gendarme cape See CAPES, CLOAKS, AND SHAWLS: FRENCH POLICEMAN'S CAPE.

genoa cloak See CAPES, CLOAKS, AND SHAWLS: ITALIAN CLOAK.

Glengarry cape ∞ Three-quarter-length cape worn by women in the 1890s made with a tailored collar and single-breasted closing. A hood, sometimes plaid lined, was attached at

neckline under the collar. Also called *cawdor cape*.

glocke (glok′-ka) Medieval poncho-type outer garment made of LODEN CLOTH, with a hole in center of large circle of fabric. Still worn today, especially in mountainous Alpine regions of Europe. *Der.* German, "bell."

half-compass cloak See CAPES, CLOAKS, AND SHAWLS: FRENCH CLOAK.

Inverness cape ∞ (in-ver-ness) Man's full cape, usually long, and made of wool or worsted. Was close-fitting at neck and fell loose from shoulders—often made in plaid patterned fabric.

Irish mantle See CAPES, CLOAKS, AND SHAWLS: BRATT.

Isabella (The) ∞ Hip-length collarless cape of mid-1850s made with slashes for arms and extra capelets at dropped shoulders to cover arms.

Italian cloak ∞ Short hooded cloak worn by men in the 16th and 17th c. Also called *Spanish cloak* or *Genoa cloak*.

Jocelyn mantle ∞ Knee-length, double-skirted, sleeveless woman's mantle of 1852 made with three capes trimmed with fringe.

lacerna ∞ Semi-circular knee-length cape fastened in center front or on right shoulder by a fibula (pin). Worn by ancient Romans from 2nd c. B.C. to A.D. 5th c. Made of wool in white, natural, amethyst, and purple decorated with gold.

lapponica Poncho of plaid wool with fringed edges imported from Finland. Colorful plaids are of all varieties, some being in large squares of color; some being more complicated similar to the STEWART TARTANS (see PLAIDS AND TARTANS); and some in smaller checks similar to glen plaid (see PLAIDS AND TARTANS: GLEN URQUHART PLAID).

limousine ∞ Full-length circular woman's evening cape of late 1880s with shirring around neck so fullness falls in folds over the arms, forming sleeves.

Maintenon cloak ∞ (mant-nown′) Woman's wide-sleeved, black velvet coat of 1860s sometimes embroidered and usually trimmed with a wide pleated flounce covered with GUIPURE LACE (see under LACES). *Der.* Named for the *Marquise de Maintenon,* mistress and second wife of Louis XIV of France.

manteau (man-tow′) See CAPES, CLOAKS, AND SHAWLS: FRENCH CLOAK.

mantelet ∞ **1.** A short cape mentioned by Chaucer in 1386. **2.** Small cloak worn by women in 18th c. **3.** Scarf of fur, lace, or silk worn around shoulders, crossed over chest, and ends tied in back from 1814 to 1835. **4.** 19th-c. woman's rounded shoulder cape with long end tucked under belt in front. Also spelled *mantelot, mantlet.*

mantilla (man-til′-ah) **1.** Shawl or veil worn by Spanish women, usually of black lace—white lace worn for festive occasions. Worn draped over head, sometimes over a high comb placed in hair, wrapped around neck, and falling over shoulders. This shawl has influenced 20th-c. fashions. **2.** ∞ Lightweight shawl of silk, velvet, or lace worn by women from 1840s to 1880s. Shawl hung long in back and had long ends in front. Also spelled *mantella.* *Der.* Diminutive of Spanish *manta,* "shawl."

mantle ∞ **1.** Long, loose, cape-like cloak originally cut square, oblong, or as a part of a circle. Worn from 12th through 16th c. by men and women. Mantles could be either **open mantles,** one length of fabric fastened by a pin or clasp on one shoulder, at the center, or tied at the neck, or **closed mantles** with openings for the head to slip through. **2.** In 14th c. usually a ceremonial cape. Sometimes lined and called a double mantle. **3.** By 19th c. term for a cape without sleeves. **4.** Wrap for infants in 17th and 18th c. *Der.* Latin, *mantellum,* "covering."

open mantle 13ᵗʰ c.

mantlet Matilda/mantlet Matilde ∞ Type of shawl-like woman's garment trimmed with fringe or taffeta in front, worn in 1850s.

manton de manilla See CAPES, CLOAKS, AND SHAWLS: SPANISH SHAWL.

Maud ∞ Woman's fringed wrap of plaid fabric worn in mid-1850s.

maxi cape Any ankle-length cape.

midi cape Any calf-length cape.

Moldavian mantle ∞ Full-length woman's mantle of mid-1850s with long capes over the shoulders forming "elephant sleeves."

montpensier mantle ∞ (mon-pon-see′-ay) Woman's capelike garment of 1840s, long in back, with front ending in a point, and slit up sides, leaving arms free.

Mother Hubbard cloak ∞ Woman's or girl's three-quarter-length cloak of 1880s made of brocade, velvet, satin, or cashmere with quilted lining, high collar tied at neckline, full sleeves—often in DOLMAN (see under SHOULDERS AND SLEEVES) style with shirring over shoulders. Sometimes the back section was draped over a *bustle* and tied with ribbon bow.

mousquetaire mantle ∞ (moose-key-tare′) Braid-trimmed black velvet mantle of mid-19th c. with short deep cuffs lined with quilted satin. Worn by women in 1847. *Der.* From cape worn by French musketeers or royal bodyguards of Louis XVIII in 17th c.

mozetta See CLERICAL DRESS.

muleta cape Descriptive term for a Spanish-type midi cape made of felt, sometimes scarlet, and trimmed with wool tassels around the neck, down front, and around hem. Featured in late 1960s for women.

Normandie cape ∞ Lightweight, hip-length woman's cape of late 1890s made with ruffles extended down center front, around the hem, sometimes around yoke, and a standing collar or a double-tiered ruff at the neck.

nurse's cape Three-quarter-length cape of navy-blue wool trimmed with brass buttons and lined in red. At one time worn by nurses when they wore traditional uniforms.

officer's cape Three-quarter-length cape in navy-blue worsted with small standing collar; part of dress uniform of officers in U.S. Navy.

opera cape ∞ Man's full, circular calf-length black worsted cape, sometimes lined in red satin. Worn for formal occasions with TAIL COAT (see COATS AND JACKETS) and TOP HAT (see HEADWEAR). *Der.* In the 19th c., it was fashionable attire with the high silk hat for the opera. Also favored by magicians and circus ringmasters.

opera wrap ∞ Term used in early 1900s for women's full-length opera cape usually made of elaborate fabric trimmed with fur or feathers.

paenula ∞ (pay′-new-la) Hooded cape or poncho-shaped garment, made of heavy woolen fabric or leather. Worn by ancient Romans for traveling or inclement weather.

paisley shawl See CAPES, CLOAKS, AND SHAWLS: CASHMERE SHAWL #2.

palatine See CAPES, CLOAKS, AND SHAWLS: TIPPET.

palatine royal ∞ A fur cape of 1851 with a quilted hood and short ends in front. Also called *victorine.*

paletot-cloak ∞ (pal-ah-tow′ or pal-tow′) Man's hip-length cape of the 1850s made in single- or double-breasted style with armhole slits.

paletot-mantle ∞ (pal-ah-tow′ or pal-tow′) Woman's three-quarter-length cloak with hanging sleeves and a cape collar worn in late 1860s.

palla ∞ Rectangular shawl-like garment resembling ancient Greek HIMATION. Worn by Roman women draped around body, sometimes with one end draped over head.

palla and stola

pallium ∞ Rectangular shawl worn by Roman man. Also see HIMATION.

paludamentum ∞ (pa-lu-da-men′tum) **1.** Purple mantle of rich fabric fastened with clasp at shoulders. Worn by Roman emperors and military officers. **2.** Same item worn by upper class Byzantine men, the emperor, and the empress but

paludamentum #2

changed to ankle-length by 5th c. This garment had a large, square decoration called a TABLION at the open edge over the breast.

pelerine ∞ (pel-er-reen′) **1.** Woman's short shoulder cape of fur, velvet, or other fabric worn from 1740 to end of 18th c. Sometimes worn with long scarf ends crossed and tied around waist. **2.** A wide collarlike cape, sometimes permanently attached, made of lace or fabric worn over a dress or PELISSE (see under COATS AND JACKETS) that was especially popular from c. 1820 to 1850.

peplum rotonde ∞ Woman's waist-length circular cloak, made with back vent and fringed border, worn in 1871.

piano shawl See CAPES, CLOAKS, AND SHAWLS: SPANISH SHAWL.

Pierrot cape ∞ (pee-ehr-oh′) Woman's three-quarter-length cloak of 1892 with additional shoulder cape and satin ruff at neckline similar to that worn with Pierrot costume.

Polish mantle ∞ Knee-length woman's cloak of mid-1830s with attached cape made of satin edged with fur.

polonaise ∞ (pol-on-nays′) In 1750s a cape or small hooded cloak drawn back like a polonaise dress (see POLONAISE #1). Also called *polonaise pardessus* (pol-on-nays′ par-de′-soo).

poncho 1. Fashion item shaped like a square or a small oblong blanket with hole in center for the head. Frequently fringed around the edges. Popular in late 1960s and after. **2.** Utilitarian garment consisting of waterproofed fabric with a slash in the center for the head. When worn, it was used as a rain cape; when not worn could be used as a tarpaulin or a blanket. **3.** Square of nylon fabric, 54″ × 80″, laminated with polyvinyl chloride, that slips over the head and snaps closed at the sides to make a partial sleeve. One size fits everyone. Usually styled with an attached hood. Originally made of a rubberized fabric and worn by policemen on a

poncho #1

rainy day. Also called a *rain poncho* or *all-purpose poncho*. **3.** ∞ Woman's loose three-quarter-length cloak worn in the 1860s with buttons from neck to hem, a small standing collar, full sleeves—narrower at the wrist—with capes over the sleeves.

rain cape **1.** A lightweight plastic cape that may be folded, placed in a small envelope, and carried for use when it rains. **2.** A cape of any fabric treated for water repellency.

rain poncho See CAPES, CLOAKS, AND SHAWLS: PONCHO #3.

rebozo (re-bow'-zho) An oblong shawl made of native fabric worn originally by South American Indians and introduced as a fashion item in late 1960s.

ripple cape ∞ In the 1890s a woman's short ruffled cape extended beyond the shoulder by shirring three layers of fabric or lace onto a yoke trimmed with ribbon.

roquelaure ∞ (roke'-ay-lore) Man's knee-length to full-length heavy cloak of 18th c. often fur-trimmed and lined with bright-colored silk. Usually made with cape collar and back vent for riding horseback. *Der.* From Antoine Gastone Jean-Baptiste, le duc de Roquelaure (1656–1738), minister of wardrobe under Louis XIV. Also spelled *roculo, roccelo, rocklo.*

rotonde ∞ Woman's short or three-quarter length circular *cape* of 1850s and 1860s made of lace or of same material as dress.

sagum ∞ (sa'-goom) Red woolen rectangle of cloth worn pinned on the right shoulder as a cape by Roman soldiers and by all Roman citizens in time of war. The phrase "to put on the sagum" was synonymous with saying "to go to war."

serape (say-rah'-pay) Bright-colored oblong rectangle worn by Mexicans over the shoulder. Handmade in horizontally striped patterns, it resembles a small blanket. Usually made with fringed ends.

shale ∞ French shawls, with handspun warp and machine-spun merino filling, made in Rheims.

shawl See under category heading for CAPES, CLOAKS, AND SHAWLS: SHAWL.

skoncho A do-it-yourself style poncho made from a brushed wool plaid blanket or striped with a fringe on two ends, similar to a blanket used at a football game. A 16″ slash is cut diagonally in the center. May also be worn as a skirt.

soccus ∞ Ceremonial and coronation cape fastened on the right shoulder worn during Middle Ages by kings and dignitaries. Also spelled *socq.*

sontag ∞ (sonn'-tag) Woman's small cape of 1850s and 1860s worn for warmth, often knitted or crocheted with ends crossed in front and worn under a cloak. *Der.* Named for German opera singer, Henriette Sontag.

sortie de bal ∞ (sor'-tee de bal) Woman's evening *cloak* with attached hood worn from 1850s to 1870s. Made of silk or cashmere and lined with a quilted fabric.

space blanket Insulated blanket with one side aluminized, the other brightly colored. Worn on one side to insulate from the cold, the other side protects from the heat of the sun. Folds to pocket size for easy carrying. *Der.* Developed for NASA space program in late 1960s.

Spanish cloak See CAPES, CLOAKS, AND SHAWLS: ITALIAN CLOAK.

Spanish shawl Large embroidered silk shawl usually made in China then shipped to Spain where the long silk fringe was added. When such a shawl was shipped by way of Manilla in the Philippines, it was known as a *manton de manilla*. When used as a wrap, the shawl was folded diagonally with the point in center at the back and the ends thrown loosely over the shoulders. A fashionable accessory of the early 20th c., it was revived in the late 1960s and early 1970s and becomes fashionable periodically. Also called *piano shawl,* because in the early 20th c. this type of shawl was draped on the top of grand pianos.

Spanish shawl 1926

Spencer cloak ∞ Woman's cloak of early 19th c. made of embroidered net with elbow-length sleeves.

stole **1.** See SCARVES. **2.** See CAPES, CLOAKS, AND SHAWLS: FUR STOLE.

tabard ∞ Short heavy cape of coarse cloth worn outdoors in 19th c. by men and women.

tablet mantilla ∞ Watered or plain silk wrap of mid-1850s made with a yoke that falls low on the shoulders. Trimmed with cut-turret (tab-shaped) edging, narrow braid, and fringe.

Talma ∞ **1.** Woman's long cape or cloak, frequently hooded, worn in 1860s. **2.** Woman's knee-to-hip–length cape of embroidered satin, lace, or velvet with fringe at hem used as an outer garment from 1850s to mid-1870s. **3.** In 1890s, a woman's full-length coat with loose sleeves and lace cape or deep velvet collar. **3.** Knee-length man's cape with a turned-over collar and silk lining, worn for evening in 1850s. *Der.* Named for François Joseph Talma (1763–1826), a French tragic actor of Consulate and Empire period. Also called *Talma mantle.*

tebenna ∞ (te-bain′-ah) Etruscan semicircular cloak in purple, white, or black (for funerals) worn by a king and important citizens—short at first, later knee-length, and finally full-length. The Roman toga is thought to have developed from this cloak.

templar cloak See COATS AND JACKETS: CABAN.

tippet ∞ **1.** Shoulder cape of fur or cloth worn by women from 16th c. on. In the 1840s, such a small fur or lace shoulder cape of the 1840s with long flat ends in front reaching below the waist was called a **palatine. 2.** See CAPES, CLOAKS, AND SHAWLS: FUR STOLE.

tudor cape ∞ Woman's short circular cape of 1890s, usually using embroidered fabric. Made with pointed yoke front and back, and epaulet on each shoulder, and velvet Medici collar.

venetian cloak ∞ Woman's black satin cloak of late 1820s with collar, cape, and wide hanging sleeves.

victorine See CAPES, CLOAKS, AND SHAWLS: PALATINE ROYAL.

visite ∞ (vee-zeet) General term for woman's loose cape-like outdoor garment worn in last half of 19th c.

waterproof cloak ∞ Outergarment with small tasselled hood worn by women from 1867 to 1870s, made of waterproof fabric. Later became an ankle-length semi-fitted coat with princess lines buttoned down the front. Also see CAPES, CLOAKS, AND SHAWLS: ESMERALDA CLOAK.

Watteau cape ∞ (wat-toe′) Knee-length cape of the 1890s worn by women. Styled with collar fitted on neck then turned over. Made with single box pleat in back, and gathered to neckline in front. Made with separate pieces gathered over the shoulders to form capes over the arms. *Der.* Named for the artist Antoine Watteau (1684–1721).

witchoura mantle ∞ **1.** Woman's cloak, worn from 1808 to 1818, made with long fur-trimmed cape. **2.** An 1830s' name for a woman's winter mantle with standing collar, large sleeves, and lined or trimmed with fur.

---

cape à l'espagnole See CAPES, CLOAKS, AND SHAWLS: CAPA.

cape coat See COATS AND JACKETS.

cape collar See NECKLINES AND COLLARS.

cape hat See HEADWEAR.

capelet See BLOUSES AND TOPS and CAPES, CLOAKS, AND SHAWLS.

capeline See ARMOR and HEADWEAR.

Cape May diamond See GEMS, GEM CUTS, AND SETTINGS.

cape ruby See GEMS, GEM CUTS, AND SETTINGS.

capeskin See LEATHERS.

cape sleeve See SHOULDERS AND SLEEVES.

Capezio® See FOOTWEAR: BALLET SLIPPERS.

capless wig See WIGS AND HAIRPIECES.

cap of dignity See HEADWEAR: CAP OF MAINTENANCE.

cap of estate See HEADWEAR: CAP OF MAINTENANCE.

cap of maintenance See HEADWEAR.

capot See COATS AND JACKETS: CAPOTE.

capote **1.** See CAPES, CLOAKS, AND SHAWLS. **2.** See COATS AND JACKETS. **3.** See HEADWEAR.

capot-ribot See HEADWEAR.

cappuccio See HEADWEAR: CHAPERON.

caprice See COATS AND JACKETS.

Capri-length panty girdle See UNDERGARMENTS: GIRDLES.

caprioll See HEADWEAR: CABRIOLE HEADDRESS.

Capri pants See PANTS.

caps See HEADWEAR.

cap sleeve See SHOULDERS AND SLEEVES.

Capucci, Roberto * See APPENDIX/DESIGNERS.

capuche See HEADWEAR: CAPUCHE and CAPUCHIN.

Capuchin See HEADWEAR.

Capuchin collar See NECKLINES AND COLLARS.

capuchon 1. See HEADWEAR: CAPUCHIN. 2. See CAPES, CLOAKS, AND SHAWLS.

capucine See HEADWEAR: CAPUCHIN.

Capulet See HEADWEAR.

caraco See COATS AND JACKETS.

caraco corsage See COATS AND JACKETS: CARACO #2.

caracul 1. See FURS: KARAKUL. 2. See KARAKUL CLOTH in alphabetical listing.

carat See GEMS, GEM CUTS, AND SETTINGS.

caravan See HEADWEAR.

caravan bag See HANDBAGS: SAFARI BAG.

carbatina See FOOTWEAR.

carbuncle See GEMS, GEM CUTS, AND SETTINGS.

carcaille See NECKLINES AND COLLARS.

car coat See COATS AND JACKETS.

carded yarn † Yarn made from short fibers, known in the textile industry as staple fibers, that have been subjected to the process of carding. Carding is the first step in making staple fibers into yarns. The fibers are separated, straightened out somewhat, and formed into a weblike mass, after which the web is drawn out and given a greater or lesser degree of twist to form a yarn. Carded yarns have more fibers on the surface and are not so smooth as COMBED YARNS.

cardigan An adjective used to describe collarless garments with round or V-necklines that button down the front. The name is derived from that of James Thomas Brudenell, 7th Earl of Cardigan (1797–1868), the lieutenant general in the British Army during the Crimean War who led the famous charge of the Light Brigade. Needing an extra layer of warmth for the cold Crimean winter, he wore a sleeveless knitted woolen vest under his uniform. Present-day cardigans do not resemble the original garment. See COATS AND JACKETS: CARDIGAN, NECKLINES AND COLLARS: CARDIGAN, SHIRTS: CARDIGAN, and SWEATERS: CARDIGAN. Shown at SWEATERS: CARDIGAN.

cardinal See CAPES, CLOAKS, AND SHAWLS.

cardinal pelerine See NECKLINES AND COLLARS.

carding See CARDED YARN.

Cardin, Pierre * See APPENDIX/DESIGNERS.

care label Permanently attached label for apparel required by a Federal Trade Commission ruling of 1972. The label must provide care and maintenance directions. Exceptions include hats, gloves, and footwear; articles selling for less than $3; items that would be defaced by attaching a label; or items not requiring cleaning.

careless See COATS AND JACKETS.

cargo Adjective used to describe apparel that has cargo pockets. See POCKETS: CARGO. Also see CARGO JUMPSUIT, PANTS: CARGO PANTS, and SHORTS: CARGO SHORTS.

carmagnole See COATS AND JACKETS.

carmeillette See CAPES, CLOAKS, AND SHAWLS: CAPUCHON.

Carnaby cap See HEADWEAR: NEWSBOY CAP.

Carnaby dress Simple beltless dress made in fabrics of unusual color combinations with a large white collar. *Der.* Named for Carnaby Street, in London, England, where "mod" fashions originated in 1960s.

Carnaby look Look adopted first in London in connection with the MOD LOOK. Introduced in the United States in 1964, it featured such items as miniskirts; capes for men; polka dot shirts with large flat white collars; low-slung, bell-bottomed trousers; newsboy caps; and wide vinyl neckties one day—string ties the next. A major factor in the trend for young men to move away from traditional styling, it also influenced skirt lengths for women, and styling of children's wear. *Der.* After Carnaby Street, a London back street, behind the grand shopping thoroughfare of Regent Street, where the mod look first appeared in many small boutiques catering to avant-garde young customers. Also see NECKLINES AND COLLARS: CARNABY COLLAR.

Carnegie, Hattie * See APPENDIX/DESIGNERS.

carnelian   See GEMS, GEM CUTS, AND SETTINGS.

carnival collar   See NECKLINES AND COLLARS.

carnival lace   See LACES: BRIDAL LACE.

Caroline corsage ∞ Woman's evening bodice of 1830s made with lace ruffles forming a V in front, extended around shoulders into small cape.

Caroline hat   See HEADWEAR.

Caroline sleeve   See SHOULDERS AND SLEEVES.

carpenter   *Adj.* Describes clothing modeled after or influenced by clothing worn by carpenters. See PANTS: CARPENTER PANTS and APRONS: CARPENTER APRON.

carpenter's apron   See APRONS.

carpet bag   See HANDBAGS AND RELATED ACCESSORIES.

carpet slipper   See FOOTWEAR.

carpincho   See LEATHERS.

carriage boot   See FOOTWEAR.

carriage dress ∞ A woman's dress or costume suitable for riding in a carriage. The term was in use from about 1820 to the end of the 19th c. The specific style conformed to current fashions and was frequently trimmed with fur.

carriage parasol   See UMBRELLAS AND PARASOLS.

carriage suit   Three-piece set for infant, consisting of jacket, pants, and hat. Worn outdoors in baby carriage since the late 1920s.

carriage trade   Term coined by merchants (c. 1890–1910) to refer to affluent customers who arrived at the stores in their own carriages. Still sometimes used in reference to upscale customers.

carrick   See COATS AND JACKETS.

Carrickmacross lace   See LACES.

carryall   See HANDBAGS AND RELATED ACCESSORIES: TOTE.

carryall clutch   See HANDBAGS AND RELATED ACCESSORIES.

carrying frocks   See LONG CLOTHES.

carryover   Apparel styles in a line from one season that are repeated to the next season. See COLLECTION.

Cartier's   Famous New York City retail store that sells jewelry. Alfred Cartier and his son, Louis, established the firm in 1898 and by the beginning of the 20th c., they had become the most prestigious jewelers in the world. Among their clients were the king of Portugal, Grand Dukes and Princes of Russia, the Brazilian royal family, and other royalty and celebrities throughout the world.

cartoon apron   See APRONS.

cartoon fashions   Apparel imprinted with images of comic strip and cartoon characters. Part of the trend toward LICENSING.

cartoon T-shirt   See SHIRTS.

cartoon watch   See WATCHES.

cartridge belt   See BELTS.

cartridge pleats   See CLOTHING CONSTRUCTION DETAILS.

cartwheel   *Adj.* Describes apparel that has the shape of a large, round wheel like those used on carts. For examples see HEADWEAR: CARTWHEEL HAT; SHOULDERS AND SLEEVES: CARTWHEEL SLEEVES; and NECKLINES AND COLLARS: CARTWHEEL RUFF.

casaque   See COATS AND JACKETS: CASAQUE and COATS AND JACKETS: CASSOCK #3.

casaquin   See COATS AND JACKETS: CARACO.

casaquin bodice ∞ Tight-fitting bodice for daytime dress, similar in cut to man's tail coat (see COATS AND JACKETS: SWALLOW TAIL COAT), closing with buttons down front and worn in 1878.

casaweck   See COATS AND JACKETS.

cascade   **1.** Ruffles bias-cut from fabric, in circular manner, that fall in folds. **2.** Trimming used in the 19th and early 20th c. made by cutting a narrow piece of fabric on BIAS and pleating it to form repeated shell designs. **3.** ∞ Jet pendants of beads with a zigzag edge used at waistline or bodice in 1860s. **4.** See NECKLINES AND COLLARS.

cased body ∞ **1.** Man's sleeveless jerkin worn over DOUBLET in second part of 16th c. **2.** Woman's bodice of early 19th c. with series of horizontal pleats or rows of SHIRRING (see CLOTHING CONSTRUCTION DETAILS) across the front.

cased sleeve   See SHOULDERS AND SLEEVES.

casentino   See COATS AND JACKETS.

cashambles   See CHAUSSEMBLES.

cashgora † Fiber obtained from goats bred in New Zealand that are a cross between female cashmere goats and angora males. The fiber is fine, soft, and strong, has a low to medium luster, and dyes well.

Cashin, Bonnie * See APPENDIX/DESIGNERS.

cashmere † **1.** A fine, soft, downy wool undergrowth produced by the cashmere goat, which is raised in the Kashmir region of India and Pakistan and parts of northern India, Tibet, Mongolia, Turkmenistan, China, Iran, and Iraq. Similar goats can now be raised in the United States. **2.** Cloth woven from this wool fiber. Synonyms include PASHMINA.

cashmere shawl See CAPES, CLOAKS, AND SHAWLS.

cashmere sweater See SWEATERS.

cashmere work See EMBROIDERIES AND SEWING STITCHES.

casing See CLOTHING CONSTRUCTION DETAILS.

casque See HEADWEAR.

casquette See HEADWEAR.

Cassini, Oleg * See APPENDIX/DESIGNERS.

cassock See COATS AND JACKETS and CLERICAL DRESS.

cassock mantle See CAPES, CLOAKS, AND SHAWLS.

Castelbajac, Jean Charles de * See APPENDIX/DESIGNERS.

castellated ∞ (kas-tell-ay′-ted) Adjective describing a garment with "squared scallops" at edges, particularly the edge of sleeves or hem. Used in 14th and 15th c. Similar to DAGGING. Also see BATTLEMENT.

caste mark Red mark usually worn in center of forehead by women of India that originally symbolized and identified caste or class membership but which now serves a decorative function. Paste-on caste marks were introduced in U.S. as body jewelry for women in 1968.

Castle, Irene American ballroom dancer, married to her dancing partner, Vernon Castle. Together they made tea-dancing the rage in pre–World War I. By 1914 she had started many fashion fads—short earlobe-length hair brushed back off forehead in loose weaves, Dutch lace caps, slashed HOBBLE SKIRTS (see under SKIRTS), and dancing shoes with BALLET LACES (see under FOOTWEAR).

castor See HEADWEAR.

casual wear Clothing designed to be worn for occasions that do not require more formal dress. Over time, casual wear has been widely accepted for many activities, including some work situa-tions. See CASUAL FRIDAY. Related terms include LEISURE WEAR, SPORTSWEAR.

casual work days/casual Friday Working days identified by business or industry when employees can wear casual dress to work. For many companies, the selected day is Friday.

casual Friday look

casula See CLERICAL DRESS: CHASUBLE.

catagan See HAIRSTYLES: CADOGAN and WIGS AND HAIRPIECES: CLUB WIG.

catalog showroom Setting like a warehouse in which merchandise is sold from a catalog or floor samples.

catcher's mask See MASKS.

catch stitch See EMBROIDERIES AND SEWING STITCHES.

category killer A specialty discounter that "kills" the competition by concentrating on having the best selection at the best price of a single product. Smaller independent stores that carry the same type of merchandise are generally unable to compete with a "category killer."

cater cap See HEADWEAR.

Catherine II Married in 1745 to Peter III of Russia, who ascended the throne in 1762, was deposed, and his crown usurped by Catherine. A major fashion influence of her time, one of her dresses, worn to receive the Turkish ambassador in 1775, was trimmed with many diamonds and 4,200 magnificent pearls. During her reign, coiffures were limited in height to about 36″.

Catherine-wheel farthingale See FARTHINGALE.

catogan wig See WIGS AND HAIRPIECES: CLUB WIG.

cat's eye See GEMS, GEM CUTS, AND SETTINGS.

cat stitch See EMBROIDERIES AND SEWING STITCHES: CATCH STITCH.

cat suit See ACTIVEWEAR.

cattlehide See LEATHERS.

caudebec See HEADWEAR.

caul 1. See HEADWEAR. **2.** See WIGS AND HAIRPIECES.

cauliflower wig See WIGS AND HAIRPIECES.

caution fee Fee paid by American designer or manufacturer to attend showing of a Paris couturier. That fee, which may be equal to cost of one or two items, can be applied to purchases.

cavalier *Adj.* Describes apparel derived from or inspired by clothing worn by partisans of King Charles I of England (1625–1649). Among the styles favored by cavalier men

cavalier style 1630

were long, curled hairstyles, large-brimmed hats decorated with feathers, wide, flat collars decorated with lace, wide cuffed boots, and full hip-length capes. For examples see HEADWEAR: CAVALIER HAT, NECKLINES AND COLLARS: CAVALIER COLLAR, and SHOULDERS AND SLEEVES: CAVALIER SLEEVE.

cavu shirt See SHIRTS.

cawdebink See HEADWEAR: CAUDEBEC.

cawdor cape See CAPES, CLOAKS, AND SHAWLS: GLENGARRY CAPE.

caxon See WIGS AND HAIRPIECES.

ceint (sant) ∞ Man's or woman's belt or girdle worn in the 14th and 15th c. Also spelled *seint*.

celata See ARMOR: SALETT.

cellophane Generic name, once a trademark, for thin transparent film made of acetate. Used in ribbon-sized strips to cover paper fibers imitating straw or used alone as synthetic straw for hats, handbags, etc.

celluloid collar See NECKLINES AND COLLARS.

cellulose Basic substance, a carbohydrate, contained in all vegetable fibers, and certain manufactured fibers, including ACETATE and RAYON.

cervellière See ARMOR.

ceryphalos See HEADWEAR.

CFDA See COUNCIL OF FASHION DESIGNERS OF AMERICA.

CGMM See COMPUTER GRADING AND MARKER MAKING.

chaconne See TIES.

chaddah See CHADOR #1.

chador/chaddar/chadri **1.** An all-enveloping shapeless cape worn by women in some Muslim countries. The exact cut and how it is worn varies from country to country. In some cases, it is worn with a head scarf, or it may cover the wearer from head to toe and have netting over the eyes. In Afghanistan, this garment is called a *burka*. Also spelled *chadder, chaddah, chadur, chadar, chudder, chuddar*. **2.** An Indo-Iranian shawl or mantle about three yards in length. Also called *uttariya*. **3.** Indian shawls wrapped around the shoulders or waist by Hindu men.

chaddar or burka

chadur See CHADDAR #1.

chaffers See HEADWEAR: ENGLISH HOOD.

chain **1.** Series of connected loops or links made of metal, plastic, or tortoise shell used for closings or worn as an ornamental accessory in the form of necklace, bracelet, or belt. Chains are called by various names

chain   rope chain

according to shape of links—**cobra chain** is composed of two rows of triangular-shaped links that alternate in a flat effect. **Herringbone chain** is made of small slanting links giving a flat effect. **Roped chain** is composed of two (or more) pieces of chain twisted and wound together like rope. **2.** Adjective used to describe items of apparel that incorporate chains into their design. See BELTS: CHAIN BELT, CLOSURES: CHAIN CLOSURE, HEADWEAR: CHAIN HAT, FOOTWEAR: LOAFER, JEWELRY: CHAIN BRACELET and CHAIN NECKLACE.

chain mail See ARMOR: MAIL.

chain store Centralized retail organization that owns and operates a number of retail outlets in different locations that are similar in the lines of merchandise they sell and in their methods of operation.

chainse ∞ (shens) Medieval garment of the 11th and 12th c. that was worn over a CHEMISE (see UNDERGARMENTS) and may have been worn as a house dress or perhaps as a summer garment, as it was made of washable, lightweight fabric, probably white linen.

chain stitch See EMBROIDERIES AND SEWING STITCHES.

chainstitched embroidery See EMBROIDERIES AND SEWING STITCHES.

chalcedony See GEMS, GEM CUTS, AND SETTINGS.

chalk stripes See PRINTS, STRIPES, AND CHECKS.

challis † (shal'-lee) Soft, plain weave fabric made of wool, rayon staple, cotton, or manufactured fiber blends. Supple and lightweight, it is often printed in small floral patterns. Generally used for women's dresses and sportswear, infant's wear, and robes.

chamarre ∞ (shah-mar) An academic robe made like a long full coat with sleeves full at the shoulders—usually fur-lined and decorated with braid and passementerie. Introduced about 1490 in England; later referred to a judge's gown. Also spelled *chammer, chymer, samarra, samarre, shamew.* Also see CLERICAL DRESS: SIMAR.

chambord mantle/chambard mantle See CAPES, CLOAKS, AND SHAWLS.

chambray † (sham'-bray) A broad class of plain weave fabrics made with colored yarns in the lengthwise direction and white yarns in the crosswise direction. May be a plain color, striped, or checked. Usually made of cotton, manufactured fibers, or a blend of the two.

Chambre Syndicale de la Couture Parisienne (sham'-br san'-dee-kale de lah koo'-ture pah-ree-zee-en) An association of Parisian couturiers founded in 1868 as an outgrowth of medieval guilds that regulates its members in regard to piracy of styles, dates of openings for collections, number of models presented, relations with press, questions of law and taxes, and promotional activities. Formation of the organization was brought about by Charles Frederick Worth. An affiliated school was organized in 1930 called L'Ecole de la Chambre Syndicale de la Couture. Since 1975, this organization has worked within the FÉDÉRATION FRANÇAISE DE COUTURE, DU PRÊT-À-PORTER DES COUTURIERS ET DES CRÉATEURS DE MODE.

Chambre Syndicale de la Mode (sham'-br san'-dee-kale de lah mode) French official organization of milliners operating like the CHAMBRE SYNDICALE DE LA COUTURE PARISIENNE.

Chambre Syndicale de la Mode Masculine (sham'-br san'-dee-kale de lah mode mas'-ku-leen) Organization of couture and men's ready-to-wear designers formed in 1975 as another vehicle for promotion working within the FÉDÉRATION FRANÇAISE DE COUTURE, DU PRÊT-À-PORTER DES COUTURIERS ET DES CRÉATEURS DE MODE.

Chambre Syndicale des Paruriers (sham'-br san'-dee-kale deh pa-roo'-yer) An association comprised of accessory houses in Paris that produce bags, belts, feathers, flowers, gloves, and umbrellas.

Chambre Syndicale du Prêt-à-Porter (sham'-br san'-dee-kale duh pret ah por-tay') Organization of couture and women's ready-to-wear designers formed in 1975 as another vehicle for promotion working within the FÉDÉRATION FRANÇAISE DE COUTURE, DU PRÊT-À-PORTER DES COUTURIERS ET DES CRÉATEURS DE MODE.

chammer See CHAMARRE.

chamois See LEATHERS.

chamois cloth † (sham-wah') Soft cotton fabric that is either knitted or woven. Made with a fine soft nap in imitation of chamois-dyed sheepskin. Should not be shortened or confused with CHAMOIS (See under LEATHERS), as this refers to leather and a leather-tanning process.

chamois tanning See LEATHERS.

chandelier earrings See JEWELRY.

Chanel bag See HANDBAGS AND RELATED ACCESSORIES.

Chanel, Gabrielle * See APPENDIX/DESIGNERS.

Chanel suit Classic women's suit style originated by Gabrielle Chanel in the 1920s and revived in the 1960s. It had a collarless, CARDIGAN-style jacket, and the 1960s version was frequently made of plaid fabric with a braid trim.

Chanel suit 1960s

changeable earrings See JEWELRY.

changeable effect † An iridescent effect in fabric that is achieved by using lengthwise and crosswise yarns dyed different colors. Usually made in silk or lustrous manufactured fibers in fabrics such as TAFFETA to achieve the most dramatic effect. Synonyms: *glace* (glahs-ay'), *shot.*

changeable taffeta See CHANGEABLE EFFECT.

change pocket See POCKETS: TICKET POCKET.

change purse See HANDBAGS AND RELATED ACCESSORIES.

channel setting See GEMS, GEM CUTS, AND SETTINGS.

Chantilly lace See LACES.

chapeau See HEADWEAR.

chapeau à la Charlotte See HEADWEAR: CHARLOTTE.

chapeau bras See HEADWEAR.

chapeau claque See HEADWEAR: OPERA HAT.

chapeau cloche See HEADWEAR.

chapel cap See HEADWEAR: CHAPEL VEIL.

chapel de fer See ARMOR.

chapel-length train See LENGTHS.

chapel veil See HEADWEAR.

chaperon See HEADWEAR.

chaperone See HEADWEAR: CHAPERON.

chapiney See FOOTWEAR: CHOPINE.

chaplet See HEADWEAR.

chaps See PANTS.

Charlie Chaplin **1.** See COATS AND JACKETS **2.** See FOOTWEAR: CHARLIE CHAPLIN TOE.

Charlotte See HEADWEAR.

Charlotte Corday cap See HEADWEAR.

Charlotte Corday fichu See SCARVES.

charm See JEWELRY.

charm bracelet See JEWELRY.

charm necklace See JEWELRY.

charro pants See PANTS.

Chase, Edna Woolman Editor-in-chief of American *Vogue* magazine from 1914 to 1952; also editor of British *Vogue*, first published in 1916, and French *Vogue*, 1920. Considered one of the most able and competent fashion authorities. One of her outstanding achievements was the introduction in 1914 of a society-sponsored fashion show with live models called "Fashion Fête," the beginning of her long promotion of American designers.

chasembles See CHAUSSEMBLES.

chasing See JEWELRY.

chasseur jacket See COATS AND JACKETS.

chastity belt Beltlike device worn by women in the Middle Ages to ensure marital fidelity.

chasuble See CLERICAL DRESS.

chatelaine (shat'-eh-lane) **1.** Ornamental device of oxidized silver, silver-plated metal, or cut steel suspended at woman's waistline or hooked to belt to hold small items such as scissors, thimble case, tape measure, penknife, watch, keys, or buttonhook. Worn in last half of 19th c. See CORDELIÈRE. **2.** Antique silver or plated scent bottle worn around neck on a long chain in 1980s. *Der.* French, "lady of the castle." Also see JEWELRY and WATCHES.

chatelaine bag See HANDBAGS AND RELATED ACCESSORIES.

chatelaine #1

chatelaine watch See WATCHES.

chati cat See FURS: SPOTTED CAT.

chatoyancy See GEMS, GEM CUTS, AND SETTINGS.

chausembles See CHAUSSEMBLES.

chausons ∞ (show-son') French equivalent of the English under pants, called BRAIES (see UNDERGARMENTS), worn from the 5th through the 13th c.

chausse ∞ (shos) **1.** See ARMOR. **2.** Stockings and trunks cut in one piece similar to contemporary tights. First worn in Norman period (1066–1154). Later in the Middle Ages, they fastened to the upper garment (a DOUBLET) by means of lacers called POINTS. **3.** About mid-16th c. chausses were divided into two parts—upper part then called haut de chausses, later called TRUNK HOSE and upper stocks. Lower part was called **bas de chausses** (ba deh shos), then hose and finally stockings. **4.** See CAPES, CLOAKS, AND SHAWLS: EPITOGA #2. *Der.* French, "bottom of hose." Also see LOWER STOCKS.

chaussembles ∞ (show'-som-bl) Man's cut-and-sewn hose with attached soles of leather or whalebone worn in Middle Ages. Probably cut on the BIAS to provide some degree of stretch, they were somewhat baggy and ill-fitting as compared to later knitted HOSIERY. Also spelled *chausembles, chasembles, cashambles.*

chaussembles
15th c.

chausses en bourse ∞ (shos on boorce) Breeches padded so they were fuller at bottom—making a flattened balloon shape—worn in 17th c. *Der.* French, "bag breeches."

chausses en tonnelet See TRUNK HOSE.

chaussures à crics See FOOTWEAR.

cheat ∞ **1.** Man's waistcoat or vest of 17th c. with expensive fabric on front and poorer quality in back. **2.** 19th-c. term for man's false shirt front with collar attached worn instead of a full shirt.

chechia See HEADWEAR.

check See PRINTS, STRIPES, AND CHECKS.

checked gingham See GINGHAM.

checkerboard checks See PRINTS, STRIPES, AND CHECKS.

checkerboard hose See HOSIERY.

checkered-apron man ∞ English barbers of 16th c. distinguished by the checked pattern of their aprons. Also see BLUE-APRONED MEN and GREEN-APRONED MEN.

checks See PRINTS, STRIPES, & CHECKS.

cheek wrappers See HEADWEAR: DORMEUSE.

cheeks-and-ears See HEADWEAR.: COIF #6 and ORRELET.

cheetah See FURS.

chef's apron See APRONS.

chef's hat See HEADWEAR.

Chelsea look Styles worn by the Chelsea Set, young people who frequented a London area called Chelsea that was popular with artists and writers. Trends changed from time to time and were usually copied in other countries as items chosen by this group had wide influence on general fashion trends. In the late 1940s and 1950s, the look was tight jeans from U.S; in the late 1960s, old uniforms including nurses' or policemen's uniforms, red guardsmen's tunics, and navy overcoats were all featured. Also see NECKLINES AND COLLARS: CHELSEA COLLAR and FOOTWEAR: BEATLE BOOT.

chemise (shem-ees′) **1.** See UNDERGARMENTS. **2.** Dress style that derives from the style of the undergarment called a chemise. Chemise-type dresses are characterized by a loose fit. If they are belted, belts are generally located at hipline or under the bust and the dress is unfitted at the anatomical waistline. Periods in which such styles were worn by women included the Directoire and Empire periods (c. 1795–1820), the 1920s, chemise #2 1959

the 1960s, and the 1990s. Also called "*the sack.*" Der. French "shift" or "shirt."

chemise gown See PERDITA CHEMISE in alphabetical listing.

chemise slip See UNDERGARMENTS.

chemisette (shem-ee-zet′) **1.** See SCARVES. **2.** See BLOUSES AND TOPS. **3.** See VESTEE. **4.** See SHIRTS: HABIT SHIRT.

chemisette à jabot ∞ (ah zha′-bo) Embroidered or pleated ruffle of 1850s and 1860s worn as a fill-in at front opening of a REDINGOTE (see COATS AND JACKETS: REDINGOTE #5) showing from neck to waist.

chemisette garter ∞ Vertical supporter for hose attached to the corset in 1830s and 1840s.

chemise tucker See SCARVES: CHEMISETTE.

chenille † Fabrics made from chenille yarns. These yarns have a fuzzy surface with short fibers projecting on all sides. Chenille fabrics may be woven or knitted. When woven, they are usually made with the chenille yarns in the crosswise direction.

chenille embroidery See EMBROIDERIES AND SEWING STITCHES.

chenille lace See LACES.

cheongsam Chinese woman's dress originating in Shanghai, China, in the late 1930s in an attempt to blend traditional Chinese and Western styles. It has a high, close-fitting collar, diagonal front opening that closes with frogs or buttons, short sleeves, a snug fit, and a side slit running from the bottom of the hem and reaching, in more daring versions, as high as the thigh. Used as a basis for Western designs, most notably in housecoats and dresses. cheongsam Synonyms: *qi pao, Chinese dress,* and *mandarin dress.*

Cheruit, Madeleine * See APPENDIX/DESIGNERS.

cherusse See NECKLINES AND COLLARS.

chesterfield See COATS AND JACKETS.

Chesterfield, 6th Earl of A British fashion leader in the 1830s and 1840s after whom the CHESTERFIELD OVERCOAT (see under COATS AND JACKETS) was named.

chest-high boot See FOOTWEAR: WADERS.

chesticore See COATS AND JACKETS: JUSTAU-CORPS.

chest measurement **1.** Men: distance around body at fullest part of upper torso, one of the measurements by which suits are sold. **2.** Women: measurement around the body taken with tape in front placed across front of body from arm-hole seam to armhole seam at point above bust and across the back. Differs from the **bust measurement** taken at fullest part of bosom.

cheviot † (shev′-ee-ott) **1.** Rough surfaced, hairy fabric made in a plain or twill weave from wool, manufactured fibers, or blends. Does not hold a crease well and, therefore, is generally used for casual clothing. **2.** Cotton shirting woven with fairly heavy yarns in checked, striped, or small figured patterns.

chevron **1.** Motif consisting of two straight lines meeting to form an inverted V. **2.** Badge of these V stripes worn on sleeve by policemen, firemen, and the military to indicate rank.

chevrons ∞ Trimmings for women's clothes intro-duced in mid-1820s, usually a zigzag band near hem of skirt.

chic **1.** *n.* The quality of being very much in style. **2.** *Adj.* Smart, sophisticated, stylish.

chicken skin See LEATHERS.

chicken-skin gloves See GLOVES AND GLOVE CONSTRUCTIONS.

chiffon † **1.** Thin transparent fabric made in a plain weave. It drapes well and is made from tightly twisted or CREPE YARNS. Originally made in silk; now also made in manufactured fibers. Dyed solid colors or often printed in floral designs. Used for sheer dresses, blouses, and scarves. **2.** A trifle or bit of feminine finery. *Der.* French, *chiffe,* "rag."

chignon See HAIRSTYLES.

chignon cap See HEADWEAR.

chignon strap See HEADWEAR.

chill mask See MASKS: HOT MASK.

chimere/chimer See CLERICAL DRESS.

chimney-pot hat See HEADWEAR: TOP HAT.

China doll hairstyle See HAIRSTYLES.

china grass See RAMIE.

China mink See FURS.

China ribbon **1.** Narrow ribbon, about ⅛″ wide, woven with a plain edge popular in mid-19th c.

for China ribbon embroidery. See EMBROIDERIES AND SEWING STITCHES: ROCOCO.

China silk † Soft, lustrous silk fabric in a plain weave that may have slight texture due to use of irregular yarns. Made in China and Japan; origi-nally handmade in China as early as 1200 B.C., the name is also applied to machine-made fab-rics of a similar type.

chinchilla See FURS.

chinchilla cloth † Thick, heavyweight coating fabric of all wool, or wool and cotton distin-guished by curly nubs on the surface. **1.** Woven as a double cloth with a plain back and a satin face. Extra crosswise yarns added to the face of fabric are loosely floated over the surface. When napped and rubbed into curled tufts, these yarns form distinctive nubs on the surface. Less expen-sive fabric is not woven in the same manner and may have a different surface effect. **2.** A similar fabric made by knitting and brushing surface yarns into nubs.

chin cloak See SCARVES.

chiné See PRINTS, STRIPES, AND CHECKS: WARP PRINT.

Chinese collar See NECKLINES AND COLLARS.

Chinese design Design composed of motifs such as dragons, lanterns, clouds, and moun-tains, in style typical of Chinese paintings and embroideries.

Chinese dog See FURS.

Chinese dress See CHEONGSAM.

Chinese embroidery See EMBROIDERIES AND SEWING STITCHES.

Chinese jacket See COATS AND JACKETS: COOLIE COAT.

Chinese knot Ornamental knot of covered cord used as trimming on apparel. Copied from traditional ornaments on Chinese robes.

Chinese lamb See under FURS: KARACUL.

Chinese look Adaptations of Chinese styles in U.S. including items such as COOLIE COATS and HATS, CHINESE PAJAMAS, MANDARIN COATS, MAN-DARIN NECKLINES, and Chinese dresses with side slit called CHEONGSAM. When China opened its doors to West in early 1970s, there was a revival of interest in Chinese fashions resulting in such styles as the basic worker's suit—or MAO SUIT,—quilted jackets, the CHINESE SHOE, and denim coolie coats. St. Laurent featured Chinese ensembles in 1977 that included small versions of red coolie hats, coolie-type jackets of red and gold brocade with frog closings and mandarin collars; and pants tapered to hem worn with boots having flared tops.

Chinese lounging robe See SLEEPWEAR AND LOUNGEWEAR.

Chinese pajamas See SLEEPWEAR AND LOUNGE-WEAR.

Chinese Raccoon See FURS: USSURIAN RACCOON.

Chinese shoe See FOOTWEAR.

Chinese slipper See FOOTWEAR: KAMPSKATCHA SLIPPER.

chinner See SCARVES: CHIN CLOAK.

chino † (chee'-no) Durable cotton, firmly woven with a fine steep twill and dyed a yellowish-tan or khaki color. Contemporary versions are also dyed in many colors. Originally used for summer uniforms for the U.S. Army, by the 1950s the fabric had been adopted by teenagers for school and general wear, particularly for pants. Now used for a wide variety of casual clothing.

chinoise, à la (shin' waaz, ah lah) French phrase meaning "from the Chinese." Often used as an English fashion term to describe items of apparel that show Chinese influences.

chinoiserie (shin-waaz-ze-ree') Those designs in textiles, fashion, and the decorative arts that derive from Chinese styles.

chinos See PANTS.

chin stays See HEADWEAR.

chintz † Medium-weight cotton or blended fabric with a glazed or shiny finish that may be a plain color or printed with floral, bird, or other designs. Originally a fabric for slipcovers and draperies; now also used for variety of items such as beachwear, shorts, blouses, skirts, dresses, and rainwear. *Der.* Indian, *chint,* name for a gaudily printed fabric of cotton.

chip See GEMS, GEM CUTS, AND SETTINGS.

chip bonnet See HEADWEAR.

chip straw Wood or straw cut in fine strips for hats or baskets. Used for women's hats in 18th c. and for women's CHIP BONNETS (see under HEAD-WEAR) in the 19th c.

chique-tades See SLASHINGS.

chiton ∞ (ki'-tawn) Garment worn in ancient Greece that consisted of a rectangle of fabric wrapped around the body and fastened at the shoulders with one or more pins. A number of variations of this basic style were worn at different points in Greek history. They were as follows: (1) **chitoniskos** (ki-tawn-iss'-kos): Worn by men from about 800 to 550 B.C., usually short, made of patterned wool, and fitted closely to the body; (2) **doric peplos:** Worn by women from about 800 to 550 B.C., usually reaching to the ankles, pinned at the shoulder with a large pin, made of patterned wool, and fitted closely to the body; (3) **ionic chiton** (eye-ohn'-ik ki'-tawn): Worn from 550 B.C. to 480 B.C. and less often from 480 B.C. to 300 B.C.

chitoniskos   doric peplos

ionic chiton worn under a shawl   doric chiton

helenistic chiton   exomis

by men and women, either short (for men) or long, made of lightweight wool or of linen and pleated. More fully cut than earlier chitons, it had long, full sleeves fastened with many small brooches at the shoulder; (4) **doric chiton:** Worn from 400 B.C. to 100 B.C. by men and from 450 B.C. to 300 B.C. by women and made of wool, linen, or silk, the doric chiton was generally short when worn by men and long when worn by women. More narrowly fitted than the ionic chiton, and sleeveless, it was fastened at each shoulder with a single pin. (5) **helenistic chiton:** Worn by women from 300 to 100 B.C., similar to the doric chiton but narrower, and often belted below the bosom, this chiton was worn long and made of lightweight wool, linen, or silk; (6) **exomis:** Worn by working-class men and slaves in all Greek periods, this chiton was short and fastened over one shoulder and probably made from sturdy, durable wool fabric.

chitoniskos See CHITON.

chitterlings ∞ (chit-er-lings) Popular term used in the 18th and 19th c. for frills or ruffles on front of man's shirt.

chlaine See CAPES, CLOAKS, AND SHAWLS.

chlamydon ∞ (kla′mee-don) A type of outer garment for women in ancient Greece that was pleated to a band of fabric and worn under the left arm and over the right shoulder.

chlamys See CAPES, CLOAKS, AND SHAWLS.

Chloé * See APPENDIX/DESIGNERS: KARL LAGERFELD and STELLA MCCARTNEY.

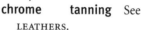
chlamydon

chlorspinel See GEMS, GEM CUTS, AND SETTINGS: SPINEL.

choir-boy collar See NECKLINES AND COLLARS.

choir robe Ankle-length closed robes similar to academic gowns worn by singers in church choirs. See ACADEMIC COSTUME.

choker Term used for accessories and clothing that fit high on the neck. See NECKLINES AND COLLARS and JEWELRY.

choli See BLOUSES AND TOPS.

choori-dars See PANTS.

chopine See FOOTWEAR.

chou (shoo) **choux** (pl.) **1.** Frilly pouf of fabric used at neckline. **2.** Large rosette used to trim gowns in late 19th and early 20th c. **3.** See HEADWEAR. **4.** See HAIRSTYLES: CHIGNON. *Der.* French, "cabbage."

christening dress Any dress or suit worn by infants for their baptism. Until the mid-20th c. both boys and girls wore extremely long white dresses, elaborately trimmed with tucks, lace,

and hand embroidery. In recent decades, boys have been dressed either in white suits or in dresses. Dresses for both boys and girls today may be shorter, but would usually cover the feet.

christening dress 1898

chrome tanning See LEATHERS.

chronograph See WATCHES.

chronometric watch See WATCHES.

chrysoberyl See GEMS, GEM CUTS, AND SETTINGS.

chrysolite See GEMS, GEM CUTS, AND SETTINGS: PERIDOT.

chrysoprase See GEMS, GEM CUTS, AND SETTINGS.

chubby See COATS AND JACKETS.

chuddah/chudder See CHADDAR.

chukka (chuh′-ka) Periods in the game of polo. Used to describe modern clothes and accessories similar to those worn when playing polo. See FOOTWEAR: CHUKKA BOOTS, HEADWEAR: CHUKKA HAT, SHIRTS: POLO SHIRT.

chunky heel See FOOTWEAR.

chunky shoe See FOOTWEAR.

chymer See CHAMARRE.

ciclaton See CYCLAS.

CIM See COMPUTER INTEGRATED MANUFACTURING.

cinch **1.** See BELTS. **2.** See WAISTLINES: CHINCHED WAISTLINE.

cinch buckle/cinch closing See CLOSURES: D-RING CLOSING.

cincture **1.** See BELTS. **2.** See CLERICAL DRESS.

cinglation See CYCLAS.

cingulum **1.** See BELTS. **2.** See CLERICAL DRESS.

Cipullo, Aldo * See APPENDIX/DESIGNERS.

Circassian round robe ∞ (ser-kash′-yan) Early 1820s evening dress of gossamer gauze made with low square-cut neckline, short sleeves, high waistline, and skirt elaborately decorated down the front and above the hem with festoons of knotted ribbon. *Der.* Caucasian tribe of Circassia, a historical region between the western end of the Caucasus range and the Kuban River, north of the Black sea.

Circassian wrapper ∞ (ser-kash′-yan) Loose wrap, cut somewhat like a nightgown, worn by women for daytime in Empire Period, 1813. *Der.*

Caucasian tribe of Circassia, a historical region west of the Caucasus mountains and north of the Black Sea.

circassienne ∞ Late-18th c. version of the polonaise (a draped skirt) worn by women just before French Revolution. *Der.* French, "circassian."

circle/circular Adjective used to describe garments that are shaped round, like a circle. See CAPES, CLOAKS, AND SHAWLS: CIRCULAR, SKIRTS: CIRCLE, SLEEVES: CIRCLE, and POCKETS: ROUND POCKET.

circular See CAPES, CLOAKS, AND SHAWLS.

circular hem See CLOTHING CONSTRUCTION DETAILS.

circular knit † Fabric knitted in a tubular shape with no SELVAGES. Made either by hand or machine. Hose knitted in this manner have no seams.

circular ruffle Ruffle cut from circle of fabric rather than straight across the grain, making graceful folds less bulky than a gathered ruffle. Also see CASCADE RUFFLE.

circumfolding hat See HEADWEAR: OPERA HAT.

ciré † (sear-ray′) Finishing process or the fabric produced by the process in which wax or other compounds are applied to the surface of a fabric, after which a hot roller is passed over the surface to produce a high polish. If the fibers in the fabric are heat sensitive, the fibers will fuse and the effect will be permanent.

ciselé velvet † (seez-el-ay′) A fabric with a raised pattern of velvet figures on a satin ground formed by cut and uncut loops—with the cut pile being higher.

citrine See GEMS, GEM CUTS, AND SETTINGS.

city boots See FOOTWEAR.

city pants/city shorts Terms coined by the fashion-industry newspaper *Women's Wear Daily* in 1968 for women's pants or shorts suitable for town wear. Also see PANTS: CITY PANTS.

civet cat See FURS.

Claiborne, Liz * See APPENDIX/DESIGNERS.

clamdiggers/Clamdiggers® See PANTS.

claque See HEADWEAR.

Clara Bow hat See HEADWEAR.

Clarence See FOOTWEAR.

Clarissa Harlowe bonnet/hat See HEADWEAR.

Clarissa Harlowe corsage ∞ Evening-dress bodice with off-the-shoulder neckline, folds caught at the waist by band of ribbon, and short sleeves trimmed with two or three lace ruffles. Worn in late 1840s. *Der.* From heroine in novel *Clarissa, or the History of a Young Lady,* by Samuel Richardson, published in 1747–48.

classic Apparel made in a style that continues to be fashionable over a long period of time, and that may return to high fashion at intervals. When revived, classic fashions retain the basic line of the original style, but are sometimes altered in minor details, e.g., COATS AND JACKETS: CARDIGAN, BLAZER, TRENCHCOAT, and POLO COAT, or CHEMISE, SHIRTWAIST DRESS.

classic look See BROOKS BROTHERS® and PREPPY LOOKS.

classic pull-back See HAIRSTYLES.

classification (class) A general type of merchandise that is housed within an individual department. Examples: sportswear, eveningwear, or lingerie.

class ring See JEWELRY.

claw-hammer coat See COATS AND JACKETS.

clayshooter's vest See VESTS.

clean-stitched seam See CLOTHING CONSTRUCTION DETAILS.

cleats See FOOTWEAR.

cleavage 1. See GEMS, GEM CUTS, AND SETTINGS. 2. Separation between a woman's breasts, made more obvious when a low neckline is worn.

clerical cape See CAPES, CLOAKS, AND SHAWLS.

clerical collar See CLERICAL DRESS.

CLERICAL DRESS

Items of clothing worn by members of the clergy either during rituals being celebrated or as a means of identifying their clerical status within their religion. Also called *ecclesiastical dress*. These entries do not include religious garb or symbols worn by lay members of a religion. Such entries will be found in the alphabetical listing.

clerical dress: priest

orphrey
chasuable
maniple
stole
alb

alb Full-length long-sleeved LITURGICAL ROBE (see ROBE #2) with drawstring neckline or cowl hood worn by priests at Mass. Originally of white linen, now often of blended cotton and man-made fibers. *Der.* Latin, "white."

amice (am′ees)   A strip of linen placed around the shoulders and tied in position to form a collar worn by priests saying mass.

bäffchen   See CLERICAL DRESS: GENEVA BANDS.

biretta (bi-ret′-tah) **birretta/berrette/barrette**
1. Stiff square clerical cap with three or four upright projections on top radiating from center, sometimes finished with a pompon. **2.** 16th-c.: a round cap that later became square on top when hatters learned to use a rigid frame. Worn by clergy today, e.g., cardinals and bishops.

calotte (ka-loht′) **calot/callot**   Tiny, close-fitting skullcap cut in shaped gores often with a tab at center of top worn by Roman clergy, priests, and monks in early Christian orders—now worn by the Pope. Also called *zucchetto* (zook-ket′-toe).

camauro (ka-mao′-row)   Red velvet, ermine-trimmed cap slightly larger than a skullcap formerly worn by Pope of Roman Catholic church.

campagus (kam-pa′-gus)   Shoe worn by bishops in Western Church, particularly Roman Catholic, sometimes Episcopal.

capuche   See HEADWEAR.

cassock   **1.** Full-length liturgical robe, made like a coat with standing collar, worn by clergy, altar boys, and choirs, sometimes under white SURPLICE or COTTA (see under CLERICAL DRESS). Also called *soutane* (soo-tahn′). **2.** Short front buttoned jacket worn by clerics.

cassock

casula (kas-oo′-lah)   Latin name of CHASUBLE (see under CLERICAL DRESS).

chasuble (chaz′-yu-behl)   Sleeveless clerical garment, shaped somewhat like a PONCHO (see under CAPES, CLOAKS, AND SHAWLS), with round neckline and open sides. Sometimes has a Y-shaped band from neck to hem called the ORPHREY (see under CLERICAL DRESS). Worn as part of vestments at the cele-

bration of Mass in the early Christian church, now worn by priests over the cassock. *Der.* Latin, *casula*, "cloak."

chimere (she′-mar) **/chimer**   Full-length sleeveless robe, similar to an academic robe worn by Anglican bishops. Extra full lawn sleeves were attached to armholes.

cincture (sink′-cher)   Twisted rayon, silk, or rope belt—approximately eight feet in length—worn by clergy with the ALB (see under CLECRICAL DRESS). It is worn doubled, with one end pulled through the loop and the long ends hanging free. With tassels on the end, called **traditional;** when knotted at the end, called **contemporary.** Shown at COPE.

cingulum (sin-goo′-lum)   Belt worn with liturgical garments since Middle Ages.

clerical cape   Three-quarter-length cape of wool MELTON with satin lining, small velvet collar, and braided frog closing worn by clergy.

clerical collar   Stiff white standing band collar worn by clergy with suit or with liturgical robes. May be fastened in back as a **Roman collar** or have a narrow opening in front. White collar is sometimes half covered by a similar black collar which may be attached to the CASSOCK or to a biblike RABAT (see under CLERICAL DRESS). Also see CLERICAL DRESS: GENEVA BANDS.

clerical front   An adjustable shirt front worn by clergymen with a black business suit or under a pulpit robe. Fits around the neck usually with black collar on top of a white collar. Ties secure the garment at the waist. Usually made in black faille or wool with or without a center pleat down the front. Also called *shirt front.*

clerical shirt   Black or gray shirt with short or long sleeves styled with a fly-front and standing CLERICAL COLLAR (see under CLERICAL DRESS) worn by clergymen. A second collar of white may be inserted inside the neckline. Frequently has white cuffs. Formerly made of lightweight wool, now made in wash-and-wear fabrics.

colobium (koh-lo′-bee-um)   A liturgical garment derived from a Roman secular garment consisting of a long linen tunic, either sleeveless or with short sleeves. It was replaced by the DALMATIC.

cope Ornately embroidered semi-circular mantle, fastened across the chest with an elaborate clasp arrangement worn on ceremonial occasions by the Pope and dignitaries of the Roman Catholic Church and by priests offering the Benediction.

cope
cincture

cope and cincture

cotta (coat'-tah) Clerical surplice made like a full, short, white overtunic, gathered into a narrow rounded yoke with long, full bell-shaped sleeves. Worn by clergy over cassock and by choir members over long robes.

dalmatic See DALMATIC in alphabetical listing.

ecclesiastical vestments Garments worn by the clergy for religious services.

fanons Two decorative LAPPETS attached to back of miter worn by the Pope, which hung down over the shoulders. These may originally have been used to hold the miter on the head. See CLERICAL DRESS: MITER.

ferraiolo (fair-ay-o'-lo) A full-length black circular cape worn as an outer garment by clerics over other vestments for ceremonial occasions such as receptions, academic occasions, or banquets.

fisherman's ring Gold ring used at investiture of the Pope of the Roman Catholic Church. The figure of St. Peter in a fisherman's boat is engraved on the ring along with name of the Pope.

Geneva bands Collar consisting of two short white linen tabs hanging down from the neckline, attached to a string tied around the neck. Worn mainly by clergy. Also called *short bands* and *bäffchen* (bef'-ken). *Der.* Originated by Swiss Calvinist clergy in Geneva, Switzerland.

Geneva gown Black clerical gown worn by Calvinists and later by other Protestant clergy, similar to an academic robe and often worn with two vertical white linen bands at the neck called Geneva bands.

Geneva hat ∞ Wide-brimmed, high-crowned hat worn in late 16th and early 17th c. by Puritan ministers and others.

liturgical robe See ROBE #2.

maniple Narrow ornamental band about 3½′ long, worn by Catholic priests on the left arm near the wrist.

mantelletta (mahn-tell-et'-tah) Sleeveless thigh-length circular-cut garment that opens in front and has a small collar. Worn by prelates of Roman Catholic Church over the ROCHET, it is made of silk or wool with two vertical slits for arms. For cardinals it is red, purple, or rose-colored. See CLERICAL DRESS: ROCHET.

mantellone (mahn-tell-own'-nay) Purple ankle-length ecclesiastical mantle, worn over the CASSOCK (see under CLERICAL DRESS) by lesser prelates of Papal court of the Roman Catholic Church.

miter Very tall ornamental headpiece, worn by Catholic and Episcopal church dignitaries, with high separate pointed arches in front and back.

miter

mozetta (mo-zet'-tah) Elbow-length cape with ornamental hood hanging in back, worn by cardinals and church dignitaries. *Der.* Italian *mozzare*, "to cut short."

orphrey (or'-free) Y-shaped band of embroidery decorating the CHASUBLE (see under CLERICAL DRESS) that extends from each shoulder meeting vertical stripe in center front and back. Also spelled *orfray, orfrey.*

pallium A narrow band of white wool that was worn by popes and archbishops. Prelates wore the band with one end falling to the front and the other to the back.

parament (pa'-ra-ment) Synonym for an ornamental Ecclesiastical vestment.

pileolus/pilleolus (pil-eh'-oh-lus) Skullcap worn by Catholic priests and pope under the MITER and TIARA (see under CLERICAL DRESS). *Der.* Latin, "skullcap."

rabat (rab-e; ra-bat) Black dickey or shirt front to which the white CLERICAL COLLAR is attached (see under CLERICAL DRESS). Worn with suits or with liturgical robes by Catholic and Protestant clergy.

rochet (rash'-et) Similar to a SURPLICE (see under CLERICAL DRESS) and worn especially by bishops and abbots.

Roman collar See CLERICAL DRESS: CLERICAL COLLAR.

shirt front See CLERICAL DRESS: CLERICAL FRONT.

short bands See CLERICAL DRESS: GENEVA BANDS.

simar (si-mar´) Clerical robe, similar to full-length CASSOCK (see under CLERICAL DRESS), but having short button-on false sleeves and a shoulder cape that does not fasten in front. Worn at home or on the street, but not worn for high church services, particularly by prelates of the Catholic church. Made of white wool for the Pope, black wool with scarlet trimmings for Cardinals, black wool with amaranth red or purple trim for Penitential or mourning days for Bishops, and ash-gray wool for Franciscans. Also worn by seminarians without the false sleeves (thus indicating inferior dignity). Also see CHAMARRE.

soutane See CLERICAL DRESS: CASSOCK #1.

stole Long narrow scarf, part of CLERICAL VESTMENTS worn over the COTTA (see under CLERICAL DRESS) by clergymen.

surplice Loose white overblouse, either waist- or knee-length, gathered to flat yoke with full open sleeves worn by clergy, acolytes, and choir singers. Also see CLERICAL DRESS: COTTA.

tiara (tee-ar´-a) An ancient headpiece, worn by the Pope of the Roman Catholic church, consisting of three coronets placed one on top of the other, each successively smaller.

ventilated collar Stiff white standing collar punctured with holes around the sides and back. Used to support the black CLERICAL COLLAR, creating a white trim at center front and around the edge.

vestments See CLERICAL DRESS: CLERICAL VESTMENTS.

zucchetto See CLERICAL DRESS: CALOTTE.

clerical front See CLERICAL DRESS.

clerical shirt See CLERICAL DRESS.

clip See JEWELRY.

clip-back earring See JEWELRY.

clip closure See CLOSURES.

clip hat See HEADWEAR: BICYCLE CLIP HAT.

clip-on sunglasses See EYEWEAR.

clip-on tie See TIES.

cloak See introduction to CAPES, CLOAKS, AND SHAWLS.

Cloak and Suit Industry Name given manufacturers of coats and suits when first U.S. census of the clothing industry was made in 1860. This category made up half the total of manufacturing establishments. Originally called *Cloak and Mantilla Manufacturers,* later called *Coat and Suit Industry.*

cloak bag breeches ∞ Full oval-shaped man's breeches fastened above or below the knee with decorative points or bows. Worn in early 17th c. Also see BREECHES.

cloche See HEADWEAR.

clock 1. See HOSIERY: CLOCKED HOSE. 2. Triangular gore inserted into a stocking, cape, or collar to make it wider with embroidery over the joined seams. Worn from 16th c. on. Also see HOSIERY.

clog See FOOTWEAR.

cloisonné (kloi-zeh-nay´) An enameling technique in which small areas of colored enamel separated by thin metal bands form the design. Popular in 1980s for necklaces, bracelets, earrings, pins, and belt buckles. *Der.* French, "partitioned." Also see under JEWELRY: CLOISONNÉ NECKLACE.

close coat See COATS AND JACKETS.

closed display/closed back display See WINDOW DISPLAYS.

closed dress/closed gown See ROUND DRESS.

closed island displays Display in which merchandise is visible but enclosed behind glass. Often used for especially valuable objects. See SHOWCASE DISPLAY.

closed seam See FOOTWEAR.

closeout Merchandise that remains unsold from a seasonal line. Usually all these remaining items are sold at a discount.

closeout store A discount store to which a retailer sends merchandise from its regular-price store that has been slow to sell or has reached the end of its season.

close-plate buckle See CLOSURES.

close stitch See EMBROIDERIES AND SEWING STITCHES: BUTTONHOLE STITCH #3.

closing 1. Manner in which an item of apparel fastens. Early clothing was draped and held together by belts or pins called FIBULAE. Later lacing was used, then buttons—with men's clothing buttoning left to right and women's buttoning right to left. **2.** The type of device by which a garment or part of a garment is secured. See CLOSURES: CLOSURE.

CLOSURES

closure A device used to close or fasten shoes or a garment. Synonym: *closing*.

abalone button (ah-bah-low-nee′) Type of pearl button made from shell of a mollusk called an ear shell, or sea-ear, found off Pacific coast of the United States.

asymmetric closing Garment closing that fastens at the side or diagonally rather than at the center of the garment.

asymmetric closing

barred buttonhole See CLOSURES: WORKED BUTTONHOLE.

barrel snaps ∞ Tubular-shaped gilded-metal fasteners, used for cloaks and pelisses from 1800 to 1830. Also see COATS AND JACKETS: BAROUCHE COAT.

basket button ∞ Fashionable metal button in embossed basket weave pattern, used on men's coats in 18th and 19th c.

belt buckle Any ornamental or functional device, usually plastic or metal, used to fasten a belt.

blazer button Distinctive brass or gold-plated brass button with a monogram, a coat-of-arms, or a crest embossed or engraved on top. Usually sold by the set, which includes three large and four small sleeve buttons. Specifically used on blazers. See COATS AND JACKETS: BLAZERS.

blind eyelet Shoe-industry term for metal eyelet concealed in the inner surface of leather while the outside layer has a punched hole through which shoestring is pulled.

bound buttonhole Buttonhole with edges finished with separate strips of fabric or leather binding.

bound buttonhole

brass button Gilt button made of brass or of other metals or plastic gilded to simulate brass. Brass buttons embossed with a large eagle are used on jackets and coats worn by U.S. armed forces. Brass buttons are also used by civilians on various types of apparel.

breasts ∞ Term used on tailors' bills in the 18th c. for waistcoat buttons. Coat buttons were listed as **coats**.

buckle A decorative or functional clasp, usually of metal, wood, or plastic. Consists of a rectangular or curved rim, often with one or more movable tongues. Also a clip device fixed to end of a strap used to fasten to other end of belt or to another strap. Used since earliest times for belts, shoes, and knee breeches.

buckles d'Artois ∞ Shoe buckles of enormous size worn from 1775 to 1788. *Der.* Named after the Comte d'Artois, later Charles X of France.

button **1.** A decorative ornament used for trimming or a functional fastener. Usually made with holes punched in center or a shank on the back, they close by slipping through a buttonhole or loop. Introduced in the 13th c. as trim, buttons became functional by the 14th c.; by the 16th c., buttons of all types were used. *Der.* French, *bouton*, a round object, a bud, a knob. **2.** See GLOVES AND GLOVE CONSTRUCTIONS.

buttonhole Opening for button to go through in order to secure the garment. Generally classified as either a BOUND or a WORKED buttonhole (see under CLOSURES). The use of buttonholes dates from about the 15th c.

button hooks See CLOSURES: SPEED LACING.

calico button ∞ Metal ring covered with calico, sometimes with metal eyelets in center, used mainly for underclothes from 1840s on.

chain closure Laced closing using a metal chain instead of a lacer. Used on vests and blouses, it was a novelty of the late 1960s.

cinch buckle/cinch closure See CLOSURES: RING BUCKLE.

clip closure Metal fastener with a spring-backed device on one side of garment and a ring, eyelet, or slotted fastener on other side. Used mainly on raincoats, jackets, and car coats.

close-plate buckle ∞ Shoe buckle of late 1660s to 1680s made of tutania—an alloy of tin, antimony, and copper—cast in a mold by a street peddler in about fifteen minutes.

coats See CLOSURES: BREASTS.

collar button See CLOSURES: STUD.

covered button Ball or disk-type button covered with fabric either matching or contrasting with garment. Kits of various-sized disks to be covered may be purchased by the home sewer. First used in latter part of 16th c. The button industry in the United States was started in 1826 by Mrs. Samuel Williston, wife of a storekeeper in East Hampshire, Mass., who first covered wooden buttons by hand. Later she invented a machine for this purpose and her factory was credited with one-half of the world production of buttons.

covered zipper Zipper made with fabric tape covering teeth so that teeth do not show when zipper is closed.

crocheted button Shank-type buttons made by crocheting over a disk, a ball, or a barrel-shaped object. Sometimes used on sweaters and formerly used on dresses and coats in Victorian era and early 19th c.

cuff button **1.** Small button, usually of mother-of-pearl, sewed on shirt cuff to fasten it. Introduced in 19th c. and used in lieu of *cuff links.* **2.** ∞ Late 17th c.: used to describe two metal disks connected by links used to replace earlier CUFF STRING (see under CLOSURES).

cuff string ∞ String pulled through eyelets on cuff to fasten it. Used in lieu of a button in the 17th c. Also called *sleeve string.*

cut-steel buckle Popular buckle of early 20th c. made of polished steel with jewel-like facets. Used on silk or moiré afternoon or evening shoes and on belts.

death's head button ∞ Domed 18th-c. button covered with metal thread or mohair forming an X on top like the cross of the skull and crossbones.

Dorset thread button ∞ Brass wire ring covered with cotton threads radiating from center to form a flat button; used on underwear from about 1700 to 1830.

double-breasted closing See DOUBLE-BREASTED in alphabetical listing.

D-ring closure **1.** See CLOSURES: RING BUCKLE. **2.** Closings on footwear that are D-shaped through which shoe laces are threaded.

fly-front closing Buttonholes, or zipper, inserted under a placket. Developed in latter half of 19th c. for overcoats, particularly the chesterfield, and used on men's or women's trousers.

foil button ∞ Silk pasted on paper and glued to reverse side of glass button; patented in 1774.

French portrait buttons ∞ Buttons worn about 1790 with profiles of famous people in light color mounted against a black silk background and surrounded with a rim of tin (e.g., profiles of Lafayette, Mirabeau, and Louis XVI).

frog Ornamental fastener using cording or braid through which a soft ball made of cording or a button is frog pulled. Used for closing garments, especially military uniforms and some Chinese clothes. When introduced in the West from China in last quarter of 18th c., they were named **Brandenburgs** after braid-trimmed uniforms worn by Brandenburg troops of Prussia during the Napoleonic War. Also called *olivettes.*

galosh closure Closing with a metal hook on one side that clips into a metal fastener with several slots in order to adjust the degree of tightness. A closing used for such garments as raincoats, coats, and jackets. *Der.* Similar to closings for galoshes in the early 20th c.

glitter button Any type of button set with rhinestones or imitation gems. Also see CLOSURES: RHINESTONE BUTTON.

glove button Tiny buttons, usually round and often pearlized, used to button long gloves.

gold button Any type of gold colored button, formerly solid gold or plated. Henry VIII had jeweled gold buttons made to match his rings. A record of the 15th c. notes 25 golden buttons, each set with seven pearls, at a cost of 200 gold pieces. In the 16th c., gold buttons set with diamonds and other precious stones were frequently used.

gripper closure Metal fastener in the shape of a large snap used on some types of jackets and raincoats. Also used on children's and infants' clothing, particularly at crotch of pajamas, panties, and pants to enable them to be put on more easily.

hasp ∞ Decorative silver fastening, similar to HOOK AND EYE (see under CLOSURES). Used for fastening coats in 17th and 18th c.

hip buttons ∞ Term used from late 17th to end of 19th c. for pair of buttons placed on either side of center back pleats of man's suit coat.

hook and eye Closing using a small metal hook on one side and either an embroidered loop or a small metal loop on the other side. Used extensively for shirtwaists and dresses with back closings in late 19th and early 20th c. Almost entirely replaced by the zipper on contemporary clothing.

hook and loop closure See CLOSURES: VELCRO®.

industrial zipper See CLOSURES: ZIPPER.

laced closing Leather thong or cord laced through small metal or embroidered eyelets. Popular method of fastening garments in Middle Ages and in late 1960s. Also used for shoes from 18th c. on. Also see POINTS in alphabetical listing.

lacing studs See CLOSURES: SPEED LACING.

latch buckle Round, square, or oblong metal plates attached to each end of a belt and closed over one another. A swivel from one end of the belt slips through a slot in the other end and turns to fasten.

Leek button ∞ Shank-type button with metal edge surrounding a metal shell or mold of pasteboard made at Leek, England, and patented in 1842.

loop and button Closing with a series of corded loops on one side and covered or round buttons on the other side. Used for its decorative effect. Sometimes used on wedding dresses.

machine-made buttonhole Buttonhole made on a sewing machine with a zig-zag stitch or by a special attachment.

mother-of-pearl button Button made from nacre, the inside shell of the oyster. First manufactured in U.S. in 1885 from imported mollusks and later from domestic oysters found in Chesapeake Bay.

neck button ∞ Decorative button of mid-17th c. worn at neck of doublet and held closed by loop on opposite side to reveal the fine shirt underneath.

olive button Long, oval-shaped, silk-covered button worn from mid-18th c. on.

olivette See CLOSURES: FROG.

pearl button Classic button for almost any use, originally made from shells. Sometimes called "ocean pearl" until development of plastic in the 1930s, after which imitation pearl buttons were widely used. Also see CLOSURES: MOTHER-OF-PEARL BUTTON.

piped buttonhole Buttonhole similar to BOUND BUTTONHOLE in which PIPING (see under CLOTHING CONSTRUCTION DETAILS) is used around the opening.

poker chip button Extra-large round, flat button with a shank on the back. *Der.* From size and shape of a poker chip.

rhinestone button Any button set with stones, made of glass or PASTE (see under JEWELRY), that simulates a diamond.

ring buckle Two rings on one end of belt through which opposite belt end threads—first through both, then back through one—and pulls tight. When rings are made in the shape of a "D," called a **D-ring buckle.** Also called *cinch buckle* or *cinch closing.* Borrowed from fastenings on horse bridles and saddle straps and used mainly on belts and cuffs of sleeves.

self-covered button See CLOSURES: COVERED BUTTON.

shank button Button with metal or plastic loop on the back.

shirt button Small mother-of-pearl or imitation pearl button with four holes and a ridge around the edge. Originally used on men's shirts.

shoe buckle Buckles worn on the shoe were very popular in France and Italy about 1660 and in England during reign of Charles II (1660–1685). Also fashionable in colonial America until about 1770. At first intended to hold shoe in place, the buckle was small in size and worn with a BUTTERFLY BOW (see under FOOTWEAR), later reached larger dimensions. Also see CLOSURES: BUCKLE and PINCHBECK. Revived in 1870s and at end of 19th and early 20th c., but limited to women's shoes. Revived for both men's and women's shoes in late 1960s.

single-breasted closing See SINGLE-BREASTED in alphabetical listing.

sleeve button **1.** Button at wrist to close cuff or sleeve. **2.** Decorative trim used on sleeves of man's suit coat consisting of two or three buttons placed on outside of cuff. This particular fashion originated in the 18th c. when large cuffs were worn buttoned back to the sleeve.

sleeve string See CLOSURES: CUFF STRING.

slide fastener See CLOSURES: ZIPPER.

snail button ∞ Covered button ornamented with FRENCH KNOTS (see EMBROIDERIES AND SEWING STITCHES) used on men's coats and waistcoats in 18th c.

snap closure Metal fastener used to close a garment at places where there is little strain. Replaced almost entirely in contemporary garments by ZIPPERS and GRIPPERS (see under CLOSURES).

speed lacing Closing on boot consisting of metal hooks replacing eyelets for upper part of lacing. Used particularly on ice skates, ski boots, and hiking boots. Also called *button hooks* or *lacing studs*.

storm flap Large flap that covers a zipper and has buttons and buttonholes to keep the flap in place.

stud Small ornamental closure used since the mid-18th c. that is not fastened to the shirt. Consists of a broader section, a short post, and a smaller buttonlike end that is inserted through an eyelet to fasten a shirt front, neckband, or cuffs. Also called *collar button*.

surplice closing See CLOSURES: WRAP CLOSING.

tab/tabbed closing An extra flap, strap, or loop of fabric, used with buttonhole, buckle, or snap to close coats, collars, sleeves, and cuffs. Popular closing for car coats from mid-1960s.

tailored buttonhole See CLOSURES: WORKED BUTTONHOLE.

tied closing **1.** Type of closing used on a wrap-style garment (e.g., a sash used on bathrobes, wrap dresses, and skirts to hold the garment closed). **2.** Series of ties used to fasten a garment.

toggle closure Rod-shaped button, usually of wood, attached by rope loop on one side of garment and pulled through similar loop on opposite side. Also see COATS AND JACKETS: TOGGLE COAT.

Velcro® Trademark for a tape woven with minute nylon hooks that mesh with loops on opposite tape. Used on children's and adults' clothing, sportswear, and shoes. First used by astronauts. Generic term for this type of closure is *hook and loop*.

wooden button Made in all sizes and shapes—may be in ball shape with shank on back or disk-shaped. In the late 1930s, larger saucer-shaped buttons tied on with matching corded fabric were used on women's coats.

worked buttonhole Buttonhole made by covering the raw edges of a slit in the fabric with hand or machine stitches. In hand-worked buttonholes, first the slit is made, then the raw edges are covered by embroidering them with a buttonhole stitch. Machine-made worked buttonholes are stitched first, then cut open. A stitch similar to the buttonhole stitch is made by the sewing machine. The shapes of worked buttonholes may vary as follows: **barred** or **rectangular buttonhole** Worked buttonhole with straight bar, called a bar tack, embroidered across the ends. 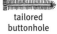 **oval buttonhole** Worked buttonhole with fan-shaped arrangement of stitches at both ends. **tailored buttonhole** Worked buttonholes with a bar tack at one end and a fan-shaped arrangement of stitches at the other end. **keyhole buttonhole** Worked buttonhole with a bar tack at one end and an area of much enlarged fan-shaped stitches at the

barred buttonhole

oval buttonhole

tailored buttonhole

other so as to allow a place for the button shank to rest.

wrap closing Closing by wrapping one side of garment over the other and holding with a belt, sash, button, or snap.

zipper Although the name "zipper" was coined and registered as a trademark by B. F. Goodrich Co. in 1925, the forerunner of this device was invented in 1891 by Witcomb B. Judson. He called it a *clasp locker*. The design was improved by Gideon Sundback who manufactured *Hookless Fasteners* used for corsets, gloves, sleeping bags, money belts, and tobacco pouches. Goodrich used zippers in "Zipper boots." By the 1930s zippers were so widely used in garments ranging from handbags to men's trousers that "zipper" became a generic term applied to any toothed, slide fastener. This device consists of parallel rows of metal or nylon teeth on adjacent edges of an opening, interlocked by sliding tab. Teeth may be covered by fabric tape and almost invisible or made in various lengths to use on necklines, skirt plackets, coat and jacket fronts, or handbags and pockets. Large-sized zippers, originally used for upholstery and industrial uses, were adopted for decorative trim on clothing in mid-1960s and were called **industrial zippers.**

clot See FOOTWEAR.

cloth Synonym for TEXTILE FABRIC.

clothe **1.** To put on garments. **2.** To provide with clothing.

cloth embroidery See EMBROIDERIES AND SEWING STITCHES.

clothes Collective term for all items of apparel worn on the body by men, women, and children. *Der.* Anglo-Saxon, *cläthas,* plural of *cläth,* "cloth." Synonyms: *apparel, attire, clothing, costume, dress, garb, garment, raiment, vestments.*

CLOTHING CONSTRUCTION DETAILS

clothing construction The process of making a garment by hand or machine sewing or both. Mass production generally relies on machine processes while made-to-order cloth-

ing uses more hand sewing. See EMBROIDERIES AND SEWING STITCHES for specific stitches used.

details The individual components within the structure of a garment that are combined in order to create the final, functional garment.

dress with various construction features

accordion pleats Folds in fabrics that are named for their resemblance to the folds of the musical instrument called an accordion. Smaller at the top but larger at the bottom, the lower edge of the hem shows a zigzag pattern. An accordion-pleated skirt takes a full circle of fabric. First used in the late 1880s. Synonyms: *sunburst pleats* and *fan pleats.*

accordion pleats

asymmetric hem Hem of uneven length—may be long in back and short in front or slanted diagonally from one side to the other. The latter has been popular since the late 1960s. All types of uneven hemlines were popular in the 1980s.

backing Layer of fabric placed underneath the outer fabric of a garment. Its function is generally to support the outer fabric.

asymmetric hem 1920

barred buttonhole See CLOSURES: WORKED BUTTONHOLE.

bias pleats Pressed-down pleats made in fabric cut on the diagonal, usually stitched down a few inches at top to make them hang better.

binding Narrow fabric strips used to cover seams or raw edges of clothing. May be cut on the BIAS or on STRAIGHT GRAIN.

bound An adjective describing a raw edge of a garment or part of a garment that has been finished either with band of machine stitching, bias binding, or tape.

bound buttonhole See CLOSURES.

bound seam Edges of plain seam bound with bias binding (see CLOTHING CONSTRUCTION DETAILS: BINDING). Used particularly on seams of unlined jackets and around necklines, armholes, and jackets in contrasting color for decoration.

bound seam

box pleat Pleat made by making two folds in fabric, the edges of which face in opposite directions. Sometimes box pleats may be stitched down for some distance before the fullness is released.

box pleats

broad-stitched seam See CLOTHING CONSTRUCTION DETAILS: TOP-STITCHED SEAM.

buttonhole See CLOSURES.

cartridge pleats Small rounded pleats, like very large gathers. Used quite extensively for gathering skirts in the mid-1800s. *Der.* from their resemblance to cartridge loops on military belts.

casing Fabric stitched in such a way as to form a tunnel through which elastic, a cord, or a drawstring is drawn. Types of casings include (1) **fold-down casing,** formed by turning down and stitching an extension at the edge of a garment. (2) **applied casing,** formed by folding a separate strip of fabric, stitching it to form a tunnel, and then applying it to some part of a garment.

circular hem Hem put in a full circular or gored skirt. If narrow, hem is machine-stitched or hand-rolled. Deeper hems have fullness worked in with tiny DARTS or GATHERS or may have a FACING applied. (See cross references under CLOTHING CONSTRUCTION DETAILS).

clean-stitched seam Plain seam pressed open on wrong side of garment with the raw edges turned under and stitched so they will not ravel.

clean-stitched seam

cluster pleats Pressed or unpressed pleats arranged in groups. Usually consisting of a large BOX PLEAT with several small KNIFE PLEATS on either side. See under CLOTHING CONSTRUCTION DETAILS.

corded seam Plain seam with cord inside bias binding inserted in seam before the seam is stitched so that covered cord appears as decoration along the seam. This technique was widely used in clothing construction in the early through the mid-19th c.

corded seam

crystal pleats Very fine, heat-set ridges usually used in sheer nylon or polyester fabrics. Also see CLOTHING CONSTRUCTION DETAILS: MUSHROOM PLEAT.

dart Sewing term for V-shaped tuck used to make garment conform to the body. Used frequently at shoulders, waist, or in side seam under the arm.

darts diagram

double ruffle Strip of fabric stitched in the center and gathered to form a ruffle on either side of stitching.

double-stitched seam See CLOTHING CONSTRUCTION DETAILS: TOP-STITCHED SEAM.

ease **1.** *v.* The process of joining a slightly larger garment piece to a smaller garment piece by evenly distributing the fullness along the seam where the pieces are joined. **2.** *n.* The fullness produced when garment pieces are eased.

ease

envelope pleats Large INVERTED PLEAT (see under CLOTHING CONSTRUCTION DETAILS) placed at the side seam of dress skirt and reveals a pocket underneath when one edge is pulled aside.

eyelet See in alphabetical list.

faced hem Use of another piece of fabric, usually lighter in weight and bias cut, sewed on at base of hem, turned up, and finished like a plain hem. Usually used when dress or pants are to be made longer or the garment is very flared.

faced hem

facing Fabric piece attached to the raw edge of some part of a garment in order to finish that edge. Facings are used in areas such necklines, armholes of sleeveless dress, and openings at the front or back. Hems may also be faced. The verb *to face* describes the act of applying a facing.

fan pleats See CLOTHING CONSTRUCTION DETAILS: ACCORDION PLEAT.

feather boning See CLOTHING CONSTRUCTION DETAILS: STAY #1.

facings at armhole, neck, and front closing

fell seam See CLOTHING CONSTRUCTION DETAILS: FLAT-FELLED SEAM.

flat felled seam Seam created by placing the undersides of garment pieces together and stitching a seam of about ⅝″ wide that appears on the right sides. One edge of the seam is then cut off to ⅛″ and the other edge folded over cut edge. Both are then pressed flat in the same direction and the folded edge is top-stitched. As a result, two rows of stitching appear on outside. This creates a very durable seam. Also called *fell seam.*

flat-felled seam

flat pleats See CLOTHING CONSTRUCTION DETAILS: KNIFE PLEATS.

fluted hem Tiny hem finished with picot edge (see PICOT #2) in a sheer nylon fabric which is set in crystal pleats. The edge gives a serpentine effect winding outward and inward.

french seam Seam created by placing the undersides of garment pieces together and stitching a seam that appears on the right sides. This seam is trimmed, then the fabric is folded so that the outsides of the fabric pieces are together. A seam is then stitched that encases the previously stitched seam. This seam is mostly used on transparent and lightweight fabrics that ravel.

french seam

fused hem Hem created with special tape that when pressed with a hot iron melts and adheres to the fabric. Sometimes loosens when garment is washed or dry cleaned. Introduced in the 1960s.

fused seam Seam made in plastic or vinyl by heating edges to be joined. Also called *welded seam.*

gathering Drawing up fullness along several threads in a row of stitching. Also see CLOTHING CONSTRUCTION DETAILS: SHIRRING.

gathers

gauging See CLOTHING CONSTRUCTION DETAILS: SHIRRING.

godet (go-day′) Triangular piece, sometimes rounded at top and flaring at the base, set into a skirt or sleeve to give added fullness. See CLOTHING CONSTRUCTION DETAILS: GORE and GUSSET.

godet

godet pleats ∞ (go-day′) Pleats that hang in a series of rolls forming a gored skirt, popular in 1890s. Also called *pipe-organ pleats.*

gore **1.** Skirt section, wider at hem than top, providing fullness and shaping to waist without using darts. A four-gore skirt has seams at sides, center front, and center back; six-gore skirt has side-front and side-back seams as well as side seams. There may be as many as twenty-four gores in a skirt. **2.** In sewing, a triangular insert of fabric that creates fullness, greater width, or desired shape. Used in skirts and bell-bottom pants. Also used in gloves at wrist, to make a flared cuff and facilitate opening. Also called *godet.*

six gored skirt

gusset **1.** Diamond-shaped piece of fabric inserted under the arm of sleeve or in the crotch seam to permit greater movement. **2.** Triangular piece used at sides of handbag, at sides of men's shirttails, and sides of shoes for wider opening.

gusset #1

handkerchief hem Hem that falls in points similar to when a handkerchief is held in the center and allowed to fall.

heading Small hem through which elastic is pulled.

handkerchief hem

hem The lower edge of an item of clothing, such as a skirt or blouse, or of sleeves.

C

inverted pleat Pleat formed by bringing two folds to a center line and pressing them. Reverse side of several inverted pleats will look like box pleats.
inverted pleats

kick pleats Single flat pleat or one KNIFE PLEAT (see under CLOTHING CONSTRUCTION DETAILS) at the back or front of a narrow skirt to make walking easier.

kilt pleats Flat pleat covering half of next pleat, all folded in the same direction as in a Scottish kilt.

knife pleats Pressed in pleats, usually placed ½″ to 1″ apart. All pleats go in the same direction. Also called *flat* or *side pleats*.
knife pleats

lapped seam Simple seam used on interfacing and also in shoe and glove construction. One layer of material is placed on top of another and topstitched. Excess material is trimmed away.

lettuce edging Narrow-hemmed finish for edges of garments that creates the appearance of a curly lettuce leaf.

lingerie hem Rolled hem with overcast stitches at intervals forming minute puffs between stitches. Handmade hem popular in the 1920s and still used occasionally.
lingerie hem

machine-made buttonhole See CLOSURES.

miter To finish a square corner with a diagonal seam.
mitered corner

mushroom pleats Very fine, heat-set pleats similar to CRYSTAL PLEATS (see under CLOTHING CONSTRUCTION DETAILS). *Der.* From appearance of the inside cap of the mushroom.

nun's tucks Tucks, usually of 2″ or more in width, placed around the hem of a dress or used on sleeves in a series of three, five, or seven.

open-welt seam See CLOTHING CONSTRUCTION DETAILS: TUCKED SEAM.

overcast seam **1.** Plain seam pressed open on wrong side and each raw edge finished by hand or machine overcast stitches to prevent raveling. **2.** Seam made on inside of garment with both raw edges overcast together either by hand or machine.
overcast seam

overlapped seam See CLOTHING CONSTRUCTION DETAILS: LAP SEAM.

petal hem Hem that falls in rounded sections similar to petals of a flower.

picot hem Hem finished with a row of machine hemstitching—then cut apart—used on ruffles to reduce bulkiness. Popular in the 1920s. See EMBROIDERIES AND SEWING STITCHES: HEMSTITCH #2.

pinked Describes seams or other fabric areas that have been finished by trimming raw edges with a pinking shears, which makes saw-toothed edges to prevent raveling.
pinking

pin tucks See CLOTHING CONSTRUCTION DETAILS: TUCKS.

piped buttonhole See CLOSURES.

pipe organ pleats See CLOTHING CONSTRUCTION DETAILS: GODET PLEAT.

piping A folded piece of bias binding. Piping may be inserted between two layers of fabric before stitching to create a decorative effect as, for example, in piped seams. Piped seams are similar to corded seams but have a flat rather than a rounded edge.

placket Word used since the 16th c. for slit at neck, side, front, back, or wrist in dress, blouse, pants, or skirt to facilitate taking garment on and off. Fastened in early times by lacings, buttons, or hooks and eyes; since 1930s by zippers, and since 1970s by *Velcro®*. A **side placket** is an opening placed in side seam of a dress or blouse to facilitate putting on a fitted dress. It extends about 4″ above and below waistline. Originally fastened with SNAPS (see under CLOSURES), later side plackets closed by a special type of zipper. Most dresses had this type of opening from 1930s to 1950s. Replaced by long back zippers extending from neckline to hips.
placket

plain hem Hem folded up and hand-sewn. The edge of the hem may be finished to prevent raveling by various means such as turning the hem edge under and machine stitching,

plain hem

pinking (see CLOTHING CONSTRUCTION DETAILS: PINKED), or sewing tape to the edge by machine after which hand stitches are used to finish the hem.

plain seam Simple seam stitched on wrong side of garment usually pressed open. Used on a fabric that will not ravel.

pleat/plait **1.** *n.* Fold of fabric usually pressed flat but sometimes left unpressed. When used in a skirt, blouse, or dress, it is sometimes stitched down at the top of the garment to make it hang better. In polyester and nylon fabrics, pleats may be put in permanently with a heat-setting process. **2.** *v.* To set in folds.

rolled hem Handmade hem used on sheer and delicate fabrics. First rolled between the fingers, then sewed with tiny stitches. Used for chiffon evening gowns of the 1920s and 1930s, and still used occasionally.

rolled hem

saddle-stitched seam See FOOTWEAR.

saw-toothed hem Faced hem made with pointed edges.

scalloped hem Faced hem made with rounded edges simulating a shell design.

seam The place at which two or more layers of textile material or leather are sewn together. A variety of stitches and techniques can be utilized in creating seams. See individual types of seams listed under CLOTHING CONSTRUCTION DETAILS and GLOVES AND GLOVE CONSTRUCTIONS.

seam binding Narrow tape woven on the straight used at hem of garment to cover raw edge. Also stitched to seams on wrong side to prevent stretching. Sometimes used to bind cut edges of raveled seams.

shirring Three or more rows of *gathers* made by small running stitches in parallel lines. Used to produce fullness at tops of gloves, skirts, sleeves, and swimsuits. Also called *gauging*. May be made

shirring

by using a large stitch on the sewing machine and then pulling the bobbin thread to form gathers or by using elastic thread on the bobbin.

shoulder dart V-shaped dart, extending from mid-shoulder seam to bust, or from shoulder seam to shoulder blade in back.

side placket See CLOTHING CONSTRUCTION DETAILS: PLACKET.

side pleats See CLOTHING CONSTRUCTION DETAILS: KNIFE PLEATS.

slot seam Seam created by folding under the edge of each of two garment pieces, laying the edges facing each other over a tape or strip of fabric, and topstitching the folded

slot seam

edges through the underlying fabric. This technique is often used to create a contrast in color or fabric between the underlying fabric and the top garment fabric.

stay **1.** Strip of material, originally whalebone but now usually thin metal or plastic, placed behind or within seams or darts and used to stiffen such garments as corsets, bodices, collars, or belts. Light boning used particularly at hem of skirt to extend it is called **feather boning**. **2.** Piece of fabric stitched under pleats or gathers to hold fullness in place.

strap seam Plain seam stitched with wrong sides together, thereby making the seam on the outside of the garment. The seam is pressed open. Bias tape, with the edges folded under, is laid over the open seam and top-stitched into place.

strap seam

stud See CLOSURES.

sunburst pleats See CLOTHING CONSTRUCTION DETAILS: ACCORDION PLEAT.

sunburst tucks Used in a series, these are darts that taper to nothing. May be arranged around the neckline of a dress, on the front of the blouse, or at the front of the waistline. Provide a decorative effect and reduce fullness without gathers. Also called *fan tucks*.

tailored buttonhole See CLOSURES: WORKED BUTTONHOLE.

topstitching Stitching visible from the outer or "top" side of a garment that consists of one or more rows of machine stitching made through all layers of fabric.

topstitched seam Plain seam pressed open and stitched on either side of seam on right side of garment or pressed to one side and stitched on reverse side. Also called *double-stitched seam* or, when double rows of stitching are placed on either side of the seam, *broad-stitched seam.*

top stitched seam

tuck A means of controlling fullness in a garment in which part of the garment piece is made smaller by folding the fabric and stitching a line parallel to the fold. At the place where the tuck ends, fullness is released. Often tucks are arranged in a series and designated by width (e.g., 1″, ½″, ¼″, or **pin tucks**; the latter are only wide enough for a row of stitching).

tucked seam Seam finished with tucks stitched about ¼″ to 1″ from either side of seam and pressed to meet over seam. Also called *open-welt seam.*

umbrella pleats Similar to ACCORDION PLEATS (see under CLOTHING CONSTRUCTION DETAILS) but larger, like the folds of an umbrella.

venetian-blind pleats A pleat formed by a wide-stitched tuck made in the fabric. Each tuck slightly overlaps the previous one in the fashion of Venetian blind slats.

Watteau pleats Box pleats hanging free from back shoulder yoke to hem of dress or dressing gown. *Der.* From the name of an 18th-c. French painter who often depicted women wearing dresses with this style pleat. The term was coined in the 19th c. Shown at WATTEAU BACK.

welded seam See CLOTHING CONSTRUCTION DETAILS: FUSED SEAM.

welt seam Plain seam stitched on underside of the fabric, one edge is trimmed, then both edges are pressed in same direction with the narrower edge under the wider. Finally the seam is topstitched at a point close enough to the seam to catch wider edge. This is a very durable seam finish and

welt seam

may also be used for decorative effects if the color of the top stitching contrasts with the fabric.

worked buttonhole See CLOSURES.

clothing industry See APPAREL INDUSTRY.
clouded cane See CANE.
clout-shoen See FOOTWEAR: CLOT.
cloverleaf lapel See NECKLINES AND COLLARS: LAPEL.
clown suit Popular fancy dress costume for children or adults consisting of a jumpsuit with full pant legs with ruffles at cuffs and ankles. A large unstarched RUFF (see NECKLINES AND COLLARS) is worn at the neckline. Made of two colors, divided down center front and back, and trimmed with pompons. Worn with tall tapered DUNCE'S CAP (see HEADWEAR).
club bow tie See TIES.
club wig See WIGS AND HAIRPIECES.
Cluny lace See LACES.
cluster curls See HAIRSTYLES.
cluster earring See JEWELRY.
cluster pleats See CLOTHING CONSTRUCTION DETAILS.
cluster ring See JEWELRY.
clutch coat See COATS AND JACKETS.
clutch purse/bag See HANDBAGS AND RELATED ACCESSORIES.
CMT See CUT, MAKE AND TRIM.
coachman's coat See COATS AND JACKETS.
coal-scuttle bonnet See HEADWEAR.
coat-dress Dress fastened down front from neck to hem, like a coat, in single- or double-breasted style, either belted or unbelted. A classic since the 1930s.
coated fabrics † Fabrics sometimes made nonporous and water repellent through coating with various substances such as lacquer, varnish, pyroxlin, rubber, polyethylene, or plastic resin.
coatee See COATS AND JACKETS.
coat jumper See JUMPERS.
coat of mail See ARMOR: HAUBERK.
coat set See COATS AND JACKETS.
coat shirt See SHIRTS.
coats See CLOSURES: BREASTS.

COATS AND JACKETS

coat Sleeved outerwear that ranges from hip-length to full-length, it is designed to be worn over other clothing either for warmth or as a decorative element of the costume. Although a coat with set-in sleeves was worn in ancient Persia, MANTLES and CAPES (see under CAPES, CLOAKS, AND SHAWLS) were more generally worn as the outermost garment until the end of the 18th c. when the REDINGOTE and PELISSE were introduced (see under COATS AND JACKETS). *Der.* From "cloak" in use by mid-19th c., and not changed to "coat" until the late 19th c.

jacket For men: used in English to describe a garment, often sleeveless, that was worn over a DOUBLET in France and England in 15th c. and into the early 17th c. It was also called a *jerkin.* In 18th c. worn by country people, laborers, seafarers, and apprentices, thus becoming a mark of social inferiority. In mid-19th c. accepted by gentlemen, replacing the suit coat for some occasions. For women: In the 17th c. the jacket was a type of BODICE that was more loosely fitted than more formal wear and was also called either a doublet or waistcoat. In the 19th c., when women adopted dresses made up of separate bodices and skirts, the separate bodice was referred to as a JACKET BODICE (see in alphabetical listing), whereas the term "jacket" alone as used today (see #1 below) was applied to separate garments such as the ZOUAVE JACKET (see COATS AND JACKETS). In the 20th c., many styles, for both formal and informal occasions, were introduced for both men and women. Present-day usage defines jackets as follows: **1.** An item of apparel, usually shorter than hip-length, designed to be worn over other clothing either indoors or outdoors. Some are made with double-breasted or single-breasted closings; others have no closing, and some are closed with a zipper. **2.** Part of a suit that covers the upper part of the body—a *suit jacket. Der.* Old French, *jackquette,* the diminutive of *jacque,* a coat.

admiral coat Double-breasted REEFER-style coat (see under COATS AND JACKETS), frequently with gold buttons. *Der.* Adapted from coats worn by U.S. Navy officers.

Afghanistan jacket Jacket of lambskin, tanned with hair left on, made with leather side out, giving a shaggy border around edge, sometimes embroidered on the smooth side. Popular in late 1960s as part of trend toward ethnic clothes.

Albert driving cape ∞ Not a true cape, but a single- or double-breasted, loose, CHESTERFIELD-style coat (see under COATS AND JACKETS) of 1860 usually made with no back seam. Also called *driving sac.*

Albert jacket ∞ Man's single-breasted jacket of 1848. It was made with or without waistline seam side pleats, and and had no breast pocket.

Albert overcoat ∞ Man's loose-fitting midcalf overcoat with fly front, small shoulder cape, flapped hip pockets, long back vent, and vertical slit breast pockets; worn in 1877.

Albert riding coat ∞ High-buttoned single-breasted man's coat of 1841 with front cut away in slanted style. Made with broad collar, narrow lapels, and hip pockets.

Albert top frock ∞ Men's heavy overcoat styled like a FROCK COAT (see under COATS AND JACKETS), made with wide velvet collar, flap pockets, wide cuffs, and lapels; worn from 1860s to 1900.

A-line coat Coat made close and narrow at the shoulders, flaring gently from under arms to hem; shaped like letter **A**, made in single- or double-breasted style with or without a collar. Introduced in 1955 by Paris designer Christian Dior.

all-weather coat Waterproofed or water-repellent coat sometimes made with zip-in lining to adapt to various temperatures.

all-weather raincoat Raincoat that can be worn year-round as it is made with a zip-out lining, usually of acrylic pile.

almain coat/jacket ∞ (al′man) Jacket worn by men over DOUBLET in second half of 15th and early 16th c. Made close fitting with short, flared skirt and long hanging sleeves, and slashed at front seams.

Alpine jacket ∞ **1.** Waist-length jacket worn with LEDERHOSEN (see under SHORTS) as part of a Tyrolean mountain climber's costume. **2.** Englishman's jacket similar to a NORFOLK JACKET (see under COATS AND JACKETS), made double-breasted with vertical flap pockets and pleat down center back. Worn buttoned to neck, often without a vest, in 1876.

American coat ∞ British term for man's single-breasted full-length coat, usually black, made with narrow lapels, wide collar, and full skirt; worn in 1829.

angle-fronted coat ∞ Variation of man's MORNING COAT (see under COATS AND JACKETS), cut away diagonally on each side to reveal triangles of waistcoat; worn from 1870 to 1880. Also called *university coat.*

anorak (an'-nah-rack) Hip-length jacket made of water-repellent fabric, sometimes lined with fur, which has a zip-front and draw-string hem and is worn for winter sports. Introduced in World War II for pilots. *Der.* Eskimo word for a hooded waist-length jacket of sealskin or printed cotton worn for warmth by Greenland Eskimos.

anorak

Armenian mantle ∞ Loose-fitting pelisse (see under COATS AND JACKETS) without a cape, enriched with PASSEMENTERIE made of braid, worn by women in 1847

ascot jacket ∞ Loose-fitting man's jacket with rounded hems in front and matching fabric belt pulling in the waistline, worn in 1876.

automobile coat See COATS AND JACKETS: DUSTER.

balmacaan (bal-ma-kan) Raglan-sleeved, loose-fitting style coat that buttons up the front to the neck and has a small,

balmacaan

turned-down collar. Frequently made of tweed or water-repellent fabric. *Der.* Named after Balmacaan, Invernessshire, Scotland.

Balmoral jacket ∞ **1.** Woman's jacket of 1867 that buttoned to neck with front and back points below waist. **2.** Woman's belted double-breasted semi-fitted jacket with lapels and small gauntlet cuffed sleeves, similar to coat of riding habit, worn c. 1870.

barn coat See COATS AND JACKETS: FIELD COAT.

barouche coat ∞ (bar-roosh) Woman's tight-fitting three-quarter-length outdoor coat with full sleeves, fastened in front with gold barrel-shaped snaps and an elastic-type belt with buckle, worn in 1809.

baseball jacket Waist-length zippered or snap-closed jacket with ribbed cuffs and waist styled after those worn by Major League and Little League baseball players. While those used in professional and amateur sports are made in team colors with team name on the front and player's number on the back, those for general wear are made in a wide variety of colors and fabrics and may or may not have team logos or other decorations. Also called *varsity jacket.*

baseball or varsity jacket

base coat ∞ Man's jacket or *jerkin* with short sleeves, square neckline, and skirts, or BASES, hanging in tubular unpressed pleats to just above the knees; worn from 1490 to 1540.

basquine ∞ (bas-keen') **1.** Woman's coat with pagoda sleeves, fringed trimming, and long extension below the waistline, worn in 1857. **2.** Outdoor jacket worn in 1860s. Also spelled *basquin, basquine.*

Battenberg jacket ∞ Woman's loose-fitting outdoor jacket with large buttons and a turned-down collar worn in 1880s.

battle jacket Waist-length Army jacket worn in World War II, having two breast pockets, fitted waistband, zippered fly-closing, and

battle jacket

turn-down collar with revers. Also called *Eisenhower jacket* after Allied forces Commander-in-Chief General Dwight D. Eisenhower, who wore this style.

beach coat See ACTIVEWEAR: BEACH ROBE.

Beaufort coat ∞ Man's suit jacket of 1880s with single-breasted, four-button closing, narrow straight sleeves, and seams often double-stitched. Also called *jumper coat.*

beer jacket ∞ Short, boxy cotton jacket with patch pockets and brass buttons originally worn by upper classmen at Princeton University in 1930s, and copied by other students.

bellboy/bellhop jacket Waist-length jacket with standing collar, two rows of brass buttons on front in V-style, frequently connected with gold braid. Originally worn by messenger boys, pages, and bellboys at hotels. Now used mainly for band uniforms and occasionally adapted for men's, women's, and children's wear.

bench coat See COATS AND JACKETS: BENCHWARMER JACKET.

benchwarmer jacket Hooded knee-length jacket slipped over head and zipped at neck. Copied for young people from jackets worn by football players waiting on the bench. Also called *bench coat.*

benjamin ∞ Overcoat, generally white, worn by working men in the 19th c. Also called *benny* or *lily benjamin.*

big coat Long, full, sometimes-ankle-length voluminous coat with long full sleeves. Worn belted, unbelted, or with a belt in the back to confine the fullness.

bike jacket Waist-length sport jacket. Styling varies but is often similar to a WINDBREAKER or BATTLE JACKET (see under COATS AND JACKETS).

bi-swing Suit or sport jacket with set-in belt in back and deep pleats extending upward to each shoulder to give freedom of movement. Has single-breasted closing and conventional notched collar with lapels. Popular in the 1930s for men and women.

blade jacket Man's business jacket of the 1930s made with extra fullness at upper arm and back, or shoulder blades, giving broad-shouldered look and freedom of movement.

blazer Sport jacket in a solid color or striped. Originally single breasted, and with patch pockets, now made double-breasted as well and with varying types of pockets. Generally worn with trousers or skirt of contrasting color. *Der.* Earliest uses of this term seem to have been for bright (blazing) red jackets worn for sports.

blazer

blouse coat Coat with V-shaped neckline, *dolman* or *kimono* sleeves, and single-button closing at waistline; frequently made with slightly flounced skirt and lavish, high fur collar; popular in the 1920s.

blouson jacket (blue′-zohn) Jacket with a bloused effect at a normal or low waistline, either gathered into knitted waistband or pulled in by drawstring. *Der.* French, "blouse."

bobtailed coat ∞ Short-tailed man's coat with narrow REVERS (see NECKLINES AND COLLARS) worn at end of 18th and early 19th c.

body coat ∞ In 19th-c. men's tailoring, used to distinguish a suit coat from an outdoor coat or overcoat.

bolero Waist-length or above-the-waist jacket, usually collarless and often sleeveless, with rounded front, and no fastenings. Copied form the Spanish bullfighter's embroidered jacket and worn by women since late 19th c. *Der.* From name of a Spanish dance and also music for the dance.

bolero

bomber jacket See COATS AND JACKETS: FLIGHT JACKET.

box coat 1. Woman's straight coat with wide shoulders, popular in late 1920s and 1930s. Also see COATS AND JACKETS: CARRICK. 2. ∞ Heavy, warm overcoat with single or multiple shoulder capes worn throughout 19th c. particularly by coachmen and travelers riding outside coach on the "box." Also called *driving coat* and *curricle coat* (kur′-eh-kul). 3. ∞ Hip-length woman's double-breasted jacket styled like a REEFER (see COATS AND JACKETS), worn in early 1890s. 4. ∞ Unfitted large sleeved jacket coming to below waist-line, styled with standing collar and side closing. Worn in mid-1890s. **5.** See COATS AND JACKETS: EMPIRE JACKET #2. **6.** ∞ Three-quarter-length unfitted coat of early 1900s, made with shawl collar, unfastened in front. Sometimes trimmed lavishly with braid. **7.** Double-breasted girl's coat sometimes made with shawl collar, or an extra cape, worn in early 20th c.

box jacket Any straight unfitted jacket, waist-length or longer.

boy coat Double-breasted coat with long, notched collar and set-in sleeves.

Brandenburg/Brandenbourg/Brandenburgh ∞ Man's long, loose winter coat made in military style with frog closings, worn in last quarter of 17th c. *Der.* Named for braid-trimmed uniforms worn by Brandenburg troops of Prussia during the Napoleonic War who fought for a state located in the eastern part of Germany.

Breton jacket ∞ (bret-ohn′) Fitted hip-length woman's jacket buttoned on either side to a front panel, with tailored collar and lavishly trimmed with wide braid. Frequently shorter in center back. In the late 1870s, when worn with matching skirt, called a *Breton costume.*

British warm British army or navy officers' heavy double-breasted overcoat, knee-length or shorter, copied for civilian wear in 1950s and 1960s.

Bronx jacket See COATS AND JACKETS: PERFECTO JACKET.

bucksain ∞ Man's padded overcoat with wide sleeves, worn in 1850s.

buckskin jacket Western-style jacket of sueded DOESKIN or SHEEPSKIN (see LEATHERS) trimmed with long fringe. A standard style in the American West from colonial days, it was adapted for citywear in the late 1960s.

buff coat ∞ Man's leather jacket made of ox or buffalo hides. Sometimes with shoulder wings and sleeves of fabric, sometimes sleeveless. Worn in 16th and 17th c. Originally a military garment worn during civil wars in England, adopted by civilians and American Colonists. Also called *buff jerkin* or *leather jerkin.*

bulletproof jacket Any jacket that is con-structed with strong, bullet-resistant fiber such as Kevlar® aramid. One example is a lightweight jacket with zipper front and three bulletproof panels—two in front and one in back—that slip into pockets in the lining.

Burberry® Trademark of Burberry's Interna-tional, Ltd., London, for an expensive unisex trenchcoat-type raincoat. Made in lightweight polyester and cotton fabric with an optional plaid zip-out lining. Skirts, scarves, and um-brellas are made to match the lining. Details include handstitching on collar, handmade buttonholes, and D-rings on belt for holding objects. First used by British officers in 1914. Also see alphabetical listing.

bush jacket/bush coat Jacket originally worn in Africa on hunting expeditions, where it was made of khaki-colored cotton with peaked lapels, single-breasted front, belt, and four large bel-lows pockets. Adapted for fashionable wear and made in all types of fabrics and worn by men, women and children. *Der.* From clothes worn on

bush jacket or safari jacket

hunting trip into the African bush country. Also called *bush coat* or **safari jacket,** which is similar in all respects to the bush jacket, but called by this name in the mid- and late 1960s when introduced as a fashion item for women by Dior, the French couturier. Newer versions in 1980s styled without belt, sometimes with epaulets. *Der.* From name of African hunting trip, *safari,* for which similar style jacket is worn.

caban ∞ Man's loose outdoor garment of the 1840s that had wide, bell-like sleeves, some-times had a small cape at the shoulders, and a hood. Also known as *templar cloak.*

Camargo ∞ (ka-mar′-go) A woman's jacket with draped fullness, pannier-style, around hips worn over waistcoat or vest in late 1870s. *Der.* After Marie Ann de Cupis Camargo (1710–1770), celebrated dancer.

Cambridge coat ∞ Three-button, single- or double-breasted man's suit coat of 1870, made with three seams in back and a center vent.

Cambridge paletot ∞ (pal-ah-tow′ or pal-tow′) Man's knee-length overcoat of mid-1850s cut with wide cape collar, large turned-back cuffs, and wide lapels extending almost to hem.

campaign coat ∞ Originally a long military overcoat worn by the rank and file from about 1667, and later adopted by men for civilian wear in late 17th c.

canadienne (ka-nah′-dee-en) Woman's hip-length, double-breasted, belted coat designed in Paris during the 1940s, copied from coats worn by Canadian soldiers.

cape coat **1.** Coat with sleeves and an attached or separate cape. **2.** Combination of cape and coat with the back falling like a cape, the front having sleeves and looking like a coat. Also see COATS AND JACKETS: DOLMAN.

capote/capot ∞ (kah-poat) **1.** Man's loose coat with turn-down collar and cuffs worn in 18th c. **2.** Hooded coat or cloak worn from Middle Ages on.

caprice ∞ (ka-preece) Loose short sleeveless woman's evening jacket of mid-19th c. that tapered to rounded point below the waist in back.

caraco (kar′-a-ko) **1.** Fitted hip-length suit jacket with peplum made by French designer Yves Saint Laurent in 1969, said to derive from jackets depicted in Toulouse-Lautrec paintings. **2.** ∞ Thigh-length fitted jacket, flaring below waist, made with no waistline seams and popular for women from late 18th through 19th c. Also called *caraco corsage*.

car coat Sport or utility coat made hip- to three-quarter length, which is comfortable for driving a car. First became popular with the station-wagon set in suburbia in 1950s and 1960s and has become a classic style since then. Some of the styles in which car coats have been made include BENCHWARMER, DUFFEL COAT, RANCH COAT, MACKINAW JACKET, STADIUM COAT, TOGGLE COAT. See these under COATS AND JACKETS.

cardigan coat/cardigan jacket Collarless coat or jacket made with plain round neckline and buttoned down center front and which may have binding around the neckline and down the front. *Der.* Named for 7th Earl of Cardigan, who needed an extra layer of warmth for his uniform during the Crimean War, 1854.

careless ∞ Man's loose-fitting caped overcoat with spread collar and no seams at waistline, worn in 1830s.

carmagnole ∞ (car′-man-yole) Jacket or short-skirted coat with wide collar, lapels, and rows of metal buttons. Worn with black pantaloons and red LIBERTY CAP (See HEADWEAR) by French Revolutionaries in 1792 and 1793.

carrick ∞ Man's or woman's full-length duster worn from 1877 on. Styled like a box coat with three capes and similar to an ulster (see under COATS AND JACKETS: ULSTER #1 AND #2).

casaque ∞ (ka-sack′) **1.** Fitted jacket buttoned down the front, worn by women from mid-1850s to mid-1870s. Early types had extensions of the bodice (basques) to the hips or sometimes longer; later types had skirts draped in POLONAISE style. **2.** French term for jacket worn by jockeys, usually made in bright colors of their respective stables. **3.** Girl's coat cut on princess lines worn in 1860s. **4.** See COATS AND JACKETS: CASSOCK #1.

casaweck ∞ (kasa′-wek) Woman's short, quilted outdoor mantle made with close-fitting velvet or silk collar and sleeves. Frequently trimmed with fur, velvet, or lace. Worn from mid-1830s to mid-1850s. Also see COATS AND JACKETS: POLKA and VARENS.

casentino (ca-zen-tee-no) Red overcoat with a green lining worn by coachmen in Casentino, a section of Italy. Later adapted for winter sportswear.

cassock **1.** ∞ Long loose overcoat with a cape collar. Worn from late 16th through 17th c. by men and women for hunting, riding, and by foot soldiers. Also called a *casaque* (ka-sack′). **2.** See CLERICAL DRESS.

Charlie Chaplin coat Ankle-length, full-shouldered, oversized coat with baggy sleeves ending in wide-buttoned cuffs and huge patch pockets. Introduced by Claude Montana, French couturier, in spring collection of 1985.

Der. Named after Charlie Chaplin, an early silent-film comedian.

chasseur jacket ∞ Fitted, hip-length, military-inspired women's jacket of 1880s made with standing military collar, slashings at hem, and elaborately trimmed with braid and BRANDENBURGS (see CLOSURES: FROGS).

chesterfield coat Semi-fitted, straight-cut classic man's or woman's overcoat in single- or double-breasted style, with black velvet collar. Single-breasted style usually has a fly-front closing. Originally an overcoat introduced in 1840s for men. Popular

chesterfield coat

in late 1920s through 1940 and worn at intervals since. *Der.* Named after the 6th Earl of Chesterfield, a fashion leader in 1830s and 1840s.

Chinese jacket See COATS AND JACKETS: COOLIE COAT.

chubby Woman's straight-cut waist- to hip-length jacket of long-haired fur, made collarless, with straight sleeves. Popular in late 1930s and revived in early 1970s.

claw-hammer coat ∞ Colloquial name for the SWALLOW-TAILED COAT (see under COATS AND JACKETS) named for shape of coat-tails with ends cut straight across resembling claws of a hammer.

close coat ∞ Term used in 18th and 19th c. for a buttoned coat.

clutch coat Woman's coat with no fasteners in front worn open or held clutched together. Originally introduced in the mid-1920s as a low-waisted evening wrap with bagpipe sleeves and large fur collar and also for day wear. Revived periodically.

coachman's coat Double-breasted coat with large, wide lapels, fitted waistline, and flared skirt. Frequently has a

clutch coat

cape collar and brass buttons. Copied from English coachmen's coats of 19th c.

coatee ∞ Short close-fitting coat with short skirt, flaps, or coattails. Fashionable in mid-18th c. and also in 1860s.

coats See CLOSURES: BREASTS.

coat set Child's coat made with matching hat, or matching pants, sold together since 1940s.

coattail Portion of coat below the back waistline, especially the long back portions of a SWALLOW-TAILED coat or a CUTAWAY (see under COATS AND JACKETS).

coachman's coat, 1775

cocoon Wrap coat with very large shoulders, deep cuffed batwing sleeves, and standing collar that may be rolled down. Envelops the figure, tapering to the hem, like a cocoon. Used as a *rain or shine coat.* Originally introduced by Yves Saint Laurent in spring 1984 as an evening coat in velvet, it reached to thigh in back and tapered in cutaway fashion in the front.

Codrington ∞ Man's loose-fitting single or double-breasted overcoat resembling a CHESTERFIELD (see under COATS AND JACKETS) worn in 1840s. *Der.* After Sir Edward Codrington, British admiral, who led fleet to victory at Navarino in 1827.

coin de feu ∞ (kwan′ de fuh′) Short coat with high neck and wide sleeves made of silk, velvet, or cashmere usually worn indoors over a home dress in mid-19th c.

combing jacket ∞ Woman's loose jacket, usually waist-length, worn in the bedroom when brushing hair or applying makeup, in late 19th and early 20th c.

coolie coat Short boxy coat reaching slightly below waist with standing collar, KIMONO SLEEVES (see SHOULDERS AND SLEEVES) and FROG FASTENERS (see CLOSURES). Worn by Chinese workmen and frequently copied as beach or lingerie coat. *Der.* Chinese, *kuli,* "unskilled workman."

coureur ∞ (koor-er′) Tight-fitting CARACO jacket (see COATS AND JACKETS: CARACO #2), with short PEPLUM or BASQUES worn by women during French Revolution.

C.P.O. See SHIRTS.

Cubavera jacket White cotton sport jacket with four patch pockets similar to BEER JACKET (see under COATS AND JACKETS). Worn with lightweight slacks for sportswear by men from 1940 to 1950.

curricle coat ∞ (kur′-eh-kul) **1.** Woman's fitted full-length coat with lapels worn in early 19th c. Cut away in front from chest to waist, sloping to the back; sometimes called *gig coat.* **2.** Synonym for *box coat* that was used in the mid-19th c. See COATS AND JACKETS: BOX COAT #2.

cutaway ∞ 19th c. man's coat style that was known by a number of different names throughout the century. It originated as a **riding coat**, worn from 1825 to 1870s and was made with skirt slanting from waist to thigh in back that was made by cutting away the front of a FROCK COAT

cutaway coat c. 1895

(see under COATS AND JACKETS) instead of folding the skirts back for horseback riding. From the riding coat the **Newmark** or **Newmarket coat** evolved. This name, used c. 1838 and after, also has a connection to riding, as New Market, England, was a horse racing center. This was a long-tail coat made single- or double-breasted with front skirts cut away and rounded, often with flap pockets and cuffed sleeves. By the 1850s, this basic style was known as a "cutaway" and worn for more formal occasions. It was usually a black, one-button jacket with peaked lapels and skirt cut away from the waist in front, tapering to knees in back, in a slanting line. It had a back vent topped by two buttons and was worn with a waistcoat and striped trousers in daytime. By the 1870s the same style was more likely to be called a **morning coat.**

cutaway frock ∞ Man's suit coat almost knee-length—similar to a FROCK COAT (see under COATS AND JACKETS)—and cut away from waistline to each side seam in rounded curve. Worn in 1890s and early 1900s. As the **dress frock coat** worn in 1870s and 1880s, this coat was double-breasted and exposed the shirt in front.

cutaway sack ∞ Man's loose-fitting suit jacket reaching to hips cut away in rounded lines in front to side seams. Worn in 1890s and early 1900s.

cycle jacket See COATS AND JACKETS: MOTORCYCLE JACKET.

deck jacket Short hooded water-repellent jacket, sometimes made with nylon pile lining, which closes with zipper and has attached ribbed, knitted trim at wrists and neck. Worn onboard sailboats and other craft.

denim jacket Any jacket made of blue denim fabric.

dinner jacket **1.** Man's white semiformal jacket worn in summer. **2.** See COATS AND JACKETS: TUXEDO.

Directoire coat ∞ (dir-eck′-twa) Woman's coat having ankle-length skirt in back and coming only to waistline in front, worn in late 1880s.

Directoire jacket ∞ (dir-eck′-twa) Woman's waist-length jacket of late 1880s. Similar to DIRECTOIRE COAT (see under COATS AND JACKETS), worn as top of a daytime dress.

dirndl coat (durn′-dul) Woman's coat cut with fitted torso, and skirt gathered at a low waistline, popular in the mid-1960s. *Der.* From gathered skirt and fitted bodice of the Tyrolean peasant dress called a *dirndl.*

dolman (dole′-man) Woman's short mantle or full-length wrap that gives the appearance of a cape from the back, but is sleeved in front. Worn from 1870s through the 1880s, revived in early 20th c., and returns to current fashion frequently in coat collections. The **peplum dolman,** a variation with

dolman c. 1882

long points hanging at sides, was worn by women in the early 1870s. A crocheted dolman that fastened at neck with large bow

C

of ribbon worn in the 1890s was called a **dolmanette.**

d'Orsay coat ∞ Man's overcoat of late 1830s—similar to a PILOT COAT (see under COATS AND JACKETS), but fitted at waist with darts. Made with a small collar, slashed or flapped pockets, plain sleeves trimmed with three or four buttons, and no pleats or hip buttons in the back. *Der.* Named for Compte d'Orsay, a 19th-c. arbiter of fashion.

d'Orsay habit-coat ∞ Fitted, man-tailored, three-quarter-length coat for women, somewhat resembling man's CUTAWAY (see under COATS AND JACKETS) style, made double-breasted with large REVERS (see NECKLINES AND COLLARS). Introduced in early 1880s.

doublet See in alphabetical listing.

douillette ∞ (do-yeh′) Woman's winter coat worn from 1818 to 1830s. Over this time, the style changed with the current fashions, the earlier form being a quilted PELISSE (see under COATS AND JACKETS) and the later style consisting of a coat of cashmere, merino wool, or figured satin with a pelerine (a short cape) and having very large sleeves. Also spelled *donnilette.*

down jacket **1.** Usually a zippered jacket with long sleeves, knitted cuffs and waistband, interlined with DOWN quilted to the outer fabric and lining. Worn for warmth and popular for everyday use and sportswear in the 1970s and after. **2.** A similar jacket with zip-off sleeves can also be worn as a vest.

dress coat See COATS AND JACKETS: SWALLOW-TAILED COAT.

dress frock coat See COATS AND JACKETS: CUTAWAY FROCK COAT.

dressmaker coat A woman's coat designed with softer lines and more details than the average coat. May have a waistline and unusual details, e.g., tucks or pleats. *Der.* Styled more like a dress.

driving coat See COATS AND JACKETS: BOX COAT #2.

dressmaker coat

driving sac See COATS AND JACKETS: ALBERT DRIVING CAPE.

Du Barry mantle ∞ Dolman-style (see COATS AND JACKETS: DOLMAN) wrap of early 1880s with smocked yoke front and back, fur collar, and large full cuffs. Lavishly trimmed with ribbon bows and streamers at neck, below yoke, sleeves, and at center back. *Der.* Named for Comtesse Du Barry, mistress of King Louis XV of France.

duck-hunter ∞ Striped linen jacket worn by English waiters about 1840s.

duffel coat Car coat or a shorter-length coat fastened with toggles rather than buttons, introduced during World War II, and worn by men in British navy. In 1950s it was adopted as a sport coat. *Der.* From the original fabric used—a heavy napped wool originally made in Duffel, Belgium. Same as *toggle coat* although sometimes toggle coats are made with a hood.

duffle coat or toggle coat

duo-length coat See COATS AND JACKETS: ZIP-OFF COAT.

duster 1. ∞ Tan or brown lightweight full-length coat worn when riding in an automobile in early 20th c. to protect clothing from dust. Worn with AUTOMOBILE VEIL. See HEADWEAR. **2.** Big-shouldered, big-sleeved, big-pocketed classic coat with smocked back, treated for water repellency and introduced in 1984. **3.** Lightweight clutch coat with full swing at hem and small rolled collar usually made in black bengaline or faille worn in the 1950s. **4.** Fitted coat with long skirt slashed up back to waist worn when riding horseback. Has buttons and buttonholes for closing the slashed skirt. **5.** See SLEEPWEAR AND LOUNGEWEAR: DUSTER. **6.** ∞ Man's summer overcoat of 1870s.

duster 1905

Dutch coat see COATS AND JACKETS: MUFF'S CLOAK

Edwardian coat Man's knee-length, usually double-breasted and black, topcoat or overcoat with large high-rolled, deep-notched collar, nipped-in waistline, and deep vent in in back. Worn with a high silk hat and a cane in Edwardian period, 1901–1910. Versions of this style were revived in the 1960s. *Der.* Inspired by coats of Edwardian era in England.

Edwardian jacket Fitted jacket made with some flare at back and sides and vents at sides or center back. Styled with double- or single-breasted closing and NAPOLEON or REGENCY COLLAR. (See NECKLLINES AND COLLARS.) Introduced in the 1960s, it was similar in cut to jackets of the Edwardian period. *Der.* After Edward VII, King of England, 1901–1910.

Edwardian jacket c. 1967

Eisenhower jacket See COATS AND JACKETS: BATTLE JACKET.

Empire coat ∞ (em′-pire or ohm-peer) Woman's three-quarter to full-length coat of early 1900s worn for traveling or evening wear. Made with a full skirt of large unpressed pleats attached to a high waistline. Bodice is cut somewhat like an ETON JACKET (see under COATS AND JACKETS) with large lapels and a standing MEDICI COLLAR (see NECKLINES AND COLLARS).

Empire jacket (em′-pire or ohm-peer) **1.** Jacket name coined by Women's Wear Daily for a jacket designed by Karl Lagerfeld in 1992 that was banded under the bosom. **2.** ∞ Square-yoked woman's jacket of mid-1890s made with MEDICI COLLAR (see NECKLINES AND COLLARS), large box pleats in front and back, and large balloon sleeves. Also called a *box coat.*

English coat ∞ **1.** Woman's double-breasted three-quarter-length jacket of 1890s made somewhat like a PEA JACKET (see under COATS AND JACKETS) with lapels and flapped pockets. **2.** Full-length coat of 1890s sometimes made with elbow-length cape.

English walking jacket ∞ Woman's jacket of mid-1870s made in single-breasted style with lapels. Unfitted in front but fitted at waistline in back flaring to form a PEPLUM. Sleeves with large turned-back cuffs.

English wrap See COATS AND JACKETS: PALETOT.

Eton jacket Straight-cut jacket with collar and wide lapels worn unbuttoned or with only top button closed, reaching to waist or a little below. Adapted from jackets worn by underclassmen

Eton jacket c. 1896

at Eton preparatory school in England until 1967, popular for women in early 1890s, revived periodically, and a perennial style for small boys. Also see ETON SUIT.

Eton jacket bodice ∞ Woman's waist-length jacket similar to boy's ETON JACKET (see under COATS AND JACKETS) worn open in front over a waistcoat in 1889. In the late 1890s, the front was trimmed with braid and frogs and rounded at waistline.

Eugénie paletot ∞ (yoo-je′-nee) **1.** Tailored three-quarter-length woman's coat of 1860s made in unfitted double-breasted style with notched collar and bell sleeves having false cuffs. The sides of cuffs and rounded patch pockets were decorated with buttons. **2.** Shorter length sack-type jacket, collarless or with a small collar, closing at neck with one button. *Der.* Named for Eugénie, Empress of France (1853–71).

evening wrap Any coat of fabric or fur designed to be worn primarily for formal occasions. It may be a coat designed to match or contrast with an evening dress. Very popular in the 1920s in clutch style. In 1930s, popular in black velvet in a full length with leg-of-mutton sleeves and in hip-length with batwing sleeves.

fake fur coat See COATS AND JACKETS: FUR FABRIC COAT.

fearnothing jacket ∞ Man's jacket similar to a waistcoat with sleeves worn by sailors, sportsmen, laborers, and apprentices in the 18th and early 19th c. Made of heavy woolen fabric called **fearnaught.**

fencing jacket Close-fitting, waist-length jacket, usually padded or quilted, made with high-standing collar and fastened diagonally to right side with a red heart embroidered on left chest. Worn for sport of fencing and sometimes copied for general wear.

field coat Hip-length coat usually made of cotton canvas that buttons down the front. Generally has large pockets on either side of the front near the hem. Often made with corduroy or leather collar in contrasting color. **Barn coat** is similar in style, but made in various types of materials, including suede.

Figaro jacket ∞ Variation of the ZOUAVE or BOLERO JACKET (see under COATS AND JACKETS), with or without shoulder epaulets, worn by women in 1860s and again in 1890s.

fishing parka Knee-length slip-on jacket styled with attached hood and one large KANGAROO POCKET (see POCKETS) across the chest. Made of waterproof fabric and worn for fishing in inclement weather.

flight jacket Waist-length jacket, sometimes made of leather. First worn as part of their uniform by U.S. Army Air Corps pilots in World War II, then adapted for sportswear in 1960s. In early

flight or bomber jacket

1980s and after made in a variety of styles, mainly of nylon, with standing collar, ribbed or elastic waistband, patch or slot pockets, and zip-front. Also called *bomber jacket.*

flyaway jacket Very short jacket, with a full back worn by women in the late 1940s and early 1950s.

fold-up raincoat Any raincoat that folds to small size, specifically a lightweight raincoat frequently of clear vinyl which folds to pocket size. Introduced as early as 1850 and then called POCKET SIPHONIA (sih´-foh´-nee-ah). See under COATS AND JACKETS: SIPHONIA.

French frock See COATS AND JACKETS: FROCK COAT #1.

frock coat ∞ **1.** Suit coat of the 18th c. that was looser and shorter than dress coats. Single- or double-breasted, it buttoned to the waistline. At first it had a full skirt, flapped pockets, and a vent in back with two buttons at waist-

frock coat #1 1895

line, and a flat, turned down collar and no lapels. Initially considered suitable for country wear, but after 1770 was accepted for more formal wear as well. The **French frock** coat, for example, was worn from 1770 to 1800 for full dress and usually trimmed with gold embroidered buttons. As the silhouette of men's coats grew narrower, the frock coat skirt also narrowed. Less popular during the Empire period, the frock coat was important from 1816 until the end of the 19th c., after which it was worn by dignitaries and older men. The specific cut varied depending on the current fashionable silhouette, but the 19th c. coat always had a fitted waist attached with a waistline seam to a knee-length skirt that fell straight and met at the center front. Among the variations of the frock coat was the **jemmy frock,** described as fashionable in the 18th c., but by the 19th c. the **jemmy** had become a man's shooting coat styled like a many-pocketed short frock coat. **2.** Hip-length fitted tailored jacket worn by women in 1890s.

frock greatcoat ∞ Man's coat worn from 1830s on, similar in cut to a FROCK COAT (see under COATS AND JACKETS) but usually double-breasted, longer, and styled for outdoor wear. Also see COATS AND JACKETS: TOP FROCK.

frock overcoat ∞ Boy's calf-length overcoat, worn in late 1880s and 1890s, made with fitted lines, usually with a large CAPE COLLAR (see under NECKLINES AND COLLARS).

fur fabric coat Coat made of fabric that simulates fur, e.g., MODACRYLIC pile fabric, sometimes colored with stripes to imitate mink; sometimes stenciled to look like leopard, giraffe, tiger, and zebra. Incorrectly called a *fake fur coat.*

gaberdine/gabardine ∞ (gab-er-deen) Believed to have been the first fitted European coatlike garment with sleeves. Of Arabian origin, it was introduced from the East by way of Vienna in the mid-14th c. and was popular throughout the 15th c. It had a closed front and wide sleeves with the underarm seam open. Sometimes worn with a belt and was sometimes made of felt. Worn particularly by fashionable men until 1560, and by commoners until early 17th c. *Der.* Eastern *gaba*, "coat." Also called *caban*.

Garibaldi jacket ∞ (gar-ih-bawl′-dee) Woman's square-cut waist-length jacket of 1860s made of red cashmere trimmed with black braid. *Der.* Inspired by clothes worn by Italian patriot Giuseppe Garibaldi.

gascon coat See COATS AND JACKETS: JUPE.

gendarme jacket (zhahn′-darm) Conventional jacket buttoned and adorned with brass buttons on sleeves, pockets, and down center front. Inspired by jackets worn by French policemen. *Der.* French, *gendarme*, "an armed policeman."

Gladstone ∞ Man's short double-breasted overcoat of 1870s made with shoulder cape and borders of Persian lamb. Also see COATS AND JACKETS: ULSTER.

golf jacket Short waist-length jacket with zip-front, worn for playing golf. Often styled with a pleat in the back to allow for freedom of movement when swinging a golf club.

greatcoat Heavy voluminous overcoat worn by men and women, originally made with fur lining and styled similar to an ULSTER (see under COATS AND JACKETS). Term has been used from 19th c. to present.

guardsman coat Double-breasted, half-belted coat made with inverted box pleat in back, slashed pockets, and wide collar. *Der.* Adapted from coats of British guardsmen. Also called *officer's coat*.

hacking jacket Single-breasted fitted jacket similar to man's suit coat, made with slanting flap pockets and center back vent. Used for informal horseback riding and for general casual wear.

happi coat See SLEEPWEAR AND LOUNGEWEAR.

Henrietta jacket ∞ Loose three-quarter-length woman's jacket of 1890s with large collar falling over chest in front, frequently lined with quilted satin.

hunt coat See COATS AND JACKETS: PINK COAT.

hussar jacket ∞ Woman's short jacket of 1880s fastened with FROGS (see under CLOSURES) and trimmed with braid and worn over waistcoat. Inspired by uniforms of British troops returning from a campaign in Egypt.

imperial ∞ Man's coat worn in 1840s similar to loose-fitting, fly-front PALETOT overcoat (see under COATS AND JACKETS).

incroyable coat ∞ (on-kwai′-abla) Woman's coat of 1889 made with long coattails and wide lapels. Worn with lace *jabot* and waistcoat for afternoons. Adapted from the SWALLOW-TAILED COAT (see under COATS AND JACKETS). *Der.* Copied after styles of INCROYABLES (see DIRECTOIRE # 2).

inner-vest jacket Short jacket, sometimes with hood, snapped or buttoned-down front. Attached to the side seams in front is a vest usually similar to a sweater with front zipper.

insulated jacket Lightweight jacket usually made of tightly woven high-count 70 denier nylon, frequently quilted with padding of POLYESTER fiberfill. Usually made with zip-front and rib-knit at neck and wrists, and frequently given soil-resistant and water-repellent finish.

Inverness coat (in-ver-ness) ∞ **1.** Man's loose-fitting overcoat with below-elbow removable cape, introduced in 1859. In 1870s, sometimes had a separate cape over each shoulder. In 1880s, the sleeves were sometimes omitted. In 1890s, armholes were very large and a "sling" was used to support or rest arm. **2.** Knee-length coat with long removable cape or half-capes over the shoulders, like those worn by men in late-19th c. *Der.* From county of Invernessshire, Scotland.

Irene jacket ∞ Short, fitted, collarless woman's jacket of late 1860s cut away in front above waistline and sloping to below waistline in center back. Lavishly trimmed with braid around neckline, on sleeves, and in back.

jemmy See COATS AND JACKETS: FROCK COAT.

Joseph ∞ **1.** Woman's green riding coat worn in the mid-18th c. **2.** Woman's outdoor wrap worn from 1800 to 1810 with loose sleeves, similar to long tunic worn by Jewish men.

journade ∞ (zhur-naad) Short circular jacket with large full sleeves, or with sleeves long and slit. Worn in 14th and 15th c. for riding. Also spelled *jornade.*

judo jacket See ACTIVEWEAR: KARATE CLOTHING.

jump ∞ **1.** Thigh-length 17th-c. soldier's coat, buttoned down front with long sleeves and vent in back, adopted by civilians. Also called *jumpcoat* and *jumpe.* **2.** British name for woman's jacket.

jump coat Thigh-length coat for casual wear. Also see COATS AND JACKETS: CAR COAT.

jumper coat See COATS AND JACKETS: BEAU-FORT COAT.

jupe ∞ (zhoop) 16th- and 17th-c. British term for woman's riding coat worn with protective skirt or *safeguard.* Also called *gascon coat* and *jupon.*

justaucorps ∞ (zhust-o-kor′) **1.** Man's tight-fitting, knee-length coat worn over waistcoat. Borrowed from a military coat and worn from mid-17th to early 18th c. in England and France. **2.** Woman's riding coat, styled like a man's frock coat, worn from mid-17th to early 18th c. Also called *demi-riding coat* and *habit à la française.* Also spelled *justacor, juste, justico, just-au-corps.* justaucorps c. 1690

karate jacket An indoor jacket styled like a Japanese kimono but short in length. Worn when engaging in sport of karate and also adopted for at-home wear by men and women in late 1960s. *Der.* Named for sport for which it is used. Also see ACTIVEWEAR: KARATE CLOTHING.

laboratory coat/smock Single-breasted coat, usually with turned-down collar and REVERS (see NECKLINES AND COLLARS), made of white cotton or manufactured fiber. Worn to protect street clothes while working in chemical or medical laboratory. Also called *lab coat.*

leather jerkin See COATS AND JACKETS: BUFF COAT.

Leicester jacket ∞ Englishman's suit or lounge jacket with RAGLAN SLEEVES (see under SHOULDERS AND SLEEVES). Worn in 1857.

lily benjamin See COATS AND JACKETS: BENJAMIN.

Lindbergh jacket Waist-length heavy woolen or leather jacket with large pockets, lapels, and rolled collar. Made with waistband and cuffs of stretchable rib-knit wool. *Der.* Type of jacket worn by Colonel Charles A. Lindbergh, who made the first solo flight from New York to Paris across the Atlantic in 1927.

London Fog® Trademark for London Fog, a manufacturer of men's and women's raincoat of classic style.

Louis XV basque ∞ Woman's fitted tailored jacket of 1890s worn open down center front, revealing waistcoat or vest. Usually hip length with a standing collar and cut tabs extending from waistline to hem. *Der.* Named after Louis XV, who ruled France from 1710 to 1774.

Louis XVI basque ∞ Woman's fitted jacket of late 1890s made with a point in front at waistline. Had a standing lace-edged MEDICI COLLAR (see under NECKLINES AND COLLARS) extending to two squared lapels and moderate-sized leg-of-mutton sleeves with cuffs that fell over the wrists. Skirt flared over hips, had pleats in center back, and was open at center front. *Der.* Named for Louis XVI of France (1754–1793).

lounging jacket See COATS AND JACKETS: SMOKING JACKET and SACK JACKET.

lumber jacket/lumberjack Waist-length jacket with a bloused effect and rib-knitted bands at waist and cuffs. Made of woven plaid wool fabric. Originally worn by woodsmen in the lumbering trade. Introduced for sportswear in the late 1920s and worn by both adults and children. Reintroduced in early 1980s.

Macfarlane ∞ Man's overcoat made with separate cape over each sleeve and side slits to permit access to pockets of inner garment. Worn from 1850s to end of 19th c.

mackinaw jacket/mackinaw coat Hip-length sport jacket of heavy wool woven in patterns similar to those used for blankets. Improvised in the winter of 1811 when Captain Charles Roberts, a British officer, became stranded with his patrol on St. Martin's Island in the Straits of Mackinac. When reinforcements failed to reach him, warm coats were made from blankets of wide strips and various patterns. Became popular for explorers and woodsmen of the north and continued in popularity to present. *Der.* Named after Mackinaw City, Michigan, located at tip of Michigan facing the Straits of Mackinac.

mackinaw jacket

Mackintosh 1. ∞ Loose-fitting, waterproof coat made of patented India rubber cloth of olive drab or dark green with waterproof straps over the seams. Introduced in 1836 and named for the inventor, Charles Macintosh, who patented fabric in 1823. **2.** British slang for various types of raincoats, often abbreviated to *mac.* **3.** ∞ Long coat with single or double detachable cape introduced for women at end of 19th c. for a raincoat. Made either of "single texture" with printed or woven fabric on outside and heavy rubber coating on inside or "double texture" with a layer of rubber between two fabrics. *Der.* Named after Charles Macintosh, who first invented the rubberized fabric in 1823.

mandarin coat Straight-lined coat with Chinese neckline.

mandarin jacket Jacket with standing-band collar copied from styles of Chinese Mandarin costume. Shows some similarites to NEHRU JACKET (see under COATS AND JACKETS).

mandilion/mandeville ∞ (man-dill´-yun) Loose hip-length jacket with narrow long sleeves worn by men from late 16th to early 17th c. Often worn COLLEY WESTONWARD (e.g., worn by soldiers around shoulders as a cape, with sleeves hanging free). Later worn with short sleeves, sometimes slit, for LIVERY.

man-tailored jacket 1. Woman's suit jacket tailored similar to a man's suit jacket and made in fabrics of pinstripes, tweeds, and other men's wear fabrics. Style may be made with one, two, or three buttons or may be double-breasted. **2.** First jackets with mannish-type tailoring were introduced for women as suit jackets in the late 19th c., and the suits were called TAILOR-MADES. Continued in various styles as a type of jacket suitable for working women.

mantee ∞ Woman's coat of 18th c. worn open in front showing STOMACHER (#2) and PETTI-COAT (#2) underneath.

mantelet See COATS AND JACKETS: PARDESSUS.

marlotte ∞ 16th-c. woman's outer garment, similar to short *mantle,* open in front with back falling in folds. Made with short puffed sleeves and a STANDING COLLAR or RUFF (see NECKLINES AND COLLARS).

marquise mantle ∞ (mar-keez´) Short lace-trimmed taffeta woman's mantlet of mid-1840s with short sleeves. Made with fitted back and flounce below the waist. Also called *marquise.*

masher dust wrap ∞ Tight-fitting man's INVERNESS COAT (see under COATS AND JACKETS) of 1880s having large armholes with a separate cape over each shoulder.

maxi coat Term for any ankle-length coat first used in 1969 and thereafter. At the time these coats represented a radical change from MINI COAT styles. See COATS AND JACKETS: MINI COAT.

mess jacket 1. White waist-length jacket made with large REVERS (see NECKLINES AND COL-LARS) in front and no buttons. Back section is cut in three pieces with center section extending to shoulders in a modified "T," center waistline pointed in back. Worn by busboys and waiters. Formerly worn in white as a summer semiformal jacket for men. Originally worn as part of naval formal evening dress. *Der.* From Naval "mess room." **2.** ∞ Waist-length jacket with standing collar and LEG-OF-

MUTTON SLEEVES (see under SHOULDERS AND SLEEVES) worn by women in 1890s.

Metternich sack ∞ (mett´-er-nik) Woman's collarless, knee-length wrap of mid-1860s made of black velvet with three BOX PLEATS (see under CLOTHING CONSTRUCTION DETAILS) at center back. Trimmed at neck, front, shoulders, and cuffs with wide velvet ribbon embroidered with white cord. *Der.* Named for Prince von Metternich, Austrian statesman of the mid-19th c.

Michael Jackson jacket Red leather jacket designed by Claude Montana for Michael Jackson in the video "Beat It." Copied in polyurethane, buttoning down the front in windbreaker-style with stand-up collar and as many as twenty-seven short zippers placed in unusual places (e.g., three placed diagonally on each side of chest and on shoulder blades in back, vertically at midriff, two placed at armholes so that sleeves are detachable). Trademarked and licensed for sale by Stadium Management Corp. and introduced in 1984. *Der.* Named for Michael Jackson, popular singer.

midi coat (mid´-ee) Mid-calf-length coat introduced in 1967 in radical contrast to thigh-length MINI COAT (see under COATS AND JACKETS). Made in many styles. *Der.* From term coined by *Women's Wear Daily.*

military coat Any coat that borrows details from military coats and jackets (e.g., braid trim, epaulets, gold buttons, or high-standing collar). Usually a fitted double-breasted coat with slightly flared skirt.

military frock coat ∞ Man's FROCK COAT (see under COATS AND JACKETS), worn from early 1820s on, made with standing collar, no lapels, and no flaps on pockets. Later styles had rolled collars and lapels.

military tunic ∞ **1.** Term used first in France in 1670 for long tunic worn by soldiers over a full, sleeved waistcoat. **2.** Man's long tubelike coat with skirts lapped over in front; adopted by British army in 1855.

mini coat Thigh-length coat introduced in mid-1960s and made in any number of styles.

monkey jacket ∞ Short jacket made of heavy fabric like a PILOT COAT (see under COATS AND JACKETS). Worn by sailors in rough weather from 1850s on.

morning coat See COATS AND JACKETS: CUT-AWAY.

Moscow wrapper ∞ Man's loose-fitting overcoat of 1874 with PAGODA SLEEVES (see under SHOULDERS AND SLEEVES), fly front, narrow turned-down collar of astrakhan fur, and other fur trimming.

motorcycle jacket Close-fitting black leather jacket waist-length, fastened to one side of center front with zipper, snap fasteners, or buttons. Popular in the 1960s and worn by both children and adults, continuing into the present. Very much like the PERFECTO JACKET (see under COATS AND JACKETS). Also called a *cycle jacket.*

muff's cloak ∞ Man's coat of late 16th and early 17th c. Same as *Dutch coat.* (Note: The "Dutch" in this case means "German" and is a mistranslation of the word *Deutsch,* meaning German.)

Napoleon coat ∞ Woman's man-tailored hip-length jacket of mid-1890s with standing MILITARY COLLAR (see under NECKLINES AND COLLARS), full LEG-OF-MUTTON SLEEVES (see under SHOULDERS AND SLEEVES), military braid down the front, and fastened with large BRANDENBURGS (see CLOSURES: FROGS). *Der.* Named for Napoleon, who wore a similar style during his military career.

Nehru jacket/Nehru coat (nay´-roo) Single-breasted jacket or coat, slightly fitted, with a standing band collar introduced in late 1960s. Adapted from type of coat worn by Indian maharajahs. *Der.* From wearing of this type of coat by Jawaharlal Nehru, Prime Minister of India, 1947–1964. Shown at NEHRU SUIT.

Newmark/Newmarket coat See COATS AND JACKETS: CUTAWAY.

Newmarket jacket ∞ Woman's close-fitting hip-length jacket with turned-down collar, silkfaced lapels, flapped pockets, and cuffed sleeves. Frequently part of the "masculine" TAILOR-MADE fashions of the 1890s.

Newmarket overcoat ∞ **1.** Man's long single-breasted overcoat of 1880s similar to a FROCK OVERCOAT (see under COATS AND JACKETS). Usually made with velvet collar and cuffs and frequently made of HOMESPUN. **2.** Woman's long single or double-breasted winter coat with velvet collar, lapels, tight sleeves, cuffs, and flapped pockets. Made of heavy fabric for winter from mid-1880s to 1890s.

Newmarket top frock ∞ Man's overcoat of 1895 similar to a FROCK COAT (see under COATS AND JACKETS), made of rough CHEVIOT fabric with velvet collar, pockets on waist seams, and the lower part lined with checked fabric—upper part with silk or satin.

norfolk jacket Belted hip-length jacket with two box pleats from shoulders to hem, on front and back. Matching fabric belt is either threaded through slots under pleats or worn over them. Worn by men for sport and travel since 1880s and associated with the character Dr. Watson of Sir Arthur Conan Doyle's Sherlock Holmes stories. Popular for young boys from 1890s to about 1920 and revived periodically. See NORFOLK SUIT in alphabetical listing.

Norfolk jacket

norfolk shirt ∞ Man's lounging jacket styled like a shirt made of rough tweed with box pleat down center back and two box pleats on either side of front. Worn with matching belt. Had a tailored collar and bands at wrist. Worn from 1866 to 1880.

officer's coat See COATS AND JACKETS: GUARDSMAN COAT.

oriental wrapper See COATS AND JACKETS: ZOUAVE COAT.

overcoat Man's coat, heavier than a topcoat, designed for very cold weather. Sometimes lined with fur or modacrylic pile and made in any of a variety of styles.

Oxonian jacket ∞ Two- or three-button single-breasted tweed jacket worn by men in 1850s through 1860s. Made with many pockets and a back shaped by three seams. Also called *Oxford coatee.*

paddock coat Man's long semi-fitted overcoat worn from 1892 on, made with single- or double-breasted fly-front closing, large pockets, and pleat-covered back vent.

paletot ∞ (pal-ah-tow′ or pal-tow′) Generally meaning an outdoor coat or overcoat. Used for a number of different coat styles for men and women from approximately the 1830s to end of century. For men there were these variations. **1.** In 1830s, the paletot was a short overcoat made without a waistline seam and with or without a short back vent. Sometimes pleated at side seams. **2.** The **paletot-sac** was single- or double-breasted, cut short and straight, sometimes made with a collar, sometimes with a hood and worn in 1840s and 1850s, whereas the **English wrap** was a double-breasted paletot sac worn in 1840s and similar to a loose CHESTERFIELD COAT (see under COATS AND JACKETS). Women's paletots had these variations. **1.** Late 1830s to end of 19th c., a woman's caped three-quarter-length cloak that hung in stiff pleats from the shoulders. By mid-1840s it had three capes and armholes trimmed with flaps. **2.** From 1860s to 1880s, a woman's short paletot was also called a *yachting jacket.* **3.** From mid-1860s to mid-1880s, it was a long fitted outdoor coat—reaching to below the knees, frequently trimmed with lace and having tight sleeves. **4.** **paletot-redingote** (red′-in-gote), of late 1860s, was also long and fitted and made in Princess style with no seam at the waistline. It had buttons down the front and revers and was sometimes made with circular shoulder capes. **5.** Another paletot worn in 1870s had wide cuffed sleeves and WATTEAU PLEATS (see under CLOTHING CONSTRUCTION DETAILS) in the back. *Der.* Dutch *paltrok,* from *pals,* "palace" and *rok,* "garment."

paletot-redingote See COATS AND JACKETS: PALETOT.

paletot-sac See COATS AND JACKETS: PALETOT.

palmerston wrapper ∞ Man's single-breasted, loose-fitting SACK OVERCOAT (see under COATS AND JACKETS) of mid-1850s made with wide collar and lapels. Sleeves were full at wrists with no cuffs and pockets had side flaps. *Der.* Named after British statesman 3rd Viscount Palmerston, Henry John Temple, who was prime minister of England between 1855 and 1865.

pardessus ∞ (par-de´-soo)　1. French term for man's overcoat. **2.** Generic term used from 1840s to end of 19th c. for woman's outdoor garment of half or three-quarter length. Made with sleeves, fitted waistline, and frequently with a cape trimmed with lace or velvet. Also called *mantelet* and *paletot. Der.* French, "for on top."

parka　Loose-fitting pull-on jacket made with an attached hood that is sometimes trimmed with real or synthetic fur. Worn originally by the Eskimos and introduced during the 1930s for winter sportswear (e.g., ski-

parka

ing and skating). Still worn in all cold climates. *Der.* Russian-Aleutian, "pelt."

patrol jacket ∞ **1.** Men: Jacket of military cut made with five-button single-breasted closing and Prussian collar. Worn in late 1870s with tight knee pants for bicycling. **2.**Women: Tight-fitting hip-length jacket of late 1880s trimmed with military braid across front. Also had a standing collar at neck and tight-fitting sleeves finished with cuffs.

pea jacket/pea coat **1.** Copy of U.S. sailor's hip-length, straight, double-breasted navy-blue wool coat with notched lapels, vertical slash pockets, and vent in back. Inspiration for coats de-

pea jacket #1

signed by Yves Saint Laurent in Paris in 1960s and a classic coat style for men, women, and children. Also called *pea coat* and formerly

called a *pilot coat.* **2.** ∞ From 1830s on, man's double-breasted, unfitted thigh-length jacket with wide lapels and notched collar. Worn either as an overcoat or as a suit jacket. In 1850s had large buttons, usually six. Also called a *pilot coat. Der.* So called because it was made of "pilot cloth." From 1860 known as a *reefer.*

peasant coat　Mid-length coat lavishly trimmed down front with embroidery, sometimes with fur borders and cuffs, fashionable in late 1960s.

pelisse ∞ (peh-leese´)　Meanings and spellings of this term evolved over time. Its earliest forms involve some use of fur. Later it becomes a warm, winter outdoor garment. **1.** In the Middle Ages a **pelice** or **pelicon** (pel´-ees-sohn) referred to any of a number of fur-trimmed garments. **2.** In the 18th c., for women it was a caped, or hooded, three-quarter-length cloak with armhole slits and entire collar, hem, and front usu-

pelisse #3, 1819

ally edged with fur, sometimes with silk or satin. **3.** In the early 19th c. it was generally full-length, often made of handsome silk fabrics with a padded or quilted lining for warmth. Sometimes it had one or more shoulder capes. It was fitted and followed the current fashionable SILHOUETTE. Out of fashion by 1850. **4.** Revived in the late 1800s, for women it was a full-length winter mantle gathered on the shoulders and having loose sleeves, often made of silk, velvet, or satin. **5.** For men in the late 19th and early 20th c., the term was applied to a heavy fur-lined coat with fur collar, worn particularly with formal clothes. Also spelled *pellice.*

pembroke paletot ∞ (pal-ah-tow´ or pal-tow´) Man's calf-length, long-waisted overcoat worn in mid. 1850s made with wide lapels, double-breasted with eight buttons and easy-fitting sleeves with turned-back cuffs. Also had flapped side pockets and vertical breast pocket.

perfecto jacket　Black leather jacket, originating during World War II and worn by Marlon Brando in the 1954 film *The Wild One,* that became a symbol of rebellious youth and went on to become part of mainstream fashion. Synonym: *Bronx jacket.*

Petersham frock coat ∞ FROCK COAT (see under COATS AND JACKETS) of 1830s with slanted flapped pockets on hips and collar, lapels, and cuffs of velvet. *Der.* Named for Viscount Charles Petersham.

perfecto jacket

Petersham greatcoat ∞ Man's overcoat, with short shoulder cape, worn in 1830s. *Der.* Named for Viscount Charles Petersham.

pilot coat See COATS AND JACKETS: PEA JACKET.

pink coat Crimson-colored hunting jacket styled like a man's one-button suit coat with peaked lapels, back vent, and black velvet collar. Worn by men and women for fox-hunting. Also called *hunt coat.*

pocket siphonia See COATS AND JACKETS: SIPHONIA.

Polish greatcoat ∞ Full-length tight-fitting man's coat with collar, cuffs, and lapels of Russian lambskin. Closed with FROG fasteners (see under CLOSURES) or loops. Worn with evening dress in early 19th c.

Polish jacket ∞ Woman's waist-length jacket made with REVERS (see under NECKLINES AND COLLARS) and collar. Sleeves were wide at wrist, squared off, and slit to elbow on inside seam. Usually made of cashmere lined with quilted satin. Worn outdoors for informal occasions in mid-1840s.

polka ∞ **1.** Woman's short outdoor jacket of mid-1840s made with full sleeves, cashmere or velvet fabric and lined with silk. A variety of CASAWECK (see under COATS AND JACKETS). **2.** Woman's knitted close-fitting jacket.

polo coat Double- or single-breasted camel, vicuña, or camel-colored wool coat with notched collar and tied with a sash. Introduced in 1920s for men's spectator sports,

polo coat

for women in 1930s, this became a classic coat style that is made in many colors and fabrics.

polonaise ∞ (pol-on-nays′) **1.** Man's jacket of early 1770s, also called a *polonese frock.* **2.** In 1830s a military redingote, usually of blue fabric worn by civilians. Also called a *redingote.*

pommel slicker ∞ Raincoat worn when riding horseback in early 20th c. Similar to other raincoats but with long vent in back. Also called a *saddle coat.*

postillion coat ∞ (pos-till′-yon) Double-breasted fitted GREATCOAT (see COATS AND JACKETS) with flap pockets, high REGENCY COLLAR, and broad REVERS (see under NECKLINES AND COLLARS). *Der.* From clothes worn by *postillions,* "men on horseback accompanying carriages."

Prince Albert coat ∞ **1.** Double-breasted long FROCK COAT (see under COATS AND JACKETS) worn in late 19th c., with flat collar, usually of velvet. Worn for formal occasions (e.g., weddings and funerals) until about 1920. **2.** Adaptation of this coat for women worn in late 1890s—a double-breasted fitted, knee-length coat with turned-down collar and *revers,* flared skirt seamed at waistline, with two unpressed pleats with button trim at center back. *Der.* Named for Prince Albert of Saxe-Coburg-Gotha, consort of England's Queen Victoria.

Prince of Wales jacket ∞ Man's jacket of late 1860s similar to REEFER (see under COATS AND JACKETS). Cut in double-breasted style with three pairs of buttons. Named for Edward VII of England before he became king.

Prince Rupert ∞ Woman's full-length fitted coat of late 19th c. made of velvet or plush, worn with a blouse and skirt. *Der.* Named after Prince Rupert (1619–82), son of a Bohemian king, who supported Charles I in the English Civil War and became a councilor to Charles II after the restoration of the monarchy. His biography was published in 1899.

princess coat Woman's fitted coat cut in long panels that flare at hem. Has no seam at the waistline and usually made single-breasted. A classic style. *Der.* Style claimed to have been introduced by Worth about 1860 in a morning dress for Empress Eugénie.

Prussian collar coat ∞ Man's coat with narrow standing collar of 19th c. with ends nearly meeting in front, or worn turned down.

PVC jacket Hip-length simulated leather-look jackets made with conventional styling including a convertible collar, sometimes a yoke, buttoned- or zip-front, long sleeves, and tied or buckled belt. Made of polyvinyl chloride, a leather substitute that is soft and supple, washable, and water resistant.

pyramid coat Tent-shaped woman's coat of late 1940s and early 1950s made with narrow shoulders and wide hem.

raccoon coat Long bulky coat of raccoon fur with large rolled collar worn originally by college men in the 1920s. Popular again in the mid-1960s and usually purchased from thrift shops.

racing jacket Lightweight two-ply nylon jacket with zip-front and drawstring hem. Made in various official colors with a wide stripe outlined with two narrow stripes of red, running from shoulder to hem on left side. Jacket is wind-resistant and water-repellent. Originally worn for auto stock racing, now available for men and women. Usually has a patch printed on right chest with automobile brand emblems.

raglan cape/raglan coat Fly-front or double-breasted overcoat first worn in 1857. It had slit pockets and wide RAGLAN SLEEVES (see under SHOULDERS AND SLEEVES) that extended in V-shaped form to neck rather than having a seam at the shoulder. The name was subsequently applied to any long, loose coat with raglan sleeves. *Der.* Named for Lord Raglan (see RAGLAN, LORD).

raincoat Clothing originally designed to be worn in rainy weather, now also worn as *top coat* in fair weather. Made of waterproof material or given a special surface finish to make it water repellent. Raincoats were introduced in 1830 after the perfection of a rubberized fabric by Charles Macintosh in 1823. Original fabric was waterproof but had an objectionable odor. TRENCHCOATS (see under

COATS AND JACKETS) were introduced in World War I. Modern technology in the development of water-repellent finishes in recent years has made it possible to use a greater number of fabrics for raincoats. Another innovation is GORE-TEX®. Also see COATS AND JACKETS: SIPHONIA.

rain or shine coat Fabric coat treated with water-repellent finish so that it can be worn as an all-purpose coat.

rajah jacket **1.** *Men:* similar to NEHRU JACKET (see under COATS AND JACKETS). **2.** *Women:* usually a tunic-length jacket, with standing collar that is usually worn with pants. *Der.* Shortened form of "maharajah."

ranch coat Leather car coat or jacket made in western style with leather side uppermost, sometimes made of or lined with shearling (see LEATHERS).

redingote (red′-in-gote) Men: **1.** ∞ A full overcoat having a large collar worn for riding in France about 1725. **2.** ∞ In 1830 a greatcoat of blue cloth in military style closed with frogs, had sloping pockets, and a fur collar. Also called a *polonaise.* Women: **3.** ∞ Coat adapted from man's coat in 1790s in lighter-weight fabrics and worn as part of a dress rather than an outdoor coat. **4.** During the Empire period, it was an outer coat. **5.** ∞ From 1820s on, it was a dress cut like a coat either fastening down all the way down the front or with the skirt open to show an underskirt. **6.** ∞ In 1890s became an ensemble with matching coat and dress, with the coat usually being cut a little shorter than the dress. **7.** Contemporary: A matching or contrasting coat and dress worn together as an ensemble. *Der.* French, "mannish woman's frock coat" or English, "riding coat."

reefer **1.** Man's double-breasted, thigh-length boxy jacket called a *pea jacket* or *pilot coat* from 1830s to 1860s and taking on the name "reefer" about 1860.

reefer #5

See COATS AND JACKETS: PEA JACKET #2. **2.** ∞ Women's and children's short jacket of 1890s and early 20th c., frequently worn with matching skirt as a suit. Made with unfitted double-breasted front and fitted back. **3.** Since 1960s, a short double-breasted car coat. **4.** In 1930s and 1940s, a woman's single-breasted fitted coat with large lapels, revived in 1983 and in use as basic coat style after this.

Regency coat Double-breasted coat for man or woman made with wide lapels and high-rolled REGENCY COLLAR (see NECKLINES AND COLLARS.) Sometimes has large cuffs. Man's coat has nipped waist and deep vent in back. *Der.* Inspired by coats of the Regency period.

reversible jacket **1.** Any jacket that can be worn on either side. **2.** Short down-quilted nylon jacket with zip-out sleeves and zip-front made with knitted cuffs and waistband. Reverses to a knitted jacket with removable sleeves.

riding coat **1.** Tailored fitted jacket worn for horseback riding, similar in cut to PINK COAT, but in other colors or plaids. Also see COATS AND JACKETS: HACKING JACKET and PINK COAT. **2.** See COATS AND JACKETS: CUTAWAY.

sack jacket Loose, comfortable man's jacket, introduced in the late 1840s, that had no waistline, a straight front, center vent in back, sleeves without cuffs, and a small collar with short lapels. Called a *lounging jacket* in England, this jacket is a forerunner of tuxedo jackets and contemporary men's sport jackets.

sack overcoat ∞ Man's above-the-knee, loose-fitting overcoat worn from 1840s to about 1875. Made with sleeves wide at wrist, WELT POCKETS (see under POCKETS), and back cut in one piece with center slit. The edges of coat were double-stitched or bound. In 1860s closed higher and styled with three or four-button closing, narrow lapels, optional pockets, and sometimes trimmed with velvet at collar, cuffs, and lapels.

sack jacket 1840s

saddle coat See COATS AND JACKETS: POMMEL SLICKER.

safari coat See COATS AND JACKETS: BUSH JACKET.

Sardinian sac ∞ Loose-fitting single-breasted man's overcoat of mid-19th c. Made with square-cut collar, no lapels, and full bell-shaped sleeves. Worn flung over shoulders and secured by cord with tassel in front.

Scarborough ulster ∞ Caped and hooded man's ULSTER (see under COATS AND JACKETS) without sleeves worn in early 1890s.

señorita ∞ Woman's waist-length, bolero-style jacket of mid-1860s made with three-quarter- or full-length sleeves and lavishly trimmed with braid, fringe, buttons, or lace. Worn over a blouse with full sleeves. Also called a *Spanish jacket.*

shearling jacket Jacket made of a sheepskin tanned with wool attached. Leather side is sueded or buffed and used for the outside of the coat, with woolly side worn inside. Collar is made with wool side out. Also called *sheepskin jacket.*

sheepskin jacket See COATS AND JACKETS: SHEARLING JACKET.

shirt-jac See SHIRTS.

shooting coat ∞ Term used from 1860s to 1890s for morning coat. See COATS AND JACKETS: CUTAWAY.

shortie coat Woman's short coat, about finger-tip length, made in boxy fitted or semi-fitted styles, worn in 1940s and 1950s. Revived periodically.

show coat Longer style riding jacket or suit coat with hacking pockets (pockets with flaps placed at an angle), fitted waist, narrow lapels, three-button closing, inverted pleats at sides, and long slash in center back. Worn for semi-formal showing of horses.

simar ∞ (si-mar´) Woman's loose-fitting jacket with side flaps, or skirts, extending to knees, sometimes worn over petticoat to make a dress in 17th and 18th c. Also spelled *samarre.*

siphonia ∞ (sy-fo-ni-a) Long weather-proof overcoat worn by men in 1850s and 1860s. The **pocket siphonia** was short and thin enough to be rolled up and carried in case of rain.

skeleton waterproof ∞ Woman's full-length front-buttoned raincoat of 1890s made with large armholes, instead of sleeves, covered by a hip-length circular cape.

ski jacket Any type of wind-resistant jacket worn when skiing. Conventional type zips up front and may be made of nylon, wool, fur, or quilted fabric. Frequently has an attached hood. Usually made waist or hip length with zippered pockets.

slicker **1.** Bright-yellow oilskin coat, or similar coat of rubberized fabric in other colors, usually fastened with clips in front. Originally worn by sailors, now often worn with SOU′WESTER HAT (see HEADWEAR) by fishermen and children. **2.** A type of yellow rubber raincoat with slash in back to waist and extra insert so that each side can be fastened around legs to form protection when riding horseback in rainy weather.

sling-duster ∞ British term for coat worn by women in mid- and late 1880s. Made with DOLMAN or SLING SLEEVES (see SHOULDERS AND SLEEVES). Frequently made of black-and-white checked silk.

smoking jacket **1.** Man's jacket of velvet or other luxurious cloth, or with velvet or satin shawl collar. May be with or without buttons, sometimes has a sash, and is worn at home for informal entertaining, since 1850. **2.** English version of American TUXEDO JACKET (see under COATS AND JACKETS), a short black semiformal dinner jacket made with satin lapels, called by the French "le smoking." Adapted for women by Paris designer, Yves Saint Laurent, in mid-1960s.

smoking jacket #1 1893

snorkel jacket Warm hooded parka, made with front-opening zipper extending up over the wearer's chin, giving the hood the look of a "snorkel" (a submarine's air-intake or exhaust tube). Made hip- to knee-length usually of water-repellent nylon satin or taffeta with quilted or pile lining and fake-fur edging around hood. Characterized by an inside drawstring waistline and knitted inner cuffs. Also has a multiplicity of zippered and snapped pockets, including one for pencils on the sleeve and a flap fastened with buttons and loops to keep snow out of the front zipper. Very popular in early 1970s for men, women, and children.

Spanish jacket ∞ **1.** See COATS AND JACKETS: SEÑORITA. **2.** Short sleeveless jacket worn in 1862, somewhat similar to a bolero with no fasteners in front. Sometimes has a collar attached to a low neckline and often has rounded edges at hem in front.

spencer Short open jacket, usually ending at or above the waistline. A version with lapels and long sleeves was reintroduced in mid-1980s for women. Thought to have been first worn by a British peer, Lord Spencer, and worn by men from 1790 to 1850 and by women from 1790 until about 1820. Three different stories of the origin of the style are told: (a) Lord Spencer burned one of the coattails of his jacket and cut off the other; (b) He was out riding and tore one of the coattails, so tore off the other; and (c) He made a wager he could start a new fashion and proceeded to cut off the coattails of his jacket, thus creating a new popular fashion.

spencer c. 1810

spencerette ∞ Woman's fitted jacket with low-cut neckline edged with lace worn at end of Empire Period, about 1814.

sport jacket **1.** Conventional tailored jacket made in tweed, plaid, or plain colors worn with contrasting pants for business and general wear since 1920s. Also see COATS AND JACKETS: BLAZER. **2.** Outerwear worn for school and general wear in place of coat during warmer weather or on informal occasions. **3.** Outerwear designed for specific sports, e.g., golf, skiing, and cycling, sometimes accepted for general wear.

sport jacket #1

stadium coat **1.** Car coat of three-quarter length sometimes made with SHEARLING collar (see FURS and LEATHER) and TOGGLE closing (see under CLOSURES) introduced in early 1960s. By 1980s sometimes made with inner-zipper VEST SWEATER (see under SWEATERS) in front. **2.** In early 1980s three-quarter-length reversible jacket made of waterproof vinyl with drawstring hood, two large pockets, and fastened with grippers at sleeves and front. *Der.* Worn at football stadiums.

storm coat Heavy coat sometimes quilted and made with water-repellent finish. May be styled with SHEARLING (see under FURS), pile or quilted fabric lining and collar. By 1980s entire coat was made of quilted nylon.

stroller jacket ∞ A semiformal man's suit jacket similar to a TUXEDO JACKET with satin lapels and peaked collar. Also called a SACK JACKET (see cross-references under COATS AND JACKETS).

suburban coat Same as COATS AND JACKETS: CAR COAT.

sultane jacket ∞ (sul-tane′) Very short, sleeveless bolero-type woman's jacket worn in late 1880s. Similar to ZOUAVE JACKET (see under COATS AND JACKETS).

surtout (ser-too′) **1.** Contemporary French and British term for man's cloak or overcoat. *Der.* French, literally "over all." **2.** Synonymous with a number of different overcoat styles in the 17th to the 19th c. See listings under COATS AND JACKETS for BRANDENBURG, WRAP-RASCAL, GREATCOAT, and WRAPPER #2. **3.** Caped coat worn by women in late 18th c.

swagger coat Pyramid-shaped woman's coat with flared bias back. Usually with raglan sleeves and large saucer-shaped buttons attached by fabric cord. Popular in 1930s, revived in 1970s.

swallow-tailed coat Man's formal evening coat that does not button in front, and is cut with peaked lapels trimmed with satin or grosgrain. Made waist-length in front with two

swallow-tailed coat
c. 1895

long tails in back. *Der.* Back resembles the "tail of a swallow." Also called *tails*.

sweater coat Knitted, often cardigan-style, coat.

sweat jacket Garment similar to a sweatshirt but open down the front and closing with buttons or a zipper. Made of cotton knit jersey with cotton fleece lining. Originally gray-colored, but now made in any color.

Taglioni (tal-yoh-nee′) Man's fitted GREAT-COAT (see under COATS AND JACKETS) reaching to knees, worn from 1839 to 1845. Usually double-breasted with wide turned-back lapels, large flat collar, and cuffs of satin or velvet. Also had a back vent and slit pockets bound with twill fabric. *Der.* Named after Italian ballet master Filippo Taglioni (1777–1871).

Taglioni frock coat Man's single-breasted FROCK COAT (see under COATS AND JACKETS) worn from 1838 to 1842, made with short full skirt, broad notched collar, slashed or flapped pockets, and back vent. *Der.* Named after Italian ballet master Filippo Taglioni (1777–1871).

tail coat/tails See COATS AND JACKETS: SWALLOW-TAILED COAT.

Tallien redingote ∞ (tal-ee-en′ red′-in-gote) Outdoor coat worn by women in late 1860s, created by French couturier Worth. Matched to dress or made of black silk, coat had a heart-shaped neckline, full back, and a sash tied in large bow with long ends in back. Small bows were tied to ends of sash. *Der.* Named for Theresa Tallien, Princess de Chimay (1773–1835), a fashionable woman who is said to have owned 30 wigs of different colors.

Talma lounge ∞ A jacket worn by men in 1898 made with raglan sleeves, straight fronts, and curved or slanted pockets. Worn as an informal jacket. *Der.* Named for François Joseph Talma (1763–1826), a French tragic actor of Consulate and Empire period.

Talma overcoat ∞ Raglan-sleeved greatcoat with large armholes worn by men in 1898. *Der.* Named for François Joseph Talma (1763–1826), a French tragic actor of Consulate and Empire period.

teddybear coat ∞ Bulky coat of natural-colored alpaca-pile fabric worn by men, women, and children in 1920s. *Der.* Named after the teddy bear, a child's toy of early 20th c., which was named for President Theodore Roosevelt.

templar cloak See COATS AND JACKETS: CABAN.

tent coat Woman's pyramid-shaped coat, widely flared at hem, popular in 1930s, 1940s, and in mid-1960s. Revived periodically.

three-decker ∞ Term used from late 1870s on for man's or woman's triple-caped ULSTER (see under COATS AND JACKETS).

three-seamer British tailoring term for man's jacket with center back seam and two side seams, contrasted with coat having SIDE BODIES and five seams. Used from 1860 on.

toggle coat See COATS AND JACKETS: DUFFEL COAT.

topcoat **1.** Man's or woman's lightweight coat in any style, designed to wear over suit jacket or dress. See COATS AND JACKETS: OVERCOAT. **2.** ∞ Woman's tailored, full-length, straight-cut coat worn in 1890s, with moderate LEG-OF-MUTTON SLEEVES (see under SHOULDERS AND SLEEVES), tailored collar, and fly-front closing. Had large flap pockets on hips and small ticket pocket above.

top frock ∞ Man's overcoat cut like a FROCK COAT (see under COATS AND JACKETS) but longer, worn from 1830 on. Usually double-breasted and intended to be worn without a suit coat.

topper coat Woman's hip-length coat, often made with a flared silhouette, popular in early 1940s.

toreador jacket (tor-ay´-ah-dor) Waist-length woman's jacket with epaulet shoulder trimming frequently braid-trimmed and worn unfastened. Adapted from jackets of bullfighters in Spain and Mexico.

tow coat Three-quarter-length coat similar to a *toggle coat* or *duffel coat,* designed for winter sports.

trench coat Coat created by Thomas Burberry during World War I for soldiers that was made of a chemically finished, water-repellent cotton gabardine. After the War the style became an all-purpose civilian coat made of a water-repellent fabric in double-breasted style with a convertible collar, large

lapels, epaulets, fabric belt, slotted pockets, and a vent in the back. Over the shoulders in back it had an extra hanging yoke and an extra flap hung from the front right shoulder. In the 1940s women adopted the trench coat, which has become a classic style.

trench coat

tuxedo jacket Man's semiformal jacket made in one-button style with shawl collar usually faced with satin or faille. Until the late 1960s, it was conventionally black or navy for winter and white for summer. Now styled in any color or pattern (e.g., red, green, blue, or plaid fabrics, sometimes with notched collar). Introduced in 1886. *Der.* After Tuxedo Park Country Club, Tuxedo Park, New York, where it was first worn by Griswold P. Lorillard. Also called a *dinner jacket.*

tweed jacket **1.** Man's conventional sport jacket of tweed wool fabric or a wool blend usually made with traditional single-breasted styling. **2.** Women's jacket of almost any style made out of yarn-dyed wool of a textured nature and usually worn with matching skirt or pants. Popular in the 1920s and 1930s for women as suitable for the "country" rather than town wear.

ulster **1.** ∞ Man's heavy overcoat introduced in late 1860s. Usually made in single- or double-breasted style with a belted back or with a complete belt and detachable hood. By the 1870s, a cape was more usual. About 1875, a TICKET POCKET (see POCKETS) was placed in left sleeve above cuff, and by 1890 a *fly-front* closing was used. Length varied, the coat being ankle length in 1870s. **2.** ∞ Woman's coat similar to man's worn from late 1870s on. When made with a triple cape, it was called a CARRICK. Sometimes made of waterproof fabric, sometimes with a train. *Der.* Named after a northern province of Ireland in which the cities of Belfast and London-derry, manufacturing centers for heavy coats, are located. **3.** British name for a long, loose-fitting overcoat.

varens ∞ Woman's short outdoor jacket of 1847 with loose sleeves. Made of cashmere or velvet with silk lining, a variation of the CASAWECK and POLKA (see under COATS AND JACKETS).

vareuse ∞ (vah-reuz′) Rough woolen over-blouse or jacket, similar to COATS AND JACKETS: PEA JACKET.

varsity jacket See COATS AND JACKETS: BASEBALL JACKET.

vinyl raincoat (vine′-ul) **1.** Waterproof raincoat usually made of heavy clear vinyl. Special attention must be paid to sewing the seams, or it will tear where the sewing machine perforates it. **2.** Fabric given a vinyl finish and used to make a raincoat.

waistcoat paletot ∞ (pal-ah-tow′ or pal-tow′) Woman's knee-length coat of 1884 in tailored style buttoned only at neckline, made with hip-length waistcoat showing in front.

walking coat Knee-length single-breasted coat with a notched collar.

wamus (wah′-muss) Heavy outdoor jacket or cardigan of coarse cloth, buttoned at collar and wrists worn in the United States. Also spelled *wammus, wampus.*

watch coat Short, heavy, windproof coat worn by sailors on watch. Also see COATS AND JACKETS: PEA COAT.

Watteau coat ∞ (wat-toe′) Lady's princess-style coat of the 1890s made in fitted unbuttoned style with waistcoat showing in front. Usually had a standing collar, wide lapels, and turned-back cuffs with characteristic single or double box pleat in center back. *Der.* Named for the artist Antoine Watteau (1684–1721).

Wellesley wrapper Above-the-knee double-breasted sack-like coat, worn in 1853 by men and fastened in front with BRANDENBURGS (see CLOSURES: FROGS).

western jacket Jacket like those worn by American cowboys, made of buckskin or fabric with breast pockets, a yoke, and sometimes having a fringe of leather on yoke, sleeves, and hem.

windbreaker/Windbreaker® Formerly a trademark and continues in common usage for a warm lightweight nylon jacket zipped up front with close-fitting waistband and cuffs, often made with attached hood. Trademark now applies to a wide variety of apparel items.

wraparound coat Woman's coat made without buttons or fasteners in front and held closed with long self-fabric sash. Also called *wrap coat.*

wrapper ∞ **1.** Man's loose overcoat, worn in 1840s, either single- or double-breasted. Sometimes used to indicate a CHESTERFIELD (see under COATS AND JACKETS). **2.** In the 1850s, man's loose thigh-length overcoat, with shawl collar, that wrapped in front, sometimes worn with evening dress.

wrap-rascal ∞ Man's loose-fitting overcoat made of heavy fabric, worn from about 1738 to 1850. The 19th-c. type usually referred to coats worn when traveling on the outside of a coach. Also worn in the country.

yachting coat ∞ Woman's hip-length, square-cut jacket worn from 1860s to 1880s. Made single- or double-breasted with large buttons and loose sleeves. Also called *short paletot.* See COATS AND JACKETS: PALETOT.

yachting jacket Double-breasted four-button man's jacket with lapels and collar, usually styled in navy-blue wool with brass buttons. Made similar to U.S. Naval uniforms with black braid instead of gold, and yacht club buttons instead of Navy buttons; worn on board by yacht club members.

Zhivago coat (zhi-vah′go) Mid-calf-length coat, lavishly trimmed with fur at neck, cuffs, and hem, sometimes with frog closing. Inspired by costumes worn in *Dr. Zhivago*, 1965 film of Boris Pasternak's novel about the 1917 Russian Revolution.

zip-off coat Long coat styled to be used in two or three lengths, achieved by placing zippers at mini and midi lengths. When made to have only two lengths, may be called a *duo-length coat.*

Zouave coat ∞ (zoo-ahv′) Man's cloak of mid-1840s with velvet collar and cuffs and quilted silk lining. Used for riding, walking, or worn to the opera. Same as the *oriental wrapper.* *Der.* Arabic, *Zouaova*, a Kabyle tribe, one of the Berbers, living in Algeria or Tunisia.

Zouave jacket ∞ (zoo-ahv′) **1.** Woman's waist-length, bolero-type jacket fastened at the neck and with curved sides in front. Had three-quarter-length sleeves cut rather full. Showed military influence in the trim inspired by Algerian Zouave troops and an American Northern Troop of the Civil War. Fashionable 1859 to 1870 and revived in the 1890s. **2.** Similar jacket worn by little boys in the 1860s. *Der.* Arabic, *Zouaova*, a Kabyle tribe, one of the Berbers, living in Algeria or Tunisia.

zouave jacket #1

Zouave paletot ∞ (zoo-ahv′ pal-ah-tow′ or pal-tow′) Waterproofed llama-wool coat worn by men with or without a suitcoat in 1840s. *Der.* Arabic, *Zouaova*, a Kabyle tribe, one of the Berbers, living in Algeria or Tunisia.

---

coat-style pajamas See SLEEPWEAR AND LOUNGE-WEAR.

coat sweater See SWEATERS.

coattail See COATS AND JACKETS.

cobbler Shoemaker, a term first used in Middle Ages. Also called a *cordwainer*.

cobbler's apron See APRONS.

cobra chain See CHAIN.

cocarde See COCKADE #1.

cock ∞ Term used from end of 17th to early 19th c. for turning up a hat brim. Given various names for manner of turn-up. Also see HEAD-WEAR: COCKED HAT.

cockade **1.** Ornamental rosette or bow of ribbon, usually made flat around a center button. Sometimes worn as a part of a uniform or badge of office, e.g., tricolor cockade of red, white, and blue worn on side of hat as patriotic symbol during French Revolution. Also called *cocarde.* **2.** Feather trimming. See FEATHERS. **3.** See FANS.

cocked hat See HEADWEAR.

cockers See FOOTWEAR.

cock feather See FEATHERS.

cockle See HAIRSTYLES.

cockle hat See HEADWEAR.

cockscomb See COXCOMB.

cocktail Adjective applied to clothing and accessories worn at cocktail parties, social gatherings where various short alcoholic drinks are served before dinner. See COCKTAIL DRESS, APRONS: COCKTAIL APRON, GLOVES AND GLOVE CONSTRUCTION: COCKTAIL GLOVES, and JEWELRY: COCKTAIL RING.

cocktail dress Contemporary term for short evening dress with décolleté neckline made in luxury fabrics. Suitable for formal late-afternoon or cocktail parties; popular in the 1950s.

coconut straw/coco straw Braided straw, usually tan or light brown, made from coconut-palm leaves.

cocoon See COATS AND JACKETS and SLEEPWEAR AND LOUNGEWEAR.

cocurs See FOOTWEAR: COCKERS.

codovec See HEADWEAR: CASTOR.

codpiece ∞ **1.** Triangular flap at front of crotch of men's trunk hose large enough for a pocket, frequently padded and decorated, worn during 15th and 16th c. Shown at TRUNK HOSE and DOUBLET. **2.** By early 17th c. term applied to front fastening of BREECHES. Also called a *cod placket.* Compare with BRAYETTE.

cod placket See CODPIECE #2.

Codrington See COATS AND JACKETS.

coffer headdress See HEADWEAR.

coggers See FOOTWEAR: COCKERS.

coif (kwaf) **1.** Short for coiffure. French, "hairstyle." See HAIRSTYLES. **2.** (verb) To style or dress the hair. **3.** See HEADWEAR.

coiffe de mailles See ARMOR.

coiffette See ARMOR.

coiffure (kwa′-fure) French term used in English since 18th c. for hairdressing or arrangement of hair. *Note: coiffeur* (m.) (kwa′-fuhr) and *coiffeuse* (f.) (kwa′-fuhz) are the French words for hairdressers.

coiffure à l'Agnès Sorel See HAIRSTYLES.

coiffure à la Grecque See HAIRSTYLES: GREEK COIFFURE.

coiffure à la hérisson See HAIRSTYLES: HÉRISSON.

coiffure à la indépendance See HAIRSTYLES.

coiffure à la Maintenon See HAIRSTYLES.

coiffure à la mouton See HAIRSTYLES.

coiffure à la Ninon See HAIRSTYLES: NINON COIFFURE.

coiffure à la Sévigné   See HAIRSTYLES.

coiffure à la Titus   See HAIRSTYLES.

coiffure à la zazzera   See HAIRSTYLES.

coiffure à l'enfant   See HAIRSTYLES.

coiffure en bouffons   See HAIRSTYLES.

coiffure en bourse   See HAIRSTYLES and WIGS AND HAIRPIECES: BAGWIG.

coiffure en cadenettes   See HAIRSTYLES.

coiffure en raquette   See HAIRSTYLES.

coiled bracelet   See BRACELETS.

coin de feu   See COATS AND JACKETS.

coin dot   See PRINTS, STRIPES, AND CHECKS: DOTS.

coin necklace   See JEWELRY.

coin purse   See HANDBAGS AND RELATED ACCESSORIES: CHANGE PURSE.

coin silver   Strong silver alloy, containing 90% silver and 10% copper; used for jewelry. The only silver available to early American Colonists, obtained by melting down silver coins.

cointise ∞ (kwan-teez′)   **1.** Cut-out decoration used on the overgarment, worn from 13th and 14th c., also the garment itself. **2.** See ARMOR.

cokers   See COCKERS.

Colbert embroidery   See EMBROIDERIES AND SEWING STITCHES.

Colbertine lace   See LACES.

cold mask   See MASKS: HOT MASK.

collar   **1.** See introduction to NECKLINES AND COLLARS. **2.** See FOOTWEAR: QUARTER.

collar and cuff set   Women's separate collar and cuffs usually made of linen, lace, organdy, or other sheer fabrics—often white, trimmed with lace, insertion, embroidery, or tucks. Popular from early 15th c. until 1930s and used occasionally since.

collar button   See CLOSURES: STUD.

collaret   **1.** See NECKLINES AND COLLARS. **2.** See ARMOR.

collarette à la Lyon   See NECKLINES AND COLLARS: CHERUSSE.

collar necklace   See JEWELRY.

collar pin   See JEWELRY.

collar stay   Narrow strip of plastic or metal inserted in point of man's collar from the underside to ensure a crisp unwrinkled look.

collection   Term used by couture, ready-to-wear, or manufacturer's designer for clothing and accessories offered to customers for a specific season.

Originally used only for high-priced couture clothing. Also called **line.**

Colleen Bawn cloak   See CAPES, CLOAKS, AND SHAWLS.

collegians   See FOOTWEAR: OXONIAN BOOT.

colley-westonward ∞ 16th-c. slang meaning "worn awry" or "crooked," usually applied to the MANDILION JACKET (see COATS AND JACKETS), which was worn without putting arms through sleeves and turned sideways so that one sleeve hung in front, the other in back. *Der.* From a Cheshire, England, saying for "anything that goes wrong."

colobium   **1.** See UNDERGARMENTS. **2.** See CLERICAL DRESS.

Colonial shoe/pump   See FOOTWEAR.

Colonial tongue   See FOOTWEAR.

color blocking   Use of large geometrical areas of contrasting color in dresses, blouses, jackets. Shown at MONDRIAN DRESS.

color forecasting   Predictions of color preferences developed through research carried out by color forecasting companies, textile, and apparel companies.

color-graded glasses   See EYEWEAR.

colorway   The three or four color choices available of a solid or printed fabric for a garment style produced in more than one color.

columnar heel   See FOOTWEAR.

comb   **1.** An article—often of tortoise shell, ivory, plastic, wood, or metal—with a row of narrow teeth that is drawn through the hair or beard to arrange or untangle it. **2.** Combs of precious metals or those decorated with jewels are often placed in women's hair to hold it in place and as decorations, especially at sides of head or in back when hair is set in a twist. Earliest combs are from late Stone Age.

combat boot   See FOOTWEAR.

combed yarn   † Yarn made from short fibers, known in the textile industry as STAPLE FIBERS, that have been subjected to the process of combing. Combing is an optional step in the spinning of yarns in which fibers that have been carded are subjected to further straightening and alignment, formed into a strand of fibers, and given a greater or lesser amount of twist to form them into a yarn. Combed yarns have fewer fibers on the surface, are smoother, and can be finer yarns than those that have only been carded. See CARDED YARNS.

combination last See FOOTWEAR: LAST.

combinations See UNDERWEAR: COMBINATIONS.

combination tanning See LEATHERS.

combing See COMBED YARN.

combing jacket See COATS AND JACKETS.

comb morion See ARMOR: MORION.

comedy mask See MASKS.

comfort collar See NECKLINES AND COLLARS.

comforter See SCARVES.

commander's cap See HEADWEAR.

commercial match A color match between components of a style that are provided by a contractor and that is satisfactory to the manufacturer.

Commes des Garçons * See KAWAKUBO, REI under APPENDIX/DESIGNERS.

commissionaire Middleman who operates in foreign countries buying merchandise for American retailers.

commode See HEADWEAR: FONTANGE.

commodore cap See HEADWEAR.

commodore dress ∞ Dress with nautical braid trim worn by girls and young ladies in early 1890s. Typical dress might have a wide braid trimmed sailor collar and gathered skirt with braid trim near the hem. Usually worn with a flat SAILOR HAT or a COMMODORE HAT. (See HEADWEAR.)

Common sense heel See FOOTWEAR.

Communion dress Clothing customarily worn by children when taking their first Communion in the Catholic church. Girls' dress generally consists of a white dress worn with a short white veil. Boys generally wear a white suit. Also see HEADWEAR: COMMUNION VEIL.

compact Cosmetic container used to hold powder, rouge, eye shadow, and sometimes lipstick. Made of metal or plastic with mirrored lid.

compass cloak See CAPES, CLOAKS, AND SHAWLS: FRENCH CLOAK.

competition stripes See SHIRTS and CHECKS, PRINTS, AND STRIPES.

computer-aided design (CAD) Computer hardware and software systems for designing apparel and implementing their manufacture. This technology can significantly decrease errors and save time because the effects of changes in design can be seen on the computer screen without making actual samples.

computer-aided design/computer-aided manufacturing (CAD/CAM) The linking of computer systems for creating designs with those for pattern creation, GRADING, and MARKER in order to coordinate the steps in production.

computer-aided manufacturing (CAM) Computer hardware and software systems that GRADE and make MARKERS electronically. They may also have the capability to do computer-controlled cutting, use lasers for specialized cutting, and employ robotics in manufacturing. These systems lower the use of manual labor, but because of the initial high capital investment it is generally only large manufacturers that utilize this sophisticated technology to the maximum.

computer dress Dress made from discarded computer chips hooked together, sometimes made in one-shoulder style with asymmetric hemlines. Chips are collected from computers, TVs, and other electronic machines. Dresses sold in 1984 by Panages, from $2,000 to $50,000.

computer grading and marker making (CGMM) The computer hardware and software systems that process the pattern grading and marker-making segments of a garment pattern for production.

computer integrated manufacturing (CIM) The production of a finished product by integrating various computer-aided processes (such as CAD, CAM, CGMM) that can link information and equipment throughout the manufacturing process.

computer pattern Sewing pattern developed in 1960s, made to fit the individual. Salesperson in store takes customer's measurements, which are then sent to a pattern company and fed into a computer to produce a custom-cut pattern for garment.

conch ∞ (conk or consh) Sheer, gauzelike veil of the late 16th c. extending from shoulder to floor and worn capelike over the shoulders.

conch 16th c.

At the back of the neck, it was attached to a winglike construction that stood up like a high collar behind the head.

concierge   See HAIRSTYLES: POMPADOUR.

conductor's cap   See HEADWEAR.

coney/cony   See FURS.

confidants   See HAIRSTYLES.

congress boot   See FOOTWEAR.

Connolly, Sybil   * See APPENDIX/DESIGNERS.

considerations   See UNDERWEAR: PANNIERS.

consignment   Goods stocked by a retailer but not paid for until they are sold. After selling the goods, the retailer pays the person or firm that provided the goods a price agreed-upon at the time of consignment.

constable   See CANE.

Consumer Product Safety Commission (CPSC)   A U.S. federal government agency that oversees product safety and, as part of its responsibilities, monitors flammability regulations for apparel and home furnishings.

continental   Adjective applied to garments thought to have originated in one of the countries on the continent of Europe. See CONTINENTAL SUIT, PANTS: CONTINENTAL PANTS, and POCKETS: CONTINENTAL POCKETS.

continental hat   See HEADWEAR: COCKED HAT.

continental heel   See FOOTWEAR.

continental stitch   See EMBROIDERIES AND SEWING STITCHES.

continental suit   Man's suit with natural shoulderline, easy fitting jacket, and narrow tapered trousers with no belt. Pockets in trousers are slanted from waistline to side seams. Style originated in Italy in 1950s.

continuous filament yarn   † Manufactured yarns made by pushing the spinning fluid through a nozzle, or spinerette with tiny holes, producing strands of indefinite length. When only one strand is produced, a **monofilament yarn** is formed; when many strands are produced, a MULTIFILAMENT YARN is formed.

contour belt   See BELTS.

contour bra   See UNDERGARMENTS.

contour clutch   See HANDBAGS AND RELATED ACCESSORIES.

contractor   A person or firm that agrees to construct apparel for a manufacturer or retailer.

contractual retailer   Retailer that has made contractual arrangements with other retailers, with a manufacturer, or with a wholesaler that may be advantageous in simplifying management and increasing market impact. Examples of contractual arrangements include FRANCHISES and LEASED DEPARTMENTS.

control   Describes garments such as women's girdles, foundations, or pantyhose made with elastomeric yarns (see ELASTOMER), which provide support. See HOSIERY: CONTROL PANTYHOSE, UNDERGARMENTS: CONTROL BRIEF, and CONTROL PANTS.

controls   In retailing, refers to the methods used by a retailer to monitor business operations and evaluate the effectiveness of merchandising strategies. Also see MAZUR PLAN.

convenience goods   Products that require relatively little evaluation before their purchase by consumers. Compare with SHOPPING GOODS and SPECIALTY GOODS .

conversation bonnet   See HEADWEAR: POKE BONNET.

converted goods   † Textile fabrics processed by a CONVERTER.

converter   † In the textile industry, a middleman, either a firm or an individual, that takes woven goods in an unfinished state and applies finishing processes (e.g., dyeing, bleaching, waterproofing). After processing, fabrics are suitable for the clothing manufacturer or the yard goods retailer.

convertible   Adjective applied to articles of clothing that can be changed in appearance or form by some means. Example: NECKLINES AND COLLARS: CONVERTIBLE.

cookie   See FOOTWEAR: ARCH CUSHION.

coolie   Unskilled Asian laborer who wears distinctive clothing and hat often copied by fashion designers. See COATS AND JACKETS and HEADWEAR.

coolie hat   See HEADWEAR.

coonskin cap   See HEADWEAR: DAVY CROCKETT CAP.

co-op advertising   A type of advertising strategy whereby companies share the cost of an advertisement that features a number of companies.

cooperative buying office   See ASSOCIATED BUYING OFFICE.

cope See CLERICAL DRESS and CAPES, CLOAKS, AND SHAWLS.

copotain See HEADWEAR.

copped shoe See FOOTWEAR: CRAKOW.

copper toe See FOOTWEAR.

copyist Person in the apparel trade who makes replicas of designs—translating a high-priced item to a lower price for a manufacturer.

coq feathers See FEATHERS.

coquette parasol See UMBRELLAS AND PARASOLS: MARQUISE.

coral See GEMS, GEM CUTS, AND SETTINGS.

corazza See SHIRTS.

cord † **1.** The result of twisting together two or more ply yarns. **2.** A surface effect in fabrics that creates ridges running in the lengthwise direction. **3.** See LACE: CORDONNET.

cordé handbag See HANDBAGS AND RELATED ACCESSORIES.

corded seam See CLOTHING CONSTRUCTION DETAILS.

cordelière ∞ (kor′-deh-lyare′) Long chain, often of gold, that hung from belt, or girdle, and used to hold a cross, scissors, or other small items worn by women in the 16th c. *Der.* French, "cord or girdle worn by Franciscan friar." Also spelled *cordilier.* Also see CHATELAINE.

cording **1.** Trimming made by inserting a soft ropelike cord into a strip of bias-cut fabric. **2.** Full-rounded trimming used for frogs and loops made by pulling the cord through a seamed tube of BIAS fabric to cover cord completely.

cordonnet See LACE.

cordovan See LEATHERS.

corduroy † (kohr′-duh-roy) Strong durable woven fabric with vertical stripes of cut pile that are formed by an extra system of crosswise yarns. The lengthwise stripes may be made in various widths. Those that are very narrow are called **pinwale** . Usually made of cotton or a cotton blend. The name is thought to derive from the French *corde du roi,* meaning "cord of the king."

corduroy knit † Knitted fabric made with stripes of cut pile in imitation of woven corduroy fabric.

cordwainer ∞ Obsolete term for a shoemaker. Originally signified one who worked in cordovan leather (from Cordova, Spain), making shoes and other leather items. See LEATHER: CORDOVAN.

cord yarn † Heavy yarn made by twisting together two or more PLY YARNS. Used in BENGALINE, OTTOMAN, and BEDFORD CORD fabrics. Called *cable yarn* in Great Britain.

cordyback hat See HEADWEAR: CAUDEBAC.

core yarn † Yarn made with a heavy center cord around which are wrapped finer yarns of different fibers (e.g., synthetic rubber core wrapped with rayon, cotton, or silk) to improve absorption and feel. Also see ELASTOMERIC YARNS.

cork **1.** Outer bark of oak, *Querous suber,* grown in Mediterranean countries. Stripped, dried, and boiled to remove sap and tannic acid, then used for fillers in shoes, for clogs, for tropical hats, and for other items that require low weight, resilience, moisture resistance, and insulation against heat. **2.** FOOTWEAR: GALOSH.

corkies See FOOTWEAR: WEDGE HEEL.

cork lace See LACES.

cork rump See UNDERGARMENTS.

corkscrew curl See HAIRSTYLES.

corkscrew wig See WIGS AND HAIRPIECES.

cornalia See VEILS: ORALIA.

corned shoe See FOOTWEAR.

cornercap See ACADEMIC COSTUME: MORTARBOARD.

cornet **1.** See HEADWEAR: HENNIN. **2.** See HEADWEAR. **3.** See SKIRTS.

cornet sleeve See SHOULDERS AND SLEEVES.

cornrows See HAIRSTYLES.

cornu See HEADWEAR: ORALIA.

coronal See CORONET.

coronation braid See BRAIDS.

coronation robes **1.** Three capes worn by British king or queen for coronation at various times during the ceremony: (a) a red cape lined with white, (b) an ecclesiastical COPE (see under CLERICAL DRESS), and (c) a purple velvet cloak trimmed with ermine. **2.** Ermine trimmed robes worn by British nobility attending the coronation with trains of prescribed lengths according to rank. Worn with various types of CORONETS (see HEADWEAR) according to rank. Also called *robes of state.*

coronet See HEADWEAR.

corps (cor) 17th-c. French term for BODICE.

corps à baleine See UNDERGARMENTS: CORPS PIQUÉ #2.

corps piqué See UNDERGARMENTS.

corsage (cor-sahge′) **1.** Small floral arrangement of flowers worn fastened to woman's shoulder or waist, sometimes attached to specially designed wristband and worn on wrist. Worn on special occasions or for formal events. Also see BOSOM FLOWERS. **2.** ∞ Term used in the 18th and 19th c. for a woman's bodice.

corsage à la Du Barry See DU BARRY CORSAGE.

corsage à la Maintenon ∞ (cor-sahge′ ah lah man-teh′-nah) Fitted bodice of 1830s and 1840s trimmed with bow knots down center front. *Der.* For Marquise de Maintenon, second wife of Louis XIV of France.

corsage en corset ∞ (cor-sahge on corseh) Tight-fitting evening bodice of 1830s and 1840s cut in sections with seams similar to those on a corset.

corse ∞ **1.** Tight-fitting underbodice, of metal or leather with center front lacings, worn under tunic by men in 12th and 13th c. **2.** BALDRICK (see under BELTS) for carrying a bugle used by men in 16th c.

corselet **1.** ∞ Variant of word CORSET, in 14th and 15th c. **2.** See BELTS. **3.** See ARMOR. **4.** See UNDERGARMENTS. **5.** See PEASANT BODICE. **6.** See WAISTLINES.

corset **1.** See UNDERGARMENTS. **2.** ∞ In 11th c. a leather bodice stiffened with wood or metal. **3.** ∞ From 16th to 18th c., a stiffened bodice called STAYS (see under UNDERGARMENTS). **4.** ∞ Woman's gown laced up back and lined in fur, worn in 14th and 15th c. **5.** ∞ Man's surcoat, with or without sleeves, worn in Middle Ages.

corset à la ninon See UNDERGARMENTS.

corset bikini See SWIMWEAR: BIKINI.

corset cover See UNDERGARMENTS: CAMISOLE #1.

corset frock ∞ Dress of late 18th c. made with bodice of three gores of white satin in front and lacing in back, similar to a corset.

Corsican tie See TIES: NAPOLEON NECKTIE.

corundum See GEMS, GEM CUTS, AND SETTINGS.

cosmonaut look Jumpsuits and helmets reflecting this look influenced by the attention drawn to the first space astronauts. Featured by St. Laurent in 1963. Started the trend toward pantsuits and jumpsuits for women. *Der.* Russian, "astronaut." Also see LUNAR LOOK.

Cossack Pertaining to garments or styles derived from those worn by people inhabiting the Caucasus, an area between the Black and Caspian Seas. Men were particularly noted for their horsemanship, and wore distinctive clothing. See BLOUSES AND TOPS: COSSACK BLOUSE, HEADWEAR: COSSACK FORAGE HAT and COSSACK HAT, NECKLINES AND COLLARS: COSSACK COLLAR, PANTS: COSSACKS, SHIRTS: COSSACK SHIRT, and SLEEPWEAR AND LOUNGEWEAR: COSSACK PAJAMAS.

cosse See FEATHERS.

cost (wholesale cost, or cost to manufacture) The total cost to manufacture a garment. Derived from the total of the costs of materials, FINDINGS, labor, shipping, packaging, and duty, if applicable.

costing marker The layout of the pattern pieces for the PROTOTYPE of a new style in order to ascertain the yardage required.

costume **1.** Dress, coat, or suit with coordinated accessories, an ensemble. **2.** Fancy dress for masquerade parties, Halloween, costume and masked balls. **3.** Dress from a certain period in history, generally referred to as historic costume. **4.** Theatrical dress worn on stage. **5.** Native dress worn for festivals and specific occasions. **6.** ∞ In the 1860s term used for outdoor day dress or afternoon dress with a long train.

costume à la constitution Red, white, and blue striped or flowered dress of muslin or lawn worn with a vivid red sash and helmet-shaped cap. Symbolized the tricolor of the French Revolution and was worn by patriots. Also called *dress à la constitution.*

costume jewelry See JEWELRY.

cote ∞ (koht) Used in the 13th c. and after for an undertunic worn by men and women during the Middle Ages. Spelled *cotte* in France, this garment was worn over a shirt or chemise and under a **surcote** (ser′-koht), or outer tunic. This word is the source of the modern word *coat.* For women, *kirtle* is sometimes used as a synonym.

cote and sideless surcote 1390

cotehardie/cote-hardy/cote-hardie ∞ (coat′-har′-dee) **1.** A variant of the *surcote,* or outer tunic, for men. The same term seems to have had different applications in different countries. In France, it was identified as either a short garment with long sleeves for outdoor wear, at first simple and later more elegant and fur-trimmed; a gown; or an outergarment open in front and buttoned at the sides. In England, it was a buttoned outergarment fitted through the body to the waist or below where it flared out into a usually knee-length skirt.

cotehardie #1

The sleeves ended at the elbow in front while hanging down at the back in a shorter or longer flap. With time, some versions of the garment became quite decorative. A decorative belt was often worn low on the hip. **2.** Woman's close-fitting dresslike garment of same period, made of rich fabric and laced up back or front. Had long tight sleeves and slits in sides of skirt called fitchets. Said to have been introduced by Anne, wife of Richard II of England.

cothurnus See FOOTWEAR.

cotorinas See VESTS.

cotta See CLERICAL DRESS.

cottage bonnet See HEADWEAR.

cottage cloak See CAPES, CLOAKS, AND SHAWLS.

cottage dress ∞ High-waisted straight dress of early 1820s with long apron in front made of same fabric. Necklines varied—some low with FICHU (see SCARVES), others with white collars either trimmed with frills or V-shaped edging. Sleeves were fitted. Hem of skirt was usually decorated with a tubular-shaped trimming stitched at regular intervals to create puffs of fabric.

cottage front ∞ Daytime bodice with LACERS in front for decorative effect. Worn over a HABIT SHIRT (see SHIRTS), or CHEMISETTE (see SCARVES), in early 19th c.

cottage pants See PANTS: COTTAGE PANTS.

cotte See COTE.

cotton † Soft white vegetable fiber from ½" to 2" long that comes from the fluffy boll of the cotton plant. Grown in Egypt, India, China, and southern United States. American cottons include *acala, upland, peeler, pima,* and *Sea Island.* Composed largely of cellulose, cotton fibers are absorbent, comfortable, and washable; therefore, they are used in a wide variety of clothing items.

cotton batting See BATTING.

Coty American Fashion Critics Awards Annual awards sponsored by Coty, Inc., international cosmetics and perfume company, from 1942 to 1985, given for outstanding fashion design. Judges were magazine and newspaper fashion editors, broadcasters, and fashion retailers. The *Winnie* was awarded each year to a designer who contributed to American design and had significant effect on fashion. Originally awards were given to designers of women's fashions. In 1968 the Coty Menswear Fashion Awards were established. A designer receiving a *Winnie* or Menswear Award three times was accepted into the *Hall of Fame.*

couched embroidery See EMBROIDERIES AND SEWING STITCHES.

couching stitch See EMBROIDERIES AND SEWING STITCHES.

couel **1.** See HEADWEAR. **2.** Synonym for COWL (see NECKLINES AND COLLARS) in England.

Council of Fashion Designers of America A nonprofit organization with a membership of the foremost American designers, founded in 1962 with Norman Norell as the first president. Membership is by invitation only. Accomplishments include: (a) recognition for American designers both here and abroad; (b) created the National Endowment for the arts with recognition of fashion as an art form; (c) presents costume exhibitions annually; (d) hosts the "party of the year" at the Metropolitan Museum of Art in New York City; (e) contributes annually since 1963 to the Costume Institute of the Metropolitan Museum; (f) supports recognized costume institutes throughout the country, including the costume wing of the Smithsonian; (g) was instrumental in founding the Fashion Institute of Technology in New York City. Since 1985 an annual "awards evening" is given to honor individuals who have made an outstanding contribution to fashion and fashion journalism. Also abbreviated to CFDA.

counted cross-stitch embroidery See EMBROIDERIES AND SEWING STITCHES.

counted thread embroidery See EMBROIDERIES AND SEWING STITCHES.

countenance See COUTENANCE.

counter See FOOTWEAR.

counter book See PATTERN BOOK.

counterfeit goods Unauthorized illegal copies of goods with registered tradenames, trademarks, or logos.

counter fillet See HEADWEAR.

counter sample See SEW BY.

countertop display Merchandise shelf or table-top displays that allow customers to touch and self-select products.

country-western look **1.** Look initiated by country-western musicians at the Grand Ole Opry® in Nashville, Tennessee, that ranges from overalls, straw hats, and gingham dresses to ultra dressy rhinestone and sequin-studded western garb as displayed by Dolly Parton, Barbara Mandrell, and Kenny Rogers. *Der.* From style of music. See WESTERN LOOK for individual items. **2.** The costumes worn by square dancers in the rural United States that feature women in dresses and skirts (sometimes gingham) with many petticoats, and men in western pants, plaid or fringed shirts, and neckerchiefs (e.g., as seen on characters in the musical *Oklahoma*). *Der.* Type of dancing originating in rural United States, usually done to the music of a fiddler.

coureur See COATS AND JACKETS.

courier bag See HANDBAGS AND RELATED ACCESSORIES: MESSENGER BAG.

Courrèges boot See FOOTWEAR.

Courrèges hat See HEADWEAR.

Courrèges fashions/Courrèges look (coor-rej) Clothes and accessories introduced by Paris designer André Courrèges (see APPENDIX/ DESIGNERS) that included above-the-knee skirts worn with white calf-length boots. Cut of dress or skirt had hard geometric lines, standing away from the body in A-line shape in fall of 1963. The next year his whole collection was done in shorter-length skirts. Responsible for starting the general trend in the United States toward shorter-length skirts and wearing of boots; however, this trend actually originated with the MOD and CARNABY LOOKS.

Courrèges flower sock See HOSIERY: KNEE-HI SOCK.

Courrèges glasses See EYEWEAR.

courrier dummies See MODEL DOLLS.

course See KNIT.

court dress Costume and items of apparel required to be worn for daily functions and ceremonial occasions in the presence of ruling monarchs. Also see CORONATION ROBES and COURT HABIT.

courtepye/courtepy ∞ (kor'-tay-pih) Very short overgarment worn in 14th and 15th c. similar to surcoat. Made in a circle with round neckline, high collar, and slashed at the sides. Frequently PARTI-COLORED or embroidered with gems.

court habit ∞ Term for men's clothing worn only at French court in 17th and 18th c. Called **grand habit** for women.

court plasters See PATCHES.

court shoe See FOOTWEAR.

court tie See FOOTWEAR.

coutenance/countenance Small muff carried in late 16th and early 17th c.

coutes See ARMOR.

couture (koo'-ture) French term for the business in which original apparel designs are created by designers and the items are manufactured in the couture house using exceptionally fine sewing and tailoring and expensive fabrics. Also see HAUTE COUTURE.

Couture Group, New York See NEW YORK COUTURE BUSINESS COUNCIL, INC.

couture lace See LACES.

couturier (ko-tour'-ee-ay) French term for male designer or proprietor of a couture house.

couturière (ko-tour'-ee-air) French term for female designer or proprietor of a couture house.

coverall One-piece jumpsuit worn over other clothes by mechanics and other workmen. Originally worn by gas station attendants in the 1920s. Restyled and fashionable for sportswear from the late 1960s on.

coverchief See HEADWEAR.

coverall 1942

covered button   See CLOSURES.

covered heel   See FOOTWEAR.

covered placket   See CLOTHING CONSTRUCTION DETAILS.

covered yarn   See CORE YARN.

covered zipper   See CLOSURES.

covert cloth   † **1.** An extremely firm durable twill weave fabric with a characteristic mottled look achieved by twisting lengthwise yarns spun from two strands—one dark and the other light. Crosswise yarns are the same or of a dark color. Used for men's and women's suits and coats. **2.** Imitated in all cotton, covert is used for work clothes, caps, uniforms, and trousers.

cover-up   See ACTIVEWEAR: BEACH WRAP-UP.

cowboy/cowgirl   Term originally used for a man or woman in the western United States who herds or tends cattle, usually going about on horseback. In fashion, may be used as an adjective to describe apparel that is derived from styles associated with cowboys or cowgirls. See BELTS: COWBOY BELT, FOOTWEAR: COWBOY BOOT, HEADWEAR: COWBOY HAT, and SHIRTS: COWBOY SHIRT.

cowboy suit   Child's suit worn when playing, an imitation of the regular cowboy's costume. Consists of a shirt, pants, leather bolero, and sometimes CHAPS. Gunbelt and a wide-brimmed cowboy hat with chin cord are worn and toy guns are carried. The girl's costume is called a cowgirl's suit and sometimes has a short fringed skirt.

cowhide   See LEATHERS: CATTLEHIDE.

Cowichan sweater   See SWEATERS.

cowl   See NECKLINES AND COLLARS.

cowpunk   An uncoordinated medley of PUNK and WESTERN LOOKS appearing in Los Angeles in 1986. Style includes western fringed jackets or leather jackets worn over miniskirts, chain jewelry, three western belts worn at same time, Boy George hats and hairstyles, ragged-looking shirts, all type of hairstyles including spiky, mini braids, mohawk, and Indian braids. *Der.* Combination of cowgirl and punk looks.

coxcomb/cockscomb   **1.** See HAIRSTYLES. **2.** See HEADWEAR. **3.** See DANDY.

C.P.O. jacket/shirt   See SHIRTS.

CPSC   See CONSUMER PRODUCT SAFETY COMMISSION.

crab-back bathing suit   See SWIMWEAR.

Crafted with Pride in the U.S.A. Council   Organization of textile and apparel industry firms (formed 1984) that promotes domestically manufactured textiles and apparel.

Crahay, Jules-François   * See APPENDIX/DESIGNERS.

crakow/crakowe/cracow   See FOOTWEAR.

crampons   See FOOTWEAR.

crants   See HEADWEAR.

crapaud   See WIGS AND HAIRPIECES: BAGWIG.

crape   See CREPE #2.

crash   † Coarse, loosely woven fabric made in a variety of weights with irregular yarns giving it an uneven texture. Usually made in plain weaves of cotton, cotton blends, or linen.

craunce   See HEADWEAR: CRANTS.

cravat   See TIES.

cravate cocodes   See TIES.

cravat strings   See TIES.

crawcaw   See FOOTWEAR: CRAKOW.

crawlers   See PANTS.

crease resistance   † The ability of a fabric to recover from wrinkling. Manufactured synthetic fabrics usually have higher wrinkle recovery than natural fiber fabrics, but special finishes can be applied to natural and regenerated fiber fabrics to aid wrinkle recovery.

Creed, Charles   * See APPENDIX/DESIGNERS.

creedmore   See FOOTWEAR.

creel backpack   See HANDBAGS AND RELATED ACCESSORIES.

creepalong set   Infant's or toddler's two-piece suit usually consisting of a knit shirt with overall-type pants. Also called CRAWLERS (see under PANTS).

creepers   **1.** See PANTS: CRAWLERS. **2.** See FOOTWEAR.

creeping apron   ∞ Infant's garment of early 1900s cut long and gathered at hem into a band through which a cord was drawn. Could be pushed up above knees for a romper effect.

Cremona cravat   See TIES.

crepe   † (krape) **1.** A general classification of fabrics made from almost any fiber and characterized by a broad range of crinkled or grained surface effects. **2.** In the 18th and 19th c. a heavy crepe fabric dyed black and worn for mourning. Often spelled **crape**.

crepe-back satin † (krape) Lightweight fabric with a smooth, lustrous, shiny finish on the face and a dull crepe appearance on the back. May be used with either side as the exterior. Made in a satin weave with silk, rayon, or manufactured fiber for the lengthwise yarns, and a crepe twist crosswise yarn. The fabric has twice as many lengthwise as crosswise yarns. Used for dresses, blouses, and lingerie. Also called *satin-back* and sometimes called *satin-faced crepe.*

crepe de chine † (krepp deh sheen) **1.** Fine, lightweight silk fabric with a crepe texture that is made by using highly twisted yarns in the crosswise direction and more lengthwise than crosswise yarns. It is piece-dyed or printed and used for dresses and blouses. **2.** Crepe-textured fabric made with silk lengthwise yarns and worsted crepe-twisted crosswise yarns. *Der.* French, "crepe of China."

crepe georgette See GEORGETTE.

crepe-soled shoes See FOOTWEAR.

crepe yarn † (krape) Yarn that is given a high twist during spinning. The yarn is stiff, wiry, and contracts during finishing giving pebbled surface to fabrics.

crepida See FOOTWEAR: KREPIS.

crescent Motif copied from shape of moon in its first quarter. Also called a *lunette.* See FOOTWEAR: CRESCENT TOE.

Crete lace See LACES.

crève-coeur See HEADWEAR.

crevés (krev-ay) See SLASHING.

crew cut See HAIRSTYLES.

crew neckline See NECKLINES AND COLLARS.

crew-neck shirt See SHIRTS.

crew-neck sweater See SWEATERS.

crew socks See HOSIERY.

crewel work See EMBROIDERIES AND SEWING STITCHES.

crewel yarn † Two-ply, loosely twisted, fine worsted yarn used for embroidery.

criardes See UNDERGARMENTS.

crimmer See FURS: LAMB.

crimp/crimping **1.** † *n.* Natural or machine-made bending or waviness in a fiber making yarn resilient, less shiny, bulkier, and suitable for knitting. **2.** *v.* To curl the hair with a hot iron.

3. *v.* To shape leather by a machine that uses heat and pressure.

crin French for horsehair. See BRAIDS: HORSEHAIR BRAID.

criniere (cran-yere′) See WIGS AND HAIRPIECES.

crinkle crepe Same as PLISSÉ.

crinolette See UNDERGARMENTS.

crinoline † (krin′-uh-lyn) **1.** Heavily sized (see SIZING), open weave cotton fabric. **2.** See UNDERGARMENTS: CRINOLINE.

crinoline and tournure See UNDERGARMENTS: BUSTLE.

crinoline era (krin′-uh-lyn) Used by costume historians to designate the period from 1850 to 1870 when crinoline petticoats (see UNDERGARMENTS: CRINOLINE) or hoops (see UNDERGARMENTS: HOOPS) were used to support full skirts.

crisp **1.** See VEILS. **2.** See HAIRSTYLES.

crispin See CAPES, CLOAKS, AND SHAWLS.

crispine See HEADWEAR.

crispinette See HEADWEAR: CRISPINE.

crochet (kro-shay′) **1.** † Fabric made from a continuous series of loops of yarn made with a single hooked needle. Originally developed in the 16th c. as an inexpensive method of creating a lacelike fabric. Modern textile machinery can create fabrics that have the appearance of crochet. **2.** Adjective used to describe apparel made by crocheting. See CAPES, CLOAKS, AND SHAWLS: CROCHETED SHAWL, CLOSURES: CROCHETED BUTTON, and HEADWEAR: CROCHETED HAT. **3.** Term used from 14th to 17th c. for a hook or fastener, e.g ., a hook attached at woman's waist for suspending a pomander, or a fastener on a shoe.

crochets and loops See CLOSURES: HOOKS AND EYES.

crocodile See LEATHERS.

Cromwell Adjective used in the 18th c. to describe clothing inspired by or derived from clothing items worn at the time Oliver Cromwell ruled as Lord Protector of England, 1653 to 1658. See NECKLINES AND COLLARS: CROMWELL COLLAR and FOOTWEAR: CROMWELL SHOES.

Cromwell collar See NECKLINES AND COLLARS.

Cromwell shoe See FOOTWEAR.

crooked shoe See FOOTWEAR.

crop-doublet See DOUBLET.

cropped   Term denoting shortened, or cutoff, when referring to clothing or hair. See BLOUSES AND TOPS: CROPPED TOP and PANTS: CROPPED PANTS.

cropping   See SHEARING.

croquet boot   See FOOTWEAR.

croquis (kro´-key)   A French term used in fashion illustration that refers to a rough sketch of a figure used as a base on which to show garment design ideas. Also called a *lay figure.*

cross   **1.** A depiction, stylized or realistic, of an instrument used by Romans for executing individuals. An actual cross would have been made from an upright post of wood with a cross piece near the top, a form that is known as a **Latin cross.** Crosses have been worn by Christians as a symbol of their religious belief from the early days of Christianity and as a badge on the clothing worn by Crusaders during the Middle Ages. Different representations of crosses in badges, jewelry, or as motifs of various kinds have developed and have been given such names as (1) **ansate cross** See ANKH. (2) **Eastern Orthodox cross** With two cross pieces more than half way up the central post and a diagonal cross piece a short distance from the bottom. (3) **Greek cross** With the cross piece the same length as the vertical piece and located at its center. (4) **Maltese cross** With four arms of equal length that are shaped like arrowheads decreasing in size as they approach the center. (5) **St. Andrew's cross** With diagonal arms, like an X. (6) **tau cross** With the cross piece at the top of the post, like the Greek letter *tau.* **2.** European term for BIAS, or diagonal cut—called fabric cut "on the cross."

cross-boarded   See LEATHERS.

cross body bag   See HANDBAGS AND RELATED ACCESSORIES.

crosscloth   See HEADWEAR.

crosses   See FURS.

cross-country skiing   See PANTS: KNICKERS #1.

cross fox   See FURS.

cross gaitering   See CROSS GARTERING.

cross gartering   ∞ **1.** Binding or holding the leg-coverings, *broc* of Anglo-Saxon, or *braies,* of the French (see BRAIES), close to the leg by criss-crossing strips of leather around legs on top of pants. **2.** Used from mid-16th to early 17th c. to describe the style of gartering hose by using a ribbon around leg below the knee, crossing in back, and tying with bow above knee in front or at side of knee when stockings were worn over CANIONS.

cross-gartering #1

cross girdling   ∞ Style of wearing the girdle, or sash, crossed at the chest and then wrapped around the waist by ancient Greeks. Also see BELTS: GREEK BELT.

crossover bra   See UNDERGARMENTS.

crossover collar   See NECKLINES AND COLLARS.

crossover thong sandals   See FOOTWEAR: THONG #3.

cross Persian lamb   See FURS: LAMB.

cross stone   See GEMS, GEM CUTS, AND SETTINGS: FAIRY STONE.

cross-stitch   See EMBROIDERIES AND SEWING STITCHES.

crotch   Place in a garment where the legs meet. British term is *crutch.*

crown   **1.** See HEADWEAR. **2.** See GEMS, GEM CUTS, AND SETTINGS.

crown hats   See HEADWEAR.

crown sable   See FURS: SABLE.

cruches   See HAIRSTYLES.

crusader hood   See HEADWEAR.

crusader's cross   See JEWELRY.

crush hat   See HEADWEAR: CHAPEAU CLAQUE.

crushed leather   See LEATHERS.

crusher hat   See HEADWEAR.

crutch   British term for CROTCH.

cryptocrystalline   See GEMS, GEM CUTS, AND SETTINGS.

crystal   See GEMS, GEM CUTS, AND SETTINGS.

crystal bracelet   See JEWELRY.

crystalline structure   See GEMS, GEM CUTS, AND SETTINGS.

crystal pleats   See CLOTHING CONSTRUCTION DETAILS.

cuaran   See FOOTWEAR.

Cuban heel   See FOOTWEAR.

Cubavera jacket   See COATS AND JACKETS.

cube heel See FOOTWEAR.

Cubic Zirconia® See GEMS, GEM CUTS, AND SETTINGS.

cue See HAIRSTYLES.

cue peruke See WIGS AND HAIRPIECES.

cuff bracelet See JEWELRY.

cuff button See CLOSURES.

cuffed Describes the bottom edge of a garment that has been given a wide hem that has been turned back to form a cuff. Examples of garments that are often cuffed are shorts and pants.

cuffed trousers See PANTS: PRE-CUFFED TROUSERS.

cuff link See JEWELRY.

CUFFS

cuff **1.** Finish for a sleeve consisting of a separate sewed-on piece or a turned-back extension of a sleeve. **2.** The turned-over or stitched-on piece at the top of a glove. **3.** A turned-back piece at the hem of trousers; a trouser cuff. **4.** A turned-over or stitched-down band at the top of a boot. **5.** See JEWELRY.

band cuff Simplest type of cuff made from a separate piece of fabric and applied to the bottom of a sleeve. The band is cut from a straight piece of fabric. Such cuffs are made in varying widths and sometimes may have attached ruffles or pieces of elastic pulled through the bands.

barrel cuff See CUFFS: SINGLE CUFF.

boot cuff ∞ Large turned back cuff, reaching nearly to elbow. Popular for men's coats from 1727 to about 1740, used on a BOOT SLEEVE (see under SHOULDERS AND SLEEVES).

detachable cuff Cuff cut out of an additional piece of fabric rather than being an extension of the sleeve and which may be taken off, washed, and reattached to the sleeve.

double cuff See CUFFS: FRENCH CUFF.

elbow cuff ∞ Turned-back cuff attached to woman's elbow-length sleeves in first half of 18th c.—wide on outside of arm and fitting more closely at elbow.

French cuff Large band cuff that doubles back on itself and is usually fastened with a cuff link. Also called *double cuff*.

French cuff

fringed cuff Leather band at the wrist that has long hanging fringe at the end. A fashion innovation of the late 1960s.

gauntlet cuff Wide turned-back cuff that slants away from the arm, flaring wide at top and tapering to wrist.

gauntlet cuff

hand fall/hand cuff ∞ Term for lace-trimmed, turned-back, flared starched *cuff* frequently made double. Worn by men and women in 17th c. with FALLING BAND, FALLING RUFF, and STANDING BAND (see under NECKLINES AND COLLARS).

hounds' ears ∞ Large turned-back cuffs with rounded corners used on men's coats from 1660s to 1680s.

knit cuff Cuffs made with a rib knit stitch that gives a tight fit but is elastic enough to slip over hand easily.

mariner's cuff ∞ Man's coat cuff, worn in second half of 18th c., consisting of a small turned-back cuff decorated on outside with a curved flap, similar to a pocket flap, and three or four buttons that matched those of the coat.

mousquetaire cuff ∞ (moose-ke′-tare) **1.** Deep, wide cuff flaring above the wrist, used on men's coats in early 1873. **2.** Sleeve of mousquetaire-type worn in late 1880s with flaring top and cuff sometimes trimmed with vandykes (see VANDYKING). *Der.* From uniform of French musketeers or royal bodyguards of Louis XIII in 17th c.

parament (pa-ra′-ment) Ornamental cuff at wrist, turned up over sleeve and stitched. Also spelled *parement*.

pendant cuff Cuff that hangs down from the sleeve.

pendant cuff

roll-up cuff Extension of the sleeve that is folded over several times to form a cuff. Sometimes fastened with a tab. See SHOULDERS AND SLEEVES: BUTTON-TAB SLEEVE.

single cuff Band cuff that, in contrast to a French cuff, has no section doubled back on itself.

roll-up cuff

This cuff is stitched to the sleeve and usually closes with one or more buttons.

turned-back cuff Turned-back extension of the sleeve. Sleeve is cut longer and a section is turned up to form a cuff.

turned-back cuff

cuff string See CLOSURES.

cuff-top girdle See UNDERGARMENTS: GIRDLES.

cuirass ∞ (kwe-rass′) **1.** See ARMOR. **2.** Plain, close-fitting waist worn by women in early 1900s. *Der.* French, *cuirasse,* "breastplate."

cuirass bodice/cuirasse bodice ∞ (kwe-rass′) Extremely tight, boned women's daytime bodice of mid-1870s extending down over hips to mold the body. Frequently made in fabric different from the dress.

cuirasse tunic/cuirasse tunic ∞ (kwe-rass′) Tight-fitting tunic skirt worn with the CUIRASS BODICE by women in mid-1870s.

cuirass bodice 1881

cuir savage See LEATHER LOOK and WET LOOK.

cuisse See ARMOR.

culet **1.** See GEMS, GEM CUTS, AND SETTINGS. **2.** See ARMOR.

culotte dress (ku-lot′) Dress that combines pants and blouse into one garment, usually without a waistline seam, popular in 1967 and after. Also called a *pantdress.*

culottes (ku-lotz′) **1.** Garment that hangs like a skirt, but is actually pants (i.e., a divided skirt). *Der* French, "breeches, trousers, tights, and knickers." When used as an adjective, indicates a garment with culotte-type construction. See CULOTTE DRESS, SLEEPWEAR AND LOUNGE-WEAR: CULOTTE PAJAMAS, SKIRTS: CULOTTES, and UNDERGARMENTS: CULOTTE SLIP. **3.** ∞ Term first used for tight, below-the-knee pants worn during reign of Henry III of France, 1574–1589. **4.** ∞ Synonym for PETTICOAT BREECHES.

cultured pearl See GEMS, GEM CUTS, AND SETTINGS.

Cumberland corset See UNDERGARMENTS: APOLLO CORSET.

Cumberland hat See HEADWEAR.

cummerbund See BELTS.

Cummings, Angela * See APPENDIX/DESIGNERS.

cupola coat See UNDERGARMENTS: BELL HOOP.

cuprammonium rayon † Cellulosic fiber regenerated from wood pulp or from cotton fibers too short to spin into yarns. This fiber is no longer manufactured in the United States because it produces high levels of water pollution, but is manufactured abroad and may be found in imported goods. Used in women's dresses, blouses, and scarves.

curch See HEADWEAR.

curls See HAIRSTYLES.

curlyhead See HAIRSTYLES.

curricle coat See COATS AND JACKETS.

curricle dress ∞ (kur′-ee-kul) Women's thigh-length, short-sleeved, open-front tunic usually of net worn from 1794 to 1803 over a full-length dress.

curtain drapery ∞ American term for HIP BAGS.

curtains See HEADWEAR: LAMBALLE BONNET.

cushion cut See GEMS, GEM CUTS, AND SETTINGS.

cushionet See UNDERWEAR.

cushion headdress See HEADWEAR.

cushion pad See UNDERGARMENTS: BUSTLE.

cushion sole **1.** See FOOTWEAR. **2.** See HOSIERY.

cushion-style embroidery See EMBROIDERIES AND SEWING STITCHES: BERLIN WORK.

custom designer Designer who creates an original garment that is executed by skilled seamstresses who drape the fabric on a dress form conforming to the customer's special measurements. Clothes produced by such designers are known as *custom-made* or *made-to-measure.*

custom-made Adjective describing garments made by tailor or couture house for an individual customer. The correct size is achieved either by fitting on a dress form adjusted to the customer's measurements or by several personal fittings.

customs broker A U.S. agent licensed by the Customs Office to assist apparel manufacturers in gaining clearance through customs for the importation of goods produced OFFSHORE.

cutaway coat/jacket See COATS AND JACKETS.

cutaway frock See COATS AND JACKETS.

cutaway sack See COATS AND JACKETS.

cut-finger gloves See GLOVES AND GLOVE CONSTRUCTION.

cut, make and trim (CMT) Apparel contractor that performs the operations necessary to cut, make, and trim garments for an apparel manufacturers.

cut-offs See SHORTS.

cutout dress Any dress with cutout portions revealing the body. May have enlarged armholes or be cut out at the midriff, hips, or back. An innovation of the 1960s.

cutouts Ornamental holes of different sizes and shapes cut from apparel. See SWIMWEAR: CUT-OUT SWIMSUIT, FOOTWEAR: CUTOUTS, GLOVES AND GLOVE CONSTRUCTIONS: ACTION GLOVES.

cut-steel beads See JEWELRY.

cut-steel buckle See CLOSURES.

cutter Garment-production term for the person who cuts the fabric with an electric knife.

cutting-up trade Jargon used by textile industry for clothing manufacturers.

cut-up trade Manufacturers who make belts that are added to pants, skirts, and dresses by apparel manufacturers.

cut velvet A fabric that has a fairly complex woven pattern consisting of velvet figures on a background of a relatively sheer fabric. A very decorative fabric, it is used for women's apparel, especially dressy clothing.

cut wig See WIGS AND HAIRPIECES.

cut work/cut-work 1. See EMBROIDERIES AND SEWING STITCHES. 2. ∞ Used in mid-14th through 15th c. to refer to DAGGING, or a dagged border of a garment. Motifs such as leaves, flames, and scallops were used.

cyberpunk See PUNK LOOK.

cyclas ∞ 1. Sleeveless outer tunic that apparently began as a garment worn over armor in early 14th c.—extending to waist in front and to knees in back—slashed up sides and then laced. When it became part of civilian clothing, it appears to have been the same as the SURCOTE. Also spelled *ciclaton, cinglaton*. Shown at COTE. 2. Wrapped garment similar to a toga that was worn in ancient Rome. 3. Rich elaborate overgarment, sometimes fur- or silk-lined, made of a large piece of cloth with round opening for head. Worn in medieval times on ceremonial occasions by both men and women (e.g., at the coronation of Henry III of England in the 13th c.).

cycle jacket See COATS AND JACKETS: MOTORCYCLE JACKET.

cycling suit/cycling costume See ACTIVEWEAR.

cymophane See GEMS, GEM CUTS, AND SETTINGS.

Czechoslovakian embroidery See EMBROIDERIES AND SEWING STITCHES.

D 1. Shoe size: Letter indicating a width; widths run from AAAAs to EEEEE with AAAAs being the narrowest and EEEEEs being the widest. **2.** Pajama size: Men's regular height (5′8″–5′11″) size corresponding to 45″–48″ chest measurement. For other sizes, see BIG, EXTRA-TALL, REGULAR, and TALL. **3.** Shirt size: For men's extra-tall size with 18–18½ collar measurement. **4.** Bra cup size. Standard sizes run AAA, AA, A, B, C, D, the A sizes being the smallest and the D the largest. There is no industry agreement on cup sizes larger than D. Different manufacturers use different designations.

Daché, Lilly   * See APPENDIX/DESIGNERS.

dadaism (da′-da′-ism)   Movement in art and literature flourishing during and immediately after World War I that attempted to discredit all previous art and culture. Dadaism rejected existing moral, social, and aesthetic codes—substituting the incongruous and accidental. Figures were distorted and the beautiful made ugly. The movement flourished in Paris, Berlin, and Zurich, where it began. Jean Arp, Marcel Duchamp, and Max Ernst were among the artists who were its best-known exponents.

dagging ∞ Ornamental borders cut on garments in shapes of leaves, tongues, and scallops. Originating in the 1340s, these decorations remained fashionable for hems of gowns, sleeves, and garment edges until the end of the 15th c. Also

dagging

called *cut work, dag, dagges, foliated, jags,* and *jagging.* Also see CASTELLATED.

Dali, Salvador (dah′-lee) (1904–1989)   Spanish artist, one of leading exponents of surrealism in painting, noted for his jewelry designs in fantastic shapes. His paintings influenced fashion, display, and advertising.

dalmatic ∞ (dal-ma′-tic)   Long, extra wide-sleeved, loose-fitting tunic trimmed with two vertical stripes in front. Worn by men and women in Byzantine period. Later worn as a clerical vestment by cardinals, abbots, and bishops, and as part of the coronation robes of Great Britain. *Der.* From *tunica dalmatica,* worn by Romans in 2nd c., starting in Dalmatia.

dalmatic

damaging-out   Repairing of tears or holes in fur pelts and garments.

damascene/damascening   See JEWELRY.

damascene lace (dam-ah-seen)   See LACES.

damask † A broad group of fabrics with elaborate woven floral or geometric designs that are distinguished from the background by contrasting luster and/or color and which are reversible. Woven on a JACQUARD loom, the design of the fabric is often made in a satin weave. Because of their decorative aspects, damask fabrics are often used for evening wear.

dance set   See UNDERGARMENTS: STEP-INS.

dance skirt   See SKIRTS.

dandizette ∞ (dan-dee-zet′) Term used from 1816 to 1820 for a female *dandy* conspicuous for her GRECIAN BEND, or the manner in which she walked.

dandy **1.** Term used from about 1816 on for a man excessively fond of and overly concerned with clothes, exemplified by Beau BRUMELL, Lord PETERSHAM, and Count D'ORSAY, who greatly influenced men's fashions in England and France. Synonyms: *beau,* or, in excessive cases, *fop.* **2.** Adjective used to describe apparel based on styles worn by 19th c. dandies. See BLOUSES AND TOPS: DANDY BLOUSE and SHIRTS: DANDY SHIRT.

dandy hat See HEADWEAR.

dandy look Similar to the EDWARDIAN LOOK but characterized by ruffles at neck and wrists. Worn by both men and women in the late 1960s and early 1970s. Complete costume might include an EDWARDIAN SUIT with regency collar (see under NECKLINES AND COLLARS) and shirt with ruffled front and cuffs.

Danish trousers See PANTS.

darning Method of reweaving threads by hand to repair a hole in a sock or garment. May also be done on sewing machine. Also see EMBROIDERIES AND SEWING STITCHES and LACES: DARNED LACE.

dart See CLOTHING CONSTRUCTION DETAILS.

dashiki Short to full-length garment inspired by a central African style. The American version is cut straight and loose-fitting, is collarless and slips on over the head, has bell-shaped or kimono sleeves, and is usually made of an African-inspired distinctive panel or border print. The style was introduced in United States in

dashiki

late 1960s for general wear and was particularly popular among African-Americans.

Davy Crockett cap See HEADWEAR.

day cap See HEADWEAR.

day sheer hose See HOSIERY: SHEER HOSE.

daywear Apparel that is generally worn during the day, as compared with eveningwear, worn for evening events, or sleepwear, worn for sleeping.

d.b. British tailors' 19th c. slang term for DOUBLE-BREASTED (see under CLOSURES).

death's head button See CLOSURES.

De Bevoise brassière See UNDERGARMENTS.

debutante slouch ∞ Posture fashionable for young sophisticated women, starting about 1917 and very popular in 1920s, with shoulders drooping forward giving a flat-chested appearance.

decal Picture or design that can be transferred from specially prepared paper to the skin or other surface such a textile.

decalcomania **1.** The process of transfering a decal to another surface. **2.** Fad for wearing designs from decals of butterflies, flowers, and other motifs on legs and arms, which was especially popular in mid-1960s and after. Also see TATTOO.

decatur ring See JEWELRY.

deck Adjective used to describe clothing and accessories derived from or inspired by clothing used for nautical sports. See COATS AND JACKETS: DECK JACKET, FOOTWEAR: BOATING SHOE, and PANTS: DECK PANTS.

décolletage (deh-coll′-eh-tahzh) French noun sometimes used in English to indicate bare shoulders or a low-cut neckline. Also used as an adjective to describe apparel with a low neckline. See NECKLINES AND COLLARS: DÉCOLLETÉ COLLAR and UNDERGARMENTS: DÉCOLLETÉ BRA.

deconstructionists Designers of the 1990s. who took elements of garment construction and put them together in unusual ways. For example, putting garment seams on the outside of clothing and leaving them unfinished or using experimental dyeing techniques.

découpage (deh-coo-pahg′) The art of decorating items with cutout pictures of paper or fabric pasted to surfaces and shellacked. This technique was especially popular in mid- and late 1960s for decorating handbags. *Der.* French, "cutout."

deep See ASSORTMENT: DEPTH.

deerskin See LEATHERS: BUCKSKIN.

deerstalker See HEADWEAR.

de Joinville teck See TIES.

de la Renta, Oscar * See APPENDIX/DESIGNERS.

Delhi work See EMBROIDERIES AND SEWING STITCHES.

Delineator, The Fashion magazine originating in 1872, self-described as a "Journal of Fashion

Culture and Fine Arts." Associated with the Butterick Pattern Company, this journal had many illustrations of apparel for women and children printed with the pattern number so that a consumer could order tissue paper patterns and make her own clothing. By the 1920s and 1930s the publication had become a more general women's magazine but continued to show fashions from patterns until it ceased publication in 1937.

Dell'Olio, Louis   See APPENDIX/DESIGNERS.

Delphos dress   Women's dress made by a new system patented by designer Mariano Fortuny in 1909. The front and back of the dress were laced together, rather than being stitched down the sides. Styles were reminiscent of ancient Greek dresses. Beautiful fabrics were used and the entire dress was minutely pleated thus molding the body like a Greek statue. Many women wore these dresses, which did not conform to the usual mode of the era, as tea gowns or at home styles. Fortuny continued to make the same general style until his death in 1949.

Delphos dress
c. 1910

demantoid   See GEMS, GEM CUTS, AND SETTINGS: ANDRADITE GARNET.

demi-boot   See FOOTWEAR.

demi-bra   See UNDERGARMENTS.

demi brassard   See ARMOR.

demi-castor   See HEADWEAR: CASTOR.

demi-coronal   See HEADWEAR.

demi-corset   See UNDERGARMENTS.

demi-gigot   See SHOULDERS AND SLEEVES.

demi-habillement   See HALF ROBE.

demi-jamb   See ARMOR.

demi-maunch   See SHOULDERS AND SLEEVES: DEMI-SLEEVE.

demimondaines (demi-mon-dan´)   French term for mistresses of wealthy men who were dressed by famous Parisian couturiers and greatly influenced fashion from the Second Empire in France through the Edwardian era. *Der.* French, "those of the half-world."

demi-riding coat   See COATS AND JACKETS: JUSTAUCORPS.

demi-sleeve   See SHOULDERS AND SLEEVES.

demi-toilette   See HALF DRESS.

demi-vambrace   See ARMOR.

demographic segmentation   The practice of identifying markets by demographic characteristics such as age, education, gender, and income on the assumption that certain items and styles will appeal to those who fit into specific segments of the market.

Demorest, Madame   Operator of Demorest's Emporium of Fashion from the 1870s to 1890s. Showrooms and a factory were located at Union Square, New York, where ladies came to select home-sewing patterns. From 1865 to 1899 her husband published *Demorest's Monthly Magazine* and *Demorest Fashions,* a weekly newspaper. Both were profusely illustrated with fashions.

Demeulemeester, Ann *   See APPENDIX/DESIGNERS.

denier † (den-yer´)   International textile and hosiery system used for numbering silk and manufactured filament yarns—the low numbers represent finer yarns, the higher numbers the heavier yarns. *Der.* From old French coin, the weight used as a measure of size and number of silk.

denim †   Sturdy, serviceable fabric woven in the TWILL WEAVE, traditionally made with indigo-blue or brown lengthwise yarns and white crosswise yarns, however now made in many color variations and in novelty striped and figured patterns. Used for sportswear, work clothes, pants, jackets, and occasionally in high fashion items. *Der.* French, *serge de Nimes,* a fabric made in Nimes, France. Also called *dungaree.*

denim look   With the acceptance of jeans for daytime and schoolwear in early 1970s, denim fabric was used in matching skirts, jackets, and shorts, as well as men's tailored suits and women's dresses. Although denim was originally a cotton fabric, polyester and stretch fibers were combined to give a more comfortable feel and in order that pants could be worn skin tight. *Der.* From name of fabric used. Also see PANTS: JEANS and COATS AND JACKETS: DENIM.

Denmark cock   See HEADWEAR: COCKED HAT.

dentelle lace   See under LACES: DIEPPE POINT and DENTELLE DE LA VIERGE.

dentil   Term for a Greek motif consisting of a series of toothlike scallops used as a border.

department   In retailing, that segment of a retailing establishment that groups together items of merchandise that are complementary to one another, such as a junior department or an active sportswear department.

department store   Large retail establishment that organizes its functions and merchandise into departments.

depth   See ASSORTMENT.

de Rauch, Madeleine   * See APPENDIX/ DESIGNERS.

derby   See HEADWEAR.

desert boot   See FOOTWEAR.

desert fatigue cap   See HEADWEAR.

deshabillé (des-hah-bee′)   French word meaning wrapper, dressing gown, or negligée that is sometimes used in English (and spelled *dishabillé*) to refer to being partially dressed or dressed in nightclothes.

designer   Person engaged in creating original clothing and accessories in various areas of the fashion industry. Some designers own their businesses; others are employed by manufacturers to develop collections of merchandise in ready-to-wear, couture, lingerie, millinery, footwear, accessories, and jewelry.

designer brand   A designer name used as a BRAND name. Also called *signature brand*.

designer collection/designer line   See COLLECTION.

designer jeans   See PANTS.

designer label   See LABEL.

designer scarf   See SCARVES.

Design Industries Foundation for AIDS (DIFFA)   Organization of the fashion industry in the United States that raises funds to assist those suffering from AIDS.

Dessès, Jean   * See APPENDIX/DESIGNERS.

destination store   A type of retailer patronized by a customer because only it provides specific products or services that the customer wants. Customers seek out destination stores.

detachable collar   See NECKLINES AND COLLARS.

detachable cuff   See CUFFS.

detachable pantyhose   See HOSIERY.

detached chain stitch   See EMBROIDERIES AND SEWING STITCHES: LAZY DAISY STITCH.

Dettigen cock   See HEADWEAR: COCKED HAT.

development bundle system   See BUNDLE SYSTEM.

devotional ring   See JEWELRY.

dhoti   See PANTS.

dhoti shorts   See SHORTS.

diadem   See HEADWEAR.

diadem cap   See HEADWEAR.

diadem comb   See HAIR ACCESSORIES.

diadem fanchon bonnet   See HEADWEAR.

Diaghilev, Sergei Pavlovich (dee-ah-gehlef′) (1872–1929)   Russian aristocrat and avant-garde creator of the Ballets Russes, who produced *Scheherazade*, 1910, with costumes by Leon Bakst. The brilliant colors and new concept of stage design started a wave of Orientalism in Paris that affected the whole couture, particularly the work of PAUL POIRET, and banished somber Victorian fashions.

diagonal stitch   See EMBROIDERIES AND SEWING STITCHES.

diagonal weave   See TWILL WEAVE.

diamanté (dya-mahn-tay′)   Adjective that indicates a sparkling effect as that of the reflection of gemstones. *Der.* French, "made of diamonds." See DIAMANTÉ DRESS, BLOUSES AND TOPS: DIAMANTÉ TOP, BRAIDS: DIAMANTÉ BRAID, and HEADWEAR: DIAMANTÉ HEADBAND.

diamanté dress (dya-mahn-tay′)   Dress made almost entirely of sparkling beads, sequins, or paillettes, giving a glittering effect, very popular in mid-1980s. Although Norman Norell designed dresses in 1968 made entirely of sequins, they were not referred to as diamanté dresses until the mid-1980s. *Der.* French, "made of diamonds."

diamond   See GEMS, GEM CUTS, AND SETTINGS.

diamond bracelet   See JEWELRY.

diamond earring   See JEWELRY.

diamonds by the yard   See JEWELRY.

diamond watch   See WATCHES.

Diana Vernon hat   See HEADWEAR.

diaper cloth   See BIRD'S-EYE # 1.

D

dickey **1.** Separate fill-in used inside woman's low neckline with or without an attached collar. May be knitted or woven and have many types of collars. Also see BLOUSES AND TOPS: BLOUSETTE. Also spelled *dicky, dickie.* **2.** Man's false shirt front with attached collar, worn over a flannel shirt in the 19th c., not considered proper attire for gentlemen. **3.** Pinafore, or bib, for a child. **4.** See UNDERGARMENTS.

die cutting Method of cutting garment pieces using a sharp-edged piece of metal (the die), similar to a cookie cutter, that is made in the exact dimensions and shape of the pattern piece. The die is positioned over the fabric to be cut, then a pressurized plate is applied to the die, and this causes it to cut through the fabric layers.

Dieppe point lace See LACES.

Dietrich, Marlene German actress and entertainer, considered the supreme example of a glamorous film star, who was a significant fashion influence in the 1930s and 1940s. She was particularly famous for her legs, arched plucked eyebrows, and screen wardrobe (designed by Travis Banton who utilized many clinging chiffons and feather boas). Dietrich was credited with making mannish slacks and fedora hats popular for women.

diffusion line A less expensive line produced by a high fashion designer. Examples include Armani X, DKNY. *Der.* A French fashion term that is equivalent to a BRIDGE LINE.

digital watch See watches.

digitizer A table that enables a pattern to be entered into a computer. The table is embedded with sensors that relate to the *X* (horizontal) and *Y* (vertical) coordinates of a grid, allowing the pattern piece to be traced and entered into the computer.

dimensional stability † Ability of fabric to return to its original shape and size after wear, washing, or dry cleaning.

dimity † A range of lightweight, sheer fabrics usually made of cotton or a cotton blend characterized by lengthwise cords made by bunching or grouping several yarns together. Less often, a checked effect is made by grouping cross-wise yarns together as well.

dink/dinky See HEADWEAR: SKULLCAP.

dinner dress Full-length dress suitable for a formal dinner. Introduced in the 1930s, a dinner dress was distinguished from an evening gown by having the shoulders covered for dinner. Such dresses were frequently made with a coordinated jacket that, when removed, revealed a formal dress.

dinner jacket See COATS AND JACKETS.

dinner ring See JEWELRY: COCKTAIL RING.

Dior, Christian * (dee-ore) See APPENDIX/DESIGNERS.

dip ∞ Term used in 1890s and early 20th c. for the point of a waistline that was lower in front than back.

dip belt ∞ See BELTS: CONTOUR BELT.

diplax ∞ Large piece of fabric, nearly square, worn folded double as a mantle by Greek women. It was shown on Greek and Roman statues as either draped under right arm and pinned together on left shoulder or draped around hips.

diploidion ∞ (dip-ploy-dion) (pl. *diplois*) Mantle worn by ancient Greeks made out of a square or oblong piece of fabric folded double with the fold placed under the left arm and fastened on the right shoulder. Also see DIPLAX.

dip-top boots See FOOTWEAR: COWBOY BOOTS.

direct marketing channel See MARKETING CHANNEL.

Directoire (dir-eck´-twa) **1.** Period in French history from 1795 to 1799, following the French Revolution, when France was ruled by the Directory (in French, *Directoire*), a five-man executive body. **2.** Adjective used, especially in the 19th c., to describe apparel styles that were inspired by or derived from styles popular during the Directoire period in France. For women these were high-waisted, narrow-skirted muslin dresses with low necklines that were frequently worn with spencer jackets; flesh-colored stockings, shoes similar to laced ballet slippers, and ostrich plumes in the hair or on turbans. Men were more likely to wear coats cut short in front and with tails in back that were

Directoire #2: incroyable and merveilleuse

D

left open in front to show a waistcoat, tightly fitted breeches, stockings, low shoes or high boots, and top hats flaring at the top. Men who affected the most exaggerated of these styles were called **incroyables** (an-kwai´-ab-leh) (meaning "the incredible ones"). They contrived a careless appearance with loosely tied cravats wound high on the neck, unkept hair, and ridiculously large lapels. Women who were known as **merveilleuses** (mer-vay-use´), or "the marvelous ones," wore few undergarments, extremely low-cut and very sheer dresses, short and shaggy hairstyles, and huge jockey caps or poke bonnets. **3.** Styles of late 1880s to 1895 inspired by Sardou's drama *La Tosca* starring Sarah Bernhardt in 1887. Some of these styles have no relationship to the styles of the Directoire Period.

Directoire bonnet   See HEADWEAR.

Directoire coat   See COATS AND JACKETS.

Directoire gown   ∞ **1.** Woman's dress of muslin or similar sheer fabric with high waistline and narrow skirt. Sometimes has an overskirt forming a train in back, an extremely low neckline, and elbow-length or long sleeves. Frequently worn with a SPENCER JACKET (see under COATS AND JACKETS) during the French *Directoire Period* (1795–1799). **2.** Slim coat-style dress with wide lapels, gauntlet-cuffed sleeves, and high-sashed waist. Worn by women in late 19th c.

Directoire jacket   See COATS AND JACKETS.

Directoire skirt   See SKIRTS.

Directoire waistline   See WAISTLINES.

dirndl (durn´-del) **1.** Adjective used to describe various styles in which a full skirt or pant is gathered into a waistline. See COATS AND JACKETS: DIRNDL COAT, PANTS: DIRNDL PANTS, SKIRTS: DIRNDL SKIRT, and UNDERGARMENTS: DIRNDL PETTICOAT. **2.** Dress with gathers at the waistline that derives from a full-skirted Tyrolean peasant costume originating, and still worn, in Austrian and Bavarian Alps. Specific versions have varied in shape, with those worn in 1980s having a slightly belled shape to the skirt while the 1940s and 1950s version had a fuller skirt with more gathers at the waist to produce a more bouffant effect. The skirt is usually attached to tight-fitted bodice.

discharge print   See PRINTS, STRIPES, AND CHECKS.

disco clothes   Glittery fashions in bright, glowing colors styled in unrestrained fabrics. Usually made with short skirts for vigorous evening dancing at discotheques. *Der.* French, *discothéque,* "record library," as dancing is done to records rather than live music.

discount   See REDUCTIONS.

discount store   Retailer that sells brand name merchandise at below traditional retail prices.

dishabille   See DESHABILLÉ.

dishrag shirt   Loosely knitted man's sport shirt with placket closing at neck worn in 1930s. *Der.* Resemblance of knit to knitted dishrags of that period.

disposable swimsuit   See SWIMWEAR.

distressed   See STONE WASHED.

distribution centers   Centralized locations used by apparel companies or retailers to prepare merchandise for distribution to retail stores.

distribution strategy   System used by businesses to assure that apparel is placed in stores that sell to the target market for whom the merchandise was designed and manufactured.

ditto suit   ∞ Man's suit of the second half of the 18th c. in which the same fabric is used for pants, jacket, vest, and, sometimes, a cap.

divided skirt   **1.** See SKIRTS: CULOTTES. **2.** See SKIRTS: DIVIDED SKIRT.

division   A breakdown of merchandise in the business organization within a retail store that is the largest unit. Examples of divisions include women's, children's, or men's wear, which are, in turn, subdivided into DEPARTMENTS, CLASSIFICATIONS, and SUB-CLASSIFICATIONS.

ditto suit
18th century

djellaba/djellabah/jellaba   See SLEEPWEAR AND LOUNGEWEAR. Also see CAFTAN.

dobby attachment   See DOBBY WEAVE.

dobby fabric   Fabric made in the DOBBY WEAVE. *White-on-white broadcloth* is an example of a dobby fabric.

dobby weave   Weave forming small repeat geometric patterns that is made on plain loom with **dobby attachment,** a mechanical or electronic device that enables a loom to produce small repeat designs of not more than 8 to 30 rows of

D

crosswise yarns. More complex and larger patterns can be made on a JACQUARD loom.

Dr. Denton's® See SLEEPWEAR AND LOUNGEWEAR.

Doc Martens See FOOTWEAR.

doctor's gown See ACADEMIC COSTUME.

doctor's hood See ACADEMIC COSTUME.

Doctor Zhivago See ZHIVAGO.

doeskin **1.** See LEATHERS. **2.** Misnomer for doeskin fabric.

doeskin fabric † Any of several types of fabric made to simulate the texture and appearance of sueded doeskin leather. The fabrics may be made from napped wool, rayon, manufactured, or cotton fibers and woven or knitted.

doeskin glove See GLOVES AND GLOVE CONSTRUCTION.

dogaline ∞ Loose-fitting, straight-cut gown with very wide sleeves—lower edge turned up and fastened to shoulder—revealing sleeve of the undergown. Worn by men and women during the Middle Ages and 16th c.

dog collar **1.** See COLLARS AND NECKLINES: DOG COLLAR and HALTER NECKLINE. **2.** See JEWELRY: DOG COLLAR.

dog collar scarf See SCARVES.

dog's-ear collar See NECKLINES AND COLLARS.

Dolce and Gabbana * See APPENDIX/DESIGNERS.

dollar plan A type of planning utilized in some retail establishments in which a forecast of merchandising activities is used to generate a money budget expected to cover purchases of stock to be sold over a specified period.

dollar-round toe See FOOTWEAR.

Dolley Madison hood See HEADWEAR.

doll hat See HEADWEAR.

Dolly 1. See BABY-DOLL LOOK.

dolly look British term for BABY-DOLL LOOK.

Dolly Varden polonaise ∞ Type of woman's costume—inspired by Charles Dickens' character Dolly Varden in *Barnaby Rudge*—consisting of a fitted bodice and a draped overskirt of chintz, cretonne, or foulard with silk underskirt either plain, flowered, or quilted (or cashmere in winter). Worn with wide straw hat trimmed with flowers and ribbon and tied under the hair, which was worn in a CHIGNON (see under HAIRSTYLES). Popular in 1870s.

dolman (dole-man) **1.** See COATS AND JACKETS. **2.** See SHOULDERS AND SLEEVES. **3.** SWEATERS.

dolmanette See COATS AND JACKETS: DOLMAN #2.

dolman sweater See SWEATERS.

dome hat See HEADWEAR: BUBBLE HAT.

dome ring See JEWELRY.

dome umbrella See UMBRELLAS AND PARASOLS: BELL UMBRELLA.

domestic market The sale of goods within the 50 states of the United States. See INTERNATIONAL MARKET and REGIONAL MARKET.

domestic sourcing Obtaining of merchandise from sources available within the United States. See INTERNATIONAL SOURCE/SOURCING and SOURCING.

domino **1.** See CAPES, CLOAKS, AND SHAWLS. **2.** See MASKS.

Dom Pedro shoe See FOOTWEAR.

donegal tweed **1.** Medium- to heavyweight tweed made in Ireland. Originally handwoven in the county of Donegal and made in plain or twill weave, usually of coarse yarns with a single colored warp and a blend of colors in the filling yarn. Used for coats, suits, skirts, trousers, and jackets. Synonym: *Irish tweed.* **2.** A term for tweeds made from Yorkshire yarns spun and dyed in Donegal, Ireland. **3.** Imitations of the original Irish Donegal Tweeds.

donnilette See COATS AND JACKETS: DOUILLETTE.

don't mentions See INEXPRESSIBLES.

doo rag See HEADWEAR.

door knocker See JEWELRY.

dorelet See HEADWEAR.

dormeuse/dormouse See HEADWEAR.

dorm shirt See SLEEPWEAR AND LOUNGEWEAR.

Dorothée Bis * See APPENDIX/DESIGNERS.

Dorothy cloak See CAPES, CLOAKS, AND SHAWLS.

d'Orsay coat See COATS AND JACKETS.

d'Orsay, Count See ORSAY, COUNT D'.

d'Orsay habit-coat See COATS AND JACKETS.

d'Orsay pump See FOOTWEAR.

d'Orsay slippers See FOOTWEAR.

Dorset thread button See CLOSURES.

dots See PRINTS, STRIPES, AND CHECKS.

dotted swiss † Crisp lightweight fabric ornamented with regularly spaced dots that are created either by clipped sections of extra crosswise yarns that interlace with lengthwise yarns or flocked dots of fiber glued to the fabric surface.

double besom pocket See POCKETS: WELT POCKET.

double-breasted Describing the front opening of a garment lapped over double and fastening with two rows of buttons. Originally both rows were functional, now one row is usually decorative. Also called *d.b.,* in British tailors' 19th-c. slang. Shown at COATS AND JACKETS: BLAZER.

double chignon See HAIRSTYLES.

double cloth † Heavy fabric consisting of two separate fabrics woven at the same time and having another, binder yarn that moves from one layer to another to hold them together. Such fabrics are usually reversible, in which case they are referred to as DOUBLE-FACED.

double collar See NECKLINES AND COLLARS.

double cuff See CUFFS: FRENCH CUFF.

double dress Two dresses designed to be worn one over the other. Often the outer dress may be of sheer fabric while the under dress is of an opaque fabric.

double entry pocket See POCKETS.

double-faced satin ribbon † Ribbon woven with satin face on both sides.

double-girdled ∞ Describing the ancient Greek fashion of wearing a long narrow sash, or two separate sashes, wound around waist and crossed over chest to adjust fullness of garment.

double dress

double knit † Knit fabric in which face and back of the fabric have a similar appearance. Made in a rib knit construction using double sets of needles, the resulting fabric is heavier, has greater dimensional stability, and less tendency to sag or lose its shape than single knit fabrics.

double mantle See CAPES, CLOAKS, AND SHAWLS: MANTLE #2.

double ombré stripe See PRINTS, STRIPES, AND CHECKS.

double-puffed sleeve See SHOULDERS AND SLEEVES.

doubler See FOOTWEAR.

double ruffle See CLOTHING CONSTRUCTION DETAILS.

double-running stitch See EMBROIDERIES AND SEWING STITCHES.

double stitchdown See FOOTWEAR: STITCHDOWN SHOE CONSTRUCTION.

double-stitched seam See CLOTHING CONSTRUCTION DETAILS: TOPSTITCHED SEAMS.

doublet (dub′-let) **1.** ∞ Main garment for upper part of man's body worn from late 14th c. to 1670 and styled like a close-fitting short jacket of various lengths. Worn with either TRUNK HOSE or BREECHES. This garment seems to have evolved from garments used by the military such as the **gambeson** (gam′-bay-sohn), a sleeveless, padded and sometimes quilted cloth or leather garment worn under armor

doublet 1300s

in the Middle Ages. By the 14th c. the gambeson had become civilian costume and was more often referred to as a **juppe** (zhup), **gipon** (gee′-pon), or **pourpoint** (poor′-pwan, a French term for the stuffed and quilted jacket worn by men from 14th to 17th c.). The **jack** was a padded tight-fitting military doublet worn from the late 13th to the late 15th c. that was sometimes made of 30 layers of fabric and worn over the HAUBERK (see ARMOR). As worn by civilians in 14th c., the jack was a short jacket made of rich fabrics. **Peascod-bellied doublet** had a false front stuffed with cotton into a projection over the waistline that was shaped like the breast of a peacock. It was introduced into France from Spain and popular from 1570 to 1600,

peascod belly

codpiece

paned trunk hose

doublet with peascod belly, paned trunk hose, and codpiece 1542

though it seems originally to have been a Dutch style. It, too, may have had a military origin and is said to have been in imitation of the CUIRASSE (see ARMOR) to deflect bullets. Also called *bellied doublet, goose-bellied doublet, kodpeased doublet, long-bellied doublet,* and *shotten-bellied doublet.* Civilian doublets included the **hanseline** (han-sa-lyn) (also spelled *anslet, hanslein, haunse-leyns, hense lynes,* and *henselyns*), an extremely short garment, fashionable in late 14th and early 15th c. that some authorities equate with the **paltock.** All that seems to be known with certainty, however, of the paltock is that it was a very short men's garment which served as an anchor for HOSE. The **jerkin** was similar to the doublet with a slightly longer skirt, sometimes with HANGING SLEEVES (see under SHOULDERS AND SLEEVES), and worn from 1450 to 1630. By the 16th and 17th cs. the jerkin had become a sleeveless jacket, with WINGS on the shoulders. A **crop-doublet** was short-waisted and popular about 1610. **2.** ∞ Part of woman's riding habit from 1650 to 1670. **3.** See JEWELRY. **4.** Jacket of Scots HIGHLAND DRESS.

double-zipper foundation See UNDERGARMENTS.

Doucet, Jacques * See APPENDIX/DESIGNERS.

douillette See COATS AND JACKETS.

doupioni † (doop-ee´-on-ee) Yarn or fabric made from silk yarn reeled from double cocoons, or two interlaced cocoons in which the silk is intertwined. Yarn has uneven slubs, rather than being smooth, giving a decorative texture to the fabric. Also spelled *douppioni, doppione.*

doup weave See LENO WEAVE.

down See FEATHERS.

down jacket See COATS AND JACKETS.

down vest See VESTS.

downy calves See FALSE CALVES.

drain-pipe trousers See PANTS.

drape **1.** *n.* The degree to which fabric falls into graceful folds when hung or arranged in different positions. **2.** *v.* The act of creating fashion designs by manipulating, pinning, and cutting muslin or other fabric over a dress form. In this technique, the draped garment is then used to create a pattern from which a garment can be made.

draped heel See FOOTWEAR.

draped skirt See SKIRTS.

draping See DRAPE #2.

drawers See UNDERGARMENTS.

drawn fabric work See EMBROIDERIES AND SEWING STITCHES.

drawn thread work See EMBROIDERIES AND SEWING STITCHES.

drawstring Ribbon or cord inserted through a band of fabric, pulled and tied to form a closing. See BLOUSES AND TOPS: DRAWSTRING BLOUSE, HANDBAGS AND RELATED ACCESSORIES: DRAWSTRING BAG, NECKLINES AND COLLARS: DRAWSTRING NECKLINE, PANTS: DRAWSTRING PANTS, SHIRTS: DRAWSTRING SHIRT, SHORTS: DRAWSTRING SHORTS, and WAISTLINES: DRAWSTRING.

Dr. Denton Sleepers® See SLEEPWEAR AND LOUNGEWEAR.

dreadlocks See HAIRSTYLES.

dreadnought See COATS AND JACKETS: FEARNOTHING JACKET.

Drécoll * See APPENDIX/DESIGNERS.

Dresden point See EMBROIDERIES AND SEWING STITCHES.

dress **1.** *n.* Collective term for all clothing (e.g. the dress of Spain, the dress of an ethnic group). Synonyms: *apparel, clothes, costume.* **2.** *n.* In the field of textiles and apparel, a widely accepted definition of dress is ". . . the total arrangement of all outwardly detectable modifications of the body itself and all material objects added to it" (Roach and Musa, 1980, 11). **3.** *n.* General term for a one-piece outer garment that varies in length but extends at least to below the hips and ends in a skirt. In Western costume history, traditionally worn by women. The term dress as presently used did not come into common usage until the late 18th c., before which the terms *robe* or *gown* were used. Fashion terms for various dress styles have developed and are generally formed by placing an adjective describing the apparel in front of the word "dress." Examples: COAT DRESS, DROP WAIST DRESS, SHIRT DRESS, SWING DRESS, SWEATER DRESS. **4.** *v.* To put on a garment. **5.** *v.* To arrange the hair. **6.** *v.* To tan and finish hides for leather uses. **7.** *adj.* Describes an item of apparel intended to be worn for more formal occasions, e.g., dress shoes, dress shirt.

dress à la constitution See COSTUME À LA CONSTITUTION.

dress alikes Women who were friends and wore exactly the same dress or costume, a popular fashion in 1984.

dress clip/dress holder ∞ Device used for holding up woman's skirt that has been fashionable periodically. In the 1840s a metal hook was attached at the waistline or belt to lift the skirt when walking. In the 1870s this was an elaborate device made with two pendant chains and clips used for holding up skirts. Also see PAGE.

dress coat See COATS AND JACKETS: SWALLOW-TAILED COAT.

dress elevator See PORTE-JUPE POMPADOUR.

dress form Dressmaking form in shape of human body on which the designer or home sewer drapes fabrics or clothes while sewing. Also called *dressmaker's dummy, dressmaker's form, model form.*

dress frock coat See COATS AND JACKETS: CUT-AWAY FROCK COAT.

dress holder See DRESS CLIP.

dress improver See UNDERGARMENTS: BUSTLE.

dressing gown/robe See SLEEPWEAR AND LOUNGEWEAR.

dressing sacque See SLEEPWEAR AND LOUNGEWEAR.

dress lounge British term for an early version of the dinner jacket. See COATS AND JACKETS: DINNER JACKET.

dressmaker 1. Person, usually a woman, who makes clothing for private customers. From 1850 through 1920s, before ready-to-wear, dressmakers often worked in customer's homes to prepare seasonal wardrobes for the family. Also called a *seamstress.* 2. See TAILORED.

dressmaker coat See COATS AND JACKETS.

dressmaker pin Fine STRAIGHT PIN with head used when sewing on delicate fabrics. Also called *silk pin.*

dressmaker's brim See HEADWEAR.

dressmaker's dummy See DRESS FORM.

dressmaker suit Woman's suit made with soft lines and fine details, as contrasted with man-tailored styles that have the sharply defined lines of a man's suit made by a tailor. Fashionable in 1950s and revived in the mid-1980s.

dressmaker swimsuit See SWIMWEAR.

dress shield Protective device placed inside a dress under the arm to prevent staining of the garment by perspiration. The earliest dress shields (c. 1840s) were made of leather covered by fabric. Later versions were of fabric-covered natural or synthetic rubber.

dress shirt See SHIRTS.

dress shoe See FOOTWEAR.

dress socks See HOSIERY.

dress Wellington See FOOTWEAR.

dressy casual Coined in 2001 to describe clothing appropriate for workers in management positions that was replacing CASUAL WEAR styles that had been accepted in the 1990s. The return to more formal business suits seemed to come as a result of an economic downturn. Also see CASUAL FRIDAY.

drill † Durable cotton fabric made in a twill weave and similar to DENIM.

D-ring belt See BELTS.

D-ring closing See CLOSURES.

drip-dry See DURABLE PRESS.

driving cape/sac See COATS AND JACKETS: ALBERT DRIVING CAPE.

driving coat See COATS AND JACKETS: BOX COAT.

driving glove See GLOVES AND GLOVE CONSTRUCTION.

drop earring See JEWELRY.

drop-front See PANTS.

dropped shoulders See SHOULDERS AND SLEEVES.

dropped skirt See SKIRTS.

dropping See FURS: LETTING OUT.

drop waist/dropped waist/dropped waistline See WAISTLINES: DROPPED WAISTLINE.

drum farthingale See FARTHINGALE.

drum major's hat See HEADWEAR.

dual or multi channel distribution System of merchandise distribution in which manufacturers sell their products through manufacturer-owned retail stores and also through other independent retailers.

Du Barry Adjective derived from the name of Marie Jeanne Bécu, Contesse Du Barry (1746–1793) and the last mistress of King Louis XV of France. This adjective was used to describe 19th-c. garments inspired by or derived from clothing items thought to have been worn by Madame Du Barry and her contemporaries. See DU BARRY CORSAGE, COATS AND JACKETS: DU BARRY MANTLE, SHOULDERS AND SLEEVES: DU BARRY SLEEVE.

Du Barry corsage ∞ Bodice with a wide V-shaped front, worn by women from the 1830s to

1850, adapted from the style worn by Comtesse Du Barry (1746–1793), last mistress of Louis XV of France. Also called *corsage à la Du Barry*.

Du Barry costume ∞ Style of dress worn by Marie Jeanne Bécu, Comtesse Du Barry (1746–1793), last mistress of Louis XV of France. Consisted of a fitted bodice with low décolletage, long V to bodice front filled with lace RUCHING, elbow-length sleeves, and a full skirt.

Du Barry mantle See COATS AND JACKETS.

Du Barry sleeve See SHOULDERS AND SLEEVES.

Dubinsky, David See UNION OF NEEDLETRADES, INDUSTRIAL, AND TEXTILE EMPLOYEES.

duchess See HAIR ACCESSORIES.

duchesse † Lightweight lustrous satin fabric made of silk or rayon and dyed solid colors. Also called *duchesse satin*.

duchesse lace See LACES.

duchesse pleat ∞ Term used in mid-1870s for back pleats of a skirt, usually two *box pleats* on either side of center-back placket or seam.

duchesse satin See DUCHESSE.

Duchess of Windsor (1896–1986) The former Wallis Warfield Simpson, an American divorcée who married Edward VIII of England. In order to marry Mrs. Simpson, the king abdicated and assumed the title of Duke of Windsor in 1936. World famous for her impeccable taste and conservative fashion leadership, and usually dressed by French couture, the duchess' wedding gown, designed by designer Mainbocher in Paris, became the most copied dress in the world—available at every price level.

duck † A broad term for a wide range of strong, firm, plain weave fabric that is usually made of cotton, linen, or cotton blended with manufactured fibers.

duckbills See FOOTWEAR.

duckbill solleret See ARMOR: SABATON.

duck-hunter See COATS AND JACKETS.

ducks See PANTS.

duck's-foot fan See FANS.

Duck Shoe® See footwear.

ducktail haircut See HAIRSTYLES.

dude **1.** American term used at a Western ranch for someone from the city or the East Coast. Also see COWBOY/COWGIRL. **2.** ∞ Term used in 1890s for a dandy, an affected or fastidious man.

dude jeans See PANTS: WESTERN PANTS.

duds Slang for clothes in general.

dueling blouse/shirt See BLOUSES AND TOPS and SHIRTS.

duet pin See JEWELRY.

duffel bag See HANDBAGS AND RELATED ACCESSORIES.

duffel coat See COATS AND JACKETS.

Duke of Windsor (1894–1973) Edward VIII, king of England, who reigned briefly in 1936 until he abdicated in order to marry Wallis Warfield Simpson, an American divorcée. He was henceforth known as the Duke of Windsor. As the Prince of Wales he strongly influenced men's fashions in the 1920s and is credited with introducing such styles as the large Panama hat, tab collar, Windsor knot tie, double-breasted jacket with long roll lapel, Fair Isle sweater, white waistcoat worn as dinner jacket, guard's overcoat, seashore resort-type sportswear, and brown buckskin shoes.

dummy See DRESS FORM.

dunce cap See HEADWEAR.

dungarees See PANTS.

dunstable See HEADWEAR.

duo-length coat See COATS AND JACKETS: ZIP-OFF COAT.

duplex print See PRINTS, STRIPES, AND CHECKS.

duplicate In retailing, a sample copy of the manufacturer's PROTOTYPE that is used by sales representatives in selling styles in the line to retail buyers. Also called *sales sample*.

duppioni See DOUPIONI.

durable finish † Any fabric finish that will withstand laundering, drycleaning, and wear for a reasonable period of time.

durable press † (DP) The name given to a special finish that provides garments with shape retention, durable pleats and creases, durably smooth seams, and wrinkle resistance during use and after laundering. Some of the first fabrics that did not require ironing were called **drip-dry** fabrics.

dust cap See HEADWEAR.

duster **1.** See COATS AND JACKETS. **2.** See SLEEPWEAR AND LOUNGEWEAR: BRUNCH COAT.

dust gown ∞ 18th-c. term for an overskirt worn by women to protect the dress when riding horseback.

dust ruffle ∞ Ruffle inside of hem of full-length dress or petticoat to protect dress from becoming soiled when walking outdoors in late 19th and early 20th c. Also called *balayeuse* and *sweeper.*

Dutch Adjective used to describe various types of clothing and accessories derived from or inspired by styles worn in the Netherlands.

Dutch bob See HAIRSTYLES: BUSTER BROWN.

Dutch boy cap See HEADWEAR.

Dutch boy heel See FOOTWEAR.

Dutch cap See HEADWEAR.

Dutch coat ∞ Man's short jacket worn in late 14th and 15th c., later called a jerkin. (From 14th to 16th c., "Dutch" usually meant German.)

Dutchman See FOOTWEAR.

Dutch neckline See NECKLINES AND COLLARS: SQUARE NECKLINE.

Dutch waist ∞ Woman's bodice without a point in center front worn with the wheel farthingale about 1580 to 1620. See FARTHINGALE.

Duvillier wig See WIGS AND HAIRPIECES.

dux collar ∞ Man's narrow standing collar, with front corners turned down, worn from 1860s on.

dyeable shoe See FOOTWEAR.

dyed sable See FURS: SABLE.

dyeing/dyes † Coloring of fibers, yarns, fabrics, furs, and leather with natural or synthetic coloring agents, called dyes, that are relatively permanent.

D

E Shoe size: Letter indicating a width; widths run from AAAAs to EEEEEs, with AAAA being the narrowest and EEEEE the widest.

ear band See JEWELRY.

earclip See JEWELRY: EARRING.

earmuffs **1.** See HEADWEAR. **2.** See HAIRSTYLES.

earring See JEWELRY.

ear string ∞ Black ribbon, or strands of silk, worn through pierced left ear by men from latter part of 16th c. to about 1610.

earthquake gown ∞ Woman's warm gown, suitable for wear outdoors, made in England in 1750 in anticipation of a third earthquake after two earlier quakes had taken place in London.

ease **1.** *n.* Factor taken into consideration when drafting a pattern—allowing extra measure at bust, waist, and hips, so garment will fit comfortably, not skintight. **2.** See CLOTHING CONSTRUCTION DETAILS.

Easter bonnet See HEADWEAR.

Eastern Orthodox cross See CROSS #1.

Easter Parade **1.** Term coined for promenading in new spring clothes on Easter Sunday. A traditional event in New York City since March 25, 1883. People originally rode in carriages and strolled on Fifth Avenue after church. Later activities centered on areas around St. Patrick's Cathedral, at 50th Street and Fifth Avenue extending north to Central Park and south to 42nd Street. The idea of dressing in new spring finery on Easter Sunday dates back to Biblical and Roman times. **2.** Title of film and song starring Judy Garland and Fred Astaire produced in 1948 featuring New York City's Easter Parade. **3.** See HEADWEAR.

ecclesiastical vestments See CLERICAL DRESS.

écharpe See SCARVES.

echelles ∞ (eh-shell′) Decorative trim on front of woman's bodice made with braid, lace, or ribbon bows arranged in ladderlike effect. Popular from end of 17th to end of 18th c. *Der.* French, "ladder." Shown at ENGAGEANTES.

Eclipse Tie See FOOTWEAR.

eco-friendly Apparel made from natural fibers that were grown without pesticides and finished with nonpolluting substances, or from manufactured fibers produced using less polluting processes, or from renewable resources or recycled materials such as plastic bottles. Also called *green clothes.*

écrasé See LEATHERS.

edge **1.** See FOOTWEAR. ∞ **2.** A late 15th- and early 16th-c. term for an ornamental border, usually made by a goldsmith, used on a headdress. Also spelled *neyge, age, oegge, egge.*

edging Narrow decorative border of lace, embroidery, braid, or fringe used for trimming on clothing, particularly at hem, sleeve, or neck.

EDI See ELECTRONIC DATA INTERCHANGE.

Edwardian/Edwardian look Fashions based on a revival of elements of styles of the early 1900s, including nipped waistlines, regency collars, capes, and neck ruffles worn by both men and women. Such fashions were especially popular in the 1960s. *Der.* From period 1901–1910, when Edward VII was king of England.

Edwardian coat/Edwardian jacket See COATS AND JACKETS.

Edwardian Period From 1901 to 1910, when Edward VII, first son of Queen Victoria, was King of England. Popular styles that have been revived in later years include fitted frock or suit coats, top hats for men, and HOURGLASS SILHOUETTE in dresses for women, which were often worn with large decorative hats.

Edwardian suit Man's suit with close-fitting fingertip-length jacket, with high notched lapels and narrow stovepipe pants. Copied from styles of 1900 to 1911, reign of Edward VII, and popular in exaggerated form by London TEDDY BOYS in late 1950s. Made in velvet for women in late 1960s and early 1970s.

eelskin masher trousers See PANTS.

eelskin sleeve See SHOULDERS AND SLEEVES.

eel skirt See SKIRTS.

egge See EDGE #2.

Egham, Staines, and Windsor See HEADWEAR.

egret feathers (e-grit) See FEATHERS: AIGRETTE.

Egyptian collar See JEWELRY.

Egyptian cotton † High-quality long-staple, strong lustrous cotton produced along the Nile River with staple averaging $\frac{1}{8}''$ to $1\frac{1}{2}''$. Imported to make threads, laces, and fine fabrics.

Egyptian lace See LACES.

Egyptian sandal See FOOTWEAR.

Egyptian styles (ancient) Dress of the ancient Egyptian Civilization (c. 3000 to 300 B.C.) was generally draped from rectangles of linen fabric. Although changes in dress can be seen over this time period, styles remained remarkably consistent for almost 3,000 years. Among the basic costumes types used throughout Egyptian history were a LOIN CLOTH, a skirtlike garment called a SCHENTI, that wrapped around the waist, and a closely fitted, tubular wrapped dress often mistakenly called a KALASIRIS by costume historians but more accurately described as a **sheath dress**. In the period after 1575 B.C., new garments such as

Egyptian boy in schenti

kalasiris

tunics and more elaborate garments made of sheer accordion-pleated fabric were added.

Egyptian wig See WIGS AND HAIRPIECES.

eiderdown See FEATHERS.

eighths See FOOTWEAR.

eight-point cap See HEADWEAR.

Eiseman, Florence * See APPENDIX/DESIGNERS.

sheath dress   pleated robe

Eisenhower jacket See COATS AND JACKETS: BATTLE JACKET.

elastic **1.** † *n.* Stretchable fiber, yarn, or tape. Generally elastics are made from natural or synthetic rubber or ELASTOMERS such as SPANDEX and frequently are covered with some other fiber, yarn, or fabric. **2.** *adj.* Describing any fiber, yarn, fabric, or garment that is stretchable. Synonym: *elasticized*. See FOOTWEAR: ELASTIC-SIDED BOOT, HEADWEAR: ELASTIC ROUND HAT, JEWELRY: ELASTIC BRACELET, NECKLINES AND COLLARS: ELASTICIZED NECKLINE, UNDERGARMENTS: ELASTIC-LEG BRIEF, and WAISTLINES: ELASTICIZED WAISTLINE.

elasticity † Ability of fabric or yarn to stretch and return to its original shape when tension is released. Very important for hose and pantyhose.

elasticized See ELASTIC.

elastomer † A synthetic material which has the excellent stretchability and recovery of natural rubber. SPANDEX, an elastomeric fiber, is an example.

elbow cuff See CUFFS.

elbow-length sleeve See SHOULDERS AND SLEEVES.

electric *adj.* Apparel or accessories powered by electricity.

electric dress Novelty dress decorated with electric lights wired to a battery at the waist, designed to be worn to discothèques in the late 1960s.

electric mole See FURS.

electric-processed rabbit See FURS: ELECTRIC MOLE and ELECTRIC SEAL.

electric seal See FURS.

electric sock See HOSIERY.

E

electric vest See VESTS.

electrified lambskin See FURS.

electronic data interchange (EDI) Electronic transfer of information from one point to another by way of computers. For example, transmission of purchase orders from retailer to manufacturer, allowing more rapid response to consumer demands.

electronic game watch See WATCHES.

electronic retailing Sale of merchandise through electronic media. Television sales and shopping on the Internet are examples.

elephant-leg pants See PANTS.

elephant sleeve See SHOULDERS AND SLEEVES.

elevator heel See FOOTWEAR.

Elevator shoe See FOOTWEAR.

Elizabethan styles
Garments and accessories worn during the reign of Elizabeth I of England, 1558–1603. Men's costume usually consisted of SLASHED and PANED TRUNK HOSE, DOUBLET, and variations of the RUFF (see under NECKLINES AND COLLARS). Women's dress in the latter part of

Elizabethan styles: woman wearing a wheel farthingale and man in trunk hose and canions.

the period usually had barrel-shaped skirt, called a FARTHINGALE, and a standing lace collar. Costume of this period is sometimes also called *Shakespearean costume*.

elkhide See LEATHERS.

elliptic collar See NECKLINES AND COLLARS

Ellis, Perry * See APPENDIX/DESIGNERS.

embossed leather See under LEATHERS: LEATHER in category heading.

embossing † A process to produce a raised design or pattern in relief on fabrics by passing the cloth between hot, engraved rollers that press the design into the fabric. In heat-sensitive fabrics, embossing is permanent. In other fabrics, resin finishes are used to give fabrics a durable effect. Velvet or plush fabrics are embossed either by shearing or by pressing certain areas flat.

embroidered braid See BRAIDS.

embroidered sweater See SWEATERS.

EMBROIDERIES AND SEWING STITCHES

embroidery Fancy needlework or trimming using colored yarn, embroidery floss, soft cotton, silk or metallic thread. Usually done by hand, but may be made on a sewing machine or on mechanized machines such as a SCHIFFLI MACHINE (see under EMBROIDERIES AND SEWING STITCHES). In primitive times, straws or grasses were used to embroider with a bone needle; gold embroidery was first made by Assyrians; later copied by Egyptians, Greeks, and Romans. Each country in Europe developed its own type of embroidery. Needlework has been a popular craft for women since medieval times.

sewing stitches Utilitarian stitches made by hand or by sewing machine in the construction of apparel.

afghan stitch Simple crochet stitch made with a long hooked needle and yarn in various colors used to make garments and afghans. Also called *tricot stitch* (tree´-co), *Tunisian crochet, railway,* and *idiot stitch.*

aloe thread embroidery Straw-like ALOE fibers satin-stitched, forming a raised effect. Popular in England in the late 19th c.

Anglo-Saxon embroidery Long surface stitches couched with metal or silk threads in an outline effect. See EMBROIDERIES AND SEWING STITCHES: COUCHED EMBROIDERY. *Der.* Done by Anglo Saxons in ancient times.

antique couching See EMBROIDERIES AND SEWING STITCHES: ORIENTAL COUCHING.

Appenzell embroidery (ap-en´-tsell) Fine Swiss DRAWN WORK (see under EMBROIDERIES AND SEWING STITCHES) used chiefly on handkerchiefs and fine muslin, a cottage industry in Switzerland. *Der.* Named for town in Switzerland where it originated.

appliqué See in alphabetical listing.

Arrasene embroidery (ar-a´-seen) Embroidery with simple stitches to create a velvetlike effect made by using Arrasene thread of silk or wool, which resembles CHENILLE. Introduced in the 1880s. *Der.* Named for town of Arras, France.

arrowhead stitch/arrowhead Embroidery consisting of two stitches slanted to form an arrow, used singly or filled in with the satin stitch. Often used as reinforcement or decorative element at top of a pleat or pocket, where it is called an **arrowhead**. First seen in Eastern embroideries.

arrowhead stitch

Assisi embroidery (ahs-si′-si) Cross-stitch embroidery in which the design image is outlined and the background is worked solidly in cross-stitch. Originated in the Assisi area of northern Italy. See EMBROIDERIES AND SEWING STITCHES: CROSS-STITCH.

Aubusson stitch See EMBROIDERIES AND SEWING STITCHES: REP STITCH.

Ayrshire embroidery Scottish form of embroidery on fine muslin with open filling stitches. Evolved from 18th c. DRESDEN and TAMBOUR embroidery techniques. See cross-references under EMBROIDERIES AND SEWING STITCHES and also see MADEIRA EMBROIDERY.

back stitch Stitch used for hand sewing to prevent seam from ripping out. Also used for embroidery, where it may serve as a basis for forming BLACKWORK embroidery patterns (see under EMBROIDERIES AND SEWING STITCHES). Each stitch goes back over space left by previous stitch, giving the appearance of a machine stitch.

back stitch

backstitch Sewing term for reversing stitch on sewing machine. Used to secure threads at the beginning and ending of seams. Also called *staying a seam* or *stay.*

backstitch embroidery Outline embroidery similar to HOLBEIN work (see under EMBROIDERIES AND SEWING STITCHES), but single-faced instead of double.

ballpoint embroidery See EMBROIDERIES AND SEWING STITCHES: LIQUID EMBROIDERY.

bargello stitch (bar-gel′-low) Stitch worked vertically on canvas or scrim over a given number of

bargello stitch

threads to form a zigzag pattern. Visual impact results from color usage and stitch length variations. Also called *flame* and *Florentine stitch.*

bar tack Embroidery detail used either to reinforce an area, such as the end of a buttonhole, or as a decorative device. Made by taking several parallel stitches of the same size, then passing another thread around the parallel threads on the surface of the fabric. This latter thread is attached to the fabric only at the ends.

basket stitch Embroidery stitch resembling series of overlapped cross-stitches used to fill in backgrounds.

basket weave stitch Needlepoint stitch in which a series of diagonal stitches (see EMBROIDERIES AND SEWING STITCHES: CONTINENTAL STITCH) is most often used to fill background.

baste *v.* To stitch fabrics together either by hand or with large machine stitches to hold in place prior to sewing final seams. After stitching, bastings are removed.

basting *n.* Loose running stitches, often alternating long and short, used to hold sections of garment together before machine stitching.

beading **1.** embroidery in which beads of various kinds are sewn onto dresses, handbags, wedding dresses, sweaters, or blouses. **2.** Lines of small embroidered eyelets as seen in WHITEWORK embroidery (see under EMBROIDERIES AND SEWING STITCHES).

Beauvais embroidery (bo-vay′) Tapestrylike embroidery done in many colors. *Der.* Named after city in France where it originated.

Berlin woolwork Allover type of needlepoint embroidery (see EMBROIDERIES AND SEWING STITCHES: NEEDLEPOINT #1) done on canvas, primarily using the cross-stitch. *Der.* Name dates from 1820, when Berlin wool was used. Also called *canvas* or *cushion style* embroidery.

blackwork Embroidery originally done in black silk on white linen, fashionable from 16th to 17th c. Sometimes worked in an all-over continuous scroll design and used to decorate collars, cuffs, smocks, and

blackwork

E

handkerchiefs. In modern times the technique has evolved to geometric pattern stitching executed on an even-weave textile. When reversible, called HOLBEIN WORK (SEE UNDER EMBROIDERIES AND SEWING STITCHES). Also called *Spanish blackwork*.

blanket stitch Embroidery stitch that looks like a series of connected Us. Originally used to finish edges of binding on blankets, now for decorative effect. Also called *purl stitch* or *open buttonhole stitch*.

blanket stitch or open buttonhole stitch

blind stitch See EMBROIDERIES AND SEWING STITCHES: SLIP STITCH.

bonnaz (bo-nahz') Machine embroidery, sometimes worked on canvas-based cloth, with all types of designs possible as the operator can make the machine go in any direction. Used on sweaters, dresses, hats, gloves, and handbags. *Der.* Named after J. Bonnaz, a French inventor.

Breton work Peasant embroidery in colored silk and metallic threads made in floral and geometric designs, largely done in chain stitch. Also called *Brittany work*. *Der.* Originated in Brittany.

brick stitch/brickwork Blanket stitch used on flat fabric in continuous rows resembling brick wall. Also called *long and short stitch, featherwork, Irish stitch, tapestry shading stitch*.

Brittany work See EMBROIDERIES AND SEWING STITCHES: BRETON WORK.

brocade embroidery Embroidery made by needlework done over the designs of brocade fabric.

broderie anglaise See EMBROIDERIES AND SEWING STITCHES: MADEIRA EMBROIDERY.

broderie russe See EMBROIDERY AND SEWING STITCHES: RUSSIAN EMBROIDERY.

bullion embroidery (bull-yawn') Embroidery done with fine gold wire, also embroidery done with gold or silver threads, or cords, originating with the Phrygians (a region of what is now central Turkey) in ancient times.

bundle Embroidery stitch resembling a small bow knot. Made by taking 3 or 4 long loose stitches

bundle stitch or sheaf stitch

side by side, then placing a small stitch across at the center, drawing them together.

Bunka embroidery Japanese embroidery done with chain stitch with machine-made knitting yarn (frequently polyester) that is unraveled to reveal its textured effect. This yarn is threaded through a special needle, held like a pencil, and punched into the fabric (similar to making a hooked rug). Usually used to make scenes depicting figures, animals, birds, and floral patterns.

buttonhole stitch Embroidery stitch similar to BLANKET STITCH (see EMBROIDERIES AND SEWING STITCHES) worked close together with an extra purl at the edge. Used for worked buttonhole. The basic stitch for NEEDLEPOINT LACE (see under LACES) and the most commonly used stitch for edging design areas in cutwork. Also called *close stitch*.

Byzantine embroidery Appliqué work combined with decorative stitches done in the 19th c.

Byzantine stitch Slanting embroidery stitch, similar to SATIN STITCH (see EMBROIDERIES AND SEWING STITCHES), worked on canvas as a background filler over 3 or 4 vertical and horizontal threads in diagonal pattern.

cable stitch **1.** Embroidery stitch, similar to chain stitch, with extra stitch connecting the links. See EMBROIDERIES AND SEWING STITCHES: CHAIN STITCH #2. **2.** Hand-knitting stitch that produces a vertical cable pattern by crossing groups of knitting stitches over each other. **3.** Type of stitch used for smocking, that consists of extra stitches between the dots.

California embroidery **1.** Contemporary term used for leather stitching and braiding. **2.** Primitive pre-Spanish embroidery made in California by Indians using fishbone needle and animal substance for thread.

candlewick embroidery Tufts made with thick loosely twisted cotton yarn called *candlewicking* and a large needle. Several stitches are taken in the same place making loops that are cut to form a fluffy tuft.

canvas embroidery See EMBROIDERIES AND SEWING STITCHES: BERLIN WORK and NEEDLEPOINT #1.

Carrickmacross See under LACES.

cashmere work Rich, varicolored embroidery, frequently inlaid APPLIQUÉ done in India, with complicated needlework covering almost entire surface, used for shawls.

catch stitch Loose stitch, like a series of Xs crossed near their top, used for bulky hems and for pleats in linings. Also called *cat stitch*.

catch stitch

cat stitch See EMBROIDERIES AND SEWING STITCHES: CATCH STITCH.

chain stitch **1.** Embroidery stitch making connected loops that form a chain on the front. **2.** Machine stitch made by a commercial sewing machine done with a single thread, forming a chain on the back, used for hems and shoes—easy to remove. **3.** Basic crochet stitch.

chain stitch #1

chainstitched embroidery Machine embroidery worked in different designs using a chain stitch. Used lavishly at necklines, cuffs, and hems of blouses imported from India in 1980s.

chenille embroidery (shen-neel´) Embroidery originating in France using fine CHENILLE yarn with flat stitches producing a soft, velvetlike pattern.

china ribbon embroidery See EMBROIDERIES AND SEWING STITCHES: ROCOCO EMBROIDERY.

Chinese embroidery Single- or double-faced embroidery that usually covers entire robe or gown with motifs of cherry blossoms, birds, butterflies, and dragons. Done in satin, chain, French knots, feather, and other stitches with silk, gold, or silver threads in an elaborate and intricate design. Originally floss and metal threads were worked over a painted design.

close stitch See EMBROIDERIES AND SEWING STITCHES: BUTTONHOLE STITCH.

Colbert embroidery (col-bare´) Embroidery made with colored threads outlining the designs and background covered with an all-over pattern done in the satin stitch.

continental stitch Diagonal stitch used on canvas worked over 2 threads used to make the pattern or to fill in needlepoint backgrounds. Also called *tent stitch*. Shown at EMBROIDERIES AND SEWING STITCHES: NEEDLEPOINT.

couched embroidery/couching Decorative embroidery made by laying a long piece of yarn or embroidery floss flat while tiny stitches are worked around this yarn at intervals to fasten it tightly. Couching is often used to hold metal threads in place in METAL THREAD EMBROIDERY (see under EMBROIDERIES AND SEWING STITCHES).

couching

counted cross-stitch embroidery Embroidery done on an even weave textile, using cross-stitch and usually worked with embroidery floss. Design is usually executed following a graph pattern.

counted thread embroidery A category of embroidery. For specific types see EMBROIDERIES AND SEWING STITCHES: COUNTED CROSS-STITCH, BLACKWORK, ASSISI EMBROIDERY, NEEDLEPOINT, and DARNING.

crewel work Embroidery made with heavy, colored, crewel yarns, usually of loosely twisted two-ply worsted, on a linen fabric or ground. Motifs are filled in with many types of stitches.

crochet See CROCHET # 1 in alphabetical listing.

cross-stitch Decorative stitch that forms an X worked in various colored yarns on a plain background. Also used in NEEDLEPOINT, CREWEL EMBROIDERY, BLACKWORK, and ASSISI EMBROIDERY (see under EMBROIDERIES AND SEWING STITCHES).

cross-stitch

cross-stitch embroidery Embroidered Xs made in a colored pattern on a plain ground.

cushion-style embroidery See EMBROIDERIES AND SEWING STITCHES: BERLIN WORK.

cutwork (*opus scissum*) (oh´-puss siss´-um) Embroidery made by embroidering the edges of a design with BUTTONHOLE STITCHES (see under EMBROIDERIES AND SEWING STITCHES) and cutting out the background fabric around the designs. BARS or BRIDES (see under LACES) are frequently used to connect the larger cut-out areas.

cutwork

Czechoslovakian embroidery Bright-colored cotton, silk, or wool threads worked in geometric designs on linen. Made by counting stitches or using a traced pattern.

E

darning   Vertical stitches woven through horizontal stitches in a one-to-one checkerboard pattern to resemble plain woven cloth. Used for mending holes or as an embroidery stitch to fill in backgrounds.

Delhi work   Chain- and satin-stitch embroidery made in India with metal and silk threads on satin or other fabrics.

detached chain stitch   See EMBROIDERIES AND SEWING STITCHES: LAZY DAISY STITCH.

diagonal stitch   Embroidery stitch worked diagonally over double threads of canvas with stitches varying in lengths.

double-running stitch   A basic BLACKWORK stitch (see under EMBROIDERIES AND SEWING STITCHES) that is a tiny running stitch, worked and then reversed, so that new stitches fill spaces and make a pattern similar to machine stitch. Also called *line stitch, square stitch, stroke stitch, two-sided stitch, Holbein stitch,* and *Italian stitch.*

drawn fabric work   Various embroidery stitches are executed with a fine thread and pulled tightly on canvas or an even weave textile, thereby compressing the yarns of the textile together to produce an open lacelike appearance. Also known as *pulled fabric work* or *pulled thread embroidery.*

drawn thread work (opus tiratum) (oh′-puss tir-ah′-tuhm)   Open lacelike-appearing design resulting from withdrawing yarns from an even woven textile. The remaining yarns are bundled together, stitched over, or folded back on each other to create pattern. For techniques used in drawn threadwork, see EMBROIDERIES AND SEWING STITCHES: HEMSTITCHING, HARDANGER EMBROIDERY, HEDABO EMBROIDERY, AND NEEDLEWEAVING. Also called *withdrawn thread work* or *withdrawn fabric embroidery.*

drawn thread work

Dresden point   German lace of drawn work type introduced in the late 16th c., on linen. Some of the threads are taken out and some left to form a pattern. Others were worked to form square meshes. After the pattern was made, it was embroidered with intricate stitchery. Also called MORAVIAN WORK.

English work   Excellent quality of embroidery done by Anglo-Saxon women from 7th to 10th c. Highly prized in England and on the Continent. Also called *opus Anglicum* (oh′-puss ang′-lee-kum), term usually applied to clerical embroidery done in silk and metal threads.

eyelet embroidery   Holes punched out and embroidery worked around the hole, by hand or on a Schiffli machine. Also see EMBROIDERIES AND SEWING STITCHES: MADEIRA EMBROIDERY.

fagoting   1. Stitch, similar to single FEATHER STITCH (see under EMBROIDERIES AND SEWING STITCHES), used to join two edges of fabric together in decorative openwork effect. **2.** Open-work embroidery done by drawing out horizontal threads of a fabric, then tying the vertical threads in groups to produce open spaces. **3.** Method of joining two fabric edges together by means of embroidery stitches to produce a lacelike effect. Fagoting is part of a group of techniques known as insertions. Also see EMBROIDERIES AND SEWING STITCHES: HEMSTITCHING and INSERTIONS. British spelling is *fagotting.*

fagoting #1

feather stitch   Decorative stitch that looks like a double row of Vs, branching out first to one side then to the other in a continuous line, which is a line stitch based on a buttonhole or chain stitch variation. See EMBROIDERIES AND SEWING STITCHES: BUTTONHOLE STITCH and CHAIN STITCH #1.

feather stitch

featherwork   See EMBROIDERIES AND SEWING STITCHES: BRICK STITCH.

figure stitch   See EMBROIDERIES AND SEWING STITCHES: ORIENTAL COUCHING.

filling stitch   Any type of embroidery stitch used to fill in a design, which may be outlined if desired. Also used to refer to couched grid stitches that are used to fill in a design (see EMBROIDERIES AND SEWING STITCHES: COUCHED EMBROIDERY).

fishbone stitch   Embroidery stitch resembling the backbone of fish, made with a long diagonal stitch crossed at one end with a small diagonal stitch worked in the opposite direction. Stitches usually branch out from a center line. Similar to FEATHER STITCH (see under EMBROIDERIES AND SEW-ING STITCHES), but worked closer together.

fishbone stitch

flame embroidery   See EMBROIDERIES AND SEW-ING STITCHES: FLORENTINE EMBROIDERY.

flame stitch   See EMBROIDERIES AND SEWING STITCHES: BARGELLO STITCH.

Florentine embroidery   Embroidery done on canvas in zigzag patterns and in shaded colors. Also called *flame embroidery,* from the effect it achieved, or *Hungarian point embroidery.*

Florentine stitch   See EMBROIDERIES AND SEW-ING STITCHES: BARGELLO STITCH.

free motion machine embroidery   Creation of machine embroidery by using decorative thread and dropping the device in the sewing machine that moves the fabric. The embroiderer creates abstract or realistic designs by moving the fabric in various directions.

French knot   Decorative stitch used for embroidery. Embroidery floss is looped around the needle, usually 2 times, needle is pulled through the material, forming a small nub or ball of yarn on the surface.

French knot

Genoese embroidery   Embroidery done by buttonhole-stitching over a cord on muslin or then, cutting fabric away from between parts of the design, much like the whitework technique called Madeira work. Formerly used for dress and undergarment trimmings. See EMBROIDERIES AND SEWING STITCHES: BUTTONHOLE STITCH and MADEIRA WORK.

gimped embroidery   Embroidery where the design is achieved by arranging cord or vellum on fabric and covering with silk or gold threads. Obsolete name for this work is *laid embroidery.*

grass embroidery   Native American and Caribbean embroidery using colored grasses as threads usually done on deer skins or textiles.

gros point (groh pwanh)   See EMBROIDERIES AND SEWING STITCHES: PETIT POINT.

ground   The base fabric on which embroidery is applied.

hardanger embroidery (hard-ahn′-ger)   Open form of needlework made in diamond or square patterns on even-weave cotton or linen cloth. The material is stitched with satin stitch type squares called kosters blocks. This technique is native to the Hardanger region of Western Norway.

Hedebo (head-day′-bow)   Danish form of WHITEWORK that incorporates CUTWORK (see under EMBROIDERIES AND SEWING STITCHES) and NEEDLEPOINT LACE (see LACES).

hemming stitch   Long, loose slanting stitch placed through hem and caught to fabric with a very small stitch.

hemstitch   **1.** Ornamental stitch made by drawing out several parallel threads, then fastening together groups of vertical threads at regular intervals, making hourglass shapes. Used as borders on blouses, handkerchiefs, etc. **2.** Machine hemstitching done with a special attachment on sewing machines to give the same effect as above. When cut through the middle, each edge forms a PICOT EDGE (see PICOT #2).

hemstitch #1

hemstitching   Embroidery in which several parallel yarns are removed from the fabric and fine stitches used to catch group of three or four cross threads at regular intervals giving an even openwork arrangement. This type of embroidery, done at the edge of the hem, holds and decorates at the same time.

herringbone stitch   Name of the CATCH STITCH (see EMBROIDERIES AND SEWING STITCHES), when used for embroidery work. Also *Russian stitch, Russian cross-stitch,* and *witch stitch.*

Holbein stitch   See EMBROIDERIES AND SEW-ING STITCHES: DOUBLE-RUNNING STITCH.

Holbein work (hole′-bine)   Delicate reversible outline embroidery, done in double-running stitch using exact geometrical or conventional designs, that is part of the embroidery technique called blackwork. Popular for trimming in the 16th c. *Der.* Named after the painter Hans Holbein (1465–1524) because design was so frequently shown on his

E

paintings. Also called *Rumanian embroidery.* Also see EMBROIDERIES AND SEWING STITCHES: BLACKWORK.

holy work/hollie work Fancy work in lace, cutwork, and embroidery carried out in religious subjects. Used in late 16th c. and by Puritans mainly in the 17th c. to decorate shirts, smocks, wristbands, and neckbands.

honeycomb stitch 1. Similar to BRICK STITCH (see EMBROIDERIES AND SEWING STITCHES). **2.** Machine or hand zigzag stitch used for smocking, mending, overcasting, attaching elastic, stretch lace, and blanket binding. Looks like 3 rows of diamond-shaped stitches.

huckaback stitch/huckaback embroidery Darning stitch worked horizontally on huck toweling, a fabric with ridges at intervals. Stitches are worked underneath the ridges across the fabric to make geometrical motifs. Also called *huck weaving, huck embroidery.*

Hungarian embroidery 1. Brightly colored peasant garments and linens embroidered in conventional designs in flat or chain stitch traditionally used on Hungarian peasant costumes. **2.** A type of APPLIQUÉ done on blue, scarlet, or ecru linen.

Hungarian point See EMBROIDERIES AND SEWING STITCHES: FLORENTINE EMBROIDERY.

Indian embroidery Oriental embroidery done by Southeast Asian natives on cloth. May use small glass mirrors decoratively stitched to the fabric. For techniques employed see EMBROIDERIES AND SEWING STITCHES: CASHMERE WORK, QUILTING and CHAINSTITCH.

insertions Open, straight-line areas on fabric created either by joining two lengths of fabric with lace-type stitching, or by withdrawing threads from fabric and either hemstitching across or drawing ribbon through the voids. Most often found on infants' garments or lingerie.

inverted-T embroidery See EMBROIDERIES AND SEWING STITCHES: MATHILDE EMBROIDERY.

inverted-Y embroidery See EMBROIDERIES AND SEWING STITCHES: MATHILDE EMBROIDERY.

Irish stitch See EMBROIDERIES AND SEWING STITCHES: BRICK STITCH.

Italian stitch See EMBROIDERIES AND SEWING STITCHES: DOUBLE-RUNNING STITCH.

janina stitch See EMBROIDERIES AND SEWING STITCHES: ORIENTAL COUCHING.

Japanese embroidery Elaborate embroidery worked with colored silk or metallic threads in satin stitch forming an intricate design or scene. Also includes padded and shaded embroidery.

laid embroidery See EMBROIDERIES AND SEWING STITCHES: GIMPED EMBROIDERY.

laid stitch Embroidery stitch made by first placing yarn or floss on area and then working small stitches over it to hold it in place. Similar to filling stitches used in CREWEL EMBROIDERY (see under EMBROIDERIES AND SEWING STITCHES.

lazy daisy stitch Single chain stitch used in embroidery with extra stitch added at outer edge to hold loop in place to form a petal. Also called *detached chain stitch.*

lazy daisy stitch

liquid embroidery Not actually embroidery, but color applied to fabric with ballpoint-shaped paint tubes in special colors. Paint is squeezed from the tube to outline designs on a cloth. Creates a permanent and washable design resembling colored-thread embroidery. When seen at a distance, gives the general effect of embroidery.

lock stitch Machine stitch done with one thread coming across the top of the machine around the tension and through the needle. Other thread comes from a bobbin on the underside of the machine.

long and short stitch See EMBROIDERIES AND SEWING STITCHES: BRICK STITCH.

Madeira embroidery (ma-deer′-a) Eyelet embroidery cut or punched and then overcast. Made with openings arranged in floral or conventional designs on fine lawn or linen. Also called *broderie anglaise* (brod-e′-ree onh-glase′), *Ayrshire, English, Moravian work,* or *Swiss embroidery. Der.* From Island of Madeira, where work was originally done by nuns using very pale blue thread on a white ground.

mark stitch See EMBROIDERIES AND SEWING STITCHES: TAILOR'S TACKS.

Mathilde embroidery Wide vertical band of embroidery used on front of woman's dress in early 19th c. Later a band added around hem of dress and the combination with vertical band called an *inverted-*T or *inverted-*Y.

metal thread embroidery Embroidery stitched in gold, silver, copper, or other metal and metallic threads. Often combined with silk thread embroidery and utilized in Oriental embroidery, clerical embroidery, and military emblems and badges.

Moravian work See EMBROIDERIES AND SEWING STITCHES: MADEIRA EMBROIDERY.

Mountmellick work Irish coarse WHITEWORK that uses cotton thread in raised stitches. For stitches used see EMBROIDERIES AND SEWING STITCHES: BUTTONHOLE, CHAIN #1, CABLE #1, and PADDING #1.

needlepoint **1.** Allover wool embroidery worked on open canvas or scrim with yarn in a variety of stitches. Used for household articles, fashion items, and decorative art. Regular-sized stitches called *gros point,* small stitches called *petit point.* Also called *canvas work.* **2.** Lace made with a needle and thread. See LACES: NEEDLEPOINT LACE.

needlepoint #1: continental stitch

needle tapestry work Embroidery worked in variety of stitches on canvas to resemble woven tapestries.

needleweaving Figure-eight stitching around the remaining lengthwise yarns of a textile after the crosswise yarns have been withdrawn. The grouping of the stitched threads can form lacelike patterns. Also called *Swedish weaving, Swedish darning.*

net embroidery See EMBROIDERIES AND SEWING STITCHES: TULLE EMBROIDERY.

open buttonhole stitch See EMBROIDERIES AND SEWING STITCHES: BLANKET STITCH.

openwork Embroidery made by drawing, cutting, punching, or pulling aside threads of fabric to form open spaces in the design. For various forms of openwork see EMBROIDERIES AND SEWING STITCHES: DRAWN FABRIC WORK, HARDANGER, AND MADEIRA WORK.

opus Anglicum See EMBROIDERIES AND SEWING STITCHES: ENGLISH WORK.

oriental couching Series of long straight stitches placed side by side, with each stitch intersected in center by short diagonal stitch. Also called *Rumanian stitch, janina stitch, figure stitch,* and *antique couching.*

outline stitch Variation of STEM STITCH (see under EMBROIDERIES AND SEWING STITCHES). Used to outline stems, leaves, and other motifs in embroidery.

overcasting **1.** By hand: diagonal edging stitch that enters the fabric always from the same side and goes around raw edge to keep it from fraying. **2.** By machine: a similar finish for raw edges made by a special sewing-machine attachment or a serger.

overcasting #1

padding stitch **1.** Running stitch sometimes used in rows to provide a base for embroidery stitches (e.g., satin stitch) worked on top. **2.** Diagonal rows of basting stitch. Used in tailoring to hold interfacing in place.

petit point Canvas embroidery worked from right to left, working over single threads through large meshes. The same stitch worked over double threads is called **gros point.**

Philippine embroidery Handmade embroidery done in dainty floral motifs by native women in the Philippine Islands. Used on lingerie.

picot stitching **1.** See EMBROIDERIES AND SEWING STITCHES: HEMSTITCH. **2.** Stitch used in lacemaking that forms loops of thread extending from the edges.

piqué embroidery (pee-kay′) Embroidery worked on firm fabric with white thread using corded outlines and various filling stitches. Used formerly for children's garments.

plain knitting stitch Basic stitch used in knitting. Made by putting one needle through a previous stitch, putting yarn around needle to form a new stitch, and pulling the new stitch through the old.

popcorn stitch Knitting or crocheting stitch that projects like a round pompon.

pulled fabric work/pulled thread embroidery See EMBROIDERIES AND SEWING STITCHES: DRAWN FABRIC WORK.

punch/punched work Embroidery of open-work type made by pulling certain threads aside with a needle or stiletto and securing them with embroidery stitches. Also called *Rhodes work.*

purl stitch **1.** Hand knitting stitch that is the opposite of a knit stitch. Ribs can be formed through the selective use of knit and purl stitches. Making only purl stitches produces a fabric with a nubby surface that is the same on both sides. Alternating rows of knit and purl stitches produces a jersey fabric. See JERSEY #1. **2.** See EMBROIDERIES AND SEWING STITCHES: BLANKET STITCH. **3.** Double purl stitch is used in making buttonholes and is formed by throwing thread over the needle as it crosses.

quilting See alphabetical listing.

raised embroidery/raised work Embroidery done in the satin stitch over padding stitches to give a raised effect in the design. Used for monograms, scallops, etc. If heavily padded called STUMP WORK (see under EMBROIDERIES AND SEWING STITCHES).

rep stitch Needlepoint half-stitch worked vertically on double thread canvas. Also called *Aubusson stitch* (o-buss'-sohn).

Rhodes work See EMBROIDERIES AND SEWING STITCHES: PUNCH WORK.

rococo embroidery (row-cok'-oh) Type of embroidery made with very narrow ribbon, often called *China ribbon embroidery* or *silk ribbon embroidery.*

Romanian embroidery See EMBROIDERIES AND SEWING STITCHES: HOLBEIN WORK.

Romanian stitch See EMBROIDERIES AND SEWING STITCHES: ORIENTAL COUCHING.

running stitch Very tiny even stitches placed close together and used for seams, tucking, gathering, and quilting. Stitches and spaces between them should be equal in length.

Russian embroidery **1.** Embroidery done mainly in outline designs on Holland linen. **2.** Cloth and canvas embroidered with wool. Then canvas is removed to leave embroidery on background of cloth. Also called *broderie russe.*

saddle stitch Running stitch made in contrasting or heavy thread. Frequently used for trim on coats, sport dresses, and gloves.

satin stitch Embroidery stitch with straight, usually long, stitches worked very close together either vertically or slanted to fill in a large area (e.g., leaf or flower).

satin stitch

Schiffli embroidery A form of shuttle embroidery done by a Schiffli machine that can embroider the entire width of fabric at one time, in either elaborate or simple designs. Both eyelet and quilted designs may be made in many colors simultaneously.

seed embroidery Type of German embroidery done with seeds for floral motifs and chenille yarn for stems and leaves, formerly used for handbags.

seed stitch Embroidery stitch consisting of tiny individual back stitches, worked at random to fill background.

shadow embroidery/shadow work Embroidery worked with a catch stitch on the wrong side of transparent fabric.

shell stitch **1.** Stitch taken at intervals on a tuck to produce scalloped effect. **2.** A crochet stitch forming a shell design.

Sicilian embroidery See EMBROIDERIES AND SEWING STITCHES: SPANISH EMBROIDERY #2.

silk ribbon embroidery See EMBROIDERIES AND SEWING STITCHES: ROCOCO EMBROIDERY.

slip stitch Small almost invisible stitches with connecting thread hidden under fabric. Used to join an edge to a single layer (e.g., a hem or facing). Also called *blind stitch, blind hemming, invisible hemming.*

slip stitch

smocking Decorative needlework used to hold gathered cloth together. The stitches catch alternate folds in elaborate honeycombed designs. Used especially on infants' and children's yokes and on waists and sleeves of dresses in late 19th and early 20th c., revived in early 1970s.

smocking or honeycomb stitch

Spanish blackwork See EMBROIDERIES AND SEWING STITCHES: BLACKWORK.

Spanish embroidery **1.** Muslin worked with herringbone filling stitches. **2.** Lacelike embroidery made on muslin or cambric with braid and closely placed buttonhole stitches. Also called *Sicilian embroidery.*

stem stitch **1.** Embroidery stitch with overcast stitches placed close together making a rounded, raised, ropelike effect. **2.** Outline stitch used in CREWEL WORK (see under EMBROIDERIES AND SEWING STITCHES).

stump work Embroidery in high relief due to much padding, sometimes using horsehair, covered with satin stitches. Subjects are historical, Biblical, or allegorical scenes in grotesque shapes carried out with complicated stitchery. Also called *raised embroidery.*

Swedish weaving/Swedish darning See EMBROIDERIES AND SEWING STITCHES: NEEDLEWEAVING.

Swiss embroidery See EMBROIDERIES AND SEWING STITCHES: MADEIRA EMBROIDERY.

tack To sew together lightly with invisible stitches or to join by sewing loosely at just one point.

tailor's tack Large stitch taken through 2 thicknesses of fabric with a loop left between the layers. The layers are cut apart, leaving tufts in each piece to be used for guide marks in clothing construction. Also called *mark stitch.*

tailor's tacks

tambour work (tam-boor´) Embroidery worked with a hooked needle and a stitch on a double drum-shaped frame. The stitch is similar to the chain stitch. Originally used in Eastern embroideries, replaced by CHAINSTITCHED EMBROIDERY (see under EMBROIDERIES AND SEWING STITCHES).

tapestry shading stitch See EMBROIDERIES AND SEWING STITCHES: BRICK STITCH.

tapestry stitch Short vertical stitches used in canvas work to imitate tapestry fabric.

tent stitch See EMBROIDERIES AND SEWING STITCHES: CONTINENTAL STITCH.

top-stitch Machine stitching showing on the right side of the garment (e.g., the edge of a shirt collar).

tricot stitch See EMBROIDERIES AND SEWING STITCHES: AFGHAN STITCH.

tulle embroidery (tool) Floss silk used on tulle, a netlike fabric, either by darning or by using embroidery stitches on a traced paper design. Formerly used for trimming party dresses. Also called *net embroidery.*

two-sided line stitch See EMBROIDERIES AND SEWING STITCHES: DOUBLE-RUNNING STITCH.

venetian ladder work Outline embroidery done with two parallel lines of buttonhole stitches connected with cross-stitches at intervals in ladder-style. Used mainly for border work in conventional designs.

whip stitch Short overcast stitch used on rolled or raw edges.

whitework Embroidery executed in white thread on a white textile.

Yugoslavian embroidery Bright-colored wool used on coarse linen in geometrical designs, done by counting threads, mainly in cross-stitch, double-purl, slanting, or satin stitch. Also spelled *Jugoslavian.*

zigzag stitch Sewing machine stitch giving a saw-toothed effect used to connect 2 flat pieces of fabric together. Also used on edges of fabric to eliminate fraying.

---

emerald See GEMS, GEM CUTS, AND SETTINGS.

emerald cut See GEMS, GEM CUTS, AND SETTINGS.

emperor shirt See SHIRTS.

empiecement Trimming effect with outer fabric cut away and edges embroidered to show a sheer fabric underneath. Popular in late 19th and early 20th c.

Empire (em´-pire or ohm-peer´) Adjective used to describe styles worn the First Empire in France (c. 1800–1814) or those derived from or inspired by styles of this period.

Empire bodice ∞ (em´-pire or ohm-peer´) Dress bodice of late 1880s giving a short-waisted effect by arranging several silk scarfs around the waist and tying them on one side or in the back.

Empire bonnet See HEADWEAR.

Empire coat See COATS AND JACKETS.

Empire coiffure See HAIRSTYLES.

Empire cone hairstyle See HAIRSTYLES.

Empire dress (em′-pire or ohm-peer′)
1. Dress with a high waistline located just under the bosom. The
waistline is defined by an inserted
piece of fabric or a seam. The style
derived from the type of dresses that
were popular during the DIRECTOIRE
and EMPIRE periods in France. Other
features included a neckline lowcut
in front and back, small puffed
sleeves, ankle-length and a relatively
straight skirt. For court wear, a train
usually hung from the shoulders. **2.** Any contemporary dress with high waistline, usually
with a narrow skirt. *Der.* From First Empire in
France, 1804–1814.

Empire dress #1

Empire house gown ∞ (em′-pire or ohm-peer′)
NEGLIGÉE COSTUME of mid-1890s with high collar and tucked yoke crossed with ribbons tied in
a bow at the center front. Floor-length, the gown
fell in folds from a yoke and had three-quarter
length sleeves that were trimmed with ruffle at
the wrist.

Empire jacket See COATS AND JACKETS.

Empire jupon See UNDERGARMENTS: HOOPS.

Empire Period See EMPIRE STYLES.

Empire petticoat See UNDERGARMENTS: HOOPS.

Empire skirt See SKIRTS.

Empire stays See UNDERGARMENTS.

Empire styles (em′-pire or ohm-peer′) France
had two Empire periods. The First Empire (1804–
1815), under the reign of Napoleon Bonaparte
and the Second Empire under the reign of Louis
Napoleon (1852–1871). **1.** During the first Empire the predominant styles for men consisted
of tight-fitting breeches or trousers; double-
breasted jackets with high collars, short, single-
breasted waistcoats—cut straight at hem—and
cravats or neck cloths. Women wore dresses
like those described under EMPIRE DRESS #1,
often with short jackets (see COATS AND JACKETS:
SPENCER), and BONNETS (see under HEADWEAR).
2. During the Second Empire men wore various
types of coats (see COATS AND JACKETS: FROCK
COAT, MORNING COAT, DRESS COAT) and trousers
of a moderately loose fit with TOP HATS (see
HEADWEAR). Women's dresses had a natural
waistline, were closely fitted through the bodice,
and had extremely full skirts that were supported
by hoops after 1857. The Empress Eugénie (see
EUGÉNIE, EMPRESS) was an important fashion
influence.

empire waistline See WAISTLINES.

Empress Eugénie hat See HEADWEAR: EUGÉNIE
HAT.

Empress Josephine See JOSEPHINE, EMPRESS OF
FRANCE.

Empress Josephine gown ∞ High-waisted dress
with a bodice that closes by wrapping one side
over the other, full sleeves, sash ends hanging
from inserted belt, and gathered skirt. Worn in
the 1890s with a FIGARO JACKET (See COATS AND
JACKETS), the style was inspired by dresses of the
first Empire in France (see EMPIRE STYLES).

Empress petticoat See UNDERGARMENTS.

end **1.** † An individual lengthwise yarn, which
may be either SINGLE, PLY, or CORD YARN. **2.** A
remnant or short piece of fabric.

endangered species Animals and birds that are
becoming rare because of slaughter of animals
for clothing, accessories, adornment, and other
reasons. Animals include tigers and certain types
of reptiles. Birds include the egret and eagle.
Several states and the U.S. federal government
have passed protective laws. For protective legislation concerning furs, see FURS: FUR #1 under
category heading. Also see AUDUBON PLUMAGE
LAW.

endorsement Use of individuals, usually celebrities, or organizations that state in advertising or
in public their approval and preference for a
particular product. Generally those making en-
dorsements are paid.

engageantes ∞ (ahn-gahj′-
eh-ahnt) **1.** French for
two or three tiers of lace,
or sheer-fabric ruffles, used
as cuffs on sleeves from end
of 17th through 18th c.
2. Detachable undersleeves,
of white fabric edged with
lace or embroidery, worn
by women from 1840s until about 1865. Also see
SHOULDERS AND SLEEVES: ISABEAU SLEEVE.

engageantes and echelles
on an 18th c. dress

engagement ring See JEWELRY.

engineer's boot See FOOTWEAR.

engineer's cap See HEADWEAR.

English coat See COATS AND JACKETS.

English cottage bonnet See HEADWEAR: BIBI BONNET.

English drape **1.** Style used for man's single- or double-breasted long suit jacket in 1930s and 1940s. Distinguished by fullness at top of tapered sleeve, width through the chest, and fitted waist. Worn with trousers made with high-rise waistline and pleats at side front. **2.** Similar style jacket adopted for women's suits in 1930s and 1940s; revived in 1980s.

English drape suit #1

English embroidery See EMBROIDERIES AND SEWING STITCHES: MADEIRA EMBROIDERY.

English farthingale See FARTHINGALE.

English hood See HEADWEAR.

English rib sock See HOSIERY.

English thumb See GLOVES AND GLOVE CONSTRUCTION.

English walking jacket See COATS AND JACKETS.

English work See EMBROIDERIES AND SEWING STITCHES.

English wrap See COATS AND JACKETS: PALETOT.

ensemble (ahn-sahm´-bl) **1.** An entire costume, including accessories, which is worn together. **2.** More than one item of clothing designed and coordinated to be worn together, such as a dress and coat.

en tablier (ahn-tahb´-lee-yeh) Trimming arranged in crosswise rows of lace or ribbon spaced down front panel of dress, sometimes from neck to hem or from waist to hem. Used particularly in 19th c. *Der.* French, *tablier,* "apron."

en tous cas See UMBRELLAS AND PARASOLS.

entre deux (on´-tray dew) Fine narrow open-work insertion set into the seams of dainty lingerie used from late 19th c. until mid-1930s.

envelope combination See UNDERGARMENTS.

envelope handbag See HANDBAGS AND RELATED ACCESSORIES.

envelope pleat See CLOTHING CONSTRUCTION DETAILS.

environmentally friendly Describes products that are manufactured using methods and materials which do not harm the natural environment.

envoy hat See HEADWEAR.

epaulet/epaulette (ep´-oh-let) **1.** Ornamental shoulder trim used on military uniforms, originally consisting of gold braid looped to form fringe around the edge. **2.** Shoulder trim used in 19th c., very popular in 1860s. **3.** Flat band of fabric, sometimes fastened with a button on shoulders of uniforms; also used on military-style civilian coats and jackets (e.g., trenchcoats). Very fashionable in 1980s on blouses, coats, dresses, shirts, and jackets. **4.** See ARMOR: EPAULIÈRE.

epaulets #2

epaulet shirt See SHIRTS.

epaulet sleeve ∞ See SHOULDERS AND SLEEVES.

epaulière See ARMOR.

ephebi (ef-he´-bee) Military cape similar to the CHLAMYS, worn by Greek soldiers.

epitoga See CAPES, CLOAKS, AND SHAWLS.

equestrienne costume (ee-kwes-tree-enn´) Riding habits for women, which were called by this name from about the 1840s, consisted of a full-length gathered skirt worn with a tailored jacket, sometimes double-breasted with REVERS and a PEPLUM. Accessories included a tall top hat with veiling hanging down the back, a tailored shirt, and necktie or stock. In the early 20th c., the skirt was uneven in length—shorter on right side, longer on left—looped up when walking, let down when mounted sidesaddle. By 1908 drill breeches and boots were worn under a short skirt. A DERBY, FEDORA, TRICORN, or SAILOR HAT (see under HEADWEAR) was worn over a braided club hairstyle. By 1910 or 1912, women rode astride wearing a divided skirt that buttoned closed in front. Also see RIDING HABIT under ACTIVEWEAR. *Der.* Latin, "woman skilled in horsemanship."

equipage See ETUI.

ermine See FURS.

ermine cap See HEADWEAR: LETTICE CAP.

erogenous zone theory (e-raj´-ah-nas) Theory expounded by James Laver, noted British authority on historic costume, who believed that emphasis in dress tends to shift from one eroge-nous zone of the body to another (e.g., when short hemlines are worn, the legs are in focus; when plunging necklines are worn, the bosom or breasts are emphasized). In Laver's theory, the cycle lasts about seven years between shifts of interest from one zone to another and is respon-sible for fashion change.

Erté (ehr′-tay) (1892–1990) Fashion designer and costume illustrator of timeless, daring, flam-boyant creations touched with fantasy. Strongly influenced public taste in feminine beauty dur-ing period 1915 to 1936 by designing 240 covers for *Harper's Bazaar*. Styles were sometimes bizarre and romantically inviting, but always highly imag-inative, theatrical, and unique. Faded to obscu-rity and returned to high popularity in 1980s by designing an imaginative line of limited edi-tion knitwear for MagiFrance® in 1985. Born Romain de Tirtoff in St. Petersburg (Leningrad), he settled in Paris in 1912, where he took his professional name from pronunciation of his initials in French: "air-tay."

escarelle ∞ (es-ka-rel′) Pouch or purse attached to a waist or hip belt in the 14th and 15th c. into which a knife was frequently thrust.

esclavage See JEWELRY.

Esmeralda cloak See CAPES, CLOAKS, AND SHAWLS.

espadrille See FOOTWEAR.

etched-out fabric See BURN-OUT FABRIC.

eternity bracelet See JEWELRY: SLAVE BRACELET.

eternity ring See JEWELRY.

Ethiopian shirtdress Simple shift, with slit at neckline trimmed with embroidery, imported from Ethiopia or made domestically in same style in late 1960s.

ethnic/ethnic look In fashion, the adoption of clothing and accessories derived from or in-spired by native or national styles of many coun-tries or regions, including clothing from Africa, Asia, South America, Europe, and of Native Americans. Became a trend in the 1960s and is periodically a fashion influence for designers.

Eton cap See HEADWEAR.

Eton collar See NECKLINES AND COLLARS.

Eton crop See HAIRSTYLES.

Eton jacket See COATS AND JACKETS and ETON SUIT.

Eton jacket bodice See COATS AND JACKETS.

Eton suit Uniform worn by junior schoolboys at Eton College, Eton, Buckinghamshire, England, from 1798 until 1967, that consisted of a waist-length square-cut jacket with wide lapels and small turned-down collar. It was worn with a white shirt having a white starched collar, nar-row dark tie, and single-breasted vest. The jacket was originally blue or red, became black in 1820 when England went into mourning for George III. Trousers were usually gray. The basic style was adapted as a dress-up suit for very young boys in the United States and England from late 19th through early 20th c. and elements, such as the jacket, cap, and tie are revived periodically.

etui ∞ (a-twe) An ornamental case worn hang-ing from the waist by women in the 17th and 18th c. to hold thimble, scissors, or scent bottle. Also called *equipage*.

EU See EUROPEAN UNION.

Eugénia, The See CAPES, CLOAKS, AND SHAWLS.

Eugénie collarette See NECKLINES AND COLLARS.

Eugénie dress ∞ (yoo-je′-nee) Full-skirted dress of 1850s made with three-tiered skirt, tight-fitting waist, and short or pagoda style sleeves. *Der.* Named for Eugénie, Empress of France.

Eugénie, Empress (yoo-je′-nee) Marie Eugénie de Montijo de Guzmán (1826–1920), Spanish wife of Napoleon III, and Empress of France (1853–1871), who exerted great influence on fashion during the Age of Crinoline. CHARLES WORTH was her couturier and is credited with designing the PRINCESS-STYLE DRESS for the Empress.

Eugénie hat See HEADWEAR.

Eugénie paletot See COATS AND JACKETS.

Eugénie petticoat See UNDERGARMENTS: BUSTLE.

European Union (EU) Major trading bloc consist-ing of European countries that petition to join and meet specified economic criteria.

even checks See PRINTS, CHECKS, AND STRIPES: CHECKERBOARD.

evening Adjective used to describe attire worn primarily in the evening, especially for formal and informal occasions. See FOOTWEAR: EVENING SLIPPER, SKIRTS: EVENING SKIRT, UNDERWEAR: EVENING PETTICOAT and EVENING SLIP.

evening gown See FORMAL ATTIRE.

E

eveningwear Used in the retail industry to refer to clothes worn primarily in the evening for formal or informal occasions.

evening wrap 1. Wrap worn for formal functions, may be styled like a shawl, a cape, a stole, or a coat. **2.** See COATS AND JACKETS.

even plaid See PLAIDS AND TARTANS.

even priced Prices for goods that end with an even number. Such endings as .95 or .99 are often assigned to sale merchandise, while .00 or easily divisible numbers are used for nonsale prices.

Everett See FOOTWEAR.

examining gown Simple wraparound gown or one slit up the back and fastened with ties, used by patients in doctors' offices. Originally made in coarse muslin, most are now of disposable, nonwoven materials.

exclusive contractor A supplier that contracts to work for just one retail company.

exclusive orders Merchandise orders that, through a special arrangement between vendor and retailer, are sold only to one particular store or buyer.

exercise sandal See FOOTWEAR: EXERCISE SANDAL and SCHOLL'S® EXERCISE SANDALS.

exercise shorts See UNDERWEAR: ATHLETIC SHORTS.

exercise suit See ACTIVEWEAR: SAUNA SUIT.

expandable bracelet See JEWELRY.

export agent A representative in a foreign country who assists a U.S. apparel manufacturer with exportation of products produced in that country.

express stripe See PRINTS, STRIPES, AND CHECKS.

extended marketing channel See MARKETING CHANNEL.

extended shoulder/extended sleeve See SHOULDERS AND SLEEVES.

extra-large 1. Size range used along with SMALL, MEDIUM, and LARGE for women's sweaters, housecoats, nightgowns, panties, girdles, and panty girdles. **2.** Size for men's sport shirts, sport jackets, sweaters, and robes.

extra-long knit shirt See SHIRTS.

extra small Size designation used along with SMALL, MEDIUM, LARGE, and EXTRA LARGE for men, women, and children in such categories as sweaters, knit and sport shirts, sport jackets, nightgowns and pajamas, robes, gloves, girdles and panty girdles. Abbreviated XS.

extra-tall Men's size corresponding to a chest measurement of 38″–48″ and a height of 6′3″–6′6½″.

eye agate See GEMS, GEM CUTS, AND SETTINGS: AGATE.

eye candy Something that is visually exciting. In fashion, most often applied to jewelry, lingerie, or other decorative garments.

eyeglass case See EYEWEAR.

eyeglass chain See EYEWEAR.

eyeglasses See introduction to EYEWEAR.

eyelet 1. Circular metal ring clamped on fabric or leather through which a lacer is pulled; first used about 1828. Also see CLOSURES: BLIND EYELET. **2.** Holes punched in fabrics for lacings or as decoration which are embroidered around the edges to keep them from fraying. **3.** See EMBROIDERIES AND SEWING STITCHES: EYELET EMBROIDERY.

eyestay See FOOTWEAR.

EYEWEAR

eyewear Accessories worn over the eyes to improve the vision or to protect the eyes from the glare of the sun. The most common form of eyewear is called **eyeglasses** or **glasses**. Conventional eyeglasses are made with plastic or glass lenses that fit into metal or plastic frames with temples (see TEMPLE under EYEWEAR) that extend over top of ears. **Photochrome® lens**, which darkens as the light increases and vice versa, was one of the innovations of the 1980s. Glasses were first introduced in Italy in the late 13th c., where they were an indication of wisdom as few people could read. During the 17th c. colored lenses were introduced for protection from the sun. In the 1960s glasses suddenly became a fashion item. Originally called *spectacles*.

antireflective coating A coating applied to lenses so that reflection of light from the lens is eliminated thereby improving vision, reducing eye fatigue, and making the eyes more visible.

aviator's glasses Sunglasses with lens wider at sides of face and sloping toward nose. Made in imitation of goggles worn by early airplane pilots. Also called *flyboy glasses*. *Der.* From style worn by aviator pilots.

Ben Franklin glasses Small elliptical, octagonal, or oblong lenses with delicate metal frames, worn perched on the middle of the nose. A fad started in 1965 imitating the glasses seen in paintings of Benjamin Franklin, U.S. statesman. Also called *granny glasses.*

Ben Franklin glasses

bifocals Glasses with lenses divided in two parts for near vision and distance. The line dividing the two fields of vision was made invisible in the early 1980s.

bow See EYEGLASSES: TEMPLE.

bug-eyed glasses Bulging convex sunglasses shaped like the eyes of an insect. Some glasses are made of a solid piece of plastic shaped to head and face. Unusual colors such as red are sometimes used to give a psychedelic appearance to viewer. An innovation of the late 1960s.

butterfly glasses Large rimless sunglasses with lenses made in the shape of a butterfly's wings, a fashion of the late 1960s.

clip-on sunglasses Sunglasses without frames made with a clip at the center or on either side that allows them to attach over the top of prescription glasses. Some, called **flip-up glasses**, have a hinge which permits them to flip up.

color-graded glasses Tinted glasses with the lens color varying from light at the bottom to dark at the top. Designed for use in a car; maps can be read through the clear section at bottom.

Courréges glasses Sunglasses, introduced by Andrè Courréges in 1966, made of a strip of opaque plastic that circled the face extending to the ears. Through the center of the plastic was a tinted horizontal sliver of glass or plastic. Copied widely, they became known by the name of the French couturier who originated the style.

eyeglass case Container for storing eyewear when it is not in use. May be plain or decorative.

eyeglass chain/eyeglass cord Chain or cord that has loops that slip over the temples of glasses so that when glasses are not being used, they can be worn around the neck. May be decorated with crystals, pearls, beads, and the like or plain.

eyeglasses See category introduction to EYEWEAR.

flip-down glasses Ben Franklin-type glasses with separate hinged lenses that pull down so that eyeshadow or mascara can be applied. Also used for inserting contact lenses.

flip-up glasses See EYEWEAR: CLIP-ON SUNGLASSES.

flyboy glasses See EYEWEAR: AVIATOR'S GLASSES.

folding glasses Glasses with both folding bridge and temples that condense to a 3″ size for easy carrying.

glasses See category introduction to EYEWEAR.

goggles Protective glasses, usually with impact resistant lenses in wide frames wrapped around temples, held on by strap around head and worn by auto racers, skiers, etc. Goggles for underwater swimming are watertight.

goggles

granny glasses See EYEWEAR: BEN FRANKLIN GLASSES.

half-glasses Glasses for reading with shallow lenses, allowing wearer to look over top for distance viewing.

half-glasses

harlequin glasses (har′-lee-kwin) Glasses with diamond-shaped lenses. Eyeglasses slanting up to corner peaks.

horn rims/horn-rimmed glasses Eyeglasses with heavy frames of dark horn or mottled brown plastic imitating horn, very popular in the 1940s and 1950s.

instant sunglasses Lightweight, impact-resistant shaped plastic that is placed behind regular glasses when outdoors.

Lennon specs Sunglasses with circular metal-rimmed lenses and thin metal temples. *Der.* John Lennon, member of the English rock group, The Beatles, made this style popular. Originally English workmen's sunglasses.

lifestyle eyewear Used in retailing eyeglasses to describe frame and lens selections that emphasize personal image and/or specific use such as computer, sports, career, and evening eyewear.

lorgnette (lorn-yet′) A pair of eyeglasses attached to a handle, or a pair of opera glasses, similarly mounted; usually hinged so eyeglasses may be folded when not in use. Used since late 19th c. *Der.* French *lorgner,* "to spy or peep."

louvre sunglasses (loo′-vra) Molded plastic sunglasses made with tilted slats similar to Venetian blinds. Introduced from France in mid-1980s.

monocle Man's single eyeglass used for one eye held in place by cheek and forehead muscles. When not in use, suspended on a ribbon around the neck. Dandies of c. 1820 called this device a **quizzing glass** and had the glass fixed in the head of a cane.

monocle

opera glasses Small binoculars used to provide close-up view at the opera or theater. Usually a fashionable accessory decorated with mother-of-pearl, gold, brocade, etc.

owl glasses Extra-large sunglasses with very wide heavy rims that give the look of a surprised owl.

Photochrome lens® See category introduction to EYEWEAR.

pince-nez (pants-nay′) Eyeglasses without ear pieces, kept in place by spring gripping the bridge of the nose. *Der.* French "nose-pincher."

pince-nez

Polaroid® glasses Trademark for special sunglasses with lenses that polarize light, especially effective in cutting down glare.

progressive lens Lens that gradually adds focal power across its surface so that the same lens permits distant, intermediate, and close viewing. No lines are visible at the point where the focus changes.

quizzing glass See EYEWEAR: MONOCLE.

rimless glasses Lenses attached to metal nose piece and ear pieces but not outlined by a frame. Popular from 1930s to 1940s, and revived in 1960s and after.

safety glasses Glasses made of impact resistant lenses and safety frames worn by industrial workers. Also called GOGGLES (see under EYEWEAR).

shades Slang for sunglasses.

specs Slang for SPECTACLES. See category introduction to EYEWEAR.

spectacles See category introduction to EYEWEAR.

sunglasses Eyeglasses with dark-colored lenses to cut glare invented about 1885, made popular by movie stars in Hollywood in 1930s and 1940s, prevalent fashion from 1960s to the present in various shapes and sizes. Some made with mirrored lenses.

temple Shaft attached to side of glasses, curved at one end to fit over the ear. Also called *bow.*

tortoise-shell glasses Glasses with frames made from imitating tortoise shell, which is an attractive, brown, speckled material, obtained from the shell of the hawksbill turtle. The turtle has been hunted to near-extinction, and the use of the natural material has been banned. Heavy tortoise shell frames became popular in the 1930s, 1940s, and 1950s, replacing metal frames and rimless glasses worn earlier.

trifocals Prescription glasses worn to correct vision, made similarly to BIFOCALS (see under EYEGLASSES), but with three sections. The lowest section for reading; the middle section for intermediate vision for drawing, playing the piano, or playing cards; and the uppermost section for distance.

wraparound glasses Sunglasses made of a molded piece of plastic shaped like a headband that is cut out for insertion of the lenses. Similar to COURRÉGES GLASSES (see under EYEGLASSES) but with a wider viewing area.

E

fabala See FURBELOW.

Fabergé, Carl (1846–1920) (Russian name Karl Gustavovich) Russian goldsmith, jeweler, and brilliant designer, who used precious and semi-precious gems (e.g., jade, lapis lazuli, and malachite—plus gold and silver) to make conventional jewelry and gift objects of fantasy, including celebrated Easter eggs commissioned by Czars Alexander III and Nicholas II of Russia. Also made ingenious and exquisite masterpieces of flowers, figure groups, animals, and ornamental trinkets. Established workshops in Moscow, Kiev, and London. Inherited family business in 1870, which he operated until Russian Revolution of 1917. Died in exile in Switzerland.

fabric See TEXTILE FABRIC.

fabric count † In the textile-industry refers to the number of lengthwise (warp) and crosswise (filling) yarns in a square inch of woven fabric. Expressed by first writing the number of warps then number of fillings (e.g., 72 × 64 would mean 72 warps and 64 fillings per square inch).

face **1.** † *n.* Right side of fabric with better appearance—as opposed to back, or reverse side. Some fabrics are reversible and may be used on both sides. **2.** *v.* See CLOTHING CONSTRUCTION DETAILS: FACING.

face cone ∞ Long megaphone-type cone held over face while wig was being powdered in 18th c. Also see POWDERING JACKET.

faced hem See CLOTHING CONSTRUCTION DETAILS.

facet See GEMS, GEM CUTS, AND SETTINGS.

facing See CLOTHING CONSTRUCTION DETAILS.

factoring A business in the apparel industry in which an agent (the factor) buys the manufacturer's receivables (the money owed) at a discounted rate and then collects the full amount of the money owed from the retailer. This helps to maintain a steady cash flow to the manufacturer.

factory outlet A store owned by a manufacturer in which closeouts, overruns, canceled orders, discontinued and irregular items can be sold.

factory outlet mall A shopping center in which several FACTORY OUTLET STORES are located.

fad Short-lived fashion that becomes suddenly extremely popular, remains for a short period of time, and fades quickly.

fade See HAIRSTYLES.

fading † Loss of color in fabrics from exposure to light from washing, dry cleaning, or from contact with ordinary household fumes.

fagoting See EMBROIDERIES AND SEWING STITCHES.

faille † (file) Fabric with a flat-ribbed effect running crosswise that is flatter and less pronounced than GROSGRAIN. Lengthwise yarns are finer and there are more of them in order to cover the heavier filling yarns. Originally made in silk—now made of silk, wool, cotton, manufactured yarns, or combinations of yarns. Used for women's suits and dresses, robes, trimmings, and hats.

Fair Isle sweater See SWEATERS.

fairy stone See GEMS, GEM CUTS, AND SETTINGS.

fake fur See SYNTHETIC FUR.

fake fur coat See COATS AND JACKETS: FUR FABRIC COAT.

falbala See FURBELOW.

falbala wig See WIGS AND HAIRPIECES: DUVILLIER WIG.

faldetta See CAPES, CLOAKS, AND SHAWLS.

fall **1.** ∞ The front opening of men's breeches or trousers, so named from about 1730 on. **Whole falls** were square-shaped flaps that extended across the front to the side seams. **Small** or **split falls** meant a smaller central flap that covered only the center front of the garment. After 1840, the fall was also called a *spair*. **2.** See WIGS AND HAIRPIECES. **3.** See NECKLINES AND COLLARS: FALLING BAND.

fall closing at the front of men's 18th c. knee breeches (fall #1)

fal-lals Term for any trifling decoration on a garment or accessory (e.g., ribbons and bows, used from 17th c. on).

falling band See NECKLINES AND COLLARS.

falling ruff See NECKLINES AND COLLARS: RUFF.

falling tucker See NECKLINES AND COLLARS: TUCKER.

fall lift Dome-shaped piece of wire mesh placed under the hair, frequently used when wearing a hairpiece called a FALL (see under WIGS AND HAIRPIECES). Much used in the late 1960s.

fallout The fabric remaining in the spaces between pattern pieces after a garment style is cut. Such fabric pieces may be used in recycled textiles.

false bosoms See FALSIES.

false calves ∞ Padding inserted in men's stockings to make legs more shapely—worn during 17th, 18th, and 19th c. Also called *downy calves*. Called **parchment calves** when the padding was made of parchment.

false calves

false doublet See JEWELRY.

false eyelashes Eyelashes made of synthetic fibers or animal hair attached to a very narrow band that is fastened to the eyelid with adhesive. Each lash may also be glued in place by a skilled technician.

false face See MASKS.

false gown **1.** ∞ 18th-c. woman's dress style, borrowed from dresses worn by little girls in France, featuring a tight bodice, gathered skirt, and wide ribbon sash. **2.** Dress worn during French Revolution made without PANIERS (see under UNDERGARMENTS) and having a tight bodice with a skirt that was not split in front.

false hanging sleeve See SHOULDERS AND SLEEVES: HANGING SLEEVE #2.

false hips See UNDERGARMENTS: PANIERS.

false rump See UNDERGARMENTS: RUMP FURBELOW.

falsies Bust pads, usually foam-filled, that are inserted into a bra to give a fuller appearance and were especially popular in the 1950s, when a large bosom was fashionable. Devices intended to give the bosom a fuller appearance went by different names in different time periods: in the early 1800s, they were called **false bosoms**; in 19th c., some were made of lace ruffles and sometimes called **fluffy ruffles** or **gay deceivers**; and in the late 18th and early 19th c., **bosom friends** made of wool flannel or fur were worn both to protect the chest from cold and to enlarge the bosom.

family ring See JEWELRY.

fan-back dress Evening gown with slim-fitting front and back of contrasting fabric made of accordion pleats caught a little below the waistline with a bow. Pleats extend upward and downward in fan shape. Featured by Guy Laroche in black and fuchsia in fall 1986 collection.

fanchon **1.** See HEADWEAR. **2.** See SCARVES.

fanchon cap See HEADWEAR.

fancies **1.** See HOSIERY. **2.** ∞ Used from 1650s to 1670s for ribbon trimmings used on men's petticoat breeches or other types of open-legged breeches.

fan collar See NECKLINES AND COLLARS.

fancy diamond See GEMS, GEM CUTS, AND SETTINGS.

fancy leather See LEATHERS.

fancy sapphire See GEMS, GEM CUTS, AND SETTINGS: CORUNDUM.

fancy work See EMBROIDERIES AND SEWING STITCHES.

fan hoop See UNDERGARMENTS.

fanny pack See HANDBAGS AND RELATED ACCESSORIES.

fanny sweater See SWEATERS.

fanons See CLERICAL DRESS.

F

fan parasol See UMBRELLAS AND PARASOLS: MARQUISE.

fan pleat See CLOTHING CONSTRUCTION DETAILS: ACCORDION PLEAT.

FANS

fan A hand-held implement for creating a breeze. Some are made rigid—wedge-shaped, round, or flat. Others are pleated, collapsible, and attached to a handle. Made of carved ivory in early Egypt, China, and Japan, fans have been in common use by women in the Western world from mid-16th c. Materials used range from paper, fabric, lace, tortoise shell, feathers, hand-painted silk, to woven palm. The fan was considered a weapon for coquetry with definite rules for flirtation from 17th through 19th c.

aide memoire fan (ade mem'-whar) Fan on the back of which instructions for dance steps, words and music of songs, or other useful information was printed. Used in the late 18th and the 19th cs.

cockade fan A folding fan generally mounted on two sticks that opens to a full 360-degree circle. A **parasol fan** is similar but generally has a single stick.

duck's-foot fan ∞ Early folding fan that opened to one-fourth of a circle. Made of alternate strips of mica and vellum with an ivory handle, this fan was introduced to France from Italy by Catherine de Medici in mid-16th c.

folding fan

folding fan Half- or quarter-circle fan pleated to close narrowly. Introduced to France in mid-16th c. by Catherine de Medici.

parasol fan See FANS: COCKADE.

parasol or cockade fan

fantail hat See HEADWEAR.

fantail wig See WIGS AND HAIRPIECES.

fan tucks See CLOTHING CONSTRUCTION DETAILS: SUNBURST TUCKS.

farmer John See ACTIVEWEAR: WETSUIT.

farthingale/fardingale ∞ The name for a support for 16th and early 17th-c. women's skirts

and the term used to describe the shape of the skirt it supported. The supporting device was variously made of hoops of wood, wire, whalebone, or cane set into a coarse linen fabric. From its introduction in Spain in the second half of the 1400s until it went out of fashion in the first quarter of the 1600s, it changed shapes several times. Its various forms were: (1) **Spanish farthingale,** or *verdugado.* The earliest Spanish form consisted of cane hoops sewn to the outside of skirts to maintain a cone-shape to the skirt. By the time it spread to France from Spain, the hoops were worn under the skirt. This shape was variously spelled as *verdugale, verdugalle, verdugado, verdugo.* (2) **drum** or **wheel farthingale** (shown at ELIZABETHAN STYLES), a drum-shaped farthingale produced by using a wheel-shaped piece of whalebone to support the skirt at the waist. The skirt rested on this platelike support, then fell straight to the ground. Also called *Italian farthingale, English farthingale, Catherine-wheel farthinggale, drum-shaped farthingale, tambour farthingale.* (3) **French farthingale** Similar to the wheel farthingale but slightly flatter in front. Sometimes supported by a padded roll, called a **bum roll,** rather than a frame. (4) **roll farthingale** Tubular-shaped skirt supported by means of a BUM ROLL (see under UNDERGARMENTS) tied around the waist. Also see GUARDINFANTE.

farthingale sleeves See SHOULDERS AND SLEEVES.

fascinator See SCARVES.

fashion *n.* A sociocultural phenomenon in which a preference is shared by a large number of people for a particular style that lasts for a relatively short time, and then is replaced by another style. Fashion change in the Western world is generally considered to have begun in the Middle Ages and although it is evident in many different kinds of material goods, it is particularly pronounced and rapid in apparel. By the 20th c., an enormous **fashion industry** had grown up to design, produce, distribute, and sell fashionable goods both domestically and internationally.

fashion babies See MODEL DOLLS.

fashion boot See FOOTWEAR.

fashion calendar **1.** General term for a schedule for the current year that indicates the market weeks, or dates, when the designers' or manufacturers' new lines may be seen by buyers. **2.** Retail store schedule listing all fashion promotions for the store, including fashion shows, advertising, and special promotions.

fashion cycle   The lifespan of a fashion product or of an overall fashion trend consisting of three stages: beginning, when it is first being adopted; peak, when it reaches the greatest popularity; and decline, when its popularity is decreasing. The first group of consumers to adopt new fashions are generally known as **fashion leaders** while consumers who adopt a new fashion after the fashion leaders are called **fashion followers** or *fashion emulators.*

fashion director   That person in a retailing business who provides buyers with information on current fashion trends so that buyers can select appropriate items.

fashion dolls   See MODEL DOLLS.

fashion followers   See FASHION CYCLE.

fashion forecast   Prediction of the colors and styles of apparel and accessories that the majority of people will want to buy at a given time and place.

fashion forward   Describing designers, retailers, consumers, and merchandise that represent the newest, most fashionable styles.

fashion goods   New, in demand, or currently popular apparel. More financially risky than BASICS because they are less stable and have a short life span.

Fashion Group International, The   An international professional association of those who work in fashion manufacturing, marketing, retailing, communication, and education. Founded in 1931 with Mary Brooks Picken as the first president. Originally formed to promote more careers for women in fashion and serve as a clearinghouse for information and ideas. The Fashion Group circulates information among its members and to students considering fashion careers by means of fashion shows, exhibits, speeches, career courses, and discussion panels, and also sponsors an annual Night of Stars Award Gala.

fashion helmet   See HEADWEAR.

fashion industry   See FASHION.

fashionista   A woman who is an avid follower of high fashion.

fashion jewelry   See JEWELRY.

fashion leaders   See FASHION CYCLE.

fashion marks   The marks seen in seamed or full-fashioned hosiery, particularly at the back of the leg or in knitted garments where stitches have been increased or decreased to shape the item to fit. fashion marks

fashion plate   ∞ **1.** An illustration depicting the prevailing or new styles in clothing and accessories. First introduced in last quarter of 18th c., hand-colored, engraved fashion plates became important features in women's magazines of the 19th c. **2.** An individual who consistently dresses in the latest fashions.

fashion press   Reporters and/or periodicals specializing in reporting news on fashion for trade or consumer magazines, newspapers, and broadcast media.

fashion promotion   Sales promotion of fashion merchandise in a retail store accomplished by newspaper and magazine advertising, window and interior display, publicity, fashion shows, and broadcast media.

fashion research   Conducting of fashion counts, consumer surveys, and the study of past performance of an item in order to forecast the demand for various types of fashion merchandise.

fashion season   Use of such terms as spring, summer, fall, holiday, and resort to name COLLECTIONS that correspond to seasons of the year when consumers would most likely wear the merchandise.

fashion show   An exhibition of fashion merchandise sponsored by a retail store, a designer, or a manufacturer. Apparel is usually shown on live models on a runway or stage, and the show may serve to introduce the clothes for a new season or may be a benefit performance for charity. Synonym: *style show.* The first American fashion show with live models was staged by *Vogue* magazine editor Edna Woolman Chase in November 1914, and this started the idea of fashion shows for charity, which spread over the country. Current trends in fashion shows include TV, videotapes, film, and the Internet.

fashion trend   Direction in which styles, colors, fabrics, and designs are tending to change.

F

Political events, films, personalities, dramas, social, and sports events often influence fashion trends.

fashion victim A person who, in trying to keep up with fashion changes, succeeds only in wearing the most tasteless of available fashions.

fashion watch See WATCHES.

fast-color † Describing dyed fabric that will not fade when subjected to sunlight, washing, dry cleaning, perspiration, or atmospheric fumes.

fastener Synonym for CLOSURES.

Fastskin® † Registered trademark of Speedo Company for fabric used in swimwear that is designed to reduce drag and turbulence in the water in order to improve athletic performance. Approved for competitive swimming in 1999.

Fath, Jacques * See APPENDIX/DESIGNERS.

fatigue cap See HEADWEAR.

fatigues Military clothing worn when doing chores at camp. Some items have been adopted for wear by civilians. For examples, see PANTS, SWEATERS, and HEADWEAR: FATIGUE CAP.

Fauntleroy See LITTLE LORD FAUNTLEROY SUIT.

fausse montre ∞ (fowss mont-tr′) At end of 18th c. the appearance of wearing two watches, one of which was actually a snuff box disguised as a watch. *Der.* French, "false watch."

fausse Valenciennes See LACES.

Faust slipper See FOOTWEAR: ROMEO.

faux (fo) *adj.* French for false or counterfeit, imitation; used in English in connection with gems, pearls, furs, and leathers.

faux jewels See JEWELRY.

favorite/favourites **1.** See HAIRSTYLES. **2.** See BEARD.

FDA See FOOD AND DRUG ADMINISTRATION.

fearnaught See COATS AND JACKETS: FEARNOTHING JACKET.

fearnothing jacket See COATS AND JACKETS.

FEATHERS

feather Individual unit from a bird's plumage. A feather is composed of a horny stem, the **quill**, which has a smooth front and a grooved back. The flat portion of the feather is called the **vane** and is

feather fan

composed of many individual, small, parallel filaments called **barbs.** At the base of the feather are fluffy, fuzzy filaments called **flues** or **fluff.** Used from earliest times as decorative hair ornaments, necklaces, or body ornaments. Also used for fans or to decorate hats from 16th c. on. In late 1960s and 1970s whole dresses, pants, shawls, and jewelry were made of feathers. Songbird and eagle feathers, as well as other wild bird feathers, are not permitted by law to be used for clothing or accessories in the United States.

aigrette feather (ay-gret′) **1.** Extremely long, delicate, white feathers with plume at the tip, from the egret, a member of the heron family—a long-legged wading bird that became almost extinct from the demand for these feathers. Popular in the 1920s, it is now illegal in the United States to use these feathers on clothes or accessories. Also spelled *aigret.* **2.** Jeweled ornament imitating feathers, attached to a headband worn in the 1920s.

amazon plume Early term for an ostrich feather, generally taken from the wing of the bird with the tips of the barbs curled so shaft is concealed.

barbs See introduction to FEATHERS.

biot (bee-oh) Long strip of short, stiff feathers created by stripping the vane from the stem.

bird-of-paradise feather Long plume brilliantly colored, often golden-orange. Taken from beneath the shoulder or tail of full-grown male birds of paradise. Used on hats or headdresses. Illegal to import into the United States. Introduced on evening wear by Yves Saint Laurent in 1969.

cockade Tuft of feathers used as trim.

cock feather Long curly feathers from the tail of the rooster, often black, blue, and green with iridescent highlights.

coq feather (cok) French for "cock or chicken feathers."

cosse Any short, stiff feather.

down Material used to pad winter jackets and coats to increase warmth. Genuine down comes from fluffy soft fibers under the feathers of water fowl (e.g., geese and ducks). Used as interlining for insulation and warmth in vests, jackets, and coats. The term is sometimes incorrectly applied as an adjective to describe garments insulated with synthetic fiberfill.

egret feather See FEATHERS: AIGRETTE.

eiderdown (eye-der-down′) Soft fine under feathers from the eider duck. Also called *down*. *Der*. From the feathers of the *eider duck*.

flues See introduction to FEATHERS.

fluff See introduction to FEATHERS.

grebe feather Feathers from a waterfowl, similar to ducks that are ivory-colored, flecked with brown, and were used for millinery in early 20th c.

guinea feather (gin′-ee) Small, flat feathers from the guinea hen that are characterized by black-, white-, and gray-striated markings. Used in 1960s for pants and stoles.

hackle Commercial term for rooster feathers.

herl Short, delicate, stiff fronds of peacock feather that have been removed from the stem and are bundled together and used as trimming.

jabiru (jab-ih′-roo) Soft, fuzzy plumage from a storklike South American bird. The white, pale smoke-colored, and black-and-white feathers were popular for trimming on women's hats, muffs, and collars in early 20th c.

marabou Delicate, fluffy, fine feathers from tail and wing of a species of stork made into trimmings that sell by the yard in black, white, and all colors. Popular in the 1920s and 1930s for trim on lingerie and boudoir slippers. Also used for trim on dresses or cape collars, sleeves, and hems. Returned to fashion in early 1980s. Because of the expense of these feathers, less expensive feathers such as turkey feathers are sometimes substituted.

osprey feather Feathers from the osprey or fish hawk, the breast feathers white, other feathers brown or gray-brown crossed by brown bars, used for trimming on hats in early 20th c.

ostrich feather Long, curly plume feathers from the ostrich, a native African bird. Natural color of the feathers from the female bird is beige, barred with white. Most feathers are dyed in colors. Popular decoration on hats for men and women in time of the Cavaliers, Louis XIV, and in Edwardian era for women, and used in 1960s for whole dresses, capes, stoles, or pants.

paradise feather See FEATHERS: BIRD-OF-PARADISE FEATHERS.

peacock feather Long, thin dark feather with brilliantly marked "eye" in greenish-blue at the tip, from upper tail of peacock. Individual feathers became a fad of the hippies, carried in the hand, in the late 1960s.

pheasant feather **1.** Long, stiff tail feather from the domestic game bird, with striated markings of orange, black, and brown. **2.** Small, soft body feathers of the same bird, sometimes used to cover hats or hatbands.

plumage The mass of feathers that come from the bird's neck and chest area.

plume A single, large feather. Plumes most often used are from ostriches.

quill Long stiff shaft of a feather with many thin projections called *barbs*. Used as ladies' hat trim, especially in 1940s. Also see introduction to FEATHERS.

rhea feather (ray′-ah) Either of two South American *ratite* birds, resembling *African ostrich*, having long draping feathers.

schlappen Rooster tail feathers that are small, narrow, and pointed.

swan's down/swansdown Soft underfeathers of swans, used to trim negligées, dresses, and cloaks, especially in late 19th and early 20th c. Compare with MARABOU (see under FEATHERS).

vane See introduction to FEATHERS.

weepers ∞ Ostrich feathers, worn in late 19th c.

---

feather boa See scarves.

feather boning See CLOTHING CONSTRUCTION DETAILS: STAY #1.

featherbrush skirt See SKIRTS.

feather cut See HAIRSTYLES.

feathering See FURS.

feather stitch See EMBROIDERIES AND SEWING STITCHES.

featherwork See EMBROIDERIES AND SEWING STITCHES: BRICK STITCH.

Federal Trade Commission (FTC) Regulatory agency that oversees legislation important to the apparel industries including labeling requirements for apparel under the Textile Fiber Products Identification Act, the Permanent Care Labeling Act, and legislation covering fur and wool products labeling. The FTC also monitors the legal aspects of business advertising.

Fédération Française de Couture, du Prêt-à-Porter des Couturiers et des Créateurs de Mode (fed-err-ats´-yohn fran´seys deh koo´-toor duh pret ah por-tay´ dey koo´-toor-ee-yair ay dez kreat´-tuhr de mode) An umbrella organization consisting of three French trade organizations that regulate activities of the French COUTURE. These organizations are the CHAMBRE SYNDICALE DE LA COUTURE PARISIENNE, the CHAMBRE SYNDICALE DU PRÊT-À-PORTER, and the CHAMBRE SYNDICALE DE LA MODE MASCULINE. A fourth organization, **Union Nationale Artisanale de la Couture et des Activitiés Connexes** (oon-yon´ nas´-yon-ee-ahl ar-tiz´-ahn-ahl´ deh la koo´-toor ay dey ak-tiv´-ee-tay´ kon-eks´) (the National Couture Craft Industry and Related Activities Union, composed of couture dressmakers from outside of Paris), is a corresponding member of the federation.

fedora See HEADWEAR.

fee buying office See INDEPENDENT BUYING OFFICE.

feed bag See HANDBAGS AND RELATED ACCESSORIES.

feldspar See GEMS, GEM CUTS, AND SETTINGS.

fell seam See CLOTHING CONSTRUCTION DETAILS: FLAT-FELLED SEAM.

felt † Nonwoven fabric made by compressing wool and hair fibers with heat and steam into sheet form. In true felt, no adhesives are used. Some felts are left hard and smooth; others are napped to give a softer hand. When used for hats, the felt is shaped into an object called a hood (see HEADWEAR: HOOD #1), which has a crown and a floppy shapeless brim. Hats are made by placing the hood in a metal mold. Steam and pressure are used to achieve desired shape. Felt is also used for apparel, handbags, bedroom slippers, and trimming. *Der.* Anglo-Saxon, *filt,* "filter."

felted wool See FULLED WOOL.

felts See FOOTWEAR.

femoralia/feminalia ∞ (fem-or-al´-ah/fem-in-al´-ee-ah) Short pants or drawers, reaching from waist to knees, worn by Roman troops in northern climates; probably imported by Emperor Augustus from Gaul. Also called *Roman leggings.*

fencing Sport of fighting with foils or other types of swords. Special clothing is worn that has sometimes inspired fashionable styles. See ACTIVEWEAR: FENCING SUIT, COATS AND JACKETS: FENCING JACKET, MASKS: FENCING MASK, and SHIRTS: FENCING SHIRT.

Fendi * See APPENDIX/DESIGNERS.

fermail/fermayll/fers ∞ (fer´ mail) In 15th c., buckles or pins used to hold slashes (see SLASHING) of the garments together (e.g., as on sleeves and DOUBLETS).

Ferragamo, Salvatore * See APPENDIX/DESIGNERS.

ferraiolo See CLERICAL DRESS.

Ferré, Gianfranco * See APPENDIX/DESIGNERS.

Ferris waist See UNDERGARMENTS.

ferronnière See JEWELRY.

fers See FERMAIL.

festoon Garlands of flowers, braid, or other decorative trimmings arranged in loops.

fetishistic clothing Fashions inspired by styles associated with aberrant sexual practices such as sado-masochism. These include stiletto heels, thigh-high boots, corsets, and garments made of leather, rubber, and PVC plastic.

fez See HEADWEAR.

fiber † Basic component from which textile yarns or fabrics are made. These may be either short natural materials such as cotton, wool, silk, or linen; or manufactured materials such as rayon, acetate, or polyester, which are made in long continuous filaments. See MONOFILAMENT and MULTIFILAMENT.

fiberfill † Generic term for a material consisting of fluffy short fibers. Frequently made of polyester and used between two layers of fabric to make quilted fabrics, padded bras, less expensive coats, and quilted vests.

fiber lace See LACES.

fibula ∞ (pl. *fibulae*) (fib-you´-lah) Pin or brooch shaped like a long straight STILETTO, or hinged like a SAFETY PIN. Used by the Greeks and Romans to secure garments, espe- cially at the shoulder.

fibula

fichu **1.** See SCARVES. **2.** See NECKLINES AND COLLARS.

fichu lavaliere See SCARVES: FICHU #1.

fichu menteur See SCARVES.

fichu-pelerine See CAPES, CLOAKS, AND SHAWLS.

fichu-robings ∞ Term used in 1820s for flat trimming used on the bodice of gown from shoulders to waist to give the effect of a FICHU (see SCARVES).

field coat See COATS AND JACKETS.

field pants See PANTS: FATIGUES #1.

fiesta shirt See SHIRTS.

fifties look Fashions based on revival of styles popular in the 1950s. Especially notable in the mid-1970s and mid-1980s, when important features included nipped-in waistlines, swing skirts, ruffled petticoats, strapless bodices, high-heeled shoes, and hats. The slim SHEATH silhouette was also popular. Shown at RETRO.

Figaro jacket See COATS AND JACKETS.

fig leaf See APRONS.

figure improver See UNDERGARMENTS.

figure skate See FOOTWEAR.

figure stitch See EMBROIDERIES AND SEWING STITCHES: ORIENTAL COUCHING.

filament fiber **1.** † Long continuous textile fiber of indefinite length. Silk is the only natural filament fiber. Manufactured fibers can be made in filament lengths or cut into short, STAPLE FIBERS. **2.** See MONOFILAMENT and MULTIFILA-MENT YARNS.

filament yarn See YARNS.

filet **1.** † Net with a square mesh formed by knotting at right angles. **2.** Embroidery thread made of fine raw silk fibers twisted together. **3.** See LACES.

filet de Bruxelles See LACES: BRUSSELS NET.

filigree See JEWELRY.

filigree ring See JEWELRY.

filled gold See JEWELRY: GOLD-FILLED.

filler See FOOTWEAR: SOLE.

fillet **1.** See HEADWEAR. **2.** See HAIRSTYLES.

filleting ∞ Term used in 17th c. for narrow tape used as trimming.

filling Crosswise yarn of a woven fabric that runs at right angles to the SELVAGE. Also called *pick,* *woof,* or *weft.* Opposite of WARP, the vertical yarns.

filling stitch See EMBROIDERIES AND SEWING STITCHES.

findings In the garment industry or in sewing, all the smaller items and trimmings that complete a garment (e.g., buttons, hooks, bindings, laces).

fine jewelry See JEWELRY.

fineness **1.** † A measure of the diameter of yarns or fibers. Also see DENIER. **2.** The purity of gold. **3.** Number of sewing machine stitches per inch.

Finger-Free® gloves See GLOVES AND GLOVE CONSTRUCTION.

fingering yarn **1.** † Combination of woolen and worsted yarn, usually two or more ply, used for hand-knitted garments. **2.** Loosely twisted wool yarn used in Great Britain for BERLIN WORK (see EMBROIDERIES AND SEWING STITCHES).

fingerwave See HAIRSTYLES.

finish **1.** † *n.* Any of a number of chemical or mechanical processes that affect the appearance, hand, or performance of textile fibers, yarns, or fabrics. Finishes are generally applied during the manufacturing process to produce fabrics ready for manufacture into apparel or household products. **2.** † *v.* To apply such a process. **3.** *v.* To trim threads, press, or otherwise prepare a garment for shipping after its construction is complete.

finished width † Measurement in inches across woven cloth after all operations have been completed.

fins See FOOTWEAR: FLIPPERS.

fire opal See GEMS, GEM CUTS, AND SETTINGS.

fishbone braids See HAIRSTYLES.

fishbone stitch See STITCHES.

fisher See FURS.

fishing/fisherman's Adjective used to describe various items of clothing derived from or inspired by clothing worn by fishermen for the sport of fishing. See COATS AND JACKETS: FISHING PARKA, FOOTWEAR: FISHING BOOT and HIP BOOT and WADERS, SWEATERS: FISHERMAN'S SWEATER and VESTS: FISHERMAN'S VEST.

fisherman's ring See CLERICAL DRESS.

fishmouth lapel See NECKLINES AND COLLARS: LAPELS.

F

fishmouth toe   See HOSIERY.

fishnet   **1.** † Coarse mesh fabric made in LENO WEAVE. Major uses include dresses, scarves, and trimming. **2.** Adjective describing apparel made of fishnet fabric. See CAPES, CLOAKS, AND SHAWLS: FISHNET PONCHO, HOSIERY: FISHNET HOSE, SHIRTS: FISHNET SHIRT, and UNDERGARMENTS: FISHNET UNDERWEAR.

fishtail   See GEMS, GEM CUTS, AND SETTINGS and SKIRTS.

fishwife costume   ∞ Blouson dress of 1880s made with shawl collar, dickey insert, and full sleeves. Double skirt was gathered at waistline with overskirt turned up revealing a lining of contrasting fabric. Underskirt made of a third fabric, frequently striped to match dickey. Imitated a dress worn with several petticoats by Portuguese fishermen's wives.

fitch   See FURS.

fitchet   ∞ (fich′-ett) French term used from 13th to mid-16th c. for vertical slit made in side front of skirt of the gown to enable woman to reach her pocket, which was a separate undergarment.

fit model   A live model whose body dimensions correspond to the company's sample size so that he or she can wear the sample in order that the designer can assess the fit, styling, and overall look of a new PROTOTYPE.

fitted   *adj.* Describing a garment that conforms closely to body lines.

fitted sleeve   See SHOULDERS AND SLEEVES.

fitting   *n.* Dressmaker's or tailor's session with customer for altering garment to fit the figure.

Fitzherbert hat   See HEADWEAR.

five-language watch   See WATCHES.

flame embroidery   See EMBROIDERIES AND SEWING STITCHES: FLORENTINE EMBROIDERY.

flamenco dress   Dress with long torso top and skirt made with a series of circular-cut flounces. In the late 1960s adaptations were accepted for general wear. *Der.* Inspired by dresses worn by flamenco dancers in Spain.

flame resistance   † Fabric treated with a flame retardant. Fabric will burn only when placed in a flame, but self-extinguishes rapidly when the ignition source is removed. Also see FLAMMABLE FABRICS ACT.

flame stitch   See EMBROIDERIES AND SEWING STITCHES: BARGELLO STITCH.

Flammable Fabrics Act   † Legislation enacted in 1953 that prohibits the sale of highly flammable fabrics or wearing apparel that does not meet established standards, which are revised periodically. Amended in 1967 to include carpets, mattresses, and items of children's sleepwear. The act is enforced by the Consumer Products Safety Commission.

flammeum   ∞ (flow-may′-oom) Dark, flame-colored, full-length wedding veil worn by Roman brides. Removed by bridegroom when couple arrived at new home.

flandan   See HEADWEAR.

flange heel   See FOOTWEAR.

flange shoulder   See SHOULDERS AND SLEEVES.

flannel   † Fine soft fabric made in tightly woven twill or plain weave and finished with a light napping. May be made of wool or other fibers or blends and is often used for women's and girls' coats, suits, and dresses or men's trousers and sport shirts. *Der.* Welsh, *Gwlanen,* from *Gwlan,* "wool."

flannelette   † Name often given to cotton flannel that is used in sleepwear and sports shirts. See FLANNEL.

flannel nightgown   See SLEEPWEAR AND LOUNGEWEAR.

flannel petticoat   See UNDERGARMENTS.

flannel shirt   See SHIRTS.

flannel skirt   See UNDERGARMENTS: FLANNEL PETTICOAT.

flapped besom pocket   See POCKETS: WELT POCKET.

flapper   Fashionable young woman in her late teens and early twenties who adopted the unfitted styles, short skirts, and bobbed hair of the 1920s. Suggested origins for this term vary and include: the practice of these young women of wearing open, flapping galoshes or overshoes in bad weather, the hair bows worn by young girls in the post–World War I period, or the flapping of the wings of young birds as they learn to fly. This latter origin is given greatest credence, as the parallel is made between these young women "trying their wings" as young adults, but the usage may have been reinforced by the flapping galoshes they wore.

flapper dress Short-skirted unfitted, long torso dress first worn in the late 1920s and revived in the 1960s and 1990s.

flapper dress 1920s

flapper look Revivals of styles inspired by or derived from clothing of the 1920s. Typical dresses were knee-length, long-waisted blouson- and chemise-types, often lavishly decorated with beads for evening. Coats were without waistlines, or long-waisted, wrap-style, many with large fur collars. Hair was cut in a short bob, frequently a brow band and long ropes of pearls were worn. Also called *twenties style.*

flap pocket See POCKETS.

flared leg panty See UNDERGARMENTS.

flares See PANTS.

flashdance look Various items of dancewear designed by Michael Kaplan for the 1983 movie *Flashdance,* and contemporary fashions adapted from these designs. Typical items were loose oversized shoulder-baring sweatshirts, tank tops, cardigans, dresses, and exercise pants. Also see BLOUSES AND TOPS: FLASHDANCE TOP.

flashdance look 1983

flashy nightshirt See SLEEPWEAR AND LOUNGEWEAR.

flat In fashion sketching, refers to drawings of clothing without a human figure.

flat-felled seams See CLOTHING CONSTRUCTION DETAILS.

flat front pants See PANTS.

flat heel See FOOTWEAR.

flat-knit hose See HOSIERY: FULL-FASHIONED HOSE.

flat pattern A design process in which a base block, or SLOPER, is used to create a pattern for a new style.

flat pleats See CLOTHING CONSTRUCTION DETAILS: KNIFE PLEATS.

flats/flatties See FOOTWEAR.

flat-top See HAIRSTYLES: CREW CUT.

flax † Fiber from the stem of the flax plant. Linen fabrics are made from flax fibers.

flea fur See SCARVES.

flea-market Market held continuously or occasionally in such locations as barns, buildings, or in the open. All types of clothing, either used or new, are sold (e.g., shirts, shorts, and dresses purchased in job lots from manufacturers). Flea market shops opened in Paris and England in late 1960s and have been a source of vintage clothing.

flea market look The wearing of old clothing and accessories from former eras sold and worn as contemporary items of clothing that look as if they might have been purchased in a flea market. See VINTAGE LOOK.

fleece **1.** † Wool sheared from the sheep usually taken off in one piece. **2.** † A fabric with a thick, heavy, fleecelike surface; it may be a PILE fabric, or simply one with a NAP, and may be woven or knitted. **3.** See SHEARLING under FURS and LEATHERS.

fleece-lined fabric † Soft fabric with a heavily napped surface on one side. May be woven but more often knitted with floats on back that are brushed to form a NAP. Used for sweatshirts, sweatpants, and jogging suits.

Flemish hood See HEADWEAR: BEGUIN.

fleshing **1.** See LEATHER. **2.** See FURS.

fleur-de-lis See PRINTS, STRIPES, AND CHECKS.

flexible manufacturing system (FMS) "Any departure from traditional mass production systems of apparel toward faster, smaller, more flexible production units that depend upon the coordinated efforts of minimally supervised teams of workers" (AAMA Technical Advisory Committee, 1988, as cited in Hill, 1992, p. 34).

flight Adjective used to describe apparel that is inspired or influenced by clothing or accessories used in flying. Examples: flight bag, flightsuit.

flight bag See HANDBAGS AND RELATED ACCESSORIES.

flight deck cap See HEADWEAR: ASTRONAUT'S CAP.

flightsuit One-piece garment of a design based on suits worn by pilots in the Armed Forces. Generally made with long sleeves, long legs, and zipping up the front to close. Similar to JUMP-SUIT (see under ACTIVEWEAR).

flip   See HAIRSTYLES.

flip-chip dress   Make-your-own dress of colored plastic chips or squares and connecting fasteners put together in any pattern, similar to a LINKED DRESS.

flip-down glasses   See EYEWEAR.

flip-flops   See FOOTWEAR.

flippers   See FOOTWEAR.

flip-tie blouse   See BLOUSES: STOCK-TIE BLOUSE.

flip-up eyeglasses   See EYEWEAR: CLIP-ON SUNGLASSES.

float   **1. †** *n.* Lengthwise or crosswise yarn in a woven fabric that extends over several rows without being interlaced. **2. †** *n.* In knitting, a yarn that extends for some distance across back of fabric without being interlaced. **3.** *adj.* Describes dress that falls free from shoulders and neckline with a full sweep at the hem, giving a tent shape that is either dress- or full-length with accordion pleats, or cut on bias. May have various types of sleeves and necklines. Style is sometimes used for leisurewear and hostess gowns.

floater necklace   See JEWELRY.

floating pedestal wedge   See FOOTWEAR.

floats   See FOOTWEAR.

flocked print   See PRINTS, STRIPES, AND CHECKS.

flocked ribbon   **†** Ribbon given a pilelike surface by means of FLOCKING, an electrostatic process, rather than woven in a pile weave like VELVET ribbon.

flocking   **† 1.** Short lengths of fiber that are used in printing designs on fabrics or to cover the surface of a fabric to create surface texture. **2.** Method of applying short fibers overall or in a design by first printing fabric with an adhesive and then causing minute pieces of fibers to adhere to the design. When a design is produced the method is known as **flock printing.**

Flohpelzchen   See SCARVES: FLEA FUR.

flokati   See FOOTWEAR.

floor ready merchandise (FRM)   Merchandise received by the retailer with hangtags, labels, and price information affixed so that the goods can be placed on the selling floor immediately.

floral print   See PRINTS, STRIPES, AND CHECKS.

Florentine embroidery   See EMBROIDERIES AND SEWING STITCHES.

Florentine neckline   See NECKLINES AND COLLARS.

Florentine stitch   See EMBROIDERIES AND SEWING STITCHES: BARGELLO STITCH.

Florodora costume   ∞ (flor-oh′-dora) Dress with tight-fitted lace-trimmed bodice with bishop sleeves and long full skirt trimmed with ruffles. Worn with an off-the-face picture hat trimmed with ostrich feathers. *Der.* worn by chorus of the musical, *Florodora,* a hit of 1900.

flotation vest   See VESTS.

flounce   **1.** Piece of material either circular and bias-cut or straight-cut and gathered. Used on skirt of dress, usually at hem, singly or in series. First introduced in 16th c. **2.** See FURBELOW.

flouncing   **1.** Decorative lace or embroidered fabric usually gathered at upper edge. **2.** See LACES.

flower bottle   **1.** ∞ Fresh flower in small bottle of water worn in buttonhole and held in place under lapel by broad ribbon. Worn by men in the mid-1860s. **2.** See BOSOM BOTTLES.

flowered mink   See FURS.

flower-pot hat   See HEADWEAR.

flow-flow   ∞ Term used in mid-1880s for bodice trimming consisting of a graduated cascade of ribbon loops.

flues   See introduction to FEATHERS.

fluff   See introduction to FEATHERS.

fluffy ruffles   See FALSIES.

flush setting   See GEMS, GEM CUTS, AND SETTINGS: CHANNEL SETTING.

fluted hem   See CLOTHING CONSTRUCTION DETAILS.

fluting   Tiny pleats in sheer fabrics that give a corrugated effect. Those set in manufactured fabrics may be permanently heat-set. A late 19th-c. trimming popular again in 1960s through 1980s. Also called GOFFERING.

flutter sleeve   See SHOULDERS AND SLEEVES.

flyaway jacket   See COATS AND JACKETS.

fly-boy glasses   See EYEWEAR: AVIATOR GLASSES.

fly cap   See HEADWEAR: BUTTERFLY CAP.

fly-fringe   ∞ 18th-c. fringe, consisting of strands of silk floss knotted in clumps, used for trimming a gown.

fly front   See CLOSURES.

flygirls   See HIP-HOP.

flying panel skirt See SKIRTS.

FMS See FLEXIBLE MANUFACTURING SYSTEM.

fob See WATCH FOB.

fob pin See JEWELRY: CHATELAINE.

fob pocket See POCKETS.

fob ribbon ∞ Term used from 1740s to 1840s for ribbon attached to watch carried in the FOB POCKET (see under POCKETS). The ribbon end hung outside of pocket and held a fob, seals, or watch key. Worn only with BREECHES or pantaloons (see PANTS: PANTALOONS #2).

Fogarty, Anne * See APPENDIX/DESIGNERS.

foil button See CLOSURES.

foil dress Disposable dress made in various colors of aluminum foil, sometimes quilted. Introduced in 1968 along with PAPER DRESSES, and reintroduced in 1986 in creative, imaginative designs.

folding/fold-up Adjective describing an item of apparel that bends over itself in order to become smaller. See COATS AND JACKETS: FOLD-UP RAINCOAT, EYEWEAR: FOLDING GLASSES, FANS: FOLDING FAN, FOOTWEAR: PULLMAN SLIPPER, HANDBAGS AND RELATED ACCESSORIES: FOLD-OVER CLUTCH, and HEADWEAR: FOLD-UP HAT.

folette See SCARVES.

foliated See DAGGING.

follow-me-lads See HEADWEAR.

folly bells ∞ Tiny bells suspended from chains used to decorate belts, shoulder belts, or neckbands in 15th c.

Fontana Sorelle * See APPENDIX/DESIGNERS.

fontanges See HEADWEAR.

fontanges hat See HEADWEAR.

Food and Drug Administration (FDA) A federal agency that is responsible for regulating the safety of cosmetics as well as food and drugs.

fool's cap See HEADWEAR.

football helmet See HEADWEAR.

football jersey See SHIRTS.

footed pajamas See SLEEPWEAR AND LOUNGEWEAR.

footie See HOSIERY: FOOTSOCK.

footing ∞ Trimming used on edges of garments (e.g., elaborate ruffles, pleating, lace, net, insertion, and ribbon). Widely used on women's dresses and undergarments in late 19th and early 20th c.

foot-mantle See SKIRTS.

footsock See HOSIERY.

footwarmers See HOSIERY: BED SOCKS.

FOOTWEAR

footwear Outermost covering for the foot that serves to protect the foot but frequently is also a decorative element of the costume. The category of FOOTWEAR is often divided among different named basic styles of footwear. The definitions of these types of footwear may be found under the category of

man's oxford shoe (balmoral style) with stacked heel

woman's pump with stiletto heel

FOOTWEAR in these entries: BOOT, CLOG, MOCCASIN, MULE, OXFORD, PUMP, SANDAL, and SLIPPER. SHOE has become a general term referring to any footwear that does not extend to above the ankle. Individually named examples of various types (e.g., saddle shoe, loafer, sneaker) of footwear each have a separate entry in the category. Definitions of parts of footwear (e.g., COUNTER, HEEL, QUARTER, SOLE, TOE, TONGUE, UPPER, VAMP) are also included in the FOOTWEAR category.

Achilles tendon protector See FOOTWEAR: A.T.P.

acrobatic slipper Soft flexible slipper made out of sueded splits of leather (see SUEDED and SPLITS under introduction to LEATHERS). Vamp comes up high in center front and a piece of elastic connects it to the quarter or back of shoe. Worn by dancers and gymnasts and also adopted by avant-garde for streetwear in the 1960s.

adelaide boot ∞ Woman's ankle-high side-laced boot with patent-leather toe and heel, sometimes with fur or fringed trimming at top. Worn in the United States from about 1830s to 1860s.

aerobic shoe Laced shoe of nylon mesh with suede outside counter, toe band, and trim. Somewhat higher cut than a sneaker, with shock-absorbing midsole and nonskid rubber sole.

after-ski boot See FOOTWEAR: APRÈS-SKI BOOT.

Alaska ∞ In early 20th c., an overshoe or storm rubber with a high tongue over the instep.

Albert boot ∞ Man's side-laced boot with fabric top and patent-leather toe, frequently decorated down front with mother-of-pearl buttons; worn from 1840s on. *Der.* From fashion made popular by *Prince Albert,* the consort of England's Queen Victoria.

Albert slipper Slipper with a VAMP (see FOOTWEAR) that extends up to form a tongue that rests on the instep.

all-weather boot Calf-high boot made with fleece-lined upper attached to molded waterproof rubber sole with low heel.

alpargata (ahl-par-gah′-ta) Sandal worn in Spain and South America with rope sole and canvas upper only around the heel. Fastened to foot by cord coming from sole in front, crossing at instep, threaded through holes in upper and fastened around ankle.

alpine boot ∞ Ankle-high shoe of early 1900s designed with bent nails on a sturdy sole to give mountain climbers a secure footing. Also see FOOTWEAR: HIKING BOOT.

American buskins ∞ Shoes with stout leather soles and knee-high cloth uppers, or leggings, fastened with lacings, worn by American Colonists. Similar to STARTUPS.

ankle boot See FOOTWEAR: DEMI-BOOT, GEORGE, and PANTS BOOT.

ankle-jack ∞ Man's ankle-high boot, laced up front with five pairs of eyelets. Popular in East End of London in 1840s.

ankle-strap shoe/sandal Shoe, frequently of the sandal-type, having a strap attached at the top of the heel and going around the ankle. Shown at D'ORSAY PUMP. Frequently made with platform sole. Very popular in the 1930s and 1940s, revived in late 1960s, and very popular in 1980s and after.

antigropolis ∞ (an-te-grop′-oh-lis) Man's long GAITER (see under FOOTWEAR), usually leather; coming over thigh in front, but cut away to knee in back; worn in mid-19th c. for walking or riding.

après-ski boot (app-reh skee) Bulky insulated boot often calf-length and made of long-haired shaggy fur worn for warmth after skiing. *Der.* French, "after ski." Also called *after-ski boots.*

après-ski slipper Same as SLIPPER SOCKS.

apron tongue See FOOTWEAR: TONGUE.

arch cushion Pad for support of the arch of the foot. Also called *cookie.*

arctics **1.** Waterproof rubber boot worn over regular shoes usually with zipper closing, popular in 1940s, revived in 1970s. **2.** See FOOTWEAR: GALOSH #1.

athletic shoes A broad category of shoes worn for any of a wide variety of athletic activities. This term is often used interchangeably with SNEAKERS (see under FOOTWEAR), although it seems to be preferred within the footwear industry over the older term.

A.T.P./Achilles tendon protector (a-kil′-ees) Padding placed at the back of the heel collar of some athletic shoes to protect the Achilles tendon. Also called *heel horn.*

baby boot ∞ An infant's soft fabric or leather shoe with a high top of the second half of 19th c. Usually made of fabric or felt, and elaborately trimmed with embroidery. Also see FOOTWEAR: BOOTIE #2.

baby-doll shoe Low-heeled shoe with wide rounded toes similar to MARY JANE shoe (see under FOOTWEAR), sometimes with straps over instep, popular for women in 1960s with miniskirts for little-girl look. Popularity enhanced by film *Baby Doll* (1956). *Der.* Term used to refer to clothing and accessories used for children's dolls and infants' clothes in the early part of the 20th c.

baby Louis heel See FOOTWEAR: LOUIS HEEL.

backstay Reinforcement of the vertical seam at the back of a shoe with a narrow piece of leather.

bagging shoe See FOOTWEAR: START UP.

bal/Balmoral (bahl-mor′-al) Basic style of OXFORD with the TONGUE cut in a separate piece from the VAMP of the shoe and joined with stitching across the vamp (see cross-references under FOOTWEAR). *Der.* First

bal/balmoral shoe

worn at Balmoral Castle in Scotland in early 1850s.

ballerina shoe   **1.** Soft, low kid shoe with thin sole and flat heel, sometimes made with drawstring throat. Inspired by shoe worn by ballet dancers. Popular in 1940s for school girls. Also see FOOT-WEAR: BALLET SLIPPER. **2.** Plain, low-cut pump made with flat or wedge heel and a crepe or synthetic sole, introduced in 1980s.

ballerina shoe

ballet laces (bal′-lay)   Wide satin ribbons used as lacings for ballet slippers, crisscrossing at intervals around ankle and calf and tied in a bow. Worn in 1870s on bathing slippers and during World War I with high-heeled pumps. Reintroduced in 1980s.

ballet slipper (bal′-lay)   **1.** Soft flexible slipper made of kid. Upper is pulled around to form part of the sole, which is very thin and has no heel. Worn by ballet dancers and children for dancing and in late 1940s for streetwear. Most slippers for professional dancers have been made since 1887 by Capezio, trademark of Capezio Ballet Makers, a division of U.S. Shoe Corp. **2.** Any similarly styled slipper worn indoors or outdoors usually with a heavier type sole. Reintroduced in 1984 with outer sole for streetwear styled in leather or fabric and sometimes worn with ballet laces.

ball heel   Spherical heel made of wood or Lucite. Popular since 1960s.

ball heel

Balmoral boot ∞ (bahl-mor′-al)   Short black boot worn by women from 1850s to 1870s with a walking dress. Made with front lacings, sometimes colored. *Der.* Name of Queen Victoria's castle in Scotland that was often used as an adjective when describing certain fashionable items of Victorian apparel.

bamberges ∞ Shin guards worn during Carolingian Period, mid-8th to 11th c.

basketball shoe   High or low oxford made of canvas or army duck with nonslip molded rubber sole. The shoe laces to the toe and is frequently made with reinforced toe and COUNTER (see under FOOTWEAR). Originally used only for sports, in 1970s accepted for school wear. In

basketball shoe

1980s and after, sometimes made in leather with a padded collar added at top.

Bass Weejun®   Trademark of G.H. Bass & Co. for a high-quality moccasin-type loafer with tasseled bow in front using the same type last since 1936. Originally copied from a Norwegian-type moccasin. *Der.* Word originally from shortened form of Norwegian-Injun.

bathing slipper   Woman's flat fabric shoe, sometimes laced up leg similar to ballet slipper, worn while swimming and popular in late 19th c. After 1920s similar shoes without lacing, frequently of rubber, were worn on beach and in water.

batt   ∞ Heavy laced low shoe used for country wear in England in 17th c., sent to New England Colonists in 1630s.

Beatle boot   Ankle-high boot with pointed toe and side gores of elastic styled for men. Probably the first fashionable ankle-high shoe to be worn by men for general wear in place of oxfords since World War I period. *Der.* Introduced in the 1960s by the Beatles, an avant-garde rock-music group from Liverpool, England. Also called *Chelsea boot*.

Beatle boot with winkle-picker toe 1964

bedroom slipper   An older term used for footwear made of fabric, felt, or leather, usually in heelless style and intended for indoor wear.

belgrave shoe   ∞ Woman's evening shoe cut like a PUMP, but coming up high in the back, fastened in front with GILLIE lacings; worn in 1870s. See FOOTWEAR: GILLIE and PUMP.

bell-bottom heel   See FOOTWEAR: LOUIS HEEL.

bellows tongue   See FOOTWEAR: TONGUE.

bicycle bal   ∞ Shoe with protective toe cap and a circle stitched over ankle joint. Closed with laces extending toward the toes. Designed for bicycling in latter part of 19th c. and later adopted for other sports.

Blake   See FOOTWEAR: McKAY METHOD.

blind eyelet   See CLOSURES.

block heel   See FOOTWEAR: CUBAN HEEL.

blucher (bloo′-cher or bloo′-ker)   **1.** Basic oxford type with the tongue and vamp cut in one piece. See FOOTWEAR: OXFORD, TONGUE, and VAMP. **2.** Man's ankle-length riding boot

F

that laces up center front through six pairs of eyelets. Worn from 1820 to 1850.

blucher #1

Der. Named after Field Marshal Gebhard Leberecht von Blucher, Prussian commander at battle of Waterloo (1815), who devised this type of shoe for army wear in 1810.

blucher bal (bloo′-cher or bloo′-ker) Modified BLUCHER oxford (see under FOOTWEAR) with VAMP stitched over QUARTER at sides, but not stitched over TONGUE (see cross-references under FOOTWEAR).

boating shoe Canvas shoe similar to TENNIS SHOE, but made with a special nonskid rubber sole for walking on slippery boat decks. Also called *deck shoes.* Also see FOOTWEAR: SPERRY TOPSIDERS®.

body boot See FOOTWEAR: STOCKING BOOT.

boot garters ∞ 18th-c. term for straps attached to back of man's boot, which wound around the leg above knee over top of the breeches.

boot hook **1.** ∞ 19th-c. term for leather loop attached to back or sides of boot at top, used to aid in pulling on boots. Also called *boot strap.* **2.** Long L-shaped piece of metal with a handle used to pull boots on.

bootie/bootee ∞ **1.** Bedroom slipper edged with fur or fake fur. **2.** Infant's fabric or knitted footcovering. **3.** Type of sock worn by astronauts in flight.

boots Shoe that extends to the ankle or above. Boots have been worn since Anglo-Saxon times in various lengths. More popular during some eras such as Louis XIII period and Regency period. From 1820s to 1880s, ankle-high dainty boots were worn outdoors by women. In 1890s, calf-high boots, either buttoned or laced, with medium heel were worn. In mid-19th c. very fashionable for children. Now classified as **utility boots** and used for various purposes (e.g., skiing, skating, hunting, mountain climbing, etc.), or as **fashion boots,** intended to be worn

utility boot: hiking boot

fashion boot

indoors and out in place of shoes. Made as a fashion item, and not intended to be waterproof, such boots became very fashionable in the mid- and late 1960s and after in all lengths and in many fabrics as well as leather.

boot strap See FOOTWEAR: BOOT HOOK #1.

botews See FOOTWEAR: BUSKINS #2.

bottine ∞ (bow-teen′) Woman's knee-high riding boot of 16th c.

boudoir slipper (bood-war′) Early 20th-c. term usually referring to slippers without backs made in fancy fabrics, and sometimes trimmed with marabou. Also see MULES.

boulevard heel Sturdy high heel similar to a CUBAN heel that is tapered at sides and back, has straight front, and a flange where heel joins with sole.

boulevard heel

bowling shoe Soft, supple shoe of oxford or other type with cushioned insole for comfort. Made with hard rubber sole and heel with an added leather tip on the sole of the right shoe (or left, for left-handed bowlers).

bracelet-tie shoe Woman's ankle-strap shoe with loop extending on rim in center back to hold the strap; worn in 1930s and 1940s, and again in early 1970s.

breasted heel Any heel made with a curved section where it attaches to the sole of the shoe at the *shank.*

brodekin/brodkin/brotike ∞ Lightweight shoe worn in Middle Ages inside boots.

brogan Originally men's ankle-length shoe worn in Scotland. Made of leather and fastened to foot by side flaps either buckled or tied over short tongue.

brogue Heavy walking shoe, a type of OXFORD (see under FOOTWEAR), originally made for men, that usually has a wing tip decorated with heavy perforations and pinkings. Frequently worn for golf but also for city wear. *Der.* From coarse heelless shoe of untanned hide, with hair left on, worn by men in Ireland in 1790.

brogue 1916

bucket-top boot See FOOTWEAR: FRENCH-FALL BOOT.

buck oxford   A BLUCHER-type oxford (see under FOOTWEAR) made with sueded split-leather upper. Typically has a red cushion-crepe rubber sole. When made of white leather, called **white bucks.**

built-up heel   See FOOTWEAR: STACKED HEEL.

bulldog toe   Bulbous toe popular on a man's buttoned ankle-high shoe before World War I. Similar to FOOTWEAR: KNOB TOE.

bumper   Rubber strip attached across the front of the toe in some athletic footwear.

buskins   1. See FOOTWEAR: COTHURNUS. **2.** ∞ High, sometimes knee-length, boots often made of patterned silk and worn from 14th to 17th c. Also called *botews* (bot'-toos). **3.** ∞ Leather riding boots worn in 17th c. for traveling. **4.** Women's low-cut shoe with elasticized gores at sides of instep worn in the early 20th c. **5.** See FOOTWEAR: AMERICAN BUSKINS.

Buster Brown®   Comic strip character of the early 20th c. whose haircut, collars, suit, and shoes were widely copied for children's wear. The name became a trademark for children's shoes and is currently a trademark for a wide variety of products.

butterfly bow   ∞ Length of stiffly starched lace, resembling outstretched butterfly wings, fastened to front of shoe at end of 17th c.

buttoned shoe   ∞ Shoe with a three- or four-button diagonal closing and a BULL-DOG TOE (see FOOTWEAR) or a conventional toe. Worn by men in early 1900s.

button shoes   ∞ Short boots buttoned up outer side with black glossy or mother-of-pearl buttons. Worn from 1837 to early 20th c. by men, women, and children. When the shoe came to ankle or above and closed to side of center front with a row of small shoe buttons, it was called a **high button shoe.** These were worn by both men and women from late 19th through early 20th c.

cack   Heelless shoe with soft leather sole, made for infants in sizes one to five.

calamanco shoes   ∞ (kal-ah-man'-ko) Heavy shoes made from a twilled cotton fabric called calamanco, which were worn by American women in Colonial days. Fabric is also spelled *calimanco, callamancoe, calliman, callimanco, calmanco.*

calcarapedes   ∞ (kar-kara'-ped-eez) Self-adjusting rubber galoshes worn by men in the 1860s.

calceus   ∞ Roman boot coming to below ankle with long straps wrapping around leg, reaching to calf and sometimes the knee. Lower part was slit down each side to permit easy access. When worn by Roman senators, called **calceus patricius.**

calk   1. Device on heel, or sole, of shoe or boot to prevent slipping or give longer wear; may be a metal plate with sharp points. **2.** ∞ In Colonial America, term used for CLOG (see under FOOTWEAR) with spiked sole.

cameleons   ∞ (ka-me'-le-on) Women's shoes and boots of late 1850s made with cutouts to show colored stockings underneath.

campagus   ∞ (kam-pah'-gus) **1.** Shoe worn by bishops in Western Church, particularly Roman Catholic, sometimes Episcopal. **2.** Shoe worn during Byzantine period and the Middle Ages, high in back to the ankle and fastened with ribbon or strap over instep.

carbatina   ∞ (kar-batt'-ee-nah) Ancient Roman sandal made of single piece of untanned hide as sole, overlapping sides of foot, and held on by leather thongs. Copied since 1950s as barefoot summer sandal.

carpet slipper   19th-c. informal slip-on house slipper made of carpeting, cut in pump style with a standing rounded tongue cut in one piece with toe and soft padded leather sole with flat heel made in one piece. Style still made in other fabrics and in felt. Also see FOOTWEAR: FELTS.

carriage boot   ∞ Woman's fur-trimmed winter boot usually of fabric, sometimes of leather, worn over other shoes to keep feet warm in unheated carriages or automobiles in early 20th c.

chain loafer   See FOOTWEAR: LOAFER.

Charlie Chaplin toe   Wide round toe used on a Mary Jane shoe. Featured by Courrèges in his spring 1967 collection. Also see FOOTWEAR: MARY JANE.

F

chaussures à crics ∞ (show-sur′ ah kree) Shoes with high heels worn in the 17th c. *Der.* French, "shoes on lifts." Also called *chaussures à Pont-Levis.*

Chelsea boot See FOOTWEAR: BEATLE BOOT.

chest-high boot See FOOTWEAR: WADERS.

Chinese shoe Fabric flat-heeled crepe-soled shoe of MARY JANE type (see under FOOTWEAR) made with one strap and rounded toe. Made in many colors, sometimes with embroidery. The national shoe of China, it was imported by the U.S. and sold first at Oriental and later at other stores in late 1970s and 1980s and since.

Chinese slipper See FOOTWEAR: KAMPSKATCHA SLIPPER.

c h o p i n e / c h o p i n / c h a p i n e y ∞ (sho-peen′) Wooden or cork CLOG, covered with leather, sometimes 18″ high, fitted with toe cap and used as a patten, or overshoe; worn in 16th and 17th c. See FOOTWEAR: PATTEN.

chopine 16th c.

chukka boot (chuh′-ka) Men's and boys' ankle-high boot laced through two sets of eyelets, made of splits of unlined sueded cowhide. Has thick crepe-rubber sole. Originally worn by polo players and adopted for general wear in 1950s. *Der.* From *chukka,* a period in polo games. A **desert boot,** introduced in 1960s, differs from a chukka boot in that it is usually lined and has a rubber sole. **Floats,** also introduced in early 1960s, have thick crepe soles and a thick pile lining, but are otherwise like chukka and desert boots.

chunky heel High or medium heel that has exaggerated width—a shoe fad of late 1960s and early 1970s.

chunky heel

chunky shoe Shoes of all types made in exaggeratedly heavy shapes with bulbous toes and massive heels, often with very thick platform soles. A fad in late 1960s and early 1970s and fashionable again in the 1990s.

chunky shoe

city boots Women's boots of a more tailored or dressy style that are suitable for wear with business or more formal daytime dress.

Clarence ∞ Man's laced ankle-high boot of 19th c. made of soft leather with triangular gusset at the side, forerunner of ELASTIC-SIDED BOOT (see under FOOTWEAR).

cleats Projections attached to soles of sport shoes, made of plastic, wood, rubber, or metal. Used particularly on football, golf, and baseball shoes to prevent slipping.

clog **1.** See FOOTWEAR: PATTEN. **2.** ∞ Woman's leather-soled overshoes with instep straps generally matching the shoe, worn outdoors in 17th and 18th c. **3.** Wooden shoe. See FOOTWEAR: SABOT.

closed seam Shoe seam, similar to a simple fabric seam, stitched on the inside and edges pressed back. Usually used for joining the shoe at center back.

clot ∞ Heavy shoe with thin iron plates on the sole worn by workmen in the 15th c. Also called *clout-shoen.*

cockers **1.** ∞ High boots, crudely made, worn by laborers, sailors, country people, and shepherds from 14th to 16th c. Also called *okers.* **2.** ∞ In 17th c. boots worn by fishermen. **3.** From 18th c. a term used for leggings buttoned or buckled at the side with straps under the instep. Word still used today in the North of England. Also spelled *cokers, cocurs, coggers.*

collar See FOOTWEAR: QUARTER.

collegians See FOOTWEAR: OXONIAN BOOTS.

colonial shoe Medium-heeled slip-on shoe with stiffened tongue standing up over instep, frequently decorated with large ornamental buckle. Worn in the 17th and 18th c. in the United States and revived often.

Colonial tongue Stiffened shoe tongue that extends up from vamp of Colonial shoe and is frequently trimmed with ornamental buckle.

columnar heel High circular-styled heel graduating from wide width at sole of shoe to small base.

combat boot Ankle-high laced boot worn by U.S. armed forces made of special retanned leather designed to be waterproof. Adopted as fashionable footwear in the 1980s and 1990s.

combination last See FOOTWEAR: LAST.

common-sense heels Low heel used on children's or infants' shoe made by increasing size of OUTSOLE at heel. See FOOTWEAR: SOLE.

congress boot/congress gaiter ∞ Ankle-high shoe with leather or cloth top and elastic gore inset on each side that was popular from Civil War to early 20th c. Served as the pattern for ROMEO SLIPPERS for men and JULIET SLIPPERS for women (see under FOOTWEAR).

Continental heel High narrow heel made straight in front with square corners at base and slight curve at back. Has a slight edge extending forward where it joins the sole. Exaggeratedly high and narrow version is called a SPIKE HEEL.

continental heel

cookie See FOOTWEAR: ARCH CUSHION.

copped shoe See FOOTWEAR: CRAKOW.

copper toe ∞ Metal cap placed on children's shoes to keep them from scuffing and wearing out. Used at the turn of the 20th c.

cork See FOOTWEAR: GALOSH #2.

corkies See FOOTWEAR: WEDGE HEEL.

corned shoe ∞ Broad-toed shoe worn from 1510 to 1540.

cothurnus ∞ (ko′-thur-nus) Ancient Greek and Roman calf-high boot laced up the front, made of colored leather with thick soles, sometimes of cork if wearer wished to appear taller. Worn by upper classes, huntsmen, and tragedians on stage in ancient Greece. Also called *buskin*. Also spelled *kothornus*.

cothurnus or buskin

counter Extra cup-shaped reinforcement placed at heel of shoe upper, between outer upper and lining, to add stiffness.

Courrèges boot (Koor′-rej) White calf-length low-heeled fashion boot introduced by French designer André Courrèges in fall of 1963 for wear with miniskirts.

court shoe 1. See TENNIS SHOE. 2. British term for PUMP (see under FOOTWEAR).

court tie 1. British term for a man's low-cut oxford, generally of patent leather, worn as part of ceremonial COURT DRESS in England. 2. ∞ British term for a woman's laced oxford of early 20th c. made with two or three pairs of eyelets in blucher style.

covered heel Heel of wood or plastic covered with leather or another plastic.

cowboy boot High-heeled dip-top calf-high boot of highly ornate tooled or appliquéd leather, often two tone. First worn by cowboys of the western United States, now adapted for women and children. Also called *dip-top boot* and *western boot*.

cowboy boot

crakow/crakowe/cracow/krakow ∞ (kra′-kow) Long-toed shoe of soft material—either a separate shoe or cut in one piece with the hose—introduced from Poland during reign of Richard II in England. During the 14th and 15th cs., toes of shoes became so long that they were stuffed and fastened by gold and silver chains to bracelets below the knees. Also called *copped, piked* or *peaked shoe. Der.* After Cracow, Poland. Later called **poulaine** (pooh-lane′). Also spelled *poulain, pullayne.*

crakow

crampons Iron plates with spikes on the bottom that fasten onto shoes or boots so as to facilitate walking or climbing on ice.

creedmore 1. Calf-high, laced work boot with two buckled straps at top. Worn during last part of the 19th and early 20th c. 2. Ankle-high shoe with buckled strap over instep.

creepers Small plates of metal set with spikes fastened over soles of shoes by straps. Worn when walking on ice and snow to prevent slipping.

crepe-soled shoe Shoe made with crepe rubber sole and heel. Originally worn for sportswear, they were so comfortable that they were adopted for everyday wear, particularly by men and schoolchildren. Fashionable for women since early 1970s.

crepida (pl. *crepidae*) See FOOTWEAR: KREPIS.

crescent toe Narrow-toed shoe ending with a curved rather than a NEEDLE TOE (see under FOOTWEAR).

Cromwell shoe ∞ Woman's shoe with large buckle-trimmed tongue worn in late 1860s for croquet parties. Reintroduced in 1888 with

F

high-cut vamp and large bow trim for day-time wear. *Der.* Named for Oliver Cromwell, Lord Protector of England, 1653–1658.

crooked shoe ∞ Shoe cut specifically to fit left or right foot, first produced in volume about 1850, superseding shoes that were straight-cut and fit either foot.

crossover thong sandal See FOOTWEAR: THONG SANDAL #3.

croquet boot ∞ Woman's shoe of mid 1860s made of MOROCCAN LEATHER (see under LEATHERS), frequently trimmed with fancy toe-cap, laced with colored ribbon, and trimmed with tassels. *Der.* Named for the game of croquet, a fashionable pastime of this era.

cuaran ∞ (kwar'-ahn) Knee-length boots of horsehide or cowhide held up by thongs—originally "early Scottish bands made of rawhide." Worn by Scots Highlanders around 1500.

cuban heel Medium to high broad heel with slight curve in back, popular in 1930s and 1940s. The **block heel** is a similar straight heel, but set further back and approximately the same width at top and base.

cube heel Square-backed heel made of leather or Lucite.

cushion sole Cork, felt, or foam rubber used under the insole of shoe as shock absorber when walking.

cutouts Shoe-industry term for tiny patterns shaped like diamonds, teardrops, squares, and other shapes cut out of the upper part of shoe to give open-air effect.

deck shoe See FOOTWEAR: BOATING SHOE.

demi-boot Short boot reaching just to the ankle. Also called *half-boot.*

desert boot See FOOTWEAR: CHUKKA BOOTS.

dip-top boot See FOOTWEAR: COWBOY BOOT.

discotheque shoe A sole with a small heel, fastened to the foot by means of a few narrow straps. Popular for dancing at discotheques in the mid- and late 1960s. *Der.* French *disc,* "record," and *-otheque,* "library."

Doc Martens Laceup boots with air pocket soles to ease pressure on the feet. The boots, first marketed in 1959, were adopted by skin-heads and punks in the 1960s and 1970s and subsequently became widely popular among young people.

dollar-round toe ∞ Old trade term for a toe of a shoe whose shape coincided with the rounded edge of half a silver dollar.

Dom Pedro shoe ∞ Ankle-high man's heavy work shoe fastened with laces and one buckled strap over center of lacing worn in early 1900s. *Der.* Introduced by Dom Pedro of Brazil.

d'Orsay pump/d'Orsay slipper Pump with closed heel and toe, cut down to the sole at the sides, leaving shank bare. Often made with high heel. Popular in 1940s as evening slipper or at-home shoe. Revived periodically. *Der.* Named for *Count d'Orsay.* See ORSAY, COUNT D' in alphabetical listing.

double-needle toe See FOOTWEAR: NEEDLE TOE.

doubler Extra layer of soft fabric placed between the leather and the lining of shoe to make leather look plumper.

double stitchdown See FOOTWEAR: STITCH-DOWN SHOE CONSTRUCTION.

draped heel Heel on woman's shoe with leather or fabric from COUNTER (see under FOOTWEAR) arranged in folds over the back.

dress shoe **1.** Man's or woman's shoe worn for formal occasions, general wear, and business. Does not include sport shoes or crepe-soled shoes. **2.** Girl's shoes worn on Sunday or for special occasions, not for school or sportswear.

dress wellington ∞ Fitted stocking reaching to the knee, attached to a shoe similar to an EVENING SLIPPER (see under FOOTWEAR) and worn under the dress trousers or PANTALOONS (see PANTS). Worn by men with evening clothes from 1830 to 1850.

duckbills ∞ Modern term for broad-toed flat shoes worn in England from about 1490 to 1540—shown in paintings of Henry VIII.

Duck shoe® Trademarked oxford or slip-on style shoe usually made in two colors (e.g., brown with tan, navy with yellow) of manufactured waterproof materials with chain-tread rubber soles. Also called *rubber moccasin.*

Dutch boy heel Low heel with medium-sized base, back slants slightly and inside edge is slanted toward front, where it joins the edge.

Dutchman Triangular wedge placed between insole and outsole of shoe to improve posture of wearer. Also used between layers of a built-up heel to adjust heel pitch.

dyeable shoe Shoe made of white fabric such as satin, faille, or silk that may be dyed to match a dress, worn primarily for evening parties or weddings.

Eclipse Tie ∞ Trade name for woman's shoe made with one pair of eyelets and a pointed tongue usually coming up high on the instep. Worn in late 19th and early 20th c.

edge Shoe-industry term for part of shoe that is visible around outside of front of shoe sole—may be rounded, beveled, or square.

Egyptian sandal ∞ Thong-type sandal with T-strap coming up over instep to join two straps attached to both sides of sole. Worn by ancient Egyptians (e.g., sandal found in King Tut's tomb made entirely of gold).

eighths Height of heels of shoes are measured in eighths of an inch (e.g., a ¹⁶⁄₈ths heel is a 2″ heel, a ⅘th heel is ¹⁄₂″ high).

elastic-sided boot ∞ Ankle-high boot, introduced for men and women about 1837, with India-rubber insert on each side, and patented by James Dowie.

elevator heel Man's heel worn to make him appear taller. Inside of shoe is built up at the heel, making the outside of shoe appear lower than it is. Attached heel lift is higher than average.

Elevator shoe Trademark, now expired, for a man's shoe with a wedge inserted inside the shoe toward the heel to make the man appear taller. Usually made to order.

engineer's boot Man's 12″ high, straight-sided boot with low heel and leather strap buckled across the instep. Also has buckle and strap over elastic gore set in the top.

espadrille (ess-pa′-dril) **1.** Rope-soled shoe with canvas upper. Some versions tied on with long

espadrille #1

shoelaces threaded through top of shoe, crossed, and tied around the ankle. Originally worn for bathing shoe and later for sportswear. Popular in 1940s, reintroduced in 1970s, and fashionable periodically since. **2.** Restyled in 1980s as an oxford, or pump cut high and straight across instep with medium-high wedge heel covered with jute, made with crepe sole, and no lacers. *Der.* French, shoe made of canvas with cord sole.

evening shoe/evening slipper Delicate shoe worn with evening clothes. Women's styles include pumps or sandals in gold, silver or metallic kid or luxurious fabrics; men's style is usually a patent-leather pump or slipper.

Everett Man's house slipper with low back and high tongue curving over instep.

exercise sandal Vinyl sandal held on with two straps. Foot rests on sole made up of tiny rounded projections that massage the foot. Introduced in early 1980s. Also see FOOTWEAR: SCHOLL'S® EXERCISE SHOE.

eyestay Section of footwear that reinforces the holes used for lacing.

fashion boot See FOOTWEAR: BOOT.

Faust slipper See FOOTWEAR: ROMEO SLIPPER.

felts Slippers with soft sole and upper frequently made of felt.

figure skate Fancy skating boot with reinforced instep and counter, laces to above the ankle with speed lacing to the top. Color is usually white for woman, black for men.

filler See FOOTWEAR: SOLE.

fishing boot See FOOTWEAR: HIP BOOT and WADERS.

flange heel Heel that flares or angles to make a wider base.

flat heel Broad low heel originally used on children's shoes, now popular on flat heel women's shoes. Shoes with this heel are called *flats* or *flatties.*

flat/flatties See FOOTWEAR: FLAT HEEL.

flip-flops Sandal made with sponge rubber sole fastened to the foot by two straps that come up between the first and second toes and fasten to the side of the sole. Copied from the original Japanese *zori,* which is a sandal.

F

flippers Rubber extensions, shaped like a duck's webbed foot, that fit over the feet and attach with straps around heels. Worn for scuba diving, underwater swimming, and water sports. Also called *fins*.

floating pedestal wedge Medium broad heel similar to a wedge, but cut out under the arch, making it wider at the base of the heel and slanting toward the sole.

floats See FOOTWEAR: CHUKKA BOOT.

flokati (flow-kat′-ee) Handcrafted Greek slipper sock in above-ankle length, made of fuzzy wool in bright colors and used as after-ski slipper. See FOOTWEAR: SLIPPER SOCKS.

folding slipper See FOOTWEAR: PULLMAN SLIPPER.

foxing **1.** Extra fancy-cut piece of leather sewed on at the top of the back seam of the shoe for reinforcement and decoration. **2.** Strip of rubber fastened to the upper and the shoe that goes all around the shoe.

French-fall boot ∞ Leather boot of 17th c. with extravagantly wide top crushed down to reveal elaborate lace cannons. Also called *bucket-top boots*. Also see HOSIERY: BOOT HOSE.

French heel High heel that curves inward at back then flares slightly outward at base.

french heel

French seam Shoe seam that starts with a simple or closed seam, restitched on either side on the outside. Used for closing back of shoe.

fringed tongue Shoe tongue finished with sawtoothed edge at top.

Frye® boot Boot of WELLINGTON type (see under FOOTWEAR), first manufactured in 1863 for Union soldiers. A registered trademark of John A. Frye Co. and now produced in a variety of boot styles.

gaiter Cloth or leather covering for leg and ankle, buttoned or buckled at side, often held on by straps under foot. Worn by men from end of 18th to early 20th c. and fashionable for women from 1820s to 1840s, and from 1890s to early 20th c. Revived in 1960s in vinyl, leather, or cloth. Fashionable in 1980s and after in water repellent fabrics for cross-country skiing. Also called *leggings*. Also see FOOTWEAR: SPATS.

gaiter boots ∞ Woman's buttoned or elastic-sided, ankle-high leather shoes worn from 1835 to 1870. Made with cloth tops and fastened at side—simulating shoe worn with GAITERS (see under FOOTWEAR).

galosh **1.** Waterproof ankle-high boot worn over the shoe, fastened with a snap, buckle, or zipper. Rubber galoshes were patented in 1842. Also spelled *goloshe, golosh*. Also called *arctics*. See CLOSURES: GALOSH CLIP. **2.** ∞ Wooden platform elevating foot above street, worn in 15th and 16th c. Also called a *patten*. Called a **cork** when a man's galosh of 15th c. had a cork rather than wooden sole. **3.** ∞ In the 17th c. also called *boxes*. **4.** ∞ In 16th and 17th c. wooden-soled low overboots. **5.** ∞ In 17th c. became "covers for shoes." **6.** ∞ In 18th c. called CLOGS. Also spelled *galoche, galage, galoss, galossian*; plurals: *galloses, galloshes, gallotives*.

Ganymede sandal (gan-e-meed) Open sandal derived from Ancient Greek style, with vertical straps from the sole extending up the legs and crossed at intervals around the leg with additional straps. Introduced in 1960s to wear with minidresses. *Der.* Named for the beautiful boy who was the cupbearer of the gods in Greek mythology.

George boot Ankle-high boot made with one-buckle fastening similar to JODHPUR BOOT (see under FOOTWEAR). Widely accepted for general wear by men in late 1960s.

geta Japanese sandal elevated by means of wooden blocks under the sole and fastened to foot by two straps, meeting between first and second toes, curved to fasten at sides of sole. Adapted for beachwear in 1960s.

gillie/ghillie (gil′-ee) **1.** Laced shoe, usually without a tongue, with rounded lacer pulling through leather loops and fastened around the ankle. Worn with Scottish kilt, therefore also called *kiltie* (see FOOTWEAR: KILTIE OXFORD). *Der.* Popularized by Edward VIII and sometimes called *Prince of Wales shoe*. **2.** Many adaptations of this style, particularly for women's shoes, include some styles with high heels. *Der.* Scottish, *gille*, "an attendant or personal servant to a Highland chieftain."

F

gladiator sandal   Flat sandal with several wide cross straps holding sole to foot, and one wide strap around ankle. Introduced in late 1960s. *Der.* Copied from sandals worn in Roman arena by "gladiators."

go-go boot   Calf-length white boot, similar to Courrèges boot (see under FOOTWEAR). *Der.* Named because worn by go-go dancers.

golf shoe   Oxford-style shoe made of oil-treated leather usually given a water-repellent finish, and having a foam-cushioned inner sole. Original shoes had replaceable golf spikes, located on heel and sole, attached to two metal sole plates. Popular in 1920s in a two-toned black-and-white style that returned to fashion in late 1960s and early 1970s. In the 1980s and after, soles of shoes were made with solid rubber sole with rubber spikes.

granny boot   Women's boots laced up the front in imitation of high-topped shoes of 19th c.

Gucci® loafer   See FOOTWEAR: LOAFER.

gumshoe   Colloquial term for sneaker or rubber overshoe. From this comes the slang term meaning a detective or private investigator, alluding to the quiet tread of *sneakers,* which is useful in confidential work.

half-boot   See FOOTWEAR: DEMI-BOOT.

half-jack boot   See FOOTWEAR: JOCKEY BOOT.

Harlow pump   Sabot-strap pump with high chunky heel popular in early 1970s. *Der.* Named after shoes worn by Jean Harlow, Hollywood actress of the 1920s and 1930s.

Harlow slipper   Boudoir slippers, similar to toeless SLIDES (see under FOOTWEAR) with medium to high heel, trimmed with marabou. Copied from slippers worn by Jean Harlow, the Hollywood actress, in the late 1920s and 1930s.

heel   Part of the shoe that elevates the back of the foot. Heels may be flat, medium, or high and are measured in $1/8''$ (e.g., a 1% heel is $2''$ high). Inside edge of heel is called the **breast** of the heel. Extra replaceable piece on bottom is called the **heel lift.** Heels may be made of wood, plastic, Lucite, or metal.

heel horn   See FOOTWEAR: A.T.P.

heel lift   See FOOTWEAR: HEEL.

Hessian boot ∞ (hesh′-an)   Man's black leather riding boot, calf-length in back, curving up-ward to below the knee in front and ending in a point decorated with a tassel. Often made with narrow top border of another color. Worn from 1790s to 1850s.

heuse ∞ (huse)   Mid-thigh length leather riding boot with thick sole, fastened with buttons, buckles, or straps on outer side of leg. Worn by men from 1240s to end of 15th c. Later called *housel* or *huseau.*

high button shoe   See FOOTWEAR: BUTTON SHOE.

high cut   Footwear that extends over the ankle.

hiking boot   Above-the-ankle boot with padded collar, and soft leather lining. Uppers are made of various materials including leather, GORE-TEX®, or MANUFACTURED FIBER FABRIC. Laced up front through riveted D-RINGS with SPEED LACING (see CLOSURES) at top. Usually has a cushioned insole and padded quarter and tongue. Heel and lug-type outsole are made of VIBRAM® (a durable synthetic rubber blend—see under FOOTWEAR) welded to upper. Also called *hikers* and *mountain climbing boot.* Shown at FOOTWEAR: UTILITY BOOT.

hip boot   Rubber fishing boot, thigh-length with straps at sides to fasten to belt at waist. Usually insulated and made with a cushioned innersole, steel shank, semihard toe cap, and cleated sole. Also see FOOTWEAR: WADERS.

hobnailed boot   Boot with a sole into which short nails with large heads have been set. The nailheads serve to prevent wear on the soles.

hockey skate   Skate rounded in front attached to boot with reinforced toe. Sometimes has a strap across the instep, worn for ice hockey.

hooded heel   Heel slanting into shank of shoe, usually covered in one piece with upper.

housel   See FOOTWEAR: HEUSE.

house slipper   Older term for any type of slippers worn indoors.

huarache (wah-rah-chee)   Mexican sandal consisting of closely woven leather thongs forming vamp, made with sling back and flat heel. Popular casual shoe in the United States for all ages and both sexes.

huseau   See FOOTWEAR: HEUSE.

Hush Puppies®   Trade name initially used for casual oxford or slip-on shoes with sueded leather uppers and crepe soles. Popular for men, women, and children. The trademark has now been extended to other shoe styles.

hussar boots ∞ (hoo-zar′) Man's calf-length boots coming to a slight point in front, sometimes having turnover tops and iron soles. Style borrowed from the military and worn by men from 1800 to 1820.

ice cube heel Low, square-cut heel of clear Lucite® introduced in 1970. *Der.* The shape and size of an ice cube.

Indian moccasin See FOOTWEAR: MOCCASIN.

inlay Shoe-industry term for piece of leather or fabric placed underneath a cut-out layer of leather and stitched into place for a decorative effect.

insole Inside of shoe on which sole of foot rests; usually covered by SOCK LINING (see under FOOTWEAR).

instep The inside arch area of the shoe.

insulated boot Any boot with a lining for protection against cold, rain, snow, and bad weather. May be lined with fur, acrylic pile, wool, or foam-bonded fabric.

Italian heel Shoe heel worn from 1770s on that curved inward at back, similar to LOUIS HEEL (see under FOOTWEAR). Also had a wedge-shaped extension at top of heel extending under the sole nearly to ball of foot.

jack boot ∞ **1.** Man's heavy leather riding boot made with square toes and heels with expanded bucket tops extending over knees. Worn by cavalry and civilians from 1660 to 18th c. **2.** Lightweight boots of 18th c. made of soft leather, sometimes laced or buttoned on outside. Also called *light jack boots*. For HALF-JACK BOOT see FOOTWEAR: JOCKEY BOOT #3.

jack boot #1
mid-18th c.

jazz oxford Flat-heeled OXFORD made with VAMP line (see under FOOTWEAR) curved and stitched extending downward to arch. The remainder of shoe is cut in one piece with front lacing.

jellies/jelly beans Molded footwear of soft plastic or rubber made in many styles (e.g., wedgies, multistrapped sandals, flat-heeled thongs, high-heeled pumps, and booties). Some have cut-out "portholes" or lattice strips, and are worn with bright-colored contrasting socks. All are made in a great variety of bright colors and were high fashion in 1983–84. Originally introduced for children, they were imported from Brazil, China, Japan, Greece, and Mexico and were also made in the United States. The style was basically a practical fisherman's sandal made of soft plastic. *Der.* Named for soft translucent look of jelly in jelly-bean colors.

jemmy boot ∞ 18th-c. term for man's lightweight riding boot, a fashionable type of JOCKEY BOOT (see under FOOTWEAR).

jockey boot **1.** High leather boot similar to RIDING BOOT (see under FOOTWEAR), worn by jockeys in horse races. **2.** ∞ Child's high boot of 19th c. often with cuff of contrasting material trimmed with a tassel. **3.** ∞ Man's below-the-knee boot with turned-down top of soft light-colored leather with loops on either side of top to aid in pulling on. Worn from 1680s to end of 18th c. Also called *half-jack boot*. After 1780s, called *top boot*.

jodhpur boot (jod′-poor) Ankle-high boot fastened with one buckle on the side, worn for horseback riding and for general wear. Similar to GEORGE BOOT (see under FOOTWEAR). *Der.* Named for Jodhpur, a city in India.

Juliet slipper Woman's slipper with a high front and back, and V-shaped elastic gores at the sides. *Der.* Named for heroine of William Shakespeare's play *Romeo and Juliet*.

jungle boot Combat boot used for U.S. Army in Vietnam. Made with heavy steel SHANK (see under FOOTWEAR) and tiny drainage holes in sides and heel.

kalso Danish open sandal with platform sole, carved from laminated mahogany, finished with rubber walking sole and held on with two wide straps—one over instep and one around heel.

kampskatcha slipper ∞ (kamp-skat′-cha) Woman's shoe of late 18th c. with pointed upturned toe, moderately high VAMP, and low curved FRENCH HEEL (see under FOOTWEAR) frequently made of Spanish leather with fur lining. Also called *Chinese slipper.*

Keds® See FOOTWEAR: SNEAKERS.

kiltie flat A low-heeled shoe with a fringed tongue and shoelace tied over top in a bow usually made with crepe sole. Compare with FOOTWEAR: KILTIE OXFORD.

kiltie oxford Laced shoe with a shawl or fringed tongue projecting over front of shoe through which laces may be tied. Adopted from Scottish type shoes and popular in 1930s, 1960s, and 1980s.

kiltie oxford with wing tip toe

knob toe Bulbous toe introduced in the early 1970s. Similar to BULLDOG TOE (see under FOOTWEAR).

kolhapuri sandal/kolhapure/kolhapur (ko'-lap-poor') Leather thong-type sandal imported from India, made of hand-tooled water buffalo hide. When sandals are first worn in the shower, the leather becomes permanently shaped to the sole of the foot. Also spelled *kolhapure, kolhapur.*

kothornus See FOOTWEAR: COTHORNUS.

krakow See FOOTWEAR: CRAKOW.

krepis ∞ (kray-pees') Man's toeless sandal with sides and straps crossing in center front, worn in ancient Greece. Similar to Roman sandal called *crepida.*

landlady shoe See FOOTWEAR: WOOLWORTH® SHOE.

landrine/ladrine ∞ (lon-dreen') Louis XIII boot with wide flared cuff reaching halfway up leg with top turned up for riding horseback. Also called *lazarine.*

last Carved wooden or molded plastic form on which a shoe is made. There is a right and left form for each pair in each size. A **combination last** has heel of narrower width than toe.

lasting boots ∞ Term for late 19th c. boots made with black wool uppers.

latchet ∞ Term used from Middle Ages on for strap used to fasten a shoe.

lazarine See FOOTWEAR: LANDRINE.

lift The replaceable part on the bottom of the heel of the shoe. Also called *heel lift.*

lineman's boot High-top or above-the-ankle leather boot, usually black with laces up the center front, made of retanned leather. May have eyelets at the bottom and hooks for SPEED LACING (see CLOSURES) near the top.

lining Leather or fabric that covers part or all of the interior of footwear.

Littleway shoe construction Process of shoe construction or manufacturing that uses a staple to attach the insole to the upper. The outsole may be sewed on with a lock stitch or cemented to the insole.

loafer Slip-on shoe of moccasin-type construction with a slotted strap stitched to the VAMP (see under FOOTWEAR). Introduced first for wear by college girls in the 1940s, now a classic worn by adults and children. Variations include **chain loafer,** trimmed with metal links or hardware trim over the instep. A classic shoe since the 1960s. A variant of the chain loafer is the **Gucci® loafer** (goo'chee), the most popular of the fine shoes sold by Italian firm Gucci in the United States since early 1960s. It has a distinctive gold-metal harness hardware decoration across vamp. Man's shoe has low heel, woman's, a medium heel. Widely copied throughout the 1960s and early 1970s. The **penny loafer** has a slot in the strap across each vamp into which a coin is sometimes inserted. Pennies were originally inserted, but dimes and quarters are now more generally used. Originally in brown but featured in colors beginning in 1980s. The **tassel-top loafer** has a leather tassle on instep.

penny loafer

Louis heel Heel of medium height curved sharply inward around sides and back, then flared slightly at base, similar to heels worn in Louis XV period. Low version is called **baby Louis heel,** and a **bell-bottom heel** is an exaggerated version with a chunky medium heel, curved inward and then flaring at the bottom.

Louis heel

bell-bottom heel

lounger Pull-on boot for cold weather with full grain cowhide upper stitched to rubber shoe. Made with cushioned innersole vulcanized to chain-tread crepe outer sole. Sometimes lined and insulated with wool pile and sheepskin innersole.

lug sole Shoe or boot sole with rubber ridges or cleats to provide additional traction.

F

low cut Footwear cut below the ankle.

lumberman's overboot Man's heavy laced 10″ high boot with oiled-leather top, rubber vamp, and sole worn over felt inner boot. Worn by men in early 20th c., especially when working in lumber industry. *Der.* Boot originally worn in lumbering trade.

Maine hunting boot Waterproof boot consisting of leather uppers sewn to waterproof, vulcanized rubber bottoms. Developed by Leon Bean, owner of L.L. Bean Company of Maine, and first sold by his firm in 1913.

majorette boot Calf-high white boot worn by majorette or cheerleader at athletic events since the 1940s. Some have long white tassel attached to front.

Mamma shoe Retail store and trade name for shoes worn by older women that stress comfort rather than style. Usually made in an oxford style with medium-high broad heel.

mary jane/Mary Jane® **1.** Low-heeled slipper made of patent leather with blunt toe and single strap over the instep that buttons or buckles at center or side. First used as a trademarked shoe for children in 1927, the style has remained popular ever since although currently the trademark is applied to a wide variety of apparel. **2.** In 1980s a *flattie* or *wedgie* in pump style with buckled strap coming high over the instep. *Der.* Named for shoes worn by character Mary Jane in comic strip *Buster Brown*, drawn by R. F. Outcault in early 1900s. Compare with FOOTWEAR: BABY-DOLL SHOE.

mary jane #1

McKay shoe construction Shoe manufacturing process in which the upper is pulled around the last and fastened to the insole by means of tacks. The outsole may be attached by stitching or by cementing. Invented by Lyman Blake in 1861.

medallion In the shoe-industry, an ornamental pattern punched in leather in center of man's wing-tip oxford.

Mexican wedding boot Soft white leather above-the-calf boot made in moccasin style fastened down the outside with four large buttons. Colorful embroidery extends from VAMP (see under FOOTWEAR) up to top of boot.

midsole See FOOTWEAR: SOLE.

military heel Medium to low heel with a broad base. Slants slightly in back and usually has an attached rubber lift. Used on comfort shoes and walking shoes for women.

military heel

Miranda pump Platform pump with high, heavy, flared heel worn in 1969. *Der.* Named after Carmen Miranda, a popular movie star of the late 1930s and 1940s.

moccasin Heelless shoe in which the sole is made of leather and comes up to form the QUARTER and part of the VAMP (see under FOOTWEAR). A tonguelike curved piece is hand-stitched to complete the vamp. Thong is threaded around the collar of the slipper and ties on the instep. Frequently is fleece-lined. May have fringe, beadwork, or tassel trim. Sometimes called *Indian moccasin* because this footwear was worn originally by Native Americans.

moccasin

moccasin-type shoe Shoe construction based on the MOCCASIN (see under FOOTWEAR), in which the UPPER starts under the sole of the foot and forms the quarter, with the toe stitched to an oval VAMP (see under FOOTWEAR). Hard soles, sometimes of rubber, are added to produce a more durable shoe than the soft Indian moccasin.

mod boot Various types of boots worn by boys and girls in mid-1960s in imitation of English mod fashions (e.g., see FOOTWEAR: BEATLE BOOT).

moile/moyle/mowle See FOOTWEAR: MULE.

molded boot A ski boot, sometimes of glass fiber, closed with buckles, made with entire sole and part of shoe molded in one piece. Introduced for skiwear in the late 1960s.

monk shoe Closed shoe with wide buckled strap over tongue at instep rather than lacings. Popular for women in 1940s and for men during World War II when this style was favored by U.S. Army Air Corps officers. Revived in late 1960s and early 1970s.

monk shoe

F

monster shoe Clumsy bulky shoe with wide bulbous toe and large clunky heel. Popular in 1968.

mountain climbing boot See FOOTWEAR: HIKING BOOT.

mousers Women's leather stocking-pants reaching to the waist with attached chunky-type shoes made of shiny wet-look leather. Introduced by Mary Quant, British designer, in 1969.

mukluk **1.** Boot reaching to lower calf worn by Alaskan Eskimos made of walrus hide or sealskin in moccasin construction, tanned with the hair left on. Copied for winter wear for men, women, and children in same style since 1960s. **2.** Slipper socks made in MOCCASIN construction (see under FOOTWEAR).

mule High-heeled slipper or shoe with vamp but no back often made of fancy leathers and fabrics. Name has been used since 16th c. Also spelled *moile, moyle, mowle*.

mule

museum heel Medium-height heel with front and back curving inward and then outward to make a flared base. Also called *shepherdess heel*.

Napoleons ∞ Long military boots, reaching above knee in front, with piece cut out in back. Worn by civilians on horseback in 1850s. *Der.* Named for Napoleon III, Emperor of France, 1851–1871.

needle toe Long narrow extremely pointed toe. Narrower and more pointed variations are called *double-needle* and *triple-needle toes*. Also see FOOTWEAR: WINKLE PICKERS.

Nike® waffle trainers First true running shoe developed in 1974 by Bill Bowerman (Oregon track coach) who in seeking a way to get more traction without increasing the weight of shoes experimented with making the soles in a waffle iron. Subsequently this textured sole was incorporated into a running shoe manufactured by a then-new company called Nike.

oker See FOOTWEAR: COCKER.

open-back shoe See FOOTWEAR: SLINGBACK SHOE.

open-shank sandal High-, medium-, or low-heeled sandal shaped like a D'ORSAY PUMP (see under FOOTWEAR) with a strap around the ankle or over the instep frequently heelless and toeless. Popular style since the late 1930s.

open shank shoe Woman's shoe with closed toe and heel portions but open on sides down to sole; sometimes with side straps connecting vamp and quarter. Also see FOOTWEAR: D'ORSAY PUMP.

open-toed shoe Women's shoe with the toe section cut out.

opera pump Plain, undecorated woman's pump with medium to high heel. Upper is cut from a single piece of leather or fabric. Introduced in 1920s and a basic style since then.

opera slipper Man's bedroom slipper similar to D'ORSAY SLIPPER (see under FOOTWEAR) but front and back sections overlap at shank.

outsole See FOOTWEAR: SOLE.

oval toe Woman's shoe toe, narrower than a round toe but not an extreme point.

overboot ∞ Crocheted or fabric woman's boot of 1860s worn over the shoes for warmth in carriages in winter. Also used as bedsocks for warmth in winter.

overlay A piece of leather or other material stitched on shoe in decorative manner. Usually made of a contrasting color or a textured leather such as lizard or snakeskin.

overshoe Waterproof fabric or rubber shoe worn over other shoes in inclement weather. Also called *rubbers*. Also see FOOTWEAR: ARCTICS, GALOSHES, and RAIN BOOTS.

oxford **1.** Originally a shoeman's term to differentiate low-cut shoes from boots. Now a basic style of low shoe usually fastened with shoe laces, but may be closed with buckles, Velcro®, or other type of fasteners. Shown at definition of FOOTWEAR. **2.** ∞ Historically was a half-boot introduced in England about 1640 and worn by university students. *Der.* Named for Oxford University.

Oxford button-overs ∞ Men's shoes of 1860s, covering the instep and closed with buttons instead of laces.

Oxonian boots ∞ Man's short black boots worn in 1830s and 1840s often made of patent

F

leather with wedge-shaped portion cut out of either side at top so they pull on easily. Also called *Oxonians* or *collegians.*

Oxonian shoe ∞ High-laced shoe with seam at instep worn by men in 1848.

pac boot Laced boot coming to the lower calf of the leg, sometimes made with traction-tread for sole and heel. Insulated and pile-lined, sometimes made in rubber. Basic type boot originally made in MOCCASIN-type construction (see under FOOTWEAR) worn by sportsmen, hunters, and workmen.

paddock boot A less formal type of riding boot that laces to close in order to provide adjustable ankle support.

pantofle (pan-tof´-l) **1.** ∞ Heelless slipper worn from end of 15th to mid-17th c. by men and women. Also spelled *pantoffle, pantoffel.* **2.** Overshoe similar to a patten, with a cork sole worn in late 16th c. Also spelled *pantables, pantacles.* **3.** Term used for bedroom slippers. *Der.* French, *pantoufle,* "slipper."

pants boot Ankle-high shoe-boot designed to wear with pants.

patten **1.** ∞ Overshoe worn over regular shoes to raise feet above muddy streets. One type had a wooden sole with top portion indented for the heel and was patten #1 18th c. secured by strap fitting over regular shoe. Another consisted of a wooden sole raised about three inches with bands of iron forming the walking surface. Worn by men and women from 14th to mid-19th c. Also called *clog.* Also see FOOTWEAR: CHOPINE. **2.** Shoe fitted with iron blades for skating in Middle Ages.

peaked shoe See FOOTWEAR: CRAKOW.

penny loafer See FOOTWEAR: LOAFER.

perforations Small holes punched through leather of shoe to achieve decorative effect. Used particularly for SPECTATOR PUMPS and BROGUES (see under FOOTWEAR). Also called *perfs* in shoe trade slang.

perfs See FOOTWEAR: PERFORATIONS.

piked shoe See FOOTWEAR: CRAKOW.

pinafore heel Flat leather or rubber heel made in one piece with the sole having a curve under

arch of the shoe. Made in the same manner that rubber heels and soles are joined on SADDLE OXFORDS (see under FOOTWEAR).

pinking Saw-toothed trimming on edges of leather used in contrasting color on extra pieces applied to toes and heels of SPECTATOR and GOLF SHOES (see under FOOTWEAR) for a decorative effect.

pinson/pinsnet ∞ Lightweight indoor slipper, often furred, worn from end of 14th to end of 16th c. by men and women. From 17th c. referred to as PUMP (see under FOOTWEAR).

platform sandal Open-type sandal with platform sole usually made with high heel. Popular in 1940s, 1970s, and periodically since.

platform shoe Shoe with thick mid-sole, usually made of cork and covered so that the wearer appears taller. Popular for women in 1940s and revived by Paris designer Yves Saint Laurent in 1960s. Worn by men in 1970s. Revived periodically.   platform shoe

platform sole Mid-sole of shoe, often made of cork or sponge rubber, raising the foot off ground on a platform varying in height from $1/2''$ to $3''$. Popular in 1940s for women's shoes, reintroduced in late 1960s by Roger Vivier in Paris, and popular in the United States from early 1970s.

platypus toe Squared-off tip of toe shaped like a duck's bill. *Der.* Named for animal with snout shaped in this manner.

plug/plugged oxford Low-laced shoe cut with VAMP and QUARTERS (see under FOOTWEAR) in one piece and a separate lace stay (e.g., FOOTWEAR: SADDLE OXFORDS).

point shoe See FOOTWEAR: TOE SLIPPER.

police boot Black leather boot reaching to below the knee made in shiny, stiff leather. Similar to a RIDING BOOT (see under FOOTWEAR). Worn by motorcycle police, some state police, and by mounted police in the United States and Canada.

Polish boot ∞ Woman's high front-laced boot of 1860s decorated with colored high heel and tassel in front.

poulaine/poulain/pullayne See FOOTWEAR: CRAKOW.

pre-walkers Infant's shoe with very soft soles worn before child begins to walk.

Prince of Wales shoe See FOOTWEAR: GILLIE.

Pullman slipper Man's lightweight, glove leather flat slipper that folds into small envelope for traveling. Also made in patterned stretch fabrics for women. *Der.* Named for railroad sleeping cars designed by George Pullman and Ben Field in 1858–59 and owned since 1864 by Pullman Palace Car Co.

pump Slip-on shoe with low-cut, rounded, or V-shaped THROAT, a heel that may be of any height and may be covered with the same material as the UPPER. Toes vary from rounded to pointed depending on the current style. Sometimes made with open toe and/or open heel in SLINGBACK style. A classic style for women for day or evening since 1920s. Shown at definition for FOOTWEAR. Also see SPECTATOR PUMP, COURT SHOE, and OPERA PUMP. See cross-references under FOOTWEAR. *Der.* Pump replaced the word *pinson* used in 17th c.

pyramid heel Medium-high heel with squared base flaring toward the sole—like an inverted pyramid.

pyramid heel

quail-pipe boot ∞ Man's high soft leather boot worn pushed down and wrinkled on the leg. Fashionable in late 16th and early 17th c.

quarter Back portion of shoe upper covering the sides and back of the foot. In athletic footwear the top line of the quarter, called the **collar**, is sometimes padded.

racing shoe See FOOTWEAR: RUNNING SHOE.

raglan boot ∞ Thigh-length, soft black leather boot worn by men for hunting in late 1850s. *Der.* Named after Lord Raglan. See RAGLAN, LORD.

rain boot **1.** Lightweight plastic or rubber stretch galoshes that may be folded and carried in the purse. See FOOTWEAR: TOTES®. **2.** Clear fold-up plastic coverings extending to ankle with zip front. Made with hole at heel through which high-heeled shoe can be worn.

rand A leather strip placed between the shoe UPPER (see under FOOTWEAR) and the sole.

riding boot High boot coming to below the knee made of high-quality leather, usually custom-ordered to fit leg. Worn with breeches

for horseback riding. May have boot straps at top for ease in dressing.

roller blades An updated version of roller skates consisting of shoes with wheels attached.

roller skate Above-the-ankle boot made with polyurethane wheels, rubber toe stop, closed with eyelets and speed lacing. Worn for roller skating.

Romeo slipper Man's pull-on, boot-type slipper with elastic side gores. Also called *Faust slipper*. *Der.* Named for hero of William Shakespeare's play *Romeo and Juliet.*

rubber boot Molded rubber waterproof boot with or without insulated lining but usually fabric-lined, worn over the shoe (especially by children) or in place of the shoe as protection against rain or snow. In mid-1980s and after made in many colors (e.g., red, yellow or purple).

rubbers Waterproof lightweight shoes that pull on over regular shoes in inclement weather. Also called *overshoes*. Also see FOOTWEAR: STORM RUBBERS and TOE RUBBERS.

rubber shoe/rubber moccasin See DUCK SHOE® under FOOTWEAR.

Ruby Keeler shoe Low-heeled pump tied across instep with ribbon bow similar to tap shoes. Popular for teenagers in early 1970s. *Der.* Named after tap dancer Ruby Keeler, popular star of 1930s' films who made a stage comeback on Broadway in 1971 in a revival of the 1917 musical *No, No Nanette.*

running shoe Sport shoe with crepe or rubber sole and upper made of two or three colors of contrasting leather or fabric. Sometimes laced to the toe and sometimes styled like a regular oxford. Style inspired by the track shoes worn by athletes, which sometimes have contrasting stripes of colored leather on the sides of the shoe. Also called *racing shoe*.

sabot (sa-bo') **1.** Shoe carved from one piece of wood, worn by peasants in France, Belgium, Spain, and Portugal. Also worn with Dutch national costume. **2.** Clog shoe with thick wood sole and open heel, made with closed leather vamp or leather bands across instep.

sabot-strap shoe (sa-bó) Woman's shoe with a wide strap across instep, usually buckling to one side. May be used on a SPECTATOR PUMP (see under FOOTWEAR) type of shoe.

saddle Extra piece of leather sewed over instep of a shoe, usually of contrasting color or texture (e.g., black or brown on white shoes).

saddle oxford/saddle shoe Sport or school shoe usually made of white buck calf with a brown or black leather "saddle" shaped section over the middle of the shoe. Usually made with rubber soles, it has been a basic style since the 1920s, very popular in the 1940s, and still worn.

saddle oxford

saddle seam Hand or machine-stitched seam used on shoes when two raw edges of leather stand up on outside, as on the VAMP of a MOCCASIN (see under FOOTWEAR).

safety shoe Work shoe with a heavy metal reinforced toe, or another protective feature, worn by industrial workers.

safety toe Steel toe box inserted between shoe upper and lining. Used on shoes worn by workmen in industrial plants for protection.

sandal Shoe held on the foot by means of straps or a projection between the toes. Usually made with an open shank and frequently toeless and heel-less, or consisting of a sole held to the foot with straps. Worn since earliest times—gold sandals have been found in Egyptian tombs. Greeks and Romans wore many types of sandals. During the Middle Ages, sandals were worn only by peasants. In the 16th c., worn by monks in monastic orders, pilgrims, and by sovereigns at coronations. During the 1920s and 1930s, introduced for evening wear, sportswear, and day wear. *Der.* Greek, *sandalon.*

sandal

Scholl's® exercise shoe A trademark for a wooden sandal with sole shaped to fit foot and special carving underneath the ball of the foot for gripping the foot when walking; made with only one wide strap over front of foot, buckled to adjust the size, and an outer sole of ridged rubber. Action of foot on carved sole when walking provides healthful exercise. Introduced in late 1960s, continuing into the present.

scuff Open-back, sometimes open-toe, slipper with flat heel. May be of fur, shaggy fabric, lightweight kid, terrycloth, or other fabrics.

sculptured heel Broad medium-high heel made with a see-through center, introduced in 1960s. Similar to some freeform pieces of sculpture. Used on wooden clogs in late 1970s.

semi cut Shoe cut just to or slightly over the ankle. Also called *three-quarter cut.* Compare with FOOTWEAR: HIGH CUT and LOW CUT.

set-back heel Heel with straight back joined to the sole as far back as possible.

set-back heel

set-under heel Heel with outside edge curving forward under heel.

set-under heel

shank 1. The narrow part of the shoe under the arch of the foot between the heel and the ball of the foot. 2. The narrow strip of metal or other reinforcement inserted under arch of shoe between INSOLE (see under FOOTWEAR) and outer sole to give strength to the arch.

shawl tongue See FOOTWEAR: TONGUE.

shell See FOOTWEAR: SKIMMER.

shepherdess heel See FOOTWEAR: MUSEUM HEEL.

shoe/shoes Outer covering for the foot that does not reach higher than the ankle. Shoes are basically made up of the sole, or part under the foot; the vamp, or front part of the shoe; the quarter or back of the shoe, and the shank or portion under the instep. Shoes may be of the slip-on variety or closed with laces or buckles. VELCRO® (see under CLOSURES) was introduced in the early 1980s for closings.

shower shoe Plain heel-less pump with upper of fishnet and sole of rubber or crepe. Worn at home, in the shower, or at the beach.

side-gore shoe Slip-on shoe, usually with high vamp, that has triangular insertions of elastic at sides.

side-laced oxford Oxford laced at side front rather than center front, made with low wedge heel, reinforced counter, side perforations near sole for ventilation, and cushioned arch support. Often made in white and popular with nurses.

skating boot See FOOTWEAR: FIGURE SKATE, HOCKEY SKATE, and ROLLER SKATE.

ski boot Waterproof, thick-soled ankle-high boot of leather or molded plastic, closed with laces or buckles. Sometimes has an inner boot or foam lining. Attaches to ski by clamp that grips the sole. Also see FOOTWEAR: MOLDED BOOT. Sometimes has a strap and buckle at ankle, tread soles, and removable felt liners of 80% wool and 20% rayon for warmth. Worn for skiing.

skimmer Very low-cut women's pump with shallow sides set on low or flat heels, usually made of very soft leather. Also called *shell*.

slant/slanted toe Rather wide toe that slants diagonally toward the little toe.

slap-sole ∞ Woman's or man's high-heeled boot or shoe of the 17th c. that had a flat sole attached at the toe underneath the shoe but not at the heel. This secondary sole kept the heel from sinking into mud. *Der.* From the slapping sound made by the sole while walking.

boot with slap-sole c. 1630

slide Toeless open-back sandal with WEDGE HEEL (see under FOOTWEAR) of various heights or regular heel made of wood or leather in all heights.

slingback shoe Any shoe with an open back and a strap around the heel of the foot to hold it in place. May be made in pump or sandal style.

slingback shoe

slingback thong sandal See FOOTWEAR: THONG SANDAL #2.

sling pump See FOOTWEAR: SLINGBACK SHOE.

slip-on shoe Any shoe that stays on the foot without using straps or fasteners (e.g., a PUMP, LOAFER, or MOCCASIN) (see under FOOTWEAR). Also called a *step-in shoe*.

slipper 1. Low shoe usually worn indoors. 2. In 16th c. the word meant a low shoe easily slipped on and off as differentiated from BOOTS and OXFORDS (see under FOOTWEAR). 3. Sometimes used to refer to some delicate types of shoes (e.g., evening slipper).

slipper socks Bulky knit socks, frequently handmade with lightweight leather or ure-thane soles, worn after skiing or around the house. Also called *after-ski slippers, après-ski slippers, mukluk slippers,* and *flokati.*

slip-shoe Man's MULE (see under FOOTWEAR) worn from 16th to mid-18th c. Made with flat heel that produced a shuffling step from which came the word "slip-shod."

slop ∞ 15th-c. slipper.

sneakers Formerly used to refer to gym shoes or tennis shoes of white canvas. Now refers to a type of low shoe similar to tennis shoes or a high canvas shoe worn by men, women, and boys for school, sportswear, or gym. They originated in 1868 when canvas uppers were added to rubber soles creating "croquet sandals." These were renamed "sneakers" in 1873. In 1917 U.S. rubber introduced Keds®. (The name derived from the combination of the words "kids"—for whom the first ones were made—and "ped"—Latin for foot.) See also FOOTWEAR: ATHLETIC SHOES.

upper, eyelet, toe box, lace, lining, sole, eyelet stay — sneaker with parts labeled

snowmobile boot Waterproof boot with an attached nylon top tightened with drawstring around calf of leg.

soccus ∞ (pl. *socci*) (soke-oos′) Light slip-on slipper worn in ancient Greece, especially the low shoe worn by the comic actors on the stage. Compare with COTHURNUS, worn by Greek tragic actors.

sock lining Sole-shaped piece of leather or fabric covering shoe INSOLE (see under FOOTWEAR).

sole Bottom part of the shoe, under the foot, usually consisting of three parts—**outsole**, which touches the ground; **midsole**, also called the *filler*, which fills the space between the out-sole and the innersole; and INSOLE (see under FOOTWEAR), which is the part under the foot.

solea ∞ (pl. *soleae*) (sol-eh′-ah) Simple form of sandal worn by the Romans consisting of a wooden sole held on with thongs or a cord.

solers ∞ Early form of slippers used from the 12th c. on. Made of leather or cloth in various unlined styles, worn strapped on the foot. *Der.* Roman, *solea.*

soulette/solette ∞ (soo-let′) Early 17th-c. term for leather band crossed over instep and under arch of foot to hold the patten to the shoe (see FOOTWEAR: PATTEN #2). Fitted over a **surpied,** a quatrefoil (a four-leafed design motif) of leather, used as trimming on the instep of boot.

Space® shoe Trademarked name for side-laced leather orthopedic shoes, with extra moving space for each toe, custom-made over casts of the wearer's feet. Made with thick crepe soles and low wedge heels for comfort.

Spanish heel High heel with a curve similar to a FRENCH HEEL (see under FOOTWEAR) but has a straight inside edge.

spats Short cloth or leather GAITER (see under FOOTWEAR) reaching over ankle, buttoned at sides, and held on by strap under instep. First worn by the military, later adopted by civilian men in 1878 to wear with MORNING COAT (see under COATS AND JACKETS) in white, tan, or gray. Also worn by women from 1914 to 1920. Reintroduced at intervals, including the late 1960s for women. Also see FOOTWEAR: SPAT-TERDASHES. Shown at SAILOR SUIT.

spatterdashes High leggings worn by men from 1670s on, made mainly of leather or canvas reaching to knees. Fastened down outside of leg with buttons or buckles.

spectator pump Two-toned pump frequently made in contrasting colors of black, navy, red, or brown on white. Extra sewed-on toe and heel pieces of another color sometimes have perforations and are pinked at edges. Introduced in 1920s.

spectator pump

Sperry Topsiders® Trademark for shoes with a specially designed rubber sole that provides good traction on a wet boat deck; often made in loafer or sneaker style with canvas upper. This type of shoe is often referred to simply as a **topsider.** The trademark now applies to a wide variety of footwear.

spiked shoe Shoe with metal appendages on the soles. Used as early as 1861 for playing cricket.

spike heel High curved slender heel with tiny base; usually 3″ to 3¹/₂″ high. Also see FOOT-WEAR: CONTINENTAL HEEL.

spit-boot ∞ Man's boot combining shoe and GAITER (see under FOOTWEAR), worn in northern England from 18th to mid-19th c. Closed down outside of leg with interlocking fasteners. The last fastener was an iron spike or "spit" that fastened through an iron socket.

sports sandals Sandals for hiking, running, walking, and other forms of exercise. Invented in 1982 by Mark Thatcher who wanted to devise a shoe that could be used in wading through streams and walking over rough terrain. He used a basic THONG SANDAL (see under FOOTWEAR) with a sturdy rubber sole, and added sturdy nylon straps to hold it on the foot. This sandal was marketed under the trademark Teva®. Other companies have adapted the concept to make a wide variety of sports sandals.

spring heel Low broad heel with extra layer of leather inserted between heel and sole. Used primarily on children's shoes.

squaw boot Below-the-knee boot made of buckskin with fringed turned-down cuff at top, soft sole, and no heel. Originally worn by Native American women, it became a fashion item in late 1960s.

stacked heel Heel built up of horizontal layers of leather. Also called *built-up heel.* Shown at definition for FOOTWEAR.

stadium boot Calf-high sheepskin-lined boot popular to wear to football games in the 1950s. One of the first boots designed to be worn on the foot by women, not over the shoe.

startup ∞ High shoe reaching above the ankle, worn by country men, American colonists, and sometimes by women in late 16th and early 17th cs. Frequently laced or buckled on outside of leg, made of untanned leather, and worn for sports or by country people. Sometimes had velvet or silver trim for women. When loose-fitting, it was called a *bagging shoe.* Also spelled *startop, styrtop, stertop.*

step-in shoe See FOOTWEAR: SLIP-ON SHOE.

stiletto heel (stil-et′-tow) Narrow set-back heel that ends in a tiny rounded base, usually fitted with a metal tip. As the walking surface is small, there is an enormous amount of weight on the heel. Used mainly from 1950s until mid-1960s and revived in the 1990s. Shown at definition for FOOTWEAR.

stitchdown shoe construction Manufacturing process for shoes that involves turning of the shoe UPPER to the outside rather than around and under the LAST (see cross-references under FOOTWEAR). The outer sole is stitched to the extended edge around the shoe. Simple flexible low-cost shoe construction used primarily for infants' shoes, now used for all types of shoes. Sometimes made with two soles and called **double stitchdown.** Sometimes made with three soles and called **triple stitchdown.**

stocking boot Fashion boot made of stretch vinyl, leather, or fabric with no zipper, fitting the leg closely like a stocking. Sometimes reached to thigh with attached panties in late 1960s. Also called *body boot.*

stocking shoe Shoe covered with knitted fabric and attached to a long stocking. Introduced in late 1960s by shoe designer Beth Levine.

storm boot Any type of boot worn in inclement weather. Also see FOOTWEAR: ALL-WEATHER, RAIN, and RUBBER BOOTS.

storm rubbers Waterproof overshoes with rounded flap coming up over the instep.

straights Soles of shoes that are not shaped to fit right and left feet. This style prevailed from c. 1600 to c. 1825, and can be found even as late as 1900.

stretch boot See FOOTWEAR: TOTES.®

surpied See FOOTWEAR: SOULETTE.

taj toe Tiny pointed and turned-up oriental-type toe used on a shoe.

tango shoe A woman's shoe that is cut high in the back with an ankle strap that buckles or ties. Popular from the late 1880s until the 1920s and revived periodically.

tap shoe Any shoe worn by a tap dancer. Made with metal plates at tip of toe and back edge of heel to increase sound when dancing. Men's style is usually a patent-leather pump or oxford; women's is usually a low-heeled patent-leather pump with ribbon tie at instep. Also see FOOTWEAR: RUBY KEELER SHOE.

tassel-tie Bows ending in tassels on moccasins, wing-tip oxfords, and loafers.

tassel-top loafer See FOOTWEAR: LOAFER.

tatamis (tah-tahm'-is) Thong-type sandal with nonflexible rubber sole having a slight wedge. Top of sole is made of woven straw matting. Thong straps are made of wide pieces of durable velvet. *Der.* Japanese, *tatami,* "woven straw mat."

tennis shoe Canvas or drill low-cut oxford with a circular cut vamp. Made with special type of rubber sole for use on tennis courts. Also see FOOTWEAR: SNEAKERS. Also called *court shoe.*

Theo tie An open-throated, tongueless shoe, with ribbon or cord lacings, introduced in early 20th c.

thong sandal 1. Flat, often heelless sandal, held to the foot by narrow strips of leather coming up between first and second toes and attached to sole at either side. Popular for beachwear since 1960s. 2. In early 1980s strap was added around heel, then called **slingback thong. 3.** Thong sandal with complete strap around big toe is called **crossover thong sandal.**

three-quarter cut See FOOTWEAR: SEMI-CUT.

throat The open area at the top of the VAMP in front of the INSTEP. See under FOOTWEAR.

toe Front portion of the shoe covering the toes. In the Middle Ages, toes of shoes became extremely long and pointed. In the 16th c., extremely wide toes were worn on duckbilled shoes. Fashion fluctuates between the extremes. For example, while in the early 1960s very narrow needle toes were worn, by the mid-1960s broad-toed shoes had become fashionable.

toe rubbers Overshoes, worn by women, that fit over the toes and have either a strap around the heel or snap together over the instep.

toe slipper Lightweight kid slipper reinforced with a hard shank and toe and usually tied on with satin ribbons crisscrossing across the instep and around the ankle. Worn by ballerinas and toe dancers. Made by Capezio, trademark of Capezio Ballet Makers, a division of U.S. Shoe Corp. Also known as a *point shoe.*

toe spring The distance between the flat surface on which a shoe stands and the toe end of the shoe.

tongue Part of OXFORD shoe (see under FOOTWEAR) under the lacing. A **shawl tongue** is an extra-long tongue folded over the lacing, sometimes made with decorative fringed end, a style made fashionable when Prince of Wales wore it with kilts in Scotland in mid-1920s. Shoe with shawl tongue sometimes called KILTIE SHOE (see under FOOTWEAR). A similar construction consisting of an extra long leather tongue, often fringed at end, is called an **apron tongue**. It fits behind lacing, then flops over, covering laces completely. A **bellows tongue** is stitched to sides of vamp of shoe and pleated so it expands across instep. In shoes or boots for outdoor wear, it serves to keep out snow.

top boot See FOOTWEAR: JOCKEY BOOT.

topline The opening in the shoe around the ankle.

topsider See FOOTWEAR: SPERRY TOPSIDER®.

Totes® Trademark name for lightweight, fold-up unlined rubber boot, worn over shoes. Also called *stretch boot* or *rain boot*. The trademark also applies to a wide variety of other apparel products.

triple-needle toe See FOOTWEAR: NEEDLE TOE.

triple stitchdown See FOOTWEAR: STITCHDOWN SHOE CONSTRUCTION.

T-strap shoe/sandal Shoe made with a strap coming up from the vamp to join second strap across the instep, forming a **T**. May have high or low heel with open or closed shank. Popular since 1920s.

t-strap shoe
1928

turned shoe construction Lightweight shoe, usually in pump style, constructed by stitching sole to upper inside-out, then "turning" to right side with seams on inside.

tuxedo pump Low-heeled pump with rounded toe, usually made of patent leather with grosgrain trim around the collar of the shoe and a broad flat grosgrain bow on the vamp. Introduced in mid-1980s.

upper Shoe industry term for all parts of shoe above the sole. Includes the COUNTER, QUARTER, VAMP, and LINING (see under FOOTWEAR).

utility boot See FOOTWEAR: BOOT.

vamp Front part of shoe, covering toes and instep. The term has been used used since 15th c., and was formerly called the *vamprey.*

veldtschoen construction Method of making shoes in which the UPPER (see FOOTWEAR) is turned out at the bottom edge, **cemented,** and stitched to the sole.

Vibram® A durable synthetic rubber usually used as a lug-type sole on hiking boots. *Der.* From the first syllables of the name of its inventor, *Vi*tale *Bram*ani, who wanted to make climbing shoes for Alpinists that would be useful not only at lower altitudes but also on the rocky surfaces encountered near the peaks.

vulcanized shoe construction Shoe construction that involves bonding a rubber outsole and heel to a shoe. Upper is tacked or stapled to insole and cement is applied to the shoe bottom. Sole is then inserted into a mold that was previously prepared for individual widths, sizes, and sole pattern. Heat and pressure hold the soling compound to the shoe.

waders Pants and boot in one piece reaching to above waist with suspenders over shoulders. Made of lightweight, flexible vinyl pressed to cotton jersey or rubber, welted to seamless boots with felt liners and cleated nonskid soles. Also called *fishing boot.* Also see FOOTWEAR: HIP BOOTS.

waist The narrow part of footwear between the toe and heel.

walkers Ankle-high laced shoe, usually made of white leather, with man-made or leather soles. Worn by children when first learning to walk.

walking shoe Any comfortable shoe with a relatively low heel, sometimes made with a cushion or crepe sole, worn more for comfort than style.

walled toe Deep toe cap with vertical edge at least ³/₄″ high.

wedge heel Slanted heel made in one piece with the sole of the shoe. Comes in low, medium, and high heights. Introduced in 1930s. Some heels are cut in one piece with a slight platform sole and are usually covered with jute,

wedge heel

fabric, urethane, or leather. Some are made of cork and called *corkies.*

wedgies Shoes with WEDGE HEELS (see under FOOTWEAR) completely joined to soles under arches, made in all styles and heel heights. Popular for women in late 1940s, revived for women and also worn by men in 1970s. Originally made with high wedge, now also made with low- and medium-sized wedges.

Wellington boot Calf-length or below-the-knee boot with a seam below ankle making it look like a top has been joined to a man's low shoe with a long tongue-like projection at vamp. Seams also extend down the sides of the boot to the ankle with boot loops at top. Usually made of water-repellent leather with oak-tanned soles and rubber heels, sometimes leather-lined. *Der.* Named for Duke of Wellington, British military hero who defeated Napoleon in the battle of Waterloo in 1815. Also see WELLINGTON STYLES in alphabetical listing.

welt Narrow piece of leather stitched to shoe upper lining and INSOLE before being attached to OUTSOLE (see FOOTWEAR: SOLE) with seam concealed. A method of shoe construction that permits shoe to be resoled.

western boot See FOOTWEAR: COWBOY BOOT.

white bucks See FOOTWEAR: BUCK OXFORD.

wilderness boot Ankle-high laced boot with reinforced rubber toe, reinforced counter, and strap stitched diagonally from arch over ankle to aid in arch support. Made with LUG SOLE (see under FOOTWEAR) and upper of olive-drab cotton duck backed with cotton drill for quick drying. Worn for mild-weather hiking, wading streams, canoeing, or in African bush country.

wing-tip Decorative leather cap sewn to toe of shoe. Sometimes curved with center point and perforated in patterns. Shown at FOOTWEAR: KILTIE OXFORD. See FOOTWEAR: WING-TIP OXFORD.

wing-tip oxford Laced shoe decorated at toe with wing-shaped overlay perforations, sometimes trimmed with perforations.

winkle pickers British slang for exaggeratedly pointed shoes worn by TEDDY BOYS and Teddy girls in early 1950s. *Der.* From suggestion that

the pointed toes can dig out snails, or periwinkles, from the sand. Shown at FOOTWEAR: BEATLE BOOT.

Woolworth® shoe Shoe sold in millions by Woolworth® stores. Made of cotton canvas, in sandal style, in red, navy, paisley, black, or white. This shoe had sold for 50 years and has been entered in the permanent collection in the Metropolitan Museum of Art Costume Collection. Also called *landlady shoe.*

zori See FOOTWEAR: FLIP-FLOPS.

---

fop Term used to describe a vain man preoccupied with the exquisiteness of his dress or showiness of his person (e.g., affected eccentricities such as the carrying of fans in the late 16th and late 18th c.). *Der.* Middle English *foppe,* "fool." Also see DANDY.

forage cap See HEADWEAR.

ford Apparel industry slang for a style that has mass acceptance. *Der.* From the similarity to mass appeal of the inexpensive early Ford automobiles.

Ford, Tom ∗ See APPENDIX/DESIGNERS.

fore-and-after cap See HEADWEAR: DEERSTALKER.

forecasting The predictions of styles and trends that are made to assist retailers in making both long and short-term merchandising decisions.

forehead cloth See FRONTLET #2 and HEADWEAR: CROSSCLOTH #2.

forepart ∞ **1.** From 16th c. to 1630: a decorative panel made of expensive or elaborate fabric sewed to an underskirt of coarse fabric. The expensive fabric showed through the split skirt of the gown. **2.** 19th c.: the part of a man's waistcoat extending across the chest.

foresleeve See SHOULDERS AND SLEEVES.

foretop See WIGS AND HEADPIECES: TOUPEE #2.

forks See GLOVES AND GLOVE CONSTRUCTION: FOURCHETTES.

formal attire Clothes worn by men and women at formal social functions. Women's dresses designed for formal occasions are often called *formal gowns, evening gowns,* or *ball gowns.*

formaldehyde tanning See LEATHERS.

formal shirt See SHIRTS.

formal suit See TUXEDO and FULL-DRESS SUIT.

Fortuny, Mariano ∗ See APPENDIX/DESIGNERS.

F

foulard † Soft lightweight silk or manufactured fiber fabric, usually made in a twill weave and surface printed in a small design. Used for scarves, neckties, and dresses. Also see SCARVES: FOULARD.

foundation See UNDERGARMENTS.

foundation pattern See SLOPER.

foundling bonnet See HEADWEAR.

fourchettes See GLOVES AND GLOVE CONSTRUCTION.

four-gore slip See UNDERGARMENTS.

four-in-hand tie See TIES.

fourragère (foor-ah'-zher) Braided cord worn usually draped around left shoulder as a military award or decoration. Compare with AIGUILLETTE.

fourreau dress See PRINCESS DRESS.

fox See FURS.

foxing See FOOTWEAR.

fraise See SCARVES.

fraise à la confusion See NECKLINES AND COLLARS: FALLING RUFF.

frame See HANDBAGS AND RELATED ACCESSORIES.

framing See HANDBAGS AND RELATED ACCESSORIES.

France, point de See LACES.

franchise A contractual arrangement between a franchisor (the entity selling its name) and a franchisee (the buyer). In return for using a well-known company name, and sometimes, management assistance, the franchisee, who is an independent owner, pays royalties to the franchisor.

fraternal ring See JEWELRY.

fraternity See JEWELRY.

Frazer tartan See PLAIDS AND TARTANS.

free-form ring See JEWELRY.

free motion machine See EMBROIDERIES AND SEWING STITCHES.

freight forwarding company A company that ships goods to the United States from the country that produced the goods.

frelan See HEADWEAR.

French antelope lambskin See LEATHERS.

French back Back of dress made with three seams—one in center and one on either side curving into the armhole. Fashionable in late 19th and early 20th cs. and still used. Also see SIDE BODIES.

French beret See HEADWEAR: BERET #2.

French boa See SCARVES.

French bottoms See PANTS.

French bra See UNDERGARMENTS.

French braid See HAIRSTYLES: FISHBONE BRAID.

French cinch See UNDERGARMENTS.

French cloak See CAPES, CLOAKS, AND SHAWLS.

French corsage ∞ Woman's BASQUE waist worn in 1860s with wide tight-fitting CORSELET (see BELTS), extending to middle of bust and made of different fabric. Bodice had a boat-shaped neckline and double ruffled sleeves. Skirt was of contrasting fabric.

French crepe † Originally a silk fabric with a flat smooth surface made in France of crepe-twisted yarns. Now applied to a large group of similar plain woven fabrics called *lingerie crepes,* made of rayon and other manufactured fibers.

French cuff See CUFFS.

French drawers See UNDERGARMENTS.

French dress ∞ Little girl's long-waisted dress, worn in late 19th and early 20th cs. Usually made with square or round neckline accented with a large bertha collar. Sleeves may be short, ruffled or puffed, or of long leg-of-mutton style. Skirt was full with wide ribbon sash at low waistline.

French-fall boot See FOOTWEAR.

French farthingale See FARTHINGALE.

French frock See COATS AND JACKETS.

French gigot sleeve See SHOULDERS AND SLEEVES: LEG-OF-MUTTON SLEEVE.

French gores ∞ Term used in 1807 for panels introduced into skirts to eliminate gathers at the waist.

French heel See FOOTWEAR.

French hood See HEADWEAR.

French hose See TRUNK HOSE.

French jacket See PETENLAIR.

French kid See LEATHERS.

French knot See EMBROIDERIES AND SEWING STITCHES.

French lace See LACES.

French lock See HAIRSTYLES: LOVE LOCK.

French maid sleeper See SLEEPWEAR AND LOUNGEWEAR.

French nightcap See HEADWEAR: DORMEUSE.

French opening vest See VESTS.

French panties See UNDERWEAR.

French policeman's cape   See CAPES, CLOAKS, AND SHAWLS.

French polonaise   See IRISH POLONAISE.

French portrait buttons   See CLOSURES.

French purse   See HANDBAGS AND RELATED ACCESSORIES.

French Revolution styles   Just before the French Revolution of 1789, styles in dress had simplified somewhat and the conflict did not usher in immediate major style changes; however, certain visible costume symbols were associated with the Revolution. Patriotic Frenchmen and women were expected to wear the Revolutionary colors of red, white, and blue. The red cap of liberty (see *BONNET ROUGE* under HEADWEAR), the trousers that replaced knee breeches among the working classes and revolutionaries (their wearers were called *SANS CULOTTES* or "without knee breeches"), and the *CARMAGNOLE* (see under COATS AND JACKETS) a short woolen or cloth jacket with a full back were probably the most important symbolic items. Jewelry was made from the stones of the Bastille, the prison that was pulled down at the beginning of the Revolution. Once the worst excesses of the Revolution were over and the DIRECTOIRE PERIOD began, styles changed radically from the prewar wide-skirted dresses and elaborate suits to much simpler styles.

man's clothing of the French Revolutionary Period

French roll   See HAIRSTYLES.

French ruff   See NECKLINES AND COLLARS: RUFF.

French sailor dress   ∞ Girl's long-waisted tailored dress of early 20th c. with BLOUSON effect, short pleated skirt, and SAILOR COLLAR (see under NECKLINES AND COLLARS).

French sailor hat   See HEADWEAR.

French seam   **1.** See CLOTHING CONSTRUCTION DETAILS. **2.** See FOOTWEAR.

French skirt   See SKIRTS: CORNET.

French sleeves   See SHOULDERS AND SLEEVES.

French thumb   See GLOVES AND GLOVE CONSTRUCTIONS.

French twist   See HAIRSTYLES.

French vest   See VESTS.

French wig   See WIGS AND HAIRPIECES: FULL-BOTTOM WIG.

freshwater pearls   See GEMS, GEM CUTS, AND SETTINGS: PEARLS.

fret   **1.** See HEADWEAR. **2.** ∞ Trelliswork sometimes used to ornament a garment in a lattice design in the 16th c. *Der.* French, "trelliswork." **3.** Greek design consisting of a series of incompleted rectangles in a repeat design. Also called the *Greek key, Greek fret,* or *Grecian border.*

friendship bracelet   See JEWELRY: WOVEN FRIENDSHIP BRACELET.

friendship pin   See JEWELRY.

friendship ring   See JEWELRY.

frigate cap   See HEADWEAR.

frileuse   See CAPES, CLOAKS, AND SHAWLS.

frill   Narrow piece of fabric or lace gathered to form a ruffle and attached as trimming to a dress or blouse. Term used since the 16th c.

frilling   ∞ Ruffles of gathered, stiff, white muslin worn at the wrist and neck, specifically on widows' dresses of 1870s and 1880s.

fringe   **1.** Ornamental trim used since medieval times, consisting of loose strands of thread, yarn, or beads, fastened to a band. **2.** Fabric or leather slashed into narrow strands, used for trim.

fringed cuff   See CUFFS.

fringed tongue   See FOOTWEAR.

friponne   See JUPE #1.

frisette   See HAIRSTYLES.

frisk   See UNDERGARMENTS.

frizzle   See NECKLINES AND COLLARS.

frizz-wig/frizze/frizzle   See WIGS AND HAIRPIECES.

frizzy   See HAIRSTYLES.

FRM   See FLOOR-READY MERCHANDISE.

frock   Origin and usage of this term is unclear and it has at various times been applied to such garments as a woman's undergarment, a priest's gown, and a loose-fitting riding coat. Among the specific usages are these: **1.** Synonym for a woman's dress. Specific usage has varied. In 16th and 17th c. a general term for an informal gown; by 19th c. usually meant a dress of thin fabric; and in 20th c. was often used for a child's dress as well as to refer to women's dresses generally. **2.** From medieval times, a man's loose-fitting, sleeved outer garment of coarse fabric, derived from a monk's HABIT and worn by farm workers or laborers. Also called *smock frock* and in some areas was decorated with smocking. See SMOCK. **3.** See COATS AND JACKETS: FROCK COAT.

frock coat   See COATS AND JACKETS.

frocked jacket   See COATS AND JACKETS: FROCK #2.

frock greatcoat   See COATS AND JACKETS.

frock overcoat   See COATS AND JACKETS.

frog   **1.** See CLOSURES. **2.** See LEATHERS.

front   See WIGS AND HAIRPIECES.

fronts   See HIP-HOP.

frontayl/frontel   See FRONTLET #2.

front-closure bra   See UNDERGARMENTS.

frontier pants   See PANTS: WESTERN PANTS.

frontlet   **1.** ∞ See HEADWEAR. **2.** A brow band covered with face cream, worn at night in the 18th c. to remove wrinkles. Also called *forehead cloth* or *crosscloth* or spelled *frontayl, frontel.*

front-zipper foundation   See UNDERGARMENTS.

froufrou   Fluffy trimmings such as ruffles, ribbons, and laces. *Der.* French, "rustle" or "swish."

froufrou dress   ∞ (froo′-froo′)   Daytime dress of 1870 made with low-necked bodice and worn under a short muslin tunic. Skirt was cut away in front, revealing a silk underskirt trimmed with many tiny pinked flounces. *Der.* From the name of the comedy *Froufrou*, written by Henri Meilhac and Ludovic Halévy in 1869.

froufrou mantle   See CAPES, CLOAKS, AND SHAWLS.

frouting   ∞ In the 17th c.: process of rubbing perfumed oil into a garment to freshen it.

frouze   See WIGS AND HAIRPIECES.

Frye boot®   See FOOTWEAR.

FTC   See FEDERAL TRADE COMMISSION.

full-bottom wig   See WIGS AND HAIRPIECES.

full dress   Formal attire consisting of formal evening dress for women and white tie and tails for men.

full-dress suit   Man's formal suit consisting of SWALLOW-TAILED COAT (see under COATS AND JACKETS) frequently trimmed with satin lapels, and matching trousers with satin stripes down side of pants. Worn with formal shirt, white vest, and white tie. Also called *white tie and tails.*

fulled wool   † Woolen or worsted fabrics that have been subjected to the finishing process called **fulling**, which consists of compressing or shrink-ing the fabric by use of heat, moisture, pressure, and friction to produce a dense appearance somewhat like felt. Contemporary fashion promotions often use the terms *boiled wool* or *felted wool* to refer to these fabrics.

full fashioned   Knit garment or garment pieces in which shaping is provided by increasing or decreasing the number of stitches.

full-fashioned hose   See HOSIERY.

full grain   See LEATHER.

fulling   See FULLED WOOL.

full length   See LENGTHS.

full lining   Finishing of the inside of the garment with a complete lining, so that no seams of the outer fabric are showing. Used mainly for coats, jackets, and sometimes dresses.

full piqué/full P.K. seam   See GLOVES AND GLOVE CONSTRUCTIONS.

full skirt   See SKIRTS.

full tee   See SHIRTS.

full top grain   See LEATHER.

fully let-out   See FURS.

fume fading   † Fading of acetate fabrics caused by acid gases in the atmosphere.

fun furs   See FURS.

funky look/funk fashion   **1.** Styles inspired by the funk music played by African-Americans, which gained popularity in the 1970s. Patchwork leather coats, platform shoes, wide-legged pants, or LAMÉ jumpsuits of satin or gold, large jewelry, and glittery stage makeup worn by performers were imitated by fans. **2.** In 1983, the designer Kenzo used "funky factor" to describe hobo styles and baggy oversized suspender pants worn with clown-like makeup.

funnel   Adjective used for accessories and parts of apparel made in the shape of a flaring cone. See HEADWEAR: FUNNEL HAT, NECKLINES AND COLLARS: FUNNEL NECKLINE.

funnel sleeve   See SHOULDERS AND SLEEVES.

FURS

fur   **1.** Pelt of an animal, raw or processed, with the hair attached—as differentiated from leather, which is tanned without the hair. All furs usually have dense short hairs called **underfur**, and much longer, silky hairs called **guard hairs**. Best, or **prime pelts**, are secured in coldest time of year with the exception of beaver, a water animal, where water is coldest in early spring from melting snow. Furs were used since earliest times for clothing, preceding woven cloth. Popular for trim and linings in the Middle Ages, with certain furs reserved for the nobility. Often used in the latter half of the 19th and early 20th cs. for matching collar and cuffs on full-length coats. From 1900 through 1950s fur scarves with head, tail, and feet of animal were fashionable, and in the early 1930s all types of furs were worn. During the 1940s, mink became the most generally used fur, with the fur stole increasing in popularity. In 1964, FUN FURS (see under FURS) were introduced. Later, furs worked in herringbone, grooved, plaid, and tweed patterns were introduced. In the mid-1980s full-length coats of long-haired furs, e.g., lynx, fox (including silver fox), fisher, fitch and tanuki were popular, along with mink and sheared beaver. Lightweight KNITTED FURS (see under FURS), made by a lazer-cutting technique, were in style in 2002. According to **Federal Fur Products Labeling Act of 1952,** furs must be labeled as to name of fur; proper origin; processing (sheared, dyed, etc.); and a Label Authority Tag must be attached stating that product was made by a manufacturer who supports code of Fair Labor Standards. In 1969, U.S. Congress passed **Endangered Species Act,** which banned importation and sale of pelts of some animals. Some individual states have also passed laws restricting sale of furs from endangered animals and in 1975 a Convention on International Trade in Endangered Species of World Fauna and Flora was established. See entries under FURS for definitions of specific furs and fur processing techniques. **2.** An item of wearing apparel, accessory, or trimming made from such pelts (e.g., a fur coat, scarf, hat, or muff).

Alaskan seal See FURS: FUR SEAL.
American marten Least expensive marten with long guard hair and underfur ranging in color from blue-brown to dark brown.

antelope Stiff flat hair, similar to calf, in beautiful soft brown color; rarely used for fur as the number of antelopes is very limited.
Armur raccoon See FURS: USSURIAN RACCOON.
Australian opossum Woolly type fur usually gray in color; best quality comes from Australia and Tasmania.
Austrian seal ∞ Term used in early 20th c. for rabbit fur. Used prior to the Fur Labeling Act, it is no longer correct.
badger Heavy, warm, durable fur with long silvery gray guard hairs and dense white or tan underfur.
Baltic seal/Baltic tiger ∞ Term used in early 20th c. for rabbit fur; considered incorrect terminology since Fur Labeling Act of 1938.
baum marten Medium-length brown guard hairs and yellow-brown underfur; resembling sable, but guard hairs are coarser, shorter, and not as lustrous. Best pelts are obtained from Europe. Used primarily for jackets, scarfs, and trimmings. Fair to good durability; expensive. Also see FURS: MARTEN and STONE MARTEN.
bearskin Pelt of a bear.
beaver Rich velvety brown fur that, when sheared, reveals a wide silvery stripe down the center. Preferred color is blue-brown; sometimes left natural or bleached beige for "blonde beaver." Most beaver is sheared and coarse guard hairs are plucked out. Pelts are large, requiring only five to seven for a *let-out* coat. Best qualities from Canada, particularly the Laurentian Valley in Quebec, and the United States, including Alaska. *Der.* From Middle English *bever,* "brown."
beaverette ∞ Term used in the early 20th c. for rabbit fur; considered incorrect since Fur Labeling Act of 1938.
black fox Fur with long silky guard hairs and thick underfur, a color phase of the RED FOX belonging to the same genus. SILVER FOX and PLATINUM FOX are color phases of the black fox. It is possible to raise all types by fur farming with the best qualities obtained from this source as well as from Alaska, eastern Canada, and northern Europe. See cross-references under FURS.

Blackglama® American Legend Cooperative Association trademark for very dark MUTATION MINK (see under FURS).

blanket **1.** Fur-industry term for small pieces of fur sewn to form a pattern, making a piece large enough for a fur coat, e.g., mink in brown and white, used to form herringbone, window pane, or checkerboard patterns. Usually imported from Greece. **2.** Fur-industry term for extra large beaver skins.

blending Fur-industry term for lightly applying dye to tips of hairs of furs, such as mink and sable, to improve the coloring.

blue fox Dark brown fur with a bluish cast, long silky guard hairs, and thick underfur. Some pelts also have silvery hairs. This fox is a color phase of the Arctic WHITE FOX (see under FURS), but its habitat is more southerly. Best qualities from Alaska and Greenland. It is possible to dye the white fox this color.

blue pelt Fur pelt taken in early fall, too soon to be prime, or best, pelt.

broadtail lamb Natural, unsheared, flat moiré pattern, with silky texture. Colors may be natural brown, grays, or black or possibly dyed.

brush Bushy tail of an animal, usually a fox, used as trimming.

bucky pelts Fur pelts taken in spring months when skins are not fully furred and tend to be tough and unyielding. Also called *springy pelts.*

burunduki (bur-oo′-duke-ee) Usually small, lightweight delicate skins with nine alternate stripes of white and black on a yellow or orangish background. Skin obtained from rodent native to Russia similar to American chipmunk. Frequently imported in PLATES (see under FURS). Used for linings and trimmings.

caging Fur-cleaning process, in which furs are revolved in cagelike wire drums that permit the sawdust, used for cleaning, to fall out through the wire mesh.

calf/calfskin Flat, short, stiff-haired fur from young cattle, usually brown spotted with white, also may be black and white, all black, or brown. Used for trimmings, handbags, belts, shoes, and vests.

caracul See FURS: KARAKUL.

chati cat See FURS: SPOTTED CAT.

cheetah Flat fur from the cat family from Africa or Southern Asia, with black spots on a tawny ground. Hair is softer and lighter than leopard. Used for coats, jackets, hats, etc. No longer permitted by law to be used in the United States.

China mink Yellowish mink found in China dyed to imitate North American mink, which is much more expensive. Also see FURS: KOLINSKY.

chinchilla Silky-haired fur with a very delicate skin. Best quality has slate-blue underfur and guard hairs that are white and darker at the tips, center back is gray. This small rodent is native to the Andes Mountains in South America. May also be raised on fur ranches. Mutation colors are now available.

Chinese dog Fur with long guard hairs and thick underfur from Mongolia and Manchuria. Used as trimming on inexpensive coats. Sewed into mats for shipment.

Chinese lamb See FURS: KARACUL.

Chinese raccoon See FURS: USSURIAN RACCOON.

civet cat Spotted fur characterized by elongated black marks against a dark gray background with a greenish cast. Not widely used. Comes from southern China and the Malay Peninsula. The little spotted skunk of South America is sometimes incorrectly called the civet cat.

coney Synonym for RABBIT (see under FURS). The word "rabbit" originally meant "the young of the coney." This term is accepted as a synonym for rabbit for proper fur labeling. Coats may be labeled as beaver-dyed coney or beaver-dyed rabbit.

crimmer See FURS: LAMB.

crosses Fur term for small pieces of fur, such as paws and gills, sewn together to make a large piece that is cross-shaped—used particularly on varieties of lamb.

cross fox Fur with long silky guard hair and dense underfur in a dark reddish color. Named for the marking between the gills in the shape of a "cross" rather than a product of cross breeding. It is a color phase of the RED FOX (see under FURS).

dropping See FURS: LETTING OUT.

dyed sable See FURS: SABLE.

electric mole ∞ Incorrect terminology used in early 20th c. for RABBIT FUR (see under FURS) prior to the Fur Labeling Act of 1938. Correct terminology is *electric-processed rabbit*.

electric-processed rabbit See FURS: ELECTRIC MOLE and ELECTRIC SEAL.

electric seal ∞ Incorrect terminology for *rabbit* that is sheared and then carved in ridges. Correctly called *electric-processed rabbit*.

electrified lambskin Lambskins tanned with hair intact and given an electrical treatment that gives the hair a silky texture.

ermine Pure white fur from weasel family with short guard hairs and silky soft underfur. Best quality from the far north—Siberia, in particular. As the animal roams further south, it develops protective coloration of light shades of brown. Traditionally used by royalty since Middle Ages and still used on ceremonial robes of British peerage.

feathering Applying extra dye delicately to guard hairs of fur by means of a feather dipped in dye. Used to improve appearance of the fur.

fisher Color shading from brown to blackish tones with long guard hairs and dense underfur. Used primarily for scarfs and jackets usually in its natural state. Best quality pelts come from Labrador. Very good durability; fairly scarce and expensive.

fitch Moderately priced fur, with yellow underfur and black guard hairs with a silky texture; found in Europe. *White fitch,* another type, is found in Ural Mountains of southern Russia. Used for coats, jackets, and trimmings. Durability is very good; relatively inexpensive. Color ranges from ecru with black markings to orange tones.

fleshing Hand process of smoothing reverse side of fur by scraping with a sharp knife.

flowered mink Term used to describe a mink coat worked in a floral design, usually consisting of a six-petal arrangement (e.g., a daisy). Used in color or white against colored background. An innovation of the late 1960s.

fox Fur with long lustrous guard hairs and deep dense underfur. There are four primary types of foxes and many miscellaneous types. Main groups are: (a) *red fox*—includes black, silver, platinum, and *cross fox* (yellowish with a black cross marking) as color phases; (b) *white fox*—with blue fox a color phase; (c) *gray fox;* and (d) *kit fox.* Northern kit fox is protected by Canadian government. Found in every continent except South America, and also raised on fur farms. Used for coats, jackets, scarfs, muffs, jackets, and trimmings. See other fox furs listed separately under FURS: BLACK, BLUE, CROSS, GRAY, PLATINUM, RED, SILVER, and WHITE FOX.

fully let-out Fur industry term for a fur coat with pelts cut so that one let-out strip goes from neck to hem of coat. Also see FURS: LETTING-OUT.

fun furs Term originated in 1965 for long-haired and unusual furs worked in an interesting manner into a coat or other garment suitable for sports or informal occasions.

fur farming Raising and scientific breeding of animals for their pelts. Originated in the 1920s with raising of SILVER FOXES; later same method was used to raise RANCH MINK and MUTATION MINK. See cross-references under FURS.

fur seal Soft velvety fur from the genuine Alaska seal. All pelts are sheared and dyed either black or brown and other colors. Sealing is controlled by the U.S. government with pelts coming from the Pribilof Islands, off the coast of Alaska. Used for coats, jackets, hats, and muffs. Durability is high. Expensive because of the limited quantity available. Argentina and Ecuador protect species.

golden muskrat Side portions of the southern muskrat pelt. Also see FURS: MUSKRAT.

gray fox Long-haired fur with silky guard hairs and dense underfur of a gray color. Used mainly for trimmings; best qualities are from the United States.

gray muskrat The belly part of the southern muskrat. Also see FURS: MUSKRAT.

grooving See alphabetical listing.

guanaco (gwa-nak´-ko) Reddish-brown fur from the young guanaco or guanaquito found in Argentina. Inexpensive and not durable, it is used for jackets and trimmings, and is the only member of the llama family used for fur.

guard hairs   See FURS in category heading.

hair seal   Stiff rather short-haired fur with a natural blue-black or blue-and-black mottled effect that may be dyed various other colors. Comes from two varieties of seals, the *harp seal* and the *hooded seal,* whose habitat is the North Atlantic. Baby hair seals are white in color, and used to make sealskin leathers as the fur is slightly woolly.

hamster   Small soft golden-brown pelts of rodent found in the Rhine River Valley and in Siberia. Similar in appearance to the American muskrat. Used most often for linings. Rarely used in America.

hare   Soft short-haired fur, similar to rabbit but with more tendency to mat. Arctic hare from northern Europe and Asia has a long guard hair and is sometimes used to imitate the Arctic fox. Durability is low but higher than rabbit fur.

harp seal   See FURS: HAIR SEAL.

hooded seal   See FURS: HAIR SEAL.

Hudson Bay sable   See FURS: MARTEN.

Hudson seal   Proper name is *Hudson seal-dyed muskrat.* Also see FURS: MUSKRAT.

jaguar   Flat spotted fur with dark rosette markings with two dots in centers against tawny background. Popular for coats and two-piece suits for women in the early 1960s. In comparatively short supply. No longer permitted by law to be used in the United States.

Jap/Japanese mink   Muddy yellow-colored mink from Japan that is always dyed in imitation of more expensive American mink.

Jap fox   See FURS: USSURIAN RACCOON.

Jap raccoon   See FURS: USSURIAN RACCOON.

karakul/caracul (kar′-ah-kul)   Lamb pelt with a moiré appearance (see under FURS)—best pelts are the flattest. Majority of skins are white and may be dyed; or may be rusty brown, dark brown, or black. Best quality from Russia. When skins are from China, called *Chinese lamb* or *Mongolian lamb.* Used for coats, jackets, and trimmings. Durability is moderate.

kidskin   Short-haired flat gray fur with wavy pattern, inexpensive fur with low durability.

The best pelts come from young goats of India, China, Ethiopia, and South America.

kit fox   See FURS: FOX.

knitted fur   Fur that is cut into quarter-inch strips and the skin sanded to reduce bulk, after which the strips are knitted into fur garments. First done in 1960s by artisans and avant garde designers; such garments tended to be stiff. New laser-cutting techniques make construction of light, soft, warm garments possible.

knuckle curl   Fur-industry term for tight natural curl in *Persian lamb.*

kojah   See FURS: MUTATION MINK.

kolinsky   Brownish fur with medium-length silky guard hair and slightly yellowish underfur. Best qualities from Manchuria. Used primarily for scarves and trimmings, and used in imitation of American and Canadian mink. Durability is fair. Also see FURS: CHINA MINK.

krimmer   See FURS: LAMB.

lamb   Many types of lamb are processed for fur, but three main types stand out: *Persian lamb, broadtail lamb,* and *karakul lamb*—differentiated by luster, and tightness of the fur curl. Other lamb variations include *Afghan, Astrakhan, Argentine, Bessarabian, Iranian, Kalgan, Soviet Union, India, China,* and *Southwest Africa.* Crimean lamb is called *crimmer* or *krimmer.* Also see FURS: BROADTAIL, KARAKUL, MOUTON, and PERSIAN LAMB.

lapin (la-pan′)   French word for rabbit. Not used in the United States except in a descriptive form (e.g., lapin-processed rabbit).

leathering   Fur-industry term for using narrow strips of leather between strips of fur in order to make the fur less bulky and give it a more graceful hang.

leopard   Spotted jungle-cat fur judged by: (a) flatness; (b) contrast between spots and background; (c) shape of rosettes or spots. There is no underfur in the best qualities, and better qualities have shorter hair. Best quality is from African Somaliland. Although leopard fur was used as early as Egyptian times, it was not popular for women's wear until after World War I. Good durability; very limited in supply and expensive. No longer permitted by law to be used in the United States.

lettice ∞ (let'-ees) Term used for ERMINE or MINIVER (see under FURS), specifically white ermine or other white or gray fur, in 16th and 17th cs.

letting-in Fur-industry term for process of intricate cutting and resewing a fur skin to make it shorter and broader.

letting-out Fur-industry term for process of intricate cutting and sewing a fur skin to make it longer and narrower. The pelt is cut down center back, slit into tiny diagonal pieces, and each piece dropped when joined to next pieces. Process makes the pelt long enough that a skin may extend from neck to hem of the garment. Also called *dropping*.

lynx Long silky-haired delicately spotted fur. Colors vary from white, blue gray, pale gray, and brown. Best quality of white comes from the Hudson Bay area and Alaska. Pelts also come from other parts of Canada, Scandinavia, and Siberia. Used for coats, jackets, and trimming. Spain protects the *Spanish lynx*.

lynx cat Differs from lynx, being darker in color with darker spots and shorter guard hairs, similar to the American wildcat. Best qualities are from Nova Scotia, other qualities from Canada and the United States. Used extensively in coats and jackets and for trimmings.

marguay See FURS: SPOTTED CAT.

marmot Fur with guard hair and underfur similar to MUSKRAT and MINK (see under FURS). Blue-black color is preferred, other pelts are dyed brown and frequently processed to simulate mink; moderately priced. Marmot comes mainly from the Soviet Union, Manchuria, and China. Used mainly for coats, jackets, and trimmings for cloth coats. No longer permitted by law to be used in United States.

marten Soft, rich fur with fairly long guard hair and thick underfur similar to sable; blue-black or brown colors preferred, but ranges to canary yellow. Best qualities found in eastern Canada and the Hudson Bay area. Incorrectly called the *Hudson Bay sable*. Also see FURS: BAUM MARTEN, STONE MARTEN, and AMERICAN MARTEN.

miniver **1.** ∞ White or spotted gray and white fur, used for linings and trimmings in the Middle Ages. **2.** White fur, especially ermine, used to trim "robes of state" in various countries. Also see FURS: LETTICE and VAIR.

mink Fur with silky to coarse guard hairs and dense, soft underfur. Best qualities of the dark pelts are lustrous with the guard hairs giving off a blue reflection. Originally only WILD MINK was available, with best qualities coming from eastern Canada; northeastern U.S. pelts ranked second. Animal also exists in Europe, but pelts are usually of less value. Zoological name is *Mustela vison* and animal is from the weasel family. *Vison* is the European name for mink. Since the 1940s, much mink is raised by fur farming in the United States. Many color variations are now available due to the development of new strains, or MUTATIONS, on ranches (see MUTATION MINK). Most mink is used in the natural color, and the fur is of good durability. In the 1930s, the mink coat became a status symbol. With the growth in popularity of the stole during the 1950s, and the production of more pelts by fur farming, mink became available to the masses. In mid-1960s, patterned and patchwork minks became fashionable. These were made of paws, gills, and small bits pieced together to form *blankets* of flowered, herringbone, plaid, tweed, and windowpane patterns from which a garment was cut. In the late 1960s and early 1970s painted, sheared, hand-screened, and tie-dyed mink became fashionable.

moiré pattern (mwa-ray') Fur term for appearance of Persian broadtail and American processed broadtail—flat furs with a wavy surface.

mole Extremely soft gray fur, rather flat with a wavy appearance, and a very delicate skin. Best qualities come from Asia. Popular for jackets and trimmings in early 1900s. Poor durability. Always dyed to avoid white skin showing through.

Mongolian lamb See FURS: KARACUL.

monkey Very long, lustrous black fur with no underfur. Used for trimmings and jackets. Obtained primarily from the colobus monkey on the east and west coasts of Africa.

F

mouton-processed lamb Woolly fur with a dense pile, made by shearing the merino sheep rather than "hair" sheep. Used for coats, jackets, and hats. Inexpensive, warm, and durable. Generally dyed brown, frequently water-repellent.

muskrat Fur with long guard hairs and dense underfur, processed three different ways: (a) dyed and striped to resemble mink and sable; (b) sheared and dyed to imitate Alaskan seal and called *Hudson seal-dyed muskrat;* and (c) left natural and finished to improve the coloring. Best qualities of northern muskrat, which is brown or black, are used for Hudson seal-dyed muskrat and come from the Great Lakes region in the United States. Southern pelts, which vary in color, are used for natural muskrat coats. Durability is moderate to high. Natural muskrat skins are split into five parts, each part used separately as "back coats," "golden sides coats," and "silver belly coats."

mutation mink Strains of mink developed scientifically on fur farms by carefully mating the animals. Original wild pelts were brown. From mating the odd animals, many new colors were produced. Also during the 1960s, mink with longer hair was produced through breeding. A trade name for this type was *kojah.* In order to market pelts, associations of mink breeders were formed.

nailing See FURS: STAPLING.

natural mink Mink that has not been dyed or colored in any manner.

nutria Fur with a velvety appearance after long guard hairs have been plucked, with color ranging from cinnamon brown to brown with gray stripes. Fur is similar to beaver although not as thick, lustrous, and rich in color. Animal is a water rodent of northern Argentina. Usually wild but some attempts at breeding were made in 1950s. Used for coats, linings, and trimmings. Durability is moderate. Sometimes kept in natural state with long guard hairs and short underfur in lustrous brown. When produced on a ranch, it is bluish-beige in color and slightly coarser. May also be dyed.

ocelot Spotted fur with elongated dark markings against a tan background. Flatter-haired pelts were the best qualities and came from Brazil and Mexico. Used mainly for coats and jackets. Now on the endangered list and not available.

opossum Long, straight guard hairs and dense underfur that in the natural color is either black or gray. Best qualities come from Australia and the United States. Used for coats, linings, trimmings, or dyed to imitate other furs such as skunk and fitch; moderately priced. Australian varieties have short, dense, plush-like fur ranging from yellow-gray to blue-gray.

otter Relatively short-haired fur with silky lustrous guard hair and dense underfur—the most durable fur for the weight and thickness. Preferred color has blue-brown guard hairs and underfur slightly lighter with the base being gray to white color. Best qualities come from eastern Canada. Some otter is sheared and plucked. Also see FURS: SEA OTTER.

paw Fur term for small pieces of fur from paws of animals.

pelt Skin of an animal with the hair attached used for making fur garments and accessories. Also called a *peltry.*

Persian lamb Curly lustrous fur that is usually black but occasionally brown or white. Dark colors are always dyed to color the white skin. Quality is determined by the tightness of the "knuckle" curl and formation of interesting patterns called "flowers." Best quality comes from Bokara, Russia, from Karakul sheep. Others come from Afghanistan, Southwest Africa, and Iran. Popular for coats and trimmings. Durability is high. Now available in new mutation colors. Also see FURS: LAMB.

Persian paw Fur of the Persian lamb that is left after a coat is made—the paws, head, and gills. Small pieces are sewed together to make larger pieces called *plates.* Another coat, collar or garment is then cut from the *plate.*

plates Small pieces of fur joined together to make a larger unit (e.g., Persian lamb plates made from paws and gills that are left over from other garments).

platina See FURS: PLATINUM FOX.

platinum fox Silvery long-haired fur with long guard hairs and dense black underfur. The reverse of the silver fox, it has much silvery hair and little black hair. First discovered in 1935, and later raised on fur farms in the U.S. and Norway, where the trade name is *Platina*. Originally one of the rarest furs.

plucking   Fur-industry term for the process of removing some of the longer *guard hairs*, which may mar the beauty of the final product.

pony   Short-haired flat fur with a wavy moiré appearance. Used in natural color, bleached, or dyed pale colors. Best quality comes from Poland and Russia. Durability good, but short bristly fur has a tendency to wear "bald."

prime pelt   Fur term for a best quality pelt. Animals must be hunted during the season when the pelt is the most fully furred. For most animals, this is during the coldest winter months. *Beaver*, being a water animal, has a fuller pelt in the early spring when the streams are cold with water from melting ice and snow. *Marmot* pelts are best before animal hibernates for the winter.

rabbit   Soft light fur in a variety of colors used in natural state or can be dyed or processed as follows: (a) striped to imitate muskrat, (b) sheared to imitate beaver, and (c) sheared and stenciled to resemble leopard. Best qualities come from Australia and New Zealand. Poor durability; inexpensive. Also see CONEY.

raccoon   Long light-silvery guard hair and dark-brown underfur. Lighter weight peltries from the southern part of the United States are used for coats. The northern United States provides heavy-skinned pelts used primarily for hats and trimmings. Popular for men's and women's coats in 1920s, revived in 1960s. Also see SHEARED RACCOON.

Raccoon dog   See FURS: USSURIAN RACCOON.

ranch mink   MINK (see under FURS) in which the color ranges from true rich brown to brownish-black.

red fox   Fur with long silky guard hairs and dense underfur, which is red-orange in color. As the fur becomes more yellowish, it is less valuable. A red fox may have different colored foxes in its litter (e.g., BLACK, SILVER, or CROSS FOX). Best qualities come from Alaska, Siberia, and Labrador.

rosette   Spotted marking on leopard fur, resembling a paw mark.

Russian crown sable   See FURS: SABLE.

sable   Luxurious fur with lustrous long silky guard hairs and soft dense fluffy underfur; preferred color, a blue-black-brown. Skins that are light brown in color are tipped, blended, and called *dyed sable*. Used for coats or scarfs, with best quality, called *Russian crown sable*, coming from Siberia. Animal is also found in Canada, China, Korea, and Japan. Durability is good and very expensive. Golden sable in amber tone is less expensive.

seal   See FURS: HAIR SEAL and FUR SEAL.

sea otter   Fur with silky guard hairs and silky underfur in a deep blue-black or brown with sprinklings of white hairs. Having exceptionally soft, dense, and luxurious pelts, sea otters were hunted almost to extinction for their fur. Now protected in the United States, these animals can no longer be hunted and their fur cannot be used.

sheared raccoon   Velvety-textured fur similar in appearance to beaver, but not as soft or silky and more cinnamon brown in color with lighter stripes. Raccoon is processed by plucking and shearing. Durable fur, much less expensive than beaver.

shearing   Process used on furs (e.g., beaver, lamb, muskrat, raccoon, and seal) to cut hairs to same length to give them a velvety appearance.

shearling   Pelts from "wool" lambs that have been processed with the hair intact, therefore classifying them as "fur" rather than "leather." Used for jackets, collars, and coats. Usually sueded on the leatherside.

silver fox   Black long-haired fur with long, silky silvery guard hairs and dense underfur. Best quality has the greatest amount of "silver" in it. Silver fox may be found in litters of the red fox. Also raised by fur farming.

skunk   Black fur with long guard hairs and thick underfur with characteristic white stripe down back. Quality of fur depends on ability of the underfur to remain black rather than take on a brownish or rust-colored appearance. For an all-black fur, pelts have white streaks

F

removed and are dyed to darken the skin. Used extensively in the 1930s for jackets and coats; best qualities are from the Dakotas and Minnesota. Also found in Canada and South America. Better U.S. types have high durability. Zorina South American skunk is similar, with flatter fur and silky texture.

snow leopard Spotted long silky guard hair with long underfur in a pale yellow-gray color with white belly and markings that are more like spots than rosettes. Found in high altitudes of the Himalaya Mountains of central Asia. No longer permitted by law to be used in the United States.

spotted cat Variety of spotted fur that comes from three main types of South American cat: the *chati cat,* the *marguay* (mar'-gay), and *long-tailed cats.* Markings are more rounded than those of the OCELOT; fur is less expensive.

springy pelts See FURS: BUCKY PELTS.

squirrel Very soft gray or brown relatively short fur that takes dye readily and may be made any color or worked into a two-toned pattern. Best qualities come from Europe, Asia, Russia, Poland, Finland, and Canada. Used mainly for jackets, capes, and trimmings. Low durability; moderately priced.

stapling A fur industry term used for wetting, blocking, and fastening pieces of a fur garment to a board to make them conform to the shape called for in the pattern. Formerly, this process was called **nailing** because nails were used. Now staples are used because of their smaller size.

stone marten Fur with brown guard hairs and grayish-white underfur judged for quality by the contrast of two colors. Best qualities come from Europe, particularly Russia. Used primarily for scarfs. Also see MARTEN.

tanuki Japanese name for raccoon-dog, which must be labeled and sold under name *Ussurian raccoon* in United States according to Federal Trade Regulations. Also see FURS: USSURIAN RACCOON.

tawning The process of finishing furs, making the pelts pliable and water resistant.

tipping Fur-dyeing process in which only the tips of the guard hairs are colored.

underfur/underhair Short fur fiber of animals such as mink, muskrat, and fox as contrasted with the GUARD HAIRS, which are long and silky. Formerly called *fur fiber.* See under FURS.

Ussurian raccoon Long-haired, yellowish-brown pelt with shoulder and tail tipped with black, slightly coarse guard hair and long, dense underfur. May be dyed, sheared, or used in natural state mainly for collars and trim. Comes from a species of dog that resembles a raccoon in appearance. The Japanese species, known as TANUKI, has the most silky, fully furred pelt (but is not the largest). Other qualities come from Manchuria, Korea, Siberia, and parts of Europe. Also called *raccoon dog, Armur raccoon, Chinese raccoon, Jap fox, Jap raccoon.* These names cannot be used when merchandising pelts in the United States. Color is similar to red fox with distinctive cross markings.

vair ∞ Name for highly prized fur worn by kings and magistrates in 13th and 14th c., used for linings and trimmings. Thought to have been a type of squirrel with dark back and white underside.

vertically worked Term for fur skins that are first let out, and then sewn together so that each skin runs from top of fur coat to hem.

vison See MINK.

weasel Soft silky short guard hairs and silky underfur similar in texture to ERMINE (see under FURS), a close relative. Color varies with the seasons—winter, white; spring, yellowish; summer, streaked with brown or gray; and brown all year in southern climates.

white fitch See FURS: FITCH.

white fox Pure white fur with long silky guard hairs and dense underfur. Comes from the *Arctic fox,* which lives north of the timberline and remains white the entire year. The BLUE FOX (see under FURS) is a color phase of this fox living south of the timberline.

wild mink Skins procured from animals that run wild in the forest. Very expensive because skins must be matched in color. Under controlled conditions on a mink farm, color is more uniform and is usually brown.

wolf Long-haired fur with long silky guard hairs and dense underfur. Pale-colored skins are sometimes stenciled to imitate LYNX; others are used in natural state or dyed brown, black, or gray. Quality depends on fluffiness and density of underfur that supports the long guard hairs. The best quality comes from the timber wolf of Canada. Used for coats, capes, jackets, trimmings, and scarfs. The red wolf is protected in the United States.

wolverine Coarse fur with long brown guard hairs and dense gray underfur. Very durable; best qualities found in the Arctic regions, also found in the Rocky Mountains and Siberia. Used mainly for sportswear and trimming. Used in the far north to trim the edges of parkas as moisture will not condense on it.

worked in the round Method of joining fur skins together horizontally so that skins continue around coat or garment.

zebra Flat, stiff fur with wide, black irregularly shaped stripes against a light-colored background. Comes from Africa; used infrequently for coats. Calf is sometimes stenciled to imitate zebra.

zorina See FURS: SKUNK.

---

furbelow (foor´-beh-low) **1.** ∞ Skirt ruffles used as trim on women's skirts and scarfs in the 18th c. Usually made of same fabric or lace. Also called *falbala* or *fabala*. **2.** In contemporary usage generally refers to useless, ostentatious trimming.

furbelow wig See WIGS AND HAIRPIECES: DUVIL-LIER WIG.

fur blended yarn † Any yarn made from FUR FIBER blended with other fibers (e.g., wool or nylon, used for knitted or woven clothing).

fur boa See SCARVES: BOA.

fur fabric coat See COATS AND JACKETS.

fur farming See FURS.

fur felt Best grade of felt obtained from UNDERFUR (see under FURS) of beaver and rabbit and is used for hats. Also see HEADWEAR: BEAVER HAT.

fur fiber Fibers obtained from the pelts of fur-bearing animals. See FURS: UNDERFUR in introduction to category.

Fur Labeling Act See FURS: FUR #1 in category heading.

fur lining Lining a garment with fur for warmth and fashion appeal. If the garment is meant to be reversible, the sleeves are lined; otherwise sleeves are not fur-lined in order to reduce bulkiness.

fur scarf See SCARVES.

fur seal See FURS.

fur stole See CAPES, CLOAKS, AND SHAWLS.

fused collar See NECKLINES AND COLLARS.

fusible fabric † Nonwoven fabric made up of some fibers that have a low melting point. When heat and pressure are applied, the heat-sensitive fibers melt and the fabric can bond to another fabric or surface.

fused hem See CLOTHING CONSTRUCTION DETAILS.

fused ribbon Ribbon made of acetate or other heat-sensitive manufactured fibers and woven like piece goods. It is then cut with a hot knife, thereby melting the edges enough to keep them from fraying.

fused seam See CLOTHING CONSTRUCTION DETAILS.

gabardine † (gab′-uhr-deen) Durable, closely woven fabric with diagonal ridges created by a warp-faced TWILL WEAVE and made from wool, rayon, or other fibers and blends. Wool gabardine has a firm hand, is made with worsted yarns, and given a clear finish. Used for tailored suits and coats for men and women, pants, sportswear, and riding breeches. *Der.* From word used for a cloak or mantle in the Middle Ages.

gaberdine See COATS AND JACKETS.

gable bonnet/hat See HEADWEAR.

gable headdress See HEADWEAR: ENGLISH HOOD.

Gabrielle dress ∞ (ga-bree′-el) **1.** Daytime dress of 1865 with bodice and front of skirt cut in one piece. Back was made with two large box pleats on either side and another in center. **2.** Girl's jumper-type dress of early 20th c. made in princess style and worn over bracelet-length, full-sleeved, high-necked blouse.

Gabrielle sleeve See SHOULDERS AND SLEEVES.

Gabrielle waist See BLOUSES AND TOPS.

Gainsborough hat See HEADWEAR.

gaiter See FOOTWEAR.

gaiter boots See FOOTWEAR.

galage See FOOTWEAR: GALOSH.

Galanos, James * See APPENDIX/DESIGNERS.

galatea fichu See SCARVES.

galatea hat See HEADWEAR.

Galitzine, Princess Irene * See APPENDIX/ DESIGNERS.

gallants ∞ Small ribbon bows worn in hair or on sleeve, bodice, or skirt in mid-17th c.

Galliano, John * See APPENDIX/DESIGNERS.

galligaskins ∞ (gal-lee-gas′-kins) **1.** See TRUNK HOSE. **2.** 19th-c. term for gaiters of leather worn by sportsmen.

Gallo-Greek bodice ∞ Bodice style of 1820s made with narrow flat trim running diagonally from shoulders to waist in front and back.

galloon See BRAIDS.

gallowses See BRACES.

galosh See FOOTWEAR.

galosh closure See CLOSURES.

galuchat See LEATHERS.

gambeson See DOUBLET.

gamin See HAIRSTYLES.

gaming purse See HANDBAGS AND RELATED ACCESSORIES.

gamp See UMBRELLAS AND PARASOLS.

ganges See LEATHERS.

gangster suit Wide-shouldered, single- or double-breasted suit with wide lapels, inspired by movie *Bonnie and Clyde* in 1967. Usually made of black or gray pinstriped flannel; re-creation of 1930s man's fashion.

Ganymede look (gan-e′-meed) Fashions derived from or inspired by styles of Ancient Greece that became popular in 1969. Generally consisted of a short tunic with a one-shoulder neckline worn with unusual sandals that reached nearly to the knee. *Der.* From the Greek myth about a Greek boy, named Ganymede, carried off by an eagle to become a cupbearer for Zeus. Also called *Greek boy look.*

Ganymede sandal See FOOTWEAR.

garb See APPAREL #1.

Garbo, Greta Swedish-born film star of great beauty who gave unforgettable performances from 1925 to 1939 in such movies as *Mata Hari* (1932), *Grand Hotel* (1932), *Anna Karenina* (1935), *Camille* (1936), and *Ninotchka* (1939). At age 36, she retired to a secluded life in New York City. Publicity shy, she was frequently seen in trenchcoat, slacks, and slouch hat, the latter now called by her name. See HEADWEAR: GARBO HAT.

garcette See HAIRSTYLES.

garçon See HAIRSTYLES: BOYISH BOB.

garde-corps/gardcors ∞ (gard′ cor) An outdoor garment worn by men and women in 13th and early 14th c., which consisted of a full, unbelted outer tunic with a hood and long full hanging sleeves that was frequently worn with the arms passed through slits above elbows. The **herigaut** appears to have been a similar garment.

garde-corps

garden hat See HEADWEAR.

Garibaldi jacket See COATS AND JACKETS.

Garibaldi shirt/blouse See BLOUSES AND TOPS.

Garibaldi suit ∞ (gar-ih-bawl′-dee) **1.** Little boy's collarless suit of 1860s consisting of thigh-length overblouse with dropped shoulders, belted at waistline, and worn with calf-length trousers. Trimmed with braid, rickrack, and buttons down center front, around hem of blouse, at sleeves, and down sides of trousers. **2.** Little girl's collarless two-piece dress of 1860s with full blouse, sleeves set into dropped shoulders, and a full skirt. Trimmed at neck, down front, around waist, wrists, and hem with bands of leather and steel buttons.

garland Wreath of flowers or foliage. Sometimes worn on the head as ornament or as an honor.

garment See APPAREL #1.

garment dyed † Apparel produced as white or colorless goods, constructed into a garment, then dyed during the finishing process.

garment specification sheet Information such as garment sketch, fabric swatch, specific fabrics for all areas including interfacings, all findings, and construction specifications that are essential for the garment style. Size specifications (dimen-

sions) may also be included. Also called a garment *spec sheet.*

garment purchase agreement (GPA) A contract that describes a quantity of goods to be purchased, along with the price, dates, terms, and conditions of the purchase.

garment trade See APPAREL INDUSTRY.

garnache ∞ Outdoor garment worn from 13th to mid-14th c. that was a long cloak with capelike sleeves, often lined or collared with fur. Sides were either joined at the waist, from waist to hem, or left open. The garment had two flat, tongue-shaped lapels at the neck. Similar to **housse** (hoos).

garnache

garnet See GEMS, GEM CUTS, AND SETTINGS.

garniture ∞ Term used in 19th and early 20th c. for trimmings (e.g., ruffles, lace, ribbons, and bows).

garrison cap See HEADWEAR.

garter **1.** Elastic supporters attached to girdle or garter belt, used to hold up hose. **2.** Since Medieval times through the 18th c., a strip of fabric worn by men that tied around the leg or buckled below knee. **3.** Band of elastic worn below the knee to hold up hose. **4.** Round elasticized band worn around the sleeve to shorten it.

garter belt **1.** See UNDERGARMENTS. **2.** See HOSIERY.

garter briefs See UNDERGARMENTS.

gascon coat/gaskyn See JUPE #3.

gaskins See GALLIGASKINS.

gathered skirt See SKIRTS.

gathering See CLOTHING CONSTRUCTION DETAILS.

gaucho/goucho look (gow′-cho) *adj.* Used to describe styles derived from or inspired by clothing and accessories worn by South American cowboys called gauchos. A gaucho look, consisting of calf-length full CULOTTE-type pants (see PANTS: GAUCHO) usually worn with a full-sleeved blouse, bolero, and distinctive broad-brimmed GAUCHO HAT (see HEADWEAR) became popular in

gaucho look

G

the 1960s and 1970s. This style trend was influenced by an Andalusian riding suit worn by Jacqueline Kennedy on her trip to Spain in 1966. *Der.* Spanish, "cowboy" of Argentina, Chile, and Uruguay. Also see BELTS: GAUCHO BELT.

gaucho suit (gow'-cho) Woman's pantsuit with wide-legged calf-length CULOTTES (see PANTS) and a matching BOLERO (see COATS AND JACKETS), frequently made in leather. A full-sleeved blouse is usually worn under the sleeveless bolero. Introduced in mid-1960s. *Der.* Spanish, "cowboy" of Argentina, Chile, and Uruguay.

gauge † (gayj) Knitting term for number of stitches per unit of width and length in a knitted fabric.

gauging See CLOTHING CONSTRUCTION DETAILS: SHIRRING.

Gaultier, Jean-Paul * See APPENDIX/DESIGNERS.

gauntlet 1. See ARMOR. 2. See CUFFS. 3. See GLOVES AND GLOVE CONSTRUCTION.

gauze † (gawz) 1. Sheer, open-weave fabric used for trimmings and costumes made in the LENO or PLAIN WEAVE of silk, cotton, rayon, and other MANUFACTURED FIBER fabrics. 2. Plain openweave fabric, similar to lightweight muslin made of loosely twisted cotton yarns. Sometimes given a crinkled finish, used for blouses, and worn unpressed. *Der.* From Gaza, a city in the Middle East.

gauze weave See LENO WEAVE.

gay deceivers See FALSIES.

Gay 90s Period from 1890 to 1900 when society began to relax from some of the conservative social conventions of the Victorian era. Socioeconomic trends such as the movement of more women into the work force, increased participation in active sports by women, and a less formal life style resulted in fashion trends such as tailored clothes for women; divided skirts for bicycling and special clothing for yachting, tennis, canoeing, and swimming; as well as less formal clothes for men.

gay 90s style

Gay 90s swimsuit See ACTIVEWEAR.
Gaze, point de See LACES.
gele See SCARVES.
gem-cutter See LAPIDARY.
gemel ring See JEWELRY.

GEMS, GEM CUTS, AND SETTINGS

gem Mineral that is rare, beautiful, durable, and is in demand because of fashion. It must also be portable and suitable for personal adornment. Divided into PRECIOUS STONES, SEMIPRECIOUS STONES, ORNAMENTAL STONES, and MARINE GEMS. Gems are classified as TRANSPARENT, SEMITRANSPARENT, or OPAQUE. Also classified as to CRYSTALLINE, CRYPTO-CRYSTALLINE, or AMORPHOUS. See definitions of the foregoing cross-references under GEMS, GEM CUTS, and SETTINGS. Only a qualified gemologist can determine accurately the name of a gem. This is done by testing the gem for hardness, specific gravity, light reflection, and crystalline structure. The **Mohs' scale** is used to rate the degree of hardness of precious gems. The diamond, the hardest gem, has a hardness of 10 and will scratch any gems that rate below it. A set of minerals used to test gems was invented by Friedrich Mohs and is as follows:

MINERAL	HARDNESS
Talc	1
Gypsum	2
Calcite	3
Fluorite	4
Apatite	5
Orthoclass (feldspar)	6
Quartz	7
Topaz	8
Sapphire	9
Diamond	10

gem cut Method of cutting gemstones to be mounted into gold and other metals (e.g., rings, bracelets, necklaces, tiaras, etc.).

gem setting The manner in which a stone is mounted in an article of jewelry. Metals used for genuine jewelry are usually 14k or 18k gold, silver, or platinum. COSTUME JEWELRY (see JEWELRY) uses any type of metal, sometimes gold-washed or gold-plated.

agate Variety of CHALCEDONY quartz (see under GEMS, GEM CUTS, AND SETTINGS) consisting of bands of color either arranged in curved or wavy parallel bands and thus called *banded agate* or in widening circular rings and called *eye agate.* Also with fern or foggy effect called *moss agate* or *mocha stone.*

alexandrite Transparent or translucent variety of the mineral CHRYSOBERYL (see under GEMS, GEM CUTS, AND SETTINGS), which appears one color in daylight and another color under artificial light. May appear emerald green in daylight and columbine-red at night. Found in Russia in 1833 on the same day that Czar Alexander II celebrated his attainment to majority and named after him.

almandite garnet Transparent to opaque semiprecious garnet in deep-red, violet-red, brownish-red to almost black. Includes the CARBUNCLE (see under GEMS, GEM CUTS, AND SETTINGS).

amber An amorphous fossil resin that was exuded from prehistoric trees found in deposits along the southern coast of Baltic Sea in Poland. Also found in marine deposits in Eastern Germany, Rumania, Sicily, and Myanmar. Exists in colors and is translucent. Most popular is called "clear" and is yellow; other colors vary from colorless to brownish-red.

amethyst Transparent purple or violet-colored quartz of the crystalline variety. Rated as a semiprecious stone because it exists in large quantities. Best qualities are a clear even color in the darker tones. The finest qualities come from Uruguay, Ural Mountains, and Brazil. Other sources include Sri Lanka, Japan, South America, and Mexico.

amorphous A property of gems meaning without a crystalline structure. Semiprecious or ornamental gems such as the opal and turquoise are amorphous, as opposed to the diamond, ruby, and amethyst, which are crystalline.

andradite garnet Transparent to opaque garnets called by various names: **topazolite,** yellow and transparent; **demantoid,** grass-green and transparent also known erroneously as *olivine* and as *Ural emerald;* **melanite,** black opaque garnets formerly used for mourning jewelry.

aquamarine Transparent variety of BERYL (see under GEMS, GEM CUTS, AND SETTINGS) from which the emerald comes. Has the same crystalline structure and hardness, but color is aqua rather than green. Comes from Ural Mountains, Brazil, and Madagascar. One large aquamarine found in Minas Gerais, Brazil, weighed 243 pounds.

Arizona ruby See GEMS, GEM CUTS, AND SETTINGS: RUBY.

asterism Ability of a gemstone to project a star-shaped pattern as in rubies and sapphires. Produced synthetically in trademarked LINDE STAR® and HOPE® sapphires.

baguette cut (ba-get´) Small stones cut in oblong shape with facets. Usually placed horizontally along the side of a larger center diamond. *Der.* French, "rod."

balas ruby See GEMS, GEM CUTS, AND SETTINGS: SPINEL.

banded agate See GEMS, GEM CUTS, AND SETTINGS: AGATE.

base Lower portion of a BRILLIANT-CUT stone (see under GEMS, GEM CUTS, AND SETTINGS).

beryl Mineral from which the EMERALD is obtained (see under GEMS, GEM CUTS, AND SETTINGS).

bevel Slanted cut on gemstone, to give light reflection, especially on square-cut gemstones.

bezel See GEMS, GEM CUTS, AND SETTINGS: CROWN.

birthstone Precious or semiprecious stone assigned to the month of birth, often worn in a ring. Although the breastplate of Jewish high priests (worn first by Aaron) contained 12 stones, and there were in ancient times 12 stones for the signs of the Zodiac, the custom of a birthstone for each month is comparatively recent. Became popular among the Hebrews in Poland in the 18th c., reaching its greatest popularity in the 20th c. Popular

G

birthstones are: January—garnet; February—amethyst; March—aquamarine, bloodstone; April—diamond, white sapphire; May—emerald; June—alexandrite, moonstone, pearl; July—ruby; August—peridot, sardonyx; September—sapphire; October—opal, tourmaline; November—citrine (yellow quartz), topaz; December—lapis lazuli, turquoise, zircon.

bloodstone Opaque variety of the mineral quartz characterized by red spots on a dark green background. The early church frequently used it to engrave sacred objects, the red spots simulating the blood of Christ. Found in India and Siberia. Also called *heliotrope.*

Borazon® Trademark for General Electric's industrial artificial diamonds. First made in 1957, now tons are produced yearly. More suitable than natural diamonds for some industrial purposes.

Brazilian emerald Misleading term for a green TOURMALINE (see under GEMS, GEM CUTS, AND SETTINGS) used as a gemstone.

Brazilian peridot Misleading term for a yellow-green TOURMALINE (see under GEMS, GEM CUTS, AND SETTINGS) used as a gemstone.

Brazilian sapphire Misleading term for a blue TOURMALINE (see under GEMS, GEM CUTS, AND SETTINGS) used as a gemstone.

brilliant cut A faceted cut used particularly for diamonds and transparent gems cut with 58 facets, which may be increased to 64, 72, and 80 facets. It usually appears with a flat surface on top, called the **table,** sloping outwardly to the **girdle** or widest point, and tapered to a point at bottom, where a small facet called the **culet** (kue'-lit) is cut. When mounted, only about one-third of gem is visible. The number of facets and the expertise in cutting increase the brilliancy of the stone. It can be round, oval, pear, marquise, or heart-shaped.

cabochon cut (ka-bow-shown') **1.** Type of cut used for gemstones that involves rounding off the top of the stone so that it is higher in the center and slopes to the rim. Used particularly for star rubies and sapphires. **2.** A **high cabochon** cut is a stone with a flat base and a higher elongated top. Also called a *tallow top cut.*

cairngorm Popular stone in Scotland. See GEMS, GEM CUTS, AND SETTINGS: SMOKY QUARTZ.

cameo cut A raised design carved out of a stone (e.g., onyx or banded sardonyx), which has more than one layer. The foreground color is carved away, leaving a white design exposed on a colored surface, usually of black or orange. Also see CAMEO in alphabetical listing.

canary diamond Fancy diamond in a definite yellow color. As differentiated from diamonds that have a yellow tinge, genuine yellow diamonds are rare and expensive.

Cape May diamond Misleading term for rock crystal from Cape May, New Jersey.

cape ruby Gem from the GARNET (see under GEMS, GEM CUTS, AND SETTINGS) group, ruby red to black in color and found in deposits with diamonds in Africa. No relationship to genuine ruby.

carat Unit of weight used for gemstones. Fractions of a carat are divided into 10 points. Thus, a 1½ c. stone would be 1.5, or 1 carat and 5 points. In actual weight 1 carat equals 200 milligrams or 2 grams (16 grains). Not to be confused with KARAT, which is related to the quality of gold. (The abbreviation used is c.) See also GRAIN #2.

carbuncle Variety of ALMANDITE GARNET (see under GEMS, GEM CUTS, AND SETTINGS) that varies from deep red and violet-red to brownish-red and black. Transparent red varieties are used for gems. Before scientific testing, often believed to be a RUBY or SPINEL.

carnelian Transparent to translucent reddish variety of CHALCEDONY (see under GEMS, GEM CUTS, AND SETTINGS) that may be pale red, deep clear red, brownish-red, or yellow-green. Also called *sard. Der.* Latin, "flesh-colored."

cat's eye **1.** Variety of opalescent greenish CHRYSOBERYL that is CHATOYANT when cut CABOCHON style. Light seems to fluctuate lengthwise across the stone as it is turned under the light. Also called *cymophane* and *oriental cat's eye.* **2.** Variety of QUARTZ, also CHATOYANT, that is grayish, brownish, or green in color. Not as valuable as #1. See cross references under GEMS, GEM CUTS, AND SETTINGS.

chalcedony (kal-say-doe´-nee) Transparent to translucent varieties of quartz known by different names for each color. Red is called carnelian, apple green called chrysoprase, dark green with red spots is called bloodstone or heliotrope, black-and-white banded is called onyx, and brown banded with white called sardonyx.

channel setting Grooves of metal used to hold stones. Also called *flush setting*.

chatoyancy (sha-toy´-an-see) Optical properties in certain gems produced when stone is cut. As stone turns, a single streak of light reflects from needlelike crystals arranged parallel to one another (e.g., CAT'S EYE or TIGER'S EYE. See under GEMS, GEM CUTS, AND SETTINGS). *Der.* French, *chatoyer,* "to change luster," as a cat's eye.

chip **1.** Term used for single-cut MELEE, a small ROSE-CUT diamond, or an irregularly shaped diamond (see under GEMS, GEM CUTS, AND SETTINGS). **2.** Term used for a break on the edge of a larger diamond.

chlorspinel See GEMS, GEM CUTS, AND SETTINGS: SPINEL.

chrysoberyl A mineral with a hardness of 8.5 from which the following gems are obtained: ALEXANDRITE, ORIENTAL CAT'S EYE, and CHRYSOLITE (see under GEMS, GEM CUTS, AND SETTINGS).

chrysolite See GEMS, GEM CUTS, AND SETTINGS: PERIDOT.

chrysoprase Apple-green variety of CHALCEDONY quartz (see under GEMS, GEM CUTS, AND SETTINGS) that comes from California, Oregon, and Silesia.

citrine (sit-reen´) Yellow crystalline quartz that resembles TOPAZ (see under GEMS, GEM CUTS, AND SETTINGS) in color and transparency, sometimes erroneously sold as topaz. Comes from Brazil.

cleavage Ability of gemstone to break along the crystalline structure lines; especially important when cutting valuable diamonds.

coral Translucent substance made up of calcareous skeletons secreted by tiny marine animals found in tropical seas. Precious coral of red or pink "grows" in branchlike formations. Used for necklaces, rosaries, and bracelets; may also be cut into beads.

corundum Extremely hard mineral, rating 9 on Mohs' scale, that produces the precious gems RUBY and SAPPHIRE (see under GEMS, GEM CUTS, AND SETTINGS). Also comes in other colors, but these are not so valuable and are called *fancy sapphires.* All red corundum gems are called rubies.

cross stone See GEMS, GEM CUTS, AND SETTINGS: FAIRY STONE.

crown Upper portion of a brilliant-cut faceted stone (e.g., a diamond). Also called *bezel.*

cryptocrystalline Term describing a gem with very fine crystalline structure only visible with X rays.

crystal **1.** Genuine rock crystal, a mineral. See GEMS, GEM CUTS, AND SETTINGS: QUARTZ. **2.** Beads or simulated gems of faceted glass resembling rock crystal.

crystalline structure Property possessed by most minerals and thus used as a means of identifying gems under a microscope. Principal systems are variations of hexagonal, cubic, tetragonal, orthorhombic, monoclinic, and triclinic. Minerals with no crystalline structure are called AMORPHOUS (see under GEMS, GEM CUTS, AND SETTINGS).

cubic zirconia Man-made synthetic stone made to imitate the diamond.

culet See GEMS, GEM CUTS, AND SETTINGS: BRILLIANT CUT.

cushion cut Variation of the BRILLIANT CUT (see under GEMS, GEM CUTS, AND SETTINGS), shaped square with the corners cut off and rounded at the widest part of the stone or girdle. Used particularly for large diamonds and transparent stones.

cymophane See GEMS, GEM CUTS, AND SETTINGS: CAT'S EYE.

diamond Transparent variety of nearly pure carbon. This is the hardest mineral known and very brilliant when faceted. Colorless stones are most generally known, but diamonds also come in yellow, brown, green, red, and blue. Diamonds are graded according to color, cut,

G

weight, clarity, and brilliance. Originally found only in India, now many come from Brazil and South Africa, with 95% coming from the latter.

emerald Precious gem from the mineral BERYL (see under GEMS, GEM CUTS, AND SETTINGS). Hardness is 7½ to 8. Best stones are transparent to translucent green, and large stones of clear color are rare, thus making them very valuable. Comes from Colombia and Brazil, also found in Ural Mountains and Australia.

emerald cut A type of STEP CUT (see under GEMS, GEM CUTS, AND SETTINGS) with all four square corners cut off diagonally. Used particularly for emeralds and large diamonds. Also see GEMS, GEM CUTS, AND SETTINGS: CUSHION CUT.

eye agate See GEMS, GEM CUTS, AND SETTINGS: AGATE.

facet Jewelry term for a small plane cut in a gemstone to enhance its ability to reflect light—the more facets, the more brilliance.

fairy stone Mineral frequently found in the shape of a cross caused by twin crystals. Usually reddish-brown in color and translucent to opaque. Used for crosses for the clergy or for curiosity items. Also known as *staurolite* and *cross stone.*

fancy diamond Any diamond with a distinctive color and high degree of transparency. May be yellow or brown, with green, red, or blue being the most rare.

fancy sapphires See GEMS, GEM CUTS, AND SETTINGS: CORUNDUM.

feldspar A transparent to opaque mineral with vitreous to pearly luster and a hardness of 6½. Various colors of gem varieties are called by the following names: opalescent called *moonstone* comes from Switzerland, Elba, and Sri Lanka; green, called *amazon stone,* comes from the Urals and Pennsylvania; blue, called *Labradorite,* comes from Labrador; yellow, called *orthoclase,* comes from Madagascar; and reddish, called *sunstone* or *aventurine,* comes from Norway and Siberia.

fire opal Semitransparent to transparent variety of opal that is yellow, orange, or red in color. May show a play of color.

fishtail setting Series of scallops (like fish scales) holding stone in place.

flush setting See GEMS, GEM CUTS, AND SETTINGS: CHANNEL SETTING.

garnet Gems, with a hardness of 6½ to 7½, that exist in too large a quantity to be considered precious gems. Exists in all colors except blue and ranges from transparent to opaque. Varieties include ANDRADITE and ALMANDITE (see under GEMS, GEM CUTS, AND SETTINGS).

gem cuts See introduction to GEMS, GEM CUTS, AND SETTINGS.

gem setting See introduction to GEMS, GEM CUTS, AND SETTINGS.

golden beryl Yellow semiprecious transparent variety of the mineral BERYL (see under GEMS, GEM CUTS, AND SETTINGS).

gold filled Gold of 10–22 karats fused to a base metal (e.g., nickel, silver, or brass). Layer of gold should weigh at least one twentieth of the entire metal used. One tenth 18k means that the gold used is 18 karat and that it represents one tenth of the weight of the metal. Compare with JEWELRY: ROLLED GOLD.

goshenite Colorless transparent variety of the mineral BERYL (see under GEMS, GEM CUTS, AND SETTINGS).

grain Measure used to determine the weight of pearls or approximate that of diamonds, equal to slightly more than 50 milligrams or ¼ carat. Not the same as the troy grain. Also see GEMS, GEM CUTS, AND SETTINGS: CARAT.

harlequin opal (har-lay′-kin) White opal that displays uniform patches of colors resembling a mosaic.

heart-shaped cut Variation of the BRILLIANT CUT (see under GEMS, GEM CUTS, AND SETTINGS) in heart shape, used for large diamonds.

helidor Yellow transparent variety of the mineral BERYL (see under GEMS, GEM CUTS, AND SETTINGS) from southwest Africa.

heliotrope See GEMS, GEM CUTS, AND SETTINGS: BLOODSTONE.

hematite Iron mineral that is opaque black, or black with red streaks and metallic luster. Comes from England, Norway, Sweden, and Lake Superior region.

Herkimer diamond Misleading term for ROCK CRYSTAL (see under GEMS, GEM CUTS, AND SETTINGS).

Hope Star® Trademark for a synthetic star sapphire.

hyacinth Name used for clear transparent zircons of yellow, orange, red, and brown varieties. Also called *jacinth*.

imitation gems Reproductions of fine gemstones in colored glass or other inexpensive material as distinguished from man-made SYNTHETIC GEMS (see under GEMS, GEM CUTS, AND SETTINGS). The latter, although man-made, are chemically identical to gems occurring in nature.

intaglio/intaglio cut (in-tal′-yo) Method of cutting gems by engraving design into the surface. Compare with CAMEO carving (see under GEMS, GEM CUTS, AND SETTINGS).

jacinth See GEMS, GEM CUTS, AND SETTINGS: HYACINTH.

jade Includes two minerals of similar appearance, **nephrite** and **jadeite**. The former is the most common variety with hardness of 6 to 6½, and color variations from white to leaf green. Often found in China, Turkestan, Siberia, and Alaska. Jadeite is lustrous, transparent to opaque, and more rare with a hardness of 6½ to 7. Color is white or greenish white to emerald green, translucent to opaque, and found in upper Burma, Yunnan in southern China, Tibet, Mexico, and South America. In 1965, boulders weighing as much as 10,000 pounds containing gem-quality jade (nephrite) were found in Alaska. Popular in China for centuries either carved into objects or used for jewelry.

jargon See GEMS, GEM CUTS, AND SETTINGS: ZIRCON.

jasper Form of opaque QUARTZ (see under GEMS, GEM CUTS, AND SETTINGS) available in brown, dark green, grayish-blue, red, or yellow colors.

jet An opaque mineral made largely of carbon, a variety of lignite or coal, which polishes easily. Comes from England, Spain, France, and the United States. Black varieties of quartz, obsidian, and glass also masquerade as this mineral. All were used for pins, earrings, and beads in mourning jewelry during Victorian era.

Lake George diamond Misleading term for ROCK CRYSTAL (see under GEMS, GEM CUTS, AND SETTINGS).

lapis lazuli Translucent to opaque mineral in tones of blue, deep blue, azure blue, Berlin blue, and greenish-blue. It is a mixture of lazurite and other minerals. Comes from Afghanistan, Siberia, and Chile. In contemporary times, used for beads, brooches, pendants, and cuff links.

Linde Star® Trademark for a synthetic gem that imitates the star sapphire.

malachite Ornamental opaque stone that exists in too large a quantity and is too soft to be a precious or semiprecious gem, mainly from Ural Mountains. May have irregular rings of various tones or be banded. Primary color is green—from emerald green to grass green.

marcasite (mar-ka′-sight) Mineral with a metallic luster having the same composition as iron pyrite, but crystals are different. Cut material sold as marcasite is usually pyrite.

marine gems Gems found primarily in the sea, e.g., PEARLS, AMBER, and CORAL.

marquise cut (mar-keez′) Variation of the BRILLIANT CUT (see under GEMS, GEM CUTS, AND SETTINGS), basic shape is oval with pointed ends. Introduced during reign of Louis XV, and named for his mistress Marquise de Pompadour.

mauve diamond (mowv) Fancy diamond of a purplish hue.

melanite See GEMS, GEM CUTS, AND SETTINGS: ANDRADITE GARNET.

melee (may-lay′) A collective term for small, brilliant-cut diamonds usually .20 to .25 carats. *Der.* French, "confused mass."

mocha stone See GEMS, GEM CUTS, AND SETTINGS: AGATE.

Mohs' scale See under category heading GEMS, GEM CUTS, AND SETTINGS.

moonstone Opalescent gem variety of FELDSPAR, which is cut CABOCHON style (see under GEMS, GEM CUTS, AND SETTINGS).

morganite Transparent pink to rose variety of the mineral BERYL (see under GEMS, GEM CUTS,

G

AND SETTINGS). *Der.* Named after J.P. Morgan, financier and collector of gems.

moss agate See GEMS, GEM CUTS, AND SETTINGS: AGATE.

nephrite See GEMS, GEM CUTS, AND SETTINGS: JADE.

obsidian Volcanic glass rather than a mineral. Usually black in color, but also comes in red, brown, and greenish black. Attractive colors are cut as gems. Comes from Mexico, Greece, California, and Wyoming.

off-color diamond Trade term used in America for a diamond with a tinge of an undesirable color, particularly yellow or brown, which is easily discernible.

old mine cut Brilliant cut of the 19th c. that retained much of original stone and had a larger CULET and smaller TABLE when compared to modern cuts. See BRILLIANT CUT.

olivine The gemologists' term for PERIDOT (see under GEMS, GEM CUTS, AND SETTINGS).

onyx Variety of CHALCEDONY quartz that consists of parallel straight bands of black and white. Used for cameos and stones for rings. A popular ring for many years is composed of a large onyx with small diamond mounted on it.

opal Transparent to opaque gem that is AMORPHOUS and has a pleasing play of color, or opalescence, when cut CABOCHON (see under GEMS, GEM CUTS, AND SETTINGS). Comes in many colors, including the valuable dark gray, blue, and black colors called *black opal.* Also see GEMS, GEM CUTS, AND SETTINGS: FIRE OPAL and HARLEQUIN OPAL.

oriental cat's eye See GEMS, GEM CUTS, AND SETTINGS: CAT'S EYE.

ornamental stones Gems that exist in such large quantities that they are not considered precious or semiprecious gems (e.g., CORAL and TURQUOISE) (see under GEMS, GEM CUTS, AND SETTINGS).

oval cut Variation of the BRILLIANT CUT (see under GEMS, GEM CUTS, AND SETTINGS) made in oval shape.

paste See JEWELRY.

paste setting Stone is glued in place; method used for inexpensive stones.

pavé (pah-vay′) A jewelry term for a setting of stones placed close to each other so that no metal shows between them.

pavilion Jewelry industry term for lower portion below the GIRDLE of a brilliant-cut gem. Also called the *base.*

pear cut Variation of the BRILLIANT CUT, similar to MARQUISE CUT (see under GEMS, GEM CUTS, AND SETTINGS), but with one pointed and one rounded end. Shaped somewhat like a pear. Used particularly for large diamonds.

pearl Divided into three groups: **genuine pearls, cultured pearls,** and **simulated pearls. 1. genuine pearls** are secured from oysters that have made a deposit over a grain of sand. The grain of sand is an irritant to the oyster, which secretes a deposit over it, making a pearl. Very expensive and rare, pearls must be matched in size and color. They are translucent to opaque, are most often white or faintly yellowish or bluish, but they may be pink, yellow, purple, red, green, blue, brown, or black. Genuine pearls also include: (a) *baroque pearls,* which are irregular in shape; (b) *freshwater pearls* of chalk-white color found in mussels in freshwater streams in the United States and not as lustrous as Oriental pearls; (c) *Oriental pearls,* the most beautiful and expensive natural pearls from Japan, Pacific Islands, Persian Gulf, Australia, Venezuela, and Panama; (d) *seed pearls,* tiny irregular-shaped real pearls. Formerly used in necklaces, now used primarily for embroidery on sweaters or wedding dresses. **2. cultured pearls** are secured by artificially implanting oysters with a tiny round piece of mother-of-pearl, placing oysters in cages, and lowering them into the ocean. Pearls are formed around the irritant. Pearls formed this way do not have many layers of coating, and can only be distinguished from genuine pearl by X ray. **3. simulated pearls** are not gems, but plastic or glass beads coated with a solution called "pearl essence" made from an adhesive combined with fish scales giving an iridescent luster.

peridot (pehr′-ee-dot) Transparent gem that is bottle green to olive green in color and comes from Myanmar, Ceylon, and Brazil. Also called *chrysolite.* Called OLIVINE (see under GEMS, GEM CUTS, AND SETTINGS) by minerologists.

precious stone Term applied to a gem that is not only beautiful, durable, and portable, but also rare—diamonds, rubies, sapphires, and emeralds fall into this category.

pronged setting Stone held in place by narrow projecting pieces of metal.

quartz Mineral used for gems that exists in both crystalline transparent varieties, and cryptocrystalline, transparent, or opaque varieties. Crystalline varieties include *rock crystal, amethyst, rose quartz, smoky quartz, citrine, tiger's eye,* and *cat's eye.* Cryptocrystalline quartz appears to the unaided eye to be amorphous, but revealed as crystalline under the microscope. Usually regarded as chalcedony although various colors go by different names (e.g., *carnelian* or *sard, chrysoprase, bloodstone* or *heliotrope, agate, onyx, sardonyx, jasper.*)

rhinestone A colorless transparent artificial gem made of glass or PASTE (see JEWELRY) usually cut like a diamond and used widely for costume jewelry and buttons. *Der.* Originally made in Strasbourg, France, on the Rhine River. Also see under CLOSURES.

rock crystal Clear transparent crystalline variety of the mineral QUARTZ (see under GEMS, GEM CUTS, AND SETTINGS). Exists in such large quantities that it is inexpensive. May be carved for beads. May also be imitated by glass poured into molds to make beads.

rose cut Simple faceted cut, used for inexpensive gems.

rose quartz Transparent crystalline variety of QUARTZ (see under GEMS, GEM CUTS, AND SETTINGS) in rose pink color.

rubicelle See GEMS, GEM CUTS, AND SETTINGS: SPINEL.

ruby Transparent precious gem that comes from the mineral CORUNDUM. Pigeon's blood red is the preferred color. Some stones have an asterism and are called STAR RUBIES. Best quality comes from Burma. The terms *cape ruby* and *Arizona ruby* are misleading and refer to garnets. The term *balas ruby* is misleading and refers to a spinel (see under GEMS, GEM CUTS, AND SETTINGS).

sapphire All precious transparent corundum mineral of a color other than red. Preferred color is cornflower blue and called "Kashmir blue." Other sapphires may be white, pink, or yellow. May also be asterated and then called a STAR SAPPHIRE. Rates next to the diamond in hardness.

sapphirine See GEMS, GEM CUTS, AND SETTINGS: SPINEL.

sard See GEMS, GEM CUTS, AND SETTINGS: CARNELIAN.

sardonyx Variety of CHALCEDONY quartz that is composed of banded layers of sard or CARNELIAN, and layers of white (see under GEMS, GEM CUTS, AND SETTINGS).

semiprecious gems/stones Gems too plentiful to be considered rare, e.g., TOPAZ, GARNET, TOURMALINE, AMETHYST, and QUARTZ (see under GEMS, GEM CUTS, AND SETTINGS).

simulated gems Term applied to copies of precious gems made of PASTE, or other inexpensive materials. See under JEWELRY. Sometimes confused with synthetic gems, which are manmade but chemically identical to natural gems.

smoky quartz Transparent variety of *crystalline quartz* in smoky yellow to dark brown. The national gem of Scotland. Also called CAIRNGORM. Sometimes mistaken for TOPAZ. See cross-references under GEMS, GEM CUTS, AND SETTINGS.

spinel Transparent to opaque semiprecious mineral that closely resembles the ruby. Softer and lighter in weight than a ruby with hardness of 8 on MOHS' SCALE (see in introduction to GEMS, GEM CUTS, AND SETTINGS category). Preferred color is deep ruby red; comes in a great variety of other colors including violet and purple. Misleading terms for the above include: *balas ruby, rubicelle, almandine, sapphirine,* and *chlorspinel.* Properly spinels should be identified by color name. A large red stone on the English Crown, called the Black Prince's ruby, was later proved to be a spinel.

square cut See GEMS, GEM CUTS, AND SETTINGS: EMERALD CUT.

square setting Four prongs forming corners for EMERALD-CUT stones (see under GEMS, GEM CUTS, AND SETTINGS).

G

star ruby Genuine ruby from corundum mineral; shows a five- or six-pointed star, or ASTERISM, when cut CABOCHON style (see under GEMS, GEM CUTS, AND SETTINGS).

star sapphire Genuine sapphire from corundum mineral, it shows a five- or six-pointed star, or ASTERISM, when cut CABOCHON (see under GEMS, GEM CUTS, AND SETTINGS). Color varies from blue to gray and transparent to translucent. The 116-carat Midnight Star Sapphire and the 563-carat Star of India, the largest star sapphire in the world, were recovered after a jewel robbery at the Museum of Natural History in New York City in 1965.

staurolite See GEMS, GEM CUTS, AND SETTINGS: FAIRY STONE.

step cut Rectangular stone cut with facets that are oblong and placed in horizontal positions in steps, or rows, both above and below the girdle, or widest part of the stone.

synthetic gem Gem manufactured in a laboratory having the same physical and chemical properties as genuine gems. Virtually all types of gems can be manufactured, including synthetic diamonds, emeralds, and sapphires. These gems are used in watches and sold for fine jewelry when mounted in necklaces, bracelets, and rings.

table See GEMS, GEM CUTS, AND SETTINGS: BRILLIANT CUT.

tallow top cut See GEMS, GEM CUTS, AND SETTINGS: CABOCHON #2.

tanzanite First discovered in the foothills of Mount Kilimanjaro in Tanzania, Africa. In 1968 was confirmed to be blue zoisite by gemologists—the first ever found. Name was changed by Tiffany's of New York to tanzanite, from place where it was found. Not a precious stone, but beautiful when cut. Changes color when held in light to a blue, richer than a sapphire; purple, similar to amethyst; and pinkish salmon brown. One gem found was 2,500 carats and when cut weighed 360 carats.

Tiffany setting High pronged setting for solitaire stone introduced by Tiffany & Co., New York jewelers, in 1870s and often imitated. In 1971, Tiffany introduced a modernized version of its famous setting.

tiger's eye Semiprecious variety of QUARTZ is CHATOYANT when cut CABOCHON (see under GEMS, GEM CUTS, AND SETTINGS). Yellowish brown, bluish, or red in color. Found in South Africa.

topaz Transparent gem of which the most precious is wine-yellow in color. Other colors include colorless, yellowish brown, gray, pale tints of green, blue, lavender, and red. With a hardness of 8, only the diamond, ruby, sapphire, and chrysoberyl are harder; the emerald and spinel are of equal hardness. Found in Europe, South America, Sri Lanka, Japan, Mexico, Utah, Colorado, and Maine.

topazolite See GEMS, GEM CUTS, AND SETTINGS: ANDRADITE GARNET.

tourmaline Transparent semiprecious mineral that comes in many colors: achroite, colorless; rubellite, rose-red; siberite, violet; indicolite, dark blue, green, blue, and yellowish green. Sometimes erroneously called *Brazilian emerald, Brazilian peridot* (pehr'-ee-dot), *Brazilian sapphire,* and *peridot of Ceylon.*

turquoise Opaque amorphous ornamental stone that comes in sky blue, greenish blue, or apple green. Used for jewelry, but exists in too large a quantity to be rare. Popular for jewelry made by Native Americans of Arizona and Mexico; usually set in silver for bracelets, necklaces, pins, and earrings.

Ural emerald See GEMS, GEM CUTS, AND SETTINGS: ANDRADITE GARNET.

zircon Transparent gem with a luster approaching the diamond when brilliant cut is used. White colorless stones resembling diamonds are sometimes referred to as *matura diamonds,* a misleading term. Yellow, orange, red, and brown zircons are called *hyacinth* or *jacinth;* all other colors, including colorless gray and smoky, are called *jargons,* while blue are called *blue zircon.* An 103-carat zircon is in The Smithsonian Institution in Washington, D.C.

gendarme (john-darm) *adj.* Used to describe clothing and accessories inspired by or derived from the uniform of a French policeman, a *gendarme.* See CAPES, CLOAKS, AND SHAWLS: FRENCH

G

POLICEMAN'S CAPE and COATS AND JACKETS: GENDARME JACKET.

General Agreement on Tariff and Trade (GATT) See MULTIFIBER ARRANGEMENT.

generation X The population group born following the baby boomers.

generic fiber categories † Common or family name for natural or manufactured fibers as defined by the Federal Trade Commission.

Geneva bands See CLERICAL DRESS.

Geneva gown See CLERICAL DRESS.

Geneva hat See CLERICAL DRESS.

Genoa cloak See CAPES, CLOAKS, AND SHAWLS: ITALIAN CLOAK.

Genoese embroidery See EMBROIDERIES AND SEWING STITCHES.

George See FOOTWEAR and HAIRSTYLES.

genouillère See ARMOR: POLEYN.

genuine pearl beads See GEMS, GEM CUTS, AND SETTINGS: PEARLS.

geometric design See PRINTS, STRIPES, AND CHECKS.

georgette/georgette crepe/crepe georgette † Fine sheer silk fabric made in the plain weave with twisted or creped yarns in both lengthwise and crosswise directions. Used for dresses, evening gowns, blouses, and nightgowns.

German gown See SACK #1.

German helmet See HEADWEAR.

German hose See TRUNK HOSE.

Gernreich, Rudi * See APPENDIX/DESIGNERS.

gertrude/gertrude skirt See UNDERGARMENTS.

geta See FOOTWEAR.

ghillie See FOOTWEAR.

Gibson, Charles Dana (1867–1944) American illustrator, master of black-and-white drawings published in *Scribner's, Harper's,* and *Century* magazines depicting the idealized American girl of the 1890s and early 1900s.

Gibson girl/Gibson girl look The idealized young woman drawn by Charles Dana Gibson became known as the Gibson girl. In subsequent fashion revivals of the styles

Gibson girl look

of the 90s and 1900–1910 those garments, accessories, and hairstyles derived from or inspired by those worn by the Gibson girl were known as the Gibson girl look. Features of these revivals included high-necked collars, tucked and lace-trimmed blouses with LEG-OF-MUTTON SLEEVES (see SHOULDERS AND SLEEVES), gathered skirts or hair worn in the POMPADOUR style (see HAIRSTYLES). *Der.* For Charles Dana Gibson's magazine sketches of fashionable women of the 1895–1910 era.

Gibson pleat Wide 2″ pleat at the shoulder of blouse in front and back covering the armhole seam and sloping to waistline to give a narrow-waisted effect. *Der.* Named after Charles Dana Gibson, who portrayed "The Gibson girl."

Gibson waist See BLOUSES AND TOPS.

gibus See HEADWEAR: OPERA HAT.

gig coat See COATS AND JACKETS: CURRICLE COAT.

gigot sleeve See SHOULDERS AND SLEEVES: LEG-OF-MUTTON SLEEVE.

gilet 1. See VESTS. 2. See PLASTRON.

gillie See FOOTWEAR.

gills/shirt gills ∞ Colloquial term for upstanding points of men's shirt collars in the 19th c.

gimmel ring See JEWELRY: GEMEL RING.

gimp 1. See BRAIDS. 2. See HEADWEAR: WIMPLE.

gimped embroidery See EMBROIDERY AND SEWING STITCHES.

gingham 1. † Yarn-dyed checked or plaid fabric made of cotton or cotton blended with polyester. May be made of coarse yarn or of combed yarns in a high count fabric. **Checked ginghams** are two-colored effects made by using two colors, or one color and white, for groups of yarns in both the lengthwise and crosswise. **Plaid ginghams** are yarn-dyed designs of several colors. **Zephyr ginghams** are made with fine, silky, mercerized yarns. Used for dresses, children's wear, sportswear, swimsuits, blouses, and beachwear. 2. See UMBRELLAS AND PARASOLS.

gipcière See HANDBAGS AND RELATED ACCESSORIES: ALMONIERE.

gipon/gippon See DOUBLET.

gipser See HANDBAGS AND RELATED ACCESSORIES: ALMONIERE.

girdle 1. See UNDERGARMENTS. 2. See BELTS. 3. See GEMS, GEM CUTS, AND SETTINGS.

girdles See UNDERGARMENTS.

girls' sizes Size range from 4 to 6X and from 7 to 16.

Givenchy, Hubert de * See APPENDIX/DESIGNERS.

glacé See LEATHERS.

gladiator sandal See FOOTWEAR.

Gladstone See COATS AND JACKETS.

Gladstone collar See NECKLINES AND COLLARS.

glam rock/glam **1.** Styles worn by rock stars such as David Bowie in the early 1970s. Male singers wore makeup, platform shoes, and glittery silver fabrics. **2.** A heavy metal music style of the 1980s performed by either bare-chested macho singers or those of ambiguous sexuality.

glasses See introduction to EYEWEAR.

glazed kid See LEATHERS.

glazing † Process of pressing fabric with heated rollers to give it a high gloss. Finish may be permanent or nonpermanent.

glen check/glen Urquhart check See PLAIDS AND TARTANS.

glengarry See HEADWEAR.

Glengarry cape See CAPES, CLOAKS, AND SHAWLS.

glen plaid See PLAIDS AND TARTANS: GLEN URQUHART.

glitter button See CLOSURES: BUTTONS.

glitter hose See HOSIERY.

glocke See CAPES, CLOAKS, AND SHAWLS.

glove band/glove string ∞ Ribbon or plaited horsehair band tied near elbow to keep a woman's long glove in place. Used from 1640 to about 1700.

glove button See CLOSURES: BUTTONS.

glove length See GLOVES AND GLOVE CONSTRUCTION.

glover's stitch See EMBROIDERIES AND SEWING STITCHES: WHIPSTITCH and SADDLESTITCH.

GLOVES AND GLOVE CONSTRUCTION

glove A covering for the hand, usually divided into separate stalls for the thumb and fingers, worn as a decorative accessory, for warmth in cold weather, or as protection for workers. Gloves were known to ancient Egyptians, Greeks, and Romans but did not become an important accessory until the Middle Ages. By the beginning of the 17th c., leather, fabric, and knitted gloves were all available. Throughout the Victorian era and early 20th c., gloves were the mark of a lady or gentleman. In the 1960s, gloves declined in use for social occasions and by 1970s were very seldom worn except for protection from the cold. Also see GLOVES AND GLOVE CONSTRUCTION: MITTS and MITTENS. *Der.* Origin of the word is disputed, believed to have been from Anglo-Saxon, *glof,* "palm."

fourchette, gusset or quirk, thumb, glove

action glove Gloves with cutouts on back of hand or over knuckles to increase flexibility. Originally used for sports such as golf or racing car driving, adopted for women's daytime wear in mid-1960s. Also called *cutout gloves* or *racing gloves.*

bandelet/bandelette (ban-day'-lay or ban-day'-let) Wide hem at wrist of a glove. Also called *bord.*

Berlin glove ∞ **1.** Sturdy leather gloves produced in Germany. **2.** Sturdy white cotton glove worn in the 1830s.

biarritz glove Slip-on glove with no VENT, usually of two- or four-button length.

bicycle glove Wrist-length knitted glove with leather palm padded with two layers of foam for comfort. Mesh knit is used for remainder of glove, leaving the tips of the fingers and thumb exposed.

binding Glove term for reinforcement or piping of leather or fabric around wrist and placket.

Bolton thumb See GLOVES AND GLOVE CONSTRUCTION: ENGLISH THUMB.

bord See GLOVES AND GLOVE CONSTRUCTION: BANDELET.

bracelet length Gloves ending above the wrist.

button The length of the glove. One button is equal to one French inch (approximately ½ inch longer than American inch), with the measurement starting at base of thumb. A 1-button glove is wrist length, a 6-button glove is about halfway to elbow, and a 16-button glove is a formal length.

chicken-skin glove ∞ Thin, strong leather glove treated with almonds and spermaceti worn, at night as cosmetic aid to keep hands soft and white, by women from the end of 17th to early 19th c.

cocktail glove Dressy suede glove with wide stand-up accordion-pleated taffeta cuffs. Worn in the 1930s and after.

cut-fingered gloves **1.** ∞ Gloves slashed to show rings on fingers, worn in late 16th c. **2.** Women's gloves with tips of fingers cut off, worn in early 18th c. Revived as a fad in 1985.

cutout glove See GLOVES AND GLOVE CONSTRUCTION: ACTION GLOVE.

doeskin glove **1.** Glove made of suede-finished sheepskin. Properly it should be "doeskin-finished sheepskin," but the term doeskin is permissible. **2.** Glove made from the skin of the female deer frequently sueded. As there are few deerskins available for commercial usage, real doeskins usually come from areas where deer are plentiful (e.g., northern Michigan and where skins are usually processed on Native American reservations).

driving glove Knitted gloves with leather palms made for a good grip on the steering wheel of the car.

English thumb Glove thumb construction in which the thumb and QUIRK (see under GLOVES AND GLOVE CONSTRUCTION) are cut in a single piece in order to provide freedom of movement. Considered the strongest and best-fitting thumb. Also called *Bolton thumb.*

Finger-Free® glove Trademark for gloves made with one long strip of material forming all the fourchettes between fingers. Designed by Merry Hull in 1938 for greater flexibility. See GLOVES AND GLOVE CONSTRUCTION: FOURCHETTE.

forks See GLOVES AND GLOVE CONSTRUCTION: FOURCHETTE.

fourchette (foor-shet′) Narrow piece forming the sides of the fingers of gloves ending in points at tips of fingers and joining the back to the front of the glove. Also called *forks.*

French thumb Glove thumb construction in which a small diamond-shaped piece (the quirk) is inserted in the arch of the thumb, allowing freedom of movement.

full-piqué/full P.K. seam Used on expensive kid gloves, all fourchettes are inserted with one piece of leather lapped over the other and stitched on the right side. See GLOVES AND GLOVE CONSTRUCTION: FOURCHETTE. Also called *kid seam* and *overlapped seam.*

gauntlet (gawnt′-let) Above-the-wrist glove with wide flaring cuff. The cuff may be cut in one with the glove or as a separate piece that is sewn to the glove.

glove length Glove term indicating the length of a glove. Measured in BUTTONS. See under GLOVES AND GLOVE CONSTRUCTION.

glove seam Manner in which gloves are stitched together. Seams must be flexible and sturdy. The body of the glove is cut in one piece and the fourchettes (or pieces for the sides of the fingers) and quirks (small pieces for base of fingers and thumb) are stitched to it by various seams. See GLOVES AND GLOVE CONSTRUCTION: FOURCHETTE and QUIRK. Various glove seam types are defined in separate entries under GLOVES AND GLOVE CONSTRUCTION.

half-piqué/half P.K. seam Finger seams on the palm side of the hand are stitched with seams turned to the inside while those on the outside of hand are made in piqué manner, with one piece of leather lapped over the other and stitched on the outside, thereby giving the appearance of a more expensive glove.

igloo mitt Shaggy fur mitten, frequently with leather palm, worn for sportswear.

inseam Gloves stitched together inside out and then turned so that no stitching shows on the right side. Used on sheer nylon, lace, and cotton gloves.

insert thumb Glove thumb construction in which thumb is cut in one piece and extends all the way to the cuff edge of the glove.

insulated glove Glove lined for protection against cold. Lining may be fur, fleece, wool or acrylic knit, or laminated foam.

jessamy gloves/jasmine gloves ∞ Perfumed gloves given by bride and groom as wedding presents in 17th c.; jasmine being most popular scent.

kid glove Gloves made of genuine kidskin and also of sheepskin. Originally all were kid and as the leather became more scarce, other leathers were used. Fashionable from early 19th c. and still used.

kid seam See GLOVES AND GLOVE CONSTRUCTION: FULL-PIQUÉ GLOVE SEAM.

lace glove Made by hand or machine in white and used for dress-up summer wear.

laying off Final step in the construction of leather gloves in which the glove is placed on a metal hand of the selected size and heated to shape the glove to the correct size.

Limerick gloves ∞ Short or long lambskin gloves made from very young or unborn lambs. Worn by women during latter half of 18th and first half of 19th c.

mittens **1.** Gloves with a thumb and one other compartment for fingers; worn mainly by children and skiers for warmth. So called since 14th c. **2.** See GLOVES AND GLOVE CONSTRUCTION: MITTS.

mitten #1

mitts Fingerless gloves, reaching to or above wrist. Often of kid, net, lace, or sheer fabric and sometimes worn with bridal dresses. Also called *mittens*.

mitt

money mitt Knitted glove with fingers and thumb made with vinyl palm and back. Has zippered slot in center of palm for keys or money.

mousquetaire glove (moos-keh´-tare) Woman's long loose glove made in pull-on style or with buttoned slit at wrist in 14- or 16-button length. Worn crushed down or with hand out of slit, remainder of glove crushed up to elbow with formal evening dress.

opera glove Long-length glove, sometimes made without a thumb.

outseam Glove seams stitched by machine on the right side, leaving edges exposed. Used on sport gloves (e.g., pigskin and sometimes cotton gloves).

outseam

overlapped seam See GLOVES AND GLOVE CONSTRUCTION: FULL-PIQUÉ GLOVE SEAM.

overseam Gloves stitched on the right side with an OVERCAST STITCH (see under EMBROIDERIES AND SEWING STITCHES) that covers the two raw edges. Used on men's gloves. Also called *round seam*.

overseam

Oxford glove ∞ Perfumed glove, worn from mid-16th to mid-17th c., scented with Earl of Oxford's favorite perfume.

piqué/P.K. seam See GLOVES AND GLOVE CONSTRUCTION: FULL-PIQUÉ and HALF-PIQUÉ GLOVE SEAMS.

pointing Ornamental stitching on back of glove, usually in three rows. Same as *silking*.

prix seam/PXM seam (pree) Outseam stitched on a flat machine that moves horizontally instead of vertically. Used on heavier gloves instead of piqué seam. See GLOVES AND GLOVE CONSTRUCTION: OUTSEAM.

pull-down cutting The process of cutting gloves by die cutting the pieces.

pull-on Glove that slips easily over the hand and is made without placket or fastening. Also called *slip-on gloves*.

quirk Small triangular insert placed in glove at base of each finger and at thumb. Used to give a close fit yet permit flexibility.

racing glove See GLOVES AND GLOVE CONSTRUCTION: ACTION GLOVES.

reverse glove Glove thumb construction in which the thumb is set in with a QUIRK (see under GLOVES AND GLOVE CONSTRUCTION) in such a way that the glove is perfectly flat and can be worn on either hand.

round seam See GLOVES AND GLOVE CONSTRUCTION: OVERSEAM.

saddle-stitched seam Small running stitches visible on the outside of glove that are used to close fingers of the glove.

set-in thumb Glove thumb construction in which the thumb is cut in one piece and set into a round opening.

shorty glove Any two-button glove coming to the wrist.

silking See GLOVES AND GLOVE CONSTRUCTION: POINTING.

slip-ons   See GLOVES AND GLOVE CONSTRUCTION: PULL-ON GLOVE.

slit trank   Trade term used in glove production. Piece of leather large enough for one glove is called a trank. When a die is pressed on the trank to cut out the glove, the process is called "slitting the trank."

snowmobile glove   Similar to SNOWMOBILE MITT (see under GLOVES AND GLOVE CONSTRUCTION) made with fingers.

snowmobile mitt   Water-repellent gloves with polyester fiberfill or down as insulation. Made with suede-leather palms, rubberized nylon back, knitted cuffs, and leather pull-on tabs.

table-cut glove   TRANKS (see under GLOVES AND GLOVE CONSTRUCTION) from which these gloves are cut are hand-pulled to determine the amount of stretch in the leather and then cut. Women's fine kid gloves are made in this manner to ensure proper stretch but no bagginess.

thermal glove   Short gloves made of glacé leather with silk lining and inner lining of polyfoam. Worn for warmth, especially for riding or driving.

trank   Leather piece from which a glove is cut.

wrist length   Short gloves ending at the wristbone.

York-tan gloves   ∞ Gloves of soft fawn-colored suede worn mainly by women from 1780 to 1820s.

wrist length glove

---

glove seams   See GLOVES AND GLOVE CONSTRUCTION.

glove string   See GLOVE BAND.

goatee   See BEARD.

goatskin   See LEATHER.

gobelin corselet   See BELTS.

gob hat   See HEADWEAR: SAILOR HAT.

godet   See CLOTHING CONSTRUCTION DETAILS.

godet pleat   See CLOTHING CONSTRUCTION DETAILS.

godet skirt   See SKIRTS.

Godey, Louis Antoine   See GODEY'S LADY'S BOOK.

Godey's Lady's Book   The first American periodical for women, published by Louis Antoine Godey. Distributed monthly, it contained stories, music, needlecraft, poetry, and fashions. Each month there was a hand-colored engraving showing fashions as well as many black-and-white illustrations. Started in 1830 as the *Lady's Book,* it was later called *Godey's Lady's Book.* Edited by Sarah Josepha Hale from 1837 to 1877. Publication ceased in 1898.

goffer (goff´-er)   **1.** An ornamental pleating used for frills and borders as on women's caps. **2.** To press ridges or narrow pleats into a frill.

goffered veil   See HEADDRESS.

goggles   See EYEWEAR.

go-go   Coined in late 1960s for a dancer at a discotheque called a go-go dancer, then extended to mean "flashy" or "hip" accessories of this era. Example: FOOTWEAR: GO-GO BOOTS, WATCHES: GO-GO WATCH.

go-go watchband   See WATCHES: GO-GO WATCH.

going frocks   See LONG CLOTHES.

gold   **1.** *n.* Precious metal that in its pure state is too soft to be durable. It is usually made into alloys called *karat gold* and used for *plating,* or gold-washed jewelry items. See JEWELRY. **2.** *adj.* Used to describe anything the color of gold metal.

gold button   See CLOSURES.

golden beryl   See GEMS, GEM CUTS, AND SETTINGS.

golden muskrat   See FURS.

gold filled   See JEWELRY.

gold hose   See HOSIERY: GLITTER HOSE.

gold leaf   Pure gold hammered so thin it takes 300,000 units to make a stack 1″ high. Used for jewelry and gold leather.

gold-plated   See JEWELRY.

gold-washed   See JEWELRY.

gole   See HEADWEAR: CHAPERON.

golf clothes   Apparel that is derived from or inspired by clothing worn for the sport of golf. By 1890s, golf was a sport enjoyed by both men and women. Men wore KNICKERS, a NORFOLK JACKET (see COATS AND JACKETS), and a cap with a visor; by the 1920s they wore PLUS FOURS (see PANTS) and a sweater. Women in the early days wore a version of the Norfolk jacket, the GLENGARRY CAP (see HEADWEAR), and sometimes shorter skirt or a divided skirt. In pre–World War I days, a coat sweater was worn; in the 1930s an ACTION-BACK DRESS was introduced. See COATS AND

G

JACKETS: GOLF JACKET, FOOTWEAR: GOLF SHOE, and VESTS: GOLF VEST.

gondolier's hat See HEADWEAR.

gonel ∞ (gohn'-el) Synonym for GOWN #1 in 14th c.

goose-bellied doublet See DOUBLET.

Gordian knot Decorative square knot used as trimming in the last half of 18th c.—sometimes on bracelets, sometimes a length of false hair used as a CHIGNON (see under HAIRSTYLES). *Der.* From Greek mythological founder of Phrygia (now Turkey) called *Gordius*. An oracle pronounced that he would be master of Asia until the knot he tied was undone. Alexander the Great severed the knot with one blow of his sword.

gore See CLOTHING CONSTRUCTION DETAILS.

gored skirt See SKIRTS.

gorge In men's tailoring used to indicate seam where collar meets lapel—may be either high or low.

gorget (gor'-jet) **1.** See ARMOR. **2.** See HEADWEAR: WIMPLE. **3.** See HEADWEAR: CHAPERON. **4.** See NECKLINES AND COLLARS. **4.** See JEWELRY.

Gore-Tex® fabric † Trademark owned by W. L. Gore and Associates Inc. for a porous membrane that repels water but allows for the passage of moisture vapor. Widely used for garments for outdoor sports.

goshenite See GEMS, GEM CUTS, AND SETTINGS.

goth/goth look A style, originating in a London club called the Batcave in 1981, that was inspired by the gothic literary works of the 19th c. such as *Dracula*. Followers mixed black, bloodred, and purple colored velvet and lace with fishnet and leather. Hair was dyed black and makeup featured black accents at the eyes and lips.

Goth look

Gothic costume Styles in dress that were worn in Western Europe from the 13th to mid-14th c. (early Gothic) and from the mid-14th through mid-15th c. (Late Gothic).

gown **1.** From 11th c. used to refer generally to a woman's dress. From the late 18th century, "gown" is most often used to refer to a floor length, more formal, skirted garment, while "dress" is used for less formal, skirted garments. **2.** Loose-fitting, wide-sleeved outer garment or robe worn by judges, scholars, clergy, and for ceremonial occasions. **2.** See DRESS #3.

gown à la française ∞ (ah lah frahn'-saiz) Dress, fashionable in 18th c., made with a bodice that fits closely in front and loosely at the back. The front closing was filled in with decorative STOMACHER, and two wide box pleats fell from shoulders to hem in back. *Der.* French, "French gown." Also called *robe à la française* and, in the 19th c., referred to as a WATTEAU GOWN. Shown at WATTEAU BACK.

gown à la levantine ∞ (ah lah leh-van'-teen) A loose open robe worn in the last quarter of the 18th c. Fastened at the chest with a pin or ties, the opening revealing a waistcoat and petticoat of contrasting color and fabric. Wrist-length undersleeves matched the petticoat. The overdress had a wide turned-back collar and wide draped sash with long hanging ends, sometimes fur-trimmed. Also called *levite gown*.

gown à l'anglaise ∞ (ah long'-glaze) Dress, close-fitting in both front and back, that was worn in late 18th c. without PANNIERS (see UNDERGARMENTS). The bodice was shaped to long point in back and closed in front. Skirt was either closed or slashed in front to show matching petticoat. *Der.* French, "English gown." Also called *robe à l'anglaise.*

gown à l'anglaise

gown à la polonaise See POLONAISE #1.

gown à la sultane See SULTANE.

gown à la turque ∞ (ah lah toork') Dress, worn c. 1780, with a tight-fitting bodice, turned-down collar, flared sleeves at wrist, and draped large sash knotted on one hip with long hanging ends. Worn over contrasting petticoat. *Der.* French, "Turkish gown."

Grace Kelly bag See HANDBAGS AND RELATED ACCESSORIES: KELLY BAG.

grading See PATTERN GRADING.

grade rules Guidelines giving not only the amounts of increase or decrease but also their locations on a pattern in order to create different sizes.

graduation dress White dress worn for graduation. In the early 20th c., young girls were expected to make their graduation dresses in sewing classes. This practice ended after World War II.

graffiti/graffiti look (graf-fee'-tee) Abstract designs used for clothing and accessories made by drawings on fabric, leather or vinyl; piecing bits of fabric, leather, and vinyl together and studding with fake jewels or dabbing with blobs of paint, used for jackets, blouses, shoes, handbags, and belts. Developed from copying street-art forms painted or scratched on buildings. *Der.* Latin, *graffito*, a drawing or writing scratched on a wall or surface.

grain **1.** See LEATHERS. **2.** See GEMS, GEM CUTS, AND SETTINGS. **3.** † In textile usage, yarn direction, either lengthwise or crosswise.

grande-assiette sleeve ∞ (grawn ahs-ee'-ette) Extra cap sleeve, crescent shape, extending over top curve of shoulder on the DOUBLET from 14th to mid-15th c.

grand habit See COURT HABIT.

grand vair See FUR: VAIR.

granite weave † Weave characterized by pebbly effect somewhat similar to crepe. Such fabrics are called granite cloth. Also called *momie weave* and *pebble weave*.

granjamers See SLEEPWEAR AND LOUNGEWEAR.

granny Adjective used to describe apparel items of the type that might have been worn in the era of one's grandmother. Generally has the connotation of styles worn in the late 19th or early 20th c. See GRANNY DRESS, EYEWEAR: BEN FRANKLIN GLASSES, FOOTWEAR: GRANNY BOOT, HEADWEAR: GRANNY BONNET, PRINTS, STRIPES, AND CHECKS: GRANNY PRINT, and SKIRTS: GRANNY SKIRT.

granny dress Ankle-length dress styled with a high round or choker neckline, long or short sleeves, high waistline, and slightly gathered skirt—sometimes with a ruffle at the hem. Frequently made of CALICO

granny dress

fabric in a small print and trimmed with ruffles. Worn by a child or young person and popular in the 1960s. *Der.* Copied from style worn by her grandmother, or "granny."

granny blouse/granny waist See BLOUSES AND TOPS: VICTORIAN BLOUSE.

grass embroidery See EMBROIDERIES AND SEWING STITCHES.

graundice See HEADWEAR: CRANTS.

gray flannel See OXFORD GRAY FLANNEL.

gray fox See FURS.

gray goods/greige goods † Unfinished fabrics as they come from the loom. Some fabrics may be mill-finished but most are sent to CONVERTERS for the finishing processes. *Der.* French, *grege*, "raw."

gray market goods Merchandise that, while not exactly illegal, is an unauthorized import. Often such goods are sold at discounters with no warranty or with older dates than those through authorized channels. There is an ongoing campaign to make gray-market goods illegal.

gray muskrat See FURS.

greatcoat See COATS AND JACKETS.

greave See ARMOR.

grebe feathers See FEATHERS.

Grecian bend ∞ Stance affected by fashionable women from 1815 to 1819 and again from 1868 to 1870 in which the body was tilted forward while a bustle under the skirt emphasized the back.

Grecian border See FRET.

Grecian curls See HAIRSTYLES.

Grecian sandal See FOOTWEAR: GANYMEDE SANDAL.

Greek belt See BELTS.

Greek boy look See GANYMEDE LOOK.

Greek coiffure See HAIRSTYLES.

Greek cross See CROSS #1.

Greek fisherman's cap See HEADWEAR.

Greek fret See FRET #3.

Greek handbag See HANDBAGS AND RELATED ACCESSORIES.

Greek key See FRET #3.

Greek lace/Greek point lace See LACES: RETICELLA.

Greek lounging cap See HEADWEAR: LOUNGING CAP.

green-aproned men ∞ London porters of 18th c. distinguished by green aprons worn by members of this trade. Also see BLUE-APRONED MEN.

Greenaway, Kate See KATE GREENAWAY COSTUME.

green clothes See ECO-FRIENDLY.

greenery-yallery See AESTHETIC DRESS.

gregs See TRUNK HOSE.

greige goods See GRAY GOODS.

Grès, Alix * See APPENDIX/DESIGNERS.

grey goods See GRAY GOODS.

gripper closure See CLOSURES.

grommet See CLOSURES.

grooving Method of shearing a deep pile of fabric or furs in lines that have a shorter pile than the rest of the surface.

grosgrain † (groh′-grayn) Fabric with a large rib that is made by grouping several crosswise yarns together. Made originally in silk, now made mostly with rayon or acetate warp and cotton or rayon filling. Also made entirely of cotton. Used for ribbons, sashes, trim on dresses, bows, neckwear, hatbands, and millinery trimming.

gros point (groh pwanh) See EMBROIDERIES AND SEWING STITCHES: PETIT POINT and LACES.

gross margin The difference between the net sales and cost of goods sold and usually an indicator of profit.

Grosvenor gallery costume See AESTHETIC DRESS.

ground 1. General term for the plain base or background part of a decorated textile fabric. 2. In pile fabrics, the lengthwise and crosswise yarns that support the pile. 3. See LACES. 4. See EMBROIDERIES AND SEWING STITCHES.

group Items within an apparel COLLECTION that use a limited number of colors and fabrics so that they can be coordinated.

grow bag Synonym for a BABY BUNTING.

grow sleepers See SLEEPWEAR AND LOUNGEWEAR.

grunge A style of dressing in which clothing items look worn, are either too large or too small, and frequently are purchased from thrift shops. Included among the more popular items of grunge style are heavy work boots and checked shirts.

G-string Narrow band, worn low on the hips, with a decorative ornament on front. Originally worn by striptease dancers.

guanaco/guanaquito See FURS.

guarantee Issued by a manufacturer, it ensures that a product will perform as it is supposed to. See WARRANTY.

guard hair See introduction to FURS.

guardinfante ∞ (gard-in-fahn′-tay) Variation of the FARTHINGALE, worn by Spanish royalty in the 17th c. after the style had been given up in the rest of Europe. It was wider from side-to-side and had a long, wide extension of the bodice below the waistline that extended over

guardinfante

the top of the skirt. The bodice shoulderline was horizontal and sleeves were full and slashed, ending in fitted cuffs.

guards ∞ 16th-c. term for decorative bands of rich fabrics, plain or embroidered, used to conceal garment seams.

guardsman coat See COATS AND JACKETS.

guayabera shirt See SHIRTS.

Gucci * See APPENDIX/DESIGNERS.

Gucci® loafer (goo-chee) See FOOTWEAR: LOAFER.

guepiere See UNDERGARMENTS.

guiches See HAIRSTYLES.

guimpe 1. See BLOUSES AND TOPS. 2. Piece of fabric draped around the face falling over the neck and chest. Worn by women in the 14th and 15th c., particularly by widows and nuns and still worn by some nuns. Also spelled *guimp*.

guimpe dress/guimpe costume ∞ Jumper-dress with *guimpe* or blouse under short-sleeved, low-necked dress. Worn from 1880s to early 20th c.—first by children, later by older girls and women. Sometimes took the form of a suspender-type jumper with blouse called GUIMPE (see BLOUSES AND TOPS) underneath.

guimple See HEADWEAR: WIMPLE.

guinea feathers See FEATHERS.

guipure/guipure de Bruges See LACES.

guleron See HEADWEAR: CHAPERON.

gumshoe See FOOTWEAR.

gun-club checks See PRINTS, STRIPES, AND CHECKS.

gusset See CLOTHING CONSTRUCTION DETAILS.

gym bloomers See ACTIVEWEAR: GYM SUITS.

gymnasium costume See CALISTHENIC COSTUME.

gymnastic suit See ACTIVEWEAR.

gym sock See HOSIERY: SWEATSOCK.

gym suit See ACTIVEWEAR.

gypsy look **1.** Colorful garments in bright shades—full skirts, blouses, scarves, boleros, shawls, head scarfs, and hoop earrings—characteristic apparel of nomadic tribes called gypsies in Europe. A popular style for Halloween costumes since mid-19th c. and high fashion in late 1960s. *Der.* Originally worn by gypsies, a nomadic people of Europe, Asia, and North America. **2.** Adjective used to describe apparel derived from or influenced by the dress of gypsies. See BLOUSES AND TOPS: GYPSY BLOUSE and JEWELRY: GYPSY EARRING.

gypsy stripe See PRINTS, STRIPES, AND CHECKS: BAYADÉRE STRIPES.

G

haberdashery A store that sells men's apparel and accessories.

habiliment (heh-bil'-eh ment) Synonym for clothing, garb, attire, or dress. *Der.* French, *habillement,* "clothing."

habit Characteristic apparel of a calling, rank, or function (e.g., clerical clothes, court dress or riding habit).

habit d'escalier ∞ (ah-beet' des-kahl'-yaye) Late 18th and early 19th c. evening dress made with an overtunic or HALF ROBE. The short sleeves were slit open and trimmed with ribbons tied in ladderlike fashion.

habit-redingote ∞ (red'-ing-gote) Woman's dress of 1879 made in princess style with front closed from neck to knees. Lower front of skirt was cut away and rounded to reveal the underskirt.

habit shirt See SHIRTS.

hacking Riding for pleasure, as opposed to riding to hounds, for which a specific type of clothing is worn. Sometimes used as an adjective to describe clothing used for riding. See COATS AND JACKETS: HACKING JACKET, POCKETS: HACKING POCKET, and SCARVES: HACKING SCARF.

hackle See FEATHERS.

haincelin See HOUPPELANDE.

HAIR ACCESSORIES

anadem/anademe ∞ (ahn'-ah-dem) Wreath or garland of leaves or flowers, worn on hair by women in late 16th and early 17th c.

barrette (ba-ret') Clip worn in the hair. May be small and worn one on either side of head, or larger and worn in back or at nape of the neck. Made of plastic, metal, wood or other materials in various shapes (e.g., bar or bow knot). *Der.* French, diminutive of *barre,* "bar." Also spelled *barret, barette.*

bobby pin Small flexible piece of metal bent in half with prongs held together by the spring of the metal; worn to keep hair in place or to set hair in pin curls. See HAIRSTYLES: PIN CURLS #2.

diadem comb ∞ (dye'-ah-dem) High, wide, curved comb with ornamental top worn for evening by women in the 1830s.

duchess ∞ Knot or bow of ribbon worn as part of the FONTANGE hairstyle (see under HEADWEAR) in the late 17th c.

hairband **1.** From 15th to 17th c. a ribbon for the hair or fillet. See HEADWEAR: FILLET #2. **2.** See HEADWEAR: HEADBAND #1 and #2.

hairpin A two-pronged device usually of plastic or metal. Used to hold the hair in place, especially hair styled in a bun, knot, updo, or French twist. The classic hairpin is a wire bent double with crimps halfway down each side to give flexibility. Pins of very fine wire tinted to match hair are called **invisible hairpins**. Decorated hairpins are worn as jewelry and made of exotic materials or jeweled. Also see HAIR ACCESSORIES: BOBBY PIN.

hair sticks Long stiletto-like pieces of wood, plastic, or metal worn for decorative effect. Usually thrust through hair knotted at the back of the head.

papillotte comb ∞ (pahp'-ee-laut) Decorative tortoise shell comb, 3″–4″ long, used on either side of head to puff out hair by women in late 1820s. *Der.* French, *papilloter,* "to flutter," and *papillon,* "butterfly."

peigne Josephine ∞ (pahn) Woman's high comb, ornamented with small gilt balls. Worn at the back of head for evening in 1842.

pompon ∞ Hair or cap ornament composed of feathers, tinsel, butterflies, etc., worn in center part of hair by women from 1740s to 1760s, originally called *pompadour* (pohm'-pah-dure).

rat Sausage-shaped padded roll of nylon mesh (formerly of hair or felt) worn by women under natural hair to create high pompadour effect in early 20th c. and since. Also see HAIRSTYLES: POMPADOUR #1.

roll/rowle ∞ 16th and 17th c. term for pad used to raise the front hair up from forehead.

scrunchy Elastic band covered with fabric for confining ponytails.

Spanish comb Comb with ornamental top, sometimes 5″ high, worn at crown of head to support a MANTILLA (see under HEADWEAR) or separately for decorative effect.

scrunchy

toque ∞ A triangular cushion worn from 1815 to 1820 by women on top of the head to extend the hair.

---

haircut Trimming and shaping of hair with scissors or razor. See HAIRSTYLES.

hairdo See HAIRSTYLES.

hair fibers † Fibers obtained from the fleece or pelt of an animal.

hair jewelry See JEWELRY.

hairline stripe See PRINTS, STRIPES, AND CHECKS.

hair net See HEADWEAR.

hairpiece See introduction to category WIGS AND HAIRPIECES.

hairpin See HAIR ACCESSORIES.

hairpin lace See LACES.

hair seal See FURS.

hair sticks See HAIR ACCESSORIES.

HAIRSTYLES

hairstyle Manner in which the hair is worn. Also called *hairdo, coiffure, coif.* Elaborate hairstyles were popular in ancient times, particularly with the Greeks and Romans. The complexity of hairstyles varied throughout history with some of the most elaborate styles being worn in 18th c. France. First permanent wave was introduced in about 1909. Hair spray came into general use in the 1950s, thus making possible more elaborate hair arrangements. Hairstyles from the 1960s on revived many old styles as well as introducing totally new ones. Styling gel and mousse were in general use by 1980s.

abstract cut Straight short geometric haircut, often asymmetric, with one side of hair cut different from other. Introduced by English hairstylist Vidal Sassoon in mid-1960s.

abstract cut

Afro Style adopted for African-Americans in 1960s in which hair that had a natural tight curl was cut and allowed to assume its natural shape with no attempt made to straighten the hair. The size of the hair style varied with the length of hair. There are many interesting variations of this style.

afro

Afro puffs Afro hairstyle variation made by parting hair in center, pulling to sides, tying near ears, and teasing to form puffs over ears.

aggravators ∞ Term used for semicurls near the eye or temple, worn by men from 1830s to 1850s.

Agnès Sorel coiffure ∞ Woman's hairstyle with ribbon bands in front and a knot in back; worn from 1830s to 1850s. Named for AGNÈS SOREL.

American Indian braids See HAIRSTYLES: AMERICAN INDIAN HAIRSTYLE.

American Indian hairstyle Hair worn straight and long—below shoulder length—and parted in center. A headband worn low on the brow is usually added. The long hair may be tied in two pony tails, made into braids, or hang

H

free. When braided called **American Indian braids.**

ape drape See HAIRSTYLES: SHAG.

apollo knot ∞ Woman's elaborate evening hairstyle, worn from 1824 to 1832, made with wired loops of false hair, projecting up from crown of head, and finished with decorative comb, flowers, or feathers.

artichoke Short, back-combed layered hair, not too bouffant, popular in early 1960s.

back-combing Hairdressing technique of lifting each strand of hair and combing or brushing lightly toward the scalp to increase bulk; used widely in 1950s and 1960s for BOUFFANT and BEEHIVE hairdos (see under HAIRSTYLES). Also called *teasing.*

bandeau d'amour ∞ (ban'-doe dahm-moor') Woman's hairstyle or wig with high slanting and hanging curls worn in 1770s and 1780s.

banging chignon ∞ (sheen'-yon) Women's hairstyle of 1770s with wide flat loop of ribbon tied hair, hanging from crown of head to nape of neck.

bangs Hair combed forward over forehead and cut straight across, with the remainder left smooth or waved. Called *fringe* in England.

Bardot hair (bar-doe') Long hair, loosely curled and arranged in tousled disarray with loose tendrils around face. Popular after being seen on French film star Brigitte Bardot in 1959.

barrel curls Full, round large curls frequently grouped at crown or back of the head.

Beatle cut Man's haircut worn full with SIDEBURNS (see under HAIRSTYLES) and well down the neck in back. The first 20th c. style to revive longer hairstyles for men, it was introduced in the 1960s by the Beatles, an avant-garde rock music group from Liverpool, England.

Beatle cut

beehive High, exaggerated bubble hair shape, achieved by backcombing into a rounded dome. First worn by Teddy girls in London in late 1950s, popular until mid-1960s. Also called *bubble bob.*

beehive

Benoiton coiffure ∞ (ben-waa'-tone) Women's elaborate coiffure of 1866 with hair parted in center, smooth on top, chignon and curls in back. Three gold chains were worn over the top of the head and hung in dangling loops under the chin; sometimes garlands of flowers were used instead of chains. *Der.* Named after *La Famille Benoiton,* a play by Victorien Sardou, 1865.

bingle British term for very short haircut. *Der.* Combination of the words BOB and SHINGLE (see under HAIRSTYLES).

bob Short blunt-cut hair, either with bangs or bared forehead, introduced in 1920s by Irene Castle. Also called *Twenties bob.* Also see HAIRSTYLES: BOYISH BOB.

Boldini (bol'-dee-nee) See pompadour #1. Also called *Belle Epoque* (bell eh'-puck), *concierge* (cohn'-see-ehrj), and *onion. Der.* For Italian society painter Giovanni Boldini (1845–1931), who often painted women wearing this style.

bouffant (boo-fahnt') Hair exaggeratedly puffed out by means of back-combing (see under HAIRSTYLES) and held there by use of hair spray. Fashionable in early 1960s for medium-length and long hair. *Der.* French, "full" or "puffed."

bowl crop ∞ Men's hairstyle of 15th c. with hair shaved at back and sides, and longer hair hanging from crown of head in round basin-shaped fashion; a fashion revived in 1970 for young men when it was called a BOWL CUT (see under HAIRSTYLES). Also called *pudding-basin cut.*

bowl crop
15th c.

bowl cut Modern version of the BOWL CROP (see under HAIRSTYLES) that looks as if a bowl was placed over the head and then all the hair that can be seen around the edges of the bowl was cut. As a result, hair on top "under the bowl" is fairly long and that below can range in length from being shaved to being cut very short. Variations of this cut include the **dipped mushroom,** or **dipped bowl cut,** that dips several inches lower at the back of the head and the **under cut,** in which the underneath layer of hair under the bowl is cut with clippers for an additional inch or two. As a result, when the head is shaken, the bowl cut returns to its original shape.

boyish bob   Woman's extremely short hairstyle, shingled (see HAIRSTYLES: SHINGLE) in back and short on sides. Originally popularized by Beatrice Lillie, British actress in the mid-1920s, and worn since at intervals. Also called *Eton crop, gamin,* and *garçon.*

boyish bob or garçon haircut

braids   Hairstyle made by plaiting three sections of hair together. Braids may be worn hanging down on shoulders, looped up, tied or pinned together, wound around the head in a coronet, or wound in a BUN (see under HAIRSTYLES) at the nape of the neck. Popular style for children in the early 20th c., also very popular in the 1960s and early 1980s.

brush cut   See HAIRSTYLES: CREWCUT.

Brutus head/wig   ∞ Man's own hair worn closely cropped or brown unpowdered wig, both worn disheveled. Popular from about 1790 to 1820 and inspired by the French Revolution.

bubble bob   See HAIRSTYLES: BEEHIVE.

bubble curls   Very loose curls, back-combed slightly and turned under, appearing on head as series of rounded bumps.

bull head/bull tour   ∞ Woman's hairstyle with fringe of thick curls across forehead worn in late 17th c. Also called *taure* (tawr). *Der.* French, *tauteau,* "bull."

bun   Large mass of hair confined neatly at crown of the head or at the nape of the neck.

bun

bush cut   See HAIRSTYLES: CREW CUT.

business man's cut   Men's moderately short haircut, long enough to be parted or brushed back.

Buster Brown   Straight short hairstyle with bangs over forehead. *Der.* Named for early 20th-c. comic-strip character and popular for little boys. Also called **dutch bob,** especially if worn by girls.

bustle curls   Long curls worn dangling at back of head.

burr cut   See HAIRSTYLES: INDUCTION CUT.

butch cut   See HAIRSTYLES: CREW CUT.

buzz cut   See HAIRSTYLES: CREW CUT.

cadogan/catagan   (ka-do'-gan)   **1.** ∞ Hairstyle with cluster of ringlets or braids of hair hanging at back of head, tied at nape of neck with wide ribbon. Worn as natural hair or as a wig by men in the 18th c. (see WIGS AND HAIRPIECES: CATOGAN WIG) and by women in 1870s. **2.** ∞ Same style worn by women with riding habit in 18th c. Hair usually pulled back, looped up, and tied with a ribbon or the hair itself formed the band. **3.** Hair pulled back with a bow at the nape of neck; a style revived by French couturière Gabrielle Chanel in 1960s. Also see HAIRSTYLES: GEORGE. *Der.* British General, First Earl of Cadogan (1675–1726).

cadogan #1, 18th c.

Caesar cut   Contemporary men's haircut in the style shown on Roman busts of Julius Caesar. Moderately short, the hair is layered to about one or two inches and brushed forward to a short bang over the forehead.

chignon   (sheen'-yon)   Large roll of hair twisted into a circle or figure eight on the back of the head or at the nape of the neck, often enclosed in decorative net or held by fancy hairpins. Classic style in 1860s, in 1920s, 1930s, and revived in 1980s. In the late 17th c., was sometimes called a *chou* (choo).

chignon

China doll hair   Typical Chinese hairstyle with short straight hair, sometimes shingled in back, and bangs at forehead.

chou   See HAIRSTYLES: CHIGNON.

classic pull-back   Long hair worn combed neatly to the back and tied with a ribbon. In the 1940s worn with a barrette in the back. Also see HAIRSTYLES: GEORGE.

cluster curls   Groups of false ringlets or sausage curls, mounted on netting to be pinned in place as part of an elaborate coiffure.

cockle   ∞ Term used for woman's curl or ringlet in the 17th c.

coif   (kwaf)   Another name for hairstyle or shortened form of the world coiffure (kwaf-foor').

coiffure   See HAIRSTYLES: COIF.

coiffure à l'Agnès Sorel   See HAIRSTYLES: AGNES SORÈL COIFFURE.

H

coiffure à la Grecque See HAIRSTYLES: GREEK COIFFURE.

coiffure à la hérisson See HAIRSTYLES: HÉRISSON.

coiffure à la indépendance ∞ French hairstyle with a sailing-ship model perched on top of wavy locks and curls. Worn in 1778 to honor Benjamin Franklin's appearance at the French court for negotiation of a treaty between the U.S. and France. Also called *Triumph of Liberty.*

coiffure à la Maintenon ∞ (ah la manta-naw′) Woman's coiffure of late 17th and early 18th c. with hair parted in the center, curled, and piled high. *Der.* After the Marquise de Maintenon, second wife of Louis XIV of France.

coiffure à la mouton ∞ (ah la moo-ton′) Short hairsyle fringed over forehead and crimped on sides. *Der.* French, "sheep."

coiffure à la Ninon See HAIRSTYLES: NINON COIFFURE.

coiffure à la Sévigné ∞ (say-veen′-yay) Women's hairstyle of 1650 parted in center, puffed out over the ears, hanging in waves and curls to the shoulders with decorated bow at ear level. *Der.* After Marie, Marquise de Sévigné (1626–1696), a witty correspondent and writer of the time.

coiffure à la Titus See HAIRSTYLES: TITUS.

coiffure à la zazzera ∞ (zatz-zeh′-rah) Man's long hairstyle with ends curled under—originally worn by Romans and revived by Venetians in 15th c.

coiffure à l'enfant ∞ (ah lon-fon′) Woman's hairstyle of 1780s, bobbed short like a child's.

coiffure en bouffons ∞ (on buff-on′) Woman's hairstyle with tufts of crimped or curled hair arranged over the temples, and the forehead covered with fringe of hair called *garcette* (gar-cett′). Worn in the Louis XIII period.

coiffure en cadenettes ∞ (on ka-dey′-net) **1.** A hairstyle worn by men and women of Louis XIII period with two long locks—called **moustaches**—falling on either side of face, wound with ribbons, and tied with bows. **2.** 17th-c. term for masculine hairstyle with two long locks pulled back and tied with a ribbon.

coiffure en raquette ∞ (on ra-ket′) Woman's hairstyle with hair brushed up, puffed over the temples, and supported by a wire hoop. Worn in last quarter of 16th c. *Der.* French, "racket."

cold wave See HAIRSTYLES: PERMANENT WAVE.

concierge See HAIRSTYLES: POMPADOUR #1.

confidants ∞ Woman's clusters of curls placed over the ears in late 17th c.

corkscrew curls Free hanging curls that appear coiled, frequently lacquered to hold the shape.

corkscrew curls

cornrows Hair braided in horizontal rows by adding more hair after each plait to the braid. *Der.* From African styles worn by African-Americans in the South in the 19th c., revived in early 1970s by fashionable African-Americans, then copied by others.

cornrow braids

coxcomb/cockscomb Woman's upswept coiffure with hair brushed to the back and pinned to form a vertical row of ringlets down center back.

crève-coeur ∞ (krev-kur′) Term used at end of 17th c. for curls at nape of woman's neck. *Der.* French, "heartbreaker."

crew cut Man's hair closely cropped so that hair on crown of head stands erect. Front hair is usually a little longer than the back. Originally worn by oarsmen to keep hair out of eyes. Adopted by college men in 1940s and 1950s. At that time it was similar to Army haircuts. Also worn by some women in 1980s and after. When very short and even length all over, called a **butch cut** or a **buzz cut.** Slightly longer versions of the crew cut include the **brush cut,** so named because it stands up like the bristles of a brush, and the **ivy league cut** with hair longer at the front of the head so it can be brushed up or down or parted. Also see HAIRSTYLES: FLATTOP.

crew cut

crisp ∞ 17th-c. term for a curl of hair worn by a woman.

cruches ∞ (kroosh) Late 17th-c. term for small curls worn on the forehead.

cue ∞ 18th-c. spelling of QUEUE (see under HAIRSTYLES), the hanging tail of a wig, which first appeared for civilian wear about 1720.

curlyhead See HAIRSTYLES: POODLE CUT.

D.A. See HAIRSTYLES: DUCKTAIL HAIRCUT.

dipped bowl cut/dipped mushroom cut See HAIRSTYLES: BOWL CUT.

double chignon ∞ Woman's hairstyle of 1860s with two large rolls of hair, one above the other, at the nape of the neck. Sometimes artificial hair was used.

dreadlocks/Rasta dreadlocks   Hair arranged in many long hanging twists that was first worn by Rastafarian (a religious sect) reggae musicians from Jamaica. During the 1980s

dreadlocks

and 1990s some young African-American men and women and some Caucasians adopted the style. Sometimes hair spray is used to make locks stand up on top of head in a tousled mass. *Der.* From the style worn by Rastafarians, a sect from Jamaica, founded in 1930 when Ras Tafari (Haile Selassie) became emperor of Ethiopia.

ducktail haircut Short hairstyle combed to come to a point at the nape of the neck. Worn by both men and women in the 1950s. Also called *D.A.*, slang for "duck's ass."

ducktail haircut

dutch bob See BUSTER BROWN HAIRSTYLE.

earmuffs Hair parted in center, braided on each side, and wound around to form buns over the ears.

Empire coiffure ∞ (ohm-peer) Hairstyle worn in 1860s with curls in Greek manner around the face, and a band of narrow ribbon wrapped three times around the head. The back is done in a large CHIGNON (see under HAIRSTYLES) with narrow ribbon wrapped around it several times, ending with two ribbon streamers down the back.

Empire cone hairstyle Cone-shaped ornament, frequently wound with braids, and placed on crown of head. Hair is pulled back smoothly from the forehead, brought through the cone, and allowed to hang in a ponytail from top of cone or wound into a cockscomb spike.

Eton crop Variation of BOYISH BOB (see under HAIRSTYLES) worn in England.

fade A hairstyle popular in the 1990s that originated with young African-American men in which the hair was cut very short on the sides, and long on the top. Sometimes words, names, or designs were shaved on the scalp.

favourites ∞ Women's curls worn near the temples from 1690 to about 1720.

feather cut Short lightly curled woman's bob, cut in layers, popular in 1950s and 1960s.

fillet 19th-c. evening hairstyle made by wrapping a satin band, embroidered with pearls, spirally around the head.

fingerwave Short hair set in flat waves by means of setting lotion and held until dry by bobby pins, or sometimes by combs. Popular in 1930s and revived in early 1970s. Also called *water wave.*

fishbone braid Hair is braided so that the interlacing of hair down center back looks similar to the spine of a fish with small bones on each side. Also called *French braid.*

fishbone or French braid

flattop General category of hairstyles usually for men, in which the top of the hair is cut to a flat surface. Lengths may vary. The head being round, when the hair is cut flat, the scalp on the top of the head is close to the surface, and may be visible. This is known as a **landing strip.** When the hair is cut so short on top that the only remaining hair forms a horseshoe-shaped ridge on the upper sides and across the front, the cut is called a **horseshoe flattop.** In another version called **white walls,** the back and sides are shaved clean.

flip Medium-length woman's hairstyle with hair turned up on ends to form an incomplete curl. Front is often cut in bangs.

French braid See FISHBONE BRAID.

French lock See HAIRSTYLES: LOVE LOCK.

French roll/twist Upswept hairstyle with side and back hair combed and twisted in roll at the center back. Popular in 1940s and classic style since.

French roll or French twist

H

fringe See HAIRSTYLES: BANGS.

frisette ∞ (frih-zet′) **1.** 19th-c. term for crimped bangs of hair, either real or false, worn on the forehead. **2.** In the 1860s a sausage-shaped pad over which back hair was rolled.

frizzy Describing hair in many tight small curls.

gamin (gam′-in) Short boyish cut with shingled back and sides and irregularly cut bangs, popular in 1940s. Also called *urchin* and *garçon. Der.* French, "street urchin." Also see HAIRSTYLES: BOYISH BOB.

garcette (gar-cett′) See HAIRSTYLES: COIFFURE EN BOUFFONS.

garçon/garçonne (gar-sohn′) See HAIRSTYLES: BOYISH BOB.

George Long hair pulled back and secured at the nape of the neck with a twist of hair, ribbon, or scarf. Named for hairstyle as seen in 18th-c. portraits of U.S. President George Washington. George hairstyle Classic style for women, adapted by men in early 1970s. Also called a *cadogan* or *catagon.* Also see HAIRSTYLES: CADOGAN #3.

Gibson Girl Hair worn in high puffy POMPADOUR (see under HAIRSTYLES) with small bun on top of head. Fashionable in 19th and early 20th cs., made popular in drawings of Charles Dana Gibson. Revived occasionally.

Grecian curls **1.** ∞ Hairstyle of the 1860s with rows of curls hanging down the back from the nape of the neck. Sometimes arranged in two rows, one shorter than the other. **2.** Small curls around the face, copied from Napoleonic era that in turn looked to Greece for inspiration. Used in the 1960s with helmet-style headwear. See HEADWEAR: HELMET.

Greek coiffure Womans's hairstyle of 1860s with center part, hair braided and wrapped around the crown of the head, made to form three hanging loops in back and wound around the loops at nape of neck. Also called *coiffure à la Grecque.* Also see HAIRSTYLES: GRECIAN CURLS.

guiche (gweesh) Few strands of hair made into curl in front of ear. Also called *kiss curl.* When curled back toward the ear instead of forward, called a *reverse guiche.*

hairdo See introduction to HAIRSTYLES.

hérisson/coiffure à la hérison ∞ (air-ee′-sonh) **For women:** Late 18th-c. short hairstyle with loose curls in back and frizzed ends at front and sides. **For men:** Same cut in front, but worn with a CADOGAN or PIGTAIL (see under HAIRSTYLE) in back. *Der.* French, "bristly, shaggy."

highlights Naturally or artificially produced lighter areas of the hair that provide a contrast with darker areas.

hurluberlu ∞ (er-loo-bare′-loo) Woman's hairstyle with short curls all and over and long ringlets in back, first worn by Madame de Montespan about 1671.

induction cut An even length of stubble across the head. This is the cut given to male recruits to the U.S. Armed Services. Also called *burr cut.*

Irene Castle bob ∞ Short bob with hair brushed back off the forehead and hanging in loose waves. *Der.* After Irene Castle, the ballroom dancer who made bobbed hair fashionable prior to World War I.

ironed hair Long straight hair, achieved by placing hair on an ironing board and pressing with a warm iron to remove all waves; a fad with young girls in the late 1960s. Now flat irons are used to achieve super-sleek hairstyles.

ivy league cut See HAIRSTYLES: CREW CUT.

jumbo curls Very large curls similar to BARREL CURLS (see under HAIRSTYLES).

kiss curl See HAIRSTYLES: GUICHE.

kolbe ∞ (kol-be′) Man's hairstyle worn in mid-16th c. with bangs in front and hair the same length at sides and back, usually above the ears. Also called *kolbenschmitt.*

La Belle Époque See HAIRSTYLES: POMPADOUR.

La Goulue See HAIRSTYLES: POMPADOUR.

landing strip See HAIRSTYLES: FLATTOP.

layered cut Hair cut in graduated lengths in a horizontal fashion around the head.

lion's tail A long piece of hair or a switch, hanging down the back, twined with cord to about 6″ from the bottom, thus appearing like a lion's tail. Also called *queue de lion.*

love lock/long lock ∞ Long lock of curled hair brought forward from nape of neck and worn hanging over chest, popular from 1590 to 1650s for men and sometimes women. Also called a *Bourbon lock, French lock, heart breaker.*

Maintenon coiffure ∞ (man-te′-non kwa-foor′) Woman's hairstyle of early 1860s with two long hanging curls at either side of face, tiny curls on the forehead, and a *chignon* at the back of the neck. Filmy lace decorated with foliage and flowers went over the crown of the head and hung down each side to shoulders in form of LAPPETS (see under HEADWEAR). The MAINTENON TOUPET (see under WIGS AND HAIRPIECES) could be added to secure proper effect of curls on the forehead. *Der.* Named for the *Marquise de Maintenon,* mistress and second wife of Louis XIV of France.

Mandinko Exaggerated MOHAWK-type hairstyle (see under HAIRSTYLES) with sideburns connected to beard and moustache, as worn by Mr. T., television star of early 1980s.

marcel wave ∞ Artificial wave put in woman's hair with heated curling irons, devised by hairdresser Marcel of France in 1907 and popular in the 1920s.

mini-mini braids/mini-plaits Extremely minute braids introduced in 1968. Natural hair may be styled in this manner or a hairpiece attached.

Mohawk Style in which entire head is shaved except for upstanding fringe of hair, about 3″ high and 2″ or more wide, running from brow to the nape of the neck. Sometimes left long and made to stand up in "spikes" with gel. See hairstyles: PORCUPINE. *Der.* Adapted from style worn by Mohawk Indians.

Montague curls ∞ (mon′-ta-ghu) Woman's evening hairstyle with a fringe of crescent-shaped curls pasted to the forehead in 1877.

Ninon coiffure ∞ (nee-nonh′ kwa-foor′) Hairstyle with ringlet curls over the forehead, shoulder-length curls at sides (sometimes wired), and back hair pulled into a knot. Introduced in England in mid-17th c. *Der.* Style was later given this name after Anne de Lenclos (1620–1705), known as Ninon de Lenclos, a legendary courtesan and Parisian fashion leader.

onion See POMPADOUR #1.

oreilles de chien ∞ (or-ray de she-en) Nickname for two long curls worn at either side of face by men from 1790 to 1800. *Der.* French, "dog's ears."

pageboy Straight hair shoulder length or shorter, with ends curled under at back and sides very smoothly. A classic hairstyle. *Der.* From hair of medieval "pages." pageboy

pannier curls (pann-yeh′) Curls worn at sides of face in front of the ears.

permanent/permanent wave Waves or curls that last until hair is cut off, originally created by chemicals and heated rollers, later by means of chemicals alone. First permanent wave was invented by Charles Nestlé in 1906. First machine wave, introduced in beauty shops, required electrical wiring to each roller. In 1930s, new machineless wave used chemicals and heated rollers. In the early 1940s, the first *cold wave,* in which chemicals curled the hair without heating it, was introduced. This made home permanents possible. In 1960s a soft version called a body wave gave hair more fullness for noncurly coiffures. Popular for men in late 1970s. In slang, called **perm.** Also SEE HAIRSTYLES: MARCEL WAVE.

pigeon-wings See WIGS AND HAIRPIECES.

pigtails **1.** Hair worn in two side braids, sometimes with ribbon bow tied on ends. Popular style for young girls since 1940s. **2.** Child's hairstyle for short hair with tiny, ribbon-tied braids all over head.

pin curls **1.** Curls used on forehead or sides of face made by winding hair around the finger then set with bobby pins. When pins are removed, curl is left tightly twisted. **2.** Method of setting the hair by making tiny curls all over the head and securing them with bobby pins. May be combed out into either waves or curls.

pixie haircut Short hairstyle cut in layered style close to head and combed in points around forehead and face.

pompadour (pohm′-pah-dure) **1.** Woman's hair brushed up high and smooth from forehead and temples, sometimes teased or rolled over false stuffing and tucked into a small bun

H

on top of head. Copied from style worn in late 19th and early 20th c. See GIBSON GIRL. Variations of this style called *La Belle Epoque, concierge, onion, Boldini,* and *La Goulue* in late 1960s. **2.** Hair rolled up in front with back worn straight and curled on ends, popular in 1940s. **3.** Man's hair worn rather long and brushed straight up and back from forehead with no part. Also see HAIRSTYLES: QUIFF. **4.** See HAIR ACCESSORIES: POMPON. *Der.* From Marquise de Pompadour, mistress of Louis XV of France.

pompadour #1

ponytail **1.** Hair pulled to crown or center back of head and tied with a ribbon or held with an elastic band. Ends left hanging loose like a horse's tail. **2.** Hair parted in the center and two ponytails made—one on either side of the face near the ears.

ponytail #1

poodle cut All over short curled effect similar to hair of a poodle. Also called *curlyhead.*

porc-epic See HAIRSTYLES: PORCUPINE HEADDRESS.

porcupine hairstyle Man's 1985 hairstyle with center portion from forehead to neck left longer with even longer strands about 8″ in length made to stand up on top of head with gel or mousse.

porcupine headdress ∞ Man's hairstyle, with short hair standing up like bristles, worn at end of 18th c. Also called *porc-epic.*

pouf See HAIRSTYLES: BOUFFANT.

pouf au sentiment ∞ (poof o sont-eh′-mont) Extravagantly high hairstyle elaborately decorated with flowers and other objects, worked over a framework of gauze. Worn by women in 18th c. before the French Revolution.

psyche knot (si-kee) Copy of Greek hairstyle for women with hair pulled back and twisted to form a knot at back of head. *Der.* Named for Greek mythological maiden, Psyche, the lover of Cupid, made immortal by Jupiter.

pudding-basin cut See HAIRSTYLES: BOWL CROP.

puffs Women's hair when BACK-COMBED (see under HAIRSTYLES) to form bouffant effect at sides of face in early 20th c.

punk hair A variety of unusual hairstyles including MOHAWK, PORCUPINE, and SPIKY HAIRSTYLES (see under HAIRSTYLES), sometimes dyed a variety of colors.

punk hairstyle

queue (kew) Long single braid hanging down the back. Similar to hairstyle worn by Chinese men. Also spelled *cue.*

queue de lion See HAIRSTYLES: LION'S TAIL.

quiff Hairstyle brushed forward first, then back, giving a somewhat *pompadour* effect in front. Similar to style affected by Elvis Presley, a rock-music superstar of the 1950s and 1960s.

Rasta dreadlocks See HAIRSTYLES: DREADLOCKS.

razor cut Haircut that is done using a razor blade rather than a scissors.

Rècamier hairstyle ∞ (ray-cahm′-ee-ay) Hairstyle of 1870s and 1880s arranged with *chignon* high on back of head and curls at neck. *Der.* Named after hairstyle worn by Madame Rècamier.

reverse guiche See HAIRSTYLES: GUICHE.

ringlets Loose curls that hang in dangling fashion.

ringlets

romeo Modified PAGEBOY cut (see under HAIRSTYLES) with bangs falling to eyebrows, sides cut sloping backward to reveal the face as an oval, and hair gently turned under at back and sides.

Sassoon Short, straight boyish hairdo, combed forward from crown, cut in low bangs, shaped to points in front of ears, and shingled in back to deep V. *Der.* First ABSTRACT CUT (see under HAIRSTYLES), designed by British hairdresser Vidal Sassoon in 1964.

sausage curl Tightly rolled horizontal curl usually arranged in layers around sides or back of head from ear level to nape of neck. Popular in late 1930s, early 1940s, and revived in 1980s.

sculptured hair Hair covered with mousse so that it may be arranged in fan-shaped design

H

or brushed straight up from face and cut in scalloped design at top. Styles were introduced by Patti LaBelle, a rock singer in mid-1980s.

shag Longish bob, layered for a shaggy look, with bangs and "shaggy" in front of ears. An innovation of the late 1960s. Also called *ape-drape.*

shingle Tapering of hair up back of head, and sometimes around to the sides, in imitation of a man's conventional haircut. Style introduced in 1920s for women, achieving new popularity in the 1960s and 1980s and after. Also see HAIRSTYLES: BINGLE.

sideburns That part of a man's hair and whiskers that extends from his hairline to below the ears.

spiky hair Short or medium-length hair, segmented and twisted to form pointed projections that are stiffened with hair spray, gel or mousse. Sometimes dyed different colors (e.g., blue, orange, and pink).

sideburns

spit curls Separate ringlets formed flat against the forehead or cheek often held in place by water, setting lotion, or lacquer. Popular in 1930s, and revived in 1970s and 1980s. Also see HAIRSTYLES: GUICHE.

Statue of Liberty hair Outré hairstyle of 7 spikes of hair, sprayed to stand erect, framing face like Statue of Liberty crown. *Der.* Inspired by the July 4, 1986, celebration of the restoration of the Statue of Liberty in New York harbor.

tapered haircut The hair is cut progressively shorter down the back of the head to nape of the neck. The length of the hair being tapered can vary depending on the style.

taure See HAIRSTYLES: BULLHEAD.

teasing See HAIRSTYLES: BACK-COMBING.

teddy boy cut See TEDDY BOY in alphabetical listing.

tendrils Long loosely curled strands of hair worn hanging at the forehead, sides, or nape of neck, popular with the pompadour hairstyle (see HAIRSTYLES: POMPADOUR #1).

tipping Hand-painting the tips of sections of the hair.

Titus ∞ Coiffure, worn in late 18th c. after the French Revolution, that resembled the way a man condemned to the guillotine wore his hair, cut short and brushed forward over forehead. Also called *Titus hairstyle. Der.* From hairstyle of Roman Emperor, Titus, A.D. 79–81.

topknot Hair twisted into a knot or bun at the crown of the head.

twenties bob See HAIRSTYLES: BOB.

under cut See HAIRSTYLES: BOWL CUT.

upsweep/updo Popular 1940s woman's hairstyle with medium-long hair brushed upward from the sides and nape of neck, then secured on top of the head in curls or a pompadour (see under HAIRSTYLES: POMPADOUR #1).

upsweep

urchin See HAIRSTYLES: GAMIN.

Veronica Lake hairstyle Long hair parted on side with heavier section hanging down almost covering one eye. Worn by film star Veronica Lake in 1940s, revived after interest for older movies in 1960s.

wash-and-wear hair **1.** Hair worn in a tousled mass, achieved by washing hair and allowing it to hang uncombed. First popular in early 1980s. **2.** Any hair style that is cut so as to allow the hair to be washed and worn without any additional styling.

waterfall ∞ Woman's hairstyle of the 1860s and 1870s, usually made with a piece of false waved hair hanging down in back in a confined mass or in form of loose chignon with braid pulled tight at center, making two loops of hair.

water wave See HAIRSTYLES: FINGERWAVE.

wedge Hair is tapered close to the head at the nape of the neck, almost to a V. Above this the hair is full and all one length. The front and sides are all one length, squared off at middle of ear, and short bangs are informally styled. *Der.* Popular after it was worn by Dorothy Hamill, an Olympic figure skating champion in 1976.

white walls See HAIRSTYLES: FLATTOP.

wind-blown bob Popular 1930s woman's hairstyle that was cut short and shingled, so that

H

hair fell softly about the face as if blown by the wind.

Hale, Sarah Josepha See *GODEY'S LADY'S BOOK.*

half Adjective used for smaller or incomplete items of apparel or accessories. The prefix **demi** is a synonym. See APRONS: HALF APRON, BELTS: HALF BELT, EYEWEAR: HALF GLASSES, FOOTWEAR: DEMI-BOOT, HOSIERY: HALF HOSE, SHIRTS: HALF SHIRT, SHOULDERS AND SLEEVES: HALF SLEEVE, UNDERGARMENTS: DEMI-BRA and HALF SLIP.

half-compass cloak See CAPES, CLOAKS, AND SHAWLS: COMPASS CLOAK.

half coronet See HEADWEAR: DEMI-CORONAL.

half dress ∞ Late 18th and 19th-c. term for daytime or semiformal evening dress. Also called *half-toilette* or *demi-toilette.*

half gaiters See FOOTWEAR: SPATS.

half gown See HALF ROBE.

half handkerchief See SCARVES.

half-jack boot See FOOTWEAR: JOCKEY BOOT.

half kirtle See KIRTLE.

half lining Lining of only part of the garment (e.g., front completely lined but only the shoulders lined in the back). Frequently used in men's jackets and topcoats.

half mask See MASKS: DOMINO.

half-moon pocket See POCKETS.

half mourning See MOURNING DRESS.

half-piqué/half P.K. seam See GLOVES AND GLOVE CONSTRUCTION.

half robe ∞ Low-necked, short-sleeved, thigh-length tunic worn over long gown with fullness pulled in at waist by narrow ribbon. Worn from late 18th to early 19th c. Also called *half-gown* or *demi-habilliment.*

half sizes Women's garments cut for a fully developed figure: short-waisted in back, larger in waist and hips, height about 5'2" to 5'8"—usually sized 10½ to 24½.

half-toilette See HALF DRESS.

Hall of Fame See COTY AMERICAN FASHION CRITICS' AWARD.

halo hat See HEADWEAR: PAMELA.

Halston * See APPENDIX/DESIGNERS.

halter Strap encircling the neck used to support front of a garment, leaving shoulders and back bare. Popular in 1930s and 1940s, revived in early 1970s and periodically since then. Used on blouses, dresses, evening wear and swimsuits. See BLOUSES AND TOPS: HALTER TOP, NECKLINES AND COLLARS: HALTER NECKLINE.

Hamburg lace See LACES.

hamster See FURS.

hand † Characteristics of a fabric that are revealed through sense of touch (e.g., crispness, softness, smoothness, drape, resilience, fineness, and the like).

HANDBAGS AND RELATED ACCESSORIES

handbag Accessory carried primarily by women and girls to hold such items as money, credit cards, and cosmetics. Comes in many styles and made of a variety of materials (e.g., leather, fabric, vinyl, metal, plastic, canvas, straw, and patent leather). The word is often shortened to *bag.* Also called a *purse* or POCKETBOOK. From 13th to 16th c. the AULMONIERE, a small leather pouch, was worn suspended from man's girdle in order to have alms for the poor. From late 19th to early 20th c., women carried a small elongated bag called a RETICULE. In late 19th c., various types of handbags began to be carried mainly for traveling. By 1920s it was a necessary accessory. In 1968 the MANBAG was introduced for men. See cross-references under HANDBAGS AND RELATED ACCESSORIES.

accordion bag Bag made like an expandable filing envelope that is narrow at the top and pleated at sides and bottom. Usually made with a handle and frequently with a zipper compartment in the center. *Der.* From resemblance to pleats on the musical instrument of this name.

American Indian bag See HANDBAGS AND RELATED ACCESSORIES: SQUAW BAG.

Apache bag See HANDBAGS AND RELATED ACCESSORIES: SQUAW BAG.

attaché case See HANDBAGS AND RELATED ACCESSORIES: BRIEFCASE #1.

aulmoniere ∞ (all-mon-yehr') Medieval pouch of silk or leather suspended from girdle worn by nobles from the 13th c. until the Reformation to carry alms. Also used by women in 14th c. to carry mirrors and tweezers for their hair. Also spelled *aumoniere, aulmonier, almoner.* **Gipser** was such a bag worn by men in late Middle Ages. Also spelled *gipcière, gypsire.*

backpack Bag with straps fitting over shoulders so that it can be worn on the back. Term *backpack* has largely replaced KNAP-SACK (see under HANDBAGS AND RELATED ACCESSORIES) in describing bags worn on the back. Used since 1970s to carry books and sometimes used in place of a handbag in the 1980s and after. Usually made of nylon or other MANUFACTURED FIBERS and sometimes of real or synthetic leather. Variations now include a backpack designed to be carried over one shoulder and called a **one-shoulder backpack.**

backpack

bag See HANDBAG in introduction to HANDBAGS AND RELATED ACCESSORIES.

baguette bag (bah-get′) Popular woman's handbag originated by Italian design house of Fendi. An extended oblong shape, the bag closes with a flap over the front and may have both a shoulder strap and handles. It is made in a wide variety of materials. *Der.* Named after a long, narrow loaf of French bread.

ballentine See HANDBAGS AND RELATED ACCESSORIES: RETICULE.

barrel bag Handbag shaped like a stubby cylinder with a zipper closing and handles attached to the sides. *Der.* From the shape similar to a small barrel.

barrel bag

basket bag Applies to many types of handbags. Originally woven only of reed in typical basket shapes. Now made of reed, straw, cane, inter-woven plastic strips, or other mate-rials such as leather or plastic in the shape of a basket. One popular style resembles a small picnic hamper. Sometimes decorated with shells, beads, sequins, brass, or leather.

basket bag

beaded bag Any ornate small bag entirely cov-ered with varicolored pearls or glass beads or a fabric bag, often satin, with a design worked in beads. Beaded bags were used for daytime and evening through-out the 19th c. but were limited to more formal wear by the 20th c.

beaded bag

One type popular in the early 1900s was usu-ally hand-crocheted in small elongated pouch style with a drawstring top and a beaded tassel at the bottom. Another style, made in France, was oblong in shape with beaded fringe on the bottom and sterling silver frame and handle. This latter type was revived in 1968.

belt bag **1.** A small bag worn at waist having slots in the back through which a belt is drawn. Usually has a flap closing and is worn with sportswear. **2.** A pouch bag with handle through which a belt is drawn.

billfold See HANDBAGS AND RELATED ACCES-SORIES: WALLET.

book bag Slim oblong bag the size of a note-book cinched around center with strap that forms loop handle; introduced in 1970s.

bourse ∞ (boorce) Large purse or bag worn from 1440 until mid-18th c. Later spelled *burse.*

box bag Handbag with rigid frame, similar to small suitcase or lunchbox, made in leather, metal, or vinyl.

bracelet bag Type of handbag with one or two BANGLE BRACELETS (see under JEWELRY) as handles. May be a soft pouch bag made of leather or fabric, or it may be made with a frame.

briefcase **1.** Large, usually flat case with a carry-ing handle, most often made of real or synthe-tic leather and is large enough or can expand sufficiently to hold documents, books, and the like. Also called *attaché case.* **2.** Handbag of briefcase size for woman executive that features small outside pockets for personal items.

bucket bag Round handbag made in the shape of a bucket.

budget ∞ Wallet or extra pocket hanging from belt used in 17th c.

canteen bag Circular-style bag frequently made with a shoulder strap and zipper clos-ing. Made in the shape of a flat canteen used to carry water in dry climates.

caravan bag See HANDBAGS AND RELATED ACCESSORIES: SAFARI BAG.

H

carpet bag Handbag made of patterned carpeting or heavy tapestry, in a large satchel style. Popular in 19th c., late 1960s, and revived in mid-1980s in lighter-weight fabrics. *Der.* From carpet valises popular with Northerners for travel just after the Civil War. Southerners alluded to the travelers by the derisive term "carpetbaggers."

carpet bag

carryall See HANDBAGS AND RELATED ACCESSORIES: TOTE BAG.

carryall clutch Woman's wallet designed to hold coins, bills, photographs and credit cards. Usually the size of U.S. paper money, with snap closing on long edge and purselike sections for coins.

Chanel bag Handbag designed by French couturiere Gabrielle Chanel that has become a classic. Of quilted leather with gold chain handles, it has a gold House of Chanel logo on the front.

Chanel bag

change purse Small purse that closes by a snap clasp on the rigid frame or by a zipper. Usually carried inside handbag to hold coins and made in leather, clear plastic, or matched to the larger handbag. Also called a *coin purse.*

chatelaine bag (shat′-eh-lane) Small handbag that hung from waist by ornamental chain and hook, popular from 1850s to the end of the century.

chatelaine bag

clutch bag/clutch purse **1.** Regular-sized handbag without a handle. **2.** Type of handbag frequently used for an evening bag. Sometimes has a strap on back through which hand may be inserted, or a fine gold chain attached in such a manner that it is of optional use. Frequently made in envelope style, in which case it is called an **envelope bag.** *Mini-clutch* bags are tiny versions of this style.

clutch purse

coin purse See HANDBAGS AND RELATED ACCESSORIES: CHANGE PURSE.

contour clutch WALLET similar to a CLUTCH purse, but curved on top edge, sometimes with attached leather carrying loop at one end. See HANDBAGS AND RELATED ACCESSORIES: WALLET and CLUTCH BAG. Also called *swinger* or *swinger clutch.*

cordé bag (kor-day′) Any type of handbag made out of a fabric composed of rows of gimp (see under BRAIDS) stitched to a background fabric to make a pattern. Popular style in the 1940s and still used.

cordé bag

courier bag See HANDBAGS AND RELATED ACCESSORIES: MESSENGER BAG.

cross body bag Handbag with long strap designed to be worn with the strap over one shoulder and the bag on the other side of the body, which causes the strap to cross the chest. A variation of the shoulder bag (see under HANDBAGS AND RELATED ACCESSORIES) that developed when women started placing shoulder straps across the body in order to make the bag more secure.

doctor's bag Large handbag shaped like the bag traditionally carried by a physician. It has two handles, one on either side of hinged top opening.

drawstring bag Any handbag that is closed by pulling a cord, usually of pouch type.

duffel bag **1.** Large barrel-shaped canvas bag with a drawstring top. Used originally by sailors and soldiers to transport their clothing and other items. When used by sailors, called a *sea bag.* **2.** Copied in various sizes for handbags, beach bags, and luggage. May have an extra piece of fabric on outside that forms large pockets around outside of bag. Generally closes with a zipper. **3.** Small taffeta evening bag in pouch style with large ruffled top closed with tasseled drawstring.

duffel bag #2

envelope bag See HANDBAGS AND RELATED ACCESSORIES: CLUTCH BAG.

fanny pack An envelope or pouchlike bag mounted on a strap that fastens around the waist. Intended to be worn with the bag in the back, resting on the hips (or in slang, *fanny*), the bag is made in materials ranging from sturdy nylon to leather and in many sizes. Originally a day pack for hiking, by 2000 it had become acceptable daytime street wear and is especially popular with travelers.

feed bag Cylindrical leather or canvas bag with flat round bottom and top handles copied from canvas bags used for feeding horses. Forerunner of many open tote bags.

flight bag **1.** Soft canvas satchel with zippered top closing and two handles, copied from standard carryall issued by airlines to passengers when air travel was less common. **2.** Any handbag used for traveling, larger than a handbag and smaller than a suitcase. Also called a *travel bag.*

fold-over clutch Small envelope bag that may be open at the top or with zippered closing. Bag is folded over double and carried in the hand or under arm.

frame **1.** *n.* Metal top of handbag around which the bag is constructed. **2. framing** *v.* Securing the frame to the handbag. Material and lining are fitted into frame and secured permanently by machine.

French purse Foldover wallet for bills. One half incorporates a change purse with metal clasp closing at the top that is actually one end of the wallet.

gaming purse ∞ Drawstring bag of kid, velvet, or embroidered fabric used in 17th c. Made with flat stiffened circular base and pleated sides. *Der.* Used to hold counters and coins when "gaming" (e.g., playing cards for money).

gipser See HANDBAGS AND RELATED ACCESSORIES: AULMONIERE.

Grace Kelly bag See HANDBAGS AND RELATED ACCESSORIES: KELLY BAG.

Greek bag Square or rectangular wool opentop bag. Handwoven in Greek-key designs, trimmed around edge with cable yarn that also forms the handle.

hatbox bag Handbag made to look like a HATBOX.

hippie bag See SQUAW BAG.

Indian bag See SQUAW BAG.

indispensible See HANDBAGS AND RELATED ACCESSORIES: RETICULE.

interchangeable bag Complete handbag with extra covers that snap or button over frame to change colors.

inverted frame Handbag industry term for type of frame covered with fabric or leather so metal frame does not show at top of bag.

Kelly bag Handbag favored by Princess Grace of Monaco (actress Grace Kelly) in the 1950s. After Grace Kelly was seen frequently carrying an alligator TOTE (see under HANDBAGS AND RELATED ACCESSORIES) made by the design firm Hermès, the firm began to call this bag the Kelly bag. It has since become a classic style, and variations of the bag are now made by many manufacturers.

Kelly bag

Kikuyu Open-top straw tote bag with leather handles. Handwoven of natural sisal in horizontal strips of red and blue alternating with natural color. Made by Kikuyu craftsmen of Kenya.

knapsack A carryall made in heavy fabric that had shoulder straps and was worn by soldiers and hikers to carry necessary gear. Now more likely to be called a BACKPACK (see under HANDBAGS AND RELATED ACCESSORIES) and made in a wide variety of materials for many purposes.

lunchbox bag Identical in shape to the traditional deep lunchbox with a curved lid. Introduced from Italy in 1967, it was first made in papier-mâché and later in metal. Distinctive feature is a collage effect of decorative pictures pasted on the outside and then shellacked. Later do-it-yourself DÉCOUPAGE kits were marketed.

manbag Handbag, usually a shoulder bag style or with a wrist strap, that is carried by a man. A fashion that gained in popularity in early 1970s as an outgrowth of wide use of camera bags by men.

manbag

mesh bag Tiny links of metal joined to make a flexible bag. Popular in early 1900s in small size with sterling silver top and chain with the metal frequently enameled in a floral design. In the 1940s, mesh handbags were made with larger white enameled links and white plastic frames.

messenger bag Large bag with an envelope-like main compartment that usually closes with a zipper and has a large flap over the front that fastens with a buckle or snap. May have either shoulder straps or handles. Inspired by bags carried by messengers. A smaller version with a more tailored, square appearance is called a **courier bag.**

minaudiere (min-oh′-dee-yehr′) Small, rigid metal evening bag made in oval, oblong or square shapes and used to hold cosmetics. Carried in hand or by short chain. Decorated by engraved designs or set with jewels, this expensive jeweler's product gained popularity when sold by Cartier in New York. *Der.* French, *simper,* "to smirk."

mini bag Small bags that became important in the 1960s with the introduction of miniskirts. Tiny bags were introduced in all styles. Some had double and triple frames, usually with attached shoulder chains or straps.

mini-clutch bag See CLUTCH BAG.

miser's purse ∞ Small tubular purse closed at each end, with a slit in center, and two movable rings to keep money at one end or other. Carried from latter half of 17th through 19th c.

miser's purse

Constructed either by netting, knotting, or knitting and often beaded, the bags varied in size with 18th c. and Victorian period purses being larger than those of the early 19th c. Also called *wallet, ring purse, stocking purse,* or *Victorian long purse.*

Moroccan bag **1.** Tooled leather handbag made in Morocco of Moroccan leather. Decorated with elaborate designs and color combinations, such as saffron and wine. **2.** Handbag made with stitched allover design in saffron on wine-colored leather.

muff bag Basically a muff, an accessory used to keep the hands warm, frequently styled in fur. In the 1930s a zippered compartment to hold small items was added to the muff, and this became a classic item used by little girls.

newsbag TOTE BAG style (see under HANDBAGS AND RELATED ACCESSORIES) with separate section on the outside to slip in a rolled magazine or newspaper.

one-shoulder backpack See HANDBAGS AND RELATED ACCESSORIES: BACKPACK.

pannier bag (pan-yeh′) A bag with zipper compartment in the center and two open compartments on either side. A single broad handle extends from one side to the other on the outside of the bag at the middle.

pianta bag (pee-ahn′-tah) Small evening bag introduced from Italy in mid-1960s resembling a tiny umbrella made from a square of fabric with four corners folded to the center and a looped center handle.

pocketbook Originally an envelopelike container for written materials and paper money carried by men in the 17th and 18th c. Made of leather and often tooled or decorated or of silk or wool worked in colored or metal yarns. Eventually became a synonym for women's handbag.

pokey Small drawstring pouch made of sueded leather, sometimes with tiny pocket on front. Popular in the late 1960s. *Der.* Copied from a small leather bag used by '49ers to carry gold nuggets and gold dust.

pompadour bag ∞ Drawstring bag in circular or oblong shape, popular in mid-1880s, made of satin, plush, or velvet with floral embroidery heightened by edgings of gold or silver thread. *Der.* Named after Marquise de Pompadour, mistress of Louis XV of France.

porte-monnaie ∞ (port-mohn′ay) Embroidered handbag carried by women in the 1850s, made with metal frame; sometimes with chain handle, sometimes in clutch styles. *Der.* French, "purse."

pouch Basic style originally made of soft shirred leather or fabric with a drawstring closing. Now also made with a frame and handles.

pouch

purse See introduction to HANDBAGS AND RELATED ACCESSORIES.

reticule ∞ (ret-ih-kewl′) Woman's small purse made of satin, mesh, velvet, red morocco leather, and other materials. Took many shapes, e.g., shaped like an envelope, an urn, a lozenge, a circle, a shell, or a basket. Used from 19th to early 20th c. When first introduced sometimes made fun of and called a *ridicule*. Also called *indispensible, ballantine*.

reticule
19th c.

ring purse See HANDBAGS AND RELATED ACCESSORIES: MISER'S PURSE.

saddle bags Pair of soft leather bags joined to central strap handle. *Der.* From large bags thrown over horse's saddle to carry provisions.

safari bag Double-handled bag made like a small flight bag with a zippered closing. Characteristic features are the small pockets placed low on the outside of the bag. One of the most popular bags of the late 1960s and now a classic style. Also called *caravan bag*.

safari bag

Sally Jess® bag Trademarked by English designer Sally Jess, this bag was a favorite with British younger set in the 1960s. Made of fabric in simple tote design with fabric handle and two cut-out crescent sections at the top.

satchel Leather bag with a rigid flat bottom. The sides slope upward to close on metal frame hinged about halfway down the bag. Often fastened with extra snap locks and with metal reinforcements at corners. Sides are usually recessed. Handle is generally rigid and curved. Similar to a DOCTOR'S BAG (see under HANDBAGS AND RELATED ACCESSORIES).

sea bag See HANDBAGS AND RELATED ACCESSORIES: DUFFEL BAG.

shigra Handmade handbag of tote type sold to American tourists or exported to the United States from Ecuador, made from fibers taken from the leaves of the cabuya plant. Artisans use a looping system done with a needle to form distinctive patterns with natural and colored yarns. Originally used for storage of grain and flour. Made in patterns characteristic of different communities in Ecuador.

shoulder bag Handbag in any shape or size with long chain or strap to place over the shoulder. Some types of shoulder straps con-

vert to double chain handles, others may be shortened by unbuckling a section of the strap.

signature bag Handbag of leather or canvas with designer's initials or signature stenciled or printed in an allover repeat pattern. Originating with Louis Vuitton in Paris, later copied by Hermés, Saint Laurent, Mark Cross, Gucci, etc., and considered a fashion status symbol.

Vuitton©
signature bag

sovereign purse ∞ Small, round, half-inch diameter purse on a curved metal clasp for holding small coins. Carried in the 18th and 19th c.

sporran bag (spo'-an) Adaptation for women of sporran (see HIGHLAND COSTUME) as worn by the Scots Highlander. Shoulder bag is made of leather with long strands of horsehair hanging from it. The frame is metal.

squaw bag Handbag inspired by bags used by Native Americans. May be made of genuine doeskin in natural color or made of tiny geometric contrasting patches of colored leather. Most bags are trimmed with fringe. Popular handbag of the late 1960s. Also called *American Indian bag, Apache bag,* and *hippie bag*. *Der.* Name by which settlers called Native American woman.

stocking purse See HANDBAGS AND RELATED ACCESSORIES: MISER'S PURSE.

suitcase bag Handbag made of metal and shaped like a miniature suitcase complete with lock and reinforced corners.

swagger pouch Bag with double handles and two open sections on either side of zippered compartment. Classic style since the 1930s.

swinger bag See HANDBAGS AND RELATED ACCESSORIES: CONTOUR CLUTCH.

tooled leather bag Typical Western-type handbag made of natural colored cowhide with handstamped pattern. Each individual character is stamped with a metal die.

tote bag 1. Utility bag, large enough to carry small packages, sometimes with inner zippered compartment for

tote bag

H

money. Copied from shape of common paper shopping bag. Made with open top and two handles, sometimes with outside loop to hold umbrella. **2.** Any large bag with open top and two handles.

travel bag   See FLIGHT BAG.

travelling bag   ∞ Large handbag consisting of two somewhat circular pouches made of fabric fringed around the edges and joined together at the top. Used when traveling in the 1860s.

triplex/triple-framed bag   Triple-framed bag with three separate clasps. Each section is an individual compartment. Introduced in 1967, many were styled as tiny mini bags (see under HANGBAGS AND RELATED ACCESSORIES).

umbrella tote   **1.** TOTE BAG (see under HANDBAGS AND RELATED ACCESSORIES), but with a pocket at side for holding an umbrella. **2.** Bag shaped like a briefcase with a zipper around it and the umbrella attached to the side with a plastic loop. **3.** Conventional satchel-type bag with zippered compartment at bottom for umbrella.

vanity bag   Stiff-framed box-shaped bag usually fitted with a large mirror and sometimes other grooming accessories.

Victorian long purse   See HANDBAGS AND RELATED ACCESSORIES: MISER'S PURSE.

wallet   **1.** Accessory used to carry money, credit cards, and photographs. Sometimes with change purse attached and/or space for checkbook and note pad. Originally used only by men, now also used by women and children. Also called a *billfold* when designed to hold paper money, credit or other cards and photos, and made to fold in center. **2.** In 1980s smaller sizes, closed with VELCRO,® were introduced to wear on wrist, ankle, or belt, primarily when engaging in sports (e.g., jogging). **3.** See HANDBAGS AND RELATED ACCESSORIES: POCKETBOOK. **4.** See HANDBAGS AND RELATED ACCESSORIES: MISER'S PURSE.

Zouave pouch   ∞ (zoo-ahv′)   Small handbag of various shapes—sometimes rectangular, sometimes triangular—finished with tassels and hung by a hook from the waistband placed underneath the Zouave jacket. Worn by women in 1860s. *Der.* Arabic, Zouaova, a Kabyle tribe, one of the Berbers, living in Algeria or Tunisia.

---

hand-blocked print   See PRINTS, STRIPES, AND CHECKS: BLOCK PRINTING.

handcoverchief/hand cloth   See HANDKERCHIEF.

hand cuff   See CUFFS: HAND FALL.

hand fall   See CUFFS.

handkerchief   Square of cotton, linen, or silk, sometimes edged with lace or embroidered, carried and used for wiping the face or nose. Men's are usually larger than women's. Often colored for day use, they might be black or black-bordered for mourning. In 1870, plain white cambric was correct for day or evening. In 1890s, it was fashionable to wear in the cuff of the left sleeve, a practice copied from the military. Modern handkerchiefs are made in a wide variety of colors and sizes, although white predominates. Called a *napkin* in 16th c.

handkerchief dress   ∞ Dress of the 1880s with a tunic made from, or resembling, a bandanna handkerchief. Two were arranged diagonally on the front of the dress with one point reaching nearly to the hem of dress. A long-skirted jacket with shaped REVERS (see under NECKLINES AND COLLARS) and waistcoat comprised the bodice of the dress. Also see HANDKERCHIEF TUNIC.

handkerchief hem   See CLOTHING CONSTRUCTION DETAILS.

handkerchief linen   ∞ Lightweight, sheer fine fabric used for handkerchiefs and infants' wear.

handkerchief skirt   See SKIRTS.

handkerchief sleeve   See SHOULDERS AND SLEEVES.

handkerchief tunic   ∞ Dress of 1917 with peplum made from large square of fabric, like a handkerchief. Made with center opening for waist and pointed ends hanging down over skirt.

hand knitting   Knitting apparel, accessories, or trimming made entirely by hand as opposed to machine knitting.

hand-painted print   See PRINTS, STRIPES, AND CHECKS.

hand-screened print   See PRINTS, STRIPES, AND CHECKS: SILK-SCREEN PRINT.

hand sleeve   See SHOULDERS AND SLEEVES.

handspun yarn † Yarn made with different types of spindles or hand-spinning wheels—making yarn that is less regular in appearance than machine-made yarns, which adds texture and interest to the woven fabric.

hang *Colloquial* **1.** The way in which fabric drapes on the figure after it is sewn. **2.** Marking the hem of a skirt with pins or chalk so it can be straightened.

hanging sleeve See SHOULDERS AND SLEEVES.

hank See SKEIN.

hanseline See DOUBLET.

happi See SLEEPWEAR AND LOUNGEWEAR: HAPPI COAT.

happy face Stylized face made up of a yellow circle with black dots for eyes and nose and a single black line for mouth. Used on *sweatshirts,* buttons, jewelry, and in prints, since early 1970s.

hardanger embroidery See EMBROIDERIES AND SEWING STITCHES.

hard goods See SOFT GOODS.

hard hat See HEADWEAR.

Hardwick, Cathy * See APPENDIX/DESIGNERS.

hare See FURS.

harem/harem look Simulation of the costumes of the Near East primarily using full ankle-length harem pants gathered at the ankle combined with blouse and bolero or in bare-midriff effect. Sandals are generally worn; jewelry and chains complete the costume. Appeared in the late 1960s to 1980s. Also called *Arabian Nights look.* Also used as an adjective to describe apparel derived from clothing thought to have been worn by Middle Eastern women. See HAREM DRESS, PANTS: HAREM KNICKERS, PANTS: HAREM PANTS, SKIRTS: HAREM SKIRTS, and SLEEPWEAR AND LOUNGE-WEAR: HAREM PAJAMAS.

harem dress Symmetrically or asymmetrically draped dress falling in loose folds to the hem where it is turned under and fastened to a lining giving the hem a draped appearance. Usually made of soft, clinging fabric. In styles of the early 20th c., often made as a harem

harem dress 1913

skirt worn under a tunic overskirt. *Der.* An adaptation of Middle Eastern dress introduced by Paris designers Paul Poiret and Drécoll in 1910 and revived at intervals.

harlequin (hahr'-leh-kwin) **1.** Traditional theatrical costume made of varicolored diamond-shaped patches on tunic and tights, a flaring brimmed black BICORNE hat (see under HEADWEAR) decorated with pompons, and a black mask. **2.** See PRINTS, STRIPES, AND CHECKS. **3.** See EYEGLASSES. **4.** See HEAD-WEAR. *Der.* From *Harlequin,* a part played by an actor in 16th to 18th c. Italian performances called *commedia dell'arte.* **5.** See PRINTS, STRIPES, AND CHECKS: HARLEQUIN CHECK.

harlequin #1

harlequin opal See GEMS, GEM CUTS, AND SETTINGS.

harlot/herlot ∞ Garment, similar to tights, worn by men in England in the late 14th c. Stockings and pants were made in one piece and tied to the upper and outer garments by strings known as points.

Harlow, Jean See HARLOW LOOK.

Harlow look Adaptation of styles of late 1920s and early 1930s including bias-cut dresses, wide-legged cuffed trousers for women, shoes, and slippers of this era. These styles were revived in the 1960s. See FOOTWEAR: HARLOW PUMP and HARLOW SLIPPER, and PANTS: HARLOW PANTS. *Der.* Named for Jean Harlow, platinum blonde Hollywood star of the late 1920s and 1930s who wore such styles on and off the screen.

Harper's Bazaar Womens' fashion magazine that started in 1867 as a weekly tabloid-style newspaper containing many fashion engravings. It became a monthly magazine in 1901 and was bought by William Randolph Hearst in 1913. Among its best-known editors were Edna Woolman Chase, Carmel Snow, and Diana Vreeland.

harp seal See FURS: HAIR SEAL.

Harris Tweed® Trademark of Harris Tweed Association for tweed fabric. Defined by the British Board of Trade and Federal Trade Commission as handwoven woolen fabric from the Hebrides Islands, off the coast of Scotland, consisting of Harris, Lewis, Uist, Barra, and other smaller islands. There are two types a) made from hand-spun yarn, and b) made from machine-made yarn. Used mainly for women's coats styled in a classic manner.

Hartnell, Sir Norman * See APPENDIX/DESIGNERS.

harvest hat See HEADWEAR.

hasp See CLOSURES.

hat See HEADWEAR.

hatband Decoration, usually of ribbon, around the base of the crown of a hat. In former years, men wore black hatbands for mourning.

hatbox **1.** Initially a circular-shaped item of luggage with a strap handle and flat bottom that was originally made to carry large hats in the 1920s. Now carried by fashion models or used by stores when selling a hat. These boxes may be round, oval, hexagonal, or square in shape. **2.** See BANDBOX.

hatbox bag See HANDBAGS AND RELATED ACCESSORIES.

hat cap See HEADWEAR.

hat mask See MASKS.

hat pin See HEADWEAR.

hauberk See ARMOR.

haunseleyns See DOUBLET.

hausse-cul See BUM ROLL.

haut de chausses See CHAUSSES.

haute couture (oat koo′-toor) **1.** As defined by the CHAMBRE SYNDICALE DE LA PARISIENNE, firms that create models that may be sold to private customers or to other segments of the fashion industry who also acquire the right to reproduce the designs. Designers show at least two collections a year of original designs to the public. An **original design** is not the only one of its kind, but means only that the garment was designed and made in the atelier of the designer. **2.** As currently used in the United States and in the fashion press, refers to the latest and most advanced fashions; high fashion.

haut ton See UNDERGARMENTS.

havelock See HEADWEAR.

havelock cap See HEADWEAR: AUTOMOBILE CAP.

Hawaiian shirt See SHIRTS.

Hawes, Elizabeth (1903–1971) American designer and an author who is best known for her autobiography *Fashion Is Spinach,* which provided insights about the construction of clothing as done by a Parisian couture house.

headband See HEADWEAR.

head cloth See HEADWEAR: KERCHIEF.

headdress Synonym for HEADWEAR.

heading See CLOTHING CONSTRUCTION DETAILS.

head rail See HEADWEAR: KERCHIEF.

HEADWEAR

headwear Covering for the head, a *headcovering.* Headwear may be decorative or utilitarian or both. It may also serve as a symbol of status, e.g., a CROWN (see under HEADWEAR). The category of headwear is often divided among different-named types of headwear. The definitions of types of headwear are found under the category of HEADWEAR in the following entries: BONNET, CAP, HAT, HELMET, VEIL. It is often difficult to assign a head covering to one type, so individually named items each have a separate entry. The components of bonnets, caps, hats, and helmets generally include the **brim,** which is the rim of hat and may be narrow to wide—worn level, turned down, up, or to a variety of angles, and the **crown,** which is the portion that covers the top of the head.

poke-type bonnet

almuce ∞ (al′-mus) A cowl-like hood, frequently of fur or fur-lined, introduced in the 13th c., when it was worn by the clergy for church services in inclement weather.

Alpine hat Various types of hats adapted from Bavarian and Austrian Tyrolean hats. **1.** One contemporary version for men is of fur felt, with a slight PILE, a slightly peaked crown with a crease in the center, and an upturned brim in the back. Popular since 1940s as a man's sport hat, it was first introduced in the late 1890s. Also called a *Tyrolean hat.* **2.** ∞ Woman's hat with high crown and medium-sized brim worn in

alpine hat #1

1890s. *Der.* Named for alpine Tyrol region in Austria and Bavaria where this type hat is worn by natives.

American Indian headband Narrow band of leather, fabric, or beadwork placed low on the forehead and tied at side or back, sometimes with feather in back, worn by American Indians and adopted by HIPPIES in the 1960s.

anglesea hat ∞ (angle-see′) Man's hat with flat brim and high cylindrical-shaped crown, worn about 1830.

Angoulême bonnet ∞ (ahn-goo′-lem) Straw bonnet of 1814 made with high pleated crown, broad front brim narrowed at sides, and tied with bow at side. Worn by women in French Empire period, and named for Duchesse d'Angoulême, daughter of Marie Antoinette.

apex ∞ Originally, the spike of olive wood on the peak of a cap worn by a Roman *flamen*, a priest of some particular deity. Later the entire cap was known by this name.

applejack cap See HEADWEAR: NEWSBOY CAP.

army cap Caps worn by U.S. Army. See HEADWEAR: FATIGUE, OVERSEAS and SERVICE CAPS.

astronaut's cap Cap similar to a BASEBALL CAP (see under HEADWEAR) with elaborately embroidered gold braid on visor, band of gold braid around edge of crown, gold button on top of crown, and adjustable back strap. Copied from caps worn by astronauts and World War II naval commanders, the gold braid is sometimes facetiously called "scrambled eggs." Also called *commander's cap* and *flight deck cap.*

atef ∞ Headdress consisting of tall white cap with two plumes, or feathers, arranged at the sides. Symbolic headdress of certain Egyptian gods, particularly Osiris, also depicted as worn by Egyptian kings.

atours ∞ (a-toor′) Padded, horned headdress worn by women in 14th and 15th c.

attifet ∞ (at-tee′-fet) Woman's headdress of 16th c. arched on either side of forehead to form a "widow's peak" and draped completely with a veil as seen in paintings of Mary Stuart, Queen of Scots. Also see MARIE STUART BONNET.

attifet 16th c.

attire ∞ Used since the 15th c. for woman's headdress of gold and gems worn on state occasions, later shortened to *tire.*

automobile cap ∞ Cap and hood of waterproof fabric worn by women for automobile riding in early 1900s that consisted of a flat-topped cap with brim rolled down in front and up in back, worn over a tight-fitting hood exposing only the face. Also see HEADWEAR: HAVELOCK CAP.

automobile veil ∞ Wide, sheer, long veil placed over wide-brimmed hat and tied under chin with ends flowing over front of duster; worn for motoring in early 1900s. Most often made of gauze or chiffon. Also called *motoring veil.*

aviator's helmet **1.** helmet made of high-impact plastic, sometimes fitted with an oxygen mask, worn by a pilot and crew of planes flying at high altitudes. **2.** ∞ World War I helmet fitting the head snugly and fastened under the chin. Made of leather with wool or shearling lining for warmth. Goggles were worn on top. Also called *Red Baron helmet* after a famous World War I ace.

babet bonnet/babet cap ∞ **1.** Small cap for evening worn by women in 1838. Usually made with wide side frills and flattened top, sometimes of tulle. **2.** Woman's morning cap of muslin with ribbon trimming, covering ears and part of cheeks; worn from 1836 to 1840s.

baby bonnet Infant's cap, often made of batiste and lavishly trimmed with lace and ribbons, that is fitted to shape of head and tied under chin.

baby Stuart cap ∞ Classic type of infant's close-fitting cap with narrow chin band, illustrated in portrait of Charles II painted by Van Dyck in 1634.

bag bonnet ∞ Woman's bonnet with soft crown fitted loosely over back of head, worn in early 19th c.

bag cap ∞ Man's cloth cap, sometimes made of velvet, shaped like a turban, trimmed with fur or ornamental band; worn in 14th and 15th c.

bagnolette ∞ (ban′-yo-let) Woman's wired hood standing away from face, covering shoulder; worn in 18th c.

H

balaclava (bal-ah-kla'-vah) Hood covering the head and shoulders exposing the face, made of knitted wool. Worn by soldiers in 1890s and in World War I and II in cold weather. Now worn by mountain climbers and skiers. *Der.* Named for Crimean War, Battle of Balaklava, fought October 25, 1854.

balaclava

balloon hat ∞ Woman's hat with wide brim and large puffed-out crown, of gauze over a wire or straw foundation. Fashionable from 1783 to 1785. Inspired by balloon flight of Lunardi. Also called *Lunardi hat* and *parachute hat*.

Balmoral cap/bonnet Flat Scottish beret somewhat similar to a TAM-O-SHANTER (see HEADWEAR: TAM) with wide checked band around head. Usually dark blue with a red or blue pompon on top, with feather and badge of the clan on one side. Worn with *kilts* in Scotland.

bambin/bambino hat (bam-been) Woman's hat with a halo-shaped brim rolling away from the face, worn in the 1930s.

bandeau (band-oh') Narrow piece of ribbon or fabric, sometimes decorated, worn around head as substitute for a hat.

bandore and peak ∞ Widow's black headdress with heart-shaped brim and black veil, draped in back; worn from 1700 to about 1830.

barbe ∞ Long piece of white linen fabric, pleated vertically, worn encircling the chin with a black hood and long black veil by widows and mourners from 14th to 16th c.

barbette/barbet (bar-bet') Used in the 13th and first half of 14th c. for the linen chin band worn pinned on the top, or sides, of the head, and worn with a small white fillet or COVERCHIEF (see under HEADWEAR). The barbette and coverchief formed the wimple (see under HEADWEAR: WIMPLE #1) in France.

barrette (ba-ret) **1.** ∞ Brimless hat with round flat top worn by Jewish men and boys. Clement VII on June 13, 1525, ordered all Jews to wear a yellow barrette. Later revoked, but Pope Paul IV in 1555 ordered all Jews to wear a green barrette. Same style worn for synagogue dress until early 19th c. by Jewish men.

Also spelled *beret*. **2.** See CLERICAL DRESS: BIRETTA #2.

baseball cap Cap with dome-shaped crown, sometimes made with alternate panels of nylon net for coolness, and an adjustable band or elastic at the back. May have any type of "patch," slogan, or picture on front, e.g, major league football, baseball and Little League team names, makes of cars or trucks, sports insignia, soft-drink brands, cartoon characters, and the like. When first introduced, cap fit more closely to the head like a skullcap. In the 1990s wearing these caps backward became a fad among the young. Also see HEADWEAR: BATTER'S CAP.

baseball cap

basket ∞ Woman's hat resembling a wicker basket, 1½' high; worn in second half of 16th c.

basque beret See HEADWEAR: BERET #1.

bathing cap Tight-fitting cap made of rubber or ELASTOMERS, with or without strap under chin. May be elaborately decorated with rubber flowers, fringe, or other trimmings. Worn to protect hair while swimming.

battant l'oeil ∞ (bah-tan' loy) Woman's cap, worn in 1770s, with sides projecting forward over temples, eyes, and cheeks in exaggerated fashion.

batter's cap/batter's helmet Duck-bill visored cap with hard crown for protection worn by baseball players when taking turn at bat.

bavolet ∞ (ba-vo'-lay) A ruffle or piece of cloth extended down from the back of woman's bonnet to shade the neck, worn from 1830 on.

beach hat Hat used as a sunshade on the beach or at a resort, usually made of bright-colored straw, either natural or synthetic, in a variety of shapes. Frequently has a wide brim, conical crown, and sometimes decorated with felt, sequins, or shells.

beanie See HEADWEAR: SKULLCAP.

bearskin cap Tall cylindrical cap of black bearskin with a chain or strap under lower lip or the chin. Worn by some personnel of the British army, also by military guards of Buckingham Place in London and Parliament buildings in

Ottawa, Canada. Also see HEADWEAR: DRUM MAJOR'S HAT.

beaver hat 1. ∞ Hat worn from 14th c. by men and women. Originally made of beaver skins, later with beaver-hair nap felted over wool and rabbit hair base. Also see HEADWEAR: CASTOR. **2.** Man's tall hat made of silk in imitation of beaver fur, fashionable in 17th and 18th c. In the 19th c. called *silk hat, opera hat,* and *top hat.*

bebe bonnet ∞ Tiny outdoor bonnet of 1877 trimmed with ribbons, flowers, and tulle worn with brim turned up showing a cap underneath.

bebop cap See HEADWEAR: NEWSBOY CAP.

becca See HEADWEAR: ROUNDLET.

beefeater's hat Distinctive hat worn by Yeomen of the Guard in England, consisting of a narrow brim and soft high crown pleated into headband with crown flaring slightly at the top. Also see BEEFEATER'S UNIFORM.

beehive hat 1. ∞ Woman's hat with large bubble-shaped crown and narrow brim trimmed with ribbon tied under chin; worn in 1770s and 1780s. Also called *hive bonnet.* **2.** Same style decorated to look like a beehive and fashionable about 1910.

beguin ∞ (bay-gan') Early 16th-c. headdress made from stiffened rectangle of white linen creased in center over the forehead and draped to form a heart-shaped opening for the face. The back was caught together at nape of neck and remainder was folded symmetrically to form a wide streamer that hung from top of head down the back. *Der.* French, *beguine,* "nun." Also called a *Flemish hood.*

bellboy/bellhop cap Small fabric pillbox, often trimmed with gold braid, sometimes with chin strap, worn by hotel or restaurant bellboys.

benjy ∞ British slang term for straw hat with a wide brim.

beret (beh-ray') General name given to a round, flat hat, usually synonymous with tam (see under HEADWEAR). Some specific types include. **1. basque beret** (bask beh-ray') Round, flat, soft woolen

French or pancake beret

cap worn by Basque peasants who inhabit the western Pyrenees region of France and Spain. **2. pancake beret** Flat molded felt tam. Worn tilted to one side of the head and associated with the dress of an artist. Also called a *French beret.* **3. bubble beret** Large bouffant beret, usually without a brim, worn tilted to side of head in the early 1960s. **4.** ∞ A headcovering with a large flat halo crown with elaborate trim, worn from the 1820s to the 1840s.

bergère hat (ber-zher') Woman's straw hat with low crown and a wide floppy-type brim, sometimes tied under chin. Worn from 1730 to 1800, revived in 1860s and currently used to describe similar hats. Worn by Marie Antoinette (1755–1793), wife of Louis XVI of France, when she played at farming on the grounds of the palace at Versailles. Also called *milkmaid hat* or *shepherdess hat. Der.* French, "shepherdess."

bergère hat

berretino See HEADWEAR: ROUNDLET #1.

Bewdley cap See HEADWEAR: MONMOUTH CAP.

bibi bonnet ∞ (bee-bee bun-neh) Small woman's bonnet worn in 1830s with sides flaring upward and forward around the face and tied with lace-trimmed ribbons. Also called *English cottage bonnet.*

bicorne/bicorn ∞ (by'-korn) Man's hat of the Napoleonic era in shape of a crescent, with front and back brims pressed against each other, making points on either side. Frequently trimmed with a COCKADE. *Der.* Latin, *bicornis,* "two-horned."

bicorne

bicycle-clip hat Tiny half-hat fastened over crown and side of head by piece of springy metal. Often used for a child's hat of fur. *Der.* From metal clip worn around leg when riding a bicycle to keep trousers from catching in chain or wheel spokes.

bicycle helmet Helmet not covering the ears, with dark adjustable visor and air inlets for ventilating and cooling, held on by a strap under the chin. Shell is high-impact PVC plastic lined with polystyrene, and foam-lined for comfort.

H

biggin/biggonet/biggon ∞ (big-in/big-on-net) **1.** 16th- and 17th-c. term for woman's or child's cap similar to COIF (see under HEADWEAR). **2.** Man's nightcap, worn from second half of 16th through 17th c. **3.** Large MOB CAP (see under HEADWEAR). Made without chin ties, worn in early 19th c. *Der.* French, *beguine*, "nun."

bill See HEADWEAR: VISOR.

billiment/billment ∞ (bee-leh-mahn′) **1.** 16th-c. term for the decorative jeweled border on French hoods, sometimes made by goldsmiths. **2.** Head ornament worn by brides in 16th c. Also called *habillement (habiliment), abillements,* or *borders.*

billycock/billicock ∞ 19th-c. colloquial term for man's soft, wide, curved-brimmed hat with low crown. *Der.* From either (1) bully-cocked hat of 18th c., or (2) hat first worn by Mr. William (Billy) Coke for shooting parties at Holkham, England.

bird cage Dome of stiff wide-mesh veiling pinned to crown of head covering face and ears. Worn in place of hat, especially in late 1950s.

biretta (bih-ret′-ah) **1.** See CLERICAL DRESS. **2.** 16th-c. round cap that later became square on top when hatters learned to use a rigid frame. Worn by clergy today. Also called *barrette.* Also spelled *birretta, berrette.*

birlet See HEADWEAR: BOURRELET.

bluebonnet Small-sized Scotch TAM (see under HEADWEAR), of blue wool with narrow TARTAN (see PLAIDS AND TARTANS) band fitting around head, black streamers in back, and colored pompon on top. Originally made in leather for protection when fighting. Also called *bonaid. Der.* Scottish, "bonnet."

boater **1.** Man's flattopped flat-brimmed straw hat with an oval 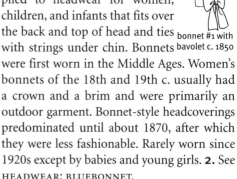 crown, worn from 1880s to 1930s. Introduced about 1865 for children, later adopted by women. The **Henley boater,** popular since 1894, was a blue or gray felt hat of similar shape, named for Henley-on-Thames, England, site of boat races. Used for summer wear until about 1930. Also called *canotier.*

boater #1

2. Style copied in plastic for wear at political conventions.

bobby's hat Hat with domed high crown and narrow turned-down brim worn by English policemen. *Der.* From slang British term "bobbies," meaning policemen.

bolero toque ∞ (bow-ler′-oh toke) Woman's small draped hat of fabric or fur, with black trimming extending up over the crown, worn in 1887.

bollinger ∞ Man's hat, worn from 1858 to late 1860s, having bowl-shaped crown with knob in center and narrow circular brim. First worn by British cab drivers, later adopted by gentlemen for country wear. Also called *hemispherical hat.*

bonaid See HEADWEAR: BLUEBONNET.

bongrace ∞ (bohn-gras′) **1.** Stiffened oblong woman's head-covering with drapery in back; worn in 16th and early 17th c. over a coif. **2.** Pendant flap in back of French hood, which was brought up over crown and fastened so as to project forward over forehead. Also called *burn grace.*

bongrace #1

bonnet **1.** Sometimes used as a generic term for headcovering, however is more specifically applied to headwear for women, children, and infants that fits over the back and top of head and ties with strings under chin. Bonnets were first worn in the Middle Ages. Women's bonnets of the 18th and 19th c. usually had a crown and a brim and were primarily an outdoor garment. Bonnet-style headcoverings predominated until about 1870, after which they were less fashionable. Rarely worn since 1920s except by babies and young girls. **2.** See HEADWEAR: BLUEBONNET.

bonnet #1 with bavolet c. 1850

bonnet à bec ∞ (bon-neh′ ah beck) Woman's early 18th-c. bonnet that covered top of head and had a peak over the forehead. Lower edge touching the hair was called the *papillon.* Also called *bonnet en papillon* (bon-neh′ on pah-pee′-yon).

bonnet babet See HEADWEAR: BABET BONNET.

H

bonnet en papillon See HEADWEAR: BONNET À BEC.

bonnet rouge ∞ (bon-neh′ rooje) Red wool peaked-top cap, symbol of liberty, worn by patriots in French Revolution of late 18th c. *Der.* French, "red bonnet." Also called *liberty cap*.

bosses ∞ Decorative snoods of gold or linen covering thick coils of braided hair arranged at each side of face with a coverchief, or veil, over entire headdress. Worn from late 13th to end of 14th c. **Templers** were a 15th c. style of ornamental bosses that conceal the hair. Sometimes connected by band above forehead, sometimes part of headdress. Also spelled *templettes, temples.*

boudoir cap ∞ (boo′-dwar) Soft lace-trimmed cap with gathered crown and ruffled edge worn over woman's hair in bedroom in 19th and early 20th c.

Bourbon hat ∞ (boor′-bon) Blue satin hat decorated with pearls in a fleur-de-lis pattern. Popular in 1815 to celebrate Napoleon's defeat at Waterloo and return of King Louis XVIII, a member of the Bourbon royal family, to the throne.

bourrelet ∞ (boor′-lay) 15th-c. term for padded sausage-shaped roll worn by men and women for headdress, or as base of headdress. Also spelled *birlet, burlet.*

bourrelet 15ᵗʰ c.

bowler See HEADWEAR: DERBY.

breton (breh′-ton) Woman's off-the-face hat made with medium-sized rolled-back brim worn on back of head. Copied from hats worn by peasants of Brittany, France.

breton

bridal veil Traditionally a length of white net, lace, tulle, or silk illusion reaching to waist, hips, ankles, or floor in back. Chest length in front and worn over face during wedding—turned back after ceremony.

brim See in introduction to category: HEADWEAR.

broadbrim ∞ Wide-brimmed, low-crowned hat worn by members of the Society of Friends, called Quakers. "Broadbrim" therefore became a nickname for Quakers.

brow band Ribbon, fabric, beaded band, or braid of hair around head worn low on forehead.

bubble beret See HEADWEAR: BERET #3.

bubble hat Puffed-out felt or straw hat, usually stiff rather than soft, made with tiny brim in early 1960s. Worn perched on top of head over bouffant hairstyles. Also called a *dome hat.*

bucket hat Casual hat made of fabric that has moderate-sized, sloping brim that may be stitched in concentric circles and is attached to flattopped, slightly cone-shaped crown.

bully-cocked See HEADWEAR: COCKED HAT.

bumper **1.** ∞ Cap worn in the Netherlands by children, fitted at back of head, with wide thick roll of yarn around the face for protection. Also see child's PUDDING under HEADWEAR. **2.** Hat with a BUMPER BRIM (see under HEADWEAR).

bumper brim Thick rolled-back brim, surrounding various styles of crowns. Used in various widths on different styles of hats.

burlet See HEADWEAR: BOURRELET.

burnet/burnette ∞ 17th-c. hood or headdress.

burngrace See HEADWEAR: BONGRACE.

busby Tall cylindrical black fur or feathered military hat with cockade at top of center front. A bag-shaped drapery hangs from crown and is draped to the back. Worn by Hussars and certain guardsmen in the British army.

bush hat Large-brimmed Australian-type hat worn turned up on one side. Worn in Australia and in Africa for safaris, also worn as part of uniform by Australian soldiers in World War II. Also called *caddie or caddy.*

bush hat

bustle back Puffs of ribbon or bows at back of hat, popular in 1930s.

butterfly cap ∞ Woman's small lace cap wired in shape of a butterfly, worn perched above forehead with lappets, jewels, and flower trimmings frequently added for court wear. Worn in 1750s and 1760s. Also called *fly cap.*

H

butterfly headdress ∞ 16th-c. term for a 15th-c. towering head-dress made of sheer gauze wired to stand out like wings, and supported by a fez-shaped cap. Worn after this period by an order of nuns in Normandy, France.

butterfly headdress

bycocket/bycoket **1.** ∞ High-crowned hat with a wide brim peaked in front, and turned up in back worn by men in the Middle Ages. **2.** Similar hat called a *student bycocket* worn by Italian students in mid-20th c.

cabas (kah-bas′) Version of Phrygian cap (see under HEADWEAR), made of beaver or velour, draped across forehead to conceal hair and ornamented in back. Created by New York milliner Sally Victor in 1956.

cabriole headdress ∞ (kab′-ree-oll) Rare fashion of about 1755, lasting only a few years, consisting of a miniature coach-and-six, or post chaise, worn by women on head instead of a cap. Coach was made of gold thread with six dappled gray horses made of blown glass. Also spelled *caprioll*. *Der.* French, "two-wheeled carriage."

cabriolet bonnet ∞ (kab-ree-o-leh′) Large bonnet, popular from the late 18th to mid-19th c., made with brim extending forward framing the face like a carriage top, but cut away in back to show hair. *Der.* French, "two-wheeled carriage."

cache-peigne ∞ (cash payn) Snood of net and ribbon worn by women to hold hair back, in the 1850s and 1860s. *Der.* French, "hide-comb."

caddie/caddy See HEADWEAR: BUSH HAT.

cadogan net See HEADWEAR: SNOOD.

cake hat ∞ Man's soft felt hat of 1890s with a low oval crown creased in manner similar to Alpine hat (see under HEADWEAR).

calash/calèche ∞ (ka-lash′) Large hood worn from 1720 to 1790 and revived 1820 to 1839, made with hinged arches of whalebone or cane covered with fabric in manner similar to folding top of convertible car. Stands away from head, protecting bouffant hairstyles. *Der.* After hood of "French carriage" called *calèche*.

calash

calotte (ca-lot′) **1.** A SKULLCAP (see under HEADWEAR) frequently made of leather or suede with a small matching projection like a stem on center top. **2.** See CLERICAL DRESS. **3.** Woman's small skullcap worn in 1940s and 1950s, sometimes with large jeweled pin. **4.** A cap worn by schoolboy, called a beanie (see HEADWEAR: SKULLCAP).

camargo hat ∞ (kam-are′-go) Small woman's evening hat with brim raised in front; worn in mid-1830s. *Der.* After Marie Ann de Cupis Camargo (1710–1770), celebrated dancer.

camelaurion ∞ (kamel-loh′-ree-yon) Coronet with closed crown, worn by Roman Caesars and by Byzantine emperors.

campaign hat Broad-brimmed field hat with high crown first worn by Union soldiers in Civil War and later issued to entire U.S. army. Worn by soldiers in World War II with four dents in top of crown. Same as Mountie's hat (see under HEADWEAR).

canotier See HEADWEAR: BOATER.

cap Head covering fitting more snugly to the head than a hat, frequently made with a visor-type front. Usually made of felt, leather, or fabric and worn for sports or informal occasions. In the 16th c., caps were worn by servants and apprentices; in the 19th c., gentlemen began to wear caps in the country or for sports, but not in town. From 1500 to 19th c., ladies wore caps indoors. After the mid-19th c., indoor caps were worn only by female servants and the elderly. See HEADWEAR: DAY CAP. *Der.* Latin, *cappa*, "a hooded cloak."

cap

cape hat Woman's half-hat made by attaching felt or fabric capelet to a springy metal clip that crosses the head from ear to ear, letting capelet fall over back of head.

capeline (cap-leen′) **1.** See ARMOR. **2.** ∞ Second half of 18th c. woman's feather-trimmed wide-brimmed hat. **3.** ∞ Hood with attached cape worn in 1863 by women in rural areas. **4.** Wide floppy brimmed hat with small round crown worn since 1920s.

cap of maintenance Cap carried on a cushion before British sovereigns in coronation processions; sometimes used for mayors. Usually

H

made of scarlet velvet with ermine trim and symbolizing high rank. Also called *cap of dignity* and *cap of estate.*

capote ∞ (kah-poat′)   Popular bonnet of 1830s with stiff brim framing the face, soft gathered crown, and ribbon bows tied at side or under chin. By 1890, worn mostly by older women.

capot-ribot ∞ (ka-poh′ ree′-bow)   Black velvet hat with long "curtain" (or veil), hanging below shoulders at sides and back. Popular in France after Napoleonic campaign in 1798.

capuche ∞ (cap-poosh′)   **1.** Sharp-pointed, pyramid-shaped hood worn by an order of monks, the Capuchins. **2.** See HEADWEAR: CAPUCHIN. **3.** Woman's hood attached to cloak worn in 17th c. **4.** Woman's silk-lined sunbonnet of mid-19th c.

Capuchin ∞ (kap′-yoo-shen)   **1.** Hood worn outdoors in 16th, 17th, and 18th c. **2.** Hood and shoulder cape or long cloak, sometimes lined in colored or striped silk, called a *redingote* (red′-in-gote), worn by women in 18th c. for traveling. *Der.* From *capuche,* "cowl worn by Capuchin monks of Franciscan order." Also spelled *capuchon, capucine, capuche.*

capuchon ∞ (ka-poo-shon′)   **1.** See HEADWEAR: CAPUCHIN. **2.** Tiny bonnet made of flowers. Worn in 1877.

Capulet (cap-yew-let′)   Small hat conforming to shape of head and placed back from brow, sometimes with cuffed brim in front. *Der.* For cap worn by Juliet Capulet, heroine of Shakespeare's play *Romeo and Juliet.*

caravan ∞   Small type of collapsible bonnet of 1765 similar to the CALASH (see under HEADWEAR). Made of semicircular hoops that, when opened, drop a veil of white gauze over the face.

Carnaby cap   See HEADWEAR: NEWSBOY CAP.

Caroline hat ∞ Man's hat made of Caroline beaver, imported from Carolinas in the British Colonies, worn in England from 1680s to mid-18th c.

cartwheel hat   Woman's hat with extra wide stiff brim and low crown frequently made of straw.

casque (cask)   Hat shaped like a helmet. *Der.* French, "helmet."

cartwheel hat

casquette ∞ (kass-ket′)   **1.** Cap with visor, similar to military officers' caps, adapted for women's headwear. **2.** Woman's straw cap worn in 1863 and 1864 similar to a GLENGARRY (see under HEADWEAR) with additional short brim front and back. Trimmed with black velvet ribbon and ostrich feathers.

castor ∞ Hat made entirely of beaver fur popular in 17th and 19th c. If rabbit fur was added, it was called a **demi-castor.** The 17th-c. trade term for a man's castor hat in the 17th century was **codovec.**

cater cap ∞ (kay-ter)   Used in 16th and 17th c. to describe a square cap worn at universities, now called *mortarboard.* See ACADEMIC COSTUME.

caudebec ∞ (kawd′-ee-bek)   An imitation beaver hat made of felt worn from end of 17th throughout 18th c. Also called *cawdebink* or *cordybeck hat.*

caul ∞ (kol)   **1.** Mesh cap that encloses the hair and is often the work of a goldsmith. Frequently called a *fret* in medieval times. Also see HEADWEAR: BOSSES and CRISPINE. Usually worn by unmarried girls and by women of high status during the medieval period. **2.** See WIGS AND HAIRPIECES. **3.** In 18th and 19th c. used to describe soft crown of bonnet or cap.

caul #1

cavalier hat   **1.** A wide-brimmed velvet hat trimmed with ostrich plumes. **2.** Brimmed hat with one side turned up worn by Theodore Roosevelt and his Rough Riders in Spanish American War.

ceryphalos ∞ (ser-rif-ah′-los)   Wide head band or fillet worn by women in ancient Greece.

chaffers   See HEADWEAR: ENGLISH HOOD.

chain hat   Decorative close-fitting cap made with lengths of chain—some linked together, others dangling. Decorative item of body jewelry introduced in the late 1960s.

chapeau (cha-po′)   French word meaning hat or cap.

chapeau à la Charlotte   See HEADWEAR: CHARLOTTE.

chapeau bras ∞ (sha-po′ bra)   **1.** Man's flat three-cornered hat, evenly COCKED (see under

HEADWEAR) or crescent-shaped, made expressly to be carried under arm; from 1760s to 1830s in France, England, and United States. By 1830, generally called *broken hat.* Also see HEADWEAR: OPERA HAT. **2.** Woman's crush bonnet, or CALASH (see under HEADWEAR), that folded small enough to be carried in handbag or under the arm. Worn to concerts and opera in early 19th c. England. *Der.* French, "arm-hat."

chapeau claque (sha-po′ klack) See HEADWEAR: OPERA HAT.

chapeau cloche ∞ Small crowned hat with wide drooping brim worn by women in 1860s to protect face from the sun.

chapel cap Small round cap that fits on the back of the head, sometimes lace-trimmed, matched to choir robes, and worn by women of choir for church services.

chapel cap/chapel veil Small circle of lace or tulle, frequently edged with a ruffle, worn by women over top of head while inside a church.

chaperon ∞ (shap′-er-ohn) **1.** Used as general designation for a hood during the Middle Ages. Worn largely by men but also occasionally by working-class women. **2.** Anglo-French term for a fitted hood cut in one with a shoulder cape (called a *gole, collet, gorget,* or *guleron*), which was worn from the late 12th c. until the mid-15th c. The hood had a long pendant tail called a **liripipe** (lir′-ee-peep) in 14th c.

chaperon #2
with liripipe

3. Draped version of the chaperon popular in the 15th c. in which the cape was rolled and tied with the extended tail of the hood to form a turbanlike headress. **4.** Woman's soft hood in the 17th c. Also spelled *chaperone, chaperonne.* Also called *cappuccio.*

chaplet **1.** ∞ Originally a garland of flowers for the head worn by Anglo-Saxon men and women on festive occasions. **2.** In 15th c. such a garland was worn only by a bride. **3.** Circlet, or metal band set with gems, worn by both men and women in 14th, 15th, and 16th c. Also called a *coronal of goldsmithry.* **4.** In late 14th and 15th cs., a headband of twisted silk or satin wound around a padded roll. **5.** 17th-c. term used for a short rosary or set of beads worn on the neck.

Charlotte ∞ Very large brimmed hat with lace ruffle at edge, worn drooping over forehead, sometimes worn over a lacy cap. Crown richly decorated with wide loops and bows of ribbon. Worn in mid-1780s. *Der.* Named for Queen Charlotte of England (1744–1818), married to George III of England. Style later returned to popularity somewhat modified in late 19th and early 20th cs. Both styles also called *chapeau à la Charlotte.*

Charlotte Corday cap ∞ Indoor cap worn in daytime in 1870s, made with puffed muslin crown gathered into a band, sometimes had a ruffle around edge, sometimes with lappets. *Der.* Named for Charlotte Corday, who assassinated Marat, a leader of the French Revolution.

chechia Adaptation for women in the late 1930s and early 1940s of a felt hat with a tassel—similar to a fez but more peaked in shape—that was worn by Algerian and Moroccan children.

cheek wrappers See HEADWEAR: DORMEUSE.

chef's hat Tall, white full-crowned fabric hat starched to stand up stiffly. Set into the headband with 100 pleats, which originally indicated that the chef could cook eggs 100 ways. Also called *hundred pleater.* The more important the chef—the taller the hat.

chignon cap Small cap made in a variety of colors and fabrics worn over the chignon in the 1930s and 1940s. Popular again in the 1960s and 1970s—usually made of crocheted wool—and called a *bun-warmer* or *bun snood.*

chignon strap Band of ribbon fastened to woman's hat that passes around back of head and under the chignon to hold hat firmly. Worn in the 1860s and 1870s, again in the 1940s and 1950s.

chimney pot hat See HEADWEAR: TOP HAT.

chin stays ∞ Term used in 1830s for ruffles of tulle or lace added to bonnet strings forming a frill when tied under chin. Synonym: *mentonnieres* (men-ton-yehr′).

chip bonnet ∞ Coarse, inexpensive straw bonnet made of strips or shavings of wood, or

H

woody material, imported from Italy and used for millinery in the 19th c.

chou (shoo) **choux** (*pl.*) Soft, crushed-crown hat similar to MOBCAP (see under HEADWEAR). *Der.* French, "cabbage."

chukka hat (chuh´-ka) Domed hat with small brim copied from hats worn by polo players. Similar to, but not as high as, English policeman's hat. *Der.* Named for divisions of polo game called chukkars.

circumfolding hat See HEADWEAR: OPERA HAT.

claque See HEADWEAR: OPERA HAT.

Clara Bow hat ∞ Trademark for various styles of felt hats for women in late 1920s. The beret and cloche styles were the most popular. *Der.* Named after *Clara Bow,* famous movie star of the 1920s.

Clarissa Harlowe bonnet/hat ∞ Pictured in 1857 as a wide-brimmed, lace-trimmed hat with drooping sides and a small rounded crown with large ostrich plume placed so it curved from the crown over the back brim of hat. In 1879, described as a bonnet made of leghorn straw (see HEADWEAR: LEGHORN HAT) with a large brim lined with velvet, worn tilted on the forehead—popular until 1890s. *Der.* From heroine in novel *Clarissa, or the History of a Young Lady,* by Samuel Richardson, published in 1747–48.

clip hat See HEADWEAR: BICYCLE-CLIP HAT.

cloche (klohsh) Deep-crowned hat with very narrow brim or brimless, fitting head closely, almost concealing all of the hair. Worn pulled down almost to eyebrows, fashionable in 1920s and again in 1960s. *Der.* French, "bell."

cloche

coal-scuttle bonnet ∞ Bonnet of mid-19th c. with a large, stiff brim with peak in center front. *Der.* Shaped like the scoop called a scuttle that was used to pick up coal and put it into the fire.

cocked hat ∞ **1.** Man's hat worn from late 17th to early 19th c. with wide brim. To avoid weather sag and deterioration, it became the fashion to turn up brim, which

cocked hat

was sometimes fastened with buttons and loops to crown—first one side, then two sides, and eventually three sides forming a tricorne. Many variations developed, each involving individual details. Named types include: (1) **bully-cock,** an 18th-c. term for a broad-brimmed, three-cornered cocked hat; (2) **continental hat,** a three-cornered hat with a wide upturned brim worn with the point placed at center front. Worn by the Continental army during the American Revolution. Rank of officers was denoted by various colors of cockades worn on the left side of the hat; (3) **Denmark cock** Man's three-cornered hat of the second half of the 18th c. with three sides of the hat turned up, the back higher than the front; (4) **Dettigen cock** Man's cocked hat of the 18th c. with the brim turned up equally in three sections; (5) **Kevenhuller cock** Man's three-cornered hat worn from 1740s to the 1760s, cocked with the front forming a peak and turned up higher in back. (6) **Monmouth cock** Broad-brimmed hat of the second half of the 17th c. turned up or cocked in back. Also see HEADWEAR: TRICORNE. **2.** Contemporary hat inspired by any of the historic versions of a cocked hat.

cockle hat ∞ Hat trimmed with a scallop shell, worn by pilgrims returning from the Holy Land during the crusades in the 11th to 13th c. *Der.* French, *coquille,* "shell."

coffer headdress ∞ Woman's small box-shaped headdress of 14th c. usually worn over top of hair with coiled braids over the ears.

coif (kwaf) **1.** White headdress worn by nuns of some orders under the veil. **2.** ∞ From 12th to 15th c., linen headcovering similar to a baby's bonnet tied under chin. Art of the period

coif #2 13th c.

shows it to have been worn by individuals from many levels of society and by soldiers and knights under metal helmets. By the 16th c. it was more likely to be worn by the aged and the learned professions. Coif may be a modern term applied to this headwear. **3.** ∞ From 16th to 19th c., an under cap worn mainly by women. In the late 16th c. and early 17th c. the cap was sometimes embroidered, with sides

H

curved forward to cover the ears. These were called *cheeks-and-ears*. Similar caps were called *orrelets*, or *round-eared caps*. **4.** Also see HEADWEAR: BIGGIN.

commander's cap See HEADWEAR: ASTRONAUT'S CAP.

commode 1. ∞ A silk-covered wire frame of the late 17th and early 18th c. that was used to support the high FONTANGES headdress (see under HEADWEAR). Also called *mont la haut* (mont lah hoh) and *palisade*. **2.** English name for the fontages headdress.

commodore cap ∞ Flattopped cap with a visor fashionable for women for boating and sports, including bicycling, in 1890s. Similar to YACHTING CAP (see under HEADWEAR).

communion veil A sheer net elbow-length veil worn by girls for first communion in the Catholic Church.

conductor's cap Cap with crown shaped like a pillbox with visor-shaped brim, frequently trimmed with braid around the crown and an insignia in front. Worn placed straight on forehead by train conductors.

continental hat See HEADWEAR: COCKED HAT #2.

conversation bonnet See HEADWEAR: POKE BONNET.

coolie hat 1. Chinese hat made of straw that may take many forms—mushroom-shaped with knob at top, bowl-shaped, conical flared shape, and a flared shape with a peak in the center. All are made of bamboo, palm leaves, or straw, and stand away from the head, forming almost a parasol against the sun. **2.** Copies of the above styles made in felt and straw for general wear. *Der.* Chinese, "kuli," an unskilled worker.

copotain ∞ (ko-poh-tan′) Man's or woman's hat with a high conical crown rounded at top and medium-sized brim usually turned up at the sides and back. Made of beaver, fur, or leather trimmed with wide band. First mentioned in 1508, but very fashionable from 1560 to 1620. Revived in 1640s to 1665; then called the **sugarloaf hat** due to its resem-

copotain or sugarloaf hat

blance to a loaf of sugar. Also called *pantile*. Also spelled *copatain, copintank, coppintanke, copytank, coptank.*

cornet 1. See HEADWEAR: HENNIN. **2.** ∞ Dark-colored velvet cap similar to a BONGRACE (see under HEADWEAR) worn from 17th to 19th c. **3.** ∞ Day cap with rounded caul; tied under the chin, in first half of 19th c. (see HEADWEAR: CAUL #1). Also spelled *cornette*. **4.** Synonym for MORTARBOARD (see under ACADEMIC DRESS).

coronet (kor′-o-net) **1.** Crown that denotes rank below that of sovereign. Nobility of Great Britain have seven different styles of crowns for prince of the blood, younger son, nephew, duke, marquis, earl, viscount, and baron. **2.** Band or wreath worn by women on the head like a TIARA (see under HEADWEAR). **3.** ∞ 14th-c. term for open crown worn by nobility. Also spelled *coronal*.

cossack forage cap Visored cap with soft crown set on band worn toward back of head rather than pulled down on forehead. Made in napped suede fabric in natural, black, or loden green. Adapted from caps worn by Russian Cossacks and accepted for general wear by men and women in the late 1960s. Also see FORAGE CAP.

cossack hat Tall brimless hat of fur worn by Russian horsemen and cavalrymen. Copied for men's winter hat in the United States and England in 1950s and 1960s.

cottage bonnet ∞ Straw bonnet fitting head closely with brim projecting beyond the cheeks worn from 1808 to 1870s. Early styles were worn over a cap. Later styles had upturned pleated brim with satin lining.

couel ∞ British turban headdress of 15th c. in red for commoners, and black for nobility.

counter fillet ∞ Late 14th and early 15th c., the fillet or band securing a woman's veil.

Courrèges hat (Koor′-rej) Fashion helmet shaped similar to World War I aviator's helmet. Introduced in 1964 by French couturier André Courrèges as a result of universal interest in astronauts.

coverchief/couverchief/couverchef ∞ Norman term meaning **head rail**, a draped Saxon head covering made of different fabrics and colors worn by women of all classes from medieval times to the 16th c.

cowboy hat Large wide-brimmed felt hat with crown worn creased or standing up in cone shape with the brim rolled up on both sides and dipping in front. Sometimes with hatband of leather and silver. Worn in the United States by Western cowboys to shade face and neck. Also called **ten-gallon hat** when extra tall and uncreased. Also see HEADWEAR: SOMBRERO and STETSON.®

cowboy hat: ten gallon type

coxcomb/cockscomb ∞ Hood trimmed with strip of notched red cloth at the apex worn by licensed court jesters in 16th and 17th cs.

crants ∞ Garland of flowers or chaplet made of gold and gems worn by women from Medieval times to 18th c. Also spelled *craunce, graundice.*

crisp ∞ 16th-c. term for a woman's VEIL (see under HEADWEAR).

crispine ∞ (kris'-pihn) An extra band at the forehead used during the late 14th c. to keep the elaborate net (see HEADWEAR: CAUL or FRET) in place. A veil draped over the crispine and caul was referred to as a **crispinette** (kris'-pin-ett).

crispinette See HEADWEAR: CRISPINE.

crocheted cap (kro-shade') Any type cap that is hand-crocheted. Styles vary—some are helmet-shaped—others made like TAMS (see under HEADWEAR). Some styles are trimmed with metal or plastic PAILLETTES attached at intervals.

crosscloth **1.** ∞ Triangular KERCHIEF of 16th and 17th cs. worn by women with a COIF or CAUL tied under chin or at back of head. Frequently embroidered to match the coif. (See cross-references under HEADWEAR.) **2.** A brow band worn in bed to prevent illness, or as a beauty aid to remove wrinkles. Worn by men and women from 16th to 18th c. Also called *forehead cloth.* Also see FRONTLET.

crown **1.** See in category heading: HEADWEAR. **2.** Circlet of precious metal and gems worn by kings and queens. **3.** Bridal headpiece worn with veil. **4.** A garland or wreath worn on the head as an ornament or sign of honor.

crown hats Hats of African inspiration that are round, flat-topped, and sometimes have leather medallions with maps of Africa in the colors of African and West Indian countries. Worn by African-Americans in late 1980s and 1990s.

crusader hood Snug-fitting hood cut in one piece with a small shoulder cape. Originally made of chain mail—later copied in knits for winter sportswear.

crusher hat Comfortable man's snap-brim felt hat that can be made into a compact roll to fit in pocket or pack for travel. Introduced about 1900 and popular in the 1920s and again in the 1980s and after.

Cumberland hat ∞ Man's hat with 8″ high tapered crown and small brim turned up at the sides, worn in 1830s. Also called *hat à la William Tell.*

curch ∞ Untrimmed close-fitting woman's cap worn in Colonial America. Also spelled *kerche.*

cushion headdress ∞ 19th-c. term for large padded roll worn as headdress by women in first half of the 15th c.

dandy hat Woman's high-crowned, roll-brimmed hat decorated with jet embroidery, feathers, and a veil. Introduced by New York milliner Sally Victor in mid-1950s.

Davy Crockett cap Coonskin (raccoon fur) cap with tail of animal hanging down back. Worn in Colonial America by woodsmen and pioneers and named after David Crockett, frontiersman and politician, who fought and died at the Alamo in Texas in 1836. Popular for young boys in 1950s and 1960s after wide exposure on television programs, at which time the term was copyrighted. Copyright now applies to a wide variety of apparel.

day cap ∞ Muslin cap worn by adult women indoors and sometimes under bonnets outdoors in the 18th and 19th c. By the second half of the 19th c., only elderly women continued to wear these caps.

day cap, first half of 19th c.

deerstalker Checked or tweed cap with visor on both front and back and ear laps that can be buttoned or tied to top of crown, worn from 1860s on. Associated with pictures of Sherlock Holmes, the fictional detective created by Sir Arthur Conan Doyle. *Der.* Originally worn in England for hunting, including "stalking deer." Also called *fore-and-after.*

deerstalker

demi-castor   See HEADWEAR: CASTOR.

demi-coronal   See HEADWEAR: TIARA.

Denmark cock   See HEADWEAR: COCKED HAT.

derby   American name for a hat, called a **bowler** in England, first worn about 1860, made of hard felt with a domed crown and narrow stiff brim rolled up on the sides. Usually black, but brown and fawn colors were worn with NORFOLK JACKET (see under COATS AND JACKETS). *Der.* The British version was named for the hatter William Bowler, about 1850 to 1860, although shape dates from 1820s. The American version was named for Earl of Derby and an English horse race called the Derby; pronounced *darby* in England.

derby or bowler

desert fatigue cap   Visor cap of cotton poplin made with soft crown set on wide band, worn with top crushed down at sides. Copied from German forage cap worn in World War II and accepted for general wear in late 1960s.

diadem (dy′-ah-dem)   **1.** A crown. **2.** Decorative headdress resembling a crown.

diadem cap ∞ (dy′-ah-dem)   Bathing cap of 1870s usually of oiled silk shaped like a shower cap with a band and upstanding ruffle in front and ties under the chin.

diadem fanchon bonnet ∞ (dy′-ah-dem fan′-shon)   Lace and velvet bonnet of late 1860s with brim forming a halo. Made with two sets of bonnet strings—one tied under CHIGNON (see under HAIRSTYLES) in back, the other, trimmed with RUCHING, loosely tied under the chin.

diamanté headband (dya-mahn-tay′)   Band of fabric set with artificial sparking jewels (example: rhinestones) and worn around head, low on forehead during Edwardian period (1890–1910) and in late 1920s.

Diana Vernon hat/Diana Vernon bonnet ∞   Wide-brimmed, shallow-crowned straw bonnet of the late 1870s with one side of the brim turned up and trimmed with a rosette. Wide streamers came from underside of brim to tie under the chin. *Der.* Named for the heroine of *Rob Roy,* 1817 English novel by Sir Walter Scott.

dink/dinky   See HEADWEAR: SKULLCAP.

Directoire bonnet ∞ (dir-eck′-twa)   Bonnet tied under the chin, fitting close over the ears, with a high flaring front brim. Worn in late 1870s through early 1880s. Inspired by hats worn during the French *Directoire Period* (1795–1799), but not known by this name at that time.

Dolley Madison hood ∞ Lace-trimmed opera hood resembling a DUST CAP (see under HEADWEAR) with a deep ruffle of lace falling around the face and neck. Worn toward back of head and secured under chin with broad ribbon ties. Popular at end of 19th c. Also spelled *Dolly. Der.* Named after Dolley Madison, wife of James Madison, President of the United States, 1809 to 1817.

doll hat   Miniature hat worn in different ways at different time periods. In the late 1930s, pushed forward on the head and held on with an elastic band around back of head. Popular after being worn by Jacqueline Kennedy when she was First Lady in early 1960s, when it was attached to the back of head with combs or pins and sometimes had a veil. Reintroduced in 1984 to perch on the front of the head in various shapes—square, round, etc.

dome hat   See HEADWEAR: BUBBLE HAT.

doo rag   Headcovering with the appearance of a head scarf tied in the back with long, hanging tail. Usually made from brightly colored fabrics or leather.

dorelet ∞ (dor-reh′-lay)   Term used in Middle Ages for woman's hair net ornamented with jewels. Also spelled *dorlet.*

dormeuse/dormouse (dor-muse′)   Ribbon-trimmed white cap with a puffed crown and falling lappets (see under HEADWEAR) trimmed with lace, called *wings,* popularly known as **cheek wrappers.** Worn in the house by women

H

in second half of 18th c. Also called a *French nightcap*.

dressmaker's brim Hat brim, usually on a fabric hat, that has closely spaced rows of machine stitching or stitched tucks around the brim.

drum major's hat Very tall hat with chin band, frequently made of fur in black or white, worn by the leader of a band or drum major for parade functions. Similar to BEARSKIN CAP (see under HEADWEAR).

dunce cap Tall conical cap, sometimes marked with a D, formerly worn in school by students who failed in their lessons. Sometimes wrongly called FOOL'S CAP (see under HEADWEAR).

dunstable Hat of plaited straw originally made in Dunstable, England.

dust cap ∞ Cap made of handkerchief or circular piece of fabric hemmed on outer edge and gathered by elastic, worn by women or maids for housework from 19th to early 20th c.

Dutch-boy cap Cap with visor and soft wide crown usually made of navy blue wool.

Dutch cap Cap worn by women and girls in Volendam, Holland, made of lace or embroidered muslin fitted to the head with a slight peak at the crown and flaring wings at sides of face. Made fashionable by *Irene Castle*, famous ballroom dancer in 1920s. Sometimes used as bridal cap. Also called *Dutch bonnet*.

earmuffs **1.** Two disks of wool, fur, felt, or other fabric worn to keep the ears warm in winter. Disks may be fastened to a strap that goes overhead and ties under the chin, or fastened to a springy metal band that fits over top of the head. **2.** A pair of flaps on sides of a cap that may be turned up and buttoned at top of cap, or left down to cover the ears.

Easter bonnet Another name for an Easter hat. May be any type of hat, not necessarily tied under the chin. Also see EASTER PARADE.

Egham, Staines, and Windsor ∞ Nickname used in early 19th c. for three-cornered TRICORNE HAT (see under HEADWEAR). *Der.* From geographical location of three English towns that form a triangle on map.

eight-point cap Policeman's cap, or utility cap, with soft crown and a stiff visor in front. Crown is made by sewing together eight straight-edged wedges of fabric making an octagon-shaped crown.

elastic round hat ∞ Patented collapsible hat of 1812, which could be flattened by releasing steel spring and carried under the arm. Forerunner of the Gibus (see under HEADWEAR: OPERA HAT).

Empire bonnet/Empire cap ∞ (em'-pire or ohm-peer') Small outdoor bonnet of 1860s shaped like a baby's cap with no veil or curtains in back.

engineer's cap Round cap with visor worn by railroad workers, usually of blue-and-white striped cotton. The crown is box-pleated onto the band. Adopted in 1960s by young people for sportswear.

English cottage bonnet See HEADWEAR: BIBI BONNET.

English hood ∞ Woman's headdress worn from 1500s to 1540s, sometimes made of black fabric wired to form a peak or gable over the forehead with long velvet lappets at side and the back draped in thick folds over the shoulders. When these lappets were embroidered, they were called **chaffers** (chaf'-ers). After 1525, the back drapery became two long pendant flaps. Also called *gable* and *pediment headdress,* by 19th-c. writers.

English hood

envoy hat Man's winter hat similar to COSSACK HAT (see under HEADWEAR) with leather or fur crown and fur or fabric edge. Popular in late 1960s.

ermine cap See LETTICE CAP.

Eton cap Close-fitting cap with a short visor, modeled after those worn at Eton College in England. Popular in fabrics to match coats for young boys in the United States in 1920s and 1930s.

Eugénie hat (yoo-je'-nee) Small hat, with brim rolled back on either side, worn by Greta Garbo in a film about the Empress Eugenie and popular in the 1930s. Worn tilted sideways and to the front, and often trimmed with one long ostrich plume

Eugenie hat

H

in the side roll. *Der.* Named for Eugénie, Empress of France.

fanchon ∞ (fan-shon') Small lace-trimmed head scarf, or the lace trimming on sides of an outdoor bonnet or day cap, worn from 1830s on.

fanchon cap ∞ (fan-shon') Small indoor cap of tulle or lace with side pieces covering the ears, worn by women from 1840s to 1860s.

fantail hat ∞ Three-cornered hat with wide brim, cocked or turned up at sides, with point in front; the back, somewhat-shaped semicircular, resembled a fan. Worn in the last quarter of 18th c. by men and women for horseback riding.

fashion helmet Any helmet designed as a fashion item rather than for protection. May be made of leather, fabric, fur, plastic, or other materials. Types include *Courrèges*, *Paco Rabanne*, *Pucci*, and *chain helmets*.

fatigue cap U.S. armed forces cap usually made of twill fabric in style similar to ENGINEER'S CAP (see under HEADWEAR).

fedora Felt hat with medium-sized brim and high crown with lengthwise crease from front to back. Originally worn by men but now also styled for women with turned-up back brim. *Der.* Popular for men after Victorian Sardou's play *Fedora* was produced in 1882. Now a classic men's hat style.

fedora

fez **1.** Red felt hat shaped like truncated cone with long black silk tassel hanging from center of crown worn by Turkish men until 1925; also worn in Syria, Palestine, and Albania. Also worn by the "Shriners," an auxiliary order of the Masons. **2.** Basic shape, without tassel, copied for women's hats in the West. *Der.* Named for town of Fez in Morocco.

fillet **1.** Narrow band tied around the hair, usually as a brow band, worn from 13th to 19th c. **2.** ∞ Stiffened band of linen worn with the BARBETTE, FRET, or both in 13th and 14th c. (see under HEADWEAR). **3.** See HEADWEAR: HEADBAND # 1 and #2.

Fitzherbert hat ∞ Modified form of BALLOON HAT (see under HEADWEAR), with wide oval brim and low crown of puffed fabric, worn by women in mid-1780s.

flandan ∞ (flahn'-dahn) Late 17th-c.: a PINNER or LAPPET (see under HEADWEAR) fastened to woman's day cap.

Flemish hood See HEADWEAR: BEGUIN.

flight deck cap See HEADWEAR: ASTRONAUT'S CAP.

flower-pot hat ∞ Man's hat of 1830s with crown shaped like a truncated cone, or upside-down flower pot, with large turned-up brim. Also called *turf hat*.

fly cap See HEADWEAR: BUTTERFLY CAP.

fold-up hat Straw sun hat with pleated brim and crown that folds to a 6″ roll for carrying in pocket or purse.

follow-me-lads ∞ Long ribbon streamers of 1850s and 1860s hanging from back of girl's bonnet.

f o n t a n g e s ∞ (f a w n ' - t a n j z) **/fontange** Woman's starched, pleated, lace-and-ribbon headdress placed on top of upswept hairstyle in late 17th and early 18th c. Said to have originated about 1679 when Marie Angélique de Scorraille de Roussilles, la Duchesse de Fontanges, a favorite of Louis XIV who was out riding with the King, used her lace and jeweled garter to fasten back her hair, which had become disarranged. Also called *tower headdress* and *high head*. The COMMODE (see under HEADWEAR) was used to support the headdress.

fontanges

fontanges hat ∞ (fawn'-tanjz) Tiny hat covering crown of head trimmed with lace, ribbon, and flowers with a sheet veil or curtain in back. A band of ribbon, edged with fluting, went under the chin. Featured in *Godey's Magazine* in 1876.

fool's cap Of three types: (a) forward-curved peaked cap with donkey's ears; (b) a cockscomb in place of peak and without ears; (c) two hornlike peaks at sides of head. Bells were added to each style. Also called *jester's cap*. Also see JESTER'S COSTUME.

football helmet Molded plastic helmet that conforms closely to the head, covering the ears. Made with nose guard, consisting of curved plastic strips attached to sides, and decorated with symbols indicating team. Worn by all contact football players.

forage cap **1.** Cap with a visor adapted from the military for small boys in first half of 19th c. Made with circular felt crown, head band stiffened with cane, a tassel from center of crown, and sometimes glossy black leather straps under the chin. **2.** Small cap similar to a KEPI (see under HEADWEAR), formerly worn by soldiers in U.S. Army.

fore-and-after See HEADWEAR: DEERSTALKER.

foundling bonnet ∞ Small, soft-crowned, stiff-brimmed bonnet of 1880s usually made of plush and fastened with ties under chin.

frelan ∞ Late 17th-c. term for woman's BONNET and PINNER (see under HEADWEAR) worn together. Also spelled *freland, frelange*.

French beret See HEADWEAR: BERET #2.

French hood ∞ Woman's headdress, consisting of a small bonnet over a stiffened frame, worn at back of head and trimmed with RUCHING. Front border was curved forward to cover the ears and had two ornamental gold bands or BILLIMENTS. A back flap either enclosed the hair or was folded forward over head, projecting above forehead (see HEADWEAR: BONGRACE). Fashionable from 1521 to 1590 and worn by some until 1630.

French hood
c. 16ᵗʰ c.

French sailor hat Large navy blue or white cotton TAM (see under HEADWEAR), stitched to stiff navy blue headband and trimmed with red pompon at center of crown. Originally worn by French seamen pulled down on forehead with top exactly horizontal.

fret ∞ Mesh snood or skullcap made of gold mesh or fabric worked in an openwork lattice design and sometimes decorated with jewels. Worn by women from the 13th to early 16th c. Also called a *caul.*

frigate cap Utility visored cap of mid-20th c. with flat top slanting toward back. Made of water-repellent black silky rayon with cord and buttons on front for trim. Copied from caps worn by merchant seamen in the 19th c.

frontlet ∞ Decorative BROW BAND worn in medieval times under a COVERCHIEF or VEIL. Also

worn in 16th and early 17th c. with COIF or CAUL. (See cross-references under HEADWEAR.)

funnel hat Brimless tall conical hat of felt or fabric worn by women in the 1930s and 1940s.

gable bonnet/hat ∞ Woman's hat of 1884 with front brim angled like a Gothic arch.

gable headress See HEADWEAR: ENGLISH HOOD.

Gainsborough hat Large, graceful brimmed hat worn from late 1860s to 1890s and copied periodically since. Made of velvet, straw, or beaver, frequently turned up on one side and trimmed with ostrich plumes. *Der.* Named after the 18th-c. British painter *Gainsborough,* who painted many portraits of ladies in this type of hat, including portrait of *Duchess of Devonshire.*

galatea hat ∞ (gal'-ah-teh-ah) Child's hat of plaited straw with sailor crown and turned-up brim worn in 1890s.

Garbo hat Slouch hat worn so frequently by Greta Garbo in the 1930s that it is sometimes called by her name. See HEADWEAR: SLOUCH HAT. Also see GARBO, GRETA.

garden hat **1.** ∞ Woman's hat of 1860s made of muslin with flat top cut in oval shape. Ruffles or long pieces of muslin hung down to protect the wearer from the sun. Hat was frequently made with ribbon trim. **2.** Large-brimmed floppy hat of horsehair or straw worn in 1920s and 1930s for afternoon teas and garden parties. **3.** Large-brimmed straw hat currently worn when gardening to protect face from the sun.

garrison cap See HEADWEAR: OVERSEAS CAP.

gaucho hat (gow-cho) Wide-brimmed black felt hat made with medium-high flat crown. Fastened under chin with leather thong. Originally worn by South American cowboys, it was adapted for women in late 1960s and worn with gaucho pants (see under PANTS). Also called *sombrero córdobes* (som-brer'-oh kordob'-ehs). *Der.* Spanish "cowboy" of Argentina, Chile, and Uruguay.

German helmet Metal helmet made with small visor and a spike on the top decorated with large gold eagle on front. Worn by Germans in World War I and adopted by teenage boys in the late 1960s. Also called a *pickelhaube.*

H

Gibus See OPERA HAT.

glengarry cap Military cloth cap creased to fold flat like an OVERSEAS CAP (see under HEADWEAR) usually with tartan band at edge, regimental badge at side front, and two black ribbon streamers in back. Part of the uniform of Scottish Highland regiments, and adapted for sportswear by women and small boys in mid-19th c. *Der.* After Glengarry, a valley in Invernessshire, Scotland.

gob hat See HEADWEAR: SAILOR HAT.

goffered veil ∞ 19th-c. term for linen headdress, with fluted or GOFFERED frill surrounding the face. Has back drapery to shoulders, worn from 1350 to 1420. *Nebula headdress* is a 19th-c. synonym.

gondolier's hat (gon-doh-leer') Straw hat with a medium-sized brim and a shallow, slightly tapered crown with a flat top. Wide ribbon trims the crown and long streamers extend down the back; the color of the ribbon denoted length of service. Worn formerly by gondoliers of Venice, Italy. Often purchased as a tourist souvenir by visitors to Venice.

granny bonnet ∞ Child's bonnet of early 1890s with ribbon ties under the chin, broad flaring brim, and gathered conventional crown decorated with ribbons. *Der.* Styled after the bonnets that grandmothers wore.

Greek fisherman's cap Soft cap of denim or wool with crown higher in front than in back. Elaborately trimmed with braid on visor and at seam where visor meets crown. Styled in black wool, blue denim, or white and worn for sportswear or boating in 1980s by both men and women.

hair net Fine cap-shaped net worn over the hair to keep it in place. Sometimes made of knotted human hair and nearly invisible. Also made of chenille, gold, or silver threads and worn as decoration. Also see HEADWEAR: SNOOD.

halo hat See HEADWEAR: PAMELA.

hard hat Protective covering for the head. Made of metal or hard plastic in classic PITH HELMET shape or similar to a baseball BATTER'S CAP (see under HEADWEAR). Held away from the head by foam lining to absorb impact. Worn by construction workers and others subject to work hazards. In late 1960s, the term "hard hat" took on political connotations when U.S. construction workers expressed their sentiments against peace advocates.

harlequin Hat with brim, wide at sides and cut straight across front and back, worn in 1938. *Der.* From *Harlequin,* a part played by an actor in 16th to 18th c. Italian comedies called *commedia dell'arte.*

harvest hat Believed to be the term used for the first straw hats worn by farmers in the United States.

hat Sometimes used as a generic term for headwear, however the term is more specifically applied to headwear that consists of a crown and a brim and that usually does not tie under the chin. A decorative accessory or one worn for warmth, hats can be made of felt, straw, fur, fabric, leather, or synthetic materials. The Greek petasos (see HEADWEAR: PETASOS #1) was among the earliest of brimmed hats. Medieval hat styles included the COPOTAIN (see under HEADWEAR) and until c. 1660 men wore hats indoors as well as out and in church. Women did not generally wear hats except for traveling until after the late 16th c., when they wore either hats or bonnets for outdoors and for church. From the late 1950s, bouffant hairstyles, and later the use of wigs and falls, made it difficult to wear hats and although hats have been periodically fashionable since then, they are worn much less frequently than in the past.

Hat à la William Tell See HEADWEAR: CUMBERLAND HAT.

hat cap ∞ 18th-c. term for a day cap worn under a hat mainly by women. Also called *undercap.*

hat pin Straight pin from 3″ to 12″ long with bead or jewel at top. Used by women to secure their hats in late 19th through early 20th c., becoming less common after hair was bobbed in the 1920s.

havelock 1. Cloth covering for military cap extending to shoulders in back in order to protect the neck from sun. *Der.* Named for Sir Henry Havelock, British general in India. 2. See HEADWEAR: AUTOMOBILE CAP.

headband **1.** Strip of leather, cord, or fabric bound around the head horizontally across the forehead. Also called a *brow band*. **2.** Band worn over top of the head from ear to ear as an ornament or to keep hair in place since ancient times. **3.** Band at bottom edge of hat crown.

head rail See HEADWEAR: COVERCHIEF.

head wrap In 1980s, a scarf, bandanna, ribbon, or piece of fabric worn in carefree manner around the head to frame the face or as a BROW BAND (see under HEADWEAR).

heart-shaped headdress ∞ Rolled woman's headdress of 1420 to 1450, forming a heart-shaped peak in center front. Raised on sides to show netting coming down over the ears. Usually worn with a long veil. The style was called a **miter** by 19th-c. writers.

helmet Protective covering for the head worn primarily to prevent injury, particularly by armed forces and for various sports. First worn by Greeks and Romans with feathered crests; *chain mail* was used during the Crusades; cast metal used from 14th c. on for knights' helmets, which usually had a visor. In the late 1950s, space helmets were introduced for astronauts, and in the 1960s helmet-shaped hats were introduced as a fashion accessory. Also see ARMOR: BURGONET and MORION.

hemispherical hat See HEADWEAR: BOLLINGER.

Henley boater See HEADWEAR: BOATER.

hennin ∞ (hen'-in) Woman's tall steeple-shaped headdress worn in Burgundy during the second half of 15th c. Supported by a wire frame and worn tilted back with a long sheer veil hanging from tip down to floor, or caught up as drapery at waist. SUMPTUARY LAWS regulated the size of these hats. Princesses could wear hats a yard high; however, those of noble ladies could be only 24″ or less. Also called *steeple headdress* and *corner. Der.* From an old French word meaning "to inconvenience,"

hennin, 2nd half of the 15th c.

a reference to the inconvenience such a headdress would cause.

heuke ∞ (hyuke) Veil enveloping wearer to knees or ankles—sometimes with the top stiffened by wire—worn over head forming a cage. Worn in Flanders in 16th and 17th c. Also spelled *hewke, heyke, hewk.*

high hat See HEADWEAR: TOP HAT.

hive bonnet See HEADWEAR: BEEHIVE HAT #1.

homburg Man's hat of rather stiff felt with narrow rolled brim and lengthwise crease in the crown worn from 1870s on for formal occasions. Made fashionable by Prince of Wales, later Edward VII, who visited Bad Homburg in Germany many times. Revived after President Dwight Eisenhower wore one to his inauguration in 1952. *Der.* Homburg, Prussia.

homburg

hood **1.** Preliminary, shaped piece of FELT or straw from which the milliner works. Has a high rounded nondescript crown and an extra large floppy brim. **2.** Accessory worn on the head and sometimes the shoulders that is frequently attached to a jacket or coat. Differs from a hat in that it has no specific shape and usually covers the entire head, sometimes tying under the chin. Popular item for winter wear, it is made in all types of fabrics and fur. Although there are a great variety of styles, there are no specific names for these items. Worn from 11th c. on but replaced generally by caps in 1860s and 1870s, and for winter sportswear in the 1920s and 1930s. Very popular from late 1960s and after.

horned headdress ∞ Headdress consisting of two horns extending horizontally at either side of face or curved upward. A veil was draped over top and hung down the back. Worn from 1410 to 1420, and, rarely, to 1460.

horned headdress 15th c.

hundred pleater See HEADWEAR: CHEF'S HAT.

hunt cap Cap cut in six segments with small visor, elastic chin strap, and button on center top, sometimes of cloverleaf shape. Worn with riding habit, it is sometimes made with a plastic shell covered with velvet or velveteen and a padded lining.

hunt derby Stiff protective DERBY (see under HEADWEAR) made with reinforced strong plastic shell covered with black felt worn with riding habit.

hunting cap Bright-orange visored cap, sometimes fluorescent, enabling hunter to be seen in the woods.

Jenny Lind cap ∞ Crocheted band crossing the crown of the head coming down over ears and around to the back, where it fastened. Sometimes made of scarlet and white wool. Worn as a woman's MORNING CAP in late 1840s and early 1850s. *Der.* Copied from style worn by Jenny Lind (1820–1887), famous coloratura soprano called the "Swedish Nightingale."

Joan ∞ Woman's small, close-fitting indoor cap shaped like baby's bonnet tied under chin with narrow frill of muslin or lace around face. Worn from 1755 to 1765. Also called *Quaker cap.*

jockey cap Visored cap with crown usually of bicolored sateen cut in gores, similar to BASEBALL CAP (see under HEADWEAR) but with deeper crown, worn by racetrack jockeys. Similar caps worn by women in mid-1960s.

Juliet cap SKULLCAP (see under HEADWEAR) of rich fabric worn for evening or with wedding veils. May also be made entirely of pearls, jewels, or chain. *Der.* Medieval costume of Juliet in Shakespeare's play *Romeo and Juliet.*

kepi High-crowned, flattopped visored cap frequently worn with HAVELOCK (see under HEADWEAR) in back as protection from sun. Worn by French Foreign Legion and French General and statesman Charles de Gaulle. Also called *Legionnaire's cap.*

kerchief **1.** In current usage, a large triangle of cloth, or square folded in triangular fashion, worn as a headcovering or around the neck. Also see SCARVES: KERCHIEF and NECKERCHIEF. **2.** ∞ Covering for the head from Medieval times to end of 16th c. Also spelled *karcher, kercher, kercheve, kersche.* In 16th and 17th c., called a HEAD RAIL. See HEADWEAR: COVERCHIEF.

kevenhuller hat See HEADWEAR: COCKED HAT.

kiss-me-quick ∞ Popular name for tiny bonnet fashionable in late 1860s.

lamballe bonnet ∞ (lam-bahl′) Saucer-shaped straw bonnet of mid-1860s worn flat on head with sides pulled down slightly and tied under chin with large ribbon bow. Some had lace LAPPETS (see under HEADWEAR), others had small veils in back called "curtains."

Langtry hood ∞ Detachable hood on woman's outdoor garment of 1880s with a colored lining. *Der.* Named after actress *Lillie Langtry.*

lappets Long, ribbonlike strips of fabric that extend from a headdress. Particularly used in the 18th and 19th cs. to refer to such strips, often lace trimmed, when they hang at sides or back of an indoor cap.

leghorn hat/leghorn bonnet Woman's hat or bonnet in leghorn straw, a fine, smooth straw braid plaited with thirteen strands. Made from the upper part of wheat stalks grown near Livorno, a town in Tuscany, Italy. Fashionable at intervals since latter half of 19th c. *Der.* Named for place of export for the straw, Livorno, Italy. The British anglicized the name of the city to "Leghorn."

Legionnaire's cap See HEADWEAR: KEPI.

lettice cap/bonnet **1.** ∞ 16th-c. term for woman's outdoor cap or bonnet of triangular shape that covered the ears. Made of lettice, a fur resembling ermine. **2.** In 16th and 17th c., man's nightcap of lettice fur worn to induce sleep. Also called *ermine cap* or *miniver cap.*

liberty cap **1.** See FRENCH REVOLUTION STYLES. **2.** See HEADWEAR: BONNET ROUGE. **3.** See HEADWEAR: PHRYGIAN CAP.

liripipe **1.** ∞ Long pendant tail of the CHAPERONE (see under HEADWEAR), a hood worn in 14th and 15th c. **2.** Part of a hood worn by university graduates from 1350 to 15th c. Also spelled *liripipium, lirapipe, liripoop.* Also called *tippet.*

long hood See HEADWEAR: PUG HOOD.

Louis XV hat ∞ Woman's hat of mid-1870s with large high crown and wide brim turned up on one side. Fastened to crown with velvet bows and trimmed elaborately with ostrich feathers. *Der.* Named for Louis XV of France (1710–1774).

H

lounging cap ∞ Gentleman's at-home cap, worn in mid-1860s, made in pillbox or dome shape with silk tassels fastened at center. Also called *Greek lounging cap.*

lunardi See HEADWEAR: BALLOON HAT.

mafors ∞ Long narrow veil worn by women from 6th to 11th c. that usually covered head and draped over shoulders.

Mameluke turban ∞ (mama-luke′) White satin woman's turban of 1804 trimmed with one large ostrich feather, with the front rolled back like a hat brim over a dome-shaped crown. *Der.* Mamelukes were originally non-Arab slaves brought to Egypt, later trained as soldiers. Ruled Egypt from 1250 to 1517 and remained powerful until 1811 under Turkish viceroys. The Mameluke army was defeated by Napoleon Bonaparte during his Egyptian campaign in 1798.

Mandarin hat ∞ Woman's black velvet PORK PIE HAT (see under HEADWEAR) of early 1860s with feather trim over the back of the flat crown. Design inspiration may have been an ancient Chinese court hat with wide, flaring, upturned brim and decorative button at crown (indicating rank of wearer), made of fur and satin for winter and decorated with a peacock feather.

mantilla (man-til′-ah) Large oblong, fine lace veil, usually in rose pattern of black or white, worn wrapped over head and crossed under chin with one end thrown over shoulder. Frequently worn to church instead of a hat in Spain and South America. Popular after it was worn in early 1960s by U.S. first lady Jacqueline Kennedy.

Marie Stuart bonnet/cap ∞ Bonnet with heart-shaped peak or brim projecting over center of forehead, popular from 1820 to 1870, especially for widows. A derivative of the ATTIFET headdress (see under HEADWEAR) worn by Mary, Queen of Scots, also called Mary Stuart (or Stewart) (1542–1587).

Marie Stuart hood ∞ Separate hood of 1860s with heart-shaped peaked brim in front extended over the face with crown cut round and gathered at edge. Tied with ribbons under chin and lavishly trimmed with RUCHING, embroidery, braid, and ribbon.

marin anglais bonnet ∞ (mar′-ahn an-glayz′) Woman's bonnet worn on the back of the head like a child's sailor hat in 1870s. Trimmed with ribbon and feathers and tied under chin. *Der.* French, "English sailor cap."

marmotte bonnet ∞ (mar′-mowt) Tiny bonnet of early 1830s with narrow front brim similar to BIBI BONNET. See under HEADWEAR.

marmotte cap ∞ (mar′-mowt) Triangular handkerchief, placed on back of head and tied under chin, worn indoors by women in early 1830s.

marquis ∞ (mar-kwiss′ or mar-kee′) A three-cornered hat worn by women.

Mary, Queen of Scots cap ∞ Indoor cap worn by women, mainly matrons and widows, from 1750s to 1760s. Made with a heart-shaped peak in center front edged with beads, may have side frills and lappets. Also called *Mary cap.*

matador hat (mat-ah-door) Hat shaped like the top of a bull's head—rounded over forehead with two projections like bull's horns covered with black tufts of fabric, with the center of crown of embroidered velvet. Worn by bullfighters in Spain and Mexico.

mazarin hood ∞ (maz′-ah-rhan) Woman's hood worn in the last quarter of the 17th c. *Der.* Named after the Duchesse de Mazarin, niece of Cardinal Mazarin (1602–1661), minister to Louis XIV.

Mecklenburg cap ∞ Turban-style indoor cap worn by women in 1760s. *Der.* Named after Charlotte of Mecklenburg, who married George III of England in 1761.

mentonnières (mahn-toe nyehr′) See HEADWEAR: CHIN STAYS.

Merry Widow hat Very wide-brimmed hat, sometimes a yard across, frequently of velvet and ornately trimmed with ostrich plumes. *Der.* Named for 1905 light opera *The Merry Widow,* with music by Franz Lehár.

Milan bonnet ∞ (mee-lan′) Man's cap of first half of 16th c., usually black with soft puffed crown. Rolled-up brim was sometimes slit on the sides and trimmed with crimson satin lining pulled through slashes.

milkmaid hat See HEADWEAR: BERGÈRE.

H

miner's cap Stiff cap with short duck-billed visor and battery-powered light attached to front of crown.

mistake hat ∞ Woman's hat with tall flat-topped crown and brim cut in blunt point in front and turned up. Back brim was turned down. Worn on the back of the head in 1804.

miter **1.** ∞ Woman's headband worn in ancient Greece. **2.** See HEADWEAR: HEART-SHAPED HEADDRESS.

Moabite turban ∞ (mo'-ab-ite) Woman's crepe turban draped in many folds and trimmed with an aigrette feather on one side. Worn tilted to back of head in early 1830s.

mob cap Woman's indoor cap of 18th and 19th cs. made of white cambric or muslin with gathered crown and ruffled edge forming a bonnet. Had side LAPPETS (see under HEADWEAR), called *kissing strings* or *bridles,* which tied under the chin.

mob cap
18th c.

mod cap Cap similar to NEWSBOY CAP (see under HEADWEAR), popular in the United States in the mid-1960s.

molded felt Hat industry term for the felt HOOD made into hat shape by placing over a wooden block shaped like a head. See HEADWEAR: HOOD #1.

Monmouth cap ∞ Man's knitted cap with high rounded crown and small turned-down brim worn by soldiers, sailors, and civilians. Listed as necessary item for new settlers in America. Most common in 17th c. although also worn from 1570s to 1625. Made at Monmouth and Bewdley in Worcestershire, England. Also called *Bewdley cap* and worn by country folk by that name as late as 19th c.

Monmouth cock See HEADWEAR: COCKED HAT.

Montespan hat ∞ (mon-tes-pan') Woman's small round velvet evening hat of 1843 with brim turned up in front, trimmed with plume. *Der.* Named for Marquise de Montespan (1641–1707), mistress of Louis XIV of France.

Montgomery beret Military cap, a bit larger than the conventional BASQUE BERET (see HEADWEAR: BERET) but set on a band like a Scottish *tam-o-shanter* and decorated with reg-

imental insignia. Popular after being adopted by field marshal Bernard Law Montgomery, 1st Viscount Montgomery, commander of British ground forces in World War II.

mont-la-haut See HEADWEAR: COMMODE.

morning cap ∞ Dainty cap of muslin, lace, tulle, and ribbon worn on the back of the head indoors in the morning by women from 1820s to end of 19th c. Also called a *breakfast cap.*

mortarboard See ACADEMIC COSTUME.

motorcycle helmet ∞ Molded plastic helmet with foam lining worn when riding a motorcycle. Usually has a large dark-colored plastic shield that snaps on to protect eyes and face.

motoring veil See HEADWEAR: AUTOMOBILE VEIL.

Mountie's hat Wide-brimmed hat with high crown creased into four sections with a small peak at the top. Similar to World War I army hat worn with dress uniform. Worn by state policemen, Forest Rangers, and by the Royal Canadian Mounted Police.

mourning bonnet ∞ Any black bonnet worn to complete a mourning costume—especially in the 1870s and 1880s. An off-the-face bonnet, sometimes with a heart-shaped brim, it was made of black silk, lavishly trimmed with RUCHING and ribbon, and tied under the chin. The veil was arranged over the face or allowed to hang down the back.

mourning veil Semi-sheer black veil to the shoulders, usually circular, sometimes edged with wide band of black fabric worn under or over hat at funerals or during periods of mourning.

mousquetaire hat ∞ (moose-ke-tare') **1.** Wide-brimmed hat usually trimmed with three ostrich plumes. Also called *Swedish hat. Der.* From hats worn by French musketeers or royal bodyguards of Louis XIII in 17th c. **2.** Brown mushroom-shaped woman's straw hat edged with black lace hanging from the brim worn in late 1850s.

muffin hat ∞ Man's fabric hat with round flat crown and narrow standing brim used for country wear in 1860s.

Muller cut-down ∞ Man's hat of 1870s made like top hat with crown cut to half the height. *Der.* Named after English murderer whose hat led to his arrest in 1864.

mushroom hat Woman's straw hat with small round crown and downward-curved brim, shaped like the cap of a mushroom. Worn in 1870s and 1880s, trimmed with ribbons, flowers, and birds. Worn again in early 1900s and in the 1930s and 1940s usually made of felt.

napkin-cap Man's 18th-c. house cap or plain NIGHTCAP (see HEADWEAR: NIGHTCAP #2) worn at home when wig was removed.

Neapolitan bonnet ∞ (nee-a-poll'-i-tan) LEG-HORN bonnet of 1800 (see under HEADWEAR) trimmed with straw flowers and matching ribbons attached at the crown and loosely tied over the chest. *Der.* Greek, *Napolis,* "old town," present-day Naples.

Neapolitan hat (nee-a-poll'-i-tan) Sheer lacy conical hat made in Naples of horsehair braid. Later, any hat made of this braid. *Der.* City in which it originates: Naples.

Nebula headdress See HEADWEAR: GOFFERED HEADDRESS.

necked bonnet ∞ Lined or unlined cap with wide flap fitted around back of neck worn by men in first half of 16th c.

newsboy cap Soft fabric cap with flat bloused crown and visor that sometimes snaps to the crown. Formerly worn by newsboys and made famous by child actor Jackie Coogan in silent films of the 1920s. Revived in exaggerated form in 1960s and 1970s. Also popular in 2000 and after. May be referred to by various names (e.g., Carnaby, bebop, soul, applejack cap).

night coif ∞ (kwaf) Woman's cap worn with NEGLIGEE costume or in bed in 16th and 17th c. Frequently embroidered and usually worn with FOREHEAD CLOTH (see HEADWEAR: CROSSCLOTH #2).

man's nightcap 18th c.

nightcap **1.** Plain washable cap worn in bed by men and women from earliest times, sometimes made like stocking cap of knitted silk with tassel on top. In 19th c. called a *jellybag.* Also see HEADWEAR: BIGGIN #2. **2.** ∞ 14th- to mid-19th-c. skullcap with upturned brim, worn indoors by men when wig was removed. **3.** See HEADWEAR: NAPKIN CAP. **4.** See HEADWEAR: MOB CAP.

Norwegian morning cap/Norwegian morning bonnet ∞ Woman's cerise and white-striped Shetland wool, knitted kerchief-shaped head covering of 1860s. Tied under the chin with a ribbon and trimmed with bows over crown and back of the head.

nurse's cap White stiffly starched fabric cap received by nurses at graduation. At one time, but no longer, worn pinned to the crown of the head when dressed in uniform and on duty in hospitals. Each school of nursing has an individual style of cap.

obi hat ∞ Woman's hat of 1804 with high flat-topped crown and narrow brim rolled up in front. Ribbons come over crown and brim of hat, tying under chin.

octagonal hat ∞ Cap shaped like a TAM (see HEADWEAR) made of six wedges stitched together, forming an octagonal-shaped crown. Sometimes made of two contrasting fabrics and usually trimmed with two short streamers hanging in back. Popular for girls and young women in mid-1890s.

open-crown hat Woman's hat made without a crown—may be of the HALO or TOQUE hat type (see under HEADWEAR).

opera hat ∞ **1.** Small tricorne hat carried under the arm rather than worn from mid-18th c. on. Also called *chapeau bras.* **2.** Bicorne hat worn from 1800 to 1830 with a crescent-shaped brim front and back that could be compressed and carried under the arm. Also called a *military folding hat.* **3.** Man's tall silk hat with collapsible crown worn formerly for full dress occasions. Also worn by ring-masters, magicians, and performers. Differs from a TOP HAT (see under HEADWEAR) by being completely collapsible and made of dull, rather than shiny, fabric. Also called a **gibus** (jy-bus) and made with sides containing metal springs that snapped open to hold it upright. *Der.* From Antoine Gibus, who invented the hat in 1823, patented in 1837. Similar styles

H

were called *chapeau claque, circumfolding hat,* and *elastic round hat.*

oralia ∞ (or-ahl'-yuh)   Early medieval term for pointed veil. By first quarter of 14th c., known as *cornalia* or *cornu.* Also spelled *orales. Der.* Latin, "veil."

orrelet ∞ (or-let')   Term used in later half of 16th c. for hanging side pieces of woman's coif that covered ears. Also called *cheeks-and-ears.* Also spelled *oreillett, orillette, orilyet.* See HEADWEAR: COIF #3.

overseas cap   Flat folding cloth cap of khaki or olive drab fabric worn by men and women in the armed services. Has a lengthwise pleat from front to back in center of crown to enable it to fold flat. Worn overseas in World Wars I and II. Also called *garrison cap.*

Paco Rabanne hat   (pak'-oh rah'-bahn) Unusual cap fitted to conform to the head and covered with tiny diamond-shaped mirrors linked together. Introduced in late 1960s and named for French couturier *Paco Rabanne.*

padre hat   Shovel-shaped hat with turned-up brim on the sides and long square cut brim in front and back. Worn by some orders of Catholic priests. *Der.* Italian, "father."

painter's cap   Lightweight duck-billed fabric cap made with a round, flat-topped crown. Sometimes imprinted with school name, team name, or resort on front of crown. *Der.* From cap worn by house painters.

palisade   See HEADWEAR: COMMODE.

pamela   **1.** ∞ Straw bonnet worn from 1845 to late 1860s, made of a "saucer-shaped" piece of straw or fabric placed on top of the head. Fastened with bonnet strings that bent it into a U-shape around the face. Trimmed on

pamela or halo hat

top with foliage, flowers, or feathers. **2.** Continued to be a basic hat style with a rounded crown and wide brim and now often called a **halo hat.**

Panama hat   **1.** Hat made of fine, expensive straw obtained from the leaves of the *jipijapa* plant hand-woven in Ecuador. Very popular at the end of 19th and beginning

panama hat

of 20th c. Worn in different styles from 1855 on. A large Panama hat was worn by the Prince of Wales in 1920s at Belmont Park, Long Island, where more than 50,000 people were gathered, thus reviving the wearing of Panama hat. **2.** By extension, any man's straw summer hat regardless of type of straw.

pancake beret   See HEADWEAR: BERET #2.

pantile   See HEADWEAR: COPOTAIN.

papillion   See HEADWEAR: BONNET À BEC.

parachute hat   See BALLOON HAT.

Peruvian hat   ∞ Woman's rain hat made from plaited palm leaves, worn in early 19th c.

petasos ∞ (pet'-ah-soss)   **1.** Felt hat with a large floppy brim and nondescript crown worn in ancient Greece when traveling. Also worn in ancient Rome. **2.** Close-fitting winged cap as seen in representations of Roman god, Mercury. Also spelled *petasus.*

Peter Pan hat   Small hat with brim extended in front and turned up in back. Made with a conical crown trimmed with long feathers. *Der.* Named after the hat worn by actress Maude Adams in 1905 when starring in J. M. Barrie's play *Peter Pan.*

Phrygian cap/Phrygian bonnet   (frij'-ee-an) **1.** Cap with high rounded peak curving forward with lappets hanging at sides, sometimes made of leather. Worn in ancient Greece from 9th to 12th c. and copied from 18th c. on as BONNET ROUGE (see under HEADWEAR). **2.** See PILEUS #2.

pickelhaube   See HEADWEAR: GERMAN HELMET.

picture hat   Hat with large brim framing the face, frequently made of straw. Also see HEADWEAR: LEGHORN HAT.

pileus ∞ (pi'-lay-uss)   /pilleus **1.**   Ancient Roman skullcap worn at games and festivals. **2.** Felt brimless cap with peak folded over, similar to PHRYGIAN CAP (see under HEADWEAR), worn by freed Roman slaves. Also see PILOS. *Der.* Latin, "skullcap."

pillbox hat   Classic round brimless hat that can be worn forward or on the back of the head. Introduced in late 1920s

pillbox hat

H

and worn since with slight variations. *Der.* From small round pillboxes formerly used by chemists or druggists.

pilos (pi′-los) Conical cap worn by Greek peasants or fishermen, derived from those worn by ancient Greeks and Romans, similar to PILEUS (see under HEADWEAR). *Der.* Latin, "skullcap."

pinner ∞ A lappet, strip of fabric hanging from a woman's indoor cap, when worn pinned up and, by extension, term for cap itself in 17th to mid-18th c.

pipkin ∞ Woman's small hat, worn about 1565 to 1600, made with flat crown pleated into narrow brim. Usually trimmed with a narrow jeweled band and feathers. Also called *taffeta pipkin.*

pith helmet See TOPEE.

planter's hat Wide-brimmed white or natural handwoven straw hat with high dented crown, banded with dark ribbon. Worn by Southern gentlemen in the United States and popular for women in late 1960s.

plug hat See HEADWEAR: TOP HAT.

poke bonnet ∞ Bonnet of 19th c. made with very wide brim slanting forward from small crown to frame and shadow the face. Also called *poking bonnet.* When made with rolled brim—one side extending beyond the cheek, the other side rolled back from face, it was called a **conversation bonnet,** a style worn in 1803.

Polish toque ∞ Woman's hat of mid-1860s somewhat similar to *pillbox,* trimmed in front with foliage and in back with a large bunch of velvet ribbon loops.

polka ∞ Woman's cap of cream-colored tulle with crocheted edges appliquéd with lace floral designs, with LAPPETS (see under HEADWEAR) covering ears, and tied under chin.

polo hat See HEADWEAR: CHUKKA HAT.

pork-pie hat **1.** Classic snap-brim man's hat, flat on top with crease around edge of crown, made of fabric, straw or felt. Worn in 1930s and copied for women in the 1940s. Still a basic hat for men. **2.** ∞ Introduced in 1860s as a hat for women made of straw or velvet

pork pie hat
#1

with a low flat crown and turned-up narrow brim.

postboy hat ∞ Woman's small straw hat of 1885 styled with high flat crown and narrow brim sloping down all around. Trimmed with plume in front and worn perched on top of head.

postillion (pohse-til′-yohn) Hat with tall tapered crown and narrow brim, usually beaver, worn by women for riding. *Der.* From clothes worn by *postillions,* "men on horseback accompanying carriages."

pot hat See HEADWEAR: TOP HAT.

prayer veil Small triangular lace veil worn instead of hat for church services.

profile hat Woman's hat with brim turned down sharply on one side, silhouetting the profile, popular in late 1930s.

Pucci hat (pooch′-ee) Plastic glass bubble with cut-out for the face that stands away from the head to keep hair from blowing. Designed by Emilio Pucci, Italian couturier, as part of wardrobe for airline stewardesses.

pudding ∞ Small, round padded cap or padded band worn by infants and small children to serve as shock absorber in a fall. Synonym: *bumper.*

pudding
17th c.

pug hood ∞ Woman's soft hood of 18th c. with pleats radiating from back where it fitted the head. Made with or without an attached cape. Usually black with colored turned-back lining and tied under the chin with matching ribbons. Same as *short hood.* A **long hood** was similar, but with long tabs on the sides to facilitate tying under the chin.

pultney cap ∞ Woman's heart-shaped indoor cap of 1760s with wired peak, worn on the back of the head.

Puritan hat Black, stiff, tall-crowned man's hat with medium-wide straight brim trimmed with wide black band and silver buckle in center front. Worn by Puritan men in America in early 17th c. and copied for women in 1970s.

Quaker bonnet ∞ Small close-fitting, undecorated woman's bonnet with a puffed crown and stiff brim tied under the chin. Made in same fabric as the dress (often gray) or in straw, and worn over a ruffled white muslin

H

cap. In 17th through 19th c. prescribed for women of Quaker faith by the Society of Friends.

Quaker cap   See HEADWEAR: JOAN CAP.

Quaker hat   **1.** ∞ TRICORNE HAT with open cock and tall crown, worn in 18th c. **2.** Hat with large, slightly rolled brim, low crown, and no ornamentation worn in the 19th c. by Quaker men.

quartered cap   ∞ Boy's cap with flat circular crown divided into four segments and attached to stiff band. Made with or without a visor from mid-18th to mid-19th c.

rain bonnet   Accordion-pleated plastic covering for head that ties under chin. Folds up to fit in purse when not in use.

rain hat   Any waterproof hat worn in the rain. Some hats are made of vinyl and styled with a high crown and a floppy brim. Also see HEADWEAR: SOU'WESTER.

ranelagh mob   ∞ Woman's cap of 1760s made with a KERCHIEF (see under HEADWEAR) folded diagonally and placed over the head with two long ends tied under chin. The ends were pulled back and pinned or left to hang down.

ranger's hat   See HEADWEAR: MOUNTIE'S HAT.

Red Baron helmet   See HEADWEAR: AVIATOR'S HELMET.

red crown   ∞ Outward flaring crown with long extension up back worn by kings of Upper Egypt in ancient times. When kingdom became united both the *red crown* and the WHITE CROWN (see under HEADWEAR) were worn together.

reticulation   ∞ (re-ti'-cu-lay-shun)   Decorative netting holding hair on either side of face worn with horned headdress by women in 15th c. See HEADWEAR: CAUL #1.

Rex Harrison hat   Man's snap-brim hat of wool tweed with narrow brim and matching tweed band. Popular after being worn by actor Rex Harrison in his role as Professor Henry Higgins in the musical *My Fair Lady,* in 1956.

Robin Hood hat   Hat with high peaked crown, brim turned up in back, down in front, and trimmed with one long feather. *Der.* From hat in illustrations of books about Robin Hood, legendary British outlaw of the 12th c.

roll   ∞ 15th-c. term for the circular pad made when converting the man's chaperon into a hat. Also see HEADWEAR: BOURRELET.

roller   Hat with close-fitting crown and narrow curved brim worn rolled up or with the front turned down. Popular for women and girls in 1930s and 1940s, revived in early 1970s.

round-eared cap   ∞ Woman's white cambric or lace indoor cap worn from 1730s to 1760s. It curved around face and was finished with a ruffle. The shallow back was pulled together with a drawstring. Sometimes with side LAPPETS (see under HEADWEAR) pinned up or tied loosely under chin. Sometimes called *coif.*

roundlet   ∞ **1.** 17th-c. term used to describe the roll of the 15th-c. CHAPERONE, worn with a stuffed roll encircling the head and tail, called a **becca,** which was a long strip of fabric hanging forward that was sometimes worn slung over the shoulders. This style was very popular in the reign of Henry VI of England and was also called a **berretino. 2.** Man's small round hat of the 18th c. with attached streamer for carrying it over shoulder.

Rubens hat   ∞ High-crowned woman's hat of 1870s and 1880s with brim turned up on one side, sometimes trimmed with feathers and bows. *Der.* Named for hats painted by Flemish master Peter Paul Rubens (1577–1640).

safari hat   ∞ Lightweight straw or fabric hat shaped somewhat like a shallow soup dish with medium-sized brim. Hat is somewhat similar to a TOPEE (see under HEADWEAR) with a shallower crown. Worn to deflect heat in warm weather. *Der.* Shape of hat is similar to those worn on African hunting trips called "safaris."

sailor hat   **1.** Hat worn by naval enlisted personnel made of white duck fabric with gored crown and stitched up-turned brim worn either on the back of the head or tilted over the fore-head. Also called *gob hat* and *tennis hat.* **2.** Women's straight brimmed hat with shallow flat crown worn since 1860s. Very popular in 1890s for sportswear and bicycling and worn intermittently since. **3.** Popular hat for small boys in the 1880s, sometimes em-

sailor hat #1

broidered with fictitious name of a ship on a ribbon band at the base of the crown, similar in style to the brimless FRENCH SAILOR HAT (see under HEADWEAR).

Saint Laurent hat Cap designed by French couturier Yves Saint Laurent in 1966, made of leather studded with nailheads and styled similar to World War I aviator's helmet.

Salvation Army bonnet High-crowned black straw bonnet with short front brim raised off forehead to show a pale-blue lining. Has dark-blue ribbon around crown and ties under chin; worn by women of the Salvation Army, a religious and charitable organization.

scarf cap Long tubular knitted or crocheted scarf with opening for head in one end, similar to STOCKING CAP (see under HEADWEAR).

scarf hat **1.** Woman's soft fabric hat made by tying a scarf over a lining or base, sometimes shaped like a PILLBOX (see under HEADWEAR), and sewed in place. **2.** A triangular piece of colorful print or plain fabric quilted on long side. Worn with quilted part in center front and tied on the head like a KERCHIEF (see under HEADWEAR).

scoop bonnet ∞ Bonnet popular in 1840s with wide stiff brim shaped like a flour scoop attached to soft crown. *Der.* From old-fashioned "flour scoop."

scottie A brimless hat styled somewhat like the GLENGARRY (see under HEADWEAR) with narrow recessed crown. Veiling, ribbon, or feathers are sometimes placed on top toward the back.

sempstress bonnet ∞ Woman's bonnet of 1812 with long, wide ribbons crossing under chin and brought up to top of crown, where they tied in a bow.

service cap Army cap worn with dress uniform, made with a stiff, round, flat top and stiff visor of leather or plastic.

shade ∞ Piece of knitted or woven fabric usually attached to a hatband and arranged to fall over the back of the head and neck to prevent sunburn. Worn by women in 1880s.

shako (shay'-ko) Cylindrical stiff tall cap with attached visor. Top is sometimes tapered, sometimes flared, with feather cockade in front. Worn by marching bands, it was adapted from a style of military cap worn formerly. Also see HEADWEAR: DRUM MAJOR'S HAT.

shepherdess hat See HEADWEAR: BERGÈRE.

shoe hat Hat designed by Elsa Schiaparelli in the 1930s that looked like a woman's shoe. This design was reflective of the designer's interest in SURREALISM.

shoe hat 1930s

shower cap Plastic or waterproof cap, usually shirred into an elastic band, worn to keep the hair dry when taking a shower.

silk hat ∞ High cylindrical-shaped hat with flat top and silk-plush finish used by men on formal occasions and with formal riding dress by men and women. Invented by John Hetherington, a haberdasher of London, provoking a riot when first worn by him on January 15, 1797. He was charged in court for "breach of peace" for frightening timid people. Hat subsequently became the TOP HAT (see under HEADWEAR) in 1830.

skimmer SAILOR HAT or BOATER (see under HEADWEAR), with exaggerated shallow crown and wide brim.

skullcap Gored cap, usually made in eight sections, which fits tightly to crown of the head, often part of ecclesiastical garb or national costume. A **beanie** is a skullcap cut in gores to fit the head. Worn by children and by freshmen students as a part of hazing by upperclassmen, this is also called a *dink* or *dinky.* A **yarmulka** (yahr-muhl'-kuh) is a skullcap made of plain, embroidered, beaded, or crocheted fabric that is worn by Orthodox Jewish males for day wear and in the synagogue. Worn by other Jewish men for special occasions and religious services. Also see HEADWEAR: CALOTTE and CLERICAL DRESS: CALOTTE.

sleep bonnet Any net, snood, or cap worn to bed to protect hairstyle.

slouch hat Woman's hat similar to a man's FEDORA (see under HEADWEAR) made with a flexible brim that may be turned down in front. Also called a GARBO HAT (see under HEADWEAR).

slouch hat

H

snap-brim hat Man's or woman's hat with the brim worn at several different angles according to the preference of the wearer. Also see HEADWEAR: REX HARRISON HAT.

snood Hairnet made from chenille, mesh, or other material worn at the back of the head and nape of neck to confine the hair—sometimes attached to a hat. In 15th and 16th c., nets decorated with pearls and jewels were worn. During the Second Empire (1852–1870) snoods of chenille or fine silk cord decorated with steel beads were worn over the CHIGNON (see under HAIRSTYLES). A **cadogan net** was a snood, popular in late 1870s and early 1880s particularly for young women and girls, that was sometimes made of knotted silk yarn, worn over crown of head and enclosing the hair that hangs down the back. Also spelled *catagan.* Snoods are revived periodically.

snood

sombrero (som-brer′-oh) Mexican hat with a tall, slightly tapered crown and large upturned brim. Worn in Mexico by peons in straw and by wealthier citizens in felt lavishly trimmed around the edge, sometimes with silver lace. Also worn in Spain and the southwestern United States, where it is made of felt and somewhat similar to a *ten-gallon hat. Der.* Spanish, *sombre,* "to shade."

sombrero córdobes See HEADWEAR: GAUCHO HAT.

soul cap See HEADWEAR: NEWSBOY CAP.

sou'wester/southwester Rain hat made with a dome-shaped sectioned crown and broad stitched brim—larger in back. Originally made of yellow oiled silk—now made of any waterproof fabric for children's rainwear and fishermen. *Der.* First worn by fishermen in New England where a wind from the southwest meant rain.

space helmet Helmet made of molded plastic covering the head and neck completely and fastening to collar around the top of the space suit. Front section is made of see-through plastic with mirror-like reflective finish.

splyter-hat ∞ 16th-c. term for hat made of braided split pieces of straw rather than whole rounded stalks. Also spelled *splinter.*

spoon bonnet ∞ Small-crowned bonnet of early 1860s with brim narrow at sides and projecting upward above forehead in elliptical shape.

Statue of Liberty visor Headband with seven spikes and visor in front worn during "Liberty Weekend" in 1986 in celebration of the renovation of the Statue of Liberty in New York harbor.

steeple headdress See HEADWEAR: HENNIN.

stephane ∞ **1.** Decorated crescent-shaped headdress worn in ancient Greece and Rome by brides, or as a badge of office or wreath used as a symbol of victory. **2.** Ancient Greek term for anything that encircles the head; a *coronal, diadem,* or the brim of a helmet. **3.** Crown sent by Byzantine Emperors to other monarchs and important dignitaries. Also spelled *stephanos.*

Stetson® Trade name for a man's hat manufacturer of all types of hats, but often used to mean a wide-brimmed Western-style hat, especially the COWBOY style (see under HEADWEAR).

stocking cap A knitted or crocheted cap with a long pendant tail worn hanging down the back or side frequently with a tassel on the end. Also called *toboggan cap.*

stovepipe hat See HEADWEAR: TOP HAT.

stocking cap

stroller Casual mannish felt hats worn by women for town and spectator sports in 1930s and 1940s.

sugarloaf hat See HEADWEAR: CAPOTAIN.

sun bonnet Wide-brimmed fabric bonnet tied under chin especially worn by infants and children for protection against the sun. Often made with pockets into which pieces of cardboard or other firm material could be slipped in order to provide stiffness to the brim. Worn originally by early pioneers on western treks across the United States for protection against the sun. Revived for Centennial celebrations throughout the United States.

swagger hat Informal sports hat, often felt, with medium-sized brim turned down in front. Popular in 1930s and 1940s for men and women.

sweatband **1.** Band, usually made of sheepskin leather, placed around the inside of a man's hat where crown joins the brim, to protect hat from sweat. **2.** A stretch terrycloth band worn around the head during exercise to absorb sweat.

tam/tam-o-shanter **1.** "Tam" is a shortened form of the Scottish "tam-o-shanter" used in the United States. It is a flat cap made in several ways: (a) out of two circles of fabric—one complete and one with hole cut in center—sewed together at the outer edge; (b) crocheted with pompon on top for trim; (c) made out of piece of circular molded felt and also called a BERET (see under HEADWEAR). **2.** Genuine Scottish tams are frequently made out of long, shaggy striped wool fabric and cut in segments so that stripes form a pattern on the top. Usually larger than other tams with a pompon at center of crown. *Der.* From the name of the main character of Scottish poem written by Robert Burns about 1791 called "Tam O'Shanter."

tam

tea-cozy cap Cap introduced in late 1960s that fits head closely to cover hair completely. *Der.* Quilted padded cover for teapots used to keep the tea hot at the table.

templers/temples/templettes See HEADWEAR: BOSSES.

ten-gallon hat See HEADWEAR: COWBOY HAT and SOMBRERO.

terai hat ∞ Riding hat of fur or felt with red lining, shaped somewhat like a DERBY (see under HEADWEAR), with large brim that had a metal vent in the crown. Made with two hats sewed together at edges of brims and worn by British women, sometimes men, in tropical climates since 1880s.

Thérèse/Teresa ∞ (ter-eece′) Large hood, held out with wire, designed to go over tall bonnets and hairstyles. Worn in France from mid-1770s to 1790, later with an attached shoulder cape.

three-storeys-and-a-basement ∞ Amusing name given to woman's hat of 1886 with very high crown.

thrum ∞ **1.** Short tufts of wool left on loom after fabric is cut away, which was knitted into workmen's caps in the United States, and England in 18th c. **2.** Long-napped felt hat worn in 16th c. Also called a *thrummed hat.*

tiara (tee-ar′-ah) Curved band, often of metal set with jewels or flowers, worn on top of woman's head from ear to ear, giving effect of a crown. Sometimes used to hold a wedding veil. Also called *demi-coronal.*

tilbury hat ∞ Man's small hat with high tapered flat-topped crown and narrow rounded brim worn in 1830s.

toboggan cap See HEADWEAR: STOCKING CAP.

topee/topi Tropical helmet shaped more like a hat with a wide brim, originally made of cork ½″ thick. Worn particularly in the jungles as a protection from the sun. Does not fit close to the head, because constructed with an air space between head and helmet. Also called *pith helmet. Der.* Name refers to European cork.

top hat Man's tall hat made of shiny silk or beaver cloth with narrow brim. Differs from an OPERA HAT (see under HEADWEAR) in that the latter is always collapsible and made of dull silk. Term used since about 1820 for a high crowned hat with a flat top and narrow brim, sometimes slightly rolled at the sides. Also called a **chimney-pot hat** from the 1830s, when it replaced the beaver hat. After this it was made by felting rabbit hair on top of silk and applying steam and pressure to make a smooth and shiny surface. Also see HEADWEAR: SILK HAT. Also called *plug hat* (American term for top hat), *pot hat, stovepipe hat* (because of its resemblance to a stove pipe), or *topper.*

top hat

topper See HEADWEAR: TOP HAT.

toque (tok) **1.** A basic hat type that has a high crown and is generally brimless or may have a very small brim. Can be made in various shapes, often turban-like. **2.** ∞ Woman's coif or head scarf worn in the 16th and early 17th cs.

toque #1

H

toquet ∞ (toe-ket′) Woman's small draped evening hat worn on back of head in 1840s. Made of satin or velvet with small turned-up brim in front and trimmed with ostrich feather.

toreador hat (tor-ayah′-dor) **1.** See HEADWEAR: MATADOR HAT. **2.** ∞ Woman's hat of the 1890s with flat, shallow circular crown made of felt or straw and worn tilted. Inspired by the opera *Carmen,* starring Emma Calve.

torsade ∞ (tor-sahd′) Coronet of pleated velvet or tulle with long LAPPETS (see under HEADWEAR) worn for evening by women in 1864.

touring cap Leather or fabric cap with snap-down visor, frequently treated for water repellency. Popular in the 1980s, it is copied from earlier cap worn when "touring" in early 20th-c. automobiles.

Trafalgar turban ∞ British woman's evening turban of 1806 embroidered with Admiral Nelson's name. *Der.* Named for British naval victory near Cape Trafalgar, off Spanish coast, in 1805.

trencher hat ∞ Woman's silk hat with triangular brim coming to point above forehead, worn in first decade of the 19th c.

tricorne (try′-korn) 19th-c. term for variation of the cocked hat (see under HEADWEAR), turned up to form three equidistant peaks with one peak in center front. Also spelled *tricorn.*

tricorne

trilby ∞ Man's soft felt hat with supple brim worn from 1895 on. *Der.* Inspired by George de Maurier's 1894 novel *Trilby.* The following year, *Trilby* was made into a play in which Beerbohm Tree played the character Svengali, in this type of hat.

trooper cap Man's or boy's cap of leather or leatherlike plastic with fur or pile lining and a flap around sides and back. Flaps can be folded down to keep ears warm or up to reveal lining. *Der.* Originally worn by state police or "troopers," now used by mail carriers, police officers, etc.

turban **1.** Man's headdress of Moslem origin consisting of long scarf of linen, cotton, or silk wound around the head. Sometimes with one loose end hanging down, or decorated with a jewel in center front. Sometimes consists of fabric wrapped around a FEZ (see under HEADWEAR) with crown showing. **2.** Adaptation of this draped hat for women has become a classic style.

turban #2

Turkey bonnet ∞ Term used in the 15th and 16th-c. for man's or woman's tall cylindrical hat without a brim introduced to Italy, France, and England from the East. Woman's style was shaped like inverted flower pot with veil from crown passing under chin. Also called *Turkey hat.*

tutulus ∞ (toot-too′-luss) Tall cone-shaped hat worn by ancient Etruscan women with, or without, upturned brim across the front.

Tyrolean hat See HEADWEAR: ALPINE HAT.

ugly ∞ British term for collapsible brim worn from late 1840s to mid-1860s over a *bonnet* as a sunshade to protect weak eyes or when traveling. Made of series of cane half-hoops covered with silk. When not is use, folded up like a *calash.*

umbrella brim Brim of woman's hat set in *umbrella pleats,* opens out to resemble an umbrella.

under cap ∞ **1.** Indoor cap made like a skull-cap worn under hat by elderly men in 16th c. **2.** Woman's indoor cap usually shaped like a COIF (#3) worn under outdoor hat from 16th to mid-19th c.

Valois hat ∞ (val-wa′) Velvet or beaver hat with brim of equal width all around worn by women in 1822.

veil **1.** Decorative accessory usually made of lace, net, tulle, or sheer fabric placed on the head and usually draped down the back. May also drape over the face and shoulders. **2.** Piece of net or tulle attached to a hat. Introduced in medieval times and called a *coverchief.* From late 18th to end of 19th c. a piece of net, lace, or gauze worn attached to an outdoor bonnet or hat worn by women. Arranged to cover part or the entire face or draped to back as trimming. From 1890s veils extended to the chin. Worn intermittently since, mostly as trim. Particularly worn in 1930s, 1940s, and 1950s.

visor   Stiffened part of a semicircle attached to a headband or to front of a cap to protect eyes from the sun. Also called **bill.**

vulture-winged headdress   ∞ Egyptian queen's headdress with two wings hanging down on either side of the face with the uraeus, or cobra design of the sacred asp, usually attached to center front. The vulture wings are a symbol of protection used by the Egyptians.

watch cap   Knitted cap, fitting closely over head with turned-up cuff, made of navy-blue wool yarn. Worn by sailors on watch, for other work duty, or as a replacement for white duck hat. Adapted in other colors for sportswear by men, women, and children.   watch cap

Watteau hat   ∞ (wat-toe′)   Small hat for the seashore shaped like an upside-down saucer, worn by women in 1866. Trimmed with ribbons radiating from crown to edge of brim. Sometimes had a rosette with attached streamers on right side. *Der.* Named for the artist WATTEAU.

welding cap   Cap similar to a baseball cap but with a relatively short VISOR (see under HEADWEAR).

Wellington hat   ∞ Tall beaver hat worn by men in the 1820s and 1830s with a crown at least 8″ high and flared at the top. *Der.* Named for the first Duke of Wellington, British military hero who defeated Napoleon in the Battle of Waterloo in 1815.

western hat   High-crowned hat with a flat top and wide brim frequently trimmed with a leather thong pulled through holes punched at regular intervals around the crown. Has a leather adjustable strap worn under the chin to secure the hat, or permit it to hang down the back. Similar to GAUCHO HAT (see under HEADWEAR).

white crown   ∞ Crown of ancient upper Egypt made in tall cylindrical shape tapered in at top and ending with a knob. When Egypt became

united, this crown was worn together with the red crown of lower Egypt.

wide-awake   ∞ Man's 19th c. broad-brimmed low-crowned hat of felt or other material used for country wear.

widow's peak   ∞ Small cap wired in heart-shaped form with peak in center of forehead. Originally worn by Catherine de Medici as a widow's bonnet and much worn by Mary, Queen of Scots. Also see HEADWEAR: MARIE STUART BONNET.

wig hat   Soft hat, often crocheted, that fits tightly around the face but blouses in the back. Some hats are entirely covered with feathers, some with flowers. No hair shows from beneath the hat. Popular in mid-1960s.

William Penn hat   Medium-sized brim with high-rounded crown worn forward on the head. Introduced in late 1960s. *Der.* Similar to hat worn by William Penn (1644–1718) when he colonized Pennsylvania.

wimple   **1.** Cloth worn to cover the chin of a woman in the Middle Ages. During the 14th c., it gradually became a part of the customary dress of widows, who wore it with a dark hood and veil. It also became a part of the habits of some orders of nuns. Also called a *barbe.* **2.** ∞ Gauze veil of 1809 worn with evening dress.

wind bonnet   Lightweight foldup covering for head made of net, point d'esprit, or chiffon to protect hair.

World War I helmet   Cast metal helmet, with a shallow crown and narrow brim, that did not cover the ears or conform to the shape of the head, held on by a chin strap.

World War II helmet   Cast metal helmet conforming closely to the shape of the head with slightly upturned edge. When worn in battle, sometimes covered with a piece of multi-colored fabric for camouflage.

yachting cap   Cap, usually white, with flat crown and black or navy blue visor, decorated with yacht-club emblem. Styled similar to a naval officer's cap, and also worn by yacht-club members on boats.

yarmulka   See HEADWEAR: SKULLCAP.

H

yeoman hat ∞ Woman's fabric hat with puffed crown gathered into wide band, sometimes with upturned brim worn with WALKING DRESS from 1806 to 1812.

zucchetto See CLERICAL DRESS: CALOTTE.

---

head wrap See HEADWEAR.

heart breaker See HAIRSTYLES: CRÈVE-COEUR and LOVE LOCK.

heart-shaped cut See GEMS, GEM CUTS, AND SETTINGS.

heart-shaped headdress See HEADWEAR.

heather effect † Appearance of fabric achieved by blending dyed fibers with white fibers to produce a mottled appearance. First made in lavender tones similar to the flowers of the heather plant, but now made in many different colors.

heat setting † Process used to set, by applying heat and pressure, permanent pleats or creases in fabrics made of manfactured fibers such as nylon, polyester, and acetate.

Hedebo See EMBROIDERIES AND SEWING STITCHES.

hedgehog See HAIRSTYLES: COIFFURE À L'HERISSON.

heel 1. See FOOTWEAR. 2. See HOSIERY.

heel horn See FOOTWEAR: A.T.P.

heelless hose See HOSIERY.

heel lift See FOOTWEAR: HEELS.

heels See FOOTWEAR.

Heim, Jacques * See APPENDIX/DESIGNERS.

heliodor See GEMS, GEM CUTS, AND SETTINGS.

heliotrope See GEMS, GEM CUTS, AND SETTINGS: BLOODSTONE.

helmet See HEADWEAR.

hem See CLOTHING CONSTRUCTION DETAILS.

hematite See GEMS, GEM CUTS, AND SETTINGS.

hemispherical hat See HEADWEAR.

hemming stitch See EMBROIDERIES AND SEWING STITCHES.

hemp † A coarse, strong, lustrous fiber from the stem of the hemp plant. Cultivation of hemp plants is illegal in the United States because the plant is from the same family as marijuana; however, sale of hemp fabrics and fibers is legal and the fiber is used for making apparel.

hemstitch/hemstitching See EMBROIDERIES AND SEWING STITCHES.

Henley boater See HEADWEAR.

Henley neckline See NECKLINES AND COLLARS.

Henley shirt See SHIRTS.

henna 1. Orange-colored dye, one of the earliest dyes discovered, comes from the plant by the same name. Egyptians used it to dye their fingers to the first joint, simulating our nail polish. Also used on toes in some Eastern countries in early days. Used to dye fabrics in primitive times. 2. Basic hair dye or rinse. 3. An orange color.

hennin See HEADWEAR.

Henrietta jacket See COATS AND JACKETS.

Henry II collar See NECKLINES AND COLLARS.

Henry IV collar See NECKLINES AND COLLARS.

hense lynes/henselyns See DOUBLET.

Hercules braid See BRAIDS.

herigaut See GARDECORPS.

hérisson See HAIRSTYLES.

Herkimer diamond See GEMS, GEM CUTS, AND SETTINGS.

herl See FEATHERS.

herlot See HARLOT.

Herman, Stan * See APPENDIX/DESIGNERS.

Hermés * See APPENDIX/DESIGNERS.

heroin chic Term applied to fashion advertising and magazine photography style of the late 1980s and 1990s in which models appear emaciated, pale, and unkempt, with large circles under their eyes; an appearance likened to that of hard-drug addicts.

Herrera, Carolina * See APPENDIX/DESIGNERS.

herringbone Pattern made of short, slanting parallel lines adjacent to other rows slanting in reverse direction, creating a continuous V-shaped design like the bones of a fish. Used in tweeds, embroidery, and in working of fur skins.

herringbone chain See JEWELRY.

herringbone stitch See EMBROIDERIES AND SEWING STITCHES: CATCH STITCH.

herringbone weave † Chevron pattern produced in a fabric by using the twill weave for several rows in one direction, then reversing the direction. Usually made of yarns of two colors in yarn-dyed woolen fabric with thick yarns producing a large pattern. Also called *broken twill weave*.

Hessian boot See FOOTWEAR.

heuke See HEADWEAR.

heuse See FOOTWEAR.

H

hickory stripes See PRINTS, STRIPES, AND CHECKS.

hidden rivets jeans Jeans with rivets hidden inside the pockets, manufactured by Levi Strauss between 1937 and about 1960.

high button shoe See FOOTWEAR.

high cut See FOOTWEAR.

high fashion Apparel of advanced design available from innovative designers and/or firms. It is usually more expensive.

high hat See HEADWEAR: TOP HAT.

high head See HAIRSTYLES.

Highland dress Traditional man's costume of Scots Highlander, consisting of KILT; PLAID over one shoulder fastened by brooch; scarlet jacket; wide belt with SPORRAN attached; feather bonnet or GLENGARRY CAP (see under HEADWEAR); plaid-top socks; and buttoned gaiters over shoes. Costume was forbidden by law from 1747 to 1782. Also see PLAIDS AND TARTANS.

Highland suit Boy's suit of 1880s and early 1890s consisting of jacket, kilt, GLENGARRY CAP (see under HEADWEAR), and plaid socks copied from *Highland dress.* Also called a *Scotch suit.*

highlights See HAIRSTYLES.

high-rise pants See PANTS.

high-rise waistline See WAISTLINES.

high tech fabrics/hi-tech fabrics Fabrics made from manufactured fibers with special performance characteristics (e.g., water repellence, strength, stretch, heat resistance). Such fabrics have been used for fashion goods, especially in the area of clothing for active sports. Also called *high performance fibers.*

hikers See FOOTWEAR.

hiking boot See FOOTWEAR.

hiking costume ∞ Costume worn by women in 1890s consisting of serge or lighter-weight bloomers, pleated or gathered at the waist and pulled down below the knee. Worn with a tight-fitting Eton-type jacket with large lapels; a white shirt; man's necktie; serviceable shoes with flat heels worn with PUTTEES (see under FOOTWEAR) or high-top laced boots to below the knee; and hat similar to a cowboy hat with high uncreased crown and wide brim. Worn for mountain climbing and hiking.

Hilfiger, Tommy * See APPENDIX/DESIGNERS.

himation ∞ (he-matt'-ee-own) Greek mantle in the form of a rectangular shawl, 3½ to 4 yards long and about 1½ yards wide that was worn alone or over a tunic by men and women in ancient Greece. Made of wool or linen—usually white with border—it was usually draped over the left shoulder and wrapped under the right arm; sometimes one end was pulled over the head.

himation

hinged bracelet See JEWELRY.

hip bags ∞ Slang term in 1883 for folds of skirt forming PANNIERS at hips. Also called *curtain drapery* in the United States and *pompadour* in England.

hip boot See FOOTWEAR.

hip buttons See CLOSURES.

hip-hop A style of dancing associated with rap music that began in the Bronx in New York City. **B-boys** (break boys) of 1970s (their female followers were called **flygirls**) developed an athletic dance style. When this music and dance became part of the mainstream in the 1980s, fans imitated styles worn by B-boys and flygirls and wore bright, baggy clothes, football or baseball shirts, baseball caps turned backward, and high running shoes with untied shoe laces, designer sportswear, athletic shoes, and large-scale gold jewelry. In the 1990s, mainstream fashion designers such as TOMMY HILFIGER incorporated hip-hop styles into their lines, and hip-hop influences permeated styles worn by the young. Around 2001, fans of rap music began to wear clip-on covers for their teeth, called **fronts,** made of gold and set with diamonds or other gems. When a person wearing these devices smiled, it was said that his or her smile had **bling.**

hip-hugger Contemporary term for low-slung pants, skirt, or belt worn below normal waistline, resting on hip bones.

hip length See LENGTHS.

Hiplets® See HOSIERY.

hippie/hippie look Term coined in mid-1960s for young person who defied established customs and adopted an unconventional mode of dress

H

(e.g., long uncombed hair, aged blue jeans, miscellaneous tops, fringed jackets, strings of beads, symbolic pendants, pouch bags, bare feet, or sandals). Started a trend toward ethnic fashions and unusual mixtures of dress.

hippie look

hip-rider swimsuit See ACTIVEWEAR.

hipsters **1.** See PANTS: HIP-HUGGERS. **2.** Fans of Bebop music, played by Dizzy Gillespie in the 1940s, who wore berets, colorful, wide scarves, sunglasses, and goatees (see BEARDS).

hi-rise girdle See UNDERGARMENTS.

his and hers look Garments that look alike but that are specifically made one for a man, the other for a woman—as distinct from "unisex-look," where garments were actually interchangeable. Popular for pajamas during the 1950s. During the late 1960s, popular for all types of clothing, particularly pantsuits with matching vest, caped coats, shirts, and sweaters. Also see UNISEX LOOK.

hive bonnet See HEADWEAR: BEEHIVE HAT #1.

H-line Straight silhouette, or dress, marked by a low horizontal belt or seam and called H by Paris designer Christian Dior in 1957.

hobble skirt See SKIRTS.

hockey skate See FOOTWEAR.

hogger/hoker See FOOTWEAR: OKER.

holbein stitch (hole-bine) See EMBROIDERIES AND SEWING STITCHES: DOUBLE-RUNNING STITCH.

Holbein work (hole-bine) See EMBROIDERIES AND SEWING STITCHES.

Hollywood top slip See UNDERGARMENTS.

holoku (hoh-low′-koo) Traditional Hawaiian garment derived from the EMPIRE DRESS styles worn by American missionary women when they arrived in Hawaii in the early 1880s. Hawaiian royalty asked the missionaries to make them dresses, and the resulting gowns were altered slightly to accommodate the larger size of the Hawaiians and the climate. The full-length garment had a YOKE from which the dress fell in a loose fit, a high neck, and long sleeves. Over the years these garments have changed somewhat as fashions changed, but retain these basic lines in either more or less fitted versions and are still worn for formal occasions by women of Hawaiian descent.

holster pockets See POCKETS.

holy work/hollie work See EMBROIDERIES AND SEWING STITCHES.

homburg See HEADWEAR.

home fashions Textile products used for home end uses such as towels, bedding, draperies, and table linens, and which exhibit style changes over time in response to changing fashion trends.

home party See PARTY PLAN.

homespun † Fabrics made from handspun yarns and woven on a hand loom. Most are plain weave, loosely constructed, heavy wool fabrics made of coarse, uneven yarns. Contemporary versions are now made with automatic looms from manufactured and wool blends and imitate the texture and appearance of the handmade fabrics.

honeycomb † Any fabric that forms a series of recessed squares similar to a waffle and is made either in a honeycomb weave or knit. Cotton fabrics are frequently called *waffle-cloth*. They are sometimes erroneously called *waffle piqués*.

honeycomb stitch See EMBROIDERIES AND SEWING STITCHES.

Honiton gossamer skirt See UNDERGARMENTS.

Honiton lace See LACES.

hood See HEADWEAR.

hooded heel See FOOTWEAR.

hooded seal See FURS: HAIR SEAL.

hook and eye See CLOSURES.

hook-and-loop closure See CLOSURES: VELCRO.®

hoop bracelet See JEWELRY: BANGLE BRACELETS.

hoop earrings See JEWELRY: GYPSY EARRINGS.

hoop petticoat See UNDERGARMENTS: HOOPS.

hoops See UNDERGARMENTS.

hoop skirt See SKIRTS.

Hoover apron See APRONS.

Hope Star® See GEMS, GEM CUTS, AND SETTINGS.

Hopi bracelet See JEWELRY.

hopsacking † A broad classification of fabrics made in loosely constructed plain weave of coarse uneven yarns. The fabric was originally found in sacks made from coarse undyed jute or hemp into which hops were put during harvesting. Made in cotton, spun rayon, and manufactured fibers. Coarse varieties also called BURLAP.

hoqueton/houqueton See ARMOR: ACTON.

horizontal integration The production by a business of products competitive with other products it makes. For example, a knitted fabric producer that makes various types of knitted fabrics. Also see VERTICAL INTEGRATION.

Horn, Carol * See APPENDIX/DESIGNERS.

horned headdress See HEADWEAR.

horn rims See EYEWEAR.

horsehair 1. † Hair fiber obtained from the mane or tail of a horse. 2. Fabric made from this fiber used in combination with mohair, linen, cotton, and other fibers woven in an openwork weave. Used for interfacing in suits, coats, and also for stiffening.

horsehair braid See BRAIDS.

horsehide See LEATHERS.

horseshoe Term for U-shape, used as neckline or yoke on blouses, sweaters, and dresses.

horseshoe collar/horseshoe neckline See NECKLINES AND COLLARS.

horseshoe jumper See JUMPERS.

hose See HOSIERY.

HOSIERY

Knitted item of wearing apparel covering the foot and/or leg. Includes apparel also called STOCKINGS and SOCKS (see under HOSIERY). For forerunners of knitted hosiery, see CHAUSSES and CHAUSSEMBLES in the alphabetical listing. A machine for knitting stockings was invented in the late 1500s, and the inventor presented Queen Elizabeth I with a pair of knitted silk stockings. Hosiery was made from cotton, linen, wool, and silk yarns. Among the innovations in the development of hosiery were "flesh-colored," or beige, silk hosiery in the 1920s, the introduction of NYLON hose in 1940, textured hose in the 1960s, and PANTYHOSE (see under HOSIERY) in the 1960s. Synonym: HOSE (see under HOSIERY). *Der.* Anglo-Saxon *hosa.*

all-in-one pantyhose See HOSIERY: PANTYHOSE.

all-sheer pantyhose Sheer nylon pantyhose made with no reinforcements. Also called *sheer pantyhose.*

ankle-length hosiery Sock-length hosiery made out of conventional nylon yarn. Worn by women with full-length slacks or pants.

ankle sock Short sock reaching only to the ankle; may be worn turned down or have elastic top on the cuff. Introduced for women in 1920. This caused a sensation when they were first worn at Forest Hills, New York, for an amateur tennis match in 1931 by Mrs. Fearnley-Whittingstall. Worn today by women and children and infrequently by men. Also called *anklet.* Also see HOSIERY: BOBBY SOCK.

anklet See HOSIERY: ANKLE SOCK.

anti-embolism stocking A stocking specially constructed with graduated compression that aids blood flow and prevents blood clots from forming. Also called *surgical stockings.*

argyle socks Sock knitted in a diamond pattern of several colors by hand or on a jacquard loom. Heel, toe, and top areas are of solid color while the other part is of a multicolored, diamond-patterned plaid. *Der.* Tartan of Duke of Argyle and Clan Campbell of Argyll, a county in West Scotland. Also spelled *argyll, argyl.*

Art Deco hose Hose printed with geometric designs derived from Art Deco styles, which underwent a revival in the late 1960s. *Der.* French, *art decoratif,* "decorative art."

Art Nouveau hose Stylized single or multiple printed designs placed on the calf or climbing the leg, usually on opaque or colored hose, based on Art Nouveau designs. An innovation of the late 1960s. *Der.* French, "new art."

astrolegs hose Hose imprinted with signs of the zodiac, introduced in the late 1960s.

athletic sock See HOSIERY: SWEATSOCK.

bed sock Knit sock worn when sleeping to keep foot warm. Often hand-knit in a variety of fancy stitches. Also called *foot warmer.*

bikini pantyhose Pantyhose with low-slung top for wear with bare-midriff dresses, hip-hugger skirts, or low-slung pants.

blazer sock Boys' and girls' socks decorated with bands of color. Similar in effect to competitive stripes on knit shirts.

bobby sock Ankle sock, usually with turned-down cuff, worn by children and so universally popular with female teenagers during 1940s and 1950s that young girls were called "bobby soxers."

bodyshaper pantyhose See HOSIERY: PANTY-HOSE.

boot That part of pantyhose or stocking that extends from the panty or welt to the toe.

boot hose ∞ Long stockings of coarse linen with flared tops. The tops sometimes had decorated borders made of gold or silver lace, ruffled linen, or fringed silk, which were called **boot hose tops.** When made with no foot, fitted with a strap under arch of foot and laced through eyelets at top to connect with breeches, they were called **stirrup hose.** Worn by men from mid-15th to 18th c. to protect silk stockings under heavy boots. Also called *boot stocking.*

boot hose tops See HOSIERY: BOOT HOSE.

bootie See FOOTWEAR: BOOTIE #2.

checkerboard hose Hose knitted in a checked design with some squares sheer and some opaque, or knitted in two colors.

clocked hose Hose or stockings that have designs running part way up the sides of the legs. First worn in the 16th c. and intermittently since. Designs may be knitted in or embroidered on after hose are knitted.

clocked hose

control pantyhose See HOSIERY: PANTYHOSE.

Courrèges flower sock See HOSIERY: KNEE-HI SOCK.

crew sock Heavy sock extending to lower calf with foot knitted in plain stitch, upper part with rib stitch. Originally white and worn for rowing and other sports. Now made in colors, especially for men and boys.

cushion-sole sock Sock worn for active sports knit with a special sole that keeps the foot from blistering—often a layer of cotton and stretch-nylon terry cloth. Frequently given a special finish to help protect the foot from fungus, bacteria, and odor.

detachable pantyhose Three-piece pantyhose made with patented bands on panties to attach replacement stockings.

dress sock Man's sock in lightweight, silky type, nonbulky yarns in conservative colors.

electric sock Heavyweight knee-high sock, usually made of a combination of fibers, with a specially designed heating element operated by a battery held on by strap around the leg. Worn by spectators at winter sports events. Trademarked by Timely Products Corp. and called *Lectra-Sox.*®

English rib sock Man's sock knit with a wide rib or wale and a narrow depression between the wales (see WALE #2).

fancies Men's socks in multicolor designs.

finger band In all nude pantyhose, a reinforcement just under the waistband to protect against fingernail punctures.

fishmouth toe Method of closing a nonreciprocating toe (see HOSIERY: RECIPROCATING CONSTRUCTION) in which the seam runs parallel to the bottom of the foot rather than across the top of the toe.

fishnet hose Openwork hose in a diamond-shaped pattern.

flat-knit hose See HOSIERY: FULL-FASHIONED HOSE.

footsock/footie Sock that ends below the ankle bone. When these socks have a pompon sewn on at the back, they may be called **poms.**

foot warmers See HOSIERY: BED SOCK.

full-fashioned hose Hose knit in flat pieces and seamed up the back, leaving fashion marks where knitting is increased or decreased. Also called *flat-knit hose.*

garter belt hose Hose attached to two elastic strips that connect at waistline to an elastic band around waist.

glitter hose Hose made of shiny yarn—some made with metallic yarn that reflects silver, gold, and copper tones. Introduced to wear with minidresses in the 1960s. Also called *glimmer, silver, gold* or *metallic hose.*

gold hose See HOSIERY: GLITTER HOSE.

gym sock See HOSIERY: SWEATSOCK.

half-hose Standard-length stocking for men that ends halfway between the ankle and the knee.

heel Portion of the hose that fits the heel of the foot.

heelless hose Hosiery without a double reinforcement at the heel.

hose Synonym for STOCKINGS (see HOSIERY) and HOSIERY (see introduction to HOSIERY). Current usage suggests that hose tends to be used when referring to the more transparent and decorative varieties of hosiery, while "stockings" is used for heavier varieties of a more utilitarian nature.

jacquard hose (ja-kard′) Hosiery knit on a jacquard knitting machine that permits much variation in colors and patterns. Argyle and herringbone designs would be examples of jacquard patterns. Popular in the 1920s for children, and fashionable since.

jeweled pantyhose Sheer pantyhose with embroidery at ankle trimmed with rhinestones. Introduced in 1986.

knee-high hose Hose of conventional nylon yarn or of nylon and SPANDEX that come to just below the knees and are finished at the top with elastic. First made in beige and worn when dresses were long, now worn with various types of pants and after the 1980s featured in black, white, and colors. Sometimes abbreviated to *knee-hi.*

knee-hi sock Sock that reaches to below the knee. Worn by boys in early 1900s with knickers and accepted for girls in 1920s and 1930s and after. Adopted by teenagers and adult women in the 1960s as the popularity of the MINI increased. Featured by the French couturier Courrèges in his collection in 1965. In 1967 he introduced a variation called the **Courrèges flower sock** (coor-rej′), a dainty feminine sock coming to several inches below the knee usually styled in white with lacy top, embroidered with flowers. Also called *knee sock, trouser sock.*

knee high socks

knee sock See HOSIERY: KNEE-HI SOCK.

lace hose Knitted lace in rose, Chantilly, and Spanish lace patterns used to make hosiery. Introduced in 1960s and popular for children and women in 1980s.

lace pantyhose Pantyhose made of patterned stretch lace in openwork styles.

legwarmer Knitted covering for legs extending from the ankle to the knee or above. Originally worn by ballet and toe dancers when exercising and in the 1980s became a fashion item.

leg warmers

lisle hosiery (lyle) Socks and hose made of cotton LISLE YARN, smooth, lustrous cotton yarn. Nearly as fine as silk, usually white, brown, or black, lisle hosiery was worn by men, women, and children throughout 19th and early 20th c. until replaced by silk in 1920s and nylon in 1940s. Revived in the 1960s when longer opaque socks were popular. See HOSIERY: OPAQUE HOSE. *Der.* Early spelling of Lille, France.

mesh hose Nylon hose knit with a milanese stitch, forming tiny diamond designs that make hose run-resistant. See MILANESE KNIT.

metallic hose See HOSIERY: GLITTER HOSE.

mini-pane hose See HOSIERY: WINDOWPANE HOSE.

mock seam Hosiery industry term for seam sewed into circular-knit hose to give appearance of FULL-FASHIONED HOSE (see under HOSIERY).

neats Solid color socks ornamented with small, evenly spaced designs such as dots.

neon sock Ankle- or knee-length sock styled with ribbed tops in extremely bright colors of 100% nylon.

nonreciprocated See HOSIERY: RECIPROCATED CONSTRUCTION.

novelties Women's hosiery that has unusual patterns, designs, or coloring.

nylons Now synonymous with women's hose because of the almost universal use of NYLON in dress hose for women. Trademarked nylon yarn was introduced in 1939, making possible a much sheerer type of hose that was also more durable than the silk hosiery worn previously. In great demand during World War II, nylon hosiery became a "black market" item.

nude heel Women's pantyhose or nylon stockings that have no reinforcement at the heel. Popular for wear with backless or sling-back shoes.

opaque hose/opaque pantyhose (oh-pake′) Textured or plain hose or pantyhose that are

H

not sheer and come in all colors. Opaque nylon pantyhose are 40 DENIER or more in weight.

over-the-knee socks Sock or stocking with an elastic top that reaches above the knee. Elastic top holds up the stocking without a garter.

pantyhose Hosiery, made with textured and sheer nylon yarns, that follows the design of tights, having stockings and panties cut in one piece. In 1958 the firm called Societé de Bonneterie De Tergnier in France patented a brand of sheer pantyhose called *mitoufle* (mitt-oof′-luh) (or tights). Mary Quant, British designer, also was influential in trying to find a suitable hose and girdle combination for wear with her short-skirted dresses of early 1960s. Panty-hose were introduced in the United States about 1963. First made in sizes for tall, medium, and petite heights, and later made in larger sizes, pantyhose were introduced for men in fall 1970. In the mid-1980s interest in unusual pantyhose was revived and currently they are made in many patterns, colors, and textures. Those pantyhose with a knitted-in panty of heavier weight nylon or cotton are known as **all-in-one pantyhose. Control pantyhose** are those in which the panty portion is knit of nylon and stretch yarns (see ELASTOMERS) to provide the control of a lightweight girdle. **Bodyshaper pantyhose** are control pantyhose with the control section extending to cover the thighs in addition to abdomen and hips. Also see HOSIERY: TIGHTS.

panty hose

patterned hose Hosiery woven in a design, usually on a Jacquard knitting machine, e.g., point d'esprit, checkerboard, and argyle hose.

Peds® Registered trademark of American Corporation for a broad range of hosiery products of varying types and uses. Also see HOSIERY: SOCKLET.

poms See HOSIERY: FOOTSOCK.

point d'esprit hose (pwan des-pree′) Netlike machine-manufactured hose of cotton or nylon with some of the holes made solid to form a decorative pattern.

proportioned hose Hosiery designed to fit different types of legs (e.g., extra long, full above-the-knee, long, short, and average).

quarter socks Sock, shorter than ankle length, made of acrylic and nylon with colored terry knit top in colors.

reciprocated construction In the making of a stocking, which begins at the top and moves toward the toe, a semicircular or "recipro-cating" motion of the machine shapes a pocket for the heel. A toe may also be formed. A **nonreciprocated** stocking has no shaped heel or toe. (See HOSIERY: TUBE SOCK and FISHMOUTH TOE.)

replaceable legs Waist-length garment in which one or both legs can be replaced. Made either as a separate panty to which legs attach at the bottom or as two separate legs, each with a half panty and a full waistband.

ribbed hose Textured hose knit with vertical wales.

rollups ∞ Man's stockings pulled up over knee of breeches and folded over in wide band. Worn in late 17th to mid 18th c. Also called *rollers, rolling stockings,* or *hose.*

run See RUN in alphabetical listing.

run-resistant hosiery See RUN-RESISTANT in alphabetical listing.

sandalfoot hose Hosiery with no reinforce-ment at the toe. Popular for wearing with open-toed shoes or sandals.

sandalfoot pantyhose Sheer pantyhose with no reinforcements at toes or heels. May have an opaque panty portion, or be sheer to the waist.

sanitary sock An athletic sock, usually white, worn under a STIRRUP SOCK (see under FOOT-WEAR) as part of an athletic uniform.

seamed hose **1.** Full-fashioned hose with a seam up the back, originally made by the flat-knit process and sewed together. Popular type hose generally worn until the 1960s, when tex-tured yarns were invented with more "stretch" making it possible to make well-fitting hose without the seam. By 1968, very few seamed hose were sold. **2.** Reintroduced in 1970s but made in circular knits usually with black lines up the back.

seamed pantyhose Conventional pantyhose with black seam up the back.

seamless hose Circular-knit hose without seam in back. See CIRCULAR KNIT in alphabetical listing.

sheer hose Nylon hose made with a fine or low denier yarn, thus making them more translucent. **Ultra sheer** hose are made with exceptionally fine yarns; **day sheer** or **business sheer** hose are less sheer and more durable.

sheer pantyhose See HOSIERY: ALL-SHEER PANTYHOSE.

silver hose See HOSIERY: GLITTER HOSE.

slipper sock Crocheted or knit sock attached to soft, moccasin-type sole.

slouch sock Anklet with shirred tricolored top, made of acrylic and stretch nylon, designed to be pushed down and gathered around the ankle.

sneaker sock Type of **socklet** (see under HOSIERY) that is shaped higher in front to conform to laced instep of the sneakers. Worn instead of sock for the bare-legged look.

socklet Very low-cut sock usually lightweight and not visible above pumps or other shoes, styled to keep feet comfortable while maintaining bare-leg look in summer. **Peds®** (see under FOOTWEAR) is a trademark for the first widely available socklet made in a number of fibers and styles.

socks Now generally applied to knitted coverings for the foot and part of the leg that end somewhere around the ankle or above. Also see under HOSIERY: STOCKINGS. The term derives from the Latin *soccus*, which was a soft Roman shoe that covered the foot and ankle.

stay-up hose Regular hose knitted with a special top that holds the hose up without garters. Also called *stretch top*.

stirrup hose **1.** Hosiery in which the foot portion is fashioned without a heel or toe but which has a strap that fits under the instep of the foot. Often this construction is part of an athletic uniform. **2.** See HOSIERY: BOOT HOSE.

stockings Generally applied to knitted coverings for the foot and most of the leg. The distinction between socks and stockings is not entirely clear-cut, although socks are generally thought of as shorter and stockings as longer. The term derives from a type of leg covering called STOCKS that was worn in the 15th and 16th cs. and covered the foot and leg, extending to the waist. The upper section was called the upper stocks and the lower section, the lower stocks. When the garment was eventually divided into two separate parts in the 16th c., the lower part, which extended to the knee or above, became known as a stocking.

stretch hose Hosiery made with textured nylon stretch yarns. When such hose are not on the leg, they look very small.

stretch socks Socks knitted with textured yarns. Made so flexible that one size usually fits any size foot. Also made for men, women, and children.

support legwear Hosiery for men or women knitted of stretch nylon combined with spandex yarns to provide support to the muscles and veins of the legs. These fabrics keep pressure on the blood vessels so they will not dilate. This improves the circulation and prevents leg fatigue. They are made as hose and pantyhose for women and socks or stockings for men.

surgical stocking See HOSIERY: ANTI-EMBOLISM STOCKING.

sweatsock Sock made of combination of fibers (e.g., wool, acrylic, cotton, sometimes with cushioned sole). When this type of sock was first worn, it was always white and made of coarse cotton yarns that stretched out of shape easily. The cotton versions were known as **gym socks,** which were worn instead of wool socks for active sports and gym classes because of their washability. Blends now make these socks more washable and shape retentive. Usually they have a ribbed top and plain foot. Also called *athletic sock.*

tattoo pantyhose Very sheer pantyhose with legs painted in twining floral designs that appear at a distance to be tattooed on the leg.

textured hose Any style of hose patterned with thick and thin sections (e.g., lace, striped, or windowpane hose). First introduced by Rudi Gernreich in 1964 and later shown by other couturiers such as Givenchy in 1969.

thermal sock Heavy boot-length sock worn for winter activities; made of fibers with good insulating qualities.

thigh highs Nylon or nylon and spandex stockings that end at the top of the thigh and usually have elastic lace tops.

tights Knitted pants and stockings made in one piece, usually of opaque textured yarns. Worn originally by athletes and dancers, later worn by children. In the early 1960s worn primarily by women and girls as a substitute for hose. In 1980s also worn with leotards for dancing, exercising, etc.

toelet Hosiery designed to cover only the toe portion of the foot. Worn with heelless shoes such as mules or clogs.

tights

trouser sock See HOSIERY: KNEE-HI SOCK.

tube sock Calf or knee-length sock made of stretch yarn that does not have a knitted-in heel or toe.

ultra-sheer pantyhose See HOSIERY: SHEER PANTYHOSE.

U seams Pantyhose in which one leg is sewn to the other with a continuous U-shaped seam, As a result, they have no crotch.

welt That part at the top of a stocking that is reinforced so that it is strong enough to fasten a support device. It may be a separate piece of fabric machine sewn to the top of the stocking or may be knitted in heavier yarn and folded double.

windowpane hose Textured hose made in geometric squares in thin and thick sections. Heavier part looks like the frame of the window, sheerer section looks like the glass. **Mini-pane** hose have smaller squares. Made in white, black, and all colors (e.g., shocking pink, chartreuse, and orange). Popular in the mid-1960s.

---

hostess Adjective used to describe informal apparel worn at home while entertaining. Also called

at-home wear. See SLEEPWEAR AND LOUNGEWEAR: HOSTESS CULOTTES and HOSTESS ROBE.

hot mask See MASKS.

hot pants/HotPants See SHORTS.

hounds' ears See CUFFS.

hound's-tooth/houndstooth check See PRINTS, CHECKS, AND STRIPES.

houppelande ∞ (hoop′-land)
1. Man's voluminous outer robe of late 15th and 16th c., introduced by Richard II of England, made with high funnel-shaped neckline—later V-shaped. Sleeves were long, full, and DAGGED at edge or of BAGPIPE-type (see under SHOULDERS AND SLEEVES). Varied from thigh-length to trailing on the ground when worn as ceremonial robe.

houppelande #2

2. Woman's dress worn from late 14th through the 15th c. with fitted bodice, V-neckline with REVERS (see NECKLINES AND COLLARS) and dickey, or scooped neckline. Sleeves were long and tight-fitting or voluminous with fur lining. Frequently trained in back and so long in front that skirt had to be lifted when walking. **3.** A short houppelande with embroidery on both sleeves was known as a **haincelin** (ayn-cell-ihn) and named after Haincelin Coq, jester of Charles VI of France.

hourglass silhouette The shape of a woman's dress that has a full bust, pinched-in waist, and full, curving hips, a shape not unlike that of an hourglass. Illustrated at SILHOUETTE.

housecoat See SLEEPWEAR AND LOUNGEWEAR.

housedress A simple inexpensive dress made of washable fabric, worn while doing household chores. In the early 20th c., it was called a *wrapper.* One of the first items made by the garment industry in mass production, the wrapper evolved from a woman's dressing gown.

housel See FOOTWEAR: HEUSE.

house slipper See FOOTWEAR.

housedress
c. 1930s

H

housse See GARNACHE.

howling bags See PANTS.

huarache (wa-rach-ee) See FOOTWEAR.

Hubbard blouse See BLOUSES AND TOPS.

huckaback embroidery See EMBROIDERIES AND SEWING STITCHES.

huckaback stitch See EMBROIDERIES AND SEWING STITCHES.

Hudson Bay sable See FURS: MARTEN.

Hudson seal See FURS: MUSKRAT.

hug-me-tight See VESTS.

huke See HUQUE.

hula skirt See SKIRTS.

human hair wig See WIGS AND HAIRPIECES.

hundred pleater See HEADWEAR: CHEF'S HAT.

Hungarian Embroidery See EMBROIDERIES AND SEWING STITCHES.

Hungarian point See EMBROIDERIES AND SEWING STITCHES: FLORENTINE EMBROIDERY.

Hungarian suit ∞ A boy's belted double-breasted tunic, worn from late 1860s with a small turned-down collar and fastened on the side in a double-breasted manner. Trimmed with braid down the side front, on the flapped pockets, and cuffs. Worn with matching full or fitted trousers to below the knees with JOCKEY BOOTS (see under FOOTWEAR).

hunt Adjective used to describe clothing and accessories used by equestrians when hunting on horseback. See ACTIVEWEAR: HUNT BREECHES, COATS AND JACKETS: PINK COAT, HEADWEAR: HUNT CAP and HUNT DERBY.

hunter's pink See COATS AND JACKETS: PINK COAT.

hunter's watch See WATCHES.

hunting calf British term for REVERSE CALF. See LEATHERS.

hunting cap See HEADWEAR.

hunting necktie See TIES.

hunting plaid See PLAIDS AND TARTANS.

hunting shirt See SHIRTS.

hunting stock See TIES.

hunting vest See VESTS.

hunt look **1.** Overall appearance, popular around 1984, that consisted of the wearing, for daytime or evening, of either full attire or individual items of apparel worn when riding or for a formal fox hunt (e.g., jodhpurs or stirrup pants in tweeds or flannels with a stock shirt or any other type blouse; Derby worn with stock tie, weskit [sometimes with sleeves], pleated trousers, and a full-length coat similar to a Chesterfield; a narrow midi-length skirt with side slit worn with boots and hacking or velvet jacket). **2.** Riding habit as worn for a formal fox hunt or hacking in Great Britain, Massachusetts, or Virginia.

huque/huke ∞ Man's flowing outergarment, worn throughout 15th c., generally calf-length—sometimes longer or shorter—slashed up sides, and fur-trimmed around edges. Sometimes slashed up front and back for ease in riding horseback.

hurluberlu See HAIRSTYLES.

huseau See FOOTWEAR: HEUSE.

Hush Puppies® See footwear.

husky sizes Boys' sizes—8 to 20—cut with more generous proportions.

hussar boots See FOOTWEAR.

hussar jacket See COATS AND JACKETS.

hyacinth See GEMS, GEM CUTS, AND SETTINGS.

H

I

ice cube heel   See FOOTWEAR.

Icelandic sweater   See SWEATERS.

I.D./identification bracelet   See JEWELRY.

igloo mitt   See GLOVES AND GLOVE CONSTRUCTIONS.

ikat † (ee′-kat)   **1.** A method of yarn dyeing in which selected areas are knotted or tied so the dye will not penetrate. **2.** Fabrics woven from ikat yarns. The resulting design has a blurry or indistinct appearance. *Der.* Malayan, *mengikat,* "to tie, bind, knot or wind around." Also see PRINTS, STRIPES, AND CHECKS: WARP PRINT.

ikat fabric

I.L.G.W.U.   Abbreviation for INTERNATIONAL LADIES' GARMENT WORKERS' UNION. See UNION OF NEEDLETRADES, INDUSTRIAL, AND TEXTILE EMPLOYEES (UNITE).

image   A term used to describe the perception customers have of a company or product.

imbecile sleeve   See SHOULDERS AND SLEEVES.

imitation gems   See GEMS, GEM CUTS, AND SETTINGS.

imitation leather   Fabrics such as drill, sateen, and duck that have been coated, dyed, and embossed to simulate leathers such as alligator, snakeskin, or lizard. Coatings used include rubber, pyroxlin, nitrocellulose compounds, or vinyl resins.

imitation moleskin   See MOLESKIN FABRIC.

imitation pearls   See under GEMS, GEM CUTS, AND SETTINGS: PEARL.

imperial   **1.** See COATS AND JACKETS. **2.** See BEARD.

imperial skirt   See UNDERGARMENTS: HOOPS.

import   **1.** *n.* Merchandise bought offshore and brought into another country to sell. **2.** *v.* The act of importing.

importer/packager   Company that arranges with foreign contractors for the development and manufacture of full lines of apparel. The lines are sold to U.S. retailers to sell as private label merchandise.

impulse buying   Consumer purchasing of goods with little or no planning.

inchering   ∞ 18th c.: taking measurements of a person in order to make a garment.

incroyable bow   ∞ (an-kwai′-ab-leh)   Large bow of lace or transparent, light-weight silk worn at the neck by women in 1889 with revival of DIRECTOIRE costume.

incroyable coat   See COATS AND JACKETS.

incroyables   See DIRECTOIRE # 2.

incrustation   **1.** Set-in piece of embroidery, lace, or trimming on women's and children's garments. **2.** Covered or studded with gems.

independent buying office   A firm with retailers as clients that performs such services as buying goods, forecasting trends; assists with finance, personnel, advertising, and promotion; may consult on a variety of issues, including the manufacture of private-label merchandise. Also called *salaried* or *fee buying office.*

independent store   A retailing unit that is not part of any chain of stores.

Indian   **1.** *adj.* Describes articles of clothing and accessories copied from or inspired by North

American Native American tribes. **2.** Adjective used to describe styles from the Indian subcontinent in southern Asia.

Indian beadwork See AMERICAN INDIAN BEADWORK.

Indian embroidery See EMBROIDERIES AND SEWING STITCHES.

Indian gown/Indian nightgown See BANYAN.

Indian handbag See HANDBAGS AND RELATED ACCESSORIES: SQUAW BAG.

Indian headband See AMERICAN INDIAN HEADBAND.

Indian lamb See FURS: LAMB.

Indian meditation shirt See SHIRTS: MEDITATION.

Indian moccasin See FOOTWEAR: MOCCASIN.

Indian necktie See TIES.

Indian print See PRINTS, STRIPES, AND CHECKS.

Indian wedding blouse See BLOUSES AND TOPS.

indigo † Blue dye made since earliest time from stems and leaves of *Indigofera tinctoria, Indigofera anil,* and woad plants; a similar synthetic dye now made from coal tar.

indispensible See HANDBAGS AND RELATED ACCESSORIES: RETICULE.

induction cut See HAIRSTYLES.

industrial mask See MASKS.

industrial zipper See CLOSURES: ZIPPER.

ineffibles See INEXPRESSIBLES.

inexpressibles ∞ Late 18th- and early 19th-c. polite term for men's BREECHES OR TROUSERS. Also called *ineffibles, don't mentions, nether integuments, unmentionables,* and *unwhisperables.*

infanta style (in-fahn'-tah) Costumes as in paintings by Velásquez of Philip IV of Spain's daughter showing extremely wide VERTUGALE (see FARTHINGALE). Used as inspiration for evening gowns by *Lanvin* in the 1920s and *Balenciaga, Givenchy,* and *Castillo* in 1950s. Also see GUARDINFANTE.

informal habit See ACTIVEWEAR.

initial cost estimate Approximation of the cost of a new style. Developed from the cost of materials, FINDINGS, labor, shipping, and any import duty required.

initial ring See JEWELRY: SIGNET RING.

inlay See FOOTWEAR.

inner-vest jacket See COATS AND JACKETS.

innerwear Trade term used to describe underwear or lingerie.

innocente See SACK #1.

inseam **1.** The seam in men's trousers, from the crotch to the hem. Leg length for men's pants is measured by this seam. **2.** See GLOVES AND GLOVE CONSTRUCTION.

insertion Trimming made in straight bands and set between pieces of fabric in a garment. Especially popular from 1890 to 1910 when bands of beading, embroidery, braid, or lace were often set in between rows of tucks and ruffles. Used particularly on white lawn dresses, blouses, petticoats, and drawers.

insertions See EMBROIDERIES AND SEWING STITCHES.

insert thumb See GLOVES AND GLOVE CONSTRUCTION.

insole See FOOTWEAR.

instant sunglasses See EYEWEAR.

instep See FOOTWEAR.

instita ∞ (in-stee'-tah) The distinctive dress of a Roman matron. Costume historians differ as to precisely what it was. Some consider it to have been a flounce or narrow ruffle on the lower edge of a Roman matron's STOLA, while others identify it as the *stola* itself and describe it as a dress suspended from sewed on straps.

insulated Describing a garment constructed to protect against cold. Materials used to insulate include down, foam, fiberfill, wool, and sheepskin. See COATS AND JACKETS: INSULATED JACKET, FOOTWEAR: INSULATED BOOT, and GLOVES AND GLOVE CONSTRUCTION: INSULATED GLOVE.

intaglio See GEMS, GEM CUTS, AND SETTINGS.

intarsia † (in-tar'-sea-a) Decorative colored motifs knitted into a solid color fabric, giving an inlay effect. Patterns on both sides of fabric are identical.

intellectual property Designs, inventions, literary works, and other creations that have been patented, copyrighted, or trademarked. Use by unauthorized persons is illegal.

interactive kiosks Computerized units in retail stores that allow customers to ascertain whether the company has a particular size in stock. The customer can place an order and have the product delivered to the store or to their home.

interchangeable bag See HANDBAGS AND RELATED ACCESSORIES.

interfacing † Canvas of linen, linen and hair, unbleached muslin; crinoline fabric; or nonwoven fabric inserted between the outside and the facing of a garment to give body and shape.

interior product displays Showing merchandise in locations such as countertops, showcases, ledges, aisles, or at point of purchase or in open selling displays, and closed-island displays. Such displays help customers locate merchandise and may provide examples of how the merchandise is used or worn.

interlining † 1. Fabrics used between the lining and the outer fabric of a coat, collar, or suit to give shape to the garment. Best types have permanent stiffening and will dry clean or wash (e.g., tailor's canvas, linen canvas, or nonwoven fabrics). Unbleached muslin and crinoline fabric are used in less expensive garments and will not wash or clean satisfactorily. Same as INTERFACING. 2. Open weave woolen or cotton fabric used between the lining and outer fabric in a winter coat to give warmth.

interlock † Knit made on a machine having alternate units of short and long needles. Thicker than plain rib knits with good lengthwise elasticity, firm texture, and less tendency to curl at the edges. Similar to jersey but both the face and back of the fabric look alike.

International Ladies Garment Workers Union See UNION OF NEEDLETRADES, INDUSTRIAL, AND TEXTILE EMPLOYEES (UNITE).

international market A market that could be located anywhere in the world. Paris, London, Milan, and Tokyo are just of few of the larger international markets. See DOMESTIC MARKET and REGIONAL MARKET.

international source/sourcing Buying goods from or manufacturing goods in countries other than the United States. (see IMPORT, DOMESTIC SOURCE/SOURCING, SOURCING). As the number of imports in the fashion industry has increased, international sourcing has played a significant role in the related businesses.

Internet An on-line, worldwide network of computers that is used for the exchange of information. The Internet is being used by retailers to market and advertise products, as well as to sell them. This technology ultimately works in much the same way as a store; however, it is generally used by the consumer on a home computer. Shopping on the Internet is the newest technological retail format of on-line retailing.

in-the-white See LEATHERS.

intimate apparel Department-store term for lingerie and underwear.

inventory 1. *n.* A current record made by a retailer or manufacturer of its goods or stock. 2. *v.* To generate such a record.

Inverness 1. See COATS AND JACKETS. 2. See CAPES, CLOAKS, AND SHAWLS.

inverted frame See HANDBAGS AND RELATED ACCESSORIES.

inverted leg-of-mutton sleeve See SHOULDERS AND SLEEVES.

inverted pleats See CLOTHING CONSTRUCTION DETAILS and SKIRTS.

inverted-T/-Y embroidery See EMBROIDERIES AND SEWING STITCHES: MATILDE EMBROIDERY.

invisible necklace See JEWELRY: FLOATER NECKLACE.

invisible zipper See CLOSURES: ZIPPER.

Irene Castle bob See HAIRSTYLES.

Irene jacket See COATS AND JACKETS.

Iribe (1883–1935) Paul Iribarnegaray, a Parisian illustrator and designer who was an important figure in artistic and fashionable circles of Paris in the early 20th c. In 1908 he illustrated *Les Robes de Paul Poiret,* a limited edition of the couturier's oriental fashions. His original and imaginative style changed the type of drawings used as illustrations in magazines. In 1914, he came to the United States and in 1919 worked in Hollywood. In Paris in 1906 he published the newspaper *Le Démoin,* which failed and was later revived in the 1930s. Also see LEPAPE.

iridescent fabric † Any fabric made with yarns of one color in the lengthwise direction and another color crosswise. Reflects both colors in the light, e.g., chambray.

iridium See JEWELRY.

Irish crochet See LACES.

Irish knit † Hand-knit in traditional patterns usually including cables, bobbles, and unusual stitches. Knit on large needles with natural wool yarns (without the oil removed from yarn). Used for Irish fishermen's bulky sweaters imported by the United States for general sportswear in 1950s and 1960s. Also, similar knits of manufactured yarns imitating the authentic Irish knits. Also see under SWEATERS: FISHERMAN'S SWEATER.

Irish linen † Fine quality of linen fabric woven from flax grown mainly in Northern Ireland. Used for handkerchiefs and apparel.

Irish mantle See CAPES, CLOAKS, AND SHAWLS: BRATT.

Irish point lace See LACES: YOUGHAL.

Irish polonaise ∞ (po-lo-nayz) Woman's dress worn from 1770 to 1775 with square-cut neckline, bodice buttoned to waist, fitted at back, and elbow-length sleeves. A long pleated skirt, split in front to show shorter underskirt and caught up at waist by buttons or vertical cords into puffed sides. Also called *Italian nightgown* or *French* or *Turkish polonaise.*

Irish stitch See EMBROIDERIES AND SEWING STITCHES: BRICK STITCH.

Irish tweed See DONEGAL TWEED.

ironed hair See HAIRSTYLES.

iron ring See JEWELRY.

Isabeau bodice ∞ Black or colored silk, woman's evening bodice of 1869, ending at the waistline with a wide ribbon sash having long ends and large bow in front. Made with low square neckline, short puffed sleeves, and trimmed with two lace ruffles.

Isabeau corsage ∞ (is-ah-bow′ kor-saj′) Bodice worn in mid-1840s made like a jacket with the front cut away just below the hips. Also had a high neckline with a falling collar; long sleeves with open short oversleeve below each shoulder; and was trimmed with horizontal bands of *galloon lace,* braid, and silk buttons.

Isabeau sleeve See SHOULDERS AND SLEEVES.

Isabeau style dress ∞ (is-ah-bow′) Daytime dress of 1860s cut in PRINCESS STYLE and trimmed down front with a row of buttons or rosettes.

Isabella (The) See CAPES, CLOAKS, AND SHAWLS.

Isabella peasant bodice ∞ Close-fitting decorative corselet bodice decorated with long strands of beads hanging down from waistline. Worn over a dress in early 1890s.

Isabella skirt See UNDERGARMENTS: HOOPS.

Italian bodice ∞ Corselet bodice laced up the front with straps over shoulders, flat fitted collar, and embroidery in front. Worn over a blouse in early 1870s.

Italian cloak See CAPES, CLOAKS, AND SHAWLS.

Italian collar See NECKLINES AND COLLARS.

Italian corsage ∞ Woman's low-cut BASQUE bodice of mid-1860s, laced up the front and worn over a blouse. PEPLUM was made up of decorative tabs. Sleeves of bodice were slashed and trimmed with bows of ribbons pulled through openings.

Italian farthingale See FARTHINGALE.

Italian heel See FOOTWEAR.

Italian hose See VENETIANS.

Italian nightgown See IRISH POLONAISE.

Italian stitch See EMBROIDERIES AND SEWING STITCHES: DOUBLE-RUNNING STITCH.

item house Contractor that makes one specialized category of apparel or accessories. Examples: logo-printed T-shirts, baseball caps.

ivory 1. Hard opaque substance—creamy white to pale yellow—from the tusks of elephants and other mammals, living and extinct (e.g., hippopotami, walruses, whales, warthogs, boars, and mammoths). Ivory from elephants is now in scarce supply because of over-hunting and international restrictions have been imposed on trade in elephant ivory, in some other types of ivory from endangered animals, and in objects made from ivory. As a result the horns and teeth of many animals, such as elk, are also called ivory and some nuts are used to produce **vegetable ivory.** Only antique ivory from restricted species that is more than 100 years old and for which the buyer has documentation proving its age can be brought into the United States. Carved for fans, jewelry, and other ornaments for many centuries. 2. The color of ivory—a creamy white.

Ivy League look Styles based on those worn first in the 1940s and 1950s by college men at Eastern universities that were members of the intercollegiate sports association called the Ivy League (Brown, Columbia, Cornell, Dartmouth, Harvard, University of Pennsylvania, Princeton, and Yale). The style consisted of a slim-cut suit jacket with natural shoulders, narrow lapels, and skinny sleeves; slim-cut pants. *Der.* The name was originally popular slang alluding to the old and ivy-covered buildings on these campuses. See IVY LEAGUE SUIT, PANTS: IVY LEAGUE PANTS, and SHIRTS: IVY LEAGUE SHIRTS.

Ivy League look

Ivy League suit   Man's suit with natural shoulders, narrow lapels, three-button closing, and narrow trousers. Popular in 1950s, spreading from the eight Eastern college campuses in the Ivy League as reaction against exaggeratedly wide padded shoulders and wide trouser legs of the 1940s.

jabiru feathers See FEATHERS.

jabot (zha-bo′) Ruffle of lace, embroidery, or sheer fabric made in a cascade (see cascade #1), attached to front of dress, blouse, or a cravat-like neckpiece (see TIES: CRAVAT). Popular in 18th c. for men and revived for women in late 19th c., 1930s, 1940s, and 1980s. Also see BLOUSES AND TOPS: JABOT BLOUSE and NECKLINES AND COLLARS: JABOT.

jabot

jacinth See GEMS, GEM CUTS, AND SETTINGS: HYACINTH.

jack See DOUBLET.

jack boot See FOOTWEAR.

jack chain See JEWELRY.

jacket dress Dress with a matching or contrasting jacket. The dress is usually sleeveless or bares the shoulders. With the jacket, it is suitable for business or afternoons. Popular since the 1930s.

jacket earring See JEWELRY.

jackets See COATS & JACKETS.

jacket dress

Jackson, Michael See MICHAEL JACKSON LOOK.

jack tar suit See SAILOR SUIT.

jack tar trousers See PANTS.

Jacobs, Marc * See APPENDIX/DESIGNERS.

jacquard † (ja-kard′) **1.** A system of weaving that, because of a pattern-making mechanism of great versatility, permits the production of woven designs of considerable size. Invented by Joseph Marie Jacquard in France in 1801, the loom controls each lengthwise yarn separately by use of a pattern on a punched card or, in newer looms, by an electronic device. Some of the most widely used jacquard fabrics are BROCADE, DAMASK, and TAPESTRY. **2.** Elaborately patterned knitted fabric produced on a knitting machine that makes a wide variety of stitches. **3.** Fabrics made by jacquard weaving or knitting. See HOSIERY: JACQUARD HOSE and SWEATERS: JACQUARD SWEATER.

jade See GEMS, GEM CUTS, AND SETTINGS.

jadeite See GEMS, GEM CUTS, and SETTINGS: JADE.

Jaeger underclothes See UNDERGARMENTS.

jagging/jags See DAGGING.

jaguar See FURS.

Jamaica shorts See SHORTS.

jamb/jambe See ARMOR: GREAVE.

jambeau See ARMOR.

jamboy See ARMOR: TONLET.

James, Charles * See APPENDIX/DESIGNERS.

janina stitch See EMBROIDERIES AND SEWING STITCHES: ORIENTAL COUCHING.

Japanese embroidery See EMBROIDERIES AND SEWING STITCHES.

Japanese look/Japanese style **1.** Clothing and accessories worn in Japan many of which have been adopted in the Western Hemisphere. **2.** Styles introduced by Japanese designers such as Rei Kawakubo and Issey Miyake in the 1980s that became a major fashion influence worldwide. Typical designs use few seams, and are not

Japanese style #2

fitted to the body—sometimes one size fits everyone. Although the basic Japanese kimono is not used, its "EASE" is borrowed. Emphasis is also on originality of fabrics, sophisticated colors, and dramatic simplicity. Most styles are bulky, such as the 1983 style of very full harem pants shirred in front from ankle to knee, worn with a big top that has large kimono-cut sleeves, or an oversized knee-length coat of bulky fabric that is draped in front rather than buttoned. Some styles have asymmetric necklines, collars, and hems. **3.** Style of the Japanese kimono as adapted by U.S. and European designers for dresses, robes, and sportswear. A style for negligées used since the 19th c.

Japanese mink See FURS.

Japanese parasol See UMBRELLAS AND PARASOLS.

Japanese print See PRINTS, STRIPES, AND CHECKS.

Japanese sandals See FOOTWEAR: ZORI.

Japanese wrapper See SLEEPWEAR AND LOUNGE-WEAR.

Jap fox/Jap raccoon See FURS: USSURIAN RACCOON.

jargon See GEMS, GEM CUTS, AND SETTINGS: ZIRCON.

jasey (jay-see) See WIGS AND HAIRPIECES.

jasmine gloves See GLOVES AND GLOVE CONSTRUCTION: JESSAMY GLOVES.

jaspé † (jas-pay′) Cotton or cotton blend fabric with narrow woven stripes of coloring that shade from light to dark or a knitted fabric with crosswise ribs, which achieve this effect.

jasper See GEMS, GEM CUTS, AND SETTINGS.

Java lizard See LEATHERS.

jazerant See ARMOR.

jazz garter Elaborate, wide, round-elastic garter covered with colored satin and sometimes trimmed with lace rosettes. Worn for decorative effect with very short skirts in the late 1920s. *Der.* From jazz music of this era.

jazz oxford See FOOTWEAR.

jazz suit Narrow shouldered, tight-waisted three-button jacket made with long 12″ center vent and vertical slashed pockets. Worn with pipestem pants by men in post–World War I era. *Der.* From jazz music of this era.

jean † Durable fabric made of carded yarns, primarily of cotton or cotton blend, in a twill weave. It may be bleached, dyed solid colors, or printed. Used in blue for overalls and work pants, such pants were given the name of *blue jeans*. Used for uniforms, slacks, shoe linings, and sportswear.

jeanette ∞ Women's necklace of 1836 made of a narrow braid of hair or velvet from which a small heart or cross is suspended.

jeans See PANTS: BLUE JEANS.

jellaba See DJELLABA.

jellies/jelly beans See FOOTWEAR.

jellybag See HEADWEAR.

jemmy See COATS AND JACKETS: FROCK COAT.

jemmy boot See FOOTWEAR.

jemmy frock See COATS AND JACKETS: FROCK COAT.

Jenny Lind cap See HEADWEAR.

Jenny Lind dress Hoop-skirted dress of mid-19th c. with three lace ruffles on skirt and off-the-shoulder neckline. *Der.* Copied from style of dress worn by Jenny Lind (1820–1887), coloratura soprano known as the "Swedish Nightingale."

jerkin **1.** See DOUBLET. **2.** See VESTS. **3.** Synonym for WAISTCOAT.

jersey **1.** † Classification of knitted fabrics that are made in a plain stitch without a distinct rib. Originally made of wool but now made of many natural and manufactured yarns, some textured. Also called *plain knit. Der.* From Isle of Jersey, off the coast of England, where it was first made. **2.** Synonym for knitted shirts worn by seamen, or for sport, from 1860s on—called *football jersey* in 1870s. **3.** See JERSEY COSTUME. **4.** See SHIRTS: KNIT SHIRT.

Jersey costume ∞ Long, tight-fitted blouse reaching to the thigh that was worn over a serge or flannel pleated skirt. Top was made of red or blue knitted silk or wool jersey. This fashion became popular about 1879 when worn by actress **Lillie Langtry** (1852–1929)—famous British actress and beauty born on the Isle of Jersey, located in English Channel, who was also called the "Jersey Lily." Many other items of apparel were also named after her.

jessamy gloves See GLOVES AND GLOVE CONSTRUCTION.

jester's costume An ensemble associated with court jesters of the Middle Ages and Renaissance that consists of a DOUBLET and tights worn with a FOOL'S CAP (see HEADWEAR) having bells attached to peak. Bells are also sometimes worn on garters below knee or attached to dangling sleeves. Usually the entire costume is of PARTI-COLORED fabric. See HEADWEAR: FOOL'S CAP, HOSIERY: TIGHTS.

jet See GEMS, GEM CUTS, AND SETTINGS.

jewel **1.** Precious stone that has been cut and polished—a gem. See GEMS, GEM CUTS, AND SETTINGS. **2.** Natural or synthetic precious stone used as a bearing in a watch. See WATCHES.

jeweled pantyhose See HOSIERY.

jeweled watch See WATCHES.

jewel neckline See NECKLINES AND COLLARS.

JEWELRY

jewelry A purely decorative accessory (e.g., bracelet or necklace) made of precious or plated metal or of genuine or simulated stones mounted in precious or plated metals. Jewelry of less precious materials is called costume jewelry (see under jewelry). Also see jewelry: fashion jewelry.

adjustable ring Ring made with band with overlapping ends so that it can be fitted to any finger size. Usually an inexpensive ring.

Afro choker Necklace made of strand of springy metal wound around the neck many times, *Der.* Copied from necklaces worn by Ubangi tribe in Africa. Also called *Ubangi necklace.*

American Indian beads **1.** Tiny opaque beads of various colors used to make necklaces and belts. Also used for embroidery on moccasins, headbands, belts, and other Native American clothes. **2.** Shell beads used by Native Americans in 16th c. as money and called *wampum.* The amount of trimming on garments indicated wealth of individual.

American Indian necklace **1.** Long, flat necklace made with tiny glass beads of various colors, usually woven on small loom. **2.** Necklace of tiny colored beads worked in rope effect with Native American motif as center pendant, also made by Native Americans. American Indian jewelry was popular in late 1960s and early 1970s.

ankh ring (angk) Gold or gold-finished ring made in the shape of the ankh, the ancient Egyptian symbol of life—a cross with a loop at the top.

ankle bracelet Ornament worn around the ankle; may be a chain or I.D. bracelet. Worn in Eastern countries and Egypt since earliest times. Also called *anklet.*

ankle bracelet

anklet See JEWELRY: ANKLE BRACELET.

ansate cross See ANKH.

armband Bracelet for the upper arm frequently made of a band of metal. Fashionable in matching sets with anklets in ancient Egypt and reintroduced in 1969.

Art Deco earring Earring made in geometrical forms. Derived from patterns of the 1920s shown in the 1925 Paris Exhibition and revived in the late 1960s. See ART DECO.

armband and bangles

aurora borealis crystal (aw-ror'-ah bore-ee'-al-is) Glass beads coated with a solution that causes them to reflect rainbow colors.

Austrian crystal Lead crystal made with 32% lead oxide, faceted and polished to give full spectrum light reflection in sunlight or artificial light. Usually colorless but may be coated on back to reflect a color (e.g., red or blue, or both colors if coated on both sides). Made in village of Innsbruck, Austria.

baby bracelet Tiny beads with letters on them. Originally used in hospitals to spell out the name of the newborn child on a bracelet. Now used for personalized bracelets, barrettes, and necklaces.

ball earring Earring in the shape of a round bead usually suspended from a tiny linked chain, made of gemstones, plastic, glass, or other material.

bangle bracelet Narrow, round, rigid bracelet of metal, plastic, wood, or other material, worn singly or several at a time. Popular since 1900s and originally worn in sets that jingled when the arm moved. Also called *hoop bracelet.* Shown at JEWELRY: ARMBAND.

baroque pearls See GEMS, GEM CUTS, AND SETTINGS: PEARLS.

bar pin Long, narrow pin secured by back fastener the same length as the pin. Fashionable since early 20th c.

bar drop pin Long narrow pin made with attached pendants.

bayadere Seed pearl necklace made up of multiple strands twisted together.

bead/beads **1.** A piece of glass, plastic, wood, crystal, gem, or other material bored through the center and strung on leather, cord, thread or chain to wear as necklace, bracelet, anklet, headband, or used for embroidery. Usually round but may be cylindrical, square, disc-shaped, pendant-shaped, oblong, etc. **2.** A string of beads, synonym for necklace, made and worn since earliest recorded history. Egyptians used carved beads of lapis lazuli, amethyst, feldspar, and agate. Romans wore ropes of pearls. Manufacture of glass beads started in Venice in 14th c.

beaded necklace See JEWELRY: AMERICAN INDIAN NECKLACE.

beggar beads Hand-carved ornamental gemstones in elongated shape strung on necklace between gold beads. Stones include MOSS AGATES, GREEN JASPERS, BLOODSTONES, BROWN or ORANGE CARNELIANS, and other nonprecious stones. (See specific stones under GEMS, GEM CUTS, AND SETTINGS.) Originally worn in India for good luck.

betrothal ring ∞ 16th-c. ring, broken in half after wedding ceremony and halves given to bride and groom.

bib necklace Necklace fitting close to base of neck and extending in the shape of a child's bib. Sometimes made of linked metal, looking like a short triangular scarf, sometimes made of several irregular strands of beads or chains arranged like a fringe.

bib necklace

birthstone necklace **1.** Medium-length fine-linked chain with individualized birthstones in the form of a bead placed about every three to four inches. Also see JEWELRY: DIAMONDS BY THE YARD. **2.** A short fine-linked chain with an attached pendant containing a colored gem representing an individual birthstone. Also see GEMS, GEM CUTS, AND SETTINGṢ: BIRTHSTONE.

birthstone ring Ring set with a stone representing the birth month of the wearer (e.g., an amethyst for February). Also see GEMS, GEM CUTS, AND SETTINGS: BIRTHSTONE.

body jewelry See JEWELRY: BODY-PIERCING.

body-piercing Making a hole at some place in the body through which an item of jewelry can be fastened. Ear lobes have long been pierced for the insertion of earrings and in the late 1990s a fashion for piercing almost any part of the body spread, especially among young people. The jewelry for insertion in these openings is called **body jewelry.**

boot bracelet Linked bracelet, sometimes with dangling charms, worn either around the ankle or calf of the boot.

bracelet Decorative band or circlet worn on the arm, wrist, or ankle as an ornament. Made of metal, chain, plastic, wood, leather, or Lucite, either in one piece or in links. *Der.* Latin, *bracum,* "arm."

bracelet ring See JEWELRY: SLAVE BRACELET.

breastplate Solid metal bra or metal breast ornaments worn by women as body jewelry in late 1960s.

bridal set Matching engagement ring and wedding band.

bridge jewelry Umbrella term for several types of jewelry, including those made from silver, gold (14K, 12K, 10K), and less expensive stones; jewelry designed by artists using a variety of materials.

brooch See JEWELRY: PIN.

bubble bracelet Oversized spherical beads, often hollow, popular for choker necklaces in 1950s and revived in mid-1960s.

bugle beads Long tubular-shaped glass beads, often black, white, or silver, popular for trimming dresses from last half of 19th c. to present.

button earring Round flat earring shaped like a button. Made in various sizes of materials such as imitation pearls, metal, wood, or plastic.

byzance (bi-zance′) Beads alternat- button earring ing with chain in long necklace with dangling ends similar to a rosary. Created by Christian de Gasperi (nephew of former prime minister of Italy) and given this name by Pierre Cardin in 1968 when it became popular at the Riviera resort of St. Tropez, France.

cameo See GEMS, GEM CUTS, AND SETTINGS.

chain See CHAIN in alphabetical listing.

chain bracelet One or more chains of varying width worn on the wrist.

chain necklace Necklace consisting of links of metal sometimes interspersed with gems or imitation stones. May be short or long and looped around neck several times. Worn at intervals since 16th c. and very popular during the late 1960s and 1980s. See alphabetical listing for types of CHAIN.

chandelier earring Long dangling oversized earring made of metal or beads hanging like crystals on a chandelier.

chandelier earring

changeable earring Earring usually made with a selection of colored plastic disks that may be snapped into metal circlet. Parts of the PEEK-A-BOO EARRING (see under JEWELRY) can also be interchanged.

charm Small amulet, usually of metal, consisting of all sorts of mementos (e.g., heart, disk, or zodiac signs worn on bracelet or necklace).

charm bracelet A metal (often gold or silver) chain bracelet on which one or more matching metal charms (e.g., disks, zodiac signs, or hearts) are hung, often to commemorate personal events. Popular in 1940s and 1950s.

charm bracelet

charm necklace **1.** Gold- or silver-toned chain worn around the neck with a cluster of metal objects attached in center front (e.g., hearts, initials, animals, sports motifs, some engraved with slogans or names). **2.** Young girls' plastic chain necklace with dangling miniature plastic replicas of keys, telephones, tennis rackets, roller skates, pencils, and other ornaments.

chasing Jewelry term for fine lines engraved on metals.

chatelaine (shat-len′) Pin worn on the lapel or chest with hook on back to secure a watch, or two decorative pins joined by a chain. Also

called *fob pin. Der.* Keys worn at the waist on a chain by medieval mistress of the castle or "chatelaine."

choker Necklace fitting snugly around base of neck, may be one or more strands of beads, a suede or ribbon band, or a dog collar. Popular in 1930s and also in 1960s.

choker

chute A single strand of pearls.

class ring High school or college ring of individual design for each school with class year included. Sometimes uses large stones, crests, or individual initials. Also called a *school ring.*

clip Ornament similar to a pin but with spring clasp on back that snaps closed over the edge of fabric. Set with diamonds or rhinestones. Introduced in 1930s and 1940s.

clip-back earring Earring that fastens to the ear by means of a spring clip that snaps against back of the ear to secure it; an innovation of the 1930s.

cloisonné necklace **1.** A medallion made of brass enameled with luminous colors and fired. Usually attached to a braided cord of silk, nylon, or polyester with an additional cord pendant hanging from base of medallion. **2.** Necklace of beads with some of the beads being made in the cloisonné manner.

cluster earring Groups of pearls, gems, or beads fastened together to make a large earring.

cluster ring Type of ring set with many large and small stones grouped together. Sometimes made of precious stones, frequently diamonds.

cocktail ring Large showy ring, either a piece of costume jewelry or made of fine jewelry, set with precious or semiprecious stones. Sometimes called *dinner ring.*

coiled bracelet Bracelet made from a long gold- or silver-tone finished strip of metal curled like a spring to fit the arm.

coin necklace Antique coin (e.g., a five-dollar gold piece, a silver dollar, an Indian head penny, or a buffalo nickel) worn on a chain around the neck, sometimes enhanced by a circlet of gold, silver, or other metal around edge.

collar necklace **1.** Necklace shaped and fitted to neck like a collar. Frequently of metal and

J

popular in late 1960s. **2.** Tiny beads interlaced to form a separate collar.

collar pin 1. Pin placed through holes embroidered into the points of shirt collars. **2.** Stud first used in late 19th c. by men for attaching separate shirt collar.

costume jewelry Jewelry not made of genuine gems or precious metals. Introduction is credited to French couturière Gabrielle Chanel, who showed imitation pearls, emeralds, and rubies for daytime in the 1920s—copies of her own real jewels. In the late 1970s new terms were introduced to describe costume jewelry. See JEWELRY: FAUX JEWELS and FASHION JEWELRY.

cross See CROSS in alphabetical listing.

crusader's cross Name given in 1960s to a large Maltese cross (see CROSS) used as a pendant for a necklace. Also called *St. George cross.*

crystal bracelet Beads carved out of genuine transparent quartz. Popular from late 19th c. to about 1930s. Not used today because of the expense of making them. Glass is usually substituted for genuine crystal.

cuff bracelet Oval-shaped rigid bracelet styled with opening in back. May be wide or narrow and usually made of metal.

cuff link Decorative jewelry consisting of two buttons or disks, joined by a link or short chain, worn to close the FRENCH CUFF (see under CUFFS) of a shirt. May be metal, engraved, set with stones, or made in wide variety of materials. Worn originally by men and adopted by women. Also see CLOSURES: CUFF BUTTON.

cultured pearls See GEMS, GEM CUTS, AND SETTINGS: PEARL.

cut-steel beads Tiny faceted steel or other metal beads, similar in appearance to MARCASITE (see under GEMS, GEM CUTS, AND SETTINGS), popular in last half of the 19th and early 20th c.

damascene ring (dam'-ah-sehn) Blackened metal inlaid with fine gold-tone wire to form a delicate design.

damascening (dam'-ah-sehn-ing) Engraving steel, bronze, or iron and filling up the incision with gold or silver wire. An inferior style of damascening can be made by etching the pattern on steel then depositing gold or silver in the engraved lines electronically. *Der.* Named for Damascus, where the technique was formerly used.

Decatur ring Gold band, similar to a wedding ring, with two inset bands of black enamel. Copied from ring given to Stephen Decatur, American naval officer, by Lieutenant Richard Somers in 1804 as a friendship ring. Original ring is in the Smithsonian Institution, Washington, D.C.

devotional ring ∞ Bronze, gold, or ivory ring with ten spherical projections around the band used in Middle Ages for saying the Creed.

diamond bracelet Bracelet made of expensive metals (e.g., gold or platinum, set with many small faceted diamonds and other precious gems. Also worn as watch bracelet with diamond watch. Fashion started in 18th c. and very popular in late 19th and early 20th c.

diamond earring Earring made with single diamond attached to a post for pierced ears or long strings of diamonds with larger stones set at the top. The former has been a popular wedding gift for the groom to give to the bride. Marie Antoinette, Queen of France in the late 18th c., had a famous pair of the latter type. Elaborate types of diamond earrings were popular from the 1920s on for evening wear.

diamond necklace 1. Any necklace made of genuine diamonds. May be single or large diamonds set in pavé fashion in a band of precious metal, or diamonds set in precious metals and mounted in medallions linked together with chains of the same metal. **2.** Single large diamond suspended from a chain.

diamonds by the yard Chain of 18k gold interspersed with a diamond at intervals, sold by the yard. Worn wrapped around the neck, wrist, or waist. Introduced in 1974 by Elsa Peretti of Tiffany's, New York City. In 1984, sold for $2,500 per yard depending on size of diamonds. Also made of rubies, emeralds, or sapphires.

dinner ring See JEWELRY: COCKTAIL RING.

dog collar 1. Wide CHOKER (see under JEWELRY), similar to a dog's collar, often consisting of pearls or of a band of metal set with diamonds or rhinestones. Introduced in early 20th c., popular in 1930s, and again in 1960s at which time it was also called *throat belt*. **2.** Band of colored suede or leather worn tightly around neck, popular in early 1970s.

dome ring Ring with a high rounded top, similar to a dome, usually set with many stones or made of metal.

door knocker earring Elongated hoops hanging free from ear clips—may be interchangeable.

doublet Jewelry term for two pieces of glass or gems cemented together to form one large stone.

drop earring Any earring in which the lower part swings free. One of the earliest styles, and one that was popular for single genuine gemstones or pearls, was called a **pendant earring**.

duet pins Two pins worn together as a set.

ear band Earring that clips on middle edge of ear with dangling portion.

ear clip Synonym for JEWELRY: EARRING.

earring Decorative jewelry accessory worn on the ear. Ear may be pierced and small wires or posts inserted. For unpierced ears, types include SCREW- or CLIP-BACKS (see under JEWELRY). Mentioned in the Bible and visible on carvings of ancient monarchs, earrings have been worn by kings, nobles, and soldiers, as well as women in early times. Pirates have been depicted wearing one earring. Popular during the 16th and 17th c., earrings were worn by Henry III of France, and Charles I of England went to his execution wearing a drop pearl in his right ear. After this time, the fashion of earrings for men ended until the 1980s, whereas women have worn earrings from Biblical times to present. Mid-19th-c. earrings were also available in "sets" with matching necklace, brooch, and bracelet. In late 1950s, piercing of ears was revived, even for preschool children. In early 1980s, double and triple piercing became a fashion with two and three sets of earrings being worn at the same time on either one or both ears. While in the 1960s, earrings were often tiny, in the 1980s they became quite large and sometimes dangled to the shoulders. Also called an *earclip*.

Egyptian collar Wide flat necklace made in ancient Egypt of beads, shells, seeds, faïence, or semiprecious stones in various colors. Sometimes mounted in gold or made of

Egyptian collar

papyrus or fabric with geometrical lotus designs embroidered in colored wool.

elastic bracelet Bracelet made of beads or sectional motifs of various types strung on elastic that slips over the hand.

engagement ring Ring given to a woman by a man signifying that they plan to be married—for many years a diamond SOLITAIRE (see under JEWELRY)—now most any type of ring.

esclavage (ess-kla-vasj′) Mid-18th-c. term for a necklace composed of several rows of gold chain that fell in swags over the bosom. *Der.* French, "slave."

eternity bracelet See JEWELRY: SLAVE BRACELET.

eternity ring Full or half circlet of diamonds, rubies, or sapphires set in a narrow band of gold or platinum, sometimes given by husband to wife as a pledge of love on a special occasion (e.g., birth of a child or wedding anniversary). This tradition started in England in 1930s.

expandable bracelet Spring-link metal bracelet that stretches and needs no clasp. Since 1940s frequently used as watch bracelet.

facet See GEMS, GEM CUTS, AND SETTINGS.

false doublet Stone made from two pieces cemented at the girdle (circumference of largest portion of faceted stone) in which a genuine stone makes up the crown or top, and a cheaper stone or glass is used for the pavilion or bottom part.

family ring Rings for all members of the family (i.e., father, mother, daughter, grandmother, etc.). Rings are of various sizes and shapes, but all incorporate several birthstones representing birthdays of various members of the family.

fashion jewelry Term coined in 1980s for high-quality, expensive costume jewelry. Styles include pavé collars (see GEMS, GEM CUTS, AND SETTINGS: PAVÉ), flashy brooches, lapel pins, necklaces, earrings, and hat pins made of imitation gems. Identical imitation of precious stone jewelry is called **paste.** See JEWELRY: COSTUME JEWELRY, FAUX JEWELS, PASTE.

faux jewels (foh) Term used for fashion jewelry when it is obviously fake.

ferronnière (fehr′-ohn-yair′) **1.** Delicate chain worn as band across the brow with single jewel hanging in center of forehead. Fashion originated by La Belle Ferronnière, a favorite of Francis I (1515–1547), as shown in a portrait attributed to Giovanni Boltraffio or Leonardo da Vinci. **2.** Narrow brow band, with jewel in center, worn on the forehead with evening dress by women in the 1830s. Also called *La Belle Ferronnière.*

ferronnière

filigree (fill′-ee-gree) Ornamental metalwork for jewelry or accessories made of fine silver, gold, or copper wire intricately arranged—or similar pierced metal openwork.

filigree ring (fill′-ee-gree) Gold or silver wire twisted in a lacy intricate pattern to make a ring, usually protruding upward to make a dome.

fine jewelry Jewelry made only from precious metals and precious and semiprecious stones.

floater necklace Necklace of beads or pearls strung on a cord that is almost invisible, such as nylon fishing line, so that the beads seem to "float" on the skin of the wearer. Also called *invisible necklace.*

fob pin See CHATELAINE.

fraternal ring Emblematic ring only used by members of fraternal organizations (e.g., Masons, Elks, and Knights of Columbus). Frequently made of gold or silver with an onyx setting on which symbols of the organization are placed in gold, silver, and gems.

fraternity pin Pin selected and specially made for a high school or college fraternity group. Usually contains the Greek letters of the fraternity in gold on an onyx background. Tiny pearls may be mounted around the edge. Sometimes a small guard chain is attached with individual symbol.

free-form ring Contemporary ring that may be almost any shape other than the conventional round ring. Frequently made of a long piece of metal shaped to the finger but having the two ends lapped over each other, often made with gemstones at the ends. *Der.* From free-form sculpture.

freshwater pearls See GEMS, GEM CUTS, AND SETTINGS: PEARLS.

friendship bracelet See JEWELRY: WOVEN FRIENDSHIP BRACELET.

friendship pin Tiny colored beads threaded on small safety pin and worn fastened to shoelaces. Exchanged as tokens of friendship or love, colors of the beads have various meanings (e.g., red, best friend; pink, sweetheart; green, enemy; purple, good friend; yellow, pal; blue, going steady). A school fad of the 1980s.

friendship ring An older term for a simple metal ring exchanged by good friends and worn for sentimental value. Formerly called a *talisman ring.*

fronts See HIP-HOP.

gemel ring A ring fashionable in the Middle Ages that was really two identical rings joined together and worn together. Popular style had clasped hands on the front. Traditionally the rings were separated at betrothal—the man and woman each wearing one. After marriage the rings were joined together and worn by the woman. Later, triple and quadruple rings of this style were worn. Revived in the mid-1980s. *Der.* From the Italian word *gemelli,* or Latin, *gemini,* "twins." Also spelled *gemmel, geminal, gimmel.*

genuine pearls See GEMS, GEM CUTS, AND SETTINGS: PEARLS.

girdle See GEMS, GEM CUTS, AND SETTINGS: BRILLIANT CUT.

gold beads **1.** 14k-gold beads sometimes purchased one at a time and added to a chain for necklace. **2.** Beads plated with gold. **3.** Costume jewelry with different bases and gilt finishes.

gold filled Gold of 10 to 22 karats fused to a base metal (e.g., nickel, silver, or brass). Layer of gold should weigh at least 1/20th of the entire metal used. Gold of 1/10 18k means that it's 18 karat and represents 1/10th of the weight of the metal.

gold-plated Describing jewelry with a thin surface of gold electrolytically plated to a base metal.

gold-washed Describing jewelry with a thin coating of gold applied to a base metal by dipping or washing it in a solution of gold.

gorget ∞ (gorge-et′) Chain with crescent-shaped ornament worn around the neck by officers during 17th and 18th c. as a badge of rank.

grain See GEMS, GEM CUTS, AND SETTINGS.

gypsy earring Large hoop earring usually of brass or gold-colored metal, worn in pierced ear, inspired by plain brass circles worn by gypsies. For unpierced ears, hoop is suspended from a small button top that clips to the back of the ear.

hair jewelry ∞ Jewelry made with or from human hair. During the early 19th c., some locks of hair of a deceased loved one were often incorporated into jewelry as a memento; however, by the latter part of the century, ready-made hair jewelry could be purchased.

hat pin See HEADWEAR.

hinged bracelet Any bracelet with a hinge allowing it to open wide for removal.

hippie beads Beads adopted by hippies, an avant-garde group of young people in the United States in the mid-1960s. For necklaces, usually small beads worn chest-length by both sexes. Influenced conventional men to adopt the fashion of wearing chains or medallion necklaces. Also called *love beads*. See HIPPIE/HIPPIE LOOK.

hoop bracelet See JEWELRY: BANGLE BRACELET.

hoop earring **1.** Circlet (or oval) of metal, plastic, or wood that swings free from a small button. Also see JEWELRY: GYPSY EARRING. **2.** Incomplete circlet that fastens around the earlobe. May be hinged and clip into place.

hoop earring

Hopi bracelet Narrow sterling silver cuff bracelet with symbols of Hopi Native American tribe in black. *Der.* From Hopi Indians of the southwestern United States.

I.D./identification bracelet Bracelet of large links attached to oblong metal plaque engraved with name or initials. First used by soldiers in wartime, later adapted for adults and children.

imitation pearls See GEMS, GEM CUTS, AND SETTINGS: PEARLS.

initial ring See JEWELRY: SIGNET RING.

iridium (ih-rid′-ee-em) Metal frequently alloyed with platinum to make a more durable metal for use in jewelry.

iron ring ∞ Finger ring worn by ancient Romans, with gold rings being reserved for badges of civil and military rank.

jack chain ∞ Chain made of links like a figure eight, worn as an ostentatious decoration by men in 17th c.

jacket earring Earring consisting of post plus various shaped separate pieces with holes in top that may be interchanged by placing post through hole. "Jackets" may be in shape of shells, roses, hearts, butterflies, etc. Introduced in early 1980s.

jet jewelry See GEMS, GEM CUTS, AND SETTINGS: JET.

kilt pin See SAFETY PIN #3.

lampshade bracelet Short lengths of tiny strung beads, hung in a fringe from a ribbon tied close to neck, worn in early 1970s. *Der.* Beaded fringe on lampshades popular in late Victorian era and 1920s.

langettes ∞ (lan-get′) Term for string of beads in 16th c.

lapel pin Woman's pin originally worn on the lapel of a suit. Almost all medium-sized pins are now called lapel pins.

lariat necklace **1.** Long strand of beads or metal, sometimes ending in tassels, that is not fastened by a clasp. Worn looped into a knot or uses a slide so that the two ends hang free. **2.** Man's short necklace (or tie) usually made of leather that has a silver slide and two ends tipped with silver hanging free.

lavaliere (lav-al-yer′) Pendant, sometimes set with precious stones, worn as a necklace on a fine chain. *Der.* Named after Louise de la Baume Le Blanc La Vallière, mistress of Louis XIV of France.

locket Chain necklace with a gold or silver disk that opens to reveal picture of loved one or lock of hair. Very popular from mid-19th

J

to early 20th c. and still worn, especially by children.

love beads See JEWELRY: HIPPIE BEADS.

Mali bracelet Handmade bracelet made of leather approximately 1″ wide and decorated with very small European glass beads (called *American Indian beads* in the United States) in a variety of colors and designs. Introduced from the Republic of Mali in Africa in 1980s.

matinee-length necklace Bead necklace, usually of pearls or simulated pearls, 30″ to 35″ long.

medallion necklace Heavy chain necklace with large disk as a pendant, worn by women during various eras and introduced for men in late 1960s.

medic alert bracelet Bracelet worn to indicate blood type and allergies to certain drugs.

mesh bracelet Metal bracelet made of minute links or a continuous piece of woven metal. Used in gold for expensive watches and bracelets.

mizpah medallion necklace (miz′-pah) Large medallion with a quotation from Genesis cut in half in zigzag fashion to form "his" and "hers" medals worn on a chain.

mobile earring (mo-beel) Delicate wire drop earring like small mobile sculpture carefully balanced so it is constantly in motion.

mourning jewelry ∞ Jet and black-enameled jewelry worn by women of the mid-19th through early 20th c. instead of regular jewelry during a mourning period. Also see JEWELRY: HAIR JEWELRY.

mourning ring ∞ Massive ring, frequently black, later blue enamel, sometimes given to guests at funerals. Sometimes included portrait of deceased, emblems, motto (e.g., "be prepared to follow me"), or hair of the departed plaited in a design.

mouse jewelry **1.** ∞ Bracelets, brooches, rings, and earrings made of metal and decorated with replicas of mice, worn by women during the 1880s. Bracelet consisted of a metal ring with three mice placed along the outer edge, their tails winding around the ring of metal. **2.** In the late 1960s and early 1970s, jewelry for children was made with enameled metal or plastic mice, usually to look like Mickey Mouse®, a Walt Disney creation.

neck-chain ∞ Decorative gilded brass or gold chain worn by men from Middle Ages to mid-17th c. Sometimes worn by travelers in Middle Ages who used a few links of it for money. For late 17th-c. variation, see JEWELRY: JACK CHAIN.

necklace Decorative accessory worn around the neck. Frequently made of beads or chain and sometimes of real or imitation gems set in gold, silver, or other metals. Primitive people wore necklaces of seeds, nuts, shells, teeth and claws of animals strung on grass or thong. A TORQUE (see under JEWELRY) was a twisted metal collar or necklace worn by ancient Teutons, Gauls, and Britons of the Bronze Age. Egyptians wore amulets such as the SCARAB and the UTCHAT (oot-shat′), a representation of a sacred eye. Greeks wore metal necklaces with a "fringe" of small vaselike drops of diamonds, sapphires, garnets, etc. Romans introduced the rope pearl necklace. From 16th c. on, heavy chains and all types of necklaces were worn. In contemporary times, an expensive necklace is frequently a status symbol.

neck ring Single narrow band of springy metal worn as choker, sometimes with dangling ornament. An innovation of late 1960s.

necktie pin See JEWELRY: STICKPIN.

nugget ring Ring with stone made from a piece of metal in its natural shape (e.g., a gold nugget).

opera-length necklace Necklace of beads, usually of pearls or simulated pearls, 48″ to 120″ long, usually worn wrapped twice around the neck. Originated in 1890s for wear to the opera or for other formal occasions. Also see JEWELRY: ROPE NECKLACE.

Oriental pearls See GEMS, GEM CUTS, AND SETTINGS: PEARLS.

ouch ∞ Term used from 13th to 15th c. for a collection of jewels or a jeweled clasp or buckle. Also spelled *nouch.*

parure (pah-roor′) Matched set of jewelry that may consist of a necklace, earrings, pin, or bracelet. *Der.* French, "adornment."

paste   Highly reflective transparent types of flint glass faceted or molded to make imitation gems. One variety is called **strass,** named for Josef Strasser, a German jeweler. Used in making replicas of expensive jewelry. Also see JEWELRY: FAUX JEWELS and FASHION JEWELRY.

pavé   See GEMS, GEM CUTS, AND SETTINGS.

peace ring   Simple ring designed of metal with "peace symbol" consisting of a circle intersected with straight bar down the center and Y-shaped bars to the outer edge.

pearl beads   PEARLS (see GEMS, GEM CUTS, AND SETTINGS: PEARLS) all of one size or graduated in size. Usually strung on thread, often with a knot after each bead, made in a variety of lengths and worn in single strand or several strands. A classic fashion for many centuries.

peek-a-boo earring   Earring for pierced ears with small object or stone showing where ear is pierced and three or four stones showing at lower edge of ear. The latter group is attached to back of earring.

pendant earring   See JEWELRY: DROP EARRING.

pendant necklace   Ornament such as a locket, medallion, or single jewel suspended around neck from a chain, thong, or cord. Worn since the Renaissance.

pendant pin   Pin with a clasp at back and a hook at center top so it can be worn on a chain, cord, etc., as a necklace or a pin.

pendicle   ∞ Single pendant earring worn by men in 17th c.

perfume ring   Large ring that is hinged under the stone so that solid perfume may be placed inside.

pierced earring   Earring designed to be worn in pierced ears. A wire or post is inserted through the ear lobe and should be made of gold or surgical steel rather than plated metals to prevent infection. Until the introduction of screw-back earrings, all types of earrings were made for pierced ears.

pierced-look earring   Earring designed for unpierced ears. Has a delicate band of metal coming under the ear to the front giving the appearance that it goes through the ear.

pin   Ornamental jewelry made with pin fastener on back that may have a safety catch. Made in all types of materials (e.g., gold, silver, plated metals, and frequently set with gems or imitation stones). In Anglo-Saxon, Greek, and Roman times used to fasten clothing. See PENANNULAR BROOCH and FIBULA. Later became more decorative. The word *brooch* is a synonym.

plated   As applied to jewelry, e.g., gold-plated, a thin film of precious metal applied to an inexpensive base metal—usually by electrolysis.

platinum   Rare white metal used for mounting jewels, usually alloyed with 10% iridium to increase hardness.

plummet   ∞ Term used in 17th c. for pendant earrings. See JEWELRY: DROP EARRING and PENDICLE.

poison ring   1. Finger ring worn from Roman period through the 17th c. that was designed to hold a dose of poison. Made in Roman times with the setting a mere shell and the poison behind it. Cesare Borgia's ring, dated 1503 and still in existence, has a small sliding panel that opened into a small cavity in which poison was placed. 2. Similar novelty item of the late 1960s, sometimes used to contain perfume.

posts   See JEWELRY: STUDS.

posy/poesy ring   Plain gold band, sometimes with small decorative design in center, given as a love token. Inside was inscribed "let love endure" or "faithful and true." Popular in the 16th c., revived in the 1980s.

regard rings   ∞ Rings worn in 16th c. set with stones having initials spelling out such words as L-O-V-E or name of the beloved.

religious medal   A pendant necklace worn by Christians of various sects (e.g., the St. Christopher medal worn predominantly by Catholics).

rhodium   White-colored metal of the platinum group used for plating jewelry.

ring   Decorative jewelry worn on the finger, sometimes on the thumb, and infrequently on one of the toes. Before the mid-1960s, rings were worn on the third finger and the little finger. After this time, it was fashionable to wear rings on any of the fingers. This was a revival of styles of the 16th c. when many rings were worn and two rings were sometimes worn on the same finger. Since earliest times a ring has been a pledge or a seal of faith, and also used as a stamp of authority. See JEWELRY: DEVOTIONAL RING, FISHERMAN'S RING, GIMMEL RING, and POISON RING.

ring bracelet See JEWELRY: SLAVE BRACELET.

rolling ring Bands of three circlets of gold in different colors of gold—rose, yellow, and white—interlocked to make a ring. Designed and made by Cartier since the 1920s. Also made with six interlocking circles.

rondella (rohn-del′-ah) Round, small metal disk that is placed between beads. It may be plain or ornamented with stones.

rope necklace Extra-long beaded necklace, usually of pearls, that may be wrapped around neck several times or worn long and knotted. Very popular in 1920s and worn continuously since then.

safety pin An item of jewelry shaped like a utilitarian safety pin that may have beads hanging suspended from the long bar or decorating the head.

sautoir (so-twar′) Pendant-type necklace with a dangling piece in front that may appear to be fringed at base. *Der.* French, woman's watch chain or a medal of honor worn around the neck.

scarab bracelet Bracelet made of several oval semiprecious stones (e.g., lapis lazuli or chalcedony) engraved to look like beetles, outlined in gold, and connected by gold links. *Der.* Ancient Egyptian sacred beetle. See SCARAB in alphabetical listing.

scarf pin See JEWELRY: STICKPIN.

school ring See JEWELRY: CLASS RING.

screw-back earring Earring for unpierced ears, with screw behind the ear that can be tightened to hold it in place. An innovation of the early 20th c. that enabled people without pierced ears to wear earrings.

seed bead necklace Necklace in various styles that is made from very small beads.

seed-pearls See GEMS, GEM CUTS, AND SETTINGS: PEARLS.

serpent ring Ring shaped like snake curled around the finger. Similar rings were worn in ancient Rome.

signet ring **1.** Ring with large stone cut INTAGLIO (See GEMS, GEM CUTS, AND SETTINGS). Formerly used to make an impression in sealing wax to seal letters. **2.** Ring with king's seal used by ancient Egyptians.

silk pin See DRESSMAKER PIN.

simulated-pearls See GEMS, GEM CUTS, AND SETTINGS: PEARLS.

slave bracelet **1.** Ring connected by a chain to a bracelet worn around the wrist. Also called a *bracelet ring*, a *ring bracelet*, and more recently an *eternity bracelet*. Originally copied from bracelets worn in Eastern countries for centuries. Popular in 1880s and the 1990s. **2.** A *toe-ankle chain* is also called by this name.

slave bracelet #1 or ring bracelet

sleeve bracelet Ornate bracelet worn around upper arm over full sleeve to make a double puffed sleeve. Fashionable in England in late 1960s.

slide bracelet Bracelet with small piece of pierced metal through which fine flat chains are threaded. Needs no clasp as it is adjusted by pulling the chains. Popular in late 19th c., and revived by using antique watch chains in 1960s.

snake bracelet Metal bracelet in form of a serpent worn coiled around the arm. Worn by ancient Greeks and fashionable in 1880s and in late 1960s.

solitaire Ring set with a single stone, frequently a diamond, sometimes a pearl or another gem.

solitaire

sorority pin Similar to FRATERNITY PIN (see under JEWELRY), but worn by high school and college girls as an emblem of their club or sorority.

spoon ring The handle of a small sterling silver spoon molded to wrap around the finger to form a ring.

spring bracelet Beads strung on flexible wire in a spiral that expands to permit entry of hand.

squash blossom necklace Traditional necklace made of tiny pieces of turquoise set in sterling silver. Stones are mounted in a manner to imitate flowers with many petals. *Der.* Handcrafted by Zuni Native Americans of the southwestern United States. Some necklaces are in the collections of the Museum of Natural History and the Smithsonian Institution.

squash blossom necklace

Statue of Liberty earring Dangling earring with head of Statue of Liberty enclosed in circle. *Der.* Inspired by the July 4, 1986, celebration in New York harbor of the restoration of the Statue of Liberty.

sterling silver Metal containing 92.5 parts silver and 7.5 parts copper, a standard set by law. Used for jewelry, it is "silvery" in color and lustrous. One disadvantage is that it tarnishes. This can be easily remedied with silver polish.

St. George cross See JEWELRY: CRUSADER'S CROSS.

stickpin 1. Straight stiletto-type pin with an ornamental top worn by a man to secure a four-in-hand necktie or ascot. Popular from late 19th c. to 1930s. Now *tie tacks* are more usually worn. Also called *scarf pin* and *tie pin*. 2. Same type of pin styled as a lapel pin for women.

stickpin

strass See JEWELRY: PASTE.

studs 1. Earrings similar to posts designed for pierced ears. One part of earring goes through the ear and back screws into the "post." Basic type of earring for pierced ears. Some studs are secured by pushing back piece onto straight post, notch in post secures back. 2. See CLOSURES: STUD.

talisman ring (tahl´-iss-mahn) "Charm" ring worn in Ancient Greece and the Middle Ages to ensure the wearer of good health, the strength of ten, love, wealth, and happiness. Worn in recent times as a pledge of friendship. Also see JEWELRY: FRIENDSHIP RING.

tassel necklace Long linked chain necklace with cluster of as many as twelve short chains forming a tassel at the end.

tethered studs ∞ Man's evening jewelry of 1830s and 1840s consisting of three ornamental shirt studs joined with small chains.

throat belt See JEWELRY: DOG COLLAR.

tie clasp/clip Jewelry consisting of a decorative metal bar bent double that slides over a man's tie and behind his shirt front placket clipping the tie in place. May also have spring-clip back.

tie pin See JEWELRY: STICKPIN.

tie tack Small ornament with a sharp-pointed back worn pierced through both parts of a man's necktie to hold them together. Back portion is usually screwed into a round metal stud.

toe-ankle chain Unusual ankle bracelet with chain attached to toe ring, worn in 1970. Also called SLAVE BRACELET (see under JEWELRY).

toe ring Any ring worn on one of the toes, usually the big toe. In 1967 plastic, papier-mâché, or felt rings were popular. Also see JEWELRY: TOE-ANKLE CHAIN.

torque/torc ∞ (tork) An incomplete circle of metal that fit around the neck that was worn by the Celtic people of Western Europe. Some were ornamented by twisting or working the metal or inlaying colored enamel.

torsade Several strands of pearls, chains, or beads twisted together to form a single necklace.

Ubangi necklace See JEWELRY: AFRO CHOKER.

utchat See JEWELRY: NECKLACE.

washed gold Thin coating of gold applied to a base metal by dipping or washing it in a solution of gold salts.

watch bracelet Band, strap, or other device attached to wristwatch made of all types of metals, leather, plastic, or fabric that holds the watch on the wrist.

wedding band/wedding ring Used in wedding ceremony and traditionally a band of gold in any of various widths worn by both men and women on the third finger of the left hand. Although worn since Egyptian times, not adopted by Christians until the second half of the 9th c. The plain gold band of modern times dates from the time of Mary Tudor and her marriage to Phillip II of Spain in 1554.

J

wedding band earring Wide gold hoop earring similar in style to a wide gold wedding ring.

wedding trio Woman's engagement ring and wedding band—plus men's wedding band, similarly styled and sold together. Also see BRIDAL SET.

Wedgwood® cameo Usually blue in color with the head of a woman in raised design on the surface. Made by casting Wedgwood pottery material. Can be distinguished from cut cameos by the tiny air bubbles on the surface. *Der.* Made by the Wedgwood China Company in England.

wires Earrings for pierced ears that have a thin curved wire, usually gold, that passes through the ear. Usually dangling objects are attached to the wire or the wires may be worn separately.

worry beads Short string of beads, often made of semiprecious stones. Originally carried in hand to fidget with by men in Middle Eastern countries, Greece, and Turkey. Popular in America in late 1960s. *Der.* From string of 33 beads used to count the 99 names of Allah during prayers in Moslem countries.

woven friendship bracelet Bracelet made from different colored strands of yarn woven, knotted, or plaited together.

wrist strap Wide band of leather buckled around wrist, usually trimmed with metal studs. Introduced in late 1960s.

zodiac necklace Any necklace, usually of the pendant type, with medallion engraved with a personal sign of the zodiac. Popular in late 1960s and early 1970s.

Zuni jewelry Beautiful exotic and unusual bracelets, pins, necklaces, and rings of sterling silver set with genuine turquoise gems. *Der.* Made by the Zuni, a Native American tribe inhabiting the largest of the Indian pueblos in western New Mexico.

Zuni snake eye ring Sterling silver ring set with 25 turquoise stones, mounted 5 to a row in 5 rows, alternating with rounded silver beads. Copied from ring in the Smithsonian Institution. *Der.* Originally made by Zuni, Native Americans of the southwestern United States.

---

jiffy dress 1. Sew-it-yourself dress with limited number of pieces that can be stitched together in a short time. 2. A dress knitted quickly on jumbo needles from a kit or from separately purchased yarn.

jiffy-knit sweater See SWEATERS.

jigger button ∞ 19th-c: a button concealed under lapel on man's double-breasted coat that was used to fasten back a wide lapel.

JIT See JUST-IN-TIME.

Joan See HEADWEAR.

Joan-of-Arc bodice ∞ Woman's tight-fitting bodice worn in 1875, reaching to hips and covered with jet or steel beads. Made with tight-fitting sleeves and ruffles at wrists.

jobber An agent in the apparel industry that sells CLOSEOUTS and JOB LOTS or carries inventories of apparel immediately available to retailers.

job lot Odds and ends of remaining styles that a manufacturer wants to dispose of. Often made up of broken sizes, colors, and/or styles and if purchased as a group can be bought for a considerable discount.

Jocelyn mantle See CAPES, CLOAKS, AND SHAWLS.

jockey Adjective used to describe apparel derived from or inspired by the clothing worn by professional jockeys in horseracing. See ACTIVEWEAR: JOCKEY PANTS, FOOTWEAR: JOCKEY BOOT, HEADWEAR: JOCKEY CAP, SHIRTS: JOCKEY SHIRT, and VESTS: JOCKEY WAISTCOAT.

jockey shorts® See UNDERGARMENTS.

jockey silks Costume of racehorse rider who wears a colorful shirt and cap to designate stable that owns his horse. Also called *racing silks*.

jodphur boot See FOOTWEAR.

jodhpurs See ACTIVEWEAR.

jogging shorts See SHORTS: SWEAT SHORTS.

jogging suit See ACTIVEWEAR.

Mr. John * See APPENDIX/DESIGNERS.

johnny collar See NECKLINES AND COLLARS.

Johnson, Betsey * See APPENDIX/DESIGNERS.

joinville See TIES.

Joop, Wolfgang * See APPENDIX/DESIGNERS.

jornade See COATS AND JACKETS: JOURNADE.

Joseph See COATS AND JACKETS.

Josephine knot Ornamental knot used for trimmings—made by looping two ribbons leaving the four ends hanging free.

journade See COATS AND JACKETS.

jours See LACES.

judo clothing See ACTIVEWEAR: KARATE CLOTHING.

judo jacket See ACTIVEWEAR: KARATE CLOTHING.

Jugoslavian embroidery See EMBROIDERIES AND SEWING STITCHES: YUGOSLAVIAN.

juive tunic ∞ (zweeve) Hip-length princess-style OVERDRESS (see OVERDRESS #1) of 1875 made with large armholes, V-neck front and back, and overskirt forming a train in back. Worn over regular dress as outdoor costume. *Der.* French, "Jewish."

Julian, Alexander * See APPENDIX/DESIGNERS.

Juliet *adj.* Used to describe fashions thought to be similar to those that might have been worn by the heroine of Shakespeare's drama *Romeo and Juliet.* Often these styles derive from clothing used in popular films or theatrical presentations of the play. See JULIET DRESS, FOOTWEAR: JULIET SLIPPER, HEADWEAR: JULIET CAP, SHOULDERS AND SLEEVES: JULIET SLEEVE, and SLEEPWEAR AND LOUNGEWEAR: JULIET GOWN.

Juliet dress Dress in medieval style with high waistline and puffed-topped sleeves that are fitted at the lower arm. *Der.* Inspired by the film of Shakespeare's play *Romeo and Juliet,* made by Franco Zeffirelli in 1968.

jumbo curl See HAIRSTYLES.

jump See COATS AND JACKETS.

jumper coat See COATS AND JACKETS: BEAUFORT COAT.

jumper dress One-piece dress with sleeves and collar of a contrasting color, giving the appearance of a two-piece blouse and jumper. Also called a *jumper shift.*

JUMPERS

jumper **1.** A sleeveless garment, generally for women or children, worn over a sleeved blouse, sweater, or shirt. May be belted or beltless. Fashion terms for various jumper styles have developed and are generally formed by placing an adjective describing the apparel in front of the word "jumper." Examples: apron jumper, back belt jumper. **2.** See SWEATERS. **3.** See BLOUSES AND TOPS.

A-line jumper Jumper styled similar to a sleeveless A-LINE DRESS, it can be worn with or without a blouse or shirt underneath.

bib jumper Jumper styled similar to a skirt, with the front extending up to form a bib similar to the top of overalls. Straps are attached to the bib, extend over the shoulders, cross in the back, and attach to the skirt.

bib jumper

buckled jumper Bib-type jumper with two buckles placed at the neckline through which straps coming over the shoulder from the back are fastened.

buckskin jumper Made similar to a sleeveless fringed AMERICAN INDIAN DRESS, fastened with a laced closing in center front.

coat-jumper Single- or double-breasted jumper styled similar to a sleeveless COAT-DRESS.

horseshoe jumper Jumper made with a very low horseshoe neckline in front and back and large armholes. The straps that extend over the shoulders are cut in one piece with the skirt of the garment.

painter's jumper Jumper design inspired by painters' work clothes.

pantjumper **1.** Jumper similar to a sleeveless PANT-DRESS, worn with or without a blouse. **2.** Jumper worn over a long sleeved blouse combined with full-length pants.

pinafore jumper Similar to a BIB JUMPER (see under JUMPERS). Also see APRONS: PINAFORE APRON.

horseshoe jumper

sandwich-board jumper A jumper made by joining two oblong pieces of fabric at the shoulders and at the waistline. So called because it resembles a sign previously worn over the shoulder with advertising copy in front and back called a "sandwich-board sign."

shift jumper Jumper similar to a sleeveless shift dress, may be worn with or without a blouse.

suspender jumper Any jumper with straps extending over the shoulders usually hooked to waistband of the skirt. A popular style for young girls. Also see SKIRTS: SUSPENDER SKIRT.

shift jumper

tunic jumper Thigh-length jumper worn over a blouse. Usually made with matching full-length pants. Can be worn as a MINIDRESS or as a PANTSUIT.

wrap jumper A jumper that fits over the head, wraps around the body, and ties in front or back. Also called *apron jumper.*

wrap jumper

jumper shift See JUMPERS: SHIFT JUMPER.

jumper suit Jumper dress with matching jacket.

jumps Unboned bodice of 18th c. worn by women for comfort or during pregnancy.

jumpshorts See SHORTS.

jumpsuit See ACTIVEWEAR.

jumpsuit pajamas See SLEEPWEAR AND LOUNGEWEAR.

jungle boot See FOOTWEAR.

jungle print See PRINTS, STRIPES, AND CHECKS.

junior petite sizes Women's garments cut for adult, well-proportioned figure, about 5′ to 5′1″ tall. Usually sized 3JP to 13JP.

junior sizes Women's garments cut for a well-proportioned adult figure, about 5′4″ to 5′5″ tall and short-waisted. Usually sized 5 to 15.

jupe **1.** See SKIRTS. **2.** See DOUBLET. **3.** See COATS AND JACKETS.

jupel See DOUBLET.

jupon **1.** See DOUBLET. **2.** See SKIRTS. **3.** See UNDERGARMENTS: Empire jupon. **4.** See COATS AND JACKETS: JUPE.

juppe See DOUBLET.

justaucorps See COATS AND JACKETS.

just-in-time (JIT) Manufacturing system designed to lessen costly inventories of textiles and apparel. Electronic communications allow suppliers to produce and supply materials to manufacturers "just in time" for production.

jute † A fiber from the stem of the jute plant, grown in Bangladesh, India, China, and Thailand. Soft, fine, lustrous, and pliable, it becomes weak and brittle when exposed to moisture. It is used in making fabrics such as BUCKRAM and BURLAP.

J

K   Abbreviation for KARAT.

kabuki (ka-boo′-kee)   Adjective used to describe clothing derived from or inspired by traditional costumes worn by actors in Japanese *kabuki theater*. See KABUKI DRESS, SHOULDERS AND SLEEVES: KIMONO SLEEVE, and SLEEPWEAR AND LOUNGE-WEAR: KABUKI ROBE.

kabuki dress (ka-boo′-kee)   Collarless wrap-around dress with KIMONO SLEEVES (see under SHOULDERS AND SLEEVES), held closed by a sash. *Der.* Copied from traditional dress of actors in Japanese popular *kabuki theater,* which began in early 17th c. with women dancers and actors. In mid-17th c. (1652) the government decreed that there should only be men as actors—doing all the female parts, too. Plots fall in three groups: historical plays, domestic plays, and dance drama performed in stylized acting. Costumes used are elaborate and include exaggerated brocaded KIMONOS, wide jeweled belts, wigs, and masklike face makeup.

kaffiyeh-agal (ka-fee′-yeh ah-gal) Headdress consisting of a large square of plain or striped cotton folded diagonally and placed on head. Sometimes has hanging tassels at cor-ners, and held by a circlet of twisted cord called **agal.** Worn by Arabs in Middle East. Also spelled *kaffiyah, kaffieh, keffiyeh, kuffieh.*

kaffiyeh-agal

kaftan   See CAFTAN.

Kahn, Robin   *   See APPENDIX/DESIGNERS.

kalasiris ∞ (kah-lah-seer′-iss)   Egyptian garment sometimes inaccurately described as a long, tight-fitting sheath-type dress, but based on the description of Herodotus, a Greek historian, more likely to have been a linen tunic. Also see EGYPTIAN DRESS. Also spelled *calasiris.*

Kalgan lamb   See FURS: LAMB.

kalso   See FOOTWEAR.

kalyptra ∞ (ka-lip-tra)   Sheer veil worn over head and face by women in ancient Greece.

Kamali, Norma   *   See APPENDIX/DESIGNERS.

kampskatcha slipper   See FOOTWEAR

kangaroo   See LEATHERS and POCKETS.

kangaroo skirt   See SKIRTS.

kapa   See TAPA CLOTH.

Karaca sweater   See SWEATERS.

karakul   See FURS: KARAKUL.

karakul cloth † (kar′-ah-kul)   Heavyweight pile fabric, similar to ASTRAKHAN, woven in imita-tion of BROADTAIL fur or PERSIAN LAMB (see under FURS).

Karan, Donna   *   See APPENDIX/DESIGNERS.

karat   Relates to the quality or fineness of gold, especially that used in jewelry. Gold of 24K is 100% gold with no alloys added; however, gold of this quality is too soft for jewelry. When alloys are added to gold, the resultant alloys are labeled as 12K, 14K, or 18K gold meaning that 12/24, 14/24, or 18/24 of the metal is gold, the remain-der is the alloy. The letter K is used as an abbre-viation. Compare with CARAT, which is the weight of a gemstone.

K

karate clothing   See ACTIVEWEAR. Also see COATS AND JACKETS: KARATE JACKET and SLEEPWEAR AND LOUNGEWEAR: KARATE PAJAMAS.

karcher   ∞ Medieval spelling for KERCHIEF. See under HEADWEAR.

kasuri   † Handwoven Japanese textile made by tie-dyeing yarns in a method similar to IKAT. Traditionally made of cotton with irregularly shaped white dots on a dark blue background. A technique often used by craftpersons for WEARABLE ART.

Kate Greenaway costume   Children's dress, popular in 1880s and 1890s, inspired by illustrations of children in empire costumes drawn by Kate Greenaway, the popular British children's book illustrator of late 19th c. Typical costumes were made of lightweight fabric printed with flowers and styled with a high waistline, puffed sleeves, and ankle-length skirts trimmed with narrow ruffles, worn with ribbon sashes, PANTALETTES (see UNDERGARMENTS) showing, and MOB CAPS or POKE BONNETS (see under HEADWEAR). These dresses were widely copied for children's wear through end of 19th c. and are still a fashion inspiration. *Der.* Named after the artist Kate Greenaway (1846–1901).

Kate Greenaway costume

Kawakubo, Rei   * See APPENDIX/DESIGNERS.

Keds®   See FOOTWEAR: SNEAKERS.

keffieh   See KAFFIYEH-AGAL.

Kellerman, Annette   See SWIMWEAR: ANNETTE KELLERMAN.

Kelly bag   See HANDBAGS AND RELATED ACCESSORIES.

kemes/kemise/kemse   See UNDERGARMENTS: CHEMISE.

kente cloth   † Fabric with woven or printed designs characterized by narrow, brightly colored bands with randomly placed geometric patterns. These fabrics are derived from traditional silk fabrics and their designs made by the Asante people of Ghana.

kente cloth

Kenzo   * See APPENDIX/DESIGNERS.

kepi   See HEADWEAR.

kercher/kercheve/kersche   Medieval spelling of KERCHIEF. See HEADWEAR: KERCHIEF #1.

kerchief   1. See HEADWEAR. 2. See SCARVES.

kevenhuller hat   See HEADWEAR: COCKED HAT.

keyhole neckline   See NECKLINES AND COLLARS.

key pocket   See POCKETS.

key resource list   See VENDOR MATRIX.

keystone markup   See MARKUP.

khaki   † (ka-key)   Fabrics of a dull, yellowish tan color, whether serges, drills, or whipcords, are called by this name. Used by the Armed Services of France, England, and the United States as far back as 1848. After World War I, the United States added an olive drab tint that is now government issue for Armed Forces. *Der.* Hindu, "dust color or earth color."

Khanh, Emmanuelle   * See APPENDIX/DESIGNERS.

kick pleat   See CLOTHING CONSTRUCTION DETAILS.

kid/kidskin   See FURS, GLOVES AND GLOVE CONSTRUCTION and LEATHERS.

kiddie couture   The production of expensive clothing for children by well-known designers.

kidney belt   See BELTS.

kid seam   See GLOVES AND GLOVE CONSTRUCTION: FULL PIQUÉ.

Kieselstein-Cord, Barry   * See APPENDIX/DESIGNERS.

kikuyu   See HANDBAGS AND RELATED ACCESSORIES.

kilt   See SKIRTS.

kiltie dress   Dress style adapted from the Scottish KILT (see SKIRTS) in which the front of the skirt is plain with wrapped side closing fastened with a safety pin, the remainder of skirt is knife-pleated and joined to a simple tailored top. Introduced in the late 1960s.

kiltie look   Clothing and accessories derived from those worn by Scots Highlanders. First adopted for boys in about 1880, revived at intervals, and fashionable since late 1960s. Elements include wearing of skirts cut like kilts, knee socks, TAMS (HEADWEAR), plaid fabrics, and GILLIE SHOES (FOOTWEAR), in imitation of Scots Highlanders' garb. Also see FOOTWEAR: KILTIE FLAT and KILTIE OXFORD.

kilt pin   See SAFETY PIN # 3.

kilt pleat   See CLOTHING CONSTRUCTION DETAILS.

kimono   (keh-mo′-no)   1. A traditional costume of Japan, either in dark colors for men or in bright colors and floral patterns for women, that is a loose, straight-cut cotton or silk robe made in various lengths and sashed at waist with a belt called an OBI (see under BELTS). Loose straight sleeves are either cut on or set-in at right angles. Adapted for fashionable wear in the United States. **2.** See SLEEPWEAR AND LOUNGEWEAR.

kimono dress (keh-mo'-no) Wrap-around dress held in place with a sash. Made with *kimono sleeves*, usually cut in one piece with the front and the back of the dress. There are no armhole seams. *Der.* Adapted from the *Japanese kimono,* first used as a dressing robe and adapted for a dress in late 1960s.

kimono #1

kiosk See INTERACTIVE KIOSK.

kip/kipskin See LEATHERS.

kipper See TIES.

kirtle **1.** From 9th to end of 14th c., a knee-length tunic with sleeves worn by men. **2.** Full-length sleeved garment worn by women from 10th to 16th c. as basic garment over the smock and under the gown. May appear as a synonym for COTE. **3.** In the 16th c., applied also to an under-skirt that is part of a dress, but by the mid-16th to mid-17th c., it was more likely to be called **half-kirtle** and, eventually, a PETTICOAT. **4.** Short jacket worn in 18th and 19th cs. **5.** An outer petticoat worn when riding.

kiss curl See HAIRSTYLES: GUICHE.

kiss-me-quick See HEADWEAR.

kitsch Styles considered to be overly sentimental or pretentious. Also used as an adjective to describe such styles.

kit fox See FURS: FOX.

Klein, Anne * See APPENDIX/DESIGNERS.

Klein, Calvin * See APPENDIX/DESIGNERS.

knapsack See HANDBAGS AND RELATED ACCESSORIES.

knee breeches ∞ Garment worn on lower half of the body by men from 1570s to about 1820. Extending from waist to slightly below the knee, they fit the leg, bloused slightly below knee, where they fastened with a button on outside of leg. From end of 17th c. on, buckles were usually worn as closures.

knee cop See ARMOR: POLEYN.

knee-fringe ∞ Fringe of ribbons around bottom edge of open-style breeches, worn by men from 1670 to 1675.

knee-high/knee-hi See HOSIERY.

knee length See LENGTHS.

knee pants See PANTS: KNICKERS.

knee-piece **1.** Upper part of BOOT HOSE (see under HOSIERY). **2.** See ARMOR.

kneesock See HOSIERY: KNEE-HI SOCK.

knee-string ∞ Drawstring used in 17th and 18th c. for tightening breeches below knee.

knee warmers Pair of knitted cuffs that slip on over legs to cover knees and may be worn under or over hose in winter or when participating in active sports.

knickerbockers **1.** ∞ Loose breeches gathered or pleated into buckled band at knee that were introduced for men about 1860, originally for country wear. **2.** ∞ Worn by women for bicycling in early 1890s. Also called RATIONALS (see under ACTIVEWEAR). **3.** Used by men for golf and sportswear in late 19th and early 20th c. Also see PANTS: PLUS FOURS. **4.** Short, full pants ending at the knee that were worn by young boys from 1860s to the early 1940s. Typically boys were dressed in short pants until school age, then in knickers until adolescence, and after this, in full-length, adult-style pants. In the early 20th c., boy's knee-length pants were usually called *knickers.*

knickers or knickerbockers #4

knickers **1.** See KNICKERBOCKERS. **2.** See UNDERGARMENTS. **3.** See PANTS.

knife pleats See CLOTHING CONSTRUCTION DETAILS and SKIRTS.

knightly girdle ∞ Decorative belt made of sections of metal joined together and buckled around hips with ornamental buckle in front. Worn only by nobility from about 1350 to about 1420.

knit/knitting † Process of making a fabric, or an item of apparel, by the interlacing of loops either by machine or by hand. A crosswise row of loops is called a **course,** while a vertical row is called **wale.** A great variety of stitches and yarns may be used to give textured effects and surface interest. Knitted stockings were introduced about 1530 when Queen Elizabeth I was presented with the first pair of knitted silk hose. Knits were used in colonial days but not widely used for clothing until late 1870s, when the JERSEY COSTUME was introduced by Lillie Langtry. Popular in handknits for sweaters for men from 1860s and women from early 20th c., in the 1920s, knits also became fashionable for women's dresses. Knits have also been important for lingerie and underwear since the 1880s. In the 1950s, the Italians introduced double-knit fabrics, which gave knits better shape retention.

knit corduroy † Knitted fabric made to have the appearance of CORDUROY, a pile weave fabric.

knit cuff See CUFFS.

knit shirt See SHIRTS.

knitted fur See FURS.

knitted knickers See SLEEPWEAR AND LOUNGEWEAR.

knitted velour See VELOUR.

knitting yarn † MANUFACTURED or NATURAL FIBER YARN used for making knitted fabrics or garments either by hand or by machine.

knob toe See FOOTWEAR.

knock-off An item of apparel copied from a more expensive item and generally manufactured from lower-priced components so it can sell at a lower price. Compare with LINE-FOR-LINE COPY and PIRACY.

knot 1. Interlacing of threads, cords, ribbons, and joining them together to fasten a garment or ends of a belt. **2.** Ornamental tyeing together of two or more lengths of ribbon, fabric, or lace. **3.** See HAIRSTYLES: CHIGNON.

knot stitch See EMBROIDERIES AND SEWING STITCHES: FRENCH KNOT.

knotted lace See LACES.

knuckle curl See FURS.

kodpeased doublet See DOUBLET.

kojah mink See FURS: MUTATION MINK.

kolbe See HAIRSTYLES.

kolhapuri sandals See FOOTWEAR.

kolinsky See FURS.

kolobion ∞ (ko-low´-bee-on) Shirtlike garment worn by men in ancient Greece, opening at the side seam rather than along the top. **Colobium** is a Roman variation of this term.

kolpos ∞ Greek term for blousing of fabric at waistline of the chiton. A second belt, worn at hips, made a *double kolpos.*

Korean dress National costume of Korean women, which consists of the **ch'ima,** a high-waisted pleated skirt; **chogori,** an extremely short jacket; and **chang-ot,** a full-sleeved cloak.

Kors, Michael * See APPENDIX/DESIGNERS.

kothornus See FOOTWEAR: COTHURNUS.

krakow See FOOTWEAR: CRAKOW.

krepis See FOOTWEAR.

krimmer See FURS: LAMB.

Krizia * See MANDELLI, MARIUCCIA under APPENDIX/DESIGNERS.

K

L Letter designation for size LARGE, used along with EXTRA SMALL, SMALL, MEDIUM, and EXTRA LARGE for men, women and children. See LARGE.

L-85, General Limitation Order Restrictions enacted during World War II (on March 8, 1942) by U.S. government War Production Board that placed limitations on the quantities of fabric that could be used on men's and women's clothing. Among the restrictions were limitations on length and circumference of women's skirts and jackets, numbers of pockets, width of belts, and for men shorter jackets, no vests with double-breasted suits, and no cuffs on trousers. Items exempted from the ruling included bridal gowns, maternity dresses, and burial gowns.

lab coat See COATS AND JACKETS: LABORATORY COAT.

lab dip A sample of dyed-to-match FINDINGS (i.e., fabric, zipper, button, thread, or other products needed to construct a garment) supplied by the vendor so that the garment manufacturer can check the color.

label Small piece of cloth stitched to the neck or interior seams of a garment that conveys information such as the manufacturer, size, care instructions, country of origin, whether the item was made by unionized workers, and the like. Custom of labeling started in early 1820s with men's tailored garments.

La Belle Époque (eh′-puck) Used by some fashion writers to refer to the period of time between 1871 and 1914 when peace prevailed in Western Europe. The upper classes led an active social life, and women patronized Parisian couturiers and wore elegant clothes. Also a period noted for progress in literature, the arts, and technology. *Der.* French, "the beautiful epoch." Also see HAIRSTYLES: POMPADOUR.

La Belle Ferronière See JEWELRY: FERRONIÈRE.

labels ∞ 14th-c.: Two lappets of silk or fur that were part of the hood worn with academic costume.

laboratory coat/smock See COATS AND JACKETS.

laced closing See CLOSURES.

laced foundation See UNDERGARMENTS.

lace glove See GLOVES AND GLOVE CONSTRUCTION.

lace hose See HOSIERY.

lace insertion Narrow lace finished with straight edges used on blouses, dresses, lingerie, and infants' dresses.

lace pantyhose See HOSIERY.

lacer/lace/lacing Rounded or flattened string or thong often with reinforced tips of metal or plastic. Usually threaded through eyelets as a fastener for a laced closing or shoes. Also called SHOELACE or SHOESTRING.

lace insertion

lacerna See CAPES, CLOAKS, AND SHAWLS.

LACES

lace 1. Decorative openwork fabric made by hand or machine by looping, braiding, interlacing, knitting, or twisting of thread to form a pattern. Various elements of lace structure include bars called **brides** that may be used to join motifs; heavier outline thread called a cordonnet (kor-dohn-ay′); and **picots** (pee′-koh), small loops along the edge of lace. Lace is classified according to method. **Needlepoint** or **point lace** is handmade by outlining the design with a single linen or cotton thread on parchment paper, holding it with tiny stitches to be

brides   ground
cordonnet
needlepoint lace

cut away later, then working the background entirely with a needle. **Pillow** or **bobbin lace** is handmade with small bobbins holding each yarn. A paper design is placed on a pillow, pins inserted, and yarns interlaced around pins to form a pattern. Designs may also

picots   ground
bobbin lace

be made separately and appliquéd to handmade net. **Tatting,** a knotted lace, usually narrow, is made by winding thread on small handheld shuttle with the fingers making small loops and patterns. Used for edging lingerie, handkerchiefs, etc. Lacemaking probably developed from CUT-WORK EMBROIDERY (see EMBROIDERIES AND SEWING STITCHES) in the 15th c. and was an important industry for centuries. Distinctive techniques and patterns that developed in cities and regions were named for the locality. Lace became very popular for collars, cuffs, and ruffs in 16th c. and was fashionable in 17th and 18th c. for trimmings and flounces. By early 19th c., John Heathcoat invented the BOBBINET machine and John Leavers started a factory to make lace by machine in England. First lace factory in the United States was started in Medway, Massachusetts, in 1818. Machine-made lace was used for shawls, parasols, collars, cuffs, and trimmings. In 20th c., lace is used especially for lingerie trim, collars, cuffs, and wedding veils. **2.** See CLOSURES.

ajour   See LACES: JOURS.
Alençon lace (ah-lan-sohn′)   Fine handmade or machine-made needlepoint lace with solid designs on sheer net ground outlined with cor-

donnet. First made in 1665 and called *point de France,* later in 1678 called *point d'Alençon. Der.* For town of Alençon, France.
allover lace   Term for wide lace with repeat patterns extending entire width of fabric. Lace purchased by the yard used for clothing.
aloe lace (ah′-low)   Tatting and bobbin lace made from ALOE fiber in the Philippines, Italy, South America, and the Barbados Islands.
Angleterre, point d'   See LACES: POINT D'ANGLETERRE LACE.
antique lace   Darned bobbin lace made by hand with heavy linen thread on knotted square net with large irregular or square openings. Also called *araneum, opus araneum,* and *spider work.*
Antwerp lace   1. Rare handmade bobbin lace similar to ALENÇON (see under LACES) with a vase or basket effect in design first made in 17th c. Also called *Antwerp pot lace* or *potten kant.* **2.** All Belgian laces, including MECHLIN and BRUSSELS (see under LACES), made before 17th c.
appliqué lace (app-lee-kay′)   Type of lace made by attaching previously made bobbin or needlepoint handmade designs to machine-made mesh ground. Also called *point d'appliqué.*
araneum lace   See LACES: ANTIQUE LACE.
argentan lace (ahr-jahn-tahn)   Flat-patterned French needlepoint lace of ALENÇON type (see under LACES) but with bolder designs, larger mesh background, and no CORDONNETS (see under LACE in category heading LACES). Popular for aprons, cravats, sleeve ruffles, and caps in 18th c. Also called *point d'Argentan* or *point de France.*
Armenian lace   Hand- or machine-made knotted lace made in narrow widths with saw-toothed edge.
baby Irish lace   Narrow fine hand-crocheted lace made in Ireland.
baby lace   Any narrow, fragile, dainty lace used to trim infants' garments (e.g., baby caps and baptismal gowns).
Battenberg lace   Lace made by applying a coarse linen Battenberg tape to the design and connecting tape with decorative linen stitch

by hand or machine. Similar to RENAISSANCE LACE (see under LACES), but coarser.

Bavarian lace Simple type of TORCHON LACE (see under LACES).

beading Term used in late 19th and 20th c. for narrow slotted lace, or embroidered bands, through which ribbon was pulled.

beggar's lace Inexpensive type of TORCHON LACE (see under LACES). Also called *bisette*.

Belgian lace Classification for PILLOW LACES (see under LACES: LACE in category heading) with machine-made grounds from Belgium, including ANTWERP, VALENCIENNES, BRUSSELS, and MECHLIN LACES (see under LACES).

Binche (bansh) Flemish bobbin lace similar to VALENCIENNES (see under LACES) with scroll floral patterns and snowflakes sprinkled on net ground. Used for cuffs and fichus since 18th c. *Der.* Named for town of Binche, Belgium.

bisette (bee-set′) Inexpensive narrow, coarse bobbin lace of TORCHON type (see under LACES), made in France since 17th c. Same as *beggar's lace*.

blonde de fil See LACES: MIGNONETTE LACE.

blonde lace Fine French bobbin lace with floral pattern on net ground, originally made of unbleached Chinese silk in Bayeux, Caen, and Chantilly; later bleached and dyed black or colors. Fashionable at French court from mid-18th to mid-19th c.

bobbinet (bob-in-ett′) Mesh fabric base for lace with hexagonal holes made by hand or machine.

bobbin lace See LACES: LACE under category heading.

Bohemian lace Bobbin lace characterized by tapelike designs on net ground. Originally handmade in Bohemia from old Italian patterns, now machine-made.

bone lace Bobbin lace made by fastening threads to pillow by thin fish bones when pins were scarce in Elizabethan times. See LACES: LACE under category heading.

bourdon lace (boor′-dohn) Machine-made net lace with cord outlining pattern and outer edge.

Breton **1.** Lace made by embroidering with colored yarns on net, rather than weaving de-

sign, in imitation of ALENÇON LACE (see under LACES). **2.** Net fabric with larger holes than Brussels net.

bridal lace **1.** Contemporary industry term for lace used to make a wedding dress, for trimming, or for the veil. **2.** RETICELLA-type of lace (see under LACES) worn by brides of France and Spain in the 16th and 17th c. The designs consist of heraldic devices relating to owner. Also called *carnival lace*.

brides See under LACES: LACE in category heading.

Bruges lace (broozh) Fine GUIPURE (see under LACES) tape lace of bobbin-type similar to DUCHESSE (see under LACES), but coarser. *Der.* For city of Bruges, Belgium.

Brussels lace Needlepoint lace with cords outlining designs made separately and appliquéd to fine net. Formerly handmade, now machine-made.

Brussels net Handmade BOBBINET (see under LACES), made in Belgium, with hexagonal holes, two sides of holes braided, the other four sides twisted. Also called *filet de Bruxelles*.

Buckingham lace Fine bobbin lace with simple pattern on a fine clear ground worked all in one piece. *Der.* For Buckinghamshire, England, where it was first manufactured in 16th c. Also called *Buckinghamshire lace*.

bullion (bull-yon′) Antique heavy lace made of silver or gold thread in a simple design. Also called *bullion lace*.

burn-out lace See BURN-OUT.

carnival lace/carnaval lace See LACES: BRIDAL LACE #2.

Carrickmacross lace (Kar-ik′-ma-cross) Two types of lace: (a) GUIPURE type with design cut from fine cambric or lawn and embroidered with fine needlepoint stitches connected by brides, (b) APPLIQUÉ type with designs embroidered, then superimposed on machine net. See cross-references under LACES. *Der.* Made in or near Carrickmacross, Ireland, since 1820.

Chantilly lace (shan-til′-ee or shon-tee-yee′) Delicate fragile-looking bobbin lace first made by hand in early 18th c. Later made by machine with hexagonal mesh and a design

L

of scrolls, branches, and flowers outlined with CORDONNETS (see under LACES: LACE in category heading). Made with a scalloped edge in white and used for contemporary bridal dresses. Also produced in black. Made in Caen and Bayeux during the last half of the 19th c., Chantilly lace was very fashionable for shawls and parasols. *Der.* For town of Chantilly, France, where it was first made.

chenille lace (shen-eel′) 18th-c. French needle-point lace made with hexagonal mesh and designs outlined in white chenille yarn. See CHENILLE in alphabetical list.

Cluny lace (kloo′-nee) **1.** Coarse bobbin lace, similar to TORCHON (see under LACES), usually made of heavy ivory-colored linen thread in wheel or paddle designs. **2.** Machine-made cotton lace of similar design.

Colbertine lace A coarse, French bobbin lace with a square mesh ground. Produced in France in 17th c. under royal patronage when Colbert was prime minister. Sometimes spelled *Colberteen, Colbertan.*

cordonnet See under LACES: LACE in category heading.

Cork lace Older types of Irish lace formerly made in Cork, Ireland, are identified by this term. Includes flat needlepoint lace copied after Italian laces and YOUGHAL LACE (see under LACES).

Crete lace Silk or linen bobbin lace usually made with geometrical designs on colored ground with colored chainstitch along the edge. Made in Crete.

crochet lace See CROCHET in alphabetical list.

damascene lace (damah-seen′) Lace made with sprigs and braids of lace joined together by corded bars in imitation of HONITON LACE (see under LACES).

darned lace Term applied to all filet-type lace made by pulling out groups of warps and fillings from fabric and inserting stitches with a needle. Background may also be reworked in buttonhole stitch. See LACES: FILET LACE.

dentelle de la vierge See LACES: DIEPPE POINT LACE.

Dieppe point lace (dee-epp′) French bobbin lace similar to VALENCIENNES (see under LACES) but simpler, made in 17th and 18th c., narrow variety is called **poussin** (poos-ahn′); wider type called **dentelle de la vierge** (dahn-tel′ de la veeairzh). *Der.* For town of Dieppe, France.

duchesse lace (do-shes′) Type of bobbin lace characterized by floral designs and a tapelike effect made with fine thread and much raised work. Designs are made first then connected by means of BRIDES (see under LACES: LACE in category heading) or bars. When joined together, it gives an allover look with irregularly shaped spaces between the designs. Frequently handed down from one generation to next for use on bridal dresses. Originally called *guipure de Bruges.*

Egyptian lace Knotted lace frequently made with beads placed between meshes.

fausse Valenciennes (fowss va-lahn-see-enz′) A term used for lace similar to VALENCIENNES (see under LACES) but not made in the city of Valenciennes.

fiber lace Delicate lace made of banana and aloe fibers.

filet de Bruxelles See LACES: BRUSSELS NET.

filet lace (fil-ay′) Hand-knotted lace with square holes frequently filled in with colored yarns in darning stitch. Also imitated by machine. Also called *darned filet lace.*

flouncing Lace wider than edging lace, used for ruffles or trimmings, with one straight edge, the other scalloped. Usually made with one strong thread along straight edge that can be pulled to make gathers.

French lace Machine-made lace fabrics made in imitation of handmade French lace. Included are lingerie laces of the ALENÇON, CHANTILLY, and VALENCIENNES types (see under LACES) and couture laces used for garments, grouped into: (a) re-embroidered lace, (b) CHANTILLY of the fine type, (c) GUIPURE lace, (d) veiling and tulle. See cross-references under LACES.

Greek lace See LACES: RETICELLA LACE.

gros point (groh pwanh) Venetian needlepoint lace made in large designs with high relief work. Also called *gros point de Venise* and *point de Venise.*

ground The background of lace as opposed to the designs it supports or surrounds. Two types are used: net or mesh and bar.

guipure (ghee-poor′) **1.** Heavy tape lace characterized by large showy patterns in needlepoint or bobbin fashion worked over a coarse mesh ground. **2.** Lace with designs, with or without bars or brides, to hold pattern in place. **3.** Early name for gold and silver lace.

guipure de Bruges See LACES: DUCHESSE LACE.

hairpin lace Insertion-type lace with a looped edge made by winding the thread around a hairpin. Crochet hook is used to catch the threads together.

Hamburg lace Heavy embroidered effect carried out on cambric or muslin fabric.

Honiton lace (hon′-ih-ton) Bobbin lace, similar to DUCHESSE, made in England with either motifs made first and appliquéd to machine-made net ground, or lace with round heavy motifs made of fine braid joined together like GUIPURE. See under LACES. *Der.* From town of Honiton, Devonshire, England, where lace has been made since time of Queen Elizabeth I.

Irish crochet lace Handmade lace characterized by raised designs of roses, shamrocks, or other patterns set against a coarse diamond-shaped mesh with heavy scalloped edge. Made in the chainstitch. Copied from needlepoint lace of Spain and Venice and made in Ireland originally. Later made in France, Belgium, China, and Japan. Popular for collars and cuffs in early 20th c.

Irish point lace See LACES: YOUGHAL LACE.

jours The fancy stitches used in needlepoint and bobbin lace for filling enclosed spaces.

knotted lace Lace made by hand-tied knots to form a meshlike pattern, e.g., MACRAMÉ (see in alphabetical list) and TATTING (see under LACES: LACE in category heading).

lacis (lay-sis) Original term for square-mesh net that is darned or embroidered; a forerunner of lace.

Leavers (leevers) **/levers** Term applied to all laces made on Leavers machine invented by John Leavers in 1813 and used in factories, particularly in Nottingham, England, and in the United States.

Lille lace (lihl) Fine bobbin lace of simple pattern outlined by heavy CORDONNETS (see under LACES: LACE in category heading) on net background with hexagonal holes, similar to MECHLIN LACE (see under LACES). First made in 16th c. *Der.* From town of Lille, France.

Lyons lace (lee′-yon) MALINE-type of lace (see under LACES) with pattern outlined in silk or mercerized cotton. *Der.* From British name for town of Lyons, France.

machine-made lace Any type of lace made by machine. See LACES: LEAVERS LACE and NOTTINGHAM LACE. Most contemporary laces of all types are made by machine.

macramé lace See MACRAMÉ in alphabetical list.

maline lace (mah-leen′) **1.** Stiff bobbin lace with hexagonal mesh ground similar to MECHLIN LACE (see under LACES). **2.** General term for all light Flemish laces before 1685. Also spelled *malines*.

Mechlin lace (meck′-lin) Fragile bobbin lace with ornamental designs outlined with shiny cordonnets and placed on hexagonal net ground. Used in Regency and Louis XV period; greatest vogue about mid-18th c. *Der.* From city of Mechlin, Belgium, where it was made.

Medici lace (med-ih′-chee) French bobbin lace, combining closed and open work, one edge finished in scallops similar to but finer than CLUNY LACE (see under LACES). Also spelled *Medicis* in France. *Der.* For noble Italian family in power from 14th to 18th c.

mignonette lace (min-yohn-et′) Narrow, light, fine, French bobbin lace made in linen thread and worked in small patterns on six-sided mesh ground that resembles tulle. Also called *blonde de fil*.

Milan lace (mee-lan′) Type of bobbin lace, originally made with flat tapelike circular designs connected with BRIDES (see under LACES: LACE in category heading) or bars. Popular in 17th c. and earlier made of gold, silver, and silk thread. Later, elaborate designs such as flowers, animals, and figures were used on a mesh ground and made in shaped pieces for collars. *Der.* From Milan, Italy. Also called *Milan point lace*.

Moscow lace A copy of Italian lace made in Russia.

L

needlepoint lace   See under LACES: LACE under category heading.

Northamptonshire lace   Bobbin lace with fine mesh ground imitating Flemish laces, similar to LILLE, VALENCIENNES, and BRUSSELS LACES (see under LACES). Made in England in 17th and 18th c. and popular in United States in 19th c.

Nottingham lace   **1.** Cotton lace made on Nottingham machine. Has a V-shaped mosaic-like pattern and is made in wide width. **2.** Originally a classification of machine-made laces made in Nottingham, England. Now used for laces made on Nottingham machines anywhere. *Der.* From place of origin.

opus araneum   See LACES: ANTIQUE LACE.

orris lace (or-iss′)   18th-c. lace of gold and silver. *Der.* From Arras, France. Also spelled *orrice.*

passement (pass′-mahnt)   French term used in 16th c. for all types of lace, finally developed into PASSEMENTERIE.

pillow lace   See LACES: LACE under category heading.

Plauen lace (plow′-en)   Lace made by BURNOUT method—the design is embroidered by Schif-fli machine in a fiber different from the ground fiber, so when chemically treated, the ground dissolves, leaving lace. *Der.* From Plauen, Germany, where method was invented. Also called *St. Gall* and *Saxony laces.*

point d'Alençon   See LACES: ALENÇON LACE.

point d'Angleterre (pawnh donh′-gla-tare)   Fine handmade BRUSSELS bobbin lace (see under LACES) with pattern of floral, bird, or geometrical motifs worked separately and applied to handmade mesh. Introduced into England and Belgium in 17th and 18th c. and used for collars, fichus, handkerchiefs, aprons, petticoats, fans, and to trim gloves. Revived in the 19th c. when applied to good Belgium lace, a coarse mixed Belgium lace, or a type of tape lace.

point d'appliqué   See LACES: APPLIQUÉD LACE.

point d'Argentan   See LACES: ARGENTAN LACE.

point d'esprit   (pwanh des-pree′)   Open stitch used in GUIPURE lace (see under LACES) with loops forming a pattern on a mesh ground.

point de France   Needlepoint lace similar to *Venice* and *Milan* laces of same era. Manufac-ture was encouraged by French government under supervision of Colbert, a state official who imported workers from Italy and started a factory in 1665 at Alençon. Also see LACES: ARGENTAN LACE.

point de Gaze (pwanh de gahz)   Belgian needle-point lace with flower designs appliquéd on fine bobbin net, later cut away under the designs.

point de Paris (pwanh de pa-ree′)   **1.** Narrow bobbin lace with hexagonal mesh and flat design. **2.** Machine-made lace similar to VAL LACE (see under LACES) with design outlined with GIMP (see under BRAIDS).

point de rose   See LACES: ROSE-POINT.

point de Venise (pwanh de ven-ees′)   Type of Venetian needlepoint lace made with padded, raised cordonnets, and edges of designs trimmed with many picots. By late 17th c. also made in France and England. Most sought-after lace by 17th-c. Cavaliers. Also called *gros point de Venise.*

point lace   Shortened form for NEEDLEPOINT LACE (see under LACES).

point noué (pwanh new-ay′)   French lace-makers' term for buttonhole stitch, the basis of all needlepoint lace.

potten kant lace   See LACES: ANTWERP LACE.

poussin lace   See LACES: DIEPPE POINT LACE.

princesse lace (pranh-sess′)   Imitation of DU-CHESSE LACE (see under LACES), done in a fine delicate manner with machine-made designs joined together or applied to net ground.

punto (puhn′-toe)   Term for Italian laces of 16th c. Also applied to Spanish laces. *Der.* Italian, "stitch."

Renaissance lace (ren-ay′-sonse)   Heavy flat lace made with tape laid out in pattern and joined together in a variety of stitches. First made in 17th and revived in late 19th c. for fancy work and then called BATTENBERG LACE (see under LACES).

reticella lace (reh-tee-chel′ lah)   First needle-point lace made by cutting and pulling out threads, then reembroidering. Developed from cutwork and drawn work done on linen. Early patterns were geometrical and connected by PICOT BRIDES (see under LACES: LACE in cate-

L

gory heading) or bars. First mentioned in 1493 in a Sforza inventory. Very fashionable in 16th c. and widely imitated; still made in Italy. Also called *Greek lace, Greek point, Roman lace, Roman point,* and *Venetian guipure* (ghee-poor´).

Roman lace See LACES: RETICELLA LACE.

rose-point lace Venetian needlepoint, similar to VENETIAN POINT (see under LACES) but finer and with smaller motifs of flowers, foliage, and scrolls. Has more design repeats and connecting brides, or bars, and is padded with buttonhole edges and a heavy cordonnet. Also called *point de rose.*

Saxony lace See LACES: PLAUEN LACE. *Der.* From Saxony, Germany.

shadow lace Machine-made lace that has flat surface and shadowy indistinct designs.

Shetland lace Bobbin lace made of black or white Shetland wool. Formerly used for baby covers and shawls.

Spanish blonde lace Lace characterized by heavy pattern on fine net ground. Made in Catalonia and Barcelona or frequently imported from France to Spain for use in mantillas, scarfs, and flounces.

Spanish lace **1.** Lace with a flat design of roses connected with a net background. Used for mantillas. **2.** Coarse pillow lace made with gold and silver threads.

spider work Coarse open bobbin lace, same as LACES: ANTIQUE LACE.

St. Gall lace A term for Swiss laces and embroideries, specifically PLAUEN LACE (see under LACES). *Der.* From St. Gallen, Switzerland.

stretch lace Machine-made lace of narrow or full width knitted with extra core yarns that are expandable. Used in narrow width for hems; wider widths used for girdles and foundations.

tambour work See EMBROIDERIES AND SEWING STITCHES.

tape lace A lace made of machine or handmade tape manipulated into a pattern either connected with bars or laid upon a net ground.

tatting See LACES: LACE under category heading.

teneriffe lace (ten-err-eef´) Lace with wheel designs made by winding thread around the top of a small spool about 2½″ in diameter then working back and forth across the circle with a needle and thread. Made chiefly in the Canary Islands. Sometimes called *teneriffe work.*

toile (twal) Lace-makers' term for pattern of lace as distinguished from the background. *Der.* French, "cloth."

torchon lace (tor´-shon) Coarse inexpensive bobbin lace made of cotton or linen in simple fanlike designs, produced in Europe and China. Also made by machine. Also called BEGGAR'S LACE and BISETTE LACE (see under LACES).

valenciennes lace (va-lahn´-see-enz) Handmade French fine bobbin lace first made in time of Louis XIV. Distinguished by small floral and bow designs made in one with the ground of square, diamond-shaped, or round mesh. *Der.* From Valenciennes, France.

val lace Abbreviated form for VALENCIENNES (see under LACES). This term usually applies to machine-made copies.

Venetian lace Many types of laces and embroidery from Venice including cutwork, drawn work, RETICELLA (see under LACES), raised point, and flat point.

Venetian point lace Heavy needlepoint lace with floral sprays, foliage, or geometrical designs made in high relief by buttonhole stitches with motifs connected with BRIDES (see LACES: LACE under category heading) or bars and decorated with picots. Originally made in Venice; later made in Belgium and other countries. Also called *Venetian raised point.* Also see LACES: POINT DE VENISE.

youghal lace (yoo-gahl´) Irish flat needlepoint lace inspired by Italian laces, particularly Venetian types. *Der.* First made in Youghal, County Cork, Ireland. Also called *Irish point lace.* Also see LACES: CORK LACE.

---

lacet See BRAIDS.

lacing studs See CLOSURES: SPEED LACING.

lacis See LACES.

Lacoste® See shirts.

Lacroix, Christian * See APPENDIX/DESIGNERS.

L

ladder braid   See BRAIDS.

ladrine   See JEWELRY: LANDRINE.

Lagerfeld, Karl   *   See APPENDIX/DESIGNERS.

La Goulue   See HAIRSTYLES: POMPADOUR.

laid embroidery   See EMBROIDERIES AND SEWING STITCHES: GIMPED EMBROIDERY.

laid stitch   See EMBROIDERIES AND SEWING STITCHES.

laisse-tout-faire   See APRONS.

Lake George diamond   See GEMS, GEM CUTS, AND SETTINGS.

Lalique, René   (la-leak′, Rah-nay′) (1860–1945) Jeweler who presented such unique and artistic jewelry at Salon du Champ de Mars in Paris in 1895 that he became known as the foremost *Art Nouveau* jeweler-artist. He used subjects (e.g., the snake, owl, octopus, and bat), set with blue-green colored stones including opals to carry out his highly personalized jewelry. Also used mysterious female figures in enamel, ivory, vitreous paste, or engraved glass to obtain pictorial effects.

lamb/lambskin   See LEATHERS and FURS.

lamballe bonnet   See HEADWEAR.

lamboy   See ARMOR: TONLET.

lame   See ARMOR.

lamé †   (lah-may′) Any textile fabric woven or knitted with metallic yarns to form either the background or the pattern. May be made in jacquard or rib weave. The metallic yarns are frequently coated with a fine polyester film that prevents tarnishing. *Der.* French, *lamé,* "leaves of silver or gold."

laminated fabric †   A layered fabric structure in which the outer layer is joined to the backing fabric by either heat sensitive foam or adhesive.

lampshade beads   See JEWELRY.

landing strip   See HAIRSTYLES: FLATTOP.

landlady shoe   See FOOTWEAR: WOOLWORTH® SHOE.

landrine   See FOOTWEAR.

Lane, Kenneth Jay   *   See APPENDIX/DESIGNERS.

langet   ∞ (lahn-jay′)   **1.** A thong (see THONG #2) or LACER used to fasten garments together in 15th c. Also see POINTS. **2.** Plume worn on a Knight's helmet.

langettes   See JEWELRY.

Langtry bustle   See UNDERGARMENTS: BUSTLE.

Langtry hood   See HEADWEAR.

Langtry, Lillie   See JERSEY COSTUME.

languette   ∞ (lan-get′)   Flat, tongue-shaped piece of cloth appliquéd as trimming on woman's cloak or skirt, either singly or in series. Especially seen from 1818 to 1822. *Der.* French, *langue,* "tongue."

lantern sleeve   See SHOULDERS AND SLEEVES.

Lanvin, Jeanne   *   See APPENDIX/DESIGNERS.

lanyard   Cord, usually braided in contrasting colors, used suspended around neck or from belt to hold an accessory such as a whistle or pocket knife.

lapel   See NECKLINES AND COLLARS and WATCHES.

lapel pin   See JEWELRY.

lapidary   Person who specializes in cutting of gems other than diamonds. Same as a *gem cutter.*

lapin   See FURS.

lapis lazuli   See GEMS, GEM CUTS, AND SETTINGS.

la pliant   ∞ (la plee′-awnt)   Invention of 1896 for holding out back of skirt by inserting steel strips in casings eliminating the need for many petticoats. *Der.* French, "flexible."

lapped seam   See CLOTHING CONSTRUCTION DETAILS.

lappets   **1.** See HEADWEAR. **2.** See ECCLESIASTICAL DRESS: FANONS.

lapponica   See CAPES, CLOAKS, AND SHAWLS.

large   Size used along with EXTRA SMALL, SMALL, MEDIUM, and EXTRA LARGE for men, women, and children in such categories as: gloves, girdles, knit shirts, nightgowns, pajamas, panty girdles, robes, shirts, sports jackets, and sweaters. Abbreviation is L.

lariat necklace   See JEWELRY.

Laroche, Guy   *   See APPENDIX/DESIGNERS.

last   See FOOTWEAR.

lasting boots   See FOOTWEAR.

latch buckle   See CLOSURES.

latchet   See FOOTWEAR.

latex †   Rubber, in natural or synthetic liquid form, that may be extruded or cast to form core of ELASTOMERIC yarn. May be used bare or wrapped with another textile yarn.

lattice   Decorative openwork made from crossed pieces of fabric, leather, or BIAS BINDING. Pieces are crossed at right angles to look similar to "lattice work" on old houses. Used for decorative trimming on clothing and shoes.

Laura Ashley® look Style using small Victorian floral designs on cotton fabric for everything from garden overalls to nightgowns and dresses. Designed and trademarked by Laura Ashley of England, and sold in Laura Ashley stores in France, The Netherlands, Switzerland, Great Britain, and the United States. Also see PRINTS, STRIPES, AND CHECKS: LAURA ASHLEY PRINT.

Lauren, Ralph * See APPENDIX/DESIGNERS.

lava-lava See PAREO.

lavaliere See JEWELRY.

lawn † Sheer, lightweight, high-count cotton fabric made in a plain weave of fine combed yarns. May be dyed or printed, given a soft or a starched finish, and calendered (see CALENDER).

lawn-party dress ∞ Afternoon dress suitable for an outdoor reception in 1890s, frequently made with a high, boned collar, gored full-length skirt, and sash at waist. Worn with floppy straw hat trimmed with flowers, ribbon, and veiling.

lawn-tennis apron See APRONS.

lawn-tennis costume ∞ Woman's fitted jacket and full skirt coming to boot tops made with bustle-back. Sometimes embroidered with racquets and tennis balls at hem. Worn by women for playing tennis in the 1880s. See ACTIVEWEAR for modern tennis clothing.

layaway Purchase of apparel through scheduled payment amounts on merchandise that is held by the store. When all the payments have been made, the customer takes ownership of the goods.

layered/layered look Used to describe the look of several garments worn one on top of the other, all being of different lengths. Popular from the late 1960s, early 1970s, and 1980s and after. See SKIRTS: LAYERED SKIRT.

layered cut See HAIRSTYLES.

layette Garments and accessories collected by prospective mother for a new baby.

lay figure See CROQUIS.

laying off See GLOVES AND GLOVE CONSTRUCTION.

lazarine See FOOTWEAR: LANDRINE.

lazy daisy stitch See EMBROIDERIES AND SEWING STITCHES.

L.B.D. Abbreviation for "little black dress." See BASIC DRESS.

LCD quartz watch See WATCHES.

leading strings Narrow ropelike cords attached at the shoulders of children's dresses in the 17th and 18th c. Used to guide child when learning to walk. Also called *tatas*. Also see RIBBONS OF CHILDHOOD.

leaf See NECKLINES AND COLLARS.

leased department Space within a large department store for a specialty department (such as fine jewelry, furs, shoes) so that it may provide special goods or services.

leatherette † Misnomer for fabrics made in imitation of leather.

leathering See FURS.

leather jerkin See COATS AND JACKETS: BUFF COAT.

leather look Classic tailored look of natural, sueded, or simulated leather used for coats, jackets, pants, skirts, or accessories. First introduced in 1920s for jackets, and in 1960s for coats, skirts, and pants. Not called by this name until 1968 when it started a trend toward the slick, shiny, or WET LOOK. Popular again in 1984 when it also included patchwork leather patterns in various colors. Also called *cuir savage*.

LEATHERS

leather Skin or hide of an animal with the hair removed and the grain revealed by process of tanning. Usually dyed and finished by **glazing**, applying a shiny finish applied to kid-skins by using a glass roller; **buffing**, abrading with emery wheel; **embossing**, impressing a design with engraved metal rollers to imitate another leather; or **sueding**, buffing on the flesh side to raise a slight nap. Sometimes split into several layers with top layer called the **grain**, others called **splits**. Leather has been used for shoes and clothing since primitive times. Now used extensively for all types of clothing including coats, jackets, skirts, vests, pants, suits, handbags, shoes, and other accessories. Also used as trim on fabric apparel. Fabric and vinyl used as a substitute for leather must be labeled "man-made or manufactured materials." Real leather may be labeled "genuine leather." In LEATHERS category listing also see ALUM, CHROME, COMBINATION, and VEGETABLE TANNING.

L

alligator   Leather from alligators with characteristic markings of blocks, rectangles, and circles with cross markings between. Used for shoes, handbags, and belts. Law passed by Congress in 1970 prohibited use in the United States, later rescinded.

alligator-grained   Term for alligator-skin pattern EMBOSSED (see under LEATHERS: LEATHER in category heading) or printed on cowhide, calf-skin leather, plastic, or imitation leather.

alligator lizard   Leather from a large lizard with markings like grains of rice and elongated blocks, similar in appearance to hides of small alligators.

alum tanning   Process used to produce soft, pliable, white leathers. Mainly used for gloves. Primary disadvantage is that leather is not washable.

antelope   Rare, soft velvety leather made from antelope or gazelle skins, usually SUEDED (see under LEATHERS: LEATHER in category heading.) Used for fine shoes, bags, and jackets.

antelope-finished lambskin   Soft finish applied to lambskin, calfskin, or goatskin in imitation of genuine antelope skin.

antique finish   Finish applied to leather giving a shaded effect by dyeing, buffing, wrinkling, waxing, and oiling the surface to resemble old leather.

bark tanning   See VEGETABLE TANNING.

bating   Term for processing of skins and hides to reveal grain of leather after hair has been removed.

bend   Leather term for the best section of leather cut from a whole hide.

boarded finish   Leather finish that makes the grain of the leather more pronounced. Hand-processed by folding the leather with grain sides together and rolling it back and forth while pressing it with a cork board.

box calf   Calf that has been BOARDED (see under LEATHERS) in two directions to give it squared markings on the GRAIN side (see under LEATHERS: LEATHER).

bronzed leather   Copper-colored kid or calf-skin.

brush-dyeing   Coloring of leather by placing skins flesh side down on metal table and applying dye to grain side with brush. Desirable for black kidskin gloves as inside remains white.

buckskin   **1.** Deer or elk skins with the grain given a suede finish similar to early skins cured by Native Americans. Second SPLITS (see under LEATHERS: LEATHER in category heading) of deerskin must be called *split deerskin* or *split buckskin*. **2.** Sheepskin treated to resemble true buckskin.

buffing   See under LEATHERS: LEATHER in category heading.

cabretta   Fine, smooth, tight-grained leather made from Brazilian sheepskins used mainly for women's dressy gloves.

calf/calfskin   Supple, fine-grained, strong leather from skins of cattle a few days to a few weeks old finished in many ways (e.g., GLAZED, SUEDED, BOARDED, EMBOSSED, WAXED, or made into PATENT LEATHER. Used for shoes, handbags, belts, and wallets. Best qualities come from the United States. See cross-references under LEATHERS.

capeskin   Light, flexible fine-grained leather made from skin of the South African hair sheep or from other hair sheep. *Der.* Frequently shipped from Capetown, South Africa, hence the name.

carpincho   Leather tanned from a water rodent. Often sold as pigskin and used mainly for sport gloves.

cattlehide   Heavy leather, usually vegetable-tanned, from cow, bull, and steer hides. Used for sole leather. Also called *cowhide.*

chamois   (sha´-mee, or French, shah-mawh´) Originally leather made from an Alpine goat or chamois; now undersplits of sheepskins that are oil-dressed and suede-finished are correctly called by this name. See LEATHERS: CHAMOIS TANNING.

chamois tanning   Treatment of hides by scraping the surface, saturating both sides with oil, and pounding the hide until the oil is absorbed. Also called *oil tanning.*

chickenskin   Leather of unborn calves; light in weight.

chrome tanning   A mineral type of tanning process for leather. Skins are placed in large revolving drums and are tanned in three to eight hours. The basic ingredients used are salts of chromium. This is the most used process today for tanning shoe uppers, handbags, belts, etc. Before being dyed, leather is a robin's-egg blue color.

combination tanning Leather tanned by using both CHROME and VEGETABLE TANNING methods (see under LEATHERS).

cordovan Durable, almost completely nonporous leather, made from the shell of horse-butts used for uppers of fine men's shoes. It is given a characteristic waxy finish in black and reddish-brown colors. *Der.* Named for Cordoba, Spain, where tanning of leather was highly perfected under the Arabs.

cowhide See LEATHERS: CATTLEHIDE.

crocodile Thick-skinned leather, from a large water reptile, characterized by black markings and a scaly horny surface; very similar to *alligator.*

cross-boarded Leather-industry term for skins processed to make grain more pronounced by folding leather in one direction, pressing with a cork armboard and rolling; then folding in opposite direction and repeating the process.

crushed leather Leather given a crinkled surface made by hand boarding, machine boarding, or by embossing to produce an imitation of a boarded finish. See LEATHERS: LEATHER in category heading and LEATHERS: BOARDED FINISH. Also called *écrasé leather* (eh-kras-zay), a French word for leather crushed to reveal the grain.

deerskin See LEATHERS: BUCKSKIN.

doeskin **1.** Genuine doeskin is leather made by tanning female or male deerskins by the CHAMOIS PROCESS (see under LEATHERS) and then buffed to produce a SUEDED FINISH (see under LEATHERS: LEATHER in category heading). **2.** Sheepskin or lambskin tanned by CHAMOIS or ALUM PROCESS (see under LEATHERS) and sueded. Should be called *doeskin-finished lambskin.*

écrasé See LEATHERS: CRUSHED LEATHER.

elkhide Misleading term for CATTLEHIDE (see under LEATHERS) finished to look like elk leather—should be labeled *elk-finished cowhide.*

embossed See under LEATHERS: LEATHER in category heading.

fancy leather Industry term for leather having a natural grain or a distinctive pattern, e.g., alligator, lizard, and snakeskin. Also includes embossed effects simulating reptile patterns or leathers given a decorative finish, e.g., metallic kid.

fleshing Processing the skin side of hides, with a machine that has rollers fitted with sharp spiral knives, to remove excess skin and flesh making hide appear even in thickness.

formaldehyde tanning A bleaching process that can be added to chrome or chamois tanning. Necessary if white leather is to remain white after frequent laundering. See LEATHERS: CHROME TANNING and CHAMOIS TANNING.

French antelope lambskin LAMBSKIN (see under LEATHERS), tanned in France, that has been given a lustrous suede finish to make it look like antelope skin.

French kid Originally KIDSKIN (see under LEATHERS) imported from France, now refers to any alum- or vegetable-tanned kidskin that resembles the original.

frog Leather with a distinctive grain and pattern made from the skin of a species of giant frog found in Brazil. Limited in availability and used for women's accessories and trimmings. May be simulated by EMBOSSING (see under LEATHERS: LEATHER in category heading) other leathers and called *frog-grained leathers.*

full grain/full top grain In the leather industry, the side of the skin or hide from which the hair has been removed.

galuchat (ga-lu'-chat) Leather made from tough outer layer of SHARKSKIN (see under LEATHERS). Used for handbags and novelty items.

ganges Leather embossed to imitate snakeskin.

glacé (gla-say') Shiny finish applied to kidskins by using a glass roller. Also called *glazed.* *Der.* French, "frozen."

glazé kid/glazed kid KIDSKIN (see under LEATHERS) given a very shiny surface by means of heavy rollers. *Der.* French, "shiny."

L

goatskin Leather made from the skin of the goat. Used for gloves, shoe uppers, and handbags. Also see LEATHERS: KIDSKIN.

grain Leather term for the markings that appear on the skins and hides when the hair or feathers are removed. Pigskin shows small markings in groups of three. Ostrich skins show a rosette where the quill has been removed.

horsehide A durable fine-grained leather from horses and colts. Usually imported and used flesh side up with GRAIN (see under LEATHERS: LEATHER in category heading) used for inside surface of shoe uppers. Also see LEATHERS: CORDOVAN LEATHER.

hunting calf See LEATHERS: REVERSE CALF.

"in the white" Undyed and unfinished tanned leather.

Java lizard Lizard skins with black, white, and gray coloring. Imported from Java in Indonesia, and used for handbags, shoes, and belts.

kangaroo Durable scuff-resistant leather made from kangaroo and wallaby hides. Similar to KIDSKIN (see under LEATHERS) in appearance and imported mainly from Australia.

kid/kidskin Leather made from young goat skins. Used for women's shoe uppers, handbags, belts, and fine gloves.

kip/kipskin Leather-industry term for pelts of young steers, cows, or horses that weigh between 15 and 25 pounds, as distinguished from skin or hide of older animals.

lambskin Leather made from skin of a young sheep.

lizard Reptile leather with pattern similar to grains of rice. Often named for place of origin in India and Java. Used for shoe uppers, handbags, belts, and ornamental trimmings.

mocha Fine-sueded glove leather made from skins of blackhead or whitehead sheep from Somaliland, Sudan, and Egypt. Used for women's fine gloves and shoes.

Moroccan leather Fancy goatskins with a pebbly GRAIN (see under LEATHERS: LEATHER in category heading), often dyed red. Originally tanned in Morocco and mainly used for handbags and slippers. See HANDBAGS AND RELATED ACCESSORIES.

nap finish Leather finish that creates a suede-like finish (see LEATHERS: SUEDE) on the grain side of the leather.

nappa Glove leather from sheepskins or lambskins of domestic New Zealand or South American origin that have been tanned by CHROME, ALUM, or COMBINATION METHODS (see under LEATHERS).

nubuck An imitation deerskin made from cattle hide. See LEATHERS: BUCKSKIN #1.

oil tanning See LEATHERS: CHAMOIS TANNING.

ostrich Leather with a distinctive rosette pattern caused by removal of plumes from ostrich skins. Used for fine shoes and handbags.

patent leather Leather processed on the grain side to form a bright hard brittle surface. Done by degreasing, stretching on frames, coating with paint and linseed oil, then alternately baking in the sun and rubbing with pumice stone. VINYL is used to make imitation patent leather.

pebbled finish An embossed leather finish similar to tiny cobblestones or pebbles.

peccary Leather processed from the skin of the wild boar of Central and South America. Used mainly for pigskin gloves.

Persians Leather industry term for hair-sheepskin leather tanned in India. See LEATHERS: SHEEPSKIN.

pigskin Leather made from the skin of the pig, which has groups of three tiny holes forming a distinctive pattern caused by removing the bristles.

pin seal High-grade skins from hair seal with fine pebbly grain. Imitated widely by embossing patterns on calfskin, cowhide, goatskin, and sheepskin, and then called pin-grain calfskin, etc.

python Leather processed from skin of a large nonpoisonous snake with medium-sized scales and distinctive markings. Available in black and white, tan and white. It is sometimes dyed bright red, yellow, blue, and other colors. Used for handbags, shoes, and trimmings.

rawhide Leather in natural pale beige or yellowish color made from CATTLEHIDES (see under LEATHERS) not actually tanned but dehaired, limed, stuffed with oil and grease. Used mainly for thongs (see THONG #2).

reverse calf Calfskin finished with flesh side out, GRAIN side (see under LEATHERS: LEATHER in category heading) inside. Called *hunting calf* in England.

rosette Mark left on ostrich skin when quill is removed.

Russian leather Leather tanned with birch bark, which has distinctive odor. Usually finished in brown and originally from Russia. Term now used for any similar brown calfskin.

saddle leather Natural tan leather made from vegetable tanned STEERHIDES or CATTLEHIDES (see under LEATHERS) and used for tooled-leather handbags, belts, and saddles for horses.

sealskin Leather made from genuine Alaska fur seal hides. Rare, because the Alaska fur seal is protected by the U.S. government. Also see LEATHERS: PIN SEAL.

shagreen (sha-green′) Untanned leather of the shark and similar fishes usually dyed dark green or black and highly polished. Used in 18th and 19th c. for snuff boxes, medallions, and watch cases.

sharkskin Almost scuff-proof leather made from the skin of certain species of sharks. The "outer armor," or SHAGREEN (see under LEATHERS), is removed before the skins are tanned. Used for shoes, belts, handbags, wallets, and cigarette cases. Also see LEATHERS: GALUCHAT.

shearling Short curly wool skins of sheep or lambs sheared before slaughter and tanned with the wool left on. Used for slippers, gloves, coats, and jackets, with the sueded flesh side out.

sheepskin Leather from sheep, characterized by more than average sponginess and stretchability, frequently sueded. Small skins with fine grain are called LAMBSKIN (see under LEATHERS). Used for shoes, handbags, coats, and jackets. Sheepskin tanned with wool left on is often used leather side out for coats and sport jackets. See LEATHERS: SHEARLING.

side leather CATTLEHIDES (see under LEATHERS), too large to process in one piece, are cut down center back into two parts—each part is called a **side**. Used for sole leather or for shoe uppers and belts.

snakeskin Diamond-patterned leather with overlapping scales processed from skin of a number of species of snakes (e.g., diamond-backed rattlesnake, python, cobra, or boa).

sole leather Heavy stiff leather usually CATTLEHIDE (see under LEATHERS) used for the soles and built-up heels of shoes.

split One of several layers or cuts sliced from thick CATTLEHIDE with the grade of leather determined by the split: TOP-GRAIN is the smooth hair side of the skin; other splits have a rough surface, called **deep-buff**, split, and **slab**. The latter cuts mainly used to make SUEDE. See cross-references under LEATHERS.

split buckskin/deerskin See LEATHERS: BUCKSKIN.

staking A means of making leather more pliable by passing it over a blunt metal blade.

steerhide Heavy leather from skins of castrated male cattle, usually used as SOLE LEATHER for shoes or to make SADDLE LEATHER (see under LEATHERS).

suede Leather, usually lambskin, doeskin, or splits of cattlehide (sometimes called REVERSE CALF, see under LEATHERS) that has been buffed on the flesh side to raise a slight texture. Sometimes buffed on grain side or on both sides of a split to cover small defects. Used for skirts, pants, jackets, vests, and accessories.

tanning The process of making leather from hides. Methods include: VEGETABLE TANNING with tannin, mineral tanning with CHROME or ALUM, CHAMOIS TANNING with oil, and artificial methods. See cross-references under LEATHERS.

top grain Leather-industry term for first SPLIT (see under LEATHERS) from grain side of leather. Used for shoes and handbags.

undersplit One of the underlayers of leather obtained when leather is SPLIT (see under LEATHERS).

vegetable tanning Tanning process that produces various shades of orange- and beige-colored leathers. Basic ingredients include vegetable products such as bark, leaves, nuts, tannic acid, and twigs. Great disadvantage is the length of time involved for tanning, which runs between four and six months.

vici kid **1.** Term used for all GLAZÉ KID (see under LEATHERS). **2.** ∞ Formerly trade term for a chrome tanning process.

wallaby Leather made from the skins of small species of kangaroo family. Similar to KANGAROO LEATHER (see under LEATHERS) but sometimes finer grained.

---

leavers See LACES.

Le Canned dress Trade name for a simple shift dress of printed nylon knit packaged for sale in a tin can. Briefly popular in 1967.

lederhosen See SHORTS.

le dernier cri (ler durn′-yer cree) French, "the last word," the utmost in fashion.

le dernier mode French, "the latest fashion."

Leek button See CLOSURES.

leg bandages/leg bindings ∞ Strips of woolen cloth that were wound around the leg. Worn as a leg covering from ancient times in Northern Europe, adopted by Roman soldiers, and continued in use in the early Middle Ages. Considered to be a forerunner of STOCKINGS (see under HOSIERY).

legging Covering for leg and ankle extending to knee or sometimes secured by stirrup strap under arch of foot. Worn in 19th c. by armed services and by civilian men. See PUTTEE and GAITER. Worn by women in suede, patent, and fabric in late 1960s.

leggings/leggins See PANTS #1.

leghorn See HEADWEAR.

legionnaire's cap See HEADWEAR: KEPI.

leg-of-mutton/leg-o′mutton sleeve See SHOULDERS AND SLEEVES.

legwarmers See HOSIERY.

legwear Any type of apparel worn on the legs. Examples: stockings, tights, socks. See HOSIERY.

lei Hawaiian garland of flowers, frequently orchids, worn around the neck. Often presented to visitors on arrival in Hawaii.

Leicester jacket See COATS AND JACKETS.

leisure bra See UNDERGARMENTS.

leisure suit Man's suit styled in knit or woven fabric in casual style with jacket similar to a

shirt having a convertible collar, more "sporty" buttons, and sleeves with no cuffs or with single cuffs. Popular in the 1970s.

Lelong, Lucien * See APPENDIX/DESIGNERS.

LENGTHS

length Point at which the lower edge of item of apparel ends, (i.e. the hem of a coat, jacket, skirt, or dress). Dresses were generally floor, or at least ankle, length until World War I. In the late 1920s they were knee length; after which the fashionable length varied— at some times to the ankle, at others below the knee. In the 1960s, MINI skirts ended above the knee and vied in popularity with MAXI and MIDI lengths (see under LENGTHS). Since then, skirt length has become more a matter of personal choice rather than being dictated by fashion.

leisure suit

lengths

ankle length Length that clears the floor by a few inches, reaching to the ankle. Same as MAXI LENGTH (see under LENGTHS).

ballerina length Skirt reaching to the center of the calf of the leg or a little below. Worn at one time by ballet dancers. Popular for evening dresses in the late 1940s and 1950s.

boy-leg Adjective describing a garment with a close-fitting leg that ends about half way down the thigh.

calf length Hem of skirt, dress, or coat reaching below the knee at the widest part of the calf. Compare with MIDI LENGTH (see under LENGTHS), which is longer.

chapel-length train Skirt made with back cut longer, ending in a short train of about one yard, primarily used for informal wedding dresses.

full length Term indicated floor length. Most dresses were this length until early part of the 20th c.

hip length Popular length for suit coats for men and women, ending at hip bone.

knee length Skirt or coat reaching to the middle of the knee cap or to the top of the knee.

longuette Term coined by *Women's Wear Daily* in January 1970 to describe the radically longer lengths on coats, skirts, and dresses reaching from below-the-knee to ankle-length that were an abrupt change from the miniskirts of the late 1960s. Styles were introduced simultaneously in Paris and New York. *Der.* French diminutive for "long."

maxi length Word coined in 1968 for skirts that reached the ankles. Ankle-length dresses were worn for day or evening, which was the first time since World War I that ankle-length dresses were worn as daytime dresses.

micro Coined in late 1960s as an adjective describing very short skirt lengths or any very small piece of clothing. Worn by ultra-MOD young women in the late 1960s.

micro length Dress or skirt reaching to upper thigh; an exaggerated mini.

midi length (mid′-ee) Originally described a skirt length coming to the mid-calf of the leg, but later applied to anything that length such as dresses, capes, or coats. Term coined in 1967 by *Women's Wear Daily. Der.* French, *midi,* "middy."

mini length (minn′-ee) Dresses, skirts, and coats reaching to mid-thigh, introduced in England in the early 1960s as part of MOD fashions, with credit for introduction often going to Mary Quant, the English designer. In late 1960s became an accepted fashion in the United States.

nine-tenths length Coat length made a few inches shorter than the dress or suit worn underneath.

seven-eighths length Woman's coat length made several inches shorter than the dress or

suit it covers. Popular for coats in the 1940s and 1950s.

tea length Skirt hem ending at the shin.

three-quarter length Woman's coat or jacket approximately halfway between hip and thigh.

waist length Jacket length reaching to the natural waistline. Fashionable length for suit jacket used at intervals since 1890s. Also a popular length for a jacket matched to a dress from the 1930s on.

waltz length Calf length. Usually used to describe nightgowns and robes.

Lennon specs See EYEGLASSES.

leno weave † Open weave with two lengthwise yarns locking around each crosswise yarn in a figure-eight design. Also called *doup* and *gauze weave.* Marquisette is one of the most widely used leno weave fabrics.

leopard See FURS.

leopard print See PRINTS, STRIPES, AND CHECKS: ANIMAL PRINT.

leotard See ACTIVEWEAR.

leotard shirt See SHIRTS.

Lepape (Georges) (1887–1971) An illustrator who studied at École des Beaux Arts and became famous when asked by Paul Poiret, Parisian couturier, to illustrate his publication *Les Chose de Paul Poiret* in 1911. After that, his fashion drawings were in demand by periodicals such as *Gazette du Bon Ton, Vanity Fair, Femina, Harper's Bazaar,* and *Vogue.* Did many covers for *Vogue* during the 1920s and early 1930s. Also designed sets and costumes for plays. He used bold color with original and inventive designs rather than naturalistic portrayals in his fashion illustrations. He was influenced by the *Ballets Russes* and famous artists of that time.

Leroy * See **Roy, Hippolyte** under APPENDIX/DESIGNERS.

Leser, Tina * See APPENDIX/DESIGNERS.

le smoking See SMOKING SUIT.

letter/letterman sweater See SWEATERS.

lettice See FURS.

lettice cap/bonnet See HEADWEAR.

letting-in See FURS.

letting-out See FURS.

lettuce edging See CLOTHING CONSTRUCTION DETAILS.

lettuce ruff/lettice ruff See CABBAGE RUFF.

Letty Lynton dress Dresses styled by the designer Adrian and worn by Joan Crawford in the 1932 MGM film *Letty Lynton.* One particular style was fitted to the hips with a full skirt, the outstanding feature being very full balloon sleeves covered with ruffles. Another style designed for the movie was a slim SHEATH, tight to the knees, with a HALTER neckline and flaring TRUMPET SKIRT (see SKIRTS). *Der. Letty Lynton,* a film of 1932.

Levi's® See PANTS.

Levi's 501's A lot number given to certain of Levi Strauss jeans in 1890 by the manufacturer. Used 501 jeans are now in great demand on the used-jeans market.

levite gown See GOWN À LA LEVATINE.

liars ∞ Wire framework worn during latter half of 18th c. under a scarf, to give the effect of a larger bosom. Also called *menteurs* (mon′-tur) and *trompeurs* (trom′-puhr).

Liberty® Trademark for Liberty Ltd., a London fabric manufacturer that produces cotton prints called LIBERTY PRINTS (see PRINTS, STRIPES, AND CHECKS). Also produces a Liberty SATIN, and Liberty LAWN, and some silk fabrics. All have the trademark attached.

liberty cap See HEADWEAR: BONNET ROUGE.

liberty stripes See PRINTS, STRIPES, AND CHECKS: HICKORY STRIPES.

licensed goods Apparel or other products manufactured as a result of LICENSING.

licensing The sale of the right to use an image or design by the owner (licensor) to a manufacturer (licensee), in return for payment of royalties to the licensor who continues to own the rights to the original image or design.

life mask See MASKS.

lifestyle The attitudes, values, and material possessions that characterize an individual's way of life.

lifestyle eyewear See EYEWEAR.

lift See FOOTWEAR.

light jack boots See FOOTWEAR: JACK BOOTS #2.

Lille lace See LACES.

Lilly® Trademark for a simple printed-cotton shift dress designed and sold by designer Lilly Pulitzer of Palm Beach, Florida, from late 1960s. Pulitzer began designing these printed dresses after spilling orange juice on her dress. Company was liquidated in mid-1980s; however, the trademark remains active for a wide variety of products ranging from cosmetics to clothing.

lily benjamin See COATS AND JACKETS: BENJAMIN.

Limerick gloves See GLOVES AND GLOVE CONSTRUCTIONS.

limited marketing channel See MARKETING CHANNEL.

limousine See CAPES, CLOAKS, AND SHAWLS.

Lincoln lamb See FURS.

Lindbergh jacket See COATS AND JACKETS.

Linde Star dress® Jeweled full-length evening dress sprinkled with Linde Star sapphires (synthetic sapphires) set at intervals. Novelty dress of the late 1960s.

line See COLLECTION.

line brochure/line catalog/line sheet A catalog used to market the current COLLECTION to retail buyers. It shows all the available styles.

linecloths, pair of See UNDERGARMENTS.

line-for-line copy American interpretations of Parisian and Italian couture dresses made expressly for American stores. The retail dress buyer may purchase a PROTOTYPE or pattern for the dress from the original designer in Paris. May also purchase the identical fabric, but the dress is produced and sold in America at a much lower price than the Parisian original. A popular practice in the 1950s. Compare with KNOCK-OFF.

lineman's boot See FOOTWEAR.

linen † **1.** Fibers of the flax plant that are used to make linen yarn. **2.** Fabrics made of linen yarns in many qualities and many weights. Crease-resistant finishes are frequently applied to linen fabrics. *Der.* French, *linge,* "linen."

lingerie (lan′-zha-ree) Women's underwear; sometimes called intimate apparel by the trade. *Der.* French, *linge,* "linen," as women's undergarments were originally of linen.

lingerie crepe See FRENCH CREPE.

lingerie hem See CLOTHING CONSTRUCTION DETAILS.

lining Fabric, pile fabric, or fur used to finish inside of garment. The extra layer is used for warmth, to retain shape of outer layer, or for appearance. See HALF LINING and ZIP-IN/ZIP-OUT LINING.

linked dress Dress made by linking geometrically shaped pieces of metal, leather, plastic or mirror together. Introduced by Paris couturier Paco Rabanne in 1966.

lion's tail See HAIRSTYLES.

lipstick A crayon-like stick of lip coloring, usually in a metal or plastic tube.

liquid embroidery See EMBROIDERIES AND SEWING STITCHES.

liripipe See HEADWEAR: CHAPERON #1.

lisle yarn † (lyle) A two-ply cotton yarn made of long staple fibers that are combed, tightly twisted, and sometimes given further treatment to remove all short fuzzy fiber. Also see HOSIERY: LISLE HOSIERY.

list/listing See SELVAGE.

little black dress See BASIC DRESS.

little bodkin See PONYET #2.

little-boy shorts See SHORTS.

little girl look Fashions for adults, introduced by designers in 1960s, that imitated the dress of a 12-year-old girl with an undeveloped figure. Elements included above-the-knee skirts, some knee-high socks for day and evening wear, and ankle socks worn with mary jane shoes.

Little Lord Fauntleroy suit ∞ Young boy's costume consisting of black velvet tunic and knee pants worn with wide sash. Blouse had wide white lace trimmed collar and cuffs, and was worn with black stockings, pumps, and shoulder-length hair. Worn by boys in the United States from 1886 to 1914 for special occasions. *Der.* Inspired by popularity of book *Little Lord Fauntleroy,* by Mrs. Frances Hodgson Burnett, published in 1886.

Little Lord Fauntleroy suit

Littleway shoe construction See FOOTWEAR.

Little Women dress Child's dress made with plain, fitted, front-buttoned bodice, short or long plain sleeves, small turned-down collar with ribbon bow tie, and full-gathered skirt. *Der.* Inspired by dresses described in Louisa May Alcott's book *Little Women,* published in 1868.

liturgical robe See ROBE #2.

livery Characteristic clothes or uniform worn by servants, now chiefly used in reference to chauffeurs' uniforms. In the Middle Ages and after, servants' livery was made in the colors of the family crests of their employers.

lizard See LEATHER.

llama † Fibers similar to ALPACA obtained from a member of the camel family, native to high altitudes in Andes mountains of South America. Fiber colors range from white, gray, and light brown to black. The outer coat of the animal is coarse while the underfiber is soft.

loafer See FOOTWEAR.

locket See JEWELRY.

lock stitch See EMBROIDERIES AND SEWING STITCHES.

loden cloth † Dense, water-repellent coatings and suitings woven by people of the Tyrol, a section of Austria and Germany. Made of local wool in a deep olive green color, sometimes with the addition of camel's hair, these fabrics are used for winter sportswear, skiwear, and coats.

loft † Term to describe the resiliency of fibers.

logo A compact symbol, drawing, or name for a designer, manufacturer, or other organization that is easily recognized by a target audience or market.

loincloth Under- or outer garment consisting of a length of fabric wrapped around the hips and lower abdomen. Generally worn in cultures where clothing is draped rather than cut and sewn, such as ancient Egypt. Length may range from very short to ankle-length. Specific constructions vary. Some are shaped and worn like a triangular diaper, while others may consist of a long piece of fabric that goes between legs and is brought up and pulled under a belt in front and back with part of the fabric left hanging down in front and back. Synonyms: *breechcloth, breechclout.*

London Fog® See COATS AND JACKETS.

London look See BRITISH LOOK.

long and short stitch See EMBROIDERIES AND SEWING STITCHES.

long-bellied doublet See PEASCOD-BELLIED DOUBLET.

long bob See WIGS AND HAIRPIECES: BOB-WIG.

long clothes ∞ Dresses worn by infants from the second half of the 17th c. and after. Approximately

3 feet long, usually decorated with embroidery, the dress was worn with a matching petticoat. A style still used for modern christening dresses. Worn by children who could not yet walk, they were also called **carrying frocks,** while shorter dresses worn by children who could walk were known as **going frocks.**

long Duvillier   See WIGS AND HAIRPIECES: DUVILLIER WIG.

long handles   See UNDERGARMENTS: LONG JOHNS.

long hood   See HEADWEAR.

long johns   See UNDERGARMENTS.

Long John trunks   See ACTIVEWEAR.

long-leg panty girdle   See UNDERGARMENTS.

long-line bra   See UNDERGARMENTS.

long-line bra slip   See UNDERGARMENTS.

long lock   See HAIRSTYLES: LOVE LOCK.

long stocks/long stockings   ∞ Stockings attached at thigh to TRUNK HOSE worn by men in 16th and 17th c.

long-torso   Describing a garment with waistline placed near the widest part of the hips.

longuette   See LENGTHS.

look   *n.* Used with descriptive adjectives to characterize the overall impression or appearance of a style or trend. This usage of the term began in 1947 with Christian Dior's NEW LOOK, a radical change in fashion. Since the 1950s, looks have been influenced by protest of the younger generations against traditional styles, social evolution, civil rights movements, and political events. Other looks evolved from clothes and accessories worn on stage, as well as movies and TV shows or from clothes and accessories worn by celebrities in the limelight (e.g., Jackie Kennedy Onassis and Princess Diana of England). Looks may not always be widely adopted, but general trends they represent often find their way into the mainstream of fashion.

loom   † A mechanical device on which cloth is woven. Looms may be hand-operated, now used mostly for crafts, or automated for use in the textile manufacturing industry.

loo mask   See MASKS.

loop and button closing   See CLOSURES.

looped dress   ∞ Hoop-skirted dress worn in 1860s, made with skirt in two layers. Outer layer was gracefully looped up in four, five, or six places by fabric tabs called **Lyons loops** to show the underskirt.

Lord Byron shirt   See SHIRTS.

Lord Fauntleroy suit   See LITTLE LORD FAUNTLEROY SUIT.

lorgnette (lorn-yet)   See EYEWEAR.

Louis XIV sleeve   See SHOULDERS AND SLEEVES.

Louis XV basque   See COATS AND JACKETS.

Louis XV bodice   ∞ Dress bodice of 1850s and 1860s made with long point in front tapering to waistline with a short PEPLUM in back. Had several rows of RUCHING around neck and a V-shaped neckline in front that was filled in with bows of ribbon. RUCHING also was used on the peplum and sleeves. *Der.* Similar to bodice worn by Marquise de Pompadour, mistress of Louis XV of France in mid-18th c.

Louis XV hat   See HEADWEAR.

Louis XVI basque   See COATS AND JACKETS.

Louis heel   See FOOTWEAR.

lou mask   See MASKS: LOO MASK.

lounger   See FOOTWEAR.

lounge suit   ∞ British term for man's suit worn for informal occasions from 1860s on, consisting of lounging jacket, vest, and trousers all of same fabric.

loungewear   See under category heading for SLEEPWEAR AND LOUNGEWEAR.

lounging cap   See HEADWEAR.

lounging jacket   See COATS AND JACKETS: SACK JACKET and SMOKING JACKET.

lounging pajamas   See SLEEPWEAR AND LOUNGEWEAR.

lounging robe   See SLEEPWEAR AND LOUNGEWEAR.

loup   See MASKS.

louvre sunglasses   See EYEWEAR.

love beads   See JEWELRY: HIPPIE BEADS.

love knot   ∞ **1.** Decorative bow used in 16th c. tied across puffs in vertically slashed sleeves. **2.** Ornamental knot of ribbon originally worn as a love token. Made of intertwined loops of two or more cords, the knot originally symbolized constancy of true love.

love lock   See HAIRSTYLES.

love ribbon   ∞ Gauze ribbon with narrow black-and-white satin stripes, formerly worn as a mourning band.

low cut   See FOOTWEAR.

lower stocks ∞ Stockings made of silk or wool cloth worn by men from mid-16th to 17th c. Also called *nether stocks;* formerly called *bas de chausses* (ba deh shos). Worn with upper stocks. See CHAUSSE, TRUNK HOSE.

low rise/low-slung See WAISTLINES.

lozenge front ∞ Daytime dress bodice with front trimmed with strips of net, ribbon, and lace arranged in crisscross fashion to form a diamond-shaped pattern. Worn at the end of 18th and beginning of 19th c.; similar to dresses worn by the Marquise de Maintenon, second wife of Louis XIV of France. *Der.* French, *lozenge,* "diamond shaped."

L-shaped lapel See NECKLINES AND COLLARS: LAPEL.

luau pants See PANTS.

Lucite® Trademark for transparent acrylic plastic material used for handbags, sandals, shoe heels, and jewelry.

lumberjack/lumber jacket See COATS AND JACKETS.

lumberjack plaid See PLAIDS AND TARTANS.

lumberman's over See FOOTWEAR.

Lunardi hat See HEADWEAR: BALLOON HAT.

lunar fashion/lunar look Clothes and accessories imitating those used by astronauts that were introduced after American astronauts landed on the moon July 20, 1969. During the same month Italian designers Baratta, Eleanor Carnett, and Tiziani showed metallic jumpsuits. Parisian designer Cardin showed a moon cape. Space suits were introduced for children in imitation of the astronauts' suits. *Der.* Latin, *lundris,* "of the moon." For earlier interpretations of this same look, see COSMONAUT LOOK.

lunchbox bag See HANDBAGS AND RELATED ACCESSORIES.

lunette See CRESCENT.

Lurex® † Trademark for a decorative metallic fiber and yarn made of aluminum-coated plastic to prevent tarnishing.

Lycra® See SPANDEX.

lynx/lynx cat See FURS.

lyocell † Regenerated cellulosic fiber made by a more environmentally friendly process than rayon. The Federal Trade Commission has designated lyocell as a generic fiber name but classified it as a subcategory of rayon. Trademark names for the fiber include Tencel®, made by Acordis, and Lyocell by Lenzing®.

Lyons lace See LACES.

Lyons loops See LOOPED DRESS.

L

M

M **1.** Letter designation for size *medium* used along with EXTRA SMALL, SMALL, LARGE, and EXTRA LARGE for men, women and children. See MEDIUM. **2.** Shoe width designation equivalent to a B.

mac See COATS AND JACKETS: MACKINTOSH #2.

macaroni ∞ Fashionable man of George III's reign who belonged to the *Macaroni Club,* formed in 1764 with membership based on having traveled to Italy. Style of dress did not develop until 1770s and included the macaroni suit, which had a thigh-length, tight-fitting jacket with very tight-fitting sleeves; an extremely high, tight stock or cravat and collar, breast pocket for handkerchief, and low flapped pockets; large nosegay on left shoulder; and breeches worn with hose of various colors. Shoes were low-cut with enormous buckles, and a tiny three-cornered hat was carried.

Macaroni c. 1770s

macaroni collar See MACARONI.

macaroni cravat See MACARONI.

Macbeth tartan See PLAIDS AND TARTANS.

Macclesfield tie See TIES.

MacDonell of Glengarry tartan See PLAIDS AND TARTANS.

Macfarlane See COATS AND JACKETS.

MacGregor (Rob Roy) See PLAIDS AND TARTANS.

machine knitting See KNIT.

machine-made buttonhole See CLOSURES: BUTTONHOLES.

machine-made lace See LACES.

Macintyre and Glenorchy tartan See PLAIDS AND TARTANS.

Mackie, Bob ★ See APPENDIX/DESIGNERS.

mackinaw See COATS AND JACKETS.

mackintosh See COATS AND JACKETS.

MacPherson hunting tartan See PLAIDS AND TARTANS.

macramé (mak'-rah-may)   Two, three, four, or more strands of cord, string, or yarn knotted in groups to form patterns. Craft used by sailors as a pastime, producing belts and ornaments. Revived in early 1970s by young adults making neckwear, vests, belts, and other accessories. In 1980s, used for belts, handbags, and shoes. *Der.* Turkish *magramah,* "napkin" or "facecloth."

macramé flat knot

Madeira embroidery See EMBROIDERIES AND SEWING STITCHES.

made-to-measure See CUSTOM-MADE and TAILOR-MADE.

madras † (mah-drass')   Shirting or dress fabric woven in a variety of structural patterns (e.g. stripes, cords, plaids, dobby, and Jacquard patterns from cotton or cotton blends, usually made with combed yarns and mercerized (see MERCERIZATION). Stripes and plaids are yarn-dyed and may bleed. Sometimes this is considered an asset, as it tends to soften the sharp plaid effect. Such fabrics are called **bleeding madras.** *Der.* Imported from the city of Madras in India.

mafors See HEADWEAR.

magyar sleeve See SHOULDERS AND SLEEVES.

maharatta tie (ma-ha-ra-ta) See TIES: INDIAN NECKTIE.

mail See ARMOR.

mail-coach necktie See TIES.

maillot See ACTIVEWEAR.

Mainbocher * See APPENDIX/DESIGNERS.

Maine hunting boot See FOOTWEAR.

Maintenon cloak See CAPES, CLOAKS, AND SHAWLS.

Maintenon coiffure See HAIRSTYLES.

Maintenon corsage ∞ (man-te-non) Woman's evening dress bodice of 1839 and 1840s, trimmed with ribbon bows down center front in ladder-like effect with lace ruffle at waist. *Der.* Named for the *Marquise de Maintenon,* mistress and second wife of Louis XIV of France.

Maintenon toupet See WIGS AND HAIRPIECES.

majorette boot See FOOTWEAR.

major wig See WIGS AND HAIRPIECES.

malacca cane See CANE.

malachite See GEMS, GEM CUTS, AND SETTINGS.

Mali bracelet See JEWELRY.

Malimo® See stitch-bonded fabric.

maline (mah-leen') **1.** † Extremely fine, soft silk, rayon, or cotton net with hexagonal holes used primarily for millinery. Sometimes used over feathers on hats to keep them in place. *Der.* Originally made in Maline, Belgium. **2.** See LACES.

Maltese cross See CROSS #1.

Mameluke sleeve See SHOULDERS AND SLEEVES.

Mameluke tunic (mama-luke) See tunic à la mameluke.

Mameluke turban See HEADWEAR.

Mamma shoe See FOOTWEAR.

manbag See HANDBAGS AND RELATED ACCESSORIES.

mancheron See SHOULDERS AND SLEEVES.

manchette ∞ (mon-chet) Wrist ruffle of lace worn by women on afternoon dresses from 1830s to 1850s.

mandarin collar See NECKLINES AND COLLARS: CHINESE COLLAR.

mandarin dress See CHEONGSAM.

mandarin hat See HEADWEAR.

mandarin jacket See COATS AND JACKETS.

mandarin sleeve See SHOULDERS AND SLEEVES: KIMONO SLEEVE.

Mandelli, Mariuccia * See APPENDIX/DESIGNERS.

mandilion See COATS AND JACKETS.

mandinko See HAIRSTYLES.

manikin See MANNEQUIN.

maniple See CLERICAL DRESS.

man-made fiber See MANUFACTURED FIBERS.

mannequin (man'-eh-kin) **1.** A model of the human body, used to display clothes in department stores, etc. **2.** A woman whose job is wearing clothes in FASHION SHOWS. Also spelled *manikin.*

Manon robe ∞ (man-ohn') Daytime dress of 1860s with front cut in one piece from neck to hem. Back with double BOX PLEAT or WATTEAU PLEATS (see under CLOTHING CONSTRUCTION DETAILS) hanging from under collar to hem of skirt. *Der.* Named for Manon, heroine of 1733 book by Abbé Prevost.

mant See MANTUA.

man-tailored Applied to a woman's suit or coat to imply that the garment is tailored similarly to a man's suit, coat, or shirt, as contrasted with tailoring of the softer type used in DRESSMAKER SUITS. Sometimes made in men's wear fabrics.

manteau (man-tow) **1.** See CAPES, CLOAKS, AND SHAWLS. **2.** See MANTUA.

mantee See COATS AND JACKETS.

mantelet See COATS AND JACKETS: PARDESSUS.

mantella **1.** See HEADWEAR: MANTILLA. **2.** See CAPES, CLOAKS, AND SHAWLS.

mantelletta See CLERICAL DRESS.

mantellone See CLERICAL DRESS.

mantelot See CAPES, CLOAKS, AND SHAWLS: MANTELET #4.

mantilla **1.** See HEADWEAR. **2.** See CAPES, CLOAKS, AND SHAWLS.

mantinee skirt See UNDERGARMENTS: HOOPS.

mantle See CAPES, CLOAKS, AND SHAWLS.

mantlet See CAPES, CLOAKS, AND SHAWLS: MANTELET.

mantlet Matilda See CAPES, CLOAKS, AND SHAWLS.

manto See MANTUA.

manton de manilla See CAPES, CLOAKS, AND SHAWLS: SPANISH SHAWL.

mantua ∞ (man'-tu-a) Woman's overdress or gown worn over underskirt that was made with a loosely fitted unboned bodice joined to overskirt with long train. Split in front to expose petticoat, the front edges of the overskirt were sometimes looped up at the sides to create a draped effect. Worn on social or formal occasions from mid-17th to mid-18th c. Also called *mant, manteau, manto, manton,* and *mantua gown.*

mantua 1708

mantua maker ∞ 17th and 18th-c. term for TAILOR (a man) or DRESSMAKER (a woman).

manufactured fibers † Textile fibers that are not found in nature but are produced through various chemical processes. They may be classified as either **synthetic fibers,** which are created from chemical components (e.g., ACRYLIC, NYLON, POLYESTER, OLEFINS, SPANDEX) or as **regenerated fibers,** which are created by taking natural materials, such as wood chips or very short cotton fibers that cannot be used as textile fibers in their natural form but which can be chemically processed and reformed into useable textile fibers (e.g. RAYON, ACETATE, LYOCELL). Also called *man-made fibers.*

marabou See FEATHERS.

marcasite See GEMS, GEM CUTS, AND SETTINGS.

marcel wave See HAIRSTYLES.

marguay See FURS: SPOTTED CAT.

Marguerite dress ∞ Dress of early 1890s with a scarf at the neckline, made with full sleeves gathered into a wide cuff reaching halfway to elbow. Blouse was full and gathered at neckline and worn with full gathered skirt trimmed with bands of braid. Contrasting low-necked sleeveless peasant bodice, laced up the front and back, is worn over the dress.

Marguerite girdle See BELTS.

Marie Antoinette fichu See SCARVES: ANTOINETTE FICHU.

Marie Antoinette skirt See SKIRTS.

Marie sleeve See SHOULDERS AND SLEEVES.

Marie Stuart bodice ∞ Tight-fitting, boned evening bodice ending in a deep point at waist-line worn in late 1820s. *Der.* Similar to bodice of dress worn by Mary, Queen of Scots, also called Mary Stuart (or Stewart) (1542–1587).

Marie Stuart bonnet/cap See HEADWEAR.

Marie Stuart hood See HEADWEAR.

marin anglais bonnet See HEADWEAR.

marine gems See GEMS, GEM CUTS, AND SETTINGS.

mariner's cuff See CUFFS.

Marino Faliero sleeve See SHOULDERS AND SLEEVES.

markdown Reduction of the retail price of an apparel item. Some markdowns are temporary, while others are permanent.

marker A plan for cutting the pattern pieces for a specific garment style.

market **1.** The location where a buyer, representing the retailer, and a seller, representing the manufacturer, purchase or sell goods. The site may be a MERCHANDISE MART or TRADE SHOW, or even a specific city. **2.** A time when buyers and manufacturers come together, such as the Spring market.

market calendar Itemization of the dates and locations of trade shows and markets. Also see MARKET WEEK.

market center A city that not only has marts and showrooms but is also a principal location for manufacturing and retailing industries (e.g., New York, Los Angeles, Dallas, Atlanta, Chicago).

marketing channel System through which merchandise moves from the manufacturer to the ultimate consumer. In a **direct marketing channel,** the manufacturer sells directly to the consumer (e.g., catalog sales, Internet). A **limited marketing channel** routes the merchandise from the manufacturer to the retailer, who sells it to the consumer. In an **extended marketing channel,** wholesalers obtain products from manufacturers and sell them to retailers or to jobbers who, in turn, sell them to retailers.

market niche See NICHE.

market week Any of the weeks of the year in which apparel companies show their fashion lines.

mark stitch See EMBROIDERIES AND SEWING STITCHES: TAILOR'S TACKS.

markup/markon The amount of money added to the manufacturer's cost to determine the final retail sales price. The traditional markup on the apparel doubles the cost of the merchandise and is called a **keystone markup.**

marled † Made from MARL YARN.

marlotte See COATS AND JACKETS.

marl yarn † Yarn, made from two or more different-colored strands of fiber or two or more different-colored yarns, that produces mottled or HEATHER effect in fabrics woven or knitted from this yarn.

marmot See FURS.

marmotte bonnet See HEADWEAR.

marmotte cap See HEADWEAR.

marquis See HEADWEAR.

marquise 1. See GEMS, GEM CUTS, AND SETTINGS. 2. See COATS AND JACKETS: MARQUISE MANTLE. 3. See UMBRELLAS AND PARASOLS.

marquise bodice ∞ (mar-keez) Evening bodice of mid-1870s with low heart-shaped neckline forming two large scallops and trimmed with RUCHING or lace frill. Also called *bodice en coeur.*

marquise mantle See COATS AND JACKETS.

marquisette † (mar-kee-set′) Fine, transparent netlike fabric with good durability. Made with cotton, silk, or manufactured yarns in the LENO WEAVE, which prevents the crosswise yarns from slipping. Used for evening gowns, cocktail dresses, and sheer blouses.

mart See MERCHANDISE MART.

marten See FURS.

Martha Washington fichu See SCARVES: FICHU #1.

Martha Washington waist See BLOUSES AND TOPS.

martingale See BELTS.

Mary cap See HEADWEAR: MARY, QUEEN OF SCOTS CAP.

mary jane/Mary Jane® See footwear.

Mary, Queen of Scots cap See HEADWEAR.

masher ∞ Term used for an elaborately dressed DANDY of 1880s and 1890s. Also called *Piccadilly Johnny.*

masher collar See NECKLINES AND COLLARS.

masher dust wrap See COATS AND JACKETS.

masi See TAPA.

MASKS

mask Covering for the face used as a disguise for Halloween or masquerades. Also worn as a protection for the face for active sports and industrial purposes. Some cultures use masks in rituals. Ancient Greeks used masks in the theater. In the 16th and 17th cs., masks were used for purposes of disguise when going out on the street at night. (See MASKS: LOUP.) In the American colonial period, masks were fashionable for protection of face from the sun in the daytime.

cache-laid ∞ (cash lade) Mask worn in Paris to conceal a plain or unattractive face. Fashionable about 1650 during reign of Louis XIV. *Der.* French, "hide-ugly."

catcher's mask Mask made of wire or plastic covering the face that fastens with strap around the head. Worn in baseball games by the catcher to prevent face injury.

chill mask/cold mask See MASKS: HOT MASK.

domino Small mask covering upper half of the face, leaving the mouth exposed; worn for masquerades. Also called a *half-mask.*

domino

false face See MASKS: RUBBER MASK.

fencing mask Protective mask of fine wire screening fitting over the face to prevent injury from foil when fencing.

half-mask See MASKS: DOMINO.

hat mask Hat extending partway down over the face with cutouts for the eyes. Used for beach hats and for helmet-type hats in 1960s.

hot mask Mask shaped like a DOMINO (see under MASKS) that ties at back of head. **Chill mask** is used for puffy eyes, tension, or hangover; heat mask is used to relieve sinus pain and stuffy noses. Also called *cold mask.*

industrial mask Large fiberglass mask with clear see-through window. Worn for soldering or doing dangerous industrial tasks.

life mask Mask similar to a surgical mask with carbon filter. Worn on the street as a protection against air pollution and smog.

loo mask Half mask hiding upper part of face, worn by women from mid-16th to early 18th c. on the stage or as a disguise. Also spelled *lou.* Also see LOUP and DOMINO under MASKS.

loup (loo) Black velvet mask worn during 16th and 17th c. by fashionable women on the street to protect face from sun, rain, dust, and eyes of passing men. A full mask was worn in 16th c. as a fashion item or when riding. When not being worn, the mask hung from the belt by a string. Also see MASKS: LOO MASK. *Der.* French, "wolf," because it frightened children. Also see MASKS: DOMINO.

rubber mask Mask fitting over the entire head-worn for Halloween. Molded of latex and painted various colors in a realistic representation of characters from comic strips, cartoons, stories, films, and television; of grotesque and imaginary creatures; and of animals. Also called *false face.*

scarf mask Fashion item of the early 1970s consisting of a scarf tied across the face revealing only the eyes.

scuba mask See-through mask covering eyes and nose worn when swimming underwater or for scuba diving or snorkeling.

ski mask Knitted hood fitting snugly over the head and neck with openings for the eyes, nose, and mouth. Worn for skiing, winter sports, and in cold climates to prevent frost-bite. *Der.* Inspired by similar hoods worn in the mountains of Peru.

ski mask

sleep mask Soft cushioned mask fitting closely to eyes and nose made of black fabric with an elastic band fitting around head. Worn when sleeping in daylight to block out the light.

surgical mask Sanitized cloth mask tied over nose and mouth by physicians and nurses to prevent spread of germs to patients. Sometimes used outdoors by people affected by allergies or air pollution.

mass customization The adaptation of a garment style for a specific customer by using computer technology to adjust the fit to the customer's measurements, or by offering choices of combinations of fabric, garment style, and size options.

mass fashion Fashionable goods that are produced in large quantities, and sold at moderate prices to many consumers who follow fashion. Also see FASHION CYCLE.

mass merchandiser Retailer that serves the MASS FASHION market.

mass production Manufacture in large quantities of the same item of apparel by workers using machines for production.

master pattern See SLOPER.

master's gown See ACADEMIC COSTUME.

master's hood See ACADEMIC COSTUME.

matador hat See HEADWEAR.

matador's jacket See COATS AND JACKETS: BOLERO #2.

matelassé † (mat-lass-ay´) Luxurious fabric with a blistered or embossed effect made on the JACQUARD or DOBBY loom in a double cloth weave. Front and back of cloth are actually separate fabrics, which are fastened together with extra crepe yarns that form the raised pattern. Genuine matelassé will not become flat-looking as the raised portion is woven in, and is quite different from an inexpensive embossed design (see EMBOSSING). Made from many different fibers. Cotton may have a quilted effect, others a blistered effect. Used for formal dresses, cocktail dresses, evening wraps, blouses, and robes. *Der.* French, "cushioned or padded." Also spelled *matellassé.*

maternity clothes Garments designed to be worn by pregnant women. See MATERNITY DRESS, BLOUSES AND TOPS: MATERNITY BLOUSE, PANTS: MATERNITY PANTS, SKIRTS: MATERNITY SKIRT, and UNDERGARMENTS: MATERNITY SLIP.

maternity dress Dress designed for pregnant women following the general style trends but made with more fullness in front. In the late 1990s and after, some maternity clothing fit more tightly.

Mathilde embroidery See EMBROIDERIES AND SEWING STITCHES.

Matilda ∞ **1.** In the 19th c., a velvet decoration around hem of a woman's skirt. **2.** In the 1840s, a bouquet of flowers worn in the hair by women.

matinee 1. See SLEEPWEAR AND LOUNGEWEAR. **2.** See BLOUSES AND TOPS: TEA JACKET.

matinee-length necklace   See JEWELRY.

matte finish (mat)   A dull finish. Used in the textile industry to describe fabrics and also for makeup that has no shine.

mattress ticking stripe   See PRINTS, STRIPES, AND CHECKS.

Maud   See CAPES, CLOAKS, AND SHAWLS.

mauve diamond   See GEMS, GEM CUTS, AND SETTINGS.

maxi/maxi dress   See LENGTHS.

maxi coat   See COATS AND JACKETS.

maxi fall   See WIGS AND HAIRPIECES: FALL.

maxi skirts   See SKIRTS.

Maxwell, Vera   * See APPENDIX/DESIGNERS.

mazarin hood   See HEADWEAR.

Mazur plan   The division of retail activities into four areas: (1) merchandising, which is the buying and selling of goods and services for a profit. This includes the planning, pricing, and control of sales and inventory; (2) publicity, which is concerned with promotion and advertising, display, special events, and public relations; (3) store (operations) management, which involves the operations of the retail store, selling customer service, and all such physical concerns for the store as maintenance and security; (4) accounting and control (finance), which is concerned with all the financial aspects of the business, including credit, collection, budgets, control, and bookkeeping. Although retailers may vary the configuration of their organizational charts from this four function chart to accommodate the size and type of the company and its structure, all retailers must have at least two functional areas—merchandising and store operations management.

McCardell, Claire   * See APPENDIX/DESIGNERS.

McCartney, Stella   * See APPENDIX/DESIGNERS.

McFadden, Mary   * See APPENDIX/DESIGNERS.

McKay shoe construction   See FOOTWEAR.

McQueen, Alexander   * See APPENDIX/DESIGNERS.

M-cut lapel   See NECKLINES AND COLLARS: LAPEL.

Mechlin lace   See LACES.

Mecklenburg cap   See HEADWEAR.

medallion   1. See JEWELRY. 2. See PRINTS, STRIPES, AND CHECKS. 3. See FOOTWEAR.

medic   See NECKLINES AND COLLARS and SHIRTS.

medic alert bracelet   See JEWELRY.

Medici collar   See NECKLINES AND COLLARS.

Medici dress   ∞ (meh′-dee-chee)   Trained PRINCESS DRESS of early 1870s with TABLIER front (see SKIRTS: TABLIER SKIRT) and short sleeves. Der. Inspired by clothes worn by Marie de' Medici, Queen of France c. 1600.

Medici lace   (meh-dee-chee)   See LACES.

Medici sleeve   See SHOULDERS AND SLEEVES.

Medici vest   ∞ (meh′-dee-chee)   Woman's fitted blouse of mid-1870s with double-puffed sleeves ending in three fluted ruffles at elbow and V-neck trimmed with a single pleated ruffle. Had a short BASQUE below the waistline with fullness in back. Der. Inspired by clothes worn by Marie de Medici, Queen of France c. 1600.

medieval   In a broad sense, usually refers to period 500–1450; same as Middle Ages. For historic costume study the period is sometimes divided into these periods: Byzantine (400–1100), Romanesque (900–1200), Early Gothic (1200–1350), and Late Gothic (1350–1450).

meditation shirt   See SHIRTS.

medium   Size used along with EXTRA SMALL, SMALL, LARGE, and EXTRA-LARGE for men, women, and children for such items as sweaters, knit shirts, sport jackets, nightgowns, pajamas, robes, gloves, girdles, and panty girdles. Abbreviation M.

Medusa wig   See WIGS AND HAIRPIECES.

melanite   See GEMS, GEM CUTS, AND SETTINGS: ANDRADITE GARNET.

melee   See GEMS, GEM CUTS, AND SETTINGS.

melon sleeve   See SHOULDERS AND SLEEVES.

melton   † Heavy, durable coating fabric that looks somewhat like wool broadcloth and has a hand similar to felt. Originally made of heavy woolen yarns or wool crosswise and cotton lengthwise yarns. Now made in combinations including manufactured fibers. Compactness of the fabric makes it warm and protective against wind penetration. Used by the U.S. Armed Forces as well as for men's, women's, and children's coats and snowsuits. Der. Named for Melton Mowbray, a town in Leicestershire, England.

men's wear look   Women's style of dress using men's suit and overcoat fabrics in an uncoordinated way (e.g., using stripes and different-sized plaids and checks together). Introduced in 1969, starting a trend toward mixing of fabrics previously thought not to be harmonious. In 1984, look was further implemented with oversized coats, similar to men's overcoats; man-tailored blazers; pinstriped suits; men's tailored dress shirts worn with neckties; tailored cuffed trousers in silk and linen tweed; and well-cut jodhpurs worn with a Victorian blouse.

men's wear look 1976

menteurs   See LIARS.

mentonnière   See ARMOR.

mentonnières   See HEADWEAR: CHIN STAYS.

menu vair   See FURS: VAIR.

Menzies Black and White tartan   See PLAIDS AND TARTANS.

Menzies hunting tartan   See PLAIDS AND TARTANS.

mercerization   † Finishing process with caustic soda applied to cotton yarn, fabric, or thread, which increases luster, strength, and dyeability. *Der.* Named for John Mercer, calico printer in Lancashire, England, who discovered this process in 1844.

merchandise mart   A trade center with showrooms and other facilities for showing and selling apparel lines to retail buyers. Dallas, Atlanta, and Chicago are the sites for major marts, and secondary marts are located in such smaller cities as Charlotte, Pittsburgh, and Seattle.

merino wool   † High-quality wool yarn made from fleece of merino sheep, which has short, fine, strong, resilient fibers, and takes dyes well.

mermaid sheath   Slim, fitted evening gown introduced by designer Norman Norell in late 1960s. Dress was completely covered with SEQUINS (or PAILLETTES), giving a dazzling effect. *Der.* Similar to the way mermaids are pictured (minus the tail).

Merry Widow   See UNDERGARMENTS.

Merry Widow hat   See HEADWEAR.

merveilleuse   See DIRECTOIRE # 2.

mesh   **1.** Metal links joined together to form a flat flexible unit. See JEWELRY, CHAIN MAIL, BELTS, and HANDBAGS AND RELATED ACCESSORIES.

mermaid sheath 1960s

2. † Knitted or woven fabric in an open weave, such as LENO, producing a net or a screenlike effect. Also see MILANESE KNIT.

mesh hose   See HOSIERY.

messenger bag   See HANDBAGS AND RELATED ACCESSORIES.

mess jacket   See COATS AND JACKETS.

metallic cloth   † Any type of fabric made with metallic yarns or using metallic yarns in the crosswise direction and other yarns lengthwise. Formerly yarns such as silver tarnished, but now they may be coated with a fine film of polyester that resists tarnish. Used for blouses, formal wear, cocktail dresses, and knitwear.

metallic hose   See HOSIERY: GLITTER HOSE.

metallic yarn   **1.** See LUREX.® **2.** CORE YARN made by twisting thin metal foil around another yarn.

metal thread embroidery   See EMBROIDERIES AND SEWING STITCHES.

Metternich sack   See COATS AND JACKETS.

Mexican wedding boot   See FOOTWEAR.

Mexican wedding shirt   See SHIRTS.

MFA   See MULTIFIBER ARRANGEMENT.

Michael Jackson/Michael Jackson look   Popular singer, originally a member of the Jackson Five, who became famous as an individual rock singer in 1983 and set the first record for winning eight Grammy awards. A look based on styles he wore swept the entire country, becoming almost a "must" for back-to-school students of all ages in September 1984. Elements included multizippered jackets, pants of polyurethane, white socks, and black loafers. Some students even copied his habit of wearing one white rhinestone-studded glove. Also see COATS AND JACKETS: MICHAEL JACKSON JACKET.

micro   See LENGTHS.

micro dress   Shorter version of the minidress, reaching the top part of the thigh like a tunic blouse; introduced in 1966.

microfiber   † Manufactured filament fiber that measures 1.0 denier per filament or less.

Middle Ages   See MEDIEVAL.

middleman   An agent who sees to the handling of some part of the transfer of merchandise from the manufacturer to the retailer.

middy   **1.** Blouse worn by sailors in U.S. Navy. Extended to mean dress with top styled like a

MIDDY BLOUSE (see under BLOUSES AND TOPS). Also see MIDDY SUIT and SAILOR DRESS. **2.** Adjective used to describe apparel or its elements similar to or derived from the sailor's middy top. See BRAIDS: MIDDY BRAID, NECKLINES AND COLLARS: SAILOR COLLAR, and SLEEPWEAR AND LOUNGEWEAR: MIDDY-TOP PAJAMAS.

middy suit ∞ Three-piece sailor suit for children introduced in the mid-1890s. Boy's suit had waist-length jacket with large sailor collar, close-fitting collarless blouse, and short or knee-length pants. Girl's suit had hip-length jacket with sailor collar, leg-of-mutton sleeves, and unpressed-pleated skirt.

midi See LENGTHS.

midi coat See COATS AND JACKETS.

midriff That part of a garment that covers the middle part of the torso between the chest and the abdomen.

midriff dress One-piece dress with a piece of fabric or elastic inserted at waistline, giving the effect of a cinched waist.

midriff shirt See SHIRTS.

midsole See FOOTWEAR: SOLE.

mignonette lace See LACES.

Milan bonnet See HEADWEAR.

Milanese knit † (mil′-en-aze) Machine-made warp knit with diagonal yarns at intervals giving run-resistant openwork effect. Used particularly for women's underpants and hose.

Milan lace See LACES.

Milan straw (mih-lan′) Plaited straw using seven strands in each braid. Made from lower part of a type of wheat stalk, called *pedal straw,* grown near the city of Milan in Tuscany, Italy.

military/military look **1.** Clothes and accessories, inspired by military uniforms of officers and enlisted men, frequently trimmed with brass buttons that often serve as a source of inspiration for designers. See BRAIDS: MILITARY BRAID; COATS AND JACKETS: MILITARY JACKET, MILITARY FROCK COAT, and MILITARY TUNIC; NECKLINES AND COLLARS: MILITARY COLLAR; and TIES: MILITARY STOCK. **2.** Fad starting in late 1960s with college men wearing army jackets of previous wars and sometimes helmets for daytime wear. **3.** Wearing of all types of military clothing and accessories purchased from Army/Navy surplus stores.

military folding hat See HEADWEAR: OPERA HAT #2.

milkmaid hat See HEADWEAR: BERGÈRE HAT.

milkmaid skirt See SKIRTS.

mille-fleurs (mihl-flhur) French name for a pattern of tiny flowers. *Der.* French, "thousand flowers."

Miller, Nicole * See APPENDIX/DESIGNERS.

milliner **1.** One who makes headwear for women. **2.** ∞ In the 17th c., one who traded in goods from the city of Milan in Italy. This included trimmings, buttons, and small accessories including gloves.

millinery Covering for the head, generally for women. See HEADWEAR.

minaudiere See HANDBAGS AND RELATED ACCESSORIES.

miner's cap See HEADWEAR.

mini/mini look (minn′-ee) Used to describe a skirt length reaching to midthigh or the look of short thigh-length skirts, fashionable in 1960s, that was later applied to any fashion item that is tiny or short. See COATS AND JACKETS: MINI COAT, HANDBAGS AND RELATED ACCESSORIES: MINI BAG and MINI-CLUTCH, HAIRSTYLES: MINI BRAIDS, SHORTS: MINI JEANS, SKIRTS: MINI SKIRTS, and UNDERWEAR: MINI-PETTI.

mini-clutch bag See HANDBAGS AND RELATED ACCESSORIES: CLUTCH BAG.

mini-crinoline Wide-skirted, short dress style that was popular in the 1980s.

minidress Dress with short skirt coming to midthigh or about 6″ above the knee. First introduced in early 1960s by designer Mary Quant in England as part of the "mod" fashions and became a mass fashion by end of 1960s. Reintroduced in the mid-1980s and worn since then.

mini fall See WIGS AND HAIRPIECES: FALL.

mini jupe See SKIRTS: JUPE #1.

minimal bra See UNDERGARMENTS: NUDE BRA.

minimum orders The least amount of merchandise that must be bought from a vendor in order to place an order.

mini-pane hose See HOSIERY: WINDOWPANE HOSE.

mini-pettipants See UNDERGARMENTS: PETTIPANTS.

miniver See FURS.

miniver cap See HEADWEAR: LETTICE CAP.

mink See FURS.

mi-parti See PARTI-COLORED.

Miranda pump See FOOTWEAR.

miser purse See HANDBAGS AND RELATED ACCESSORIES.

misses sizes Women's garments cut for a well-proportioned adult figure about 5′5″ to 5′6″ tall, usually sized 6–18.

Missoni * See APPENDIX/DESIGNERS.

mistake hat See HEADWEAR.

miter **1.** See CLERICAL DRESS. **2.** See HEADWEAR. **3.** See CLOTHING CONSTRUCTION DETAILS.

mitons See MOUFLES.

mitre See HEADWEAR: MITER.

mittens See GLOVES AND GLOVE CONSTRUCTION.

mitten sleeve See SHOULDERS AND SLEEVES.

mitten-sleeve gown Infant's nightgown with drawstrings at the ends of the sleeves to cover the hands to prevent scratching. In 1980s, the style was made with small mitten, with slit for hand, at end of sleeve.

mitts See GLOVES AND GLOVE CONSTRUCTION.

mix and match/mix-and-match look Use of coordinated prints or plaids with plain-colored fabrics for blouses, skirts, jackets, pants, vests, etc. Popular look in the 1950s, which resulted in increased sales of "separates" in retail stores. In the late 1960s, generally called the PUT-TOGETHER LOOK.

mixed suit Man's suit with contrasting jacket and pants. First popular in early 1930s, after which it developed into sport jacket and slacks look.

mixture † **1.** Fabric woven with yarns composed of fibers dyed different colors. Fabric may also be made of yarns that vary in luster. Preferred term is **blend. 2.** U.S. manufacturers of manufactured fibers limit the term to fabrics with lengthwise yarn of one type yarn and crosswise yarn of another (e.g., a nylon warp with a rayon filling).

Miyake, Issey * See APPENDIX/DESIGNERS.

Mizrahi, Isaac * See APPENDIX/DESIGNERS.

mizpah medallion necklace See JEWELRY.

Moabite turban See HEADWEAR.

moat collar See NECKLINES AND COLLARS: RING COLLAR.

mob cap See HEADWEAR.

mobile earrings See JEWELRY.

moccasin See FOOTWEAR: MOCCASIN-TYPE SHOE.

mocha leather See LEATHERS.

mocha stone See GEMS, GEM CUTS, AND SETTINGS: AGATE.

mockador See MUCKINDER.

mock collar See NECKLINES AND COLLARS.

mock pocket See POCKETS.

mock seam See HOSIERY.

mock turtleneck See NECKLINES AND COLLARS and SWEATERS.

moctour See MUCKINDER.

mod/mod look British slang for a pseudo-Edwardian style first adopted by the group of young men, known as the TEDDY boys, and their girlfriends about 1958. The mods opposed the ROCKERS, who wore leather jackets and other motorcycle gear. Mod styles included miniskirts for girls and long neat hair for men, along with Edwardian-style suits—exemplified by the dress of the Beatles singing group. Mary Quant, a British fashion designer with imaginative and unconventional designs, gained wide acceptance for her mod look clothes. The new styles were sold in London on side streets such as King's Row and Carnaby Street—away from Savile Row and Bond Street, the home of traditional tailoring. In England, the concept of mod was somewhat different from that in the United States. The British version consisted of close-cut hair, ankle-length skirts worn with granny boots, Edwardian suits, etc. *Der.* From word "modernist" meaning someone who appreciated the music of the times—the Beatles. Also see CARNABY LOOK.

mod dress

modacrylic † Generic category of manufactured fiber made from acrylic resins and characterized by soft hand, warmth without bulk, resistance to moths and mildew, easy care, and high wrinkle recovery. Used for sweaters, other knitwear, and fur fabrics. Trademark names include Acrilan®, Duraspun®, Creslan®, and Cresloft®.

mod boot See FOOTWEAR.

mod cap See FOOTWEAR.

mode French word meaning fashion.

model **1.** American term for person who is paid to wear a garment in a fashion show or for a

M

photograph. **2.** French term for the garment itself.

model dolls/fashion dolls Full-sized or smaller dolls made of wax, wood, or fabric that, as early as the 14th c., served as a means of sending examples of the current fashions to various places to show styles. Initially they circulated only among the courts and royalty, but by the 18th c., they were available to all who could afford to pay a fee to see them. The word "doll" was not used until about 1750—previously they were referred to as *moppets* or *courier dummies.* They appeared in America in early 18th c., where they were called *little ladies* or *fashion babies.* In the latter part of the 19th c., fashion plates replaced the dolls.

model form See DRESS FORM.

moderate-priced goods See APPAREL PRICE RANGES.

modeste See SKIRTS: JUPE.

modesty piece Piece of fabric inserted at the front of a dress in order to cover the cleavage of the bosom. Worn with décolleté bodices in 18th c. and since then.

modiste (mow-deest′) **1.** French meaning milliner. **2.** In Great Britain a *dressmaker.*

modular production Apparel production system in which employees are organized into teams of seven to nine operators who are all able to carry out production tasks. The team is responsible for the construction of a complete garment. As a result, production is more flexible than in the mass production system.

mohair † Fiber obtained from the hair of the angora goat or fabric made from that hair. The fiber is long, white, and lustrous and comparatively coarse. Durable and resilient, it is used for apparel, linings, coats, imitation furs, and knitting yarn. *Der.* Arabic, *mukhayyar,* "goat's hair."

Mohawk hairstyle See HAIRSTYLES.

Mohs' scale See introduction to GEMS, GEM CUTS, AND SETTINGS.

moile See FOOTWEAR: MULE.

moiré † (mwa-ray′) Stiff, heavy-ribbed fabric with a watered effect, made of silk or manufactured fibers. The design is applied with heated rollers that flatten some of the heavy crosswise yarns, thus changing the light reflection. The pattern is not permanent on silk, but is permanent if made with heat-sensitive fibers. Used for evening dresses, skirts, and women's coats. *Der.* French, "watered."

moiré pattern See FURS.

mokadour/moketer See MUCKINDER.

mola appliqué † (ap-plee-kay) A technique for making decorative textiles, associated with the Cuna Native American women of Panama and Columbia, that are created by tacking together two or more layers of fabric of the same size in different colors. Designs are cut out of one or more of the uppermost layers to expose brightly colored lower layers. The edges of the cut fabric are turned under and stitched down to prevent raveling.

Moldavian mantle See CAPES, CLOAKS, AND SHAWLS.

molded boot See FOOTWEAR.

molded dress Dress made with fabric that is heat-set or molded to take on a sculptured geometrical form. Introduced by Paris couturier Pierre Cardin in fall 1968 collection.

molded felt See HEADWEAR.

mole See FUR.

moleskin fabric † Durable cotton fabric with a suedelike nap in a satin weave made with coarse cotton yarns and a large number of crosswise yarns. Fabric should be called *moleskin fabric* to distinguish it from the fur by the same name. Used for sportswear and work clothes. *Der.* Arabian, *molequin,* "old fabric."

Molyneux, Edward ✳ See APPENDIX/ DESIGNERS.

Mondrian dress (Mohn′-dree-yon) Straight unconstructed dress made with blocks of color and neutrals heavily banded with black. Introduced by Yves Saint Laurent in fall 1965 collection. *Der.* Inspired by modern linear paintings of Piet Mondrian.

Mondrian dress 1960s

Mondrian, Piet (Mohn′-dree-yon, Peet) (1872–1944) Dutch painter who was an exponent of neo-plasticism. Best known for his geometrics using only vertical and horizontal lines intersecting to form compartments of color. From about 1921 on, his palette held only red, yellow, and blue colors plus neutrals of white, black, and gray. His work served as the inspiration for dress designs of Yves Saint Laurent in fall of 1965, as well as styles imitating the Saint Laurent designs.

money belt See BELTS.

money mitt See GLOVES AND GLOVE CONSTRUCTION.

Mongolian lamb See FURS: KARACUL.

monkey See FURS.

monkey jacket See COATS AND JACKETS.

monk's Adjective used for apparel and accessories worn by monks in monasteries since early Christian times and subsequently to describe items derived from or inspired by their vestments.

monk's belt 1. See BELTS. 2. See CLERICAL DRESS.

monk's dress Dress styled like a monk's robe with cowl neck, bell sleeves, and cord belt confining fullness.

monk's robe See SLEEPWEAR AND LOUNGEWEAR.

Monmouth cap See HEADWEAR.

Monmouth cock See HEADWEAR: COCKED HAT.

monobosom silhouette Shape of bodices worn in the first decade of the 20th c. Garments are cut with a full, pouched front section that makes the wearer appear to have one single, large breast.

monobosom silhouette
1904

monocle See EYEWEAR.

monofilament yarn Yarn consisting of a single strand of manufactured fiber. To be strong, this yarn must be large in diameter. Compare with MULTIFILAMENT YARNS.

monogram One or more initials embroidered, printed, or engraved on a garment, accessory, or jewelry. Usually these will be the initials of the owner, however sometimes the initials of the designer who created the garment may be used.

mono-kini See SWIMWEAR.

monster shoe See FOOTWEAR.

Montague curls See HAIRSTYLES.

Montana, Claude * See APPENDIX/DESIGNERS.

Montespan corsage ∞ (mon′-tes-pan′) Tight-fitting woman's evening bodice of 1843 with deep square-cut neckline and pointed waistline in front and back. *Der.* Named for Marquise de Montespan (1641–1707), mistress of Louis XIV of France.

Montespan hat See HEADWEAR.

Montespan pleats ∞ (mon-tes′-pan) Large, flat, double or triple BOX PLEATS used at waistband of skirt. (See under CLOTHING CONSTRUCTION DETAILS.) Popular in 1859 and 1860s. *Der.* Named for Marquise de Montespan (1641–1707), mistress of Louis XIV of France.

Montespan sleeve See SHOULDERS AND SLEEVES.

Montgomery beret See HEADWEAR.

mont-la-haut See HEADWEAR: COMMODE.

montpensier mantle See CAPES, CLOAKS, AND SHAWLS.

moonstone See GEMS, GEM CUTS, AND SETTINGS.

moppet See MODEL DOLLS.

Moravian work See EMBROIDERIES AND SEWING STITCHES.

morganite See GEMS, GEM CUTS, AND SETTINGS.

Mori, Hanae * See APPENDIX/DESIGNERS.

morion See ARMOR.

morning cap See HEADWEAR.

morning coat See COATS AND JACKETS: CUTAWAY.

morning dress 1. Formal daytime attire for men consisting of striped pants, cutaway coat, ascot tie, and sometimes top hat. 2. ∞ In the 19th c. applied to any dress suitable for wear in the morning—for visiting, shopping, or at home—as differentiated from a more formal afternoon dress. Also called *morning gown* or *morning robe*. 3. ∞ In early 20th c. referred to a HOUSE DRESS of inexpensive fabric.

morning frock coat See COATS AND JACKETS: FROCK COAT.

morning-glory skirt See SKIRTS.

morning gown 1. ∞ Long, loose dressing gown with a sash at the waist, worn indoors by men from 18th c. to 1830s. Similar to BANYAN. 2. See MORNING DRESS #2.

morning robe 1. ∞ Type of dress suitable for the boudoir or for informal occasions worn in last half of 19th c. by women. 2. See MORNING DRESS #2.

Moroccan handbag See HANDBAGS AND RELATED ACCESSORIES.

Moroccan leather See LEATHERS.

M

Morris bells ∞ Tiny bells attached to leather or ribbon trim worn for Morris dancing in 16th-c. Tudor England. Bells were attached to ribbon-trimmed garters worn below knees, hat bands, sleeves, or special leggings. These bells became part of what was considered to be the traditional dress of court jesters.

Morris, William (1834–1896) Creator of printed and painted fabrics in intricate designs first produced in the 1870s. From 1881 until 1940, they continued to be made in a large workshop in Merton Abbey, England. These prints were used in fashionable clothing of women who were associated with the Arts and Crafts movement, which its proponents promoted as a replacement for prevailing Victorian styles. Morris was an artist, an architect, social reformer, and writer—instrumental in changing Victorian taste and launching the Art Nouveau movement.

mortarboard See ACADEMIC COSTUME.

mosaic print See PRINTS, STRIPES, AND CHECKS.

moschettos See PANTS.

Moschino, Franco * See APPENDIX/DESIGNERS.

Moscow See LACES.

Moscow wrapper See COATS AND JACKETS.

moss agate See GEMS, GEM CUTS, AND SETTINGS.

Mother Hubbard/Mother Hubbard wrapper ∞ Comfortable, plain housedress or wrapper styled for girls in ankle-length, full-length for women. Usually made with a yoke with buttons or ties down the front and fitted only at the yoke. Used for morning wear at home in late 19th and early 20th c. Der. Named for nursery-rhyme character who was shown in illustrations in a similar style.

Mother Hubbard c. 1890

Mother Hubbard cloak See CAPES, CLOAKS, AND SHAWLS.

mother-of-pearl Shiny, iridescent substance lining shell of the pearl oyster, abalone, or other mollusks. Also called *nacre* (nay'-cruh). Also see CLOSURES: MOTHER-OF-PEARL BUTTON.

mothproofing † A special finish used on wool fabrics or clothing to make them resistant to moths. Can also be purchased in a spray can for use at home.

motorcycle Adjective used to describe clothing and accessories worn for motorcycling or items inspired by motorcycling clothes.

motorcycle jacket See COATS AND JACKETS.

motoring veil See HEADWEAR: AUTOMOBILE VEIL.

mouche (moosch) Der. French, "fly" or "speck." See PATCH #3.

moufles ∞ (moof'-lah) **1.** Fingerless gloves or mittens worn in Merovingian Period for hunting or working. **2.** Late 14th-c. term for extensions of sleeves covering hand. Also called *mitons*.

moulds ∞ Men's DRAWERS (see UNDERGARMENTS), padded with horsehair and other fibers, worn under wide trousers in England in latter half of 16th c. Also spelled *mowlds*.

mountain climbing boot See FOOTWEAR: HIKING BOOT.

Mountie's hat See HATS.

mountmellick work See EMBROIDERIES AND SEWING STITCHES.

mourning bonnet See HEADWEAR.

mourning clothes Clothing, usually black, worn for funerals or during the mourning period after the funeral. Etiquette for mourning was not well established until the end of the 15th c., although black had been recognized in Northern Europe as a symbol for grief since the 14th c. During 19th and early 20th c., custom prescribed not only colors and fabrics, but also stages and gradations of mourning. Men were required to wear a black armband. Widows had to wear **deep mourning,** black crape-covered dresses worn with black accessories, for a year and a day. Other female relatives wore deep mourning for varying periods of time depending on their relationship to the deceased. The next stage was **half mourning,** which usually consisted of black, gray, or purple costume with touches of white. See also MOURNING CREPE, JEWELRY: MOURNING JEWELRY, HEADWEAR: MOURNING BONNET.

mourning crape/crepe Collective term for black fabrics, usually CRAPE, worn for funerals or for mourning. During the 19th and early 20th c., deep mourning or black was worn for six months to a year after the death of a close member of the family. *Half mourning,* a purple or lavender color, was worn for six months longer.

mourning garland ∞ 17th-c: Willow hatband or garland of willow worn for mourning.

mourning jewelry See JEWELRY.

mourning knot ∞ Armlet with attached bunch of black ribbons worn on left arm for mourning by men in 18th c.

mourning ribbon ∞ 17th-c.: Black ribbon worn by men on the hat for mourning.

mourning ring See JEWELRY.

mourning scarf ∞ Scarf of lawn about 3¼ yards long presented along with hatbands to principal mourners at funerals in 17th and 18th c.

mourning tire ∞ 17th-c.: A MOURNING VEIL (see under HEADWEAR) worn by women.

mourning veil See HEADWEAR.

mouse jewelry See JEWELRY.

mousers See FOOTWEAR and PANTS.

mousquetaire collar See NECKLINES AND COLLARS.

mousquetaire cuff See CUFFS.

mousquetaire gloves See GLOVES AND GLOVE CONSTRUCTION.

mousquetaire hat See HEADWEAR.

mousquetaire mantle See CAPES, CLOAKS, AND SHAWLS.

mousseline † Transparent, light-weight fabric made in the plain weave and similar to chiffon. Often made of silk.

moustaches See HAIRSTYLES: COIFFURE EN CADENETTE.

mouton-processed lamb See FURS.

mowlds See MOULDS.

mowle/moyle See FOOTWEAR: MULE.

mozetta See CLERICAL DRESS.

muckinder/mockador ∞ **1.** A child's bib, term used from early 16th to 19th c. **2.** Handkerchief. Also spelled *mocket, mockete, muckender, muckiter, muckinger.*

muff Warm tubular covering for the hands open at each end, frequently of fur or rich fabrics—usually round or oblong in many sizes—sometimes with concealed inner pockets. Carried by women as an accessory and usually matched to

muff

material of coat or trimming. Carried by men from 2nd half of 16th to 19th c.

muff bag See HANDBAGS AND RELATED ACCESSORIES.

muffettees ∞ **1.** Pair of small wrist muffs worn for warmth or when playing cards to protect wrist ruffles by both men and women in 18th and 19th c. **2.** Pair of small muffs worn for warmth in mid-18th c., closed at one end and sometimes with separate stall for thumb. **3.** Coarse mittens of leather or wool knit worn by old men in early 19th c.

muffin hat See HEADWEAR.

muffler See SCARVES.

muff's cloak See COATS AND JACKETS.

Mugler, Thierry * See APPENDIX/DESIGNERS.

Muir, Jean * See APPENDIX/DESIGNERS.

mukluk See FOOTWEAR.

mulberry silk Silk obtained from silk worms that are fed on leaves of cultivated mulberry tree.

mules See FOOTWEAR.

muleta See CAPES, CLOAKS, AND SHAWLS.

Muller cut-down See HEADWEAR.

Multifiber Arrangement (MFA) A set of special rules under the General Agreement on Tariff and Trade (GATT) to control international trade in textiles and apparel. The MFA will be phased out by the year 2005 and will bring the textile and apparel industry under the jurisdiction of the newly formed World Trade Organization. Quotas on textiles and apparel will be phased out and tariffs reduced.

multifilament yarn † Many long, continuous manufactured fibers twisted together to form a yarn.

Munro tartan See PLAIDS AND TARTANS.

muscle shirt See SHIRTS.

museum heel See FOOTWEAR.

mushroom hat See HEADWEAR.

mushroom pleats See CLOTHING CONSTRUCTION DETAILS: PLEATS.

mushroom sleeve See SHOULDERS AND SLEEVES.

musk apples/muskballs See POMMES DE SENTEUR.

muskrat See FURS.

muslin † Plain weave cotton or cotton blend fabric made in many weights from very fine and sheer to coarse and heavy. Higher qualities have

COMBED, mercerized yarns (see MERCERIZATION) and may be either dyed or printed. Such fabrics are lustrous, long-wearing, washable, and soft to the touch. Coarser qualities have CARDED yarns, may have a variety of construction counts, and are used for sheets and pillowcases. Lightweight fabrics are used for summer dresses and blouses.

muslin pattern **1.** Complete garment made in an inexpensive fabric (e.g., muslin) usually draped on a dress form and, after muslin garment is finished, taken apart to provide a pattern for actual garment. **2.** Process used for fur designing. Also called a *toile* (twal).

mustache The hair on a man's upper lip. When it is allowed to grow, this hair may be shaved and trimmed into various shapes. One of the more common variations is the **walrus**

mustache

mustache, which has long drooping ends hanging at either side of the mouth.

mutation mink See FURS.

mu'umu'u (moo oo' moo oo') Loose-fitting, full dress worn by Hawaiian native women that was adapted from chemises given to native women by missionaries in the early 19th c. to wear under the HOLOKU, a European-derived style of outerwear. Native women wore the garment for swimming and sleeping until the 1930s when it was made in Hawaiian floral-printed fabrics and adopted for street wear. By the post–World War II period, it was made in various lengths and its use had spread to the mainland, especially for loungewear. *Der.* Hawaiian, meaning *cutoff*.

mu'umu'u

M

N Shoe width designation for a narrow shoe, equivalent to an A.

nabchet 16th-c. slang term for cap or hat.

nacre See MOTHER-OF-PEARL.

nacré velvet † (nah-cray′) Velvet fabric with an iridescent or changeable effect caused by using one color for the background yarn and another color for the pile. Used for evening wear.

NAFTA See NORTH AMERICAN FREE TRADE AGREEMENT.

nailing See FURS: STAPLING.

nap † **1.** Fiber ends protruding on the surface of one or both sides of a fabric that produce a fuzzy appearance and soft texture. Achieved by brushing the surface of a fabric with loosely twisted yarn. The nap may be brushed in one direction so that when cutting a garment with a nap, pieces of the pattern should be placed so that the nap runs in the same direction in all pieces. **2.** Used in home sewing to refer to any fabric that has either a nap or a PILE, which is formed by an extra yarn. Both require that all pattern pieces run in the same direction.

nap finish See LEATHERS.

napkin ∞ 16th and early 17th-c. term for handkerchief used for the nose.

napkin-cap See HEADWEAR.

napkin hook ∞ Ornamental hook of 17th c., attached to woman's waistband, used to suspend a handkerchief.

Napoleon Adjective used to describe apparel derived from or inspired by the clothing of Napoleon Bonaparte (1769–1821) or clothing worn in the Napoleonic period. He was the first Emperor of France and together with his wife, Josephine, influenced styles during and after his reign. See COATS AND JACKETS: NAPOLEON COAT, TIES: NAPOLEON NECKTIE, NECKLINES AND COLLARS: NAPOLEONIC COLLAR, FOOTWEAR: NAPOLEONS.

nappa leather See LEATHERS.

nappe/napperon See APRONS: NAPRON.

napping See NAP.

napron See APRONS.

narrow In retailing, describes an ASSORTMENT that consists of relatively few different styles.

narrowcasting Serving the needs of a specific customer. For example, individualized catalogs containing specifically selected merchandise can be sent to individual consumers.

narrow fabric † Any nonelastic fabric such as tape, ribbon, or webbing, not more than 12″ wide, woven on narrow looms with selvages on both sides. Bias binding and seam binding are not included in this classification.

narrow goods ∞ Once used for fabrics woven 27″ wide or less.

Nast, Condé (1874–1942) Publisher of *Vanity Fair* from 1913 to 1936 and of *Vogue* magazine, including English and French *Vogue,* from 1909 to 1942. President of The Condé Nast Publications Inc., which also published the *Vogue Pattern Book, Glamour,* and *House and Garden* during his lifetime. Other periodicals were acquired later.

National Press Week Semiannual event when newspaper fashion editors across the country are invited to New York by the *New York Couture Group* to see collections of Seventh Avenue designers. Idea originated with New York manufacturer Ben Reig in 1942.

Natori, Josie ＊ See APPENDIX/DESIGNERS.

natural bra See UNDERGARMENTS.

natural fiber † Fiber that is of animal, vegetable, or mineral origin, as opposed to manufactured fiber regenerated from natural materials or synthesized from chemicals (e.g., WOOL, LINEN, SILK, COTTON, HEMP, RAMIE, CASHMERE, and MOHAIR).

naturalistic print See PRINTS, STRIPES, AND CHECKS.

naturally colored cotton Cotton that is used in its natural color. At present, commercially available colors are limited to shades of green and brown.

natural mink See FURS.

natural shoulder See SHOULDERS AND SLEEVES.

natural straw Straw made from any vegetable plant or tree grown in the soil (e.g, bark, coconut fibers, grass, hemp, or palm-tree fibers).

natural waistline See WAISTLINES.

Naugahyde® † Trademark of U.S. Rubber Co. for a fabric with a vinyl resin coating on the face and knitted fabric back. The knitted back gives stretch to the vinyl. Used for handbags, shoes, and rainwear.

nautical/nautical look Items of clothing and motifs borrowed from navy uniforms or seamen's clothes, frequently using a red, white, and blue color scheme and symbols such as stars, chevrons, or stripes. In 1966, Saint Laurent showed clothes of this type. Used since the 1860s, particularly for boys' sailor suits, it is a classic look for yachting and boating as well as sportswear. Also see BLOUSES AND TOPS: MIDDY BLOUSE.

Navajo Native American tribe of Southwestern United States living in Arizona and New Mexico, noted for metalworking in iron, copper, and silver; blankets woven in distinctive geometric designs; and for handmade silver jewelry often set with turquoise. The latter is not only a classic fashion in the Western states, but is also popular throughout the United States.

Neapolitan bonnet See HEADWEAR.

Neapolitan hat See HEADWEAR.

neats See HOSIERY.

Nebula headdress See HEADWEAR.

neck button See CLOSURES.

neck-chain See JEWELRY.

neckcloth 1. See TIES. 2. See SCARVES: NECKERCHIEF #2.

necked bonnet See HEADWEAR.

neckerchief See SCARVES.

neckerchief slide Ring of metal, plastic, or woven braid used to hold NECKERCHIEF (see under TIES) in place, e.g., those used by Boy Scouts or cowboys.

neck handkerchief See TIES.

necklace See JEWELRY.

NECKLINES AND COLLARS

neckline Contour or shape of clothing at neck, shoulders, or above the bust—ranging from high to low to strapless. Before the 20th c., garments worn over the same time period tended to have similar styles of necklines. In the 20th c., this changed and a wide variety of different neckline styles were worn at the same time. However in both the 19th c. and 20th c., evening dresses have usually had low necklines.

collar 1. Separate piece attached to an item of clothing at the neckline in order to finish the neckline edge. May be made of matching or contrasting fabric, and may be trimmed with lace or embroidery. Shape may be flat, rolled, standing, or draped. Not to be confused with the neckline, it is an extra section attached to or turned over at neckline. 2. Separate costume element made of fabric, fur, leather, or other material that fits around the neck and is not permanently attached to the garment. Collars were not generally worn until the 15th c., when garments such as the HOUPPELANDE and DOUBLET were made with collars. Another early style of the 16th c. was the RUFF (see under NECKLINES AND COLLARS). Subsequently other styles appeared.

Many new collar styles were introduced in the 20th c.

amazon collar ∞ Standing collar, similar to a CHINESE COLLAR (see under NECKLINES AND COLLARS), with gap in center front. Used on women's blouses in early 1860s and worn with a black ribbon necktie.

angled shawl collar Collar that follows the front opening of a TUXEDO jacket. The outer edge is square cut or "angled" at the waistline.

ascot neckline/ascot collar Long scarf approximately 8″ wide attached to center back of neckline. The ends are brought around to the front and looped over. Popular in the late 1920s, reintroduced in late 1960s, and popular since for both men and women. *Der.* Fashionable horse-racing spot Ascot Heath, England. Also called *stock neckline* and *stock collar.*

ascot neckline or collar

asymmetric collar Any collar that does not appear the same on both sides of center front (e.g., large collar with slanting line to one side appearing longer on one side); popular in the 1980s.

asymmetric neckline Any neckline that appears different on either side of center front, or closes to one side of center front of blouse or shirt (e.g., a slit at left side closed with a loop and button which, when opened, makes one lapel on right).

asymmetric neckline

attached collar Any collar that is permanently attached to the clothing for which it is made. From the early 19th c. to the early 20th c., men's shirt collars were separate, fastened with STUDS (see under JEWELRY) to the neckline in back and front, and called DETACHABLE COLLARS (see under NECKLINES AND COLLARS).

ballet neckline/ballerina neckline (bal-lay′) Wide, rounded neckline that falls below the collarbone and is similar to those of ballet practice clothing.

band **1.** See FALLING BAND. **2.** CLERICAL DRESS: GENEVA BANDS.

band collar/banded collar Collar that stands up around neck and closes with buttons at front or back. A variant may also be turned down in either front or back. Also called *stand-up collar.* Also see NECKLINES AND COLLARS: CHINESE COLLAR and NEHRU COLLAR.

banded neckline Narrow band attached to neckline and buttoned in front. Introduced in early 1980s, it looks somewhat like neckbands of shirts of the 1890s and early 1900s without the ATTACHED COLLAR (see under NECKLINES AND COLLARS).

Barrymore collar DRESS SHIRT (see under SHIRTS) collar with long points in front, frequently worn with STRING TIE (see under TIES), that became popular after it was worn by the actor John Barrymore in 1930s.

bateau neckline (ba-toe′) Boat-shaped neckline wide from side-to-side over the shoulders but high in front and back. Popular neckline in 1930s and 1940s, and revived in 1980s. Also called *boat neckline. Der.* French, "boat."

bateau neck

Ben Casey collar See NECKLINES AND COLLARS: MEDIC COLLAR.

Bermuda collar Woman's shirt collar that opens in front, is small and round, and lies flat. Its corners have a right-angle shape. Popular since 1940s, mainly on blouses.

bertha Large capelike collar falling over shoulders and bodice of dress, introduced about 1839 as a lace ruffle encircling the décolleté neckline of evening dress. Fashionable in 1930s as a large cape collar, revived in 1980s. Spelled *berthe,* when first introduced.

bertha

bertha pelerine ∞ (pel-er-een′) Lace ruffle or BERTHA (see under NECKLINES AND COLLARS) open at the front where the ends extend down center front to waist. Worn in 1840s on low-necked dresses.

Betsie ruff ∞ Small RUFF (see under NECKLINES AND COLLARS) worn around the neck, with dresses having either a high or low neckline in late Empire period.

bib collar Flat, rounded, or square collar fitting over top of dress or blouse and around neck like a child's bib. Also called a *plastron*. Popular in 1980s with pleating, embroidery, or lace around edge.

bib collar

bishop collar Large collar, rounded in front, extending almost to shoulder seams.

boat neckline See NECKLINES AND COLLARS: BATEAU NECKLINE.

bolster collar Padded circlet worn around neck as a collar.

bow collar Flat stand-up band, with extended ends, that is sewn to the neckline. The ends tie in a bow in front. Introduced in the late 1920s and continued in fashion ever since.

bumper collar Large fur collar that extends to edges of shoulders when worn flat. Becomes a high rolled collar when ends are hooked in center front. Popular on fabric coats of the late 1920s, early 1930s, and mid-1980s.

Buster Brown collar Medium-sized stiffly starched round white collar first worn by boys in the beginning of the 20th c. and later adopted by women and girls. Often worn with a separate wide, soft bow tie. *Der.* Named for *Buster Brown,* a comic strip character, drawn by Richard F. Outcault in early 20th c.

butterfly collar Extremely large collar extending to sleeves at shoulders. Front hangs down in two points almost to waist with outer edge having scrolled effect to shoulders, creating the appearance of a butterfly's wings. An innovation of early 1980s.

button-down collar Shirt collar with pointed ends that are fastened to the shirt by small buttons. Popular collar of 1950s and 1960s for men and women, and part of button-down collar preppy look introduced in 1980s.

Byron collar Collar with large points and not much roll, similar to BARRYMORE COLLAR (see under NECKLINES AND COLLARS). *Der.* Named after English poet Lord Byron. Also called *Lord Byron collar* and *poet's collar.*

cabbage ruff See NECKLINES AND COLLARS: RUFF.

caftan neckline Round neckline with slit down center front and frequently edged with embroidery, beading, or diamanté bands. Fashionable in late 1960s and adapted from the African CAFTAN.

camisole neckline Neckline cut straight across above the bust with straps over the shoulders. Also see UNDERGARMENTS: CAMISOLE.

cape collar Large circular-cut collar that extends over the shoulders and upper arms. Similar to a BERTHA (see under NECKLINES AND COLLARS), but can be used with high or low neckline.

Capuchin collar ∞ Continuous roll collar on a wrap-over front bodice with a V-neckline that was used with high-waisted dresses of the late 18th and early 19th c.

carcaille ∞ (kar-kai′) 15th-c. standing collar that flared upward to the ears. Used on HOUPPELANDE and POURPOINT (see DOUBLET).

cardigan neckline Plain, round, collarless neckline on garment with a center front opening (e.g., cardigan sweater). *Der.* Named for the Seventh Earl of Cardigan, who needed an extra layer of warmth for his uniform during the Crimean War of 1854.

cardinal pelerine ∞ (pel-er-een′) Large lace BERTHA (see under NECKLINES AND COLLARS) that is open in center front, worn on evening dresses in 1840s.

Carnaby collar Collar, usually white with rounded ends in front, worn on colored, printed, or polka dot shirt in mid-1960s. *Der.* Named after Carnaby Street, London, where MOD fashions originated.

carnival collar Collar made of wide loops of bright printed fabric arranged in an unstarched RUFF (see under NECKLINES AND COLLARS) as on a clown's costume.

cartwheel ruff See NECKLINES AND COLLARS: RUFF.

cascade Circular-cut ruffle attached to neckline of blouse with a binding. The ruffle may extend to waistline in a straight or diagonal line.

cascade

N

cavalier collar Broad, flat, lace-edged collar falling over shoulders that is similar to collars worn by Cavaliers, partisans of Charles I, in early 17th c. Also called a *falling collar*.

celluloid collar ∞ Detachable shirt collar made of celluloid, a highly flammable plastic made of guncotton and camphor, that was popular for men in the early 20th c.

Chelsea collar Medium-sized flat woman's collar with pointed ends that form a low V-neckline in front; popular in late 1960s. *Der.* For borough in southwest London where it originated.

cherusse/cherusque ∞ (sher-oose′) Starched lace standing border for low-cut necklines on women's gowns. Worn during the Revolutionary period in France and later at Napoleon's court in Empire period. Also called *collarette à la Lyon*.

Chinese collar/Chinese neckline Standing BAND COLLAR that extends up on neck, not quite meeting at center front. Also called *mandarin collar* or NEHRU COLLAR (see under NECKLINES AND COLLARS).

Chinese collar

choir-boy collar Flat collar with rounded ends in front, similar to PETER PAN COLLAR (see under NECKLINES AND COLLARS), only larger; worn over choir robes.

choker collar Tight band collar that stands up high on neck almost to chin and fastens in back. Often made of sheer material or lace, it is boned, and edged with a narrow ruffle. Fashionable from 1890 to 1910 and revived in mid-1960s and 1980s. Also called *Victorian collar*.

clerical collar See CLERICAL DRESS.

collaret/collarette ∞ (kol-lar-et′) **1.** Woman's tiny separate collar of 19th c., specifically one made of lace, fur, or beads. **2.** RUCHING worn inside of high standing collar in the 16th c. **3.** In Colonial America, a ruff of ribbon ending in a bow.

collarette à la Lyon See NECKLINES AND COLLARS: CHERUSSE.

comfort collar A feature sometimes used on formal shirts in which the collar button is attached to a small tab that slides in order to provide greater range of movement and comfort.

convertible collar Rolled shirt collar that, if worn open, forms small lapels. When worn fastened with small concealed button and loop, it fits close to the neck with no lapels and has the appearance of a DRESS SHIRT (see SHIRTS).

convertible collar

cossack collar High-standing collar that closes on the side and is frequently banded with embroidery. Also called *Zhivago collar* (zhi-vah′go) and *Russian collar*.

cowl collar **1.** Large draped collar, frequently cut on the bias, that extends nearly to shoulders in circular style. Popular in 1930s and revived in 1980s. **2.** Cowl collar that drapes to form a hood that can be pulled over head. Also called a *cowl hood*. *Der.* Inspired by a monk's habit.

cowl neckline Draped neckline falling in soft folds. Blouse or dress is usually bias cut for better drape. Popular style of the 1920s, 1930s, and 1980s.

cowl neckline

crew neckline Round neckline finished with knit ribbing. *Der.* From neckline on crew-racing shirts.

crew neckline

Cromwell collar ∞ Wide turnover collar with front edges nearly meeting; worn by women in the 1880s. *Der.* Named for Oliver Cromwell, Lord Protector of England, 1653–1658.

crossover collar A convertible collar with two large lapels that, when buttoned up to the neck, overlap.

décolleté neckline (day-kohl-tay′) Any neckline cut very low. *Der.* French, "to bare the neck."

detachable collar **1.** Made with tiny buttonholes at lower edge of collar so that it can be buttoned onto a dress or blouse. **2.** A man's separate shirt collar usually fastened with a STUD (see JEWELRY) in back and a collar button in front. Popular men's collar from early 1800s until 1920s and worn later with TUXEDO and FULL DRESS. Said to have been invented by Hannah Montague, wife of a blacksmith in the 1820s, who cut the collars off her husband's shirts and washed them separately—thus he could wear the shirt several times with a fresh collar. During the 19th and early 20th c., the collar became taller and stiffer until it reached 4″, as worn by President Herbert Hoover. The Cluett, Peabody & Co. of Troy, New York, promoted it as the *Arrow*® *collar* from 1905 to 1931. J. C. Leyendecker, an artist, created advertisements in which a handsome young man called the *Arrow*® *Collar Man* appeared. He was considered the idealized male, comparable to the GIBSON GIRL.

dog collar 1. Collar that fits tightly around base of neck or higher, sometimes used with HALTER NECKLINE (see under NECKLINES AND COLLARS). Also see NECKLINES AND COLLARS: CHOKER COLLAR. **2.** From 1860s, a small, plain standing collar that overlapped in front. Formerly called an *all-rounder*. Later a name given to CLERICAL COLLAR (see under CLERICAL DRESS), which buttoned in back.

dog-collar neckline See NECKLINES AND COLLARS: HALTER NECKLINE.

dog's ear collar Flat collar of medium size with long rounded ends. *Der.* Ends shaped like a spaniel's ear. Also called *spaniel's-ear collar*.

double collar Usually a large collar styled with two identical layers of fabric—one slightly larger than the other. May also be two layers with the upper one cut in an ASYMMETRIC style.

drawstring neckline Neckline with cord threaded through a casing that can be gathered and adjusted to create either a high or low neckline. Inspired by peasant styles. Introduced for little girls in the 1930s and used intermittently since.

Dutch neckline See NECKLINES AND COLLARS: SQUARE NECKLINE.

elasticized neckline Low neckline cut very wide and finished by turning fabric over a narrow band of stretched elastic, making a wide scooped neckline in front and back. Often used for nightgowns and blouses.

elliptic collar ∞ Patented DETACHABLE MAN'S COLLAR (see under NECKLINES AND COLLARS)

of early 1850s, with the front cut higher than the back. Could be fastened either in front or in back.

Eton collar Stiffened boy's collar, similar to a man's shirt collar but twice as wide, with widespread points in front. Worn by underclassmen at Eton College in England until 1967. Also see ETON SUIT in alphabetical listing.

Eugénie collarette ∞ (yoo-je′-nee) Crocheted collar of late 1860s made in two-tone yoke effect, pointed in center back and front, and closed in center front with loops and buttons. *Der.* Named for EUGÉNIE, EMPRESS of France.

fall/falling band ∞ Large, flat turned-down collar attached to the shirt, later made as a separate collar. Usually edged with lace and worn instead of a RUFF (see under NECKLINES AND COLLARS) by men and women from 1540s to 1670s.

fall or falling band

falling ruff See NECKLIINES AND COLLARS: RUFF.

falling tucker See NECKLINES AND COLLARS: TUCKER.

fan collar ∞ Standing collar of Elizabethan times shaped like an open fan and placed at back of neck. Usually lace-edged, starched, and wired to stand up.

fichu Originally a sheer fabric or lace triangular kerchief (see SCARVES: FICHU) worn in late 18th and 19th c. with very low neckline. Reintroduced in 1968 as separate collar worn around neck, crossed in front, and tied in back of waist.

Florentine neckline Wide, square neckline extending to shoulders and cut straight across front and back. *Der.* Inspired by Florentine paintings of the Renaissance.

French ruff See NECKLINES AND COLLARS: RUFF.

frizzle See NECKLINES AND COLLARS: RUFF.

funnel collar Large, stand-up collar that stands away from the face. Generally, buttoned or zippered up the center front and used on heavy winter coats or jackets.

funnel neckline Neckline coming up high on the throat, cut in one with garment. Made with shoulder seams slanted

funnel neckline

upward toward neck in the shape of an inverted funnel.

fused collar Collar for a man's shirt made by bonding the interlining with the right side of the collar using chemical or heat-sensitive adhesive, thereby making collar easier to iron and wrinkle-free.

Gladstone collar ∞ Standing collar with sides flaring up towards cheeks. Worn with a wide black scarflike tie in latter half of 19th c. *Der.* Named for William Ewart Gladstone, prime minister of England at intervals, between 1868 and 1894, during Queen Victoria's reign.

gorget ∞ (gorge-et′) **1.** Small ruffle at neck of smock in 16th c. Also spelled *gorgette.* **2.** See NECKLINES AND COLLARS: WHISK. **3.** High collar, cut low in front, worn by women in late 19th and early 20th c.

halter neckline Sleeveless front of garment that is held in place and leaves the back and shoulders bare. A strap around neck, drawstring at neck gathered and tied in a bow, or a band like a dog collar may serve to hold the front.

halter neckline

Henley neckline Round neckline made with ribbing and front placket opening. *Der.* From crew racing shirts worn at Henley, England.

Henry II collar ∞ **1.** Small, medium, or large collar standing up high on the neck in back and rolling over to form points in front. Larger collars had a shawl-collar effect in front. Worn by women in 1890s. **2.** Medium-sized RUFF (see under NECKLINES AND COLLARS) with a large ribbon bow and ends in front worn by women in 1890s.

Henry IV collar ∞ Standing collar around which are placed loops of ribbon forming a small RUFF (see under NECKLINES AND COLLARS) worn by women in 1890s.

horseshoe collar Flat collar extending approximately three-quarters to seven-eighths the distance around the neck with ends not quite meeting in center front.

horseshoe neckline Scooped neckline made low in front in shape of a horseshoe.

Italian collar Collar cut in one piece with front of blouse or shirt, then faced and turned over.

jabot (zha-bo′) Standing band collar (see under NECKLINES AND COLLARS) with hanging ruffle attached to front of collar.

jewel neckline High round neckline made with or without binding as a simple background for jewels.

jewel neckline

johnny collar Very small collar used for woman's or girl's shirt.

keyhole neckline High round neckline made with wedge-shaped or keyhole piece cut out at center front.

lapel Turned-back front section of blouse, jacket, coat, or shirt where it joins the collar. Each side folds back to form REVERS (see under NECKLINES AND COLLARS), or lapels that are cut in various shapes. Names of the types are based on the shape of the point where the collar and lapel meet and they include: **cloverleaf**—both collar and lapel are rounded where they meet; **fishmouth**—with lapel cut slanted and collar end rounded; **L-shaped**—with lapel cut straight across a narrow rounded collar; **notched**—with lapel and collar cut slanted thereby creating a notch; **peaked**—with V-shaped ending at lapel and collar fitting into it. Other variants include an **M-cut collar,** a man's coat collar of first half of 19th c. with M-shaped notch at the lapel, a style worn for daywear that continued until 1870 for evening coats.

cloverleaf lapel
fishmouth lapel
L-shaped lapel
notched lapel
peaked lapel

leaf British term for turned-down part of a *stand-fall* or *rolled collar.*

mandarin collar/mandarin neckline See NECKLINES AND COLLARS: CHINESE NECKLINE. *Der.* the neckline used on the Chinese mandarin robes.

masher collar ∞ Extremely high collar worn by ultra-fashionable men in 1880s and 1890s.

M-cut lapel See NECKLINES AND COLLARS: LAPEL.

N

medic collar Standing BAND COLLAR (see under NECKLINES AND COLLARS) fastened on the side with a single button. Made like those used on a physician's white jacket that has a side closing. Popular after it was seen on the *Ben Casey* television show in 1961. Also called *Ben Casey collar*.

Medici collar (meh-dee-chee) **1.** Large standing fan-shaped collar, usually of net or lace wired to stand up in back, and sloping to join low square neckline in front.

Medici collar #1

Worn by Marie de' Medici (1573–1642), second wife of Henry IV of France. Not given this name until the 19th c., when it was revived. **2.** ∞ Smaller woman's standing collar of 1890s rolled over at top, sometimes nearly meeting in front.

middy collar See NECKLINES AND COLLARS: SAILOR COLLAR.

military collar Standing collar, high in front and hooked either in front or back (e.g., type used on cadet's uniform at U.S. Military Academy at West Point, New York).

moat collar See NECKLINES AND COLLARS: RING COLLAR.

mock collar/mock-turtleneck collar Single unfolded fabric band that reaches a short distance up the neck that is made to simulate a TURTLENECK COLLAR (see under NECKLINES AND COLLARS).

mock collar or mock turtleneck collar

mousquetaire collar ∞ (moose-key-tare′) Medium-sized turned-down collar, usually linen, with the front ends pointed. Fashionable for women about 1850. *Der.* From uniform of French musketeers or royal bodyguards of Louis XIII in 17th c.

Napoleonic collar Collar that rolls up high on neck in back then turns over. Extends approximately three-quarters of the way around neck with wide lapels in front and double-breasted closing. *Der.* Named for *Napoleon Bonaparte* (1769–1821) as depicted by J. L. David, court painter.

neck ruche ∞ Woman's neckpiece of early 20th c. made of frilled MOUSSELINE pleated, sewed to a ribbon, and worn around the neck with long hanging streamers of silk or ribbon in front.

neck whisk ∞ **1.** Small wired or stiffened fan-shaped man's sheer standing collar worn inside standing collar of the doublet in late 16th c. **2.** Flat round man's collar with pointed ends open in front. Worn in Spain in 17th c.

Nehru collar/Nehru neckline (nay′-roo) Standing collar similar to Chinese collar but sometimes made with rounded ends in front. Copied from the costume of Jawaharlal Nehru, Prime Minister of India 1950–1964. Also called *rajah collar*.

notched collar/notched lapel Tailored collar primarily for man's suit coat that has an indentation or "notch" cut out or formed where the lapel joins the collar.

officer's collar ∞ Woman's collar of mid-1880s with stiff standing band around neck, sometimes with frill of lace at neck. A trilayered JABOT (see under NECKLINES AND COLLARS) with vandyked edges (see VANDYKING) was worn in center front.

off-the-shoulder neckline Low neckline, usually elasticized, extending around upper part of arms baring the shoulders, sometimes with straps, sometimes without. Frequently finished with a wide ruffle around the edge. Popular for evening gowns in 1930s and 1940s, and used intermittently since for nightgowns, blouses, and evening dresses.

off-the-shoulder neckline

one-shoulder neckline Asymmetric neckline starting under one arm and continuing diagonally over opposite shoulder leaving one shoulder bare. Popular for evening dresses, swimsuits, and nightgowns. Also called *sling neckline*.

one-shoulder neckline

oval ruff See NECKLINES AND COLLARS: RUFF.

papillon collar ∞ (pa-pi-yon′) Small standing collar, decorated with pleated fabric in front to form a small butterfly, worn by women in late 1860s. Cuffs were also decorated with small pleated butterflies. *Der.* French, "butterfly."

peasant neckline Low round neckline gathered into a bias band or made with a drawstring. Sometimes worn in off-the-shoulder fashion. See NECKLINES AND COLLARS: DRAWSTRING NECKLINE.

Peggy collar Rounded collar with scalloped ends similar to PETER PAN COLLAR (see under NECKLINES AND COLLARS).

petal collar Collar made of several irregularly shaped pieces that look like petals of a flower.

Peter Pan collar Small round flat collar with rounded ends in front. Worn originally by children, later also adopted by women. *Der.* Copied from costumes worn in play *Peter Pan*, written by James M. Barrie in 1904.

Peter Pan collar

Piccadilly collar ∞ Man's detachable high wing collar of 1860s fastening to the shirt with a stud in front and a button in back. By 1895, collar was cut larger to allow a scarf to pass underneath.

pierpont collar ∞ (peer'-pont) Man's collar ending in sharp points extended over tie, worn in 1840s and 1850s. Also called *pinpoint collar.*

pierrot collar (pee-yehr-oh') Small collar made of a double ruffle or ruff. *Der.* From costume of the comedy character in French pantomime called *Pierrot* (little Peter), especially the clown in opera *Pagliacci,* who wore a clown suit with this collar.

pilgrim collar Large round collar extending to the shoulder seams at sides and ending in two long points at center front. *Der.* Copied from early Pilgrim costume.

pin collar Shirt collar fitting high on neck made with an eyelet on each side of opening through which a special collar pin is inserted.

pinpoint collar See NECKLINES AND COLLARS: PIERPONT COLLAR.

placket neckline Slit at neckline bound with bias binding, or made with a facing, sometimes in a contrasting color. Bias may continue around neck or a simple collar may be added.

placket neckline

plastron See NECKLINES AND COLLARS: BIB COLLAR.

platter collar Medium to large, round collar with large rounded ends in front, worn flat on shoulders.

plunging neckline Neckline made with low V in center front, sometimes extending to the waist or below. Fashionable for extreme styles in the 1960s and continued in popularity since.

poet's collar See NECKLINES AND COLLARS: BYRON COLLAR.

polo collar ∞ Man's white starched collar, worn in late 1890s, with points sloping toward shoulders. Could be worn either standing or turned down.

princess stock ∞ High choker collar, usually made of shirred fabric with two bows extending at sides. When a PLASTRON (see NECKLINES AND COLLARS: BIB COLLAR) was attached at center front neckline, collar was called *princess stock collarette.* Worn by women in mid-1890s.

Puritan collar Square-cut, wide, flat white collar, or FALLING BAND (see under NECKLINES AND COLLARS), that extends to shoulder seam. *Der.* Copied from early Puritan costume.

rabat (ra-bat') /**rabbi** ∞ A linen and lace collar worn over the DOUBLET in 17th c.

rabato (rah-bah'-toe) /**rebato 1.** ∞ White collar wired to stand up at back of neck, worn with low-cut neckline by women from late 16th to mid-17th c. **2.** See NECKLIINES AND COLLARS: RUFF.

rajah collar/rajah necklines See NECKLINES AND COLLARS: NEHRU COLLAR.

regency collar Similar to NAPOLEONIC COLLAR (see under NECKLINES AND COLLARS) but smaller in size.

revers (reh-veerz') Another name for lapels, actually the facing of the lapels, which fold back to show the reverse side of the collar and lapels. See NECKLINES AND COLLARS: LAPELS.

revers

ring collar Stand-away band that circles the neck at a distance about halfway to shoulder

N

seam. Also called *moat collar* and *wedding-band collar.*

Robespierre collar ∞ (robz-pee-yehr′) Man's coat collar worn about 1790, coming up high at back of neck and then turned down with jabot showing in front. Used on a double-breasted coat. *Der.* Named for Maximillian François Marie Isadore de Robespierre, French lawyer and revolutionist, executed in 1794.

rolled collar **1.** Collar extending upward from neckline and turning over, the roll higher at back than in front. **2.** Any shirt collar or other collar that has a roll to it making it stand up on neck, as differentiated

rolled collar

from a flat collar that has no roll, and lies flat at base of neck (e.g., NECKLINES AND COLLARS: NAPOLEONIC or CONVERTIBLE COLLAR). Called *stand-fall collar* in the 19th c.

rollpoint collar ∞ Similar to wing collar but overturned point is not pressed down. Worn by men in late 19th and early 20th c.

Roman collar See CLERICAL DRESS: CLERICAL COLLAR.

Rosebery collar ∞ Man's detachable collar of mid-1890s of white linen, 3″ high in back, with rounded points in front. *Der.* Named for Fifth Earl of Rosebery, British statesman, author, and prime minister, 1894–1895.

ruff Stiff white collar of varying widths, often edged in or made of lace, that projected from the neckline like a wheel around neck. Worn by men

ruff

and women from 1560s to 1640s, the ruff was one of the most characteristic features of costume of this time period. After the ruff went out of fashion, it became another alternative that could be used as a collar and has appeared in fashion periodically since the 17th c. The earliest ruffs appear to have evolved from a small ruffle at the neckline of a shirt or chemise that became a separate item of clothing and could be of enormous width. Ruffs were made in one of the following ways: (a) gathering one edge of a band of fabric to the size of the neck to form a frill of

deep folds; (b) round flat pieces of lace without depth or folds, more like a wide collar; (c) several layers of lace placed one over the other; (d) open ruffs, almost a cross between a ruff and a collar that stood behind the head and fastened in front into a square neckline. Ruffs were supported either by starching or by a **supportasse** (sup-port′-tass) or **underpropper,** a wire framework used to tilt an enormous starched ruff up on back of neck. Also called a *rabato.* Named variations of

supportasse

ruffs included the **oval ruff,** a woman's large plain ruff, oval shaped rather than round, made with large PIPE-ORGAN PLEATS (see under CLOTHING CONSTRUCTION DETAILS). Worn from about 1625 to 1650. The **cabbage ruff** was a large ruff falling in irregular folds, like leaves of a cabbage. Worn by men in early 17th c. Also called *lettuce ruff* or *lettice ruff.* The **vandyke** was a 17th-c. ruff edged with points of saw-toothed lace. A **cartwheel ruff** or **French ruff** was extremely large, starched, and set in regular convolutions and was worn from 1580 to 1610 and somewhat later in Holland. By contrast, the **frizzle** was a 17th-c. small ruff. The **falling ruff** was an unstarched ruff falling around the neck in unregulated folds. Worn in England from about 1615 to 1640 by men and women and by men in France during reign of Henry IV (1589–1610) and then called *fraise à la confusion.*

Russian collar See NECKLINES AND COLLARS: COSSACK COLLAR.

Sabrina neckline High boat neckline fastened together at shoulders with spaghetti strings that are tied in bows. Originally designed by Edith Head and worn by Audrey Hepburn in film *Sabrina* in 1950s.

sailor collar Large square collar hanging in back with front tapering to a V with dickey inserted. Trimmed with rows of braid and worn on *middy blouses* by the U.S. Navy. Popular style since 1860s, especially for children. Also called *middy collar.*

sailor collar

santon ∞ (sahn-tone´) Colored silk cravat worn with small RUFF (see under NECKLIINES AND COLLARS) by women in 1820s. Also called a *sautoir* (sew-twar´).

sautoir See NECKLINES AND COLLARS: SANTON.

scoop neckline Low curved neckline extending to shoulders or cut deep in front or back, or both. Introduced for evening wear in late 1930s, used on daytime dresses since 1950s, and blouses since late 1960s.

separate collar **1.** Any collar not permanently attached to the garment with which it is worn (e.g., collars as worn with choir robes). **2.** See DETACHABLE COLLAR.

shakespeare collar **1.** Standing collar of medium width, flaring away from face. Made of a curved pleated strip of stiffened lawn. *Der.* Similar to those shown in a portrait thought to be of 16th-c. dramatist William Shakespeare. **2.** ∞ Similar collar with longer points, sometimes trimmed with *lace* and *insertion,* worn by women in mid-1860s. **3.** ∞ Small collar with points turned down in front worn by men from 1860s on.

shawl collar **1.** Collar that follows the front opening of garment. Cut in one piece, or with seam in center back, it does not have separate lapels. It may be narrow or broad and can extend to waistline. Used on women's dresses, coats, sweaters, and men's tuxedos. See NECKLINES AND COLLARS: ANGLED SHAWL COLLAR. **2.** Women's blouse or dress collar made in one piece with low V-neck in front and hanging ends of frilly lace. Worn in early 1980s.

shawl collar #1

shirt collar Turned-down collar used on a man's or woman's shirt; specifically, a small collar fitting not too high on the neck, with medium-spread points (e.g., NECKLINES AND COLLARS: BUTTON-DOWN, CONVERTIBLE, PIN, TAB, SPREAD, and WING COLLARS).

sling neckline See NECKLINES AND COLLARS: ONE-SHOULDER NECKLINE.

spaniel's-ear collar See NECKLINES AND COLLARS: DOG'S EAR COLLAR.

split mandarin collar Similar to mandarin collar standing high on the neck. In mid-1980s called a *split mandarin collar* when it did not fasten at neckline and could be turned down to form lapels. See NECKLINES AND COLLARS: CHINESE COLLAR.

spread collar Man's shirt collar made with a wide division between points in front.

spread collar

square neckline Moderately low neckline cut square in front. Also called *Dutch neckline.*

stand-away collar Women's collar that does not hug the neck, usually of the roll-type and popular from early 1960s.

stand-fall collar See NECKLINES AND COLLARS: ROLLED COLLAR #2.

standing whisk See NECKLINES AND COLLARS: WHISK.

stand-up collar **1.** See NECKLINES AND COLLARS: BAND COLLAR. **2.** Collar similar to a band collar extending higher on the neck and sometimes finished with a frill of lace or pleating. Widely used in the late 19th and early 20th c. and revived periodically.

stand-up collar #2

stick-up collar See NECKLINES AND COLLARS: WING COLLAR.

stock collar/stock neckline See NECKLINES AND COLLARS: ASCOT NECKLINE.

strapless neckline Boned or elastic bodice that requires no shoulder straps. An innovation in the 1930s and a basic neckline style since then that has been popular for evening wear as well as sportswear.

strapless neckline

supportasse See NECKLINES AND COLLARS: RUFF.

surplice collar (sir´-pliss) Flat pointed collar fastened to a SURPLICE NECKLINE (see NECKLINES AND COLLARS). Used on a coat-style dress.

surplice neckline (sir´-pliss) Neckline of wraparound blouse, dress, or robe with one side lapping over other to form a V in center front. Introduced in 1920s and used since.

swallow-tailed collar Tailored collar with extremely long narrow points in front. *Der.* From resemblance to "the tail of a swallow."

sweetheart neckline Moderately low neckline with heart-shaped center front. Sides of neckline slant toward neck in front with back rounded. Introduced in 1930s and used intermittently since.

tab collar Shirt collar fitting high on the neck with a small flap or tab at the neckband that buttons or snaps to other side of shirt.

tab collar

Talleyrand collar (ta´-lay-rahn) Collar standing up at back of neck and turned over, similar to ROBESPIERRE COLLAR (see under NECKLINES AND COLLARS). *Der.* Named after French statesman Charles Maurice de Talleyrand-Perigord, active in politics from 1775 to 1815.

toby ruff ∞ Woman's small RUFF of 1890 (see NECKLIINES AND COLLARS: RUFF), made of two or three layers of frills tied at the throat with ribbon.

tucker ∞ Narrow strip or frill of plain or lace-trimmed fabric, used by women from 17th c. to about 1830s, to fill in low dècollétage. Also called *pinner* or *falling tucker* in 19th c. when it hung down over bodice. Also see PARTLET #2 and SCARVES: CHEMISETTE.

turndown collar Any collar that folds over on the garment or on itself, as contrasted with standing-band or stand-up type. Also see NECKLINES AND COLLARS: ROLLED COLLAR.

turnover collar Any collar that rolls and then turns over (e.g., NECKLINES AND COLLARS: A CONVERTIBLE COLLAR).

turtleneck/turtleneck collar High-band collar, usually knitted, that fits very close to the neck and rolls over, sometimes twice. Introduced in the 1860s for men, popular in the 1920s and 1930s, and revived in the late 1960s and after for men, women, and children.

turtleneck collar

turtleneck convertible collar Turtleneck collar with zipper down center front so collar may be worn high on neck or unzipped to a V.

tuxedo collar Collar that rolls over and extends down entire length of front opening in women's jacket or coat with no fasteners. Name borrowed from shawl collar of men's dinner jacket. *Der.* So named in the 1920s after the country club at Tuxedo Park, New York. Also see TUXEDO in alphabetical listing

Ubangi neckline (yoo-bang´-ee) Extremely high choker-type neckline covering the entire neck. Sometimes made of fabric, sometimes of chain or springy wire wrapped around the neck. Popular in late 1960s. *Der.* Inspired by dress of women of the Ubangi tribe of Africa.

underpropper See NECKLINES AND COLLARS: RUFF.

U-neckline See NECKLINES AND COLLARS: HORSESHOE NECKLINE.

ventilated collar See CLERICAL DRESS.

Victorian collar See NECKLINES AND COLLARS: CHOKER COLLAR.

V-neckline Neckline cut down in front or in back to a sharp point resembling the letter V.

wedding-band collar See NECKLINES AND COLLARS: RING COLLAR.

whisk ∞ **1.** Wide, flat, lace-trimmed or plain collar worn by women in 17th c., like FALLING BAND (see under NECKLINES AND COLLARS). **2.** Standing lace collar called *standing whisk*.

wing collar **1.** A tailored shirt collar with spread points. **2.** Stiff man's collar fitting high around neck with turned-down points in front; sometimes worn with man's full dress or daytime formal wear.

wing collar #2

Worn by upperclassmen at Eton College until 1967. Also called *stick-up collar*. **3.** Same type as above, introduced in 1980s of softer fabric, usually white on a colored shirt.

winker ∞ Man's collar with extremely high points reaching nearly to eyes that was worn from 1816 to 1820.

wrap collar Collar that has one end pulled around to side of neck where it buttons, introduced in 1983.

yoke collar ∞ Square or V-shaped yoke, extending wide on the shoulders, to which two gathered ruffles are attached. Worn by women in mid-1890s with high choker collar at neck.

N

Zhivago collar See Cossack collar. *Der.* From 1965 film of Boris Pasternak's novel *Dr. Zhivago*, depicting Russian Revolution of 1917.

neckpiece See scarves.

neck ring See jewelry.

neck ruche See necklines and collars.

neckstock ∞ Stiffly folded made-up cravat buckled in back worn by men in 18th and 19th c. See stock and ties: stock.

necktie See ties.

necktie pin See jewelry: stickpin.

neckwear Accessories worn around neck exclusive of jewelry. Includes neckties, scarves, and collars.

neck whisk See necklines and collars.

needle 1. Small thin spike, usually of polished steel, with one end pointed and an eye at the other end through which the thread is drawn for sewing. 2. A long implement without an eye that has a hook at one end used for knitting or for crocheting.

needlepoint 1. See embroideries and sewing stitches. 2. See introduction to laces.

needle tapestry work See embroideries and sewing stitches.

needle toe See footwear.

needle trades See apparel industry.

needleweaving See embroideries and sewing stitches.

negligée See sleepwear and loungewear.

negligée costume (neg-glee-zheh´) Informal costume, worn primarily in privacy of home or bedroom. Usually a long easy robe of supple material, ranging from simple cotton to elaborately trimmed silk. Worn by both men and women from 18th through 19th c. and developing into the tea-gown for women in last quarter of 19th c. *Der.* French, *négligée*, "neglected."

negligée shirt See shirts.

Nehru styles See Nehru under necklines and collars, coats and jackets.

Nehru suit (nay-roo) 1. A suit with a high stand-up Nehru collar (see under necklines and collars) introduced in 1967. Made in various fabrics for both men and women. 2. Woman's pantsuit with a tunic top made with Nehru collar. Top may be worn separately as a dress. *Der.*

Named after Jawaharlal Nehru, Prime Minister of India, 1950–1964.

Nehru suit #1

Nelson See undergarments: frisk.

neon colors Very bright, vibrant colors similar to those produced by neon lights.

neon sock See hosiery.

nephrite See gems, gem cuts, and settings: jade.

net See bobbinet.

net embroidery See embroideries and sewing stitches: tulle.

nether integuments See inexpressibles.

nether stocks See lower stocks.

Newgate fringe See beard.

New Look Style introduced by couturier Christian Dior in Paris in 1947. The style was a radical departure from the wartime styles, with a rounded shoulder, tightly fitted waistline, curved hipline and hemline that was almost six inches longer than prevailing styles. The fashion press called these changes "The New Look," the first time the term "look" had been used to describe an overall style.

New Look

Newmarket coat See coats and jackets.

Newmarket frock See coats and jackets: Newmarket coat.

Newmarket jacket See coats and jackets.

Newmarket overcoat See coats and jackets.

Newmarket top frock See coats and jackets.

newmarket vest See vests.

New Romantics Media-coined term for young people of the late 1970s and 1980s who, in reaction against punk fashions, wore clothing made in soft, extravagant fabrics, in dressy styles derived from historic fiction or futuristic or fantasy costumes.

newsbag See handbags and related accessories.

newsboy cap See headwear.

New Wave Punk See punk/punk look.

New York Couture Business Council, The An organization of manufacturers of ready-to-wear clothing serving as a trade council and mediating disputes between retailers and manufacturers. The promotional arm of this organization is called *The New York Couture Group* and is responsible for *National Press Week*.

neyge See EDGE #2.

niced See SCARVES: NYCETTE.

niche/niche marketing (neesh) Describes a narrowly defined group of customers and the practice of marketing to those customers. Needs of consumers in niches can be analyzed and apparel offered that appeals to this specific group.

nightcap See HEADWEAR.

night clothes An older term referring to apparel worn to bed. See SLEEPWEAR AND LOUNGEWEAR.

night coif See HEADWEAR.

nightgown 1. See SLEEPWEAR AND LOUNGEWEAR. 2. ∞ In the 18th c., a comfortable women's dress, without stays, worn either outdoors or indoors. Also see MORNING GOWN.

nightgowns & nightshirts See SLEEPWEAR AND LOUNGEWEAR.

nightie See SLEEPWEAR AND LOUNGEWEAR: NIGHTGOWN #1.

night rail See SLEEPWEAR AND LOUNGEWEAR.

nightshift/nightshirt See SLEEPWEAR AND LOUNGEWEAR: NIGHTGOWNS.

Nike® waffle trainers See FOOTWEAR.

nine-tenths length See LENGTHS.

Ninon coiffure See HAIRSTYLES.

no bra look Look accompanying the *see-through look*. Originally a sheer lightweight bra designed by Rudi Gernreich in early 1960s. Later by extension transferred to advocating of wearing nothing, or bikinis, under see-through clothes in late 1960s and early 1970s.

nomad look Look inspired by clothing worn by nomadic tribes of Middle East countries. Unusual patterned fabrics, use of shearling and embroidered leather as exemplified by the AFGHANISTAN JACKET (see under COATS AND JACKETS) and VEST popular around 1968.

nonreciprocated See HOSIERY: RECIPROCATED CONSTRUCTION.

nonseasonal Products that sell at much the same rate throughout the year.

nonwoven fabrics † Interlocking or bonding of fibers (or both) by chemical, mechanical, ther-

mal, solvent methods, and combinations to create a fabric.

Norell, Norman * See APPENDIX/DESIGNERS.

Norfolk jacket See COATS AND JACKETS.

Norfolk shirt See COATS AND JACKETS.

Norfolk suit 1. ∞ Little boy's suit with top styled like Norfolk jacket with one or two box pleats in front and back, usually worn with a belt at waist that continues under pleats. Worn with *knickerbockers* to above knee, Buster Brown collar, bow tie, and large off-the-face hat in early 1900s. 2. Man's suit with matching coat and pants, jacket styled in Norfolk manner (see COATS AND JACKETS: NORFOLK JACKET), worn from about 1912 to about 1930. Revived occasionally.

Normandie cape See CAPES, CLOAKS, AND SHAWLS.

North American Free Trade Agreement (NAFTA) Treaty that provides for the reduction and eventually elimination of trade barriers between Canada, Mexico, and the United States.

Northamptonshire lace See LACES.

Norwegian morning cap See HEADWEAR.

notched collar See NECKLINES AND COLLARS.

notched lapel See NECKLINES AND COLLARS: LAPEL.

Nottingham lace See LACES.

nouch See JEWELRY: OUCH.

novelties See HOSIERY.

novelty yarn † Yarns made with unusual or special effects such as nubs, slubs, loops, or some other variation. The preferred term in the textile industry is now *fancy yarn*.

nubuck See LEATHERS.

nub yarn † Yarn made with slubs or lumps, knots, or flecks of fibers at intervals—sometimes of different colors giving a mottled effect to the finished fabric.

nude bra See UNDERGARMENTS.

nude heel See HOSIERY.

nude look Showing large areas of the body or using beige or natural-colored body stockings that give a nude effect. Introduced in 1966 by Saint Laurent and Cardin with sheer transparent dresses worn over nude-colored body stockings. Later in the 1960s, the body stocking was not worn and this was called the **see-through look**.

nugget ring See JEWELRY.

numeral shirt See SHIRTS: FOOTBALL JERSEY/SHIRT.

nun's habit Apparel worn by nuns, women living in convents who devote their lives to their church. Many of these styles dated from the Middle Ages and usually consisted of a covered-up, ankle-length black dress, often with a white collar and belted with a long cord. Head and neck were wrapped in starched white cotton headdress like a WIMPLE (see under HEADWEAR), with the shape varying according to the convent or order and often covered by a long black veil. Many changes have been made in Roman Catholic nuns' habits since 1965, (e.g., simpler headdresses, shorter skirts, brown, navy, and gray colors added to conventional black color). Some orders have abandoned habits altogether, wearing conservative street dress instead.

nun's tucks See CLOTHING CONSTRUCTION DETAILS.

Nureyev shirt See SHIRTS.

nurse's cap See HEADWEAR.

nurse's cape See CAPES, CLOAKS, AND SHAWLS.

nutria See FURS.

nycette See SCARVES.

nylon † Generic fiber category established by the FTC for a MANUFACTURED FIBER composed of a long chain of chemicals called polyamides. Introduced in 1939 by DuPont and later produced by other manufacturers, nylon fabrics generally have a silky hand, strength, crease resistance, washability, and resistance to mildew and moths. Current trademark names include Antron®, Caprolan®, and Ultron®.

nylons See HOSIERY.

obi   See BELTS: OBI-STYLED SASH.

obi hat   See HEADWEAR.

oblong hoops   See UNDERGARMENTS: PANNIERS.

obsidian   See GEMS, GEM CUTS, AND SETTINGS.

ocelot (ah-seh-lot)   See FURS.

ocepa   See ANDEAN SHIFT.

octagonal hat   See HEADWEAR.

octagon tie   See TIES.

odd priced   Prices for goods that end with an odd number. Endings such as .95 or .99 often are assigned to sale merchandise, whereas .00 or easily divisible numbers are used for nonsale prices.

oegge   See EDGE.

off-color diamond   See GEMS, GEM CUTS, AND SETTINGS.

officer's cape   See CAPES, CLOAKS, AND SHAWLS.

officer's coat   See COATS AND JACKETS: GUARDSMAN.

officer's collar   See NECKLINES AND COLLARS.

off price   *Adj.* Merchandise or retailing of merchandise purchased at discount prices.

offshore   In U.S. apparel trade, refers to countries other than the United States. See INTERNATIONAL SOURCING and IMPORT.

offshore production   Manufacturing of apparel in countries other than the United States while using specifications that U.S. companies provide.

off the peg   See READY-TO-WEAR.

off the rack   See READY-TO-WEAR.

off-the-shoulder   See NECKLINES AND COLLARS.

oilskin   **1.** † Yellow waterproof fabric made by coating cotton with linseed oil. Used originally for raincoats worn by fishermen, sailors, and children. Term also used for fabrics given waterproof finish. **2.** Garments made of this or similar fabric (e.g., raincoats, pants, and jackets) worn by sailors in rainy weather.

oil tanning   See LEATHERS: CHAMOIS TANNING.

oker   See FOOTWEAR: COCKER.

Oldham, Todd   * See APPENDIX/DESIGNERS.

old mine cut   See GEMS, GEM CUTS, AND SETTINGS.

olefin † (oh´-leh-fihn)   Generic fiber category for a manufactured fiber composed of either polyethylene or polypropylene. Manufacturers prefer the term **polyolefin** (pol-ee´-oh´-leh-fihn). Polypropylene is used for some kinds of apparel, such as activewear products (e.g., knitted underwear and hosiery), and is also beginning to be used in other products such as lingerie, bathing suits, and children's clothing. Some trademark names include Marvess® and Polystrand®.

olive button   See CLOSURES.

Olive, Frank   * See APPENDIX/DESIGNERS.

Oliver, André   * See APPENDIX/DESIGNERS.

Oliver Twist dress   ∞ Young girl's dress worn about 1919. Made with double-breasted wrap-front and skirt pleated at sides and back and had a fluted frill at neckline and at end of three-quarter-length sleeves.

Oliver Twist suit   ∞ Little boy's suit worn about 1919, similar to girl's OLIVER TWIST DRESS. Made with wrap closing, double-breasted effect on blouse, and knee pants buttoned to blouse and had a frill at neck and sleeves.

olivette   See CLOSURES: FROG.

O

olivine   See GEMS, GEM CUTS, AND SETTINGS.

Olympics®   Sporting contests held both in the winter and summer, every four years, with participants from around the world. The various types of clothes worn for different sports frequently have an important influence on activewear. *Der.* From the games and festivals held in honor of the god Zeus on the plain of Olympia in ancient Greece, where a laurel wreath was presented to the victor.

ombré (om′-bray)   Closely related tones of color with monochromatic shading from light to dark of single color (e.g., pale pink to red, or in several colors like a rainbow). *Der.* French, "shaded." Also see PRINTS, STRIPES, and CHECKS.

one-piece bathing suit   See ACTIVEWEAR: MAILLOT.

one-shoulder back pack   See HANDBAGS AND RELATED ACCESSORIES.

one-shoulder dress   See TOGA DRESS #1.

one-shoulder neckline   See NECKLINES AND COLLARS.

one-size bra   See UNDERGARMENTS: STRETCH BRA.

onion   See HAIRSTYLES: POMPADOUR.

online retailing   See ELECTRONIC RETAILING.

on order   Goods ordered but not yet received.

onyx   See GEMS, GEM CUTS, AND SETTINGS.

opal   See GEMS, GEM CUTS, AND SETTINGS.

opaque   Term applied to gems and fabrics through which no light passes. Compare with TRANSLUCENT and TRANSPARENT. See also HOSIERY: OPAQUE HOSE and OPAQUE PANTYHOSE.

op art print   See PRINTS, STRIPES, AND CHECKS.

open-back shoe   See FOOTWEAR: SLINGBACK.

open buttonhole stitch   See EMBROIDERIES AND SEWING STITCHES: BLANKET STITCH.

open-crown hat   See HEADWEAR.

opening price point   See APPAREL PRICE RANGES.

open orders   Those orders that allow a manufacturer to ship merchandise at some point other than a set delivery date. Such orders may specify a dollar amount to be purchased, but may not require specific styles, sizes, or colors.

open robe   ∞ Term used in 19th c. for a dress with an overskirt split in front, revealing an ornamental underskirt or petticoat; most fashionable, mainly for daytime and evening wear, in 1830s and 1840s. Such skirts were worn from the 16th c. to the 18th c., but not called by this name.

open-shank   See FOOTWEAR.

open-to-buy (OTB)   A calculation based on difference between merchandise a buyer plans to order over a specified period and what has already been ordered. The open-to-buy amount can be used by the buyer to adjust orders so as to maintain inventory and profitability.

open-toed shoe   See FOOTWEAR.

open-to-ship   A calculation of the amount of merchandise needed to meet planned purchases.

open-welt seam   See CLOTHING CONSTRUCTION DETAILS: TUCKED SEAM.

open window display   See WINDOW DISPLAYS.

openwork   Knitting, weaving, or embroidery in which threads are used in such a manner that holes in fabric give a lacy effect. See EMBROIDERIES AND SEWING STITCHES.

opera   Adjective used for apparel and accessories of a type that might be worn to performances of operas or other formal public performances. See CAPES, CLOAKS, AND SHAWLS: OPERA WRAP and OPERA CAPE, EYEWEAR: OPERA GLASSES, FOOTWEAR: OPERA PUMP and OPERA SLIPPER, GLOVES AND GLOVE CONSTRUCTION: OPERA GLOVE, and HEADWEAR: OPERA HAT.

opera length necklace   See JEWELRY.

opossum   See FURS.

opus Anglicum   See EMBROIDERIES AND SEWING STITCHES: ENGLISH WORK.

opus araneum   See LACES: ANTIQUE.

oralia   See HEADWEAR.

oreilles de chien   See HAIRSTYLES.

organdy   † Light sheer cotton fabric with a permanently crisp feel. If made of manufactured fibers, it is crease resistant, but if made of natural fibers the fabric will wrinkle. Made in an open weave of fine, high-quality combed yarns, the fabric may be dyed, printed, or embroidered. Used for dresses, collars, cuffs, millinery, aprons, interfacing, and neckwear.

organic cotton   † Cotton grown without the use of pesticides and chemical fertilizers.

organza   † Lightweight, thin, transparent fabric that is stiff and wiry. Made in the plain weave of manufactured filament or silk yarns, this fabric has a tendency to crush, but is easy to press. Used for dresses, millinery, trimmings, neckwear, and blouses.

oriental cat's eye See GEMS, GEM CUTS, AND SETTINGS: CAT'S EYE.

oriental couching See EMBROIDERIES AND SEWING STITCHES.

oriental pearls See GEMS, GEM CUTS, AND SETTINGS: PEARL.

oriental stitch See EMBROIDERIES AND SEWING STITCHES.

oriental wrapper See COATS AND JACKETS: ZOUAVE COAT.

original design See HAUTE COUTURE.

orle See OURLE.

ornamental stones See GEMS, GEM CUTS, AND SETTINGS.

orphrey See ECCLESIASTICAL DRESS.

orrelet See HEADWEAR.

orris/orrice lace See LACES.

Orsay, Count d' Alfred Guillaume Gabriel (1801–1852) (ore'-say) French society leader in Paris and London at the time of William IV. A DANDY or arbiter of fashion, he is described as a wit, a sculptor, and a conversationalist, and his name is attached to fashions such as d'Orsay slippers and d'Orsay coat.

osbaldiston tie See TIES.

osprey See FEATHERS.

ostrich See FEATHERS and LEATHERS.

otter See FURS.

ottoman † Heavy luxurious fabric with broad, flat crosswise ribs or wales. Made from silk, acetate, rayon, cotton, or wool with crosswise cord yarns of cotton. Lengthwise yarns are finer and more are used so that they cover the crosswise yarns completely on both sides. Used for coats, evening wear, suits, and trimmings.

ottoman ribbed knit † Double-knit fabric with a pronounced wide crosswise rib.

ouch See JEWELRY.

ourle ∞ Term used in 13th and 14th c. for a fur border. Later spelled *orle*.

outing flannel/outing cloth † Light- or medium-weight, soft, fuzzy cotton fabric. Made with lightly twisted yarns that are napped to conceal the plain or twill weave completely. May be made in yarn-dyed stripes, piece-dyed, or printed. Used for winter pajamas, nightshirts, and gowns.

outline stitch See EMBROIDERIES AND SEWING STITCHES.

outré (oo'-tray) French adjective meaning exaggerated, strained, excessive.

outseam See GLOVES AND GLOVE CONSTRUCTIONS: GLOVE SEAMS.

outsole See FOOTWEAR: SOLE.

oval cut See GEMS, GEM CUTS, AND SETTINGS.

oval ruff See NECKLINES AND COLLARS: RUFF.

oval toe See FOOTWEAR.

oval trunk hose See BOULOGNE HOSE.

overalls See PANTS.

overblouse 1. See BLOUSES AND TOPS. 2. See ACTIVEWEAR: OVERBLOUSE SWIMSUIT.

overboot See FOOTWEAR.

overcast/overcasting See CLOTHING CONSTRUCTION DETAILS: SEAMS and EMBROIDERIES AND SEWING STITCHES.

overcoat See COATS AND JACKETS.

overdress 1. Any dress designed to be worn over another dress. 2. ∞ Transparent dress worn in late 17th c. constructed with an attached opaque underdress. 3. ∞ In 1870s, a hip-length bodice worn with a separate skirt. Some were formal in style with low-cut neckline, peplum, and fancy decorative trim of lace and ribbons. See CAGE DRESS.

overlapped seam See GLOVES AND GLOVE CONSTRUCTIONS: FULL PIQUÉ and CLOTHING CONSTRUCTION DETAILS: LAP SEAM.

overlay See FOOTWEAR.

overplaid See PLAIDS AND TARTANS.

overseam See GLOVES AND GLOVE CONSTRUCTIONS.

overseas cap See HEADWEAR.

overshirt See SHIRTS.

overshoe See FOOTWEAR.

oversized See SHIRTS and BLOUSES AND TOPS.

overskirt See SKIRTS.

overstocks See STOCKS.

over-the-knee socks See HOSIERY.

owl glasses See EYEWEAR.

oxford See FOOTWEAR.

Oxford bags See PANTS.

oxford button-overs See FOOTWEAR.

Oxford cap See ACADEMIC COSTUME: MORTARBOARD.

oxford cloth † Men's shirting fabric made in a basket weave, sometimes 2 × 2 and sometimes 4 × 2. Yarns may be all COMBED or all CARDED with crosswise yarns coarser than lengthwise. Better grades are mercerized (see MERCERIZATION). The fabric may be bleached, dyed, have yarn-dyed stripes, or small fancy designs. *Der.* Originally produced by a Scottish firm along with fabrics labeled Yale, Harvard, and Cambridge, which are no longer important.

Oxford coatee See COATS AND JACKETS: OXONIAN JACKET.

Oxford glove See GLOVES AND GLOVE CONSTRUCTIONS.

Oxford tie See TIES.

Oxonian boots See FOOTWEAR.

Oxonian jacket See COATS AND JACKETS.

Oxonians See FOOTWEAR: OXONIAN BOOTS.

Oxonian shoe See FOOTWEAR.

P See PETITE.

pac boot See FOOTWEAR.

padded sleeve See SHOULDERS AND SLEEVES.

padding Any stuffing material used between two layers of fabric or leather to give a rounded effect to clothing or accessories. At present padding is used mostly for warmth in the form of DOWN for coats and jackets or FIBERFILL for shaping in bras.

padding stitch See EMBROIDERIES AND SEWING STITCHES.

paddock coat See COATS AND JACKETS.

padre hat See HEADWEAR.

paenula See CAPES, CLOAKS, AND SHAWLS.

page ∞ Belt with long loop of ribbon, cord, or velvet placed in either side. Used to loop up overskirt of dress from 1850 to 1867. Compare with DRESS CLIP and DRESS HOLDER.

page-boy bob See HAIRSTYLES.

pagoda parasol See UMBRELLAS AND PARASOLS.

pagoda sleeve See SHOULDERS AND SLEEVES.

paillette (pay-et´) Spangle made of metal or plastic, usually a round disk larger than a SEQUIN. Used as trimming on evening clothes and handbags. *Der.* French, "speck or spangle."

painter's Used to describe clothing and accessories derived from or inspired by the dress of painters (e.g., painter's cap, painter's jumper, painter's pants).

pair of bodies See UNDERGARMENTS.

paisley print See PRINTS, STRIPES, AND CHECKS.

paisley scarf See SCARVES.

paisley shawl See CAPES, CLOAKS, AND SHAWLS: CASHMERE SHAWL #2.

pajama checks See PRINTS, STRIPES, AND CHECKS.

pajamas See SLEEPWEAR AND LOUNGEWEAR.

pajama set See SLEEPWEAR AND LOUNGEWEAR: PAJAMAS.

pajama stripes See PRINTS, STRIPES, AND CHECKS.

Pakistani vest See VESTS.

palasade See HEADWEAR: FONTANGE.

palatine 1. See SCARVES. 2. See CAPES, CLOAKS, AND SHAWLS: TIPPET.

palatine royal See CAPES, CLOAKS, AND SHAWLS.

palazzo pajamas/pants See PANTS.

paletot See COATS AND JACKETS.

paletot-cloak See CAPES, CLOAKS, AND SHAWLS.

paletot-mantle See CAPES, CLOAKS, AND SHAWLS.

paletot-redingote See COATS AND JACKETS.

paletot-sac See COATS AND JACKETS.

palisade See HEADWEAR: COMMODE.

palla See CAPES, CLOAKS, AND SHAWLS.

pallatine See SCARVES: PALATINE.

pallium 1. See CAPES, CLOAKS, AND SHAWLS. 2. See CLERICAL DRESS.

palmerston wrapper See COATS AND JACKETS.

paltock See DOUBLET.

paludamentum See CAPES, CLOAKS, AND SHAWLS.

pamela See HEADWEAR.

panache (pah-nash´) Plume or erect bunch of feathers worn on hat—originally used on military helmets.

panama hat See HEADWEAR.

pancake beret See HEADWEAR.

panel pantdress Dress with free hanging panel in front and back.

panel print See PRINTS, STRIPES, AND CHECKS.

panel skirt See SKIRTS.

panes ∞ Fabric strips cut vertically in a garment or fabric strips fastened together so that spaces appear between them. Used from 1500 to 1650s as a decorative device on sleeves, DOUBLETS, TRUNK HOSE. Shown at DOUBLET. A contrasting lining, a shirt, or chemise was visible between the panes or might be pulled out to make a puff. See PULLINGS OUT. Compare with SLASHING.

panier/paniers See UNDERGARMENTS.

paniers à bourelet See UNDERGARMENTS: PANIERS.

paniers à coudes See UNDERGARMENTS: PANIERS.

paniers anglais See UNDERGARMENTS: PANIERS.

panne satin See SATIN.

panne velvet † (pan-ay′) VELVET that has had the pile pressed down in one direction giving it a glossy appearance. Originally made with wool or silk pile and raw silk ply yarns; later with silk ground and flattened rayon pile. Used for dresses and sportswear.

pannier/panniers (pan-yehr′) **1.** See UNDERGARMENTS. **2.** Puff formed over the hip by looping up the outer skirt. *Der.* Latin, *panarium,* "a basket for bread."

pannier bag See HANDBAGS AND RELATED ACCESSORIES.

pannier crinoline See UNDERGARMENTS.

pannier curls See HAIRSTYLES.

pannier drape (pan-yehr′) **1.** See UNDERGARMENTS: PANNIER. **2.** ∞ In late 1860s, puff formed over hip by looping up the outerskirt of a dress. **3.** ∞ In 1880s, fullness of drapery on hips made by an extra piece of fabric attached to bodice or waistline draped over hips with remainder pulled to the back in polonaise style (see POLONAISE #1). **4.** ∞ In World War I era, drapery over hips sometimes made in tunic effect, or sometimes cut as part of the dress to give a PEG-TOP look.

pannier dress ∞ (pan-yehr′) Daytime dress of the late 1860s with an overskirt looped up and puffed out at back and sides. Worn over an underskirt with train trimmed with a flounce.

pannier skirt See SKIRTS.

pant An adjective used as a prefix to words when pants became accepted for the office, daytime, and evening wear in the late 1960s. Examples: pantdress, pantshift, and pantgown, pantjumper, and pantsuit.

pantalettes **1.** See UNDERGARMENTS. **2.** See PANTS.

pantaloons **1.** For men: See PETTICOAT BREECHES. **2.** See PANTS. **3.** For women: See UNDERGARMENTS: PANTALETTES.

pantdress On piece garment that has some type of pants in place of a skirt.

pantgown Full-length pantdress suitable for formal occasions popular in late 1960s and early 1970s. Sometimes made with accordion pleated pants attached to a halter top.

panties See UNDERGARMENTS.

pantile See HEADWEAR.

pantjumper See JUMPERS.

pantofle See FOOTWEAR.

PANTS

pants **1.** Clothing for the lower torso made to fit around each leg, may be any length and width; some have cuffs, some do not. In early times various styles were worn by Persian and Anglo-Saxon men, and also worn by women in China and mid-Eastern countries. Not known, however, by this name until late 19th c. when first used as a colloquial term for items worn by men and boys—now it is an all-inclusive term for all types of TROUSERS and BREECHES worn by children and adults. SLACKS (see under PANTS) for women were popular in the 1930s after Hollywood stars such as Marlene Dietrich and Katharine Hepburn wore them. They were also worn in war plants during World War II. All types of pants became very popular for women in late 1960s when pants became acceptable for business, townwear, school, and evening wear. Since that time many different styles of pants are revived periodically and a wide variety of shapes and cuts

>hip huggers

deck pants/knee pants
pedal pushers/clam-
diggers/midcalf
gaucho/calf
capri pants/ankle or
above the ankle
full length/slacks

pant lengths

in pant styles are always available to women. **2.** See UNDERGARMENTS.

accordion-pleated pants See PANTS: PARTY PANTS.

athletic pants See PANTS: SWEATPANTS.

baggy pants Pants cut fuller through hips with legs tapering and becoming narrow at ankles. Term used originally for jeans in late 1970s, adopted for all types of pants in 1980s. Also called *baggies*.

bell-bottoms **1.** Pants cut with fullness on both the outer and inner seams to give a "bell" flare at the hem. Style most generally worn by young people in late 1960s and early 1970s and revived periodically. Also called FLARES (see under PANTS). **2.** See PANTS: SAILOR PANTS.

bell bottoms #1

bib-top pants See PANTS: OVERALLS.

bleached jeans See PANTS: BLUE JEANS.

bloomers **1.** Full pants of any length that are gathered at the end of the legs. Popular for under little girls' dresses in 1920s. **2.** Black sateen pleated bloomers worn for gym and camp by women from early 20th c. to late 1920s. *Der.* Name applied in 1851 to young ladies wearing rather narrow, ankle-length pants with elastic at the bottom in imitation of costume worn by Amelia Bloomer. Shown at BLOOMER COSTUME.

blue jeans Ankle-length pants traditionally made in faded blue or indigo denim. Originally worn by farmers and workmen, pants were styled with top-stitching, two hip pockets, two side pockets, a V-shaped yoke in back, and rivets reinforcing points of strain. In the late 1960s, adapted as a general fashion with flared legs in same cut but made of many fabrics, including denim, bleached denim, printed fabrics, suede, stripes, corduroy, and even velvet. In the 1960s, **bleached jeans**, with their faded worn look, became popular, as were STONE-WASHED or acid-washed jeans in the 1980s; this process produced an uneven color.

blue jeans

In the 1970s, jeans with a small watch pocket added to carry money were accepted for school wear. Now a classic garment style, jean leg styles conform to the current mode. Also called *dungarees, Levis®, jeans, dude jeans,* and *designer jeans.* Also see PANTS: BAGGY PANTS.

boot-cut pants Refers to the width at hem of pants—cut wide enough so that pants can be pulled on over western boots with pant leg worn outside of boots.

breaker pants Straight-legged pants with zipper at side seam that shows contrasting lining when opened. May have zippered back pocket and grommet trim. *Der.* From break dancing, which requires a lot of movement.

breeches An all-inclusive term for pants reaching to below the knee, worn particularly for horseback riding. Also see BREECHES in alphabetical listing. *Der.* From word "breech," plural of Old English *broc,* "leg covering." Also see PANTS: HUNT BREECHES, RIDING BREECHES, and CANARY BREECHES.

cabin-boy breeches Tight-fitting pants laced below the knees worn for sportswear by women in the late 1940s. *Der.* After uniform worn by an employee on ocean vessel who waits on officers and passengers.

camouflage pants Pants adapted for general wear in 1980s and after that are printed with greens and browns in abstract pattern. Originally used as camouflage wear for the Army because colors blended with scenery.

canary breeches See ACTIVEWEAR: RIDING BREECHES.

capri pants (kap´-ree or kap-ree´) **1.** Tight-fitting three-quarter-length pants, with short slit on outside of leg. Worn in 1950s, revived after 2000. **2.** Tight-fitting trademarked jeans, with slit on outside of leg, called *Capri® jeans.* Worn in 1980s. *Der.* Named for Italian resort, Island of Capri, where style first became popular.

cargo pants Any pants with CARGO POCKETS (see under POCKETS).

carpenter pants Pants derived from pants traditionally worn by carpenters that not only have front and back pockets but also have a loop for a hammer and a pocket for tools on one leg.

chaps Covering for the legs worn over pants, made with legs and a front, but no seat. Originally worn by cowboys, made of leather or shearling. Adopted by women as fashion item in the late 1960s. *Der.* Shortened form of Spanish word *chaparejas,* "undressed sheepskin."

chaps

charro pants (char'-row) Wide Mexican-inspired pants in midi length, similar to GAU-CHO pants (see under PANTS). *Der.* Mexican, "rancher."

chinos Washable man's sport pants made of chino cloth, a durable close-woven khaki-colored cotton fabric. Popular in 1950s for sportswear and for schoolwear in early 1960s and after. *Der.* Adapted from Army summer uniforms made of fabric that originally was purchased in China before World War I.

choori-dars (cho-ree'-dars) Pants with full-cut top and tight-fitting legs that are extra long and worn rumpled from knee down. Worn in 1960s, increasing in popularity in 1980s. *Der.* From pants worn in India called by the same name.

citypants Term coined by fashion industry newspaper *Women's Wear Daily* in 1968 for women's trousers considered suitable for wear in town as well as at home or for sportswear. Also see SHORTS: CITYSHORTS.

clamdiggers/Clamdiggers® Trademark registered in 1946 by White Stag Manufacturing Co. for midcalf slacks and snug-fitting calf-length pants. Originating from cut-off BLUE JEANS (see under PANTS), worn while wading to dig for clams. Adopted for sportswear in 1950s. At present the trademark applies to a wide variety of apparel.

continental pants Man's trousers styled with fitted waistband and no belt. Front pockets are placed horizontally, or curved to waistband seam rather than placed in the side seams. Popular in late 1960s, the style originated in Italy.

cossacks ∞ Peg-top trousers made with double straps under the instep. Worn by men from 1814 to about 1850, these pants were derived from the full trousers worn by Cossack soldiers in the entourage of the Czar of Russia at a peace celebration in 1814.

crawlers Slacks for infants and also sizes 1–3, frequently made in bib-overall style of corduroy and other fabrics. Formerly called *creepers.*

creepers See PANTS: CRAWLERS.

cropped pants Pants cut at varying lengths between ankle and knee. The most common type was cut just below the knee. Newer versions since 1984 have been full cut, longer, and sometimes pleated into the waistband or snug-fitting.

cuffed trousers See PANTS: PRECUFFED TROUSERS.

culottes (ku-lotz') Pants of any length cut to look like a skirt. Worn from 1930s to 1940s and again in 1960s, and very popular in the 1980s and after. In 1986 some culottes were worn knee length in a pleated style, sometimes with a matching jacket. *Der.* French, *culotte,* "pants."

culottes

cut-offs See SHORTS.

Danish trousers ∞ Pants worn by young boys in 1870s that were calf-length and open at the hems. Also called *open-bottom trousers.*

deck pants Fitted pants ending below the knees; worn by men, women, and children particularly on boats in late 1950s and early 1960s.

designer jeans Jeans produced by well-known designers after blue jeans became widely worn at schools and some offices. Noted designers such as Calvin Klein and Gloria Vanderbilt produced them in higher price lines, usually attaching their names to the hip pocket and trademarking their product. Especially popular in the late 1970s.

dhoti (doe'tee) Pants with many gathers at waistband made long between the legs and tapering to ankle. *Der.* From pants worn in India called by the same name. Also see alphabetical listing.

dirndl pants (durn'-del) Culottes or pants styled with gathers at the waistline, introduced in early 1980s. Sometimes made in seven-eighths length with large pockets in side seams and decorative braided belt.

drain-pipe trousers Pants with legs cut straight, having the same diameter for the length of the garment, and with no crease.

drawstring pants Pull-on pants, usually of cotton, with drawstring at top. A unisex fashion of the late 1960s. Now a classic style. Also called *unisex pants.*

drop-front Descriptive of pants fastened by two buttoned plackets on either side of the center front allowing the front panel to drop down when unbuttoned. Used frequently on JODH-PURS, other RIDING BREECHES (see under ACTIVEWEAR), and in the past on U.S. Navy seamen's pants. An earlier version of this section of pants was call the FALL.

ducks ∞ Trousers worn by men in late 19th c. made of DUCK fabric. Also see PANTS: WHITE DUCKS.

dude jeans Similar to WESTERN PANTS (see under PANTS). Also see PANTS: BLUE JEANS.

dungarees Work pants or overalls named for the coarse blue fabric from which they are made. Also see PANTS: BLUE JEANS.

eelskin masher trousers ∞ Very tight trousers worn in mid-1880s by MASHERS, OR DANDIES. *Der.* Literally, "as tight as an eel's skin."

elephant-leg pants Trousers with extremely wide legs similar to HARLOW PANTS (see under PANTS). Introduced in late 1960s.

fatigues **1.** Pants of tough fabric worn by U.S. Army for work details. Also called *field pants.* **2.** Coveralls for work worn by Army men and WACS during World War II, sometimes made in olive drab or camouflage colors.

field pants See FATIGUES #1.

flares **1.** See PANTS: BELL-BOTTOMS. **2.** Pants with slight flare at hem.

flat front pants Pants that are made without pleats or fullness in the front.

French bottoms ∞ 19th-c. term for men's trousers flaring at the hems.

frontier pants See PANTS: WESTERN PANTS.

gaucho pants (gow'-cho) Wide calf-length women's pants, frequently made of leather, copied from pants worn by Spanish as a part of Andalusian riding suit and adapted by South American cowboys; a fashion in the late 1960s. *Der.* Spanish, "cow-boy" of Argentina, Chile, and Uruguay. Shown at GAUCHO LOOK.

harem knickers Knee-length bouffant harem pants similar to BLOOMERS (see under PANTS), introduced in late 1960s.

harem pants Bouffant pants gathered into bands at the ankles, popular at-home fashion of late 1960s. *Der.* Copied from Near Eastern styles.

harem pants

harlow pants Trousers wide from hips to hem, introduced in late 1960s. *Der.* Copied from slacks worn in 1930s by Jean Harlow, a popular film star.

high-rise pants Pants that extend to above the waistline, as opposed to HIP-HUGGERS.

hip-huggers Low-slung pants of any style starting below the normal waistline, usually with belt resting on hip bones. First popular in mid-1960s. Also called *hipsters* and *low-slung pants.*

hipsters See PANTS: HIP-HUGGERS.

howling bags ∞ Slang term for men's trousers made of colorful patterned fabrics worn in mid-19th c.

hunt breeches Riding breeches with drop front, legs cut wide from thighs to hips and tight at knees. Usually made in canary or tan cavalry twill with buckskin patches at inside of knees.

ivy league pants Type of men's trousers with "skinny" legs, usually without cuffs, cut somewhat shorter in length. Worn first by college men and introduced for general wear in 1950s. *Der.* From the group of eastern colleges called "the Ivy League."

jack tar trousers ∞ Man's trousers, close-fitting at knees, flaring widely around ankles, and worn for yachting in 1880s. *Der.* "a sailor."

jeans See PANTS: BLUE JEANS.

jockey pants See ACTIVEWEAR.

jodhpurs See ACTIVEWEAR.

knee pants See PANTS: KNICKERS.

knickers **1.** Pants of varying widths fastened below knee with buttons, buckles, or elastic; popular for boys in early 20th c. for school. Reintroduced in late 1960s for women and men. Worn for hiking and cross country skiing. **2.** See UNDERGARMENTS. *Der.* shortened form of word *knickerbockers.* Also called *knee pants.* Also see KNICKERS and KNICKERBOCKERS in the alphabetical listing.

leggings **1.** Outer pants for children worn in cold weather and usually matched to a coat making a leggings set. Made in any of several styles: with tight-fitting legs, or sometimes cut like JODHPURS (see under ACTIVEWEAR), or full to the ankle where they are held by a knitted band. Also spelled *leggins.* **2.** Ankle-length skintight pants worn in thin Lycra spandex knit fabrics. Originally worn by dancers and entertainers in brilliant colors or in regular knits with LEOTARDS (see under ACTIVEWEAR) in place of tights for exercising. Adopted by women for general wear in place of pants after the 1980s. Some have stirrup straps (see PANTS: STIRRUP PANTS) at foot.

Levis® Trademark for type of DUNGAREES or BLUE JEANS (see under PANTS). Distinguishing characteristics are a label stitched to the outside on one hip pocket, also the placing of rivets at places of most strain, and patch pockets placed at hips. First made out of cloth used for sails—later DENIM was used—by Levi Strauss in California for miners prospecting for gold in 1840s. A distinctly American fashion, it developed into a multimillion-dollar industry, with many pairs exported yearly. The Costume Institute of the Metropolitan Museum in New York and the Smithsonian Institution, Washington, D.C., have included Levis in their *Americana collection.* The trademark is also used for a wide variety of casual apparel.

low-slung pants See PANTS: HIP-HUGGERS.

luau pants (loo-ow´) Man's calf-length pants styled in colorful Hawaiian print. *Der.* From Hawaiian luau parties, where this type of pants were first worn.

maternity pants Pants worn by expectant mothers with either a cut-out section at top center front or a section of stretch fabric inserted over the abdomen.

moschettos ∞ (mos-ket´-tos) Pants similar to men's pantaloons (see PANTS: PANTALOONS #2)

of early 19th c. but fitted to leg and worn over a boot like GAITER (see under FOOTWEAR).

mousers Women's leather stocking pants reaching to waist, made of shiny wet-look leather with attached chunky-type shoes. Introduced by Mary Quant, British designer, in 1969.

overalls Pants with a bib top and suspender straps over the shoulders that cross in back. Traditionally worn by farmers in blue denim. House painters and carpenters wore them in natural or white. See PANTS: PAINTER'S PANTS. Also worn by railroad workers in striped fabrics. In late 1960s, styled in many fabrics for all occasions and worn by adults and children. Also called *bib-top pants* and *suspender pants.* **Pleated overalls** introduced in early 1980s are similar in style but cut all in one piece in front with much fullness at top, which was pleated into a band. *Der.* So called because originally worn over clothing.

overalls

Oxford bags Men's long trousers with very wide cuffed legs. Popular in the 1920s, beginning at Oxford University in England, and revived for men and women in early 1970s.

painter's pants **1.** Natural-colored or white pants styled with one or more loops on legs to hold brushes, originally worn by house painters. Adapted as a fashion item in late 1970s and worn for school and sportswear. In 1980 and after, also made in colors. **2.** See OVERALLS.

Oxford bags
1920s

pajamas See SLEEPWEAR AND LOUNGEWEAR.

palazzo pants (pah-latz´-zoh) Women's long, wide pajamas or culottes with voluminous flared legs and gathered waist. Worn for lounging or evening dress in the late 1960s and early 1970s.

pantaloons **1.** See PETTICOAT BREECHES. **2.** ∞ From 1790 to about 1850, tight-fitting pants that ending at calf until 1817. Later they extended to ankles, with strap under the instep. Known as tights about 1840. **3.** For women: See UNDERGARMENTS.

P

parachute pants Straight-legged pants with zipper (of about 6″) from hem up leg to give tight fit at ankles. Three zip pockets are placed at side of leg, and another zip pocket on hip.

party pants Name adopted in late 1960s for women's pants and pajamas made in more elaborate fabrics and sometimes accordion-pleated. Styled to wear for dining and dancing in the evening.

pedal pushers Below-the-knee straight-cut women's pants, often cuffed. Popular during World War II for bicycling; reintroduced in 1980s.

peg-top pants **1.** Pants pleated at the waistband and narrow at the ankles. **2.** ∞ Man's trousers wide and pleated at top, tapered on lower leg, and close fitting at ankles. Popular from 1857 to 1865 and revived in 1892.

Petersham cossacks ∞ Trousers worn by men from 1814, modified in 1820s, and worn into the 1830s. Very bouffant and worn spread out over the foot, drawn in with ribbon tied in bows on outside of leg, and worn with flounces at ankles. Also called *Petersham trousers. Der.* Named for Viscount Charles Petersham.

pleated overalls See OVERALLS.

plain-front pants Trousers without pleats at the waistband so that the front is smoothly fitted.

pleated-front pants Trousers with pleats at waistband in front, giving more fullness through the hips.

plain-front pants

plus fours Full baggy knickers worn for golf and other sports in the 1920s. They became stylish after they were worn by DUKE OF WINDSOR, then Prince of Wales. Generally combined with patterned wool socks and BROGUES (see FOOTWEAR). Reintroduced for men in late 1960s. *Der.* When first introduced, these knickers were 4 inches longer than usual knicker length. See KNICKERBOCKERS.

plus fours 1920s

pre-cuffed trousers Men's trousers sold in various lengths, e.g., 27″, 29″, and 31″ for inside seam, with cuff already finished. As contrasted with trousers bought with unfinished hems, tailored to length, and finished in retail store workroom.

proportioned pants Men's or women's pants in which customers are given a choice among three or four different named pant lengths. The names and specific lengths will vary somewhat from manufacturer to manufacturer. Most men's pants are sold by waist measurement and inseam length, but some may be designated as short, regular, or long. Women's pants are more likely to be sold by proportion such as petite, average, and tall sizes.

pull-on pants Stretch pants that do not have a placket but with an elasticized waistband.

push-up jeans JEANS (see PANTS) made with spandex that lift and shape the buttocks of the wearer.

railroad trousers ∞ Term for men's trousers with stripes, horizontal or vertical, worn from late 1830s to 1850.

riding breeches See ACTIVEWEAR.

sailor pants Worn by sailors in navy blue for winter and white for summer. Now made in conventional style with zip-closing. Originally made in bell-bottom style with drop-front closing having thirteen buttons for the thirteen original states. Seven buttons went across horizontally with three additional buttons extending vertically at each side. Also called *bell-bottoms.*

see-through pants Women's pants of sheer fabric or lace worn over bikini pants—a style of the late 1960s.

seven-eighths pants Any style pants coming to just below the calf of the leg.

shorts See separate category: SHORTS.

show breeches See ACTIVEWEAR: HUNT BREECHES.

skant Women's full-length pants that have a short, skirtlike layer, open at the side, that is attached at the waist.

ski pants See ACTIVEWEAR.

skort See SKIRTS.

slacks Synonym for *pants.* Term is usually applied to loose-cut casual pants, not part of a suit. In the 1930s, when women first began wearing pants for leisure activities, these garments were generally called slacks rather than pants.

slim jeans   Blue jeans cut with very narrow legs, frequently made of stretch denim worn literally "skintight."

spring-bottom trousers   ∞ Trousers of 1870s and 1880s that flare at the ankles.

stirrup pants   Pants usually made in a narrow style having an extension under the instep that can be worn inside or under the shoe.

stovepipe pants   Tight-fitting pants with narrow legs the same width from knees down. Worn by men from 1880 until 1920, reintroduced in mid-1960s, popular in 1980s, and revived periodically.

straight-cut pants   Pants straight cut from knee down. See PANTS: STOVEPIPE PANTS.

strapped trousers   ∞ Man's trousers fashionable from 1820s to 1850s made with one or two straps under the instep.

stretch pants   Pants, made from knitted stretch fabric that conform closely to the body, very popular from 1950s to mid-1960s. In 1980s popular for jeans made of stretch denim.

surfers   Close-fitting pants extending to knee, popular in early 1960s. *Der.* Introduced for beachwear and surfboard riding in California.

suspender pants   **1.** See OVERALLS. **2.** Children's pull-on pants with straps made of same fabric as pants.

sweatpants   Pants of cotton knit with fleece backing to absorb moisture. Worn by athletes before and after exercising. Also called *warm-up pants.*

tapered pants   Full-length pants with legs becoming narrower toward the ankle, popular in early 1960s and 1980s and periodically since, depending on whether wider or narrower pants are in fashion.

tights   **1.** See HOSIERY and UNDERGARMENTS. **2.** See PANTS: PANTALOONS.

toreador pants (tor-ay-ah-door´)   Tight-fitting below-the-knee pants patterned after those worn by Spanish bullfighters, popular for women in late 1950s and early 1960s.

trousers   Synonym for all full-length pants. The word origin is uncertain, probably from an Irish word for a garment similar to BREECHES. By the 17th c., seems to have been used as protective garment over breeches and in the 18th and 19th c. for loose-fitting pants worn particularly by sailors, soldiers, and town workers. By the 19th c. came to have the modern meaning of pants. *Der.* From *trouse,* a variation of *trews.*

turnip pants   ∞ Bicycling knickers that could be turned down to make full-length pants worn in 1890s.

turn-ups   ∞ British term for man's cuffed trousers first worn in House of Commons in 1893.

tuxedo pants   **1.** Men: Conventional black trousers, usually with narrow satin stripe down each side, worn with TUXEDO JACKET (see under COATS AND JACKETS) and CUMMERBUND (see under BELTS) for semiformal wear. **2.** Women: Pants made with gathers at waistline, worn with a cummerbund, and introduced in 1980s.

unisex pants   See PANTS: DRAWSTRING PANTS.

warmup pants   See PANTS: SWEATPANTS and ACTIVEWEAR: WARMUP #2.

western pants   Low-waisted, slim-fitting pants made of denim or gabardine, characterized by double-stitched seams and rivets placed at points of strain. Often with pockets opening at both top and side, producing right-angle front flaps that are buttoned at the corners. Also see PANTS: BLUE JEANS. Worn originally by ranchers and cowboys in American West. Popular for general wear since mid-1960s. Also called *dude jeans* and *frontier pants.*

white flannels   Slacks made of white wool, especially flannel, worn by men in 1980s. Reminiscent of those worn from 1890s through 1930s for sportswear with striped blazer and straw hat.

work pants   Durable full-length trousers with patches at knees, triple-stitched main seams, and rivets at points of strain. Worn by auto mechanics and other workmen. Styled with watch pocket, tool pockets on legs, and hammer loop. Made of durable washable fabric.

zippered pants Straight-legged pants with one zipper from waist to ankle and second zipper from waist to upper thigh on each leg. Snap tabs hold pants tightly at ankle.

---

pants boot See FOOTWEAR.

pantshift Simple pantdress cut like a shift dress—made with pants instead of a skirt.

pants liner See UNDERGARMENTS.

pants skirt See SKIRTS.

pantsuit Term introduced in mid-1960s for woman's suit with pants instead of a skirt, styled for town wear and evening wear. Some are of traditional styling with jackets. Others are composed of a thigh-length tunic and pants. Some formal pantsuits are styled in elaborate fabrics. Also made with matching vest or coat, and with various types of pants including knickers.

pantsuit

panty See UNDERGARMENTS: PANTIES.

panty dress Girl's dress with matching bloomers, worn in the 1920s. Also called *bloomer dress*.

panty foundation See UNDERGARMENTS.

panty girdle See UNDERGARMENTS: GIRDLE.

pantyhose See Hosiery.

pantyslip See UNDERGARMENTS.

pantywaist See UNDERGARMENTS.

paper bag waistline See WAISTLINES.

paper-doll dress/look/style Used from 1950 to 1960, particularly for dresses designed by Anne Fogarty that had tight bodies, tight waistlines, and very bouffant skirts held out with nylon net and crinoline petticoats. *Der.* From the full-skirted paper dolls children played with in the 1930s.

paper dress Classification of dresses made of various types of disposable paper or nonwoven fabrics similar to paper, a fad of c. 1968. Worn for parties and the beach, some were hand-painted and very expensive; others were inexpensive and imprinted with funny gimmicks (e.g., Yellow Pages of telephone book, a Heinz soup can, etc.). Revived in 1986 as wedding dress by Susan Lane made of a nonwoven fabric that resembles paper, selling for $140.00. Also see FOIL DRESS.

paper pattern Dress pattern made in various sizes and sold by pattern companies such as *Vogue, Butterick, McCalls,* and *Simplicity* to individuals for home sewing. First paper patterns were not made in sizes, but offered to subscribers of magazines such as *Harper's Bazaar* in supplements. Patterns for eighteen garments were sometimes placed on one large sheet of paper. Pieces for each pattern were made with different types of lines (e.g., ... or ....). To make a pattern, women copied these lines with a tracing wheel on tracing paper and enlarged the pattern to the proper size. Ebeneezer Butterick invented patterns in various sizes in 1872. These were sold through fashion magazines such as *The Delineator* and *Demorest's Magazine.*

paper taffeta † Crisp lightweight taffeta fabric.

papier-mâché/paper-mâché (pap′-yeh mah-shay′/pay′-per mah-shay′) Lightweight material molded of combination of tissue paper, bits of newspaper, or paper pulp fastened together with glue or various binders. May be painted and shellacked. Used for jewelry, particularly bracelets, beads, and pins in late 1960s. *Der.* French, "chewed paper."

papillion See HEADWEAR: BONNET À BEC.

papillon collar See NECKLINES AND COLLARS.

papillotte comb See HAIR ACCESSORIES.

Paquin * See APPENDIX/DESIGNERS.

parachute hat See HEADWEAR: BALLOON HAT.

parachute pants See PANTS.

parachute sleeve See SHOULDERS AND SLEEVES.

paradise feather See FEATHERS: BIRD OF PARADISE.

parament (pah-rah′-ment) **1.** ∞ Early term for a FACING (see under CLOTHING CONSTRUCTION DETAILS). **2.** See CUFFS. **3.** ∞ Trimming used on GOWN À LA FRANÇAISE in 18th c., usually a long decorated band, wider at hem. **4.** Synonym for an ornamental ecclesicastical vestment.

parasol See introduction to UMBRELLAS AND PARASOLS.

parasol a la Pompadour See UMBRELLAS AND PARASOLS: MARQUISE.

parasol fan See FANS: COCKADE FAN.

parasol skirt See SKIRTS.

parchment calves See FALSE CALVES.

pardessus See COATS AND JACKETS.

pareo (pah-ray'-o) Rectangular piece of colored printed cloth worn as a skirt or loincloth as the principal item of clothing for men and women of Polynesia. Adaptations popular in the United States as beach fashion in 1950s and after. Also called *lava-lava*.

pareo

Paris, point de See LACES.

parka See COATS AND JACKETS.

Parnis, Mollie * See APPENDIX/ DESIGNERS.

parti-colored Bicolored garment divided vertically with each side made of a different color—or striped on one side, plain on the other. Popular from mid-14th to mid-15th c. for hose and clothing. When hose were different colors, they might be called *pied hose*. Synonym: *mi-parti*.

parti-colored clothing

partlet/parlet ∞ (part'-let) **1.** Decorative covering for upper part of chest and neck showing under low-cut doublet worn by men in first half of 16th c. **2.** Fill-in for low-cut *bodice* worn by women in 16th and 17th c. Also called *chemisette* and *tucker*.

party Adjective describing clothes made to be suitable for parties. See SLEEPWEAR AND LOUNGEWEAR: PARTY PAJAMAS and PANTS: PARTY PANTS.

party plan Sale of apparel to invited customers at a party in the home of a host or hostess. Also called *home party*.

parure See JEWELRY.

pashm See CAPES, CLOAKS, AND SHAWLS: CASHMERE SHAWL.

pashmina † (pash-mee'-nah) Synonym for CASHMERE used in the 1990s and after to promote fine quality cashmere apparel.

passé/passé de mode (pass-ay') French term, "out of fashion," "unfashionable." Generally used in English simply as *passé*.

passement See LACES.

passementerie (pas-mahn'-tree) Trimmings, e.g., heavy embroideries, braid, tinsel, beads, lace, and gimp, used as edging in 19th c.

paste See JEWELRY.

paste setting See GEMS, GEM CUTS, AND SETTINGS.

pasties See UNDERGARMENTS.

patch **1.** Extra piece of fabric sewed or bonded by heat to clothing for mending a tear or for decorative effect (e.g., suede elbow patches on sweaters and knee patches on blue jeans). **2.** Insignia sewed to sleeve of uniform to indicate rank. **3.** From 1590s to end of 18th c., a decorative cutout of black silk or velvet shaped like moon, star, etc., applied to the face. Placement of patch denoted the wearer's mood (e.g., the "coquette" was placed on the lip); the "roguish" was placed on the nose; the "impassioned" was placed at the corner of the eye. From 1702 to 1714 in England the patch indicated the political party of the wearer. Also called *assasin, beauty spot,* or *mouche*. **4.** Flesh-colored pieces of cotton, affixed to the face with adhesive, used to cover blemishes in early 20th c., were known as *court plasters. Der.* From cutouts of black silk or velvet adhered to the face by ladies of the English and French courts beginning in late 17th c.

patches #3
17th c.

patch box Small box carried by women in 17th c. to hold various types of decorative cutouts called patches (see PATCH #3) that were applied to face.

patch pocket See POCKETS.

patchwork A method of sewing small pieces of various colors and patterns together to form a fabric or quilt.

patchwork dress/patchwork look Small pieces of various colored prints and plain colors sewed together to make the fabric from which dress or other garment is cut. Became high fashion when introduced by Saint Laurent in 1969. Old antique American patchwork quilts were found and used to make coats and skirts. Also featured in leather of different colors and patterns in 1980s. From this style, printed fabrics evolved that were made to have the appearance of actual patchwork. *Der.* From *patchwork quilt*—a country craft practiced in the United States since colonial days.

patchwork look

patchwork print See PRINTS, STRIPES, AND CHECKS.

patent Registration of an idea, product, or process with the U.S. patent office so that it is excluded from use by others for a period of 17 years. A description of the invention is published and once the patent expires, it becomes part of the public domain.

patent leather See LEATHERS.

patio dress Gay floral or abstract printed shift suitable for wearing at a backyard barbecue or at the beach.

patlet See PARTLET.

Patou, Jean * See APPENDIX/DESIGNERS.

patrol jacket See COATS AND JACKETS.

patte ∞ (pat) Earliest form of lapel, resembling a narrow collar with tabs, worn on GARNACHE in 13th and 14th c. Also called *paw*.

patten See FOOTWEAR.

pattern book Large volume issued regularly (and updated) by the publisher of paper patterns for home sewers showing all of the designs available. Available where patterns are sold for convenience of customers. Also called *counter book*.

pattern design system (PDS) Computer system used to create and store new garment and pattern styles.

pattern grading Creating a set of pattern pieces for each of the sizes listed on the garment specification sheet from the production pattern pieces made in the sample size for a style.

patterned hose See HOSIERY.

pauldron See ARMOR.

paultock See PALTOCK.

pavé See GEMS, GEM CUTS, AND SETTINGS.

pavilion See GEMS, GEM CUTS, AND SETTINGS.

paw 1. See PATTE. 2. See FURS.

paw crosses See FURS: CROSSES.

peace ring See JEWELRY.

peace symbol Circle or oval enclosing a vertical staff with two bars projecting at about a 60° angle down to left and right from center of staff. Introduced in 1960s by opponents of U.S. involvement in Vietnam War. Used for rings and medallions.

peacock feather See FEATHERS.

peacock revolution Used in 1967 to describe radical changes in men's wear from the conventional type of clothing (i.e., the gray flannel three-button suit worn with buttoned-down shirt and necktie) to clothing of a more relaxed, more creative, unconventional type. New styles accepted for men's wear included turtleneck knit shirts, Nehru jackets, flared pants, Edwardian coats, medallion necklaces, rings, perfumes, wider color ranges, and less conservative hairstyles.

peacock revolution

pea jacket/coat See COATS AND JACKETS.

peaked lapel See NECKLINES AND COLLARS: LAPEL.

peaked shoe See FOOTWEAR: CRAKOW.

pear cut See GEMS, GEM CUTS, AND SETTINGS.

pearl See GEMS, GEM CUTS, AND SETTINGS.

pearl beads See JEWELRY.

pearl button See CLOSURES.

pearl dress Novelty dress adapted from Oriental fashion consisting of draped strands of pearls at top and long hanging strands for the skirt, worn over a body stocking. Introduced by a jewelry firm Richelieu Pearls and designed by Bill Smith in 1969.

peasant bodice ∞ Woman's bodice of mid-1880s worn over a blouse. It laced up the front to the bustline and had straps extending over outermost edge of shoulder.

peasant dress/peasant look Apparel derived from or inspired by European peasant dresses that were originally costumes worn for festive occasions by peasants in various countries. Although each region had its own distinctive style, peasant dress came to be thought of as having full skirts gathered at the waist, full puffed-sleeves, and drawstring neckline trimmed with embroidery. Sometimes an apron or black-laced CORSELET (see BELTS) was added. See BLOUSES AND TOPS: PEASANT BLOUSE, COATS AND JACKETS: PEASANT COAT, NECKLINES AND COLLARS: PEASANT NECKLINE, SHOULDERS AND SLEEVES: PEASANT SLEEVE, and SKIRTS: PEASANT SKIRT.

peascod-bellied doublet See DOUBLET.

peau de soie † (po de swah′) Heavyweight satin with a fine filling ribbed effect on the reverse side made of silk or manufactured fibers. Piece-dyed and given a dull luster—better grades are reversible. Used for shoes, dresses, evening gowns, and wedding dresses. *Der.* French, "skin of silk."

pebbled finish   See LEATHERS.

peccary   See LEATHERS.

pedal pushers   See PANTS.

pediment headdress   See HEADWEAR: ENGLISH HOOD.

pedlar dolls   See MODEL DOLLS.

Pedlar, Sylvia   *   See APPENDIX/DESIGNERS.

Peds®   See HOSIERY.

peekaboo earrings   See JEWELRY.

peekaboo waist   See BLOUSES AND TOPS.

Peggy collar   See NECKLINES AND COLLARS.

peg-top   Apparel with fullness through hips that tapers to hem. See PANTS: PEG-TOP TROUSERS, SHOULDERS AND SLEEVES: PEG-TOP SLEEVE, and SKIRTS: PEG-TOP SKIRT.

peigne Josephine   See HAIR ACCESSORIES.

peignoir   See SLEEPWEAR AND LOUNGEWEAR.

pelerine   See CAPES, CLOAKS, AND SHAWLS.

pelisse   See COATS AND JACKETS.

pelisse-robe   ∞ (pe-leese')   Daytime dress in coat style, worn from about 1817 to 1840, fastened down the front with ribbon bows or with hidden hooks and eyes.

pellice   See COATS AND JACKETS: PELISSE.

pellison   ∞ (pel'-iss-ohn)   Fur-lined outer tunic or gown for men and women worn throughout 14th to 16th c. Also called *pilch.*

Pellon®   A nonwoven fabric used for interlining and made by fusing natural fibers and man-made fibers together. Retains its shape through laundering and dry cleaning. Used as interlining in collars and facings.

pelt   See FURS: PELT.

peltry   See FURS: PELT.

pembroke paletot   See COATS AND JACKETS.

penang lawyer   See CANES.

penannular brooch   ∞ A moveable pin set on a ring that was used to fasten clothing from 11th through 13th c.

pencil pocket   See POCKETS.

pencil stripe   See PRINTS, STRIPES, AND CHECKS.

pendant   An ornament that hangs or dangles. See JEWELRY and WATCHES.

pendant cuff   See CUFFS.

pendicle   See JEWELRY.

penny loafer   See FOOTWEAR: LOAFER.

pen shank shoe   See FOOTWEAR.

pentes   See SKIRTS.

peplos   See CHITON.

peplum (pep'-lum)   Extension of bodice of dress that comes below waistline, sometimes pleated, sometimes flared. Can be made in one piece with bodice, cut separately and joined to bodice by a seam, or attached to a belt. Popular in mid-1860s, 1890s, and revived periodically in the 20th c. Also see BLOUSES AND TOPS: PEPLUM BLOUSE.

peplum

peplum basque   ∞ (bask)   Woman's dress of mid-1860s with peplum attached to belt. Peplum was usually short in back and front with long hanging ends at sides.

peplum bodice   ∞ Bodice of evening dress, worn in 1870s, cut with long side panels draped to form *panniers* at hips.

peplum dolman   See COATS AND JACKETS: DOLMAN.

peplum dress   One- or two-piece dress either fitted or belted at waistline with short ruffle or circular-cut piece of fabric extending below waistline. Popular in 1930s, 1960s, and revived in 1980s.

peplum rotonde   See CAPES, CLOAKS, AND SHAWLS.

percale   † Plain-weave, lightweight fabric made in a great variety of qualities. Originally cotton, better qualities now use blended yarns of polyester staple with the cotton. Finest qualities are high count and made with combed yarns. Other percales are of low count, made of carded yarns, and sized to add body to the fabric. All types may be dyed or printed.

perdita chemise   ∞ (per-dee'-tah shem-ees')   British term for daytime dress of 1873 made with close-fitting bodice and V-neck with large falling collar, sometimes double. Also had long tight sleeves, buttons, or ribbon ties down front, and sash at waist tied with long ends in back. Also called *chemise gown. Der.* Named after Perdita Robinson, an actress.

Peretti, Elsa   *   See APPENDIX/DESIGNERS.

perfecto jacket   See COATS AND JACKETS.

perfs/perforations See FOOTWEAR: PERFORATIONS.

perfume ring See JEWELRY.

peridot See GEMS, GEM CUTS, AND SETTINGS.

periodic inventory The counting of merchandise at specified time periods. Apparel retailers often do these counts twice a year, in July and January.

periwig See WIGS AND HAIRPIECES.

permanent/permanent wave See HAIRSTYLES.

permanent markdown See MARKDOWN.

permanent press See DURABLE PRESS.

perpetual inventory A continuous record of incoming and outgoing merchandise. See POINT OF SALE.

perruque á l'enfant See WIGS AND HAIRPIECES.

perruquier ∞ (per-uke'-yay) Person who arranged and set wigs (18th c.).

Persian lamb See FURS.

Persian paw See FURS.

Persians See LEATHERS.

personalized garments Apparel items produced in single or limited quantities that are decorated with photographs or other applied designs unique to the person or organization for whom they are made.

personal shopper A retail store employee in an upscale store who works with individual customers in assisting them to select apparel.

peruke See WIGS AND HAIRPIECES: PERIWIG.

Peruvian hat See HEADWEAR.

petal collar See NECKLINES AND COLLARS.

petal hem See CLOTHING CONSTRUCTION DETAILS.

petal sleeve See SHOULDERS AND SLEEVES.

petasus See HEADWEAR.

petenlair/pet-en-l'air ∞ (pet'-en-lair) Dress worn by women from 1745 to 1770s, made with separate thigh-length bodice with fitted STOMACHER front, full back, and elbow-length sleeves. Worn with long petticoat to make a dress. Also called *French jacket*.

Peter Pan collar See NECKLINES AND COLLARS.

Peter Pan hat See HEADWEAR.

Peter Thomson dress ∞ One-piece dress with MIDDY COLLAR (see under NECKLINES AND COLLARS) and box pleats from yoke to hem. Worn as uniform by many schoolchildren and older girls (through college) from 1900 to 1920. *Der.* Named for designer Peter Thomson, who was once a tailor for the Navy.

petersham ∞ Strip of firmly woven ribbon placed in the interior of a woman's bodice that fastened around her waist in order to keep the bodice from shifting while it was worn. First used about 1870. Often had the name of the designer or manufacturing firm woven into the ribbon.

petersham belt on the interior of a dress c. 1880

Petersham cossacks See PANTS.

Petersham frock coat See COATS AND JACKETS.

Petersham greatcoat See COATS AND JACKETS.

Petersham, Viscount Charles (1780–1851) Fashionable figure from Regency period to 1850, classified between an eccentric and a true DANDY, for whom various items of men's clothing and fabrics were named (e.g., Petersham cossacks, Petersham frock coat, and Petersham greatcoat).

petit casaque See POLONAISE.

petite **1.** Size range for women who are below average height—usually sized from 6 to 16. Junior petite sizes for short-waisted women run from 5 to 15. **2.** Smallest size, along with *small, medium,* and *large* for pantyhose, bodysuits, and nightgowns. Abbreviated P.

petit point See EMBROIDERIES AND SEWING STITCHES.

petits bonshommes ∞ (peh'-tee bon-zohm') Bands of fabric with several ruffles—often of lace—used to edge sleeves of gown (e.g., gown à la française from early 1720s to 1780s).

petti Prefix used to mean little or small.

pettibockers See UNDERGARMENTS.

petticoat **1.** See UNDERGARMENTS. **2.** ∞ Term used in 17th and 18th c. for the skirt of the dress, not the underskirt. **3.** ∞ Waist-length underdoublet worn by men from last half of 15th to end of 16th c. Also called a *waistcoat.*

petticoat bodice See UNDERGARMENTS.

petticoat breeches A knee-length divided skirt, similar to modern CULOTTES, cut so full that it looked like a skirt. Fashionable court fashion for men in England and France in 1660s and 1670s, made pleated or

petticoat breeches and cannons c. 1660

P

gathered to waistband. Trimmed with ribbon loops at waistband and near hem on sides and sometimes worn with CANNONS. Worn as livery for "running footmen" until mid-18th c. Also called *Rhinegraves.*

petticulottes See UNDERGARMENTS.

pettipants See UNDERGARMENTS.

pettiskirt See UNDERGARMENTS: PETTICOAT.

pettiskirt brief See UNDERGARMENTS.

petti-slip See UNDERGARMENTS.

pheasant feather See FEATHERS.

Philippine embroidery See EMBROIDERIES AND SEWING STITCHES.

photographic print See PRINTS, STRIPES, AND CHECKS.

Phrygian cap See HEADWEAR.

physical wig See WIGS AND HAIRPIECES.

piano shawl See CAPES, CLOAKS, AND SHAWLS.

pianta bag See HANDBAGS AND RELATED ACCESSORIES.

Picadill/Piccadilly See PICKADIL.

Piccadilly collar See NECKLINES AND COLLARS.

pick See FILLING.

pick-a-devant See BEARD.

pickadil ∞ Notched edge on sleeve, bodice front, or neck opening worn from late 16th through early 17th c. Also spelled *piccadill, pickardil, Piccadilly. Der.* From Piccadilly, a street in London.

pickelhaube See HEADWEAR.

picot (pee'-ko) **1.** A row of small loops woven along selvage of ribbon or a part of the edge design on lace. **2.** Machine-made edge on fabrics produced by cutting through center of *hem-stitching,* each edge becoming a picot edge. See HEMSTITCH, under EMBROIDERIES AND SEWING STITCHES. **3.** Run-resistant loops on edge of the welt (see WELT #2) in hosiery. **4.** See CLOTHING CONSTRUCTION DETAILS: PICOT HEM.

picot stitching See EMBROIDERIES AND SEWING STITCHES.

picture hat See HEADWEAR.

piece goods † Fabric sold by the yard. Piece-good departments in retail stores sell fabrics by the yard to customers for home sewing. In the early days of retailing, few ready-made dresses were sold, so this department was one of the largest in the store. Also called *yard goods.*

pied hose See PARTICOLORED.

Piedmont gown See SACK #1.

pierced earrings See JEWELRY.

pierced-look earrings See JEWELRY.

piercing See JEWELRY: BODY-PIERCING.

Pierpont collar See NECKLINES AND COLLARS.

Pierrot ∞ (pee-ehr-oh') Close-fitting, low-necked bodice, extending to slightly below the waist worn with a matching flounced skirt from 1780s to 1790s.

Pierrot cape See CAPES, CLOAKS, AND SHAWLS.

Pierrot collar See NECKLINES AND COLLARS.

Pierrot costume (pee-ehr-oh') Clown suit worn by the comedy character in French pantomime called *Pierrot* (Little Peter) and interpreted by the Italian clown *Pagliacci* in Leoncavallo's opera. Face is whitened, the suit loose and baggy similar to clown suit, most often white with large buttons or pompons on the jacket front. Usually worn with slippers with pompons and tall hat.

Pierrot costume

pigeon-wings See WIGS AND HAIRPIECES.

pigskin See LEATHERS.

pigtails See HAIRSTYLES.

pigtail wig See WIGS AND HAIRPIECES.

Piguet, Robert ∗ See APPENDIX/DESIGNERS.

piked shoe See FOOTWEAR: CRAKOW.

pilch 1. ∞ Close fitting fur-lined outer gown worn by men and women from 14th to 16th c. in winter; later worn by clergy in drafty churches. **2.** See PELLISON.

pile † Cut or uncut loops of yarns that stand erect on fabric to form all or part of the fabric surface. Either lengthwise or crosswise yarns can be used to produce this thick soft surface. May be uncut as in *terry cloth* or cut as in VELVET, VELVETEEN, and CORDUROY.

pileolus See CLERICAL DRESS.

pileus See HEADWEAR.

Pilgrim collar See NECKLINES AND COLLARS.

pillbox hat See HEADWEAR.

pilleolus See CLERICAL DRESS: PILEOLUS.

pilleus See HEADWEAR: PILEUS.

pilling † Tendency of woven fabrics and knits, especially wool and synthetic fibers, to form surface nubs or bunches of fibers from rubbing during normal wear and washing. Pilling is caused by loosely twisted yarns unwinding and interlocking with each other.

pillow lace See introduction to LACES.

pillow-slip dress Straight-cut CHEMISE DRESS of 1920s, usually short in length with short *kimono* sleeves.

pilos See HEADWEAR.

pilot coat See COATS AND JACKETS: PEA JACKET.

pilot shirt See SHIRTS: EPAULET SHIRT.

pilot's suit ∞ Early woman's two-piece aviatrix suit of 1912 made with knee-length knickers, fitted blouse with long full sleeves at wrist, and high neckline with attached hood. Worn with bulky knee-length socks, high laced boots, and gauntlet gloves. Costume was designed by Harriet Quimby, who, on April 14, 1912, was the first woman to fly across the English Channel.

pima cotton † Fine quality long-staple cotton raised in Arizona, Texas, New Mexico, and California, a variety of American-Egyptian cotton. *Der.* From Pima County, Arizona.

pin **1.** See STRAIGHT PIN. **2.** See JEWELRY.

pinafore

pinafore Sleeveless garment like an apron worn over dress by women and children since last half of 19th c. as protection against soiling. See APRONS.

pinafore dress Dress worn with separate bib-top apron tied in back popular for children. First worn in 1870s and intermittently since. *Der.* Copied from apron worn by children. Also called *Alice in Wonderland* or *apron dress.*

pinafore heel See FOOTWEAR.

pinafore jumper See JUMPERS.

pinafore swimsuit See ACTIVEWEAR.

pince-nez See EYEWEAR.

pinchbeck Alloy, composed of five parts copper and one part zinc, used for pins and buckles cast with a surface design and then plated with a thin layer of silver or gold; frequently set with colored glass or paste. *Der.* From invention of Christopher Pinchbeck, London watchmaker, about 1700.

pin check See PRINTS, STRIPES, AND CHECKS.

pin collar See NECKLINES AND COLLARS.

pin curl **1.** See HAIRSTYLES. **2.** ∞ Term used from 1840 to 1860s for curl pinned on to underside of bonnet. Also called *pin-on curl.*

pin dot See PRINTS, STRIPES, AND CHECKS: DOTS.

pin-in bra See UNDERGARMENTS.

pink coat See COATS AND JACKETS.

pinked See CLOTHING CONSTRUCTION DETAILS.

pinking **1.** Unhemmed border of fabric cut with saw-toothed edge to prevent raveling by using special pinking scissors or shears that have saw-toothed blades. Also see CLOTHING CONSRUCTION DETAILS. **2.** ∞ Decorative effect made by cutting short slits to form a pattern in shoes or garments, in late 15th to 17th c. Also called *pouncing.* **3.** See FOOTWEAR.

pinner **1.** See HEADWEAR. **2.** See NECKLINES AND COLLARS: TUCKER.

pinning blanket See BARROW #2 and LAYETTE.

pin-on curl See PIN CURL.

pinpoint collar See NECKLINES AND COLLARS: PIERPONT COLLAR.

pin seal See LEATHERS.

pinson See FOOTWEAR.

pinstripe See PRINTS, STRIPES, AND CHECKS.

pin tucks See CLOTHING CONSTRUCTION DETAILS: TUCKS.

pinwale See CORDUROY.

pinwale piqué See PIQUÉ.

piped buttonhole See CLOSURES.

piped pocket See POCKETS: BOUND POCKET.

pipe-organ pleats See CLOTHING CONSTRUCTION DETAILS: GODET.

pipes ∞ Small rolls of clay pipe heated and used to tighten curls of man's wig in 17th and 18th c. Also called ROULETES.

piping See CLOTHING CONSTRUCTION DETAILS.

pipkin See HEADWEAR.

piqué † (pee-kay′) Group of durable fabrics characterized by corded effects either lengthwise or crosswise. (a) Plain piqués in the United States are made with lengthwise cords similar to BEDFORD CORD, by which name they could more properly be called. **Pinwale piqué** is a variation with smaller ribs. (b) Piqués made in England have cords in the crosswise direction. (c) **Waffle piqué** is made in a HONEYCOMB pattern. (d) **Bird's-eye piqué** has a diamond-shaped pattern woven-in dobby pattern. (e) **Embroidered**

piqué is plain piqué that has been embroidered with the SCHIFFLI MACHINE (see under EMBROIDERIES AND SEWING STITCHES). All types are used for dresses, blouses, pants, sportswear, handbags, and neckwear.

pique devant See BEARD.

piqué embroidery See EMBROIDERIES AND SEWING STITCHES.

piqué seam See GLOVES AND GLOVE CONSTRUCTION: FULL-PIQUÉ and HALF-PIQUÉ.

piracy Stealing of an idea for a dress by making sketches of it. Punishable as a crime in France, where dress designs are protected by the French government, it is not considered a crime in the United States unless the design is patented. Viewers at couture showings are permitted to mark their programs, but not permitted to make sketches.

pith helmet See HEADWEAR: TOPEE.

pixie haircut See HAIRSTYLES.

pizazz (pih-zazz′) Coined in 1930s to express the quality of audaciousness or daring; credited by the fashion magazine *Harper's Bazaar* to students at Harvard University.

p.j.s Abbreviation for PAJAMAS. See under SLEEPWEAR AND LOUNGEWEAR.

P.K. seam See GLOVES AND GLOVE CONSTRUCTIONS: FULL-PIQUÉ.

placard/plackard ∞ **1.** Chest piece or stomacher, used to fill in gap made by open neckline of man's DOUBLET in late 15th to mid-16th c. **2.** From mid-14th to early 16th c.: Front panel of woman's open-sided SURCOAT, often trimmed with fur and embroidery. Also spelled *placcard, placart, placcate*. Compare with PLASTRON #2.

placket See CLOTHING CONSTRUCTION DETAILS.

placket neckline See NECKLINES AND COLLARS.

PLAIDS AND TARTANS

plaid **1.** Common term for pattern woven of various colored yarns in stripes of different widths running at right angles to form blocks. *Der.* From Scottish fabrics woven to designate different clans. See PLAIDS AND TARTANS: TARTAN. **2.** Fabric design printed or woven of yarns dyed in various colors. Bands of color of different widths run both horizontally and vertically, crossing at right angles to form a series of boxes which may be slightly longer lengthwise.

tartan Each clan in Scotland has adopted a specific plaid fabric in individual colors used for the KILT, or short pleated skirt worn by men, and the *plaid,* a drapery worn hanging from the shoulders, across back, and tucked into belt. Although Scots are reported to have used stripes as early as the 5th c. and were fond of "mottled" fabrics, the real origin of the tartan is controversial. Various historians mention plaids as early as 1594 and 1645, but it was not until early 18th c. (1703) that they began to emerge as a clan symbol that designated a place of residence. After the defeat of Bonnie Prince Charles in 1747, plaids were banned by British law. Revived in 1822 when George IV visited Scotland—from that time on there were specific tartans for each clan. The better known tartans are described in this category. *Der.* Believed to have come from Flemish word *tiretaine.*

argyle plaid Made with various colored diamond-shaped designs—usually a larger diamond pattern of dark or light lines is superimposed over other solid colored diamonds. Popular in 1920s, 1940s, and revived in the late 1960s. *Der.* Tartan of Duke of Argyle and Clan Campbell of Argyll, a county in West Scotland. Also spelled *argyll, argyl.*

Balmoral tartan (bahl-mor′-al) Predominantly gray with two narrow black stripes and one red stripe grouped together and running vertically with two red stripes running horizontally plus wider stripes of black and gray used in both directions.

Black Watch tartan Very dark blue and green squares with wide and narrow black lines in both directions and no overplaid. Worn by members of the Black Watch, a Scottish regiment.

blanket plaid Very large plaid with dark colored ground and lighter overstripes, or white ground and colored overstripes used originally in woolen and cotton blankets.

Bruce tartan Bold red plaid crossed by dark green stripes of various sizes, forming a central box consisting of four green boxes out-lined with narrow green stripes. Large yellow and white overplaid encloses the design.

Buchanan tartan Intricate bold plaid consisting of dull green bands combined with red, orange, green, and yellow checks arranged in squares, having a fine overplaid of white and black.

buffalo checks See PRINTS, STRIPES, AND CHECKS.

Burberry plaid Beige, red, and black plaid named after Thomas Burberry, a mid-19th-century British tailor who specialized in waterproof gabardine raincoats lined in this plaid. The plaid is now used in a wide variety of garments and accessories. See COATS AND JACKETS: BURBERRY RAINCOAT.

Cameron tartan Predominantly bright red with four dark green stripes crossed at right angles making a central section of sixteen blocks of green. Yellow overplaid outlines each pattern.

even plaid Design that starts with a central box and repeats in the same manner on each side of the central motif. Popular for shirts, suits, and dresses because it is easier to match when sewing than an **uneven plaid,** in which designs on either side of central box are different.

even plaid

uneven plaid

Frazer tartan Similar to the CAMERON CLAN TARTAN (see under PLAIDS AND TARTANS), but smaller in size, with navy and green stripes crossing at right angles, making a central section of sixteen navy and green blocks. Also includes an overplaid in white.

gingham plaid Woven design in a cotton fabric made with stripes and boxes of various sizes in three or more colors. Gingham with only two colors is called a *gingham check.* Fabrics used for aprons, dresses, and shirts. Also see GINGHAM in alphabetical listing.

glen plaid See PLAIDS AND TARTANS: GLEN URQUHART PLAID.

Glen Urquhart plaid Woven design that pairs small checks with larger checks made with similar colored yarns in warp and filling in a combination of subdued color and white.

Used particularly for men's worsted suits. Also called *glen plaid* or *glen check. Der.* Named for Glen Urquhart, a valley in Invernessshire, Scotland.

hunting plaid Everyday version of Scottish clan's tartan made in subdued colors to blend with landscape, in contrast to dress plaid worn on ceremonial occasions.

lumberjack plaid Distinctive plaid similar to a BLANKET PLAID (see under PLAIDS AND TARTANS) but smaller in size. Usually combines tones of green and tan on a beige background. *Der.* From early plaids used for jackets by lumbermen.

Macbeth tartan A complicated patterned tartan made with cobalt blue ground and colored stripes in red, yellow, green, and black, some outlined in white.

MacDonell of Glengarry tartan Dark green and navy ground crossed with narrow red lines of two widths, making a smaller design than most tartans. Has a large overplaid in white.

MacGregor (Rob Roy) tartan Combination of vivid red blocks and wide black bands in a small block design.

Macintyre and Glenorchy tartan Red ground crossed with medium-sized bands of green and navy running vertically and horizontally with narrow bands of green and blue in between—making a squared pattern with large overplaid of light blue.

MacPherson hunting tartan Bold black block alternating with gray and beige blocks, and outlined with two narrow red stripes with bright blue stripe between them.

madras plaid (mad-dras') East Indian woven cotton in multicolor crossbar patterns with red. May bleed after washing to produce a blurred effect. Also see MADRAS in alphabetical listing.

Menzies black-and-white tartan Similar in design to MENZIES HUNTING TARTAN (see under PLAIDS AND TARTANS), but woven only in black and white.

Menzies hunting tartan Predominantly wide blocks of solid green alternating with red blocks divided into checks by green bands—other blocks are striped.

P

Munro tartan Vivid red ground plaided in dark green and navy with fine yellow lines running in both directions at intervals.

overplaid Lines of another color superimposed over a plaid or a checked design.

Ramsay tartan Brilliant red ground with wide black bands in both directions and double lines in white overplaid. Also has fine purple stripes running in both directions. Dates back to the 17th c.

Rob Roy tartan See PLAIDS AND TARTANS: MAC-GREGOR TARTAN.

Royal Stewart (Stuart) tartan Similar to STEWART DRESS tartan (see under PLAIDS AND TARTANS) with bold red ground and central box of nine squares of red outlined with green, black, and blue bands. Fine navy lines run through center of boxes with fine white and yellow overplaid.

shepherd's plaid/shepherd's check See PRINTS, STRIPES, AND CHECKS.

Stewart (Stuart) dress tartan Central box contains nine red squares outlined by wide black bands, alternating with white blocks, and green-, red-, and black-striped blocks with fine yellow and white alternating stripes defining the squares.

Stewart hunting tartan Very dark blue or green ground crossed at right angles with black bands, making a central section of sixteen blocks. An overplaid of red and yellow outlines the pattern.

tartan See under introduction for category PLAIDS AND TARTANS.

tattersall plaid Plaid consisting of narrow lines in two alternating colors, crossed to form a checked design on a plain light-colored ground, often uses red and black lines on white ground. *Der.* Named after Richard Tattersall, British horseman and founder of Tattersall's London Horse Auction Mart, established in 1776. Also called *tattersall check*.

uneven plaid See PLAIDS AND TARTANS: EVEN PLAID.

windowpane plaid See PRINTS, STRIPES AND CHECKS: WINDOWPANE CHECKS.

---

plain front See PANTS.

plain hem See CLOTHING CONSTRUCTION DETAILS.

plain knit **1.** See JERSEY #1. **2.** See EMBROIDERIES AND SEWING STITCHES: PLAIN KNITTING STITCH.

plain seam See CLOTHING CONSTRUCTION DETAILS. Also see EMBROIDERIES AND SEWING STITCHES: PLAIN KNITTING STITCH.

plain weave † Weave in which one crosswise yarn passes over the first lengthwise yarn, then under the next lengthwise yarn and continues across the width of the fabric to pass over one yarn and under another. In the next row, the crosswise yarn passes under the first lengthwise yarn, then over the next lengthwise yarn, and so on. In the third row, the pattern of the first row is repeated. The resulting interlacing of yarns is like a checkerboard pattern. Synonym: *tabby weave.*

plain weave diagram

plait (plate) **1.** *n.* See HAIRSTYLES: BRAIDS. **2.** *v.* To weave three or more strands into a single strip or braid, e.g., bands of straw for hats or ribbons for trimming. **3.** Old spelling of pleat. See CLOTHING CONSTRUCTION DETAILS: PLEAT.

planter's hat See HEADWEAR.

plastic patent † Simulated or imitation PATENT LEATHER (see under LEATHERS) made from a vinyl compound that is durable and will not split or crack like genuine patent. May have a crushed surface or be embossed with a design, e.g., alligator or snakeskin. Used for shoes and handbags and in lighter weights for jackets, coats, and trimmings. Popular from 1960s on.

plastron (plas'-tron) **1.** See ARMOR. **2.** Front center portion set into a woman's dress, usually made of a contrasting fabric for a decorative effect. Used in the 19th through the mid-20th c. and revived in the 1980s when a lacy and frilly version was called a *gilet*. In earlier centuries also called a *placard* or *stomacher*. **3.** See NECKLINES AND COLLARS: BIB COLLAR. *Der.* French, "breast-plate."

plated See JEWELRY.

plates See FURS.

platform sole See FOOTWEAR.

platina See FURS: PLATINUM FOX.

platinum **1.** See JEWELRY. **2.** Very pale silvery blond; popular shade of hair in 1930s and 1940s.

platinum fox See FURS.

platter collar See NECKLINES AND COLLARS.

platypus toe See FOOTWEAR.

Plauen lace See LACES.

playsuit See SHORTS: JUMPSHORTS and ACTIVEWEAR.

playwear Fashion business designation of casual clothing worn by children for playing.

pleat/pleated **1.** See CLOTHING CONSTRUCTION DETAILS. **2.** Apparel that utilizes pleats in its construction. See PANTS: PLEATED PANTS and PLEATED OVERALLS and SHORTS: PLEATED SHORTS.

plissé † (plee-say′) Lightweight cotton with a pebbly surface given a creped appearance by applying caustic soda with rollers, thereby causing the fabric to shrink in those areas, while the untreated areas remain the same size. The result is a crinkled appearance. Pressing will remove the crinkle. Used for pajamas, nightgowns, and children's clothing. Also known as *crinkle crepe* and *plissé crepe.*

plucking See FURS.

pluderhose See TRUNK HOSE.

plug hat See HEADWEAR.

plug/plugged oxford See FOOTWEAR.

plumage See FEATHERS.

plume See FEATHERS.

plumet petticoat See UNDERGARMENTS.

plummet See JEWELRY.

plumpers ∞ Lightweight, thin round balls of cork or wax used by women inside mouth to make cheeks look rounder from late 17th to early 19th c.

plunge bra See UNDERGARMENTS.

plunging neckline See NECKLINES AND COLLARS.

plus fours See PANTS.

plus sizes Sizes in women's apparel that are at the upper range of sizes manufactured. Generally, retailers place sizes 14 and above in this category.

ply yarn † A number of individual yarns, or singles, twisted together to form a heavier yarn.

Pocahontas dress See AMERICAN INDIAN DRESS.

pocketbook Synonym for *handbag.* See introduction to HANDBAGS AND RELATED ACCESSORIES.

pocket handkerchief See HANDKERCHIEF.

pocket hoops See UNDERWEAR: PANNIERS.

POCKETS

pocket Piece of fabric shaped to fit either on the outside or inside of clothing. Used for decorative purposes or to carry small articles, e.g., handkerchiefs or coins. From 15th c. on, small pouches were worn fastened to the belt. Men: In mid-16th c., pockets were added to TRUNK HOSE; by end of the 16th c., added to BREECHES. Waistcoat pocket introduced in early 17th c. In late 17th c., flaps were added to coat and waistcoat pockets. Women: 18th-c. tie pockets were worn suspended from waist under dress and reached by means of placket holes. In 19th c. a pouch called a *railway pocket* was worn under the dress and reached by a slit in the dress. By the 1840s small pockets were put into the waistline seams of dresses, and from midcentury on, pockets were put in dresses and shirtwaists.

angled pocket See POCKETS: HACKING POCKET.

bellows pocket Outside pocket made with center BOX or INVERTED PLEAT (see under CLOTHING CONSTRUCTION DETAILS) that expands when pocket is used. Type of pocket used on BUSH JACKET (see under COATS AND JACKETS) and SAFARI DRESS. Also called *safari pocket.*

bellows pocket

besom pocket See POCKETS: WELT POCKET.

bound pocket Interior pocket made with slit finished like a bound buttonhole on outside, providing access to inner concealed pocket. Also called *piped, slash, slit pocket.* Also see POCKETS: WELT POCKET.

breast pocket Man's pocket placed on left side of chest on suit coats and overcoats.

cargo pocket Large patch pocket used on shorts and pants. Curved top of pocket extends to waist and forms a loop through which belt is pulled.

cargo pocket

change pocket See POCKETS: TICKET POCKET.

circle pocket See POCKETS: ROUND POCKET.

continental pocket Pocket cut away at the top, usually in a curved manner, used on men's western or continental trousers. Also called a *western pocket.*

continental pocket

double-besom pocket See POCKETS: WELT POCKET.

double-entry pocket Pockets that may be entered from the top or side.

flapped-besom pocket   See POCKETS: WELT POCKET.

flap pocket   Pocket with separate piece of material covering the opening. May be of BOUND, WELT, or PATCH POCKET type (see under POCKETS).

fob pocket   Small horizontal WELT POCKET (see under POCKETS), near waistband of man's pants, designed to hold pocket watch. Popular from 17th c. until the 1920s, when wristwatches began to be fashionable. Also called *watch pocket.*

hacking pocket   Flap pocket placed on an angle used on jackets and coats, especially on hacking jackets.

half-moon pocket   Curved semicircular bound pocket used primarily on cowboy shirts. Usually reinforced at ends with embroidered arrowheads. Also called a *smile pocket.*

holster pocket   Novelty pocket shaped like a gun holster, used on sportswear.

kangaroo pocket   **1.** Extra-large pocket placed on center front of garment (e.g., a sweatshirt). **2.** Any extra-large pocket.

kangaroo pocket #1

key pocket   Small patch pocket sewn inside of larger right-front pocket in jeans-style pants, just large enough for a key or a few coins.

mock pocket   Flap sewed on outside of garment to suggest a real pocket.

patch pocket   Pocket stitched on outside of garment, either made plain or with a flap.

patch pocket

pencil pocket   Zip pocket placed on upper sleeve of sport coat or SNORKEL JACKET (see under COATS AND JACKETS), used to hold small items or a pencil.

piped pocket   See POCKETS: BOUND POCKET.

railway pocket   ∞ Flat bag with side opening tied on with tape around waist and reached by slit in skirt. Worn by women under dress when traveling, from late 1850s. A later version of the TIE POCKET (see under POCKETS).

round pocket   Full circular patch pocket bound around the edge with opening in the center, top, or side for access. Also called a *circle pocket.*

safari pocket   See POCKETS: BELLOWS POCKET.

salt-box pocket   ∞ Term used in 1790s for man's narrow rectangular flapped waistcoat pocket.

seam pocket   Pocket inserted in seam of skirt, dress, or pants that is not visible from outside.

slash pocket   See POCKETS: BOUND POCKET.

slit pocket   See POCKETS: WELT POCKET.

smile pocket   See POCKETS: HALF-MOON POCKET.

ticket pocket   British tailoring term for a small pocket, usually flapped, placed above regular pocket on right side of a man's suit coat or overcoat. Introduced in late 1850s for a railroad ticket and used at intervals since. Also called *change pocket.*

tie pocket   ∞ Large pocket sewn to a ribbon, cord, or string that tied around the waist and was used by women in the 18th and early 19th c. to carry necessary items. Often made with two pockets, one on each side of the dress. Was generally worn under the skirt and reached through a slit. When skirts were looped up and the petticoat visible, they might be worn under the petticoat. Sometimes embroidered, early American examples are frequently made of patchwork scraps of fabric. Also called *work pockets.*

tie pockets 1774

vest pocket   Welt pocket placed on side chest of waistcoat or vest, originally used to carry a pocket watch. In the Louis XV period a fashion for men to carry two watches (one was often not real) required that a pocket be made on either side of the garment. Also called a *waistcoat* or *watch pocket* or *fob pocket.*

waistcoat pocket   See POCKETS: VEST POCKET.

watch pocket   See POCKETS: FOB and VEST POCKETS.

welt pocket   An inset pocket with the lower lip finished by an upstanding welt that may be from $3/8''$ to $1''$ wide. Usually a breast pocket placed on the left front of a man's suit coat or overcoat. May be called **besom pocket** (bee´-zum) by tailors or if both edges have welts, a **double besom** pocket. If a flap is added, it is called a **flapped besom.** Also called *slit pocket.* Also see POCKETS: BOUND POCKET.

welt pocket

western pocket Same as POCKETS: CONTINENTAL POCKET.

work pocket See POCKETS: TIE POCKET.

zip pocket Any pocket closed with a zipper used particularly on sportswear.

---

pocket siphonia See COATS AND JACKETS: SIPHONIA.

pocket T-shirt See SHIRTS.

pocket watch See WATCHES.

poet's collar See NECKLINES AND COLLARS: BYRON.

poet's shirt See SHIRTS: LORD BYRON.

point Shortened form for NEEDLEPOINT. See under EMBROIDERIES AND SEWING STITCHES and introduction to LACES .

point d'Alençon See LACES: ALENÇON LACE.

point d'Angleterre See LACES.

point d'appliqué See LACES: APPLIQUÉD LACE.

point d'Argentan See LACES: ARGENTAN LACE.

point d'esprit (pwan des-pree′) **1.** † Netlike machine-made fabric of cotton or nylon that has some of the holes made solid to form a decorative pattern. Used for evening gowns and veiling. First handmade in France in 1834. Compare with BOBBINET. **2.** See LACES. **3.** See HOSIERY.

point de France See LACES.

point de Gaze See LACES.

point de Paris See LACES.

point de rose See LACES: ROSE-POINT.

point de Venise See LACES.

pointing See GLOVES AND GLOVE CONSTRUCTIONS.

point noué See LACES.

point of purchase display Merchandise displayed so that it can be handled and self-selected by the customer.

point of sale (POS) Computer program that allows retailers to track inventory and sales. Usually this is done at the cash register (the "point of sale"). Because sales data are captured instantly, they can be relayed to the vendor for automatic reordering as part of the QUICK RESPONSE system.

points ∞ Cords with metal tips used to fasten garments together from 15th to mid-17th c., e.g., TRUNK HOSE attached to DOUBLET. Also see LANGET #1.

Poiret, Paul * See APPENDIX/DESIGNERS.

poison ring See JEWELRY.

poke **1.** ∞ Large pouch used as pocket in late 16th and early 17th cs. **2.** Still used as a colloquial term for any kind of a bag in the southern United States. *Der.* French, *poche*, "bag" or "pocket."

poke bonnet See HEADWEAR.

poker-chip button See CLOSURES.

pokey See HANDBAGS AND RELATED ACCESSORIES.

poking sticks ∞ Term used in 16th c. for heated bone, wood, or metal sticks used to set pleats of a RUFF (see under NECKLINES AND COLLARS).

Polaroid® glasses See EYEWEAR.

Polartec® † Napped, knit polyester fabric made from recycled soda bottles. Used extensively for cold-weather ACTIVEWEAR because of good insulation qualities.

poleyn See ARMOR.

police boot See FOOTWEAR.

Polish boot See FOOTWEAR.

polished cotton † Most any plain-weave cotton fabric, e.g., SATEEN, CHINTZ, given a glazed finish to make it shiny and lustrous. Some finishes are permanent, particularly those of the resin-type. If the finish is made by starching and ironing with a hot roller, it is not permanent. Used for blouses, dresses, and sportswear.

Polish greatcoat See COATS AND JACKETS.

Polish jacket See COATS AND JACKETS.

Polish mantle See CAPES, CLOAKS, AND SHAWLS.

Polish toque See HEADWEAR.

polka **1.** See COATS AND JACKETS **2.** See HEADWEAR.

polka dot See PRINTS, STRIPES, AND CHECKS: DOTS.

polo Adjective used to describe clothing copied from or inspired by clothes worn for polo, a game played on horseback with long-handled wooden mallets and a ball. Periods of the game are called *chukkas*. Distinctive polo clothing has been much copied for sportswear. See BELTS: POLO BELT, COATS AND JACKETS: POLO COAT, HEADWEAR: CHUKKA HAT, NECKLINES AND COLLARS: POLO COLLAR, and SHIRTS: POLO SHIRT.

polo shirt dress See T-SHIRT DRESS.

polonaise (pol-on-nays′) **1.** Has come to refer to any overskirt pulled back and looped up at the sides to form a large drape or puff. Seems to appear first in the second half of the 18th c. when it was described as a boned bodice and overskirt looped up by drawstrings at hips and back to form three large puffs, thereby revealing the petticoat or underskirt. Worn over a separate ankle-length or trained skirt, sometimes contrasting in color, or with one skirt plain and the other striped. Disappeared from use when the silhouette narrowed at the end of the century, then revived again in the second half of the 19th c. Also called a *gown à la polonaise* and *robe à la polonaise*. The French name **petit casaque** (pe-tee′ ca-sack′) was also used in 1870s for polonaise dress. *Der.* Named after a Polish national dance and also the music for such a dance. **2.** See CAPES, CLOAKS, AND SHAWLS. **3.** See COATS AND JACKETS.

polonaise #1 18th c.

polonese frock See POLONAISE #1.

polyester † Generic fiber name for manufactured fibers made of acids and alcohols derived from petroleum. The wide variety of fabrics made from these fibers are easy care, resilient, retain their shape, and are often blended with other fibers. Current trademarks for polyester fiber include Dacron®, Hollofil®, Trevira®, Fortrel®, Micrell®, and Stay Gard®.

polyethelyne See OLEFIN.

polyolefin See OLEFIN.

polypropylene See OLEFIN.

pomander ∞ (poh′-man-der) A ball of fragrant herbs and/or flowers or the case in which these were carried. Examples of pomanders include **pommes de senteur** (pohm duh sahn′-ture), small balls of gold or silver filigree set with precious stones used to hold scent, carried or hung from belt from 1500 to 1690s (also called *musk apples, pound-box, musk balls*, and **pouncet box**, consisting of a dry-scent box that contained fragrant herbs and flower petals and was carried during the late 16th c. *Der.* French, "perfumed apples."

pommel slicker See COATS AND JACKETS.

pommes de senteur See POMANDER.

pompadour **1.** See HAIRSTYLES. **2.** See HAIR ACCESSORIES: POMPON. **3.** See HIP BAGS.

pompadour bag See HANDBAGS AND RELATED ACCESSORIES.

pompadour bodice ∞ (pohm′-pah-dure) Bodice for daytime dress worn in the 1870s with a low square neckline and tight, elbow-length sleeves trimmed with lace or ruffles. Worn as part of the POLONAISE in 1870s. See POLONAISE #1. *Der.* Named for Marquise de Pompadour, mistress of Louis XV of France.

Pompadour, Marquise de (pohm′-pah-dure, mar-kees′ deh) (1721–1764) Born Jeanne Antoinette Poisson. Mistress of Louis XV of France (1745–1764), who had great influence over him. Promoted the arts during this period. Paintings of her by Boucher epitomize the beautiful costume of this era. Many items of fashion have been named after her. Examples: pompadour hairstyle, pompadour bag, pompadour bodice, and pompadour sleeve.

pompadour sleeve See SHOULDERS AND SLEEVES.

Pompeian silk sash See BELTS.

pompey See WIGS AND HAIRPIECES: PHYSICAL WIG.

pompon/pompom **1.** Round ball of cut ends of yarn used as trimming. **2.** See HAIR ACCESSORIES. **3.** See HAIRSTYLES: TOP KNOT.

poms See HOSIERY: FOOTSOCK.

poncho See CAPES, CLOAKS AND SHAWLS.

pongee † (pon-gee′) Light- to medium-weight rough-textured silk fabric made from wild silk and usually left in natural color. Originally hand-loomed in China, later machine made. Warp yarns are finer than the filling, causing a slight rib formed by the uneven texture of the yarn. *Der.* Chinese, *penchi*, "woven at home."

pony See FURS.

ponyet ∞ **1.** Sleeve of DOUBLET that covers the lower part of arm, frequently of different fabric from upper sleeve. Worn from 14th to 16th c. Also spelled *poynet*. **2.** Long pin with decorative head worn by men in 17th c. Also called *little bodkin*.

ponytail See HAIRSTYLES.

poodle cloth † Knitted or woven fabric characterized by small curls over the entire surface. Similar to *astrakan* fabric but made with looser curls like the coat of a poodle dog.

poodle cut See HAIRSTYLES.

poor-boy Descriptive term used in mid-1960s referring to type of shrunken casual clothing based on that worn by newsboys in early 20th c. Examples: poor-boy dresses, sweaters, and NEWSBOY CAP (see under HEADWEAR).

poor-boy shift An elongated version of the poor-boy sweater. See SWEATERS.

popcorn stitch See EMBROIDERIES AND SEWING STITCHES.

Pope, Virginia (1885–1978) Fashion editor of *The New York Times* beginning in 1933. She changed fashion reporting by seeking news in the wholesale markets of New York; encouraged young American designers; and originated the *Fashion of the Times* fashion show in 1942, which featured clothes from American designers. In 1955, became fashion editor of *Parade* magazine. She also held the Edwin Goodman chair, established by Bergdorf Goodman, at Fashion Institute of Technology. Cosmopolitan, statuesque, and beautifully dressed, in her later years she became the grande dame of American fashion.

poplin † Medium-weight durable fabric with crosswise rib effect made with cotton or blends of cotton and polyester. Better qualities use combed yarns in both directions. A water-resistant or water-repellent finish may also be applied to fabrics used for raincoats. Also used for sportswear, pants, shorts, blouses, dresses, and men's shirts.

popover Denim wraparound dress with short sleeves, a large patch pocket on the front of slightly flared skirt, and trimmed with decorative double topstitching. Designed by Claire McCardell in 1942 for *Harper's Bazaar*. Intended as an inexpensive, protective, yet stylish coverup for household work. Original dress sold for $6.95, different $30 versions were shown in her collection for several years.

porcupine hairstyle/headdress See HAIRSTYLES.

porc-epic See HAIRSTYLES: PORCUPINE HEADDRESS.

pork-pie hat See HEADWEAR.

port canons See CANNONS.

porte-jupe Pompadour ∞ (port-zhupe pohm'-pah-dure) Belt worn under a dress in 1860s that was made with eight suspenders that fastened to the hem of the skirt with loops that enclosed buttons. When a tab at the front of the device was pulled, the skirt raised in much the same way as a modern Venetian blind. Also called *dress elevator*.

porte-monnaie See HANDBAGS AND RELATED ACCESSORIES.

port of entry Location in the United States. with Customs offices through which import of goods is authorized. Oakland, CA; Los Angeles, CA; New York, NY; and Miami, FL, are major entry ports.

posh British slang term meaning rich or luxurious, derived from the acronym for preferred quarters on ships sailing between Britain and India. *Der.* "Port Out, Starboard Home," i.e., the shady side of the ship.

postboy hat See HEADWEAR.

poster dress Any dress imprinted with a blown-up photograph, a brief fad in the mid-1960s. Originally made of paper, later photographs were printed on fabric. In 1984 called a *toga dress*, which had a wide-shouldered "sandwich board" effect, was sewed up the sides, and printed with posters of animals, motorcycles, and movie star faces.

postiche See WIGS AND HAIRPIECES: WIGLET.

postillion ∞ (poce-till'-yun) **1.** See HEADWEAR. **2.** ∞ Dress bodice extending below back waistline, usually with pleats or ruffles that flare outward. Worn by women in latter half of 19th c. Also called *postillion basque* (bask). *Der.* From clothes worn by *postillions*, "men on horseback accompanying carriages."

postillion basque See POSTILLION.

postillion coat See COATS AND JACKETS.

postillion corsage See BALMORAL BODICE.

posts **1.** See UNDERGARMENTS: PASTIES. **2.** See JEWELRY: STUDS.

posy/poesy ring See JEWELRY.

pot derby See HEADWEAR: DERBY.

pot hat See HEADWEAR: TOP HAT.

potholder vest See VESTS.

potten kant lace See LACES: ANTWERP LACE.

Potter, Clare * See APPENDIX/DESIGNERS.

pouch **1.** See HANDBAGS AND RELATED ACCESSORIES. **2.** ∞ Bag or purse of 12th to 16th c. worn suspended from gentleman's belt, often with dagger thrust through the pendant strap.

le pouf 1987

pouf See HAIRSTYLES: BOUFFANT.

pouf au sentiment See HAIRSTYLES.

pouf, le A wide, puffy skirt with a light, airy appearance; made in both short and longer styles around 1985, and created by Christian Lacroix, designing for Patou.

poulaine/poulain See FOOTWEAR: CRAKOW.

pouncet-box See POMANDER.

pouncing See PINKING #2.

pound-box See POMANDER.

pourpoint See DOUBLET.

poussin lace (poo-sahn) See LACES.

powdering jacket/gown ∞ A loose wrap worn by men in 18th c. to protect clothing while the wig was being powdered. Also see FACE CONE.

power suit/power dressing Used in the late 1980s and 1990s for a man's or woman's tailored suit worn for business.

poynet See PONYET.

Prada, Miuccia * See APPENDIX/DESIGNERS.

prairie look/prairie dress Introduced in early 1970s in imitation of dresses worn by pioneer women. Elements included long dresses, usually of calicolike printed fabric, styled with two-gored skirts and bodices with high neckline and long sleeves. In 1980s shown in full skirts with ruffle at hem and Victorian-styled collars. *Der.* From dresses worn by American settlers moving westward in mid- and late 19th c. Also see SKIRTS: PRAIRIE SKIRT.

prayer veil See HEADWEAR.

precious stones See GEMS, GEM CUTS, AND SETTINGS.

pre-cuffed trousers See PANTS.

predatory pricing Illegal pricing of a product below cost, the intent being to drive out any competition. Selling goods at a loss at the end of season to clear out old merchandise is not considered predatory pricing.

preliminary line sheet Internal catalog of projected styles in a line as used by a company while developing a line.

prepack An assortment of merchandise in certain quantities of sizes and/or colors of one or more styles chosen according to a manufacturer's or retailer's direction.

preppy/preppie look A style of dress derived from clothing worn by students at private, preparatory schools that emphasizes well-known trademarks from high-quality stores; clas-

preppy look 1950s

sics such as Ivy League shirts, wool and cashmere sweaters, A-line skirts, conventional-style pants in fabrics such as chino, wool, and corduroy; and shoes such as oxfords, loafers, or classic pumps in expensive leathers.

Pre-Raphaelites A society of artists founded in England c. 1850 that encouraged painting in a style they felt was characteristic of work done in the period before the time of the Italian Renaissance artist Raphael. They encouraged women associated with the movement to abandon corsets and hoopskirts. Later in the century, the clothing in which they painted women also influenced AESTHETIC DRESS.

prêt-à-porter (pret-ah′-por-tay′) French term for ready-to-wear clothes. Many haute couture designers produce special, less expensive prêt-à-porter lines of clothing in addition to their custom-made lines. *Der.* French, "ready to be carried away."

pre-walkers See FOOTWEAR.

price discrimination Selling by a vendor of identical merchandise at different prices to two or more retailers. Laws prohibit price discrimination.

price point See APPAREL PRICE RANGES.

prime pelt See FURS.

primitive print See PRINTS.

Prince Albert coat See COATS AND JACKETS.

Prince of Wales jacket See COATS AND JACKETS.

Prince of Wales shoe See FOOTWEAR: GILLIE.

Prince Rupert See COATS AND JACKETS.

princess chemise See UNDERGARMENTS.

princess coat See COATS AND JACKETS.

princess dress Fitted dress with flared skirt, frequently made like a coat-dress, styled without a waistline seam and cut in panels fitted from shoulders to hem. Original style was claimed to be designed by Worth and introduced about 1860 for Empress Eugénie. Worn intermittently since.

princesse lace See LACES.

princess slip/princess petticoat See UNDERGARMENTS.

princess stock See NECKLIINES AND COLLARS.

princess style Basic cut for women's clothing characterized by continuous

princess-style dress

vertical panels, shaped to body through torso without waistline seam. Used in dresses, coats, and slips, from about 1860 on. Called *Agnès Sorel style* and *Isabeau style* in early 1860s. French form, *princesse.*

princess waistline See WAISTLINES.

printing † Reproducing a design on fabric in color either by mechanical means or by hand. The most common methods currently in use in the textile industry are **roller printing,** using as many as 16 engraved metal rollers, and **rotary screen printing,** using perforated, round, metal screens. Handprinted designs often used in crafts include those made by BLOCK PRINTING and SCREEN PRINTS (see under PRINTS, STRIPES, AND CHECKS). Prints may be applied as overall, repeat patterns, border designs, or in large panel designs. Most countries have traditional prints native to their land.

PRINTS, STRIPES, AND CHECKS

print A design applied to a fabric by means of a mechanical or hand method of PRINTING. See entries below for named types of prints and print designs.

stripes **1.** Bands of color or texture of varying widths, making a design in a fabric, either printed on or woven in; may go in horizontal, vertical, or diagonal direction. **2.** Narrow bands of braid, bias binding, ribbon, or fabric applied in rows.

check A fabric design composed of alternate squares of colors in various sizes usually alternating with white. Design may be similar to checkerboard or any other block design that is geometrical and repeats regularly. A checked pattern may be woven or printed.

abstract print A pattern or motif not related to natural or real objects. May emphasize line, color, or geometric forms.

abstract print

African print Bold geometric designs inspired by some traditional African prints. Frequently carried out in browns, blacks, and whites.

allover print Print covering the entire surface of the fabric from selvage to selvage in a repeat design. Compare with PRINTS, STRIPES, AND CHECKS: BORDER PRINT or a PANEL PRINT.

American Indian print Bold, stylized, geometric designs from native American sources carried out in bright colors.

animal print Designs imprinted on fabrics in imitation of fur of the leopard, giraffe, ocelot, tiger, or zebra. Used on cotton, jersey, or on MODACRYLIC pile fabric to resemble furs. Popular from mid-1960s on.

apron checks A gingham fabric made in even checks of white and a color, designated as 4 × 4 or 8 × 8 according to number of yarns used in each check. Originally a fabric used for aprons, by extension, a type of check.

Art Deco print Small geometric prints, frequently outlined in black, inspired by *Exposition International des Arts Décoratifs et Industriels Modernes,* Paris, 1925; reintroduced in the late 1960s. *Der.* French, *art décoratif,* "decorative art."

Art Nouveau print Designs emphasizing curved, waving lines; stylized natural forms of plants, animals, and women; and a strong sense of motion. Inspired by early 20th-c. French art movement called *Art Nouveau.* First revived in late 1960s and seen occasionally since. *Der.* French, *nouveau,* "new art."

awning stripe Wide even bands of one or more bright colors and white, woven or printed on coarse canvas. Formerly used for window awnings, now copied in lighter fabrics for sportswear.

Aztec print Designs based on Mexican Indian geometric motifs in bright colors usually banded in black.

bandanna print (ban-dan'-nah) Designs, usually in black and white on a red or navy-blue background in imitation of bandanna handkerchiefs. *Der.* Indian, *bandhnu,* "method of tie-dyeing cloth."

batik print (baa'-teek) Designs, usually in dark blue, rust, black, or yellow, copied from Indonesian technique of painting with wax before dyeing. Also see BATIK.

batik print

bayadère stripe (by-yah-deer') Horizontal stripes of varying widths in brilliant colors of red, green, blue, and gold. Also called *gypsy* or *Romany stripes. Der.* Hindu, "dancing girl."

bend ∞ Synonym for *stripe* in Middle Ages.

blazer stripe Inch-wide bands of one or several colors alternating with white. *Der.* From striped patterns of some blazer jackets.

block print See PRINTS, STRIPES, AND CHECKS: BLOCK PRINTING.

block printing Method of hand-printing fabric by cutting separate wood or linoleum blocks for each color in relief, then inking and printing individual colored blocks. Also called HAND-BLOCKED PRINT.

bookbinder print Designs copied from multicolored abstract, swirled, and woodgrain designs used formerly on endpapers of expensively bound books.

border print Print designed so that one selvage forms a distinct border used at the hem of a dress or shirt, or worked into the garment in some other way.

buffalo checks Heavy fabrics made with large square blocks in contrasting colors, often red and black, that are used for shirts or outerwear.

burnt-out print See BURN-OUT/BURNT-OUT in alphabetical list.

calico print Allover print usually of tiny naturalistic sprigs of flowers on a colored background of red, blue, yellow, or black.

calico print

candy stripe Narrow bands of red on white background, imitating peppermint candy sticks.

chalk stripe Narrow lines of white, widely spaced, frequently used on gray, navy, or black flannel—a classic for men's business suits.

check See under category heading PRINTS, STRIPES, AND CHECKS.

checkerboard checks Even squares of two colors alternating to form a row. Succeeding rows alternate colors. *Der.* From resemblance to a checkerboard. Also called *even checks.*

chiné See PRINTS, STRIPES, AND CHECKS: WARP PRINT.

coin dots See PRINTS, STRIPES, AND CHECKS: DOTS.

competition stripe Brightly colored single or cluster stripes across front of garment bor-

rowed from competitive-sports uniforms (e.g., football jerseys).

discharge print Design made on piece-dyed fabric by applying with copper rollers chemicals that dissolve and remove the dye in the design area. A white polka-dot design on a navy ground can be made in this manner.

dots Round spots used as a pattern in regular rows or a random arrangement; e.g., **coin dots,** larger than a dime; **pin dots,** as small as the head of a pin.

double ombré stripe (om-bray′) Stripes of two colors shaded from light to dark, usually run horizontally, either printed or woven.

duplex print Fabric with same design printed on both sides to imitate a woven pattern.

even checks See PRINTS, STRIPES, AND CHECKS: CHECKERBOARD.

express stripe Twill weave fabric made with even stripes of blue and white running lengthwise. Originally used for janitors' uniforms, caps, and railroad workers' overalls. *Der.* From overalls worn by railroad workers.

fleur-de-lis (flur deh lee′) French stylized lily design used in heraldry and part of the coat-of-arms of France's former royal family. Often used in formal repeat designs.

fleur-de-lis

flocked print Design made by applying adhesive to fabric in a pattern and affixing tiny fibers. Frequently used to make border prints or flocked dotted Swiss. See FLOCKING #2.

floral print Any design using flowers in either a natural or stylized manner (e.g., a daisy, a rose, or sprigs of flowers arranged together in repeat design).

geometric print **1.** Circles, oblongs, squares, triangles, or other geometrical forms used in a printed design. **2.** Print with background broken up by using a repeat design of rectangular forms then imprinting another design within each unit.

geometric print #1

gingham checks Yarn-dyed checks of 1″, ½″, ⅛″, or 1⁄16″, made in a color alternating with white. Also called *apron check.* Also see GINGHAM in alphabetical listing.

glen/Glen Urquhart checks See PLAIDS AND TARTANS.

granny print Small floral print similar to a calico print. *Der.* Named after prints formerly worn by grandmothers for housedresses at the turn of the 20th c.

gun club checks A three-color, double-check design consisting of a large check over a smaller one used in wool and worsted fabrics.

gypsy stripe See PRINTS, STRIPES, AND CHECKS: BAYADÈRE STRIPES.

hairline stripe See PRINTS, STRIPES, AND CHECKS: PINSTRIPES.

hand-blocked print See PRINTS, STRIPES, AND CHECKS: BLOCK PRINTING.

hand-painted print Not a print at all but a pattern painted directly on fabric.

hand-screened print See PRINTS, STRIPES, AND CHECKS: SILK-SCREEN PRINT.

harlequin checks (har´-leh-kin) Check made of medium-sized, diamond-shaped colored motifs alternating with white.

hickory stripe Lengthwise stripes, usually blue and white with the blue two times the size of the white, woven in a denim-type fabric. Fancy hickory stripes are white stripes of varying widths on a blue ground. Also called *Liberty stripes* and *victory stripes*. Originally used for janitors' uniforms and workclothes, now used for sportswear.

hound's-tooth/houndstooth checks Irregular colored 1/2″ to 2″ check like a square with points at two corners. Consists of colored checks alternating with white, produced by a yarn-dyed twill weave. *Der.* From resemblance to pointed dog's tooth.

ikat See PRINTS, STRIPES, AND CHECKS: WARP PRINT.

Indian print May be a hand-blocked print or a batik as long as it originates in Madras or another city of India. Frequently made with inferior dye that *bleeds* or runs when the fabric is washed.

Japanese print Usually a scenic print featuring pagodas, foliage, and mountains, in a repeat design. Fabric is frequently used to make garments in the kimono style.

jungle print Designs using animals found in the jungle, e.g., leopards, tigers, and lions.

kente cloth print Fabric printed to imitate woven KENTE CLOTH.

Laura Ashley® print Provincial, small floral designs typically Victorian, copied from antique designs printed on cotton fabrics and wallpapers. Originally used for home furnishings, now used for clothing as well. Trademarked by Laura Ashley of England.

Liberty® print Trademark of Liberty, London, for wide range of printed fabrics. The best known are small multicolored floral designs.

Liberty stripe See PRINTS, STRIPES, AND CHECKS: HICKORY STRIPES.

mattress-ticking stripe See PRINTS, STRIPES, AND CHECKS: TICKING STRIPES.

medallion print Repeat round or oval design sometimes connected with realistic swags of foliage.

mosaic print Print introduced in early 1970s made by tiny square blocks of color arranged in a manner imitating a Byzantine mosaic.

naturalistic print Representation of flowers, shrubs, trees, and birds, arranged in a realistic manner in a repeat design.

ombré stripe Bands of color either woven or printed, usually composed of monochromatic tones of one color running from light to dark.

Op Art print Design, basically geometric, in which lines are "bent" or "warped" to give optical illusion, (e.g., a checkerboard design formed with some curved lines and squares not all of equal size). *Der.* Became popular in 1964 after an exhibit of Op Art paintings at the Museum of Modern Art in New York City.

op art print

paisley print Allover design featuring a design shaped like a tear drop, rounded at one end and with a curving point on the other. Frequently features rich colors with bold designs outlined in delicate tracery and swirls. A printed version of the pattern used in a PAISLEY SHAWL (see under CAPES, CLOAKS, AND SHAWLS: CASHMERE SHAWL #2.

paisley print

pajama checks   DIMITY woven with coarser yarns at intervals in both warp and filling forming a checked design. Used for men's underwear in 1920s and 1930s.

pajama stripes   Broad, boldly colored stripes used for PAJAMAS (see under SLEEPWEAR AND LOUNGEWEAR).

panel print   A large design intended to be used in one length, without repeating (e.g., one panel used for front—one for back of a dress). Usually made with hand-screened process and expensive.

patchwork print   A print designed to mimic a patchwork quilt design. Design is printed on fabric, not made with "patches."

pencil stripe   Vertical stripes as wide as a pencil line, with wider stripes of background color in between.

photographic print   **1.** Large design covering entire front of the garment and reproduced in such a manner as to look like a black-and-white photo. Such prints have included pictures of Beethoven and Bach imprinted on sweatshirts; rockets, tigers, and pictures of movie stars imprinted on the front of a T-shirt-type dress. **2.** Prints made by coating a photosensitive dye on fabric, then printing a design from a photographic negative.

pincheck   Check made of very tiny squares.

pin dots   See PRINTS, STRIPES, AND CHECKS: DOTS.

pinstripe   Very narrow stripes the width of a straight pin woven or printed in vertical stripes placed close together, either white stripes on dark ground or vice versa. Also called *hairline stripes*.

psychedelic print   (sy-keh-dell'-ik) Unconventional designs done in extremely vibrant, full-intensity colors (e.g., chartreuse, fuchsia, and purple in bizarre combinations forming flowing patterns on the fabric). *Der.* Inspired by the hallucinations seen when under the influence of the drug LSD.

Pucci print   (poo'-chee) Design introduced by Emilio Pucci, an Italian couturier, which is highly original and hard to imitate. Pattern is abstract and composed mainly of brilliant unusual color combinations outlined in black,

usually printed on knitted fabric. White space is also utilized but the distinguishing feature is the use of exciting and unusual color combinations. *Der.* Prints are inspired by medieval and late Renaissance designs still used in flags and costumes of the famous Palio in Siena.

rainbow stripe   Full range of the spectrum hues arranged in bands on the fabric; a multi-striped effect made by weaving or printing.

regimental stripe   Wide, even colored stripes on plain dark background. Used for men's tie fabrics. *Der.* Taken from insignia on British military uniforms in which colors of stripes identify the regiments.

resist printing   † Method of printing fabric by first applying design to fabric with chemical paste that will not take dye, and then dying the fabric. When chemical is removed, design is left white against colored background, e.g., white polka dot on navy ground.

Roman stripe   Horizontal stripes, varied in size and color, grouped together with no contrast in background.

Romany stripe   See PRINTS, STRIPES, AND CHECKS: BAYADÈRE STRIPES.

satin stripe   Satin-woven stripes alternating with bands of plain fabric.

screen printing   Printing process in which a design for each color is etched on separate pieces of pure dye silk or MANUFACTURED FIBER enclosed in wooden frames. Fabric to be printed is stretched on a long table; each screen is placed individually over the fabric; and paint, applied with a squeegee, is pushed through the etched sections. Process produces especially vibrant colors and unusual designs. When made, using silk fabric, called *silk screen printing*.

shadow stripe   Indistinct narrow stripes, all in tones of one color family, woven vertically (e.g., navy, light blue, and gray-blue used together).

shepherd's check   Small checked patterned fabric usually made of black and white or of white and another color. Made in a TWILL WEAVE of fine- to medium-quality yarns. Originated from a checked length of fabric about 4 yards long and 1½ yard wide worn in a draped manner by Scottish shepherds in Scotland. Also called *shepherd's plaid.*

silk-screen print See PRINTS, STRIPES, AND CHECKS: SCREEN PRINTING.

stenciled print Design made by using cardboard or metal cutouts over fabric, spraying paint or roller printing over them. The uncovered portions absorb the color and form the pattern.

stripes See under category heading PRINTS, STRIPES, AND CHECKS.

stylized print Ideas presented in an abstract, rather than naturalistic, manner, reducing the objects to a design.

tablecloth check Large checkerboard check, 1–3″ in size, usually in red or blue alternating with white. *Der.* Originally used for tablecloths.

tattersall Fabric with an overcheck, approximately one-half-inch square made with colored lines in both directions, on a white or contrasting ground. Also called *tattersall checks.* Sometimes called *tattersall plaid.* Used for vests, sport shirts, and coats. *Der.* Named after Richard Tattersall, English horseman, founder of Tattersall's London Horse Auction Mart established in 1776. Also see PLAIDS AND TARTANS and VESTS.

ticking stripes Narrow woven dark-blue stripes, sometimes spaced in pairs, on a white ground made in a twill weave. *Der.* Originally a heavy fabric called *ticking* used to cover mattresses, now used for sport clothes and copied in lighter weights and other colors for clothing.

tie-dyed print Handmade print created by gathering the fabric and tying at intervals, then immersing in dye that does not penetrate the tied areas. When untied, reveals a pattern of irregular designs. Method originated in Dutch East Indies and became popular as a handicraft in the United States in late 1960s and after. Used on pants, knit shirts, dresses, and even furs. Also imitated commercially by other methods. Called *bandanna* in India.

victory stripe See PRINTS, STRIPES, AND CHECKS: HICKORY STRIPE.

wallpaper print Tiny floral stripes alternating with plain colored stripes, frequently of pastel colors. *Der.* Made in imitation of 19th-c. wallpaper.

warp print Design printed on warp yarns before fabric is woven, producing a watered effect with fuzzy edges. Also called *chiné* and *ikat.*

warp print

windowpane check Dark horizontal and vertical bars crossing over light background, giving effect of a window divided into small panes. Also called *windowpane plaid.*

Priscilla apron See APRONS.

private buying office The buying office of an individual retail firm. Also called *store-owned buying office.* Compare with ASSOCIATED BUYING OFFICE and INDEPENDENT BUYING OFFICE.

private label/private label brand Apparel, produced under some degree of control by a retailer, that has a retailer's label on the product. Unlike STORE BRANDS, private label merchandise may carry not only the store name, but also names other than that of the store.

prix seam See GLOVES AND GLOVE CONSTRUCTIONS.

product data management (PDM) Computer system that joins computer to computer, and also people to people by way of E-mail. This speeds up the product development cycle and reduces the time it takes to bring products to market.

production cutting A system of cutting large numbers of apparel pieces by laying fabric open across its entire width and for a specified length, then stacking fabric in multiple layers with the marker (see PRODUCTION MARKER) resting on the top. Cutting is done either by computer or by using hand cutting machines.

production marker Full-size master cutting layout not only of the pattern pieces for a specific style, but also for all the sizes specified for production.

profile hat See HEADWEAR.

progressive bundle system See BUNDLE SYSTEM.

progressive lens See EYEWEAR.

promenade costume/dress ∞ In last half of 19th c.: clothes suitable for walking and shopping as contrasted with a carriage dress worn for riding in a carriage. Also called *walking costume* or *dress.*

promenade skirt   See UNDERGARMENTS: HOOPS.

promotional markdowns   Temporary reductions in retail price when an item first is marketed to the public.

promotional orders   Purchases from vendors at lower-than-usual prices that can be sold at lower prices to the customer.

promotional pricing   Offering apparel at reduced prices.

pronged setting   See GEMS, GEM CUTS, AND SETTINGS.

proportioned   See HOSIERY AND PANTS.

prospector's shirt   See SHIRTS.

prototype   A sample garment made for a new style that will go into a manufacturer's or designer's current line. Generally made in new or in a facsimile fabric. If made in muslin, the prototype is usually called a *toile.*

Prussian collar coat   See COATS AND JACKETS.

psyche knot   See HAIRSTYLES.

psychedelic print   See PRINTS, STRIPES, AND CHECKS.

Pucci, Emilio   * See APPENDIX/DESIGNERS.

Pucci hat   See HEADWEAR.

Pucci print   See PRINTS, STRIPES, AND CHECKS.

pudding   See HEADWEAR.

pudding basin cut   See HAIRSTYLES: BOWL CUT.

puff   **1.** *v.* To make full, to enlarge. **2.** ∞ *n.* 19th-c. term for a V-shaped gore of thin fabric, that filled in space at back of waistband of men's trousers. Lacing was used to close gap, and fabric was pulled out through laces. **3.** Also see SHOULDERS AND SLEEVES: PUFF SLEEVE.

puffball skirt   See SKIRTS.

puffs   **1.** See HAIRSTYLES. **2.** See PULLINGS OUT.

pug hood   See HEADWEAR.

Pulitzer, Lilly   * See APPENDIX/DESIGNERS and LILLY®.

pullayne   See FOOTWEAR: CRAKOW.

pullback   See SKIRTS.

pull-down cutting   See GLOVES AND GLOVE CONSTRUCTIONS.

pulled fabric work   See EMBROIDERIES AND SEWING STITCHES: PUNCH WORK.

pullings out   ∞ Decorative effect used from 16th through mid-17th c. made by drawing out colored lining fabric or an undergarment through PANES or SLASHES in the outer garment, e.g., the DOUBLET, TRUNK HOSE, or sleeves. Also called *puffs.*

Pullman slipper   See FOOTWEAR.

pull-on/pullover   A garment without full-length opening so that it must be pulled over the head or feet, e.g., a pullover sweater as opposed to a cardigan, which buttons up the front. See BLOUSES AND TOPS: PULLOVER, GLOVES AND GLOVE CONSTRUCTION: PULL-ON GLOVE, PANTS: PULL-ON PANTS, SHIRTS: PULLOVER, SHORTS: PULL-ON SHORTS, SWEATERS: PULL-ON or PULLOVER SWEATER, and UNDERGARMENTS: PULL-ON GIRDLE.

pultney cap   See HEADWEAR.

pump   See FOOTWEAR.

punched   See FOOTWEAR: PERFORATIONS.

punch work   See EMBROIDERIES AND SEWING STITCHES.

punk/punk look   **1.** Fashion originating in London in the late 1970s that was a demand for attention and a protest against the establishment by working-class teenagers, who were largely unemployed. Their idea was to scare and frighten their elders, who responded with feelings of rage, guilt, compassion, and fear. It included pasty white makeup, blackened eyes, and much lipstick; hair was cut short and dyed or painted startling colors (e.g., red, yellow, orange, green, or lavender). Clothing included black leather jackets, stud-decorated jeans, and T-shirts printed with vulgar mes-

punk look

sages or pornographic pictures. Clothing was torn and soiled, held together by safety pins. Favorite accessory was a bicycle- or dog chain worn around the neck, sometimes used to fasten one leg to the other. Punk women wore hot pants, skirts with side slits, tight sweaters, and spike-heeled sandals. **2.** American version called **New Wave Punk** was an exaggerated theatrical look not associated with the working class. Look included ripped shirts, leather clothing, and extreme hairstyles (e.g., Mohawk, wild, spiky, or frizzy hair dyed in patches of various colors; e.g., blue, orange, pink). Worn mainly by rock entertainers and their followers. *Der.* From punk rock music, popular in late 1970s and after. **3.** A spinoff of the punk movement was **cyberpunk,** which combined elements of punk style with futuristic fantasy and technological decoration. Along with black leather, rubber, and PVC (polyvinyl chloride plastics), they wore accessories made from cables and circuit boards. Also see HAIRSTYLES: PUNK HAIR.

punto lace See LACES.

pure dye silk † Soft, lustrous, high-quality silk fabric from which the gum, or impurities, have been removed. So called because less than 10% (15% for black goods) metallic salts have been added to give the fabric more weight. Pure dye silk has a very good affinity for dye and may be printed, dyed, or screen-printed. Also see WEIGHTED SILK.

puritan See NECKLINES AND COLLARS and HEADWEAR.

purl knit † A weft knit fabric in which the knitting machine can form stitches on both the front and back of the fabric so that both sides of the fabric can have the same appearance.

purl stitch See EMBROIDERIES AND SEWING STITCHES.

purse Synonym for HANDBAG. See introduction to HANDBAGS AND RELATED ACCESSORIES.

push money See SPIFFS.

push-up bra See UNDERGARMENTS.

push-up jeans See PANTS.

put-on See WIGS AND HAIRPIECES.

puttee (putt-ee′) **1.** Legging worn by U.S. Army in World War I consisting of long strip of khaki-colored wool fabric, about 4″ wide, wrapped around leg from ankle to knee. **2.** Legging worn by U.S. Army made of shaped pieces of fabric or leather, usually closed with buckles, similar to GAITER. Also see LEGGINGS.

put-together look Use of separate items such as blouse, pants, and skirt plus jewelry and accessories worn by each person in an individual manner rather than a formula for conformity. Popular in late 1960s and after.

PVC jacket See COATS AND JACKETS.

PXM See GLOVES AND GLOVE CONSTRUCTIONS.

pyjamas British variant of PAJAMAS. See SLEEPWEAR AND LOUNGEWEAR.

pyramid coat See COATS AND JACKETS.

pyramid heel See FOOTWEAR.

python See LEATHERS.

P

qiviut † (kay′-vee-ut) Underwool of the domesticated musk ox. Spun into yarn, this fine, soft fiber is knitted into a variety of apparel by Eskimo women in Alaska. Sold to tourists and by mail order.

QR See QUICK RESPONSE.

quail-pipe boot See FOOTWEAR.

quaintise See ARMOR: COINTISE.

Quaker bonnet See HEADWEAR.

Quaker cap See HEADWEAR: JOAN CAP.

Quaker hat See HEADWEAR.

quality control Inspection of the quality of products before and/or after production in order to be sure that they conform to specified quality standards.

Quant, Mary * See APPENDIX/DESIGNERS.

quarter See FOOTWEAR.

quartered cap See HEADWEAR.

quarter socks See HOSIERY.

quartz See GEMS, GEM CUTS, AND SETTINGS.

quartz crystal watch See WATCHES.

quatrefoil (kat′-rah-foyl) Geometrical four-lobed design derived from heraldry.

queen size Term used for large size women's wear; particularly used for pantyhose.

queue (kew) See HAIRSTYLES.

queue de lion (kew de le-ohn) See HAIRSTYLES.

queue-peruke See WIGS AND HAIRPIECES.

Quick Response (QR) Phrase coined for use in the American textile industry to describe streamlining of manufacture and delivery of apparel to retailers. A key component of Quick Response is ELECTRONIC DATA INTERCHANGE.

quiff See HAIRSTYLES.

quill See FEATHERS.

quilling ∞ Trimming made of narrow fluted fabric, used in 19th c.

quill work Decorative designs made on fabric and leather by Native Americans using porcupine quills.

quilting Technique of joining together layers of fabrics, sometimes with BATTING or other filling between. Done by hand or machine topstitching in crisscross lines, in diamonds, or in other patterns. Heat-sensitive manufactured fibers may be quilted electronically, with heat being used to fuse the layers together. Used to provide added bulk or warmth (e.g., quilted petticoats worn as underskirts in 18th and 19th c.). Used for robes, raincoats, sport jackets, coats, handbags, and linings.

quintise See ARMOR: COINTISE.

quirk See GLOVES AND GLOVE CONSTRUCTIONS.

quissionet See UNDERGARMENTS: CUSHIONET.

quizzing glass See EYEWEAR: MONOCLE.

quoif See HEADWEAR: COIF.

quota A limit set on the quantity of textile, fibers, yarns, fabrics, manufactured products, and the like that can be imported to the United States in a specified period of time.

Rabanne, Paco * See APPENDIX/DESIGNERS.

rabat **1.** See CLERICAL DRESS. **2.** See NECKLINES AND COLLARS.

rabato See NECKLINES AND COLLARS.

rabbi See NECKLINES AND COLLARS: RABAT.

rabbit See FURS.

raccoon **1.** See COATS AND JACKETS. **2.** See FURS.

raccoon dog See COATS AND JACKETS: FURS: USSURIAN RACOON.

racing Adjective used for items of apparel and accessories derived from or inspired by clothing worn for various forms of competitive racing (e.g., foot racing, auto racing, and horse racing). See COATS AND JACKETS: RACING JACKET, FOOTWEAR: RUNNING SHOE, GLOVES AND GLOVE CONSTRUCTIONS: ACTION GLOVE.

racing silks See JOCKEY SILKS.

rack trade Apparel industry colloquialism for manufacturers who design, produce, and market belts to retailers.

raffia † (raf′-ee-uh) Fiber from species of Madagascar palm used for making hats, bags, and fabrics.

rag business/rag trade Slang term for APPAREL INDUSTRY.

raglan boot See FOOTWEAR.

raglan cape/raglan coat See COATS AND JACKETS.

Raglan, Lord (1788–1855) Fitzroy James Henry Somerset, British General in Crimean War. After losing an arm in the Charge of the Light Brigade in 1854, had a coat designed with special sleeve, later called RAGLAN SLEEVE (see under SHOULDERS AND SLEEVES.)

raglan sleeve See SHOULDERS AND SLEEVES.

rail **1.** See SCARVES. **2.** See SLEEPWEAR AND LOUNGEWEAR: NIGHT RAIL. **3.** See HEADWEAR: HEAD RAIL.

railroad trousers See PANTS.

railway pocket See POCKETS.

railway stitch See EMBROIDERIES AND STITCHES: CHAIN and TRICOT stitches.

raiment Poetic or archaic term for clothing.

rain Adjective describing apparel intended for use in rainy weather. See CAPES, CLOAKS, AND SHAWLS: RAIN CAPE and PONCHO #3, COATS AND JACKETS: RAINCOAT, FOOTWEAR: RAIN BOOT, HEADWEAR: RAIN BONNET and RAIN HAT.

rainbow stripe See PRINTS, STRIPES, AND CHECKS.

rain dress Dress made of plastic or of fabric treated for water repellency, an innovation of the 1960s.

rain or shine coat See COATS AND JACKETS.

rainwear Clothing and accessories that are waterproofed or water-repellent.

Rainy Daisy skirt/rainy day skirt See SKIRTS.

raised embroidery See EMBROIDERIES AND SEWING STITCHES.

rajah collar See NECKLINES AND COLLARS: NEHRU.

rajah jacket See JACKETS AND COATS: NEHRU.

ramie † Strong, soft, lustrous fiber, somewhat similar to linen from inner bark of *ramie* plant, formerly imported from China. Used for dress goods and hats. Also called *rhea* or *China grass.*

Ramillies wig See WIGS AND HAIRPIECES.

Ramsay tartan See PLAIDS AND TARTANS.

ranch coat See COATS AND JACKETS.

ranch mink See FURS: MINK and MUTATION MINK.

rand See FOOTWEAR.

ranelagh mob See HEADWEAR.

ranger's hat See HEADWEAR: MOUNTIE'S HAT.

rap See HIP-HOP.

Raphael's body ∞ Woman's fitted bodice worn from late 1850s through mid-1860s with a low square neckline. Sometimes worn with a high-necked *chemisette* underneath and matching skirt.

rapolin See BRAIDS.

ra-ra skirt See SKIRTS.

raschel knit † Type of warp knitting done on a special Raschel machine that can produce a wide variety of complex knit patterns, including lace-like effects.

Rasta dreadlocks See HAIRSTYLES: DREADLOCKS.

Rasta styles Clothing adopted by reggae musicians and their followers of the 1970s and 1980s that consisted of practical jackets and trousers worn with a T-shirt of red, gold, and green (the colors of the Ethiopian flag) and a large knitted TAM (see under HEADWEAR) placed over hair dressed in DREADLOCKS (see under HAIRSTYLES).

rat See HAIR ACCESSORIES.

Ratcatcher See SHIRTS.

ratiné † (rat′-in-ay) Spongy, rough, nubby-surfaced fabric loosely constructed in a plain weave. The appearance results from the use of *ratiné yarn* with nubs or knots at intervals. In better quality fabrics, the ratiné yarn is used in both directions. In less expensive variations, it is used only in the crosswise direction. *Der.* French, "frizzy" or "fuzzy."

rationals See ACTIVEWEAR.

rat-tail braid See BRAIDS.

rat-tail comb Comb for the hair with fine teeth and a long, pointed handle used for shaping curls.

rattan **1.** Flat reedlike stem from tropical palm woven to form *basket handbags* and other items. **2.** See CANE.

ratting See HAIRSTYLES: BACK-COMBING.

rave Refers to clubs where the young danced all night—often in warehouses—that appeared first in late 1980s in Britain and then spread to other countries. The illegal drug Ecstasy became associated with some of these clubs, and some fatalities did result. Styles associated with raves included athletic shoes and T-shirts with smiling-face logos. For boys baggy jeans, T-shirts, and hooded sweatshirts, similar to HIP-HOP styles. Girls wore cropped tops (see under BLOUSES AND TOPS), HOT PANTS (see under PANTS) and MINIDRESSES. Hats, jewelry, and whistles, used to accompany the music, were designed to attract attention.

rawhide See LEATHERS.

raw silk † Silk fiber reeled from cocoon while still containing the gum or sericin that gives it a rough, slightly sticky feel. Often used to make women's summer suits.

rayon † Generic fiber name for manufactured cellulosic fibers regenerated from short cotton fibers or wood chips. First produced by Count Hilaire de Chardonnet in 1889, it was worn at Queen Victoria's funeral in 1901. Known as "artificial silk" until 1927, after which the name rayon was used. Characteristics include a silky hand, shiny lustrous appearance, good dye absorbency, and good draping qualities. Disadvantages include poor wrinkle recovery and a tendency to shrink. Used for lingerie, dresses, blouses, and shirts. *Der.* French, "ray of light."

razor cut See HAIRSTYLES.

ready-to-wear (RTW) Apparel that is mass-produced in standard sizes. Records of ready-to-wear industry tabulated in U.S. Census of 1860 included HOOP SKIRTS, CLOAKS, and MANTILLAS. From 1890 on, shirtwaists and wrappers were added; and, after 1930, dresses. In French called *prêt-à-porter* and in the United Kingdom, *off the peg*. Also called *off-the-rack*.

rebato See NECKLINES AND COLLARS: RABATO.

Reboux, Caroline * See APPENDIX/DESIGNERS.

rebozo See CAPES, CLOAKS, AND SHAWLS.

rebras ∞ (ray-brah′) 13th to 17th-c. term used when apparel or accessory was turned back to reveal lining [e.g., REVERS (see under NECKLINES AND COLLARS) of coat, upturned brim on hat, or cuff of glove].

rècamier hairstyle See HAIRSTYLES.

Rècamier, Madame (ray′-cahm-ee-ay) Jeanne Françoise Julie Adelaide (1777–1849), famous beauty of Napoleonic era. Painted by both David and Gérard, famous French artists of her time. Her mode of dress and hairstyles were widely imitated.

reciprocated construction See HOSIERY.

reclaimed wool See RECYCLED WOOL.

recycled wool Under the amendments of 1980 to the Wool Products Labeling Act of 1939: (1) wool fiber that was pulled apart from yarn or fabric that was never used by the ultimate consumer or (2) wool fiber from yarn, fabric, or products used by consumers. This term replaced the terms **reclaimed wool, reused wool,** and **reprocessed wool.** Only wool that has never been used before can be called **wool, new wool,** or **virgin wool.**

Red Baron helmet See HEADWEAR: AVIATOR'S HELMET.

red crown See HEADWEAR.

Redfern, House of * See APPENDIX/DESIGNERS.

red fox See FURS.

redingote (red´-in-gote) **1.** Ensemble consisting of a dress with matching or contrasting full-length coat. *Der.* French, "mannish woman's frock coat" or English, "riding coat." **2.** See COATS AND JACKETS.

reductions Lowering the retail price of merchandise to encourage its sale so that new goods can replace older items. MARKDOWNS, MARKUP CANCELLATIONS, and **discounts** are all types of reductions used by retailers.

reefer See COATS AND JACKETS.

regalia (re-gale´-yah) Clothing established by custom for a particular social or professional rank, position, or organization.

regard rings See JEWELRY.

regatta shirt See SHIRTS.

Regency costume **1.** Period of English history during the regency of the Prince of Wales, 1811–1820, for George III. Noted for fashions of the DANDIES and BEAU BRUMMELL (see in alphabetical listings). **2.** Adjective describing apparel inspired by or derived from Regency Period styles. See COATS AND JACKETS: REGENCY COAT, NECKLINES AND COLLARS: REGENCY COLLAR.

regenerated fibers See MANUFACTURED FIBERS.

regimental stripe See PRINTS, STRIPES, AND CHECKS.

regional market A market (see MARKET #1) that serves U.S. retailers in a geographical region. Examples include Atlanta, Dallas, and Los Angeles.

regular The ordinary size range for clothing as opposed to special sizes (e.g., regular boys' sizes as opposed to slim or husky).

regular orders Those orders placed in season for goods that are part of the usual line of a manufacturer's products.

regular pricing Prices normally charged for products.

relationship merchandising A trend for department stores to emphasize presentation, customer service, and having the right products for their target market so that they can differentiate themselves from other competing stores.

religious medal See JEWELRY.

remnant † **1.** Short length of fabric remaining after yardage has been cut off a bolt or roll of fabric. Too short to make an entire garment, these pieces are sold at a special prices. **2.** Short lengths of fabric left at mill after winding bolts to be sold at retail. Also called *mill ends.* **3.** Short lengths of lace or trimming sold at reduced prices.

remote displays Product displays not located at the actual store, but placed in locations where they can alert potential customers to the store and its merchandise.

Renaissance lace See LACES.

reorders Orders for additional quantities of a product previously purchased by the retailer.

rep † Fabric with closely spaced crosswise ribs that may be made from a variety of fibers. Used for neckties and women's wear.

replaceable legs See HOSIERY.

rep stitch See EMBROIDERIES AND SEWING STITCHES.

reprocessed wool See RECYCLED WOOL.

rerebrace See ARMOR.

reserve wig See WIGS AND HAIRPIECES.

resident buying office (RBO) An organization with offices at the MARKET that offers consultation services and procures merchandise for retailers. The two major types of resident buying offices are INDEPENDENT BUYING OFFICES and PRIVATE BUYING OFFICES.

resist dyeing † Piece-dyeing process in which some of the yarns are treated with chemicals or covered with some water-resistant substance. These yarns remain undyed while other, untreated yarns, take the dye, resulting in a two-toned fabric. Also see PRINTS, STRIPES, AND CHECKS: RESIST PRINTING.

resist printing See PRINTS, STRIPES, AND CHECKS.

retailer Individual or firm that sells merchandise to the public. In the fashion industry, that merchandise would be apparel and related products.

retail store/direct market brand Brand name on merchandise that is the same as the retailer (e.g., Gap, L.L. Bean).

reticella lace See LACES.

reticulation See HEADWEAR.

reticule See HANDBAGS AND RELATED ACCESSORIES.

retro/retro look The return to the fashion look of earlier decades (abbreviated use of the word retrospective). Used when fashions from past eras are updated and used as current styles. Sometimes the date is attached (e.g., retro-thirties, retro-forties, retro-fifties).

returns to vendor (RTV) Return of goods to a manufacturer by a retailer.

retro style of 1982 reviving 1950s style

reused wool See RECYCLED WOOL.

revers (ri-veerz) See NECKLINES AND COLLARS.

reverse calf See LEATHERS.

reverse glove See GLOVES AND GLOVE CONSTRUCTIONS.

reverse guiches See HAIRSTYLES: GUICHE.

reversible clothing Any item of clothing made so that it can be worn on either side. Usually of different color, pattern, or style on reverse side. Popular for capes, ponchos, vests, and coats.

reversible fabric Any fabric that may be used on either side (e.g., DOUBLE CLOTH or CREPE-BACK SATIN).

Rex Harrison hat See HEADWEAR.

Reykjavik sweater See SWEATERS: ISLANDIC SWEATER.

rhea See RAMIE.

rhea feathers See FEATHERS.

Rhinegraves See PETTICOAT BREECHES.

rhinestone See GEMS, GEM CUTS, AND SETTINGS.

rhinestone button See CLOSURES.

Rhodes work See EMBROIDERIES AND SEWING STITCHES: PUNCHWORK.

Rhodes, Zandra * See APPENDIX/DESIGNERS.

rhodium See JEWELRY.

rhumba/rumba Adjective used to describe clothing inspired by or derived from Latin or South American dance costumes usually using ruffles. See RHUMBA DRESS, SHOULDERS AND NECKLINES: RHUMBA SLEEVE and UNDERGARMENTS: RHUMBA PANTIES.

rhumba dress Bare-midriff dress worn with full-length skirt split up the front, tight through the hips, flaring with a mass of circular cut ruffles from hips to hem. Popular after it was worn by movie star Carmen Miranda in 1940s, revived at intervals. *Der.* Named for South American dance.

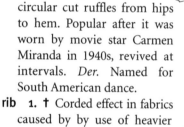

rhumba dress 1940s

rib 1. † Corded effect in fabrics caused by by use of heavier yarns in either lengthwise or crosswise directions (e.g. BENGALINE, GROSGRAIN, OTTOMAN, or FAILLE or on the diagonal by weaves such as TWILL). 2. Individual strip of metal that forms part of frame of umbrella (e.g., there are usually six to sixteen ribs in an umbrella). 3. See RIB KNIT.

riband ∞ (rib'-and) 1. The border of an item of apparel from 14th to 15th c. 2. Narrow band of decorative material or silk from 16th c.

ribbed hose See HOSIERY.

ribbon † Long narrow strip of silk, cotton, or rayon woven with selvages on both sides. Also made of acetate or other heat-sensitive fiber and then sliced into narrow strips with heated knives that fuse the edges. Used mainly for trimming and for tying hair. Made in a variety of weaves: (a) cross-ribbed, called GROSGRAIN; (b) with looped edges, called PICOT; (c) cut-pile surface, or VELVET (sometimes satin-backed); (d) SATIN; very narrow pink or blue satin is called BABY RIBBON.

ribbons of childhood Broad ribbon or tube of fabric attached to the shoulders of children's dresses in the 17th and 18th c. Some costume historians consider these to be the same as LEAD-

ING STRINGS, however others consider them to be a stylized form of Medieval hanging sleeves that were retained in the dress of upper-class children as a symbol of childhood.

ribbons of childhood
c. 1690

rib knit † Knitted fabric that shows alternate lengthwise rows of ribs and wales on both sides. (See RIB # 1 and WALE # 2.) More elastic, heavier, and durable than plain knitting. Used frequently on cuffs and necklines of sweaters and sport jackets.

rib-tickler Term used to describe short top that just reaches to ribcage—similar to BARE MIDRIFF top. Also see SWIMWEAR: RIB TICKLER SWIMSUIT.

Ricci, Nina * See APPENDIX/DESIGNERS.

rice braid See BRAIDS.

rich peasant look Designs from the late 1960s made in midi-length, of elaborate prints or plain colored silks, velvets, and rich fabrics ornately decorated with colorful embroidery and rich bands of braid. Yves Saint Laurent, Oscar de la Renta, and Giorgio Sant' Angelo designed many clothes of this type.

rickrack See BRAIDS.

ridicule See HANDBAGS AND RELATED ACCESSORIES: RETICULE.

riding Adjective describing apparel used for or derived from dress used for horseback riding. See ACTIVEWEAR: RIDING BREECHES, RIDING HABIT, RIDING SKIRT, and RIDING SMALLS; COATS AND JACKETS: RIDING COAT; and FOOTWEAR: RIDING BOOTS.

riding coat dress ∞ Woman's dress cut in coat-style worn from 1785 to 1800 with buttons down front, large collar and lapels, long tight sleeves, and skirt with slight train.

riding stock See TIES: STOCK.

rimless glasses See EYEWEAR.

ring See JEWELRY.

ring and pin See JEWELRY: ANNULAR and PENANNULAR BROOCHES.

ring bracelet See JEWELRY: SLAVE BRACELET.

ring buckle See CLOSURES.

ring collar See NECKLINES AND COLLARS.

ringlets See HAIRSTYLES.

ring purse See HANDBAGS AND RELATED ACCESSORIES: MISER'S PURSE.

ring watch See WATCHES.

ripple cape See CAPES, CLOAKS, AND SHAWLS.

ripple skirt See SKIRTS.

rise Men's tailoring term for distance from crotch to top of waistband in pants [e.g. HIP-HUGGER PANTS (see under PANTS) have a low rise].

robe **1.** Informal clothing usually styled like a loose coat; may be sashed, buttoned, zipped, or hang loose. Worn over pajamas or nightgown, at the beach, or for informal entertaining at home. Current meaning of the word is a shortened form of the word BATHROBE or DRESSING ROBE. See individual entries under SLEEPWEAR AND LOUNGEWEAR. **2.** Ceremonial garment made in long, loose, flowing style (e.g., academic robe, clerical robe, or coronation robe). **3.** In Middle Ages a long loose flowing gown or tunic worn as an outergarment. **4.** From 1817 to 1830, an outergarment or wrap; synonym for the PELISSE (see under COATS AND JACKETS). *Der.* Originally the robe meant all furniture and personal effects belonging to a person. Later it meant his collection of clothes; still later a GOWN. **5.** *v.* To put on a garment. Generally used in donning a ceremonial garment.

robe à la française See GOWN À LA FRANÇAISE.

robe à l'anglaise See GOWN À L'ANGLAISE.

robe à la Piedmontese See SACK #1.

robe à la polonaise See POLONAISE #1.

robe battante See SACK #1.

robe de chambre ∞ (robe de sham'-bra) **1.** 17th-c. term for man's informal style of dressing intended for occasions other than court functions, receptions, and ceremonies. Considered a DESHABILLE style of dress. **2.** 19th-c. term for woman's dress suitable for informal occasions or in the boudoir. Also called a *breakfast wrapper* in 1880s.

robe de style Evening dress of the 1920s with a dropped waistline and a full skirt, Originated by designer Jeanne Lanvin, this gown

robe de style 1920s

was an alternative to the tubular silhouette of the period.

robe gironnée ∞ (jir-own-nay′) Loose-fitting dress worn in 15th c. with PIPE-ORGAN PLEATS (see CLOTHING CONSTRUCTION DETAILS: GODET PLEATS) at waistline.

robe redingote ∞ Dress of 1830s and 1840s with collar and lapels on bodice, and skirt opening in front to show an underskirt.

robes of state See CORONATION ROBES.

Robespierre collar See NECKLINES AND COLLARS.

robe volante See SACK #1.

robin front ∞ 19th-c. term for bodice with trimming from shoulder to waist forming a deep V.

robings/robins ∞ Wide flat trimmings used in 18th and 19th c. around neck and down front of woman's bodice, sometimes continued down sides of open overskirt.

Robin Hood hat See HEADWEAR.

Rob Roy tartan See PLAIDS AND TARTANS: MAC-GREGOR TARTAN.

roc ∞ Loose-fitting gown of the late Middle Ages in which the bodice is cut with a round neckline from which a cascade of gathers or pleats falls at the very center of the front and back. Worn unbelted, the gown was made with either long or short sleeves and worn over an underdress that is sometimes visible at the neck or sleeves. Most often seen in Flemish and German art.

roc 2nd half 15th c.

roccelo See CAPES, CLOAKS, AND SHAWLS: ROQUELAURE.

Rochas, Marcel ✱ See APPENDIX/DESIGNERS.

rochet See EMBROIDERIES AND SEWING STITCHES.

rock crystal See GEMS, GEM CUTS, AND SETTINGS.

rocker/rocker look Styles associated with tough young British men in late 1950s, mixture of storm trooper and motorcyclist costume with crash helmet, tight jeans or DRAIN-PIPE TROUSERS (see under PANTS), black leather jacket, and knee-length boots or short boots with high heels. Rockers liked rock-and-roll music and admired Elvis Presley, movie star and singer, imitating his hairstyle.

rocklo See CAPES, CLOAKS, AND SHAWLS: ROQUELAURE.

rococo embroidery See EMBROIDERIES AND SEWING STITCHES.

roculo See CAPES, CLOAKS, AND SHAWLS: ROQUELAURE.

rodeo suit See ACTIVEWEAR.

Rodriguez, Narciso ✱ See APPENDIX/DESIGNERS.

roll **1.** See HEADWEAR. **2.** See HAIR ACCESSORIES.

rolled collar See NECKLINES AND COLLARS.

rolled hem See CLOTHING CONSTRUCTION DETAILS.

roller See HEADWEAR.

roller blades See FOOTWEAR.

roller print See PRINTING.

rollers See HOSIERY: ROLLUPS.

roller skate See FOOTWEAR.

roll farthingale See FARTHINGALE.

rolling ring See JEWELRY.

rolling stockings/hose See HOSIERY: ROLLUPS.

rollio See ROULEAU.

roll point collar See NECKLINES AND COLLARS.

roll sleeve See SHOULDERS AND SLEEVES.

roll-up **1.** See CUFFS. **2.** See SHOULDERS AND SLEEVES.

rollups See HOSIERY.

Roman collar See CLERICAL DRESS: CLERICAL COLLAR.

Romanian embroidery See EMBROIDERIES AND SEWING STITCHES: HOLBEIN WORK.

Romanian stitch See EMBROIDERIES AND SEWING STITCHES: ORIENTAL COUCHING.

Roman lace See LACES: RETICELLA

Roman leggings See FEMORALIA.

Roman stripe See PRINTS, STRIPES, AND CHECKS.

romantic **1.** Adjective used to describe feminine styles for women, and sometimes men, often decorated with lace, frills, and ribbon and made in soft fabrics. **2.** Styles associated with the Romantic period (c. 1820–1850) in art, literature, and music in Western European and American culture.

romantic look Return to frilly, fluffy ruffles, choker-necked Victorian blouses, and softer fabrics in 1967 after the rigid lines and geometric look of the Courréges style. Also see NEW ROMANTICS and EDWARDIAN LOOK.

romany stripes See PRINTS, STRIPES, AND CHECKS: BAYADERE STRIPES.

555

Romeo hairstyle See HAIRSTYLES.
romeo slipper See FOOTWEAR.
rompers **1.** Bloomer-type short pants introduced for children's playwear during World War I period. **2.** Similar styles for adult women in one-piece sport suits or in sleepwear consisting of shirt and shorts or bloomers, joined by waistline seam. **3.** See SLEEPWEAR AND LOUNGEWEAR.
rondella See JEWELRY.
ropa ∞ A woman's outer gown made either sleeveless or with sleeves that fell from the shoulders, unbelted in an A-line to the floor. Originating in Spain in the first part of the 16th c., it then spread throughout Europe.
roped chain See CHAINS.
rope necklace See JEWELRY.
roquelaure See CAPES, CLOAKS, AND SHAWLS.

ropa 2nd half 6th c.

rosary String of beads arranged on a chain with a pendant cross. Used by Roman Catholics for counting the prayers of the Rosary.
Rosebery collar See NECKLINES AND COLLARS.
rose cut See GEM, GEM CUTS, AND SETTIINGS.
rose-point lace See LACES.
rose quartz See GEMS, GEM CUTS, AND SETTINGS.
rosette (ro-zet′) **1.** Ornament arranged like a rose, usually ribbon arranged in standing loops or flattened into a formal pattern. Used to trim shoes in 17th c. and from then on to trim dresses and hats. See SHOE ROSES. **2.** See FURS. **3.** See LEATHERS.
rotary screen printing See PRINTING.
rotonde See CAPES, CLOAKS, AND SHAWLS.
rouche See RUCHING.
Rough Rider shirt See SHIRTS.
rouleaux ∞ (roo-low′) Tubular-shaped trimming stitched at regular intervals to make puffs of fabric. Used around hems of women's skirts in the 1820s. Also called *rollio.*
roulettes See PIPES.
round dress/round gown In 18th to mid-19th c., a full-length dress that did not open at the front to show a petticoat. Sources differ as to whether these gowns did or did not have TRAINS. Also called a *closed robe* or *closed gown.*

round-eared cap See HEADWEAR.
round hose See TRUNK HOSE.
roundlet See HEADWEAR.
round pocket See POCKETS.
round seam See GLOVES AND GLOVE CONSTRUCTIONS: OVERSEAM.
rowle See HAIR ACCESSORIES: ROLL.
roxalane bodice ∞ Term used from late 1820s on for low-necked bodice trimmed with wide pleated folds meeting at an angle at the waistline. Bodice had a central bone that held pleats in place.
roxalane sleeve See SHOULDERS AND SLEEVES.
roxburgh muff ∞ Woman's muff carried in 1816 made of swansdown fabric sometimes gathered at intervals and trimmed with bands of white satin.
Roy, Hippolyte * See APPENDIX/DESIGNERS.
royal George stock See TIES.
royal Stewart tartan See PLAIDS AND TARTANS.
RTV See RETURNS TO VENDOR.
RTW Abbreviation for the READY-TO-WEAR clothing industry.
rubber boot See FOOTWEAR.
rubber mask See MASKS.
rubbers See FOOTWEAR.
rubber shoe/rubber moccasin See FOOTWEAR: DUCK SHOE.®
Rubens hat See HEADWEAR.
rubicele See GEMS, GEM CUTS, AND SETTINGS: SPINEL.
ruby See GEMS, GEM CUTS, AND SETTINGS.
Ruby Keeler shoe See FOOTWEAR.
ruching (roosh′-ing) **1.** Trimming made by pleating a strip of lace, ribbon, net, fine muslin, or silk so that it ruffles on both sides. Made by stitching through the center of pleating. Also spelled *rouche, ruche.* **2.** Contemporary usage also applies the term to clothing with large rippled areas formed by gathers.

ruching #1

ruff See NECKLINES AND COLLARS.
ruffle Strip of cloth, lace, or ribbon gathered along one edge or cut in a curve to produce a ripple. Used to trim neckline, wrist, or hem of apparel. Also see FLOUNCE.

rug   See WIGS AND HAIRPIECES.

rugby shirt   See SHIRTS.

rugby shorts   See SHORTS.

rumba   See RHUMBA.

rummage sale clothes   Used and antique clothing usually gathered and sold under sponsorship or some organization such as a church. Sales are usually held in spring and fall for fundraising.

rump furbelow   See UNDERGARMENTS.

run   A flaw that may develop in jersey (see JERSEY #1) knit fabrics, especially hosiery, when a stitch breaks and the stitches connected to it unravel vertically. Also called a *ladder* because the flaw has the appearance of a ladder.

running shoe   See FOOTWEAR.

running shorts   See SHORTS: ATHLETIC SHORTS.

running stitch   See EMBROIDERIES AND SEWING STITCHES.

run proof   Hosiery and knit term for items made with specially interlocked stitches that withstand runs.

run resistant   Hosiery and knit term for stitches with locked or displaced loops that inhibit runs, but do not prevent them.

Russell, Lillian   (1861–1922) American singer and actress noted for her spectacular costumes, which had fitted, narrow waistlines, full bosoms and hips—also for her large hats. She represented the fashion ideal at the turn of the 20th c.

Russian blouse   See BLOUSES AND TOPS: COSSACK BLOUSE.

Russian blouse suit   ∞ **1.** For boys: A long belted blouse with box pleats in front, sometimes made with a sailor collar, sometimes with a turndown collar. Worn with knickers that came below the knees. **2.** For girls: A long overblouse, sometimes with Russian styling, worn over a full circular skirt. Worn during the early 20th c.

Russian braid   See BRAIDS: SOUTACHE BRAID.

Russian collar   See NECKLINES AND COLLARS: COSSACK COLLAR.

Russian crown sable   See FURS: SABLE.

Russian embroidery   See EMBROIDERIES AND SEWING STITCHES.

Russian leather   See LEATHERS.

Russian look   In fall-winter 1976–77 Saint Laurent introduced a collection of Russian dresses—evening dresses had long sleeves and tight-fitting bodices to a little below hips; usually made in black with bouffant gathered skirt in colored satins (e.g., red, green). A coat with high waistline made of elaborate gold brocade was also shown with fur Russian Cossack hat. Also see ZHIVAGO LOOK.

Russian shirtdress   Dress with high neckline banded in braid and closed on the side made with slightly full sleeves and banded at the wrist. Also called *Zhivago dress,* from clothes worn in 1965 film of Russian novel *Dr. Zhivago,* by Boris Pasternak.

Russian style dress   ∞ Two-piece dress of 1890s with knee-length tunic over full-length skirt, high COSSACK COLLAR (see under NECKLINES AND COLLARS), and embroidery trim around neck, cuffs, down side of blouse front, and around hem. Also see RUSSIAN SHIRTDRESS.

Russian styles   Clothing and accessories copied from those worn in pre-Revolutionary Russia. See BLOUSES AND TOPS: COSSACK, NECKLINES AND COLLARS: COSSACK COLLAR, HEADWEAR, and ZHIVAGO LOOK.

Rykiel, Sonia   * See APPENDIX/DESIGNERS.

S Letter designation for small size used along with EXTRA SMALL, MEDIUM, LARGE, and EXTRA LARGE for men, women and children. See SMALL. Also see SHORT.

S.A. **1.** Abbreviation for *Seventh Avenue*, an allusion to New York City garment district, coined by trade newspaper *Women's Wear Daily*. **2.** A 1940s' term for sex appeal, as exemplified by glamorous Hollywood film stars.

sabaton See ARMOR.

sable See FURS.

sabot See FOOTWEAR.

sabot sleeve See SHOULDERS AND SLEEVES.

sabot-strap shoe See FOOTWEAR.

Sabrina neckline See COLLARS AND NECKLINES.

sack/sac/saque/sack gown **1.** ∞ Applied from the 16th to the 18th c. to various styles of women's dresses. In the 16th c. seems to have referred to a loose-fitting gown for country wear. It is mentioned in *Pepy's Diary* in 1669, but its lines are not clear. Much used in the 18th c., this dress was fashionable in France at beginning of 18th c. (about 1704) and popular until 1755. Popular in England from 1720 to 1780. Its main feature was the full back or **sack-back** (called a WATTEAU BACK in the 19th c.) with two large box pleats stitched from neckband to shoulders

sack #1, 18th c.

and then hanging free to make a full skirt. In its earliest form, it was unbelted and loose in front and back from shoulder to floor and was also called *robe battante* (bah-tahnt'), *robe volante* (voh-lahnt'), or *innocente* (ahn'-oh-sahnt). From 1720 to 1730 the bodice was fitted at sides and front, loose in back. After 1750, the skirt was split up the front to reveal an underskirt. From 1770s pleats in back were sometimes stitched to the waist as in ROBE À L'ANGLAISE, or loose as in ROBE À LA PIEDMONTESE or *Piedmont gown*. The **Brunswick gown**, worn from 1760 to 1780, was sack-backed with a front-buttoned bodice and long sleeves and also known as the *German gown*. Also called *Adrienne*. **2.** ∞ Woman's or child's loose-fitting jacket of 1896. **3.** See CHEMISE #2.

sack-back See SACK #1.

sack coat See COATS AND JACKETS: STROLLER.

sack dress See CHEMISE # 2.

sack jacket See COATS AND JACKETS.

sack overcoat See COATS AND JACKETS.

sack suit Man's single-breasted daytime suit of early 20th c. Made with unfitted long jacket having wide shoulders. Pants were cut wide in legs and at hems. The earliest example of the modern business suit.

sacque (sack) **1.** See SACK. **2.** Layette item of late 19th and early 20th c. for an infant. Styled like a small jacket usually having ribbon ties for closing. **3.** See SLEEPWEAR AND LOUNGEWEAR: DRESSING SACQUE.

sack suit

saddle See FOOTWEAR, HANDBAGS, AND RELATED ACCESSORIES, CLOTHING CONSTRUCTION DETAILS: SEAMS, SHOULDERS AND SLEEVES, and EMBROIDERIES AND SEWING STITCHES.

saddle coat See COATS AND JACKETS: POMMEL SLICKER.

saddle leather See LEATHERS.

saddle shoulder See SHOULDERS AND SLEEVES.

saddle stitch See EMBROIDERIES AND SEWING STITCHES.

saddle-stitched seam **1.** See GLOVES AND GLOVE CONSTRUCTIONS. **2.** See FOOTWEAR: SADDLE SEAM.

safari *adj.* Describing garments adapted from, or similar to the BUSH JACKET (see under COATS AND JACKETS) and other clothes worn in South Africa by hunters on safaris. See BELTS: SAFARI BELT, HANDBAGS AND RELATED ACCESSORIES: SAFARI BAG, HEADWEAR: SAFARI HAT, POCKETS: BELLOWS POCKET, and SHIRTS: SAFARI SHIRT.

safari dress/safari look Restyling for daytime wear, in 1967 by Dior, of African bush jacket—a belted hunting jacket buttoned down the front, two bellows pockets with flaps on chest, and two toward hem. In 1980s this look resurfaced with popularity of film *Out of Africa*, 1986, starring Meryl Streep and Robert Redford. *Der.* From name for an African hunting trip.

safeguard **1.** See SKIRTS: FOOT MANTLE. **2.** See APRONS. **3.** See SWADDLING CLOTHES.

safari dress

safety See EYEWEAR and FOOTWEAR.

safety pin **1.** Utilitarian elliptical pin with covered head to sheath the point, introduced from Denmark in late 1870s. **2.** Similar shaped pin used on front of kilt. Also called *kilt pin.* **3.** See JEWELRY.

sagum See CAPES, CLOAKS, AND SHAWLS.

sailcloth † Durable canvas fabric made in a rib weave. When made in medium weight in cotton or a cotton blend, it is used for sportswear.

sailor Adjective, in use since 1860s, describing clothes and accessories inspired by uniforms worn by British, French, and U.S. Navy. See HEADWEAR: SAILOR HAT, NECKLINES AND COLLARS: SAILOR COLLAR, PANTS: SAILOR PANTS, SCARVES: SAILOR SCARF, SHORTS: SAILOR SHORTS, and TIES: SAILOR'S TIE and SAILOR'S REEF KNOT.

sailor dress Dress with sailor collar or MIDDY-BLOUSE (see under BLOUSES AND TOPS) effect trimmed with rows of braid in nautical style. The style was very popular for girls from 1890 to 1930, and for women from 1890 on.

sailor suit Boy's suit, introduced in 1860s, that was inspired by French and British sailors' uniforms. It consisted of MIDDY BLOUSE (see under BLOUSES AND TOPS) with braid-trimmed square collar in back, plus either baggy KNICKERS or DANISH TROUSERS (see under PANTS). Called a *jack tar suit* when made with bell-bottom trousers (younger boys wore knickers) in 1880s and 1890s. Has continued as a popular children's style.

sailor suit

Saint George cross See JEWELRY: CRUSADER'S CROSS.

Saint Laurent, Yves * See APPENDIX/DESIGNERS.

salaried buying office See INDEPENDENT BUYING OFFICE.

sallet See ARMOR.

Sally Jess® bag See HANDBAGS AND RELATED ACCESSORIES.

salon de couture (koo-ture′) Haute couture designer's showroom.

salon dresses Department-store term for expensive dresses made by well-known designers sold in a special room in department store. Dresses are not hung on view in salesroom but brought out by salespeople and sometimes shown on live models.

salt-box pocket See POCKETS.

Salvation Army bonnet See HEADWEAR.

samarra/samarre See CHAMARRE.

Sam Browne belt See BELTS.

sample cut Fabric of three to five yards in length obtained by the apparel manufacturer from a textile mill to use for making a PROTOTYPE garment.

sample sewer/sample hand A person with excellent sewing skills who constructs the PROTOTYPE garment using equipment and production processes similar to those that would be used in the manufacturing process.

Sanchez, Fernando * See APPENDIX/DESIGNERS.

sandal See FOOTWEAR.

sandalfoot hose/sandalfoot pantyhose See HOSIERY.

Sander, Jil * See APPENDIX/DESIGNERS.

sandwich-board jumper See JUMPERS.

Sanforized® † Registered trademark of The Sanforized Company, a division of Cluett, Peabody & Co., Inc., appearing on fabrics with a residual shrinkage of not more than one percent, despite repeated laundering.

sans culottes ∞ (sahn koo-lowt′) Nickname for those opposing the monarchy during the French Revolution, [i.e., those who wore trousers (the common people) instead of BREECHES, worn by the aristocrats]. *Der.* French, literally "without breeches."

Sant'Angelo, Giorgio * See APPENDIX/DESIGNERS.

santon See NECKLINES AND COLLARS.

saphirine See GEMS, GEM CUTS, AND SETTINGS: SPINEL.

sapphire See GEMS, GEM CUTS, AND SETTINGS.

sard See GEMS, GEM CUTS, AND SETTINGS: CARNELIAN.

Sardinian sac See COATS AND JACKETS.

sardonyx See GEMS, GEM CUTS, AND SETTINGS.

sari (sah′-ree) Woman's outer garment consisting of a long length of cotton, silk, or manufactured fiber fabric wrapped around the waist and pleated at the side to form a skirt. One end is thrown over shoulder or used to cover the head. Worn with bare midriff blouse called a CHOLI (see under BLOUSES AND TOPS). Western adaptations of the garment have been worn since the early 1940s. Also spelled *saree.*

sari

sarong/sarong dress (sar-ong′) Long, straight wraparound skirt made of bright-colored tropical design fabric with deep fold in front, held on by scarf around waist. Worn by men and women of the Malay Archipelago. Adapted as a beach dress style with wraparound skirt draped to one side and strapless top first designed by Edith Head for Dorothy Lamour film *Hurricane,* in 1937. Worn by Lamour in many films of the 1930s and 1940s. *Der.* Copied from Indonesian native dress. Also used to describe garments based on the sarong style. See SWIMWEAR: SARONG SWIMSUIT, SKIRTS: SARONG SKIRT, and UNDERGARMENTS: SARONG®.

sarong

sarong swimsuit See SWIMWEAR.

sash See BELTS.

sash ring ∞ Large ring on a chain suspended from a belt at the hip in late 1860s. Overskirt was pulled through ring to drape the skirt.

Sassoon hairstyle See HAIRSTYLES.

satchel See HANDBAGS AND RELATED ACCESSORIES.

sateen † Smooth glossy cotton fabric made in the SATEEN WEAVE (see under SATIN WEAVE) with floating crosswise yarns on the right side, given a lustrous finish, and used mainly for linings. Formerly spelled *satine.*

sateen weave See SATEEN.

satin † Smooth lustrous silk fabric woven with floating yarns in the warp in many variations: (a) woven with a crepe back, and called CREPE-BACK SATIN; (b) finished to be rather stiff in texture and called **panne satin;** (c) finished with a dull nubbed surface (see NUB YARN) and a satin back and called **antique satin.** Usually made of FILAMENT YARNS. *Der.* Name derived from *Zaytoun,* now Canton, China, from which fabrics were shipped in the Middle Ages.

satin back See CREPE-BACKED SATIN.

satin-backed ribbon See RIBBON.

satine See SATEEN.

satin-faced crepe See CREPE-BACKED SATIN.

satin stitch See EMBROIDERIES AND SEWING STITCHES.

satin stripe See PRINTS, STRIPES, AND CHECKS.

satin weave A basic weave in which the lengthwise, and sometimes the crosswise yarns, float over five to eleven yarns before interlacing. As a result the surface has a smooth feel and a lustrous appearance. When floats are in the crosswise direction, fabric is called *satin weave*

SATEEN and this construction is sometimes called a **sateen weave**.

sauna suit   See ACTIVEWEAR.

sausage curl   See HAIRSTYLES.

sautoir (sow-twar)   **1.** See JEWELRY. **2.** See NECKLINES AND COLLARS: SANTON.

Savile Row   Street in London's West End where many of the finest men's custom tailoring shops have been located since Henry Poole & Co. opened in 1843. They cater to wealthy internationals, stressing quality and conservatism.

Savile Row look   See BRITISH LOOK.

saw-toothed hem   See CLOTHING CONSTRUCTION DETAILS.

Saxony lace   See LACES: PLAUEN LACE.

Scaasi, Arnold   *   See APPENDIX/DESIGNERS.

scabilonians   See UNDERGARMENTS.

scaling hose   See TRUNK HOSE.

scallop   **1.** The shell of a mollusk used in ornamentation. See HEADWEAR: COCKLE HAT. **2.** One of series of curves or circle segments—like one edge of the scallop shell—forming an ornamental edge on fabric, lace, or garment edges. See CLOTHING CONSTRUCTION DETAILS: SCALLOPED HEM.

scallop #2

scalpette   See WIGS AND HAIRPIECES.

scarab (skar'-ab)   A beetle, regarded as the symbol of immortality by the ancient Egyptians, used in stylized designs on fabrics or carved from gemstones with inscriptions on the undersides. Semiprecious stones carved with scarabs are still used in rings and bracelets, and were especially popular in the United States in the late 1940s.

scarab bracelet   See JEWELRY.

Scarborough ulster   See COATS AND JACKETS.

scarf cap   See HEADWEAR.

scarf hat   See HEADWEAR.

scarf mask   See MASKS.

scarf pin   See JEWELRY: STICKPIN.

scarf slide   See NECKERCHIEF SLIDE.

SCARVES

scarf (pl. *scarfs* or *scarves*)   **1.** Decorative or utilitarian accessory worn draped around the shoulders, the neck, or over the head for warmth or adornment. May be square, oblong, or triangular and made of knitted, crocheted, or woven fabric. **2.** A decorative sash worn diagonally from shoulder to opposite hip, like a BALDERICK. **3.** See TIES.

Antoinette fichu   See SCARVES: FICHU #1.

apache scarf (ah-patch'-ee or ah'-pash)   Man's small square or triangular scarf introduced in late 1960s for wear instead of a necktie. Worn knotted or pulled through a slide. *Der.* French slang for gangster or thug, especially as depicted by French nightclub dancers. The French word taken from the southwest American Indian tribe, thought to be very fierce.

ascot scarf   Oblong scarf, frequently white, lapped over and worn loosely around the neck by men and women. Reintroduced in late 1960s by Saint Laurent, the Paris couturier, who emblazoned it with his initials, making it a status symbol. *Der.* Named for a scarf worn at Ascot racetrack in England. Shown at TIES: ASCOT.

babushka (bah-boosh'-ka)   Triangular-shaped scarf or square folded diagonally, worn draped over head and tied under chin in manner of Russian peasant woman. *Der.* Russian, "grandmother." So called because it was worn by older Russian immigrants to the United States. Also called a *kerchief.*

bachlick   ∞ Woman's FICHU (see under SCARVES) of CASHMERE edged with SWANSDOWN, with a hoodlike point finished with tassel in back. Worn over daytime dresses in late 1860s.

bandanna (ban-dan'-nah)   Large square cotton handkerchief, either red or blue with distinctive black and white design. Worn in late 19th and early 20th cs., tied around the head or neck by workmen, and later adopted in all colors for wear with sport clothes.

bandelet   ∞ (ban'-duh-let)   16th-c. term for any type of scarf.

bayadère (by-yah-deer')   Long narrow scarf of silk or lace worn in early 19th c. *Der.* Costume of Indian *bayadère* or "dancing girl."

blue billy   Neckcloth made of blue fabric with white polka dots; introduced by the fighter

William Mace and worn from about 1800 to 1820.

boa (bow′-ah) Round, narrow, long scarf worn from 1829 on, and especially fashionable in 1890s, 1920s, and 1970s. Made of feathers, pleated silk, fur, or swansdown. Also called *French boa*.

boa

breast kerchief ∞ Scarf worn under doublet or gown, wrapped around neck and shoulders for warmth, in late 15th to mid-16th c.

buffon ∞ (boof′-own) Woman's large scarf or neckerchief of gauze or fine linen draped around neck, shoulders, and puffed out over the chest. Sometimes supported by wire framework in 1780s. Also spelled *buffont*.

buffon

calligraphic scarf Letters of the alphabet arranged to form a pattern in much the same manner a picture is "drawn" on a typewriter by using Xs and other characters. Introduced in late 1960s.

Charlotte Corday fichu See SCARVES: FICHU #1.

chemisette ∞ (shem-ee-zet′) Scarf or FICHU (see under SCARVES) of cambric, tulle, or muslin fabric worn as fill-in for low-necked gown in 18th and 19th cs. Also see PARTLET and NECKLINES AND COLLARS: TUCKER. Also called a *chemise tucker*.

chin cloak ∞ From about 1535 to 1660s a synonym for MUFFLER or SCARF (see under SCARVES). Also called *chin clout, chin cloth,* and *chinner*.

comforter Woolen scarf worn around the neck in cold weather, so named from 1840 on.

designer scarf Scarf made in an elaborate design using beautiful or unusual colors. In the late 1960s, it became popular to print the name of a famous company or designer on the pure silk scarves, which were then called **signature scarves**. The fashion started in Paris with Balenciaga, Dior, and Saint Laurent—spread to Italy and United States as a status symbol for most prestigious designers.

dog collar scarf Triangular or oblong scarf folded to go around neck twice, bringing ends back to the front where they are knotted or looped over.

écharpe (eh′-sharp) Synonym for scarf. *Der.* French, "scarf."

fanchon See SCARVES: HALF HANDKERCHIEF.

fascinator Large long woolen scarf made in a lacy knit worn over the head or around the shoulders by women. First fashionable in the early 1890s and worn at intervals since.

feather boa See SCARVES: BOA.

fichu ∞ (feesh′-u) **1.** Neckwear usually consisting of a large square of muslin folded diagonally to form a triangle and worn in the 18th c. As time progressed became more elaborate—shaped to fit the neck, trimmed with ruffles, lace, and RUCHING. Frequently fastened or tied in front with hanging ends. Continued to be worn until about 1871. Variations in the style were often named after women of the 17th c. and 18th c. and included the **Antoinette fichu** or *Marie Antoinette fichu* (1850s), draped around the neck and crossed at the waistline to form two long cords that fall to the hips; the **Charlotte Corday fichu** (mid 1860s), made of grenadine trimmed with a ribbon threaded through a wide hem, which crossed in front, and tied in back; **fichu lavalliere** (fish-u la-va-leer) (1868), with sides not crossed in front and fastened with a button. Named after the Duchesse de La Vallière, a mistress of King Louis the 14th; **Martha Washington fichu** (mid-1890s), large and draped, extending to shoulders with pointed ends fastened by a rosette of lace in front, and two wide ruffles of lace extended around the edge (*Der.* An adaptation of style worn by Martha Washington, wife of the first U.S. president, George Washington). *Der.* French, "handkerchief." **2.** A triangle of net edged in lace worn in early 19th c. as a capelet.

fichu #1

fichu lavalliere See SCARVES: FICHU #1.

fichu menteur ∞ (feesh′-u mahn-ture′) Scarf worn by women in 1780s at neck of coat or low bodice. Draped so it puffed out to increase apparent size of bust. Also see SCARVES: BUFFON.

flea fur ∞ Fur scarf made of any small animal with head, tail, and paws attached to a jeweled muzzle and chain. Worn by women during late 16th c. as decoy for obnoxious insects. *Der.* From fact that "fleas" were attracted to it. Also called *Flohpelzchen* (flow-pelz´-ken).

Flohpelzchen See SCARVES: FLEA FUR.

folette/follette ∞ (fall-et) Loose scarf or FICHU (see under SCARVES) in triangular shape of soft light-colored fabric, worn during first half of 18th c. Ends were tucked into neckline of bodice.

foulard scarf (foo-lahr´) **1.** Scarf of silk twill, called FOULARD, often made with small designs printed on plain ground. Originally imported from India.

fraise ∞ (fraze) **1.** Embroidered muslin scarf, folded across the chest and kept in place by an ornamental pin, worn by women in 1836 with a carriage dress. **2.** Fashionable neckpiece worn by women from about 1877 to 1885. Had a FRILLING or RUCHING around a high neckline which continued down front of dress nearly to waistline, trimmed with bow and frilled at edges.

French boa See SCARVES: BOA.

fur scarf Neckpiece made of several skins of a small animal such as *mink,* or one large fox skin complete with head, tail and paws. Popular in the 1930s in black, platinum, or silver fox. In the late 1940s and early 1950s made of MINK, SABLE, FISHER, KOLINSKY, and BAUM MARTEN (see under FURS). A fashion revived in 1973, continuing into 1980s and periodically since.

galatea fichu ∞ (gal-ah-tay´-ah feesh´-u) Large ruffled FICHU (see under SCARVES) of mid-1890s with unpressed vertical pleats ending at center front waistline in a point and two ruffles around the outside edge.

hacking scarf Long oblong scarf doubled and placed at back of neck. Both ends are then pulled through loop and hang down in front. *Der.* Long scarf, originally 72″ worn by four-in-hand coach drivers in Old England; popular at Oxford and Cambridge Universities in England in 1931 when it was worn by Prince of Wales, becoming a fad for U.S. college students in 1932.

half handkerchief ∞ Neck or head scarf worn by women in 18th and early 19th c. made of decorative fabric in triangular shape. From 1830s on, called **fanchon.**

kerchief Scarf worn as head or neck covering, usually a square folded into triangle with crossed ends fastened on chest. Also called *neckerchief.* Originally spelled *kerchner, kercheve, karcher.* See SCARVES: NECKERCHIEF.

mantilla See HEADWEAR.

Martha Washington fichu See SCARVES: FICHU #1.

muffler **1.** Long scarf approximately 12″ wide; usually knitted or woven of plaid or plain-colored wool, silk, or rayon. Worn from 19th c. to present. Fashionable for men when made out of FOULARD, tie silk, and white silk for evening wear from 1920s to 1940s. **2.** See SCARVES: CHIN CLOAK.

neckcloth See SCARVES: NECKERCHIEF #2.

neckerchief **1.** Triangular scarf, either cut in shape of a triangle or a square folded diagonally, worn by men and women in late 1960s and early 1970s. Worn from 19th c. on by cowboys instead of a necktie. Also worn by Boy Scouts with uniforms. **2.** ∞ Late 14th to early 19th c., a square or oblong of fabric folded around the neck and worn by women. Called a *neckcloth* pior to the 16th c. **3.** ∞ A 19th-c. term sometimes used for a large silk *cravat* worn by men and women.

neckpiece BOA or SCARF (see under SCARVES), usually of fur.

nycette ∞ Late 15th and early 16th c. term for light scarf worn at neck. Also spelled *niced.*

Paisley scarf **1.** Square or oblong scarf made with paisley designs that are shaped like a tear drop, rounded at one end and with a curving point, and delicate tracery, done in rich reds, rusts, beiges, and browns. Usually made in an allover design. **2.** Unusual scarf featuring a shell design with elongated blocks around edge, Paisley print inside, and plain cream-colored center sprinkled with a few designs. Comes in 18″ x 62″ size and is copied from shawl in National Museum of American History's Costume Division of the Smithsonian Institution.

palatine ∞ (pal′-ah-tyne) Fill-in or small scarf of tulle worn around the neck to cover the low neckline of dresses of mid-17th c. *Der.* Named after Princess Charlotte of the Palatine (Liselotte), who tried to induce more modesty in dress at the French court. Also spelled *pallatine.*

rail ∞ Folded *neckerchief* worn like a shawl around neck by women from late 15th to late 17th c. See SCARVES: NECKERCHIEF # 2.

ring scarf Oblong scarf with ends stitched together to form a circle. Worn with jewelry to form a collar on a dress in early 1950s.

sailor scarf Square NECKERCHIEF (see under SCARVES) folded diagonally, worn under sailor collar and slipped through loop front of blouse or tied in a knot. Also called *sailor tie.*

shade ∞ Sheer scarf of lace, net, or gauze worn by women over the bosom of a low-necked bodice. Sometimes had a small ruff attached at the neck. Worn from latter half of 18th to early 19th c.

signature scarf See SCARVES: DESIGNER SCARF.

solitaire ∞ Narrow colored scarf, worn by women in mid-1830s, loosely tied with ends hanging to knees—usually worn with a white dress.

souvenir scarf Large square scarf imprinted with scene, picture, symbol, or words depicting a special place, e.g., Miami, Paris. Usually bought by tourists to remind them of a special holiday spent at that place.

stock Oblong scarf worn loosely lapped over rather than tied. During 1968 introduced to be worn instead of *neckties* by men. Also see TIES.

stole **1.** Long wide scarf, often fringed at ends, made of fabric, knit, or fur worn since 19th c. as woman's wrap **2.** Long wide scarf matched in fabric to woman's dress worn with baretop dress in 1950s, especially in the evening.

stole

sultana scarf ∞ Scarf of oriental colors worn in mid-1850s

that tied below waistline with long hanging ends.

tasseau ∞ (tass-oh′) Triangular scarf, usually black, used to fill in the low bodice neckline worn by women in the late 15th c. Also called *tassel. Der.* Latin, *tassa,* "clasp."

Thérèse ∞ (ter-eece) Scarf of light gauze fabric often worn over an indoor cap in the 1770s and 1780s.

zendado ∞ (zehn-dah′-doh) Scarf, usually of black fabric, covering head and falling to waist in front, where it tied. Fashionable in France and Venice in second half of 18th c.

---

scavilones See UNDERGARMENTS: SCABILONIANS.

scenic print See PRINTS, STRIPES, AND CHECKS.

schenti ∞ (shen′-tee) Ancient Egyptian man's garment with the appearance of a skirt that ranged in length from above the knee to the ankle. Styles varied over time; some were pleated at center front. Often they were worn with an elaborate belt. Also spelled *shendot, shenti, shendyt, skent.* Shown at EGYPTIAN STYLES.

Schiaparelli, Elsa * See APPENDIX/DESIGNERS.

Schiffli embroidery (sif-lee) See EMBROIDERIES AND SEWING STITCHES.

schlappen See FEATHERS.

Scholl's® exercise sandals See FOOTWEAR.

school ring See JEWELRY: CLASS RING.

school sweater See SWEATERS: LETTER SWEATER.

scissoring See SLASHING.

scoop bonnet See HEADWEAR.

scoop neckline See NECKLINES AND COLLARS.

scooter shorts/skirt See SKIRTS: SKORT.

Scotchgard® † Registered trademark of Minnesota Mining and Manufacturing for a fluoride-based finish used on fabrics to repel grease and water stains.

Scotch plaid Yarn-dyed fabrics woven in plaids that represent the various clans of Scotland. See PLAIDS AND TARTANS.

Scotch suit See HIGHLAND SUIT.

Scottie See HEADWEAR.

Scottish Highlander costume See HIGHLAND DRESS.

scrambled eggs See HEADWEAR: ASTRONAUT'S CAP.

scratch wig See WIGS AND HAIRPIECES.

S

screen print See PRINTS, STRIPES, AND CHECKS.

screen print top See BLOUSES AND TOPS.

screw-back earrings See JEWELRY.

scrub suit/scrubs Pants and tunic top with round or V-neck and short or long sleeves. Worn with matching pants. Adapted from garments worn by physicians when operating on patients, and now used for casual wear by men.

scrub suit

scrunchies See HAIR ACCESSORIES.

scuba mask See MASKS.

scuba suit See ACTIVEWEAR: WET SUIT.

scuff See FOOTWEAR.

sculptured hair See HAIRSTYLES.

sculptured heel See FOOTWEAR.

scye (sigh) See ARMHOLE.

sea bag See HANDBAGS AND RELATED ACCESSORIES: DUFFEL BAG.

seal/sealskin 1. See FURS: FUR SEAL and HAIR SEAL. 2. See LEATHERS.

sea legs See ACTIVEWEAR.

seam See CLOTHING CONSTRUCTION DETAILS.

seam binding/seam tape See CLOTHING CONSTRUCTION DETAILS.

seamed hose/pantyhose See HOSIERY.

seamless hose See HOSIERY.

seamless knit See CIRCULAR KNIT.

seam pocket See POCKETS.

seamstress Same as DRESSMAKER.

sea otter See FURS.

seasonal goods Merchandise that has its best sales during either the fall or spring season.

secondary line A less expensive version of a design originated by a manufacturer and sold by that manufacturer in different markets, different stores, and to a different group of customers than the original design.

seconds Merchandise with slight flaws that is sold at lower prices.

secrete See SKIRTS: JUPE #2.

seed bead necklace See JEWELRY.

seed embroidery See EMBROIDERIES AND SEWING STITCHES.

seed pearl See GEMS, GEM CUTS, AND SETTINGS.

seed stitch See EMBROIDERIES AND SEWING STITCHES.

seersucker † Medium-weight fabric made with lengthwise crinkled stripes alternating with plain woven stripes. Puckering is achieved by releasing the tension at intervals on the lengthwise yarns. Effect is permanent and will not wash out.

see-through/see-through look Fashion started by American designer Rudi Gernreich in 1964 with sheer blouses over bare skin. In 1966, sheer dresses with bands of glitter at strategic places, usually worn with body stockings underneath, were shown by Paris designers Pierre Cardin and Yves Saint Laurent. In 1968 transparent blouses were seen and by the late 1960s, there were transparent voile shirts for men. These fashions were part of a general trend toward greater acceptance of nudity. Also see PANTS: SEE-THROUGH PANTS and SHIRTS: SEE-THROUGH SHIRT.

seggard See SKIRTS: SAFEGUARD.

seint See CEINT.

self-covered Used in sewing when belts and buttons are made in fabric that matches the garment on which they are placed. See BELTS: SELF-COVERED and CLOSURES: COVERED BUTTON.

self-edge See SELVAGE.

self sash See BELTS: SELF-COVERED BELT.

self-winding watch See WATCHES.

selham See CAPES, CLOAKS, AND SHAWLS: BURNOOSE.

sell through A percentage computed from a comparison of the number of items sold to the number of items purchased from a particular line. A higher percentage would indicate a more successful line.

seloso A long, flowing African dress worn by women, similar to the BUBA, introduced in 1969.

selvage/selvedge (sehl′-vudge) Term used since 14th c. for narrow tightly woven band on either edge of fabric parallel to the warp that prevents fabric from raveling. Originally called *self-edge.* Also called *list* and *listing.*

semi cut See FOOTWEAR.

semiformal suit Suit appropriate for semiformal occasions. For men, a tuxedo or dinner jacket is required. For women: any type of dressy suit or dress made in a more elaborate style or fabric that would be suitable for semiformal dinners, dances, or weddings.

semiprecious gems See GEMS, GEM CUTS, AND SETTINGS.

sempstress bonnet See HEADWEAR.

señorita See COATS AND JACKETS.

separate collar See NECKLINES AND COLLARS.

separates In retailing, sportswear items—shirts, blouses, sweaters, and pants—designed to wear in combination with other items from same line.

sequin (sea'-qwin) Small shiny iridescent disk of metal or plastic pierced in the center and sewn on garments in a decorative design or in rows to cover a portion or the entire surface. Often used for evening dresses or sweaters. Also see PAILLETTE.

serape See CAPES, CLOAKS, AND SHAWLS.

serge † (serj) Suiting fabric made in an even twill with worsted yarns. Occasionally some woolen yarn is used to provide greater softness. Generally piece-dyed and given a clear finish that becomes shiny with wear. Used for suits, skirts, and pants. *Der.* Latin, *serica,* "silk," indicating it was first a silk fabric; later Italian, *sergea,* "cloth of wool mixed with silk," probably appearing as early as the 12th c.

serpentine belt See BELTS.

serpentine skirt See SKIRTS: MORNING-GLORY SKIRT.

serpent ring See JEWELRY.

service cap See HEADWEAR.

set-back heel See FOOTWEAR.

set-in 1. See SHOULDERS AND SLEEVES. 2. See WAISTLINES.

set-in thumb See GLOVES AND GLOVE CONSTRUCTION.

setting See GEMS, GEM CUTS, AND SETTINGS.

set-under heel See FOOTWEAR.

seven-eighths See LENGTHS and PANTS.

seven-fold tie See TIES.

seventeen-jeweled watch See WATCHES.

Seventh Avenue Nickname for garment district of New York City, roughly from 40th to 34th streets and from Avenue of the Americas (6th Ave.) to 9th Ave., where much of American ready-to-wear is produced. Abbreviated *S.A.*

sew To join together by hand or machine stitching.

sew by A sample garment sewn and submitted to the apparel manufacturer for approval by a contractor. Sewn production goods are compared to the sample to check quality. Also called a *counter sample.*

sewing machine Machine for stitching that was first patented in the 1830s in France and in the United States in the 1840s. Use of sewing machines in making Civil War Uniforms helped to demonstrate their usefulness, and home use expanded in the postwar period. Through innovative manufacturing and marketing, I. M. Singer captured much of the growing market for sewing machines, which were responsible for much of the rapid growth of the READY-TO-WEAR garment industry.

shade 1. Color term for hues with black added to darken (e.g., navy blue is correctly called a "shade of blue"). Light blue, however, with white added is called a "tint of blue." 2. See SCARVES. 3. See HEADWEAR.

shades See EYEWEAR.

shadow See EMBROIDERIES AND SEWING STITCHES, LACES, and PRINTS, STRIPES, AND CHECKS.

shadow-panel slip See UNDERWEAR.

shag See HAIRSTYLES.

shagreen See LEATHERS.

shahtoosh Exceptionally soft, fine, and rare wool taken from a Tibetan antelope, the chiru, which is an endangered species. The animals must be killed in order to obtain their wool, and it is illegal in the United States to buy or sell products made from this fiber. Shahtoosh shawls sell for as much as $15,000 on the black market.

shaker knit A heavyweight rib knit fabric. Used for sweaters. Developed by members of the Shakers, an American religious sect.

shakespeare collar See NECKLINES AND COLLARS.

Shakespearean costume See ELIZABETHAN STYLES.

shakespeare vest See VESTS.

shako (shay-ko) See HEADWEAR.

shale See CAPES, CLOAKS, AND SHAWLS.

shallow Characterizes a merchandise assortment that has styles in relatively few sizes and colors.

sham See SHIRTS: HALF SHIRT.

shamew See CHAMARRE.

S

sham hanging sleeve See SHOULDERS AND SLEEVES: HANGING SLEEVE.

shank See FOOTWEAR.

shank button See CLOSURES.

shantung † (shan-tung´) Medium-weight fabric woven with irregular, elongated slubs (see SLUB YARN) in the crosswise direction caused by yarns of uneven diameter throughout. Originally made of TUSSAH SILK yarn that varied in thickness, texture is now imitated with yarn of various fibers. Used for dresses, sportswear, and a wide variety of items.

shapewear See UNDERGARMENTS: BODYSHAPERS.

sharkskin **1.** † Worsted fabric woven in a TWILL WEAVE with alternating black and white yarns in both the directions to give a grayed effect. Characteristic feature is the smooth, sleek, clear finish. Used for men's suits. **2.** † Lightweight acetate (sometimes rayon) sharkskin uses filament yarns in a plain, basket, or sometimes jacquard weave to get a smooth sleek appearance. Usually made in white but sometimes dyed, used for sportswear and uniforms. **3.** † See LEATHERS.

shave coat See SLEEPWEAR AND LOUNGEWEAR.

Shaver, Dorothy President from 1946 to 1959 of Lord & Taylor, a specialty store in New York City, one of the first women to hold such a position. A backer of American designers during World War II, when French couture was in eclipse. An important person in the development of clothing design in the United States.

shawl See introduction to CAPES, CLOAKS, AND SHAWLS.

shawl collar See NECKLINES AND COLLARS.

shawl-collared cardigan See SWEATERS: TUXEDO SWEATER.

shawl tongue See FOOTWEAR: TONGUE.

shawl waistcoat See VESTS.

sheared raccoon See FURS.

shearing **1.** See FURS. **2.** † Textile process of clipping nap of fabric to desired length.

shearling **1.** See FURS. **2.** See LEATHERS. **3.** See COATS AND JACKETS.

sheath **1.** Straight, narrow fitted dress usually with no waistline but shaped to body by vertical darts, or with set-in waistline. Ease of skirt obtained by

sheath #1

inverted pleats at sides or center back. **2.** Tight-fitting dress with regular waistline seam or set-in waistline and sheath skirt that is very narrow at hem and slashed at back to facilitate walking. Both styles were popular in 1950s and early 1960s. Revived periodically.

sheath skirt See SKIRTS.

sheath swimsuit See SWIMWEAR.

sheepskin See LEATHERS and COATS AND JACKETS.

sheer † **1.** Adjective describing any fabric that is fine and transparent or semitransparent. **2.** See HOSIERY.

shell See categories of BLOUSES AND TOPS, FOOTWEAR: SKIMMER, SWEATERS, TIES, and ZIP-IN/ZIP-OUT LINING in alphabetical listing.

shell cameo See CAMEO.

shell lining Lining for only part of a coat or jacket, similar to a HALF-LINING. Also see ZIP-IN/ZIP-OUT LINING.

shell stitch See EMBROIDERIES AND SEWING STITCHES.

shenti/shendot/shendyt See SCHENTI.

shepherdess hat See HEADWEAR: BERGÈRE HAT.

shepherdess heel See FOOTWEAR: MUSEUM HEEL.

shepherd's check/shepherd's plaid See PRINTS, STRIPES, AND CHECKS.

sheriff tie See TIES.

sherte See UNDERGARMENTS.

shetland † **1.** Soft suiting fabric made of fine wool from Shetland sheep of Scotland. Usually woven in HERRINGBONE WEAVE, the term refers to the type of wool used. **2.** Knitted fabric or item such as a sweater, made from Shetland wool. Also see LACES and SWEATERS.

shibori † (she-bor´-ee) Japanese fabric ornamentation technique often used by artists in creating WEARABLE ART. Created by stitching gathers into fabrics before dyeing. After dyeing the stitched areas may be released to display complex patterns in the areas protected by the stitching.

shift #1

shift **1.** Straight-lined basic dress of 1960s, hanging away from body, similar to CHEMISE DRESS of 1957. The shift dress introduced a diagonal upward dart from the side seam that improved the fit. **2.** See UNDERGARMENTS: CHEMISE.

shigra See HANDBAGS AND RELATED ACCESSORIES.

shillelagh See CANE.

shingle See HAIRSTYLES.

shirring See CLOTHING CONSTRUCTION DETAILS.

shirt button See CLOSURES.

shirt collar See NECKLINES AND COLLARS.

shirt-drawers See UNDERGARMENTS.

shirtdress Straight-lined dress buttoned down the front cut similar to a man's shirt, worn with or without a belt. Side seams are often slashed and the hem rounded, similar to the tail of a man's shirt. Popular in 1967, it was a variation of the classic coat-dress or shirtwaist and is revived occasionally.

shirt front Term used from 1860s on for a man's backless false shirt, which had a complete front but tapered into a band in back and buttoned in center back of collar. Also see CLERICAL DRESS: CLERICAL FRONT.

shirtings † Fabrics traditionally used for men's shirts, and now for women's shirts as well, such as broadcloth, chambray, madras, oxford, and poplin. Now also used for women's shirts.

shirt-jac See SHIRTS.

SHIRTS

shirt **1.** Clothing for the upper part of the body that is usually more tailored than a blouse. May be closed in front or back or pulled on over the head; some are worn tucked in while others are worn outside of the lower garment. For women and girls: worn with pants, skirt, shorts, jumper, or suit, and buttoned right over left. For men and boys: worn with pants, shorts, or suit and buttoned left over right. Worn since early Middle Ages, the shirt originally slipped on over the head, was worn next to the skin; and was considered an undergarment. Collarless at first, a neckband was added in the 14th c.; a standing collar in the 15th c.; and embroidery, frills, and lace in 17th and 18th c. Innovations of the 19th c. included shirts that buttoned down the front and removable collars and cuffs. Usually white, although colors, including pink, were introduced in mid-19th c., printed shirts with white collars in 1860s, and stripes in the late 19th c.

In the 20th c., the white shirt became the standard for wear with business suits until the 1960s when colors were accepted. The attached collar gained popularity in 1920s and today detachable collars are seen only rarely for formal wear. **2.** In 1890s term applied to a summer blouse worn by women. See BLOUSES AND TOPS: SHIRTWAIST. In 1920s and 1930s, shirts became popular for sportswear for women.

Afghanistan wedding tunic/shirt 18th c.-style velvet tunic-blouse, lavishly decorated with gold embroidery, worn in early 1970s by men in the United States in both original and copied styles.

aloha shirt See SHIRTS: HAWAIIAN SHIRT.

apache shirt (ah-patch′-ee) Overblouse or tuck-in shirt of pullover type. Neckline is cut in low V, sometimes laced, sometimes with Italian collar (see under NECKLINES AND COLLARS). Sleeves are sometimes long, full, and gathered into band at the wrist. *Der.* Named for Native American tribe of the southwestern United States.

A-shirt See SHIRTS: ATHLETIC SHIRT.

athletic shirt Sleeveless shirt with large armholes and scooped neckline, worn for track and active team sports, copied for men and women in 1960s and early 1970s. Also called TANK TOP or *A-shirt*. Also see UNDERGARMENTS.

athletic shirt

barong tagalog (ba′-rohn teh-gah′-log) Man's *overblouse*-type shirt worn in the Philippines for informal occasions. Made with no buttons and a vent at the neckline of fine sheer fabric and frequently trimmed with embroidery; introduced for casual wear in United States in late 1960s. Sometimes called *barong*.

baseball shirt/baseball jersey Knit shirt with three-quarter-length RAGLAN SLEEVES (see under SHOULDERS AND SLEEVES) that are usually made in contrasting color to the body of the shirt. May have a round neckline bound with contrasting color or slit neckline with buttons. Became popular in 1980s. *Der.* From shirt worn by major league baseball players under uniforms.

basque shirt (bask) Striped, wide CREWNECKED (see under NECKLINES AND COLLARS) shirt popular in the 1930s.

Ben Casey shirt See SHIRTS: MEDIC SHIRT. *Der.* Named for television series *Ben Casey*, popular in early 1960s.

big shirt See SHIRTS: OVERSIZED SHIRT.

big T-shirt Extremely large mini-length shirt with placket neckline, tailored collar and all-in-one sleeve. Worn as a beach coverup. Can also be worn as a minidress or tunic over pants. Also called *oversized shirt.*

bodyshirt 1. Shirt fitted by shaping side seams to conform to body lines, introduced in early 1960s. Also called *tapered shirt.* 2. Long shirt with rounded tails worn by girls over short shorts in 1960s. 3. Woman's leotard or bodysuit combination often made with a snap crotch. Introduced in 1960s in stretch fabrics. Also see SHIRTS: LEOTARD SHIRT.

bodyshirt #3

boiled shirt See SHIRTS: FORMAL SHIRT #3.

bosom shirt 1. Man's formal white shirt with starched bib front. 2. ∞ Shirt worn in late 19th and early 20th c., made with collar and bib front of shirt fabric and rest of shirt of an inferior fabric, sometimes knitted.

bowling shirt Shirt designed to be worn by men and women for bowling—personalized with name of individual on front and team name on back.

bush shirt See SHIRTS: SAFARI SHIRT.

button-down shirt See SHIRTS: IVY LEAGUE SHIRT.

calypso shirt (kal-ip'-soh) Tailored collar or V-neck shirt that ties in center front, giving a bare-midriff effect. *Der.* Style of music characteristic of the West Indies, where shirt was originally worn.

camp shirt Conventional front-buttoned shirt with a notched collar. Usually made of woven cotton and polyester blends in solid colors, prints, or blocks of color.

camp shirt

cardigan shirt Collarless, front-buttoned shirt with round or V-neckline that is identical to cardigan sweater, but usually made in lighter-weight knits. *Der.* Named for the Seventh Earl of Cardigan, who needed an extra layer of warmth under his uniform during the Crimean War in 1854.

cartoon T-shirt Conventional T-shirt with round neck, short sleeves, and screen-printed with slogan or cartoon.

cavu shirt Long-sleeved man's sport shirt, popular from 1940 to 1950, with single pocket on the left and pointed collar. Closed diagonally from under collar almost to right side seam.

chemisette See SHIRTS: HABIT SHIRT.

chukka shirt See SHIRTS: POLO SHIRT.

clerical shirt See CLERICAL DRESS.

coat shirt Shirt that buttons down front like a coat. Introduced in the United States in 1890s for men; now the conventional-type shirt. Formerly all shirts were pullover placket style.

competition-striped shirt Sport shirt designed with wide colored stripes alternating with white. Also see SHIRTS: RUGBY SHIRT.

corazza ∞ (kor-ats'-zah) Man's shirt with close-fitting sleeves, buttoned down the back, tapered to fit the body and worn from 1845 on. Usually made of cambric or cotton.

Cossack shirt 1. Russian-type shirt with standing collar and neck placket placed to one side. Often made with braid trimming at neck, down front, and at cuffs. 2. Similar style with TURTLENECK (see NECKLINES AND COLLARS) called **turtleneck Cossack shirt.**

cowboy shirt Shirt with a convertible collar sometimes worn with a NECKERCHIEF (see SCARVES) or a STRING TIE (see TIES), often closed with GRIPPERS (see under CLOSURES). May have pockets in front and V-shaped yoke in front and back that is sometimes made of contrasting fabrics. Originally worn by cowboys in the western United States and now worn by men, women, and children in all parts of this and some foreign countries. Also called a *western shirt.*

cowboy shirt

S

C.P.O. Navy blue shirt of lightweight wool worn by chief petty officer in U.S. Navy, made with buttoned front and patch pockets. Adapted for civilian wear, sometimes in wool plaids, and worn open as a jacket over shirt or T-shirt by men, women, and children in late 1960s and after.

crew-neck shirt Plain pullover knit shirt, usually made with short sleeves and a CREW NECKLINE (see under NECKLINES AND COLLARS). *Der.* From knit shirts worn by members of a "crew" of a racing shell.

dandy shirt Shirt with lace or self-ruffles down front and at cuffs, popular in late 1960s for women and worn with dinner suits in evening by men. *Der.* From shirts worn by BEAU BRUMMELL and other 18th- and 19th-c. dandies.

dishrag shirt ∞ Net shirt that first became popular on the French Riviera in the 1930s.

drawstring shirt Hip-length shirt with drawstring at bottom giving a bloused effect. Designed to be worn over a bathing suit and frequently made of terrycloth or cotton knit. Introduced in 1940s and 1950s and still used.

dress shirt **1.** Traditional buttoned-down-the-front shirt usually worn by men with a necktie and a traditional suit. Made in tuck-in style with TAB, SPREAD, BUTTONED-DOWN, or PIN COLLAR (see under NECKLINES AND COLLARS) and with conservative sleeves with SINGLE OR FRENCH CUFFS (see under CUFFS). Popular for men since 1920s, when it replaced shirt with separate collar. Originally made in woven cotton, now made in cotton/polyester blends, and in fine knitted nylons and polyesters. **2.** See SHIRTS: FORMAL SHIRT.

dueling shirt Man's full-sleeved shirt of slip-on type sometimes worn with long stock around the neck. *Der.* Named after full-sleeved shirts shown in movies depicting era of the Three Musketeers. Similar to SHIRTS: FENCING SHIRT.

emperor shirt ∞ A country gentleman's shirt of red flannel worn in the 1850s and 1860s.

epaulet shirt (ep′-ah-let′) Shirt possessing long sleeves, buttoned front, convertible collar, patch pockets with bellows pleats, and buttoned-down flap. The characteristic feature is a sep-arate epaulet tab on each shoulder with button near neckline. Also called *pilot shirt*. Shown at EPAULET.

extra-long knit shirt T-shirt to knee or below, styled with ribbed or placket neckline in plain or striped fabric worn with below-the-calf matching skirt.

fencing shirt Unisex shirt with large full sleeves and pointed collar, frequently laced at neck. *Der.* Similar to those worn in old swashbuckling movies by Errol Flynn and Tyrone Power. Similar to SHIRTS: DUELING SHIRT.

fiesta shirt (fee-ess′-tah) Man's white cotton sport shirt trimmed with a wide band of eyelet embroidery down either side of front. Popular vacation wear from Acapulco, Mexico, in late 1960s. Also see SHIRTS: MEXICAN WEDDING SHIRT.

fishnet shirt Round-necked, raglan-sleeved shirt made of a loose, openwork, diamond-shaped knit. Designed to keep warm air next to skin, but allow perspiration to evaporate. Undershirt originally used by Norwegian army made of 100% cotton for protection against 0 degree cold and 90 degree heat.

flannel shirt Shirt of colored or plaid flannel fabric with one or two patch pockets and conventional or convertible neckline. Worn originally by woodsmen, later for sports (e.g., hunting). From early 1960s popular in lighter-weight washable fabrics for general wear. In the early 1980s a lining might be added and shirt was frequently worn as a jacket.

football jersey/football shirt **1.** Knit shirt with round neck, long or short sleeves set on dropped shoulders, and large numerals printed on front and back. Copied from shirts worn by football players and popular for children and teenagers in 1960s. Also called *numeral shirt*. **2.** In early 1980s and after made with very long dropped shoulders in short rib-tickler style of mesh fabric. **3.** ∞ Shirt worn for football games in 1870. Made with long sleeves of knitted jersey with horizontal stripes.

formal shirt **1.** Man's conventional white shirt with pleated front, WING COLLAR and long sleeves, usually finished with FRENCH CUFFS. Worn with TUXEDO JACKET and black BOW

S

TIE, or TAILS and WHITE TIE. See cross references under NECKLINES AND COLLARS, CUFFS, COATS AND JACKETS, and TIES. **2.** A similar men's shirt styled with ruffles made in white or colors. Fashionable particularly for weddings or semiformal wear since late 1960s. **3.** ∞ Formerly a shirt with highly starched bib front and detachable stiff starched collar and called a *boiled shirt.*

formal shirt #1

full tee Shirt cut out of a circular piece of fabric gathered into waistband in front and back and stitched at the sides to form deep dolman-like sleeves. Finished with a wrapped peplum below waistline. Design originated with Paris couturier Pierre Cardin in mid-1980s.

guayabera shirt (gwah-ya-bare'-a) **1.** Lightweight overshirt made with convertible collar, short sleeves and four large patch pockets. Has two sets of pin tucks in front running from small shoulder yokes to hem, and three sets of pin tucks in the back from yoke to hem. Small white pearl buttons are used for the front closing, pocket flaps, and at the top and bottom of the sets of tucks. Copied from shirts worn by the well-dressed businessmen in pre-Castro Havana. **2.** Another style is similar with embroidered stripes down front instead of tucks styled for men and women. *Der.* Shirt worn in Cuba by guava-tree growers.

habit shirt ∞ **1.** Linen shirt with standing collar, ruffled front, and wrist ruffles. Worn under a vest as part of woman's RIDING HABIT (see ACTIVEWEAR) in 18th and 19th c. **2.** Shirt worn as fill-in under low necklines in early 19th c. Also called *chemisette.*

half shirt ∞ Man's short shirt, with decorated panel down front, worn over plain or soiled shirt from 16th to 18th c. Also called *sham.*

Hawaiian shirt Man's sport shirt printed with colorful Hawaiian floral or other local designs. Made

Hawaiian shirt

with a CONVERTIBLE COLLAR (see NECKLINES AND COLLARS) and worn outside of trousers. Appears to have been introduced in the late 1930s for local wear, adopted by tourists and military men stationed in Hawaii, and gradually more widely seen on the Mainland after World War II. In 1951, President Harry Truman appeared on the cover of *Life* magazine in an Hawaiian shirt. Continues to be a staple wardrobe item in Hawaii and is periodically very popular on the Mainland as well. Also called *aloha shirt.*

Henley shirt Lightweight knit shirt with buttoned PLACKET (see under CLOTHING CONSTRUCTION DETAILS) at neckline, made in striped or plain knits with contrasting lining at placket and around ribbed neck. Popular in early 1960s and has become a classic knit shirt style for men, women, and children. *Der.* Copied from shirt worn originally by rowers in crew races at Henley, England. Also see SHIRTS: WALLACE BEERY SHIRT.

Henley shirt or Wallace Beery shirt

hunting shirt Bright-red wool shirt worn by hunters, so they are visible for long distances in woods.

Ivy League shirt Traditional shirt with buttoned-down collar, front buttoned, and styled with a YOKE in back with a loop at center of yoke. Worn first by college men in the 1950s and later by girls and boys. *Der.* Named for the group of eastern colleges called "the Ivy League."

jersey See SHIRTS: KNIT SHIRT.

jockey shirt Woman's shirt with contrasting colored inserts, similar to JOCKEY SILKS. Introduced as sportswear in late 1960s after first woman was accepted as a professional jockey.

knit shirt Sport shirt made of knitted fabric usually in pullover style. First introduced in mid-19th c. and called a **jersey.** Made of worsted wool and so-called because the fabric was first knitted on the Isle of Jersey, off the coast of England. Early shirts were worn for

S

football, rowing, and for other sports. In 1920s worn for tennis. In 1930s knit shirts with placket necklines and convertible collars were introduced for casual wear at resorts for men. In the 1950s and 1960s and after, knit shirts increased in popularity for men, women, and children due to improvements in knitting and acceptance of less formal style of dress.

Lacoste® An internationally recognized trademark used extensively on apparel as well as other goods. The term originally identified the knit shirts manufactured by La Chemise Lacoste of Paris, marked with a small alligator symbol on left front. The shirts were designed of piqué knit with the shirt tail being slightly longer in back so that it would not pull out when worn during active sports. *Der.* René Lacoste, an international tennis champion, nicknamed "le Crocodile" by French sportswriters in the 1920s. Lacoste had his friends in a textile company produce a new style of short-sleeved cotton knit shirts that he designed and sold to replace the uncomfortable long-sleeved woven shirts then worn by tennis players. He adopted the alligator symbol as the logo for knit shirts of this design because of his nickname.

leotard shirt (lee′-ah-tard′) Fitted shirt with a long tail that snaps between the legs making a leotard-type garment.

Lord Byron shirt Shirt with full sleeves and long pointed collar worn open at neck in shape of a V. Popular in 1920s and late 1960s. Also called *poet's shirt. Der.* Named for Lord George Gordon Byron, early 19th-c. English poet.

medic shirt White shirt-jacket with standing-band collar and shoulder closing worn by members of medical profession. Also called *Ben Casey shirt.*

meditation shirt Loose, open-sleeved, pullover tunic, usually made of Indian printed cotton or of solid colors and banded with embroidery around slit neck, across shoulders, and at hem. *Der.* Part of late 1960s ethnic look inspired by eastern gurus.

Mexican wedding shirt Tailored shirt of a crisp white fabric usually made with wide bands of embroidery down either side of front and on collar, popular in Acapulco, Mexico, for men and women in late 1960s. *Der.* Inspired by shirts worn by Mexican peasant grooms at weddings. Also see SHIRTS: FIESTA SHIRT.

midriff shirt Shirt for women cut to just below bustline, revealing rib cage. Often improvised from a conventional shirt by tying the tails in a knot under the bosom.

muscle shirt **1.** Descriptive term for a tight-fitting knitted shirt usually made in black or dark color, banded with white around the neck, short sleeves, and on underarm seams. Popular in late 1960s. **2.** Later version is sleeveless with rib-knit band around upper arm. Made in white and colors with printed designs or words on front. *Der.* Fitted tightly to reveal "muscles" of upper arm.

negligée shirt ∞ (neh′-glee-zheh) Term used for a man's shirt, either white or striped, with white stiff separate collar and white cuffs. Worn from early 1900s to about 1925.

nightshirt See SLEEPWEAR AND LOUNGEWEAR.

numeral shirt See SHIRTS: FOOTBALL SHIRT.

Nureyev shirt (noor-ay′-ef) Shirt with long full sleeves gathered in bands at wrists and a low round neckline finished with bias binding, popular in late 1960s. *Der.* Named for Rudolf Nureyev, ballet performer who defected from his native Russia to the West in 1961.

overshirt Any shirt styled to be worn outside of trousers or skirt, rather than tucked in.

oversized shirt Shirt cut extra large and extra long, usually made with button closing and convertible collar. Also called *big shirt.*

pilot shirt See SHIRTS: EPAULET SHIRT.

pocket T-shirt Simple knit shirt worn for sports with crew neck and tiny rounded pocket on left breast.

poet's shirt See SHIRTS: LORD BYRON SHIRT.

polo shirt A knitted shirt with PLACKET NECK-LINE and collar (see under NECKLINES AND COLLARS) usually made with short sleeves and originally used when playing polo in 1920s, then introduced for men's sportswear in the 1930s. Now a classic shirt style.

polo shirt

prospector's shirt Shirt worn next to the skin made of knitted silk fabric that insulates. Similar in style to WALLACE BEERY knit shirt (see under SHIRTS).

pullover Any light knit shirt without neck placket or fastening (e.g. SHIRTS: T-SHIRT or FOOTBALL SHIRT).

regatta shirt ∞ (re-gaht′-tah) Man's cambric or oxford striped shirt with plain front. Worn as informal summer wear in 1840s.

Rough Rider shirt Khaki shirt buttoned down the front and made with standing collar, breast pockets with flaps, and epaulets. *Der.* Similar to shirts worn by Theodore Roosevelt, Leonard Wood, and their volunteer cavalry regiment in Cuba during Spanish-American War in 1898.

rugby shirt Knit shirt with broad stripes in two contrasting colors with small white rib knit collar and cuffs. The PLACKET NECK-LINE (see under NECK-LINES AND COLLARS)

rugby shirt

closed with a zipper or buttons. *Der.* So called in imitation of shirts worn in Great Britain when playing rugby.

safari shirt African-inspired shirt introduced by Dior in mid-1960s for women. Styled with lapels, buttoned center-front closing, and four large pockets—usually of bellows-type. Same as *bush shirt. Der.* Named after an African hunting trip.

see-through shirt **1.** Woman's shirt of transparent fabric worn without undergarments. Introduced by Parisian couturier Saint Laurent in spring 1968 and popularly accepted in 1969 and 1970. Presented by Rudi Gernreich in 1964 for "at-home" wear but not called by this name at that time. Also called *see-through blouse.* **2.** Voile and sheer fabric shirts as worn by men in the late 1960s and early 1970s.

sham See SHIRTS: HALF SHIRT.

shirt-jac Front-buttoned shirt worn outside the trousers for sportswear. May have side slits, FLAP POCKETS (see POCKETS), and sometimes worn open over another shirt or knit shirt. *Der.* Combination of words "shirt" and "jacket."

skivvy Knit shirt, copy of undershirt worn by sailors, made with bound neckline and tiny placket opening in front. Often used in the plural, **skivvies,** to refer to men's underwear. *Der.* Scot-Gaelic, *skivvy* or *skivvies,* slang for sailors' underwear.

sport shirt **1.** Any type of shirt worn without a necktie by a man. At first a woven-fabric shirt with a CONVERTIBLE COLLAR (see under NECKLINES AND COLLARS) worn outside or tucked in trousers, popular in mid-1930s. Now any shirt, other than a DRESS SHIRT (see under SHIRTS), whether it is woven or knitted. **2.** Tailored or knitted shirt worn by women as sportswear since 1940s.

stock-tie shirt Plain shirt with ASCOT NECK-LINE (see under NECKLINES AND COLLARS). Also called *stock-tie blouse* and *flip-tie blouse.*

sweatshirt Long-sleeved, fleece-backed, cotton-knit pullover or zipped-front knit shirt made with rib-knit CREW NECK (see under NECK-LINES AND COLLARS), rib-knit cuffs and waist-band. Sometimes has attached hood and often worn with matching sweatpants, as a SWEAT-SUIT (see under ACTIVEWEAR). Originally worn after exercising to prevent chilling. In late 1960s adopted for jogging. Became more popular in 1980s and after for school and sportswear, sometimes with cartoon pictures, slogans, or name of school or club printed on front or back.

tank top Similar to ATHLETIC SHIRT (see under SHIRTS), but styled in colors. Also see BLOUSES AND TOPS.

tapered shirt See SHIRTS: BODYSHIRT #1.

tchamir (cha-meer) Moroccan shirt or over-blouse with heavily embroidered caftan neck-line. Imported as a current style in late 1960s for men and women in black with white embroidery and white with multicolored embroidery.

tee shirt See T-SHIRT.

Tom Jones shirt Pullover shirt made with STOCK-TIE (see TIES: STOCK), yoke, full body, and full sleeves with ruffled wristband gathered into dropped shoulders. Some adaptations omit yoke and have slit neckline with pointed collar. *Der.* Inspired by costumes worn in *Tom Jones,* 1963 film of Henry Fielding's novel, about an 18th-c. hero.

T-shirt/tee shirt Originally a white undershirt worn by men with round neck and set-in sleeves, this knitted pullover sport shirt is now made in any color, frequently screen-printed with names, slogans, or cartoons. In early 1980s became so popular that some were trimmed with lace, embroidery, and ruffles. The name in 1980s was extended to include simple woven blouses. Also see T-SHIRT DRESS. Shown at UNDERGARMENTS: T-SHIRT.

tuxedo shirt **1.** See SHIRTS: FORMAL SHIRT #1 and #2. **2.** Women's version made with bib front frequently tucked, becoming popular in the early 1980s. Sometimes worn with a black bow tie and a version of the man's tuxedo jacket. Also called *tuxedo blouse.*

unisex shirt Shirt designed to be worn by a man or woman. Has no buttons, and is usually laced at neckline.

Wallace Beery shirt Narrow rib-knit HENLEY-style shirt for men and women with self-binding at neck and buttoned placket closing. (See SHIRTS: HENLEY SHIRT.) Copied after government surplus underwear. *Der.* Called by this name because a shirt of this type was sometimes worn by the Hollywood actor Wallace Beery in films of the 1930s.

Western dress shirt Elaborately decorated western shirt and worn by cowboys for important rodeos. May be trimmed with fringe, elaborate embroidery, leather, beads, or sequins. Also see SHIRTS: COWBOY SHIRT.

Western shirt See SHIRTS: COWBOY SHIRT.

Zhivago shirt See SHIRTS: COSSACK SHIRT. *Der.* Inspired by costumes worn in *Dr. Zhivago,* 1965 film of Boris Pasternak's novel, set in Revolutionary Russia in 1917.

Zouave shirt ∞ (zoo′-ahv) Back-buttoned shirt with small banded collar with small standing frill and long full puffed sleeves. Decorated down the front with a panel, sometimes made of sheer gathered fabric crossed by bands of lace and trimmed with lace at cuffs and neck. Worn by women under Zouave jacket in 1860s. *Der.* Arabic, Zouaova, a Kabyle tribe, Berbers living in Algeria or Tunisia.

---

shirt sleeve See SHOULDERS AND SLEEVES.

shirtwaist See BLOUSES AND TOPS.

shirtwaist dress Dress with top styled like a tailored shirt, usually buttoned from neck to waist, and made with either a full or straight skirt. Introduced in the 1930s, very popular in 1940s, and now a classic.

shirtwaist dress

shoe buckle See CLOSURES.

shoe button See CLOSURES.

shoe cloth † Any fabric used in making of fabric shoes, shoe linings, or any other part of the shoe. SILK, COTTON, WOOL, and MANUFACTURED FIBERS are all used to make fabrics such as BROCADE, TAPESTRY, SLIPPER SATIN, FAILLE, NYLON MESH, CREPE, and SHANTUNG. Many of these fabrics are used to make white dyeable shoes. Better shoes are lined with leather, while DRILL and similar fabrics are used for less expensive shoes.

shoe hat See HEADWEAR.

shoelace **1.** Synonym for SHOESTRING since 19th c. When jogging-type shoes became popular, shoelaces became more decorative and included such woven designs as small hearts, animals, or strawberries. Also called a *lacer.* **2.** See TIES: BOLO TIE.

shoe rose ∞ Large ornamental rosette of lace or ribbon, frequently jeweled, used by men and women to trim shoes in 17th c. Sometimes also used on garters and hat bands.

shoes See FOOTWEAR.

shoestring Lace for tying a shoe. At first not acceptable to society—some invitations stated that shoe buckles were required—but fashionable by the end of 17th c. when made of ribbon. From mid-19th c. on, term SHOELACE was more commonly used.

shoestring tie See TIES.

shooting coat See COATS AND JACKETS.

shopping goods Merchandise, such as most apparel, that is more carefully assessed before purchase than CONVENIENCE GOODS.

shopping the market Investigating retail fashion trends that may influence an upcoming line.

short Woman's size group for various proportioned garments along with AVERAGE and TALL. Abbreviated S.

shortalls See SHORTS.

short bands See CLERICAL DRESS: GENEVA BANDS.

short bob See WIGS AND HAIRPIECES: BOB-WIG.

short hood See HEADWEAR: PUG HOOD.

short gown ∞ Garment similar to a jacket or overblouse worn with a skirt by working class and rural women of the 18th and early 19th c.

shortie/shorty See COATS AND JACKETS, GLOVES AND GLOVE CONSTRUCTIONS, SLEEPWEAR AND LOUNGEWEAR.

shortie pajamas See SLEEPWEAR AND LOUNGEWEAR.

short gown 18th c.

short markup A markup that creates a retail price less than double the cost of the goods to the merchant. Also see MARKUP.

short paletot See COATS AND JACKETS: YACHTING COAT #1.

short range forecasting Determining the demand for new styles and fashion trends through research and estimating when, what, and how much should be manufactured.

SHORTS

shorts 1. Two-legged garment ending above, at, or slightly below the knee that is mainly worn by adults and children for sportswear. Worn by little boys from late 19th c. but not called by this name until 1920s. See PANTS: KNEE-PANTS. In early 1930s worn by children and adults for camping. In 1933 worn by Alice Marble for a professional tennis

short shorts/
upper thigh

boy shorts

Jamaica shorts/
mid thigh

Bermuda shorts
above the knee

variations in shorts lengths

match. Later became generally accepted for tennis and sportswear for women. In 1940s became a children's-wear item—an alternative to dresses and rompers. In 1950s Bermuda shorts were accepted by men for leisure and city wear but not for business. In the late 1980s accepted for school wear and accepted as day wear but not for business. In 1986 the shorts suit was introduced with jackets matched to various types of shorts worn with contrasting tops giving the appearance of a minidress. **2.** See UNDERGARMENTS: BOXER PANTS #2.

athletic shorts Pull-on cotton twill men's shorts with elastic top worn for gym and exercise. Also called *exercise shorts, running shorts,* and *track shorts.*

balloon shorts Wide shorts set into waistband with large pleats and gathered at the legs into wide bands. Similar to PANTS: BLOOMERS.

Bermuda shorts Just-above-the-knee shorts that fit close to leg. First worn with knee socks as streetwear by men on the island of Bermuda, introduced in the United States in early 1950s, as sportswear for women, later adopted by men for summer casual wear both in country and in town. Also called *walking shorts.*

bib shorts Women's and children's shorts made with a bib top and straps over the shoulders attached to pants at the back of waist. Popular for women in 1940s and again in 1960s and 1980s and after. For women and children in the 1980s and after the word

bib shorts or
shortalls

shortall (a combination of the words shorts and overalls) was used for this type of shorts.

bike shorts 1. Thigh-length shorts of durable fabric with fitted waistband, inside drawstring, and zip-fly closing with button at waist. Cut to fit snugly, but not to restrict movement, seat has an extra lining of terrycloth with back cut higher to prevent shirt from pulling out. Also have specifically designed pockets on sides of legs for wallet and maps. **2.** Tight-fitting shorts knitted with SPANDEX. *Der.* Shortened form of word *bicycle*.

body shorts Woman's tight-fitting shorts cut to top of leg, like leotards, with horseshoe-shaped straps in front and back. Worn with a knit shirt for dancing and exercising.

boxer shorts 1. Shorts made with elastic in a casing around waist, similar to those worn by prize fighters. Worn as underwear and for sportswear. 2. See UNDERGARMENTS: BOXER SHORTS.

camp shorts 1. Shorts with large patch pockets on the front and back. Belt is run through tunnel loops formed by tops of pockets. Also called *trail shorts*. 2. Any shorts worn at a summer camp by children and counselors, sometimes of a required style or color constituting a uniform.

camp shorts

cargo shorts Thigh-length shorts similar to CAMP SHORTS with two very large patch pockets in front—extending almost to hem and up and over belt in a tunnel loop; has one large box-pleated pocket in back with buttoned flap. Usually made in twill fabric in a blend of polyester and cotton.

cityshorts Term coined in 1969 by fashion-industry newspaper *Women's Wear Daily* for women's tailored shorts worn instead of skirt with matching jacket for town wear.

cut-offs Full-length pants, often BLUE JEANS (see under PANTS), cut off above knee and fringed. Fad among teenagers in early 1960s. Became so popular that stores began selling this style shorts.

cut-offs

dhoti shorts (doe'tee) Thigh-length shorts with many gathers at waistband that hang longer between the legs. *Der.* From Indian loincloth of the same name.

drawstring shorts Pull-on shorts fastened with a drawstring at the waist similar to short pajama pants, introduced in late 1960s.

exercise shorts See SHORTS: ATHLETIC SHORTS.

hip-huggers Low-slung shorts resting on hips rather than coming to waistline.

hot pants Slang term coined by fashion-industry newspaper *Women's Wear Daily* in early 1971 to describe women's short shorts made of luxury fabrics and leather, worn with colored tights and fancy tops as evening wear and on city streets.

hot pants

Jamaica shorts Shorts ending at mid-thigh, shorter than Bermudas. *Der.* Named for shorts worn in resort areas on island of Jamaica.

jogging shorts See SHORTS: SWEATSHORTS.

jumpshorts JUMPSUIT with legs reaching to knee or above, worn in late 1960s. Similar to style worn in 1930s and 1940s called a PLAYSUIT (see under ACTIVEWEAR).

lederhosen (laid-err-hose'-en) Leather shorts usually made with bib top, originally a Tyrolean style, adopted for children and young people in the United States in late 1960s. *Der.* German plural of *Lederhose*, from *leder*, "leather" and *hose*, "trousers."

little-boy shorts Short-length shorts made with turned-back cuffs. Popular in early 1960s for sportswear and bathing suits.

mini-jeans Very short shorts made by cutting off BLUE JEANS (see PANTS). Introduced in late 1960s.

playsuit See SHORTS: JUMPSHORTS and ACTIVEWEAR.

pleated shorts 1. Woman's shorts styled to resemble a short skirt with inverted pleats in front and back and knife pleats in between. 2. Shorts with several small, unpressed pleats in front for added fullness.

pull-on shorts Shorts made with an elasticized waistband.

rugby shorts Thigh-length shorts precisely cut for unrestricted leg movement with elastic waistband only over hips, inner drawstring, lap-over closing with fly-front, and double-stitched side pockets. Made in colors and white of strong cotton twill. *Der.* Inspired by British shorts worn when playing rugby.

running shorts See SHORTS: ATHLETIC SHORTS.

sailor shorts 1. Shorts that fasten up back with lacings made with square buttoned flap closing in front like *sailor pants*. 2. Woman's

S

shorts with a zipper at front or side and a decorative, but not functional, lacing in back.

scooter shorts Shorts made with a panel attached in front, making them appear like a skirt. Also called a *scooter skirt*. Also see SKIRTS: SKORT®.

shortall See SHORTS: BIB SHORTS.

short shorts Very brief shorts.

shorts suit Suits accepted for city wear with longer jackets and shorts ending above-the-knee in a variety of styles.

skort See SKIRTS.

suspender shorts Any style shorts worn with suspenders of felt, fabric, or other material. Style was inspired by Tyrolean costume. Also see SHORTS: LEDERHOSEN.

sweatshorts Pull-on shorts made of cotton fleece fabric, used for running and jogging in warmer weather. Also called *jogging shorts*.

tear-away shorts Shorts with side snaps that can be pulled open very quickly.

tennis shorts Conservative type of shorts, traditionally white, worn for playing tennis and general sportswear. Colored shorts were promoted in the late 1960s, but white was still first choice on the courts. Originally women players wore skirts but when length of skirts got longer in the 1930s, Señorita de Alvares played in a below-the-knee divided skirt in 1931, and in 1933 Alice Marble appeared in the above-the-knee shorts. Tennis shorts are currently available in a wide range of colors and styles, and white is still much used.

track shorts See SHORTS: RUNNING SHORTS.

trail shorts See SHORTS: CAMP SHORTS and CARGO SHORTS.

trunks Man's brief loose shorts worn (originally over tights) for swimming, boxing, and track.

walking shorts See SHORTS: BERMUDA SHORTS.

western shorts Shorts styled like dungarees with zipper fly in front, patch pockets on hips, and tight-fitting legs. Popular in late 1960s.

---

short shorts See SHORTS.

shorts suit **1.** See ACTIVEWEAR. **2.** See SHORTS.

shorty glove See GLOVES AND GLOVE CONSTRUCTIONS.

shot cloth/shot silk See CHANGEABLE EFFECT.

shotten-bellied doublet See DOUBLET.

shoulder bag See HANDBAGS AND RELATED ACCESSORIES.

shoulder belt See BELTS: SAM BROWNE BELT.

shoulder cop See ARMOR.

shoulder dart See CLOTHING CONSTRUCTION DETAILS.

shoulder heads ∞ British term for shoulder straps of low-cut dresses used from 17th c. on.

shoulder knot **1.** ∞ Ribbon loops, sometimes jeweled, worn by men on right shoulder from 1660 to 1700. **2.** ∞ 18th-c. decoration used on footman's livery. **3.** ∞ One of a pair of detachable flaps, decorated with braided metallic cord insignia, worn on the shoulder by commissioned and warrant officers of the U.S. Armed Forces to designate rank.

shoulder pad Triangular-shaped or rounded pad, filled with wool, cotton, synthetic foam, or MANUFACTURED FIBER, tacked to the shoulder seam of clothing such as coats, dresses, and blouses so as to create the illusion of broad or square shoulders. Introduced in late 1930s and also popular in 1940s, 1980s, and after.

SHOULDERS AND SLEEVES

shoulder Manner of cutting an item of apparel in order to achieve a desired fit over the shoulder. Variations of fit across the shoulder were often achieved through the cut of the SLEEVE. In most early historical periods, shoulders of garments followed normal body lines; however, in the late 15th c., shoulder lines began to show greater variations as sleeves were less likely to be cut in one with the garment. Periods of considerable shoulder width occurred in the late 15th and the 16th c., in the 1830s, the 1890s, 1930s and 1940s, and the 1980s and 1990s. These effects were often aided by the use of padding placed in sleeves or at the shoulder of the garment.

sleeve That part of an item of clothing that covers the arm. In early times sleeves were cut as part of the main garment pieces. In the late Middle Ages, clothing construction techniques became more sophisticated and sleeves were cut separately and set into the armhole of the garment. In 16th and 17th c., sleeves were puffed, padded, or slashed (see SLASHING); in 18th c., women wore plain, elbow-length sleeves ending in ruffles, and coat sleeves for men were made with large turned-back cuffs. In early 19th c., sleeve styles varied a good deal, with short puffed sleeves worn by women being especially popular, and tailored plain set-in sleeves for men. Sleeves of the 1830s were enormous and after 1845, they subsided with a dropped shoulder being achieved by setting the sleeve well below the shoulder. By the 1870 to 1890 period, armhole placement returned the shoulder, and by 1890s, sleeves grew huge once more. Sleeves of the 20th c. showed considerable variation, but rarely did daytime clothing have extremely large sleeves.

all-in-one sleeve Sleeve with no armhole. Front and back of bodice and sleeve front and back are cut in one piece. The pieces are sewn together down the inside and outside of the arm. Resembles the BATWING SLEEVE and KIMONO SLEEVE but not cut as full under the arm. May be combined with a RAGLAN or SET-IN sleeve with the front cut in either manner and the back cut all-in-one. See cross-references under SHOULDERS AND SLEEVES.

amadis sleeve ∞ **1.** Sleeve with tight cuff, buttoned at the wrist, worn in 1830s. **2.** Revived in 1850s when the sleeve was buttoned to elbow and the upper sleeve was full and pleated into armhole. *Der.* Said to have originated by an opera singer to cover her unattractive arms.

angel sleeve Any type of long flowing sleeve. May fit smoothly into the armhole or be gathered. Sometimes split up outer arm to shoulder like a HANGING SLEEVE (see under SHOULDERS AND SLEEVES).

angel sleeves ∞ Long square panels from shoulders reaching nearly to floor. Used on women's mantles of 1889.

baby-doll sleeve Another name for a tiny PUFFED SLEEVE (see under SHOULDERS AND SLEEVES).

bagpipe sleeve ∞ Full sleeve gathered like a pouch on outer side of arm, ending in wide band at wrist. Worn in 15th c. by men and women primarily in the garment called the HOUPPELANDE. *Der.* From shape of Scottish bagpipe.

balloon sleeve Very large puff sleeve extending to elbow set into a regular armhole and frequently made of crisp fabrics. Popular in 1890s and since for evening and wedding dresses.

banded sleeve Full sleeve bound in to fit the arm at intervals, thereby creating a series of puffs.

barrel sleeve Sleeve that fits at armhole and at wrist but is full at the elbow.

batwing sleeve Long sleeve cut with deep armhole almost to waist, made tight at wrist, giving winglike appearance when arm is extended. A variation of the dolman sleeve. See SHOULDERS AND SLEEVES: DOLMAN.

bellows sleeve ∞ Full sleeve, gathered into cuff at wrist, with vertical slit from upper arm to below elbow; could be worn as short hanging sleeve in 14th and 15th cs.

bell sleeve Sleeve made narrow at the top, set into normal armhole, and flaring at lower edge like a bell. Introduced in the second half of 19th c.

bell sleeve

beret sleeve Short sleeve, often used on evening dresses, made from two circles of fabric seamed at outer edges with holes cut in centers for armhole and arm. Usually lined to stand out stiffly. Popular from 1820 to 1850 and again in 1930s. Also called *melon sleeve*.

Bernhardt sleeve ∞ Long, fitted sleeve made with a point extending over the hand; worn in the latter part of 19th c. *Der.* Named after Sarah Bernhardt, a famous French actress of the period.

bishop sleeve **1.** Full sleeve set into normal armhole and gathered into band at wrist. **2.** Sleeve full and large to wrist where it is gathered into a cuff, worn in the 1850s and called **full bishop**. **3.** In the 1890s same style but much smaller and called **small bishop**.

bishop sleeve #1

boot sleeve ∞ Man's coat sleeve with boot cuff (see CUFFS); popular from 1727 to about 1740.

bouffant mécanique ∞ (boo-fant′ mek-can′-eek) Sleeve created by hidden spring attached to corset neckline and projected into sleeve to extend it, worn in 1828.

bracelet sleeve Three-quarter-length fitted cuffless sleeve, allowing a bracelet to show.

brassart ∞ (brass′-are) **1.** 15th-c. French term for part of the sleeve extending from wrist to elbow attached by ribbons to upper sleeve called MANCHERON (see under SHOULDERS AND SLEEVES) **2.** Fur-lined half sleeve.

butterfly sleeve Wide flaring sleeve set in smoothly at armhole, extending to elbow or wrist, giving a caped effect.

button-tab sleeve A long convertible roll-up sleeve. Sleeve is rolled up and fastened by attaching a button on the exterior to a button-holed tab sewn on underside of sleeve.

cannon sleeve ∞ Woman's padded and boned sleeve large at shoulder and tapering to wrist, giving appearance of shape of a cannon. Used in women's gowns from about 1575 to 1620. Also called *trunk sleeve*.

cape sleeve **1.** Shoulder cut in shape of a cape with the sleeve set-in at a dropped shoulder-line to give more freedom of movement. Used on sport jackets in mid-1980s. **2.** Circular or semi-circular piece placed over each shoulder and stitched to the blouse, giving a caped effect over each arm. **3.** Flared piece of fabric cut to extend to neck in raglan style. Introduced in 1920s and featured in late 1960s for cape coats (see COATS AND JACKETS: CAPE COAT #2).

cape sleeve #1

cap sleeve Small extension cut on the front and back sections of a blouse that covers the shoulder. Has a seam at the shoulder and under the arms fastening front and back of garment together but no set-in sleeve. Popular in the 1940s and worn at intervals since. In the 1980s, flat turn-over cuffs were sometimes added to this type of sleeve.

cap sleeve

Caroline sleeve ∞ Woman's daytime dress sleeve worn in 1830s, full from shoulder to elbow and fitted to wrist.

cartwheel sleeve Short sleeve composed of two circles joined together around the outer edge. One circle fits into armhole, the other fits around the arm. Copied from the BERET SLEEVE (see under SHOULDERS AND SLEEVES). Also called *circle sleeve*.

cased sleeve ∞ Woman's long sleeve of about 1810 to 1820, made from sections of fabric alternating with bands of lace insertion.

Cavalier sleeve ∞ Sleeve slashed and fastened along outer edge by ribbon bows, full at shoulder, and close-fitting on forearm used on women's daytime dresses in 1830s. Modeled after the sleeves of dresses and jackets of the 1600s in England by those supporting King Charles II during the English Civil War.

circle sleeve See SHOULDERS AND SLEEVES: CARTWHEEL SLEEVE.

cornet sleeve (kor′-net) Close-fitting sleeve ending in a trumpet-shaped flounce.

demi-gigot (demee′ jhee′-goh) Sleeve, tight from wrist to elbow but full at shoulder and upper arm. Worn from 1825 to 1830, revived in early 1890s and again by young designers in England and Scandinavia in the early 1970s. *Der.* French, "half leg-of-mutton."

demi-sleeve/demi-maunch ∞ Full, elbow-length sleeve of 16th c.

dolman sleeve Sleeve fitted at wrist but cut with deep arm-hole so that it somewhat re-sembles a cape from the back. So called because it looks somewhat like sleeve in origi-nal DOLMAN coat (see under COATS AND JACKETS). Also called *batwing sleeve*.

dolman or batwing sleeve

double-puffed sleeve Full sleeve with band around arm that divides it into two puffs. In 1960s, a bracelet was sometimes worn around upper arm over full sleeve to give same effect.

dropped shoulder/dropped sleeve Shoulder of garment extended over upper arm. Sleeve seam comes on the upper arm rather

dropped shoulder

than at the natural armhole. Style was very popular from 1835 to 1870, used occasionally since, becoming fashionable again in the mid-1980s.

Du Barry sleeve ∞ Double puffed sleeve, one puff above elbow and another below, worn in mid-1830s. *Der.* Named for Comtesse Du Barry, Marie Jeanne Bécu (1746–1793), the last mistress of King Louis XV of France.

eelskin sleeve ∞ Tight-fitting lace-trimmed sleeve worn by women in the 17th c.

elbow-length sleeve Any sleeve that stops at elbow. Popular length used for dresses in 1940s and 1960s.

elephant sleeve ∞ Large sleeve of early 1830s usually made of sheer fabric—full at the shoulder, hanging down somewhat in the form of an elephant's ear, and close-fitting at the wrist.

epaulet sleeve (ep′-oh-let) Sleeve with yoke across top of shoulder cut in one piece with sleeve. It is decorated with an epaulet (ep′-oh-let), which is a wide flat band extending along top of shoulder to sleeve seam and is frequently trimmed with braid. *Der.* Borrowed from military uniforms. Shown at EPAULET in alphabetical listing.

extended shoulder/extended sleeve Plain shoulder seam extending down over arm to form a cap sleeve of longer length. Very popular in 1980s.

false hanging sleeve See SHOULDERS AND SLEEVES: HANGING SLEEVE #2.

farthingale sleeves ∞ Sleeves cut wide above and narrow below that are held out with wire, reed, or whalebone. Worn in late 16th and early 17th c. by men and women.

fitted sleeve Full-length, bracelet, or three-quarter-length sleeve cut to fit the arm closely and set into the normal armhole.

flange shoulder Extension of shoulders over armhole seam. Top sometimes made by using a wide band at edge, sometimes by making a deep pleat in front of blouse at the shoulders.

foresleeve Sleeve covering the arm from wrist to elbow. Also see SHOULDERS AND SLEEVES: HALF SLEEVE.

French gigot sleeve See SHOULDERS AND SLEEVES: LEG-OF-MUTTON SLEEVE.

French sleeves ∞ Detachable sleeves worn by men in England in second half of 16th c.

funnel sleeve See SHOULDERS AND SLEEVES: PAGODA SLEEVE.

Gabrielle sleeve ∞ (ga-bree-el′) **1.** Type of sleeve used in SPENCER JACKETS (see under COATS AND JACKETS), and dresses in 1820s and early 1830s. Made with a small oversleeve or epaulet at shoulder, full to elbow, narrowed to wrist, and ending in a deep cuff. **2.** Sleeve composed of series of puffs extending from shoulder to wrist worn from late 1850s to 1870s.

half sleeve ∞ **1.** Protective sleeve covering the sleeve on forearm, held on by an elastic garter. Worn in early 20th c. particularly by clerical workers. **2.** Sleeve covering forearm made of richer material than rest of garment, attached by lacings. Worn from late 14th to mid-17th c. Also called *foresleeve.*

handkerchief sleeve Sleeve made with square piece put over shoulder in such a manner that it falls in points like a handkerchief.

hand sleeve ∞ 16th-c. term for lower part of sleeve.

hanging sleeve **1.** Any long sleeve with an opening in the sleeve at the shoulder, at the upper arm, or at the elbow through which the arm can be put. The remainder of the sleeve hangs down at the back of the arm. Sometimes made open from upper arm to wrist with a cuff. Also see SHOULDERS AND SLEEVES: ANGEL SLEEVE. **2.** ∞ Sham hanging sleeve or a **false hanging sleeve** is a variant in which a long hanging pendant piece of fabric is attached to a short sleeve or set in the armhole in back. This piece sometimes reached ankle-length (1560s to 1630s). In 17th and 18th c., pendant fabric became more like a ribbon streamer. See RIBBONS OF CHILDHOOD.

hanging
sleeve #1

imbecile sleeve/idiot sleeve ∞ Very full balloon sleeve set in at a dropped shoulder and gathered to narrow cuff at wrist. Worn from late 1820s to

imbecile sleeve

S

mid-1830s. Also called *sleeve à la folle*. *Der.* Named after the garments used to confine patients in insane asylums, which had very large sleeves.

inverted leg-o'-mutton sleeve ∞ Woman's sleeve of early 1900s with tiny darts at shoulder, close-fitting at upper arm, bouffant on lower arm, and a tight-fitting cuff. Compare with LEG-OF-MUTTON (see under SHOULDERS AND SLEEVES).

Isabeau sleeve ∞ (Iz-ah-bow′) Triangular-shaped sleeve of 1860s with one point at the shoulder and widening to wrist. Used as an oversleeve with ENGAGEANTES (see entry #2) on dresses, on the PARDESSUS (see under COATS AND JACKETS), and on the MAINTENON CLOAK (see under CAPES, CLOAKS, AND SHAWLS).

Juliet sleeve Long sleeve with short puffed top, fitted on lower arm. *Der.* Named after heroine of William Shakespeare's tragedy *Romeo and Juliet.*

kabuki sleeve See SHOULDERS AND SLEEVES: KIMONO SLEEVE.

kimono sleeve **1.** Wide sleeve cut in one piece with front and back of the garment and seamed down outer- and underarm like a Japanese KIMONO. Also called *kabuki sleeve* and *mandarin sleeve.* **2.** A 1984 version of kimono sleeve was made with wide hanging piece under the arm, tapering to close-fitting at wrist.

kimono sleeve #1

lantern sleeve Sleeve plain at top and wrist but balloons out halfway between the wrist and the elbow. Cut in two pieces with a seam going around the sleeve at the fullest part.

leg-of-mutton sleeve/leg-o'-mutton sleeve Sleeve with full top gathered or pleated into armhole and tapered to wrist where it looks like a regular sleeve. Size may vary—in 1895, very full sleeves requiring a yard or two of fabric were popular. Also called a *French gigot sleeve* which derives from French, for "leg of lamb." Shown at TAILOR-MADE.

Louis XIV sleeve ∞ Women's oversleeve, flared as it descends from the shoulder and edged with rows of fluting. Worn with undersleeve or ENGAGEANTES in 1850s. *Der.* Named after Louis XIV, who ruled France from 1639 to 1715.

magyar sleeve ∞ (mag′-yar) Name assigned by costume historians to a sleeve worn in the 13th c. that was cut in one with the body of the garment with additional fullness under the arm. Similar to BATWING SLEEVE (see under SHOULDERS AND SLEEVES).

Mameluke sleeve ∞ (mam′-eh-luke) Full sleeve finished with a large cuff of thin fabric used in daytime dresses of the late 1820s. *Der.* Mamelukes were originally slaves brought to Egypt, later trained as soldiers. Ruled Egypt from 1250 to 1517 and remained powerful until 1811 under Turkish viceroys.

mancheron ∞ (man-cher-own′) **1.** Late 15th and early 16th c. half sleeve reaching from elbow to shoulder, lower part of sleeve called *brassart*. Two parts held together with pins and ribbons. **2.** 16th-c. false sleeve attached only at shoulder and worn hanging down back. **3.** 19th-c. very short oversleeve, similar to a large epaulette, worn by women. Term replaced by word EPAULETTE in 1860s.

mandarin sleeve ∞ See SHOULDERS AND SLEEVES: KIMONO SLEEVE.

Marie sleeve ∞ Full sleeve tied at intervals to form several puffs. Worn from about 1813 to mid-1820s and revived in the early 1870s—then called the *Marie Antoinette sleeve.*

Marino Faliero sleeve ∞ (mar-ee′ fahl-yer′-oh) Full hanging sleeve of first half of 1830s secured with ribbon band at elbow, and long point hanging to wrist. *Der.* After drama of the same name written by Lord Byron.

Medici sleeve ∞ (meh′-dee-chee) Full sleeve, puffed to elbow and tight from there to wrist worn by women in 1830s. *Der.* Inspired by clothes worn by Marie de' Medici, Queen of France c. 1600.

melon sleeve See SHOULDERS AND SLEEVES: BERET SLEEVE.

mitten sleeve ∞ Woman's tightly fitted sleeve of lace or net reaching to the knuckles; used in the early 1890s in theater and dinner dresses.

Montespan sleeve ∞ (mon′-tes-pan) Woman's puffed sleeve of early 1830s made with upper part caught in band at elbow and lace VANDYKE ruffle falling down from the band. *Der.* Named for Marquise de Montespan (1641–1707), mistress of Louis XIV of France.

mushroom sleeve ∞ Woman's short sleeve pleated into the armhole with the lower edge trimmed with lace. Used in evening dresses of the mid-1890s.

natural shoulder Follows body lines with sleeve set in at natural armhole without padding. Fashionable for men's suits in 1950s and 1960s.

padded sleeve Pads sewn inside garment to make shoulder appear broader. Introduced for women in 1930s by Schiaparelli and also popular in mid-1980s.

pagoda sleeve (pah-gode´-ah) Funnel-shaped outer sleeve flaring at wrist, falling over a puffed undersleeve. *Der.* Named for the shape of a Far Eastern temple's flaring roof. Also called *funnel sleeve.*

pagoda sleeve

parachute sleeve Long full sleeve made without a cuff with the lower edge gathered to a lining cut shorter than the sleeve.

peasant sleeve Full sleeve gathered at top and bottom. May be either short and puffed or long and full.

peg-top sleeve ∞ Sleeve worn by men from 1857 to 1864, full at shoulder and tapered to wrist. A modified form of the LEG-OF-MUTTON SLEEVE (see under SHOULDERS AND SLEEVES).

petal sleeve Short sleeve curved at hem and overlapping to give a petal-shaped effect in front.

pompadour sleeve ∞ (pohm´-pah-dure) Adaptation in 1830s and 1840s of elbow-length sleeve edged with ruffle worn by the Marquise de Pompadour, mistress of Louis XV of France.

puff/puffed sleeve Short sleeve gathered, either at the armhole or at the cuff band or both, producing a rounded shape. Popular in 1920s and 1930s, revived

puff or puffed sleeve

in late 1960s, and still used for babies and children's wear.

raglan sleeve Sleeve that extends to neckline, set in by seams slanting from underarm front and back. Used since mid-1850s. A variation is made with an additional seam down outside of arm called a **three-seamed raglan. Saddle sleeve** or **saddle shoulder,** raglan sleeve another raglan variation, has a shoulder with small yoke made by not bringing the raglan sleeve to the neck in a point, but by widening it so that it is 3–4″ in width at the neck, thus forming a "saddle" over the shoulder. *Der.* Lord Raglan, or Fitzroy James Henry Somerset, British General in saddle shoulder Crimean War, who, after losing an arm in the Charge of the Light Brigade in 1854, had a coat designed with a special sleeve.

rhumba sleeve Barrel-shaped sleeve covered with rows of small horizontal ruffles. *Der.* From shirts worn by men dancing South American rhumba.

roll/roll-up sleeve Sleeve, approximately elbow length, finished only with a narrow hem, designed to be folded—or rolled up—at least twice in lieu of a cuff. Popular for women's tailored shirts in 1950s and 1960s, an outgrowth of earlier fad for wearing long sleeves folded up in this manner.

roxalane sleeve ∞ (rok-so-lane´) Bouffant sleeve worn from the late 1820s on made by tying a fringed band around a long full sleeve above the elbow—dividing it into two puffs.

sabot sleeve ∞ (sa-boh´) **1.** Sleeve used on 18th-c. dresses tight-fitting to elbow, flared below elbow and trimmed with ruffles. **2.** Sleeve with single or double puff above elbow used on women's evening dresses from late 1820s to 1836. Also used from 1836 to 1840 on day dresses and then called *Victoria sleeve.*

saddle shoulder/saddle sleeve See SHOULDERS AND SLEEVES: RAGLAN SLEEVE.

set-in sleeve Any type of sleeve which is sewed into an armhole.

sham hanging sleeve   See SHOULDERS AND SLEEVES: HANGING SLEEVE #2.

shirt sleeve   Tailored wrist-length sleeve made with FLAT-FELLED SEAMS (see under CLOTHING CONSTRUCTION DETAILS) and set smoothly into the armhole. Sometimes has one or two small unpressed pleats where it joins the cuff. Basic sleeve for men's shirts since late 19th c. and may have SINGLE OR FRENCH CUFF (see CUFFS)—women's style may have a band at cuff.

slashed sleeve   See SHOULDERS AND SLEEVES: SPANISH SLEEVE.

sleeve à la folle   See SHOULDERS AND SLEEVES: IMBECILE SLEEVE.

sleeve hand   ∞ 17th-c. term for opening in sleeve through which hand is thrust.

sling sleeve   ∞ Sleeve cut in one with upper part of garment like a cape, frequently with attached horizontal piece of fabric, similar to a *sling*, on which to rest the arm. Worn by women in mid-1880s and used in sling-duster coat.

Spanish sleeve   ∞ Puffed sleeve, with vertical slashes revealing colored silk lining, worn by women from 1807 to 1820 and in late 1850s and 1860s. Also called a *slashed sleeve*.

suit sleeve   Sleeve cut in two pieces—one for under the arm and one for the top of the arm. Cut to allow for the bend at the elbow, it is generally used for tailored suits for men and women. A popular style in the 1850s for women's dresses.

suit sleeve

sultana sleeve/sultan sleeve   ∞ Full hanging sleeve (see SHOULDERS AND SLEEVES: HANGING SLEEVE #1) of late 1850s slit open down outside. Sometimes fastened with ribbons around upper and forearms.

three-quarter sleeve   Sleeve ending between elbow and wrist.

three-seamed raglan sleeve   See SHOULDERS AND SLEEVES: RAGLAN SLEEVE.

Tom Jones sleeve   Full sleeve, gathered into cuff or ruffle, used on men's shirts, sometimes set into dropped shoulder. *Der.* Named for style of shirts worn in 18th c. made popular by costumes worn in 1963 film of Henry Fielding's 1749 novel *Tom Jones.*

trumpet sleeve   Sleeve fitting into natural armhole, falling straight to elbow where it flares in the shape of a trumpet.

trunk sleeve   See SHOULDERS AND SLEEVES: CANNON SLEEVE.

tulip sleeve   Set-in sleeve with bell shape made in several pieces like petals on a flower.

venetian sleeve   ∞ Full sleeve of late 1850s fitting into armhole, slashed nearly to shoulder, worn by women over puffed undersleeves.

Victoria sleeve   See SHOULDERS AND SLEEVES: SABOT SLEEVE.

virago sleeve   ∞ (veer-ahg'-goh) Puffed sleeve worn by women in first half of the 17th c. made with many panes that are tied together at intervals to the wrist. Sometimes tied only at elbow and wrist, making two large puffs.

virago sleeve

wearing sleeves   ∞ Term used in 17th c. for sleeves worn on the arms as compared with hanging sleeves (see SHOULDERS AND SLEEVES: HANGING SLEEVES #1).

---

shoulder wing   ∞ Decorative projection at shoulder attached at armhole seam like a wing covering the POINTS (laces) by which the sleeve is fastened to the armhole. Worn from 1545 to 1640 by both men and women.

show   **1.** See COATS AND JACKETS. **2.** See ACTIVEWEAR: HUNT BREECHES.

showcase displays   Display of merchandise in glass cabinets. When used for expensive items, such display cases are usually locked. See CLOSED ISLAND DISPLAY.

shower   Adjective describing clothes designed to be worn in the shower. Examples: shower cap, shower slippers. See FOOTWEAR: SHOWER SHOE.

showing horn   See SHOE HORN.

showroom   Location where manufacturers or designers present their current lines to retail buyers.

shrink   See SWEATERS.

shrinkage control   † Fabrics woven and finished with processes that make them have less tendency to reduce their dimensions after washing and dry cleaning.

shrug   See SWEATERS.

Sicilian bodice   ∞ The upper part of an evening dress of mid-1860s made with square décolletage and four knee-length panels attached—two in front and two in back—giving tunic effect. See TUNIC #2.

Sicilian embroidery   See EMBROIDERIES AND SEWING STITCHES: SPANISH EMBROIDERY #2.

side   ∞ 15th to 16th-c. term for the term "long," e.g., a "side gown" is a long gown.

side boards   ∞ Slang for side whiskers.

side bodies   In tailoring, the two side pieces in the back of a man's coat. The seams that join these side panels to the center back piece curve outward at the shoulder blades, ending at the armhole seams. This construction gives better fit and flexibility than a one- or two-piece back and was used from 1840s on.

sideburns   See HAIRSTYLES.

side-channel frame   See HANDBAGS AND RELATED ACCESSORIES: FRAME.

side-gore shoe   See FOOTWEAR.

side-laced shoes   See FOOTWEAR: SIDE-LACED OXFORDS.

side leather   See LEATHERS.

sideless surcote   See SURCOTE.

side placket   See CLOTHING CONSTRUCTION DETAILS: PLACKET.

signature   Practice started by Parisian couturiers in late 1960s of using their own name printed on scarves and handbags. See HANDBAGS AND RELATED ACCESSORIES and SCARVES: DESIGNER SCARF.

signet ring   See JEWELRY.

silhouette   Contour or outline as shown in solid black on a white background. Similar to a black shadow cast on a white wall. Formerly a term widely used to indicate trend in length and general outline of garments for the coming seasons. *Der.* Named after French author and statesman Étienne de Silhouette, (1709–1767), who first

hourglass silhouette

made portraits in black with no background details.

silk   † Fiber obtained from the cocoon of the silkworm. Noted for its resiliency, elasticity, strength, and luster. Often used to make luxurious fabrics.

silk hat   See HEADWEAR.

silk illusion   † Very fine net, similar to TULLE, used for wedding veils.

silking   See GLOVES AND GLOVE CONSTRUCTIONS: POINTING.

silk pin   See DRESSMAKER'S PIN.

silk ribbon embroidery   See EMBROIDERIES AND SEWING STITCHES: ROCOCO EMBROIDERY.

silk-screen printing   See SCREEN PRINTING and PRINTS, STRIPES, AND CHECKS: SILKSCREEN PRINTING.

silver fox   See FURS.

silver hose/pantyhose   See HOSIERY: GLITTER HOSE.

silver-streakers   The population group age 50 and over.

simar (si-mar´)   **1.** See COATS AND JACKETS. **2.** See CLERICAL DRESS.

simplex knit   A reversible warp knit, double-faced fabric with the same appearance on both sides. Used for gloves.

Simpson, Adele   * See APPENDIX/DESIGNERS.

simulated gems   See GEMS, GEM CUTS, AND SETTINGS.

simulated pearls   See GEMS, GEM CUTS, AND SETTINGS: PEARL.

single-breasted   Conventional closing for suits, jackets, blouses, and coats. Abbreviated S.B. May be closed with buttons that are aligned down center front of garment. Lap is not as great as in a DOUBLE-BREASTED CLOSING.

single cuff   See CUFFS.

single-hand system   A garment production method, used primarily for couture or very high-priced, limited production apparel and for sewing PROTOTYPES, in which one sewer makes an entire garment. Compare with BUNDLE SYSTEM.

single yarn   † Refers to one strand of yarn. When two single yarns are twisted together the result is a two-ply yarn. Also see PLY YARN.

siphonia   See COATS AND JACKETS.

S

siren suit British one-piece COVERALL worn during World War II. Designed for fast dressing in case of emergencies signaled by air-raid sirens.

Siwash sweater See SWEATERS: COWICHAN SWEATER.

size specification Measurements at particular locations on a garment that are established by the manufacturer for each of the sizes in which the style will be made.

size standards The amount of proportional increase or decrease in garment measurements that a ready-to-wear apparel company requires for each of the sizes it produces.

sizing **1.** Measurements of body used as guide for cutting garments to fit a variety of body types. **2.** † Nonpermanent finishing process applied particularly to cotton fabrics to increase weight, crispness, and luster by means of starch, gelatin, oil, and wax. When done at home or in a commerical laundry, the process is called **starching**.

skant See PANTS.

skating See FOOTWEAR and SKIRTS.

skating dress Originally a close-fitting long-sleeved bodice with brief thigh-length skirt flaring from a natural waistline as worn by Norwegian skating star Sonja Henie in films of 1930s. Newer versions with long torsos and flared micro-skirts are worn by current popular figure skaters and Olympic® champions.

skating dress

skating skirt See SKIRTS.

skein † (skane) Unit by which knitting yarn is sold, usually comes packaged in loosely coiled form. Also called a *hank*.

skelton skirt See UNDERGARMENTS.

skeleton suit ∞ Boy's suit worn from 1790 to 1830, consisting of a short, tight jacket and ankle-length trousers buttoned to the jacket at waist.

skeleton waterproof See COATS AND JACKETS.

ski clothing See ACTIVEWEAR: SKI PANTS and SKI SUIT, COATS AND JACKETS: SKI JACKET, FOOTWEAR: SKI

skeleton suit

BOOT, SLEEPWEAR AND LOUNGEWEAR: SKI PAJAMAS, and SWEATERS: SKI SWEATER.

ski mask See MASKS.

skimmer **1.** A-LINE dress or SHIFT that hangs away from the body. **2.** See FOOTWEAR. **3.** See HEADWEAR.

skirt belt See BELTS.

SKIRTS

skirt **1.** Lower part of dress or long garment without legs: the section below the waistline. Dresses can be made with separate skirts and bodices or with skirt and bodice joined by a waistline seam. After the late Middle Ages, it became customary in the Western world for women to wear only garments with skirts and for men (unless their professions required wearing robes) to wear BIFURCATED GARMENTS, a practice that ended only in the 20th c. **2.** Separate item of clothing starting above, below, or at natural waistline. **3.** Term used for lower part of a coat or jacket, particularly in Great Britain.

accordion-pleated skirt Skirt made from a full circle of fabric with pressed-in pleats that are wider at the hem and taper to waistline, giving a flare to skirt. When the body is in motion, pleats flare at the hem like the bellows of a half-open accordion. Introduced in late 1880s by Loie Fuller for "skirt dancing" and popular at intervals since. Also called *sunburst-pleated skirt* or, in a usage of the 1880s, a **sunray skirt**.

A-line skirt Slightly flared skirt introduced in the early 1960s. In silhouette, it appears like the letter A.

A-line skirt

asymmetric skirt Any skirt that differs on either side of an imaginary line drawn down the center front. Sometimes has ruffles or flounces attached diagonally across center front from waist to hip; frequently has an ASYMMETRIC hemline.

baby skirt Short flared or pleated skirt worn over bathing suit or playsuit during 1930s and 1940s.

ballet skirt ∞ Tiered skirt of evening dress worn in 1880s, made with three or four layers of tulle in a variety of lengths attached to a silk foundation. Top layer was sprinkled with stars, pearls, or beetle wings.

balloon skirt See SKIRTS: BUBBLE SKIRT.

bell skirt Skirt usually gathered at waistline, making it full over hips and flared at hem. Popular from the 1830s to late 1860s and sometimes worn with crinoline or hoops underneath. Popular for evening gowns.

bell skirt

bias skirt Any skirt cut on the diagonal or BIAS of the fabric. The bias cut was introduced by Madeleine Vionnet in 1920s and was popular through the 1930s, worn at intervals since.

bouffant skirt (boo-fahnt′) Any full skirt; more specifically a gathered skirt.

box pleated skirt Two flat folds meeting underneath to form box pleats that extend around the waist, alternating with inverted pleats. Popular in 1940s and 1950s, and at intervals since.

broomstick skirt Full skirt that, after washing, is tied tightly with a string around a broomstick. When dry, it contains vertical ridges or wrinkles. Popular in the 1940s and somewhat revived in the late 1960s.

bubble skirt Skirt gathered to small waistline, ballooning out and tapered in at hem, popular in 1950s. Also called *balloon skirt, tulip skirt.* Shown at BUBBLE DRESS.

bustle-back skirt Any skirt with puffed fullness, ruffles, or large bow in the center back. Starting in late 1860s skirt fullness was pulled to the back but skirt was full. During the late 1870s skirt became slim with accent in back. In mid-1880s, skirt was full with large bustle. Style was somewhat revived in the 1930s, 1940s, and 1980s. When used it is usually in evening or bridal gowns.

circle/circular skirt Skirt made by cutting a semicircle out of a piece of fabric folded lengthwise. The selvages are then joined to make a full circle. Popular for skating and general wear in the 1930s, it has remained a basic type of skirt, becoming very popular in mid-1980s.

cornet skirt ∞ Woman's skirt of early 1890s cut straight and fitted in front, and with back cut on the bias with small train. Also called *French skirt.*

crinoline See UNDERGARMENTS.

culottes (koo-lotz′) Skirt divided into two sections so that it is actually a pair of pants but looks like a skirt when not in motion. Also called *split skirt, pantskirt, divided skirt, scooter skirt,* or *skort. Der.* French, *culotte,* "knee breeches"; *des culottes,* "trousers." Shown at PANTS: CULOTTES.

dance skirt Short skirt worn over leotard and tights by dancers for practicing.

Directoire skirt ∞ (dir-eck′-twa) Skirt cut in seven gores worn from late 1880s through early 1900s. The back four gores were lined, stiffened, and fluted into PIPE-ORGAN or GODET PLEATS (see under CLOTHING CONSTRUCTION DETAILS)—the hem being four to six yards wide around. A name patented for this style by *The Delineator* magazine.

dirndl (durn′-del) Full, gathered skirt. The style derives from Tyrolean peasant costume originating, and still worn, in the Austrian and Bavarian alps.

dirndl

divided skirt **1.** See SKIRTS: CULOTTES. **2.** ∞ Wide trousers that hang like a skirt, introduced in England in 1882 by Lady Harberton for bicycling. Same as *pantskirt* or *culottes.*

draped skirt Any skirt with additional fullness pleated or gathered into one side seam or forming a drapery that hangs down.

dropped skirt **1.** Skirt set on a low waistline; also called a *torso skirt.* **2.** ∞ Sewing term in late 19th and early 20th c. for a skirt made separate from the lining. Both are attached to the same seam at waist.

eel skirt ∞ Woman's gored skirt of late 1890s cut on the bias, fitting very snugly over the hips, and flared slightly from the knees to hem.

Empire skirt Straight skirt starting at a high waistline under the bust. Originated in *Empire Period,* 1804–1815, and worn at intervals since.

evening skirt Any type of separate skirt worn for a formal or semiformal occasion.

S

featherbrush skirt ∞ Daytime skirt of sheer material, with overlapping flounces below knees, worn in 1898.

fishtail skirt Skirt with additional stitched on free-hanging panel in front or back, simulating the tail of a fish.

flying panel skirt Complete skirt made with an extra panel, attached at the waistline, that hangs free. Basic type skirt for dresses in 1940s and 1950s, and revived with pants-type dress of late 1960s.

foot-mantle/fotemantle ∞ **1.** An outer, or extra, woman's skirt, worn in American Colonial days to keep dress clean when riding horseback. **2.** An overskirt worn by country women when riding horseback in the 14th c. Called a *safeguard* from 16th to 18th c.

French skirt See CORNET SKIRT.

friponne See SKIRTS: JUPE #2.

full skirt Any skirt made with several widths of fabric, may be cut in a complete circle, made with many gores, or gathered.

gathered skirt Skirt made straight with panels of fabric sewed together, shirred (or gathered) at the top, and attached to a waistband or bodice of dress. Popular at intervals since 1830.

godet skirt (go-day´) A triangular piece of fabric inserted upward from the hem of the skirt to give more fullness. Popular in 1930s and used occasionally since.

godet skirt

gored skirt Skirt that fits through the waistline and flares at the hem. May be made of from four to twenty-four shaped sections. Dates from 14th c. and much used in 19th c. Very popular in the late 1860s, mid-1890s, early 20th c., 1930s, 1940s, and now worn as a classic skirt style.

gored skirt

granny skirt Full-length gathered skirt usually with a ruffle at hem introduced in 1960s. *Der.* Worn by a young girl in imitation of skirt worn by her grandmother, or "granny."

handkerchief skirt Skirt with hemline cut to fall in points as if made of handkerchiefs. Popular in 1920s, 1960s, and 1980s and after.

harem skirt Draped skirt with hem gathered, turned up, and fastened to lining. Worn in the Near East and introduced to the West by Paris designer Paul Poiret in 1912. Revived periodically.

hip-hugger skirt Any skirt, usually belted, that rides low on hips below the natural waistline, popular in late 1960s and later.

hobble skirt ∞ Woman's skirt rounded over hips, tapered to ankle so narrowly that walking is impeded. Fashion designed by Paris designer *Paul Poiret* about 1912. For a variation, see SKIRTS: PEG-TOP SKIRT.

hobble skirt

hoop skirt A skirt held out with crinoline, a stiffened underskirt, or hoops. May be bell-, cone-, or pyramid-shaped. Very fashionable from 1850 to 1870 and worn at intervals since, particularly for evening and bridal gowns.

hula skirt Mid-calf-length skirt, made of long grasses fastened together at low waistline, worn in Hawaii for hula dances performed for tourists. Copied in plastic strips for costumes.

inverted pleated skirt Skirt made by bringing two folds of fabric to a center line in front and/or back. May be cut straight at sides or be slightly flared. Has been a basic type of skirt since 1920s.

jupe ∞ (zhoop) **1.** French word for skirt. A **mini-jupe** is a miniskirt. Used in 1960s as a synonym for skirt. **2.** From late 17th c.: a woman's skirt, sometimes in three layers: *modeste* on top, *friponne* in middle, and *sècrete* underneath.

jupon (zhoo´-pown) Woman's *underskirt* that contrasted or matched fabric of bodice, worn between 1850 and 1870.

kangaroo skirt Term used for maternity skirt designed by Elsie Frankfurt in early 1940s with a circular cutout in center top front. This portion was not filled in with stretch fabric as in later maternity skirts.

kick-pleated skirt Straight skirt with only one pleat in either front or back to make walking

S

easier. Popular when narrow silhouettes are worn.

kilt Scottish skirt made in wraparound style. Center front is plain with KNIFE PLEATS (see CLOTHING CONSTRUCTION DETAILS) starting at side front and wrapping around to other side or front. Hanging end may be fringed and fastened with a large decorative safety pin. Originally worn by Scots Highlander men in various tartans. See also PLAIDS AND TARTANS: TARTAN. Copied for children and women at times since the 1860s.

kilt

knife-pleated skirt **1.** Skirt made with single pleats about 1″ wide all going in the same direction completely around the skirt. **2.** Skirt made with single pleats starting from a center *box pleat* and going around to center back, where they form an INVERTED PLEAT (see CLOTHING CONSTRUCTION DETAILS). Both are basic types of skirts introduced in the 1920s. Also popular in 1940s and late 1960s and after when heat-set pleating was introduced.

layered skirt Skirt made of tiers in varying lengths, placed one on top of the other.

Marie Antoinette skirt ∞ (mah′-ree an-twan-ett′) Skirt worn from 1895 on made with seven gores—three in front, four in back—with two back panels pleated in large BOX PLEATS (see CLOTHING CONSTRUCTION DE-TAILS) stitched down to hips, making the skirt 4–6 yards wide at the hem. Named for Marie Antoinette (1755–1793), wife of Louis XVI of France.

maternity skirt Skirt worn by expectant mothers with either a cut-out section at top center front or a section of stretch fabric inserted over the abdomen.

maxi skirt Term used for ankle-length daytime skirt, popular with women in late 1960s as reaction against miniskirts.

midi skirt (mid′-ee) Skirt with hem halfway between ankle and knee, below the widest part of the calf. Introduced by designers in 1967 as a reaction to very short miniskirts.

milkmaid skirt ∞ Term used from 1885 to 1895 for double skirt with plain overskirt gathered and pulled up on one side by cord or loop at waistband to reveal a striped underskirt.

mini-jupe See SKIRTS: JUPE #1.

miniskirt Term used for extremely short skirt, any length from 4 to 12″ above the knee. Popular for day and evening in the 1960s, credited to London designer Mary Quant.

modeste See SKIRTS: JUPE #2.

morning-glory skirt Gored skirt of early 20th c. fitted through hips, then flaring in trumpet fashion. Also called *serpentine skirt.*

overskirt **1.** A second skirt or drapery often looped up or split at sides, front, or back. Also an entire skirt of a sheer fabric constructed over a more opaque *underskirt.* **2.** See POLON-AISE #1.

panel skirt See SKIRTS: FLYING PANEL SKIRT.

pannier skirt ∞ (pan-yehr′) **1.** Skirt extended at the sides but frequently narrow from front to back. Popular in the 18th c. and again in the 1870s. **2.** Skirt with an overskirt draped at the hips to form puffs, popular in the 1850s and 1860s, and again in the 1880s. Also called a *pannier puff.*

pantskirt Synonym for *culottes, split skirt, Skort®, divided skirt,* and *scooter skirt.* All popular since mid-1960s.

parasol skirt ∞ Skirt cut with many gores, stitched in same manner as seams in a parasol. Worn by women in late 19th and early 20th c.

peasant skirt **1.** Full gathered skirt that may be trimmed with bands of embroidery; plain gathered skirt; or skirt worn with an embroi-dered apron. **2.** In the 1960s referred to skirt decorated with bands of embroidery rather than style of skirt. *Der.* Adopted from national costume of European countries.

peg-top skirt **1.** Basic skirt cut full at the waistline with darts, gathers, or small un-pressed pleats used at waistline. From hips to hem skirt tapers inward becoming very narrow at hem. Sometimes made with center front seam with each panel rounded at hem. Usually made with a KNIFE PLEAT (see CLOTHING CONSTRUCTION DETAILS) or slit on

peg-top skirt #1

S

center back seam. Popular in 1950s and 1960s, used occasionally since. **2.** Skirt made with fullness from waistline to hips, tapering narrowly to hemline. Popular about 1912 to end of World War I and revived at intervals. *Der.* Name borrowed from boy's cone-shaped spinning top.

pentes ∞ (pahn) Distinctive woman's skirt of mid-1880s cut in two layers. The overskirt was draped to reveal an underskirt trimmed with alternating silk and velvet strips that were pyramid-shaped and graduated in size.

poodle skirt Full circle skirt very popular with adolescents of the late 1940s and early 1950s that was often made of felt and decorated with an appliquéd poodle dog. Revived in the 1990s.

poodle skirt

prairie skirt Flared skirt gathered at the waistband with one or two ruffles at the hem made in plain or calico-patterned fabrics. *Der.* Adapted from skirts worn by women traveling West on the wagon trains.

puffball skirt Christian Lacroix design of 1986 that resembled a short, puffed-out ball of fabric. Similar to the MINI-CRINI.

pullback ∞ Skirt of 1880s, with the fullness drawn to the back and draped.

rainy daisy skirt/rainy day skirt ∞ Tailored, ankle-length walking skirt fashionable from about 1902. Also worn for roller skating. *Der.* A nickname given to women who were members of the "Rainy Day Club" and wore skirts of this type.

ra-ra skirt Style of the 1980s derived from the skirts worn by cheerleaders that was mid-thigh length with full flounces or tiers.

ripple skirt ∞ *Gored* skirt worn in 1890s sometimes with as many as eleven gores. Fitted snugly over hips but flared at hem to a width of six yards or more. Lined with horsehair stiffening and pressed to hang in rounded PIPE-ORGAN PLEATS (see under CLOTHING CONSTRUCTION DETAILS).

safeguard See SKIRTS: FOOT MANTLE.

sarong (sar-ong′) Wrapped skirt, usually made of bold floral-print cotton, used as beach coverup. Popular after actress Dorothy Lamour wore one in film *Hurricane*, late 1930s. *Der.* Copied from Indonesian native dress.

scooter skirt See SKIRTS: SKORT.®

secrete See SKIRTS: JUPE #2.

sheath skirt Straight skirt with no flare. Usually has a kick pleat or slit in back or side to facilitate walking. Popular style in the 1950s and early 1960s and revived when straight skirts are fashionable.

skating skirt Very short full circular skirt. First popular in late 1930s after films by Norwegian-American ice-skater Sonja Henie.

skort Miniskirt with shorts, popular in late 1960s and after. Also called *scooter skirt*. *Der.* Combination of words "skirt" and "shorts."

slit skirt Straight-lined skirt with slashes on each side seam to knee or thigh. Copied after styles worn by Chinese and Vietnamese women. Also see CHEONGSAM.

split skirt Synonym for *pantskirt, divided skirt,* or *culottes.*

square-dance skirt Full skirt with large ruffle at hem. Popular in rural areas for square dancing and barn dances.

squaw skirt Full skirt, set with tiny pleats, that may have horizontal embroidered bands at intervals and a ruffle at hem. Originally worn by American Indian women with embroidered blouse. In late 1960s accepted for wear by other women.

St. Tropez skirt Ankle-length full skirt made with diagonal bands of various printed and plain-colored fabrics—may be as many as eight different fabrics used.

straight skirt Any slim skirt without fullness.

sunburst-pleated skirt See SKIRTS: ACCORDION PLEATED SKIRT.

sunray skirt See SKIRTS: ACCORDION PLEATED SKIRT.

suspender skirt Any skirt with attached suspenders. Frequently worn by young girls.

swing skirt Flared skirt, circular or cut in gores, fitted at hips with a wide flare at the hem.

S

Popular in the late 1930s, and at intervals since. Very popular in mid-1980s.

swirl skirt   Skirt made from bias-cut strips of multicolored fabrics that were often from India.

tablier skirt ∞ (tab-lee-eh′)   Skirt worn from 1850s to 1870s with decorated freehanging panel in front, suggesting an apron. Sometimes trimming was applied directly to skirt. *Der.* French, "apron."

tie-back skirt ∞   Skirt with a train pulled back and looped to form puffs at sides by means of a drawstring inserted through tapes. Gave a silhouette flat in front and puffed at back and hips. Worn from mid-1870s through early 1880s.

tiered skirt   Straight-lined skirt with a series of flounces cut either in circular style, or on the straight of the material. Each flounce is usually cut larger than the previous one. Popular in the 1840s, 1860s, 1930s, and at intervals since.

torso skirt   Pleated or gathered skirt attached to a yoke at hips.

trouser skirt ∞   Tailored skirt split at side front to reveal matching bloomers attached at waistline. Worn from 1910 to 1920 by avant-garde women.

trumpet skirt   Straight skirt that flares at the hem like an inverted trumpet. The flare is created either by cutting greater fullness at the hem or by attaching a large circular flounce.

trumpet skirt

tulip skirt   See SKIRTS: BUBBLE SKIRT.

tunic skirt   Double-layered skirt with the overskirt cut shorter than the underskirt. Originally introduced in the 1850s as a ball dress with the upperskirt trimmed with lace and underskirt with a deep flounce. Popular in slim style in the 1880s, 1910 to 1920, and worn intermittently since.

tunic skirt

umbrella-pleated skirt   Circular-cut or gored skirt with widely spaced pleats similar to accordion pleats only larger, simulating folds in an umbrella.

underskirt   Simple basic skirt over which an overskirt, or drapery, hangs.

waterfall back ∞   Skirt of mid-1880s worn over bustle made with series of cascading puffs down center back. Fullness was held in place with series of drawstrings inside dress.

wrap skirt   A skirt, open from waist to hem, that wraps around the body and fastens with buttons or ties, usually lapped across the front or back.

yoke skirt   Skirt with small fitted piece, sometimes straight, pointed, or scalloped attached at waistband. Lower part of skirt attached to yoke may be gathered or gored. Yoke may be placed at front or back of skirt, or both.

Zouave skirt ∞ (zoo′-ahv)   Style of the 1860 made by gathering the full skirt at the hem and attaching it to an inside lining to make it appear like baggy trousers worn by the French Zouaves. *Der.* Arabic, Zouaova, a Kabyle tribe, one of the Berbers, living in Algeria or Tunisia.

skirt supporter   See UNDERGARMENTS.

skivvies   See UNDERGARMENTS.

skivvy   **1.** See UNDERGARMENTS. **2.** See SHIRTS.

skoncho   See CAPES, CLOAKS, AND SHAWLS.

skort   See SKIRTS.

SKU   See STOCK KEEPING UNIT.

skullcap   See HEADWEAR.

skunk   See FURS.

slacks   See PANTS.

slammerkin ∞   Loose-fitting, unboned gown worn at home in the morning without hoops by women from 1730 to 1770. If worn outdoors, hoops were added. Also called *trollopee.*

slant/slanted toe   See FOOTWEAR.

slap-shoe   See FOOTWEAR.

slashed sleeve   See SHOULDERS AND SLEEVES: SPANISH SLEEVE.

slashing   15th and 16th-c. term for slits deliberately made in clothing that enabled a garment under-

slashing on 16th c. doublet

neath or contrasting lining to be pulled through. Slashes could be any length and run in any direction of the cloth, unlike PANES, which were vertical. Used on DOUBLETS sleeves, and TRUNK HOSE. Also called *scissoring, chiquetades,* and *creves.* Called *blistered* during late 16th and 17th c.

slash pocket   See POCKETS: BOUND POCKET.

slave bracelet   See JEWELRY.

sleep bonnet   See HEADWEAR.

sleep bra   See UNDERGARMENTS: LEISURE BRA.

sleep coat   See SLEEPWEAR AND LOUNGEWEAR.

sleep mask   See MASKS.

sleep set   See SLEEPWEAR AND LOUNGEWEAR.

sleep shorts   See SLEEPWEAR AND LOUNGEWEAR.

SLEEPWEAR AND LOUNGEWEAR

sleepwear   Department-store term for clothing used for sleeping or for preparig to go to bed.

loungewear   Clothes designed to be worn primarily at home when relaxing or entertaining.

baby-doll nightgown   Bouffant hip-length nightgown made with short puffed sleeves and matching bloomers. Usually made of sheer fabric, and popular in 1940s and 1950s.

baby-doll nightgown

baby-doll pajamas   Very short, micro-mini or mini-length pajamas consisting of a tent-shaped top, usually gathered into the neckline or yoke, worn with brief panties.

bare-midriff pajamas   Two-piece pajamas with a brief top worn by women since late 1960s for lounging or sleeping.

bathrobe   **1.** Wraparound robe usually styled with long sleeves, a shawl collar, and held closed with a sash. Worn by men, women, and children, popular styles are often made of plaid fabrics, plain wool, velour, fleece, or terrycloth. **2.** Synonym for various types of robes.

bathrobe #1

bedgown   ∞ Dressing gown with loose sleeves worn only in bedrooms by men and women in 18th c.

bed jacket   Waist-length jacket worn when sitting up in bed for breakfast or when recuperating from an illness. May match or contrast with nightgown. Popular in 1920s and still used.

blanket sleepers   Children's winter pajamas made in two pieces or in one piece with front buttoned or zippered, of napped fabric similar to that used for blankets.

breakfast coat   Contemporary name for BRUNCH COAT or DUSTER (see under SLEEP-WEAR AND LOUNGEWEAR).

brunch coat   Knee- or mid-calf-length, front-buttoned robe often in printed cotton worn in the daytime at home, popular since 1950s. Also called *duster* or *breakfast coat. Der.* Named for meal combining "breakfast" and "lunch".

brunch coat

bubble coverup   Loose-fitting, mini-length blouson-type gown gathered below hips into wide band, forming a very short shirt.

bunny suit   Form-fitting knitted jumpsuit buttoned or zippered down the front and made in footed-pajama style. Sometimes made in wide crosswise stripes of red and white.

caftan   See under alphabetical listing.

Chinese lounging robe   ∞ Full-length lounging robe with standing Chinese collar, full kimono sleeves flaring at wrist, and closing to one side in Chinese manner. Worn by women in early 1900s.

chinese pajamas   Hip- or thigh-length jacket with side seams slashed to waist, mandarin collar, and closing—sometimes diagonal with frogs—worn with straight-legged pants. *Der.* From work garments worn in China by men and women.

coat-style pajamas   Classic pajama style made like a single- or double-breasted coat with tailored convertible collar, frequently trimmed with piping, and worn with drawstring or elastic-top pants.

cocoon   Luxurious hip-length robe with large batwing sleeve and blouson back with the open front usually banded in a contrasting color.

cossack pajamas Pants plus tunic top closing at side front with standing-band collar. Introduced in 1930s and revived in late 1960s.

culotte pajamas (koo-lot′) Floor-length pajamas with wide legs, resembling a long dress, worn for dining in mid- and late 1960s and early 1970s. Also called *hostess culottes* and *party pants.*

djellaba (jel-ah′-bah) Loose garment, sometimes hooded, derived from Moroccan man's cloak. It was popular in 1960s along with the *caftan,* still worn by women as a housecoat or hostess robe.

dorm shirt Above-the-knee nightshirt made of knitted fabric and styled like a T-shirt.

Dr. Denton Sleepers® Trademark of Denton Mills, Inc., New Albany, Massachusetts, established in 1865, for one-piece knitted pajama originally worn by children that had covered feet, buttoned down the front, and with buttoned drop seat. Similar style now worn by adults called a BUNNY SUIT (see under SLEEPWEAR AND LOUNGEWEAR). This trademark is still active.

dressing gown/dressing robe 1. Men: Generally used for a man's bathrobe usually lined and styled in a silk, rayon, or nylon fabric. Made in wraparound style with long shawl collar and sash. **2.** Women: Voluminous wraparound worn in the boudoir.

dressing sacque/dressing sack ∞ Short, loose hip-length woman's jacket worn in boudoir in late 19th and early 20th c.

duster See SLEEPWEAR AND LOUNGEWEAR: BRUNCH COAT.

flannel nightgown Full-length winter nightgown made of cotton FLANNEL or a blend of cotton and polyester. Frequently styled with a square or round yoke accented with a ruffle.

flashy nightshirt Low, scoop-necked, raglan-sleeved, above-the-knee nightshirt made with curved hem split at sides. Made of sweatshirt gray poly-

flannel nightgown

ester knit. Similar to Flashdance knit shirt. See FLASHDANCE LOOK.

footed pajamas One- or two-piece child's sleeping garment with attached slipperlike coverings for the feet with soles often made of nonskid plastic.

footed pajamas

french maid sleeper Provocative two-piece pajamas consisting of a lace-trimmed sheer top, styled like a French maid's apron, with bikini panties worn underneath.

granjamer Granny-style top with yoke, a placket neckline, and ruffle trimming worn with matching pants in 1960s for sleeping.

granny gown High-necked, long-sleeved, full-length gown made with ruffle-trimmed yoke, no waistline seam, and sometimes a ruffled flounce at hem. *Der.* Worn by a young girl who copied styles worn by her grandmother, or "granny."

grow sleepers Children's pajamas with several rows of snaps at waist that extend the length as the child grows taller.

happi coat Hip-length jacket made in kimono style of brightly printed fabric, copied from knee-length jackets worn by Japanese laborers. Frequently with printed medallion on back in imitation of original Japanese jackets, which had symbol of employer on the back. Used in the United States as beach coats from 1950s to 1960s. Also spelled *happie.*

harem pajamas Very full trousers gathered at ankle, which may be paired with tunic or Oriental bolero. Fashionable for at-home wear in late 1960s.

hostess culottes See SLEEPWEAR AND LOUNGEWEAR: CULOTTE PAJAMAS.

hostess robe Full-length robe fastening in front, frequently with zipper, made in elaborate fabrics and worn for entertaining at home. Also called *hostess gown* or *hostess coat.*

housecoat Informal robe worn at home. See SLEEPWEAR AND LOUNGEWEAR: BRUNCH COAT and LOUNGING ROBE.

Japanese wrapper ∞ Woman's lounging robe of early 20th c. made in wraparound style with long wide sleeves and a square yoke.

Styled after a Japanese KIMONO (see under SLEEPWEAR AND LOUNGEWEAR).

Juliet gown   Nylon gown, usually made full length with a high or Empire waistline. May be lace-trimmed, have tiny puffed sleeves, and have ruffle at hem.

jumpsuit pajamas   Fitted pajamas in one piece, usually buttoned or zipped at center front; similar to BUNNY SUIT but lacking feet (See under SLEEPWEAR AND LOUNGEWEAR).

kabuki robe (kah-boo'-kee)   Short-length man's or woman's wraparound robe styled like a KIMONO (see under SLEEPWEAR AND LOUNGEWEAR) and closed with a sash.

karate pajamas (kah-rah'-tee)   Two-piece pajamas styled like a KARATE COSTUME, with pants and Japanese-type wrap top, introduced in late 1960s and early 1970s.

kimono (keh-mo'-no)   Type of robe cut like the Japanese kimono with KIMONO SLEEVES (see under SHOULDERS AND SLEEVES) and generally made in a scenic or floral printed fabric reminiscent of Japan. Sometimes closed with frogs rather than buttons. Very popular in the early 19th c. and used continually since. Shown at KIMONO.

knitted knickers   One-piece, sleeveless knitted pajamas with fitted top, round neck, and pants shirred at hem making a ruffle below the knee.

lounging pajamas   Full-length pajamas cut in tunic or one-piece style. Legs are wide and long, giving the appearance of a skirt when not in motion. Introduced in the 1930s and used for lounge- and beachwear. Reintroduced in mid-1960s for evening or entertaining at home. Also called *hostess pajamas.*

lounging robe   Term applied to any woman's robe, often a long one, worn informally at home for relaxation.

matinee ∞ (mah-tin-ay')   **1.** A hooded PARDESSUS (see under COATS AND JACKETS) worn with morning dress in early 1850s. **2.** Another name for a *tea jacket* worn in 1890s and early 20th c. **3.** Lace-trimmed simple jacket to hips worn only in the boudoir from about 1915 to 1930s.

middy-top pajamas   Man's two-piece pajamas styled with a slip-on top having no buttons. So named because of the resemblance to a MIDDY BLOUSE (see under BLOUSES AND TOPS).

monk's robe   Full-length, flowing robe with bell sleeve, frequently made with a hooded cowl neckline and a rope belt. *Der.* Inspired by a monk's habit.

negligée (neg-glee-zheh')   Flowing informal woman's robe of delicate fabric with trimming of lace, ruffles, etc., often worn with a matching nightgown.

nightgown   **1.** An item of apparel, styled similar to a dress, worn by men, women and children for sleeping. Sometimes abbreviated to *gown* or *nightie.* Also called a *sleeper.* Meaning of the word and use of the item dates from the early 19th c. **2.** ∞ From the 16th to the 19th c., an informal coat for men cut on contemporary lines which could be worn outdoors as well as indoors. See BANYAN in alphabetical listing.

night rail   ∞ **1.** Term originally used for a nightgown. Also spelled *night rayle.* **2.** Loose-fitting dress or robe made of plain drab-colored fabric worn in the morning by women in Colonial America. **3.** Woman's shoulder cape of lawn, silk, satin, or lace. Worn from 16th to early 18th c. as boudoir jacket or in bed.

nightshift/nightshirt   **1.** Sleeping garment worn by both men and women. Frequently made in "his or hers" style like a man's shirt in mini, knee, or calf length, usually with rounded hem and a slash at side seams. Formerly worn by men and boys before introduction of pajamas about 1880. **2.** ∞ Mid-1980s versions for women made in tank top, shirt, or T-shirt styles which can double as day wear.

nightshirt #1

pajamas/pyjamas   One- or two-piece item of apparel originally designed for sleeping; later for lounging; and in late 1960s for entertaining, evening parties, and dining out. The word pajamas is often abbreviated to **"pjs."** Originally introduced about 1880 from India for men to wear for sleeping instead of nightgowns. Introduced for women for sleeping in mid-1920s. Popular for lounge- and beachwear in the late 1920s and 1930s. *Der.* Hindustani "pajama," which came from the Persian words *pai*, "leg," and *jaman,* "a garment."

pajamas

pajama set   Tailored pajamas with a matching robe styled for men or women.

party pajamas/party pants   Type of pajamas, pants, or culottes with styling suitable to wear for dining and dancing. Also called *hostess pajamas* or *culotte pajamas.*

peignoir (pane´-war)   Feminine type of robe made in a sheer or elaborate fabric only intended for the boudoir; usually made with a matching nightgown, in which case it is called a **peignoir set.** *Der.* French, *peignoir,* "to comb," as it was originally worn when combing the hair.

peignoir set

pjs   See SLEEPWEAR AND LOUNGEWEAR: PAJAMAS.

rompers   One-piece pajamas styled like a JUMPSUIT with short legs. Usually knitted, sometimes made of terry cloth.

shave coat   Man's knee-length wraparound bathrobe frequently matched to pajamas.

shortie   Term for mini-length gown.

shortie pajamas   Two-piece pajamas with legs coming to knee. Worn primarily in summer by both men and women.

ski pajamas   Any two-piece pajamas styled with full legs gathered into knitted cuffs at the ankles.

shortie pajamas

sleepcoat   Styled like a man's pajama top but longer in length.

sleep set   Two-piece seductive sleepwear consisting of jacket or camisole-type top worn over brief bikinis. Top can also double for streetwear.

sleep shorts   Man's pull-on shorts, sometimes with two piped pockets, worn for sleeping.

slip gown   Bias-cut full-length gown made with no waistline seam and sliplike top with V-neck and narrow shoulder straps. Sometimes made of satin with matching jacket.

slouch gown   Thigh-length gown of knitted fabric styled like a long sweatshirt with a band at hem.

tailored pajamas   Any pajamas not excessively decorated or trimmed, usually finished with piping.

teddy   One-piece sleep garment with low-cut wrap-style front, high-cut legs, and elasticized waistline; sometimes with a short skirt. Often made of nylon satin or georgette trimmed with lace or ruffles. Can also be worn as an undergarment. See UNDERGARMENTS: TEDDY.

toga nightgown   Gown styled with one shoulder or with conventional top and one or both sides split to hips. Introduced in the late 1960s. *Der.* From draping of Roman toga.

toilet/toilette ∞ (twa-let´)   Term used in 18th c. for loose *wrapper* worn by women while having hair arranged. Also spelled *twillet.*

travel coat   Nylon jersey robe that packs easily and does not wrinkle.

t-shirt pajamas   Two-piece pajamas with a knitted T-SHIRT top (see under SHIRTS).

tunic pajamas   Two-piece pajamas styled with a long overblouse top. Also see SLEEPWEAR AND LOUNGEWEAR: COSSACK PAJAMAS.

twillet   See SLEEPWEAR AND LOUNGEWEAR: TOILET #1.

Watteau wrapper (wa-toe´)   Fitted full-length dressing gown worn by women in the 1880s and 1890s. Sometimes did not meet in front and tied together with sash at waistline. Had characteristic double or triple box pleats in back, sometimes ending in a train. Robes with this style back are revived periodically. *Der.* Named for the artist WATTEAU.

wraparound robe   Any robe made in wraparound style.

S

wrapper **1.** ∞ 18th-c. term for a woman's dressing gown worn in the boudoir and in bed. **2.** Synonym for *wraparound robe*.

---

sleeve See under category heading SHOULDERS AND SLEEVES,

sleeve à la folle See SHOULDERS AND SLEEVES: IMBECILE SLEEVE.

sleeve button See CLOSURES.

sleeve hand See SHOULDERS AND SLEEVES.

sleeveless blouse See BLOUSES AND TOPS.

sleeve string See CLOSURES: CUFF STRING.

sleeve tongs ∞ Ornamental metal tongs used to position large sleeves inside coat sleeves in mid-1890s.

sleevings See SLIVINGS.

slicker See COATS AND JACKETS.

slide See FOOTWEAR.

slide bracelet See JEWELRY.

slide fastener See CLOSURES: ZIPPER.

slim jeans See PANTS.

slingback shoe See FOOTWEAR.

slingback thong See FOOTWEAR: THONG SANDAL #2.

sling-duster See COATS AND JACKETS.

sling neckline See NECKLINES AND COLLARS: ONE-SHOULDER NECKLINE.

sling pump See FOOTWEAR: SLINGBACK SHOE.

sling sleeve See SHOULDERS AND SLEEVES.

slip **1.** See UNDERGARMENTS. **2.** ∞ 17th-c. lining for semitransparent dresses. **3.** ∞ Late 19th-c. term for a man's white piqué edging for a morning vest called a WHITE SLIP.

slip blouse See UNDERGARMENTS: BLOUSE-SLIP.

slip-dress Simple bias-cut dress with fitted top, straps over shoulders, and no waistline. A revival in 1966 and after of bias-cut dress of the 1920s and 1930s as worn by movie star Jean Harlow.

slip gown See SLEEPWEAR AND LOUNGEWEAR.

slip-on/slip over **1.** See PULLOVER. **2.** See GLOVES AND GLOVE CONSTRUCTIONS and FOOTWEAR.

slippage **1.** † Textile term for defects in the fabric due to shifting of yarns. Occurs because fabric is poorly constructed. **2.** Sewing term for shifting of yarns at seams of a sewed garment.

slippers See FOOTWEAR.

slipper satin † Lustrous, stiff satin fabric or made in brocaded effect. Used for formal gowns and shoes.

slipper socks See FOOTWEAR.

slip-shoe See FOOTWEAR.

slip stitch See EMBROIDERIES AND SEWING STITCHES.

slit Slashed opening in front of clothing used from 14th c. on to facilitate entry. When used at back of jacket, called a *vent*. Also see POCKETS and SKIRTS.

slit trank See GLOVES AND GLOVE CONSTRUCTIONS.

slivings See TRUNK HOSE.

slop ∞ **1.** Short jacket worn by men in 14th and early 15th c. over a DOUBLET. **2.** See FOOTWEAR. **3.** Cloak or nightgown worn by men and women in first half of 16th c. **4.** Term for laborer's *smock* worn by men in 18th and 19th c. Also see SLOPS.

sloper Basic pattern for a garment section, without style lines or seam allowances, developed from a dress form, live model, specific measurements, or manufacturer's specifications. Used to develop original patterns and create new designs. Also called *standard pattern, foundation pattern, block pattern,* and *master pattern.*

slops ∞ See **1.** TRUNK HOSE. **2.** Used until late 18th c. for sailor's trousers carried in a sea chest or "slop chest." **3.** From 17th to 19th c. a term for ready-made or old clothes and also for the bedding and supplies sold in stores known as "slop shops."

slot seam See CLOTHING CONSTRUCTION DETAILS.

slouch See HEADWEAR, SLEEPWEAR AND LOUNGEWEAR, and HOSIERY.

slub yarn † Yarn that has thicker areas alternating with thinner. When used as crosswise yarns in shantung and other fabrics, it produces an uneven appearance with elongated thickened places at intervals.

small Size used along with EXTRA SMALL, MEDIUM, LARGE, and EXTRA LARGE for men, women, and children in such categories as sweaters, knit and sport shirts, sport jackets, nightgowns and pajamas, robes, gloves, girdles, and panty girdles. Abbreviated S.

smallclothes ∞ Polite term for men's breeches used from 1770 to mid-19th c.

small falls   See FALL #1.

small slops   See TRUNK HOSE.

smile pocket   See POCKETS: HALF-MOON POCKET.

Smith, Willi   * See APPENDIX/DESIGNERS.

smock   **1.** Long-sleeved, loose-fitting garment fastened down front or back and meant to protect clothes while wearer is working. **2.** See UNDERGARMENTS: CHEMISE.

smock #1

smock blouse   ∞ Child's dress of 1880s with the top bloused below the waistline by gathering with a ribbon pulled through insertion. Knee-length skirt sometimes consisted of two ruffles.

smock dress   Dress cut with yoke that comes above the bust and straight hanging skirt attached with slight gathers to the yoke. Usually worn without a belt. Resembles the cut of a smock (see SMOCK # 1); the BABY-DOLL DRESS is similar in cut. Shown at BABY-DOLL DRESS.

smock-frock   ∞ **1.** 18th- and 19th-c.: Man's knee-length, loose-fitting homespun gown worn by farmers. Sometimes made with a sailor collar, or yoke. Usually smocked in various patterns indicating the place of residence of the worker. Also called *smock.* **2.** In 1880s, a women's garment cut like a farmer's smock.

smocking   See EMBROIDERIES AND SEWING STITCHES.

smock top   See BLOUSES AND TOPS.

smoking jacket   See JACKETS and SUITS.

smoking suit   Woman's lounging suit with jacket styled similar to man's smoking jacket, usually combined with matching velvet pants. Introduced in late 1960s, and attributed to Saint Laurent, Paris couturier. Also called *le smoking.*

smoky quartz   See GEMS, GEM CUTS, AND SETTINGS.

snail button   See CLOSURES.

snake bracelet   See JEWELRY.

snakes   See HAIRSTYLES: LOVE LOCKS.

snakeskin   See LEATHERS.

snap   See CLOSURES and UNDERGARMENTS.

snap-brim hat   See HEADWEAR.

snap pants   See UNDERGARMENTS.

sneaker   See FOOTWEAR and HOSIERY.

snip slip   See UNDERGARMENTS.

snood   See HEADWEAR.

snorkel coat/jacket   See COATS AND JACKETS.

snowboarding suit   See ACTIVEWEAR.

Snow, Carmel White (1888–1961)   Worked for *Vogue* magazine from 1921 in fashion department. Made editor of American *Vogue* from 1929 to 1932. In 1932 she became fashion editor of *Harper's Bazaar*— later becoming editor until her retirement in 1957. A personality of wit, intelligence, and strong views, she was tiny and well dressed in Parisian clothes. She had an instinct for fashion today and what would come tomorrow. Awards include 1941, Neiman Marcus Award; 1949, French Legion of Honor; 1954, Italian Star of Solidarity. Author with Mary Louise Aswell of *The World of Carmel Snow.*

snow leopard   See FURS.

snowmobile boot   See FOOTWEAR.

snowmobile gloves   See GLOVES AND GLOVE CONSTRUCTIONS: MITTS.

snowmobile suit   See ACTIVEWEAR.

snowsuit   See ACTIVEWEAR.

snuggies   See UNDERGARMENTS.

soccus (pl. socci)   **1.** See FOOTWEAR. **2.** See CAPES, CLOAKS, AND SHAWLS.

socklets   See HOSIERY.

sock lining   See FOOTWEAR.

socks   See HOSIERY.

sock suspenders   ∞ British term for men's garters (see GARTER #2), introduced in 1895, to hold up calf-length socks. Consisted of a band of elastic with attached garter clip.

socq   See CAPES, CLOAKS, AND SHAWLS: SOCCUS.

soft dressing   Loosely-fitted clothing made from soft fabrics that drape well.

soft goods   Fashion and textile merchandise (e.g., dresses, lingerie, coats, household textiles), as contrasted with **hard goods** (e.g., home appliances, hardware, or furniture).

solaret   See ARMOR: SOLLERET.

sole   See FOOTWEAR.

solea   See FOOTWEAR.

sole leather   See LEATHERS.

solers   See FOOTWEAR.

solitaire   **1.** See JEWELRY. **2.** See TIES. **3.** See SCARVES.

solleret   See ARMOR.

sombrero   See HEADWEAR.

S

sombrero Córdobes   See HEADWEAR: GAUCHO HAT.

sontag   See CAPES, CLOAKS, AND SHAWLS.

Sorel, Agnès (1422–1450) Mistress of Charles VII of France (1444–1459), called "La Dame de Beauté" (Lady of Beauty), wore jewel-studded robes, was the first commoner to wear diamonds, and made the king a waistcoat embroidered with pearls and precious stones. Acted as a model for the financier and merchant Jacques Coeur, who brought linen, silken gowns, sables, and pearls from the Orient. Painted by French artist of the time Fouquet. Many 19th-c. fashions were named after her. Examples: Agnès Sorel coiffure, Agnès Sorel corsage, and Agnès Sorel dress.

sorority pin   See JEWELRY.

sorquenie/soucanie ∞ (sor-ken-ee′) Woman's TUNIC worn from 13th to 19th c., fitted tightly over bust.

sortie de bal   See CAPES, CLOAKS, AND SHAWLS.

soucanie   See SORQUENIE.

soul   See HEADWEAR: NEWSBOY CAP.

soulette   See FOOTWEAR.

source   The vendor or supplier that sells products necessary for the production and distribution of products in the textile, apparel, or retail industries.

sourcing   The process of determining how, where, and when the materials required for textile and apparel products will be purchased.

soutache (soo-tash)   See BRAIDS.

soutane   See CLERICAL DRESS: CASSOCK #1.

Southern Colonel tie   See TIES: STRING TIE.

souvenir scarf   See SCARVES.

sou'wester/southwester   See HEADWEAR.

sovereign purse   See HANDBAGS AND RELATED ACCESSORIES.

space blanket   See CAPES, CLOAKS, AND SHAWLS.

space clothes   Since the entrance of the United States into the space program in the 1960s, the development of clothing and accessories for astronauts has been essential. New fabrics have been designed that withstand extremes of heat and cold. Velcro® was introduced for use on soles of booties and floor of space cabin to keep astronauts feet on the floor when in weightless condition. French and U.S. designers were inspired by space clothes. For examples see HEADWEAR: COURRÈGES HELMET, COSMONAUTS LOOK, and LUNAR LOOK.

space-dyed yarn † Yarns colored or dyed various colors at intervals. When woven into a fabric, they produce a random design.

space helmet   See HEADWEAR.

Space® shoe   See FOOTWEAR.

spaghetti sash   See BELTS.

spaghetti strap   Very narrow strap with cord inserted to produce a round effect, similar to a strand of spaghetti.

spaier ∞ Medieval term for vertical slash in garment, similar to a slit, used to reach pocket on inner garment.

spair   See FALL #1.

spandex † Generic fiber term for manufactured fibers, composed largely of segmented polyurethane, which are stretchable, lightweight, and resistant to body acid. Used for girdles, foundations, and bras, for bathing suits, and to make stretchable fabrics. Spandex is not used alone, but in combination with a wide variety of other fibers. Current trademarks include Lycra®, Dorlastan®, and Glospan®.

spangle   Synonym for SEQUIN or PAILLETTE.

spaniel's-ear collar   See NECKLINES AND COLLARS: DOG'S EAR COLLAR.

Spanish   See LACES and CAPES, CLOAKS, AND SHAWLS.

Spanish black work   See EMBROIDERIES AND SEWING STITCHES: BLACKWORK.

Spanish blonde lace   See LACES.

Spanish breeches ∞ Narrow high-waisted below-the-knee breeches worn by men from 1630s to 1645 and from 1663 to 1670. Loose at hems, trimmed with rosettes, buttons, and ladderlike trim. Hooked to doublet lining and similar to SMALL SLOPS (see TRUNK HOSE) but longer. Also called *Spanish hose*.

Spanish cloak   See CAPES, CLOAKS, AND SHAWLS: ITALIAN CLOAK.

Spanish comb   See HAIR ACCESSORIES.

Spanish embroidery   See EMBROIDERIES AND SEWING STITCHES.

Spanish farthingale   See FARTHINGALE.

Spanish flounce ∞ Deep gathered ruffle joined to hem of short skirt worn in late 19th and early 20th c.

Spanish heel   See FOOTWEAR.

Spanish hose   See SPANISH BREECHES.

Spanish jacket See COATS AND JACKETS.

Spanish kettledrums See TRUNK HOSE.

Spanish lace See LACES.

Spanish shawl See CAPES, CLOAKS, AND SHAWLS.

Spanish sleeve See SHOULDERS AND SLEEVES.

spats See FOOTWEAR.

spatterdashes See FOOTWEAR.

spec/specification In fashion illustration, a sketch of clothing, without a human figure, that includes various garment measurements.

special order An order for an item for a specific customer.

specialty goods BRAND-name merchandise.

specialty store Retail establishment that sells a specific type of merchandise (e.g., children's clothes, women's apparel).

specification buying Development and purchase by a retailer of private label merchandise by working directly with the sewing contractor rather than by going through an apparel manufacturer.

spectacles/specs See EYEWEAR.

spectator pump See FOOTWEAR.

speed lacing See CLOSURES.

spencer See COATS AND JACKETS.

spencer cloak See CAPES, CLOAKS, AND SHAWLS.

spencerette See COATS AND JACKETS.

spencer waist ∞ Woman's fitted blouse with a band at the waistline, worn in 1860s and 1890s.

spere/speyer ∞ Late 16th- and 17th-c. term for PLACKET (see under CLOTHING CONSTRUCTION DETAILS).

Sperry Top Siders® See FOOTWEAR.

spider work See LACES.

spiffs Incentives to motivate salespersons to sell particular items. Spiffs are provided by vendors and are sometimes called *push money.*

spiked shoe See FOOTWEAR.

spike heel See FOOTWEAR.

spike-tail Slang term for man's SWALLOWTAILED COAT (see under COATS AND JACKETS).

spiky hairstyle See HAIRSTYLES.

spinel See GEMS, GEM CUTS, AND SETTINGS.

spinning † **1.** Process of twisting fibers together to form a yarn. **2.** The formation of manufactured fibers by extruding the liquid fiber material through a spinneret, a metal disk with holes,

into a medium (air or liquid) that causes the fiber to solidify.

Spitalfield tie See TIES.

spit-boot See FOOTWEAR.

spit curls See HAIRSTYLES.

SPF See SUN PROTECTION FACTOR.

splinter-hat See HEADWEAR: SPLYTER-HAT.

split See LEATHERS.

split buckskin See LEATHERS: BUCKSKIN.

split falls See FALL #1.

split mandarin collar See NECKLIINES AND COLLARS.

split skirt See SKIRTS.

splyter-hat See HEADWEAR.

spoon back ∞ Used in mid-1880s for circular folds of drapery formed at back by the overskirt of a walking dress.

spoon bonnet See HEADWEAR.

spoon rings See JEWELRY.

sporran See HANDBAGS AND RELATED ACCESSORIES.

sport bra/Sport Bra® See UNDERGARMENTS.

sport jackets See COATS AND JACKETS.

sport set Trade term for two or more items of sportswear made to match or contrast and sold as a set (e.g., bathing suit with coverup, top with shorts or skirt, twin sweaters and skirt, child's bloomers with pinafore).

sport shirt See SHIRTS.

sports sandals See FOOTWEAR.

sport suit Clothing designed to be worn for specific sports, e.g., a suit used for horseback riding, exercising, scuba diving. Using specialized clothing when participating in active sports started at end of 18th c. with clothing for hunting. Since then, special clothing has developed for most sports. See ACTIVEWEAR for specific styles used in various sports.

sportswear **1.** Originally designated clothing worn for tennis, golf, bicycling, bathing, ice skating, yachting, and hunting in 1890s. See SPORT SUITS. **2.** By the 1920s and 1930s used for casual wear for leisure time and when participating in spectator sports (e.g., sweaters, skirts, blouses, pants, and shorts). **3.** In the post–World War II period, sportswear has become synonymous with casual wear and is worn for day or evening and even for work in some businesses. Clothing worn for active sports is designated as ACTIVE-WEAR. This has occurred primarily in the United States due to the adoption of less formal lifestyles by Americans. It has been stated that sportswear is the primary American contribution to the history of costume.

spotted cat See FURS.

spread collar See NECKLINES AND COLLARS.

spreading Unwinding large fabric rolls onto cutting tables and stacking the fabric in layers prior to cutting garment pieces.

spreading machines Equipment designed for SPREADING fabric smoothly prior to cutting.

spring-bottom trousers See PANTS.

spring bracelet See JEWELRY.

spring heel See FOOTWEAR.

springy pelts See FURS: BUCKY PELTS.

square See NECKLINES AND COLLARS and FOOTWEAR: SQUARE TOES.

square-bottom channel frame See HANDBAGS AND RELATED ACCESSORIES: FRAME.

square cut See GEMS, GEM CUTS, AND SETTINGS: EMERALD CUT.

square-dance skirt See SKIRTS.

square dancing dress Dress with puffed sleeves and a wide, full, circular skirt, frequently finished with a ruffle. *Der.* Worn for square dancing, an American type of country dancing.

square hoop See UNDERGARMENTS: PANNIERS.

square neckline See NECKLINES AND COLLARS.

square setting See GEMS, GEM CUTS, AND SETTINGS.

squash blossom necklace See JEWELRY.

squaw *adj.* Applied to clothes influenced by garments worn by Native American women. *Der.* The word "squaw" is what European settlers called Native American women, but the word was not used by Native Americans. See BLOUSES AND TOPS: SQUAW BLOUSE, FOOTWEAR: SQUAW BOOT, HANDBAGS AND RELATED ACCESSORIES: SQUAW BAG and SKIRTS: SQUAW SKIRT.

squaw dress Full-skirted minutely pleated dress with elaborate embroidery on long-sleeved bodice and in bands on skirt. *Der.* The word "squaw" is what European settlers called Native American women, but the word was not used by Native Americans.

squirrel See FURS.

stacked heel See FOOTWEAR.

stadium See FOOTWEAR and COATS AND JACKETS.

Standard Industrial Classification (SIC) codes U.S. Office of Management and Budget codes used to identify U.S. business establishments according to their general types of business activity. Both manufacturers of products such as apparel and various types of retailers are included.

standard pattern See SLOPER.

standards A shortened term for STANDARD SPECIFICATIONS.

standard specifications Defined levels of performance that products must meet in order to be considered acceptable for use.

stand-away collar See NECKLINES AND COLLARS.

stand-fall collar See NECKLINES AND COLLARS: ROLLED COLLAR.

standing whisk See NECKLINES AND COLLARS: WHISK #2.

St. Andrews cross See CROSS.

St. Gall lace See LACES.

St. Tropez skirt See SKIRTS.

stand-up collar See NECKLINES AND COLLARS.

staple fibers † Natural or manufactured fibers that are short and must be spun in order to form a yarn. Compare with FILAMENT FIBERS.

staples See BASICS.

staple yarn See YARNS.

stapling See FURS.

starcher See TIES.

starching See SIZING.

star ruby/star sapphire See GEMS, GEM CUTS, AND SETTINGS.

startup See FOOTWEAR.

Statue of Liberty **1.** See HEADWEAR. **2.** See JEWELRY. **3.** See HAIRSTYLES.

staurolite See GEMS, GEM CUTS, AND SETTINGS: FAIRY STONE.

Stavropoulos, George * See APPENDIX/DESIGNERS.

stay See CLOTHING CONSTRUCTION DETAILS.

stay hook ∞ Small ornamental hook attached to bodice in 18th c. to hold a watch. Also called *breast hook* or crochet (see CROCHET #2).

stays See UNDERGARMENTS.

stay-up hose See HOSIERY.

steeple headdress See HEADWEAR: HENNIN.

steerhide See LEATHERS.

Steinkirk See TIES.

stem stitch See EMBROIDERIES AND SEWING STITCHES.

stenciled print See PRINTS, STRIPES, AND CHECKS.

stenciling Applying dye to fur or fabric by painting through a cut-out stencil (e.g., used to make pile fabric look like leopard). In late 1960s and early 1970s applied to sheared mink and all kinds of fur and fur fabrics to simulate giraffe, tiger, leopard, jaguar, and zebra. Practice continued after this time.

step cut See GEMS, GEM CUTS, AND SETTINGS.

stephane See HEADWEAR.

step-in dress Coat-type dress that buttons or zips only three-quarters of the way down the front. Basic dress style since the 1940s.

step-ins See UNDERGARMENTS.

step-in shoe See FOOTWEAR: SLIP-ON SHOES.

sterling silver See JEWELRY.

stertop See FOOTWEAR: STARTUP.

Stetson See HEADWEAR.

Stewart dress and hunting tartan See PLAIDS AND TARTANS.

stickpin See JEWELRY.

stick-up collar See NECKLINES AND COLLARS: WING COLLAR.

stiletto (stil-let′-o) **1.** ∞ Narrow pointed stick used in ancient Greece as a hairpin. **2.** Pointed instrument similar to a large needle used to punch holes in embroidery. **3.** See FOOTWEAR.

stirrup hose See HOSIERY.

stirrup pants See PANTS.

stirrup tights See ACTIVEWEAR: AEROBIC ENSEMBLE.

stitch One complete motion of a threaded needle or other implement (e.g., a knitting needle or crochet hook), which, when used in a series, results in such decorative or utilitarian work as sewing, embroidering, knitting, crocheting, or tatting. May be made by hand or machine with thread, yarn, embroidery floss, string, straw fiber, or other material. For specific named types of stitches, see EMBROIDERIES AND SEWING STITCHES category.

stitch-bonded fabric Fabrics constructed by binding together yarns or fabric webs with stitches like those made in knitting. The earliest trademark name for this process is Malimo®.

stitchdown shoe construction See FOOTWEAR.

stitches See EMBROIDERIES AND SEWING STITCHES.

stock **1.** See TIES. **2.** From about 1590, the word *stock* was occasionally used as a synonym for stocking (see under HOSIERY). **3.** Term used for leather in shoe manufacturing. **4.** Synonym for merchandise.

stock collar/neckline See NECKLINES AND COLLARS: ASCOT.

stocking See HOSIERY.

stocking bodice See BLOUSES AND TOPS.

stocking boot See FOOTWEAR.

stocking cap See HEADWEAR.

stocking purse See HANDBAGS AND RELATED ACCESSORIES: MISER'S PURSE.

stocking shoe See FOOTWEAR.

stock keeping unit (SKU) Unit designation for inventory and record-keeping purposes that is based on style, color, size, and any other information that needs to be tracked. Only those items identical in style, color, etc., would belong to a particular SKU.

stock on hand The stock currently available in a retail store.

stocks ∞ Garment originally styled like tights. Worn on the legs from about 1400 to 1610, stocks evolved into two separate pieces. The upper part was known as TRUNK HOSE or *overstocks, haut de chausses,* or *upper stocks;* lower part was often called *bas de chausses, lower stocks, nether stocks, hose,* and later STOCKINGS (see under HOSIERY). Also see CHAUSSE and CHAUSSEMBLES.

stock-tie blouse/shirt **1.** See BLOUSES AND TOPS. **2.** See SHIRTS.

stola ∞ (stow′-la) Ancient Roman garment denoting a married, free woman. It was apparently worn as an outer layer over an undertunic and probably resembled the Doric *chiton* of ancient Greeks, being sleeveless and either pinned at the shoulder or suspended from straps. Also see INSTITA. Shown at CAPES, CLOAKS, AND SHAWLS: PALLA.

stole **1.** See SCARVES. **2.** See CAPES, CLOAKS, AND SHAWLS: FUR STOLE. **3.** See CLERICAL DRESS.

stomacher ∞ **1.** An ornamental chest piece worn by men under a V- or U-shaped doublet from late 15th to early 16th c. **2.** In women's dress, a heavily embroidered or jeweled V-shaped panel over chest, extending down to point over stomach, held in place by busks. Either a part of the dress or a separate plastron (see PLASTRON #2) worn with low-cut décolletage from late 15th c. to 1770s. **3.** Same type of inserted front panel made of shirred fabric used on dresses in first half of 19th c. Also see COTTAGE FRONT.

stone marten   See FURS.

stonewashed   † Adjective describing fabrics or garments that have been treated to produce certain color and/or texture effects by tumbling them with pumice stones or other abrasives that may have been soaked in bleaching chemicals. Where the stones come into contact with the fabric, abrasion occurs and color is removed. Synonyms include *acid washing, distressing, frosting, ice washing, snow washing, super washing,* and *white washing.*

store brand   Goods that carry the name of the retailer who not only sells but also produces and names them. See PRIVATE LABEL.

store-owned buying office   See PRIVATE BUYING OFFICE.

storm   See FOOTWEAR: STORM BOOTS and COATS AND JACKET: STORM COAT.

storm flap   See CLOSURES: STORM FLAP.

storm rubbers   See FOOTWEAR.

stormsuit   See ACTIVEWEAR.

stovepipe hat   See HEADWEAR.

stovepipe pants   See PANTS.

straight-cut pants   See PANTS.

straight pin   Functional device consisting of a sharp pointed shaft with flattened head used to pin pattern to fabric when cutting out a pattern, pinning cut out pieces together before sewing, or as a temporary fastening. Used since the 14th c., pins were scarce and sold only on January 1 and 2. Originally heads were hammered on top, after 1830 made in one piece. Also see DRESSMAKER PIN.

straights   See FOOTWEAR.

straight skirt   See SKIRTS.

strapless   See UNDERGARMENTS, NECKLINES AND COLLARS, BLOUSES AND TOPS.

strapless dress   Décolleté dress ending just at top of bosom without shoulders or straps. Top held

in place by boning, by shirring with elastic thread, or by using stretch fabric.

strapless slip   See UNDERGARMENTS.

strapped trousers   See PANTS.

strap seam   See CLOTHING CONSTRUCTION DETAILS.

strass   See JEWELRY: PASTE.

straw   A vegetable substance or a synthetic imitation used for hats, bags, shoes, and trim. Natural straw comes from dried stems of grains such as barley, oats, rye, and wheat, from stems and stalks of other plants, from leaves, and from bark. Straws may be woven into bodies of hats or made into narrow "straw braid," which is stitched together in a circular manner to make a hat. Also used for handbags, particularly of the basket type. Sometimes used for shoes.

streaking   A fad popular during the winter of 1973–74 for running across a college campus or other public place nude except for shoes and possibly a hat. "Classic" college streaker's costume consisted of knit ski mask and tennis shoes.

street style   Fashions that originate with or are inspired by clothing worn by individuals, usually young, rather than with the fashion industry, although the contemporary fashion industry draws inspiration from street style.

stretch   † **1.** Classification of fabrics of various types. (a) Knitted fabrics that stretch because of the elasticity of the knit. (b) Fabrics made with TEXTURED YARNS that have been crimped or curled. Such yarns give more resiliency and elasticity to fabrics and clothing (e.g., knit shirts, sweaters, and dresses). (c) Fabrics given special finishes that provide increased resiliency and elasticity. (d) Fabrics woven with yarns made from ELASTOMERS. **2.** Adjective used to describe apparel that exhibits the ability to extend in length or width from its original size. See BLOUSES AND TOPS: STRETCH TOP, FOOTWEAR: TOTES®, HOSIERY: STRETCH HOSE and STRETCH SOCK, LACES: STRETCH LACE, PANTS: STRETCH PANTS, UNDERGARMENTS: STRETCH BRA and GARTER BRIEF, and WIGS AND HAIRPIECES: STRETCH WIG.

stretch knit fabrics   † Fabrics knitted with textured or stretch yarns. Also see STRETCH.

stretch woven   † Woven fabric that has at least 20% stretch in either the lengthwise or crosswise direction or both.

string bikini   **1.** See UNDERWEAR. **2.** See ACTIVE-WEAR.

string tie   See TIES.

stripes   See PRINTS, STRIPES, AND CHECKS.

stroller   **1.** See COATS AND JACKETS. **2.** See HEAD-WEAR.

strophium (strof'-ee-uhm)   ∞ **1.** A band of fabric worn by women in Ancient Rome to support their breasts. **2.** See HEADWEAR: CHAPLET. *Der.* Greek *strophos*, "a swaddling band."

structural design   **1.** Used by dress designers for lines of dress that are concerned with the functional design of the dress (e.g., a zipper down the back of the dress, pleats to provide fullness) as contrasted with decorative elements of the design. **2.** † In textiles, a fabric, motif, or pattern achieved by weaving rather than surface treatment (e.g., fabric woven on a JACQUARD loom).

stud   See CLOSURES.

student bycocket   See HEADWEAR: BYCOCKET.

studs   See JEWELRY.

stump work   See EMBROIDERIES AND SEWING STITCHES.

style   **1.** *n.* In fashion, an individual and distinctive type of dress, coat, blouse, or other item of apparel or accessory. **2.** *v.* **Style, styling.** Usually used with "to" (e.g., "to style a line"). Used by a manufacturer when making or selecting the specific types of apparel for seasonal collections. **3.** *n.* "To have style," meaning to have a certain flair that is specific and individual.

style number   A coded number (usually four digits) assigned by the apparel manufacturer to a specific garment style that indicates the season/year for the style and other style information. In this way the manufacturer can keep track of the style throughout the development, marketing, and production.

style sheet   Document in which a merchandiser describes the construction and fabric of garments for import so that duty rates and quota classifications can be established by the U.S. Customs offices.

style show   See FASHION SHOW.

stylized print   See PRINTS, STRIPES, AND CHECKS.

styrtop   See FOOTWEAR: STARTUP.

subclassification (subclass)   Identifies a group of merchandise within a CLASSIFICATION (e.g.,

eveningwear) that is closely related in styling, such as full-length or short.

subcultural styles   Clothing styles originated, developed, or modified by members of groups that reject the values and mores of the dominant society. Such groups have existed in America since the founding of the European colonies, often based on religious ideals. In the post–World War II period, numerous youthful subcultures have developed that have adopted distinctive styles of dress. Some of these styles may influence high-fashion designers. For examples see TEDDY BOYS, MOD, PUNK, HIP HOP, GOTH, RAVE.

suburban coat   See COATS AND JACKETS: CAR COAT.

suede   See LEATHERS.

suede cloth   † Knitted or woven fabric of wool, cotton, or rayon having a nap on one or both sides. Used for suits, coats, vests, pants, and sportswear in imitation of genuine *suede*.

sugarloaf hat   See HEADWEAR.

Sui, Anna   * See APPENDIX/DESIGNERS.

suit   **1.** Two, three, or more items of apparel, either of matching or contrasting fabric, designed to be worn together. For women, generally consists of a jacket and skirt or pants. For men, usually consists of trousers and jacket made in single- or double-breasted style, sometimes including a vest. When the suit consists of a jacket, vest, and trousers for men or a jacket, skirt, and trousers for women, it is called a **three-piece suit.** Term used in 16th and 17th c. for DOUBLET and HOSE. Current meaning of the word suit dates from late 19th c. For some specific styles, see DITTO SUIT, ETON SUIT, LITTLE LORD FAUNTLEROY SUIT, SAILOR SUIT, TAILOR-MADE, and ZOOT SUIT in alphabetical listing.

suitcase bag   See HANDBAGS AND RELATED ACCESSORIES.

suit dress   Used in 1960s to refer to a jacket and dress ensemble that resembled a tailored suit.

suiting   † Broad and general term that applies to any fabric used for men's and women's suits. Includes worsteds and woolens, and manufactured fibers and blends made in a variety of weaves and patterns that have no specific name but tailor well.

S

suit of knots ∞ From 17th to mid-18th c., a set of matching bows, used to trim a dress or to wear in the hair.

suit of ruffs ∞ Matching neck and wrist ruffs, worn by men and women from 1560 to 1640.

suit sleeve See SHOULDERS AND SLEEVES.

suit slip See UNDERGARMENTS.

suit vest See VESTS.

sultana scarf See SCARVES.

sultana sleeve See SHOULDERS AND SLEEVES.

sultane ∞ (sul-tane′) **1.** Dress worn in the late 17th c. and again in the 1730s and 1740s, trimmed with buttons and loops. Worn for traveling. In 18th c. it was a dress with short ROB-INGS, a stomacher (see STOMACHER #2), and a plain back. **2.** PRINCESS-STYLE daytime dress of late 1870s with scarf elaborately draped to one side.

sultane jacket See COATS AND JACKETS.

sumptuary laws (sump′-too-air-ee) Laws restricting the ownership and use of luxury goods to certain social and/or economic classes. Such laws were frequently applied to clothing and its ornamentation, but were rarely obeyed or much enforced.

sun bonnet See HEADWEAR.

sunburst-pleated skirt See SKIRTS: ACCORDION-PLEATED.

sunburst pleats See CLOTHING CONSTRUCTION DETAILS: ACCORDION PLEAT.

sunburst tucks See CLOTHING CONSTRUCTION DETAILS.

Sunday clothes/Sunday best In the 19th and early 20th c., clothing worn especially for church and special occasions, as opposed to WORK CLOTHES.

sundress Dress in strapless or halter style with matching or contrasting jacket, worn in warm weather.

sunglasses See EYEWEAR.

Sun Protection Factor (SPF) A number that indicates the ability of a sunscreen or fabric to protect the skin from the harmful effects of the sun. The higher the SPF number, the greater the ability to block ultraviolet (UV) radiation. An SPF of 15 is recommended as a minimum to block out most UV radiation.

sunray skirt See SKIRTS.

sunshade See UMBRELLAS AND PARASOLS: PARASOL.

sunsuit See ACTIVEWEAR.

super tunic ∞ Overgarment made with or without sleeves. From 9th to end of 14th c., worn by men and women. In the 13th and 14th cs., more likely to be called a SURCOTE.

supportasse See NECKLINES AND COLLARS.

support legwear See HOSIERY.

surah † Lightweight, soft silky fabric made in a twill weave of silk or manufactured yarns. May be woven in yarn-dyed plaids, printed, or dyed in solid colors. Used for dresses, scarves, neckties, and blouses.

surcingle belt See BELTS.

surcote/surcoat ∞ (ser′-koht) Outermost tunic, so called in the 13th and 14th cs., worn by men and women over an undertunic, or COTE. There were both knee-length and long versions for men; long versions for women. Some had wide or bell-shaped sleeves. Others were sleeveless and were known as **sideless surcotes.** Shown at COTE. Synonyms: *cyclas, super tunic.*

surface interest † Texture or appearance of the face or outer side of a fabric that is noteworthy in some way.

surfers See PANTS.

surfing suit See ACTIVEWEAR: WETSUIT.

surf trunks See ACTIVEWEAR.

surgical mask See MASKS.

surgical stocking See HOSIERY: ANTI-EMBOLISM STOCKING.

surpied See FOOTWEAR: SOULETTE.

surplice **1.** See CLERICAL DRESS. **2.** See NECKLINES AND COLLARS. **3.** See CLOSURES: WRAP CLOSING.

surplice bodice/surplis front ∞ (sir′-pliss) A day bodice, worn in 1881, the top of the dress wraps rather than buttons. May be plain or pleated at shoulders and waistband.

Surrealism (sur-re-al-iz′-ihm) Movement in art and literature starting in the 1930s that was greatly influenced by psychoanalysis. Art has a "dreamlike" quality, which suggests the expression of the subconscious and reflects the imagination uncontrolled by reason. *Salvadore Dali* is one of the main exponents of this style. Designers such as Elsa Schiaparelli were much influenced by the Surrealists.

surtout See COATS AND JACKETS.

suspenders **1.** Detachable straps of elasticized fabric passed over shoulders and clipped or buttoned to trousers or skirt front and back. Called *braces* by the British. **2.** British term for woman's garters for stocking attached to corset called a *suspender garter*. **3.** Shoulder straps on bodice or bib top. Also used to describe apparel with shoulder straps. See JUMPERS: SUSPENDER JUMPER, PANTS: SUSPENDER PANTS, and SHORTS: SUSPENDER SHORTS.

suspender trimming See BRETELLES #1.

sustainable design Design that takes into account the effects of textile and apparel production on the environment and seeks to eliminate negative impacts.

swaddling clothes/swadding bands ∞ Narrow strips of fabric wrapped around infants as their earliest clothing. Thought to make their bones straight and strong, the practice existed since ancient times and ended only in the early 19th century. Also called *safeguard, sweathbands*, and *swathing band*.

swaddling clothes

swag Draped folds of fabric used on women's gowns in latter part of 18th c. Any similar ornamentation.

swagger **1.** See COATS AND JACKETS. **2.** See HEADWEAR.

swagger pouch See HANDBAGS AND RELATED ACCESSORIES.

swallow-tailed **1.** See NECKLINES AND COLLARS. **2.** See COATS AND JACKETS.

swanbill corset See UNDERGARMENTS.

swan's down See FEATHERS.

swatch † Textile and sewing term for a small sample of fabric.

swathing band See SWADDLING CLOTHES.

sweatband See HEADWEAR.

sweatclothes See ACTIVEWEAR.

sweater blouse See BLOUSES AND TOPS.

sweater clasp Two decorative clasps connected with a short chain used to hold a sweater together at the neckline.

sweater coat See COATS AND JACKETS.

sweater dress **1.** Knitted dress styled like a long sweater with or without knit-in waistline intro-

duced in 1940s and revived in the 1960s. **2.** Two-piece knitted dress made of matching pull-on sweater and skirt. An innovation of the 1930s, used at intervals since.

sweater-for-two See SWEATERS.

sweater girl In 1940s slang: shapely film stars who wore tight pullover sweaters that emphasized the bosom.

sweater-knit clothing Apparel knitted and styled in the same manner as a sweater. See BLOUSES AND TOPS, COATS AND JACKETS, and VESTS.

SWEATERS

sweater Clothing for the upper part of the body worn either as an outer garment or under a coat or jacket. Hand- or machine-made by knitting or crocheting in a wide variety of patterns. The sweater first appeared as the jersey, in mid-19th c. In early 1890s, turtleneck jerseys were introduced. Later a collar was added and the jersey was worn for golf and sports. In the 1920s, accepted by students and later widely adopted for general wear. At first only made of wool, washability was improved when new yarns (e.g., acrylic and nylon) came onto the market in the 1950s and 1960s.

Aran Isle sweater Pullover with round or V-neck knit in traditional Irish designs including raised cable knit, and interlaced vertical diamond-shaped patterns. *Der.* Named for island off coast of Ireland where sweaters of this type were originally made. See SWEATERS: FISHERMAN'S SWEATER.

argyle sweater (ar´-gyle) Distinctively patterned sweater made in several colors to produce diamond-shaped designs, either knit by hand or machine, often matched to socks. Popular in 1920s and 1930s, and revived in late 1960s. See PLAIDS AND TARTANS. *Der.* Tartan of Duke of Argyle and Clan Campbell of Argyll, a county in west Scotland. Also spelled *argyll, argyl*.

argyle sweater

award sweater See SWEATERS: LETTER SWEATER.

Aztec sweater Long bulky coat sweater with shawl collar closed with matching sash. Usu-

S

ally made in white with predominantly black Jacquard-knit Aztec Indian motifs running in wide bands across chest, below waist, around upper arm, and wrist.

beaded sweater Woman's sweater with decorative beading, sometimes of seed pearls, often worn for evening in 1940s and 1950s, and worn at intervals since.

big easy sweater Extra large long sweater. One style is made in lacy bouclé knit with extended shoulder making a short sleeve in loose-fitting style with rib-knitted hem.

blazer sweater Single or double-breasted jacket-type sweater with collar that is styled similarly to BLAZER JACKET (see under COATS AND JACKETS).

blazer sweater

bolero sweater (bo-lehr'-oh) Short sweater to the waist or above, styled with rounded ends in front and no fasteners. *Der.* A Spanish dance costume worn for dancing the bolero, a lively Spanish dance; also the music for this dance.

cable sweater Knit sweater in which the effect of a heavy cord (a cable) is produced by crossing groups of knitting stitches over each other. Shown at SWEATERS: PULLOVER and FISHERMAN'S SWEATER.

cardigan sweater Coat-style sweater known by various names. **Classic cardigan** is made with CREW NECK (see under NECKLINES AND COLLARS), ribbed cuffs and hem, closed with pearl buttons.

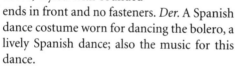

cardigan sweater

Belted cardigan is usually made in longer length, sometimes in NORFOLK style (see under COATS AND JACKETS). **Shawl collar cardigan,** also called *tuxedo sweater,* is made with a SHAWL COLLAR (see under NECKLINES AND COLLARS) and no buttons. Another type of cardigan is the COAT SWEATER (see under SWEATERS). *Der.* Named after *Seventh Earl of Cardigan,* who needed an extra layer of warmth under his uniform during the Crimean War in 1854.

cashmere sweater Sweater in any style knitted of yarn spun from the hair of the CASHMERE goat. Extremely soft and luxurious, usually imported from England or Scotland. See CASHMERE.

coat sweater Cardigan-style sweater, usually made in a longer style with or without a ribbed waistband. Frequently styled with a long V-neck and buttons. From 1930s to 1960s, usually restricted in usage to men or older people. In 1980s worn by adults and children.

Cowichan sweater (koo'-ih-chan) Sweater using North American Indian pattern—black on white or gray background—made by Cowichan Indians of Vancouver Island. Used in the late 1940s and early 1950s and revived in early 1970s. Also called a *Siwash sweater.*

cowl-neck sweater Pullover sweater with extra large rolled collar that forms a cowl drapery, popular in 1980s and after.

crew-neck sweater Pullover sweater with a round rib-knit neck. *Der.* Named for knit shirts worn by members of college rowing teams, or "crews."

dolman sweater Pullover sweater with *batwing sleeves* and with ribbing at waist. In early 1970s worn with a belt—in 1980s became loose and full with ribbed band at waist. Also see SLEEVES: DOLMAN.

embroidered sweater Sweater that is knit first and then decorated with embroidery, usually in large floral allover designs in many colors, as compared with a Jacquard-knit sweater where the design is part of the knit.

Fair Isle sweater Sweaters, both pullovers and cardigans, imported from Fair Isle off the coast of Scotland. Characterized by soft HEATHER yarns, and bright-colored knit in traditional patterns. Name

Fair isle sweater

also applied to sweaters imitating this style. Popular since the 1920s when worn by Duke of Windsor, at that time Prince of Wales, as a short-waisted sweater with V-neck, worn instead of a vest.

fanny sweater Long coat sweater coming to below the hips with ribbing or sash at waistline, introduced in early 1970s and still worn.

fatigue sweater Slip-on sweater made in firm rib knit with long sleeves, small V-shaped yoke, round turnover collar, and five-button closing. Originally worn in World War II and restyled in cotton for men and women in 1980s.

fisherman's sweater Bulky hand-knit sweater, made of natural color, water-repellent wool in characteristic patterns, in-cluding wide cable stripes, bobbles, seed stitch, and other fancy stitches—im-ported from Ireland. Popu-lar in early 1960s and widely imitated in MANUFACTURED FIBER yarns. *Der.* From Irish fishermen who wear hand-knit sweaters in a pattern indicat-ing locale in which they live.

fisherman's sweater

Icelandic sweater Hand-knit sweater in tradi-tional designs made in natural-colored wool of browns, blacks, whites, and grays. Fleece is from the rare heath sheep. Rich in lanolin, the wool is said to be almost entirely water repel-lent. Designs consist of bands around the neck in yoke fashion copied from beaded collars worn by Icelandic Eskimos. Also called *Reykjavik sweater.*

Jacquard sweater (ja-kard') Sweater knit by machine with an elaborate design in many colors. May be made of a geometrical repeat pattern or one large design, such as a deer, either on front, back, or both sides of sweater. Popular type of sweater for winter.

jiffy-knit sweater Sweater hand-knit of bulky yarn on very large needles, which takes only a few hours to knit. Popular in late 1960s.

jumper British term for pullover sweater.

Karaca sweater (ka-rah'-kah) Turtleneck pull-over sweater with elaborate Turkish embroi-dered panel down center front and lines of embroi-dery down sleeves. Imported from Black Sea region.

letter sweater Bulky coat sweater with service stripes on upper sleeves and school

letter sweater

letter on chest. Formerly given to varsity sports team members in high schools and colleges, now copied for general sportswear. Also called *award, letterman, school* or *varsity sweater.*

mock turtleneck sweater See SWEATERS: TURTLENECK SWEATER.

poor-boy sweater Ribbed knit sweater made with high round neck or turtleneck. Revived in the mid-1960s. *Der.* From type of sweater worn by newsboys of the early 20th c.

pull-on sweater See SWEATERS: PULLOVER.

pullover Sweater with round, crew, or V-neck pulled on over the head as contrasted with a cardigan or coat sweater, which opens down the front. Also called *pull-on* or *slip-on sweater.*

pullover sweater with cable pattern

Reykjavik sweater *Der.* Capital of Iceland. See SWEATERS: ICELANDIC SWEATER.

school sweater See SWEATERS: LETTER SWEATER.

shawl-collared cardigan See SWEATERS: CARDIGAN.

shell Sleeveless collarless pullover sweater usu-ally made in solid colors, worn instead of blouse. Introduced in 1950s.

Shetland sweater Originally a sweater knit of fine worsted yarn from the Shetland Islands off the coast of Scotland. Usually made in classic styles, in a medium-sized plain jersey knit stitch. By extension, name now used for same type of sweater made in MANUFACTURED FIBER yarns.

shrink Waist-length sweater sometimes made with ribbing from below bust to hem, some-times sleeveless, sometimes has short sleeves. *Der.* Entire sweater looks as if it "shrunk" when washed.

shrug **1.** Shawl and sweater combined, fitting over the back like a shawl. From elbow to wrist edges are drawn to-gether to form brief sleeves. Formerly popular at seaside resorts. **2.** Short-sleeved sweater baring mid-riff with long V-neckline and fastened with one hook under the bust.

shrug #1

S

Siwash sweater See SWEATERS: COWICHAN SWEATER.

ski sweater Classification of elaborately patterned sweaters made in jacquard knits in many colors either domestically or imported, particularly from Norway, Sweden, Switzerland, or Iceland. Worn outdoors for skiing and sometimes indoors for after-ski wear. Also see SWEATERS: ICELANDIC SWEATER.

slip-on See SWEATERS: PULLOVER.

sweater-for-two Extremely wide sweater made of stretch acrylic with wide horizontal strips. Designed with two necks, a sleeve on each side, and a single slit for arms in center. A fad of the early 1960s worn by two people for warmth at football games.

sweater set Two sweaters made to be worn together. One usually of short-sleeve PULLOVER type and the other in CARDIGAN style. Also called *twin set*.

sweater set or twin set

sweater-vest See SWEATERS: VEST SWEATER.

tennis sweater Pull-on, long-sleeved sweater sometimes made in cable-knit. Usually white and trimmed with narrow bands of maroon and navy blue at V-neck and wrists. Worn since 1930s.

tennis sweater

turtleneck sweater A pullover sweater with a very high rib-knit roll collar that folds over twice to form a flattened roll around the neck. **Mock turtleneck** may fold only once or be knitted double to give turtleneck effect without folding.

tuxedo sweater See SWEATERS: CARDIGAN.

twin set See SWEATERS: SWEATER SET.

undershirt sweater Pullover with tank top, similar to man's undershirt, sometimes tunic length. Popular in early 1970s.

varsity sweater See SWEATERS: LETTER SWEATER.

vest sweater Sleeveless coat style sweater made double- or single-breasted with a V-neck. Also called a *sweater-vest*.

vest sweater or sweater vest

wraparound sweater Hip-length cardigan-type sweater with one side lapping over the other, held closed with a matching rib-knit sash.

---

sweater set See SWEATERS.

sweater-vest See SWEATERS: VEST SWEATER.

sweath-bands See SWADDLING CLOTHES.

sweat jacket See COATS AND JACKETS.

sweat pants See PANTS.

sweatshirt See SHIRTS.

sweatshirt dress Extra large sweatshirt coming almost to knees worn as a tunic over a skirt or pants—or alone as a dress.

sweatshop Slang for a clothing manufacturing plant where workers were paid low wages and worked long hours under unfavorable conditions. Such establishments were common at the turn of the century and have been found again in recent years in large metropolitan areas where undocumented workers are willing to work under poor conditions.

sweatshorts See SHORTS.

sweatsock See HOSIERY.

sweatsuit See ACTIVEWEAR.

Swedish hat See HEADWEAR: MOUSQUETAIRE HAT.

Swedish weaving/Swedish darning See EMBROIDERIES AND SEWING STITCHES: NEEDLEWEAVING.

sweeper See DUST RUFFLE.

sweet coffers ∞ In Elizabethan times, boxes used by women to hold cosmetics.

sweetheart neckline See NECKLINES AND COLLARS.

swim bra See UNDERGARMENTS.

swimdress See ACTIVEWEAR.

SWIMWEAR

Garments for recreational bathing that originated about 1865 and consisted of knee-length dresses and ankle-length pants in woven fabric might most accurately be called **bathing dress**. The encumbering nature of these garments meant that women could do little more than get wet; they could not swim. Around 1880 a combination garment was made in one piece with top, pants, and skirt. Bathing dress grew less and less voluminous and by the mid 1920s terminology changed, with bathing suits, such as the ANNETTE KELLERMAN suit and TANKTOP suits being accepted for the beach. From then until about 1940 all bathing suits were made of knitted fabrics, preferably wool jersey, and by the late 1930s two-piece suits and elasticized bathing suits were adopted. DRESSMAKER-TYPE suits of woven fabric were popular in the 1940s and the first BIKINIS appeared at Mediterranean resorts. Men's bathing suits of the turn of century consisted of one-piece striped jersey suits with knee-length legs, sometimes short-sleeved. By the 1920s, men were wearing sleeveless knit tops and trunks and by the late 1930s only trunks. After about 1950, the general category of apparel for swimming was more likely to be called **swimwear** and the individual garments, **swimsuits.** (See SWIMWEAR: ANNETTE KELLERMAN SUIT, TANKTOP, DRESSMAKER, SWIMSUIT and BIKINI.)

Annette Kellerman One-piece knit bathing suit with short sleeves, knee-length pants, and high round neck. Originally worn under an outer bathing dress by women from late 19th c. to 1920s. Named for Annette Kellerman, the swimmer who first wore it without the bathing dress on top in early 20th c. Similar suits were worn for everyday sportswear during the summer of 1987.

apron swimsuit See SWIMWEAR: PINAFORE SWIMSUIT.

asymmetric swimsuit Swimsuit that has a strap over only one shoulder.

bandeau swimsuit (band oh′) Elasticized strapless swimsuit for women, cut straight across top, usually made without a skirt, popular in 1980s and after.

beach coat Cover-up worn over a bathing suit, styled to match or contrast with bathing suit. Frequently made of terrycloth, sometimes of lace fabric. Also called *beach toga.*

beach wrap-up Large square or rectangle of fabric frequently of terrycloth, wrapped around the body in various ways for protection after swimming or as fashion beachwear item.

bikini (bih kee′ nee) **1.** Two-piece swimsuit introduced in 1946 by designer Jacques Heim, who called it the atom because of its

small size. Soon after, a version was advertised as "smaller than the atom." The name was eventually changed to bikini after Bikini Atoll, a small coral island in the Pacific where atomic tests were made from 1946 to 1956. Worn on Riviera beaches, but not accepted on U.S. public beaches until the early 1960s. By the 1980s these suits became still smaller and a number of variations had developed. These were: **string bikini,** consisting of a minimal halter bra with bikini panties worn low on hips, and made of two triangular-shaped pieces attached to an elastic band or string ties; **teardrop bikini,** made up of bikini pants worn with a teardrop bra composed of two tiny triangles with straps at neck and around the body; **tankini** (tan′-kee-nee), a woman's bathing suit with a tank top and a bikini bottom; **corset bikini,** a top that looks like an underwire bra and a bikini bottom; **camikini,** with a camisole top and a bikini bottom. **2.** Man's very brief swim trunks.

bikini #1

string bikini

tankini

bloomer swimsuit Swimsuit made with bouffant pants gathered into elastic bands at legs that was fashionable in 1940s and also in the 1960s, particularly for little girls. Also see BLOOMER in alphabetical listing.

blouson swimsuit (blue-zone′) One- or two-piece swimsuit in which the top extends below the natural waistline in a bloused effect. The top usually has a built-in bra. Fashionable in the 1960s, then revived in 1980s and after.

bloomer swimsuit 1950s

boxer shorts swimsuit Man's swim trunks with thigh-length legs and elastic waistband, styled similarly to shorts worn by prize fighters and frequently made with three contrasting stripes down side.

boxer shorts swimsuit

boy shorts swimsuit

boy shorts swimsuit Girl's two-piece swimsuit designed with shorts or cuffed shorts and brief top.

briefers Very short swim trunks worn by men and boys that are made of elastic or knitted fabric. By the 1980s, these were often cut like bikini bottoms.

cabana set (ca-bahn'-ya) Swimsuit and short-sleeved jacket for men and boys with trunks and jacket cut out of the same fabric or made in contrasting fabrics designed to be worn together. *Der.* Spanish, *cabaña*, "a small tentlike shelter placed on the beach."

cabana set

camikini See SWIMWEAR: BIKINI.

corset bikini See SWIMWEAR: BIKINI.

crab-back bathing suit Man's swimsuit worn in 1920s and 1930s that had a top cut out very wide at armholes and a second cutout near waistline.

cutout swimsuit Fitted maillot-type of swimsuit with cutout sections that might be located at any place, including sides or center front. Sometimes fishnet is inserted in cutouts or laces may connect the cutout parts. Introduced in mid-1960s.

cutout swimsuit

dressmaker swimsuit Any swimsuit made of knitted or woven fabric and styled with a skirt. Sometimes shirred across back with elastic thread. A basic type of swimsuit since the 1940s.

Gay 90s swimsuit Two-piece, circular-striped knitted suit with knee-length pants and hip-

dressmaker swimsuit

length short-sleeved top. Offered for sale in late 1960s, it imitated jersey suits of the 1890s.

hip-rider swimsuit Two-piece swimsuit for women that has pants or skirt cut low enough to show the navel; an innovation in the 1960s.

long john trunks Man's swimsuit made with rope sash and just above-the-knee knit pants with wide stripes alternating with bright red, green, or black. *Der.* Worn in imitation of boxing trunks worn by late John L. Sullivan (1858–1918), heavyweight boxing champion (1882–1892).

maillot (my'-yo) Classic one-piece knitted or jersey swimsuit without a skirt, form-fitting and usually backless. Sometimes with detachable strap tied around neck or buttoned to back of suit. Popular since 1930s and very popular in 1980 and after with high cut legs. *Der.* French, *maillot*, "tight garment."

mono-kini Woman's TOPLESS SWIMSUIT (see under SWIMWEAR). Introduced by Rudi Gernreich in 1964.

mono-kini topless swimsuit

one-piece swimsuit Any swimsuit for women or children made all in one piece. Sometimes has an attached skirt.

overblouse swimsuit Woman's two-piece bathing suit that consists of brief trunks and a separate blouse. Often has a tank-top neckline and unfitted waist.

pinafore swimsuit Bikini swimsuit with an extra pinafore that fits tightly over bust and has a free-hanging skirt curving from sides up to center back, revealing the bikini pants underneath. Also called *apron swimsuit*.

overblouse swimsuit

rib tickler swimsuit Two-piece bare midriff suit for women, made in knits or woven fabrics.

sarong swimsuit (sar-ong') Dressmaker-type swimsuit with rounded ends on wrap skirt that drapes to one side. *Der.* Copied from dress designed by Edith

pinafore or apron swimsuit 1970

S

Head for Dorothy Lamour for film *Hurricane* in 1937, similar to Indonesian dress.

sheath swimsuit Similar to a maillot with a tiny skirt panel added in front, but not in back, usually made of stretch fabric. Classic style since the late 1930s.

sarong swimsuit

sheath swimsuit

string bikini See SWIMWEAR: BIKINI.

surf trunks Swim trunks for men longer in length than regular trunks with a hip pocket for surfboard wax. Introduced in the late 1960s.

swimdress Swimsuit that looks like a micro-mini–length dress. Synonym: *bathing dress.*

tank swimsuit Classic maillot swimsuit without skirt made with scooped neck and built-up straps. *Der.* Early indoor swimming pools were called "tanks."

surf trunks

thong swimsuit Bikini or other swimsuits cut to reveal as much of the buttocks as possible while covering the crotch.

topless swimsuit Swimsuit that starts below bust or at waist held up by two straps from the back meeting in a V in center front. Introduced by American designer Rudi Gernreich as the MONO-KINI (see under SWIMWEAR) in 1964. Forbidden on most U.S. beaches, but started topless waitress style in California nightclubs.

tank swimsuit

trunks Synonym for men's or boy's swimsuits.

tunic swimsuit Two-piece swimsuit cut like a dress with straight lines, slashed on the side seams with panties worn underneath.

swing Adjective describing a garment that is cut to hang free or to "swing" away from the body. Examples: swing blouse, swing dress, swing skirt.

swinger/swinger clutch See HANDBAGS AND RELATED ACCESSORIES: CONTOUR CLUTCH.

swing skirt See SKIRTS.

swirl skirt See SKIRTS.

Swiss belt See BELTS: CORSELET BELT.

Swiss bodice ∞ Sleeveless velvet bodice worn with SWISS BELT (see BELTS: CORSELET BELT) worn over sleeved blouse in late 1860s.

Swiss dress ∞ Child's two-piece costume worn in mid-1860s with tailored waist-length jacket and full skirt with fitted corselet at waistline.

Swiss embroidery See EMBROIDERIES AND SEWING STITCHES: MADEIRA EMBROIDERY.

Swiss girdle See BELTS: CORSELET BELT.

switch See WIGS AND HAIRPIECES.

syglaton See CYCLAS.

sylphide parasol See UMBRELLAS AND PARASOLS.

syndicated buying office A RESIDENT BUYING OFFICE owned and operated by a retail conglomerate, an organization that unites a number of different independently operated retail stores that may be located in various parts of the United States.

synthetic fiber See MANUFACTURED FIBERS.

synthetic fur Soft pile fabric made to imitate fur. Also called **fake fur**. Both terms are misnomers, as the word "fur" should not be used. The correct term would be "furlike fabric."

synthetic gem See GEMS, GEM CUTS, AND SETTINGS.

synthetic straw Manufactured fibers or materials used to make straws. See STRAW.

T

T **1.** Abbreviation designating *tall* size range. See TALL. **2.** Abbreviation designating *toddler* sizes. These range from T1 to T4. See TODDLER.

tab See CLOSURES.

tabard ∞ (tab′-erd) **1.** Overgarment constructed with loose front and back panels and short winglike sleeves, sometimes with heraldic coat-of-arms embroidered on back. Worn by heralds for tourneys and by knights over armor from 13th to 16th c. **3.** See CAPES, CLOAKS, AND SHAWLS.

tabard #1

tabbed closing See CLOSURES.

tabby weave See PLAIN WEAVE.

tab collar See NECKLINES AND COLLARS.

table See GEMS, GEM CUTS, AND SETTINGS: BRILLIANT CUT.

tablecloth check See PRINTS, STRIPES, AND CHECKS.

table-cut gloves See GLOVES AND GLOVE CONSTRUCTIONS.

tablet mantilla See CAPES, CLOAKS, AND SHAWLS.

tablier skirt See SKIRTS.

tablion ∞ (tab-lee-ohn′) Elaborate decorative oblong of gold embroidery on both the front and back of the Byzantine Imperial robes and on the PALUDAMENTUM (see under CAPES, CLOAKS, AND SHAWLS). Worn by the Emperor Justinian and his wife, Theodora, during the Byzantine period. High court officials wore a purple tablion on a white mantle. Depicted in mosaics in a church in Ravenna, Italy.

tabs ∞ In 19th c., loose-hanging pieces of fabric with a border of square or round edges forming a peplum or used as trimming. See VANDYKING and TURRET BODICE.

tack See EMBROIDERIES AND SEWING STITCHES.

taffeta † (taf′-et-tah) Crisp fabric with a fine, smooth surface made in the plain weave with a small crosswise rib. Originally made in silk, now made in manufactured filament fibers. *Der.* Persian *tuftah*, "fine, plain woven silk fabric."

taffeta pipkin See HEADWEAR: PIPKIN.

tagboard A heavy weight, durable paper, used in the fashion industry for pattern pieces. Also called *oaktag* or *hard paper.*

Taglioni See COATS AND JACKETS.

Taglioni frock coat See COATS AND JACKETS.

tail coat See COATS AND JACKETS: SWALLOW-TAILED COAT.

tailleur (tay-yure′) French for tailored costume— a suit. *Der.* French, "tailor" or "cutter."

tailor **1.** *n.* Person who makes either men's or women's clothes, mends clothing, or does alterations. Originally men did all of the commercial clothing production of men's wear, coats, and suits, especially those made of wool. **2.** *v.* To fit clothing for one individual; to fashion a garment.

tailored Adjective indicating that an item of apparel that is relatively plain and without decoration and which depends on the line and fit of the item for style. Those dresses, coats, and suits that are the opposite of tailored (i.e., have softer lines, more trimming, and are more elaborate) may be described as **dressmaker**. See BLOUSES

AND TOPS: TAILORED BLOUSE, CLOSURES: WORKED BUTTONHOLE, SLEEPWEAR AND LOUNGEWEAR: TAILORED PAJAMAS, and UNDERGARMENTS: TAILORED SLIP.

tailor-made **1.** Garment made specifically for one individual by a tailor—customer's measurements are taken and several fittings are necessary. Also called *custom-made* or *custom-tailored*. **2.** ∞ In the late 19th c., a woman's costume for morning or country wear, usually a suit consisting of a jacket and skirt made by a tailor rather than a dressmaker. Introduced by the designer Redfern in late 1870s.

tailor-made #2, 1905

tailor's tack See EMBROIDERIES AND SEWING STITCHES.

tails See FULL-DRESS SUIT.

taj toe See FOOTWEAR.

talisman ring See JEWELRY: FRIENDSHIP RING.

tall **1.** Men's size corresponding to a chest measurement of 38–48″ and a height of 5′11″–6′2½″. Also see EXTRA-TALL. **2.** Women's size range corresponding to a height of 5′8″ to 6′.

Talleyrand collar See NECKLINES AND COLLARS.

Tallien redingote See COATS AND JACKETS.

tallith (tal′-ith or tal′-iss) Prayer shawl, worn by Jewish men after age 13. Made with tassels called TSITSITH, usually blue, at the four corners. Believed to have been derived from Roman *pallium.* Took various shapes throughout the ages. Modern tallith is made of wool or silk in white with black or blue stripes. Silk types vary from 54 to 90″ long and 32 to 72″ wide. Woolen type is larger and made with two lengths joined together. Narrow silk ribbon covers place where it is pieced. At the neck is the *ata*, a narrow ribbon or band woven with silver or gold thread. Also spelled *tallis.* Also see ARBA KANFOTH.

tallow-top cut See GEMS, GEM CUTS, AND SETTINGS: CABOCHON.

Talma See CAPES, CLOAKS, AND SHAWLS.

Talma lounge See COATS AND JACKETS.

Talma overcoat See COATS AND JACKETS.

tam See HEADWEAR.

tambour farthingale See FARTHINGALE.

tambour work See EMBROIDERIES AND SEWING STITCHES.

tam-o-shanter See HEADWEAR.

tango shoe See FOOTWEAR.

tankini See SWIMWEAR: BIKINI.

tank suit See SWIMWEAR.

tank top See BLOUSES AND TOPS and SHIRTS.

tanning See LEATHERS.

tanuki See FURS.

tanzanite See GEMS, GEM CUTS, AND SETTINGS.

tapa cloth (tah′-pah) Fabric made from fibers of the inner bark of the paper mulberry tree, *Brousonnetia papyrifera,* of the tree *Pipturus albidus,* varying from a muslinlike to a leatherlike fabric. Made by natives in the South Pacific Islands by beating bark to form a weblike fabric. Before contact with the West, it was used for clothing by the natives of Pacific Islands and eastern Asia. Now made mostly for ceremonial dress and tourist items. In Hawaii called *kapa*, and in Fiji, called *masi*.

tape lace See LACES.

tapered Adjective indicating something that is wider at the top and narrower at the bottom. See HAIRSTYLES: TAPERED HAIRCUT, PANTS: TAPERED PANTS, and SHIRTS: BODY SHIRT.

tapestry **1.** † Handwoven fabric with large, mostly pictorial designs. Not used for apparel, but as decorative hangings. **2.** † Heavy fabric, usually with a pictorial design, woven of multicolored yarns on a Jacquard loom in imitation of handwoven tapestries. A heavy fabric, it is used mainly for shoes, bags, and handbags. **3.** See EMBROIDERIES AND SEWING STITCHES.

tap panties See UNDERWEAR.

tap shoe See FOOTWEAR.

target marketing/customer segmentation Using such demographic variables as age, gender, income, education, marital status, religion, family size, life-cycle stage, ethnicity, and mobility as a basis of identifying and marketing to a potential customer population.

tartan See introduction to PLAIDS & TARTANS.

tasar See TUSSAH.

tasseau (tas-oh′) **1.** ∞ Type of pin or clasp used to fasten a MANTLE (see CAPES, CLOAKS, AND SHAWLS: MANTLE #1) in late Middle Ages. **2.** See SCARVES. *Der.* Latin, *tassa*, "clasp."

tassel **1.** Bundle of threads, bound at one end, hung singly or in groups as ornament on belts, hats, shawls, etc. **2.** See SCARVES: TASSEAU. **3.** See JEWELRY.

Tassell, Gustave * See APPENDIX/DESIGNERS.

tassel-tie See FOOTWEAR.

tassel-top loafer See FOOTWEAR: LOAFER.

tasset See ARMOR.

tatamis See FOOTWEAR.

tatas See RIBBONS OF CHILDHOOD.

tattersall See PLAIDS AND TARTANS and PRINTS, STRIPES, AND CHECKS.

tattersall vest See VESTS.

tatting See introduction to LACES.

tattoo (ta-too') **1.** Permanent design made on skin by process of pricking and ingraining indelible pigment. Of Polynesian origin and practiced by aboriginal tribes. Adopted in the Western world and popular with sailors. In the late 1990s and after being tattooed became more popular among some mainstream Americans who considered tattooing a form of body art. **2.** Fashion fad in early 1970s of decorating body with transfer designs of ships, hearts, etc., imitating those tattooed on sailors' skin. Also see BODY PAINTING and DECALCOMANIA.

tattoo pantyhose See HOSIERY.

tau cross See CROSS.

taure See HAIRSTYLES: BULL HEAD.

tawning See FURS.

tchamir See SHIRTS.

tea apron See APRONS.

tea-cozy cap See HEADWEAR.

tea gown **1.** ∞ Long, informal hostess gown in pale colors worn from 1877 to early 20th c. Usually made of thin wool or silk, it might be loose-fitting and worn without a corset. **2.** Used in 1920s and 1930s to designate semiformal dress suitable for an afternoon tea or garden party.

tea gown #1 1891

tea jacket See BLOUSES AND TOPS.

tea length See LENGTHS.

tear-away shorts See SHORTS.

teardrop bikini See ACTIVEWEAR.

teardrop bra See UNDERWEAR.

teasing See HAIRSTYLES: BACK-COMBING.

tebenna See CAPES, CLOAKS, AND SHAWLS.

tech drawing An abbreviation of "technical drawing," which is a flat, rather than three-dimensional, drawing of a garment that may also include drawings of close-up details of the garment.

techno Music style of the 1980s. Fans wore leather clothing and industrial accessories.

techno stretch Fashion term used to describe high-tech fabrics that stretch. Often made from a blend of other fibers and SPANDEX.

teck scarf See TIES.

teddy **1.** See UNDERGARMENTS. **2.** SLEEPWEAR AND LOUNGEWEAR.

teddybear coat See COATS AND JACKETS.

Teddy boy/Teddy Boy look Tough young British youth from London in early 1950s who adopted styles consisting of exaggerated Edwardian jackets, high stiff collars, tight pants, pointed-toed shoes called winkle pickers, long hair carefully greased and waved, and no hats. The result was a trend to an individualized style of dress worn as a protest against the establishment by working-class teenagers. Fashion came up from the streets rather than being set by designers. *Der.* Teddy is nickname for "Edward," or Edwardian fashions. Also see FOOTWEAR: WINKLE PICKERS.

Teddy boy

Teddy girl/Teddy Girl look Female counterpart of TEDDY BOYS who also wore distinctive clothes in protest against traditional current fashions. Their preferred dress consisted of short tight skirts, high-heeled pointed-toed shoes, and high beehive hairstyles.

teen bra See UNDERGARMENTS.

teeny-bopper Young teenaged girl who follows fads in clothing and music.

tee shirt See SHIRTS: T-SHIRT.

television shopping Television programs that offer retail merchandise that can be ordered by phone or E-mail.

templar cloak See COATS AND JACKETS.

temple See EYEWEAR.

templers   See HEADWEAR.

temporary retailer   A vendor who sets up tables or carts and sells goods—often one-of-a-kind made by the seller or artist. They generally set up on street sidewalks or walkways of malls. Some larger retailers are also experimenting with temporary stores.

Tencel®   See LYOCELL.

tendrils   See HAIRSTYLES.

teneriffe lace   See LACES.

ten-gallon hat   See HEADWEAR.

tennis clothes/tennis dress   See ACTIVEWEAR and also see FOOTWEAR: TENNIS SHOES, SHORTS: TENNIS SHORTS, and SWEATERS: TENNIS SWEATER.

tensile strength   † Technical textile term for the ability of a fiber or fabric to withstand strain and resist breaking. Used in textile testing.

tent   Apparel with much fullness. See TENT DRESS and COATS AND JACKETS: TENT COAT.

tent dress   Pyramid-shaped dress with broad flaring hem, sometimes made with accordion pleats. Introduced by Pierre Cardin in the spring of 1966.

tent stitch   See EMBROIDERIES AND SEWING STITCHES: CONTINENTAL STITCH.

terai hat   See HEADWEAR.

Teresa   See HEADWEAR: THÉRÈSE.

terms of sale   In a purchase agreement between retailer and vendor, specifications for purchase that include details such as discounts, delivery, and transportation costs.

terrycloth   † **1.** Fabric made in the pile weave with uncut loops and a background weave of plain or twill. Usually made in cotton but now also made with manfactured yarns. Sometimes woven in plaid, dobby, or Jacquard patterns of two or more colors. May be yarn-dyed, bleached, piece-dyed, or printed. **2.** A similar pile weave fabric made by knitting, usually called *knitted terrycloth*. Both fabrics are used for shorts, jumpsuits, pants, beachwear, summer dresses, robes, and sport shirts.

tête de mouton   See WIGS AND HAIRPIECES and HAIRSTYLES: COIFFURE À LA MOUTON.

tethered studs   See JEWELRY.

Teva®   See FOOTWEAR: SPORTS SANDAL.

Textile/Clothing Technology Corporation (TC)²   An organization established by the textile and apparel industries and funded by industry and government to conduct research and educate apparel manufacturers, technologists, retailers, and educators about implementation and use of automated systems for manufacture and management in the textile and apparel industries. Among the outgrowths of its work are the concepts of AGILE MANUFACTURING, long-distance learning, and the VIRTUAL FACTORY.

textile fabric   † Cloth made of textile yarns by weaving, knitting, lace making, braiding, netting, or felting. Also cloth made by bonding or nonwoven methods. *Der.* Latin, *fabrica,* "workshop."

Textile Fiber Products Identification Act (T.F.P.I.A.)   † Federal law setting labeling requirements for clothing made of textiles that requires generic fiber identification, manufacturer identification, and designation of country of origin.

textured hose   See HOSIERY.

textured yarn   † Manufactured continuous-filament yarns permanently heat-set in crimped manner, or otherwise modified to improve its handle, increase bulk, or increase elasticity.

theatre suit   Woman's two-piece dressy suit suitable for late afternoon or evening. Made in two or three pieces with short jacket or regular length coat. May be made in luxurious fabrics, trimmed with beading or fur.

Theo tie   See FOOTWEAR.

Thérèse   **1.** See HEADWEAR. **2.** See SCARVES.

thermal   Adjective used to describe garments made in such a way as to insulate the wearer from cold. See GLOVES AND GLOVE CONSTRUCTIONS: THERMAL GLOVES, HOSIERY: THERMAL SOCK, and UNDERGARMENTS: THERMAL UNDERWEAR.

thermal knit   See UNDERWEAR: THERMAL.

thick and thin yarn   † Yarns, uneven size at intervals. When woven into cloth, they add interest.

Thinsulate®   † A 60% polyolefin, 40% polyester microfilament insulation providing warmth equal to down or polyester insulations of close to twice the thickness. Does not absorb water.

thigh highs   See HOSIERY.

Thirties look   **1.** Early 1930's style that featured long, lean, bias-cut dress with intricate drapery, unusual sleeves, and frequently V or round necks. **2.** In late 1930s, extremely broad shoulders were featured with small waistline and more tailored styles. Both of these styles have been revived by designers in the 1980s and 1990s.

thong **1.** See UNDERGARMENTS. **2.** Narrow strip of rawhide or other leather used for a LACER, braided into a belt, or wound around foot and leg as a fastening for sandals. Also see BELTS: THONG BELT and FOOTWEAR: THONG SANDAL.

thong swimsuit See SWIMWEAR.

thread † Smooth, tightly twisted yarn made specifically for sewing.

thread count See COUNT OF CLOTH.

threads British slang term used by young "trendy" people in 1960s for mod clothes sold on Carnaby Street, London.

three-armhole dress An easy-to-make dress promoted by pattern companies. Made in wraparound style with the left arm going through the first and third armholes, while the right arm goes through the second. An innovation of the 1960s.

three-decker See COATS AND JACKETS.

three-piece suit See SUIT #1.

three-quarter See LENGTHS and SHOULDERS AND SLEEVES.

three-quarter cut See FOOTWEAR: SEMI CUT.

three-seamed raglan sleeve See SLEEVES: RAGLAN SLEEVE.

three-seamer See COATS AND JACKETS.

three-storeys-and-a-basement See HEADWEAR.

thrift shop Secondhand clothing or fur store. In the 1960s, a popular source of fashion of earlier decades.

thrift-shop dress Term used in the 1960s for second-hand dresses found in U.S. thrift shops, in Paris flea markets, and in London's Portobello Road antique shops. Popular with the young, this type clothing influenced 1970s fashions for limp fabrics, muted-color prints, and old-fashioned trimmings. In the 1980s, antique dresses of other eras were described as *vintage*. See VINTAGE DRESS.

throat See FOOTWEAR.

throat belt See JEWELRY: DOG COLLAR.

thrum See HEADWEAR.

tiara **1.** See HEADWEAR. **2.** See CLERICAL DRESS.

Tice, Bill * See APPENDIX/DESIGNERS.

ticket pocket See POCKETS.

ticking † Sturdy durable fabric woven in a close satin weave or a twill weave with soft filling yarns. Originally used for covering pillows and mattresses, now used for sport clothes and pants.

ticking stripes See PRINTS, STRIPES, AND CHECKS.

tie-back skirt See SKIRTS.

tie clasp/clip See JEWELRY.

tied closing See CLOSURES.

tie dyeing Hand method of coloring a fabric by tying strings tightly around puffs of fabric and dipping the fabric into a dye bath to get a two-color design, Repeating the process by covering other areas and using different dye colors can add still more colors. Designs are usually circular with feathered or blended edges. A technique originating in Indonesia and popular in the 1920s mainly for scarves. Revived in 1960s and after for blue jeans, T-shirts, dresses, and furs. Also see PRINTS, STRIPES, AND CHECKS: TIE-DYED PRINT.

tie fabrics See TIE SILK.

tie pin See JEWELRY: STICKPIN.

tie pocket See POCKETS.

tiered skirt See SKIRTS.

tiers Several layers of ruffles or bias-cut sections placed one above the other and overlapping. Used mainly on skirts, full sleeves, or pants.

TIES

tie Long band made in various widths of double-thick fabric or rounded braid worn around the neck under the shirt collar and tied in various ways. May be made of fabric, suede, leather, and beads. A shortened form of the word **necktie,** the term came into use about 1820 but did not entirely replace the term "cravat" used earlier. Originally worn only by men, women adopted ties in 1890s to wear with the shirtwaist. Since 1930s, the fashionable width has varied.

bar tack stitch
loop label
shell
facing (tipping)
slip stitching
interlining
necktie

apron The wide ends at the front and back of a contemporary necktie.

ascot **1.** Wide necktie worn looped over and held in place by scarf pin. The ends are cut diagonally. Introduced in 1876 and worn since with a CUTAWAY (see under COATS AND JACKETS). **2.** Scarf looped under the chin. *Der.* Fashionable horse-racing spot, Ascot Health, England. Also see SCARVES: ASCOT.

ascot #1

ballroom neckcloth ∞ Man's pleated, starched evening neckcloth crossed over in front with ends secured to suspenders on either side. Fastened with an elaborate brooch in center front; worn in 1830s.

band bow Pre-tied bow tie on an adjustable-sized band that fastens around the neck.

bar-shaped tie FOUR-IN-HAND TIE (see under TIES) with ends of the same width that are parallel.

batswing tie ∞ Man's bow tie cut with wide flaring ends, worn in c. 1896.

Belcher handkerchief ∞ Blue neckerchief with large white polka dots, each centered with a dark blue eye; worn by men in first half of 19th c. *Der.* Named for Jim Belcher, a fighter during English Regency Period who originated style—other neckwear of the era was very formal.

bib cravat ∞ Man's wide neck piece, in shape of a bib, usually lace-edged and held on by colored CRAVAT STRING (see under TIES); popular at end of 17th c.

black tie **1.** Man's black BOW TIE (see under TIES) worn with dinner jacket or tuxedo, for semiformal occasions. **2.** Denotes type of dress expected at a semiformal occasion. "Black tie" indicates a tuxedo is required for men.

boater tie Man's FOUR-IN-HAND TIE (see under TIES), shorter than average, made with extra-large knot, and usually with square-cut ends. Introduced in late 1960s from England.

bolo tie/bola tie Western-type tie of heavy rounded braid with metal-tipped ends fastening with an ornamental slide. Also called *shoelace tie*.

bolo tie

bootlace tie See TIES: STRING TIE.

bow tie **1.** Man's tie, square-cut or with shaped ends, tied in a bow under the chin. Originally introduced in late 19th c. and worn with FULL DRESS since. See TIES: BLACK TIE and WHITE TIE. **2.** Man's tie, already tied in a bow, which clips to the collar. **3.** Short bow tied by hand on the front of a woman's dress or blouse.

bow tie #1

butterfly bow tie Bow tie with top and bottom edges that narrow at the middle of the tie to make the center about half the width of the ends. Ends may be either square or pointed. Contrast with TIES: CLUB BOW TIE.

Byron tie ∞ Short, narrow string necktie made of silk worn in the 1840s and 1850s *Der.* Named for LORD BYRON.

chaconne ∞ (shak-kon′) Ribbon CRAVAT (see TIES: CRAVAT #2) tied with ends dangling over chest. Named for dancer Pecourt, who, in 1692, danced a chaconne with his cravat tied in this manner. *Der.* Name of 17th-c. dance.

clip-on tie Tie, either pre-tied in a knot like a four-in-hand or a bow tie, that is fastened to the collarband by a metal clip.

club bow tie Bow tie in which the top and bottom edges are straight. Ends are either square or pointed. Contrast with TIES: BUTTERFLY BOW TIE.

cravat **1.** Sometimes used as a synonym for a man's wide necktie worn with morning coat and pinstriped trousers. **2.** ∞ Lawn, muslin, or silk NECKCLOTH (see under TIES) with ends tied in a bow or knot in center front, worn from 1660 to the end of the 19th c. Sometimes worn with starched collar.

cravat #2 c. 1800

cravate cocodes ∞ (kra-vat′ ko′-kod) Large bowtied CRAVAT (see under TIES) worn by women about 1863 with a HABIT SHIRT (see under SHIRTS).

cravat strings ∞ Piece of colored ribbon worn on top of the cravat and tied in a

T

bow under chin. Later a ready-made bow placed behind the loosely tied CRAVAT (see under TIES). Worn by men from 1665 to 1680s.

Cremona cravat ∞ (kre-mo´-nah kra-vat´) Plain ribbon CRAVAT (see under TIES) edged with gathers, introduced for men in 1702 after the battle of Cremona, Italy.

de Joinville teck ∞ Pre-tied man's silk or satin necktie of 1890s that was made narrow around the neck and wide like a STOCK (see under TIES) in front. It fell in graceful folds with wide, squared, fringed ends.

four-in-hand tie Long necktie that goes around the neck with one end looping over the other end twice, then pulled through loop making a slip knot. Usually made of bias-cut fabric or knit, narrow in the center back and wider at the ends. Worn continuously since the 1890s in varying widths. Also worn by women with tailored suits.

1st step

2nd step

how to tie a
four-in-hand tie:
finished tie

3rd step

final step

hunting necktie ∞ Man's broad, high necktie worn from 1818 through 1830s with three horizontal pleats on each side angled toward center front. Worn with ends brought to front, tied, and hidden by coat.

hunting stock **1.** ∞ Man's long scarf folded double, wrapped twice around neck, and tied. Worn instead of necktie for sports in 1890s. **2.** Type of wide tie or STOCK (see under TIES). Worn folded over once to fill in neckline of jacket. Used by equestrians when riding in hunt field or show ring.

Indian necktie ∞ Muslin CRAVAT (see under TIES) worn by men from 1815 to 1830s, secured in front with a sliding ring. Also called a *maharatta tie* (mah-har´-attah).

joinville ∞ Man's neckwear of mid-1840s to mid-1850s made by tying a 5" wide scarf around neck in a bow. Usually had square-cut fringed ends.

kipper Necktie 4 or 5″ wide with ends like a bow tie usually of striped or patterned fabric. Introduced from England in late 1960s.

Macclesfield tie (mak´-liz-feld) Necktie made from silk fabric of a type produced in Macclesfield, England. Fabric has small DOBBY WEAVE patterns.

maharatta tie See TIES: INDIAN NECKTIE.

mail-coach necktie ∞ Man's large scarf, sometimes a cashmere shawl, loosely folded twice around neck, tied in knot in front with ends falling over chest like a waterfall. Worn as NECKCLOTH (see under TIES) from 1818 to 1830s by dandies. Also called *waterfall necktie*.

military stock ∞ Man's made-up NECKCLOTH (see under TIES), frequently of black corded silk edged with kidskin, stiffened with cardboard or leather, and tied or buckled in back. Worn from mid-18th to mid-19th c.

Napoleon necktie ∞ Man's medium-wide necktie of about 1818 in violet color worn passed around neck, crossed over chest, and ends tied to suspenders or continued around to tie at back of neck. *Der.* Reported to have been copied from necktie worn by Napoleon on his return from Elba. By about 1830 called *Corsican necktie.*

neckcloth ∞ General term from about 1660 to mid-19th c. for any type of man's neckwear or CRAVAT wrapped around neck. See TIES: CRAVAT and STOCK.

neckerchief See SCARVES.

neck handkerchief ∞ Synonym in 18th and 19th c. for man's NECKTIE or CRAVAT.

necktie See category heading TIES.

octagon tie ∞ Man's made-up scarf or cravat worn from 1860s on with long wide piece of fabric folded to form an **X** in front and attached to a narrow band fastening at back of neck with hook and eye.

osbaldiston tie ∞ (os-bald-dis′-stun) Necktie tied in front with a barrel-shaped knot worn by men from 1830s through 1840s. Also called *barrel knot tie.*

Oxford tie ∞ Straight narrow necktie worn in 1890s by men with informal lounge suit and by women with shirtwaist.

regimental striped tie See PRINTS, STRIPES, AND CHECKS: REGIMENTAL STRIPES.

rep tie/repp tie See REP in alphabetical listing.

royal George stock ∞ Man's black velvet STOCK (see under TIES) worn in 1820s and 1830s, made with satin over the velvet at base of neck and tied in bow in front.

sailor's reef knot ∞ Common double knot or square knot used on sailor ties in U.S. Navy. Used for men's neckties from 1870 on, most fashionable in 1890s.

sailor tie Large square scarf of black silk folded diagonally and worn under square SAILOR COLLAR (see under NECKLINES AND COLLARS), and either tied in sailor knot or pulled through strap on front of MIDDY BLOUSE (see under BLOUSES AND TOPS). Formerly worn by U.S. Naval enlisted personnel, and adopted by women and children in late 19th c. and after to wear with middy blouse.

scarf 1. Extremely large CRAVAT (see under TIES) worn by men in 1830s that spread over shirt front and fastened with a decorative tie pin. **2.** Tradename for late-19th c. necktie that was narrow in back and had wide hanging ends. **3.** Also see SCARVES: SCARF #1 in introduction to category.

seven-fold tie Unlined tie made from an outer fabric that is folded over itself seven times. As a result no lining is required; however, due to the cost of such ties, they are now relatively rare.

shell Outside fabric of a necktie.

sheriff tie See TIES: STRING TIE.

shoelace tie See TIES: BOLO TIE.

shoestring tie ∞ Man's extremely narrow necktie of 1850s, tied in bow in front or fastened by pulling ends through a small ring. Also see TIES: BYRON TIE.

solitaire ∞ Necktie worn with man's bagwig from 1730s to 1770s, tied in various ways (e.g.,

in a bow under chin and pinned in place, or loosely knotted with free hanging ends).

Southern Colonel tie See TIES: STRING TIE.

Spitalfield tie (spit′-ahl-field) Necktie made from silk fabric of a type produced in the Spitalfield section of London, England. Fabric has a small, overall pattern that looks like a mosaic. It is usually made in a DOBBY WEAVE.

starcher ∞ Man's starched cravat of 19th c.

Steinkirk ∞ Long, lace-edged cravat loosely knotted under the chin that was pinned to one side, or left hanging. The ends were pulled through a buttonhole. Worn by men from 1692 to 1730 and by the unfashionable until 1770. Women wore it with their riding habits. *Der.* From the Battle of Steinkirk in 1692, when soldiers were surprised in battle before they could tie their cravats.

Steinkirk

stock ∞ Man's made-up neckcloth, sometimes stiffened with pasteboard, that fitted high on the neck and fastened in back with strings or buckles. Usually white or black, the stock sometimes had a bow at the front. At first a part of military dress, civilians soon adopted it, and it was worn from about 1735 to end of 19th c.

stock

string tie Necktie, usually not more than one inch wide, often black, worn in a bow with ends hanging down. Also called *bootlace tie, Southern Colonel tie,* and, in Britain, *sheriff's tie.*

teck scarf ∞ Man's wide necktie of 1890s somewhat shorter than average. Tied in *four-in-hand-knot* with ends cut straight across or ending in center point with slanted sides. Also see TIES: DE JOINVILLE TECK.

white tie 1. Man's white bow tie worn for formal occasions with tails, usually hand tied. **2.** Denotes a type of dress for a special occasion. "White tie" means formal dress or tails (see COATS AND JACKETS: SWALLOWTAIL COAT) for a man and a formal gown for a woman.

Windsor tie **1.** Regular man's necktie tied in four-in-hand style with a more complicated knot that is larger. *Der.* Called a *Windsor knot* after Duke of Windsor, who made it popular in early 1920s. **2.** Large flowing bow tie worn by men in 1870s and 1880s.

tie shoe See FOOTWEAR.

tie silk † Broad term for fabrics used for making neckties and scarves. Usually distinguished by small designs or stripes and woven in narrower widths than other fabrics. Since neckties are now made of fabrics with all types of fibers including cotton, polyester, and nylon, the term *tie fabrics* is more accurate.

tie tack See JEWELRY.

Tiffany, Charles Lewis (tif'an-ee) Made silverware in New York city in 1850. In 1886 introduced the Tiffany setting (see under GEMS, GEM CUTS, AND SETTINGS), a simple pronged setting used for diamonds and large stones. His son, Louis Comfort (1848–1933), was one of the most imaginative of Art Nouveau jewelers. Their store on Fifth Avenue has been a landmark for years, and noted for the finest quality gems, jewelry, and silver craftsmanship. Among his famous clients were Abraham Lincoln and Sarah Bernhardt.

tiger's eye See GEMS, GEM CUTS, AND SETTINGS.

tights **1.** See PANTS: PANTALOONS. **2.** See HOSIERY. **3.** See UNDERGARMENTS.

tilbury hat See HEADWEAR.

Tilley, Monika * See APPENDIX/DESIGNERS.

tinsel yarn Metals such as gold, silver, aluminum, or copper cut into fine strips and used alone or made into core yarn for use in brocades and glitter fabrics.

tint Color term for hues with white added to lighten (e.g., light blue and white added is called a "tint of blue"). Also see SHADE.

tippet (tip'-it) **1.** A long, narrow strip of fabric that hangs from a sleeve, hood, cape, or other areas of a garment. A particularly notable example is often shown hanging from sleeve of the COTEHARDIE, a medieval garment. Shown at COTEHARDIE. **2.** See CAPES, CLOAKS, AND SHAWLS.

tipping **1.** See FURS. **2.** See HAIRSTYLES.

tire See HEADWEAR: ATTIRE #2.

tissue † Descriptive of lightweight, semitransparent fabric (e.g., tissue gingham, tissue taffeta).

Titus coiffure/wig See HAIRSTYLES: COIFFURE À LA TITUS.

toboggan cap See HEADWEAR: STOCKING CAP.

toby ruff See NECKLINES AND COLLARS.

toddler Size range from 1 to 4 for very young children. Abbreviated T.

toe See FOOTWEAR.

toe-ankle chain See JEWELRY.

toelet See HOSIERY.

toe ring See JEWELRY.

toe rubbers See FOOTWEAR.

toe slippers See FOOTWEAR.

toe spring See FOOTWEAR.

tog ∞ Medieval term for coat. *Der.* Shortened form of *toga*.

toga ∞ Ancient Roman outer garment worn only by male Roman citizens age 16 or older. In its earliest form, it consisted of large, semicircular mantle of white wool that was draped over the left shoulder, across the back, under the right arm, and over the left shoulder again, leaving the right arm free. By the time of the Roman Empire, it had become more oval. The upper section was folded over, creating a sort of draped area at the front called the **sinus**. Although the traditional toga, called a **toga pura** (poor-ah') or **toga virilis,** was white and undecorated, there were a few significant variations. (1) The **toga praetexta** (pray-tex'-ta) had a purple border several inches wide and was worn by children of the nobility (sons until age 16 and girls until age 12) and certain adult magistrates and high priests. (2) The **toga pulla** (pooh'-lah) was black or dark colored and worn for mourning. (3) The **toga picta** was purple with gold embroidery and was assigned on special occasions to victorious generals or other distinguished persons. (4) The **toga trabea** (trah-beh'-ah), probably multicolored and striped, was worn by augurs (priests who predicted the future)

toga

and important officials. (5) The **toga candida** (kan-dee-dah′), lightened to an exceptional white, was worn by candidates for office. The word "candidate" derives from this practice.

toga dress **1.** Asymmetric dress or at-home robe styled with one shoulder bare, the other covered, an innovation of the 1960s. *Der.* From Roman toga, which covered one shoulder. Also called *one-shoulder dress.* **2.**See POSTER DRESS.

toga nightgown See SLEEPWEAR AND LOUNGE-WEAR.

toggle See CLOSURES.

toggle coat See COATS AND JACKETS.

togs Slang for clothing, especially fancy garments.

toile (twal) **1.** French term for MUSLIN pattern for a garment. Also see PROTOTYPE. **2.** See LACES. *Der.* French, "cloth."

toilet/toilette ∞ (twa-let′) **1.** ∞ Late 19th-c. referred to a woman's entire costume (e.g., afternoon toilette). **2.** Process of a woman dressing (e.g., combing her hair, applying her makeup). Used especially in 19th and early 20th c. **3.** See SLEEPWEAR AND LOUNGEWEAR.

Toledo, Isabel * See APPENDIX/DESIGNERS.

tolerance A range of acceptable variations from the dimensional measurements called for in the SIZE SPECIFICATIONS. Tolerance is stated as a + or − in inches or metric dimensions.

Tom Jones Film (1963) of Henry Fielding's novel about an 18th-c. hero that inspired clothes in mid-1960s. See SHIRTS: TOM JONES SHIRT and SLEEVES: TOM JONES SLEEVE.

tongue See FOOTWEAR.

tonlet See ARMOR.

tooled-leather See BELTS and HANDBAGS AND RELATED ACCESSORIES.

top **1.** See BLOUSES AND TOPS. **2.** See WIGS AND HAIRPIECES: TOUPÉE.

topaz See GEMS, GEM CUTS, AND SETTINGS.

topazolite See GEMS, GEM CUTS, AND SETTINGS: ANDRADITE GARNET.

top boot See FOOTWEAR: JOCKEY BOOT.

topcoat See COATS AND JACKETS.

topee/topi See HEADWEAR.

top frock See COATS AND JACKETS.

top grain See LEATHERS.

top hat See HEADWEAR.

topknot See HAIRSTYLES.

topless look The baring of the body to the waist by women. In 1964 Rudi Gernreich introduced the sensational TOPLESS SWIMSUIT (see under SWIMWEAR.) Women who attempted to wear it on American beaches were arrested, although it was accepted on the beaches of France. Topless style was accepted in nightclubs for dancers and waitresses.

topline See FOOTWEAR.

topper **1.** See HEADWEAR: TOP HATS. **2.** See COATS AND JACKETS.

tops See BLOUSES AND TOPS.

topsider See FOOTWEAR: SPERRY TOPSIDER®.

top-stitch See EMBROIDERIES AND SEWING STITCHES.

topstitching/topstitched seam See CLOTHING CONSTRUCTION DETAILS.

topweight † Fabric suitable for such garments as blouses and shirts.

toque **1.** See HEADWEAR. **2.** See HAIR ACCESSORIES.

toquet See HEADWEAR.

torchon lace See LACES.

toreador Adjective used to describe apparel inspired by or derived from the dress of Spanish bullfighters called toreadors. See COATS AND JACKETS: TOREADOR JACKET, HEADWEAR: TOREADOR HAT, and PANTS: TOREADOR PANTS.

torque See JEWELRY.

torsade 1. See HEADWEAR. **2.** See JEWELRY.

torso Adjective describing apparel that fits the body tightly from neck to hips. See TORSO DRESS, BLOUSES AND TOPS: TORSO BLOUSE, and SKIRTS: TORSO SKIRT.

torso dress Follows the line of the body to the hips, where skirt is attached to the dress. Sometimes has a belt at low waistline. May also be made in PANTDRESS style.

torsolette See UNDERGARMENTS: BUSTIER.

tortoise shell **1.** An attractive, brown, speckled material, obtained from the shell of the hawksbill turtle, which was prized for its attractive appearance. Its widespread use as a decorative material in such objects as hair ornaments, eyeglass frames, jewelry, and other trimmings caused the turtle to be hunted to near-extinction and use of the natural material has been banned. Very good imitations of genuine tortoise shell are now made of plastic and used in similar applications. **2.** Pattern similar to genuine tortoise shell used for printed fabrics and plastic eyeglass frames.

tortoise shell glasses See EYEWEAR.

tote See HANDBAGS AND RELATED ACCESSORIES.

Totes® See FOOTWEAR.

toupée See WIGS AND HAIRPIECES.

touring cap See HEADWEAR.

tourmaline See GEMS, GEM CUTS, AND SETTINGS.

tournure See UNDERGARMENTS: BUSTLE.

tournure and petticoat See UNDERGARMENTS: BUSTLE.

tournure corset See UNDERGARMENTS.

tow coat See COATS AND JACKETS.

tower See WIGS AND HAIRPIECES.

toyo (toe-yow´) Hat body material made of cellophane-coated rice paper of fine quality produced in Japan, Okinawa, and Taiwan.

track See FOOTWEAR and SHORTS: RUNNING SHORTS.

trade association Nonprofit organization that does research, promotes the interests of an industry, or provides educational services on behalf of member companies from that industry. Examples include the American Textile Manufacturers Institute, National Retail Merchants Association, or the Embroidery Council of America.

trademark Any word, name, or symbol that has been adopted and used by the owner to identify a product and distinguish it from others. When trademarks have been registered they may not be used by any other individual or firm and are written with the symbol ® or ™.

trade show Exposition sponsored by trade associations, apparel marts, and/or promotional companies that allows companies to promote their newest products to prospective customers.

Trafalgar turban See HEADWEAR.

tragedy mask Mask with corners of mouth turned down, used in Greek theatre.

trail shorts See SHORTS: CAMP SHORTS and CARGO SHORTS.

train Elongated back portion of woman's skirt that lies on the floor and is pulled along behind by wearer. Worn for formal evenings, especially in late 19th and early 20th c., and traditionally a part of bridal gowns. Dates from Middle Ages, when length of train worn only at court indicated rank.

training bra See UNDERGARMENTS: TEEN BRA.

trank See GLOVES AND GLOVE CONSTRUCTIONS.

transformation See WIGS AND HAIRPIECES.

translucent Semitransparent quality applied to gems and fabrics.

transparent Describes gems and fabrics through which light passes so that object behind may be seen clearly.

transparent dress ∞ Dress worn during the last quarter of the 17th c. consisting of a layer of lace over a complete dress of gold or brocade. Lace was usually black *point d'Angleterre.*

transparent velvet † Lightweight velvet that reflects light, thereby changing color to be somewhat iridescent. Has excellent draping qualities. Usually made with rayon pile, and given a crush-resistant finish.

trapeze dress Unfitted dress made with narrow shoulders that gradually widens, somewhat like a pyramid, to a very wide hem. Designed by Yves Saint Laurent for House of Dior in Paris in 1958. Same style resurfaced in fall of 1986.

trapeze dress

trapeze top See BLOUSES AND TOPS.

trapunto (tra-poont´-oh) Type of quilting in which design is outlined and then stuffed from the back of the fabric to achieve a raised or embossed effect.

travel bag See HANDBAGS AND RELATED ACCESSORIES: FLIGHT BAG.

travel coat See SLEEPWEAR AND LOUNGEWEAR.

traveling bag See HANDBAGS AND RELATED ACCESSORIES.

traveling wig See WIG: CAMPAIGN WIG.

trenchcoat See COATS AND JACKETS.

trenchdress Shirtwaist dress with snap front closing and cinch belt at waist. Top features epaulets and free-hanging panel to rib cage, similar to back of trenchcoat.

trencher cap See ACADEMIC COSTUME: MORTARBOARD.

trencher hat See HEADWEAR.

trend See FASHION TREND.

trend research Determining current directions for color, fabric, and fashions by reading the fashion press, subscribing to trend forecasting services, SHOPPING THE MARKET, and otherwise keeping up with the latest fashion developments.

triacetate † (try-ass'-eh-tate) Manufactured fiber regenerated through chemical treatment from wood chips or very short cotton fibers. Used for wearing apparel. Relatively little triacetate is produced at present, none in the United States.

Triangle Shirtwaist Fire A fire at the New York City women's garment manufacturing shop, Triangle Waist Co., on March 25, 1911, that took 146 workers' lives. Public opinion was consequently aroused to demand reforms for fire protection, better working conditions, sanitation, and unionization.

trickle-down theory of fashion change The idea that fashion changes result from the initial adoption of new and innovative styles by the upper socio-economic classes, and the subsequent imitation of these styles by lower socio-economic classes. Compare with BOTTOM-UP THEORY OF FASHION CHANGE.

tricorn/tricorne See HEADWEAR.

tricot (tree'-co) **1.** † Warp knit fabric made with two sets of yarns characterized by fine vertical WALES on the face and crosswise ribs on the back. When made with one set of yarns, it is called **single-bar tricot**. **Two-bar tricot**, made with yarns crossing, is run-resistant. Also called *double warp tricot, glove silk.* **Three-bar tricot** has an open-work effect. Manufactured fibers are used—with acetate tricot used frequently for backing on bonded knits. **2.** See EMBROIDERIES AND SEWING STITCHES: AFGHAN STITCH. *Der.* French, *tricoter,* "to knot."

tricot stitch See EMBROIDERIES AND SEWING STITCHES: AFGHAN STITCH.

trifocals See EYEWEAR.

Trigère, Pauline * See APPENDIX/DESIGNERS.

trilby See HEADWEAR.

triple-needle toe See FOOTWEAR.

triple stitchdown See FOOTWEAR: STITCHDOWN SHOE CONSTRUCTION.

triplex See HANDBAGS AND RELATED ACCESSORIES.

tri-suit See ACTIVEWEAR.

trollopee See SLEEPWEAR AND LOUNGEWEAR: SLAMMERKIN.

trompe l'oeil (trump' loy) Generally applied to embroidery and painting that create an optical illusion; also applied to dress and clothing. *Der.* French, "to fool the eye."

trompeurs See LIARS.

trooper cap See HEADWEAR.

tropical suiting † Lightweight fabric originally used for men's summer suits, now used for suits for all seasons. Usually tightly woven of highly twisted yarns.

tropical worsted † Lightweight WORSTED FABRIC (see WOOLEN) made in an open weave to permit circulation of air. Finished by removing surface fibers to give a clear finish. Packs well and is popular for dresses and suits for cooler days in the summer.

trousers See PANTS.

trouser skirt See SKIRTS.

trouser sock See HOSIERY: KNEE-HI SOCK.

trouses/trowses See UNDERGARMENTS.

trousses ∞ (trouz) French TIGHTS (see under HOSIERY) worn by pages and knights of king's order in 17th c.

trucker's apron See APRONS.

trumpet Adjective used to describe garments or garment parts that flare out at the bottom. Their shape is like that of the musical instrument the trumpet. See TRUMPET DRESS, SHOULDERS AND SLEEVES: TRUMPET SLEEVE, and SKIRTS: TRUMPET SKIRT.

trumpet dress Dress with flared flounce usually starting at knees. Worn in 1930s as tight-fitting dress to knees. Reintroduced in early 1980s as full-length evening gown and shift-type dress with flounce. *Der.* So called because it flares at the hem like a trumpet.

trunk hose ∞ A garment related to both BREECHES and CHAUSSE. About mid-16th c., chausses were divided into two parts— the upper part then being called *haut de chausses,* and subsequently called trunk hose or **upper stocks**. At the same time the term BREECHES was used

trunk hose: melon-shaped, c. 1572

synonymously with trunk hose, these being a man's garment covering the legs to the middle of the thigh or to the knee. The designation of trunk hose was generic, and many variations existed. Some were tight, others were loose-fitting or heavily padded with BOMBAST. Often they were PANED. Padded trunk hose included **barrel hose** that were cut very full and stuffed with horsehair or other materials and worn by men between 1570 and 1620. **Gregs** (also spelled *gregues*) were first worn in last quarter of 16th c. and were usually slashed to reveal the lining and elaborately trimmed with gold and silver. Synonyms: *gallygaskins, gally-gascoynes,* or *gaskins*. **Round hose** were described as onion-shaped and padded. In English colloquial language of the time, round hose were sometimes called *Spanish kettledrums*. **Boulogne** (boo-lawn'-yah) **hose** was an English term for round or oval trunk hose worn from 1550 to 1660. Frequently PANED and worn with CANIONS, after 1570, they were also called *bullion-hose* or *French hose*. **Venetians,** worn from 1570 to 1620 and most fashionable in 1580s, were pear-shaped, often padded, and fastened below knee by garter-ribbons. When tightly fitted, they were called **venetian galligascoines, galligaskins** or **chausses en tonnelet** (sho sawn ton-leh'). Also called *trusses* and *Italian hose*. When voluminous throughout, they were called **Venetian slops. Slops** or **slivings** were knee-length unpadded trunk hose, worn during second half of 16th and early 17th cs. Those large at the top, without a band at hem, and reaching just to knees were known as **small slops** and required for Cambridge University students in England from 1585 to about 1610. Other types included **scaling hose** or *scalings,* similar to Venetians, popular in latter half of 16th c. **A pair of buffins,** was an English colloquial term for men's trunk hose similar to slops that were worn in 16th c. **Pluderhose** were German and Swiss unpadded trunk hose worn in latter half of 16th c. Characterized by broad slashes with loose silk linings protruding, they were also called *almain hose* and *german hose*.

trunk hose:
Venetians,
c. 1582

trunks 1. See ACTIVEWEAR. 2. See TRUNK HOSE. 3. See UNDERGARMENTS. 4. See SHORTS.

trunk show A show of a complete apparel line in a retail store that is presented for customers and/or store personnel by a vendor or designer. In this way, even if the store has not chosen to buy the entire line, customers and salespersons can become familiar with the line.

trunk sleeve See SHOULDERS AND SLEEVES: CANNON SLEEVES.

truss *v.* to tie up, used from 14th c. to about 1630. Phrase "to truss the points" meant to fasten HOSE to TRUNK HOSE and DOUBLET by means of POINTS (lacers), which ended in decorative metal tip called an AGLET.

trusses See TRUNK HOSE.

T-shirt 1. See SHIRTS. 2. See UNDERGARMENTS. 3. See SLEEPWEAR AND LOUNGEWEAR.

T-shirt dress Simple knit dress styled like an elongated T-shirt, an innovation of late 1950s. Newer versions may have extended cap sleeves, spaghetti sashes, and are often printed with silk-screen designs.

tsitsith (zit-zith') Tassel, usually blue, worn on prayer shawl called TALLITH or on the ARBA KANFOTH by Jewish men. Also spelled *zizith*.

T-strap See FOOTWEAR.

tube See UNDERGARENTS: TUBE BRA, HOSIERY, and BLOUSES AND TOPS.

tubular knit See CIRCULAR KNIT.

tuck/tucks See CLOTHING CONSTRUCTION DETAILS.

tucked seam See CLOTHING CONSTRUCTION DETAILS: TUCKED SEAMS.

tucker See NECKLINES AND COLLARS.

tudor cape See CAPES, CLOAKS, AND SHAWLS.

tuft Variant of POMPON; a cluster of threads or fibers tied together to form a ball.

tulip Adjective used to describe apparel or parts of apparel that are shaped like the tulip flower. See SHOULDERS AND SLEEVES: TULIP SLEEVE and SKIRTS: BUBBLE.

tulle † (tool) Fine sheer net fabric made of silk, nylon, or rayon with hexagonal holes. Used unstarched for wedding veils and millinery, and starched for ballet costumes. In the 18th c., all hexagonal netlike fabrics were called by this name. *Der.* First made in 1768 in England by machine; in 1817, a factory was opened in the city of Tulle, France.

tulle embroidery   See EMBROIDERIES AND SEWING STITCHES.

tunic   **1.** *n.* Simple garment worn since ancient times that is T-shaped with openings for the head and arms. Lengths can vary. **2.** *n.* Garment that ends somewhere between the hip and the calf and is designed to be worn over another garment such as pants, skirt, bloomers, or dress. **3.** Adjective used to describe a garment similar to a tunic. See TUNIC DRESS, SWIMWEAR: TUNIC SWIMSUIT, BLOUSES AND TOPS: TUNIC BLOUSE, JUMPERS: TUNIC JUMPER, SKIRTS: TUNIC SKIRT, and SLEEPWEAR AND LOUNGEWEAR: TUNIC PAJAMAS.

tunic #1

tunic à la mameluke   ∞ (mah′-meh-luke′)   Woman's knee-length tunic with long sleeves fashionable at beginning of 19th c. Later called *tunique à la juive.* Inspired by Napoleon's Egyptian campaign, 1798. *Der.* Mamelukes were originally slaves brought to Egypt in 19th c., later trained as soldiers. Ruled Egypt from 1250 to 1517 and remained powerful until 1811 under Turkish viceroys.

tunic à la romaine   ∞ (ro-main′)   Tunic, worn by women in late 18th c., that was full-length, high-waisted, long-sleeved, and made of gauze or lawn.

tunic dress   **1.** Two-piece dress with a long overblouse worn over a separate narrow skirt or a one-piece dress designed to give this effect. Originally introduced in the 1850s as a ball dress with the upper skirt trimmed with lace and underskirt with a deep flounce. Popular in slim style in 1880s, 1910 to 1920, and worn intermittently since. **2.** Minidress of the late 1960s that could be worn alone or over pants to make a pantsuit.

tunic dress #1

tunnel loops   Loops of matching fabric placed at waistband of pants or skirt for belt to pull through. Loops may be 1 to 3″ wide—larger than regular belt loops.

tunnel waistline   See WAISTLINES: DRAWSTRING.

turban   See HEADWEAR.

Turkey bonnet   See HEADWEAR.

Turkey gown   ∞ **1.** Long black velvet gown bordered with lynx and decorated with 77 gold- and black-enameled buttons made for Henry VIII, who ruled England from 1515 to 1548. **2.** Long gown open in front with long narrow sleeves slit above elbow so arm could come through, remainder of sleeve hung down. Worn from 1530s on, becoming style for Puritan ministers.

Turkish polonaise   See IRISH POLONAISE.

turndown collar   See NECKLINES AND COLLARS.

turned-back cuff   See CUFFS.

turned shoe construction   See FOOTWEAR.

turnip pants   See PANTS.

turnover   Describes how many times stock is sold and replaced within a period of time.

turnover collar   See NECKLINES AND COLLARS.

turn-ups   See PANTS.

turquoise   See GEMS, GEM CUTS, AND SETTINGS.

turret bodice   ∞ Bodice with peplum, cut in square tabs below waistline, popular in early 1880s.

turtleneck   See NECKLINES AND COLLARS, and SWEATERS.

turtleneck convertible   See NECKLINES AND COLLARS.

turtleneck Cossack shirt   See SHIRTS: COSSACK SHIRT.

tussah † (tuss′-ah)   Coarse, irregular silk, from wild Asian silkworms, used to make PONGEE and SHANTUNG. The silkworm, the fiber, the yarn, and also the fabric made from the yarn are all called by this name. *Der.* Hindu, *tasar,* from the Sanskirt *trasara,* "a shuttle." Also spelled *tasar, tusser, tussas, tussus.*

tutu #2

tutu   **1.** Ballet dancer's costume designed in 1832 by Eugene Lami for Maria Taglioni, a great Italian ballerina of the Romantic period. Consisted of a tight-fitting, bare-shouldered bodice worn with a bell-shaped, sheer, white gathered skirt reaching midway between knee and ankle. **2.** Multilayered very short skirt of net or tulle. Pale pink *tights* were worn underneath and pale pink satin *ballet slippers* were worn with both versions.

tutulus See HEADWEAR.

tuxedo **1.** See COATS AND JACKETS. **2.** Man's semiformal fingertip-length jacket and pants made with satin or faille lapels and side stripes on pants. Made in black or midnight blue in winter, white jacket with dark pants in summer. Sometimes made in other colors or plaids since 1960s. Worn with CUMMERBUND (see under BELTS) and black BOW TIE (see under TIES). Abbreviated as *tux.* Also called *black tie. Der.* Worn by Griswold P. Lorillard at Tuxedo Park, NY, in 1886. **3.** Adjective used to describe garments like those worn with a tuxedo or that derive from the tuxedo style.

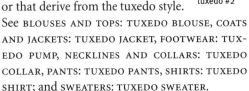
tuxedo #2

See BLOUSES AND TOPS: TUXEDO BLOUSE, COATS AND JACKETS: TUXEDO JACKET, FOOTWEAR: TUXEDO PUMP, NECKLINES AND COLLARS: TUXEDO COLLAR, PANTS: TUXEDO PANTS, SHIRTS: TUXEDO SHIRT; and SWEATERS: TUXEDO SWEATER.

tweed † Rough textured fabrics made of coarse wool in yarn-dyed effects. Made in plain, twill, or herringbone weave in various weights for coats, jackets, and suits. *Der.* Scottish, *tweed,* meaning "twill," because they were at first handloomed in homes along the Tweed River in Scotland.

twenties bob See HAIRSTYLES.

twenties look/twenties style See FLAPPER LOOK.

twillet See TOILET/TOILETTE #1.

twill fabric/twills Fabrics made with the TWILL WEAVE.

twill weave † Basic weave characterized by diagonal wales (see WALE #1) produced by staggering the points of intersection of lengthwise and crosswise yarns. Wales generally run upward from left to right, called **right-hand twill,** or from lower right to upper left, **left-hand twill.** Both make a firm, durable fabric (e.g., DENIM, TICKING, SERGE, and GABARDINE).

right-hand
twill weave
diagram

twinset **1.** See BLOUSES AND TOPS. **2.** See SWEATERS: SWEATER SET.

two-bar tricot See TRICOT.

two-ply yarn See SINGLE YARN.

two-sided line stitch See EMBROIDERIES AND SEWING STITCHES.

two-way stretch foundation See UNDERGARMENTS.

tye **1.** See WIGS AND HAIRPIECES. **2.** See APRONS.

tying contract Illegal practice in which retailers are required to buy unwanted merchandise in order to be able to purchase desired other merchandise.

Tyler, Richard * See APPENDIX/DESIGNERS.

Tyrolean hat See HEADWEAR: ALPINE HAT.

Tyrolean look (tee-roll′-ee-an) Type of dress worn by natives of Austrian Tyrol and Bavarian region, including dirndl skirts, embroidered vests, and aprons worn by women; lederhosen, knee socks, and feather-trimmed felt ALPINE HATS (see under HEADWEAR), worn by men. These styles have inspired specific items of fashionable dress such as dirndl skirts and Alpine hats. *Der.* Named for alpine region in Austria and Bavaria called the "Tyrol."

T

U

Ubangi See JEWELRY and NECKLINES AND COLLARS.

ugly See HEADWEAR.

ulster See COATS AND JACKETS.

ultrafine fiber † Manufactured filament fiber that measures 0.01 denier per filament or less.

ultra-sheer pantyhose See UNDERGARMENTS: SHEER PANTYHOSE.

ultrasonic sewing Sewing accomplished by special machines using ultrasonic sound waves that through vibrations create heat that fuses heat-sensitive fabrics together without the use of needles and thread. Advantages: eliminates use of needles and thread, also eliminates seam slippage.

Ultrasuede® † Registered trademark for luxury suedelike fabric made of 60% polyester and 40% nonfibrous urethane in a porous sheet material. Used in a wide variety of apparel.

umbrella brim See HEADWEAR.

umbrella drawers See UNDERGARMENTS.

umbrella-pleated skirt See SKIRTS.

umbrella pleats See CLOTHING CONSTRUCTION DETAILS.

UMBRELLAS AND PARASOLS

umbrella Accessory used as a protection against the rain or sun; a round flat or convex plate-like fabric canopy, originally served to shade the person beneath from the sun. It had six to sixteen collapsible ribs mounted at the top of a handle. In early Egyptian, Assyrian, Indian, and African civilizations and in the Catholic Church throughout the Middle Ages, this device was a sign of rank. By the early 16th c., it had also become a fashionable novelty to protect against the sun. Occasional mention is made in the early 17th c. of the umbrella as protection against rain, however it was only at the end of that century that waterproof umbrellas came into widespread use. By 1800 a distinction was made in English between an umbrella, which was waterproof and used against rain, and a **parasol,** which was a sunshade and often highly decorative. Parasols were very important accessories throughout the 19th c. and into the early 20th c., after which they gradually went out of fashion while the utilitarian umbrella continued to be used against the rain. *Der.* from the Italian *umbra,* meaning shade. Parasol derives from *para,* against, *sol,* the sun.

bell umbrella Dome-shaped umbrella of transparent plastic or of fabric with a plastic window through which to look, which is deeper than most umbrellas and therefore protects the face. Also called a *bell-shaped umbrella* or a *dome umbrella.*

carriage parasol ∞ Small parasol intended to be carried and used when riding in a horse-drawn carriage. It had either a folding or short handle. Compare to UMBRELLAS AND PARASOLS: WALKING PARASOL.

carriage parasol

coquette parasol See UMBRELLAS AND PARA-SOLS: MARQUISE.

dome umbrella See UMBRELLAS AND PARASOLS: BELL UMBRELLA.

en tous cas ∞ (on too′ kah) Nickname for a parasol, which could also be used as an umbrella, carried about 1870. *Der.* French, "in any case."

fan parasol See UMBRELLAS AND PARASOLS: MARQUISE.

gamp ∞ 19th-c. slang for umbrella. Named after Mrs. Sarah Gamp, character in Charles Dickens' 1843 novel *Martin Chuzzlewit.*

gingham ∞ 19th-c. colloquial term for an umbrella. So called because the less expensive types were made out of gingham fabric.

Japanese parasol Parasol or umbrella made of brightly colored glazed paper with bamboo ribs. Also made of oiled silk for wet weather.

marquise ∞ (mar-keez′) Parasol with a hinge at the top that allowed the top to be tilted in different directions. Also called *coquette* (kokett′) or *fan parasol* or, in the 1850s, *parasol à la Pompadour. Der:* Thought to have been invented by the Marquise de Pompadour, mistress of King Louis XIV of France.

pagoda parasol Parasol cover shaped like the roof of a Chinese temple (pagoda).

parasol See UMBRELLA under category heading for UMBRELLAS AND PARASOLS.

parasol à la Pompadour See UMBRELLAS AND PARASOLS: MARQUISE.

sylphide parasol ∞ (syl-feed′) Patented in 1844, this parasol had a spring at the end of the handle that allowed the shade to be closed by the hand holding it. It had a metal shaft, whalebone ribs, and a handle and point of carved ivory. The cover was usually made of silk taffeta fringed with lace.

walking parasol ∞ Parasol with a long stick or handle that was meant to be carried while walking. Compare to UMBRELLAS AND PARASOLS: CARRIAGE PARASOL.

walking parasol

umbrella tote See HANDBAGS AND RELATED ACCESSORIES.

unbleached muslin † Coarse heavily sized cotton utility fabric woven in a plain weave of carded yarns and sold in the unbleached or gray state (see GRAY GOODS). Used by fashion designers when draping garments on DRESS FORMS. After garment is designed, it is taken apart and the muslin pieces are used as a pattern. Also used for interfacings in low-quality suits and coats.

uncle Sam diamond See GEMS, GEM CUTS, AND SETTINGS.

underarm dart See CLOTHING CONSTRUCTION DETAILS: DARTS.

under cap See HEADWEAR.

underfur See FURS.

UNDERGARMENTS

undergarment Item of apparel worn under the outer garments. These garments serve many functions. They may protect the outer clothing from being soiled or provide a more comfortable layer between the skin of the wearer and the outer clothing. Those garments serving this purpose are usually made from soft, washable fabrics. Undergarments may serve to give shape to the outer garments either through constricting the body or providing support to the clothing. It is not unusual for several layers of undergarments to be worn at the same time. Although generally unseen, parts of undergarments may sometimes be a visible element of the costume. Also called *underwear.*

all-in-one See UNDERGARMENTS: FOUNDATION.

amazon corset ∞ English corset worn for riding in mid-19th c. Made with elastic lacings that shortened the garment by three inches when a hidden cord was pulled.

apollo corset ∞ Waist cincher stiffened with whalebone, worn by both men and women about 1810. When worn by English dandies of Regency period (1810–1820), sometimes called a *Brummell bodice* or *Cumberland corset.*

athletic shirt/A-shirt Man's sleeveless undershirt with low, round neckline, also worn for gym and sports.

backless bra Bra made with cups but no back. Elastic straps fasten at shoulder and at bottom of bra. These are worn crossed in back, brought around waistline, and hooked in center front. Shoulder straps may be unhooked and fastened at back of neck in halter style.

Balmoral petticoat ∞ Colored petticoat, originally red with wide decorative black band mitered to form squared half frames, which projected below a looped-up outer skirt, worn in mid-1860s.

band briefs Short underpants finished at the legs with knitted bands. Also called *band-leg panties.*

bandeau slip See UNDERGARMENTS: BRA-SLIP.

band-leg panties See UNDERGARMENTS: BAND BRIEFS.

bare bra Bra constructed of a framework of straps with sewn-in uplift bands. There is no fabric over upper part of breasts.

bearer ∞ A padded roll worn under the back of a skirt by women from second half of 17th and early 18th c. Similar to a BUSTLE (see under UNDERGARMENTS).

bell hoop ∞ Dome-shaped hoop-skirt petticoat popular in England from about 1710 to 1780. Also called *cupola coat.*

bias slip Slip cut on the diagonal of the fabric. This creates a closer fit, as the fabric stretches to conform to the movements of the body. Introduced in the 1920s, popularized in the 1930s, and a classic since.

bias slip

bikini brief Men's brief low-rise underwear made in all colors and styles of knit cotton or manufactured fiber yarns.

bikini brief

bikini panties Below-the-navel brief underpants introduced in early 1960s, modeled after BIKINI SWIMSUIT (see under SWIMWEAR).

bloomers Full panty with thigh-length leg gathered into elastic. Popular since 1920s for little girls, and worn by older women from 1930s to present. *Der.* Named for Amelia Jenks Bloomer, early-19th c. American reformer who wore full gathered pants instead of a skirt when lecturing. Also see BLOOMER COSTUME.

blouse-slip Combination slip and blouse with top cut like a blouse and lower part serving as a slip under the skirt. Also called *slip-blouse.*

bodice See UNDERGARMENTS: PAIR OF BODIES.

body briefer 1. Two-way stretch garment made in panty style without garters for hose. Usually made in SPANDEX power-net, sometimes with lace inserts for bra. 2. Lace-trimmed garment styled like a TEDDY (see under UNDERGARMENTS) with high-cut legs made of lightweight stretch fabric and with a V or camisole-type top.

body briefer

bodyshapers Fashion business designation of the of undergarments designed to control and support the figure. Also called **shapewear.**

boned foundation Foundation garment in which thin metal or plastic strips called bones have been inserted for stiffening in order to make a firm garment with more control. *Der.* So called because "bones" were originally made of whalebone. Also see CLOTHING CONSTRUCTION DETAILS: STAY #1.

bouffant petticoat (boo-fahnt′) Any full petticoat made with gores or ruffles for wearing under a wide-skirted dress.

bourrelet See UNDERGARMENTS: BUM ROLL.

boxer pants Women's and children's loose-legged underpants of pull-on type.

boxer shorts Somewhat loose-fitting, short, underpants worn by men and boys. Originally made of woven fabric, but now also made in knits. *Der.* Similar to men's shorts worn for the sport of boxing.

boxer shorts

bra/brassiere Bra is shortened form of word *brassiere,* a word first used in 1905 for a garment. A shaped undergarment worn by women to mold and support the breasts. Usually consists of two cups held in place with straps over the shoulders and elastic in center back. Also called a *bandeau* (band-oh′), although a bandeau was usally made without darts or other shaping. Also see UNDERGARMENTS: DeBEVOISE BRASSIERE.

braies See in alphabetical listing.

bra-slip Slip made with a fitted top. One garment replaces two—the bra and the slip.

U

Popular in 1960s and after. Also called *bandeau slip.*

briefs **1.** Woman's or girl's very short underpants, sometimes made of control stretch fabric with garters added. **2.** Tight-fitting short knitted underpants worn by men and boys.

Brummel bodice See UNDERGARMENTS: APOLLO CORSET.

built-in bra Bra used in swimsuits and sundresses as a part of the structure of the clothing.

built-up slip Slip, made with U-neckline, deep armholes, and wide straps. May be worn as lining for a sheer dress.

bum roll ∞ Padded roll worn around the hips to hold the skirt out into the French farthingale style, a fashion of the 16th and early 17th cs. See FARTHINGALE. Also called *bourrelet* (bour'-lay).

bum roll c. 1600

bustier (boo-ste'-yay) One-piece support garment that is a combination bra and waist cincher. Reaches to few inches below the waist or to the hips. Frequently made without straps and with or without removable garters, it has flexible boning and is sometimes lace trimmed. Also called *torsolette.*

bustier bra (boo-ste'-yay) Tight-fitted strapless bra usually waist length and often laced up the front. Sometimes used for the top of a dress.

bustle (bus'-sel) Pad, cushion, or arrangement of steel springs creating a rounded projection below the waist at the back of woman's dress. Although not called "bustle" until about 1830, skirts with back fullness had been worn earlier and were called by names such as *bum roll, cork rump, frisk, Nelson, cushion pad, cushionet,* or *rump furbelow,* which are defined under the category of UNDERGARMENTS. Bustles that resembled a small pad and tied around the waist were worn from the 1830s to the 1850s but were not used with

bustles

hoopskirts in the 1850s and 1860s. By 1870 bustles were once again used to support back fullness. Initially, they tended to use hoops and back fullness, as in the **crinolette** (krin-o-let'), a smaller form of woman's CAGE PETTICOAT (see UNDERGARMENTS: HOOPS) with steel half-hoops only in back and having CRINOLINE or HORSEHAIR ruffles forming a bustle in the back. It was worn from late 1860s to 1870s and revived in 1883. The **Eugénie petticoat** (yoo-je'-nee), worn in the early 1870s, was made full-length in back and a little below the waist in front. Semicircular steel *hoops* in the back and *bustle* held out skirt in the back. (*Der.* Named for Eugénie, Empress of France [1853–71].) A **pannier crinoline** was an 1870s underskirt for extending the dress that combined a CAGE PETTICOAT with a BUSTLE. Also called *Thomson's pannier crinoline.* The **crinoline and tournure** was a stiffened petticoat with bustle added in back worn under dresses in late 1860s. A **plumet petticoat** was a narrow, back-buttoned petticoat of 1870s with ruffles forming bustle at back and continuing to form a detachable train. The term **tournure** (toor-nure') was applied either to a bustle of early 1870s made from six rows of horsehair ruffles mounted on a calico foundation stiffened with whalebone, and attached to a band around the waist that tied in front, or, during a short period around 1876 to 1882, to a foundation piece that hung down back from waist with ruffles at hem to hold out the train of a dress. It had ties to fasten in front at intervals. In the **tournure and petticoat,** a bustle was combined with petticoat. Worn from about 1875 to 1885, some made all in one piece, some with buttons and buttonholes at hip-level so that the tournure or bustle could be used separately or removed. Bustles returned in the 1880s and were seen until the 1890s. Large bustles included the **haut ton** (oh' ton), a patented bustle of the late 1880s made of three pendant spirally coiled springs with small pad at back of waist. It was secured by a belt around the waist that fastened in the front. The **Langtry bustle** was a patented, lightweight collapsible bustle, worn in late 1880s and was made of a series of semicircular hoops fastened to a *stay* on either side. (*Der.* Named after actress *Lillie Langtry.*) As bustles diminished in size in the late 1800s, these smaller types developed: **cushion pad,** a tiny bustle stuffed with horsehair worn in late 19th c.; and the **figure improver,** a small bustle worn by women in the 1890s. Throughout the period from 1849 to the 1880s, **dress improver** was a polite term for bustle. Another synonym was *tournure.* Since 1900, back fullness in skirts has appeared occasionally, particularly for evening dress, but never again have skirts had the extreme fullness of the 19th c. bustle styles.

B.V.D.® See UNDERGARMENTS: ENVELOPE COMBINATION.

Cadoro® bra Trademark for decorative metal bra worn with scarf or bikini underneath, consisting of metal cups, frequently filigreed, held on with chains. Introduced in late 1960s as an item of body jewelry.

cage See UNDERGARMENTS: HOOPS.

cage-americaine See UNDERGARMENTS: HOOPS.

cage empire See UNDERGARMENTS: HOOPS.

cage petticoat See UNDERGARMENTS: HOOPS.

camisa See UNDERGARMENTS: CHEMISE.

camise See UNDERGARMENTS: CHEMISE.

camisette (ka-mee-sett′) Minimal support foundation with a natural bra top made close-fitting to hips with long attached garters. Sometimes worn with bikini underpants.

camisole (kam′-ih-sole) **1.** Short underbodice or vest with built-up straps worn over corset or stays. Introduced in early 1800s. Also called *chemise, corset cover,* and *petticoat bodice.* **2.** For lingerie, used to describe a waist-length, gathered, straight-cut top with straps, trimmed with lace or embroidery. Worn with a petticoat under a sheer blouse in late 19th and early 20th c.

camisole
#2

camisole slip (kam′-ih-sole) Slip with a lace or embroidery top to be worn under a sheer blouse—often cut straight across at neckline with wide straps.

cami-tap set See UNDERGARMENTS: TAP PANTIES.

Capri-length panty-girdle See UNDERGARMENTS: GIRDLES.

chemise (shem-eze′) Linen garment worn next to the skin by men and women in Middle Ages. Made with long sleeves, it was straight hanging and as long as the garment worn over it. By 14th c. a man's chemise was called *shirt* or *sherte;* and a woman's chemise, a *smock.* In 17th c. called *shift,* and by the late 18th c. the term chemise came back into English from French and continued in use in the 19th c., at which time it was generally made of cotton or linen, had a low round neck, was short-sleeved, about calf-length, and sometimes trimmed with lace and embroidered. Synonyms and alternate spellings used at various times include *camise, camisia, cames, kemes, kemise, kemse, robe linge.*

chemise
c. 1900

chemise slip Thigh-length slip of the late 1960s, it hangs straight and is not fitted.

colobium ∞ (ko-loh′-bee-um) Type of undertunic or undershirt worn in ancient Rome and during the Middle Ages; also called a *sherte* by Anglo Saxons.

combinations **1.** Underwear in which two garments (e.g., chemise and drawers or chemise and petticoat) are combined to make one. Introduced in the mid-19th c. **2.** In 1920s, name for a UNION SUIT for women. See under UNDERGARMENTS.

contour bra Rounded bra padded with fiberfill or foam.

combination
c 1880s

control-brief See UNDERGARMENTS: GARTER-BRIEF.

control pants BRIEFS, LONG-LEG PANTIES, or PANTSLINERS (see under UNDERGARMENTS) knitted with elastomeric yarns (see ELASTOMER) to provide support.

cork rump ∞ Bustle of late 18th c. made in shape of a crescent and stuffed with cork.

corps à baleine See UNDERGARMENTS: CORPS PIQUÉ #2.

U

corps piqué ∞ (cor pe-kay′) **1.** Quilted camisole with a BUSK, of varnished wood used as stiffening, first worn in France. **2.** In 17th and 18th c., a tightly laced underbodice stiffened with whalebones and held on with shoulder straps. Same as French *corps à baleine* (cor ah bah-lehn′).

corselet (kors-let′) Foundation with firm support achieved by boning, power-net side panels, and front panel of no-stretch nylon taffeta. Sometimes has an inner belt that hooks separately to help flatten abdomen. Bra top is often of nylon lace with *marquisette* (mar-kee-set′) lining and adjustable shoulder straps. Foundation is fastened by hooks underneath zipper and has six garters. Appearing first in America in 1921 and then spelled *corsellette*. Also see alphabetical listing.

corset Woman's one-piece sleeveless and often strapless garment for shaping the figure. Earlier versions laced shut, while late 19th and 20th c. corsets often closed with hooks. This term comes into use in the 19th c., is synonymous with STAYS (see under UNDERGARMENTS). The shape of the corset changes with the current fashionable silhouette. From 1820s to 1930s generally it is a heavily boned, rigid garment. Since 1940s made of lighter-weight elasticized fabrics and more likely to be called a GIRDLE or FOUNDATION GARMENT (see under UNDERGARMENTS). For named varieties see UNDERGARMENTS: AMAZON CORSET, CORSET À LA NINON, DEMI-CORSET, EMPIRE STAYS, FOUNDATIONS, and SWANBILL CORSET.

corset

corset à la ninon ∞ (ah lah nee-non′) Lightweight corset reaching to hips laced up the back and designed to wear under Empire style dresses in 1810.

corset cover See UNDERGARMENTS: CAMISOLE #1.

criardes ∞ (kree-ards) Underskirt of gummed linen puffed out at the sides, forerunner of panniers. *Der.* French, "crying or scolding" because the petticoat creaked as the woman walked.

crinolette See UNDERGARMENTS: BUSTLE.

crinoline (krin′-oh-lyn) **1.** Stiffened petticoat intended to hold out a bouffant skirt—may be made of stiff nylon, either plain or ruffled. **2.** ∞ Underskirt, worn in 1840s and 1850s, made of stiff fabric called *crinoline*. Horsehair was often incorporated into the fabric to provide stiffening. **3.** Term applied to any underskirt with hoops that support a full skirt. See UNDERGARMENTS: HOOPS.

crinoline and tournure See BUSTLE.

crossover bra Bra with reinforced straps, usually of elastic, that form an X in center front.

cuff-top girdle See UNDERGARMENTS: GIRDLES.

culotte slip (kul-lot′) Slip styled like wide underpants cut knee length or shorter.

Cumberland corset See UNDERGARMENTS: APOLLO CORSET.

cupola coat See UNDERGARMENTS: BELL HOOP.

cushionet ∞ BUSTLE (see under UNDERGARMENTS) worn with the FARTHINGALE from 1560 to 1630s that raised the back of a skirt. Also spelled *quissionet*.

cushion pad See UNDERGARMENTS: BUSTLE.

dance set See UNDERGARMENTS: STEP-INS.

DeBevoise brassiere (deh bev-waz′ brah-zeer′) Sleeveless low-necked waist, similar to a *corset cover,* reaching to waistline with a point in front and boned to support the bosom. Patented by the DeBevoise Company in Newark, NJ, in early 1900s. Although the firm used the name *brassiere,* it was only in its later models that it produced a garment more like a contemporary bra.

décolleté bra (deh-coll′-eh-tay) Low-cut bra for wear with low necklines.

demi-bra Half bra that exposes upper part of breasts, for wear with low necklines. Also called *half bra.*

demi-corset ∞ Short corset worn by women in 1830s and 1840s.

dickey Late 18th- and early 19th-c. name for under-petticoat worn by women.

dirndl petticoat (durn′-del) Petticoat flitting smoothly over hips then expanding to gathered fullness to hem. Sometimes made with tiers or ruffles. *Der.* From Austrian Tyrol full-skirted peasant costume.

double-zipper foundation Easy-to-get-into foundation garment with one zipper extending from under arm to below waist, a second zipper on opposite side extends from thigh to waistline.

drawers General term used to refer to underpants. The term probably derives from the act of drawing a garment over the lower part of the body and comes into fairly widespread use in the 16th c. Although the term was applied to both men's and women's undergarments, drawers were not universally worn by women until the 19th c. Although currently still in use as a general term for underpants, by the early 20th c., it has been replaced to a large extent by names for specific kinds of underpants.

dress improver See UNDERGARMENTS: BUSTLE.

elastic-leg brief Short panty finished with elastic around the leg rather than a band.

Empire jupon See UNDERGARMENTS: HOOPS.

Empire petticoat See UNDERGARMENTS: HOOPS.

Empire stays ∞ (em′-pire or ohm-peer′) Short high-waisted corset, forerunner of the bra, laced in back for wear with high-waisted EMPIRE DRESSES in the 1890s.

Empress petticoat ∞ Evening petticoat substituted for the cage petticoat in mid-1860s. Made in gores to fit tightly at the waist and spread to eight yards at the hem, forming a train a yard long, and finished with a full gathered flounce beginning at the knees.

envelope combination ∞ Man's *undershirt* and *drawers* combined into one garment—a type of loose-fitting UNION SUIT (SEE under UNDERGARMENTS)—with open double fold in the back. Worn in the 1920s and 1930s, **B.V.D.**® was the best-known trade name for this garment.

Eugénie petticoat See UNDERGARMENTS: BUSTLE.

evening petticoat Narrow ankle-length petticoat made with slash in center front or slashes on side seams.

evening slip Slip made to be worn under an evening dress with the cut of the back of the slip and the length conforming to the dress worn over it.

false hips See UNDERGARMENTS: PANNIERS.

Ferris waist ∞ Trade name for PANTYWAIST (see under UNDERGARMENTS).

figure improver See UNDERGARMENTS: BUSTLE.

fishnet underwear Lightweight 100% cotton string yarn in netlike weave, acting as an insulator against zero temperatures and 90° heat. Originally worn by Norwegian explorers and Norwegian Army. Worn by athletes and by general public as sportswear in 1970s and 1980s.

flannel petticoat ∞ Infant's and woman's winter petticoat worn for warmth under fancy petticoats from 1870s to early 1920s. Usually made of wool flannel, sometimes of cashmere. Also called a *flannel skirt.*

flared-leg pants Longer underpants that flare and hang loose on the leg. Introduced in the 1920s.

foundation Undergarment combining a bra and girdle in one piece to mold the figure. Made with or without straps over the shoulders and optional supporters for the hose. Frequently made with alternating panels of flexible elastic fabric and nonstretch fabric. Also called *all-in-one.* Formerly called a *foundation garment* or *garment* from about 1920 to early 1980s. Evolved from the CORSET (see under UNDERGARMENTS).

foundation

four-gore slip **1.** Slip with no waistline, cut in four panels with two side seams, one seam down center front, and another in center back. **2.** Slip with a plain top, a waistline seam, and a four-gored flared skirt made to wear with bouffant dresses.

French bra Bra that fits under bust as an uplift but has no cups, worn with low-necked dresses for natural look.

French cinch Short girdle-like garment designed to accentuate a small waist starting at the ribs and stopping above the hips with or without long garters. Consisted of a wide strip of fabric with six or eight vertically placed *bones* or *stays* that hook in front or made of ELASTOMERIC

French cinch

U

fiber. One version designed by Marcel Rochas, Paris couturier, in 1947 was called a **guepiere** (geh-pih-yair′). Also called *waist-cincher.*

French drawers ∞ Flared, knee-length underpants lavishly trimmed with lace, ruffles, and *insertion* at the hems. Set on a band at waist with ties or buttons in back to adjust the size. With split crotch, called "open," or with seam sewed, called "closed." Made of fine cambric, lawn, muslin, and worn in late 1890s and early 1900s.

French panties Short, flared, lacy underpants made of silk and cut with wide legs, worn in 1920s.

frisk ∞ Small BUSTLE worn on the exterior of the skirt by women from 1815 to 1818 to produce the Grecian bend posture. Also called *Nelson.* See UNDERGARMENTS: BUSTLE.

front-closure bra A bra that closes in the front, usually with hooks and eyes, sometimes has built-up straps.

garter belt Elasticized band, which fits either around the hips or waist, with four or six elastic garters attached to hold up hose. Some are styled like a girdle to give added support. Some are lacy and considered sexy when worn over tiny bikini underpants.

garter belt

garter briefs Short underpants with attached supporters to hold up stockings.

gertrude ∞ Infant's slip worn in early 20th c. styled with round neck, built-up shoulders, and sometimes long in length. Also called a *gertrude skirt.*

girdle Undergarment worn by women and girls designed to mold the lower torso, and sometimes the legs. May be flexible two-way stretch, or one-way stretch elastic with nonstretchable fabric panels and made with or without garters. Ends anywhere from hip- to ankle-length, when it is called a **long-leg panty-girdle,** made with longer legs to eliminate bulges. **Hi-rise girdle** extends above the waistline and the **cuff-top girdle** is a pull-on zippered girdle that extends above waistline with wide band of elastic at top. **Pull-on girdle** is made without a zipper or other

girdle

opening and is pulled on over the hips like panties. **Panty-girdle** has a closed crotch, resembling panties, and comes in lengths from hip joint to ankle. **Capri-length panty-girdle** is a very long two-way stretch panty girdle extending about 4″ below knees. Girdles were introduced in the 1930s as a rigid support garment but contemporary versions range from rigid support to, more commonly, support by means of elastic fabrics.

guepiere See UNDERGARMENTS: FRENCH CINCH.

half bra See UNDERGARMENTS: DEMI-BRA.

half-slip Straight-cut slip beginning at the waist. Introduced in 1940s, becoming a classic substitute for a regular slip. In contemporary terminology also called a *petticoat.* See UNDERGARMENTS: PETTICOAT.

haut ton See UNDERGARMENTS: BUSTLE.

hip-huggers Low-slung underpants starting at hip bone level, intended to be worn with hip-hugger pants and bare-midriff dresses.

hi-rise girdle See UNDERGARMENTS: GIRDLES.

Hollywood-top slip Slip with a fitted V-shaped top, introduced in 1920s. Previous to this time, slips were cut straight across in front or made with wider built-up straps.

Honiton gossamer skirt ∞ (hon′-ih-ton) Lightweight summer petticoat of 1850s made with strips of fabric attached to a waist belt by means of several vertical tapes as far as the hips where three circular ruffles of fabric were attached.

hoop petticoat See UNDERGARMENTS: HOOPS.

hoops A framework consisting of round or oval circles (shaped like a hoop) of whalebone, wire, or cane used to extend the skirt. Used in the 16th c. as part of the structure of the FARTHINGALE, in the 18th c. when they were called PANNIERS (see under UNDERGARMENTS), and in the 19th c. when they were called HOOPS or CRINOLINES (see under UNDERGARMENTS). Revived in 1950s, hoops are now sometimes worn with evening or bridal gowns. Fashionable in the 19th c. from c. 1857 to

hoops

1870, hoops usually consisted of a full-length petticoat made with a series of circular bands gradually increasing in size from top to hem. The hoops could be sewn into a petticoat or, as in the so-called **cage petticoat** or **hoop petticoat** or **skirt supporter,** held in place with vertical tapes making the skirt flexible enough to permit one to sit down. The following were among the most widely used named types of hoops: **cage empire** Made with graduated hoops of steel, shaped into a slight train in back, worn under a ball gown from 1861 to 1869. Also called *cage* or *artificial crinoline* and *skeleton skirt.* **cage-americaine** Hoop-skirt petticoat worn from 1862 to 1869, the upper part made of hoops connected with vertical tapes and lower part covered with fabric. **Empire jupon** (ohm´-peer zhu-pon) Gored petticoat, very full at the hem where two or three steel hoops were inserted, worn under the *Empire dress* of 1867 instead of the *cage petticoat.* Also called *Empire petticoat.* **Imperial skirt** Patented cage-type *hoop* skirt of late 1850s with as many as 32 hoops hung on fabric strips to provide a flexible, lightweight crinoline. **Isabella skirt** Underskirt worn in late 1850s with three small hoops extending one-third of the distance from waist to hem. The remainder of skirt was made with three widely spaced hoops with quilted fabric between. **matinee skirt** Woman's lightweight patented hoop skirt of 1859 made by inserting 11 lightweight hoops into a petticoat. **promenade skirt** Petticoat of 1850s with steel hoops set into muslin worn to support dress. **skirt supporter** Patented elliptical metal *hoop* of late 1850s with two moon-shaped wire metal cages inserted within the hoop—one on either side. Fitted over woman's petticoat just below the waistline to hold out a full skirt.

Imperial skirt See UNDERGARMENTS: HOOPS.

Isabella skirt See UNDERGARMENTS: HOOPS.

Jaeger underclothes (yay´-ger) Type of wool UNION SUIT (see under UNDERGARMENTS) made with hygienic principles in mind. Introduced for men and women by a German, Dr. Gustave Jaeger, in 1880s.

Jockey® shorts Trademark for knitted BRIEFS (see under UNDERGARMENTS).

knickers Woman's below-the-knee-length underpants, originating in 1890s. English term still current and synonymous with any type of underpants.

laced foundation Foundation closed by lacing through eyelets, an early method of fastening still used in some support-types of foundations.

Langtry bustle See UNDERGARMENTS: BUSTLE.

leisure bra Lightweight unconstructed bra, often of stretch lace, designed to be worn at home or when sleeping. Also called *sleep bra.*

linecloths, pair of ∞ Linen DRAWERS (see under UNDERGARMENTS) worn by men in the 15th c.

long handles See UNDERGARMENTS: LONG JOHNS.

long johns Slang term for UNION SUIT or THERMAL UNDERWEAR (see under UNDERGARMENTS) with long legs. Also called *long handles.*

long-leg panty-girdle See UNDERGARMENTS: GIRDLES.

long-line bra Bra that fits the bust or rib cage, extends to waist or below. Worn with girdle to eliminate waistline bulges. Sometimes boned and wired to be worn without straps.

long-line bra-slip A long-line bra attached to a petticoat or half-slip.

mantinee skirt See UNDERGARMENTS: HOOPS.

maternity slip Slip with an elastic panel at mid-section in the front worn by pregnant women.

merry widow Bra and short girdle combined into a minimal support garment. Made of elastic power-net, some versions are made in a lacy pattern with a ruffle and hose supporters at lower edge.

merry widow

minimal bra See UNDERGARMENTS: NUDE BRA.

mini-petti Mid-thigh-length petticoat. Introduced in late 1960s for wear with MINISKIRTS.

mini-pettipants See PETTIPANTS.

natural bra See UNDERGARMENTS: NUDE BRA.

Nelson See UNDERGARMENTS: FRISK.

nude bra Bra made of lightweight nude-colored fabric with no bones, wires, or padding. Also called *natural bra* or *minimal bra.*

oblong hoops   See UNDERGARMENTS: PANNIERS.

one-size bra   See UNDERGARMENTS: STRETCH BRA.

pair of bodies   ∞ Stays or corset worn in the 17th c. stiffened with whalebone, steel, or wood—frequently padded. Sometimes called a *bodice.*

panier/paniers   ∞ (pan-yehr′) French spelling for hoops worn to extend skirts. Worn in France from about 1718 or 1720 until the French Revolution, the earliest styles were *en coupole* (domed-shaped) and *en guéridon* (round-shaped). **Paniers à coudes** (pan-yehr a could) were French paniers of late 1720s that extended wide at the sides and were narrow from front to back. (*Der.* French, "elbows," because the woman's elbows could be rested on

paniers

them.) Toward the middle of the 18th c., paniers were made in two pieces to create a skirt that was wide from side to side. **Paniers à bourelet** (pan-yehr a boor-lay) was a French panier hoop petticoat with a thick roll at the hem to make the skirt flare. By 1750 half paniers, (called *pocket hoops* in England) were worn only for court functions while **considerations**, lightweight paniers worn to extend sides of dresses thereby eliminating need for petticoats, were worn for other occasions. **Paniers anglais** (pan-yehr′ ong′-glaze) was the French term for the English hoop petticoat. This term and the term *pannier* (English spelling) were rarely used in England in the 18th c. Also see UNDERGARMENTS: PANNIERS.

paniers à bourelet   See UNDERGARMENTS: PANNIERS.

paniers à coudes   See UNDERGARMENTS: PANNIERS.

paniers anglais   See UNDERGARMENTS: PANNIERS.

pannier crinoline   See UNDERGARMENTS: BUSTLE.

pannier/panniers   (pan-yehr′) Structure of metal, cane, wire, or wooden hoops for extending a woman's dress at both sides at hip level. Popular from about 1720 to 1789 in France. The word *pannier* (English spelling of the French word *panier*) was seldom used in England, where this garment was called "hoops." Present-day costume historians, however, tend to call all 18th c. hoops by the name panniers or paniers. **Oblong hoops** was a British term used from 1740s to 1760s for panniers on women's gowns that were flattened from front to back and projected sideways over hips and were sometimes hinged to permit passage through narrow doorways. Synonyms were *square hoops* and *false hips.* **Pocket hoops,** a British term, were very small panniers popular in early 1720s, when side hoops were coming into fashion, and in the 1770s, when the style was waning. Also refers to petticoat popular from late 1860s to 1880s. *Der.* Latin, *panarium,* "a basket for bread," so-called because they looked like baskets perched on the hips. Also see UNDERGARMENTS: PANNIERS.

pantalettes   (pan-tah-let′) Women's and girls' underpants with long straight legs ending in ruffles, tucks, and embroidery, which showed below the hem of the dress. From early 1800s to 1840 worn by women and until 1865 by girls. James Monroe's daughter, Maria Hester, is said to have been first person to wear pantalettes in Washington, D.C., in 1807 (she would have been about 8 years old). Also called *pantaloons* when worn by women. [PANTALOONS (see under PANTS) for men were an outergarment.]

pantaloons   **1.** For women, see UNDERGARMENTS: PANTALETTES. **2.** For men, see PANTS: PANTALOONS.

panties   Abbreviated term for women's and children's underpants; garments worn under outer clothing covering torso below the waist. Word came into popular usage in the 1930s. Previously called *drawers.* In the 1980s, some types of briefs and underpants were higher cut, revealing all of the leg. The word "underpants" is used in reference to men's and boys' underwear. Also called PANTY.

pants   Synonym for PANTIES and UNDERPANTS (see under UNDERGARMENTS).

pants liner   Tight-fitting control underpants coming over the knee to the calf or the ankle and worn under pants for a sleek fit.

panty-girdle   See UNDERGARMENTS: GIRDLES.

pantyslip Short petticoat with underpants attached at waistband; a popular style for little girls.

pantywaist ∞ Child's cotton undergarment worn in late 19th and early 20th c. consisting of fitted sleeveless top button-down front. Made with buttons around waistline to attach panties. Also had elastic tabs or garters to hold up long stockings suspender garters. Also called *underwaist* and sold under the trade name *Ferris waist*.

pasties 1. Cups for the breasts that have no straps or back, fastened in place with adhesive. Also called *posts*. 2. Small decorative coverings that adhere over nipples, worn by dancers.

pettibockers ∞ Ankle-length silk-jersey pantaloons worn as underwear by women in early 20th c.

petticoat Undergarment for a woman or girl similar to a slip, but starting at the waist. Depending on the overgarment, it may be full or narrow, lace-trimmed or tailored, and long or short. Originally called an *under-petticoat*, from 16th to 18th c, to distinguish it from *petticoat*, as used in 17th and 18th c. when it referred to the outer, visible skirt of a dress. Current usage dates from the 19th c. Current synonym: *pettiskirt*.

petticoat bodice ∞ 1. Petticoat joined by waistline seam to sleeveless bodice worn from about 1815 until 1890. 2. In 1890, a type of corset cover. See UNDERGARMENTS: CAMISOLE.

petticulottes (pet-tee-koo-loht') Short petticoat and underpants combined in one garment that has flared legs and an inverted pleat in center front and back, frequently lace-trimmed. Also see CULOTTES #3 in alphabetical listing.

pettipants Long dress-length underpants made of plain or bright-colored knits with ruffles and lace trimming, introduced in late 1960s. Also came in mini length, called *mini-pettipants*.

pettiskirt See UNDERGARMENTS: PETTICOAT.

pettiskirt brief Combination petticoat and short underpants joined by elastic waistband.

petti-slip Same as HALF-SLIP or PETTICOAT, (see under UNDERGARMENTS).

pin-in bra Two bra cups fastened together in the center with a piece of elastic, and with two tabs at the sides for pinning to clothing.

plumet petticoat See UNDERGARMENTS: BUSTLE.

plunge bra Bra with deep V-shaped open section in front, separated cups are attached to a band; worn with plunging necklines.

pocket hoops See UNDERGARMENTS: PANNIERS.

posts See UNDERGARMENTS: PASTIES #1.

princess chemise ∞ Woman's undergarment with corset cover and petticoat made in one piece with no waistline seam. Sometimes lavishly trimmed with lace at neckline, armholes, and hem. Worn in late 19th and early 20th c.

princess slip/princess petticoat Slip made in fitted panels from top to hem having no waistline seam, may be flared or straight cut. Called *princess chemise* in 1870s.

promenade skirt See UNDERGARMENTS: HOOPS.

pull-on girdle See UNDERGARMENTS: GIRDLES.

push-up bra Bra with low-cut front and removable foam bust pads to raise the breasts.

rhumba panties Little girls' panties with several rows of ruffles across the seat. *Der.* From ruffled costume worn for South American dance.

rump/rump furbelow ∞ Stuffed pad forming a bustle worn in the late 18th c.

Sarong® (sar-ong') Trademark for a girdle with a lapped front, giving it an appearance similar to a SARONG.

scabilonians ∞ (sca-bill-own'-ee-ans) Man's underpants worn in latter half of 16th c. Also spelled *scavilones*.

shadow-panel slip Slip made with an extra layer of fabric in a panel in front or back to diffuse the light when worn under a sheer dress or skirt.

sherte ∞ Chief male undergarment worn by men from 12th to 16th c., forerunner of modern SHIRT, which was considered an undergarment until the 20th c. Usually called *chemise* until 14th c. Also called *camise*.

shift See UNDERGARMENTS: CHEMISE.

shirt-drawers ∞ Man's combination undershirt and underpants worn in 1890s.

skelton skirt See UNDERGARMENTS: HOOPS.

skirt supporter See UNDERGARMENTS: HOOPS.

skivvies/skivvy Slang for a man's underwear, usually referring to shorts and top. *Der.* skivy, a sailor's term for an undershirt.

sleep bra See UNDERGARMENTS: LEISURE BRA.

slip **1.** Undergarment, beginning above the bust, worn by women and girls usually held in place with shoulder straps. Length is long or short in relation to the dress worn on top. Current meaning of the word dates from the early 19th c. **2.** ∞ 18th c. type of corset cover.

slip-blouse See UNDERGARMENTS: BLOUSE-SLIP.

smock See UNDERGARMENTS: CHEMISE.

snap pants Waterproof panty for infants with snaps at the crotch.

snip slip Slip finished with three rows of hemstitching around bottom. One or more rows may be cut off to adjust length.

snuggies Knee-length or over-the-knee underpants made of knitted cotton, worn for warmth with matching tank-top undershirt.

snuggies

sport bra/Sport Bra® A bra with built-up straps, coming over shoulders forming a crablike shape in back, secured by an elastic band around the body. Worn for active sports. Also a trademarked V-back bra.

sport bra

square hoops See UNDERGARMENTS: PANNIERS.

stays ∞ Earlier term for corset made very rigid with iron or whalebone. Made like a bodice laced up back with scoop neckline in front, higher in back, with shoulder straps set wide in front.

step-ins Woman's underpants with widely flared legs and narrow crotch, popular in 1920s and 1930s. Also called DANCE SET in the 1920s.

strapless bra **1.** Bra constructed so that it stays in place without straps over the shoulders. Popular since 1940s using boning or wire cups. **2.** See UNDERGARMENTS: LONG-LINE, TUBE and WIRED BRAS.

strapless slip Bra-top slip made with elastic, boning, and detachable or no straps.

stretch bra Bra made of fabric knitted with spandex. Elastic straps permit great freedom of movement. Often made in only one size, sometimes in pullover style with no fastening. Also called ONE-SIZE BRA.

stretch brief/control brief Stretch panty or girdle with detachable garters offering light control.

string bikini Minimum underpants consisting of two small triangular pieces attached to a band of elastic worn low on the hips.

suit slip Slip with white top and dark skirt worn under dark suit and sheer or white blouse.

swanbill corset ∞ Back-laced woman's corset of mid-1870s with long metal bone in front that curves outward over lower abdomen.

swimbra Molded cups, attached or separate, used inside a bathing suit to shape the bosom.

tailored slip Slip made with cording, appliqué, or tucks as trim, rather than lace. Popular in 1940s, revived in early 1970s and after.

tap panty Panty styled like short shorts with a slight flare at hem. May be made of satin or floral print with lace-trim. Frequently made with matching camisole and then called *cami-tap set.*

teardrop bra Minimal bra with triangular cups; looks like the upper part of a bikini swimsuit.

teddy **1.** Straight-cut garment of 1920s, combining a CAMISOLE (see under UNDERGARMENTS) with short slip, or long vest with underpants. Wide strap is attached to the front and back at the hem, thus making separate openings for each leg. **2.** As revived in late 1960s and 1980s and since, becoming a one-piece tight-fitting minimal garment with a low-cut front and back and high-cut leg openings.

teddy #1

tee shirt See UNDERGARMENTS: T-SHIRT.

teen bra Bra with shallow cups designed for the young girl whose breasts are not fully developed. Also called *training bra.*

tights **1.** Underpants and stockings knit in one piece, worn originally by athletes, circus performers, and dancers in late 19th c. with a LEOTARD. Now worn by women and children in variety of natural or manufactured fiber knits in many colors for all occasions. **2.** LEOTARD with legs and sometimes feet added. **3.** Women's and girl's below-the-knee underpants made fine-ribbed knit in either black or white, worn in early 20th c.

thermal underwear Long-sleeved undershirt and long-legged pants or one-piece UNION SUIT (see under UNDERGARMENTS) made of knitted cotton, wool, blends of these fibers, or polypropylene for winter, particularly for sports.

thong Rudi Gernreich design of 1975 for what was variously described as "a virtually bottomless bathing suit" or a "glorified jockstrap" cut to reveal as much of the buttocks as possible while covering the crotch. Now a common cut for underwear.

torsolette See UNDERGARMENTS: BUSTIER.

tournure See UNDERGARMENTS: BUSTLE.

tournure and petticoat See UNDERGARMENTS: BUSTLE.

tournure corset ∞ (toor-nure′) Laced foundation garment with straps over shoulders and hip-length underskirt of stiff fabric intended to hold out the skirt. Worn in late 1850s over the CHEMISE (see under UNDERGARMENTS).

training bra See UNDERGARMENTS: TEEN BRA.

trouses/trowses ∞ (trouz) Underpants or drawers worn by Englishmen under the TRUNK HOSE in 16th and 17th c.

trunks Loose-fitting underpants cut similar to men's shorts.

T-shirt/tee shirt Originally a man's undershirt with short sleeves and high round neck, forming a T-shape, usually made in white cotton knit. Adapted for sportswear by men, women, and children. Also see SHIRTS: T-SHIRT/TEE SHIRT.

T-shirt

tube bra Strapless circular stretch bra with no closing; must be put on over the head.

two-way stretch foundation Stretch garment made of SPANDEX with a satin panel in front.

umbrella drawers ∞ Women's wide bell-shaped DRAWERS of late 19th and early 20th c., trimmed with tucks, insertion, and lace.

underpants Garment for lower half of the body with separate space for insertion of each leg. Made in many different styles. Also see UNDERGARMENTS: PANTIES.

under-petticoat ∞ Term for white cambric, flannel, or skirt of poorer quality fabric worn under dress skirt or under hoops from 16th through 18th c.

undershirt 1. Man's knitted shirt, usually white cotton, with U-neckline continued into built-up straps, or with short sleeves and crew or V-neckline, worn underneath outer shirt or sweater. See UNDERGARMENTS: ATHLETIC SHIRT and T-SHIRT. **2.** Woman's knitted garment usually of cotton or cotton and wool, shaped like a man's undershirt. **3.** Infant's knitted wool or cotton shirt, in four styles: (a) double-breasted, fastened with grippers; (b) high-necked cardigan-style, usually with long sleeves; (c) similar to man's undershirt; (d) sleeved, with lapped shoulders that stretch to permit easy passage over head. Also called *vest.*

underwaist See UNDERGARMENTS: PANTYWAIST.

under-waistcoat ∞ Undergarment worn by men in last half of 18th c. for warmth. Usually made of flannel.

union suit One-piece knitted undergarment buttoned up center front, introduced in 1880s and made with short or long legs, short or long sleeves, and a drop seat. Worn for warmth. Worn by all ages until 1940s, now mainly used under ski or other winter sports' clothing. Long-legged underwear is often nicknamed *long johns* or *long-handles.* Also see UNDERGARMENTS: JAEGER SUIT, ENVELOPE COMBINATION, and THERMAL UNDERWEAR.

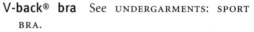
union suit

V-back® bra See UNDERGARMENTS: SPORT BRA.

vest 1. Woman's undershirt usually made of knitted rayon or nylon styled with built-up straps or a CAMISOLE top (see under UNDERGARMENTS). **2.** See UNDERGARMENTS: UNDERSHIRT #3.

V top Upper part of slip or other undergarment cut in the shape of a deep V.

U

waist-cincher   See UNDERGARMENTS: FRENCH CINCH.

waist watcher   Wide band, reaching from ribs to top of hips, made of spongy stretch fabric secured with VELCRO®. Worn by men and women to pull in the waist and as an aid in reducing the size of the waistline.

wired bra   Bra with fabric-covered wire under or over the breasts to give added support; often strapless.

zipper foundation   Foundation with zipper placed in center front rather than at side.

zippered girdle   Girdle usually made of two-way stretch and nonstretch panels closed with zippered placket for firmer support.

---

underground fashion   Clothes in bizarre colors and extreme shapes worn in 1965 by avant-garde people who attended private showings of unconventional "underground movies" of the day shown in beatnik-type bars and coffee houses.

underpants   See UNDERGARMENTS.

under petticoat   See UNDERGARMENTS.

underpropper   See NECKLINES AND COLLARS: RUFF.

undershirt   See UNDERGARMENTS.

undershirt dress   Simple knit dress similar to T-SHIRT DRESS with a bound neckline and tiny placket opening in front. Introduced by Courréges in 1969 and popularly accepted in 1970.

undershirt sweater   See SWEATERS.

underskirt   **1.** See UNDERGARMENTS: SLIP or PETTICOAT. **2.** See SKIRTS.

undersleeve   See ENGAGEANTES.

undersplit   See LEATHERS.

undervest   ∞ British term from 1840s for undershirt. See UNDERGARMENTS: UNDERSHIRT #1.

underwaist   See UNDERGARMENTS: PANTYWAIST.

under-waistcoat   **1.** See VESTS. **2.** See UNDERGARMENTS.

underwear   See UNDERGARMENTS.

undress   ∞ Ordinary or unceremonial dress for man or woman as contrasted with formal wear. Term used in 18th and 19th c., particularly in England. Also see NEGLIGÉE COSTUME.

U-neckline   See NECKLINES AND COLLARS: HORSESHOE NECKLINE.

uneven plaid   See PLAIDS AND TARTANS: EVEN PLAID.

Ungaro, Emanuel   * See APPENDIX/DESIGNERS.

uniform   **1.** Any specific type of apparel required for wear by the armed forces of any country; for a specialized occupation, by a school, or for competitive team sports such as baseball, football, and hockey. Probably originated in antiquity with costumes worn by personal bodyguards of monarchs. Worn by the Greek and Roman armies and since then by armed forces throughout the world. **2.** Worn throughout history to denote status or trade of an individual. See BLUE-APRONED MEN. **3.** Worn as LIVERY, particularly in France and England.

Union Nationale Artisanale de la Couture et des Activitiés Connexes   See FÉDÉRATION FRANÇAISE DE COUTURE, DU PRÊT-À-PORTER DES COUTURIERS ET DES CRÉATEURS DE MODE.

Union of Needletrades, Industrial, and Textile Employees (UNITE)   Labor union formed by a merger in 1995 of the Amalgamated Clothing and Textile Workers Union and the International Ladies Garment Workers Union (ILGWU). UNITE now also represents the industrial laundry industry. The ILGWU was founded in 1900 and was famous for the militancy of its early organizational drives, fight against sweatshop conditions, housing, educational, cultural programs, and medical services to members. David Dubinsky, elected president of the union in 1932, remained in office for thirty-four years and became a major figure in U.S. politics.

union suit   See UNDERGARMENTS,

unisex fashions/unisex look   Garments designed so that they may be worn by either men or women. Included shirts laced at the neckline, pants with drawstrings, and double-breasted jackets with buttons and buttonholes on both sides so they could be buttoned to the right or left. Introduced in 1968, it became a popular look, particularly with young people.

unisex look

In the 1980s, popular for sweatsuits and sweaters. Items were featured both in department stores and boutiques. Also see HIS-AND-HER LOOK. See PANTS: DRAWSTRING PANTS and SHIRTS: UNISEX SHIRTS.

unitard See ACTIVEWEAR.

UNITE See UNION OF NEEDLETRADES, INDUSTRIAL, AND TEXTILE EMPLOYEES.

United States Customs Service U.S. Department of Treasury agency responsible for the administration of import-export regulations and the implementation of tariff duties, quotas, and labeling requirements.

United States Harmonized Tariff Schedule (USHTS)/harmonized system Tariff nomenclature and categories that provide a list of all imports that are subject to tariff. Developed to simplify importing by using the same terminology and classifications for all importing countries rather than having different systems for each.

unit production system (UPS) Garment manufacturing system in which one garment at a time is transported on a conveyer belt to a sewing operator who performs one or more sewing operations, then forwards the garment to the next workstation for the next construction step.

Universal Product Code (UPC) Standard for bar-coded information on products that allows rapid optical scanning and computerized control of products. Used in management of textile and apparel merchandise and especially in QUICK RESPONSE and JUST-IN-TIME systems.

university coat See COATS AND JACKETS: ANGLE-FRONTED COAT.

university vest See VESTS.

unmentionables/unwhisperables See INEXPRESSIBLES.

UPC See UNIVERSAL PRODUCT CODE.

updated classics Apparel items that are derived from some classic style (examples: chemise, shirtwaist, cardigan, blazer) and changed in some way to give them a more contemporary appearance.

upper See FOOTWEAR.

upper garment ∞ British term used from 17th c. for outer garments such as a cloak, cassock, or gown that indicated dress of a gentleman. Without upper garment, gentleman was said to be "in QUERPO."

upper stocks See TRUNK HOSE.

UPS See UNIT PRODUCTION SYSTEM.

upsweep See HAIRSTYLES.

Ural emerald See GEMS, GEM CUTS, AND SETTINGS: ANDRADITE GARNET.

urchin cut See HAIRSTYLES: GAMINE.

usage The number of yards of fabric required to make a particular garment style.

U seams See HOSIERY.

USHTS See UNITED STATES HARMONIZED TARIFF SCHEDULE.

Ussurian raccoon See FURS.

utchat See JEWELRY: NECKLACE.

utility boot See FOOTWEAR: BOOTS.

V

vair See FUR.

Val/Valenciennes lace See LACES.

Valentino ✱ See APPENDIX/DESIGNERS.

vallancy See WIGS AND HAIRPIECES.

Valois hat See HEADWEAR.

vambrace See ARMOR.

vamp See FOOTWEAR

vamprey See FOOTWEAR: VAMP.

vandyke **1.** Adjective applied to items of clothing inspired by or copied from clothing in portraits by early 17th-c. Flemish artist Sir Anthony Van Dyke. **2.** See NECKLINES AND COLLARS: RUFF. **3.** Lace-bordered handkerchief.

vandyke beard See BEARD.

vandyking Decorative trims or lace with a pronounced V or saw-toothed edge.

vandyking

vane See introduction to FEATHERS.

vanity **1.** Small metal or plastic case, carried in woman's handbag, containing face powder and sometimes rouge or other cosmetics. **2.** See HANDBAGS AND RELATED ACCESSORIES.

varens See COATS AND JACKETS.

vareuse See COATS AND JACKETS.

variegated Having an unevenly colored, spotted, or streaked appearance.

varsity jacket See COATS AND JACKETS: BASEBALL JACKET.

varsity sweater See SWEATERS: LETTER SWEATER.

vasquine See BASQUINE.

Vassar blouse See BLOUSES AND TOPS.

V-back bra See UNDERGARMENTS: SPORT® BRA.

vegetable ivory See IVORY.

vegetable tanning See LEATHERS.

veil/veils See HEADWEAR.

veiling † Nets of various sizes made in different constructions to form open-weave fabrics that are used for trimming on hats.

Velcro® See CLOSURES.

veldtschoen construction See FOOTWEAR.

velour † (ve-loor′) Soft, velvety thick fabric with a cut pile brushed in one direction. It may be made of various fibers and yarns. Originally a woven fabric, now made by either weaving or knitting. Used for coats, warm-up suits, knit shirts, and dresses.

velvet † A fabric with a short, closely woven pile created from extra lengthwise yarns. Usually the pile is cut to create a soft, rich texture, but sometimes patterns are created by cutting some of the pile yarns and not others. Used for dressy clothing and evening wear.

velveteen † Cut-pile cotton or cotton blend fabric in which the pile is made with an extra crosswise yarn. The pile is not more than $1/8''$ high and the most durable of these fabrics have twill woven background. Used for dresses, suits, and sportswear.

vendeuse (vahn-duze′) French term for saleswoman employed at a couture house in Paris.

vendor The individual or company from which raw materials or finished goods are purchased. Synonyms: *source, supplier.*

vendor-induced incentives Inducements provided by a vendor to a retailer or store personnel (see SPIFFS) that will influence the sale of the vendor's products. These can include such services as training, TRUNK SHOWS, educational material, and contests.

vendor-managed retail inventory Programs developed between a vendor and a retailer in which retail sales and stock data are reviewed by the manufacturer and additional merchandise is provided as required.

vendor marking Provision of and attaching by the supplier of hangtags, labels, and price tags.

vendor matrix A list provided by the retail company to its buyers of approved suppliers. Also called *key resource list.*

venetian-blind pleats See CLOTHING CONSTRUCTION DETAILS.

venetian cloak See CAPES, CLOAKS, AND SHAWLS.

venetian lace See LACES.

venetian ladder work See EMBROIDERIES AND SEWING STITCHES.

venetian point lace See LACES.

venetians See TRUNK HOSE.

venetian sleeve See SHOULDERS AND SLEEVES.

venetian slops See TRUNK HOSE.

Venet, Philippe * See APPENDIX/DESIGNERS.

venise, point de See LACES.

vent Term used since 15th c. to indicate vertical slit in garment, usually from hem upward. Used, for example, in coats, gloves, jackets, shirts, and suit coats.

ventail See ARMOR.

ventilated collar See CLERICAL DRESS.

verdugale/verdugalle/verdugado/verdugo See FARTHINGALE.

veronese cuirasse ∞ (ver-o-naze′-eh kwe-rass′) Wool jersey knit bodice laced up the back that was fashionable in 1880s.

veronese dress ∞ (ver-o-naze′-e) Daytime dress of 1880s with knee-length PRINCESS-style woolen tunic ending in deep points over silk underskirt with large box pleats around hem.

Veronica Lake hairstyle See HAIRSTYLES.

Versace, Donatella * See APPENDIX/DESIGNERS.

Versace, Gianni * See APPENDIX/DESIGNERS.

vertical integration The combining under the management of one company a number of production stages that might formerly have been done by different companies. For example, a textile industry firm might produce fiber, spin yarns, weave fabrics, and manufacture apparel.

vertically worked See FURS.

vertugale Also spelled *vertugadin, verdugale, verdyngale, vertugade, vertingale.* See FARTHINGALE.

vestee ∞ Woman's decorative front or half vest attached around neck and by ties around waist. Worn under a jacket instead of a blouse in 19th c. Also called *chemisette.*

vestido See VESTS.

vestments **1.** Items of wearing apparel worn particularly for ecclesiastical services and by clergy. See CLERICAL DRESS: CLERICAL VESTMENTS. **2.** Ceremonial or official robe.

vest pocket See POCKETS.

VESTS

vest **1.** An item of wearing apparel extending to the waist or below that is similar to a sleeveless jacket. Usually worn over a blouse or shirt and sometimes under a suit jacket. Also called a *waistcoat* and *weskit.* **2.** ∞ An accessory worn by women as a fill-in for a low neckline, or as a substitute for a blouse in 19th and early 20th cs. **3.** See UNDERGARMENTS.

adjustable vest Man's front-buttoned vest that fits around the neck halter style and is held on by a band around the waist fastening in center back with a buckle. Worn by men with formal wear (e.g., dinner jacket or tuxedo).

Afghanistan vest Vest made of curly lamb tanned and worn with smooth embroidered skin side out showing edges of curly lamb. An ethnic fashion popular in the late 1960s. *Der.* Copied from vests worn by natives in Afghanistan.

bag-waistcoat ∞ Man's vest, full in front and bloused to form a pouch, worn in 1883.

benjy ∞ (ben′-gee) British slang term used in the 19th c. for a man's waistcoat or vest.

buckskin vest Vest made of sueded deerskin or sheepskin, frequently laced rather than buttoned, trimmed with self fringe at hem and shoulders. Style popular in America since colonial days.

clayshooter's vest Sleeveless jacket designed by Bob Lee with belted back, leather piping, and large side pockets; suitable for sportswear or shooting mark or clay pigeons. Main feature is a quilted leather pad at shoulder to absorb recoil of gun. Vest features a secret pocket for holding wallets and keys.

down vest Quilted vest fastened with snaps, toggles, or a zipper. Interlined for warmth with down quilted to the lining and outer fabric. Popular in late 1970s and after for general outerwear.

down vest

electric vest Vest with a lining that reflects 80% of body's heat. Special built-in electric heating system operated by batteries (concealed in left pocket) is located at the center of the lower back.

fisherman's vest Waist-length sportsman's vest usually made of khaki-colored cotton duck worn over other clothes when fishing. Has many pockets—two larger zip or snap pockets near hem and small pockets on chest to stow gear when fishing.

flotation vest Lightweight flexible vest with zip front made with shell of tear-resistant nylon filled with polyethylene foam quilted together in wide vertical panels. Worn for all recreational boating purposes as a life-saving device.

French opening vest ∞ Man's vest of 1840s cut low enough to reveal a large part of the shirt front.

French vest ∞ Man's high-buttoned vest of the 1860s with small lapels not turned over.

gilet ∞ (zhee-lay′) Vest or short waistcoat worn by men in the 1850s and 1860s.

golf vest ∞ Man's knitted, wool single-breasted vest of mid-1890s made with braid-trimming, without a collar, and with three pockets—one on each side plus watch pocket.

hug-me-tight Knitted or quilted vest with V-neck buttoned down front. Usually worn by older people under coats for extra warmth.

hunting vest Front-buttoned sportsman's vest worn over a hunting shirt. Made of cotton duck fabric with large rubber-lined game pocket.

jerkin **1.** Contemporary synonym for *vest, waistcoat,* and *weskit.* First made in buckskin by American colonists. **2.** ∞ Man's sleeved jacket worn over doublet, sometimes laced or buttoned up front, sometimes sleeveless with shoulder wings; worn from late 15th through 16th c.

jockey waistcoat ∞ Straight-hanging man's vest or waistcoat with a low standing collar, similar to Chinese collar. Worn from 1806 and revived in 1880s.

newmarket vest ∞ Plaid or checked vest, buttoned high, made with or without flapped pockets, worn by sportsmen in mid-1890s.

Pakistani vest Fitted vest with long gold-braided shawl collar, fastened in front with invisible hooks, and elaborately trimmed around edges with wide gilt braid, mirrors, and tassels. Originally called *Pakistani wedding vest*—part of fad for ethnic fashions in late 1960s.

potholder vest Handmade sleeveless crocheted vest made with built-up straps over the shoulders and crocheted "granny squares" in front and back.

reversible vest Any vest that can be worn on both sides using different fabrics on each side (e.g., plain and plaid or corduroy and paisley print). Man's four-piece suit usually has a reversible vest with each side made to match the different fabric of the two pairs of trousers.

Shakespeare vest ∞ Man's single- or double-breasted vest of mid-1870s with narrow lapels and a turndown collar similar to Shakespeare collar. See NECKLINES AND COLLARS: SHAKESPEARE COLLAR #3.

shawl waistcoat ∞ **1.** Man's vest with shawl collar worn in the 19th c. **2.** Man's vest sometimes cut out of a fabric with a printed or woven design normally used for shawls. **3.** A man's vest, sometimes actually made from a woman's shawl.

shawl waistcoat c. 1830s

suit vest Matching or contrasting vest sold with a man's suit. Usually styled with V-neck, six buttons, and two or four pockets. The back is made of lining material and has an adjustable belt. Sometimes copied for women and children.

suit vest

sweater-vest See SWEATERS: VEST SWEATER.

tattersall vest Man's vest in small checked fabric made single-breasted with six buttons, no collar, and four flapped pockets. Worn by sportsmen in mid-1890s and later worn with riding habit or with man's sport coat. *Der.* Named after Richard Tattersall, British horseman, founder of Tattersall's London Horse Auction Mart established in 1776.

under waistcoat Man's short sleeveless vest, introduced in 1790, fashionable in contrasting fabrics from 1825 to 1840, worn under the waistcoat. Survives in England for men's formal wear as waistcoat with WHITE SLIP.

university vest ∞ Double-breasted waistcoat of early 1870s made with sides cut away from lowest button and fashionable with UNIVERSITY COAT (see under COATS AND JACKETS: ANGLE-FRONTED COAT).

vestido (ves-ti'-doe) Long, handwoven wool, thigh-length vest with a fringed hem from the Southwest United States and Mexico. *Der.* Spanish and Mexican word for vest.

waistcoat/weskit See VESTS.

white vest Vest worn by men for dress under a SWALLOW-TAILED COAT (see under COATS AND JACKETS). It is cut low in front, showing the formal shirt and white tie.

---

vestsuit Pants and vest designed to be worn together. A full-sleeved blouse or shirt is worn underneath the sleeveless vest. Popular in 1960s.

vest sweater See SWEATERS.

Vibram® See FOOTWEAR.

vici kid See LEATHERS.

VICS See VOLUNTARY INTER-INDUSTRY COMMUNICATIONS STANDARDS COMMITTEE.

Victoria (1819–1901) Queen of Great Britain 1837–1901, married Albert of Saxe-Coburg-Gotha, who took the title of Prince Consort. She assumed the British throne when only eighteen and reigned for sixty-four years. Styles in fashion and the arts that are derived from or inspired by those popular during her reign are called **Victorian**. Period was noted for conservative social values and excessively decorated designs. See BLOUSES AND TOPS: VICTORIAN BLOUSE, NECKLINES AND COLLARS: CHOKER COLLAR, and SHOULDERS AND SLEEVES: SABOT SLEEVE.

Victorian See VICTORIA.

victorine See CAPES, CLOAKS, AND SHAWLS: PALATINE ROYAL.

victory stripes See PRINTS, STRIPES, AND CHECKS: HICKORY STRIPES.

vicuña † (vi-koon'-yah) Hair fiber from the vicuña, a species related to the llama, which is one of the softest fibers known. Colors range from golden chestnut to deep fawn. In spite of attempts to domesticate the animals, most of the fiber must still be obtained by hunting and killing them. The Peruvian government limits the number of animals that can be hunted, therefore the fiber supply is very limited and very expensive.

video catalog A catalog reproduced on a videocassette or disk that is sent to customers. A precursor to online shopping, customers viewed the catalog on a VCR and could telephone the retailer to place orders.

vinaigrette ∞ (vin-ay-gret') Small bottles attached to metal chains carried by women or attached to handbags in 19th c. Used to hold some aromatic (e.g., vinegar or smelling salts, used to revive women if they felt faint).

vintage look/vintage fashions Clothes and accessories from another era refurbished and sold in department stores or specialty shops (e.g., Victorian, Edwardian, and twenties dresses—plus items such as beaded bags and antique jewelry). Called by this name in 1980s. Formerly called FLEA MARKET LOOK and ATTIC LOOK.

vinyl Manufactured material that is a tough, flexible, shiny, elastic, nonporous plastic and can be made to be colored or transparent. Used for fabric coating and to produce materials resembling leather for boots, capes, gloves, raincoats, shoes, etc.

vinyl raincoat See COATS AND JACKETS.

violin bodice ∞ Long bodice, reaching to the knees in back, worn over the dress in 1874. Made in PRINCESS style with violin-shaped dark fabric insert in the back.

Vionnet, Madeleine * See APPENDIX/DESIGNERS.

virago sleeve See SHOULDERS AND SLEEVES.

virtual factory System of garment production controlled from a central computer. Electronic communications technologies make it possible

V

for different stages of production to be completed in various locations. For example, designs may be created in one location, construction in another, and the product shipped to yet another.

visa In international trade, a document provided by an exporting country that specifies country of origin of a product.

viscose rayon † (vis′-kos) Rayon fiber regenerated through the viscose process from wood pulp or cotton fibers too short to be spun. This process produces pollutants that are hard to eliminate, therefore production in the United States has been sharply reduced. The fiber is used for a wide variety of apparel because it can be dyed or printed in attractive colors and patterns, drapes well, and is comfortable to wear; however, if not given special finishes, it has a tendency to shrink and to wrinkle.

visite See CAPES, CLOAKS, AND SHAWLS.

visiting dress ∞ Used throughout the 19th c. for woman's costume worn especially for making calls in the afternoon. Also called *visiting costume* and *visiting toilette.*

vison European name for *mink.* See FURS: MINK.

visor 1. See HEADWEAR. 2. See ARMOR.

visual merchandising The visible environment of a retail store that contributes to the promotion and sale of merchandise. Included are the exterior appearance of the store, window displays, interior décor, signage, lighting, and displays of merchandise.

Viyella® † (vy′-ella) Trademark of Williams Hollins and Co. for a lightweight British fabric made of a yarn blended of 50% cotton and 50% wool. Also made in a twill weave in several weights and used for shirts, dresses, pajamas, and underwear. Also called *Viyella® flannel.*

V-look/V shape Overall style consisting of huge shoulders and oversized top tapering to a narrow skirt at the hem. Shoulders and dolman (or batwing) sleeves were sometimes cut in one piece so

V-look or V-shape

that sleeves at elbow sloped into side seam at waist. Other styles were made with extended padded shoulders and large armholes usually with sleeves of generous proportions. Introduced in 1983, causing tops of clothing to be very wide and full.

V-neckline See NECKLINES AND COLLARS.

Vogue Fashion magazine first published as a weekly in December of 1892—in 1910 became a bi-monthly. Arthur Baldwin Turnure was its founder and publisher. Bought by Condé Nast in 1909. Published both in France and Great Britain in the 1920s. Edna Woolman Chase was the editor from 1914 until 1951.

voile † (voyle) Lightweight open-weave fabric made of tightly twisted combed yarns that give it a crisp and wiry feel. Originally made only of cotton but now popular in blends of cotton/polyester. Used for dresses, blouses, and some men's shirts.

Volendam cap See HEADWEAR: DUTCH CAP.

Voluntary Inter-Industry Communications Standards Committee (VICS) Formed in 1986 by retailers and manufacturers in the textile and apparel industries to develop standardization of electronic data communication, including the use of UNIVERSAL PRODUCT CODE system and electronic data interchange formats.

Von Furstenberg, Diane * See APPENDIX/DESIGNERS.

Vreeland, Diana Dalziel (1906–1989) Dynamic fashion authority who went to work for *Harper's Bazaar* in 1937, becoming fashion editor in six months. Left to become associate editor of *Vogue* magazine in 1962, becoming editor-in-chief until 1971. After that, she acted as consulting editor to *Vogue* and consultant to the Costume Institute of Metropolitan Museum of Art, where she supervised outstanding exhibitions including subjects such as *Balenciaga, American Women of Style, The Glory of Russian Costume, Vanity Fair,* and *Yves Saint Laurent.*

V-shape See V-LOOK.

V-top See UNDERGARMENTS.

Vuitton, Louis * See APPENDIX/DESIGNERS.

vulcanized shoe construction See FOOTWEAR.

vulture-winged headdress See HEADWEAR.

W **1.** Large-size pictorial fashion magazine that covers American and couture fashions, fashionable personalities, social events, and other articles of particular interest to women. Published monthly by Fairchild Publications. **2.** Shoe width designation for a wide shoe, equivalent to a D.

wadded hem Hem that has been padded with wide band of CORDING. Used in 1820s and used occasionally on contemporary dresses and robes.

wadding Loosely connected fibers in sheet form used for shoulder pads in coats and suits. Also see FIBERFILL.

wadded hem

waders See FOOTWEAR.

waffle cloth/waffle pique † Cotton fabric made in a honeycomb weave. See HONEYCOMB.

waist **1.** Narrowest part of the torso. **2.** See BLOUSES AND TOPS. **3.** See FOOTWEAR.

waistband **1.** Band of fabric, usually faced and interfaced, seamed to waistline of skirt or pants and fastened to hold garment firmly around waist. **2.** See WAIST-LINES: SET-IN WAISTLINE

waistband #1

waist-cincher See UNDERGARMENTS: FRENCH CINCH.

waistcoat **1.** Term synonymous with VEST (see category of VESTS) in contemporary styles. Other synonyms include *jerkin* and *weskit*. **2.** ∞ From 16th c. to 1668, a man's garment either worn for warmth under the DOUBLET—it was waist-length, quilted—or worn to complete a costume, and then made of decorative fabric. Also called a *petticoat*. **3.** ∞ From 1668 on, a man's undercoat cut along the same lines as the outer coat. It was made either with or without sleeves until 1750, after which waistcoats were sleeveless. Gradually became shorter in the 18th c., becoming waist-length in 1790. Predominantly single-breasted until 1730s, then more likely to be double-breasted in 1780s and 1790s, with both styles common in the 19th c. **4.** ∞ 17th-c. Woman's bodice buttoned in front and worn with a dress. **5.** ∞ Latter half of the 18th c., woman's clothing similar in style to a man's waistcoat of the same date, worn with a riding habit. **6.** See UNDERGARMENTS. **7.** ∞ In 1851, elaborately brocaded outer-garment worn by women with a CARRIAGE DRESS. **8.** ∞ In 1880s and 1890s, a fill-in VESTEE worn by women with a suit or TAILOR-MADE costume. Also see category of VESTS.

waistcoat paletot See COATS AND JACKETS.
waistcoat pocket See POCKETS: VEST POCKET.
waist length See LENGTHS.

WAISTLINES

waistline **1.** Place on the torso where the belt is located. **2.** Horizontal seam joining the top and skirt of a dress if the garment is made in two pieces. Waistlines are not necessarily located at the anatomical waist.

cinched waistline Waistline pulled in very tightly, usually with a wide belt.
corselet waistline (kors'-let) Pulled in waistline usually made by wearing a wide belt that

generally laced in the front and was frequently used on peasant-style dresses.

Directoire waistline See WAISTLINES: EMPIRE WAISTLINE. *Der.* Named for Directoire period in France, 1795–1799.

drawstring waistline Waistline with a cord or belt drawn through a casing, heading, or beading, to gather the fullness when tightened and tied in a bow or knot. Also called *tunnel waistline.* Also see WAISTLINES: PAPERBAG WAISTLINE.

drawstring waistline

dropped waistline Waistline seam placed below the natural waistline.

elasticized waistline A waistline used for pull-on pants, skirts, and also dresses that may be made in three ways: (a) Elastic inserted through a casing. (b) Elastic sewn to the garment fabric. The elastic is stretched to the size of the fabric, sewn down with two or more rows of stitching, thereby causing the fabric to gather. (c) Elastic stitched directly to the fabric at a waistline; used mainly for dresses with a waistline seam, for panties, and for halfslips.

dropped waistline

Empire waistline (em′-pire or ohm-peer′) High-waisted effect with seam placed directly under bust. This was the predominant waistline placement from the late 18th c. to 1820s during Empire and Directoire periods in France, and has been popular periodically since then for women's dresses, coats, and lingerie. It derives from attempts to imitate the styles of the ancient Greeks and Romans.

Empire waistline

high-rise Used to describe any waistline higher than the natural waistline.

low rise/low-slung waistline Used to describe any waistline placed below the normal waistline, usually for hip-hugger skirts or pants.

natural waistline Belt or seam placed at narrowest part of the torso; the anatomical waistline.

paperbag waistline Made by inserting a drawstring through a casing placed far enough below the top edge of the garment in order to create a small stand-up ruffle around the waist. Introduced in early 1980s and used for pants, shorts, and skirts.

paperbag waistline

princess waistline Fitted waistline with no waistline seam. Garment is cut in panels from neck to hem and fitted by shaping the vertical seams. First appeared in the 1860s and popular periodically ever since. *Der.* Claimed to have been introduced about 1860 by French couturier Charles Frederick Worth in a morning dress for Empress Eugénie, hence the name "princess."

set-in waistline Horizontal panel of fabric used at waistline of dress, fitted between top and skirt, making two seams—one at or below normal waistline and one higher.

set-in waistline

tunnel waistline See WAISTLINES: DRAWSTRING WAISTLINE.

---

waist watcher See UNDERGARMENTS.

wale † **1.** Textile term for woven ridge in fabric running either vertically (e.g., in Bedford cord and corduroy); crosswise in faille; or diagonally in twills (e.g., gabardine and whipcord). **2.** Knitting term for row of loops or stitches running lengthwise.

walking Adjective used to describe items of apparel used or worn while walking. See COATS AND JACKETS: WALKING COAT, FOOTWEAR: WALKING SHOE and WALKERS, SHORTS: BERMUDA SHORTS, UMBRELLAS AND PARASOLS: WALKING PARASOL, and CANES: WALKING STICK, in alphabetical listing.

walking costume/walking dress See PROMENADE COSTUME.

walking stick See CANE.

walking suit **1.** Woman's three-quarter-length coat, sometimes fur-trimmed, worn with a matching skirt; often made of tweed. **2.** ∞ Woman's suit worn in 1901 with skirt just brushing the ground.

wallaby See LEATHERS.

Wallace Beery shirt See SHIRTS.

walled toe See FOOTWEAR.

wallet See HANDBAGS AND RELATED ACCESSORIES.

W

wallpaper print See PRINTS, STRIPES, AND CHECKS.

walrus mustache See MUSTACHE.

waltz length See LENGTHS.

wamus See COATS AND JACKETS.

Wang, Vera * See APPENDIX/DESIGNERS.

wardrobe **1.** All the clothing belonging to an individual. **2.** ∞ 15th-c. term for room where clothing was kept. **3.** From 19th c. on, piece of furniture used to contain clothing.

warehouse retailer Retailer who combines showroom, warehouse, and retail operations together in order to reduce operating expenses and offer apparel at discount prices.

warm-up jacket/warm-up pants See ACTIVEWEAR: WARM-UP.

warp/warp yarns † Lengthwise direction in fabric, or yarns that run lengthwise, parallel to SELVAGE.

warp print See PRINTS, STRIPES, AND CHECKS.

warranty/warrantee Written document that ensures the life of a product for a specific period of time. See GUARANTEE.

wash-and-wear **1.** See DURABLE PRESS. **2.** See HAIRSTYLES.

washed gold See JEWELRY.

watch bracelet See JEWELRY and WATCHES: BRACELET WATCH.

watch cap See HEADWEAR.

watch chain A decorative chain attached to a man's pocketwatch, often embellished with seals or emblems. When watch is worn in vest pocket, chain may be pulled through vest buttonhole and end tucked into pocket on opposite side.

watch coat See COATS AND JACKETS.

WATCHES

watch Timepiece usually carried in pocket or worn on a band at wrist. A fashionable accessory since 16th c. when it was usually carried in a pocket. In late 19th c. women wore watches that dangled from pins. The wristwatch was developed before World War I. In 1960s and 1970s watches were worn with novelty straps and face designs and considered to be costume jewelry. There have been many technical developments in recent decades, including watches powered by small replaceable batteries, self-winding batteries, waterproofing, and shock-resistance. Digital watches have digital displays that not only show date, time and seconds, but are also designed with alarms and other technical features which remember appointments, read pulses, and tell the temperature.

alarm watch Wristwatch that rings at a set time; sometimes the alarm is musical and called *musical alarm watch.*

ankle watch Large watch with wide band worn strapped to the ankle.

bangle watch See WATCHES: BRACELET WATCH.

bracelet watch Watch with an ornamental band with the face of the watch sometimes covered with a small hinged piece of metal. Frequently set with stones, it acts as both a decorative bracelet and a watch. Also called *bangle watch.*

bracelet watch

calculator watch Watch that, in addition to giving the time in eight different time zones of the world, is a stop watch, has an alarm, and will do mathematical problems.

calendar watch Watch that also shows month and day of year in addition to indicating time.

cartoon watch Children's watch with trademarked cartoon characters (e.g., Mickey Mouse®, Star Wars® characters, and Smurfs®) popular since 1930s.

chatelaine watch (shat'-eh-lane) Watch suspended from a lapel pin. Popular in 19th and early 20th c. and revived intermittently. Also called a *lapel watch. Der.* Keys worn at the waist on a chain by medieval mistress of the castle or "chatelaine."

chatelaine watch

chronograph A watch with features such as a perpetual calendar and moon phase repeater and that has dials which glow in the dark.

chronometric watch Watch equipped with aviation computer to calculate speed, distance, conversion of miles into kilometers or knots, and fuel consumption. Used when flying, auto racing, and boating. First used by space pioneers in flight of May 1962.

W

diamond watch **1.** Wristwatch decorated around the dial with diamonds and other precious gems. Introduced in the 1920s, the watchband was made with diamonds set in a platinum band. **2.** In the 1960s, semiprecious gems (e.g., CARNELIAN, ONYX, or TURQUOISE) (see under GEMS, GEM CUTS, AND SETTINGS) were used for the face with diamonds set around the edge.

digital watch A watch that shows the time in hours, minutes, and seconds in numbers which constantly change, rather than having a dial with hands pointing to the time.

digital watch

fashion watch Watch that is a decorative accessory as well as a functional one. In the 1950s, bracelet, pendant, and ring watches were designed, some set with jewels, others in antique mountings. Previous to this, women owned one watch—now they may own several and wear them as jewelry.

go-go watch Watch that snaps into very wide interchangeable, colorful bands, matching or contrasting with the costume. Introduced in 1966, they were at first considered a fad, but later influenced the introduction of larger-sized watches and watchbands for women.

hunter watch Large gold pocketwatch with covered face depicting a hunting scene.

jeweled watch A watch in which the metal movements have gemstone tips that prevent wear and tear, thereby prolonging the life of the watch. Seventeen jewels will produce a serviceable watch; a 23-jewel watch will outlive its owner by many years.

lapel watch See WATCHES: CHATELAINE WATCH.

LCD quartz watch Digital watch that displays time and date by Liquid Crystal Display; powered by a small replaceable battery.

pendant watch Watch suspended from a chain worn around the neck. May be decorated on the back and worn on either side or made with a hinged cover. Made in all shapes and sizes in antique as well as modern designs and in LCD calendar watches.

pocketwatch Man's watch worn either in the vest pocket or in a small watch pocket in the trousers. First worn during Louis XIV

period. Sometimes two watches were worn in small pockets of the waistcoat. By the 1840s, women were wearing pocketwatches in small pockets set into the waistline of dresses. Pocket watches remained popular until the introduction of the wristwatch in the late 1800s.

pocketwatch

quartz crystal watch A watch powered by a battery rather than by mechanical movements.

ring watch Watch in ring style—popular in 1960s and 1980s, sometimes decorated with stones and made with hinged cover. Other very simple styles were made of lucite.

self-winding watch A wristwatch that winds automatically as a result of the movement of the wrist.

seventeen jeweled watch Fine watch using genuine or imitation rubies and sapphires at points of friction inside the case. Originally stones were genuine but now synthetic stones are more frequently used.

waterproof watch A watch in a sealed case that prevents the entrance of water.

wristwatch Watch worn on the wrist. Introduced in the late 1800s and gaining in popularity before World War I. Made in all sizes and types of faces, and sometimes with interchangeable bands. Some are set with diamonds and called DIAMOND WATCHES (see under WATCHES).

wristwatch wardrobe Women's watch sold with several interchangeable watchbands in several colors.

---

watch fob Short chain, ribbon, or charm, frequently engraved with *initials,* attached to man's pocketwatch. Named for the trouser pocket in which the watch is carried, called a *fob pocket.*

watch pocket See VESTS and POCKETS: FOB POCKET and VEST POCKET.

waterfall See HAIRSTYLES.

waterfall back See SKIRTS.

waterfall necktie See TIES: MAIL-COACH NECKTIE.

waterproof † Describing clothing, usually of rubber, plastic, or heavily coated fabric, that cannot

W

be penetrated by water, especially boots and coats. Also see WATER RESISTANT/REPELLENT.

waterproof cloak See CAPES, CLOAKS, AND SHAWLS.

waterproof watch See WATCHES.

water resistant/repellent † Describing clothing of fabric or leather treated to shed water easily and dry quickly—not entirely WATERPROOF.

water wave See HAIRSTYLES: FINGERWAVE.

Watteau back (wa-toe′) Used in latter half of 19th c. and after to describe back of a dress, jacket, coat, or dressing gown with box pleats called Watteau pleats. Pleats started at the neckline and were stitched down usually to the shoulders, from which point the fabric of the back fell to the hem. This style appears most often today in dressing gowns. *Der.* Named for the artist Watteau, who portrayed such dress in his portraits. Not a term contemporaneous with the original style, when it was called a *sack back.*

Watteau back

Watteau body ∞ (wa-toe′) Daytime dress bodice, worn in early 1850s to mid-1860s, having a low square neckline trimmed with ruffles and elbow-length sleeves. Bodice did not meet in front and was fastened with a ribbon lacing, exposing a *chemisette* worn underneath. *Der.* Named for the artist WATTEAU who portrayed such dresses in his paintings.

Watteau cape See CAPES, CLOAKS, AND SHAWLS.

Watteau coat See COATS AND JACKETS.

Watteau dress ∞ (wa-toe′) Adaptations, especially in the 1850s, 60s, 80s and 90s, of 18th c. SACK DRESS similar to those painted by Watteau. One version from the 1860s was styled with a *fichu* in front and *Watteau box pleats* in back and had an overskirt that was looped up at the sides revealing the underskirt. *Der.* Named for the artist WATTEAU who portrayed such dresses in his paintings.

Watteau hat See HEADWEAR.

Watteau, Jean Antoine (Wa-toe′, Jhan An-twan′) (1684–1721) French artist who painted many scenes showing women in early 18th-c. dresses. The SACK DRESS, with box pleats set in at the neckline or yoke, was a prominent style of the time, and in 19th-c. fashion terminology, these pleats became known as Watteau pleats and imitations of the sack dress, Watteau dresses. See WATTEAU BACK.

Watteau pleat See CLOTHING CONSTRUCTION DETAILS.

Watteau wrapper See SLEEPWEAR AND LOUNGEWEAR.

wearable art A garment created as a unique work of art. Fiber artists combine a variety of techniques such as crocheting, knitting, handweaving, embroidery appliqué, layers, slashing, special dyeing techniques. They also use feathers, beads, and ribbons. This trend began in the 1970s.

wearing sleeves See SHOULDERS AND SLEEVES.

weasel See FURS.

weave † **1.** *n.* Method or pattern in which the lengthwise yarns, placed on the loom first, are interlaced with crosswise yarns to make a fabric. There are three basic weaves: PLAIN WEAVE, TWILL WEAVE, and SATIN WEAVE. All other woven fabrics use some variation or combination of these weaves. **2.** *v.* To construct a fabric by weaving on a mechanized or hand loom.

webbed belt See BELTS.

wedding band **1.** See JEWELRY. **2.** NECKLINES AND COLLARS: WEDDING-BAND COLLAR.

wedding-band collar See NECKLINES AND COLLARS: RING COLLAR.

wedding dress Any dress worn by the bride for a wedding ceremony. Since about the 1840s, brides' dresses have been traditionally white and floor-length, with or without a train. Also called a *bridal dress.*

wedding garter Decorative garter, usually blue satin trimmed with lace, worn by brides. The tradition is to toss it away at the reception to an unmarried man. The custom derived from 16th to 18th c. practice, when young men wore pieces of a bride's garter in their hats. Also called *bride's garter.*

wedding ring/wedding trio See JEWELRY.

wedding veil See HEADWEAR: BRIDAL VEIL.

wede See WEED.

wedge **1.** See HAIRSTYLES. **2.** See FOOTWEAR.

wedge dress Dress cut with very full, large shoulders and dolman sleeves. Entire dress tapers to hemline in a V or wedge shape.

W

wedgies See FOOTWEAR.

Wedgwood® cameo See JEWELRY: CAMEO.

weed ∞ Clothing of any type from medieval times to 16th c., after which meaning was limited to mourning garments of black plus veils to cover the head, usually worn by widows and then called **widow's weeds.** *Der.* Old English, *waed,* "garment or clothing." Also spelled *wede, weyd.*

weekender Woman's three- or four-piece suit including coordinated pants, skirt, jacket, and blouse suitable for weekend trips.

weepers **1.** ∞ Muslin armbands or hatbands worn by mourners in 18th and 19th c. Usually black but sometimes white if deceased was a young girl. **2.** See FEATHERS.

weft See FILLING.

weight belt See BELTS.

weighted silk/weighting † Silk fabric having metallic salts, called weighting, added to it in the finishing process to give the fabric more body so that it drapes better. Since 1938, legislation has required that weighted silk must be identified if fabric has been weighted more than 10% for colors or 15% for black fabrics. Weighting was used in excessive quantities in many silk fabrics of the late 19th and early 20th c., which caused many of these fabrics to split and crack. This damage cannot be repaired or prevented. Compare with PURE DYE SILK.

Weitz, John * See APPENDIX/DESIGNERS.

welded seam See CLOTHING CONSTRUCTION DETAILS: FUSED SEAM.

welding cap See HEADWEAR.

Wellesley wrapper See COATS AND JACKETS.

Wellington boot See FOOTWEAR.

Wellington hat See HEADWEAR.

Wellington styles ∞ Men's fashions of the early 19th c. named for the first Duke of Wellington, British military hero who defeated Napoleon in the Battle of Waterloo in 1815. Specific style was a single-breasted overcoat that buttoned to waist, had a full skirt to knees with no waistline seam, a center back vent, side pleats, and hip buttons. Worn with narrow pantaloons with slits from ankle to calf and closed with buttons, boots, a tall flared-top beaver hat, and sometimes a cape.

welt **1.** See FOOTWEAR. **2.** See HOSIERY. **3.** Term used since 16th c. for a border around edge of garment, either for decorative purposes or to reinforce edge. Also see POCKETS and SEAMS.

weskit Synonym for WAISTCOAT and VEST.

weskit dress Tailored dress, usually full sleeved, combined with a vest.

western/western look Styles worn by western U.S. cowboys, a look disseminated around the world by movies set in the old western frontier in the United States. Tight jeans, high-heeled boots, cowboy shirts, and western hats of various styles were accepted for city wear in the late 1960s and periodically since then. See COATS AND JACKETS: WESTERN JACKET, FOOTWEAR: COWBOY BOOT, HEADWEAR: WESTERN HAT, PANTS: WESTERN PANTS, POCKETS: CONTINENTAL POCKET, SHIRTS: COWBOY SHIRT and WESTERN DRESS SHIRT, and SHORTS: WESTERN SHORTS.

western look

western suit **1.** Man's or woman's suit with jacket cut longer and more fitted through waistline, worn with straight-legged pants. Reminiscent of styles of the American west in late 19th c. **2.** A suit for formal occasions styled with similar lines, called a **western formal.**

Westwood, Vivienne * See APPENDIX/DESIGNERS.

wet look Shiny, glistening fabrics—sometimes of ciré satin—worn for pants, jackets, and shirts c. 1968 and after. Frequently black with a high amount of reflection from the shiny surface, the impetus for these styles came with the adoption of black leather motorcycle jackets in 1950s. Resurfaced in the 1980s in bold neon colors (e.g., red, chartreuse, and light pastels of pink, lavender, and lime). Also called *cuir savage look.* Also see LEATHER LOOK.

wetsuit See ACTIVEWEAR.

weyd See WEED.

whalebone Pliable hornlike strips called **baleen,** obtained from upper jaw of certain whale species, and used for stiffening garments since Middle Ages (e.g., whalebone used in bodices of woman's dresses in 16th c. to the 18th c.). Under bodices called stays were also stiffened with whalebone, and were forerunners of corsets.

wheel farthingale   See FARTHINGALE.

whipcord   † Medium- to heavyweight worsted fabric with a diagonal wale caused by the steep twill weave. Yarns are hard-twisted and fabric is given a hard finish to make the weave very distinct. Also made of cotton, wool, man-made fibers, or blends. Used for men's and women's suits, coats, riding habits, and uniforms.

whip stitch   See EMBROIDERIES AND SEWING STITCHES.

whisk   See NECKLINES AND COLLARS.

white belt   See ACTIVEWEAR: KARATE CLOTHING.

white bucks   See FOOTWEAR.

white crown   See HEADWEAR.

white fitch   See FURS: FITCH.

white flannels   See PANTS.

white fox   See FURS.

white mink   See FURS: MINK.

white slip   ∞ Narrow border of white piqué along front edges of man's waistcoat, correctly worn only with MORNING COAT (see COATS AND JACKETS: CUTAWAY). A fashion introduced by Edward, Prince of Wales, in 1888.

white tie   **1.** Used to designate men's full evening dress. Compare with BLACK TIE. **2.** See TIES.

white tie and tails   See FULL-DRESS SUIT.

white vest   See VESTS.

white walls   See HAIRSTYLES: FLATTOP.

white work   See EMBROIDERIES AND SEWING STITCHES.

whole fall   See FALL #1.

wholesale price   The price charged by the apparel manufacturer for goods. This price is based on the cost to the manufacturer of producing the goods, plus profit.

wholesaler   The individual or company that sells goods in relatively large quantities to a retailer or, less often, directly to consumers. The wholesaler may be a manufacturer or a MIDDLEMAN.

wholesale selling (contact selling)   Sales directly to consumers by a manufacturer.

wide-awake   See HEADWEAR.

wide wale   Ribbed or corded fabrics with wider than average ribs (e.g., wide wale corduroy, wide wale piqué).

widow's peak   **1.** Term for hairline forming a point in center of forehead. **2.** See HEADWEAR.

widow's weeds   See WEED.

wifebeater   See BLOUSES AND TOPS.

wig hat   See HEADWEAR.

wiglet   See WIGS.

WIGS AND HAIRPIECES

wig   **1.** Hair, human or artificial, mounted on an elastic net cap or foundation of bands (called **capless wig**), worn stretched over head to conceal natural hair or baldness and styled in conventional cuts and colors, or in fancy arrangements and colors as fashion fad. **2.** Historically, human or artificial hair worn from early Egyptian times and becoming a status symbol of royalty and upper classes through 18th c. Considered a secret device to conceal baldness in 19th and early 20th cs.

hairpiece   Additional pieces of hair, either human or synthetic fibers, worn when elaborate hairstyles demanded extra hairpieces or to fill in where hair is thin or missing.

Afro wig   Very curly, short-haired wig that fits over the hair, often back-combed so that hair stands on end. Introduced in 1968 when African styles were very influential in fashion.

bag   See WIGS AND HAIRPIECES: BAGWIG.

bagwig   ∞ Man's 18th-c. wig, styled with hair pulled back and stuffed into a square black silk bag tied with bow at nape of neck. Also called *coiffure en bourse, crapaud* or *bag.*

barrister's wig   White wig with smooth top and sausage curls over ears, a small pigtail tied with ribbon in back, worn by British trial lawyers.

beach wig   Modacrylic wig sometimes attached to a bathing cap or made in amusing shapes. Worn instead of beach hats at the shore or the swimming pool.

bench wig   Tightly curled wig with flaps that hang down over the ears. Worn by British judges when they sit in court, on the "bench."

binette   ∞ (bin-ett´)   Wig of late 17th c., worn by Louis XIV, of the full-bottomed type (see WIGS AND HAIRPIECES: FULL-BOTTOMED) with three hanging locks of hair; designed by Binet, a wigmaker.

W

bob-wig ∞ 18th-c. man's informal wig without a queue, a long braid in back; a **long bob** covered back of neck, **short bob** ended at nape of neck.

bourse ∞ (boorce) 18th-c., rarely used, French term for the black silk bag of a BAGWIG (see under WIGS AND HAIRPIECES). *Der.* French, "bag." Also see WIGS AND HAIRPIECES: MAJOR WIG.

brigadier wig See WIGS AND HAIRPIECES: MAJOR WIG.

brown George ∞ Late 18th-c. colloquial term for man's brown wig said to look like coarse brown bread.

brutus wig See HAIRSTYLES: BRUTUS.

buckled wig ∞ 18th-c. man's wig with tightly rolled sausage curls arranged horizontally near ears. *Der.* French, *bouclé,* "curl."

cache-folies ∞ (cash fo-lee′) Short-haired wig worn by women in Paris in the early 19th c. to cover the cropped TITUS COIFFURE (see HAIRSTYLES) of the French Revolution.

campaign wig/campaigne wig ∞ Wig of bushy, wavy hair with center part, three ends tied together when traveling. Worn by European soldiers from 1675 to 1750—after that considered old-fashioned. Also called *traveling wig.*

catogan wig/cadogan wig See WIGS AND HAIRPIECES: CLUB WIG.

caul ∞ (kol) Late 17th- and 18th-c. foundation on which wig was made.

cauliflower wig ∞ Short-bobbed wig, with tight curls allover, worn by coachmen in latter half of 18th c.

caxon ∞ Man's wig usually white or pale yellow, sometimes black styled with curls down the back and tied with a black ribbon. Worn as an undress, or informal, wig by professional men in 18th c.

club wig ∞ Man's wig with broad, flat, club-shaped QUEUE (see under HAIRSTYLES) turned under and tied with black ribbon. Sometimes ribbon came around to front and tied in bow club wig under chin. Worn from 1760 to 1790s. Much favored by the MACARONI in 1770s. Also called *cadogan* or *catagan club wig.*

coiffure en bourse (on boorce) See WIGS AND HAIRPIECES: BAGWIG. *Der.* French, "bag."

corkscrew wig ∞ Wig in various lengths of hair which falls in "corkscrew" fashion.

crapaud See WIGS AND HAIRPIECES: BAGWIG.

crinière wig (kre-nyair′)Wig cut in Dutch boy style with bangs in front and made of red, yellow, blue, etc., in synthetic hair or modacrylic fibers. Introduced in Paris by Courrèges, spring 1969.

cue peruke ∞ (kue per-uke′) 18th-c. term for wig with hanging queue, with a long braid in back.

cut wig ∞ 18th-c. term for a man's small plain wig without a queue, a long braid in back.

Duvillier wig ∞ (doo-vee-yay′) Man's wig, worn about 1700, dressed high on top of head with long, shoulder-length hair. Named after a French *perruquier* or wigmaker. Also called *long Duvillier, falbala wig,* or *furbelow wig.*

Egyptian wig ∞ **1.** Long black wig worn by ancient Egyptians with straight bangs, square cut at bottom, and often with intricate braiding interspersed with gold links. Wig was made on a framework that elevated it from the head, creating protection from the sun. **2.** Colored short wigs in layered styles, blue or red, worn by ancient Egyptians.

falbala wig See WIGS AND HAIRPIECES: DUVILLIER WIG.

fall Long straight hairpiece fastened to head with ribbon headband or pinned in place so that it hangs down over natural hair. Popular in late 1960s. Purchased by length; short length fall is called a *mini fall;* shoulder-length fall is called a *maxi fall.*

fall

fantail wig ∞ Man's wig of early 18th c. with QUEUE (see under HAIRSTYLES) hanging loose in many small curls in back.

foretop See WIGS AND HAIRPIECES: TOUPEE #2.

French wig See WIGS AND HAIRPIECES: FULL-BOTTOM WIG.

frizz-wig/frizze ∞ Man's wig, closely crimped all over, worn from 17th to 19th c. Also called a *frizze* or *frizzle.*

front ∞ 17th-c. term for hairpiece consisting of a fringe of false hair worn on the forehead.

W

frouze/fruz ∞ (frooz)   Term used in late 17th and early 18th c. for curled false hair or wig worn to conceal baldness.

full-bottom wig   Extremely large man's wig with center part, small SAUSAGE CURLS (see under HAIRSTYLES) all over, and long locks on shoulders. Worn from 1660 to early 18th c. on formal occasions by lawyers and learned professional people. Still worn by judges in Great Britain in 20th c. for ceremonial occasions. Also called *French wig*. Also see WIGS AND HAIRPIECES: BINETTE.

full-bottom wig

furbelow   See WIGS AND HAIRPIECES: DUVIL-LIER WIG.

hairpiece   See heading of category WIGS AND HAIRPIECES.

human hair wig   Imported genuine hair wig that reacts like regular hair, therefore is harder to care for, must be set more often, and is more expensive than synthetic wigs.

jasey ∞ (jay'-zee)   Late 18th- and 19th-c. man's wig made of worsted jersey yarn.

long bob   See WIGS AND HAIRPIECES: BOB-WIG.

Maintenon toupet ∞ (mant-non' too'-pay)   Band of false curls attached to ribbon that tied at nape of neck. Worn by women in mid-1860s, pulled over the forehead to imitate the hairstyle worn by the Marquise de Maintenon. Also called *toupet Maintenon*. Also see HAIRSTYLES: MAINTENON COIFFURE. *Der.* Named for the *Marquise de Maintenon*, mistress and second wife of Louis XIV of France.

major wig ∞ Man's hairpiece consisting of a *toupée* with two *corkscrew curls* tied at the nape of neck to make a double *queue* in back. Originally a military style, but adopted by civilians and worn during latter half of 18th c. Term used in England for French **brigadier wig**.

maxi fall   See WIGS AND HAIRPIECES: FALL.

Medusa wig ∞ (meh-doo'-sa)   Woman's wig of early 19th c. made of many hanging *corkscrew curls*. *Der.* From the Greek mythical Gorgon, Medusa, slain by Perseus.

mini fall   See WIGS AND HAIRPIECES: FALL.

periwig/peruke ∞ Synonyms for wig, used in 17th and 18th c.

perruque á l'enfant/perruque naissante ∞ (pe-rook' ahl anfant/pe-rook' nay-sant)   Man's wig of 1780s with tiny curls over most of the head, larger horizontal curls above ears and neck, and long queue, a braid, hanging down back.

physical wig ∞ Short wig, brushed back from forehead, bushy at sides and back, worn by professional men during latter half of 18th c., replacing FULL-BOTTOM WIG (see under WIGS AND HAIRPIECES). Also called *pompey*.

pigeon-wings ∞ Man's hairstyle or wig with single or double horizontal curls over the ears, smooth at top and sides, worn from 1750s to 1760s. Wig also called *pigeon-winged toupée* or *aile de pigeon*.

pigtail wig ∞ Wig with a queue (a pigtail) worn by men in 18th c., interwoven with black ribbon, tied with ribbon bow at nape of neck, and smaller bow at end of queue.

pompey   See WIGS AND HAIRPIECES: PHYSICAL WIG.

postiche   See WIGS AND HAIRPIECES: WIGLET.

put-on   Thick hairpiece, sometimes 18" long, made of modacrylic matched to hair. May be worn in a multiplicity of styles (e.g., PONY-TAIL, DOUBLE BRAID, FALL, BUN, CHIGNON, WIGLET, EMPIRE CONE, and FRENCH TWIST) (see under HAIRSTYLES).

queue-peruke ∞ (kew pe-ook')   Man's small wig worn from 1727 to 1760 with fluffed or curled sides and long ends tied back with black bow to make a QUEUE (see under HAIRSTYLES).

Ramillies wig/Ramilet wig/Ramille wig ∞ Man's wig of 18th c., puffed at sides with long, tapered, braided queue (a braid) tied with black ribbon at end and nape of neck, or looped up and tied only at neck. *Der.* Named for English victory over French in Ramillies, Belgium, in 1706.

reserve wig   Man's short-haired wig worn to cover long hairstyle in 1969–70 by men enrolled in Army Reserves. *Der.* So called because men wearing the wig were in the U.S. Army Reserves.

rug   Slang for wig or hairpiece.

scalpette ∞ (scal-pet')   Term used in mid-1870s for woman's hairpiece composed of

W

extra curls attached to an invisible net worn on top of head.

scratch wig/scratch bob ∞ Man's BOB WIG (see under WIGS AND HAIRPIECES) worn from 1740 to end of 18th c. made with one long hanging curl, covering only back of head. Arranged with the natural hair brushed over top of wig. Also called *scratch bob.*

short bob See WIGS AND HAIRPIECES: BOB-WIG.

stretch wig Comfortable cool wig with synthetic hair attached to elastic bands running around and over the head in crisscross fashion.

switch Long hank of false hair that may be braided in a plait and worn as a CORONET or twisted into a CHIGNON (see under HAIRSTYLES).

tête de mouton ∞ (tate deh moo′-tone) Woman's short curly wig worn in Paris from 1730 to about 1755. *Der.* French, "sheep's head." Also see HAIRSTYLES: COIFFURE A LA MOUTON.

top See WIGS AND HAIRSTYLES: TOUPÉE #2.

toupée (too-pay′) **1.** Man's small partial wig used to cover baldness. **2.** ∞ From 1730 to end of 18th c.: front roll of hair on man's wig. Also called *toupet, foretop,* and *top.*

toupée #2

tower ∞ False curls, worn by women above the forehead from 1670s to 1710, usually with the FONTANGES headdress (see under HEADWEAR). *Der.* French, "tour."

transformation ∞ Term used in early 20th c. for a natural-looking wig or hairpiece worn by women.

traveling wig See WIGS AND HAIRPIECES: CAMPAIGN WIG.

tye ∞ 18th c. term for man's tied-back wig.

vallancy ∞ (va-lan′-see) Extremely large wig, worn in 17th c., that shaded the face.

wiglet Small hairpiece worn on the top of the head and usually combed into bangs. Worn as an aid for thinning hair by both men and women. Also a fashion item. Also called *postiche* (pos-teesh′).

---

wilderness boot See FOOTWEAR.

wild mink See FURS.

wild silk See TUSSAH.

William Penn hat See HEADWEAR.

wimple See HEADWEAR.

wind-blown bob See HAIRSTYLES.

wind bonnet See HEADWEAR.

windbreaker See COATS AND JACKETS.

window displays An important element of VISUAL MERCHANDISING. Traditional store window displays have solid backings and are called **closed displays.** They are visible when the store is open or closed. **Open displays** are common displays in malls that enable the viewer to see directly into the store through the display.

windowpane See PRINTS, CHECKS, AND STRIPES and HOSIERY.

Windsor knot/tie See TIES.

wing collar See NECKLINES AND COLLARS.

wings ∞ Term used from mid-16th to mid-17th c. for decorative pieces projecting upward from shoulders of a doublet or dress, sometimes in shape of padded rolls or crescents sewn into the armhole seam. Also called *shoulder wings.*

wing-tip See FOOTWEAR.

winkers See NECKLINES AND COLLARS.

winkle pickers See FOOTWEAR.

Winnie See COTY AMERICAN FASHION CRITICS′ AWARD.

WIP See WORK IN PROGRESS.

wired bra See UNDERGARMENTS.

wires See JEWELRY.

witchoura mantle See CAPES, CLOAKS, AND SHAWLS.

wolf See FURS.

wolverine See FURS.

women's sizes Women's garments in sizes for heavier figure than MISSES SIZE range; even-numbered bust sizes range from 38 to 50.

Women's Wear Daily (WWD) Retailer's fashion newspaper published each weekday by Fairchild Publications. It gives information about new styles, designers, foreign fashion collections, as well as information about new laws, government regulations, and foreign trade.

wooden button See CLOSURES.

woof See FILLING.

wool † **1.** Animal fiber from fleece of sheep or lambs. Fabrics made from wool are warm, resilient, have good absorption, and good affinity for dyes. Disadvantages include tendency to shrink, and poor resistance to moths unless treated. May be knitted, woven, or felted, which is possible because of a microscopic structure of scales on the surface of the fibers. May also be blended with other fibers. Used extensively for outerwear, suits, skirts, dresses. **2.** As defined by the Wool Products Labeling Act of 1939, fibers not only from sheep and lambs, but also ANGORA or CASHMERE GOATS; ALPACA, LLAMA, CAMEL, or VICUÑA.

woolen † Yarns or woven or knitted fabrics made from wool fibers that are not COMBED, but may be CARDED two or three times. **Worsteds** are made from combed and carded fibers. Generally, woolens are kinkier and softer than worsteds. Finishing processes for woolens frequently include napping or brushing as the fabrics have a fuzzy warm HAND rather than a smooth hand as do worsteds. Spelled *woollen* in England.

Wool Products Labeling Act Law passed by Congress in 1939 stating that wool products containing wool must be labeled for the consumer as either **wool, new wool,** or **virgin wool**—all of which have never been used before—or **recycled wool**—which may either have been made into products, returned to the fibrous state, but never used before, or used by consumers and returned to the fibrous state. Contents of the various types of wool must be properly stated on a label for the customer by percentage. If content is less than 5%, it need not be labeled. (Law has been amended several times.)

Woolworth® shoe See FOOTWEAR.

work apron See APRONS.

work clothes Apparel of sturdy fabric used by factory workers and other laborers (e.g., shirts, pants, overalls, coveralls, and jackets, usually made of denim, drill, chino, or duck).

worked buttonholes See CLOSURES.

worked in the round See FURS.

work in progress (WIP) The total amount of merchandise currently being constructed at a garment factory.

workout suit See ACTIVEWEAR: AEROBIC ENSEMBLE.

work pants See PANTS.

work pocket See POCKETS: TIE POCKET.

World Trade Organization (WTO) Organization that succeeds the GENERAL AGREEMENT ON TARIFFS AND TRADE (GATT) in regulating international trade in all areas, including textiles and apparel.

World War I helmet See HEADWEAR.

World War II helmet See HEADWEAR.

worry beads See JEWELRY.

worsted See WOOLEN.

Worth, Charles * See APPENDIX/DESIGNERS.

woven friendship bracelet See JEWELRY.

wrangler Western U.S. name for a cowhand.

Wrangler® Active trademark for a brand of western pants, jackets, and other clothing and accessories.

wrap **1.** *v.* To drape an outergarment around the body in various ways. **2.** *n.* A garment put on when going out of doors (e.g., a shawl, scarf, cloak, or mantle). Use of the word in this way is not as popular as it was in former years. **3.** *adj.* In contemporary usage, a shortened form of the word *wraparound,* used to describe garments that wrap. See BLOUSES AND TOPS: WRAP BLOUSE and WRAPPED TOP, CLOSURES: WRAP CLOSING, and JUMPERS: WRAP JUMPER.

wraparound Term used when apparel and accessories are not closed with fasteners, but lapped over and held with sashes that are knotted or tied in a bow. Also see COATS AND JACKETS, EYEWEAR, SLEEPWEAR AND LOUNGEWEAR, SWEATERS, and SKIRTS.

wrap cufflinks Cufflinks made with extra band extending around outside of cuff, connecting the two parts.

wrap dress Dress wrapping either to the front, similar to the kimono dress, or to the back. In either case, it has an extra lap that is approximately equal to the width of the skirt. *Der.* Term shortened from "wraparound" in late 1960s.

wrap dress

wrapper **1.** See SLEEPWEAR AND LOUNGEWEAR. **2.** See COATS AND JACKETS. **3.** See HOUSEDRESS.

wrap-rascal See COATS AND JACKETS.

wrinkle resistance † Ability of fabric to resist creasing. Many fabrics made from manufactured fibers are resistant to wrinkling. Special finishing processes can be used on fibers that wrinkle to make them more crease resistant.

W

wristband Strip of fabric, usually double, seamed to the lower edge of a sleeve and fastened around the wrist. Also see CUFFS.

wristlength See GLOVES AND GLOVE CONSTRUCTIONS.

wrist strap See JEWELRY.

wristwatch/wristwatch wardrobe See WATCHES.

WTO See WORLD TRADE ORGANIZATION.

WW Shoe width designation for a very wide shoe, equivalent to an EE.

WWD See *WOMEN'S WEAR DAILY*.

W

X Designation for size EXTRA LARGE in men's, women's, and children's clothing. XX and XXX mean successively larger.

---

yachting Adjective used to describe apparel that derives from or was inspired by items worn for the sport of boating. See YACHTING COSTUME, COATS AND JACKETS: YACHTING COAT and YACHTING JACKET and HEADWEAR: YACHTING CAP.

yachting costume ∞ Ensemble for women popular in 1890s for yachting and other sports, including canoeing and boating. Frequently consisted of a straw sailor hat or commodore hat and full-length two- or three-piece suit with nautical influence or MIDDY BLOUSE (see under BLOUSES AND TOPS.

Yamamoto, Yohji * See APPENDIX/DESIGNERS.

yard Unit of fabric measure used in the United States comprising 36″ or 3′, equivalent to 91.44 centimeters.

yard goods Fabric sold by the yard at retail stores for sewing. Also called *piece goods*.

yarmulka See HEADWEAR: SKULLCAP.

yarn † Fibers twisted together tightly enough for weaving purposes. The two basic types are **staple yarn** made from short fibers (e.g., cotton or wool carded to lie parallel, then twisted); and continuous **filament yarn** comprised of strands of indefinite length used singly or several filaments twisted together.

X-ray dress ∞ "See-through" dress made of transparent fabric worn with an opaque slip in early 20th c.

yarn-dyed † Describing fabric that is woven or knitted from yarns dyed before the fabric is constructed.

yarn number See COUNT OF YARN.

yellow diamond See GEMS, GEM CUTS, AND SETTINGS: FANCY DIAMOND.

yeoman hat See HEADWEAR.

yoke 1. Portion of garment fitted across the shoulders in front or back or both to which the lower front and back sections are attached. This piece is sometimes lined. 2. Fitted top of a skirt connected to a waistband to which the lower part of the skirt may be attached by means of SHIRRING, GORES, or PLEATS (see under CLOTHING CONSTRUCTION DETAILS).

3. Adjective used to describe apparel that incorporates a yoke. See BLOUSES AND TOPS: YOKE BLOUSE, NECKLINES AND COLLARS: YOKE COLLAR and SKIRTS: YOKE SKIRT.

yoke at neckline

York-tan gloves See GLOVES AND GLOVE CONSTRUCTIONS.

York wrapper ∞ Back-buttoned high-necked woman's morning dress made of muslin, worn in 1813. Trimmed with alternate diamond-shaped pieces of needlework in front.

Youghal lace   See LACES.

young teens   Size range between *girls* and *juniors;* includes sizes 5/6 to 15/16. Also called *young juniors.*

Yugoslavian embroidery   See EMBROIDERIES AND SEWING STITCHES.

---

zebra   See FURS.

zeitgeist (zite′gaist)   German word meaning "the spirit of the age." Used in English to refer to the thought and feeling of a particular period of time.

zendado   See SCARVES.

Zhivago/Zhivago look (zhi-vah′go)   Clothes inspired by those worn in the 1965 film *Doctor Zhivago,* based on the novel by Boris Pasternak. Introduced by Dior in 1966–67, this look featured Russian-inspired clothing and accessories such as a Russian-type overblouse with high standing collar closing at the side rather than center front. Coats were usually midi length and often lavishly trimmed with fur at neck, sleeves, and hem. Boots were also featured. *Der.* Inspired by costumes worn in *Dr. Zhivago,* which was set in Revolutionary Russia in 1917.

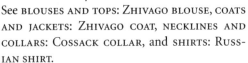

Zhivago look 1960s

See BLOUSES AND TOPS: ZHIVAGO BLOUSE, COATS AND JACKETS: ZHIVAGO COAT, NECKLINES AND COLLARS: COSSACK COLLAR, and SHIRTS: RUSSIAN SHIRT.

Zhivago dress   Same as RUSSIAN SHIRTDRESS.

zigzag stitch   See EMBROIDERIES AND SEWING STITCHES.

zip-in/zip-out lining   Completely removable lining inserted into a coat by means of a zipper around the coat facing. It starts at one side of the hem, runs up side, across back neckline, and down the other side to make a dual-purpose coat. Also called a *shell.*

zip-off coat   See COATS AND JACKETS.

zipper   **1.** See CLOSURES. **2.** Adjective used to describe apparel in which a zipper is a prominent feature. See PANTS: ZIPPERED PANTS, UNDERWEAR: ZIPPER FOUNDATION and ZIPPERED GIRDLE.

yuppies   A nickname applied to young, upwardly mobile professionals who work in fields such as the law and business. *Der.* Derived from the first letters of *y*oung *up*wardly mobile.

zip pocket   See POCKETS.

zircon   See GEMS, GEM CUTS, AND GEM SETTINGS.

zizith   See TSITSITH.

zodiac signs   Symbols of various constellations that are used in astrology. These signs sometimes appear as an ornament in apparel. See JEWELRY: ZODIAC NECKLACE.

zone (zo-knee)   **1.** ∞ A piece, used in 1770s and 1780s, that filled in an open area of the bodice of a dress. The shape corresponded to that of the exposed gap. **2.** See BELTS.

zootie   See ZOOT SUIT.

zoot suit   ∞ First adopted by teenage boys and associated with the popularity of jitterbugging (a dance style) in the early 1940s, this extreme form of the sack suit was long with excessively wide shoulders and long, wide lapels. Trousers were pleated at the waist and tight at ankle. The outfit was worn with a wide-brimmed hat, and an extra-long key chain dangling from a watch pocket with attached keys placed

zoot suit 1942

in side pocket of pants and was one of the first styles to originate at the lower end of the socioeconomic ladder. Those who adopted these styles were known as **zooties.**

zori   See FOOTWEAR.

Zouave   ∞ Adjective used to describe fashions inspired by or adapted from the costumes of Algerian troops that fought as part of the French army. During the American Civil War, a regiment called the Zouaves fought for the North and adopted, in part, the costume of the French Zouaves. The term appears in fashion as early as the 1840s and as late as the 1890s. See ZOUAVE UNIFORM, COATS AND JACKETS: ZOUAVE COAT, ZOUAVE JACKET, ZOUAVE PUFF, and ZOUAVE

PALETOT; HANDBAGS AND RELATED ACCESSORIES: ZOUAVE POUCH, SHIRTS: ZOUAVE SHIRT, and SKIRTS: ZOUAVE SKIRT.

Zouave puff ∞ (zoo ahv′) Single or double horizontal puffs at the back of the skirt, a style of the 1870s to 1880s. *Der.* Arabic, *Zouaova,* a Kabyle tribe, one of the Berbers, living in Algeria or Tunisia.

Zouave uniform ∞ (zoo-ahv′) **1.** Colorful oriental uniform consisting of a waist-length unbuttoned navy blue jacket worn over a navy blue blouse (both trimmed in red) combined with below-the-knee red trousers styled like harem pants, short black boots, and leggings. A sash of light blue is worn, and a green and red turban with a blue tassel. Worn by French infantry soldiers in Algeria, a military corps originally composed of Algerians noted for their strength and courage. **2.** Member of a military group, particularly some volunteer regiments in American Civil War, who wore a similar uniform that is same style but may vary in color *Der.* Arabic, *Zouaova,* a Kabyle tribe, one of the Berbers, living in Algeria or Tunisia.

zucchetto See CLERICAL DRESS: CALOTTE.

Zuni jewelry See JEWELRY.

Zuni snake eye ring See JEWELRY.

APPENDIX: DESIGNERS

Adolfo (Adolfo Sardiña) *American designer* (1933–)

Born in Havana, Cuba, Adolfo began as a milliner in New York in 1948. Gradually he added clothing to his line, then later switched entirely to apparel. Design interests include: men's wear, active sportswear, and accessories.

Adri (Adrienne Steckling-Coen) *American designer* (1930–)

After studying at Parsons School of Design, New York, Adri worked first at B. H. Wragge, then ANNE FOGARTY, after which she opened a small business for ready-to-wear and leisure wear. She established Adri Clotheslab, Inc. in 1983. She has said she believes that styles should evolve naturally from one collection to the next so that clients can collect, add to, and mix them freely from season to season.

Adrian, Gilbert (Gilbert Adrian Greenburgh) *American designer* (1903–1959)

Adrian designed for Metro-Goldwyn-Mayer Studios (1923 to 1939), then opened a couture and high-priced ready-to-wear retail business in Beverly Hills in 1941. It closed in 1948, and he continued in wholesale until 1953. Characteristics he was noted for included exaggeratedly wide shoulders on tailored suits; dolman sleeves; dramatic animal prints on sinuous black crepe evening gowns; asymmetric lines; diagonal closings; huge ruffle-topped sleeves.

Agnès (ah´-nyess) *French millinery designer*

A top Paris milliner of the 1920s who was a sculptress, friend of important artists of the time, including painters Léger, Mondrian, and Delaunay, whose fabric designs she used; this designer used novelty materials such as cellophane in 1935.

Allard, Linda *American designer* (1940–)

Educated at Kent State University, Allard has worked for Ellen Tracy since her graduation in 1962. Assistant designer until 1964, she then assumed the position of design director and in 1984 her name was added to the label. Her designs have been described as "career clothes that are up-to-the-minute but not over the top."

Amies, Hardy *British designer* (1909–)

London-born, Amies worked at London couture house Lachasse from 1934 to 1941 and for House of Worth in London during World War II. Opening his own house in Savile Row in 1948, he specialized in tailored suits, coats, cocktail and evening dresses. He started men's wear designing in 1959. Considered forward-thinking in his contemporary clothes, which included pantsuits for women; wide yachting pants; casual classics.

Anthony, John (Gianantonio Iorio) *American designer* (1938–)

Born in New York, Anthony worked at Devonbrook and with Adolph Zelinka before opening his own business on New York's Seventh Avenue in 1971. He was known for designs in natural fabrics, cardigan sweaters with pants, mannish shirts and ties, pullovers with skirts, dramatic easy pants, and gala dresses in soft satins with sequins and in sheer wool.

Armani, Giorgio *Italian designer* (1934–)

Born in Italy, Armani worked for seven years as assistant buyer for a large Italian department store and then went on to design men's wear for the Cerutti group. His first men's wear collection in 1974 attracted attention for his unconstructed blazer. Working on women's wear in 1975 and after and using fine tailoring techniques, he became known for easy and uncontrived shapes; masculine cuts with feminine qualities in exquisite Italian fabrics in neutral colors such as beige, black, gray, and taupe. His business includes boutiques, accessories, and perfumes for men and women. Designs under the Emporio label provide his creations in affordable prices.

Ashley, Laura *British designer* (1925–1985)

Born in Wales, Ashley formed a company in 1953 to sell household linens. She began selling simple smocks, aprons, and dresses as well in 1969. By the late 1960s, Laura Ashley retail outlets had been established in the United Kingdom and abroad.

Augustabernard (Augusta Bernard) *French designer*

After working as copyist in the region of Provence, France, Bernard opened her own house in 1919. She made unadorned, simple custom clothes for private clients in France and in New York, and for the custom departments of Henri Bendel and Bergdorf Goodman in late 1920s and 1930s. She retired in late 1930s.

Balenciaga, Cristobal (bal-lawn-see-ah′-gah) *Spanish-French couturier* (1895–1972)

After copying a Paris suit for a rich marquesa at age 14, he left his home in Spain to study clothes design. He opened his own house in Paris in 1937 and was immediately successful. His career continued until his retirement in 1968. A partial list of his innovations includes: revolutionary semi-fit jacket, 1951; middy dress evolving into chemise, 1955; cocoon coat; balloon skirt; short-front, long-back flamenco evening gown; bathrobe-wrap coat; pillbox hat. In the late 1950s and early 1960s, Balenciaga designed gowns inspired by the post-Cubist and abstract-expressionist painters of the period.

Balmain, Pierre (bal′-man, pee-yair′) *French couturier* (1914–1982)

After studying architecture, Balmain designed at Molyneux from 1934 to 1939, then was assistant to Lucien Lelong from 1940 to 1945. He opened a new house in 1945, which was an immediate success. He was known for wearable, elegant clothes, which changed little from season to season; safe daytime classics; extravagant evening gowns. The house continued with other designers after his death.

Banton, Travis *American designer* (1894–1958)

After World War I, Banton trained as a designer with LUCILE and Madame Frances. He went to Hollywood in 1924 and in the 1930s designed all of Marlene Dietrich's costumes. At the same time he was designing for several studios, he ran his own couture business for private clients.

Beaulard (bow-lahr′) *French dressmaker*

ROSE BERTIN's most serious rival at the French court as dressmaker to Marie Antoinette in the 18th-c. Credited with the invention of tall headdresses with a concealed spring that allowed them to collapse as ladies entered carriages; Beaulard is also credited with the elaborate headdresses popular in the earlier years of Marie Antoinette's reign.

Beene, Geoffrey *American designer* (1927–)

Born in Haynesville, Louisiana, Beene studied design in New York and Paris. From 1949 to 1957 he designed for Samuel Winston and Harmay and joined Teal Traina in 1958, where his name was put on the label. He opened his own business in 1962 and became known for these characteristics: simplicity, emphasis on cut and line, dressmaking details, and unusual fabrics. In late 1960s his business expanded to include furs, swimwear, jewelry, scarves, men's wear, and a boutique collection, *Beene Bag*, in 1970 as well as a variety of licensed products.

Bertin, Rose (ber-tan′) *French milliner and dressmaker to Marie Antoinette* (1744–1813)

Born Marie-Jeanne Laurent near Abbeville, France, in 1744, she came to Paris at 16 to work in a millinery shop. After becoming the court milliner and a confidante of Queen Marie Antoinette in 1772, she designed costly, fantastic, humorous headdresses from her shop, Au Grand Mogol. The first dressmaker to become celebrated and mentioned in contemporary memoirs and encyclopedias, she fled to England during the French Revolution. On her return in 1800, she sold trinkets and died in poverty in 1813.

Blahnik, Manolo (1943–)

After completing his studies, Blahnik came to London in 1971. He opened a shoe store in Chelsea (London) in 1973 and in New York in 1979. He is known for "ornate, romantic, exotic shoes in luxurious materials."

Blass, Bill *American designer* (1922–2002)

Blass studied at Parsons School of Design in New York in the early 1940s; and was employed sketching sportswear for David Crystal. After World War II, he designed for Anna Miller & Co. Miller merged with Maurice Rentner, Ltd., in 1958 and Blass was head designer and eventually vice president and then owner, after which the company name changed to Bill Blass Ltd. Noted for women's classic sportswear and glamorous evening wear, the firm's design interests include: rainwear, men's clothing, Blassport women's sportswear, loungewear, scarves, automobiles, uniforms for American Airlines flight attendants, and chocolates. Blass sold his business and retired in 1999. The firm continues with Lars Nillson as designer.

Bohan, Marc *French designer* (1926–)

Bohan worked with Molyneux, Piguet, and Madeleine de Rauch from 1945 to 1953 before opening his own business in 1953. He sold it in the same year and worked for Patou for a short time and freelanced for Originala in New York until 1958. In late 1958 he joined house of Dior, replacing Yves Saint Laurent, and continued as chief designer of couture and ready-to-wear for the Dior line until 1989.

Boss, Hugo *German design group*

Boss originally made his firm's name in men's wear, but by 2000 they were also doing women's clothing. Known for tailored suits and trim shirts that utilize feminine fabrics and touches.

Brigance, Tom *American designer* (1913–1990)

After studies at the Parsons School of Design and the National Academy of Art in New York and the Sorbonne in Paris, he became the store designer at Lord & Taylor in 1939. He opened his own business on Seventh Avenue in 1949 where he designed coats and suits, dresses for day and evening, blouses and playclothes.

Brooks, Donald *American designer* (1928–)

Brooks studied Fine Arts at Syracuse University, and at Parsons School of Design in New York. Noted for uncluttered day clothes in clear, unusual colors, careful detailing, his own designed dramatic prints, and romantic evening costumes. He also designed costumes for stage and screen. Design interests include: furs, swimwear, men's wear, shoes, costume jewelry, wigs, bed linens.

Burrows, Stephen *American designer* (1943–)

After studying at Philadelphia Museum College of Art and The Fashion Institute of Technology, Burrows and classmate Roz Rubenstein opened a boutique in 1968. Hired the next year by Henri Bendel, Burrows concentrated on design. He worked for Bendel off and on, taking some time out to design for private customers and the theater. He returned to Bendel, doing a collection of evening dresses and separates in the 1990s.

Callot Soeurs (kal′-o sir) *French couture house* (1895–1935)

This firm was founded in 1895 as a lace shop by three sisters. From 1916 to 1927, it became one of the great Paris dressmaking houses and was famous for delicate lace blouses; gold and silver lamé; Renaissance patterns; much chiffon, georgette, and organdy; rococo flower embroidery. It closed in 1937.

Capucci, Roberto (ca-puch′-ee) *Italian designer* (1929–)

First showed independently in Rome in 1952 at age 21. Moved to Paris in 1962; then reopened in Rome in 1969. Known for masterful handling of drapery, imaginative cutting, no extra ornamentation, tapered-pants jumpsuits, halter-neck hostess gowns, balloon drapes, huge bubble skirts, kimono and dolman sleeves, sculptured forms. Also designed children's wear, knits, furs, footwear, and millinery.

Cardin, Pierre (kar-dahn′, pee-air′) *French designer* (1922–)

Born in Venice, Cardin grew up in St. Étienne, France. He studied architecture in Paris and designed costumes for Cocteau's movie *La Belle et la Bête*. His work history included PAQUIN, then SCHIAPARELLI, and head of the workroom at

DIOR in 1947. He opened his own house in 1950 at age 25. A success by 1957, Cardin introduced many innovations for women and was called revolutionary for his metal body jewelry, unisex astronaut suits, helmets, batwing jumpsuits, and tunics over tights. He started designing men's wear in 1958 and was considered a leader in field of couturiers designing for both sexes. He was the first Paris couturier to sell his own ready-to-wear, designed by André Oliver, to department stores. He entered into a trade agreement with the People's Republic of China in 1979 for the establishment of factories to produce Cardin clothes.

Carnegie, Hattie *American designer* (1889–1956)

Born in Vienna, Carnegie worked in New York from 1909 to early 1950s. She took her name from that of Andrew Carnegie, "the richest man in the world." Starting in 1909 as Carnegie-Ladies Hatter; the firm became Hattie Carnegie Inc. in 1918 and expanded into resort shops, wholesale business, factories, jewelry, and cosmetics. Designer of made-to-order and ready-to-wear for society and movie stars, Carnegie was influential throughout the 1930s and 1940s. She was noted for the "little Carnegie suit." Among the noted designers who worked for her were NORMAN NORELL, JAMES GALANOS, PAULINE TRIGÈRE, and CLAIRE MCCARDELL.

Cashin, Bonnie *American designer* (1915–2000)

Cashin specialized in comfortable country and travel clothes in wool jersey, knits, tweeds, canvas, and leather and believed in functional layers of clothing, which she coordinated with her own designs of hoods, bags, boots, and belts that were influenced by her collection of ethnic fashions and fabrics. Considered one of the most innovative of American designers, she also designed for stage, ballet, and motion pictures. From 1953 on, she freelanced for sportswear houses and did bags for Coach Leatherwear. She started The Knittery in 1967, which made limited-edition collections of hand knits.

Cassini, Oleg (cass-ee′-nee) *American designer* (1913–)

Born in Paris, raised in Italy, Cassini came to the United States in 1936. He designed for films and in New York and was selected by Jacqueline Kennedy as her official designer while her husband was president in the 1960s. He was known for sheath and A-line dresses and men's turtlenecks.

Castelbajac, Jean-Charles de *French designer* (1950–)

Born in Morocco, his family moved to France when he was 5. At age 18 he was working with his mother in her clothes factory. Castelbajac designed for Pierre d'Alby, and after 1974 opened his own retail shop. He is best known for blanket plaids, canvas, quilting, rugged coats.

Chanel, Gabrielle "Coco" (shan-ell′) *French couturière* (1883–1971)

Chanel started with a hat shop in 1913. She opened her own couture house in 1914 and closed it after World War II. In 1954 she reopened again, hardly changing her original concept of simple wearability. Her business consisted of the couture house, textile, and perfume laboratories where Chanel No. 5 originated, and a costume-jewelry workshop. In the 1960s her trademark suit—braid-trimmed, collarless jacket, patch pockets, and knee-length skirt in soft Scottish tweeds—was worn with multiple gold-chain necklaces with fake jewels; chain-handled quilted handbags; beige and black slingback pumps; flat black hairbows, and a gardenia. She died in midst of preparing a collection in January 1971. The House of Chanel continued, directed by a succession of designers: Ready-to-wear was added in 1975, with Philippe Guibourgé as designer. KARL LAGERFELD has since taken over design responsibilities for both couture and ready-to-wear.

Chéruit, Madeleine (share′-oo-eet) *French couturière* (c. 1860s–unknown)

One of first women leaders of haute couture, Cheruit took over the house of Raudnitz (founded in 1873). She was first to launch simple, almost severe models in contrast to fussy clothes of the time. Not a designer, she was a critical editor of her house's designs. Louise Boulanger designed for her; PAUL POIRET sold her sketches at beginning of his career. Mme. Cheruit retired in 1923, although the house continued until 1935, when it was taken over by SCHIAPARELLI.

Cipullo, Aldo (chip-oo′-low) *American jewelry designer* (1936–1984)

Cipullo studied at University of Rome then came to New York in 1959 to attend the School of Visual Arts. After designing for David Webb, Tiffany, and Cartier, he opened his own business in 1974. His jewelry was simple, elegant, functional, and very stylish. Other design projects included silverware, textiles, china, leather goods, and desk accessories.

Claiborne, Liz *American designer* (1929–)

Born in Brussels, Belgium, Claiborne grew up in New Orleans, then studied painting in Belgium and France. In 1949, in a design contest held by *Harper's Bazaar,* she won a trip to Europe to design and sketch. On her return to the United States she worked as model sketcher, assistant to Tina Leser and others, at Youth Guild. With her husband Arthur Ortenberg as business manager, she established Liz Claiborne, Inc. in 1976. Their original interests in sportswear expanded into designs for dresses and children's wear. The business has grown so that her function became largely as editor of the work of other designers. Their philosophy: Simple and uncomplicated designs of mix-and-match separates with easy natural look; sensitive use of color; technical knowledge of fabrics; moderate price range. She and her husband retired from the company in 1989.

Connolly, Sybil *Irish designer* (1921–)

Connolly worked for Bradley's, a London dressmaker, in 1938; returned to Ireland at start of World War II and worked as buyer for Richard Alan in Dublin. She was discovered in the early 1950s by Carmel Snow of *Harper's Bazaar* magazine and The Fashion Group of Philadelphia, who were visiting Dublin. In 1957 she came to the United States with collection of one-of-a-kind designs and Irish fabrics. She then formed her own firm with a ready-to-wear boutique. Known for evening gowns with horizontally mushroom-pleated handkerchief linen skirts and ruffled blouses, finely tucked linen shirts, Carrickmacross lace, iridescent Donegal tweeds, Aran Island white homespun, striped linen dish-toweling fabric.

Courrèges, André (koor′-rej, awn-dray′) *French designer* (1923–)

Born in France, Courrèges joined BALENCIAGA and worked there from 1952 to 1960. He opened his own house in 1961; focusing on impeccably tailored suits and roomy coats. He sold his business to L'Oreal perfume company in 1965; retired for a year, dressing only private clients, then returned in 1967 with surprising see-through dresses, Cosmonaut suits, knee socks, and knit catsuits. By 1972, his designs were using feminine ruffles, color pink, and softer fabrics in evening gowns and loose pants. In 1983, Itokin, a Japanese group, purchased 65% of couture firm from L'Oreal. Widely licensed, the label appeared on products around the world.

Crahay, Jules-François *French designer* (1917–1988)

Crahay started his own fashion house in 1951, but closed within a year and became chief designer at Nina Ricci from 1954 to 1964. He went to Lanvin as head designer in 1964; retired in 1984. Known for young, uninhibited, civilized, soignée clothes. One of first to glamorize pants as evening wear.

Creed, Charles *British designer* (1908–1966)

Fifth generation of the oldest name in British fashion, an ancestor of Creed opened a men's tailoring shop in 1710. His grandfather moved it to Paris in 1750. Charles, born in Paris, studied in France and Switzerland, worked in sales in New York at Bergdorf Goodman. He had his first showing in London in 1932; reopened after World War II. He was famous for elegant suits for town and evening as well as for the country. His house closed following his death.

Cummings, Angela *American jewelry designer*

Daughter of German diplomat; Cummings graduated from art school in Hanau, West Germany; studied at an art academy in Perugia, Italy. In 1967, she joined Tiffany & Co., where she stayed until she opened her own business in 1984. Cummings's boutiques are in Bergdorf Goodman (New York), Macy's (San Francisco), and Bloomingdale's (New York). She works in classical tradition, using 18-karat gold, platinum, or sterling silver; and often combines wood, gold, and diamonds. Reviving old techniques of goldsmithing, such as damascene, she is inspired by natural and organic forms (e.g., silver jewelry in the shape of a leaf from a gingko tree).

Daché, Lilly (da-shay′) *American designer* (1904–1989)

Leading milliner in the United States from mid-1930s to early 1950s, Daché was born in France. She apprenticed at Reboux in Paris for four years. After coming to New York in 1924, she worked as a milliner and opened a small shop where she molded hats on customers and established her reputation. By 1949, she was designing dresses to go with her hats, gloves, hosiery, lingerie and loungewear, wallets, and jewelry; and by 1954 she had added perfume and cosmetics. Styles for which she is remembered include draped turbans, half-hats, war-workers' visor caps, colored snoods, romantic massed flower shapes, and, in 1949, a wired strapless bra. She closed her business in 1969.

de la Renta, Oscar (deh lah ren′-tah) *American designer* (1932–)

A native of the Dominican Republic, de la Renta studied art in Spain after which he worked for BALENCIAGA's couture house in Madrid for twelve years. He spent four years with Castillo at Lanvin-Castillo Paris; then came to Elizabeth Arden, NY, in 1963. A partner in Jane Derby in 1965, he was soon operating under his own label, Oscar de la Renta, Ltd., for luxury ready-to-wear. Noted for his use of opulent fabrics such as taffetas and tulle with sequins for sexy, romantic evening clothes and sophisticated and feminine daywear, his design interests include: signature perfume introduced in 1977 and another in 1983; boutique lines, swimwear, wedding gowns, furs, jewelry, bed linens, and loungewear. He became creative director for Balmain, becoming the first American designer to head a French couture house.

Dell'Olio, Louis (del ohl′-yoh) *American designer* (1948–)

Dell'Olio received the Norman Norell Scholarship to Parsons School of Design, where he won the Gold Thimble Award for coats and suits at graduation in 1969. He assisted Dominic Rompollo at Teal Traina from 1969 to 1971; was designer at Giorgini and Ginori divisions of Originala from 1971 to 1974; and became co-designer with DONNA KARAN for Anne Klein & Co. in 1974.

He was sole designer for Anne Klein from 1985 until 1993. His philosophy has been described as a modern sophisticated interpretation of classic Anne Klein sportswear; using easy shapes in beautiful fabrics. He also designs furs for Michael Forrest.

Demeulemeester, Ann *Belgian designer* (1961–)

Deconstructionist designer who emerged in the 1980s and made a significant success in the 1990s. An avante garde designer, she is considered to be on the cutting edge of fashion but at the same time produces wearable designs.

de Rauch, Madeleine (de-rok′) *French couturière* (1896–1985)

Renowned sportswoman of the 1920s who wanted proper sportsclothes for herself and for friends who played tennis and golf, skied, and rode horses, de Rauch started a business called "House of Friendship by Mme. de Rauch" in 1932. Aided by two sports-minded sisters, she made beautiful wearable, functional clothes, adaptable to many types of women. The firm closed in 1973.

Dessès, Jean (des-say′, zhon) *French couturier* (1904–1970)

Born in Alexandria, Egypt, of Greek ancestry, Dessès studied law in Paris; aimed at diplomatic service but switched to fashion design in 1925. After 12 years working for Jane, he opened his own house in 1937. Designing directly on the dress form, he draped the fabric himself. He was inspired by ethnic and historic garments, especially those from Greece or Egypt. His admiration for American women led him to make a lower-priced line for them in 1950, which he called "Jean Dessès Diffusion." This marked the beginning of the ready-to-wear trend in French couture. He gave up the couture in 1965 because of ill health and returned to Athens, where he ran a boutique until his death.

Dior, Christian (dee-or′, chris′-ti-ahn) *French couturier* (1905–1957)

After initially aiming at a diplomatic career, Dior operated an art gallery from 1930 to 1934. By 1938 he was sketching hat designs for AGNÈS; and designing for PIGUET, and then for LUCIEN LELONG in 1941. He opened his own house in 1947 after which he launched the revolutionary New Look, an ultra-feminine silhouette; yards of material in almost ankle-length skirt, with tiny waist, snug bodice, rounded sloping shoulders, and padded hips. In the next ten years, he devised his own inner construction to shape dresses into the "H," "A," and "Y" lines. From 1948 to 1951, the business added perfumes, scarves, hosiery, furs, gloves, and men's neckties as well as a young, less-expensive line, "Miss Dior." Having become a vast international merchandising operation, the House of Dior continued after his death in 1957 under designing leadership of his assistant, YVES SAINT LAURENT (1957 to 1960), MARC BOHAN (1958 to 1996), and JOHN GALLIANO (1996–).

Dolce and Gabbana (dohl-chay′ and gahb-bah′-nah) *Italian designers* (1958–) (1962–)
Italians Domenico Dolce and Estefano Gabbana formed a fashion consulting studio in 1982. They opened D&G in 1985, when they showed their first women's collection. By 1987 they had added knitwear, in 1989, beachwear, and in 1990, men's wear.

Dorothée Bis *French knitwear house*
A chain of Paris trend-setting boutiques from the 1960s, run by designer-buyer Jacqueline Jacobson and husband, Elie, Dorothée Bis is credited by some with starting hot pants fad in 1969. Also remembered for long pants tucked into Tibetan boots; see-through knits; mid-calf coats over miniskirts; skinny cardigans and scarves; knickers; sweetheart necklines; shrunken-crochet berets; dolman-sleeved Jacquard knits. Their trademark shop display—a life-sized rag doll slumped in chair.

Doucet, Jacques (doo-she′, zhak) *French couturier* (c. 1860–c. 1932)
One of the first couture houses in Paris in mid-19th c., the founder was the grandfather of Jacques (born c. 1860), who started his career as dress designer after the Franco-Prussian War (1870). A competitor of Worth, Doucet favored 18th-c. styles and much lace. His apprentices included Madeleine Vionnet and Paul Poiret. In 1928, firm joined Doeuillet to become Doeuillet-Doucet.

Drécoll (dreh′-caul) *French couture house*
One of most prestigious couture houses in Paris from 1900 to 1925, Drécoll's designer was Austrian Mme. de Wagner, who bought the name from Baron Christophe Drécoll, a well-known Belgian dressmaker in Vienna. Designs were architectural, of elegant line, often black and white or two colors. Drécoll sent a mannequin to the races in the first harem skirt in 1910. Her son-in-law took over business in 1925. Her daughter, Maggy, formed her own couture house under name Maggy Rouff in 1929.

Eiseman, Florence *American children's wear designer* (1899–1988)
Began to sew as a hobby following birth of her second son in 1931; and continued making clothes for her children and her neighbor's children. After samples of her work were shown to Marshall Field, Chicago, an initial $3,000 order gave birth to a clothing firm selling across the United States and abroad. Hallmarks were simple styles, children not dressed as adults, fine fabrics, excellent workmanship, high prices.

Ellis, Perry *American designer* (1940–1986)
Ellis earned a B.A. from William and Mary and an M.A. in retailing from New York University. At first a sportswear buyer, he began designing for Portfolio division of Vera in 1975. Perry Ellis Sportswear, Inc., was established in 1978 and Perry Ellis menswear in 1980. His philosophy: Fashion should not be taken seriously and individuals should not be overly concerned with clothing. He used natural fabrics; hand-knitted sweaters in silk, cotton, and cashmere, designed furs, shearling coats for men and women, shoes, legwear, scarves, Vogue patterns, sheets, towels, and blankets for Martex.

Fath, Jacques (fat, zhak) *French couturier* (1912–1954)
Fath opened his own house in 1937; stayed open during war, and for next 17 years was immensely successful, designing elegant, flattering, feminine, sexy clothes. He also operated a boutique for perfume, stockings, scarves, and millinery. He is remembered for hourglass shapes, swathed hips, plunging necklines, full-pleated skirts, wide cape collars, and stockings with Chantilly-lace tops. After his death in 1954, his business was carried on by his wife until 1957.

Fendi (fen′dee) *Italian fur house*
Founded in 1918 by Adele Fendi, the house specialized in furs, handbags, luggage, and ready-to-

wear. In 1954, after she was widowed, Signora Fendi ran business with five daughters: Paola, Anna, Franca, Carla, and Alda. She died in 1978, and her daughters and granddaughters continued to run the business. KARL LAGERFELD was hired in 1962 as designer, and he introduced new, unusual, and neglected furs such as squirrel, badger, fox as well as some unpedigreed species. Innovative design techniques: furs woven in strips, unlined, lined with silk, and the double F initials designed by Lagerfeld have become international symbols in design.

Ferragamo, Salvatore (fer-ah-gah′-moh) *Italian shoe designer* (1898–1960)

An Italian shoemaker, Ferragamo emigrated to California in 1923. He opened a cobbler's shop in Hollywood and, in 1936, a business in Florence, Italy. By the time of his death, he had ten factories in Great Britain and Italy. He is said to have originated the wedge heel, platform sole, and transparent Lucite heel. The business was carried on by his daughters, Fiamma and Giovanna, and his son Ferrucio with an emphasis on elegant, ladylike conservative styling with comfortable fit. The Ferragamo name appears on handbags, scarves, luxury ready-to-wear sold in boutiques in Europe and the United States and in major U.S. specialty stores.

Ferré, Gianfranco (fer-reh′) *Italian designer* (1945–)

Ferré studied architecture in Milan, worked with a furniture designer, and then became known for accessories design by 1970. He designed sportswear and raincoats on a freelance basis in 1972 and established his own firm in 1974. His expertise in architecture combined with fine tailoring techniques have made him one of the top European designers.

Fogarty, Anne *American designer* (1919–1981)

A designer of junior-size dresses between 1948 and 1957 for Youth Guild and Margot, Inc., and at Saks Fifth Avenue, from 1957 to 1962; the designer established Anne Fogarty Inc. in 1962. She is remembered for "paper-doll" silhouette of 1951, a revival of crinoline petticoats under full-skirted, tiny-waisted shirtwaist dresses; the "camise," a chemise gathered from a high yoke, in 1958; lounging coveralls; and slim Empire

dress with tiny puffed sleeves. In early 1970s, she showed a peasant look with ruffled shirts and long skirts with ruffled hems, and hot pants under a long quilted skirt. She had completed a spring/summer collection of sportswear and dresses at the time of her death.

Fontana, Sorelle (Fontana Sisters) (fohn-tahn′-ah sohr-rel′-ay) *Italian couture house*

This firm originated in Parma, Italy, in 1907; then moved to Rome. Headed by mother, Amabile, assisted by daughters; Micol and Zoe as designers and Giovanna in sales, the firm was noted for evening gowns, delicate handwork, asymmetric lines, interesting necklines. They showed a collection in the United States in mid–World War II. One of the leading Italian couture houses in 1950s.

Ford, Tom *American designer* (1962–)

Ford made his runway debut in 1998 and had a very quick success. By 2001 he was doing men's and women's collections for YSL and Gucci, where he was responsible for turning around a company that had been in decline.

Fortuny, Mariano (Mariano Fortuny y Madrazo) (for-too′-nee) *Italian designer* (1871–1949)

Fortuny was an innovator, inventor, photographer, stage designer, textile and dress designer. Famous for his long, slender mushroom-pleated silk teagowns, his most famous design was called the Delphos Gown, which was seen first in 1907. His clothes were considered classics all through the 1930s, and are now rare collector's items.

Galanos, James (gal′-ahn-oss) *American designer* (1929–)

Galanos studied fashion in New York. He worked at ROBERT PIGUET in Paris from 1947 to 1948, along with MARC BOHAN. After returning to the United States, he eventually started his own business in Los Angeles in 1951. His first New York show in 1952 launched him on a spectacular career. Known for luxurious day and evening ensembles and a total look for collections including hats, shoes, hosiery, accessories, hair, and makeup.

Galitzine, Princess Irene (gahl-it-zeen′) *Italian designer* (1916–)

Russian-born, Galitzine was educated in Italy and England; studied art in Rome. She worked for

SORELLE FONTANA for three years; then started her own import business in Rome in 1948. First showing her designs in 1959, she introduced silk palazzo pajamas in 1960. Also known for at-home togas, evening suits, tunic-top dresses, lingerie, bare-back or open-sided evening gowns, decorative striped stockings. Her house closed in 1968, but she revived her couture collection in 1970 and showed sporadically for several years after that.

Galliano, John (gahl-ee-ahn'-oh) *French couturier* (1960–)

Galliano finished his training in 1983 and showed his first collection in 1984. He quickly established himself as a skilled technician and imaginative designer. He moved from avant-garde creations to more sophisticated styles. Named head designer at GIVENCHY in 1995, he remained only a few seasons before moving to the House of DIOR in 1996.

Gaultier, Jean-Paul (gol-tee-yeh') *French designer* (1952–)

Gaultier presented a collection of designs to his mother and grandmother at age 13, and at 15 invented a coat with bookbag closures. In 1970 he sent his design portfolio to PIERRE CARDIN, who hired him as design assistant for two years. He also worked for Jacques Esterel and JEAN PATOU. He presented his first ready-to-wear collection with silhouettes contrary to the current designs. Inspired by London street dressing, Gaultier mixes fabrics and shapes that are unusual and controversial.

Gernreich, Rudi (gern'-rike) *American designer* (1922–1985)

Born in Vienna, Austria, Gernreich emigrated to California in 1938. He specialized in dramatic sport clothes in striking color combinations and cut, bathing suits, underwear, and hosiery—usually coordinated for total look. Remembered for maillot swimsuits with no bra and bare suits with deeply cut-out sides in the mid-1950s; the topless swimsuit and see-through blouses in 1964; "no-bra" bra in skin-color nylon net; knee-high leggings patterned to match tunic tops and tights in 1967; wrap-tied legs and dhoti dresses in 1968. He announced in 1968 that he was taking sabbatical from his fashion career and never returned to fashion design.

Gesquière, Nicholas (1971–)

After an internship with designer Agnès B., Ghesquière got his first couture job with GAULTIER at age 21. At the same time he was doing some freelance designing of knitwear. In the mid-90s he joined Balenciaga and in 1997 was made creative director. He has established a first-rate reputation and is expected to be one of the major designers of the twenty-first century.

Givenchy, Hubert de (zhee-von'-she, u-bare') *French designer* (1927–)

Givenchy studied at L'École des Beaux Arts in Paris. At age 17, he started designing at FATH, then at PIGUET and LELONG; and spent four years with SCHIAPARELLI. He opened his own house in 1952 at age 25. Noted for clothing of exceptional workmanship, masterly cut, and beautiful fabrics, his ready-to-wear was distributed worldwide through his Nouvelle Boutique. Licensing agreements include sportswear, men's and women's shirts, leathers, hosiery, furs, eyeglasses, home furnishings. He retired in 1995. Designers who succeeded him included JOHN GALLIANO, ALEXANDER MCQUEEN, and, in 2001, Julien McDonald.

Grès, Alix (gray, ah-leex') *French couturière* (1903–1993)

Grès was originally a sculptress before starting to design women's clothes. She served an apprenticeship at Premet, then started working independently under the name of Alix Barton in 1934, and showed in house called Alix until 1942, at which time it was closed by the Germans. After World War II, using her married name, Grès, she reopened. Noted for superb craftsmanship; statuesque Greek-draped evening gowns; bicolor pleated jersey gowns with crisscrossed string belts; cowled black jersey day dresses; asymmetric drapes; bias-cut caftans; loose topcoats with hoods and bat-wing sleeves; at home and beach wear. She sold her house in 1984.

Gucci (goo'-chee) *Italian leather house*

This family business in Italy established in 15th c. by ancestors of the current head, Dr. Aldo Gucci, has been manufacturing and retailing luggage and leather accessories since 1906. In 1969 they started to show collections of apparel for men and women. Known for the walking low-heeled loafer with metal harness-bit ornament across the vamp, tackroom hardware, and red and green canvas stripes used in luggage and accessories, the GG signature on bags and apparel has become a status symbol and is sold in a chain of Gucci shops throughout the world. Family court battles caused the firm difficulties, but the company was revitalized by 2000 by TOM FORD, who designs their women's and men's wear lines.

Halston (Roy Halston Frowick)   *American designer* (1932–1990)

Halston studied at Chicago Art Institute. He worked for LILLY DACHÉ in N.Y.; and designed hats for Bergdorf Goodman from 1959 to 1968, where he made news with the pillbox hat he designed for Jacqueline Kennedy to wear at the inaugural ceremony in 1961. He started his own business on East 68th Street in 1968 for private clients and opened a ready-to-wear firm, Halston Originals, in fall 1972. His formula could be described as: casual throwaway chic, using superior fabrics for extremely simple classics such as a long cashmere dress with a sweater tied over shoulders; long, slinky halterneck jerseys; wraparound skirts and turtlenecks. Though Halston died in 1990, the House of Halston continues under other designers.

Hardwick, Cathy   *American designer* (1933–)

Born in Seoul, Korea, Hardwick came to the United States at 21 and opened boutique in San Francisco. She freelanced for Alvin Duskin and other firms; then moved to New York in 1960s. There she opened Cathy Hardwick & Friends in 1972. Her philosophy: clean-cut, fluid, sensuous clothing; comfortable and useful as well as fashionable. She has also designed tableware for Mikasa and bed linens for Burlington Industries.

Hartnell, Sir Norman   *British designer* (1901–1979)

Hartnell opened a dress shop with his sister in 1923, then his own house in 1930 and became the largest couture house in London and famous as dressmaker to the British Court. He is known for Coronation gowns for Queen Elizabeth II in 1953; lavishly embroidered ball gowns, fur-trimmed suits, city tweeds.

Heim, Jacques (heym′, zhak)   *French designer* (1899–1967)

Paris-born son of Isadore and Jeanne Heim, who had founded a fur house in 1898, Jacques built this house into a world-famous couture establishment. Starting in 1923 and continuing for the next 40 years, he reflected trends rather than creating them. Known as the designer of the first bikini in 1945, he also had success with youthful clothes in his boutique, *Heim Jeunes Filles.* After his death, his son assumed direction of the firm.

Herman, Stan   *American designer* (1930–)

Designer for a number of companies, Herman has done work in hat design for John-Fredericks, at Mr. Mort (1961–71), for Henri Bendel, Youthcraft-Charmfit, Slumbertogs, and uniform houses. He has been active in the Council of Fashion Designers of America since 1967 and has served in leadership positions in this organization. He has been quoted as saying, "Fashion is one of life's nourishments which, like good food, must be grown each season to remain fresh."

Hermès (air′-mes)   *French design house*

Thierry Hermès, saddle- and harness-maker, opened a shop in 1837 in Paris, adding sporting accessories, toilet articles, boots, scarves, and jewelry. Couture began in 1920 under Emile Hermès; closed in 1952, however the firm continues to make women's and men's ready-to-wear as well as leather products.

Herrera, Carolina   *American designer* (1939–)

Herrera established her firm in 1981. She did her first fur collection for Revillon in 1984 and in 1996 produced a lower-priced ready-to-wear line called CH. She makes clothes to order for some private clients and is known for her elegant clothes.

Hilfiger, Tommy   (1952–)

Born in Elmira, NY, where he opened a retail business, the People's Store, in 1969. By 1979 Hilfiger had moved to New York and showed his first signature collection in 1984. He has been described as making "Main Street America designs" and caters to the youth culture with designs reflecting pop music and team sports. His clientele is very loyal.

Horn, Carol   *American designer* (1936–)

Horn studied fine arts at Boston and Columbia Universities and started designing junior sportswear for Bryant 9 and Benson & Partners. She opened her own company, Carol Horn Sportswear, in 1983. Clothing is uncontrived shapes made of natural fabrics and moderately priced.

Jacobs, Marc   *American designer* (1964–)

After managing his own firm from 1986 to 1988, Jacobs joined Perry Ellis, then showed under his own name after 1994. Considered a design prodigy, he was immediately successful in building a reputation as a highly original young designer. He became artistic director at Vuitton in 1997.

James, Charles   *American couturier* (1906–1978)

Born in England, James moved to Chicago and eventually operated dressmaking salons in London and Paris in the 1930s and his own custom-order business in 1940s and 1950s. Rated by his peers: "A genius . . . daring innovator in the shape of clothes . . . more of an architect or sculptor . . . independent, stormy, unpredictable, contentious." Acknowledged as an equal by the Paris couture in 1947, he is remembered for new techniques for dress patterns; new dress forms; elaborate, bouffant ball gowns in odd mixtures of colors and fabrics; batwing oval cape-coat; intricately cut dolman wraps and asymmetric shapes. He retired from couture design in 1958 to devote himself to sculpture and painting.

Mr. John   *American millinery designer* (1906–1993)

Born John Pico John in Munich, Germany, where his mother was a millinery designer, Mr. John came to New York in 1929 and designed millinery for house of Mme. Laurel. After this he formed John Fredericks with a partner, Fred Fredericks, in 1929 and subsequently started his own firm, Mr. John, Inc., in 1948. Most successful in the 1940s and 1950s, the heyday of hats, he is remembered for forward-tilted doll hats, glorified Stetsons, scarf-attached hats, skullcaps held by tight face veils, wig hats, huge flower or bushy fur toques. His business closed in 1970, although he continued designing for private clients.

Johnson, Betsey   *American designer* (1942–)

Graduate of Syracuse University; Johnson started as guest editor for *Mademoiselle* magazine, where she made sweaters for editors. These were seen by the owner of Paraphernalia boutiques, who gave her a job designing. She was one of the first American designers to design anti–Seventh Avenue fashions in early 1960s. With friends she started a boutique, Betsey, Bunky & Nini, in 1969. Her body-conscious clothes range from swimwear to bodysuits, tight pants to dance dresses. Betsey Johnson, Inc., established in 1978, manufactures sportswear, bodywear, and dresses, and operates a number of retail stores.

Joop, Wolfgang   *German designer* (1944–)

A German journalist and freelance designer, Joop showed his first fur collection in 1978. By 1981 he added Joop! ready-to-wear, in 1987 Joop! jeans. In 2000, he left his own company, which continues without him.

Julian, Alexander   *American designer*

Born and raised in Chapel Hill, North Carolina, where his father was in retailing, Julian designed his first shirt at 12; managed his father's store at 18; and owned the shop at 21. In 1975, he moved to New York, where he designs his own fabrics, interpreting traditional themes with wit and imagination. Licenses include: men's, women's, and children's wear; hosiery; home furnishings and decorative fabrics; small leather goods; pocket accessories.

Kahn, Robin   *American jewelry designer* (1947–)

Born in London, Kahn came to the United States at 5 years; graduating from the High School of Art and Design and Parsons School of Design. Trained with goldsmiths at the Haystack Mountain School of Crafts, he went on to design accessories for PIERRE CARDIN, OSCAR DE LA RENTA, and Kenneth J. Lane, and one-of-a-kind pieces for Bloomingdale's. He founded Robin Kahn, Inc. in 1978. His forms are bold, clean, and elegant; and he designs directly from metal utilizing brass, copper, and bronze; ebony, turquoise, ivory, lapis as well as leather cording and taffeta.

Kamali, Norma   *American designer* (1945–)

Born Norma Arraez and raised in New York, Kamali graduated from the Fashion Institute of Technology in 1964 as a student of illustrating. In 1969 with her husband, Eddie Kamali, she opened a tiny basement shop selling imports primarily from England and her own designs. Expanding in 1974, she began designing suits, lace dresses. In 1978, after her divorce, she established a boutique and company called OMO (On My Own). Her body-conscious and adventurous designs include: swimsuits, "parachute," and a moderate-priced collection for Jones Apparel Group using cotton sweatshirt fabric; giant removable shoulder pads. Also designed lingerie and children's wear.

Karan, Donna   *American designer* (1948–)

Attended Parsons School of Design, but after her second year dropped out to work with ANNE KLEIN, where she became associate designer in 1971; then head designer following Klein's illness in 1974. She asked former Parsons classmate LOUIS DELL'OLIO to co-design the Klein collection. In 1983 she launched a less-expensive line, Anne Klein II. She and her husband, Stephan Weiss, founded Donna Karen, New York with the support of Takihyo Corporation, Japan, Anne Klein's parent company. Very successful, the firm has many divisions, including those for men and accessories. Design principles include the classic mix-and-match sportswear concept.

Kawakubo, Rei   *Japanese designer* (1942–)

Born in Tokyo, Japan, Kawakubo graduated from Keio University in Tokyo with major in literature. After working in the advertising department of a textile firm and as a freelance stylist, she established Comme des Garçons Co., Ltd., in 1973. She first showed in Tokyo in 1975, then went on to introduce men's wear in 1978 and knitwear in 1981. In 1981 she showed for first time in Paris, after which she established offices in Paris (1982) and New York (1986). Originally designing exclusively in black and gray, she currently adds some touches of color. Designs are often asymmetrical in shape and made of cotton, linen, or canvas with tears and slashes in the designs.

Kenzo (Kenzo Takada)   *French designer* (1945–)

A trend-setting French ready-to-wear designer from early 1970s and after, Kenzo came to Paris from Japan in 1965. He opened his own boutique, Jungle Jap, in 1970. His designs were widely distributed in the United States and he opened Kenzo-Paris boutique in New York in 1983, then in 1984 went on to produce "Album by Kenzo" for The Limited. Designs are based on traditional Japanese clothing and made in spirited combinations of textures and patterns. Kenzo

retired in 2000, but the firm continues under other designers.

Khanh, Emmanuelle (kahn, e-man-u-el)   *French designer* (1938–)

Khanh entered the fashion world as mannequin for GIVENCHY. She began designing inexpensive ready-to-wear, sold in Paris and London boutiques, as a rebellion against haute couture. Attracting publicity in 1963 as a pioneer of the new wave of dress that swept the Paris streets as MARY QUANT's did in London, she is remembered for dog's ear collars, droopy revers on long fitted jackets, loose cravat closings on coats and suits. She reflected a contemporary approach to individuality symptomatic of the 1960s, and continued to design in the 1970s and after.

Kieselstein-Cord, Barry   *American jewelry designer* (1943–)

Kieselstein studied at Parsons School of Design, New York University, and the American Craft League. He did his first jewelry collection for Georg Jensen around 1972. By early 1980s his designs sold around the United States as well as abroad. In 1984, his collection included accessories in precious metals and rare woods.

Klein, Anne   *American designer* (1923–1974)

Klein has been called the all-American designer of classic sportswear for the woman 5'4" and under and was responsible for transforming "junior" clothes from fussy, little-girl type clothes to sleek sophisticated fashion clothing. In 1948, with her first husband Ben Klein, she organized the firm Junior Sophisticates, where she was the designer from 1951 to 1964. Anne Klein & Co. was formed in 1968 with her second husband. She is remembered in the 1950s for nipped waist, full skirt; unbelted chemise; "little boy" look; use of white satin with gray flannel; in the 1960s for classic blazers, shirtdresses, long midis, leather gaucho pants, Western and American Indian accessories, Turkish rug coats, hot pants; and in the 1970s she was interested in nongimmicky, interrelated wardrobe of jackets, sweaters, pants, and skirts, and slinky, hooded jersey dresses for evening. The firm continued after her death in 1974, first with DONNA KARAN and LOUIS DELL'OLIO as co-designers, and later with Dell'Olio as sole designer.

Klein, Calvin   *American designer* (1942–)

Klein attended High School of Art and Design and graduated from the Fashion Institute of Technology in 1962. With friend Barry Schwartz he formed Calvin Klein Ltd. in 1968. His designs include: women's and men's ready-to-wear; sportswear; blue jeans, furs, women's undergarments in designs similar to traditional men's undershirts and briefs, bed linens, cosmetics, skin care products, fragrances, and pantyhose; also a "couture" collection exclusively for Bergdorf-Goodman. His clothing is simple and refined and based on sportswear principles; uses luxurious natural fabrics as well as leather and suede in earth tones and neutrals.

Kors, Michael   *American designer* (1959–)

A New York native, Kors studied at Fashion Institute of Technology. In 1978 he designed and merchandised a collection for Lothar's, a New York retail store. By 1981 he was showing his own collection of luxurious and precisely cut sportswear. He joined Celine as creative director in 1997 and continues in the early 2000s to create his own line in New York and the Celine line in Paris.

Lacroix, Christian   (lah cwa′)   *French designer* (1951–)

Lacroix studied art history at Montpellier University; and in 1972 studied at L'École du Louvre in Paris. Working first as a museum curator, then as an assistant at Hermès in 1978, and at Guy Paulin, he turned to the study of fashion design in Japan. After he returned to Paris, he designed for JEAN PATOU from 1981 to mid-1987 then opened his own couture and ready-to-wear business in mid-1987. He is known for dramatic styles, often theatrical and worn with fantastic accessories. His ready-to-wear is somewhat less extreme than his couture clothes.

Lagerfeld, Karl   *French designer* (1939–)

Born in Hamburg, Germany, in 1939, Lagerfeld arrived in Paris in 1953. He worked for BALMAIN from 1954 to 1957, then in 1963 for Chloe, an upscale ready-to-wear house where he became sole designer in 1972. From 1982 he designed for CHANEL while continuing with Chloe, left Chloe in 1984 for Chanel and to begin a collec-

tion under his own label. He designed a sportswear collection specifically for the United States in 1985. He also designs furs and sportswear for FENDI. Lagerfeld creates highly original designs that are quite wearable and is always interesting and exceptionally prolific.

Lane, Kenneth Jay   *American jewelry designer* (1932–)

Lane studied at the University of Michigan and graduated from the Rhode Island School of Design in 1954. While working on the promotion staff at *Vogue* magazine, he met Roger Vivier, shoe designer, and spent part of each year in Paris working with him. He went to work for Delman shoes as assistant designer; then to Christian Dior Shoes as associate designer. At the same time, in 1963, he made some jewelry pieces that were photographed by fashion magazines and bought by some stores. He used his initials K.J.L. and by 1964 was designing jewelry full-time. He likes to see his costume jewelry worn with jewelry made of real gems.

Lanvin, Jeanne   (lahn-vahn′, zhon)   *French designer* (1867–1946)

Lanvin apprenticed at 13 and started as milliner in 1890. Designing children's clothes for her daughter and friends led to the establishment of her own business in Paris, where she remained for nearly 50 years. Remembered for *robes de style* of 18th- and 19th-c. flavor, wedding gowns, fantasy evening gowns with metallic embroideries, teagowns, dinner pajamas, dolman wraps, and capes. Her peak years were between World Wars I and II. She died at the age of 79, but the house continued under the directorship of her daughter Contesse de Polignac. After a succession of designers, the couture operation ended in 1992.

Laroche, Guy   (lah-rosh)   *French designer* (c. 1923–1990)

Son of a French cattle-farming family near La Rochelle, Laroche dabbled in hair styling and millinery; worked for three years on Seventh Avenue, eight years with JEAN DESSÈS in Paris. He showed his first collection in fall of 1957, mostly coats and suits. His greatest fame came during the early 1960s. At the time of his death, the firm had expanded into ready-to-wear, and licensing agreements (intimate apparel, furs, luggage, sportswear, rainwear, dresses, blouses, sunglasses, accessories, fragrances). He is remembered for back cowl drapes; short puffed hems for evening; schoolgirl dresses; loose lines in soft coats.

Lauren, Ralph *American designer* (1939–)
In 1967 Lauren persuaded a men's wear firm to handle made-by-hand silk neckties he had designed, thereby establishing the Polo neckwear division. Lauren was contracted to design the Polo line of men's wear for Norman Hilton. In 1968 a separate company was established that produced a total wardrobe for men. Lauren introduced women's ready-to-wear made of Harris tweeds, camel's hair, silk in 1971; followed by Polo boy's wear; Western wear; Ralph Lauren for Girls; a less expensive men's line; Polo University Club for college students and young businessmen; Roughwear, a rugged outdoor collection. Licenses include: men's and women's ready-to-wear including men's robes, swimwear, and furnishings; small leathers, furs, scarves, fragrances, cosmetics, skin care, luggage, and home furnishings.

Lelong, Lucien (leh-lohn´, luce-yen´) *French couturier* (1889–1958)
One of the great names in couture of the 1920s and through the 1940s; Lelong was famed for elegant, feminine clothes of refined taste and lasting wearability. The couture house was organized by his parents in 1886. Lucien was born in 1889. As an adult he founded his own business in 1919. Not a designer himself, he was an inspiration to a distinguished atelier of workers, including Christian Dior, Pierre Balmain, Hubert de Givenchy, and Jean Schlumberger. He started *Editions* department of ready-to-wear, forerunner of boutiques, in 1934. He was responsible for revitalizing couture after World War II. He retired in 1947, because of ill health.

Leroy See Roy, Hippolyte.

Leser, Tina *American designer* (1910–1986)
Leser studied at the School of Industrial Art and Academy of Fine Arts, Philadelphia, and at the Sorbonne, Paris. From 1936 to 1942, she lived in Hawaii, where she designed and sold her own hand-blocked floral prints in playclothes. She returned to New York in 1942 and was associated with Edwin H. Foreman, Inc. (1943 to 1952) after which she established Tina Leser Inc. in 1952. Retired in 1964; but returned to design from 1966 to 1982, Leser is remembered for sarong playclothes; water-boy pants; painted and sequined cotton blouses; wrapped pareo skirt with bandeau top; costume jewelry in cork, coral, and shells; travel-inspired Mexican, Haitian, Japanese, Indian fabrics, used in original trousers, easy coverup tops, long at-home robes. She is credited with making the first dress from cashmere.

Mackie, Bob *American designer* (1940–)
After studing art and design in Los Angeles, Mackie worked as sketcher for Jean Louis and Edith Head as well as for Ray Aghayan, his future partner. Mackie and Aghayan have designed costumes for such celebrities as Marlene Dietrich, Carol Burnett, Barbra Streisand, and Cher, and been nominated several times for Academy Awards for costume design. In mid-1980s he was successful with a ready-to-wear collection emphasizing glamorous evening clothes.

Mainbocher (man-bow-shay´) *American couturier* (1890–1976)
Born Main Rousseau Bocher in Chicago, he studied art at Chicago Academy of Fine Arts, and then in New York, Paris, and Munich. After World War I, Mainbocher supported himself as a fashion illustrator for *Harper's Bazaar* and *Vogue* and became a full-time fashion journalist in 1922 before opening his own salon in Paris in 1929. He left Paris at outbreak of World War II and opened a couture house in New York in 1939, which closed in 1971. He was noted for the Duchess of Windsor's wedding dress in 1936; Waves' (Women in the Navy) uniform in 1942; Girl Scout uniform in 1948. Among his ideas, which were widely copied, were print-bordered and lined sweaters to match dresses; beaded evening sweaters, tweed dinner suits with delicate blouses, and embroidered apron evening dresses.

Mandelli, Mariuccia *Italian designer* (mahndell´-ee) (1933–)
Founder in 1954 with her husband Aldo Pinto, of the design firm Krizia, her first show in 1957

won her excellent reviews and business boomed. Her clothes have been described as "young and original with a sense of fantasy." In the early 1970s, they established a knitwear company Kriziamaglia, which became known for animal sweaters—at each collection a different bird or beast is emphasized. Introduced hot pants in 1960s. Designs include children's wear, a boutique line, and fragrances.

Maxwell, Vera *American designer* (1903–1995)

Maxwell worked first with sportswear and coat houses, Adler & Adler and Max Milstein, before opening her own business on Seventh Avenue. She believed in a classic approach to go-together separates in finest quality Scottish tweeds, wool jersey, raw silk, Indian embroideries, etc. She was inspired by men's Harris tweed jackets and gray flannel Oxford bags. She continued to work until early in 1985, when she closed her business. In 1986 designed a collection of dresses, coats, and sportswear for the Peter Lynne Division of Gulf Enterprises but retired again soon after.

McCardell, Claire *American designer* (1906–1958)

After studying at Parsons School in New York and in Paris, McCardell worked for Robert Turk, Inc., as a model and assistant designer in 1929, then in 1931 went with Turk to work at Townley Frocks Inc. where she remained, except for two years with HATTIE CARNEGIE, until her death at the age of 52. Considered the top all-American designer of 1940s and 1950s, she specialized in practical clothes for the average working girl. Credited with originating the "American Look" (i.e., the separates concept inspired by travel needs), she was responsible for many firsts: the monastic dress with natural shoulders and tied waist; harem pajamas; the "Popover," a surplice-wrapped housedress; kitchen dinner dress; bareback summer dress; long cotton Empire dress with tiny puffed sleeves; diaper-wrap one-piece swimsuit; shoulder bolero over halter dress; balloon bloomer playsuit; signature spaghetti belts; ballet slippers for street.

McCartney, Stella *British designer* (1972–)

Daughter of former Beatle Paul McCartney and a graduate of London's Central St. Martin's College of Art & Design, this designer worked at LACROIX in Paris at age 15. Her first major success was at Chloe in 1997 at age 25. In 2001 she left Chloe and started her own label.

McFadden, Mary *American designer* (1936–)

After a varied career that included director of public relations for Christian Dior–New York from 1962 to 1964, editor of *Vogue* South Africa, and work on both the French and American *Vogue* staffs, she sold three tunics she had designed from Chinese and African silks she had collected to Henri Bendel. The silks were hand painted using resist techniques with oriental colorings. Mary McFadden, Inc. was formed in 1976 and she became known for her designs made of unique fabrics using fine pleating and quilting with ropes wrapping the body. Designs include: lingerie and at-home wear, Simplicity Patterns, scarves, eyewear, furs, shoes, bed and bath linens, and upholstery fabrics.

McQueen, Alexander *British designer* (1970–)

An art school graduate in 1992, McQueen began his design career by working in Savile Row, for Romeo Gigli, and for Koji Tasumo. He showed under his own label in 1994 and after GALLIANO left GIVENCHY, he assumed its design leadership. By 2001 he had returned to showing under his own name. He has been called "Britain's bad boy of fashion" because of his dramatic confrontational styles and his sometimes rude personal style.

Miller, Nicole *American designer*

After studying at Rhode Island School of Design and in Paris, Miller opened her own business in 1982. She has been described as "a technical master with an astute fashion sense." She makes women's and men's wear and is especially known for creative use of prints and graphics in her designs.

Missoni, Rosita & Ottavio (Tai) (miss-oh′-nee) *Italian designers* (1932–) (1921–)

Married in 1953, this couple went into business with four knitting machines. Originally they hired freelance designers such as Emmanuelle Khanh and Christiane Bailly to style their line, but currently Rosita designs clothing and Tai the knit fabrics. Colors are worked out by Tai who is always aware of distinctive patterns and stitches. Rosita drapes directly onto a model maintaining simple shapes emphasizing knit designs. Styles are so classic that their designs are difficult to date.

Miyake, Issey (me-ya'-key, ee-see) *Japanese designer* (1938–)

Born in Japan, Miyake moved to Paris in 1965 to study at La Chambre Syndicale de la Couture Parisienne. Work history included being an assistant at GUY LAROCHE and GIVENCHY from 1966 to 1968 and work with GEOFFREY BEENE in 1969. Miyake Design Studio and Issey Miyake International in Tokyo opened in 1970. He showed in Paris for the first time in 1973; established a company in Europe in 1979 and in the United States in 1982. He combines Japanese attitudes of fashion with exotic fabrics of his own designs. Miyake retired in 1997, but his firm continues under other design leadership.

Mizrahi, Isaac (miz-rah'-hee) *American designer* (1961–)

Formed his own business in 1987 after working for PERRY ELLIS, Jeffrey Banks, and CALVIN KLEIN. Mizrahi specialized in luxury sportswear for women, and also for men starting in 1990. Although his designs were considered inventive, using unexpected colors and fabrics, his business ran into difficulty and closed in 1998, after which he went into television and designed for films and theater.

Molyneux, Edward (mohl-ee'-noo) *French couturier* (1891–1974)

Born in Ireland, Molyneux was an aristocrat, sportsman, officer in the Duke of Wellington Regiment, and an art student. He started at 17 as designer, working in London, Chicago, and New York until 1914. He opened his own house in Paris in 1919, where he designed well-bred, elegant, fluid clothes and is remembered for purity of line in printed silk suits with pleated skirts; timeless, softly tailored navy blue suits, and coats. He left Paris during World War II, but returned in 1949, adding furs, lingerie, millinery, and perfumes to his lines. Because of ill health, turned over Paris house to Jacques Griffe in 1950. Persuaded to reopen in Paris, January 1965, as Studio Molyneux; he brought first ready-to-wear collection to the United States in

1965 but this venture was not successful and he retired again.

Montana, Claude *French designer* (1949–)

On a trip to London in 1971 in order to earn money to stay there, Montana designed papier-mâche jewelry encrusted with rhinestones. He stayed for a year, then returned to Paris where he went to work for a leather firm before establishing himself in his own business. Characteristics of his designs are: bold, well-defined shapes. He joined LANVIN in 1989, leaving them in 1992 to continue his own business.

Mori, Hanae (moh'-ree, hah-nah) *Japanese designer* (1925–)

Mori opened a small boutique in Tokyo, where her designs attracted members of the Japanese film industry. She designed costumes for films in 1955, and after opening another shop, went on to develop multimillion-dollar international business. Since 1977 she has shown her couture collection in Paris. Her ready-to-wear sells in fine stores around the world; her boutiques in many countries sell sportswear and accessories. She uses unusual and beautiful fabrics, with especially huge flowers, butterflies, and classic Japanese feminine motifs. Styles are Western with Oriental details; best known for evening or at-home entertaining wear.

Moschino, Franco (mos-keen'-oh) *Italian designer* (c. 1950–1994)

After studying fine arts, Moschino was hired as a sketcher with VERSACE in 1971. He went on to design for Cadette from 1977 to 1982, then worked under his own label from 1983 until his death. He was known for "wearable, sexy clothes with a sense of humor." The label continues with other designers.

Mugler, Thierry *French designer* (1946–)

Mugler made his own clothes as a teenager. His early endeavors include work for the Strasbourg ballet company as well as window-dressing for Paris boutiques. He moved to England in 1968 and then on to Amsterdam before returning to Paris two years later. His first collection in 1971 was shown under the label Café de Paris and by 1973 he designed under his own label. Characteristics include: broad shoulders and well-defined waists, and the presentations of his lines are often startling and theatrical.

Muir, Jean *British designer* (1933–1995)

Muir started her career as sketcher at Liberty, designed for six years at Jaeger; and then under her own label for Jane and Jane in 1962. She established Jean Muir, Inc. in 1966 and opened the Jean Muir Shop in Henri Bendel department store, New York, in 1967. Characteristics were: soft, classic tailored shapes in leathers or soft fabrics.

Natori, Josie *American designer* (1947–)

Born in the Philippines, Natori became a successful investment banker. She moved into the fashion world in the second half of the 1970s and became known for luxurious lingerie and evening wear.

Norell, Norman *American designer* (1900–1972)

Norell was the son of haberdashery store owner in Indianapolis. He came to New York in 1919 to study at Parsons School of Design, and his early career included theatrical and movie designing; work for Charles Armour and for Hattie Carnegie from 1928 to 1940. A partnership in the firm Traina-Norell (1941–1960) followed. He formed his own company, Norman Norell, Inc. in 1960 after Traina's death. Described as the top American designer on Seventh Avenue, the "Dean of the fashion industry," "the American Balenciaga," Norell was known for precision tailoring, dateless purity of line, conservative elegance in the finest imported fabrics. He is also remembered for trouser-suits for town and travel, widely flared day skirts, straight wool jersey chemises, slinky sequined sheaths, the sailor look. The firm continued for a short time after his death under GUSTAVE TASSELL.

Oldham, Todd *American designer* (1961–)

A self-taught designer, Oldham worked for a time in the alterations department of a Ralph Lauren Polo boutique. After going into business in Dallas, he moved to New York where he made women's shirts. His first designer collection showing was in 1990. Since then he has added work as a design consultant for other firms. His clothes have been described as "a mixture of the commercial with the offbeat."

Olive, Frank *American millinery designer* (1929–)

Olive studied art and fashion in Milwaukee and Chicago; went to California to try costume design. Arriving in New York in the early 1950s, he was hoping to design for the theater, but was advised by NORELL, who reviewed some of his sketches, to design hats. He apprenticed, sold fabrics, worked in the Saks Fifth Avenue custom hat department then established his own firm, where he presents three major hat collections: "Counterfits," mass-market; "Frank's Girl," and a moderate-priced "Frank Olive" designer label. He also designs private collections for some clients.

Oliver, André *French designer* (1932–1993)

Born in Toulouse; graduated from École des Beaux Arts in Paris, Oliver joined PIERRE CARDIN in 1955 designing men's wear. Eventually he created ready-to-wear for both men and women. His association with Cardin continued as artistic director of Cardin couture with total artistic control, sharing design responsibilities with Cardin, until Oliver's death.

Paquin, House of (pak-ann′) *French couture house*

Founded in 1891 by Mme. Paquin and her banker husband, the name Paquin was synonymous with elegance in the first decade of 20th c. Mme. Paquin was the first woman to achieve importance in haute couture. Remembered for: fur-trimmed tailored suits, furs, lingerie; evening dresses in white, gold lamé, and pale green; blue serge suit trimmed with gold braid and buttons; fine workmanship and no two dresses alike, the firm was the first to take mannequins to the opera or to the races to show their designs. They also founded the first foreign branch of a couture house in London in 1912, and later in Madrid and in Buenos Aires. Mme. Paquin retired in 1920 after selling firm, she died in 1936. The house closed in July 1956.

Parnis, Mollie *American designer* (1905–1992)

Born in New York City, Parnis was one of the most successful women designers on Seventh Avenue. She began her career in 1939 as designer for Parnis-Livingston (with husband, Leon Livingston), specializing in flattering, feminine dresses and ensembles for the well-to-do woman over

30. Her boutique collection was designed by Morty Sussman until his death in 1979. Mollie Parnis Studio collection, aimed at a younger woman, was organized in 1979. At end of 1984 she dissolved her firm to become a "part-time" consultant at Chevette Lingerie, owned by her nephew. She returned to work full-time and produced her first loungewear collection for Chevette, Mollie Parnis at Home, for fall 1985.

Patou, Jean (pa-too′, zhon)   *French couturier* (1887–1936)

One of the great names in couture of 1920s to 1930s, Patou brought glamour and showmanship to fashion. He was more of a businessman than designer, specializing in ladylike, elegant and uncluttered country-club clothes. Having opened in 1914, the firm was interrupted by World War I, then reopened in 1919 in a shop called *Parry*. After the whole first collection was bought by an American, he started a new business as Jean Patou. Remembered for the sensation caused in 1929 when he lengthened skirts to the ankle and revived a natural waistline and for long simple gowns to go with important jewels. After his death in 1936, the house remained open under Raymond Barbas with series of resident designers, among the best known of which were: MARC BOHAN (1953–1956), KARL LAGERFELD (1960–1963), and CHRISTIAN LACROIX (1982–1986).

Pedlar, Sylvia   *American lingerie designer* (1901–1972)

Pedlar studied at Cooper Union and Art Students League to be a fashion artist. She founded Iris Lingerie in 1929, and designed there for 40 years. She is remembered for reviving the peignoir and matching long-sleeved gown, the Istanbul harem-hem gown, the toga nightdress, short chemise-slip, lace-trimmed silk gowns—sometimes doubling as evening dresses. She retired in 1970.

Peretti, Elsa   *American jewelry designer* (1940–)

Born in Florence, Italy, Peretti earned a diploma in interior design and worked for an architect. After coming to New York and working for several design firms, she designed a few pieces of silver jewelry in 1969 that were used by SANT'ANGELO and HALSTON. She joined Tiffany & Co. in 1974. Her well-known designs include: heart-shaped buckles, silver horseshoe-shaped buckle on a long leather belt (also designed in horn, ebony, and ivory); pendants in the form of small vases; small open, slightly lopsided heart pendant that slides on a chain; diamonds-by-the-yard. She has designed a refillable rock crystal bottle for her perfume sold by Tiffany as well as desk and table accessories.

Piguet, Robert (pee-geh′)   *French couturier* (1901–1953)

Born in Switzerland, Piguet came to Paris at age 17 and studied design with Redfern and POIRET. He opened his own house in 1933, using freelance designers. Great couturiers of the future worked for him: GIVENCHY at age 17 and DIOR in 1937, who said Piguet taught him "the virtues of simplicity . . . how to suppress." JAMES GALANOS worked for him for three months without pay. Known for refined simplicity of black and white dresses, afternoon clothes, tailored suits with vests, fur-trimmed coats, especially styled for petite women. He closed his house in 1951.

Poiret, Paul (pwar-ay′)   *French designer* (1880–1944)

Poiret was the son of a Parisian cloth merchant. While apprenticed to an umbrella-maker, he sold sketches to couturiers and was first employed in the couture by DOUCET in 1896. After spending a short period at the house of WORTH, he opened his own house in 1904. Known as "King of Fashion" from 1904 to 1924, Poiret developed a passion for theatrical costuming and was known for his original ideas and strident colors, for banning the corset, and shackling legs with the harem and hobble skirts. His work is remembered for extreme Orientalism, the minaret skirt, kimono-sleeved tunics, exotic embroidery, barbaric jewels, and eye makeup. He was the first to travel (1912) to foreign capitals with an entourage of 12 live mannequins. After World War I he refused to change his exotic image, so faded from the fashion scene. He died in Paris after years of poverty and illness, having left his mark on the taste of two decades.

Potter, Clare   *American designer*

One of the first group of all-American designers honored by Dorothy Shaver at Lord & Taylor in late 1930s. A graduate of Pratt Institute; she majored in portrait painting; and then entered the fashion field designing embroidery. Formed own business on Seventh Avenue under name Clarepotter during 1940s and 1950s and under name Potter Designs Inc. in 1960s, and had a wholesale firm, Timbertop Inc. She was known for making classic sport, at-home, and dinner clothes. She was noted for unusual color combinations, refinement of cut, and no extraneous trimmings.

Prada, Miuccia (prah′-dah, mee-uch′-ee-ah) *Italian designer* (1950–)

Grandaughter of a leather shop proprietor in Milano, Prada opened her ready-to-wear business in 1989. She has been known both for high-quality clothing and for leather accessories.

Pucci, Emilio (poo′-chee) *Italian designer* (1914–1992)

An aristocrat (Marchese Pucci di Barsento) living in Florence, Pucci was discovered as designer of his own ski clothes by an American photographer in 1947. The following year he designed skiwear for Lord & Taylor, New York. He opened a workshop in Florence in 1949, and by 1950 had a couture house under name Emilio, with boutiques throughout Italy. He was known for brilliant heraldic prints on sheer silk jersey, made into clinging chemises, at-home robes, tights; signature scarves and dresses; resort shirts in designs from Sienese banners, Sicilian, or African motifs; the "capsula" (jumpsuit tapered to cover feet with soft boots). His house closed after his death in 1992 but reopened again in 2001.

Pulitzer, Lily *American designer* (1932–)

Socialite living in Palm Beach, Florida, when, in 1960, she designed and sold a printed-cotton shift called a Lilly, which grew into nationwide fashion in the 1960s and 1970s. She also designed a child's version called "Minnie," print slacks for men, "sneaky Pete" nightshirts, ruffled hems and short sleeves added to basic Lilly in 1970s. Her company was liquidated in mid-1980s.

Quant, Mary *British designer* (1934–)

Quant is credited with starting the Chelsea or Mod Look in the mid-1950s and making London the most influential fashion center at that time. Among the items she was associated with were body stockings, hot pants, the layered principle of dressing, and spirited, unconventional clothes.

By 1967, she started the miniskirt revolution, introduced denim, colored flannel, vinyl in "kooky" (her word) clothes, with 1920s flavor. Within ten years, she had made a less expensive line, Ginger, joined huge U.S. department-store chain J.C. Penney Co.; and designed for Puritan's Youthquake promotion in the United States

Rabanne, Paco (rah-bahn′) *French designer* (1934–)

Born in San Sebastian, Rabanne was the son of BALENCIAGA's head dressmaker. After studying architecture; he moved into designing plastic accessories and opened in Paris in 1966, age 32, causing a sensation with his metal-linked plastic-disk dresses, sun goggles, and jewelry made of plastic in primary colors. He continued the linked-disk principle in fur-patched coats, leather-patch dresses, masses of buttons laced with wire, strips of aluminum, and pioneered in fake-suede dresses in 1970; knit-and-fur coats; dresses of ribbons, feathers, or tassels linked for suppleness.

Reboux, Caroline (reh-boo′) *French millinery designer* (1837?–1927)

Reboux founded the most prestigious millinery house in Paris, both during the late 19th c. and later in the 1920s and 1930s. She created hats for leading actresses and aristocracy. After her death in 1927, her house continued leadership under Mme. Lucienne, making the head-fitting felt cloche the status symbol of fashion for many years. Noted for profile brims, dipping low on one side; forward-tilt tricorns; open-crown lamé turbans; flower bandeaus.

Redfern, House of *British couture house*

London house established in 1841 by Englishman John Redfern, dressmaker for Queen Victoria and the aristocracy. Responsible for jersey suit made for Lillie Langtry, "The Jersey Lily," in 1879. Known for sober, elegant dark blue tailored suits, the house of Redfern also designed the first woman's uniform for the International Red Cross in 1916 and also originated elaborate theater costumes.

Rhodes, Zandra *British designer* (1942–)

Textile designer who graduated from the Royal College of Art in 1966; Rhodes was producing her own designs by 1969. Her textile innovations include: hand-screened prints on soft fabrics,

Art Deco motifs, lipsticks, Teddy bears, zigzags, big splashy patterns, and punk-inspired styles. She designed soft, butterfly dresses, slit-sided chiffons, edges cut by pinking shears.

Ricci, Nina (ree′-chee, nee′-nah) *French couturier* (1883–1970)

Born Marie Nielli in Turin, Italy; she married Louis Ricci, a jeweler, Ricci began her professional life at age 13 when she came to Paris to work as seamstress. By 1905 she was designing her own models on live mannequins. The firm Nina Ricci opened in 1932 and specialized in dresses for mature, elegant women and trousseaux for brides. Styles were graceful with superb detailed workmanship. She was one of the first designers to show lower-priced models in a boutique. Since 1945 the House has been managed by her son Robert Ricci, and after 1959, other designers created the styles.

Rochas, Marcel (ro-shass, mar-sell′) *French couturier* (1902–1955)

Born in Paris, Rochas opened a couture house about 1924. He became popular after eight women appeared at same party wearing identical gowns of his design. His designs were full of fantastic ideas: special bird- and flower-patterned fabric; combinations of as many as ten colors; lots of lace, ribbon, and tulle, and a feminine, square-shouldered, hourglass silhouette several years ahead of the New Look. In 1948, he invented new corset called guépiere, which cinched the natural waist. He had a boutique for separates and accessories and designed for films.

Rodriguez, Narciso (rod-ree′-gez, nar-seeze′-oh) *American designer* (1961–)

Rodriguez came to public notice in 1996 when he designed the late Carolyn Bessette-Kennedy's wedding gown. He had worked for DONNA KAREN at ANNE KLEIN, and at CALVIN KLEIN, where he came to know Bessette-Kennedy. He was subsequently hired by Cerutti to do his own line, which is shown in Milano and also works for a Spanish leather house (Loewe). He is known for skillful tailoring and pretty, feminine designs.

Roy, Hippolyte (roy, ippo-leet) or **Leroy** *French couturier* (1763–1829)

Known to history as Leroy, Hippolyte Roy was the son of a stagehand at the Paris opera. He was

encouraged to become a tailor by ROSE BERTIN. After the French Revolution he switched to the Republican side and designed red, white, and blue patriotic dress. He became a virtual dictator of fashion for Empress Josephine and other women of the time. Directed by Napoleon to design luxurious dress to encourage French industry, Leroy reached the peak of his fame at Napoleon's coronation. He continued to work for Napoleon's second wife. His style never changed through Directorate, Consulate, and Empire periods, although he claimed he never made two dresses alike.

Rykiel, Sonia (rye-kel′) *French designer* (1930–)

Rykiel got her start by making maternity clothes for herself and designing for her husband's firm, Laura. She opened Sonia Rykiel Boutique in 1968 in the Paris department store Galeries Lafayette; and, soon after, her own boutique on the Left Bank. Known for tight, long sweaters; sheer gowns over body stockings, long, slit-sided day skirts, layered dresses and sweaters with thick, roll-back cuffs, high-rise wide pants, her liberated, unconstructed clothes range from folkloric fantasy to basic classics.

Saint Laurent, Yves (sanh la-rahn′, eve) *French designer* (1936–)

Saint Laurent won a prize for a fashion sketch in a design competition judged by DIOR, after which he was offered a position as assistant to Dior. From 1954 to 1957 he worked in the House of Dior, inheriting the top designing post at Dior's death in 1957. He opened his own house in 1961 and a series of prêt-à-porter boutiques called *Rive Gauche* in 1966. His interests expanded to designing men's wear in 1974. Licenses using the famous YSL initials include: sweaters, bed and bath linens, eyeglasses, scarves, children's wear. Saint Laurent was considered the most influential modern designer for the sophisticated woman, one who successfully interpreted the contemporary moods of fashion. Among the specific styles for which he is remembered are the trapeze line, 1958, in his first Dior collection; pea jackets and blazers; chemises divided into Mondrian-blocks of bold color; sportive leather; citypants; military jackets; the nude look in see-through shirts and transparent dresses over nude body stockings in 1966; the fantasy of the rich peasants; smoking jackets; spencer jackets; the tuxedo look. Although Saint Laurent had turned over ready-to-wear design to others, he continued to do the couture collections until 2002 when he announced his retirement.

Sanchez, Fernando   *American lingerie designer* (1930–)

Born in Spain, Sanchez studied at the École Chambre Syndicale de la Couture in Paris. He worked handling lingerie for CHRISTIAN DIOR and came to New York to work with the lines represented at Dior European boutiques. Sanchez also designed furs for Revillon for about 12 years, becoming known for such designs as the hideout mink coat. In 1973 he opened his own lingerie firm. Known for: lace-trimmed silk gowns, camisole tops, boxer shorts, bikini pants, and for developing lingerie based on sportswear principles in which he mixes color, fabrics, and lengths, he signed with Vanity Fair in 1984 to design a moderate-price line of sleep and loungewear.

Sander, Jil   *American designer* (1943–)

After studying at the University of Los Angeles, Sander worked at McCalls in Los Angeles and as a fashion journalist. A freelancer until her first women's collection was shown in 1973, her firm entered a partnership with Prada in 1999. This connection ended by her leaving the firm. She is known for "luxurious minimalism."

Sant'Angelo, Giorgio   (sant'-ahn-jell-oh, joar'-joh)   *American designer* (1936–)

Trained as an architect and industrial designer, Sant'Angelo studied art in France with Picasso; came to the United States in 1962 and created cartoons for Walt Disney. After moving to New York in 1963, he freelanced as a textile designer and stylist and served as a design consultant. He founded Sant'Angelo Ready-to-Wear in 1966 and di Sant'Angelo, Inc. in 1968, and he designs ready-to-wear and separates under the Giorgio Sant'Angelo label. His clothes are a bit out of the ordinary (ethnic themes such as the gypsy look, American Indian, Chinese; body stocking and bodysuit in brilliant bi- and tri-colors to match T-shirts and shorts), and he maintains a couture operation for a roster of celebrities.

Scaasi, Arnold   (ska'-zee)   *American designer* (1931–)

Born Arnold Isaacs in Montreal, Canada, Scaasi adopted his name spelled backward for his design work. He studied at the École Chambre Syndicale in Paris, beginning his career as an apprentice with PAQUIN. Moving to New York, he worked as sketcher for CHARLES JAMES; then, in 1957, opened his own wholesale business and, in 1960, a ready-to-wear collection. Scaasi switched to couture in 1963 and returned to ready-to-wear, with Arnold Scaasi Boutique, in 1983. Known for spectacular evening wear in luxurious fabrics, often fur- or feather-trimmed, he appealed to glamorous actresses and socialites. He has also designed costume jewelry, men's neckties and sweaters, and furs.

Schiaparelli, Elsa   (skap'-a-rell'-ee)   *French couturière* (1890–1973)

Roman-born Schiaparelli was one of the most creative, unconventional couturières of 1930s and 1940s, an innovator whose clothes and accessories were startling conversation pieces. By 1929, she had her own business *Pour le Sport,* in Paris, where she had spectacular success with avant-garde designs. As a result of her close friendship with surrealist artists, such as Dali and Cocteau, they contributed to her designs. She stopped designing in 1940 for duration of World War II, spending the time in the United States and returning to Paris after liberation. She reopened in 1945, returning to natural shoulderline, stiff peplums, and timeless black dresses. Schiaparelli had a great flair for publicity and defied tradition by using aggressive colors and rough materials. She remained a consultant for companies licensed to produce stockings, perfume, scarves, etc., under her name after closing her business in February 1954.

Simpson, Adele   *American designer* (1903–1987)

Simpson worked with her husband, textile designer Wesley Simpson, before becoming the designer for Mary Lee in 1942. They established Adele Simpson, Inc. in 1944. She was known for pretty feminine clothes in delicate prints and colors—coordinated wardrobe. Donald Hopson succeeded her as the designer of the collection.

Smith, Willi *American designer* (1948–1987)
Born in Philadelphia in 1947, Smith studied painting until 1965 when at 17 he went to New York with two scholarships to Parsons School of Design. While a student he freelanced as sketcher; then left Parsons in 1968 to work in a knitwear firm. In 1976 Smith, as a designer and vice president, formed WilliWear Ltd., and WilliWear Men in 1978. Following his death in 1987, WilliWear Ltd. continued to produce the same type of clothing that prompted Smith at one time to say, "People want real clothes. I don't think people want to walk around looking like statements with their shoulders out to there."

Stavropoulos, George (stav-row´-pole-us) *American couturier* (1920–1990)
Born in Greece and having studied dress design in Paris, Stavropoulos had a well-known custom salon in Athens from 1940 to 1960. He came to New York in 1961, opening a house there and slowly built a reputation for unusually beautiful, classically simple clothes. He was known for draped, tiered, or pleated evening gowns, asymmetric folds, wrapped coats, kimono sleeves, floating panels, capes, bias jerseys.

Sui, Anna *American designer* (1955–)
After studying at Parsons School of Design, Sui worked for various sportswear companies. She sold some of her designs to Macy's and showed her first runway collection in 1991. She is known for eclectic styling and is very popular among the young.

Tassell, Gustave (tass-ell´) *American designer* (1926–)
Born in Philadelphia in 1926, Tassell studied painting at Pennsylvania Academy of Fine Arts. He did freelance designing in New York and had a small couture business in Philadelphia, planned window displays at Hattie Carnegie; then spent two years in Paris selling his sketches. He returned to the United States in 1956 and with the help of JAMES GALANOS opened his own firm in Los Angeles, California, where he became known for refined, no-gimmick clothes with stark, clean lines. After the death of NORELL, Tassell designed under label, Norman Norell by Tassell. When Norell closed four years later, Tassell reopened his own business.

Tice, Bill *American lingerie designer* (1946–1995)
Tice arrived in New York in the mid-1960s after studying fashion design at the University of Cincinnati. He became designer for Royal Robes in 1968, for Sayour in 1974, and then to Swirl from 1975 to 1984. He introduced many at-home wear concepts such as Jersey float, quilted gypsy look, caftans, fleece robes, sundresses, sarongs, quilted silk coats worn with narrow pants.

Tilley, Monika *American swimwear designer* (1934–)
Tilley, born in Vienna, Austria, earned an M.A. degree from the Academy of Applied Arts, Vienna. She came to the United States in 1957 and worked with JOHN WEITZ; freelanced designing included skiwear and children's wear, and held design positions at: White Stag, Cole of California, the Anne Klein Studio, Mallory Leathers, and Elon of California. Establishing Monika Tilley Limited in 1970 for swim and beachwear, children's swimwear, at-home fashions and intimate apparel, she uses bias cuts, madras shirred with elastic, also a technique that angles the weave so that the fabric is molded against the body.

Toledo, Isabel *American designer* (1961–)
Cuban-born, Toledo came to the United States as a child. She was an intern for Diana Vreeland at the Metropolitan Museum before showing her first designs after 1985. She works with her husband, Ruben, a painter, sculptor, and fashion illustrator. She is considered to be a "hands on" designer whose clothes are avante-garde and sexy.

Trigère, Pauline (tree-zher´) *American designer* (1912–2002)
Born in Paris, Trigère came to New York in 1937. She worked as assistant designer to Travis Banton for Hattie Carnegie in late 1930s and started her own New York business in 1942 with brother, Robert. Specializing in coats, capes, suits, dresses, and accessories in unusual tweeds and prints, with intricate cut to flatter mature figures, her licenses include: scarves, jewelry, furs, men's neckties, sunglasses, bedroom fashions, paperworks, servingware, and fragrance. Her trademark was the turtle, which turns up in jewelry, scarf, and fabric designs. She closed her business in 1993, but continued designing jewelry for some time.

Tyler, Richard *American designer* (1948–)

Australian-born, Tyler moved to California, where he began to work. He became known for outstanding tailoring. After a short time as designer for Anne Klein, he once again made California his base.

Ungaro, Emanuel (ung'-aro) *French designer* (1933–)

Born in France to Italian immigrants, Ungaro worked with BALENCIAGA from 1958 to 1963 and then spent two seasons with COURRÈGES. He showed his first collection in 1965. In 1960s he was known for short, straight, structured dresses; high-waisted coats; diagonal seaming; A-line dresses; deeply cutout armholes; shorts and blazers. By early 1970s he showed softer lines and fabrics and his designs have become increasingly seductive, evolving into body-conscious, sensuous looks. Ready-to-wear collections are sold in Ungaro boutiques in the United States and Europe and his licenses include: furs, men's wear, sheets, wallcoverings, curtains, knitwear. In 2001 Ungaro announced his last ready-to-wear collection, but he continues to design couture.

Valentino (Valentino Garavani) (val-enn-tee'-noh) *French and Italian couturier* (1932–)

Born in Italy, Valentino went to Paris at 17 to study at Chambre Syndicale de la Couture. After working for JEAN DESSÈS in 1950 and Guy Laroche in 1958, he opened his own house, Valentino, in Rome, 1959. His designs include ready-to-wear, couture, and men's wear. He is noted for refined simplicity, elegantly tailored coats and suits—usually marked with his signature V in seams as well as in gilt V's on belts, shoes, bags, and V's woven in hosiery and silk pants. Other design interests include: Valentino Piu for gifts and interiors; bed linens, drapery fabrics, table- and cookware.

Venet, Philippe (ven-eh', feel-eep) *French designer* (1929–)

Venet started learning tailoring at age 14. He worked two years at SCHIAPARELLI (1951 to 1953), at GIVENCHY (1953 to 1962). He showed the first collection in his own house in January 1962. He is known for lean suits; rounded shoulders; round-back coats and curved seams; He also designed furs for Maximilian; and men's wear and ready-to-wear collections.

Versace, Donatella (ver-sah'-chay, dohn-ah-tell'-ah) *Italian designer* (c. 1956–)

After the death of her brother, Gianni, Donatella became the vice chairman and style and image director of the House of Versace. Initially the house declined somewhat, but by 2000 it had undergone a resurgence, and Donatella Versace earned praise for her work.

Versace, Gianni (ver-sah'-chay, gee-ahn'-ee) *Italian designer* (1946–1997)

Born in Italy to a dressmaker mother, Gianni Versace studied architecture, but became involved in his mother's couture business, eventually becoming her buyer in the late 1960s. He worked as designer for prêt-à-porter firms such as Genny and Callaghan; then presented his first solo men's wear collection in 1979. After that he designed for women and established boutiques around the world. Designs included: accessories, leathers, furs, and fragrances for men and women; costumes for La Scala and the ballet. After he was killed, his sister Donatella assumed the direction of the house.

Vionnet, Madeleine (vee-o-neh) *French couturière* (1876–1975)

One of the most creative fashion designers of the 20th c., Vionnet has been called the greatest technician of modern couture for her innovation of the bias cut. Born in Aubervilliers, France, she began dressmaking at an early age; trained in London and in Paris with Mme. Gerber at CALLOT and later at DOUCET. She opened her own house in 1912, closed during World War I; reopened in 1922, and closed permanently before World War II in 1940. Vionnet's designs were noted for classical drapery, for wide-open necklines, easy over-the-head entrance, cowl or halter neck, handkerchief-point hem; faggoted seams; Art Deco embroideries. She worked by draping and cutting designs on small wooden mannequin.

Von Furstenberg, Diane *American designer* (1947–)

Born in Brussels, Belgium, Von Furstenberg obtained a degree in economics from the University of Geneva. In 1969 she came to the United

States, where she started her career in fashion with a moderate-priced lightweight jersey wrapdress with surplice top and long sleeves. She left the fashion business in 1977, but returned in 1985 with day and evening wear based on her original wrapdress concept. Her business includes a wide variety of products including makeup and cosmetics, stationery, costume jewelry, furs, loungewear, handbags and small leather goods, raincoats, scarves, shoes, sunglasses, table linens, wallcoverings.

Vuitton, Louis (vwee′-ton, loo-ee′)   *Leather firm*

Vuitton was the founder of a firm that produces signature luggage with its yellow LV's and fleu-ron patterns on brown ground. First created for Empress Eugénie to transport her hoops and crinolines in mid-19th c., the family business is still producing luggage and leathers, making everything from wallets to steamer trunks. The firm has added lines of women's and men's wear, for which Marc Jacobs was doing the designs in 2001.

Wang, Vera   *American designer* (1949–)

Known for bridal gowns, Wang has been active and popular since the 1990s. Beginning as a fashion editor at *Vogue,* where she worked for 17 years, she moved to Ralph Lauren where she was designer and director for two years. She opened her own boutique in 1990, showed her first bridal line in 1992, and added evening dresses in 1993.

Weitz, John   *American designer* (1923–)

Born in Berlin, Weitz came to the United States in 1940. His fashion career started with Lord & Taylor after World War II, where he made bulky sweaters and jeans. One of the most versatile pioneers in design of practical clothes for sports and specific lifestyles, he is known for women's sports clothes with men's-wear look; poplin car coats; hooded, zippered-up cotton jackets; pea jackets with white pants; town pants; strapless dress over bra and shorts. In the 1960s, he devised "ready-to-wear couture," chosen from sketches and swatches. With his contour clothes for men,

inspired by Levi-Strauss jeans, cowboy jackets, fatigue coveralls, he was one of first American designers to show both men's and women's wear and one of the first to license his work.

Westwood, Vivienne   *British designer* (1941–)

A self-taught designer, Westwood first became known for antiestablishment styles. She showed in London in 1982, and also in Paris in 1983. Her 1985 mini-crini was especially influential. Her haute couture and ready-to-wear are considered to have influenced other designers. In recent years she has focused on British heritage and craftsmanship themes.

Worth, Charles Frederick   *French couturier* (1826–1895)

Born in England, Worth went to Paris to work in 1845. He became famous in the 19th c. as dress-maker for Empress Eugénie and the ladies of the court of France's Second Empire. He is considered to be the founder of the industry of *haute couture*. In 1858, the house called Worth et Bo-bergh opened. It closed during Franco-Prussian War (1870–1871), and re-opened as Maison Worth in 1874 with assistance of Worth's sons, Jean Phillipe and Gaston. For 50 years the house of Worth was a fashion leader without rivals, dressing ladies of the courts and society all over Europe and America. Worth was the innovator in the presentation of gowns on live mannequins and was the first to sell models to be copied in the United States and England. After the death of Charles, the house continued under sons and grandsons. It was sold in 1954 to Paquin.

Yamamoto, Yohji   (1943–)

Born in Japan, Yamamoto studied in Japan and later in Paris. He began designing in 1970, opened his own company in 1974 in Tokyo. He branched out with shows in Paris in 1981 and New York in 1982. His design has been described as having a "Japanese sensibility and tradition" behind it. Known for use of black fabrics, flat shoes, and layered loose garments, he does both women's and men's collections.

REFERENCES

Amaden-Crawfard *Guide to Fashion Sewing*, Third edition. New York: Fairchild Publications, 2000.

American Heritage Dictionary of the English Language, Third edition. Boston, MA: Houghton Mifflin Company, 1992.

Blair, C. *European Armour*. London: B.T. Batsford Ltd., 1972.

Boucher, E. *20,000 Years of Fashion*. London: Thames and Hudson, 1987.

Burns, L. D., and N. O. Bryant. *The Business of Fashion*, Second edition. New York: Fairchild Publications, 2002.

Callan, G. O. *Dictionary of Fashion and Fashion Designers*. New York: Thames and Hudson, 1998.

Cassell's Latin Dictionary. New York: Funk & Wagnalls Company, N.D.

Chase. D. *Terms of Adornment*. New York: Harper Collins Publishers, 1999.

Chenoune, F. *A History of Men's Fashion*. Paris: Flammarion, 1993.

Cheskin, M. P. *The Complete Handbook of Athletic Footwear*. New York: Fairchild Publications, 1987.

Clark, E. *Hats*. London: B. T. Batsford, 1982.

Collier, B. J., and P. G. Tortora. *Understanding Textiles*, Sixth edition. Upper Saddle River, NJ: Prentice Hall.

Collins, C. C. *Love of a Glove*. New York: Fairchild Publishing Company, 1947.

Cox, J. S. *An Illustrated Dictionary of Hairdressing and Wigmaking*. New York: Drama Book Publishers, 1984.

Crawford, T. S. *A History of the Umbrella*. New York: Taplinger Publishing Company, 1970.

Cudlip, E. *Furs*. New York: Hawthorn Books, Inc., 1978.

Cummings, V. *Gloves*. New York: Drama Book Publishers, 1982.

Cunnington, C. W., Cunnington, P. E., and C. Beard. *A Dictionary of English Costume, 900–1900*. London: Adam and Charles Black, 1972.

De la Haye, A., and C. Dingwall. *Surfers, Soulies, Skinheads & Skaters: Subcultural Style from the Forties to the Nineties*. Woodstock, NY: Overlook Press, 1996.

Diamond, J., and E. Diamond. *The World of Fashion*, Third Edition. New York: Fairchild Publications, 2002.

Donnellan, J. *Merchandise Buying and Management*. New York: Fairchild Publications, 1996.

Engelmeier, R., and P.W. Engelmeier. *Fashion in Film*. Prestel: New York, 1997.

Ettinger, R. *Handbags*, Second edition. Atglen, PA: Schiffer Publishing Ltd., 1998.

Ewing, E. *Underwear: A History*. New York: Drama Books, 1990.

Farrell-Beck, J., and C. Gau. *Uplift: the Bra in America*. Philadelphia, PA: University of Pennsylvania Press, 2002.

Feldman, E. *Fashions of a Decade: the 1990s*. New York: Facts on File, 1992.

Foster, V. *Bags and Purses*. London: B. T. Batsford, 1982.

Gibbings, S. *The Tie: Trends and Traditions.* Hauppauge, NY: Barron's Educational Series, Inc., 1990.

Ginsburg, M. *The Hat.* Hauppauge, NY: Barron's Educational Series, Inc., 1990.

Grass, M. N. *History of Hosiery.* New York: Fairchild Publishing Company, 1955.

Harper Collins Italian Dictionary. New York: Harper Collins, 1995.

Harrap's New College French and English Dictionary. Lincolnwood, IL: National Textbook company, 1982.

Key Moments in Fashion. London: Hamlyn, 1998.

Kopp, E., Rolfo, V., Zelin, B., and L. Gross. *Designing Apparel Through the Flat Pattern,* Sixth edition. New York: Fairchild Publications, 1992.

Kunz, G. *Merchandising Theory, Principles and Practice.* New York: Fairchild Publications, 1998.

Larousse Gran Diccionario Moderno Español Inglès. New York: Larousse, 1983.

Lawlor, L. *Where Will This Shoe Take You?* New York: Walker and Company, 1996.

Lomas, C. *20th Century Fashion: the 80s & 90s.* Milwaukee: Gareth Stevens Publishing, 2000.

Mason, A., and D. Packer. *An Illustrated Dictionary of Jewellery.* New York: Harper and Row, 1974.

Oxford English Dictionary. Oxford England: Oxford University Press, 1971.

Pattison, A. *A Century of Shoes.* Edison, NJ: Chartwell Books, 1997.

Polhemus, T. *Street Style.* New York: Thames and Hudson, Inc., 1994.

Rexford, N. E. *Women's Shoes in America, 1795–1930.* Kent, OH: Kent State University Press, 2000.

Schoeffler, O. E., and W. Gale. *Esquire's Encyclopedia of 20th Century Men's Fashions.* New York: McGraw-Hill, Inc., 1973.

Scott, M. *A Visual History of Costume: The Fourteenth & Fifteenth Centuries.* London: B. T. Batsford, 1986.

Sebesta, J. L., and L. Bonfante. *The World of Roman Costume.* Madison, WI: University of Wisconsin Press, 1994.

Stegemeyer, A. *Who's Who in Fashion,* Third edition. New York: Fairchild Publications, 1996.

Stipelman, S. *Illustrating Fashion: Concept to Creation.* New York: Fairchild Publications, 1996.

Tortora, P., and K. Eubank. *Survey of Historic Costume.* New York: Fairchild Publications, 1998.

Tortora, P., and R. Merkel. *Fairchild's Dictionary of Textiles,* Seventh edition. New York: Fairchild Publications, 1996.

Vogelsang-Eastwood, G. *Pharaonic Egyptian Clothing.* Leiden, the Netherlands: E. J. Brill, 1924.

Webster's New International Dictionary, Second edition. Springfield, MA: G. & C. Merriam Company Publisher, 1953.

Wilcox, C. *A Century of Bags: Icons of Style in the 20th Century.* Edison, NJ: Chartwell Books, 1997.